The Western Heritage

Eleventh Edition

Volume C: Since 1789

Donald Kagan
Yale University

Steven Ozment
Harvard University

Frank M. Turner
Yale University

Alison Frank
Harvard University

PEARSON

Boston Columbus Indianapolis New York San Francisco Upper Saddle River Amsterdam
Cape Town Dubai London Madrid Milan Munich Paris Montréal Toronto Delhi Mexico City
São Paulo Sydney Hong Kong Seoul Singapore Taipei Tokyo

Editorial Director: Craig Campanella
Editor-in-Chief: Dickson Musslewhite
Executive Editor: Jeff Lasser
Associate Editor: Rob DeGeorge
Director of Marketing: Brandy Dawson
Senior Marketing Manager: Maureen E. Prado Roberts
Marketing Coordinator: Samantha Bennett
Marketing Assistant: Cristina Liva
Senior Digital Media Editor: Paul DeLuca
Digital Media Editor: Lisa M. Dotson
Digital Media Project Manager: Claudine Bellanton
Managing Editor: Ann Marie McCarthy
Production/Project Manager: Barbara Mack
Full-Service Project Management and Composition: Laserwords
Art Director: Maria Lange
Interior Designer: Liz Harasymcuk
Cover Designer: Liz Harasymcuk
Cover Photo: Parachute Riggers, 1947 (oil on canvas), Clark, Paraskeva Plistik (b.1898)/© Canadian War Museum, Ottawa, Canada/The Bridgeman Art Library
Operations Manager: Mary Fischer
Operations Specialist: Alan Fischer

Credits and acknowledgments borrowed from other sources and reproduced, with permission, in this textbook appear on the appropriate page within text.

---

10 9 8 7 6 5 4 3 2 V092 16

ISBN 10: 0-205-96239-4
ISBN 13: 978-0-205-96239-6

BRIEF CONTENTS

PART 4 Enlightenment and Revolution, 1700–1850

18 The French Revolution 550
19 The Age of Napoleon and the Triumph of Romanticism 584
20 The Conservative Order and the Challenges of Reform (1815–1832) 616
21 Economic Advance and Social Unrest (1830–1850) 646

PART 5 Toward the Modern World, 1850–1939

22 The Age of Nation-States 685
23 The Building of European Supremacy: Society and Politics to World War I 715
24 The Birth of Modern European Thought 751
25 The Age of Western Imperialism 782
26 Alliances, War, and a Troubled Peace 827
27 The Interwar Years: The Challenge of Dictators and Depression 865

PART 6 Global Conflict, Cold War, and New Directions, 1939–2012

28 World War II 898
29 The Cold War Era, Decolonization, and the Emergence of a New Europe 936
30 Social, Cultural, and Economic Challenges in the West through the Present 982

CONTENTS

Documents xiii
Maps xvii
Preface xix
About the Authors xxvii
What Is the Western Heritage? xxix

PART 4
Enlightenment and Revolution, 1700–1850

18 The French Revolution 550

The Crisis of the French Monarchy 551
The Monarchy Seeks New Taxes 551
Necker's Report 552
Calonne's Reform Plan and the Assembly of Notables 552
Deadlock and the Calling of the Estates General 553

The Revolution of 1789 553
The Estates General Becomes the National Assembly 553
Fall of the Bastille 556
The "Great Fear" and the Night of August 4 557
The Declaration of the Rights of Man and Citizen 557
The Parisian Women's March on Versailles 559

The Reconstruction of France 560
Political Reorganization 561
Economic Policy 561
The Civil Constitution of the Clergy 563
Counterrevolutionary Activity 563

The End of the Monarchy: A Second Revolution 567
Emergence of the Jacobins 567
The Convention and the Role of the Sans-culottes 568

Europe at War with the Revolution 569
Edmund Burke Attacks the Revolution 569
Suppression of Reform in Britain 570
The Second and Third Partitions of Poland, 1793, 1795 570

The Reign of Terror 572
War with Europe 572
The Republic Defended 572
The "Republic of Virtue" and Robespierre's Justification of Terror 575
Repression of the Society of Revolutionary Republican Women 575
De-Christianization 576
Revolutionary Tribunals 576
The End of the Terror 577

The Thermidorian Reaction 578
Establishment of the Directory 580
Removal of the Sans-culottes *from Political Life* 580

In Perspective 582
Key Terms 582
Review Questions 582
Suggested Readings 582
MyHistoryLab Media Assignments 583

A Closer LOOK CHALLENGING THE FRENCH POLITICAL ORDER 558

COMPARE AND CONNECT **The Declaration of the Rights of Man and Citizen Opens the Door for Disadvantaged Groups to Demand Equal Civic Rights** 564

ENCOUNTERING THE PAST
The Metric System 566

19 The Age of Napoleon and the Triumph of Romanticism 584

The Rise of Napoleon Bonaparte 585
Early Military Victories 585
The Constitution of the Year VIII 586

The Consulate in France (1799–1804) 586
Suppressing Foreign Enemies and Domestic Opposition 586
Concordat with the Roman Catholic Church 587
The Napoleonic Code 588
Establishing a Dynasty 588

The Haitian Revolution (1791–1804) 588

Napoleon's Empire (1804–1814) 590
Conquering an Empire 590
The Continental System 592

European Response to the Empire 592
German Nationalism and Prussian Reform 593
The Wars of Liberation 595
The Invasion of Russia 598
European Coalition 598

The Congress of Vienna and the European Settlement 599
Territorial Adjustments 599
The Hundred Days and the Quadruple Alliance 600

The Romantic Movement 602

Romantic Questioning of the Supremacy of Reason 603
Rousseau and Education 603
Kant and Reason 603

Romantic Literature 604
English Romantic Writers 604
The German Romantic Writers 606

Romantic Art 606
The Cult of the Middle Ages and Neo-Gothicism 607
Nature and the Sublime 608

Religion in the Romantic Period 609
Methodism 609

New Directions in Continental Religion 610
Romantic Views of Nationalism and History 610
Herder and Culture 610
Hegel and History 611
Islam, the Middle East, and Romanticism 611
In Perspective 613
Key Terms 613
Review Questions 614
Suggested Readings 614
MyHistoryLab Media Assignments 614

A Closer LOOK THE CORONATION OF NAPOLEON 589

ENCOUNTERING THE PAST
Sailors and Canned Food 594

COMPARE AND CONNECT The Experience of War in the Napoleonic Age 596

20 The Conservative Order and the Challenges of Reform (1815–1832) 616

The Conservative Order 617
The Congress System 617
The Domestic Political Order 617
Conservative Outlooks 617
The Emergence of Nationalism and Liberalism 618
Nationalism 618
Early-Nineteenth-Century Political Liberalism 622
Classical Economics 624
Relationship of Liberalism to Nationalism 625
Conservative Restoration in Europe 625
Liberalism and Nationalism Resisted in Austria and the Germanies 625
Postwar Repression in Great Britain 627
Bourbon Restoration in France 631
The Spanish Revolution of 1820 632
The Conservative Order Shaken in Europe 632
Revolt Against Ottoman Rule in the Balkans 633
Russia: The Decembrist Revolt of 1825 634
Revolution in France (1830) 636
Belgium Becomes Independent (1830) 638
The Great Reform Bill in Britain (1832) 638
The Wars of Independence in Latin America 640
Wars of Independence on the South American Continent 640
Independence in New Spain 643
Brazilian Independence 643
In Perspective 643
Key Terms 644
Review Questions 644
Suggested Readings 644
MyHistoryLab Media Assignments 645

COMPARE AND CONNECT Mazzini and Lord Acton Debate the Political Principles of Nationalism 620

ENCOUNTERING THE PAST
Gymnastics and German Nationalism 628

A Closer LOOK AN UNSUCCESSFUL MILITARY COUP IN RUSSIA 635

21 Economic Advance and Social Unrest (1830–1850) 646

Toward an Industrial Society 647
Population and Migration 647
Railways 648
The Labor Force 650
The Emergence of a Wage-Labor Force 650
Working-Class Political Action: The Example of British Chartism 651
Family Structures and the Industrial Revolution 654
The Family in the Early Factory System 654
Women in the Early Industrial Revolution 656
Opportunities and Exploitation in Employment 656
Changing Expectations in the Working-Class Marriage 657
Problems of Crime, Order, and Poverty 658
New Police Forces 660
Prison Reform 661
Government Policies Based on Classical Economics 661
Early Socialism 662
Utopian Socialism 662
Anarchism 664
Marxism 664
1848: Year of Revolutions 666
France: The Second Republic and Louis Napoleon 668
The Habsburg Empire: Nationalism Resisted 671
Italy: Republicanism Defeated 673
The German Confederation: Liberalism Frustrated 674
In Perspective 676
Key Terms 676
Review Questions 677
Suggested Readings 677
MyHistoryLab Media Assignments 677

ENCOUNTERING THE PAST
The Potato and the Great Hunger in Ireland 649

COMPARE AND CONNECT Andrew Ure and John Ruskin Debate the Conditions of Factory Production 652

A Closer LOOK THE GREAT EXHIBITION IN LONDON 655

THE WEST & THE WORLD The Abolition of Slavery in the Transatlantic Economy 679

PART 5
Toward the Modern World, 1850–1939

22 The Age of Nation-States 685

The Crimean War (1853–1856) 686
Peace Settlement and Long-Term Results 687
Reforms in the Ottoman Empire 688
Italian Unification 690
Romantic Republicans 690
Cavour's Policy 690
The New Italian State 693
German Unification 696
Bismarck 697
The Franco-Prussian War and the German Empire (1870–1871) 699
France: From Liberal Empire to the Third Republic 700
The Paris Commune 700
The Third Republic 701
The Habsburg Empire 701
Formation of the Dual Monarchy 703
Unrest of Nationalities 703
Russia: Emancipation and Revolutionary Stirrings 705
Reforms of Alexander II 705
Revolutionaries 706
Great Britain: Toward Democracy 707
The Second Reform Act (1867) 707
Gladstone's Great Ministry (1868–1874) 709
Disraeli in Office (1874–1880) 709
The Irish Question 711
In Perspective 712
Key Term 712
Review Questions 712
Suggested Readings 712
MyHistoryLab Media Assignments 713

A Closer LOOK THE SUEZ CANAL 689

COMPARE AND CONNECT Nineteenth-Century Nationalism: Two Sides 694

■ ENCOUNTERING THE PAST
The Arrival of Penny Postage 710

23 The Building of European Supremacy: Society and Politics to World War I 715

Population Trends and Migration 716
The Second Industrial Revolution 716
New Industries 716
Economic Difficulties 719
The Middle Classes in Ascendancy 719
Social Distinctions within the Middle Classes 719
Late-Nineteenth-Century Urban Life 722
The Redesign of Cities 723
Urban Sanitation 724
Housing Reform and Middle-Class Values 725
Varieties of Late-Nineteenth-Century Women's Experiences 727
Women's Social Disabilities 727
New Employment Patterns for Women 729
Working-Class Women 730
Poverty and Prostitution 730
Women of the Middle Class 731
The Rise of Political Feminism 733
Jewish Emancipation 736
Differing Degrees of Citizenship 736
Broadened Opportunities 736
Labor, Socialism, and Politics to World War I 737
Trade Unionism 737
Democracy and Political Parties 738
Karl Marx and the First International 738
Great Britain: Fabianism and Early Welfare Programs 739
France: "Opportunism" Rejected 739
Germany: Social Democrats and Revisionism 740
Russia: Industrial Development and the Birth of Bolshevism 741
In Perspective 748
Key Terms 748
Review Questions 748
Suggested Readings 749
MyHistoryLab Media Assignments 749

■ ENCOUNTERING THE PAST
Bicycles: Transportation, Freedom, and Sport 721

COMPARE AND CONNECT Bernstein and Lenin Debate the Tactics of European Socialism 744

A Closer LOOK BLOODY SUNDAY, ST. PETERSBURG, 1905 747

24 The Birth of Modern European Thought 751

The New Reading Public 752
Advances in Primary Education 752
Reading Material for the Mass Audience 752

Science at Midcentury 752
Comte, Positivism, and the Prestige of Science 753
New Theories of Evolution: Lamarck, Lyell, Darwin, Wallace 753
Science and Ethics: Social Darwinism 755
Christianity and the Church Under Siege 755
Intellectual Skepticism 755
Conflict Between Church and State 758
Areas of Religious Revival 759
The Roman Catholic Church and the Modern World 759
Islam and Late-Nineteenth-Century European Thought 759
Toward a Twentieth-Century Frame of Mind 761
Science: The Revolution in Physics 761
Literature: Realism and Naturalism 763
Modernism in Literature 764
The Coming of Modern Art 765
Friedrich Nietzsche and the Revolt Against Reason 768
The Birth of Psychoanalysis 769
Retreat from Rationalism in Politics 770
Racism 771
Anti-Semitism and the Birth of Zionism 771
Women and Modern Thought 775
Antifeminism in Late-Century Thought 775
New Directions in Feminism 776
In Perspective 779
Key Terms 779
Review Questions 779
Suggested Readings 780
MyHistoryLab Media Assignments 780

ENCOUNTERING THE PAST
The Birth of Science Fiction 754
COMPARE AND CONNECT **The Debate over Social Darwinism** 756
A Closer LOOK POPULAR RELIGION AND PILGRIMAGE 760

25 The Age of Western Imperialism 782

The Close of the Age of Early Modern Colonization 783
The Age of British Imperial Dominance 784
The Imperialism of Free Trade 784
British Settler Colonies 785
India—The Jewel in the Crown of the British Empire 785
The "New Imperialism," 1870–1914 790
Motives for the New Imperialism 791
The Partition of Africa 796
Algeria, Tunisia, Morocco, and Libya 796
Egypt and British Strategic Concern about the Upper Nile 796
West Africa 799
The Belgian Congo 801
German Empire in Africa 802
Southern Africa 803
Russian Expansion in Mainland Asia 805
Western Powers in Asia 806
France in Asia 806
The United States' Actions in Asia, the Pacific, and Latin America 807
The Boxer Rebellion 808
Tools of Imperialism 810
Steamboats 810
Conquest of Tropical Diseases 810
Firearms 810
The Missionary Factor 812
Missionary Movements 812
Tensions Between Missionaries and Imperial Administrators 813
Missionaries and Indigenous Religious Movements 815
Science and Imperialism 815
Botany 816
Zoology 817
Medicine 817
Anthropology 817
In Perspective 818
Key Terms 819
Review Questions 819
Suggested Readings 820
MyHistoryLab Media Assignments 821

A Closer LOOK THE FRENCH IN MOROCCO 793
COMPARE AND CONNECT **Two Views of Turn-of-the-Twentieth-Century Imperial Expansion** 794
ENCOUNTERING THE PAST
Submarine Cables 811

THE WEST & THE WORLD Imperialism: Ancient and Modern 822

26 Alliances, War, and a Troubled Peace 827

Emergence of the German Empire and the Alliance Systems (1873–1890) 828
Bismarck's Leadership 828
Forging the Triple Entente (1890–1907) 830
World War I 832
The Road to War (1908–1914) 832
Sarajevo and the Outbreak of War (June–August 1914) 834
Strategies and Stalemate: 1914–1917 837

The Russian Revolution 847
The Provisional Government 847
Lenin and the Bolsheviks 848
The Communist Dictatorship 850
The End of World War I 851
Germany's Last Offensive 851
The Armistice 852
The End of the Ottoman Empire 852
The Settlement at Paris 854
Obstacles the Peacemakers Faced 855
The Peace 857
World War I and Colonial Empires 859
Evaluating the Peace 860
In Perspective 861
Key Terms 862
Review Questions 862
Suggested Readings 862
MyHistoryLab Media Assignments 863

COMPARE AND CONNECT **The Outbreak of World War I** 838

A Closer LOOK THE DEVELOPMENT OF THE ARMORED TANK 845

■ **ENCOUNTERING THE PAST**
War Propaganda and the Movies: Charlie Chaplin 856

27 The Interwar Years: The Challenge of Dictators and Depression 865

After Versailles: Demands for Revision and Enforcement 866
Toward the Great Depression in Europe 867
Financial Tailspin 867
Problems in Agricultural Commodities 868
Depression and Government Policy in Britain and France 868
The Soviet Experiment 869
War Communism 869
The New Economic Policy 870
The Third International 871
Stalin versus Trotsky 872
The Decision for Rapid Industrialization 872
The Collectivization of Agriculture 873
The Purges 875
The Fascist Experiment in Italy 876
The Rise of Mussolini 877
The Fascists in Power 879
German Democracy and Dictatorship 879
The Weimar Republic 879
Depression and Political Deadlock 884
Hitler Comes to Power 885
Hitler's Consolidation of Power 887
Anti-Semitism and the Police State 888
Racial Ideology and the Lives of Women 888
Nazi Economic Policy 889
Trials of the Successor States in Eastern Europe 893
Economic and Ethnic Pressures 893
Poland: Democracy to Military Rule 893
Czechoslovakia: A Viable Democratic Experiment 894
Hungary: Turn to Authoritarianism 894
Austria: Political Turmoil and Nazi Occupation 894
Southeastern Europe: Royal Dictatorships 894
In Perspective 895
Key Terms 895
Review Questions 895
Suggested Readings 896
MyHistoryLab Media Assignments 897

■ **ENCOUNTERING THE PAST**
Cinema of the Political Left and Right **886**

COMPARE AND CONNECT **The Soviets and the Nazis Confront the Issues of Women and the Family** 890

A Closer LOOK THE NAZI PARTY RALLY 892

PART 6
Global Conflict, Cold War, and New Directions, 1939–2012

28 World War II 898

Again the Road to War (1933–1939) 899
Hitler's Goals 899
Italy Attacks Ethiopia 899
Remilitarization of the Rhineland 900
The Spanish Civil War 900
Austria and Czechoslovakia 901
Munich 903
The Nazi–Soviet Pact 907
World War II (1939–1945) 907
The German Conquest of Europe 907
The Battle of Britain 908
The German Attack on Russia 909
Hitler's Plans for Europe 911
Japan and the United States Enter the War 911
The Tide Turns 912
The Defeat of Nazi Germany 916
Fall of the Japanese Empire 917
The Cost of War 919
Racism and the Holocaust 919
The Destruction of the Polish Jewish Community 920
Polish Anti-Semitism Between the Wars 920
The Nazi Assault on the Jews of Poland 921
Explanations of the Holocaust 922

The Domestic Fronts 924
Germany: From Apparent Victory to Defeat 925
France: Defeat, Collaboration, and Resistance 926
Great Britain: Organization for Victory 928
The Soviet Union: "The Great Patriotic War" 929

Preparations for Peace 930
The Atlantic Charter 930
Tehran: Agreement on a Second Front 930
Yalta 932
Potsdam 932

In Perspective 933

Key Terms 934

Review Questions 934

Suggested Readings 934

MyHistoryLab Media Assignments 935

COMPARE AND CONNECT **The Munich Settlement** 904

■ ENCOUNTERING THE PAST
Rosie the Riveter and American Women in the War Effort 915

A Closer LOOK THE VICHY REGIME IN FRANCE 927

29 The Cold War Era, Decolonization, and the Emergence of a New Europe 936

The Emergence of the Cold War 937
Containment in American Foreign Policy 938
Soviet Domination of Eastern Europe 940
The Postwar Division of Germany 940
NATO and the Warsaw Pact 941
The Creation of the State of Israel 941
The Korean War 945

The Khrushchev Era in the Soviet Union 946
Khrushchev's Domestic Policies 946
The Three Crises of 1956 947

Later Cold War Confrontations 948
The Berlin Wall 949
The Cuban Missile Crisis 949

The Brezhnev Era 949
1968: The Invasion of Czechoslovakia 949
The United States and Détente 950
The Invasion of Afghanistan 951
Communism and Solidarity in Poland 952
Relations with the Reagan Administration 952

Decolonization: The European Retreat from Empire 952
Major Areas of Colonial Withdrawal 954
India 954
Further British Retreat from Empire 955

The Turmoil of French Decolonization 956
France and Algeria 957
France and Vietnam 958
Vietnam Drawn into the Cold War 958
Direct United States Involvement 959

The Collapse of European Communism 960
Gorbachev Attempts to Reform the Soviet Union 960
1989: Revolution in Eastern Europe 963
The Collapse of the Soviet Union 964
The Yeltsin Decade 969

The Collapse of Yugoslavia and Civil War 970

Putin and the Resurgence of Russia 971

The Rise of Radical Political Islamism 974
Arab Nationalism 974
The Iranian Revolution 975
Afghanistan and Radical Islamism 975

A Transformed West 976

In Perspective 978

Key Terms 979

Review Questions 979

Suggested Readings 979

MyHistoryLab Media Assignments 980

COMPARE AND CONNECT **The Soviet Union and the United States Draw the Lines of the Cold War** 942

■ ENCOUNTERING THE PAST
Rock Music and Political Protest 962

A Closer LOOK COLLAPSE OF THE BERLIN WALL 967

30 Social, Cultural, and Economic Challenges in the West through the Present 982

The Twentieth-Century Movement of Peoples 983
Displacement Through War 983
External and Internal Migration 983
The New Muslim Population 984
European Population Trends 985

Toward a Welfare State Society 988
Christian Democratic Parties 988
The Creation of Welfare States 988
Resistance to the Expansion of the Welfare State 989

New Patterns in Work and Expectations of Women 990
Feminism 990
More Married Women in the Workforce 991
New Work Patterns 991
Women in the New Eastern Europe 993

Transformations in Knowledge and Culture 993
Communism and Western Europe 993
Existentialism 994

Expansion of the University Population and Student Rebellion 995
The Americanization of Europe 997
A Consumer Society 997
Environmentalism 997
Art Since World War II 999
Cultural Divisions and the Cold War 1001
The Christian Heritage 1003
Neo-Orthodoxy 1003
Liberal Theology 1003
Roman Catholic Reform 1004
Late-Twentieth-Century Technology: The Arrival of the Computer 1005
The Demand for Calculating Machines 1005
Early Computer Technology 1005
The Development of Desktop Computers 1006
The Challenges of European Unification 1007
Postwar Cooperation 1007
The European Economic Community 1007
The European Union 1007
Discord over the Union 1008
New American Leadership and Financial Crisis 1009
European Debt Crisis 1011
In Perspective 1012
Key Terms 1012
Review Questions 1012
Suggested Readings 1013
MyHistoryLab Media Assignments 1013

COMPARE AND CONNECT Muslim Women Debate France's Ban on the Veil **986**

ENCOUNTERING THE PAST
Toys from Europe Conquer the United States **998**

A Closer LOOK NAMELESS LIBRARY, VIENNA **1002**

THE WEST & THE WORLD Energy and the Modern World **1015**

Glossary G-1
Index I-1

DOCUMENTS

CHAPTER 18

Petition of Women of the Third Estate 553
Emmanuel Joseph Sieyès, *What Is the Third Estate?* 553
French Peasants, Cahiers de doléances (Grievances) (France), 1789 554
*The Third Estate of a French City Petitions the King 555
*The National Assembly Decrees Civic Equality in France 560
Olympe de Gouges, Declaration of the Rights of Woman and the Female Citizen 561
*Burke Denounces the Extreme Measures of the French Revolution 571
The National Convention, *Law on Suspects* (1793), and *Law of 22 Prairial Year II* (1794) 572
*A Nation at Arms 573
*The Paris Jacobin Club Alerts the Nation to Internal Enemies of the Revolution 574
Maximilien Robespierre, "Speech to National Convention: The Terror Justified" 575
*The Convention Establishes the Worship of the Supreme Being 579

CHAPTER 19

Madame de Remusat on the Rise of Napoleon 585
Louis Antoine Fauvelet de Bourrienne, *Memoirs of Napoleon Bonaparte* 586
*Napoleon Announces His Seizure of Power 587
Charles Parquin, "Napoleon's Army" 591
Carl von Clausewitz, On War, "Arming the Nation" 593
Napoleon's Exile to St. Helena (1815) 600
Jean-Jacques Rousseau, *Émile* 603
*Madame de Staël Describes the New Romantic Literature of Germany 605
Johann Wolfgang von Goethe, *Prometheus*, 1773 606
*Mary Shelley Remembers the Birth of a Monster 607
*Hegel Explains the Role of Great Men in History 612
The Rubaiyat (11th c. C.E.) Omar Khayyam 612

CHAPTER 20

*John Stuart Mill Advocates Independence 623
Adam Smith, *The Wealth of Nations* 624
Laws of Population Growth (1798) Malthus 625
David Ricardo, Excerpt from *Principles of Political Economy and Taxation* 625
*The German Confederation Issues the Carlsbad Decrees 629
The Plan of Iguala 643

CHAPTER 21

Chartist Movement: The People's Petition of 1838 651
British Parliament, "Inquiry: Child Labor" 656
Industrial Society and Factory Conditions (early 1800s) 657
*Women Industrial Workers Explain Their Economic Situation 659
Leon Faucher, "Prison Rules" 661
Robert Owen, Excerpt from *Address to the Workers of New Lanark, 1816* 663
Capitalism Challenged: *The Communist Manifesto* (1848) 665
*Karl Marx and Friedrich Engels Describe the Class Struggle 667
Metternich on the Revolutions of 1848 672
Giuseppe Mazzini, *Life and Writings of Giuseppe Mazzini, 1805–1872* 673
*A Czech Nationalist Defends the Austrian Empire 674

CHAPTER 22

An Ottoman Government Decree Defines the Official Notion of the "Modern" Citizen, June 19, 1870 688
A Letter from Bismarck (1866) 698
Fustel de Coulanges, *Letter to German Historian Theodor Mommsen, 1870* 700
*Mark Twain Describes the Austrian Parliament 702
Emancipation Manifesto (1861) 705
*The People's Will Issues a Revolutionary Manifesto 708

CHAPTER 23

*Praise and Concerns Regarding Railway Travel 720
*Paris Department Stores Expand Their Business 722
Edwin Chadwick, *Summary from the Poor Law Commissioners* 725
*A Doctor Learns How to Prevent Childbed Fever 726
Adelheid Popp, "Finding Work: Women Factory Workers" 730
George Bernard Shaw, *Mrs. Warren's Profession* 731
John Stuart Mill, *The Subjection of Women* 733
"Freedom or Death" (1913) Emmeline Pankhurst 734

*Documents preceded by an asterisk appear in the printed book. Documents without asterisks are referenced throughout the text by title and are available at MyHistoryLab.com.

*Emmeline Pankhurst Defends Militant Suffragette Tactics 735
Socialism: The Gotha Program (1875) 740
M. I. Pokzovskaya, *Working Conditions of Women in the Factories* 741

CHAPTER 24

Auguste Comte, "Course of Positive Philosophy" (France), 1830–1842 753
Origin of Species, Charles Darwin (1859) 753
Herbert Spencer, Social Darwinism, from *The Data of Ethics* (1857) 755
Matthew Arnold, Excerpt from *Dover Beach* 755
Pope Leo XIII, *Rerum Novarum (Of New Things)*, 1891 759
Sayyid Jamal al-Din al-Afghani, "Lecture on Teaching and Learning" 761
*Leo XIII Considers the Social Question in European Politics 762
Werner Heisenberg, "Uncertainty" (Germany), 1927 762
Emile Zola, *Nana* 763
Henrik Ibsen, from *A Doll's House*, Act Three 764
John Maynard Keynes, from *The End of Laissez-Faire* 764
Friedrich Nietzsche, *Beyond Good and Evil* 768
*Émile Zola Accuses the Enemies of Dreyfus of Self-Interest and Illegal Actions 772
*Herzl Advocates Jewish Nationalism 774
Ellen Key, from *The Century of the Child* 776
Virginia Woolf, from *A Room of One's Own* (Great Britain), 1929 777
*Virginia Woolf Urges Women to Write 778

CHAPTER 25

Letter to Queen Victoria (1839) Lin Zexu 785
*A Chinese Official Appeals to Queen Victoria to Halt the Opium Trade 786
Dadabhai Naoroji, *The Benefits of British Rule in India*, 1871 787
The Indian Revolt (1857) 788
Amrita Lal Roy, *English Rule in India, 1886* 788
*Gandhi Questions the Value of English Civilization 789
Karl Pearson, "Social Darwinism and Imperialism" 791
Vladimir Lenin, *Imperialism, the Highest Stage of Capitalism* 791
Arthur James Balfour, "Problems with Which We Have to Deal in Egypt," 1910 792
*Winston Churchill Reports on the Power of Modern Weaponry against an African Army 800
Carl Peters, "A Manifesto for German Colonization" 802
*General von Trotha Demands that the Herero People Leave Their Land 804
*The Russian Foreign Minister Explains the Imperatives of Expansion in Asia 807

CHAPTER 26

Borijove Jevtic, *The Murder of Archduke Franz Ferdinand at Sarajevo* (28 June 1919) 834
*The Austrian Ambassador Gets a "Blank Check" from the Kaiser 836
Bolshevik Seizure of Power, 1917 848
*The Outbreak of the Russian Revolution 849
*An Eyewitness Account of the Bolsheviks' Seizure of Power 850
Woodrow Wilson, *The Fourteen Points* (1918) 852
The Covenant of the League of Nations 857

CHAPTER 27

Irish National Identity: (a) Irish Declaration of Independence; (b) Ulster's Solemn League and Covenant; (c) Eamon de Valera, radio broadcast 869
*John Maynard Keynes Calls for Government Investment to Create Employment 870
Joseph Stalin, *Five Year Plan* 873
Benito Mussolini, "The Political and Social Doctrine of Fascism" 877
*Mussolini Heaps Contempt on Political Liberalism 878
Heinrich Hauser, "With Germany's Unemployed" 880
*Hitler Denounces the Versailles Treaty 882
Adolf Hitler, Excerpt from *Mein Kampf* 882
Heinrich Himmler, "Speech to SS Officers" 888
Gertrud Scholtz-Klink, "Speech to the Nazi Women's Organization" (Germany), 1935 889

CHAPTER 28

Adolf Hitler, *Mein Kampf* 899
Speech to Spaniards (1936) Francisco Franco 900
*Winston Churchill Warns of the Effects of the Munich Agreement 906
Adolf Hitler, "The Obersalzberg Speech" 906
Marc Bloch, from *Strange Defeat* 908
Winston Churchill, "Their Finest Hour" (Great Britain), 1940 909
An Eyewitness to Hiroshima (1945) 918
*Mass Murder at Belsen 922
Franklin D. Roosevelt and Winston Churchill, "The Atlantic Charter" 930

CHAPTER 29

Joseph Stalin, Excerpts from the "Soviet Victory" Speech, 1946 938
Winston Churchill, from the Iron Curtain Speech, 1946 938
Gamal Abdel Nasser, Speech on the Suez Canal (Egypt), 1956 947
*Khrushchev Denounces the Crimes of Stalin: The Secret Speech 948
*Gandhi Explains His Doctrine of Nonviolence 956
Frantz Fanon, from *The Wretched of the Earth* 958
Mikhail Gorbachev on the Need for Economic Reform (1987) 961
*Vladimir Putin Outlines a Vision of the Russian Future 973
Statement from Chancellor Schröder on the Iraq Crisis 977

CHAPTER 30

Justin Vaisse, from "Veiled Meaning" (France) 2004 984
Jörg Haider, from *The Freedom I Mean* (Austria), 1995 985
*Simone de Beauvoir Urges Economic Freedom for Women 992
*Sartre Discusses His Existentialism 996
Towards a Green Europe, Towards a Green World 997
*Voices from Chernobyl 1000
Pope John Paul II, from *Centesimus Annus* 1004
A Common Market and European Integration (1960) 1007
Treaty on European Union, 1992 1008
*An English Business Editor Calls for Europe to Take Charge of Its Economic Future 1010

MAPS

18–1 French Provinces and the Republic 562
19–1 The Continental System, 1806–1810 593
19–2 Napoleonic Europe in Late 1812 599
19–3 The German States after 1815 601
19–4 Europe 1815, after the Congress of Vienna 602
20–1 Centers of Revolution, 1820–1831 633
20–2 Latin America in 1830 641
21–1 European Railroads in 1850 648
21–2 Centers of Revolution in 1848–1849 668
22–1 The Crimean War 686
22–2 The Unification of Italy 692
22–3 The Unification of Germany 696
23–1 Patterns of Global Migration, 1840–1900 717
23–2 European Industrialization, 1860–1913 718
25–1 British India, 1820 and 1856 787
25–2 Imperial Expansion in Africa to 1880 797
25–3 Partition of Africa, 1880–1914 798
25–4 Asia, 1880–1914 809
26–1 The Balkans, 1912–1913 834
26–2 The Schlieffen Plan of 1905 842
26–3 World War I in Europe 843
26–4 The Western Front, 1914–1918 844
26–5 World War I Peace Settlement in Europe and the Middle East 858
27–1 Germany's Western Frontier 883
28–1 The Spanish Civil War, 1936–1939 901
28–2 Partitions of Czechoslovakia and Poland, 1938–1939 903
28–3 Axis Europe, 1941 910
28–4 North African Campaigns, 1942–1945 913
28–5 Defeat of the Axis in Europe, 1942–1945 914
28–6 World War II in the Pacific 918
28–7 The Holocaust 920
28–8 Yalta to the Surrender 932
29–1 Territorial Changes in Europe After World War II 938
29–2 Occupied Germany and Austria 941
29–3 Major Cold War European Alliance Systems 944
29–4 Israel and Its Neighbors in 1949 945
29–5 Korea, 1950–1953 946
29–6 Decolonization Since World War II 953
29–7 Vietnam and Its Southeast Asian Neighbors 961
29–8 The Borders of Germany in the Twentieth Century 965
29–9 The Commonwealth of Independent States 968
30–1 The Growth of the European Union 1008

PREFACE

The years since the publication of the Tenth Edition of *The Western Heritage* have produced significant changes that present new and serious challenges to the West and the rest of the world. The most striking of these changes is in the economy. In 2008, a serious financial crisis produced a deep recession that diminished the widespread economic growth and prosperity of the West and much of the world and threatened to produce the political instability that usually accompanies economic upheaval. By 2012, the European Union, long an economic powerhouse, felt the threat to its currency and the solvency of its weaker members. The United States also suffered a severe setback, and the recovery from its recession was the slowest in decades. There seems to be little agreement as to solutions to the problem within or among the nations of the West and even less willingness to make the sacrifices that might be necessary.

In the realms of international relations and politics, the United States and its European friends and allies pursued mixed policies. The war in Iraq, which some had thought lost, took a sharp turn in 2008 when the Americans changed their approach, that was popularly called "the surge," introducing a sharply increased military force and a new counter-insurgence strategy. It was so successful that the Western allies chose to withdraw their combat troops and leave the remaining fighting to the new Iraqi government. With fewer troops and a less clear commitment the Americans undertook a similar "surge" using a similar plan in Afghanistan. The effort met with considerable success, but the prospect of continued fighting and diminishing support by the engaged Western powers left the future of their efforts to clear the region of terrorist bases uncertain.

New challenges arose in still another area involving important Western interests: the Middle East. Insurrections against well-established autocracies in Libya and Egypt drew support in different degrees from members of NATO. Both nations succeeded in removing dictatorial rulers, but the character of the new regimes and their relationship with the West remains uncertain.

The authors of this volume continue to believe that the heritage of Western civilization remains a major point of departure for understanding and defining the challenges of our time. The spread of its interests and influence throughout the world has made the West a crucial part of the world's economy and a major player on the international scene. This book aims to introduce its readers to the Western heritage so that they may be better-informed and more culturally sensitive citizens of the increasingly troubled and challenging global age.

Since *The Western Heritage* first appeared, we have sought to provide our readers with a work that does justice to the richness and variety of Western civilization and its many complexities. We hope that such an understanding of the West will foster lively debate about its character, values, institutions, and global influence. Indeed, we believe such a critical outlook on their own culture has characterized the peoples of the West since the dawn of history. Through such debates we define ourselves and the values of our culture. Consequently, we welcome the debate and hope that *The Western Heritage*, Eleventh Edition, can help foster an informed discussion through its history of the West's strengths and weaknesses and the controversies surrounding Western history. To further that debate, we have included an introductory essay entitled "What Is the Western Heritage?" to introduce students to the concept of the West and to allow instructors and students to have a point of departure for debating this concept in their course of study.

We also believe that any book addressing the experience of the West must also look beyond its historical European borders. Students reading this book come from a wide variety of cultures and experiences. They live in a world of highly interconnected economies and instant communication between cultures. In this emerging multicultural society it seems both appropriate and necessary to recognize how Western civilization has throughout its history interacted with other cultures, both influencing and being influenced by them. For this reason, there is a chapter that focuses on the nineteenth-century European age of imperialism. Further examples of Western interaction with other parts of the world, such as with Islam, appear throughout the text. To further highlight the theme of cultural interaction, *The Western Heritage* includes a series of comparative essays, "The West & the World."

In this edition as in past editions, our goal has been to present Western civilization fairly, accurately, and in a way that does justice to this great, diverse legacy of human enterprise. History has many facets, no single one of which can alone account for the others. Any attempt to tell the story of the West from a single overarching perspective, no matter how timely, is bound to neglect or suppress some important parts of this story. Like all other authors of introductory texts, we have had to make choices, but we have attempted to provide the broadest possible introduction to Western civilization.

▾ Goals of the Text

Our primary goal has been to present a strong, clear, narrative account of the central developments in Western history. We have also sought to call attention to certain critical themes:

- The capacity of Western civilization, from the time of the Greeks to the present, to transform itself through self-criticism.
- The development in the West of political freedom, constitutional government, and concern for the rule of law and individual rights.
- The shifting relations among religion, society, and the state.
- The development of science and technology and their expanding impact on Western thought, social institutions, and everyday life.
- The major religious and intellectual currents that have shaped Western culture.

We believe that these themes have been fundamental in Western civilization, shaping the past and exerting a continuing influence on the present.

Flexible Presentation *The Western Heritage*, Eleventh Edition, is designed to accommodate a variety of approaches to a course in Western civilization, allowing instructors to stress what is most important to them. Some instructors will ask students to read all the chapters. Others will select among them to reinforce assigned readings and lectures. We believe the documents as well as the "Encountering the Past" and "A Closer Look" features may also be adopted selectively by instructors for purposes of classroom presentation and debate and as the basis for short written assignments.

Integrated Social, Cultural, and Political History *The Western Heritage* provides one of the richest accounts of the social history of the West available today, with strong coverage of family life, the changing roles of women, and the place of the family in relation to broader economic, political, and social developments. This coverage reflects the explosive growth in social historical research in the past half-century, which has enriched virtually all areas of historical study.

We have also been told repeatedly by instructors that no matter what their own historical specialization, they believe that a political narrative gives students an effective tool to begin to understand the past. Consequently, we have sought to integrate such a strong political narrative with our treatment of the social, cultural, and intellectual factors in Western history.

We also believe that religious faith and religious institutions have been fundamental to the development of the West. No other survey text presents so full an account of the religious and intellectual development of the West. People may be political and social beings, but they are also reasoning and spiritual beings. What they think and believe are among the most important things we can know about them. Their ideas about God, society, law, gender, human nature, and the physical world have changed over the centuries and continue to change. We cannot fully grasp our own approach to the world without understanding the religious and intellectual currents of the past and how they have influenced our thoughts and conceptual categories. We seek to recognize the impact of religion in the expansion of the West, including the settlement of the Americas in the sixteenth century and the role of missionaries in nineteenth-century Western imperialism.

Clarity and Accessibility Good narrative history requires clear, vigorous prose. As with earlier editions, we have paid careful attention to our writing, subjecting every paragraph to critical scrutiny. Our goal has been to make the history of the West accessible to students without compromising vocabulary or conceptual level. We hope this effort will benefit both instructors and students.

▼ The Eleventh Edition

New to This Edition

- This edition is closely tied to the innovative website, the New MyHistoryLab, which helps you save time and improve results as you study history (www.myhistorylab.com). MyHistoryLab icons connect the main narrative in each chapter of the book to a powerful array of MyHistoryLab resources, including primary source documents, analytical video segments, interactive maps, and more. A MyHistoryLab Media Assignments feature now appears at the end of each chapter, capping off the study resources for the chapter. The New MyHistoryLab also includes both eBook and Audio Book versions of *The Western Heritage*, Eleventh Edition, so that you can read or listen to your textbook any time you have access to the Internet.
- New with this Eleventh Edition: *The Western Heritage* now uses the latest release of the New MyHistoryLab, which offers the most advanced Study Plan ever. You get personalized Study Plans for each chapter, with content arranged from less complex thinking—like remembering facts—to more complex critical thinking—like understanding connections in history and analyzing primary sources. Assessments and learning applications in the Study Plan link you directly to *The Western Heritage* eBook for reading and review.
- For the Eleventh Edition, the authors welcome Alison Frank, professor of history at Harvard University. Alison Frank is interested in transnational approaches to the history of Central and Eastern Europe, particularly the Habsburg Empire and its successor states in the nineteenth and twentieth centuries. Other interests include the Eastern Alps, the Mediterranean slave trade, and environmental history.

Here are just some of the changes that can be found in the Eleventh Edition of *The Western Heritage:*

Chapter 1

- **Expanded coverage** of the eventual demise of the Hittite kingdom.
- **New Closer Look:** Babylonian World Map

Chapter 2

- **New Document:** Husband and Wife in Homer's Troy

Chapter 3

- **New Document:** Plutarch Cites Archimedes and Hellenistic Science

Chapter 5

- **New Document:** Mark Describes the Resurrection of Jesus

Chapter 6

- **Revised and reorganized the sections** on "The Byzantine Empire," "Islam and the Islamic World," and "On the Eve of the Frankish Ascendancy" to create a narrative flow that is more logical from a historical perspective.
- **Expanded coverage** of the Byzantine Empire.
- **Revised introductions** to the sections on "Islam and the Islamic World" and "Western Society and the Church" in accordance with the overall reorganization of the chapter.
- **New Documents:** Justinian on Slavery, The Carolingian Manor, The Character and "Innovations" of Justinian and Theodora

Chapter 7

- **New Document:** The English Nobility Imposes Restraints on King John
- **New feature** comparing Romanesque and Gothic architecture

Chapter 8

- **Section on schools and universities in the 12th century** has been revised with additional detail included.
- **Coverage of medieval parenting** has been revised in accordance with the most recent scholarship.
- **New Documents:** The Services of a Serf, Philip II Augustus Orders Jews out of France, Student Life at the University of Paris

Chapter 9

- **Expanded coverage** of the Black Death.
- **New Documents:** Boccaccio Describes the Ravages of the Black Death in Florence, Propositions of John Wycliffe Condemned at London, 1382, and at the Council of Constance, 1415
- **New Closer Look** feature examining a burial scene for Black Death victims from a 1349 manuscript entitled *Annals of Gilles de Muisit*

Chapter 10

- **Expanded coverage** of the art and culture of the Italian Renaissance.
- **Expanded coverage** of Northern Renaissance art.
- **Expanded coverage** of Machiavelli.
- **New Documents:** Vasari's Description of Leonardo da Vinci, Machiavelli Discusses the Most Important Trait for a Ruler, Erasmus Describes the Philosophy of Christ

Chapter 11

- **New Documents:** Calvin on Predestination, The Obedience and Power of the Jesuits

Chapter 12

- **New Document:** The Destruction of Magdeburg, May 1631

Chapter 13

- **New Document:** An Account of the Execution of Charles I

Chapter 14

- **New Document:** Man: A Mean between Nothing and Everything

Chapter 16

- **Expanded coverage** of slavery and racism as well as the wars of the mid-eighteenth century.
- **New Document:** Thomas Paine's "Common Sense"

Chapter 17

- **Extensive new coverage** of Enlightenment attitudes toward Islam and a new discussion of Immanuel Kant and his ideas.
- **Expanded coverage** of the philosophes, particularly in regard to patronage.
- **Revised discussion** of the Jewish Enlightenment.
- **New Document:** Du Châtelet Explains Happiness Scientifically

Chapter 18

- **New coverage** of U.S. attitudes toward the French Revolution.
- **Expanded coverage** of taxation by the monarchy, particularly in regard to its impact on peasants.
- **New Closer Look** feature focusing on a late eighteenth-century cartoon satirizing the French social and political structure
- **New Document:** A Nation at Arms

Chapter 19

- **Coverage of the Haitian Revolution was moved** from Chapter 20 to Chapter 19 in the new edition.
- **A new discussion** of Mary Godwin Shelley.
- **Expanded coverage** of the Romantic movement and its origins, with a particular focus on writers of the period, and expanded coverage of British naval supremacy as evidenced during the Battle of Trafalgar.
- **New Documents:** Napoleon Announces His Seizure of Power, Mary Shelley Remembers the Birth of a Monster, A Polish Legionnaire Recalls Guerilla Warfare in Spain [part of the **Compare & Connect** feature]

Chapter 20

- **The entire chapter** has been completely reorganized to create a more logical sequence of topics.
- **Coverage of Classical Economics was moved** from Chapter 21 to Chapter 20 in the new edition.
- **New coverage** of the relationship of nationalism to liberalism.
- **New Document:** John Stuart Mill Advocates Independence
- **New Closer Look** feature focusing on the painting titled *The Insurrection of the Decembrists at Senate Square, St. Petersburg on 14th December, 1825,* by Karl Kolman

Chapter 21

- **Expanded coverage** of the revolutions that occurred in 1848 and of nationalist movements.
- **New Document:** A Czech Nationalist Defends the Austrian Empire

Chapter 22

- **Expanded coverage** of the aftermath of the Crimean War and of Italian and German unification, and greatly expanded coverage of the Habsburg Empire.
- **New Map** of Crimea has been added to the chapter
- **New Map** showing nationalities within the Habsburg Empire has been added to the chapter
- **New Document:** Mark Twain Describes the Austrian Parliament
- **New Closer Look** feature focusing on a painting by Albert Rieger titled *The Suez Canal*

Chapter 23

- **New subsection** on the influence of the British Suffrage movement abroad, particularly in the United States.
- **Expanded coverage** of women and gender.
- **New Documents:** Praise and Concerns Regarding Railway Travel, A Doctor Learns How to Prevent Childbed Fever

Chapter 24

- Darwin's significance in regard to thought about **evolution and natural selection** is placed within a more realistic context by emphasizing predecessors and contemporaries that arrived at similar conclusions.
- **Expanded coverage** of the *Kulturkampf* in Germany.
- **Coverage of the Dreyfus Affair** was moved from Chapter 22 to Chapter 24 in the new edition.
- **New Document:** Herzl Advocates Jewish Nationalism
- **New Closer Look** feature examining the 19th century revival in popular religiosity, and in particular in the practice of pilgrimage

Chapter 25

- **New section on** women's involvement in missionary activity.
- **Expanded coverage** of the Berlin Conference and of U.S. efforts to acquire the rights to build and control the Panama Canal.
- **New Document:** Gandhi Questions the Value of English Civilization

Chapter 26

- **Greatly expanded coverage of World War I**, including new military technology used during the war, increased opportunities for women on the home front, and increased government involvement in domestic economies to address shortages and inflation.
- **New Document:** The Austrian Ambassador Gets a "Blank Check" from the Kaiser

Chapter 27

- **New Document:** Hitler Denounces the Versailles Treaty

Chapter 28

- **Greatly expanded coverage of the domestic front** during World War II, particularly regarding government involvement in private affairs.
- **New Document:** Winston Churchill Warns of the Effects of the Munich Agreement

Chapter 29

- **Expanded coverage** of the ideological differences between the Soviet Union and the United States that formed the basis of the Cold War.

Chapter 30

- **New section** on the European debt crisis.
- **Increased focus on women** throughout the chapter.
- **Greater emphasis** on social issues after 1991.
- **Updated and expanded coverage** of European population trends.
- **New Document:** Voices from Chernobyl

- **New Compare & Connect** feature: Muslim Women Debate France's Ban on the Veil—Mona Eltahawy Argues Women's Rights Trump Cultural Relativism and Kenza Drider Defends Her Right to Wear the Veil in Public
- **New Closer Look** feature focuses on the Nameless Library in Vienna
- A list of **Learning Objectives** now opens each chapter.
- A list of **Key Terms** has been added at the end of each chapter. These are important terms that are bold in the narrative and defined in the Glossary at the end of the book.
- **Suggested Readings were updated** throughout the text.

▼ A Note on Dates and Transliterations

This edition of *The Western Heritage* continues the practice of using B.C.E. (before the common era) and C.E. (common era) instead of B.C. (before Christ) and A.D. (anno Domini, the year of the Lord) to designate dates. We also follow the most accurate currently accepted English transliterations of Arabic words. For example, today *Koran* has been replaced by the more accurate *Qur'an*; similarly *Muhammad* is preferable to *Mohammed* and *Muslim* to *Moslem*.

▼ Ancillary Instructional Materials

Instructors using this text can visit the Instructor's Resource Center online at www.pearsonhighered.com/irc in order to download text-specific materials, such as the Instructor's Resource Manual, Test Item File, MyTest, and PowerPoint™ presentations.

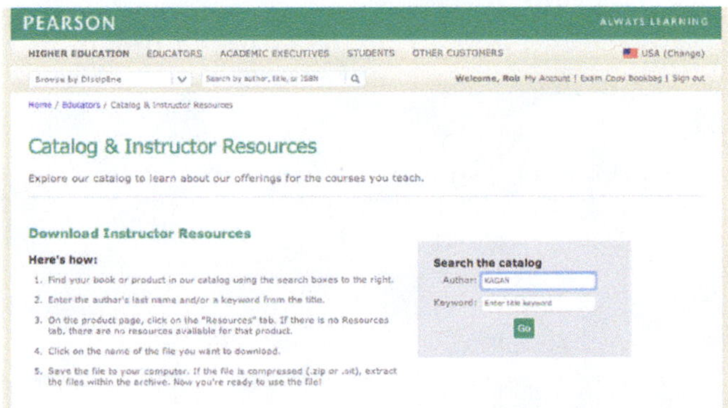

▼ Acknowledgments

We are grateful to the scholars and instructors whose thoughtful and often detailed comments helped shape this revision: Patricia Behre, Fairfield University; Hans Broedel, University of North Dakota; Dorothea Browder, Western Kentucky University; Edward Cade, Lakeland Community College; Amy Colon, Sullivan County Community College; Jean Glockler, Moraine Valley Community College; Joseph Gonzalez, Truckee Meadows Community College; Derrick Griffey, Gadsden State Community College; Sigrun Haude, University of Cincinnati; David Mock, Tallahassee Community College; Patricia O'Neill, Central Oregon Community College; Sonia Tandon, Forsyth Technical Community College; and Margarita Youngo, Pima Community College.

We would like to thank the dedicated people who helped produce this new edition. Our acquisitions editor, Jeff Lasser; our project manager, Rob DeGeorge; our production liaison, Barbara Mack; Maria Lange, our art director, and Liz Harasymcuk, who created the beautiful new interior and cover design of this edition; Alan Fischer, our operations specialist; and Karen Berry, production editor.

D.K.
S.O.
F.M.T.
A.F.

SUPPLEMENTS FOR QUALIFIED COLLEGE ADOPTERS	SUPPLEMENTS FOR STUDENTS

MyHistoryLab™

MyHistoryLab (www.myhistorylab.com)

The moment you know

Educators know it. Students know it. It's that inspired moment when something that was difficult to understand suddenly makes perfect sense. Our MyLab products have been designed and refined with a single purpose in mind: to help educators create that moment of understanding with their students.

Supplements for Qualified College Adopters	Supplements for Students
Annotated Instructor's eText Housed in the instructor's space within MyHistoryLab, the Annotated Instructor's eText for *The Western Heritage*, Eleventh Edition, leverages the powerful Pearson eText platform to make it easier than ever for instructors to access subject-specific resources for class preparation, providing access to the resources below:	**CourseSmart** www.coursemart.com CourseSmart is an exciting new choice for students looking to save money. As an alternative to purchasing the printed textbook, students can purchase an electronic version of the same content. With a CourseSmart eTextbook, students can search the text, make notes online, print out reading assignments that incorporate lecture notes, and bookmark important passages for later review. For more information, or to purchase access to the CourseSmart eTextbook, visit www.coursesmart.com
The Instructor's Resource Manual Available at the Instructor's Resource Center, at www.pearsonhighered.com/irc, the Instructor's Resource Manual contains a chapter summary, a chapter outline with references to the MyHistoryLab resources cited in the text, learning objectives from the text, key topics, class discussion questions, lecture topics, information on audiovisual resources that can be used in developing and preparing lecture presentations, and the MyHistoryLab Media Assignments feature found at the end of each chapter in the text.	***Books à la Carte*** Books à la Carte editions feature the exact same content as the traditional printed text in a convenient, three-hole-punched, loose-leaf version at a discounted price—allowing you to take only what you need to class. Books à la Carte editions are available both with and without access to MyHistoryLab.
The Test Item File Available at the Instructor's Resource Center, at www.pearsonhighered.com/irc, the Test-Item File contains a diverse set of 2,400 multiple choice, short answer, and essay questions, supporting a variety of assessment strategies. The large pool of multiple-choice questions for each chapter includes factual, conceptual, and analytical questions, so that instructors may assess students on basic information as well as critical thinking.	***Primary Source: Documents in Western Civilization* DVD** This DVD-ROM offers a rich collection of textual and visual—many never before available to a wide audience—and serves as an indispensable tool for working with sources. Extensively developed with the guidance of historians and teachers, *Primary Source: Documents in Western Civilization* includes over 800 sources in Western civilization history—from cave art, to text documents, to satellite images of Earth from space. All sources are accompanied by headnotes and focus questions and are searchable by topic, region, or theme. In addition, a built-in tutorial guides students through the process of working with documents. The DVD can be bundled with *The Western Heritage*, Eleventh Edition, at no charge. Please contact your Pearson sales representative for ordering information. (ISBN 0-13-134407-2)
MyTest Available at www.pearsonmytest.com, the MyTest program helps instructors easily create and print quizzes and exams. Questions and tests can be authored online, allowing instructors ultimate flexibility and the ability to manage assessments anytime, anywhere! Instructors can easily access existing questions and edit, create, and store using simple drag-and-drop and Word-like controls.	 Titles from the renowned **Penguin Classics** series can be bundled with *The Western Heritage*, Eleventh Edition, for a nominal charge. Please contact your Pearson sales representative for details.

SUPPLEMENTS FOR QUALIFIED COLLEGE ADOPTERS	SUPPLEMENTS FOR STUDENTS
PowerPoint Presentations Available at the Instructor's Resource Center, at www.pearsonhighered.com/irc, the PowerPoint slides to accompany *The Western Heritage*, Eleventh Edition, include a lecture outline for each chapter and full-color illustrations and maps from the textbook. All images from the textbook have captions from the book that provide background information about the image.	***Library of World Biography Series*** www.pearsonhighered.com/educator/series/Library-of-World-Biography/10492.page Each interpretive biography in the Library of World Biography Series focuses on a person whose actions and ideas either significantly influenced world events or whose life reflects important themes and developments in global history. Titles from the series can be bundled with *The Western Heritage*, Eleventh Edition, for a nominal charge. Please contact your Pearson sales representative for details.
	 ***The Prentice Hall Atlas of Western Civilization,* Second Edition** Produced in collaboration with Dorling Kindersley, the leader in cartographic publishing, the updated second edition of *The Prentice Hall Atlas of Western Civilization* applies the most innovative cartographic techniques to present western civilization in all of its complexity and diversity. Copies of the atlas can be bundled with *The Western Heritage*, Eleventh Edition, for a nominal charge. Contact your Pearson Arts and Sciences sales representative for details. (ISBN 0-13-604246-5)
	***Lives and Legacies: Biographies in Western Civilization,* Second Edition** Extensively revised, *Lives and Legacies* includes brief, focused biographies of 60 individuals whose lives provide insight into the key developments of Western civilization. Each biography includes an introduction, pre-reading questions, and suggestions for additional reading.
	A Guide to Your History Course: What Every Student Needs to Know Written by Vincent A. Clark, this concise, spiral-bound guidebook orients students to the issues and problems they will face in the history classroom. Available at a discount when bundled with *The Western Heritage*, Eleventh Edition. (ISBN 0-13-185087-3)
	***A Short Guide to Writing about History,* Seventh Edition** Written by Richard Marius, late of Harvard University, and Melvin E. Page, Eastern Tennessee State University, this engaging and practical text helps students get beyond merely compiling dates and facts. Covering both brief essays and the documented resource paper, the text explores the writing and researching processes, identifies different modes of historical writing, including argument, and concludes with guidelines for improving style. (ISBN 0-13-205-67370-8)

ABOUT THE AUTHORS

DONALD KAGAN is Sterling Professor of History and Classics at Yale University, where he has taught since 1969. He received his A.B. degree in history from Brooklyn College, his M.A. in classics from Brown University, and his Ph.D. in history from Ohio State University. During 1958 to 1959 he studied at the American School of Classical Studies as a Fulbright Scholar. He has received three awards for undergraduate teaching at Cornell and Yale. He is the author of a history of Greek political thought, *The Great Dialogue* (1965); a four-volume history of the Peloponnesian war, *The Origins of the Peloponnesian War* (1969); *The Archidamian War* (1974); *The Peace of Nicias and the Sicilian Expedition* (1981); *The Fall of the Athenian Empire* (1987); a biography of Pericles, *Pericles of Athens and the Birth of Democracy* (1991); *On the Origins of War* (1995); and *The Peloponnesian War* (2003). He is coauthor, with Frederick W. Kagan, of *While America Sleeps* (2000). With Brian Tierney and L. Pearce Williams, he is the editor of *Great Issues in Western Civilization*, a collection of readings. He was awarded the National Humanities Medal for 2002 and was chosen by the National Endowment for the Humanities to deliver the Jefferson Lecture in 2004.

STEVEN OZMENT is McLean Professor of Ancient and Modern History at Harvard University. He has taught Western Civilization at Yale, Stanford, and Harvard. He is the author of twelve books, including *When Fathers Ruled: Family Life in Reformation Europe* (1983). *The Age of Reform, 1250–1550* (1980) won the Schaff Prize and was nominated for the 1981 National Book Award. Five of his books have been selections of the History Book Club: *Magdalena and Balthasar: An Intimate Portrait of Life in Sixteenth Century Europe* (1986), *Three Behaim Boys: Growing Up in Early Modern Germany* (1990), *Protestants: The Birth of a Revolution* (1992), *The Burgermeister's Daughter: Scandal in a Sixteenth Century German Town* (1996), and *Flesh and Spirit: Private Life in Early Modern Germany* (1999). His most recent publications are *Ancestors: The Loving Family of Old Europe* (2001), *A Mighty Fortress: A New History of the German People* (2004), "Why We Study Western Civ," *The Public Interest, 158* (2005), and *The Serpent and the Lamb: Cranach, Luther, and the Making of the Reformation* (2011).

FRANK M. TURNER was John Hay Whitney Professor of History at Yale University and Director of the Beinecke Rare Book and Manuscript Library at Yale University, where he served as University Provost from 1988 to 1992. He received his B.A. degree from the College of William and Mary and his Ph.D. from Yale. He received the Yale College Award for Distinguished Undergraduate Teaching. He directed a National Endowment for the Humanities Summer Institute. His scholarly research received the support of fellowships from the National Endowment for the Humanities, the Guggenheim Foundation, and the Woodrow Wilson Center. He is the author of *Between Science and Religion: The Reaction to Scientific Naturalism in Late Victorian England* (1974); *The Greek Heritage in Victorian Britain* (1981), which received the British Council Prize of the Conference on British Studies and the Yale Press Governors Award; *Contesting Cultural Authority: Essays in Victorian Intellectual Life* (1993); and *John Henry Newman: The Challenge to Evangelical Religion* (2002). He also contributed numerous articles to journals and served on the editorial advisory boards of *The Journal of Modern History*, *Isis*, and *Victorian Studies*. He edited *The Idea of a University*, by John Henry Newman (1996), *Reflections on the Revolution in France by Edmund Burke* (2003), and *Apologia Pro Vita Sua and Six Sermons* by John Henry Newman (2008). He served as a Trustee of Connecticut College from 1996–2006. In 2003, Professor Turner was appointed Director of the Beinecke Rare Book and Manuscript Library at Yale University.

ALISON FRANK is Professor of History at Harvard University. She is interested in transnational approaches to the history of Central and Eastern Europe, particularly the Habsburg Empire and its successor states in the nineteenth and twentieth centuries. Her first book, *Oil Empire: Visions of Prosperity in Austrian Galicia* (2005), was awarded the Barbara Jelavich Book Prize, the Austrian Cultural Forum Book Prize, and was co-winner of the Polish Studies Association's Orbis Prize in Polish Studies. Her current book project, *Invisible Empire: A New Global History of Austria*, focuses on the Adriatic port city of Trieste and the Habsburg monarchy's participation in global commerce in the long nineteenth century. Other interests include the Eastern Alps, the Mediterranean slave trade, and environmental history. She is Associate Director of the Center for History and Economics at Harvard University.

WHAT IS THE WESTERN HERITAGE?

This book invites students and instructors to explore the Western Heritage. What is that heritage? The Western Heritage emerges from an evolved and evolving story of human actions and interactions, peaceful and violent, that arose in the eastern Mediterranean, then spread across the western Mediterranean into northern Europe, and eventually to the American continents, and in their broadest impact, to the peoples of Africa and Asia as well.

The Western Heritage as a distinct portion of world history descends from the ancient Greeks. They saw their own political life based on open discussion of law and policy as different from that of Mesopotamia, Persia, and Egypt, where kings ruled without regard to public opinion. The Greeks invented the concept of citizenship, defining it as engagement in some form of self-government. Furthermore, through their literature and philosophy, the Greeks established the conviction, which became characteristic of the West, that reason can shape and analyze physical nature, politics, and morality.

The city of Rome, spreading its authority through military conquest across the Mediterranean world, embraced Greek literature and philosophy. Through their conquests and imposition of their law, the Romans created the Western world as a vast empire stretching from Egypt and Syria in the east to Britain in the west. Although the Roman Republic, governed by a Senate and popular political institutions, gave way after civil wars to the autocratic rule of the Roman Empire, the idea of a free republic of engaged citizens governed by public law and constitutional arrangements limiting political authority survived centuries of arbitrary rule by emperors. As in the rest of the world, the Greeks, the Romans, and virtually all other ancient peoples excluded women and slaves from political life and tolerated considerable social inequality.

In the early fourth century C.E., the Emperor Constantine reorganized the Roman Empire in two fundamental ways that reshaped the West. First, he moved the imperial capital from Rome to Constantinople (Istanbul), establishing separate emperors in the East and West. Thereafter, large portions of the Western empire became subject to the rulers of Germanic tribes. In the confusion of these times, most of the texts embodying ancient philosophy, literature, and history became lost in the West, and for centuries Western Europeans were intellectually severed from that ancient heritage, which would later be recovered in a series of renaissances, or cultural rebirths, beginning in the eighth century.

Constantine's second fateful major reshaping of the West was his recognition of Christianity as the official religion of the empire. Christianity had grown out of the ancient monotheistic religion of the Hebrew people living in ancient Palestine. With the ministry of Jesus of Nazareth and the spread of his teachings by the Apostle Paul, Christianity had established itself as one of many religions in the empire. Because Christianity was monotheistic, Constantine's official embrace of it led to the eradication of pagan polytheism. Thereafter, the West became more or less coterminous with Latin Christianity, or that portion of the Christian Church acknowledging the Bishop of Rome as its head.

As the emperors' rule broke down, bishops became the effective political rulers in many parts of Western Europe. But the Christian Church in the West never governed without negotiation or conflict with secular rulers, and religious law never replaced secular law. Nor could secular rulers govern if they ignored the influence of the church. Hence from the fourth century C.E. to the present day, rival claims to political and moral authority between ecclesiastical and political officials have characterized the West.

In the seventh century the Christian West faced a new challenge from the rise of Islam. This new monotheistic religion originating in the teachings of the prophet Muhammad arose on the Arabian Peninsula and spread through rapid conquests across North Africa and eventually into Spain, turning the Mediterranean into what one historian has termed "a Muslim lake." Between the eleventh and the thirteenth centuries, Christians attempted to reclaim the Holy Land from Muslim control in church-inspired military crusades that still resonate negatively in the Islamic world.

It was, however, in the Muslim world that most of the texts of ancient Greek and Latin learning survived and were studied, while intellectual life languished in the West. Commencing in the twelfth century, knowledge of those texts began to work its way back into Western Europe. By the fourteenth century, European thinkers redefined themselves and their intellectual ambitions by recovering the literature and science from the ancient world, reuniting Europe with its Graeco-Roman past.

From the twelfth through the eighteenth centuries, a new European political system slowly arose based on centralized monarchies characterized by large armies, navies, and bureaucracies loyal to the monarch, and by the capacity to raise revenues. Whatever the personal ambitions of individual rulers, for the most part these monarchies recognized both the political role of local or national assemblies drawn from the propertied elites and the binding power of constitutional law on themselves. Also, in each of these monarchies, church officials and church law played important roles in public life. The monarchies, their military, and their expanding commercial economies became the basis for the extension of European and Western influence around the globe.

In his painting *The School of Athens*, the great Italian Renaissance painter Raphael portrayed the ancient Greek philosopher Plato and his student, Aristotle, engaged in debate. Plato, who points to the heavens, believed in a set of ideal truths that exist in their own realm distinct from the earth. Aristotle urged that all philosophy must be in touch with lived reality and confirms this position by pointing to the earth. Such debate has characterized the intellectual, political, and social experience of the West. Indeed, the very concept of "Western Civilization" has itself been subject to debate, criticism, and change over the centuries. © Scala/Art Resource, NY

In the late fifteenth and early sixteenth centuries, two transforming events occurred. The first was the European discovery and conquest of the American continents, thus opening the Americas to Western institutions, religion, and economic exploitation. Over time the labor shortages of the Americas led to the forced migration of millions of Africans as slaves to the "New World." By the mid-seventeenth century, the West consequently embraced the entire transatlantic world and its multiracial societies.

Second, shortly after the American encounter, a religious schism erupted within Latin Christianity. Reformers rejecting both many medieval Christian doctrines as unbiblical and the primacy of the Pope in Rome established Protestant churches across much of northern Europe. As a consequence, for almost two centuries religious warfare between Protestants and Roman Catholics overwhelmed the continent as monarchies chose to defend one side or the other. This religious turmoil meant that the Europeans who conquered and settled the Americas carried with them particularly energized religious convictions, with Roman Catholics dominating Latin America and English Protestants most of North America.

By the late eighteenth century, the idea of the West denoted a culture increasingly dominated by two new forces. First, science arising from a new understanding of nature achieved during the sixteenth and seventeenth centuries persuaded growing numbers of the educated elite that human beings can rationally master nature for ever-expanding productive purposes improving the health and well-being of humankind. From this era to the present, the West has been associated with advances in technology, medicine, and scientific research. Second, during the eighteenth century, a drive for economic improvement that vastly increased agricultural production and then industrial manufacturing transformed economic life, especially in Western Europe and later the United States. Both of these economic developments went hand in hand with urbanization and the movement of the industrial economy into cities where the new urban populations experienced major social dislocation.

During these decades certain West European elites came to regard advances in agricultural and manufacturing economies that were based on science and tied to commercial expansion as "civilized" in contrast to cultures that lacked those characteristics. From these ideas emerged the concept of Western Civilization defined to suggest that peoples dwelling outside Europe or inside Europe east of the Elbe River were less than civilized. Whereas Europeans had once defined themselves against the rest of the world as free citizens and then later as Christians, they now defined themselves as "civilized." Europeans would carry this self-assured superiority into their nineteenth- and early twentieth-century encounters with the peoples of Asia, Africa, and the Pacific.

During the last quarter of the eighteenth century, political revolution erupted across the transatlantic world. The British colonies of North America revolted. Then revolution occurred in France and spread across much of Europe. From 1791 through 1830, the Wars of Independence liberated Latin America from its European conquerors. These revolutions created bold new modes of political life, rooting the legitimacy of the state in some form of popular government and generally written constitutions. Thereafter, despite the presence of authoritarian governments on the European continent, the idea of the West, now including the new republics of the United States and Latin America, became associated with liberal democratic governments.

Furthermore, during the nineteenth century, most major European states came to identify themselves in terms of nationality—language, history, and ethnicity—rather than loyalty to a monarch. Nationalism eventually inflamed popular opinion and unloosed unprecedented political ambition by European governments.

These ambitions led to imperialism and the creation of new overseas European empires in the late nineteenth century. For the peoples living in European-administered Asian and African colonies, the idea and reality of the West embodied foreign domination and often disadvantageous involvement in a world economy. When in 1945 the close of World War II led to a sharp decline in European imperial authority, colonial peoples around the globe challenged that authority and gained independence. These former colonial peoples, however, often still suspected the West of seeking to control them. Hence, anticolonialism like colonialism before it redefined definitions of the West far from its borders.

Late nineteenth-century nationalism and imperialism also unleashed with World War I in 1914 unprecedented military hostilities among European nations that spread around the globe, followed a quarter century later by an even greater world war. As one result of World War I, revolution occurred in Russia with the establishment of the communist Soviet Union. During the interwar years a Fascist Party seized power in Italy and a Nazi Party took control of Germany. In response to these new authoritarian regimes, West European powers and the United States identified themselves with liberal democratic constitutionalism, individual freedom, commercial capitalism, science and learning freely pursued, and religious liberty, all of which they defined as the Western Heritage. During the Cold War, conceived of as an East-West, democratic versus communist struggle that concluded with the collapse of the Soviet Union in 1991, the Western Powers led by the United States continued to embrace those values in conscious opposition to the Soviet government, which since 1945 had also dominated much of Eastern Europe.

Since 1991 the West has again become redefined in the minds of many people as a world political and economic order dominated by the United States. Europe clearly remains the West, but political leadership has moved to North America. That American domination and recent American foreign policy have led throughout the West and elsewhere to much criticism of the United States.

Such self-criticism itself embodies one of the most important and persistent parts of the Western Heritage. From the Hebrew prophets and Socrates to the critics of European imperialism, American foreign policy, social inequality, and environmental devastation, voices in the West have again and again been raised to criticize often in the most strident manner the policies of Western governments and the thought, values, social conditions, and inequalities of Western societies.

Consequently, we study the Western Heritage not because the subject always or even primarily presents an admirable picture, but because the study of the Western Heritage like the study of all history calls us to an integrity of research, observation, and analysis that clarifies our minds and challenges our moral sensibilities. The challenge of history is the challenge of thinking, and it is to that challenge that this book invites its readers.

QUESTIONS

1. How have people in the West defined themselves in contrast with civilizations of the ancient East, and later in contrast with Islamic civilization, and still later in contrast with less economically developed regions of the world? Have people in the West historically viewed their own civilization to be superior to civilizations in other parts of the world? Why or why not?
2. How did the Emperor Constantine's adoption of Christianity as the official religion of the Roman Empire change the concept of the West? Is the presence of Christianity still a determining characteristic of the West?
3. How has the geographical location of what has been understood as the West changed over the centuries?

4. In the past two centuries Western nations established empires around the globe. How did these imperial ventures and the local resistance to them give rise to critical definitions of the West that contrasted with the definitions that had developed in Europe and the United States? How have those non-Western definitions of the West contributed to self-criticism within Western nations?
5. How useful is the concept of Western civilization in understanding today's global economy and global communications made possible by the Internet? Is the idea of Western civilization synonymous with the concept of modern civilization? Do you think the concept of the West will once again be redefined ten years from now?

To view a video of the authors discussing the Western heritage, go to www.myhistorylab.com

MyHistoryLab™

THE WESTERN HERITAGE

On July 14, 1789, crowds stormed the Bastille, a prison in Paris. This event, whose only practical effect was to free a few prisoners, marked the first time the populace of Paris redirected the course of the revolution. Anonymous, France, eighteenth century, Siege of the Bastille, 14 July, 1789. Musée de la Ville de Paris, Musée Carnavalet, Paris, France. Bridgeman—Giraudon/Art Resource, NY

Listen to the **Chapter Audio** on **MyHistoryLab.com**

18

The French Revolution

▼ **The Crisis of the French Monarchy**
The Monarchy Seeks New Taxes • Necker's Report • Calonne's Reform Plan and the Assembly of Notables • Deadlock and the Calling of the Estates General

▼ **The Revolution of 1789**
The Estates General Becomes the National Assembly • Fall of the Bastille • The "Great Fear" and the Night of August 4 • The Declaration of the Rights of Man and Citizen • The Parisian Women's March on Versailles

▼ **The Reconstruction of France**
Political Reorganization • Economic Policy • The Civil Constitution of the Clergy • Counterrevolutionary Activity

▼ **The End of the Monarchy: A Second Revolution**
Emergence of the Jacobins • The Convention and the Role of the *Sans-culottes*

▼ **Europe at War with the Revolution**
Edmund Burke Attacks the Revolution • Suppression of Reform in Britain • The Second and Third Partitions of Poland, 1793, 1795

▼ **The Reign of Terror**
War with Europe • The Republic Defended • The "Republic of Virtue" and Robespierre's Justification of Terror • Repression of the Society of Revolutionary Republican Women • De-Christianization • Revolutionary Tribunals • The End of the Terror

▼ **The Thermidorian Reaction**
Establishment of the Directory • Removal of the *Sans-culottes* from Political Life

▼ **In Perspective**

LEARNING OBJECTIVES

How did the financial weakness of the French monarchy lay the foundations of revolution in 1789?

How did the calling of the Estates General lead to revolution?

How did the National Constituent Assembly reorganize France?

What led to the radicalization of the French Revolution?

How did Europe respond to the French Revolution?

How did war and ideology combine to create the Reign of Terror?

What course did the French Revolution take after 1794?

IN THE SPRING of 1789 political turmoil erupted in France. By the summer it had led to a revolution that marked the beginning of a new political order in France and eventually throughout the West. The French Revolution brought to the foreground the principles of civic equality and popular sovereignty that challenged the major political and social institutions of Europe and that in evolving forms have continued to shape and reshape Western political and social life to the present day. During the

1790s the forces the revolution unleashed would cause small-town provincial lawyers and Parisian street orators to exercise more influence over the fate of the Continent than aristocrats, royal ministers, or monarchs. Citizen armies commanded by people of modest origin and filled by conscripted village youths would defeat armies composed of professional soldiers led by officers from the nobility. The king and queen of France, as well as thousands of French peasants and shopkeepers, would be executed. The existence of the Roman Catholic faith in France and indeed of Christianity itself would be challenged. Finally, Europe would embark on almost a quarter century of war that would eventually extend across the continent and result in millions of casualties.

▼ The Crisis of the French Monarchy

Although the French Revolution would shatter many of the political, social, and ecclesiastical structures of Europe, its origins lay in a much more mundane problem. By the late 1780s, thanks in large part to the expenditures associated with supporting the American revolution, the French royal government could not command sufficient taxes to finance itself. The monarchy's unsuccessful search for adequate revenues led it into ongoing conflicts with aristocratic and ecclesiastical institutions. Eventually, the resulting deadlock was so complete that Louis XVI and his ministers were required to summon the French Estates General, which had not met since 1614. Once the deputies to that body gathered, a new set of issues and problems quickly emerged that led to the revolution itself. Yet, none of this would have occurred if the monarchy had not reached a state of financial crisis that meant it could no longer function within the limits and practices of existing political institutions.

The Monarchy Seeks New Taxes

The French monarchy emerged from the Seven Years' War (1756–1763) defeated, deeply in debt, and unable thereafter to put its finances on a sound basis. French support of the American revolt against Great Britain further deepened the financial difficulties of the government. On the eve of the revolution, the interest and payments on the royal debt amounted to just over one-half of the entire budget. Given the economic vitality of France, the debt was neither overly large nor disproportionate to the debts of other European powers. The problem lay with the inability of the royal government to tap the nation's wealth through taxes to service and repay the debt. Paradoxically, France was a rich nation in which the inability to collect sufficient taxes led to an impoverished government. Peasants, who had the least to spare, bore the heaviest tax burden. They paid taxes not only to the king, but also to the church and their local lords. A bad harvest in 1788 meant that peasants were not only impoverished, but also in danger of starvation as bread prices soared. Without increased taxation on the aristocracy and the church, there was no way that taxation of peasants alone could resolve France's financial crisis.

The debt was symptomatic of the failure of the late-eighteenth-century French monarchy to come to terms with the political power of aristocratic institutions and, in particular, the *parlements*. As explained in Chapter 13, French absolutism had always involved a process of ongoing negotiation between the monarchy and local aristocratic interests. This process had become more difficult after the death of Louis XIV (r. 1643–1715) when the aristocracy had sought to reclaim parts of the influence it had lost. Nonetheless, for the first half of the century, the monarchy had retained most of its authority.

For twenty-five years after the Seven Years' War, however, a standoff occurred between the monarchy and the aristocracy, as one royal minister after another attempted to devise new tax schemes that would tap the wealth of the nobility, only to be confronted by opposition from both the *Parlement* of Paris and provincial *parlements*. Both Louis XV (r. 1715–1774) and Louis XVI (r. 1774–1792) lacked the character, resolution, and political skills to resolve the dispute. In place of a consistent policy for dealing with the growing debt and aristocratic resistance to change, the monarchy hesitated, retreated, and even lied.

Well-meaning, but weak and vacillating, Louis XVI (r. 1774–1792) stumbled from concession to concession until he finally lost all power to save his throne. Joseph Siffred Duplessis (1725–1802), *Louis XVI*. Versailles, France. Photograph copyright Bridgeman—Giraudon/Art Resource, NY

In 1770, Louis XV appointed René Maupeou (1714–1792) as chancellor. The new minister was determined to increase taxes on the nobility. He abolished the *parlements* and exiled their members to different parts of the country. He then began an ambitious program to make the administration more efficient. However, when Louis XV died of smallpox in 1774, his successor, Louis XVI, attempted to regain popular support by dismissing Maupeou, restoring all the *parlements*, and confirming their old powers.

Although the *parlements* spoke for aristocratic interests, they appear to have enjoyed public support. By the second half of the eighteenth century, many French nobles shared with the wealthy professional and commercial classes similar goals for administrative reforms that would support economic growth. Both groups regarded the lumbering institutions of monarchical absolutism as a burden. Moreover, throughout these initial and later disputes with the monarchy, the *parlements*, though completely dominated by the aristocracy, used the language of liberty and reform to defend their cause. They portrayed the monarchy as despotic—that is, as acting arbitrarily in defiance of the law. Here they drew on the ideas and arguments of many Enlightenment writers, such as Montesquieu and the physiocrats, discussed in Chapter 17.

View the **Closer Look** "Challenging the French Political Order" on **MyHistoryLab.com**

The monarchy was unable to rally public opinion to its side because it had lost much of its moral authority. Louis XVI was considered detached and ineffective. His wife, Marie Antoinette (1755–1793), was always suspect because of her Austrian background. She was viciously accused of sexual misconduct and personal extravagance in an underground pamphlet campaign that became increasingly prurient, misogynist, and xenophobic. Furthermore, Louis XVI and his family continued to live at Versailles, rarely leaving its grounds to mix with his subjects and with the aristocracy, who now, unlike in the days of Louis XIV, often dwelled in Paris or on their estates. Hence, the French monarch stood at a distinct popular disadvantage in his clashes first with the *parlements* and later with other groupings of the aristocracy.

In all these respects, the public image and daily reality of the French monarchy were much more problematical than those of other contemporary monarchs. Frederick II of Prussia and Joseph II of Austria genuinely saw themselves, and were seen by their subjects, as patriotic servants of the state. In central Europe, rulers were often themselves the generators of reform, which meant even criticism of current policy was generally combined with confidence in the monarchy's ability to correct any errors. George III of Great Britain, despite all his political difficulties, was regarded by most Britons as having a model character and as seeking the economic improvement of his nation. Frederick II, Joseph II, and George III all had reputations for personal frugality, and they moved frequently among the people they governed.

Necker's Report

France's successful intervention on behalf of the American colonists against the British only worsened the financial problems of Louis XVI's government. By 1781, as a result of the aid to America, its debt was larger, and its sources of revenues were unchanged. The new royal director-general of finances, Jacques Necker (1732–1804), did not want to admit that the situation was as bad as was feared. Necker, a Swiss banker, produced a public report in 1781 that used a financial sleight of hand to downplay France's financial difficulties. He argued that if the expenditures for the American war were removed, the budget was in surplus. Necker's report also revealed that a large portion of royal expenditures went to pensions for aristocrats and other royal court favorites. Necker was pressured to leave office not because of his dubious accounting, but because court aristocratic circles were embarrassed by his revelations. The damage had already been done: Necker's misleading assessment of French finances made it more difficult for government officials to claim a real need to raise new taxes.

Calonne's Reform Plan and the Assembly of Notables

The monarchy hobbled along without a plan for financial improvement until 1786. By this time, Charles Alexandre de Calonne (1734–1802) was the minister of finance. Calonne proposed to encourage internal trade, to lower some taxes, such as the *gabelle* on salt, and to transform the *corvée*, peasants' labor services on public works, into money payments. He also sought to remove internal barriers to trade and reduce government regulation of the grain trade. More importantly, Calonne wanted to introduce a new land tax that all landowners would have to pay regardless of their social status. If this tax had been imposed, the monarchy could have abandoned other indirect taxes. The government would also have had less need to seek additional taxes that required approval from the aristocratically dominated *parlements*. Calonne also intended to establish new local assemblies made up of landowners to approve land taxes; in these assemblies the voting power would have depended on the amount of land a person owned rather than on his social status. All these proposals would have undermined both the political and the social power of the French aristocracy. Other of his proposals touched the economic privileges of the French Church. These policies reflected much advanced economic and administrative thinking of the day.

The monarchy, however, had little room to maneuver. The creditors were at the door, and the treasury was nearly empty. Calonne needed public support for such bold new undertakings. In February 1787, he met with an Assembly of Notables, nominated by the royal ministry from the upper ranks of the aristocracy and the church, to seek support for his plan. The Assembly adamantly refused to give it. There was some agreement that reform and greater fairness in taxation were necessary, but the Assembly did not trust the information they had received from Calonne. In his place they called for the reappointment of Necker, who they believed had left the country in sound fiscal condition. Finally, they claimed that only the Estates General of France, a medieval institution that had not met since 1614, could consent to new taxes. The notables believed that calling the Estates General, which had been traditionally organized to allow aristocratic and church dominance, would actually allow the nobility to have a direct role in governing the country alongside the monarchy. The issue was less the nobility not wishing to reform tax structure than its determination to acquire power at the expense of the monarchy and to direct reforms itself.

Deadlock and the Calling of the Estates General

Again, Louis XVI backed off. He replaced Calonne with Étienne Charles Loménie de Brienne (1727–1794), archbishop of Toulouse and the chief opponent of Calonne at the Assembly of Notables. Once in office, Brienne found, to his astonishment, that the financial situation was as bad as his predecessor had asserted. Brienne himself now sought to reform the land tax. The *Parlement* of Paris, however, in its self-appointed role as the embodiment of public opinion, took the new position that it lacked authority to authorize the tax and that only the Estates General could do so. Shortly thereafter, Brienne appealed to the Assembly of the Clergy to approve a large subsidy to fund that part of the debt then coming due for payment. The clergy, like the *Parlement* dominated by aristocrats, not only refused the subsidy, but also reduced the voluntary contribution, or *don gratuit*, that it paid to the government in lieu of taxes.

As these unfruitful negotiations were taking place at the center of political life, local aristocratic *parlements* and estates in the provinces were making their own demands. They wanted to restore the privileges they had enjoyed during the early seventeenth century, before Richelieu and Louis XIV had crushed their independence. Furthermore, bringing the financial crisis to a new point of urgency, in the summer of 1788 bankers refused to extend necessary short-term credit to the government. Consequently, in July 1788, the king, through Brienne, agreed to convoke the Estates General the next year. Brienne resigned, and Necker replaced him. Some kind of political reform was coming, but what form it would take and how it would happen would be largely determined by the conflicts that emerged from summoning the Estates General.

▼ The Revolution of 1789

The Estates General Becomes the National Assembly

The Estates General had been called because of the political deadlock between the French monarchy and the vested interests of aristocratic institutions and the church. Almost immediately after it was summoned, however, the three groups, or estates, represented within it clashed with each other. The First Estate was the clergy, the Second Estate the nobility, and the **Third Estate** was, theoretically, all other adult men in the kingdom, although its representatives were drawn primarily from wealthy members of the commercial and professional middle classes. All the representatives in the Estates General were men. During the widespread public discussions preceding the meeting of the Estates General, representatives of the Third Estate made it clear they would not permit the monarchy and the aristocracy to decide the future of the nation.

Read the Document "Petition of Women of the Third Estate" on **MyHistoryLab.com**

A comment by a priest, the Abbé Siéyès (1748–1836), in a pamphlet published in 1789, captures the spirit of the Third Estate's representatives: "What is the Third Estate? Everything. What has it been in the political order up to the present? Nothing. What does it ask? To become something."[1] The spokesmen for the Third Estate became more determined to assert their role less from any preexisting conflicts with the nobility than from the conflicts that emerged during the debates and electioneering for the Estates General in late 1788 and early 1789.

Read the Document "Emmanuel Joseph Sieyès, *What Is the Third Estate?*" on **MyHistoryLab.com**

Debate Over Organization and Voting Before the Estates General gathered, a public debate over its proper organization drew the lines of basic disagreement. The aristocracy made two important attempts to limit the influence of the Third Estate. First, a reconvened Assembly of Notables demanded that each estate have an equal number of representatives. Second, in September 1788, the *Parlement* of Paris ruled that voting in the Estates General should be conducted by order, or estate, rather than by head—that is, each estate in the Estates General, rather than each individual member, should have

[1]Leo Gershoy, *The French Revolution and Napoleon* (New York: Appleton-Century-Crofts, 1964), p. 102.

one vote. This procedure would in all likelihood have ensured the aristocratically dominated First and Second Estates could always outvote the Third by a vote of two estates to one estate. Both moves raised doubt about the aristocracy's previously declared concern for French liberty. Spokesmen for the Third Estate immediately denounced the arrogant claims of the aristocracy, which seemed only concerned to protect its own privilege.

In many respects the interests of the aristocracy and the most prosperous and well-educated members of the Third Estate had converged during the eighteenth century, and many nobles had spouses from wealthy families of the Third Estate. Yet a fundamental social distance separated the members of the two orders. Many aristocrats were much richer than members of the Third Estate, and noblemen had all but monopolized the high command in the army and navy. The Third Estate had also experienced various forms of political and social discrimination from the nobility. The resistance of the nobility to voting by head confirmed the suspicions and resentments of the members of the Third Estate, who tended to be well-off, but not enormously rich, lawyers. The stance of both the reconvened Assembly of Notables and the *Parlement* of Paris regarding the composition and functioning of the forthcoming Estates General meant that the elected members of the Third Estate would approach the gathering with a newly awakened profound distrust of the nobility and of the aristocratically dominated church.

Doubling the Third In the face of widespread public uproar over the aristocratic effort to dominate composition and procedures of the Estates General, the royal council eventually decided that strengthening the Third Estate would best serve the interests of the monarchy and the cause of fiscal reform. In December 1788, the council announced the Third Estate would elect twice as many representatives as either the nobles or the clergy. This so-called doubling of the Third Estate meant it could easily dominate the Estates General if voting proceeded by head rather than by order. The council correctly assumed that liberal nobles and clergy would support the Third Estate, confirming that, despite social differences, these groups shared important interests and reform goals. The method of voting had not yet been decided when the Estates General gathered at Versailles in May 1789.

The *Cahiers de Doléances* When the representatives came to the royal palace, they brought with them *cahiers de doléances*, or lists of grievances, registered by the local electors, to be presented to the king. Many of these lists have survived and provide considerable information about the state of France on the eve of the revolution. The documents criticized government waste, indirect taxes, church taxes and corruption, and the hunting rights of the aristocracy. They included calls for periodic meetings of the Estates General, more equitable taxes, more local control of administration, unified weights and measures to facilitate trade and commerce, and a free press. The overwhelming demand of the *cahiers* was for equality of rights among the king's subjects. Yet it is also clear that the *cahiers* that originated among the nobility were not radically different from those of the Third Estate. There was broad agreement that the French government needed major reform, that greater equality in taxation and other matters was desirable, and that many aristocratic privileges must be abandoned. (See the Document "The Third Estate of a French City Petitions the King," page 555.) The *cahiers* drawn up before May 1789 indicate that the three estates could have cooperated to reach these goals. But it became clear almost from the moment the Estates General opened that conflict among the estates, rather than cooperation, was to be the rule.

Read the **Document** "French Peasants, Cahiers de doléances (Grievances) (France), 1789" on **MyHistoryLab.com**

The Third Estate Creates the National Assembly The complaints, demands, and hopes for reform expressed in the *cahiers* could not, however, be discussed until the questions of the organization and voting in the Estates General had been decided. From the beginning, the Third Estate, whose members consisted largely of local officials, professionals, and other persons of property, refused to sit as a separate order as the king desired. For several weeks there was a standoff. Then, on June 1, the Third Estate invited the clergy and the nobles to join them in organizing a new legislative body. A few priests did so. On June 17, that body declared itself the National Assembly, and on June 19 by a narrow margin, the Second Estate voted to join the Assembly.

The Tennis Court Oath At this point, Louis X VI hoped to reassert a role in the proceedings. He intended to call a "Royal Session" of the Estates General for June 23 and closed the room where the National Assembly had been gathering. On June 20, finding themselves thus unexpectedly locked out of their usual meeting place, the National Assembly moved to a nearby indoor tennis court. There, its members took an oath to continue to sit until they had given France a constitution. This was the famous Tennis Court Oath. Louis XVI ordered the National Assembly to desist, but many clergy and nobles joined the Assembly in defiance of the royal command.

View the **Image** "Oath of the Tennis Court" on **MyHistoryLab.com**

On June 27, the king, now having completely lost control of the events around him, capitulated and formally requested the First and Second Estates to meet with the National Assembly, where voting would occur by head rather than by order. Because of the doubling of its membership, the Third Estate had twice

Document

THE THIRD ESTATE OF A FRENCH CITY PETITIONS THE KING

In the spring of 1789 representatives to the Estates General brought to Versailles cahiers de doléances *which were lists of grievances generated during the election process. (See page 554.) This particular* cahier *originated in Dourdan, a city in central France, and reflects the complaints of the Third Estate. The first two articles refer to the organization of the Estates General. The other articles ask the king to grant various forms of equality before the law and in taxation. Most of the cahiers of the Third Estate included these demands for equality.*

Which of the following petitions relate to political rights and which to economic equality? The slogan most associated with the French Revolution was "Liberty, Equality, Fraternity." Which of these petitions represents each of these values?

The order of the third estate of the City . . . of Dourdan . . . supplicates [the king] to accept the grievances, complaints, and remonstrances which it is permitted to bring to the foot of the throne, and to see therein only the expression of its zeal and the homage of its obedience.

It wishes:

1. That his subjects of the third estate, equal by such status to all other citizens, present themselves before the common father without other distinction which might degrade them.
2. That all the orders, already united by duty and common desire contribute equally to the needs of the State, also deliberate in common concerning its needs.
3. That no citizen lose his liberty except according to law: that, consequently, no one be arrested by virtue of special orders, or, if imperative circumstances necessitate such orders that the prisoner be handed over to regular courts of justice within forty-eight hours at the latest.

12. That every tax, direct or indirect, be granted only for a limited time, and that every collection beyond such term be regarded as peculation, and punished as such.

15. That every personal tax be abolished; that thus the capitation [a poll tax] and the taille [tax from which nobility and clergy were exempt] and its accessories be merged with the *vingtièmes* [an income tax] in a tax on land and real or nominal property.
16. That such tax be borne equally, without distinction, by all classes of citizens and by all kinds of property, even feudal . . . rights.
17. That the tax substituted for the *corvée* be borne by all classes of citizens equally and without distinction. That said tax, at present beyond the capacity of those who pay it and the needs to which it is destined, be reduced by at least one-half.

as many members as either of the other estates that joined them. Had nothing further occurred, the government of France would already have been transformed. Henceforth, the monarchy could govern only in cooperation with the National Assembly, and the National Assembly would not be a legislative body organized according to privileged orders. The National Assembly, which renamed itself the National Constituent Assembly because of its intention to write a new constitution, was composed of a majority of members drawn from all three orders, who shared liberal goals for the administrative, constitutional, and economic reform of the country. The revolution in France against government by privileged hereditary orders, however, rapidly extended beyond events occurring at Versailles.

This painting of the Tennis Court Oath, June 20, is by Jacques-Louis David (1748–1825). In the center foreground are members of different estates joining hands in cooperation as equals. The presiding officer is Jean-Sylvain Bailly, soon to become mayor of Paris. Jacques-Louis David, *Oath of the Tennis Court, the 20th of June 1789*. Chateaux de Versailles et de Trianon, Versailles, France. Bridgeman–Giraudon/Art Resource, NY

Fall of the Bastille

Two new forces soon intruded on the scene. First, Louis XVI again attempted to regain the political initiative by mustering royal troops near Versailles and Paris. On the advice of Queen Marie Antoinette, his brothers, and the most conservative aristocrats at court, he seemed to be contemplating the use of force against the National Constituent Assembly. On July 11, without consulting Assembly leaders, Louis abruptly dismissed Necker, his minister of finance. Louis's gathering troops and dismissal of Necker marked the beginning of a steady, but consistently poorly executed, royal attempt to undermine the Assembly and halt the revolution. Most of the National Constituent Assembly wished to establish some form of constitutional monarchy, but from the start, Louis's refusal to cooperate thwarted that effort. The king fatally decided to throw in his lot with the conservative aristocracy against the emerging forces of reform drawn from across the social and political spectrum.

The second new factor to impose itself on the events at Versailles was the populace of Paris, which numbered more than 600,000 people. The mustering of royal troops created anxiety in the city, where throughout the winter and spring of 1789 high prices for bread, which was the staple food of the poor, had produced riots. Those Parisians who had elected representatives to the Third Estate had continued to meet after the elections. By June they were organizing a citizen militia and collecting arms. They regarded the dismissal of Necker as the opening of a royal offensive against the National Constituent Assembly and the city. They intended to protect the Assembly and the revolution had begun.

On July 14, large crowds of Parisians, most of them small shopkeepers, tradespeople, artisans, and wage earners, marched to the Bastille to get weapons for the militia. This great fortress, with ten-foot-thick walls, had once held political prisoners. Through miscalculations and ineptitude by the governor of the fortress, the troops in the Bastille fired into the crowd, killing ninety-eight people and wounding many others. Thereafter, the crowd stormed the fortress. They released the seven prisoners inside, none of whom was a political prisoner, and killed several troops and the governor.

On July 15, the militia of Paris, by then called the National Guard, offered its command to a young liberal aristocrat, the Marquis de Lafayette (1757–1834). This hero of the American Revolution gave the guard a new insignia: the red and blue stripes from the colors of the coat of arms of Paris, separated by the white stripe of the royal flag. The emblem became the revolutionary *cockade* (badge) and eventually the tricolor flag of revolutionary France.

The attack on the Bastille marked the first of many crucial *journées*, days on which the populace of Paris redirected the course of the revolution. The fall of the fortress signaled that the National Constituent Assembly alone would not decide the political future of the nation. As the news of the taking of the Bastille spread, similar disturbances took place in provincial cities. A few days later, Louis XVI again bowed to the force of events and personally visited Paris, where he wore the revolutionary *cockade* and recognized the organized electors as the legitimate government of the city. The king also recognized the National Guard and thus implicitly admitted that he lacked the military support to turn back the revolution. The citizens of Paris were, for the time being, satisfied. They also had established themselves as an independent political force with which other political groups might ally for their own purposes.

The "Great Fear" and the Night of August 4

Simultaneous with the popular urban disturbances, a movement known as the "Great Fear" swept across much of the French countryside. Rumors that royal troops would be sent into the rural districts intensified the peasant disturbances that had begun during the spring. The Great Fear saw the burning of *châteaux*, the destruction of legal records and documents, and the refusal to pay feudal dues. The peasants were determined to take possession of food supplies and land that they considered rightfully theirs. They vented their anger against the injustices of rural life and reclaimed rights and property they had lost through administrative tightening of the collection of feudal dues during the past century. Their targets were both aristocratic and ecclesiastical landlords.

View the **Map** "Map Discovery: Revolutionary France" on **MyHistoryLab.com**

On the night of August 4, 1789, aristocrats in the National Constituent Assembly attempted to halt the spreading disorder in the countryside. By prearrangement, several liberal nobles and clerics rose in the Assembly and renounced their feudal rights, dues, and tithes. In a scene of great emotion, they surrendered hunting and fishing rights, judicial authority, and legal exemptions. These nobles and clerics gave up what they had already lost and what they could not have regained without civil war in the rural areas. Many of them later received financial compensation for their losses. Nonetheless, after the night of August 4, all French citizens were subject to the same and equal laws. Furthermore, since the sale of government offices was also abolished, the events of that night opened political and military positions, careers, and advancement to talent rather than basing them exclusively on birth or wealth. This dramatic session of the Assembly effectively abolished the major social institutions of the Old Regime and created an unforeseen situation that required a vast legal and social reconstruction of the nation. Without those renunciations, the constructive work of the National Constituent Assembly would have been much more difficult and certainly much more limited. (See the Document "The National Assembly Decrees Civic Equality in France," page 560.)

Both the attack on the Bastille and the Great Fear displayed characteristics of the urban and rural riots that had occurred often in eighteenth-century France. Louis XVI first thought the turmoil over the Bastille was simply another bread riot. Indeed, the popular disturbances were only partly related to the events at Versailles. A deep economic downturn had struck France in 1787 and continued into 1788. The harvests for both years had been poor, and the food prices in 1789 were higher than at any time since 1703. Wages had not kept up with the rise in prices. Throughout the winter of 1788–1789, an unusually cold one, many people suffered from hunger. Wage and food riots had erupted in several cities. These economic problems fanned the fires of revolution.

The political, social, and economic grievances of many sections of the country became combined. The National Constituent Assembly could look to the popular forces as a source of strength against the king and the conservative aristocrats. When the various elements of the Assembly later quarreled among themselves, however, the resulting factions would appeal for support to the politically sophisticated and well-organized shopkeeping and artisan classes. They, in turn, would demand a price for their cooperation.

The Declaration of the Rights of Man and Citizen

In late August 1789, the National Constituent Assembly decided that before writing a new constitution, it should publish a statement of broad political principles. On August 27, the Assembly issued the Declaration of the Rights of Man and Citizen. This declaration drew on the political language of the Enlightenment and the Declaration of Rights that the state of Virginia had adopted in June 1776.

The French declaration proclaimed that all men were "born and remain free and equal in rights." The natural rights so proclaimed were "liberty, property, security, and resistance to oppression." Governments existed to protect those rights. All political sovereignty resided in the nation and its representatives. All citizens were to be equal before the law and were to be "equally admissible to all public dignities, offices, and employments, according to their capacity, and with no other distinction than that of their virtues and talents." There were to be due process of law and presumption of innocence until proof

A Closer
LOOK

View the Closer Look on MyHistoryLab.com

CHALLENGING THE FRENCH POLITICAL ORDER

THIS LATE-EIGHTEENTH-CENTURY cartoon satirizes the French social and political structure as the events and tensions leading up to the outbreak of the French Revolution unfolded. This image embodies the highly radical critique of the French political structure that erupted from about 1787 when the nobility and church refused to aid the financial crisis of the monarchy. It is one of a series of similar cartoons, most of which depict men. The caption reads "Long Live the King, Long Live the Nation. I always knew we would have our turn!" The image shows the way in which women participated in creating the new order, without addressing any specific "women's rights" agenda.

The caption expresses the separation between loyalty to the king and criticism of the abuses of the peasants blamed on the clergy and the aristocracy. Only after the calling of the Estates General was Louis XVI seen as siding with the church and nobility against the people.

Vive le Roi, Vive la Nation.
J'savois ben Qu'jaurions not tour.

Library of Congress

A peasant woman holding a distaff (a tool used in spinning) and simultaneously nursing a baby rides on the back of a noble woman. Her attire is simple and her shoes are wooden, indicating her peasant background. Her hat is adorned with a cockade in revolutionary colors.

The noblewoman clutches onto a nun for support, suggesting the collusion of aristocracy and church.

Can you tell if this image is meant to celebrate the peasantry's newfound power or lament it? What hints does the artist provide as to his or her sympathy?

Similar images involving men were very common. What does this image suggest about the role of women in the ancien régime and in the revolution?

What is the symbolic significance of the suckling infant?

The women of Paris marched to Versailles on October 5, 1789. Although they did not make any demands specific to women's rights, the mere sight of so many women expressing political demands alarmed the king and his supporters. The following day the royal family was forced to return to Paris with them. Henceforth, the French government would function under the constant threat of mob violence. Anonymous, eighteenth century, *To Versailles, to Versailles*. The women of Paris going to Versailles, 7 October, 1789. French. Musée de la Ville de Paris, Musée Carnavalet, Paris, France. Photograph copyright Bridgeman—Giraudon/Art Resource, NY

of guilt. Freedom of religion was affirmed. Taxation was to be apportioned equally according to the capacity to pay. Property constituted "an inviolable and sacred right."[2]

The Declaration of the Rights of Man and Citizen was directed in large measure against specific abuses of the old French monarchical and aristocratic regime, but it was framed in abstract universalistic language applicable to other European nations. In this respect, the ideas set forth in the declaration like those of the Protestant reformers three centuries earlier could jump across national borders and find adherents outside France. The two most powerful, universal political ideas of the declaration were civic equality and popular sovereignty. The first would challenge the legal and social inequities of European life, and the second would assert that governments must be responsible to the governed. These two principles, in turn, could find themselves in tension with the declaration's principle of the protection of property.

It was not accidental that the Declaration of the Rights of Man and Citizen specifically applied to men and not to women. As discussed in Chapter 17, much of the political language of the Enlightenment, and especially that associated with Rousseau, separated men and women into distinct gender spheres. According to this view, which influenced legislation during the revolution, men were suited for citizenship, women for motherhood and the domestic life. Nonetheless, in the charged atmosphere of the summer of 1789, many politically active and informed Frenchwomen hoped the guarantees of the declaration would be extended to them. They were particularly concerned with property, inheritance, family, and divorce. Some people saw in the declaration a framework within which women might eventually enjoy the rights and protection of citizenship. Those hopes would be disappointed during the years of the revolution and for many decades thereafter.

Nonetheless, over the succeeding two centuries the universalist language of the Declaration of the Rights of Man and Citizen would provide an intellectual framework for bringing into the realm of active civic life many groups who were excluded in the late eighteenth century. (See "Compare and Connect: The Declaration of the Rights of Man and Citizen Opens the Door for Disadvantaged Groups to Demand Equal Civic Rights," pages 564–565.)

The Parisian Women's March on Versailles

Louis XVI stalled before ratifying both the Declaration of the Rights of Man and Citizen and the aristocratic renunciation of feudalism. His hesitations fueled suspicions that he might again try to resort to

[2]Georges Lefebvre, *The Coming of the French Revolution*, trans. by R. R. Palmer (Princeton, NJ: Princeton University Press, 1967), pp. 221–223.

Document

THE NATIONAL ASSEMBLY DECREES CIVIC EQUALITY IN FRANCE

These famous decrees of August 4, 1789, in effect created civic equality in France. The special privileges previously possessed or controlled by the nobility were removed.

What institutions and privileges are included in "the feudal regime"? How do these decrees recognize that the abolition of some privileges and former tax arrangements will require new kinds of taxes and government financing to support religious, educational, and other institutions?

1. The National Assembly completely abolishes the feudal regime. It decrees that, among the rights and dues . . . all those originating in real or personal serfdom, personal servitude, and those which represent them, are abolished without indemnification; all other are declared redeemable, and that the price and mode of redemption shall be fixed by the National Assembly. . . .
2. The exclusive right to maintain pigeon-houses and dove-cotes is abolished. . . .
3. The exclusive right to hunt and to maintain unenclosed warrens is likewise abolished. . . .
4. All manorial courts are suppressed without indemnification.
5. Tithes of every description and the dues which have been substituted for [them] . . . are abolished on condition, however, that some other method be devised to provide for the expenses of divine worship, the support of the officiating clergy, the relief of the poor, repairs and rebuilding of churches and parsonages, and for all establishments, seminaries, schools, academies, asylums, communities, and other institutions, for the maintenance of which they are actually devoted. . . .
6. The sale of judicial and municipal offices shall be suppressed forthwith. . . .
7. Pecuniary privileges, personal or real, in the payment of taxes are abolished forever. . . .
8. All citizens, without distinction of birth, are eligible to any office or dignity, whether ecclesiastical, civil or military. . . .

From Frank Maloy Anderson, ed. and trans., *The Constitutions and Other Select Documents Illustrative of the History of France, 1789–1907*, 2nd ed., rev. and enl. (Minneapolis, MN: H. W. Wilson, 1908), pp. 11–13.

force. Moreover, bread remained scarce and expensive. On October 5, some 7,000 Parisian women armed with pikes, guns, swords, and knives marched to Versailles demanding more bread. They milled about the palace, and many stayed the night. Intimidated, the king agreed to sanction the decrees of the Assembly. The next day he and his family appeared on a balcony before the crowd. Deeply suspicious of the monarch and believing that he must be kept under the watchful eye of the people, the Parisians demanded that Louis and his family return to Paris with them. The monarch had no real choice. On October 6, 1789, his carriage followed the crowd into the city, where he and his family settled in the old palace of the Tuileries in the heart of Paris.

The National Constituent Assembly also soon moved to Paris. Thereafter, both Paris and France remained relatively stable and peaceful until the summer of 1792. A decline in the price of bread in late 1789 helped to calm the atmosphere.

▼ The Reconstruction of France

In Paris, the National Constituent Assembly set about reorganizing France. In government, it pursued a policy of constitutional monarchy; in administration, rationalism; in economics, unregulated freedom; and in religion, anticlericalism. Throughout its proceedings and following the principles of the Declaration of the Rights of Man and Citizen, the Assembly was determined to protect property in all its forms. The Assembly sought to limit the impact on the national life of those French people who had no property or only small amounts of it. Although championing civic equality before the law, the Assembly, with the aristocrats and middle-class elite united, spurned social equality and extensive democracy. It thus charted a general course that, to a greater or lesser degree, nineteenth-century liberals across Europe would follow.

Political Reorganization

In the Constitution of 1791, the National Constituent Assembly established a constitutional monarchy. The major political authority of the nation would be a unicameral Legislative Assembly, in which all laws would originate. The monarch was allowed a suspensive veto that could delay, but not halt, legislation. The Assembly also had the power to make war and peace.

Active and Passive Citizens The constitution provided for an elaborate system of indirect elections to thwart direct popular pressure on the government. The citizens of France were divided into active and passive categories. Only active citizens—that is, men paying annual taxes equal to three days of local labor wages—could vote. They chose electors, who then, in turn, voted for the members of the legislature. Further property qualifications were required to serve as an elector or member of the legislature. Only about 50,000 citizens of a population of about 25 million could qualify as electors or members of the Legislative Assembly. Women could neither vote nor hold office.

These constitutional arrangements effectively transferred political power from aristocratic wealth to all forms of propertied wealth in the nation. The accumulation of wealth from land and commercial property, not hereditary privilege or the purchase of titles or offices, would open the path to political authority. These new political arrangements based on property rather than birth reflected the changes in French society over the past century and allowed more social and economic interests to have a voice in governing the nation.

Olympe de Gouges's Declaration of the Rights of Woman The laws that excluded women from voting and holding office did not pass unnoticed. In 1791, Olympe de Gouges (d. 1793), a butcher's daughter from Montauban in northwest France who became a major revolutionary radical in Paris, composed a Declaration of the Rights of Woman, which she ironically addressed to Queen Marie Antoinette. Much of the document reprinted the Declaration of the Rights of Man and Citizen, adding the word *woman* to the various original clauses. That strategy demanded that women be regarded as citizens and not merely as daughters, sisters, wives, and mothers of citizens. Olympe de Gouges further outlined rights that would permit women to own property and require men to recognize the paternity of their children. She called for equality of the sexes in marriage and improved education for women. She declared, "Women, wake up; the *tocsin* of reason is being heard throughout the whole universe; discover your rights."[3] Her declaration illustrated how the simple listing of rights in the Declaration of the Rights of Man and Citizen created a structure of universal civic expectations even for those it did not cover. The National Assembly had established a set of values against which it could itself be measured. It provided criteria for liberty, and those to whom it had not extended full liberties could demand to know why and could claim the revolution was incomplete until they too enjoyed those freedoms. (See "Compare and Connect: The Declaration of the Rights of Man and Citizen Opens the Door for Disadvantaged Groups to Demand Equal Civic Rights," pages 564–565.)

Read the **Document** "Olympe de Gouges, Declaration of the Rights of Woman and the Female Citizen" on **MyHistoryLab.com**

Departments Replace Provinces In reconstructing the local and judicial administration, the National Constituent Assembly applied the rational spirit of the Enlightenment. It abolished the ancient French provinces, such as Burgundy and Brittany, and established in their place eighty-three administrative units called *départements* of generally equal size named after rivers, mountains, and other geographical features. The departments in turn were subdivided into districts, cantons, and communes. Elections for departmental and local assemblies were also indirect. This administrative reconstruction proved to be permanent. The departments still exist in twenty-first-century France. (See Map 18–1, p. 562.)

All the ancient judicial courts, including the seigneurial courts and the *parlements*, were also abolished and replaced by uniform courts with elected judges and prosecutors. Procedures were simplified, and the most degrading punishments, such as branding, torture, and public flogging, were outlawed.

Economic Policy

In economic matters, the National Constituent Assembly continued the policies Louis XVI's reformist ministers had formerly advocated. It suppressed the guilds and liberated the grain trade. The Assembly established the metric system to provide the nation with uniform weights and measures. (See "Encountering the Past: The Metric System," page 566.)

Workers' Organizations Forbidden The new policies of economic freedom and uniformity disappointed both peasants and urban workers. In 1789, the

[3]Sara E. Melzer and Leslie W. Rabine, eds., *Rebel Daughters: Women and the French Revolution* (New York: Oxford University Press, 1992), p. 88.

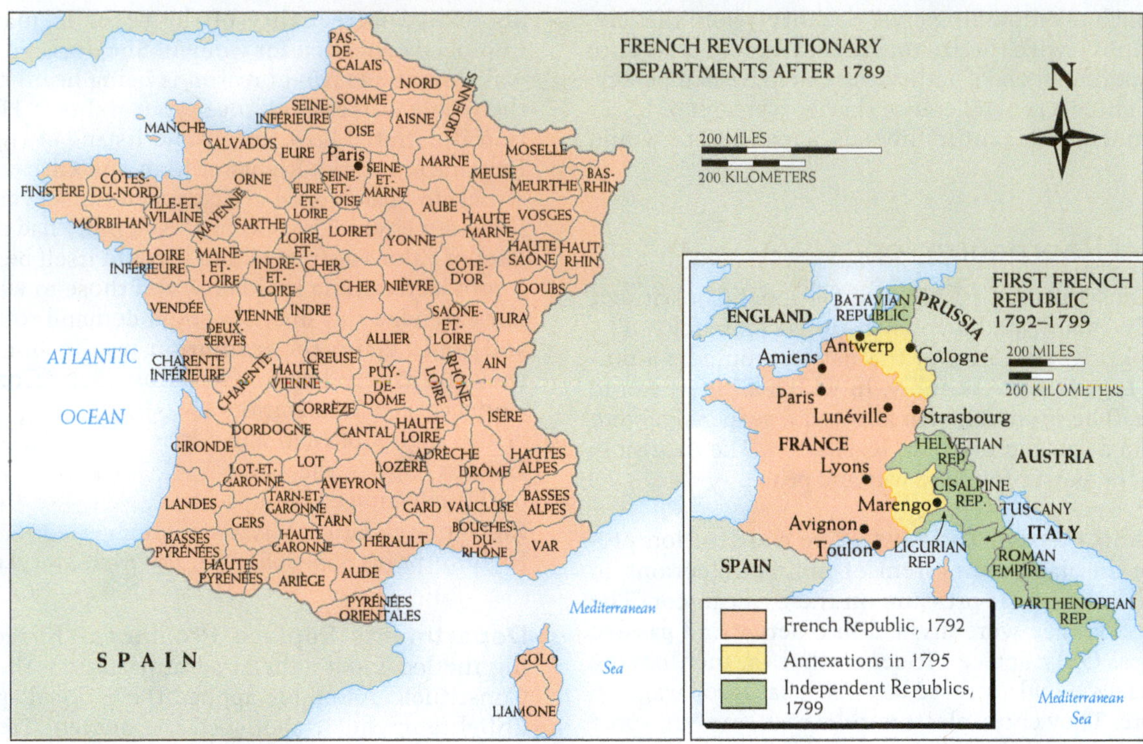

Map 18–1 **FRENCH PROVINCES AND THE REPUBLIC** In 1789, the National Constituent Assembly redrew the map of France. The ancient provinces were replaced with a larger number of new, smaller departments. This redrawing of the map was part of the Assembly's effort to impose greater administrative rationality in France.

Assembly placed the burden of proof on the peasants to rid themselves of the residual feudal dues for which compensation was to be paid. On June 14, 1791, the Assembly crushed the attempts of urban workers to protect their wages by enacting the Chapelier Law, which forbade workers' associations. The Assembly interpreted the efforts of workers to organize as a re-creation of the abolished guilds of the Old Regime and thus to oppose the new values of political and social individualism that the revolution championed. Peasants and workers were henceforth to be left to the freedom and mercy of the marketplace, without the protection of assocation.

Confiscation of Church Lands While these various reforms were being put into effect, the financial crisis that had occasioned the calling of the Estates General persisted. The Assembly did not repudiate the royal debt because it was owed to the bankers, the merchants, and the commercial traders of the Third Estate. The National Constituent Assembly had suppressed many of the old, hated indirect taxes (such as taxes on staples like salt, bread, and wine) and had substituted new land taxes, but these proved insufficient. Moreover, there were not enough officials to collect the new taxes, and many people simply evaded them in the general confusion of the day. The continuing financial problem led the Assembly to take what may well have been, for the future of French life and society, its most decisive action. The Assembly decided to finance the debt by confiscating and then selling the land and property of the Roman Catholic Church in France. The results were further inflation, religious schism, and civil war. In effect, the National Constituent Assembly had opened a new chapter in the relations of church and state in Europe.

The *Assignats* Having chosen to plunder the church, the Assembly authorized the issuance of *assignats*, or government bonds, in December 1789. Their value was guaranteed by the revenue to be generated from the sale of church property. Initially, a limit was set on the quantity of *assignats* to be issued. The bonds, however, proved so acceptable to the public that they began to circulate as currency. The Assembly decided to issue an ever-larger number of them to liquidate the national debt and to create a large body of new property owners with a direct stake in the revolution. Within a few

RÉPUBLIQUE 10000. FRANÇAISE
ASSIGNAT
de dix mille francs.
créé le 18 Nivôse l'an 3me. de la République.
Hypothéqué sur les DOMAINES NATIONAUX.
Numéro 153
10000
LA NATION RÉCOMPENSE LE DÉNONCIATEUR.
Série 224.
LA LOI PUNIT DE MORT LE CONTREFACTEUR.
10000
The *assignats* were government bonds that were backed by confiscated church lands. They circulated as money. When the government printed too many of them, inflation resulted and their value fell. Bildarchiv Preussischer Kulturbesitz

months, however, the value of the *assignats* began to fall and inflation increased, putting new stress on the urban poor. Fluctuation in the worth of this currency would plague the revolutionary government throughout the 1790s.

The Civil Constitution of the Clergy

The confiscation of church lands required an ecclesiastical reconstruction. In July 1790, the National Constituent Assembly issued the Civil Constitution of the Clergy, which transformed the Roman Catholic Church in France into a branch of the secular state. This legislation reduced the number of bishoprics from 135 to 83, making one diocese for each of the new departments. It also provided for the election of pastors and bishops, who henceforth became salaried employees of the state. The Assembly, which also dissolved all religious orders in France except those that cared for the sick or ran schools, consulted neither Pope Pius VI (r. 1775–1799) nor the French clergy about these sweeping changes. The king approved the measure only with the greatest reluctance.

The Civil Constitution of the Clergy was the major blunder of the National Constituent Assembly. It embittered relations between the French church and the state, a problem that has persisted to the present day. The measure immediately created immense opposition within the French church, even from bishops who had long championed Gallican liberties over papal domination. In the face of this resistance, the Assembly unwisely ruled that all clergy must take an oath to support the Civil Constitution. Only seven bishops and a little less than half the lower clergy did so. In reprisal, the Assembly designated those clergy who had not taken the oath as "refractory" and removed them from their clerical functions. Angry reactions were swift. Refractory priests celebrated Mass in defiance of the Assembly. In February 1791, Pope Pius VI condemned not only the Civil Constitution of the Clergy, but also the Declaration of the Rights of Man and Citizen. That condemnation marked the opening of a Roman Catholic offensive against the revolution and liberalism more broadly that continued throughout the nineteenth century. Within France itself, the pope's action created a crisis of conscience and political loyalty for all sincere Catholics. Religious devotion and revolutionary loyalty became incompatible for many people. French citizens were divided between those who supported the constitutional priests and those who, like the royal family, followed the refractory clergy.

Counterrevolutionary Activity

The revolution had other enemies besides the pope and devout Catholics. As it became clear that the old political and social order was undergoing fundamental and probably permanent change, many aristocrats, eventually over 16,000, left France. Known as the **émigrés**, they settled in countries near the French border, where they sought to foment counterrevolution. Among the most important of their number was the king's younger brother, the count of Artois (1757–1836). In the summer of 1791, his agents and the queen persuaded Louis XVI to attempt to flee the country.

Flight to Varennes On the night of June 20, 1791, Louis and his immediate family, disguised as servants, left Paris. They traveled as far as Varennes on their way to Metz in eastern France where a royalist military force was waiting for them. At Varennes the king was recognized, and his flight was halted. On June 24, a company of soldiers escorted the royal family back to Paris. Eventually the leaders of the National Constituent Assembly, determined to save the constitutional monarchy, announced the king had been abducted from the capital. This convenient public fiction could not cloak the reality that the king was now the chief counterrevolutionary in France and that the constitutional monarchy might not

The Declaration of the Rights of Man and Citizen Opens the Door for Disadvantaged Groups to Demand Equal Civic Rights

Read the **Compare and Connect** on **MyHistoryLab.com**

THE NATIONAL ASSEMBLY passed the Declaration of the Rights of Man and Citizen on August 26, 1789. The principles of the declaration were very broad and in theory could be extended beyond the domestic male French citizens to whom it applied. Within months various civically disadvantaged groups stepped forward to demand inclusion within the newly proclaimed realm of civic rights. These included free persons of color from the French Caribbean colony of St. Domingue and French women. It should be noted that during the same period French Jews also asked to have the principles of religious toleration proclaimed in the Declaration of the Rights of Man and Citizen extended to themselves.

QUESTIONS

1. **How does Raymond portray himself as free but still clearly victimized by the Assembly in St. Domingue, composed only of white members?**
2. **How does Raymond invoke the principles of the Declaration of the Rights of Man and Citizen to apply pressure on the French National Assembly?**
3. **What are the specific parallels that de Gouges draws between the rights of man and the rights of woman?**
4. **How does her declaration suggest civic responsibilities for women as well as rights?**
5. **On what grounds might the same people who championed the Declaration of the Rights of Man and Citizen in 1789 deny the extension of those rights to the various groups that soon demanded inclusion under the ideals of the declaration?**

I. A Free Person of Color from St. Domingue Demands Recognition of His Status

In the spring of 1791 Julian Raymond, a free person of color from the French Caribbean colony of St. Domingue (Haiti), petitioned the French National Assembly to recognize persons such as himself as free citizens. The National Assembly did so in May 1791 but later rescinded the decree. Only in March 1792 did the Assembly firmly recognize the civic equality of such persons. The background for the request and for the confusion of the French National Assembly over the matter was the eruption of the slave revolution in Haiti, which is discussed in Chapter 20.

Remaining to this day under the oppression of the white colonists, we dare hope that we do not ask the National Assembly in vain for the rights, which it has declared, belong to every man.

In our just protests, if the troubles, the calumnies that you have witnessed until today under the legislation of white colonists, and finally, if the truths which we had the honor of presenting yesterday to the bar of the Assembly do not overcome the unjust pretensions of the white colonial legislators who want to [proceed] without our participation, we beg the Assembly not to jeopardize the little remaining liberty we have, that of being able to abandon the ground soaked with the blood of our brothers and of permitting us to flee the sharp knife of the laws they will prepare against us.

If the Assembly has decided to pass a law which lets our fate depend on twenty-nine whites [in the colonial Assembly], our decided enemies, we demand to add an amendment to the decree which would be rendered in this situation, that free men of color can emigrate with their fortunes so that they can be neither disturbed nor hindered by the whites.

Mr. President, this is the last recourse which remains for us to escape the vengeance of the white colonists who menace us for not having given up our claims to the rights which the National Assembly has declared belong to every man. ■

From Laura Mason and Tracey Rizzo, *The French Revolution: A Document Collection* (Boston: Houghton Mifflin Company, 1999), p. 109.

II. Olympe de Gouges Issues a Declaration of the Rights of Woman

In September 1791 Olympe de Gouges published a Declaration of the Rights of Woman that paralleled in many respects the Declaration of the Rights of Man and Citizen proclaimed two years earlier. A self-educated woman and butcher's daughter, she had written widely on a number of reform topics. Radical as she was, she remained loyal to the monarchy and was eventually executed by the revolutionary government in 1793.

This is an example of the French Revolution–era clothing worn by the *Sans-culottes* or members of the poorer classes and their leaders. The outfit is comprised of the *pantalon* (long trousers), *carmagnole* (short-skirted coat), red cap of liberty, and *sabots* (wooden shoes). Dorling Kindersley Media Library/Mark Hamilton © Dorling Kindersley

Mothers, daughters, sisters [and] representatives of the nation demand to be constituted into a national assembly. . . . Consequently, the sex that is as superior in beauty as it is in courage during the sufferings of maternity recognizes and declares in the presence and under the auspices of the Supreme Being, the following Rights of Woman and of Female Citizens.

ARTICLE I

Woman is born free and lives equal to man in her rights. Social distinctions can be based only on the common utility.

ARTICLE II

The purpose of any political association is the conservation of the natural and imprescriptible rights of woman and man; these rights are liberty, property, security, and especially resistance to oppression.

ARTICLE III

The principle of all sovereignty rests essentially with the nation, which is nothing but the union of woman and man. . . .

ARTICLE IV

Liberty and justice consist of restoring all that belongs to others; thus, the only limits on the exercise of the natural rights of woman are perpetual male tyranny; these limits are to be reformed by the laws of nature and reason. . . .

ARTICLE VI

The law must be the expression of the general will; all female and male citizens must contribute either personally or through their representatives to its formation; it must be the same for all: male and female citizens, being equal in the eyes of the law, must be equally admitted to all honors, positions, and public employment according to their capacity and without other distinctions besides those of their virtues and talents. . . .

ARTICLE X

No one is to be disquieted for his very basic opinions; woman has the right to mount the scaffold; she must equally have the right to mount the rostrum, provided that her demonstrations do not disturb the legally established public order. . . .

ARTICLE XI

The free communication of thoughts and opinions is one of the most precious rights of woman, since that liberty assures the recognition of children by their fathers. Any female citizen thus may say freely, I am the mother of a child which belongs to you, without being forced by a barbarous prejudice to hide the truth. . . .

ARTICLE XIII

For the support of the public force and the expenses of administration, the contributions of woman and man are equal; she shares all the duties and all the painful tasks; therefore, she must have the same share in the distribution of positions, employment, offices, honors, and jobs. . . .

ARTICLE XVII

Property belongs to both sexes whether united or separate; for each it is an inviolable and sacred right; no one can be deprived of it, since it is the true patrimony of nature, unless the legally determined public need obviously dictates it, and then only with a just and prior indemnity.

POSTSCRIPT

Woman, wake up; the *tocsin* of reason is being heard throughout the whole universe; discover your rights. ■

From Darline Gay Levy, Harriet Branson Applewhite, and Mary Durham Johnson, eds., *Women in Revolutionary Paris, 1789–1795* (Urbana: University of Illinois Press, 1980), pp. 87–96.

ENCOUNTERING THE *Past*

THE METRIC SYSTEM

MUCH ABOUT THE era of the French Revolution seems alien to us today. One French regime followed another amidst confusion, violence, and bloodshed. Yet one thing that the revolutionaries did still touches the lives of most people in the world. In 1795, the French revolutionary government decreed a new standard for weights and measures—the metric system. The United States, Myanmar, and Liberia are currently the only countries in the world that have not officially adopted the metric system.

Inspired by the rationalism of the eighteenth-century Enlightenment, the metric system was intended to bring the order and simplicity of a system based on 10 to the chaos of different weights and measures used in the various regions of prerevolutionary France. For its adherents, the republic marked the dawn of a new era in human history in which the triumph of science would replace the reign of superstition and obscurity. A new system of uniform weights and measures would also further one of the revolutionaries' political goals: centralization. With one set of weights and measures in use throughout the country, France would be closer to becoming a single "indivisible" republic.

Astronomy, which relied on the rational application of mathematics to measure the heavens, provided the basis for the new system of distance or length. Astronomers had devised methods to measure the arch of meridians—the highest point reached by the sun—around the earth. The revolutionary authorities took the meridian in the latitude of Paris, which is 45°, as their standard for measuring the meter. The meter was to be one ten-millionth of one quarter of that meridian. All other measurements of length were then defined as decimal fractions or multiples of the meter.

1 centimeter (cm) = 10 millimeters (mm)
1 decimeter (dm) = 10 centimeters
1 meter = 100 centimeters
1 kilometer (km) = 1,000 meters

The standard for measuring weights was the gram, which constituted the weight of a cube of pure water measuring 0.01 meter on each side. Each measure of weight was defined as a decimal fraction or multiple of a gram. A kilogram is 1,000 grams.

The metric system was soon adopted by scientists, but in their everyday lives, the population of France clung to their old, familiar weights and measures. Change, however "rational," did not come easily and was resisted. In 1812, Napoleon, bowing to popular sentiment, brought back the old units, but in 1840, the French government reimposed the metric system. Thereafter, rationality—and convenience—triumphed, and by the close of the nineteenth century, the metric system was used throughout continental Europe and had been introduced into Latin America. In the twentieth century it was adopted throughout Asia and Africa.

Today, the United States remains the great exception. Despite efforts by scientists, engineers, and doctors, who all use the metric system in their work, people in the United States still prefer to measure in inches, feet, yards, and miles and to weigh in ounces and pounds.

Why did the French revolutionary government introduce the metric system?

How did the metric system reflect the ideas of the Enlightenment? Why has most of the world accepted this system?

Usage des Nouvelles Mesures.

1. le Litre (Pour la Pinte)
2. le Gramme (Pour la Livre)
3. le Mètre (Pour l'Aune)
4. l'Are (Pour la Toise)
5. le Franc (Pour une Livre Tournois)
6. le Stere (Pour la Demie Voie de Bois)

15 mars 1800

This 1800 print introduces the new measures adopted by law in France: the liter (volume), the gram (weight), the meter (length), the are (area), the franc (currency), the stere (volume). L.F. Labrousse, "Usage des nouvelles mesures," © The Art Gallery Collection/Alamy

In June 1791, Louis XVI and his family attempted to flee France. They were recognized in the town of Varennes, where their flight was halted and they were returned to Paris. This ended any realistic hope for a constitutional monarchy. © Bettmann/CORBIS

last long. Profound distrust now dominated the political scene.

Declaration of Pillnitz Two months later, on August 27, 1791, under pressure from the *émigrés*, Emperor Leopold II (r. 1790–1792) of Austria, who was the brother of Marie Antoinette, and King Frederick William II (r. 1786–1797) of Prussia issued the Declaration of Pillnitz. The two monarchs promised to intervene in France to protect the royal family and to preserve the monarchy if the other major European powers agreed. This provision rendered the declaration practically meaningless because, at the time, Great Britain would not have given its consent. The declaration was, however, taken seriously in France, where the revolutionaries saw the nation surrounded by aristocratic and monarchical foes seeking to undo all that had been accomplished since 1789.

▼ The End of the Monarchy: A Second Revolution

The National Constituent Assembly drew to a close in September 1791, having completed its task of reconstructing the government and the administration of France. The Assembly had passed a measure that forbade any of its own members to sit in the Legislative Assembly the new constitution established. That new Assembly, filled with entirely new members, met on October 1 and immediately had to confront the challenges flowing from the resistance to the Civil Constitution of the Clergy, the king's flight, and the Declaration of Pillnitz.

Emergence of the Jacobins

Ever since the original gathering of the Estates General, deputies from the Third Estate had organized themselves into clubs composed of politically like-minded persons. The most famous and best organized of these clubs were the **Jacobins** because the group met in a former Dominican priory dedicated to St. Jacques (James) in Paris. The Jacobins had also established a network of local clubs throughout the provinces. They had been the most advanced political group in the National Constituent Assembly and had pressed for a republic rather than a constitutional monarchy. They drew their political language from the most radical thought of the Enlightenment, most particularly Rousseau's emphasis on equality, popular sovereignty, and civic virtue. Such thought and language became all the more effective because the events of 1789 to 1791 had destroyed the old political framework, and the old monarchical political vocabulary was less and less relevant. The rhetoric of republicanism filled that vacuum and for a time supplied the political values of the day. The flight of Louis XVI in the summer of 1791 and the Declaration of Pillnitz led to renewed demands for a republic.

View the Image "Death of Marat" on **MyHistoryLab.com**

Factionalism plagued the Legislative Assembly throughout its short life (1791–1792). A group of Jacobins known as the *Girondists* (because many of them came from the department of the Gironde in southwest France) assumed leadership of the Assembly. They were determined to oppose the forces of counterrevolution. They passed one measure ordering the *émigrés* to return or suffer the loss of their property and another requiring the refractory clergy to support the Civil Constitution or lose their state pensions. The king vetoed both acts.

Furthermore, on April 20, 1792, the Girondists led the Legislative Assembly to declare war on Austria, by this time governed by Leopold II's son, Francis II (r. 1792–1835), and allied to Prussia. This decision launched a period of armed conflict across Western Europe that with only brief intervals of peace lasted until the final defeat of France at Waterloo in June 1815.

The Girondists believed the war would preserve the revolution from domestic enemies and bring the most advanced revolutionaries to power. Paradoxically, Louis XVI and other monarchists also favored the war. They thought the conflict would strengthen the executive power (the monarchy). The king also hoped that foreign armies might defeat French forces and restore the Old Regime. Both sides were playing a dangerous, deluded political game. The war radicalized French politics and within months led to what is usually called the second revolution, which overthrew the constitutional monarchy and established a republic.

With the outbreak of war, the country and the revolution seemed in danger. As early as March 1791, a group of women led by Pauline Léon had petitioned the Legislative Assembly for the right to bear arms and to fight to protect the revolution. Léon also wanted women to serve in the National Guard. These demands to serve, voiced in the universal language of citizenship, illustrated how the rhetoric of the revolution could be used to challenge traditional social roles and the concept of separate social spheres for men and women. Furthermore, the pressure of war raised the possibility that the nation could not meet its military needs if it honored the idea of separate spheres. Once the war began, some Frenchwomen did enlist in the army and served with distinction. Initially, the war effort went poorly. In July 1792, the duke of Brunswick, commander of the Prussian forces, issued a manifesto threatening to destroy Paris if the French royal family were harmed. This statement stiffened support for the war and increased distrust of the king.

Late in July, under radical working-class pressure, the government of Paris passed from the elected council to a committee, or *commune*, of representatives from the sections (municipal wards) of the city. Thereafter the Paris commune became an independent political force casting itself in the role of the protector of the gains of the revolution against both internal and external enemies. Its activities and forceful modes of intimidation largely accounted for the dominance of the city of Paris over many of the future directions of the revolutionary government for the next three years.

On August 10, 1792, a large crowd invaded the Tuileries palace and forced Louis XVI and Marie Antoinette to take refuge in the Legislative Assembly. The crowd fought with the royal Swiss guards. When Louis was finally able to call off the troops, several hundred of them and many Parisian citizens lay dead in the most extensive violence since the fall of the Bastille. Thereafter the royal family was imprisoned. Their quarters were comfortable, but the king was allowed to perform none of his political functions. The recently established constitutional monarchy no longer had a reigning monarch.

The Convention and the Role of the *Sans-culottes*

The September Massacres Early in September, the Parisian crowd again made its will felt. During the first week of the month, in what are known as the **September Massacres**, the Paris Commune summarily executed or murdered about 1,200 people who were in the city jails. Some of these people were aristocrats or priests, but most were simply common criminals. The crowd had mistakenly assumed the prisoners were all counterrevolutionaries. News of this event, the August massacre of the Swiss guards, and the imprisonment of the royal family spread rapidly across Europe, rousing new hostility toward the revolutionary government.

The Paris Commune then compelled the Legislative Assembly to call for the election by universal male suffrage of still another new assembly to write a democratic constitution. That body, called the **Convention** after the American Constitutional Convention of 1787, met on September 21, 1792. The previous day, the French army, filled with patriotic recruits willing to die for the revolution, had halted the Prussian advance at the Battle of Valmy in eastern France. Victory on the battlefield had confirmed the victory of democratic forces at home. As its first act, the Convention declared France a republic—that is, a nation governed by an elected assembly without a monarch.

Goals of the *Sans-culottes* The second revolution had been the work of Jacobins more radical than the Girondists and of the people of Paris known as the ***sans-culottes***. The name of this group means "without breeches" and derived from the long trousers that, as working people, they wore instead of aristocratic knee breeches. The *sans-culottes* were shopkeepers, artisans, wage earners, and, in a few cases, factory workers. The persistent food shortages and the revolutionary inflation reflected in the ongoing fall of the value of the *assignats* had made their difficult lives even more burdensome. The politics of the Old Regime had ignored them, and the policies of the National Constituent Assembly had left them victims of unregulated economic liberty. The government, however, required their labor and their lives if the war was to succeed. From the summer of 1792 until the summer of 1794, their attitudes, desires, and ideals were the primary factors in the internal development of the revolution.

The *sans-culottes* generally knew what they wanted. The Parisian tradespeople and artisans sought immediate relief from food shortages and rising prices through price controls. The economic hardship of their lives made them impatient to see their demands met. They believed all people have a right to subsistence, and they resented most forms of social inequality. This attitude made them intensely hostile to the aristocracy and the original leaders of the revolution of 1789 from the Third Estate, who, they believed, simply wanted to share political power, social prestige, and economic security with the aristocracy. The *sans-culottes'* hatred of inequality did not take them so far as to demand the abolition of property. Rather, they advocated a community of small property owners who would also participate in the political nation.

In politics they were antimonarchical, strongly republican, and suspicious even of representative government. They believed the people should make the decisions of government to an extent as great as possible. In Paris, where their influence was most important, the *sans-culottes* had gained their political experience in meetings of the Paris sections. The Paris Commune organized the previous summer was their chief political vehicle and crowd action their chief instrument of action.

The Policies of the Jacobins The goals of the *sans-culottes* were not wholly compatible with those of the Jacobins, republicans who sought representative government. Jacobin hatred of the aristocracy and hereditary privilege did not extend to a general suspicion of wealth. Basically, the Jacobins favored an unregulated economy. From the time of Louis XVI's flight to Varennes onward, however, the more extreme Jacobins began to cooperate with leaders of the Parisian *sans-culottes* and the Paris Commune to overthrow the monarchy. Once the Convention began to deliberate, these Jacobins, known as the *Mountain* because their seats were high up in the assembly hall, worked with the *sans-culottes* to carry the revolution forward and to win the war. This willingness to cooperate with the forces of the popular revolution separated the Mountain from the Girondists, who were also members of the Jacobin Club.

Execution of Louis XVI By the spring of 1793, several issues had brought the Mountain and its *sans-culottes* allies to dominate the Convention and the revolution. In December 1792, Louis XVI was put on trial as "Citizen Capet," the original medieval name of the royal family. The Girondists looked for a way to spare his life, but the Mountain defeated the effort. An overwhelming majority convicted Louis of conspiring against the liberty of the people and the security of the state. Condemned to death by a smaller majority, he was beheaded on January 21, 1793. Marie Antoinette was subsequently tried and executed in October of the same year; their son died in 1795, in prison, of disease exacerbated by neglect.

View the **Image**
"Execution of Louis XVI"
on **MyHistoryLab.com**

In February 1793, the Convention declared war on Great Britain and Holland, and a month later on Spain. Soon thereafter, the Prussians renewed their offensive and drove the French out of Belgium. To make matters worse, General Dumouriez (1739–1823), the Girondist victor of Valmy, deserted to the enemy. Finally, in March 1793, a royalist revolt led by aristocratic officers and priests erupted in the Vendée in western France and roused much popular support. Thus, the revolution found itself at war with most of Europe and much of the French nation. The Girondists had led the country into the war but had been unable either to win it or to suppress the enemies of the revolution at home. The Mountain stood ready to take up the task.

▼ Europe at War with the Revolution

Initially, the rest of Europe had been ambivalent toward the revolutionary events in France. Those people who favored political reform regarded the revolution as wisely and rationally reorganizing a corrupt and inefficient government. The major foreign governments thought that the revolution meant France would cease to be an important factor in European affairs for years.

Edmund Burke Attacks the Revolution

In 1790, however, Irish-born writer and British statesman Edmund Burke (1729–1799) argued a different position in *Reflections on the Revolution in France.* Burke condemned the reconstruction of the French administration as the application of a blind rationalism that ignored the historical realities of political development and the concrete complexities of social relations. He also forecast further turmoil as people without political experience tried to govern France, predicted the possible deaths of Louis XVI and Marie Antoinette at the hands of the revolutionaries, and forecast that the revolution would end in military despotism. As the revolutionaries proceeded to attack the church, the monarchy, and finally the rest of Europe, Burke's ideas came to have many admirers.

Thomas Paine, the hero of the American Revolution, composed *The Rights of Man* (1791–1792) in direct response to Burke and in defense of the revolutionary principles. Paine declared, "From what we now see, nothing of reform on the political world ought to be held improbable. It is an age of revolutions, in which everything may be looked for."[4] Paine's volume sold more copies at the time in England, but Burke's was influential in the long run and was immediately published widely on the continent where it became a handbook of European conservatives.

By the outbreak of the war with Austria in April 1792, the other European monarchies recognized, along with Burke, the danger of both the ideas and the aggression of revolutionary France. In the United States, no amount of gratitude for France's assistance during the revolutionary war could move Washington to offer support to France;

[4]Thomas Paine, *Political Writings*, rev. student ed., Bruce Kuklick, ed. (Cambridge, UK: Cambridge University Press, 1997), p. 153.

After the execution of Louis XVI on January 21, 1793, the executioner displayed his severed head to the large crowd. Execution of King Louis XVI of France, January 21, 1793, engraving. Musée Carnavalet Paris. CCI/The Art Archive at Art Resource, NY

throughout his presidency, Washington insisted that the new republic must resist foreign entanglements. The increasing radicalism of the French Revolution alienated even those foreign statesmen initially sympathetic to its early reformist impulses. Instead of seeing in France a positive model, one European government after another turned to repressive domestic policies in order to forestall revolutionary activity at home. (See the Document "Burke Denounces the Extreme Measures of the French Revolution," page 571.)

Suppression of Reform in Britain

In Great Britain, William Pitt the Younger (1759–1806), the prime minister, who had unsuccessfully supported moderate reform of Parliament during the 1780s, turned against both reform and popular movements. The government suppressed the London Corresponding Society, founded in 1792 as a working-class reform group. In Birmingham, the government sponsored mob action to drive Joseph Priestley (1733–1804), a famous chemist and a radical political thinker, out of the country. In early 1793, Pitt secured parliamentary approval for acts suspending *habeas corpus* and making the writing of certain ideas treasonable. With less success, Pitt also attempted to curb freedom of the press. All political groups who dared oppose the government faced being associated with sedition.

The Second and Third Partitions of Poland, 1793, 1795

The final two partitions of Poland, already noted in Chapter 17, occurred as a direct result of fears by the central and east European powers that the principles of the French Revolution were establishing themselves in Poland. After the first partition in 1772, Polish leaders had commenced reforms to provide for a stronger state. In 1791, a group of nobles known as the Polish Patriots issued a new constitution that substituted a hereditary for an elective monarchy, provided for real executive authority in the monarch and his council, established a new bicameral diet, and eliminated the *liberum veto*. Although this new constitution strengthened the monarch, it also asserted "all power in civil society should be derived from the will of the people."[5] The Polish government also adopted equality before the law and religious toleration. Frederick William II of Prussia (r. 1786–1797) promised to defend the new Polish constitutional order because he believed that a stronger Poland was in Prussia's interest against the growing Russian power. Catherine the Great of Russia also understood that a reformed Polish state would diminish Russian influence in Poland and eastern Europe.

View the Map "Map Discovery: The Partitions of Poland" on MyHistoryLab.com

In April 1792, conservative Polish nobles who opposed the reforms invited Russia to restore the old order. The Russian army quickly defeated the reformist Polish forces led by Tadeusz Kosciuszko (1746–1817), a veteran of the American Revolution. In response to the Russian invasion, Frederick William II moved his troops from the west where they were confronting the French revolutionary army to his eastern frontier with Poland. That transfer of Prussian troops proved crucial to the important later French victories in the autumn of 1792. However, rather than protecting Poland as he had promised, Frederick William reached an agreement with Catherine early in 1793 to carry out a second partition of Poland. The reformed constitution was abolished, and the new Polish government remained under the influence of Russia.

[5]*New Constitution of the Government of Poland, Established by the Revolution, the Third of May, 1791* (London: J. Debrett, 1791), Article V, p. 10.

Document

Burke Denounces the Extreme Measures of the French Revolution

Edmund Burke was the most important foreign critic of the French Revolution. His first critique, Reflections on the Revolution in France, *appeared in 1790. In 1796, he composed* Letters on a Regicide Peace, *which opposed a proposed peace treaty between Great Britain and revolutionary France. In that work, he summarized what he regarded as the worst evils of the revolutionary government: the execution of the king, the confiscation of property of the church and nobles, and de-Christianization* *(see page 576).*

To which of the major events in the French Revolution does Burke refer? Why, by 1796, would Burke and others have emphasized the religious policies of the revolution? Did Burke exaggerate the evils of the revolution? Who was Burke trying to persuade?

A government of the nature of that set up at our very door has never been hitherto seen, or ever imagined in Europe. . . . France, since her revolution, is under the sway of a sect, whose leaders have deliberately, at one stroke, demolished the whole body of that jurisprudence which France had pretty nearly in common with other civilized countries. . . .

Its foundation is laid in regicide, in Jacobinism, and in atheism, and it has joined to those principles a body of systematic manners, which secures their operation. . . .

I call a commonwealth regicide, which lays it down as a fixed law of nature, and a fundamental right of man, that all government, not being a democracy, is an usurpation. That all kings, as such, are usurpers; and for being kings may and ought to be put to death, with their wives, families, and adherents. That commonwealth which acts uniformly upon those principles . . . —this I call regicide by establishment.

Jacobinism is the revolt of the enterprising talents of a country against its property. When private men form themselves into associations for the purpose of destroying the pre-existing laws and institutions of their country; when they secure to themselves an army, by dividing amongst the people of no property the estates of the ancient and lawful proprietors, when a state recognizes those acts; when it does not make confiscations for crimes, but makes crimes for confiscations; when it has its principal strength, and all its resources, in such a violation of property . . . —I call this Jacobinism by establishment.

I call it atheism by establishment, when any state, as such, shall not acknowledge the existence of God as a moral governor of the world; . . . —when it shall abolish the Christian religion by a regular decree;—when it shall persecute with a cold, unrelenting, steady cruelty, by every mode of confiscation, imprisonment, exile, and death, all its ministers;—when it shall generally shut up or pull down churches; when the few buildings which remain of this kind shall be opened only for the purpose of making a profane apotheosis of monsters, whose vices and crimes have no parallel amongst men. . . . When, in the place of that religion of social benevolence, and of individual self-denial, in mockery of all religion, they institute impious, blasphemous, indecent theatric rites, in honour of their vitiated, perverted reason, and erect altars to the personification of their own corrupted and bloody republic; . . . when wearied out with incessant martyrdom, and the cries of a people hungering and thirsting for religion, they permit it, only as a tolerated evil—I call this atheism by establishment.

When to these establishments of regicide, of Jacobinism, and of atheism, you add the correspondent system of manners, no doubt can be left on the mind of a thinking man concerning their determined hostility to the human race.

From *The Works of the Right Honourable Edmund Burke* (London: Henry G. Bohn, 1856), 5, pp. 206–208.

In the spring of 1794, Polish officers mutinied against efforts to unite their forces with the Russian army. Kosciuszko, who had been in France and Germany since his defeat in 1792, returned to Poland to lead these troops. Initially he was successful. As the rebellion expanded, the language and symbols of the French Revolution appeared in Polish cities. Before long, Prussia, Austria, and Russia sent troops into Poland. On November 4, 1794, in the single bloodiest day of combat in the decade, Russian troops killed well over 10,000 Poles outside Warsaw. Kosciuszko ended up in a Russian prison, and the next year the three partitioning empires divided what remained of Poland among them. Polish officers and troops who escaped Poland after the last partition later fought with the armies of the French Revolution and Napoleon against the forces of the partitioning powers.

▼ The Reign of Terror

War with Europe

The French invasion of the Austrian Netherlands (Belgium) and the revolutionary reorganization of that territory in 1792 roused the rest of Europe to active hostility. In November 1792, the Convention declared it would aid all peoples who wished to cast off aristocratic and monarchical oppression. The Convention had also proclaimed the Scheldt River in the Netherlands open to the commerce of all nations and thus had violated a treaty that Great Britain had made with Austria and Holland. The British were on the point of declaring war on France over this issue when the Convention issued its own declaration of hostilities against Britain in February 1793.

By April 1793, when the Jacobins began to direct the French government, the nation was at war with Austria, Prussia, Great Britain, Spain, Sardinia, and Holland. The governments of these nations, allied in what is known as the First Coalition, endeavored to protect their social structures, political systems, and economic interests against the aggression of the revolution.

This widening of the war in the winter and spring of 1792–1793 brought new, radical political actions within France as the revolutionary government mobilized itself and the nation for the conflict. (See the Document "A Nation at Arms," page 573.) Throughout France, there was the sense that a new kind of war had erupted. In this war the major issue was not protection of national borders as such, but rather the defense of the bold new republican political and social order that had emerged since 1789. The French people understood that the achievements of the revolution were in danger. To protect those achievements, the government took extraordinary actions that touched almost every aspect of national life. Thousands of people from all walks of life including peasants, nobles, clergy, business and professional people, and one-time revolutionary leaders, as well as the king and queen, were arbitrarily arrested and, in many cases, executed. The immediate need to protect the revolution from enemies, real or imagined, from across the spectrum of French political and social life was considered more important than the security of property or even of life. These actions to protect the revolution and silence dissent came to be known as the **Reign of Terror**. (See the Document "The Paris Jacobin Club Alerts the Nation to Internal Enemies of the Revolution," page 574.)

The Republic Defended

To mobilize for war, the revolutionary government organized a collective executive in the form of powerful committees. These, in turn, sought to organize all French national life on a wartime footing. The result was an immense military effort dedicated both to protecting and promoting revolutionary ideals.

The Committee of Public Safety In April 1793, the Convention established a Committee of General Security and a Committee of Public Safety to carry out the executive duties of the government. The latter committee eventually enjoyed almost dictatorial power. All of the revolutionary leaders who served on the Committee of Public Safety were convinced republicans who had long opposed the more vacillating policies of the Girondists. They saw their task as saving the revolution from mortal enemies at home and abroad. They enjoyed a working political relationship with the *sans-culottes* of Paris, but this was an alliance of expediency for the committee.

Read the **Document** "The National Convention, *Law on Suspects* (1793), and *Law of 22 Prairial Year II* (1794)" on **MyHistoryLab.com**

The *Levée en Masse* The major problem for the Convention was to wage the war and at the same time to secure domestic support for the war effort. In early June 1793, the Parisian *sans-culottes* invaded the Convention and successfully demanded the expulsion of the Girondist members. That action further radicalized the Convention and gave the Mountain complete control. On June 22, the Convention approved a fully democratic constitution but delayed its implementation until the conclusion of the war. In fact, it was never implemented. On August 23, Lazare Carnot (1753–1823), the member of the Committee of Public Safety in charge of the military, began a mobilization for victory by issuing a ***levée en masse,*** a military requisition on the entire population, conscripting males into the army and directing economic production to military purposes.

Document

A NATION AT ARMS

On August 16, 1793, the National Convention called upon all French people, regardless of gender or age, to contribute to the war effort. Based on the notion that all citizens enjoyed political rights in the new France, the levée en masse *asserted that they also all shared responsibilities to defend their nation. Different people could fulfill those responsibilities in different ways, but no one was exempt. Somewhere between 800,000 and 1 million men were conscripted into military service, creating an army that seized the attention of all European states. According to one historian, this constituted the "first declaration of total war" as "every man, woman, child, animal and inanimate object was conscripted for the war effort."*[6]

What role are French citizens expected to play in defending France from its "enemies"? What other resources are considered rightful targets for the National Convention's call for support?

1. Henceforth, until the enemies have been driven from the territory of the Republic, the French people are in permanent requisition for army service. The young men shall go to battle; the married men shall forge arms and transport provisions; the women shall make tents and clothes, and shall serve in the hospitals; the children shall turn old linen into [bandages]; the old men shall repair to the public places, to stimulate the courage of the warriors and preach the unity of the Republic and hatred of kings.
2. National buildings shall be converted into barracks; public places into armament workshops; the soil of cellars shall be washed in lye to extract saltpeter therefrom.
3. Arms of caliber shall be turned over exclusively to those who march against the enemy. . . .
4. Saddle horses are called for to complete the cavalry corps; draught horses, other than those employed in agriculture, shall haul artillery and provisions.
5. The Committee of Public Safety is charged with taking all measures necessary for establishing, without delay, a special manufacture of arms of all kinds, in harmony with the *élan* and the energy of the French people. Accordingly, it is authorized to constitute all establishments, manufactories, workshops, and factories deemed necessary for the execution of such works, as well as to requisition for such purpose, throughout the entire extent of the Republic, the . . . workmen who may contribute to their success. . . .
7. No one may obtain a substitute in the service to which he is summoned. . . .
8. The levy shall be general. Unmarried citizens or childless widowers, from eighteen to twenty-five years, shall go first; they shall meet, without delay, at the chief town of their districts, where they shall practice manual exercise daily, while awaiting the hour of departure.
9. The representatives of the people shall regulate the musters and marches so as to have armed citizens arrive at the points of assembling only in so far as supplies, munitions, and all that constitutes the material part of the army exist in sufficient proportion. . . .
11. The battalion organized in each district shall be united under a banner bearing the inscription: *The French people risen against tyrants*. . . .

[6]Tim Blanning, *The Pursuit of Glory: The Five Revolutions that made Modern Europe, 1648–1815* (New York: Penguin, 2007), p. 628.

Document

THE PARIS JACOBIN CLUB ALERTS THE NATION TO INTERNAL ENEMIES OF THE REVOLUTION

By early 1793, the revolutionary groups in Paris stood sharply divided amongst themselves. The Girondists (also known as Brissotins), who had led the nation into war, faced military reversals. General Dumouriez, a former revolutionary commander, had changed sides and was leading an army against France. At this point, on April 5, the radical Jacobin Club of Paris sent a circular to its provincial clubs, painting a dire picture of the fate of the revolution. While Dumouriez was marching against Paris, they accused members of the government and its administrators of conspiring to betray the revolution. The circular suggested that some people were cooperating with England in the war against France. The Jacobins also portrayed as counterrevolutionaries all those political figures who had opposed the execution of Louis XVI. The Paris Jacobins then called on their allies in the provinces to defend the revolution and to take vengeance against its internal enemies. The distortion of the motives of political enemies, the appeal to a possible reversal of the revolution, and the accusations of internal conspiracy served to justify the demand for justice against enemies of the revolution. The accusations embodied in this circular and the fears it sought to arouse represented the kind of thinking that informed the suspension of legal rights and due process associated with the Reign of Terror.

How did the Jacobins use the war to call for actions against their own domestic political enemies? What real and imagined forces did they see threatening the revolution? How did this circular constitute a smear campaign by one group of revolutionaries against other groups? What actions did the Jacobins seek?

Friends, we are betrayed! To arms! To arms! The terrible hour is at hand when the defenders of the *Patrie* must vanquish or bury themselves under the bloody ruins of the Republic. Frenchmen, never was your liberty in such great peril! At last our enemies have put the finishing touch to their foul perfidy, and to complete it their accomplice Dumouriez is marching on Paris. . . .

But Brothers, not all your dangers are to be found there! . . . You must be convinced of a grievous truth! Your greatest enemies are in your midst, they direct your operations. O Vengeance !!! . . .

Yes, brothers and friends, yes, it is in the Senate that parricidal hands tear at your vitals! Yes, the counterrevolution is in the Government . . . , in the National Convention. It is there, at the center of your security and your hope, that criminal delegates hold the threads of the web that they have woven with the horde of despots who come to butcher us! . . . It is there that a sacrilegious cabal is directed by the English court . . . and others. . . .

Let us rise! Yes, let us rise! Let us arrest all the enemies of our revolution, and all suspected persons. Let us exterminate, without pity, all conspirators, unless we wish to be exterminated ourselves. . . .

Let the departments, the districts, the municipalities, and all the popular societies unite and concur in protesting to the Convention, by dispatching thereto a veritable rain of petitions manifesting the formal wish for the immediate recall of all unfaithful members who have betrayed their duty by not wishing the death of the tyrant, and, above all, against those who have led astray so many of their colleagues. Such delegates are traitors, royalists, or fatuous men. The Republic condemns the friends of kings! . . .

Let us all unite equally to demand that the thunder or indictments be loosed against generals who are traitors to the Republic, against prevaricating ministers, against postal administrators, and against all unfaithful agents of the government. Therein lies our most salutary means of defence; but let us repel the traitors and tyrants.

The center of their conspiracy is here: it is in Paris that our perfidious enemies wish to consummate their crime. Paris, the cradle, the bulwark of liberty, is, without doubt, the place where they have sworn to annihilate the holy cause of humanity under the corpses of patriots.

Following the *levée en masse*, the Convention on September 29, 1793, established a ceiling on prices in accord with *sans-culotte* demands. During these same months, the armies of the revolution also successfully crushed many of the counterrevolutionary disturbances in the provinces. Never before had Europe seen a nation organized in this way, nor one defended by a citizen army, which, by late 1794, with somewhere around a million men, had become larger than any ever organized in European history.

Other events within France astounded Europeans even more. The Reign of Terror had begun. Those months of quasi-judicial executions and murders stretching from the autumn of 1793 to the midsummer of 1794 are probably the most famous or infamous period of the revolution. They can be understood only in the context of the war on one hand and the revolutionary expectations of the Convention and the *sans-culottes* on the other.

The "Republic of Virtue" and Robespierre's Justification of Terror

The presence of armies closing in on the nation made it easy to dispense with legal due process. The people who sat in the Convention and those sitting on the Committee of Public Safety, however, did not see their actions simply in terms of expediency made necessary by war. They also believed they had created something new in world history, a "republic of virtue." In this republic, civic virtue largely understood in terms of Rousseau's *Social Contract*, the sacrifice of one's self and one's interest for the good of the republic, would replace selfish aristocratic and monarchical corruption. The republic of virtue manifested itself in many ways: in the renaming of streets from the egalitarian vocabulary of the revolution; in republican dress copied from that of the *sans-culottes* or the Roman Republic; in the absence of powdered wigs; in the suppression of plays and other literature that were insufficiently republican; and in a general attack against crimes, such as prostitution, that were supposedly characteristic of aristocratic society. Yet the core value of the republic of virtue in line with Rousseau's thought was the upholding of the public over the private good or the championing of the general will over individual interests. It was in the name of the public good that the Committee of Public Safety carried out the policies of the terror.

Read the **Document** "Maximilien Robespierre, 'Speech to National Convention: The Terror Justified' " on **MyHistoryLab.com**

The person who embodied this republic of virtue defended by terror was Maximilien de Robespierre (1758–1794), who, by late 1793, had emerged as the dominant figure on the Committee of Public Safety. This utterly selfless revolutionary figure has remained controversial from his day to the present. From the beginning of the revolution, he had favored a republic. The Jacobin Club provided his primary forum and base of power. A shrewd and sensitive politician, Robespierre had opposed the war in 1792 because he feared it might aid the monarchy. He depended largely on the support of the *sans-culottes* of Paris, but he continued to dress as he had before the revolution in powdered wig and knee breeches. For him, the republic of virtue meant whole-hearted support of the republican government, the renunciation of selfish gains from political life, and the assault on foreign and domestic enemies of the revolution. Portraying revolutionary France as endangered on all sides, he told the Convention early in 1794,

> Without, all the tyrants encircle you; within, all the friends of tyranny conspire—they will conspire until crime has been robbed of hope. We must smother the internal and external enemies of the Republic or perish with them. Now, in this situation, the first maxim of your policy ought to be to lead the people by reason and the people's enemies by terror. If the mainspring of popular government in peacetime is virtue, amid revolution it is at the same time [both] virtue and *terror:* virtue, without which terror is fatal; terror, without which virtue is impotent. Terror is nothing but prompt, severe, inflexible justice; it is therefore an emanation of virtue. It is less a special principle than a consequence of the general principle of democracy applied to our country's most pressing needs.[7]

Robespierre and those who supported his policies were among the first of a succession of secular ideologues of the left and the right who, in the name of humanity, would bring so much suffering to Europe in the following two centuries. The policies associated with terror in the name of republican virtue included the exclusion of women from active political life, the de-Christianization of France, and the use of revolutionary tribunals to dispense justice to alleged enemies of the republic.

Repression of the Society of Revolutionary Republican Women

Revolutionary women established their own distinct institutions during these months. In May 1793, Pauline Léon and Claire Lacombe founded the Society of Revolutionary Republican Women. Its purpose was to fight the internal enemies of the revolution. Its members saw themselves as militant citizens. Initially, the Jacobin leaders welcomed the organization. Members of the society and other women filled the galleries of the Convention to hear the debates and cheer their favorite speakers. The society became increasingly radical, however. Its members sought stricter controls on the price of food and other commodities, worked to ferret out food hoarders, and brawled with working market women whom they thought to be insufficiently revolutionary. The women of the society also demanded the right to wear the revolutionary *cockade* that male citizens usually wore in their hats. By October 1793, the Jacobins in the Convention had begun to fear the turmoil the society was causing and banned all women's clubs and societies. The debates

[7]Richard T. Bienvenu, *The Ninth of Thermidor: The Fall of Robespierre* (New York: Oxford University Press, 1968), p. 38.

over these decrees show that the Jacobins believed the society opposed many of their economic policies, but the deputies used Rousseau's language of separate spheres for men and women to justify their exclusion of women from active political life.

There were other examples of repression of women in 1793. Olympe de Gouges, author of the Declaration of the Rights of Woman, opposed the Terror and accused Jacobins of corruption. She was guillotined in November 1793. The same year, women were formally excluded from serving in the French army and from the galleries of the Convention. The exclusion of women from public political life was part of the establishment of the Jacobin republic of virtue because in such a republic men would be active citizens in the military and political sphere and women would be active only in the domestic sphere.

De-Christianization

The most dramatic step taken by the republic of virtue, and one that illustrates its imposition of political values to justify the Terror, was the Convention's attempt to de-Christianize France. In November 1793, the Convention proclaimed a new calendar dating from the first day of the French Republic. There were twelve months of thirty days each, with names associated with the seasons and climate. Every tenth day, rather than every seventh, was a holiday. Many of the most important events of the next few years became known by their dates on the revolutionary calendar. From summer to spring, the months of the revolutionary calendar were Messidor, Thermidor, Fructidor, Vendémiaire, Brumaire, Frimaire, Nivose, Pluviose, Ventose, Germinal, Floreal, and Prairial. In November 1793, the Convention decreed the Cathedral of Notre Dame in Paris to be a "Temple of Reason."

The legislature then sent trusted members, known as deputies on mission, into the provinces to enforce de-Christianization by closing churches, persecuting clergy and believers (both Roman Catholic and Protestant), occasionally forcing priests to marry, and sometimes simply by killing priests and nuns. Churches were desecrated, torn down, or used as barns or warehouses. This radical religious policy attacking both clergy and religious property roused enormous popular opposition and alienated parts of the French provinces from the revolutionary government in Paris. Robespierre personally opposed de-Christianization because he was convinced it would prove a political blunder that would erode loyalty to the republic.

Revolutionary Tribunals

The Reign of Terror manifested itself in revolutionary tribunals that the Convention established during the summer of 1793. The mandate of these tribunals, the most prominent of which was in Paris, was to try the enemies of the republic, but the definition of who was an "enemy" shifted as the months passed. It included those who might aid other European powers, those who endangered republican virtue, and, finally, good republicans who opposed the policies of the dominant faction of the government. The Terror of the revolutionary tribunals systematized and channeled the popular resentment that had manifested itself in the September Massacres of 1792. Those whom the tribunal condemned in Paris were beheaded on the guillotine, a recently invented instrument of efficient and supposedly humane execution. (The drop of the blade of the guillotine was certain to sever the head of the condemned at once, whereas beheading by axe or sword could, and often did, require multiple blows and cause unnecessary pain.) Other modes of execution, such as mass shootings and drowning, were used in the provinces.

The first victims of the Terror were Marie Antoinette, other members of the royal family, and aristocrats, who were executed in October 1793. Girondist politicians who had been prominent in the Legislative Assembly followed them. These executions took place in the same weeks that the Convention had moved against the Society of Revolutionary Republican Women, whom it had also seen as endangering Jacobin control.

On the way to her execution in 1793, Marie Antoinette was sketched from life by Jacques-Louis David as she passed his window. Note her cropped hair, which had recently been shorn as a symbol of her degradation. Jacques Louis David (1748–1825), Marie-Antoinette brought to the guillotine (after a drawing by David who witnessed the execution). Pen drawing. 1793. Bibliothèque Nationale, Paris, France. Bridgeman—Giraudon/Art Resource, NY

In early 1794, the Terror moved to the provinces, where the deputies on mission presided over the summary execution of thousands of people, most of whom were peasants, who had allegedly supported internal opposition to the revolution. One of the most infamous incidents occurred in Nantes on the west coast of France, where several hundred people, including many priests, were simply tied to rafts and drowned in the river Loire. The victims of the Terror now came from every social class, including the *sans-culottes*.

The End of the Terror

Revolutionaries Turn Against Themselves In Paris during the late winter of 1794, Robespierre began to orchestrate the Terror against republican political figures of the left and right. On March 24, he secured the execution of certain extreme *sans-culottes* leaders known as the *enragés*. They had wanted further measures to regulate prices, secure social equality, and press de-Christianization. Robespierre then turned against other republicans in the Convention. Most prominent among them was Jacques Danton (1759–1794), who had provided heroic national leadership in the dark days of September 1792 and who had later served briefly on the Committee of Public Safety before Robespierre joined the group. Danton and others were accused of being insufficiently militant on the war, profiting monetarily from the revolution, and rejecting the link between politics and moral virtue. Danton was executed in April 1794. Robespierre thus exterminated the leadership of both groups that might have threatened his position. Finally, on June 10, he secured passage of the Law of 22 Prairial, which permitted the revolutionary tribunal to convict suspects without hearing substantial evidence against them. The number of executions grew steadily.

Fall of Robespierre In May 1794, at the height of his power, Robespierre, considering the worship of "Reason" too abstract for most citizens, replaced it with the "Cult of the Supreme Being." This deistic cult reflected Rousseau's vision of a civic religion that would induce morality among citizens. (See the Document "The Convention Establishes the Worship of the Supreme Being," page 579.) Robespierre, however, did not long preside over his new religion.

View the **Image** "Cult of the Supreme Being, French Revolution" on **MyHistoryLab.com**

On July 26, Robespierre made an ill-tempered speech in the Convention, declaring that other leaders of the government were conspiring against him and the revolution. Similar accusations against unnamed persons had preceded his earlier attacks. No member of the Convention could now feel safe. On July 27—the Ninth of Thermidor on the revolutionary calendar—members of the Convention, by prearrangement, shouted him down when he rose to make another speech. That night Robespierre was arrested, and the next day he and approximately eighty of his supporters were executed without trial. The revolutionary *sans-culottes* of Paris did not try to save him because he had deprived them of their chief leaders. He had also recently supported a measure to cap workers' wages. Other Jacobins turned against him because, after Danton's death, they feared they would be his next victims. Robespierre had destroyed rivals for leadership without creating supporters for himself. He had also for months tried to persuade the Paris populace that the Convention itself was harboring enemies of the revolution. Assured by the Convention that Robespierre had sought dictatorial powers, Parisians saw him as one more of those internal

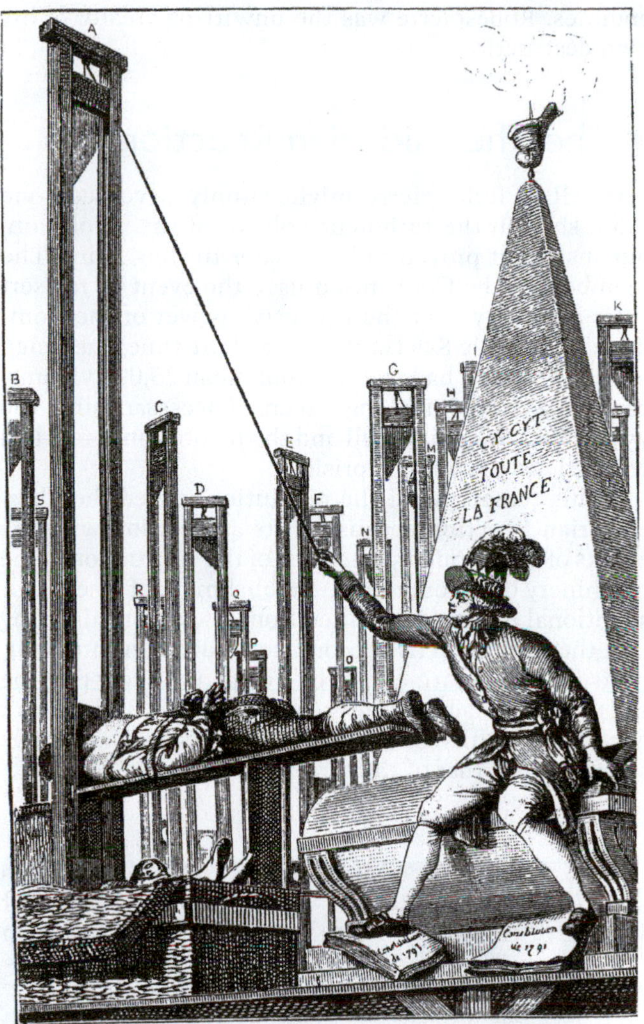

Maximilien Robespierre (1758–1794) emerged as the most powerful revolutionary figure in 1793 and 1794, dominating the Committee of Public Safety. He considered the Terror essential for the success of the revolution. In this caricature, having already guillotined all the people in France, Robespierre must himself execute the executioner. © INTERFOTO/Alamy enemies. Robespierre was the unwitting creator of his own destruction.

▼ The Thermidorian Reaction

The fall of Robespierre might simply have been one more shift in the turbulent politics of the revolution, but instead it proved to be a major turning point. The members of the Convention used the event to reassert their authority over the executive power of the Committee of Public Safety. Within a short time, the Reign of Terror, which had claimed more than 25,000 victims, came to a close. It no longer seemed necessary since the war abroad was going well and the republican forces had crushed the provincial uprisings.

This tempering of the revolution, called the **Thermidorian Reaction** because of its association with the events of 9 Thermidor, consisted of the destruction of the machinery of terror and the establishment of a new constitutional regime. It resulted from a widespread feeling that the revolution had become too radical. In particular, it displayed a weariness of the Terror and a fear that the *sans-culottes* had become too powerful. The influence of generally wealthy middle-class and professional people soon replaced that of the *sans-culottes*.

In the weeks and months after Robespierre's execution, the Convention allowed the Girondists who had been in prison or hiding to return to their seats. A general amnesty freed political prisoners. The Convention restructured the Committee of Public Safety and diminished its power while repealing the notorious Law of 22 Prairial. Some, though by no means all, of the people responsible for the Terror were removed from public life. The Paris Commune was outlawed, and its leaders and deputies on mission were executed. The Paris Jacobin Club was closed, and Jacobin clubs in the provinces were forbidden to correspond with each other.

The end of the Reign of Terror did not mean the end of violence in France. Executions of former terrorists marked the beginning of "the white terror." Throughout the country, people who had been involved in the Reign of Terror were attacked and often murdered. Jacobins were executed with little more due process than they had extended to their victims a few months earlier. The Convention itself approved some of these trials. In other cases, gangs of youths who had aristocratic connections or who had avoided serving in the army roamed the streets, beating known Jacobins. In Lyons, Toulon, and Marseilles, these so-called "bands of Jesus" dragged suspected terrorists from prisons and murdered them

The Festival of the Supreme Being, which took place in June 1794, inaugurated Robespierre's new civic religion. Its climax occurred when a statue of Atheism was burned and another statue of Wisdom rose from the ashes. Pierre-Antoine Demachy, Festival of the Supreme Being at the Champ de Mars on June 8, 1794. Musée de la Ville de Paris, Musée Carnavalet, Paris, France. Bridgeman—Giraudon/Art Resource, NY

Document

THE CONVENTION ESTABLISHES THE WORSHIP OF THE SUPREME BEING

On May 7, 1794, the Convention passed an extraordinary piece of revolutionary legislation. It established the worship of the Supreme Being as a state cult. Although the law drew on the religious ideas of deism, the point of the legislation was to provide a religious basis for the new secular French state. Article 6 outlined the political and civic values that the Cult of the Supreme Being was supposed to nurture.

How does this declaration reflect the ideas of the Enlightenment? What personal and social values was this religion supposed to nurture? How might this declaration have led to Burke's criticism of the policies of the revolution?

1. The French people recognize the existence of the Supreme Being and the immortality of the soul.
2. They recognize that the worship worthy of the Supreme Being is the observance of the duties of man.
3. They place in the forefront of such duties detestation of bad faith and tyranny, punishment of tyrants and traiters, succoring of unfortunates, respect of weak persons, defence of the oppressed, doing to others all the good that one can, and being just towards everyone.
4. Festivals shall be instituted to remind man of the concept of the Divinity and of the dignity of his being.
5. They shall take their names from the glorious events of our Revolution, or from the virtues most dear and most useful to man, or from the greatest benefits of nature. . . .
6. On the days of *décade*, the name given to a particular day in each month of the revolutionary calendar, it shall celebrate the following festivals:

To the Supreme Being and to nature; to the human race; to the French people; to the benefactors of humanity; to the martyrs of liberty; to liberty and equality; to the Republic; to the liberty of the world; to the love of the *Patrie* [Fatherland]; to the hatred of tyrants and traitors; to truth; to justice; to modesty; to glory and immortality; to friendship; to frugality; to courage; to good faith; to heroism; to disinterestedness; to stoicism; to love; to conjugal love; to paternal love; to maternal tenderness; to filial piety; to infancy; to youth; to manhood; to old age; to misfortune; to agriculture; to industry; to our forefathers; to posterity; to happiness.

much as alleged royalists had been murdered during the September Massacres of 1792.

The republic of virtue gave way, if not to one of vice, at least to one of frivolous pleasures. The dress of the *sans-culottes* and the Roman Republic disappeared among the middle class and the aristocracy. New plays appeared in the theaters, and prostitutes again roamed the streets of Paris. Families of victims of the Reign of Terror gave parties in which they appeared with shaved necks, like the victims of the guillotine, and with red ribbons tied about them. Although the Convention continued to favor the Cult of the Supreme Being, it allowed Catholic services to be held. Many refractory priests returned to the country. One of the unanticipated results of the Thermidorian Reaction was a genuine revival of Catholic worship.

The Thermidorian Reaction also saw the repeal of legislation that had been passed in 1792 making divorce more equitable for women. As the passage of that measure suggests, the reaction did not extend women's rights or improve their education. The Thermidorians and their successors had seen enough attempts at political and social change. They sought to return family life to its status before the outbreak of the revolution. Political authorities and the church were determined to reestablish separate spheres for men and women and to reinforce traditional gender roles. As a result, in at least some respects, Frenchwomen had less freedom after 1795 than before 1789.

Establishment of the Directory

The Thermidorian Reaction led to still another new constitution. The democratic constitution of 1793, which had never gone into effect, was abandoned. In its place, the Convention issued the Constitution of the Year III, which reflected the Thermidorian determination to reject *both* constitutional monarchy and democracy. In recognition of the danger of a legislature with only one chamber and unlimited authority, this new document provided for a legislature of two houses. Members of the upper body, or Council of Elders, were to be men over forty years of age who were either husbands or widowers. The lower Council of Five Hundred was to consist of men of at least thirty who could be either married or single. The executive body was to be a five-person Directory whom the Elders would choose from a list the Council of Five Hundred submitted. Property qualifications limited the franchise, except for soldiers, who were permitted to vote whether they had property or not.

Listen to the **Audio** "The Directory" on **MyHistoryLab.com**

Historically, the term *Thermidor* has come to be associated with political reaction. That association requires considerable qualification. By 1795, the political structure and society of the Old Regime in France based on rank and birth had given way permanently to a political system based on civic equality and social status based on property ownership. People who had never been allowed direct, formal access to political power had, to different degrees, been granted it. Their entrance into political life had given rise to questions of property distribution and economic regulations that could not again be ignored. Representation was an established principle of politics. Henceforth, the question before France and eventually before all of Europe would be which new groups would be permitted representation. In the *levée en masse*, the French had demonstrated to Europe the power of the secular ideal of nationhood and of the willingness of citizen soldiers to embrace self-sacrifice.

The post-Thermidorian course of the French Revolution did not undo these stunning changes in the political and social contours of Europe. What triumphed in the Constitution of the Year III was the revolution of the holders of property. For this reason the French Revolution has often been considered a victory of the bourgeoisie, or middle class. The property that won the day, however, was not industrial wealth, but the wealth stemming from commerce, the professions, and land. The largest new propertied class to emerge from the revolutionary turmoil was the peasantry, who, as a result of the destruction of aristocratic privileges, now owned their own land. Unlike peasants liberated from traditional landholding in other parts of Europe during the next century, French peasants had to pay no monetary compensation either to their former landlords or to the state.

Removal of the *Sans-culottes* from Political Life

The most decisively reactionary element in the Thermidorian Reaction and the new constitution was the removal of the *sans-culottes* from political life. With the war effort succeeding, the Convention severed its ties with the *sans-culottes*. True to their belief in an unregulated economy, the Thermidorians repealed the ceiling on prices. As a result, the winter of 1794–1795 brought the worst food shortages of the period. There were many food riots, which the Convention suppressed to prove that the era of the *sans-culottes journées* had come to a close. Royalist agents, who aimed to restore the monarchy, tried to take advantage of their discontent. On October 5, 1795—13 Vendémiaire—the sections of Paris led by the royalists rose up against the Convention. The government turned the artillery against the royalist rebels. A general named Napoleon Bonaparte (1769–1821) commanded the cannon, and with a "whiff of grapeshot," he dispersed the crowd.

By the Treaties of Basel in March and June 1795, the Convention concluded peace with Prussia and Spain. The legislators, however, feared a resurgence of both radical democrats and royalists in the upcoming elections for the Council of Five Hundred. Consequently, the Convention ruled that at least two-thirds of the new legislature must have served in the Convention itself, thus rejecting the decision the National Constituent Assembly had made in 1791 when it forbade its members to be elected to the new Legislative Assembly. The Two-Thirds Law, which sought to foster continuity but also clearly favored politicians already in office, quickly undermined public faith in the new constitutional order.

The Directory faced almost immediate social unrest. During the spring of 1796 in Paris, Gracchus Babeuf (1760–1797) led the Conspiracy of Equals. He and his followers called for more radical democracy and for more equality of property. They declared at one point, "The aim of the French Revolution is to destroy inequality and to re-establish the general welfare. . . . The Revolution is not complete, because the rich monopolize all the property and govern exclusively, while the poor toil like slaves, languish in misery, and count for nothing in the state."[8] In a sense, they were correct. The Directory intended to resist any further social changes in France that might endanger property or political stability. Babeuf was arrested, tried, and executed. This minor plot became famous decades later, when European socialists attempted to find their historical roots in the French Revolution.

[8]John Hall Stewart, *A Documentary Survey of the French Revolution* (New York: Macmillan, 1966), pp. 656–657.

THE FRENCH REVOLUTION

1787	
February–May	Unsuccessful negotiations with the Assembly of Notables
1788	
August 8	Louis XVI summons the Estates General
December 27	Approval of doubling of the Third Estate membership
1789	
May 5	The Estates General opens at Versailles
June 17	The Third Estate declares itself the National Assembly
June 20	The National Assembly takes the Tennis Court Oath
July 14	Fall of the Bastille in the city of Paris
Late July	The Great Fear spreads in the countryside
August 4	The nobles surrender their feudal rights at a meeting of the National Constituent Assembly
August 27	Declaration of the Rights of Man and Citizen
October 5–6	Parisian women march to Versailles and force Louis XVI and his family to return to Paris
1790	
July 12	Civil Constitution of the Clergy adopted
July 14	A new political constitution is accepted by the king
1791	
June 14	Chapelier Law
June 20–24	Louis XVI and his family attempt to flee France and are stopped at Varennes
August 27	The Declaration of Pillnitz
October 1	The Legislative Assembly meets
1792	
April 20	France declares war on Austria
August 10	The Tuileries palace is stormed, and Louis XVI takes refuge with the Legislative Assembly
September 2–7	The September Massacres
September 20	France wins the Battle of Valmy
September 21	The Convention meets, and the monarchy is abolished
1793	
January 21	King Louis XVI is executed
February 1	France declares war on Great Britain
March	Counterrevolution breaks out in the Vendée
April	The Committee of Public Safety is formed
June 22	The Constitution of 1793 is adopted but not implemented
July	Robespierre enters the Committee of Public Safety
August 23	*Levée en masse* proclaimed
September 29	Maximum prices set on food and other commodities
October 16	Queen Marie Antoinette is executed
October 30	Women's societies and clubs banned
November 10	The Cult of Reason is proclaimed; the revolutionary calendar, beginning on September 22, 1792, is adopted
1794	
March 24	Execution of the leaders of the *sans-culottes* known as the *enragés*
April 6	Execution of Danton
May 7	Cult of the Supreme Being proclaimed
June 8	Robespierre leads the celebration of the Festival of the Supreme Being
June 10	The Law of 22 Prairial is adopted
July 27	The Ninth of Thermidor and the fall of Robespierre
July 28	Robespierre is executed
August 1	Repeal of the Law of 22 Prairial
August 10	Reorganization of the Revolutionary Tribunal
November 12	Closing of Jacobin Club in Paris
1795	
May 31	Abolition of Revolutionary Tribunal
August 22	The Constitution of the Year III establishes the Directory
September 23	Two-Thirds Law adopted
1796	
May 10	Babeuf's Conspiracy of Equals
1799	
November 9	Napoleon's (18 Brumaire) *coup d'état* overthrows the Directory

The suppression of the *sans-culottes*, the narrow franchise of the constitution, the Two-Thirds Law, and the Catholic royalist revival presented the Directory with challenges that it was never able to overcome. Because France remained at war with Austria and Great Britain, it needed a broader-based active loyalty than it was able to command. Instead, the Directory came to depend on the power of the army to govern France. All soldiers could vote. Moreover, within the army that the revolution had created and sustained were ambitious officers who were eager for power. As will be seen in the next chapter, the instability of the Directory, the growing role of the army, and the ambitions of its leaders held profound consequences not only for France but for the entire Western world as well.

In Perspective

The French Revolution is the central political event of modern European history. It unleashed political and social forces that shaped Europe and much of the rest of the world for the next two centuries. The revolution began with a clash between the monarchy and the nobility. Once the Estates General gathered, however, the traditional boundaries of eighteenth-century political life could not contain the discontent. The Third Estate, in all of its diversity, demanded real influence in government. Initially, that meant the participation of middle-class members of the Estates General, but soon the people of Paris and the peasants made their own demands known. Thereafter, popular nationalism exerted itself on French political life and the destiny of Europe.

Revolutionary legislation and popular uprisings in Paris, the countryside, and other cities transformed the social as well as the political life of the nation. Nobles surrendered traditional social privileges. The church saw its property confiscated and its operations brought under state control. For a time, there was an attempt to de-Christianize France. Vast amounts of landed property changed hands, and France became a nation of peasant landowners. Urban workers lost the protection they had enjoyed under the guilds and became more subject to the forces of the marketplace.

Violence accompanied many of the revolutionary changes. Thousands died during the Reign of Terror. France also found itself at war with virtually the rest of Europe. Resentment, fear, and a new desire for stability eventually brought the Terror to an end. That desire for stability, combined with a determination to defeat the foreign enemies of the revolution and to carry it abroad, would, in turn, work to the advantage of the army. Eventually, Napoleon Bonaparte would claim leadership in the name of stability and national glory.

KEY TERMS

Convention (p. 568)
émigrés (p. 563)
Jacobins (p. 567)
levée en masse (p. 572)
Reign of Terror (p. 572)
sans-culottes (p. 568)
September Massacres (p. 568)
Thermidorian Reaction (p. 578)
Third Estate (p. 553)

REVIEW QUESTIONS

1. Why has France been called a rich nation with an impoverished government? How did the financial weaknesses of the French monarchy lay the foundations of the revolution of 1789?
2. What were Louis XVI's most serious mistakes during the French Revolution? Had he been a more able ruler, could the French Revolution have been avoided or a constitutional monarchy have succeeded? How much did the revolution have to do with the competence of the monarch?
3. How was the Estates General transformed into the National Assembly? How does the Declaration of the Rights of Man and Citizen reflect the social and political values of the eighteenth-century Enlightenment? How were France and its government reorganized in the early years of the revolution? Why has the Civil Constitution of the Clergy been called the greatest blunder of the National Assembly?
4. Why were some political factions dissatisfied with the constitutional settlement of 1791? What was the revolution of 1792 and why did it occur? Who were the *sans-culottes*, and how did they become a factor in the politics of the period? How influential were they during the Terror in particular? Why did the *sans-culottes* and the Jacobins cooperate at first? Why did that cooperation end?
5. Why did France go to war with Austria in 1792? What were the benefits and drawbacks for France of fighting an external war in the midst of a domestic political revolution?
6. What were the causes of the Terror? How did the rest of Europe react to the French Revolution and the Terror? How did events in France influence the last two partitions of Poland?
7. A motto of the French Revolution was "equality, liberty, and fraternity." How did the revolution both support and violate this motto? Did French women benefit from the revolution? Did French peasants benefit from it?

SUGGESTED READINGS

D. Andress, *The Terror: The Merciless War for Freedom in Revolutionary France* (2006). The best recent survey of the Reign of Terror.

N. Aston, *Christianity and Revolutionary Europe c. 1750–1830* (2002). Continent-wide survey of the impact of revolution on religion.

T. C. Blanning, *The Revolutionary Wars, 1787–1802* (1996). Essential for understanding the role of the army and the revolution.

S. Desan, *The Family on Trial in Revolutionary France* (2004). An important analysis of how the revolution impacted French domestic life.

W. Doyle, *The Oxford History of the French Revolution* (2003). A broad, complex narrative with an excellent bibliography.

A. Forrest, *Revolutionary Paris, the Provinces and the French Revolution* (2004). A clear presentation of the tensions between the center of the revolution and the provinces.

C. Hayden and W. Doyle, eds., *Robespierre* (1999). Essays evaluating Robespierre's ideas, career, and reputation.

P. Higonnet, *Goodness beyond Virtue: Jacobins During the French Revolution* (1998). An outstanding work that clearly relates political values to political actions.

D. Jordon, *The King's Trial: Louis XVI vs. the French Revolution* (1979). A gripping account of the event.

E. Kennedy, *A Cultural History of the French Revolution* (1989). An important examination of the role of the arts, schools, clubs, and intellectual institutions.

S. E. Melzer and L. W. Rabine, eds., *Rebel Daughters: Women and the French Revolution* (1997). Essays exploring the role and image of women in the revolution.

S. Neely, *A Concise History of the French Revolution* (2008). The best of the numerous brief accounts.

C. C. O'Brien, *The Great Melody: A Thematic Biography of Edmund Burke* (1992). A deeply thoughtful biography.

R. R. Palmer, *The Age of Democratic Revolution: A Political History of Europe and America, 1760–1800*, 2 vols. (1959, 1964). Still an impressive survey of the political turmoil in the transatlantic world.

M. Price, *The Road from Versailles: Louis XVI, Marie Antoinette, and the Fall of the French Monarchy* (2004). A lively narrative that brings the personalities of the king and queen into focus.

S. Schama, *Citizens: A Chronicle of the French Revolution* (1990). A lively account of the revolution that focuses on the personalities involved.

R. Scurr, *Fatal Purity: Robespierre and the French Revolution* (2007). A compelling analysis of a personality long difficult to understand.

T. Tackett, *Becoming a Revolutionary: The Deputies of the French National Assembly and the Emergence of a Revolutionary Culture (1789–1790)* (1996). The best study of the early months of the revolution.

MyHistoryLab™ MEDIA ASSIGNMENTS

Find these resources in the Media Assignments folder for Chapter 18 on **MyHistoryLab**.

QUESTIONS FOR ANALYSIS

1. How has this political cartoonist characterized the French king?

   ***Section:* The Crisis of the French Monarchy**
   View the **Closer Look** Challenging the French Political Order, p. 552

2. What were conditions like for working women around the time that this petition was written and what forms of redress do the petitioners seek from the king?

   ***Section:* The Revolution of 1789**
   Read the **Document** Petition of Women of the Third Estate, p. 553

3. What do you consider Robespierre's principal argument?

   ***Section:* The Reign of Terror**
   Read the **Document** Maximilien Robespierre, "Speech to National Convention: The Terror Justified," p. 575

4. Against whom is this complaint made?

   ***Section:* The Revolution of 1789**
   Read the **Document** French Peasants, Cahiers de doléances (Grievances) (France), 1789, p. 554

5. Why has de Gouges addressed this to Marie Antoinette?

   ***Section:* The Reconstruction of France**
   Read the **Document** Olympe de Gouges, Declaration of the Rights of Woman and the Female Citizen, p. 561

OTHER RESOURCES FROM THIS CHAPTER

The Revolution of 1789

Read the **Document** Emmanuel Joseph Sieyès, *What Is the Third Estate?*, p. 553

View the **Image** Oath of the Tennis Court, p. 554

View the **Map** Map Discovery: Revolutionary France, p. 557

The Reconstruction of France

Read the **Compare and Connect** The Declaration of the Rights of Man and Citizen Opens the Door for Disadvantaged Groups to Demand Equal Civic Rights, p. 564

The End of the Monarchy: A Second Revolution

View the **Image** Death of Marat, p. 567

View the **Image** Execution of Louis XVI, p. 569

Europe at War with the Revolution

View the **Map** Map Discovery: The Partitions of Poland, p. 570

The Reign of Terror

Read the **Document** The National Convention, *Law on Suspects* (1793) and *Law of 22 Prairial Year II* (1794), p. 572

View the **Image** Cult of the Supreme Being, French Revolution, p. 577

The Thermidorian Reaction

Listen to the **Audio** The Directory, p. 580

This portrait of Napoleon on his throne by Jean Ingres (1780–1867) shows him in the splendor of an imperial monarch who embodies the total power of the state. Jean Auguste Dominique Ingres (1780–1867), *Napoleon on His Imperial Throne*, 1806. Oil on canvas, 259 × 162 cm. Musée des Beaux-Arts, Rennes. Photograph © Erich Lessing/Art Resource, NY

Listen to the **Chapter Audio** on **MyHistoryLab.com**

19

The Age of Napoleon and the Triumph of Romanticism

▼ **The Rise of Napoleon Bonaparte**
Early Military Victories • The Constitution of the Year VIII

▼ **The Consulate in France (1799–1804)**
Suppressing Foreign Enemies and Domestic Opposition • Concordat with the Roman Catholic Church • The Napoleonic Code • Establishing a Dynasty

▼ **The Haitian Revolution (1799–1804)**

▼ **Napoleon's Empire (1804–1814)**
Conquering an Empire • The Continental System

▼ **European Response to the Empire**
German Nationalism and Prussian Reform • The Wars of Liberation • The Invasion of Russia • European Coalition

▼ **The Congress of Vienna and the European Settlement**
Territorial Adjustments • The Hundred Days and the Quadruple Alliance

▼ **The Romantic Movement**

▼ **Romantic Questioning of the Supremacy of Reason**
Rousseau and Education • Kant and Reason

▼ **Romantic Literature**
The English Romantic Writers • The German Romantic Writers

▼ **Romantic Art**
The Cult of the Middle Ages and Neo-Gothicism • Nature and the Sublime

▼ **Religion in the Romantic Period**
Methodism • New Directions in Continental Religion

▼ **Romantic Views of Nationalism and History**
Herder and Culture • Hegel and History • Islam, the Middle East, and Romanticism

▼ **In Perspective**

LEARNING OBJECTIVES

How did Napoleon come to power in France?

How did the Consulate end the revolution in France?

How did Napoleon build an empire?

Why did Napoleonic rule breed resentment in Europe?

What were the consequences of the Congress of Vienna?

How did Rousseau and Kant contribute to the development of romanticism?

How were the ideals of romanticism reflected in English and German literature and in Romantic art?

How did Romantic religious thinkers view the religious experience?

What were the Romantic views of history and national identity?

BY THE LATE 1790s, the French people, especially property owners, who now included the peasants, longed for stability. The Directory was not providing it. Only the army was able to take charge of the nation as a symbol of both order and the popular values of the revolution. The most politically astute general was Napoleon Bonaparte, who had been a radical during the early revolution, a victorious commander in Italy, and a supporter of the repression of revolutionary disturbances after Thermidor.

Once in power, Napoleon consolidated many of the achievements of the revolution. He also repudiated much of it by establishing an empire. Thereafter, his ambitions drew France into wars of conquest and liberation across the Continent. For over a decade, Europe was at war, with only brief periods of armed truce. Through his conquests Napoleon spread many of the ideas and institutions of the revolution and overturned much of the old political and social order. He also provoked popular nationalism outside of France in opposition to French domination. This new force and the great alliances that opposed France eventually defeated Napoleon.

Throughout these Napoleonic years, new ideas and sensibilities, known by the term *Romanticism*, grew across Europe. Many of the ideas had originated in the eighteenth century, but they flourished in the turmoil of the French Revolution and the Napoleonic Wars. The revolution spurred the imagination of poets, painters, and philosophers. Some Romantic ideas, such as nationalism, supported the revolution; others, such as the emphasis on history and religion, opposed its values.

▼ The Rise of Napoleon Bonaparte

The chief threat to the Directory came from royalists, who hoped to restore the Bourbon monarchy by legal means. Many of the *émigrés* had returned to France. Their plans for a restoration drew support from devout Catholics and from those citizens horrified by the excesses of the revolution. Monarchy, they thought, promised a return to stability. The spring elections of 1797 replaced most incumbents with constitutional monarchists and their sympathizers, who now commanded a majority in the national legislature.

Read the **Document** "Madame de Remusat on the Rise of Napoleon" on **MyHistoryLab.com**

To preserve the republic and prevent a peaceful restoration of the Bourbons, the antimonarchist Directory staged a *coup d'état* on 18 Fructidor (September 4, 1797). They put their own supporters into the legislative seats their opponents had won. They then imposed censorship and exiled some of their enemies. At the request of the Directors, Napoleon Bonaparte, the general in charge of the French invasion of Italy, had sent a subordinate to Paris to guarantee the success of the coup. In 1797, as in 1795, the army and Bonaparte had saved the day for the government installed in the wake of the Thermidorian Reaction.

Napoleon Bonaparte was born in 1769 to a poor family of lesser nobles at Ajaccio, on the Mediterranean island of Corsica. Because France had annexed Corsica in 1768, he went to French schools and, in 1785, obtained a commission as a French artillery officer. He favored the revolution and was a fiery Jacobin. In 1793, he played a leading role in recovering the port of Toulon from the British. As a reward for his service, he was appointed a brigadier general. During the Thermidorian Reaction, his defense of the new regime on 13 Vendémiaire won him a command in Italy.

Early Military Victories

By 1795, French arms and diplomacy had shattered the enemy coalition, but France's annexation of Belgium guaranteed continued fighting with Britain and Austria. The invasion of the Italian peninsula aimed to deprive Austria of its rich northern Italian province of Lombardy. In a series of lightning victories, Bonaparte crushed the Austrian and Sardinian armies. On his own initiative, and against the wishes of the government in Paris, he concluded the Treaty of Campo Formio in October 1797. The treaty took Austria out of the war and crowned Napoleon's campaign with success. Before long, France dominated all of the Italian peninsula and Switzerland.

In November 1797, the triumphant Bonaparte returned to Paris as a hero and to confront France's only remaining enemy, Britain. He judged it impossible to cross the Channel and invade England at that time. Instead, he chose to attack British interests through the eastern Mediterranean by capturing Egypt from the Ottoman Empire. By this strategy, he hoped to drive the British fleet from the Mediterranean, cut off British communications with India, damage British trade, and threaten the British Empire.

Napoleon easily overran Egypt, but the invasion was a failure. Admiral Horatio Nelson (1758–1805) destroyed the French fleet at Abukir on August 1, 1798. The French army was cut off from France. To make matters worse, the situation in Europe was deteriorating. The invasion of Egypt had alarmed Russia, which had its own ambitions in the Near East. Russia, Austria, and the Ottomans joined Britain to form the Second Coalition against France. In 1799, the Russian and Austrian armies defeated the French in Italy and Switzerland and threatened to invade France.

Napoleon's venture into Egypt in 1798 and 1799 marked the first major Western European assault on the Ottoman Empire. It occurred less than a quarter century after Russia, under Catherine the Great, had taken control of the Crimea in the Treaty of Kuchuk-Kainardji. (See Chapter 17.) Significantly, British, not

Ottoman forces, drove the French out of Egypt. As shall be seen in Chapter 22, after Napoleon's invasion, the Ottoman Empire realized that it had to reform itself if it was to resist other European encroachments.

Read the Document "Louis Antoine Fauvelet de Bourrienne, *Memoirs of Napoleon Bonaparte*" on **MyHistoryLab.com**

The Constitution of the Year VIII

Economic troubles and the dangerous international situation eroded the Directory's fragile support. One of the Directors, the Abbé Siéyès (1748–1836), proposed a new constitution. The author of the pamphlet *What Is the Third Estate?* (1789) now wanted an executive body independent of the whims of electoral politics, a government based on the principle of "confidence from below, power from above." The change would require another *coup d'état* with military support. News of France's domestic troubles had reached Napoleon in Egypt. Without orders and leaving his army behind, he returned to France in October 1799 to popular acclaim. Soon he joined Siéyès. On 19 Brumaire (November 10, 1799), his troops ensured the success of the coup.

Siéyès appears to have thought that Napoleon could be used and then dismissed, but he misjudged his man. The proposed constitution divided executive authority among three consuls. Bonaparte quickly pushed Siéyès aside, and in December 1799, he issued the Constitution of the Year VIII. Behind a screen of universal male suffrage that suggested democratic principles, a complicated system of checks and balances that appealed to republican theory, and a Council of State that evoked memories of Louis XIV, the new constitution established the rule of one man—the First Consul, Bonaparte. In an age of widespread interest in classical analogies, Napoleon's takeover was reminiscent of Caesar and Augustus in ancient Rome, and to the Greek tyrants of the sixth century B.C.E. From the perspective of the twenty-first century, however, Bonaparte's career points forward to the dictators of the twentieth century. He was the first modern political figure to use the rhetoric of revolution and nationalism, to back it with military force, and to combine these elements into a mighty weapon of imperial expansion in the service of his own power.

▼ The Consulate in France (1799–1804)

The **Consulate** in effect ended the revolution in France. The leading elements of the Third Estate—that is, officials, landowners, doctors, lawyers, and financiers—had achieved most of their goals by 1799. They had abolished hereditary privilege, and the careers thus opened to talent allowed them to achieve wealth, status, and security for their property. The peasants were also satisfied. They had gained the land they had always wanted and had destroyed oppressive feudal privileges. The newly established dominant classes had little or no desire to share their new privileges with the lower social orders. Bonaparte seemed just the person to give them security. When he submitted his constitution to the voters in a plebiscite, they overwhelmingly approved it.

Suppressing Foreign Enemies and Domestic Opposition

Throughout much of the 1790s, the pressures of warfare, particularly conscription, had accounted for much French internal instability. Bonaparte justified the public's confidence in himself by making peace with France's enemies. Russia had already left the Second Coalition. A campaign in Italy brought another victory over Austria at Marengo in 1800. The Treaty of Luneville early in 1801 took Austria out of the war. Britain was now alone and, in 1802, concluded the Treaty of Amiens, which brought peace to Europe.

Bonaparte also restored peace and order at home. He used generosity, flattery, and bribery to win over enemies. He issued a general amnesty and employed men from all political factions, requiring only that they be loyal to him. Men who had been radicals during the Reign of Terror, or who had fled the Terror and favored constitutional monarchy, or who had been high officials under Louis XVI occupied some of the highest offices.

Bonaparte, however, ruthlessly suppressed opposition. He established a highly centralized administration in which prefects responsible to the government in Paris managed all departments. He employed secret police. He stamped out the royalist rebellion in the west and made the rule of Paris effective in Brittany and the Vendée for the first time in years.

Napoleon also invented and used opportunities to destroy his enemies. A plot on his life in 1804 provided an excuse to attack the Jacobins, though it was the work of the royalists. Also in 1804, he violated the sovereignty of the German state of Baden to seize and execute the Bourbon duke of Enghien (1772–1804). The duke was accused of participation in a royalist plot, though Bonaparte knew him to be innocent. The action was a flagrant violation of international law and of due process. Charles Maurice de Talleyrand-Périgord (1754–1838), Bonaparte's foreign minister, later termed the act "worse than a crime—a blunder" because it provoked foreign opposition. It was popular with the former Jacobins, however, for it seemed to preclude the possibility of a Bourbon restoration. The executioner of a Bourbon was not likely to restore the royal family. The execution also seems to have put an end to royalist plots.

Document

NAPOLEON ANNOUNCES HIS SEIZURE OF POWER

On November 10, 1799 (19 Brumaire, Year VIII), the day after his successful coup, Napoleon announced his own version of what had taken place. Although he was theoretically only one of three consuls, Napoleon's proclamation showed his assumption of personal responsibility for carrying out what he considered to be the true spirit of the Revolution, and laid the groundwork for his later assumption of sole imperial power.

Which of his personal qualities does Napoleon emphasize, and how does he expect the French people to evaluate them? How does Napoleon try to present his seizure of power as legitimate? Whom does he claim to represent? Do his actions, as he describes them, defend rule by majority, or undermine it?

On my return to Paris, I found a division reigning amongst all the constituted authorities. There was no agreement but on this single point—that the constitution was half destroyed, and could by no means effect the salvation of our liberties. All the parties came to me . . . and demanded my support. I refused to be a man of any party. A council of elders invited me, and I answered to their call. [Their] plan demanded a calm and liberal examination, free from every influence and every fear. The council of elders resolved, in consequence, that the sittings of the legislative body should be removed to St. Cloud, and charged me with the disposition of the force necessary to secure its independence, I owed it, my fellow-citizens, to the soldiers who are perishing in our armies, and the national glory, acquired at the price of their blood, to accept of this command. The councils being assembled at St. Cloud, the republican troops guaranteed their safety from without; but within, assassins had established the reign of terror. . . . The majority was disorganized, the most intrepid orators were disconcerted, and the inutility of every wise proposition was made evident. I bore my indignation and my grief to the council of elders, I demanded of them to ensure the execution of their generous designs. I represented to them the maladies of their country, from which those designs originated. . . . I then repaired to the council of five hundred without arms, and my head uncovered. . . . I wished to recall to the majority their wishes, and to assure them of their power. . . . Twenty assassins threw themselves upon me, and sought my breast. The grenadiers of the legislative body, whom I had left at the door of the hall, came up and placed themselves between me and my assassins. . . . They succeeded in bearing me away. I gave orders to rescue [the president, Napoleon's brother] from their power, and six grenadiers of the legislative body brought him out of the hall. . . . The factious were intimidated, and dispersed themselves. The majority, released from their blows, entered freely and peaceably into the hall of sitting, heard the propositions which were made to them for the public safety deliberated, and prepared the salutary resolution which is to become the new and provisional law of the republic. Frenchmen! you will recognize, without doubt, in this conduct, the zeal of a soldier of liberty, and of a citizen devoted to the republic. The ideas of preservation, protection, and freedom, immediately resumed their places on the dispersion of the faction who wished to oppress the councils, and who, in making themselves the most odious of men, never cease to be the most contemptible.

From *The Annual Register, or, A View of the History, Politics, and Literature for the Year 1799* (London: Otridge & Sons, 1801), p. 253.

Concordat with the Roman Catholic Church

No single set of revolutionary policies had aroused as much domestic opposition as those regarding the French Catholic Church; nor were there any other policies to which fierce supporters of the revolution seemed so attached. When the French armies had invaded Italy, they had driven Pope Pius VI (r. 1775–1799) from Rome, and he eventually died in exile in France. In 1801, to the shock and dismay of his anticlerical supporters, Napoleon concluded a concordat with Pope Pius VII (r. 1800–1823). The agreement was possible because Pius VII, before becoming pope, had written that Christianity was compatible with the ideals of equality and democracy. The concordat gave Napoleon what he most wanted. The agreement required both the refractory clergy and those who had accepted the revolution to resign. Their replacements received their spiritual investiture from the pope, but the state named the bishops and paid their salaries and the salary of one priest in each parish. In return, the church gave up its claims to its confiscated property.

The concordat declared, "Catholicism is the religion of the great majority of French citizens." This was merely a statement of fact and fell far short of what the pope had wanted: religious dominance for the Roman Catholic Church. The clergy had to swear an oath of loyalty to the state. The Organic Articles of 1802, which the government issued on its own authority without consulting the pope, established the supremacy of state over church. Similar laws were applied to the Protestant and Jewish communities, reducing still further the privileged position of the Catholic Church.

The Napoleonic Code

In 1802, a plebiscite ratified Napoleon as consul for life, and he soon produced another constitution that granted him what amounted to full power. He thereafter set about reforming and codifying French law. The result was the Civil Code of 1804, usually known as the Napoleonic Code.

The Napoleonic Code safeguarded all forms of property and tried to secure French society against internal challenges. All the privileges based on birth that the revolution had overthrown remained abolished.

The conservative attitudes toward labor and women that had emerged during the revolution also received full support. Workers' organizations remained forbidden, and workers had fewer rights than their employers. Fathers were granted extensive control over their children and husbands over their wives. However, primogeniture—the right of an eldest son to inherit most or all of his parents' property—remained abolished, and property was distributed among all children, males and females. Married women needed their husbands' consent to dispose of their own property. Divorce remained more difficult for women than for men. Before this code, French law had differed from region to region. That confused set of laws had given women opportunities to protect their interests. The universality of the Napoleonic Code ended that.

Establishing a Dynasty

In 1804, Bonaparte seized on a bomb attack on his life to make himself emperor. He argued that establishing a dynasty would make the new regime secure and make further attempts on his life useless. Another new constitution declared Napoleon Bonaparte Emperor of the French, instead of First Consul of the Republic. A plebiscite also overwhelmingly ratified this constitution.

To conclude the drama, Napoleon invited Pope Pius VII to Notre Dame to take part in the coronation. At the last minute, however, Napoleon convinced the pope to agree that the new emperor should crown himself. Napoleon would not allow anyone to think his power and authority depended on the church. Henceforth, he was called Napoleon I.

▼ The Haitian Revolution (1791–1804)

Between 1791 and 1804, the French colony of Haiti achieved independence. This event was of key importance for two reasons. First, it was sparked by policies of

Toussaint L'Ouverture (1746–1803) began the revolt that led to Haitian independence in 1804. Library of Congress

THE CORONATION OF NAPOLEON

JACQUES-LOUIS DAVID recorded the elaborate coronation of Napoleon in a monumental painting that revealed the enormous political and religious tensions of that event, which involved the kind of ritual and ceremony associated with the monarchy of the ancien régime.

Napoleon's mother sits in a balcony-like setting and presides over her son's establishment of a new reigning dynasty in France and across Europe, through the placement of relatives on various thrones.

Napoleon is about to place a crown on the head of his wife Josephine whom he will later divorce because she and he were unable to conceive an heir for his new dynasty. He would then marry the daughter of his enemy, the Habsburg emperor Francis.

Jacques-Louis David (1748–1825), *Consecration of the Emperor Napoleon I and Coronation of Empress Josephine*, 1806–07. Louvre, (Museum), Paris, France/Scala/Art Resource, NY

To the right sits Pope Pius VII who observes the event but is not a real participant. Napoleon and the pope had signed a Concordat that restored much of the standing but by no means all of the prerevolutionary authority of the Roman Catholic Church in France. The pope understood that at that moment in France as well as throughout Europe his authority was largely subject to the wishes of the French emperor.

What tools does David use to make Napoleon's singular significance apparent?

Napoleon's mother did not actually attend the coronation. Why was it important to include her in the image?

the French Revolution overflowing into its New World Empire. Second, the Haitian Revolution demonstrated that slaves of African origins could lead a revolt against white masters and mulatto freemen. The example of the Haitian Revolution for years thereafter terrified slaveholders throughout the Americas.

The relationship between slaves and masters on Haiti had been filled with violence throughout the eighteenth century. The French colonial masters had frequently used racial divisions between black slaves and mulatto freemen to their own political advantage. Once the French Revolution had broken out in France, the French National Assembly in 1791 decreed that free property-owning mulattos on Haiti should enjoy the same rights as white plantation owners. The Colonial Assembly in Haiti resisted the orders from France.

In 1791, a full-fledged slave rebellion shook Haiti. The coordination that preceded the rebellion required that slaves place a tremendous amount of faith in one another: any conversation that could have been interpreted as advocating rebellion would have led to death if reported or overheard. François-Dominique Toussaint L'Ouverture (1743?–1803), himself a former slave, quickly emerged as its leader. The rebellion involved enormous violence and loss of life on both sides. Although the slave rebellion collapsed, mulattos and free black people in Haiti, who hoped to gain the rights the French National Assembly had promised, then took up arms against the white colonial masters. French officials sent by the revolutionary government in Paris soon backed them. Slaves now came to the aid of an invading French force and, in early 1793, the French abolished slavery in Haiti.

View the **Closer Look** "The Haitian Revolution: Guerilla Warfare" on **MyHistoryLab.com**

By this time both Spain and Great Britain were attempting to intervene in Haitian events to expand their own influence in the Caribbean. Both were opposed to the end of slavery and both coveted Haiti's rich sugar-producing lands. Toussaint L'Ouverture and his force of ex-slaves again supported the French against the Spanish and the British. By 1800, his army had achieved dominance throughout the island of Hispaniola. He imposed an authoritarian constitution on Haiti and made himself Governor-General for life, but he preserved formal ties with France.

The French government under Napoleon distrusted L'Ouverture and feared that his example would undermine French authority elsewhere in the Caribbean and North America. In 1802, Napoleon sent an army to Haiti and eventually captured L'Ouverture, who was sent back to France where he died in prison in 1803. Other Haitian military leaders of slave origin, the most important of whom was Jean-Jacques Dessalines (1758–1806), continued to resist. When Napoleon found himself again at war with Britain in 1803, he decided to abandon his American empire, selling Louisiana to the United States and withdrawing his forces from Haiti. The Haitian revolution had an anticolonial aspect, but it was most important as the first successful slave rebellion in modern history. France formally recognized Haitian independence in 1804.

▼ Napoleon's Empire (1804–1814)

Between his coronation as emperor and his final defeat at Waterloo (1815), Napoleon conquered most of Europe. France's victories changed the map of the Continent. The wars put an end to the Old Regime and its feudal trappings throughout Western Europe and forced those European states that remained independent to reorganize themselves to resist Napoleon's armies.

View the **Map** "Map Discovery: Napoleon's Empire" on **MyHistoryLab.com**

Everywhere, Napoleon's advance unleashed the powerful force of nationalism, discussed more fully in Chapter 20. His weapon was the militarily mobilized French nation, one of the achievements of the revolution. Napoleon could put 700,000 men under arms at one time, risk 100,000 troops in a single battle, endure heavy losses, and fight again. He could conscript citizen soldiers in unprecedented numbers, thanks to their loyalty to the nation and to him. No single enemy could match such resources. Even coalitions were unsuccessful, until Napoleon's own mistakes led to his defeat.

Conquering an Empire

The Peace of Amiens (1802) between France and Great Britain was merely a truce. Napoleon's unlimited ambitions shattered any hope that it might last. He sent an army to restore the rebellious colony of Haiti to French rule. This move aroused British fears that he was planning a new French empire in America because Spain had restored Louisiana to France in 1801. More serious were his interventions in the Dutch Republic, the Italian peninsula, and Switzerland and his reorganization of the German states. The Treaty of Campo Formio had required a redistribution of territories along the Rhine River, and the petty princes of the region engaged in a scramble to enlarge their holdings. Among the results were the reduction of Austrian influence and the emergence of fewer, but larger, German states in the West, all dependent on Napoleon.

British Naval Supremacy Alarmed by these developments, the British issued an ultimatum. When Napoleon ignored it, Britain declared war in May 1803. William Pitt the Younger returned to office as prime minister in 1804 and began to construct the Third Coalition. By

By the time this painting was completed in 1807, Nelson was already a hero in Britain. Here he is depicted on his deathbed aboard his ship the *Victory*, during the British defeat of French and Spanish fleets at the Battle of Trafalgar in 1805. The lighting that illuminates Nelson's suffering face evokes religious paintings and suggests martyrdom. Arthur William Devis, "The Death of Nelson." Oil on canvas. The Granger Collection, NYC—

August 1805, he had persuaded Russia and Austria to move once more against France. A great naval victory soon raised the fortunes of the allies. On October 21, 1805, the British admiral Lord Nelson destroyed the combined French and Spanish fleets at the Battle of Trafalgar off the Spanish coast. Nelson died in the battle, but the British lost no ships. Although it would take ten more years before Napoleon's final defeat, Trafalgar ended all French hope of invading Britain and ensured that Britain would be able to maintain its opposition to France for the duration of the war. Britain had endeavored to establish supremacy on the high seas for centuries; now the navy dominated global commercial shipping and seemed undefeatable in military confrontation as well. The Battle of Trafalgar not only foreshadowed Napoleon's ultimate defeat by exposing French vulnerability to British strength, but also seemed the proof of a longstanding British belief that, in the words of one historian, "concentrating resources upon the navy would render Britain 'the guardian of liberty' throughout Europe."[1] Britain's dominance of the seas would not be seriously challenged until World War I.

Napoleonic Victories in Central Europe On land the story was different. Even before Trafalgar, Napoleon had marched to the Danube River to attack his continental enemies. In mid-October he forced an Austrian army to surrender at Ulm and occupied Vienna. On December 2, 1805, in perhaps his greatest victory, Napoleon defeated the combined Austrian and Russian forces at Austerlitz. The Treaty of Pressburg that followed won major concessions from Austria. The Austrians withdrew from Italy and left Napoleon in control of everything north of Rome. He was recognized as king of Italy.

Read the **Document** "Charles Parquin, 'Napoleon's Army' " on **MyHistoryLab.com**

Napoleon also made extensive political changes in the German states. In July 1806, he organized the Confederation of the Rhine, which included most of the western German princes. Their withdrawal from the Holy Roman Empire led the current Holy Roman Emperor, the Habsburg Francis II, to dissolve that ancient political body and henceforth to call himself Emperor Francis I of Austria.

Prussia, which had remained neutral up to this point, now foolishly went to war against France. Napoleon's forces quickly crushed the famous Prussian army at Jena and Auerstädt on October 14, 1806. Two weeks later, Napoleon was in Berlin. There, on November 21, he issued the Berlin Decrees, forbidding his allies from importing British goods. Napoleon, too, recognized the connection between Britain's commercial and military strength. On June 13, 1807, Napoleon defeated the Russians at Friedland and occupied East Prussia. Having occupied or co-opted the west German states, humbled and humiliated Austria, and defeated Prussia, the French emperor was master of all Germany.

[1]David Armitage, *The Ideological Origins of the British Empire* (Cambridge, UK: Cambridge University Press, 2000), p. 185.

In this 1806 caricature by the famous English artist James Gillray, Napoleon is shown as a baker who creates new kings as easily as gingerbread cookies. His new allies in the Rhine Confederation, including the rulers of Württemberg, Bavaria, and Saxony, are placed in the "New French Oven for Imperial Gingerbread." 'Tiddy-Doll, the Great French Gingerbread Maker, Drawing Out a New Batch of Kings. His Man, Hopping Talley, Mixing Up the Dough', pub. by Hannah Humphrey, 23rd January 1806 (aquatint), Gillray, James (1757–1815). Leeds Museums and Galleries (City Art Gallery) U.K./The Bridgeman Art Library International

Treaty of Tilsit Unable to fight another battle and unwilling to retreat into Russia, Tsar Alexander I (r. 1801–1825) was ready to make peace. He and Napoleon met on a raft in the Niemen River while the two armies and the nervous king of Prussia watched from the bank. On July 7, 1807, they signed the Treaty of Tilsit, which confirmed France's gains. Prussia lost half its territory. Only the support of Alexander saved it from extinction. Prussia openly and Russia secretly became allies of Napoleon.

Napoleon established his family as the collective sovereigns of Europe. The great French Empire was ruled directly by the head of the clan, Napoleon. On its borders lay satellite states ruled by members of his family. His stepson ruled Italy for him, and three of his brothers and his brother-in-law were made kings of other conquered states. The French emperor expected his relatives to take orders without question. When they failed to do so, he rebuked and even punished them. The imposition of Napoleonic rule provoked political opposition that needed only encouragement and assistance to flare up into serious resistance.

The Continental System

After the Treaty of Tilsit, such assistance could come only from Britain, and Napoleon knew he must defeat the British before he could feel safe. Unable to compete with the British navy, he continued the economic warfare the Berlin Decrees had begun. He planned to cut off all British trade with the European continent and thus to cripple British commercial and financial power. He hoped to cause domestic unrest and drive Britain from the war. The Milan Decree of 1807 went further and attempted to stop neutral nations from trading with Britain. (See Map 19–1.) Britain responded with its own set of decrees, the Orders of Council, which in turn forbid British subjects, allies, or even neutral countries from trading with France.

Despite initial drops in exports, domestic unrest, and tension between Britain and neutral countries that resented the ban, the British economy survived. British control of the seas assured access to the growing markets of North and South America and of the eastern Mediterranean. At the same time, the Continental System badly hurt the European economies. Napoleon rejected advice to turn his empire into a free-trade area. Such a policy would have been both popular and helpful. Instead, his tariff policies favored France, increased the resentment of foreign merchants, and made them less willing to enforce the system and more ready to engage in smuggling. It was, in part, to prevent smuggling that Napoleon invaded Spain in 1808. The resulting peninsular campaign in Spain and Portugal helped bring on his ruin.

▼ European Response to the Empire

Wherever Napoleon ruled, he imposed the Napoleonic Code and abolished hereditary social distinctions. Feudal privileges disappeared, and the peasants were freed from serfdom and manorial dues. In the towns, the guilds and the local oligarchies that had been dominant for

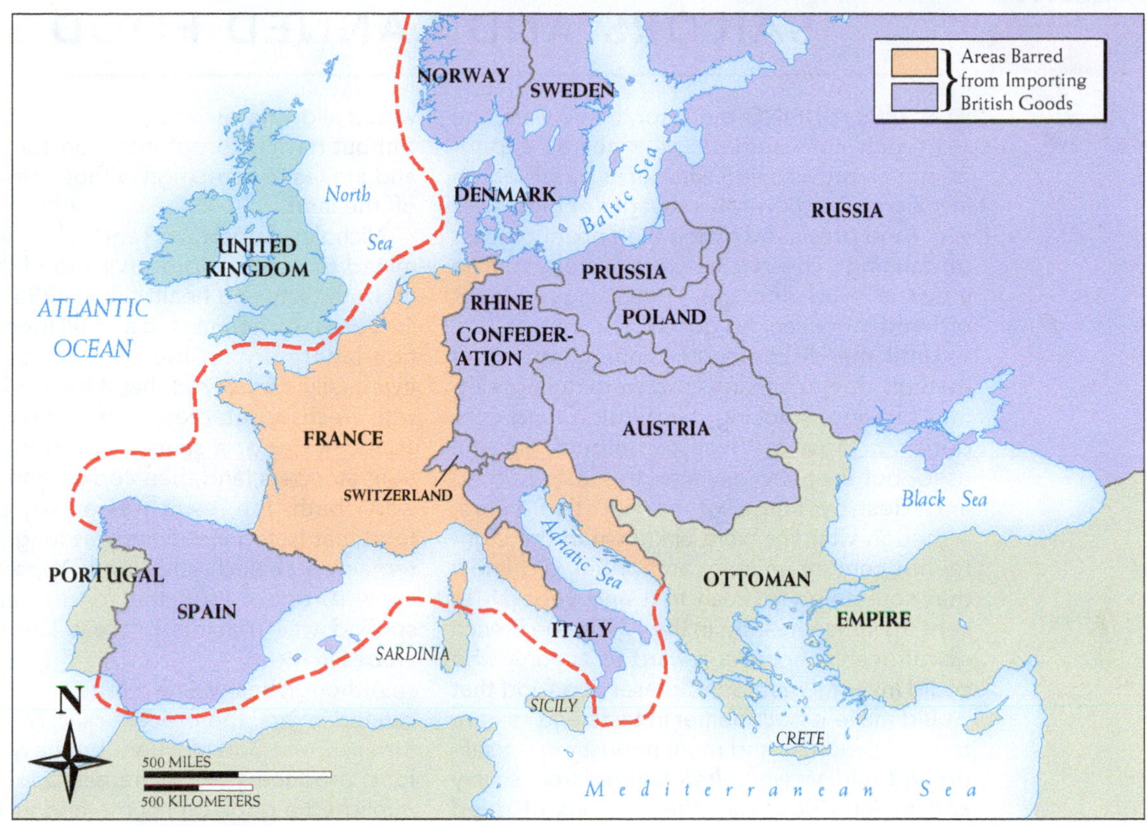

Map 19–1 **THE CONTINENTAL SYSTEM, 1806–1810** Napoleon hoped to cut off all British trade with the European continent and thereby drive the British from the war.

centuries were dissolved or deprived of their power. The established churches lost their traditional independence and were made subordinate to the state. Toleration replaced monopoly of religion by an established church. Despite these reforms, however, it was always clear that Napoleon's policies were intended first for his own glory and that of France. The Continental System demonstrated that Napoleon's rule was intended to enrich France, rather than Europe generally. Consequently, before long, the conquered states and peoples grew restive.

Read the **Document** "Carl von Clausewitz, On War, 'Arming the Nation' " on **MyHistoryLab.com**

German Nationalism and Prussian Reform

The German response to Napoleon's success was particularly interesting and important. There had never been a unified German state. The great German writers of the Enlightenment, such as Immanuel Kant and Gotthold Lessing, were neither deeply politically engaged nor nationalistic.

At the beginning of the nineteenth century, the Romantic Movement had begun to take hold. One of its basic features in Germany was the emergence of nationalism, which went through two distinct stages there. Initially, nationalistic writers emphasized the unique and admirable qualities of German culture, which, they argued, arose from the history of the German people. Such cultural nationalism prevailed until Napoleon's humiliation of Prussia at Jena in 1806.

At that point many German intellectuals began to urge resistance to Napoleon on the basis of German nationalism. The French conquest endangered the independence and achievements of all German-speaking people. Many nationalists also criticized the German princes, who ruled selfishly and inefficiently and who seemed ever ready to lick Napoleon's boots. Only a people united through its language and culture could resist the French onslaught. No less important in forging a German national sentiment was the example of France itself, which had attained greatness by enlisting the active support of the entire people in the patriotic cause. Henceforth, many Germans sought to solve their internal political problems by attempting to establish a unified German state, reformed to harness the energies of the entire people.

After Tilsit, only Prussia could arouse such patriotic feelings. Elsewhere German rulers were either under Napoleon's thumb or collaborating with him. Defeated, humiliated, and diminished, Prussia continued to resist,

ENCOUNTERING THE *Past*

SAILORS AND CANNED FOOD

IN 1803, DURING the Napoleonic wars, the French navy undertook a secret experiment—provisioning a few of its naval vessels involved in long overseas voyages or blockades with food preserved by the then novel process of canning. The results were excellent: The crews thrived and the French government ordered more canned goods.

Until the discovery of canning, the chief methods for preserving food were drying, salting, pickling, smoking, fermenting, and condensing. Most of these techniques are still used, but they strongly alter the taste of food and destroy some of its nutritive value. Although vitamins were unknown in the eighteenth century, military authorities did know that something in fresh fruit and vegetables kept their men healthy. In the 1790s, the French government offered a reward to anyone who could invent a method of preserving food that would make it both nearer in taste and texture to fresh products and more nourishing for sailors and soldiers who often suffered from scurvy and malnutrition from their rations of dried bread and salted meat. The desired food would allow naval vessels to stay at sea longer without having to put into port for fresh food and armies to campaign without having to live off the land.

Nicholas Appert, a French chef, was determined to produce preserved food that would be both tasty and healthful. In 1795, he established what amounted to a small food preservation laboratory on the outskirts of Paris. He eventually discovered that if he filled glass jars with fresh vegetables, fruit, soups, or meat, added water or a sauce, sealed the jars with tight stoppers, and then cooked them in a hot water bath, the result was a tasty preserved food that lasted indefinitely as long as the jars remained sealed. Although Appert did not know it, one reason the food remained unspoiled was that his process killed any microbes in it.

Although many fine French foods are still canned in jars, the process quickly took a new turn in Great Britain where the navy as well as food producers were interested in it. Appert published a book on his method in 1810, and by 1813 an English company began canning in tins, which were less expensive and more durable than glass jars. Soon other canning companies appeared in Europe, including those that produced canned sardines. By midcentury, millions of people, particularly in Western Europe and North America, were eating canned food. By 1900, canned goods had become what they remain today—part of everyday life around the world. The basic process used in canning is still the one Appert devised in the 1790s.

From Sue Shephard, *Pickled, Potted, and Canned: How the Art and Science of Food Processing Changed the World* (New York: Simon & Schuster, 2000).

Nicholas Appert (1749–1841) invented canning as a way of preserving food nutritiously. Canned food could be transported over long distances without spoiling. Private Collection/Bridgeman Art Library

What advantages did canning have over other methods of preserving food?

Why was the military interested in it?

How did canning become a part of everyday life?

however feebly. German nationalists from other states fled to Prussia. Once there, they called for reforms and unification that King Frederick William III (r. 1797–1840) and the Junker nobility feared and hated. Reforms came about despite such opposition because the defeat at Jena had shown that the Prussian state had to change to survive.

The Prussian administrative and social reforms were the work of Baron vom Stein (1757–1831) and Prince von Hardenberg (1750–1822). Neither of these reformers intended to reduce the autocratic power of the Prussian monarch or to end the dominance of the Junkers, who formed the bulwark of the state and of the officer corps. Rather, they wanted to fight French power with their own version of France's weapons. As Hardenberg declared,

> Our objective, our guiding principle, must be a revolution in the better sense, a revolution leading directly to the great goal, the elevation of humanity through the wisdom of those in authority. . . . Democratic rules of conduct in a monarchical administration, such is the formula . . . which will conform most comfortably with the spirit of the age.[2]

Although the reforms came from the top, they wrought important changes in Prussian society.

Stein's reforms broke the Junker monopoly of landholding. Serfdom was abolished. However, unlike in the western German states where all remnants of serfdom disappeared, in Prussia the Junkers ensured that vestiges of the system survived. Former Prussian serfs were free to leave the land if they chose, but those who stayed had to continue to perform manorial labor. They could obtain the ownership of the land they worked only if they forfeited a third of it to the lord. The result was that Junker holdings grew larger. Some peasants went to the cities to find work, others became agricultural laborers, and some did actually become small freeholding farmers. In Prussia and elsewhere, serfdom had ended, but the rise in the numbers of landless laborers created new social problems.

Military reforms sought to increase the supply of soldiers and to improve their quality. Jena had shown that an army of free patriots commanded by officers chosen on merit rather than by birth could defeat an army of serfs and mercenaries commanded by incompetent nobles. To remedy the situation, the Prussian reformers abolished inhumane military punishments, sought to inspire patriotic feelings in the soldiers, opened the officer corps to commoners, gave promotions on the basis of merit, and organized war colleges that developed new theories of strategy and tactics.

View the **Map** "Interactive Map: The Unification of Germany 1815–1871" on **MyHistoryLab.com**

[2]Geoffrey Brunn, *Europe and the French Imperium* (New York: Harper & Row, 1938), p. 174.

These reforms soon enabled Prussia to regain its former power. Because Napoleon strictly limited the size of its army to 42,000 men, however, Prussia could not introduce universal conscription until it broke with Napoleon in 1813. Before that date, the Prussians evaded the limit by training one group each year, putting them into the reserves, and then training a new group the same size. Prussia could thus boast an army of 270,000 by 1814.

The Wars of Liberation

Spain In Spain more than elsewhere in Europe, national resistance to France had deep social roots. Spain had achieved political unity as early as the sixteenth century. The Spanish peasants were devoted to the ruling dynasty and especially to the Roman Catholic Church. France and Spain had been allies since 1796. In 1807, however, a French army came into the Iberian Peninsula to force Portugal to abandon its traditional alliance with Britain. The army stayed in Spain to protect lines of supply and communication. Napoleon used a revolt that broke out in Madrid in 1808 as a pretext to depose the Spanish Bourbons and to place his brother Joseph (1768–1844) on the Spanish throne. Attacks on the privileges of the church were interpreted as attacks on Catholicism itself, and increased public outrage. Many members of the upper classes were prepared to collaborate with Napoleon, but the peasants, urged on by the lower clergy and the monks, rebelled.

In Spain, Napoleon faced a new kind of warfare. Guerrilla bands cut lines of communication, killed stragglers, destroyed isolated units, and then disappeared into the mountains. The British landed an army under Sir Arthur Wellesley (1769–1852), later the duke of Wellington, to support the Spanish insurgents. Thus began the long peninsular campaign that would drain French strength from elsewhere in Europe and hasten Napoleon's eventual defeat. (See "Compare and Connect: The Experience of War in the Napoleonic Age," pages 596–597.)

Austria France's troubles in Spain encouraged Austria to renew the war in 1809. Since their defeat at Austerlitz, they had sought a war of revenge. The Austrians counted on Napoleon's distraction in Spain, French war weariness, and aid from other German princes. Napoleon was fully in command in France, however, and the German princes did not move. The French army marched swiftly into Austria and won the Battle of Wagram. The resulting Peace of Schönbrunn deprived Austria of substantial territory and 3.5 million subjects.

Another spoil of victory was the Austrian archduchess Marie Louise (1791–1847), daughter of Emperor Francis I. Napoleon's first wife, Josephine de Beauharnais (1763–1814), was forty-six and had borne him no

COMPARE AND CONNECT

The Experience of War in the Napoleonic Age

Read the **Compare and Connect** on **MyHistoryLab.com**

THE NAPOLEONIC WARS spread violence across Europe. Different participants, writers, and artists portrayed the experience of war differently. William Napier reported his own heroism in a quite matter-of-fact manner. The German poet and historian Ernest Moritz Arndt recalled moments of intense nationalistic patriotism. The Spanish painter Goya portrayed a moment of enormous brutality suffered by the Spanish at the hands of French troops.

QUESTIONS

1. **How was the warfare in Spain different from the classic battles of the eighteenth-century? What distinguished the new "guerilla" warfare?**
2. **Why does Arndt claim each of these various groups wanted war?**
3. **How does Arndt suggest the possibility of a united nation that did not yet actually exist?**
4. **How does Goya portray Spaniards as victims of harsh, unmerciful military violence?**
5. **How do Napier's memoir, Arndt's call to arms, and Goya's painting illustrate different points of view and ways of interpreting the violence of modern warfare?**

I. A Polish Legionnaire Recalls Guerilla Warfare in Spain

Heinrich von Brandt (1789–1868), was a German-speaking Prussian who lived in territory that became part of the Duchy of Warsaw in 1807. Like many Germans his age, he was a great admirer of Napoleon's accomplishments, even if he resented his violation of Prussian sovereignty. Having first trained as a member of the Prussian military (in preparation to fight against Napoleon), he was subsequently enlisted to fight in the newly constituted Polish army, allied with Napoleon. As a member of the Vistula legion, he was sent to Spain in 1808. This excerpt from his memoirs refers to the siege of Saragossa in January and February 1809.

The more we advanced the more dogged resistance became. We knew that in order not to be killed, or to diminish that risk, we would have to take each and every one of these houses converted into redoubts and where death lurked in the cellars, behind doors and shutters—in fact, everywhere. When we broke into a house we had to make an immediate and thorough inspection from the cellar to the rooftop. Experience taught us that sudden and determined resistance could well be a trick. Often as we were securing one floor we would be shot at from point blank range from the floor above through loopholes in the floorboards. All the nooks and crannies of these old-fashioned houses aided such deadly ambushes. We also had to maintain a good watch on the rooftops. With their light sandals, the Aragonese could move with the ease of and as silently as a cat and were thus able to make surprise incursions well behind the front line. It was indeed aerial combat. We would be sitting peacefully around a fire, in a house occupied for some days, when suddenly shots would come through some window just as though they had come from the sky itself. . . .

The Spanish stopped at nothing to slow our advance down. Even when they were at last forced to abandon a building, they would scatter resin soaked faggots everywhere and set them alight. The ensuing fires would not destroy the stone buildings but served to give the besieged time to prepare their defences in neighboring houses. . . .

It was all over by the evening of 20 February. . . . [The next day] the vanguard of the famous defenders of Saragossa began to appear. A certain number of young men, aged between sixteen and eighteen, without uniforms and wearing grey cloaks and red cockades, lined up in front of us, nonchalantly smoking their cigarettes. Not long after we witnessed the arrival of the rest of the army: a strange collection composed of humanity of all shades and conditions. A few were in uniform but most were dressed like peasants. . . . Most of them were of such non-military bearing that our men were saying aloud that we should never have had so much trouble in beating such a rabble. ■

From Heinrich von Brandt, *In the Legions of Napoleon: The Memoirs of a Polish Officer in Spain and Russia, 1808–1813*, trans. and ed. Jonathan North (London: Greenhill Books, 1999), pp. 58–63.

II. A German Writer Describes the War of Liberation

Although many Germans, including Ernst Moritz Arndt (1769–1860), initially greeted the French Revolution with enthusiasm, the French Army's invasion of German territory was met with a wave of nationalist resistance. As Napoleon's army retreated from Moscow in 1813, people from virtually all German-speaking lands overcame rivalry amongst themselves to join forces against a common enemy. Arndt described the excitement of that moment in a passage subsequently reprinted in German history textbooks for more than a century.

Fired with enthusiasm, the people rose, "with God for King and Fatherland." Among the Prussians there was only one voice, one feeling, one anger and one love, to save the Fatherland and to free Germany. . . . War, war, sounded the cry from the Carpathians to the Baltic, from the Niemen to the Elbe. War! cried the nobleman and landed proprietor who had become impoverished. War! that peasant who was driving his last horse to death. . . . War! the citizen who was growing exhausted from quartering soldiers and paying taxes. War! the widow who was sending her only son to the front. War! the young girl who, with tears of pride and pain, was leaving her betrothed. . . . Even young women, under all sorts of disguises, rushed to arms; all wanted to drill, arm themselves and fight and die for the Fatherland. . . .

The most beautiful thing about all this holy zeal and happy confusion was . . . that the one great feeling for the Fatherland, its freedom and honor, swallowed all other feelings, caused all other considerations and relationships to be forgotten. ■

From Louis L., Snyder, trans., *Documents of German History*. Copyright © 1958 by Rutgers, the State University. Reprinted by permission of Rutgers University Press.

III. Francisco Goya, *The Third of May, 1808* (painted 1814–1815)

Napoleon began to send troops into Spain in 1807 after the king of Spain had agreed to aid France against Britain's ally, Portugal. By early 1808 Spain had essentially become an occupied nation. The French troops included Islamic soldiers whom Napoleon had recruited in Egypt. Many Spaniards associated French soldiers with a threat to the Catholic faith. On May 2, riots took place in Madrid between French troops and Spanish civilians. In response, the French general Murat ordered the execution of numerous citizens of Madrid, which occurred the night of May 2 and 3. The events of these two days marked the opening of the Spanish effort to rid their peninsula of French rule.

Francisco de Goya y Lucientes recorded Napoleon's troops executing Spanish guerilla fighters who had rebelled against the French occupation in *The Third of May, 1808*. PRISMA/VWPICS/© Visual&Written SL / Alamy

After the restoration of the Spanish monarchy, Francisco Goya (1745–1828) depicted the savagery of those executions in the most memorable war painting of the Napoleonic era, The Third of May, 1808.

There is one group of humble Spaniards who have already been shot, another in the process of execution, and a third group, some of whom are hiding their eyes, who will be the next victims.

The painting illustrates two forces of Napoleonic warfare confronting each other: the professional solider and the guerilla (a term coined during the Spanish resistance of this era). The guerilla must fight with what few resources he finds at his command and with few advanced weapons. By contrast, in this painting, the well-disciplined soldiers, equipped with modern rifles, carry out the execution by the light of large technologically advanced lanterns fueled by either gas or oil with which Napoleon equipped his troops. Goya succeeds in making ordinary people and very poor clergy not only the victims, but also symbolic heroes of the national war of liberation. ■

children. His dynastic ambitions, as well as the desire for a royal marriage, led him to divorce Josephine and marry the eighteen-year-old Marie Louise. Napoleon had also considered marrying the sister of Tsar Alexander, but had received a polite rebuff. The emperor of Austria, however, was in no position to refuse the match.

The Invasion of Russia

The failure of Napoleon's marriage negotiations with Russia emphasized the shakiness of the Franco–Russian alliance concluded at Tilsit. Russian nobles disliked the alliance because of the liberal politics of France and because the Continental System prohibited timber sales to Britain. Only French aid in gaining Constantinople could justify the alliance in their eyes, but Napoleon gave them no help against the Ottoman Empire. The organization of the Polish Duchy of Warsaw as a Napoleonic satellite on the Russian doorstep and its enlargement with Austrian territory in 1809 after the Battle of Wagram angered Alexander. Napoleon's annexation of Holland in violation of the Treaty of Tilsit, his recognition of the French marshal Bernadotte (1763–1844) as the future King Charles XIV of Sweden, and his marriage to Marie Louise further disturbed the tsar. At the end of 1810, Russia withdrew from the Continental System and began to prepare for war. (See Map 19–2.)

Napoleon was determined to end the Russian military threat. He amassed an army of more than 600,000 men, including a core of Frenchmen and more than 400,000 other soldiers drawn from the rest of his empire. He intended the usual short campaign crowned by a decisive battle, but the Russians retreated before his advance. His vast superiority in numbers—the Russians had only about 160,000 troops—made it foolish for them to risk a battle. Instead, they followed a "scorched-earth" policy, destroying all food and supplies as they retreated. The so-called Grand Army of Napoleon could not live off the country, and the expanse of Russia made supply lines too long to maintain. Terrible rains, fierce heat, shortages of food and water, and the courage of the Russian rear guard eroded the morale of Napoleon's army. Napoleon's advisers urged him to abandon the venture, but he feared an unsuccessful campaign would undermine his position in the empire and in France. He pinned his faith on the Russians' unwillingness to abandon Moscow without a fight.

In September 1812, Russian public opinion forced the army to give Napoleon the battle he wanted despite the canny Russian general Mikhail Kutuzov's (1745–1813) wish to let the Russian winter defeat the invader. At Borodino, not far west of Moscow, the bloodiest battle of the Napoleonic era cost the French 30,000 casualties and the Russians almost twice as many. Yet the Russian army was not destroyed. Napoleon won nothing substantial, and the battle was regarded as a defeat for him.

Napoleon underestimated the Russians' willingness to sacrifice Moscow in the interests of victory. In order to deprive French troops of food, fuel, and housing, the Russians set fire to Moscow as they abandoned the city to the invading army. Napoleon was left far from home with a badly diminished army lacking adequate supplies as winter came to a vast and unfriendly country. After capturing the burned city, Napoleon addressed several peace offers to Alexander, but the tsar ignored them. By October, what was left of the Grand Army was forced to retreat. By December, Napoleon realized the Russian fiasco would encourage plots against him at home. He returned to Paris, leaving the remnants of his army to struggle westward. Perhaps only 100,000 of the original 600,000 survived their ordeal.

European Coalition

Even as the news of the disaster reached the West, the final defeat of Napoleon was far from certain. He was able to put down his opponents in Paris and raise another 350,000 men. Neither the Prussians nor the Austrians were eager to risk another contest with Napoleon, and even the Russians hesitated. The Austrian foreign minister, Prince Klemens von Metternich (1773–1859), would have preferred to make a negotiated peace that would leave Napoleon on the throne of a shrunken and chastened France rather than see Russia dominate Europe. Napoleon might have negotiated a reasonable settlement had he been willing to make concessions that would have split his jealous opponents. He would not consider that solution, however. As he explained to Metternich,

> Your sovereigns born on the throne can let themselves be beaten twenty times and return to their capitals. I cannot do this because I am an upstart soldier. My domination will not survive the day when I cease to be strong, and therefore feared.[3]

In 1813, patriotic pressure and national ambition brought together the last and most powerful coalition against Napoleon. The Russians drove westward, and Prussia and then Austria joined them. Vast amounts of British money assisted them. From Spain, Wellington marched his army into France. Napoleon's new army was inexperienced and poorly equipped. His generals had lost confidence in him and were tired. The emperor himself was worn out and sick. Still, he waged a skillful campaign in central Europe and defeated the allies at Dresden. In October, however, the combined armies of the enemy decisively defeated him at Leipzig in what the Germans called the Battle of the Nations. In March 1814, the allied armies marched into Paris. A few days later, Napoleon abdicated and went into exile on the island of Elba, off the coast of central Italy.

[3]Felix Markham, *Napoleon and the Awakening of Europe* (New York: Macmillan, 1965), pp. 115–116.

Map 19–2 **NAPOLEONIC EUROPE IN LATE 1812** By mid-1812 the areas shown in peach were incorporated into France, and most of the rest of Europe was directly controlled by or allied with Napoleon. But Russia had withdrawn from the failing Continental System, and the decline of Napoleon was about to begin.

▼ The Congress of Vienna and the European Settlement

Fear of Napoleon and hostility to his ambitions had held the victorious coalition together. As soon as he was removed, the allies pursued their separate ambitions. Nevertheless, Robert Stewart, Viscount Castlereagh (1769–1822), the British foreign secretary, brought about the signing of the Treaty of Chaumont on March 9, 1814. It provided for the restoration of the Bourbons to the French throne and the contraction of France to its frontiers of 1792. Even more importantly, Britain, Austria, Russia, and Prussia agreed to form a Quadruple Alliance for twenty years to preserve whatever settlement they agreed on. Remaining problems—and there were many—and final details were left for a conference to be held at Vienna.

View the **Map** "Map Discovery: Europe After the Congress of Vienna, 1815" on **MyHistoryLab.com**

Territorial Adjustments

The Congress of Vienna assembled in September 1814, but did not conclude its work until November 1815. Although a glittering array of heads of state attended the gathering, the four great powers (Britain, Russia, Prussia, and Austria) conducted the important work of the conference. The only full session of the congress met to ratify the arrangements the big four made. The easiest problem the great powers faced was France. All the victors agreed that no single state should be allowed to dominate

Europe, and all were determined to prevent France from doing so again. The restoration of the French Bourbon monarchy, which was temporarily popular, and a nonvindictive boundary settlement were designed to keep France calm and satisfied.

The powers also strengthened the states around France's borders to serve as barriers to renewed French expansion. They established the kingdom of the Netherlands, which included Belgium and Luxembourg, in the north and added the important port of Genoa to strengthen Piedmont in the south. Prussia was given important new territories along the Rhine River to deter French aggression in the West. Austria gained full control of northern Italy to prevent a repetition of Napoleon's conquests there. As for the rest of the German states, most of Napoleon's territorial arrangements were left untouched. The venerable Holy Roman Empire, which had been dissolved in 1806, was not revived. (See Map 19–3.) In all these areas, the congress established the rule of legitimate monarchs and rejected any hint of the republican and democratic policies that had flowed from the French Revolution.

On these matters agreement was not difficult, but the settlement of eastern Europe sharply divided the victors. Alexander I of Russia wanted all of Poland under his rule. Prussia was willing to give it to him in return for all of Saxony, which had been allied with Napoleon. Austria, however, was unwilling to surrender its share of Poland or to see either Prussian or Russian power in central Europe grow. The Polish–Saxon question almost caused a new war among the victors, but defeated France provided a way out. The wily Talleyrand, now representing France at Vienna, suggested the weight of France added to that of Britain and Austria might bring Alexander to his senses. When news of a secret treaty among the three leaked out, the tsar agreed to become ruler of a smaller Poland, and Prussia settled for only part of Saxony. Thereafter, France was included as a fifth great power in all deliberations.

The Hundred Days and the Quadruple Alliance

Napoleon's return from Elba on March 1, 1815, further united the victors. The French army was still loyal to the former emperor, and many of the French people preferred his rule to that of the restored Bourbons. Napoleon escaped to France, and soon regained power. He promised a liberal constitution and a peaceful foreign policy. The allies were not convinced. They declared Napoleon an outlaw (a new device under international law) and sent their armies to crush him. Wellington, with the crucial help of the Prussians under Field Marshal von Blücher (1742–1819), defeated Napoleon at Waterloo in Belgium on June 18, 1815. Napoleon again abdicated and was exiled on Saint Helena, a tiny Atlantic island off the coast of Africa, where he died in 1821.

Read the **Document** "Napoleon's Exile to St. Helena (1815)" on **MyHistoryLab.com**

The Hundred Days, as the period of Napoleon's return is called, frightened the great powers and made the peace settlement harsher for France. In addition to some

In this political cartoon of the Congress of Vienna, Tallyrand simply watches which way the wind is blowing, Castlereagh hesitates, while the monarchs of Russia, Prussia, and Austria form the dance of the Holy Alliance. The king of Saxony holds on to his crown and the republic of Geneva pays homage to the kingdom of Sardinia. bpk, Berlin/Art Resource, NY

Map 19–3 **THE GERMAN STATES AFTER 1815** The German states continued to cooperate in a loose confederation, but maintained their independence. Independence was not restored to the small principalities that had been eliminated during the Napoleonic era.

minor territorial adjustments, the victors imposed a war indemnity and an army of occupation on France. Alexander proposed a Holy Alliance, whereby the monarchs promised to act together in accordance with Christian principles. Austria and Prussia signed, but Castlereagh thought it absurd, and Britain abstained. The tsar, who was then embracing mysticism, believed his proposal a valuable tool for international relations. The Holy Alliance soon became a symbol of extreme political reaction.

Britain, Austria, Prussia, and Russia renewed the Quadruple Alliance on November 20, 1815. Henceforth, it was as much a coalition for maintaining peace as for pursuing victory over France. A coalition for such a purpose had never existed in European diplomacy before. It represented an important new departure in European affairs. Unlike eighteenth-century diplomacy, certain powers were determined to prevent war. The statesmen at Vienna had seen the armies of the French Revolution and Napoleon overturning the political and social order of much of the Continent. Their nations had experienced unprecedented destruction and had had to raise enormous military forces. They knew war affected not just professional armies and navies, but entire civilian populations as well. They were determined to prevent any more such upheaval and destruction.

Consequently, the chief aims of the Congress of Vienna were to prevent a recurrence of the Napoleonic nightmare and to arrange a lasting peace. The leaders of Europe had learned that a treaty should secure not victory, but peace. The diplomats aimed to establish a framework for stability, rather than to punish France. The great powers sought to ensure that each of them would respect the Vienna settlement and not use force to change it.

Though chastened by Prussia's power and its defeat by France, Austria continued to be a powerful player in European diplomacy. Much of the credit for this goes to Metternich, who emerged as the leading statesman of Europe at the Congress of Vienna. Metternich's commitment to preventing international war by preventing domestic revolution enabled him to take the lead in a new system of cooperative conservatism that would become known as the Concert of Europe.

The Congress of Vienna achieved its goals. France accepted the new situation without undue resentment, in part because the new international order recognized it as a great power. The victorious powers settled difficult problems reasonably. They established a new legal framework whereby treaties were made between states rather than between monarchs. The treaties remained in place when a monarch died. Furthermore, during the quarter century of warfare, European leaders had come to calculate the nature of political and economic power in new ways that went beyond the simple vision of gaining a favorable balance of trade that had caused so many eighteenth-century wars. They took into account their natural resources and economies, their systems of education, and the possibility that general growth in agriculture, commerce, and industry would benefit all states and not one at the expense of others.

The Congress has been criticized for failing to recognize and provide for the great forces that would stir the nineteenth century—nationalism and democracy. Such criticism is inappropriate. At the time nationalist pressures were relatively rare; the general desire was for peace. The settlement, like all such agreements, aimed to solve past ills, and in that it succeeded. The statesmen at Vienna could not have anticipated future problems and understandably refused to yield to forces of which they disapproved and that they believed threatened international peace and stability. The measure of the success of the Vienna settlement is that it remained essentially intact for almost half a century and prevented general war for a hundred years. (See Map 19–4.)

Map 19–4 **EUROPE 1815, AFTER THE CONGRESS OF VIENNA** The Congress of Vienna achieved the post-Napoleonic territorial adjustments shown on the map. The most notable arrangements dealt with areas along France's borders (the Netherlands, Prussia, Switzerland, and Piedmont) and in Poland and northern Italy.

▼ The Romantic Movement

Reflecting on the social, political, and cultural changes within Europe from the mid-eighteenth century to the Congress of Vienna, one German writer asserted in 1818, "in the three generations alive today our own age has combined what cannot be combined. No sense of continuity informs the tremendous contrast inherent in the years 1750, 1789 and 1815."[4] The years of the French Revolution and the conquests of Napoleon saw the emergence of a new and important intellectual movement throughout Europe that has come to be called **Romanticism**. The Romantic movement was a reaction against much of the thought of the Enlightenment and the social transformation of the Industrial Revolution. Not surprisingly, given its emphasis on the individual, scholars have never been able to agree on a general definition of Romanticism. There is, however, a consensus that Romanticism represented a turn toward "absolute inwardness," in the words of Hegel: an emphasis on the artist over his or her work, on the subjective experience and potential heroism of the individual, and the inability to understand the external world through reason. Romantic writers and artists thought the imagination was superior to reason as a means to perceive the world. Instead of controlling nature, they believed, people would be awestruck by it. Many of them urged a revival of Christianity, so that it would once again permeate Europe. Unlike the philosophes, the Romantics liked

[4]Tim Blanning, *The Romantic Revolution: A History* (New York: Modern Library, 2010), p. ix.

NAPOLEONIC EUROPE

1797	Napoleon concludes the Treaty of Campo Formio
1798	Nelson defeats the French navy in the harbor of Abukir in Egypt
1799	Consulate established in France
1801	Concordat between France and the papacy
1802	Treaty of Amiens
1803	War renewed between France and Britain
1804	Execution of Duke d'Enghien
1804	Napoleonic Civil Code issued
1804	Napoleon crowned as emperor
1805 (October 21)	Nelson defeats French and Spanish fleet at Trafalgar
1805 (December 2)	Austerlitz
1806	Jena
1806	Continental System established by Berlin Decrees
1807	Friedland
1807	Treaty of Tilsit; Russia becomes an ally of Napoleon
1808	Beginning of Spanish resistance to Napoleonic domination
1809	Wagram
1809	Napoleon marries Archduchess Marie Louise of Austria
1812	Invasion of Russia and French defeat at Borodino
1813	Leipzig (Battle of the Nations)
1814 (March)	Treaty of Chaumont establishes Quadruple Alliance
1814 (September)	Congress of Vienna convenes
1815 (March 1)	Napoleon returns from Elba
1815 (June 18)	Waterloo
1815 (September 26)	Holy Alliance formed at Congress of Vienna
1815 (November 20)	Quadruple Alliance renewed at Congress of Vienna
1821	Napoleon dies on Saint Helena

the art, literature, and architecture of medieval times. They were also deeply interested in folklore, folk songs, and fairy tales. Dreams, hallucinations, sleepwalking, and other phenomena that suggested the existence of a world beyond that of empirical observation, sensory data, and discursive reasoning fascinated the Romantics. Although their specific interests, tools of expression, and priorities varied, Romantics shared an alienation from what they considered to be the cold rationalism that characterized the industrial economy and Enlightenment thought.

▼ Romantic Questioning of the Supremacy of Reason

The Romantic Movement had roots in the individualism of the Renaissance, Protestant devotion and personal piety, sentimental novels of the eighteenth century, and dramatic German poetry of the ***Sturm und Drang*** (literally, "storm and stress") movement, which rejected the influence of French rationalism on German literature. However, two writers who were also closely related to the Enlightenment provided the immediate intellectual foundations for Romanticism: Jean-Jacques Rousseau and Immanuel Kant raised questions about whether the rationalism so dear to the philosophes was sufficient to explain human nature and be the bedrock principle for organizing human society.

Rousseau and Education

Jean-Jacques Rousseau, though sharing in the reformist spirit of the Enlightenment, opposed many of its other facets (see Chapter 17). Rousseau's conviction that society and material prosperity had corrupted human nature profoundly influenced Romantic writers.

Rousseau set forth his view on how the individual could develop to lead a good and happy life uncorrupted by society in his novel *Émile* (1762). In *Émile*, Rousseau stressed the difference between children and adults. He distinguished the stages of human maturation and urged that children be raised with maximum individual freedom. Each child should be allowed to learn by trial and error what reality is and how best to deal with it. Beyond providing the basic necessities of life and warding off what was manifestly harmful, parents and teachers should stay completely out of the way.

Read the **Document** "Jean-Jacques Rousseau, *Émile*" on **MyHistoryLab.com**

To Romantic writers, this concept of human development vindicated the rights of nature over those of artificial society. They thought such a form of open education would eventually lead to a natural society. In its fully developed form, this view of life led the Romantics to value the uniqueness of each individual and to explore childhood in great detail. The Romantics saw humankind, nature, and society as organically interrelated.

Kant and Reason

Immanuel Kant (1724–1804) wrote the two greatest philosophical works of the late eighteenth century: *The Critique of Pure Reason* (1781) and *The Critique of Practical Reason* (1788). He sought to accept the rationalism of the Enlightenment and to still preserve a belief in human freedom, immortality, and the existence of God. For Kant, the human mind does not simply reflect the world around it like a passive mirror; rather, the mind actively imposes on the world of sensory experience "forms of sensibility" and "categories of understanding." The mind itself generates these categories. This meant that human perceptions are as much the product of the mind's own activity as of sensory experience.

Kant found the sphere of reality that was accessible to pure reason to be limited. He believed, however, that beyond the phenomenal world of sensory experience, over which "pure reason" was master, there existed what he called the "noumenal" world. This world is a sphere of moral and aesthetic reality known by "practical reason" and conscience. Kant thought all human beings possess an innate sense of moral duty or an awareness of what he called a **categorical imperative**. This term refers to an inner command to act in every situation as one would have all other people always act in the same situation. On the basis of humankind's moral sense, Kant postulated the existence of God, eternal life, and future rewards and punishments. He believed that reason alone could not prove these transcendental truths. Still, he was convinced they were realities to which every reasonable person could attest.

To many Romantic writers, Kantian philosophy refuted the narrow rationality of the Enlightenment. Whether they called it "practical reason," "fancy," "imagination," "intuition," or simply "feeling," the Romantics believed that the human mind had the power to penetrate beyond the limits of largely passive human understanding.

▼ Romantic Literature

The term *Romantic* appeared in English and French literature as early as the seventeenth century. Neoclassical writers then used the word to describe literature they considered unreal, sentimental, or excessively fanciful. Later, in both England and Germany, the term came to be applied to all literature that did not observe classical forms and rules and gave free play to the imagination. The Romantic Movement had peaked in Germany and England before it became a major force in France under the leadership of Madame de Staël (1766–1817) and Victor Hugo (1802–1885). (See the Document "Madame de Staël Describes the New Romantic Literature of Germany," page 605.) The first French writer to declare himself a Romantic was Henri Beyle (1783–1842), who wrote under the pseudonym Stendhal.

English Romantic Writers

The English Romantics believed poetry was enhanced by freely following the creative impulses of the mind. For Samuel Taylor Coleridge (1772–1834), the artist's imagination was God at work in the mind. Poetry thus could not be considered idle play. Rather, it was the highest of human acts, humankind's self-fulfillment in a transcendental world.

Coleridge was the master of Gothic poems of the supernatural, such as "The Rime of the Ancient Mariner," which relates the story of a sailor cursed for killing an albatross. The poem treats the subject as a crime against nature and God and raises the issues of guilt, punishment, and the redemptive possibilities of humility and penance. At the end of the poem, the mariner discovers the unity and beauty of all things. Having repented, he is delivered from his awful curse, which has been symbolized by the dead albatross hung around his neck:

O happy living things! no tongue
Their beauty might declare:
A spring of love gushed from my heart,
And I blessed them unaware . . .
The self-same moment I could pray;
And from my neck so free
The Albatross fell off, and sank
Like lead into the sea.

Wordsworth William Wordsworth (1770–1850) was Coleridge's closest friend. Together they published *Lyrical Ballads* in 1798 as a manifesto of a new poetry that rejected the rules of eighteenth-century criticism. Among Wordsworth's most important later poems is his "Ode on Intimations of Immortality" (1803). Its subject is the loss of poetic vision, something Wordsworth felt then in himself. Nature, which he had worshipped, no longer spoke freely to him, and he feared it might never speak to him again:

There was a time when meadow, grove, and stream,
The earth, and every common sight,
To me did seem
Appareled in celestial light,
The glory and the freshness of a dream.
It is not now as it hath been of yore—
Turn whereso'er I may,
By night or day,
The things which I have seen I now can
see no more.

He mourned the loss of his childlike vision and closeness to spiritual reality—a loss he believed was part of the necessary process of maturation. For Wordsworth and Coleridge, childhood was the bright period of creative imagination. Aging and urban living corrupt and deaden the imagination, making inner feelings and the beauty of nature less important.

Lord Byron A true rebel among the Romantic poets was Lord Byron (1788–1824). In Britain, even most of the other Romantic writers distrusted and disliked him. Outside England, however, Byron was regarded as the embodiment of the new person the French Revolution had created. He rejected old traditions (he was divorced

Document

MADAME DE STAËL DESCRIBES THE NEW ROMANTIC LITERATURE OF GERMANY

Anne-Louise-Germaine de Staël, known generally as Madame de Staël, was the daughter of Jacques Necker, the finance minister of Louis XVI. She was also the friend of major French political liberals and a critic of Napoleonic absolutism. More importantly for European literary life, Madame de Staël visited Germany, read the emerging German Romantic literature, and introduced it to both French- and English-speaking Europe in her book Concerning Germany *(1813). In the passage that follows, she endorses the new German literature. She points to the novelty of this Romantic poetry and then relates it to a new appreciation of Christianity and the Middle Ages. She praises the medieval troubadours, composers, and performers of lyric poetry in song.*

How does de Staël characterize the new Romantic school of poetry? How does she contrast it with the literature that had its roots in ancient Greece and Rome? What is the relationship of the Middle Ages to the new poetry and other examples of the fine arts touched by Romantic sensibilities?

The word *romantic* has been lately introduced in Germany, to designate that kind of poetry which is derived from the songs of the Troubadours; that which owes its birth to the union of chivalry and Christianity. If we do not admit that the empire of literature has been divided between paganism and Christianity, the north and the south, antiquity and the middle ages, chivalry and the institutions of Greece and Rome, we shall never succeed in forming a philosophical judgment of ancient and of modern taste.

Some French critics have asserted that German literature is still in its infancy; this opinion is entirely false: men who are best skilled in the knowledge of languages, and the works of the ancients, are certainly not ignorant of the defects and advantages attached to the species of literature which they either adopt or reject; but their character, their habits, and their modes of reasoning, have led them to prefer that which is founded on the recollection of chivalry, on the wonders of the middle ages, to that which has for its basis the mythology of the Greeks. The literature of romance is alone capable of further improvement, because, being rooted in our own soil, that alone can continue to grow and acquire fresh life: it expresses our religion; it recalls our history; its origin is ancient, although not of classical antiquity. Classic poetry, before it comes home to us, must pass through our recollections of paganism; that of the Germans is the Christian era of the fine arts; it employs our personal impressions to excite strong and vivid emotions; the genius by which it is inspired addresses itself immediately to our hearts; of all phantoms at once the most powerful and the most terrible. . . .

The new school maintains the same system in the fine arts as in literature, and affirms that Christianity is the source of all modern genius; the writers of this school also characterize, in a new manner, all that in Gothic architecture agrees with the religious sentiments of Christians. . . . It is only of consequence to us, in the present silence of genius, to lay aside the contempt which has been thrown on all the conceptions of the middle ages.

From Madame de Staël, *Concerning Germany* (London: John Murray, 1814) as quoted in Howard E. Hugo, ed., *The Romantic Reader* (New York: Viking, 1957), pp. 64–66.

and famous for his many love affairs) and championed the cause of personal liberty. Byron was outrageously skeptical and mocking, even of his own beliefs. In *Childe Harold's Pilgrimage* (1812), he created a brooding, melancholy Romantic hero. In *Don Juan* (1819), he wrote with ribald humor, acknowledged nature's cruelty as well as its beauty, and even expressed admiration for urban life.

Mary Godwin Shelley Mary Godwin (1797–1851) was the daughter of Mary Wollstonecraft, author of *A Vindication of the Rights of Woman*. Wollstonecraft died of puerperal fever shortly after Godwin's birth. At the age of 16, Godwin fell in love with Romantic poet Percy Bysshe Shelley, who was already married. Fleeing ostracism and scandal in England, they traveled through Europe, and married after the suicide of Shelley's first wife. While spending the summer of 1816 on Lake Geneva with their mutual friend, Lord Byron, Godwin conceived of the idea behind *Frankenstein: or, The Modern Prometheus*, which she published in 1818. Often considered the first science fiction novel, it tells the story of a Swiss doctor, Frankenstein, who deliberately creates a living being out of components of dead bodies. Frankenstein finds he has created not a beautiful creature, but instead an abhorrent "monster." When Godwin, by then Mary Shelley, was revealed as the author, contemporary critics complained that the gruesome subject matter was inappropriate for a young female mind.

The German Romantic Writers

Almost all major German Romantics wrote at least one novel. Romantic novels often were highly sentimental and borrowed material from medieval romances. The characters of Romantic novels were treated as symbols of the larger truth of life. Purely realistic description was avoided. Friedrich Schlegel (1767–1845) wrote the progressive early Romantic novel *Lucinde* (1799) that attacked prejudices against women as capable of being little more than lovers and domestics. Schlegel's novel reveals the ability of the Romantics to become involved in the social issues of their day. He depicted Lucinde as the perfect friend and companion, as well as the unsurpassed lover, of the hero. The work shocked contemporary morals by frankly discussing sexual activity and by describing Lucinde as equal to the male hero.

George Gordon, Lord Byron (1788–1824), chose Albanian attire for this portrait. A famous supporter of the Greek Revolution, which would cost him his life (he died of fever in Greece in 1824), Byron proudly suggested he was capable of embodying many different personalities and participating in different cultural traditions. In England, his personal life was considered scandalous. The Granger Collection, New York

Goethe Perhaps the greatest German writer of modern times, Johann Wolfgang von Goethe (1749–1832) defies easy classification. Part of his literary production fits into the Romantic mold, and part of it was a condemnation of Romantic excesses. The book that made his early reputation was *The Sorrows of Young Werther*, published in 1774. This novel, like many in the eighteenth century, is a series of letters. The hero falls in love with Lotte, who is married to another man. Eventually Werther and Lotte part, but in his grief, Werther takes his own life. This novel became popular throughout Europe. Romantic authors admired its emphasis on feeling and on living outside the bounds of polite society.

Read the **Document** "Johann Wolfgang von Goethe, *Prometheus*, 1773" on **MyHistoryLab.com**

Goethe's masterpiece was *Faust*, a long dramatic poem. Part I, published in 1808, tells the story of Faust, who makes a pact with the devil—he will exchange his soul for greater knowledge than other human beings possess. As the story progresses, Faust seduces a young woman named Gretchen. She dies but is received into heaven as the grief-stricken Faust realizes he must continue to live. At the conclusion of Part II, completed in 1832, Faust dedicates his life, or what remains of it, to the improvement of humankind. He feels this goal will allow him to overcome the restless striving that induced him to make the pact with the devil. That new knowledge breaks the pact. Faust dies and is received by angels.

▼ Romantic Art

The art of the Romantic Era, like its poetry and philosophy, stood largely in reaction to that of the eighteenth century. Whereas the Rococo artists had looked to Renaissance models and Neo-Classical painters to the art of the ancient world, Romantic painters often portrayed scenes from medieval life. For them, the Middle Ages represented the social stability and religious reverence that was disappearing from their own era.

Document

MARY SHELLEY REMEMBERS THE BIRTH OF A MONSTER

Mary Wollstonecraft Godwin Shelley thought of the idea for her most famous novel, Frankenstein, *while spending a summer on Lake Geneva with her future husband, Percy Shelley, and their friend, Lord Byron. In the 1831 edition of the novel, published after Percy Shelley's death, she reflects on the genesis of the story in a manner that emphasizes the importance of imagination and the limits of enlightenment through science.*

How does Shelley describe the creative process? How can her message be interpreted as a criticism of the Enlightenment?

My imagination, unbidden, possessed and guided me, gifting the successive images that arose in my mind with a vividness far beyond the usual bound of reverie. I saw—with shut eyes, but acute mental vision—I saw the pale student of hallowed arts kneeling beside the thing he had put together. I saw the hideous phantasm of a man stretched out, and then, on the working of some powerful engine, show signs of life, and stir with an uneasy, half-vital motion. Frightful must it be; for supremely frightful would be the effect of any human endeavor to mock the stupendous mechanism of the Creator of the world. His success would terrify the artist; he would rush away from his odious handiwork, horror-stricken. He would hope that, left to itself, the slight spark of life which he had communicated, would fade, that this thing which had received such imperfect animation, would subside into dead matter; and he might sleep in the belief that the silence of the grave would quench for ever the transient existence of the hideous corpse which he had looked upon as the cradle of life. He sleeps: but he is awakened; he opens his eyes: behold the horrid thing stands at this beside, opening his curtains, and looking on him with yellow, watery, but speculative eyes.

I opened mine in terror.

From Mary W. Shelley, *Frankenstein; or, The Modern Prometheus* (Boston: Sever, Francis & Co, 1869), pp. 11–12.

PUBLICATION DATES OF MAJOR ROMANTIC WORKS

1762	Rousseau's *Émile*
1774	Goethe's *Sorrows of Young Werther*
1781	Kant's *Critique of Pure Reason**
1788	Kant's *Critique of Practical Reason**
1798	Wordsworth and Coleridge's *Lyrical Ballads*
1799	Schlegel's *Lucinde*
1799	Schleiermacher's *Speeches on Religion to Its Cultured Despisers*
1802	Chateaubriand's *Genius of Christianity*
1806	Hegel's *Phenomenology of Mind*
1808	Goethe's *Faust*, Part I
1812	Byron's *Childe Harold's Pilgrimage*
1819	Byron's *Don Juan*
1825	Scott's *Tales of the Crusaders*
1841	Carlyle's *On Heroes and Hero-Worship*

*Kant's books were not themselves part of the Romantic Movement, but they were fundamental to later Romantic writers.

The Cult of the Middle Ages and Neo-Gothicism

Like many early Romantic artists, English landscape painter John Constable (1776–1837) was politically conservative. In *Salisbury Cathedral from the Meadows*, he portrayed a stable world in which neither political turmoil nor industrial development challenged the traditional dominance of the church and the landed classes. Although the clouds and sky in the painting depict a severe storm, the works of both nature (the trees) and humankind (the cathedral) present a powerful sense of enduring order. Constable saw the church and the British constitution as intimately related. Like many English conservatives of his day, he expected religious institutions to deter political radicalism.

View the **Closer Look** "Cult of the Unattainable" on **MyHistoryLab.com**

Constable and other Romantics tended to idealize rural life because they believed it opposed the increasingly urban, industrializing, commercial society that was developing around them. In fact, the rural landscape and rustic society that Constable depicted in his paintings had already largely disappeared from England.

The Neo-Gothic revival in architecture dotted the European landscape with modern imitations of medieval structures. Many medieval cathedrals were restored during this era, and new churches were designed to resemble their medieval forerunners. The British Houses of Parliament built in 1836–1837 were the most famous public buildings in the Neo-Gothic style, but town halls, schools, and even railroad stations were designed to look like medieval buildings, while aristocratic country houses were rebuilt to resemble medieval castles.

Nature and the Sublime

Beyond their attraction to history, Romantic artists also sought to portray nature in all of its majestic power as no previous generation of European artists had ever done. Like Romantic poets, the artists of the era were drawn toward the mysterious and unruly side of nature rather than toward the rational Newtonian order that had prevailed during the Enlightenment. Their works often sought to portray what they and others termed *the sublime*—that is, subjects from nature that aroused strong emotions, such as fear, dread, and awe, and raised questions about whether and how much we control our lives. Painters often traveled to remote areas such as the Scottish Highlands or the Swiss Alps to portray dangerous scenes from nature that would immediately grip and engage the viewer's emotions.

Romantics saw nature as a set of infinite forces that overwhelmed the smallness of humankind. For example, in 1824, the German artist Caspar David Friedrich (1774–1840) in *The Polar Sea* painted the plight of a ship trapped and crushed by the force of a vast polar ice field. In direct contrast to eighteenth-century artists' portrayal of sunny Enlightenment, Friedrich also painted numerous scenes in which human beings stand shrouded in the mysterious darkness of night where moonlight and torches cast only fitful illumination.

An artist who similarly understood the power of nature but also depicted the forces of the new industrialism that was challenging them was Joseph Mallord William Turner (1775–1851) whose painting *Rain, Steam and Speed—The Great Western Railway* of 1844 illustrated the recently invented railway engine barreling through an enveloping storm. In this scene the new technology is both part of the natural world and strong enough to dominate it.

Friedrich's and Turner's paintings taken together symbolize the contradictory forces affecting Romantic artists—the sense of the power, awe, and mastery of nature coupled with the sense that the advance of industry represented a new kind of awesome human power that could challenge or even surpass the forces of nature itself.

John Constable's *Salisbury Cathedral from the Meadows* displays the appeal of Romantic art to both medieval monuments and the sublime power of nature. Art Resource, NY. © The National Gallery, London

Caspar David Friedrich's *The Polar Sea* illustrated the power of nature to diminish the creations of humankind as seen in the wrecked ship on the right of the painting. Kunsthalle, Hamburg, Germany/A.K.G., Berlin/SuperStock

▼ Religion in the Romantic Period

During the Middle Ages, the foundation of religion had been the authority of the church. The Reformation leaders had appealed to the authority of the Bible. Then, many Enlightenment writers attempted to derive religion from the rational nature revealed by Newtonian physics, while others attacked it altogether. Romantic religious thinkers, in contrast, sought the foundations of religion in the inner emotions of humankind. Reacting to the anticlericalism of both the Enlightenment and the French Revolution, these thinkers also saw religious faith and institutions as central to human life. One of the first great examples of a religion characterized by Romantic impulses—Methodism—arose in mid-eighteenth-century England during the Enlightenment itself and became one of the most powerful forces in transatlantic religion during the nineteenth century.

Methodism

Methodism originated in the middle of the eighteenth century as a revolt against deism and rationalism in the Church of England. The Methodist revival formed an important part of the background of English Romanticism.

Joseph Mallord William Turner's *Rain, Steam, and Speed—The Great Western Railway* captured the tensions many Europeans felt between their natural environment and the new technology of the industrial age. Joseph Mallord William Turner, 1775–1851, *Rain, Steam, and Speed—The Great Western Railway 1844*. Oil on canvas, 90.8 × 121.9. The National Gallery, London/Art Resource, NY

The leader of the Methodist movement was John Wesley (1703–1791). His mother, Susannah Wesley, who bore eighteen children, had carefully supervised his education and religious development.

After studying at Oxford University to be an Anglican priest, Wesley left England for missionary work in the new colony of Georgia in America, where he arrived in 1735. While he was crossing the Atlantic, a group of German Moravians on the ship deeply impressed him with their unshakable faith and confidence during a storm. When he returned to England, Wesley began to worship with Moravians in London. There, in 1739, he underwent a conversion experience that he described in the words, "My heart felt strangely warmed."

Wesley began to preach in the open fields near the cities and towns of western England. Thousands of humble people responded to his message of repentance and good works. Soon he and his brother Charles (1707–1788), who became famous for his hymns, began to organize Methodist societies. By the late eighteenth century, the Methodists had become a separate church. They ordained their own clergy and sent missionaries to America.

Methodism stressed inward, heartfelt religion and the possibility of Christian perfection in this life. Methodist preachers emphasized the role of enthusiastic, emotional experience as part of Christian conversion. After Wesley, religious revivals became highly emotional in style and content.

New Directions in Continental Religion

Similar religious developments based on feeling appeared on the Continent. After the Thermidorian Reaction, a strong Roman Catholic revival took place in France. Its followers disapproved of both the religious policy of the revolution and the anticlericalism of the Enlightenment. The most important book to express these sentiments was *The Genius of Christianity* (1802) by Viscount François René de Chateaubriand (1768–1848). In this work, which became known as the "bible of Romanticism," Chateaubriand argued that the essence of religion is "passion." The foundation of faith in the church was the emotion that its teachings and sacraments inspired in the heart of the Christian.

Against the Newtonian view of the world and of a rational God, the Romantics found God immanent in nature. No one stated the Romantic religious ideal more eloquently or with greater impact on the modern world than Friedrich Schleiermacher (1768–1834). In 1799, he published a response to both Lutheran orthodoxy and Enlightenment rationalism, *Speeches on Religion to Its Cultured Despisers*. According to Schleiermacher, religion was an intuition or feeling of absolute dependence on an infinite reality.

Although Schleiermacher considered Christianity the "religion of religions," he also believed every world religion was unique in its expression of the primal intuition of the infinite in the finite. He thus turned against the universal natural religion of the Enlightenment, which he termed "a name applied to loose, unconnected impulses," and defended the meaningfulness of the numerous world religions. Schleiermacher interpreted the religions of the world in the same way that other Romantic writers interpreted the variety of unique peoples and cultures.

▼ Romantic Views of Nationalism and History

A distinctive feature of Romanticism, especially in Germany, was its glorification of both the individual person and individual cultures. Behind these views lay the philosophy of German idealism, which understood the world as the creation of subjective egos. J. G. Fichte (1762–1814), an important German philosopher and nationalist, identified the individual ego with the Absolute that underlies all existing things. According to Fichte, the world is as it is because especially strong persons conceive of it in a particular way and impose their wills on the world and other people. Napoleon served as the contemporary example of such a great person. This philosophy has ever since served to justify the glorification of great persons and their actions in overriding all opposition to their will and desires.

Herder and Culture

In addition to this philosophy, the influence of new historical studies lay behind the German glorification of individual cultures. German Romantic writers went in search of their own past in reaction to the copying of French manners in eighteenth-century Germany, the impact of the French Revolution, and the imperialism of Napoleon. An early leader in this effort was Johann Gottfried Herder (1744–1803), already discussed in Chapter 17 as a critic of European colonialism. In 1778, Herder published an influential essay, "On the Knowing and Feelings of the Human Soul." In it, he vigorously rejected the Enlightenment's mechanical explanation of nature. He saw human beings and societies as developing organically, like plants, over time.

Herder revived German folk culture by urging the collection and preservation of distinctive German songs and sayings. His most important followers in this work were the Grimm brothers, Jakob (1785–1863) and Wilhelm (1786–1859), famous for their collection of fairy tales. Believing each language and culture were the unique expression of a people, Herder opposed both the concept and the use of a "common" language, such as French, and "universal" institutions, such as those Napoleon had imposed on Europe. These, he believed, were forms of tyranny over the individuality of a people. Herder's writings led to a broad revival of interest in history and philosophy. Although initially directed toward identifying German origins, such work soon expanded to embrace other world cultures. Eventually the ability of the Romantic imagination to be at home in any age or culture spurred the study of non-Western religion, comparative literature, and philology.

Hegel and History

The most important philosopher of history in the Romantic period was the German Georg Wilhelm Friedrich Hegel (1770–1831). He is one of the most complicated and significant philosophers in the history of Western civilization.

Hegel believed ideas develop in an evolutionary fashion that involves conflict. At any given time, a predominant set of ideas, which he termed the *thesis*, holds sway. Conflicting ideas, which Hegel termed the *antithesis*, challenge the thesis. As these patterns of thought clash, a *synthesis* emerges that eventually becomes the new thesis. Then the process begins all over again. Periods of world history receive their character from the patterns of thought that predominate during them. (See the Document "Hegel Explains the Role of Great Men in History," page 612.)

Several important philosophical conclusions followed from this analysis. One of the most significant was the belief that all periods of history have been of almost equal value because each was, by definition, necessary to the achievements of those that came later. Also, all cultures are valuable because each contributes to the necessary clash of values and ideas that allows humankind to develop. Hegel discussed these concepts in *The Phenomenology of Mind* (1806), *Lectures on the Philosophy of History* (1822–1831), and other works, many of which were published only after his death. During his lifetime, his ideas became widely known through his university lectures at Berlin.

Islam, the Middle East, and Romanticism

The new religious, literary, and historical sensibilities of the Romantic period modified the European understanding of both Islam and the Arab world while at the same time preserving long-standing attitudes.

The energized Christianity associated with Methodist-like forms of Protestantism, on the one hand, and Chateaubriand's emotional Roman Catholicism, on the other, renewed the traditional sense of necessary conflict between Christianity and Islam. Chateaubriand wrote a travelogue of his journey from Paris to Jerusalem in 1811. A decade later, when he was a member of the French parliament, he invoked the concept of a crusade against the Muslim world in a speech on the danger posed by the Barbary pirates of North Africa.

The medieval Crusades against Islam fired the Romantic imagination. Nostalgic European artists painted from a Western standpoint the great moments of the Crusades including the bloody capture of Jerusalem. Stories from those conflicts filled historical novels such as *Tales of the Crusaders* (1825) by Sir Walter Scott (1771–1832). Although they presented heroic images of Muslim warriors, these paintings and novels ignored the havoc that the crusaders had visited on the peoples of the Middle East.

When Napoleon invaded Egypt in 1799, he met stiff resistance. On July 25, however, the French won a decisive victory. This painting of that battle by Baron Antoine Gros (1771–1835) emphasizes French heroism and Muslim defeat. Such an outlook was typical of European views of Arabs and the Islamic world. Antoine Jean Gros (1771–1835). Detail, *Battle of Aboukir, July 25, 1799*, c. 1806. Oil on canvas. Chateaux de Versailles et de Trianon, Versailles, France. Giraudon/Art Resource, NY

Document

HEGEL EXPLAINS THE ROLE OF GREAT MEN IN HISTORY

Hegel believed that behind the development of human history from one period to the next lay the mind and purpose of what he termed the World-Spirit, a concept somewhat like the Christian God. Hegel thought particular heroes from the past (such as Caesar) and in the present (such as Napoleon) were the unconscious instruments of that spirit. In this passage from his lectures on the philosophy of history, Hegel explained how these heroes could change history. All these concepts are characteristic of the Romantic belief that human beings and human history are always intimately connected with larger, spiritual forces at work in the world. The passage also reflects the widespread belief of the time that the world of civic or political action pertained to men and that of the domestic sphere belonged to women.

How might the career of Napoleon have inspired this passage? What are the antidemocratic implications of this passage? In this passage, do great men make history or do historical developments make great men? Why do you think Hegel does not associate this power of shaping history with women as well as men?

Such are all great historical men—whose own particular aims involve those large issues which are the will of the World-Spirit. They may be called Heroes, inasmuch as they have derived their purposes and their vocation, not from the calm, regular course of things, sanctioned by the existing order, but from a concealed fount—one which has not attained to phenomenal, present existence—from that inner Spirit, still hidden beneath the surface, which, impinging on the outer world as on a shell, bursts it in pieces, because it is another kernel than that which belonged to the shell in question. They are men, therefore, who appear to draw the impulse of their life from themselves; and whose deeds have produced a condition of things and a complex of historical relations which appear to be only their interest, and their work.

Such individuals had no consciousness of the general Idea they were unfolding, while prosecuting those aims of theirs; on the contrary, they were practical, political men. But at the same time they were thinking men, who had an insight into the requirements of the time—what was ripe for development. This was the very Truth for their age, for their world; the species next in order, so to speak, and which was already formed in the womb of time. It was theirs to know this nascent principle; the necessary, directly sequent step in progress, which their world was to take; to make this their aim, and to expend their energy in promoting it. World historical men—the Heroes of an epoch—must, therefore, be recognized as its clear-sighted ones; their deeds, their words are the best of that time.

From G. W. F. Hegel, *The Philosophy of History*, trans. by J. Sibree (New York: Dover, 1956), pp. 30–31. Reprinted by permission.

The general nineteenth-century association of nationalistic aspirations with Romanticism also cast the Ottoman Empire and with it Islam in an unfavorable political light. Romantic poets and intellectuals championed the cause of the Greek Revolution (see Chapter 20) and revived older charges of Ottoman despotism.

By contrast, other Romantic sensibilities induced Europeans to see the Muslim world in a more positive fashion. The Romantic emphasis on the value of literature drawn from different cultures and ages allowed many nineteenth-century European readers to enjoy the stories from *The Thousand and One Nights*, which first appeared in English in 1778 from a French translation. In 1859, Edward FitzGerald (1809–1883) published his highly popular translation of the *Rubáiyát of Omar Khayyám* of Nishapur, a Persian poet of the twelfth century.

Read the Document "The Rubaiyat (11th c. C.E.) Omar Khayyam" on **MyHistoryLab.com**

Herder's and Hegel's concepts of history gave both the Arab peoples and Islam distinct roles in history. For Herder, Arab culture was one of the numerous communities that composed the human race and manifested the human spirit. The Prophet Muhammad, while giving voice to the ancient spirit of the Arab people, had drawn them from a polytheistic faith to a great monotheistic vision. For Hegel, Islam represented an important stage of the development of the world spirit. However, Hegel believed Islam had fulfilled its role in history and no longer had any significant part to play. These outlooks, which penetrated much nineteenth-century intellectual life, made it easy for Europeans to believe that Islam could, for all practical purposes, be ignored or reduced to a spent historical force.

British historian and social commentator Thomas Carlyle (1795–1881) attributed new, positive qualities to Muhammad himself. Carlyle disliked the Enlightenment's disparagement of religion and spiritual values and was drawn to German theories of history. In his book *On Heroes and Hero-Worship* (1841), Carlyle presented Muhammad as the embodiment of the hero as prophet. He repudiated the traditional Christian and general Enlightenment view of Muhammad as an impostor. (See Chapter 17.) To Carlyle, Muhammad appeared as a person who had experienced God subjectively and had communicated a sense of the divine to others. Although friendly to Muhammad from a historical standpoint, Carlyle nonetheless saw him as one of many great religious figures and not, as Muslims believed, as the last of the prophets through whom God had spoken.

The person whose actions in the long run did perhaps the most to reshape the idea of both Islam and the Middle East in the European imagination was Napoleon himself. With his Egyptian expedition of 1798, the first European military invasion of the Near East since the Crusades, the study of the Arab world became an important activity within French intellectual life. For his invasion of Egypt to succeed, Napoleon believed he must make it clear he had no intention of destroying Islam but rather sought to liberate Egypt from the military clique that governed the country in the name of the Ottoman Empire. To that end, he took with him scholars of Arabic and Islamic culture whom he urged to converse with the most educated people they could meet. Napoleon personally met with the local Islamic leaders and had all of his speeches and proclamations translated into classical Arabic. Such cultural sensitivity and the serious efforts of the French scholars to learn Arabic and study the Qur'an impressed Egyptian scholars. (When the French sought to levy new taxes, however, the Egyptians' enthusiasm waned.)

It was on this expedition that the famous Rosetta Stone was discovered. Now housed in the British Museum, it eventually led to the decipherment of ancient Egypt's hieroglyphic writing. Napoleon's scholars also published a twenty-three volume *Description of Egypt* (1809–1828), which concentrated largely on ancient Egypt. Their approach suggested the history of the Ottoman Empire needed to be related first to the larger context of Egyptian history and that Islam, although enormously important, was only part of a larger cultural story. The implication was that if Egypt and Islam were to be understood, it would be through European—if not necessarily Christian—categories of thought.

Two cultural effects in the West of Napoleon's invasion were an increase in the number of European visitors to the Middle East and a demand for architecture based on ancient Egyptian models. Perhaps the most famous example of this fad is the Washington Monument in Washington, D.C., which is modeled after ancient Egyptian obelisks.

In Perspective

Romantic ideas made a major contribution to the emergence of nationalism, which proved to be one of the strongest motivating forces of the nineteenth and twentieth centuries. The writers of the Enlightenment had generally championed a cosmopolitan outlook on the world. By contrast, the Romantic thinkers emphasized the individuality and worth of each separate people and culture. A people or a nation was defined by a common language, history, and customs and by the possession of a historical homeland. This cultural nationalism gradually became transformed into a political creed. It came to be widely believed that every people, ethnic group, or nation should constitute a separate political entity and that only when it so existed could the nation be secure in its own character.

France under the revolutionary government and Napoleon had demonstrated the power of nationhood. Other peoples came to desire similar strength and confidence. Napoleon's toppling of ancient political structures, such as the Holy Roman Empire, proved the need for new political organization in Europe. By 1815, only a few Europeans aspired to this, but as time passed, peoples from Ireland to Ukraine came to share these yearnings. The Congress of Vienna could ignore such feelings, but for the rest of the nineteenth century, as shall be seen in subsequent chapters, statesmen had to confront the growing power these feelings had unleashed.

KEY TERMS

categorical imperative (p. 604)
Consulate (p. 586)
Methodism (p. 609)
romanticism (p. 602)
Sturm und Drang (p. 603)

REVIEW QUESTIONS

1. How did Napoleon rise to power? What groups supported him? What were his major domestic achievements? Did his rule fulfill or betray the French Revolution? What sort of challenge did the Haitian Revolution pose to France's commitment to liberty, equality, and fraternity?
2. What regions made up Napoleon's realm, and what was the status of each region within it? Did his administration show foresight, or was the empire a burden he could not afford?
3. Why did Napoleon decide to invade Russia? Why did the operation fail?
4. What were the results of the Congress of Vienna? Was the Vienna settlement a success?
5. Why did Romantic writers champion feelings over reason? What questions did Rousseau and Kant raise about reason?
6. Why was poetry important to Romantic writers? How did the Romantic concept of religion differ from Reformation Protestantism and Enlightenment deism? How did Romantic ideas and sensibilities modify European ideas of Islam and the Middle East? What were the cultural results of Napoleon's invasion of Egypt?

SUGGESTED READINGS

E. Behler, *German Romantic Literary Theory* (1993). A clear introduction to a difficult subject.

D. Bell, *The First Total War: Napoleon's Europe and the Birth of Warfare as We Know It* (2007). A consideration of the Napoleonic conflicts and the culture of warfare.

G. E. Bentley, *The Stranger from Paradise: A Biography of William Blake* (2001). Now the standard work.

T. Blanning. *The Romantic Revolution: A History* (2010). A new synthesis.

N. Boyle, *Goethe* (2001). A challenging two-volume biography.

M. Broers, *Europe under Napoleon 1799–1815* (2002). Examines the subject from the standpoint of those Napoleon conquered.

T. Chapman, *Congress of Vienna: Origins, Processes, and Results* (1998). A clear introduction to the major issues.

P. Dwyer, *Napoleon: The Path to Power, 1769–1799* (2008). A major study of the subject.

P. Dwyer, *Talleyrand* (2002). A useful account of his diplomatic influence.

S. Englund, *Napoleon: A Political Life* (2004). A thoughtful recent biography.

C. Esdaile, *The Peninsular War: A New History* (2003). A narrative of the Napoleonic wars in Spain.

A. Forrest, *Napoleon's Men: The Soldiers of the Revolution and Empire* (2002). An examination of the troops rather than their commander.

H. Honour, *Romanticism* (1979). Still the best introduction to Romantic art, well illustrated.

F. Kagan, *The End of the Old Order: Napoleon and Europe, 1801–1805* (2006). A masterful narrative.

S. Körner, *Kant* (1955). A classic brief, clear introduction.

J. Lusvass, *Napoleon on the Art of War* (2001). A collection of Napoleon's own writings.

J. J. McGann and J. Soderholm, eds., *Byron and Romanticism* (2002). Essays on the poet who most embodied Romantic qualities to the people of his time.

R. Muir, *Tactics and the Experience of Battle in the Age of Napoleon* (1998). A splendid account of troops in battle.

T. Pinkard, *Hegel: A Biography* (2000). A long but accessible study.

N. Roe, *Romanticism: An Oxford Guide* (2005). A series of informative essays.

P. W. Schroeder, *The Transformation of European Politics, 1763–1848* (1994). A major synthesis of the diplomatic history of the period, emphasizing the new departures of the Congress of Vienna.

I. Woloch, *Napoleon and His Collaborators: The Making of a Dictatorship* (2001). A key study by one of the major scholars of the subject.

A. Zamoyski, *Rites of Peace: The Fall of Napoleon and the Congress of Vienna* (2007). A lively analysis and narrative.

MyHistoryLab MEDIA ASSIGNMENTS

Find these resources in the Media Assignments folder for Chapter 19 on **MyHistoryLab**.

QUESTIONS FOR ANALYSIS

1. What is the role of the pope in this ceremony?

   ***Section:* The Haitian Revolution (1791–1804)**
   View the **Closer Look** The Coronation of Napoleon, p. 589

2. Why do you think the author felt such loyalty toward Napoleon?

   ***Section:* Napoleon's Empire (1804–1814)**
   Read the **Document** Charles Parquin, "Napoleon's Army," p. 591

3. As the German lands became absorbed into a single state, what was the general direction of that state's growth?

Section: **European Response to the Empire**

View the **Map** Interactive Map: The Unification of Germany, 1815–1871, p. 595

4. How does this author describe and rationalize Napoleon's attitudes towards Muslims in Egypt?

Section: **The Rise of Napoleon Bonaparte**

Read the **Document** Louis Antoine Fauvelet de Bourrienne, *Memoirs of Napoleon Bonaparte*, p. 586

5. How does this passage illustrate some of the tendencies of romanticism?

Section: **Romantic Questioning of the Supremacy of Reason**

Read the **Document** Jean-Jacques Rousseau, *Émile*, p. 603

OTHER RESOURCES FROM THIS CHAPTER

The Rise of Napoleon Bonaparte

Read the **Document** Madame de Remusat on the Rise of Napoleon, p. 585

The Haitian Revolution (1791–1804)

View the **Closer Look** The Haitian Revolution: Guerilla Warfare, p. 590

Napoleon's Empire (1804–1814)

View the **Map** Map Discovery: Napoleon's Empire, p. 590

European Response to the Empire

Read the **Document** Carl von Clausewitz, On War, "Arming the Nation," p. 593

Read the **Compare and Connect** The Experience of War in the Napoleonic Age, p. 596

The Congress of Vienna and the European Settlement

View the **Map** Map Discovery: Europe After the Congress of Vienna, 1815, p. 599

Read the **Document** Napoleon's Exile to St. Helena (1815), p. 600

Romantic Literature

Read the **Document** Johann Wolfgang von Goethe, *Prometheus*, 1773, p. 606

Romantic Art

View the **Closer Look** Cult of the Unattainable, p. 607

Romantic Views of Nationalism and History

Read the **Document** The Rubaiyat (11th c. CE) Omar Khayyam, p. 612

In 1830, revolution again erupted in France as well as elsewhere on the Continent. Eugène Delacroix's *Liberty Leading the People* was the most famous image recalling that event. Note how he portrays persons from different social classes and occupations joining the revolution led by the figure of Liberty. Eugène Delacroix (1798–1863), *Liberty Leading the People*, 1830. Oil on canvas, 260 × 325 cm—RF 129. Musée du Louvre, Paris, France/Scala/Art Resource, NY

Listen to the **Chapter Audio** on **MyHistoryLab.com**

20 The Conservative Order and the Challenges of Reform (1815–1832)

▼ **The Conservative Order**
The Congress System • The Domestic Political Order • Conservative Outlooks

▼ **The Emergence of Nationalism and Liberalism**
Nationalism • Early-Nineteenth-Century Political Liberalism • Classical Economics • Relationship of Liberalism to Nationalism

▼ **Conservative Restoration in Europe**
Liberalism and Nationalism Resisted in Austria and the Germanies • Postwar Repression in Great Britain • Bourbon Restoration in France • The Spanish Revolution of 1820

▼ **The Conservative Order Shaken in Europe**
Revolt Against Ottoman Rule in the Balkans • Russia: The Decembrist Revolt of 1825 • Revolution in France (1830) • Belgium Becomes Independent (1830) • The Great Reform Bill in Britain (1832)

▼ **The Wars of Independence in Latin America**
Wars of Independence on the South American Continent • Independence in New Spain • Brazilian Independence

▼ **In Perspective**

LEARNING OBJECTIVES

How did early-nineteenth-century nationalists define the nation?

What explains the strength of conservatism in the early nineteenth century?

What were the goals of the Concert of Europe?

What sparked the wars of independence in Latin America?

How did Russia, France, and Britain respond to challenges to the conservative order?

THE CONGRESS OF Vienna was followed by a decade in which conservative political forces controlled virtually all of Europe. In the international arena, these forces sought to maintain peace and to prevent the outbreak of war that would unleash destruction and disorder. They did so through unprecedented forms of cooperation and mutual consultation. Domestically, they sought to maintain the authority of monarchies and aristocracies after the turmoil the French Revolution and Napoleon had wrought. This conservative order faced new and powerful challenges. Nationalists wished to redraw the map of Europe according to the boundaries of nationalities or ethnic groups. Liberals sought moderate political reform and freer economic markets. The goals of nationalists and liberals threatened the dominance of landed aristocracies and the rule of monarchs who governed by virtue of dynastic inheritance rather than nationality. In some cases, nationalists advocated a political shift from rule in the name of God to rule in the name of the nation. In others, they advocated the independence of colonies from European states, or dependent regions on the peripheries of empires from the center.

For the first fifteen years after the Congress of Vienna, the forces of conservatism were successful within Europe, although Spain and Portugal failed to retain control of Latin America. In the late 1820s, however, the conservatives faced stronger challenges. Thereafter, certain major liberal goals were achieved when a revolution occurred in France in 1830 and a sweeping reform bill passed through the British Parliament in 1832. During the same period, Russia, Austria, Prussia, and the other German states continued to resist political and social change.

▼ The Conservative Order

At the Congress of Vienna, the major powers—Russia, Austria, Prussia, and Great Britain—had agreed to consult with each other from time to time on matters affecting Europe as a whole. Such consultation was one of the new departures in international relations the Congress achieved. The vehicle for this consultation was a series of postwar congresses, or conferences. Later, as differences arose among the powers, the consultations became more informal. This new arrangement for resolving mutual foreign policy issues was known as the **Concert of Europe**. It prevented one nation from taking a major action in international affairs without working in concert with and obtaining the assent of the others. Its goal—a novel one in European affairs—was to maintain the peace. Initially, this meant maintaining the balance of power against new French aggression and against the military might of Russia. The Concert continued to function, however, on large and small issues until the third quarter of the century. In that respect, although the great powers sought to maintain conservative domestic governments, they were taking genuinely new steps to regulate their international relations.

The Congress System

In the years immediately after the Congress of Vienna, the new **congress system** of mutual cooperation and consultation functioned well. The first congress took place in 1818 at Aix-la-Chapelle in Germany near the border of Belgium. As a result of this gathering, the four major powers removed their troops from France, which had paid its war reparations, and readmitted France to good standing among the European nations. Despite unanimity on these decisions, the conference was not without friction. Tsar Alexander I (r. 1801–1825) suggested that the Quadruple Alliance (see Chapter 19) agree to uphold the borders and the existing governments of all European countries. Castlereagh, representing Britain, flatly rejected the proposal. He contended the Quadruple Alliance was intended only to prevent future French aggression. These disagreements appeared somewhat academic until revolutions broke out in southern Europe.

View the Map "Geographic Tour: Europe in 1815" on MyHistoryLab.com

The Domestic Political Order

Despite Castlereagh's resistance to the intervention of one power in the domestic affairs of another, other European statesmen believed that preventing domestic unrest was the key to maintaining international peace. The principle proponent of this view was the chancellor of Austria, Prince Metternich (1773–1859). This devoted servant of the Habsburg emperor had been, along with Britain's Viscount Castlereagh (1769–1822), the chief architect of the Vienna settlement. It was Metternich who seemed to exercise chief control over the forces of European reaction and who, more than any other early-nineteenth-century statesman, epitomized conservatism.

Conservative Outlooks

The major pillars of nineteenth-century **conservatism** were legitimate monarchies, landed aristocracies, and established churches. The institutions themselves were

THE PERIOD OF POLITICAL REACTION

1814	French monarchy restored
1815	Russia, Austria, and Prussia form Holy Alliance
1815	Russia, Austria, Prussia, and Britain renew Quadruple Alliance
1818	Congress of Aix-la-Chapelle
1819 (July)	Carlsbad Decrees
1819 (August 16)	Peterloo Massacre
1819 (December)	Great Britain passes Six Acts
1820 (January)	Spanish revolution
1820 (October)	Congress of Troppau
1821 (January)	Congress of Laibach
1821 (February)	Greek revolution
1822	Congress of Verona
1823	France helps crush Spanish revolution

ancient, but the self-conscious alliance of throne, land, and altar was new. In the eighteenth century, these groups had often quarreled. Only the upheavals of the French Revolution and the Napoleonic era transformed them into natural, if sometimes reluctant, allies. In that sense, conservatism as an articulated outlook and set of cooperating institutions was as new a feature on the political landscape as nationalism and liberalism.

The more theoretical political and religious ideas of the conservative classes were associated with thinkers such as Edmund Burke (see Chapter 18) and Friedrich Hegel (see Chapter 19). Conservatives shared other, less formal attitudes forged by the revolutionary experience. The execution of Louis XVI at the hands of radical democrats convinced most monarchs they could trust only aristocratic governments or governments of aristocrats in alliance with the wealthiest middle-class and professional people. The European aristocracies believed that no form of genuinely representative government would protect their property and influence. All conservatives spurned the idea of a written constitution unless they were permitted to write the document themselves. Even then, some rejected the concept.

The churches equally distrusted popular movements, except their own revivals. Ecclesiastical leaders throughout the Continent regarded themselves as entrusted with the educational task of supporting the social and political status quo. They also feared and hated most of the ideas associated with the Enlightenment because those rational concepts and reformist writings enshrined the critical spirit and undermined revealed religion.

Conservative aristocrats retained their former arrogance, but not their former privileges or their old confidence. They saw themselves as surrounded by enemies and as standing permanently on the defensive against the forces of liberalism, nationalism, and popular sovereignty. They knew that political groups that hated them could topple them. They also understood that revolution in one country could spill over into another.

All of the nations of Europe in the years immediately after 1815 confronted problems arising directly from their entering an era of peace after a quarter century of armed conflict. The war effort, with its loss of life and property and its need to organize people and resources, had distracted attention from other problems. The wartime footing had allowed all the belligerent governments to exercise firm control over their populations. War had fueled economies and had furnished vast areas of employment in armies, navies, military industries, and agriculture. The onset of peace meant citizens could raise new political issues and that economies were no longer geared to supplying military needs. Soldiers and sailors came home and looked for jobs as civilians. The vast demands of the military effort on industries subsided and caused unemployment. The young were no longer growing up in a climate of war and could think about other issues. For all of these reasons, the conservative statesmen who led every major government in 1815 confronted new pressures that would cause various degrees of domestic unrest and would lead them to resort to differing degrees of repression.

▼ The Emergence of Nationalism and Liberalism

The greatest of the new pressures challenging conservative regimes in the first half of the nineteenth century were the related, but distinct, ideologies of nationalism and liberalism.

Nationalism

Nationalism proved to be the single most powerful European political ideology of the nineteenth and early twentieth centuries. It has reasserted itself in present-day Europe following the collapse of communist governments in eastern Europe and in the former Soviet Union, and in connection with anxiety about immigration in western Europe. As a political outlook, nationalism was and is based on the relatively modern concept that a nation is composed of people who are joined together by the bonds of a common language, as well as common customs, culture, and history, and who, because of these bonds, should be administered by the same government. That is to say, nationalists in the past and the present contend that political and ethnic boundaries should coincide. This was a radical, new idea; political units had not been defined or governed according to the presumptive nationality of their populations previously in European history. The idea came into its own during the late eighteenth and the early nineteenth centuries.

Opposition to the Vienna Settlement Early nineteenth-century nationalism directly opposed the principle upheld at the Congress of Vienna that legitimate monarchies or dynasties, rather than nationality, provide the basis for political unity. Nationalists objected to multinational states such as the Austrian and Russian empires. They also insisted that peoples they believed belonged to one nation, such as Germans and Italians, should all dwell in the same political units instead of being divided among smaller states. Consequently, nationalists challenged both the domestic and the international order of the Vienna settlement.

Behind the concept of nationalism usually, though not always, lay the idea of popular sovereignty, since the qualities of peoples, rather than their rulers, determine a national character. This aspect of nationalism, however, frequently led to confusion or conflict because Europe was not actually organized into groups of people sharing both one recognized nationality and one contiguous territory. Although nationalists liked to think of nations as homogeneous with easily defined boundaries, this was rarely the case. Most states included people speaking different languages and dialects, practicing different religions, and defining themselves in relation to various different groups. Nationalists claimed that they were insisting on new political rights for nations that were themselves very old. In cases where they were confronted with people who did not share their nationalist aspirations, they argued that those people were slumbering members of a nation that had to be awakened. In reality, it was the nationalists who created nations in the nineteenth century.

Creating Nations During the first half of the century, small groups of nationalist writers or other intellectual elites, using the printed word, voiced their concept of the nation. Among their first tasks was to recruit historians who could chronicle, and in some cases create, a people's past, as well as literary scholars who could establish a national literature by collecting and publishing earlier writings in the people's language. They were joined by ethnographers who collected evidence of a distinctive folk culture, including myths, fairy tales, poetry, and song, and linguists who could define what constituted their nation's formal literary language and codify grammars and dictionaries. Together, these nationalists strove to give a people a sense of their past and a literature of their own. As time passed, schoolteachers spread nationalistic ideas by imparting a nation's official language and history. These small groups of early nationalists established the cultural beliefs and political expectations on which the later mass-supported nationalism of the second half of the century would grow.

Which language to use in the schools and in government offices was always a point of contention for nationalists. In France and Italy, official versions of the national language were imposed in the schools and they replaced local dialects. In parts of Scandinavia and eastern Europe, nationalists attempted to resurrect from earlier times what they regarded as purer versions of the national language. Often, modern scholars or linguists virtually invented these resurrected languages, although they always argued for their antiquity. This process of establishing national languages led to far more linguistic uniformity in European nations than had existed before the nineteenth century. Yet even in 1850, perhaps fewer than half of the inhabitants of France spoke the official French language.

Language could become such an effective cornerstone in the foundation of nationalism, thanks largely to the emergence of the print culture, discussed in Chapter 17. The presence of a great many printed books, journals, magazines, and newspapers "fixed" language in a more permanent fashion than did the spoken word. This uniform language found in printed works could overcome regional spoken dialects and establish itself as dominant. In most countries, spoken and written proficiency in the official, printed language became a path to social and political advancement. The growth of a uniform language helped persuade people who had not thought of themselves as constituting a nation that in fact they were one.

Meaning of Nationhood Nationalists used a variety of arguments and metaphors to express what they meant by *nationhood*. Some argued that gathering, for example, Italians into a unified Italy or Germans into a unified Germany, thus eliminating or at least federating the petty dynastic states that governed those regions, would promote economic and administrative efficiency. Adopting a tenet from political liberalism, certain nationalist writers suggested that nations determining their own destinies resembled individuals exploiting personal talents to determine their own careers. Some nationalists claimed that nations, like biological species in the natural world, were distinct creations of God. Other nationalists claimed a place for their nations in the divine order of things. Throughout the nineteenth century, for example, Polish nationalists portrayed Poland as the suffering Christ among nations, thus implicitly suggesting that Poland, like Christ, would experience resurrection and a new life.

A significant difficulty for nationalism was, and is, determining which ethnic groups could be considered nations, with claims to territory and political autonomy. In theory, any of them could, but in reality, nationhood came to be associated with groups that were large enough to support a viable economy, that successfully claimed a significant cultural history, that possessed a cultural elite that could nourish and spread the national language, and that had the military capacity to conquer other peoples or to establish and protect their own independence. Throughout the century many smaller ethnic groups claimed to fulfill these criteria, but could not effectively achieve either independence or recognition. They could and did, however, create domestic unrest within the political units they inhabited. (See "Compare and Connect: Mazzini and Lord Acton Debate the Political Principles of Nationalism," pages 620–621.)

Regions of Nationalist Pressure During the nineteenth century, nationalists challenged the political status quo throughout Europe. England had brought Ireland under direct rule in 1800, abolishing the separate Irish Parliament and allowing the Irish to elect members to the British Parliament in Westminster. Irish nationalists, however, wanted independence or at least larger measures of self-government. The "Irish problem," as it was called, would haunt British politics for the next two centuries. German nationalists sought political unity for all German-speaking peoples, challenging the legitimacy

COMPARE AND CONNECT Mazzini and Lord Acton Debate the Political Principles of Nationalism

Read the **Compare and Connect** on **MyHistoryLab.com**

NO POLITICAL FORCE in the nineteenth and twentieth centuries was stronger than nationalism. It eventually replaced loyalty to a dynasty with loyalty based on ethnic considerations. It received new standing after World War I when the self-determination of nations became one of the cornerstones of the Paris Peace treaties. Still later, former European colonies embraced this powerful idea. Yet from the earliest enunciation of the principles of nationalism the concept confronted major critics who understood its potential destructiveness. In these two documents Mazzini, the great Italian nationalist, sets forth his understanding of nationalism, and Lord Acton, the distinguished nineteenth-century English historian, points to the dangers lurking behind the ideas and realities of politics based on nationalism.

QUESTIONS

1. **What qualities of a people does Mazzini associate with nationalism?**
2. **How and why does Mazzini relate nationalism to divine purposes?**
3. **Why does Acton see the principle of nationality as dangerous to liberty?**
4. **Why does Acton see nationalism as a threat to minority groups and to democracy?**
5. **How might the connection that Mazzini draws between nationalism and divine will serve to justify the repression of minority rights that Acton feared?**

I. Mazzini Defines Nationality

In 1835 Italian nationalist Giuseppe Mazzini (1805–1872) explained his understanding of nationalism. He combined a generally democratic view of politics with a religious concept of the divine destiny of nations. Once in power, however, nationalist states in Europe and the rest of the world were often not democratic states.

The essential characteristics of a nationality are common ideas, common principles and a common purpose. A nation is an association of those who are brought together by language, by given geographical conditions or by the role assigned them by history, who acknowledge the same principles and who march together to the conquest of a single definite goal under the rule of a uniform body of law.

The life of a nation consists in harmonious activity (that is, the employment of all individual abilities and energies comprised within the association) towards this single goal. . . .

But nationality means even more than this. Nationality also consists in the share of mankind's labors which God assigns to a people. This mission is the task which a people must perform to the end that the Divine Idea shall be realized in this world; it is the work which gives a people its rights as a member of Mankind; it is the baptismal rite which endows a people with its own character and its rank in the brotherhood of nations. . . .

Nationality depends for its very existence upon its sacredness within and beyond its borders.

If nationality is to be inviolable for all, friends and foes alike, it must be regarded inside a country as holy, like a religion, and outside a country as a grave mission. It is necessary too that the ideas arising within a country grow steadily, as part of the general law of Humanity which is the source of all nationality. It is necessary that these ideas be shown to other lands in their beauty and purity, free from any alien mixture, from any slavish fears, from any skeptical hesitancy, strong and active, embracing in their evolution every aspect and manifestation of the life of the nation. These ideas, a necessary component in the order of universal destiny, must retain their originality even as they enter harmoniously into mankind's general progress.

The people must be the basis of nationality; its logically derived and vigorously applied principles its means; the strength of all its strength; the improvement of the life of all and the happiness of the greatest possible number its results; and the accomplishment of the task assigned to it by God its goal. This is what we mean by nationality. ■

From Herbert H. Rowen, ed., *From Absolutism to Revolution, 1648–1848*, 2nd ed. (Upper Saddle River, NJ: Prentice Hall, 1969), pp. 277–280.

II. Lord Acton Condemns Nationalism

As well as being a historian, Lord Acton (1834–1902) was an important nineteenth-century commentator on contemporary religious and political events. He was deeply concerned with the character and preservation of liberty. In his 1862 essay "Nationality," Lord Acton's became one of the earliest voices to warn that nationalism or what he here terms "the modern theory of nationality" could endanger liberty of both individuals and people who found themselves to be a national minority within a state dominated by a different national majority. Acton's words would prove prophetic with regard to the fate of minorities within Europe for the next century. Acton also pointed out that the pursuit of nationalist goals might mean that a government would ignore the economic well-being of its peoples.

The greatest adversary of the rights of nationality is the modern theory of nationality. By making the State and the nation commensurate with each other in theory, it reduces practically to a subject condition all other nationalities that may be within the boundary. It cannot admit them to an equality with the ruling nation which constitutes the State, because the State would then cease to be national, which would be a contradiction of the principle of its existence. According, therefore, to the degree of humanity and civilization in that dominant body which claims all the rights of the community, the inferior races are exterminated, or reduced to servitude, or outlawed, or put in a condition of dependence.

If we take the establishment of liberty for the realization of moral duties to be the end of civil society, we must conclude that those states are substantially the most perfect which, like the British and Austrian Empires, include various distinct nationalities without oppressing them. Those in which no mixture of races has occurred are imperfect; and those in which its effects have disappeared are decrepit. A State which is incompetent to satisfy different races condemns itself; a State which labors to neutralize, to absorb, or to expel them, destroys its own vitality; a State which does not include them is destitute of the chief basis of self-government. The theory of nationality, therefore, is a retrograde step in history. . . .

[N]ationality does not aim either at liberty or prosperity, both of which it sacrifices to the imperative necessity of making the nation the mold and measure of the State. Its course will be marked with material as well as moral ruin, in order that a new invention may prevail over the works of God and the interests of mankind. There is no principle of change, no phrase of political speculation conceivable, more comprehensive, more subversive, or more arbitrary than this. It is a confutation of democracy, because it sets limits to the exercise of the popular will, and substitutes for it a higher principle. ■

From John Emerich Edward Dalbert-Acton, First Baron Acton, *Essays in the History of Liberty*, ed. by J. Rufus Fears (Indianapolis, IN: Liberty Classics, 1985), pp. 431–433.

The celebration of nationalism included attempts to classify different groups of people according to language, religion, and culture. Sketches of differing regional folk costumes both celebrated diversity and institutionalized difference. This mid-nineteenth-century lithograph includes images of the peasant attire of the different national groups in Hungary. From left to right, these are "Walachians" (Romanians), Hungarians, "Slavs" (Slovaks), and Germans. Costumes of Peasants, from 'Esquisses de la Vie Populaire en Hongroie' by Gabriel de Pronay, 1855 (colour litho), Veber, H. (fl.1855). Bibliotheque Nationale, Paris, France/Archives Charmet/The Bridgeman Art Library International of the Prussian and Austrian monarchies, which both contained large non-German-speaking populations. Italian nationalists sought to unify Italian-speaking peoples on the Italian peninsula and to drive out their Austrian and Bourbon rulers. Polish nationalists, targeting primarily their Russian rulers, struggled to restore Poland as an independent nation. In eastern Europe, a host of national groups, including Hungarians, Czechs, Slovenes, and others, sought either independence or, more frequently, some form of autonomy and recognition within the Austrian Empire. Finally, in southeastern Europe on the Balkan peninsula and eastward, national groups, including Serbs, Greeks, Albanians, Romanians, and Bulgarians, sought independence from Ottoman and Russian control.

Although nationalist activity in each of these areas ebbed and flowed, each of them had the potential to erupt into turmoil for much of the nineteenth century and beyond. The dominant governments often thought they needed only to repress the activity or ride it out until stability returned. Over the course of the century, however, nationalists changed the political map and political culture of Europe.

Early-Nineteenth-Century Political Liberalism

The word *liberal*, as applied to political activity, entered the European and American vocabulary during the nineteenth century. Its meaning has varied over time. Nineteenth-century European conservatives often regarded as *liberal* almost anyone or anything that challenged their own political, social, or religious values. European conservatives of the last century saw liberals as more radical than they actually were. For twenty-first-century Americans, the word *liberal* carries with it meanings and connotations that have little or nothing to do with its significance to nineteenth-century Europeans. It is therefore critical to understand nineteenth-century liberalism in its own context.

Political Goals Nineteenth-century liberals derived their political ideas from the writers of the Enlightenment, the example of English liberties, and the so-called principles of 1789 embodied in the French Declaration of the Rights of Man and Citizen. They sought to establish a political framework of legal equality, religious toleration, and freedom of the press. Their general goal was a political structure that would limit the arbitrary power of government against the persons and property of individual citizens. They generally believed the legitimacy of government emanated from the freely given consent of the governed. The popular basis of such government was to be expressed through elected representative, or parliamentary, bodies. Most importantly, free government required government ministers to be responsible to the representatives rather than to the monarch. Liberals sought to achieve these political arrangements through written constitutions. They wanted to see constitutionalism and constitutional governments installed across the Continent. They were not, however, generally advocates of universal suffrage or democracy.

These goals may seem limited, and they were. Responsible constitutional government, however, existed nowhere in Europe in 1815. Even in Great Britain, the cabinet ministers were at least as responsible to the monarch as to the House of Commons. Conservatives were suspicious of written constitutions, associating them with the French Revolution and Napoleon's regimes. They were also certain that no written constitution could embody all the political wisdom needed to govern a state.

Those who espoused liberal political structures often were educated, relatively wealthy people, usually associated with the professions or commercial life, but who were excluded in one manner or another from the existing political processes. Because of their wealth and education, they felt their exclusion was unjustified. Liberals were often academics, members of the learned professions, and people involved in the rapidly expanding commercial and manufacturing segments of the economy. They believed in, and were products of, a career open to talent. The monarchical and aristocratic regimes, as restored after the Congress of Vienna, often failed both to recognize their new status sufficiently and to provide for their economic and professional interests.

Although liberals wanted broader political participation, they did not advocate democracy. What they wanted was to extend representation to the propertied classes. Second only to their hostility to the privileged aristocracies was their contempt for the lower, unpropertied classes. They imagined an active citizenry of educated men, inspired by reason and by their own investment, through their private property, in peace and stability. Liberals transformed the eighteenth-century concept of aristocratic liberty into a new concept of privilege based on wealth and property rather than on birth. As French liberal theorist Benjamin Constant (1767–1830) wrote in 1814,

> Those whom poverty keeps in eternal dependence are no more enlightened on public affairs than children, nor are they more interested than foreigners in national prosperity, of which they do not understand the basis and of which they enjoy the advantages only indirectly. Property alone, by giving sufficient leisure, renders a man capable of exercising his political rights.[1]

By the middle of the century, this widely shared attitude meant that throughout Europe liberals had separated themselves from both the rural peasantry and the urban working class, a division that was to have important consequences.

Because the social and political circumstances of various countries differed, the specific programs of

[1]Frederick B. Artz, *Reaction and Revolution, 1814–1832* (New York: Harper, 1934), p. 94.

Document

John Stuart Mill Advocates Independence

In the early 1830s, John Stuart Mill and Harriet Taylor exchanged a series of letters on the subject of marriage and divorce. In this excerpt, Mill argues in favor of women's independence from their husbands as a matter of principle, but not one that should lead to women's equality in the workforce. As he explains why women are not yet men's equals and what must be done to redress this injustice, he reveals the basic requirements of the active citizen according to liberals. Taylor responds with a criticism of marriage and a plea in favor of women's right to divorce. Mill and Taylor married one another in 1851.

What, according to Mill, is the explanation of women's dependence on men? What sort of education do women require? How does Mill suppose education would contribute to women's independence? What are the limits of Mill's vision of equality for men and women? What does Taylor believe women will gain from the right to divorce?

Mill:

Women are so brought up, as not to be able to subsist in the mere physical sense, without a man to keep them: they are so brought up as not to be able to protect themselves against injury or insult, without some man on whom they have a special claim, to protect them, they are so brought up, as to have no vocation or useful office to fulfil in the world. . . .

There is no natural inequality between the sexes; except perhaps in bodily strength; even *that* admits of doubt: and if bodily strength is to be the measure of superiority, mankind are no better than savages. . . .

If nature has not made men and women unequal, still less ought the law to make them so. . . . A woman ought not to be dependent on a man, more than a man on a woman, except so far as their affections make them so. . . .

But this perfect independence of each other for all save affection, cannot be, if there be dependence in pecuniary circumstances. . . .

The first and indispensable step, therefore, towards the enfranchisement of woman, is that she be so educated, as not to be dependent either on her father or her husband for subsistence: a position which in nine cases out of ten, makes her either the plaything or the slave of the man who feeds her; and in the tenth case, only his humble friend. . . .

It does not follow that a woman should *actually* support herself because she should be *capable* of doing so: in the natural course of events she will *not*. It is not desirable to burthen the labour market with a double number of competitors. . . .

The great occupation of woman should be to *beautify* life: to cultivate, for her own sake and that of those who surround her, all her faculties of mind, soul, and body; all her powers of enjoyment, and powers of giving enjoyment; and to diffuse beauty, and elegance, and grace, everywhere.

Taylor:

"There is equality in nothing now—all the pleasures such as there are being men's, and all the disagreeables and pains being women's. . . . Women are educated for one single object, to gain their living by marrying. . . . To be married is the object of their existence and that object being gained they do really cease to exist as to anything worth calling life or any useful purpose. . . . I have no doubt that when the whole community is really educated, tho' the present laws of marriage were to continue[,] they would be perfectly disregarded, because no one would marry. The widest and perhaps the quickest means to do away with its evils is to be found in promoting education—as it is the means of all good. . . .

At this present time, in this state of civilization, what evil could be caused by, first placing women on the most entire equality with men, as to all rights and privileges, civil and political, and then doing away with all laws whatever relating to marriage? Then if a woman had children she must take charge of them, women would not then have children without considering how to maintain them. Women would have no more reason to barter person for bread, or for anything else, than men have—public offices being open to them alike, all occupations would be divided between the sexes in their natural arrangement. Fathers would provide for their daughters in the same way as for their sons.

John Stuart Mill, "On Marriage," *The Collected Works of John Stuart Mill*, ed. John M. Robson (Toronto: University of Toronto Press, 1984), volume XXI, pp. 41–44. Reprinted with permission of the publisher.
Harriet Taylor Mill, "On Marriage," in *The Complete Works of Harriet Taylor Mill*, edited by Jo Ellen Jacobs (Bloomington, IN: Indiana University Press, 1998), 22–23.

liberals also differed from one country to another. In Great Britain, the monarchy was already limited, and most individual liberties had been secured. With reform, Parliament could provide more nearly representative government. Links between land, commerce, and industry were in place. France also already had many structures liberals favored. The Napoleonic Code gave France a modern legal system. French liberals could justify calls for greater rights by appealing to the widely accepted "principles of 1789." As in England, representatives of the different economic interests in France had worked together. The problem for liberals in both countries was to protect civil liberties, define the respective powers of the monarch and the elected legislature, and expand the electorate moderately while avoiding democracy.

Liberals were divided on the subject of women's role in society. While some, like Harriet Taylor and her husband, John Stuart Mill, argued in favor of women's enfranchisement, most liberals were suspicious of women's education and inclination to rely on the counsel of others, including conservative priests. Women's suffrage played no role in liberal politics in the first two-thirds of the nineteenth century.

The complex political situation in German-speaking Europe was different from that in France or Britain, and German liberalism differed accordingly from its French and British counterparts. In the German states and Austria, monarchs and aristocrats offered stiffer resistance to liberal ideas, leaving German liberals with less access to direct political influence. A sharp social divide separated the aristocratic landowning classes, which filled the bureaucracies and officer corps, from the small middle-class commercial and industrial interests. Little or no precedent existed for middle-class participation in the government or the military, and there was no strong tradition of civil or individual liberty. There was also a greater tradition of reform from above than existed in France, which German rulers used to argue that they were more trustworthy and constitutions less necessary.

Most German liberals favored a united Germany and looked either to Austria or to Prussia as the instrument of unification. As a result, they were more tolerant of a strong state and monarchical power than other liberals were. They believed that unification would lead to a freer social and political order. The monarchies in Austria and Prussia refused to cooperate with these dreams of unification, frustrating German liberals and forcing them to settle for more modest achievements, such as lowering internal trade barriers.

Classical Economics

The economic goals of nineteenth-century liberals also divided them from working people. Economists whose thought derived largely from Adam Smith's *The Wealth of Nations* (1776) dominated private and public discussions of industrial and commercial policy. Their ideas are often associated with the phrase *laissez-faire* (a French phrase that means roughly "let people do as they please"). Although they thought the government should perform many important functions, the classical economists favored economic growth through competitive free enterprise. They conceived of society as consisting of atomistic individuals whose competitive efforts met consumers' demands in the marketplace. They believed the mechanism of the marketplace should govern most economic decisions. They believed most government action to be mischievous and corrupt. The government should maintain a sound currency, enforce contracts, protect property, impose low tariffs and taxes, and leave the remainder of economic life to private initiative. The economists naturally assumed the state would maintain enough armed forces and naval power to protect the nation's economic structure and foreign trade. With emphasis on thrift, competition, and personal industriousness, the political economists' voice appealed to the middle classes.

Read the **Document** "Adam Smith, *The Wealth of Nations*" on **MyHistoryLab.com**

The manufacturers of Great Britain, the landed and manufacturing middle class of France, and the commercial interests of Germany and Italy were deeply influenced by Smith's classical economics. They sought to abolish the economic restraints associated with mercantilism or the regulated economies of enlightened absolutists. They wanted to manufacture and sell goods freely. To that end, they favored the removal of international tariffs and internal barriers to trade. Economic liberals opposed the old paternalistic legislation that established wages and labor practices by government regulation or by guild privileges. They saw labor as simply one more commodity to be bought and sold freely.

Liberals wanted an economic structure in which people were at liberty to use whatever talents and property they possessed to enrich themselves. Such a structure, they contended, would produce more goods and services for everyone at lower prices and provide the basis for material progress. Liberals' commitment to the principles of classical economics set them at odds with the working class, and impeded cooperation toward social and economic reform.

Malthus on Population The classical economists had complicated and pessimistic ideas about the working class. Thomas Malthus (1766–1834) and David Ricardo (1772–1823), probably the most influential of all these writers, suggested, in effect, that nothing could improve the condition of the working class. In 1798, Malthus published the first edition of his *Essay on the Principle of Population*. His ideas have haunted the world ever since. He contended that population must eventually outstrip the food supply. Although the human population grows geometrically, the food supply can expand only arithmetically. There was little hope of averting the disaster, in Malthus's opinion, except through late marriage, chastity, and contraception, the last of which he considered a vice. It took three-quarters of a century for contraception to become a socially acceptable method of containing the population explosion.

Read the **Document** "Laws of Population Growth (1798) Malthus" on **MyHistoryLab.com**

Malthus contended that the immediate plight of the working class could only become worse. If wages were raised, the workers would simply produce more children, who would, in turn, consume both the extra wages and more food. Later in his life, Malthus suggested, in a more optimistic vein, that if the working class could be persuaded to adopt a higher standard of living, their increased wages might be spent on consumer goods rather than on begetting more children.

Ricardo on Wages In his *Principles of Political Economy* (1817), David Ricardo transformed the concepts of Malthus into the "iron law of wages." If wages were raised, parents would have more children. They, in turn, would enter the labor market, thus expanding the number of workers and lowering wages. As wages fell, working people would produce fewer children. Wages would then rise, and the process would start all over again. Consequently, in the long run, wages would always tend toward a minimum level. These arguments simply supported employers in their natural reluctance to raise wages and also provided strong theoretical support for opposing labor unions. Journals, newspapers, and even short stories, such as Harriet Martineau's (1802–1876) series *Illustrations of Political Economy*, spread the ideas of the economists to the public in the 1830s.

Read the **Document** "David Ricardo, Excerpt from *Principles of Political Economy and Taxation*" on **MyHistoryLab.com**

Relationship of Liberalism to Nationalism

Nationalism was not necessarily or even logically linked to liberalism. Indeed, nationalism could be, and often was, directly opposed to liberal political values. Conservative nationalists might seek political autonomy for their own group but have no intention of establishing liberal political institutions thereafter. Some nationalists wanted their own particular group to dominate minority groups within a particular region, denying them political rights based on nationality instead of wealth or property. This was true of the Hungarians, who sought political control over all people living within the historical boundaries of Hungary, whether they spoke Hungarian or not. Nationalists also often defined their own national group in opposition to other national groups whom they might regard as cultural inferiors or historical enemies. These nationalists would insist that becoming educated and becoming members of their own nation were the same, and that consequently only those who chose to identify with their nation deserved political rights.

Nonetheless, although liberalism and nationalism were not identical, they were often compatible. By espousing representative government, civil liberties, and economic freedom, nationalist groups in one country could gain the support of liberals elsewhere in Europe who might not otherwise share their nationalist interests. Many nationalists in central Europe and the Italian peninsula adopted this tactic. Some nationalists took other symbolic steps to arouse sympathy. Nationalists in Greece, for example, made Athens their capital because they believed it would associate their struggle for independence with ancient Athenian democracy, which English and French liberals revered.

▼ Conservative Restoration in Europe

Despite the challenges of liberalism and nationalism, the domestic political order that the restored conservative institutions of Europe established showed remarkable resilience. Not until World War I did their power come to an end. The Austrian chancellor, Prince Klemens von Metternich, masterminded the resistance to both liberal and national pressures throughout central Europe. In Britain, rapid social and economic change brought new challenges to the conservative order that were met with determined resistance. In France and Spain, the Bourbon monarchies tried to avoid binding themselves to constitutions. For the first few years after the Congress of Vienna, all these reactionary measures appeared successful.

Liberalism and Nationalism Resisted in Austria and the Germanies

Nowhere did nationalism threaten the existing order as much as in German-speaking Europe, where the creation of one single German nation-state would unseat dozens of ruling princes and destroy as many historically independent countries.

Dynastic Integrity of The Habsburg Empire The Austrian government was fundamentally threatened by the programs of liberalism and nationalism, and while it could accommodate the former to some degree, the latter threatened to undermine the basic integrity of the state.

Most Austrians did not think of themselves in national terms. Their sense of belonging was determined by their religion or by regional and local communities, combined with loyalty to the dynasty. Those Austrians who did identify with a nation could consider themselves German, Hungarian, Polish, Czech, Slovak, Slovene, Italian, Croat, Ruthenian (Ukrainian), Romanian, or Serb. Through client governments, Austria also dominated other parts of the Italian peninsula that it did not rule directly. If Austrian subjects began to privilege national identity over loyalty to the dynasty, or if they came to see their national interests as incompatible with the national interests of people who lived in the same regions but spoke different languages, the empire would be torn apart.

View the Map "Map Discovery: Nationalities within the Habsburg Empire" on **MyHistoryLab.com**

For Metternich and other Austrian officials, the recognition of the political rights and aspirations of any of the various national groups would mean the probable dissolution of the empire. If Austria permitted representative government, Metternich feared the national groups would fight their battles internally at the cost of Austria's international influence.

Although Hungarian, Czech, and Italian nationalists would later complain that they were dominated by Germans within the empire, German nationalism was, in some respects, the most threatening to the monarchy. Like German nationalists themselves, Metternich expected that the formation of a German national state would, of necessity, absorb the German-speaking core of the empire and exclude the other realms the Habsburgs governed. It was impossible to imagine a unified Germany that was compatible with Habsburg dynastic integrity. Therefore, Austria had to dominate the newly formed German Confederation to prevent the formation of a German national state. The Congress of Vienna had created the German Confederation to replace the defunct Holy Roman Empire. It consisted of thirty-nine states under Austrian leadership. Each state remained independent, but Austria was determined to prevent any movement toward constitutionalism in as many of them as possible.

Prince Klemens von Metternich (1773–1859) epitomized nineteenth-century conservatism. Sir Thomas Lawrence (1769–1830), *Clemens Lothar Wenzel, Prince Metternich* (1773–1859), © World History Archive/Alamy

Defeat of Prussian Reform An important victory for this conservative policy came in Prussia in the years immediately after the Congress of Vienna. In 1815, Frederick William III (r. 1797–1840), caught up in the exhilaration that followed the War of Liberation, as Germans called the last part of their conflict with Napoleon, had promised some form of constitutional government. After stalling, he formally reneged on his pledge in 1817. Instead, he created a new Council of State, which, although it improved administrative efficiency, was responsible to him alone.

In 1819, the king moved further from reform. After a major disagreement over the organization of the army, he replaced his reform-minded ministers with hardened conservatives. On their advice, in 1823, Frederick William III established eight provincial estates, or diets. These bodies were dominated by the Junkers and exercised only an advisory function. The old bonds linking monarchy, army, and landholders in Prussia had been reestablished. The members of this alliance would oppose the threats that German nationalists posed to the conservative social and political order.

Student Nationalism and the Carlsbad Decrees To widen their bases of political support, the monarchs of three southern German states—Baden, Bavaria, and Württemberg—had granted constitutions after 1815. None of these constitutions, however, recognized popular sovereignty, and all defined political rights as the gift of the monarch. Yet in the aftermath of the defeat of Napoleon, many young Germans continued to cherish nationalist and liberal expectations.

University students who had grown up during the days of the reforms of Stein and Hardenberg and had read the writings of early German nationalists made up the most important of these groups. Many of them or their friends had fought Napoleon. When they went to the universities, they continued to dream of a united Germany. They formed *Burschenschaften*, or student associations. Like student groups today, these clubs served numerous social functions, one of which was to replace old provincial attachments with loyalty to the concept of a united German state. Later in the nineteenth century, these clubs became increasingly anti-Semitic. (See "Encountering the Past: Gymnastics and German Nationalism," page 628.)

In 1817, in Jena, one such student club organized a large celebration for the fourth anniversary of the Battle of Leipzig and the tercentenary of Luther's Ninety-five Theses. There were bonfires, songs, and processions as more than five hundred people gathered for the festivities. The event made German rulers uneasy, for the student clubs included a few republicans.

Two years later, in March 1819, a student named Karl Sand, a *Burschenschaft* member, assassinated conservative dramatist August von Kotzebue, who had ridiculed the *Burschenschaft* movement. Sand, who was tried and publicly executed, became a nationalist martyr. Although Sand had acted alone, Metternich used the incident to suppress institutions associated with liberalism.

In July 1819, Metternich persuaded the major German states to issue the Carlsbad Decrees, which dissolved the *Burschenschaften*. The decrees also provided for university inspectors and press censors. (See "The German Confederation Issues the Carlsbad Decrees," page 629.) The next year the German Confederation issued the Final Act, which limited the subjects that the constitutional chambers of Bavaria, Württemberg, and Baden could discuss. The measure also asserted the right of the monarchs to resist demands of constitutionalists. For many years thereafter, the secret police of the various German states harassed potential dissidents. In the opinion of the princes, these included almost anyone who sought even moderate social or political change.

Postwar Repression in Great Britain

The years 1819 and 1820 marked a high tide for conservative influence and repression in western as well as eastern Europe. After 1815, Great Britain experienced two years of poor harvests. At the same time, discharged sailors and soldiers and out-of-work industrial workers swelled the ranks of the unemployed.

Lord Liverpool's Ministry and Popular Unrest The Tory ministry of Lord Liverpool (1770–1828) was unprepared to deal with these problems of postwar dislocation. Instead, it sought to protect the interests of the landed and wealthy classes. In 1815, Parliament passed a Corn Law to maintain high prices for domestically produced grain (called "corn" in Britain) by levying import duties on foreign grain. The next year, Parliament replaced the income tax that only the wealthy

In May 1820, Karl Sand, a German student and a member of a *Burschenschaft*, was executed for his murder of the conservative playwright August von Kotzebue the previous year. In the eyes of many young German nationalists, Sand was a political martyr. Bildarchiv Preussischer Kulturbesitz/Art Resource, NY

ENCOUNTERING THE *Past*

GYMNASTICS AND GERMAN NATIONALISM

TODAY CITIZENS TAKE great pride in the performance of their nations' athletes in the Olympics. This modern link between athletics and nationalism originated in early nineteenth-century Germany with the *Turnverein*, or gymnastic movement.

Friedrich Ludwig Jahn (1778–1852) was the father of the movement, which he described as "Love of the Fatherland through Gymnastics." He was also an innovator in gymnastic equipment, credited with inventing the parallel bars and improving the pommel vault.

Jahn became a fervent patriot when he saw the German states and particularly Prussia humiliated by Napoleon. He attacked what he regarded as foreign influence on German life, including that of German Jews. Jahn was convinced that Germans must cultivate their bodily strength to overcome external enemies. In 1811, he established an open-air gymnasium in a meadow near Berlin. The young men who attended this gymnasium and others that he soon founded throughout the German states saw themselves as an advanced nationalist guard.

After the defeat of Napoleon in 1815, gymnastic clubs spread across Germany, fostered nationalist sentiment, and challenged the social and political status quo. The clubs embodied social equality. All members wore plain gray exercise uniforms that Jahn had designed and addressed each other with the familiar "Du." Conservatives were suspicious. They saw these early gymnastic clubs as a state within the various disunited German states. For a time Prussia banned gymnastics and sent Jahn to prison.

During the 1840s, however, the gymnastic movement revived. Germany soon had tens of thousands of adult gymnasts, and the clubs became increasingly nationalist, often excluding Jews. After German unification in 1870, national festivals often featured gymnastic performances, and national monuments had areas for gymnastic display. Political figures from Bismarck to Hitler cultivated their links to the gymnastic societies. The connection between gymnastics and German nationalism was so strong that even liberal Germans who immigrated to the United States founded *Turnvereins* in their new homes.

Sources: Liah Greenfeld, *Nationalism: Five Roads to Modernity* (Cambridge, MA: Harvard University Press, 1992), pp. 367–370; Matthew Levinger, *Enlightened Nationalism: The Transformation of Prussian Political Culture, 1806–1848* (New York: Oxford University Press, 2000); George L. Mosse, *The Nationalization of the Masses: Political Symbolism and Mass Movements in Germany from the Napoleonic Wars through the Third Reich* (New York: New American Library, 1975), p. 128.

What factors turned Jahn to nationalism?

Why did he associate nationalism with physical strength?

How could the *Turnverein* movement spread easily in the Germanies?

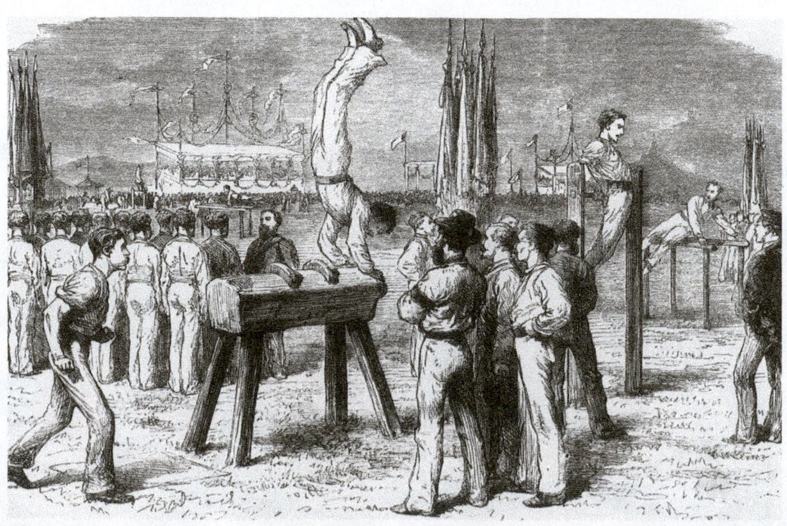

Jahn encouraged German gymnasts to use athletic equipment in their exercises. Here at a Bonn gymnastic festival in 1872 an athlete works out on a pommel horse, a piece of athletic equipment that predated Jahn, but the design of which he improved. Also note the athletic clothing, which emphasizes egalitarian social relations among the athletes.

Document

THE GERMAN CONFEDERATION ISSUES THE CARLSBAD DECREES

In 1819, following Karl Sand's assassination of playwright August von Kotzebue, the German Confederation, deeply fearful of nationalistic student activism, issued the Carlsbad Decrees under the guidance of Prince Metternich. These decrees limited the activities of German students, faculty, and publishers.

By what devices did the government attempt to replace the university discipline of students with government discipline? What kind of actions by faculty and students do these decrees forbid or discourage? How did they seek to make universities institutions of the status quo? How did all of the rules regarding universities seek to isolate students and faculty suspected of dangerous political opinions or actions? How was the censorship of newspapers to work?

REGARDING UNIVERSITY LIFE

1. There shall be appointed for each university a special representative of the ruler of each state, the said representatives to have appropriate instructions and extended powers, and they shall have their place of residence where the university is located. . . .

This representative shall enforce strictly the existing laws and disciplinary regulations; he shall observe with care the attitude shown by the university instructors in their public lectures and registered courses; and he shall, without directly interfering in scientific matters or in teaching methods, give a beneficial direction to the teaching, keeping in view the future attitude of the students. Finally, he shall give . . . attention to everything that may promote morality . . . among the students. . . .

2. The confederated governments mutually pledge themselves to eliminate from the universities or any other public educational institutions all instructors who shall have obviously proved their unfitness for the important work entrusted to them by openly deviating from their duties, or by going beyond the boundaries of their functions, or by abusing their legitimate influence over young minds, or by presenting harmful ideas hostile to public order or subverting existing governmental instructions. . . .

Any instructor who has been removed in this manner becomes ineligible for a position in any other public institution of learning in another state of the Confederation.

3. The laws that have for some time been directed against secret and unauthorized societies in the universities shall be strictly enforced. . . . The special representatives of the government are enjoined to exert great care in watching these organizations.

The governments mutually agree that all individuals who shall be shown to have maintained their membership in secret or unauthorized associations, or shall have taken membership in such associations, shall not be eligible for any public office.

4. No student who shall have been expelled from any university by virtue of a decision of the university senate ratified or initiated by the special representative . . . , shall be admitted by any other university. . . .

REGARDING THE PRESS

1. As long as this edict remains in force, no publication which appears daily, or as a serial not exceeding twenty sheets of printed matter, shall be printed in any state of the Confederation without the prior knowledge and approval of the state officials. . . .

4. Each state of the Confederation is responsible, not only to the state against which the offense is directly committed but to the entire Confederation, for any publication printed within the limits of its jurisdiction, in which the honor or security of other states is impinged upon or their constitution or administration attacked. . . .

7. When a newspaper or periodical is suppressed by a decision of the Diet, the editor of such publication may not within five years edit a similar publication in any state of the Confederation.

From P. A. G. von Meyer, *Corpus juris confoederationis Germanicae*, 2nd ed., Vol. 2 (Frankfort on Main, 1833), pp. 138 ff., as quoted and translated in Louis L. Snyder, ed., *Documents of German History* (New Brunswick, NJ: Rutgers University Press, 1958), pp. 158–160.

paid with excise or sales taxes on consumer goods that both the wealthy and the poor paid. These laws continued a legislative trend that marked the abandonment by the British ruling class of its traditional role of paternalistic protector of the poor. In 1799, the Combination Acts had outlawed workers' organizations or unions. During the war, wage protection had been removed. Many in the taxpaying classes wanted to abolish the Poor Law that provided public relief for the destitute and unemployed.

In light of these policies and the postwar economic downturn, it is hardly surprising that the lower social orders began to doubt the wisdom of their rulers and to demand political changes. Mass meetings called for the reform of Parliament. Reform clubs were organized. Radical newspapers, such as William Cobbett's *Political Registrar*, demanded change. In the hungry, restive agricultural and industrial workers, the government could see only images of continental *sans-culottes* ready to hang aristocrats from the nearest lamppost. Government ministers regarded radical leaders, such as Cobbett (1763–1835), Major John Cartwright (1740–1824), and Henry "Orator" Hunt (1773–1835), as demagogues who were seducing the people away from allegiance to their natural leaders.

The government's answer to the discontent was repression. In December 1816, an unruly mass meeting took place at Spa Fields near London. This disturbance gave Parliament an excuse to pass the Coercion Acts of March 1817, which temporarily suspended *habeas corpus* and extended existing laws against seditious gatherings.

"Peterloo" and the Six Acts This initial repression, in combination with improved harvests, calmed the political landscape for a time. By 1819, however, the people were restive again. In the industrial north, well-organized mass meetings demanded the reform of Parliament. The radical reform campaign culminated on August 16, 1819, with a meeting in the industrial city of Manchester at Saint Peter's Fields. Royal troops and the local militia were on hand to ensure order. As the speeches were about to begin, a local magistrate ordered the militia to move into the audience. The result was panic and death. At least eleven people in the crowd were killed; scores were injured. The event became known as the Peterloo Massacre, a phrase that drew a contemptuous comparison with Wellington's victory at Waterloo.

Peterloo had been the act of local officials, whom the Liverpool ministry felt it must support. The cabinet also decided to act once and for all to end these troubles. Most of the radical leaders were arrested and imprisoned. In December 1819, a few months after the German Carlsbad Decrees, Parliament passed a series of laws called the Six Acts, which (1) forbade large unauthorized, public meetings; (2) raised the fines for seditious libel; (3) speeded up the trials of political agitators; (4) increased newspaper taxes; (5) prohibited the training of armed groups; and (6) allowed local officials to search homes in certain disturbed counties. In effect, the Six Acts attempted to prevent radical leaders from agitating and to give the authorities new powers.

Two months after the passage of the Six Acts, the Cato Street Conspiracy was unearthed. Under the

The famous cartoonist George Cruikshank highlights the poverty and desperation of the British working class in the foreground of this 1819 etching, "These are the People All Tatter'd and Torn." In the background, mounted militia slash at women and children lying on the ground, in allusion to the Peterloo Massacre.

guidance of a possibly demented man named Arthur Thistlewood (1770–1820), a group of extreme radicals had plotted to blow up the entire British cabinet. The plot was foiled. The leaders were arrested and tried, and five of them were hanged. Although little more than a half-baked plot, the conspiracy helped discredit the movement for parliamentary reform.

Bourbon Restoration in France

The abdication of Napoleon in 1814 opened the way for a restoration of Bourbon rule in the homeland of the great revolution. The new king was the former count of Provence and a brother of Louis XVI. The son of the executed monarch had died in prison. Royalists had regarded the dead boy as Louis XVII, and so his uncle became Louis XVIII (r. 1814–1824). This fat, awkward man had become a political realist during his more than twenty years of exile. He understood he could not turn back the clock to 1789. France had undergone too many irreversible changes. Consequently, Louis XVIII agreed to become a constitutional monarch, but under a constitution of his own making called the Charter.

The Charter The Charter provided for a hereditary monarchy and a bicameral legislature. The monarch appointed the upper house, the Chamber of Peers, modeled on the British House of Lords; a narrow franchise with a high property qualification elected the lower house, the Chamber of Deputies. The Charter guaranteed most of the rights the Declaration of the Rights of Man and Citizen had enumerated. There was to be religious toleration, but Roman Catholicism was designated the official religion of the nation. Most importantly for thousands of French people at all social levels, the Charter promised not to challenge the property rights of the current owners of land that had been confiscated from aristocrats and the church. With this provision, Louis XVIII hoped to reconcile beneficiaries of the revolution to his regime.

Ultraroyalism This moderate spirit did not penetrate deeply into the ranks of royalist supporters whose families had suffered during the revolution. Rallying around Louis's brother and heir, the count of Artois (1757–1836), those people who were more royalist than the monarch now demanded their revenge. In the months after Napoleon's final defeat at Waterloo, royalists in the south and west carried out a White Terror against former revolutionaries and supporters of the deposed emperor. The king could do little or nothing to halt this bloodbath. Similar extreme royalist sentiment could be found in the Chamber of Deputies. The ultraroyalist majority elected in 1816 proved so dangerously reactionary that the king soon dissolved the chamber. The second election returned a more moderate majority. Several years of political give-and-take followed, with the king making mild accommodations to liberals.

In February 1820, however, the duke of Berri, son of the count of Artois and second in line to the throne after his father, was murdered by a lone assassin. The ultraroyalists persuaded Louis XVIII that the murder was the result of his ministers' cooperation with liberal politicians, and the king responded with repressive measures. New electoral laws gave wealthy electors two votes. Press censorship was imposed, and people suspected of dangerous political activity were made subject to easy arrest. By 1821, the government placed secondary education under the control of the Roman Catholic bishops.

All these actions revealed the basic contradiction of the French restoration. By the early 1820s, the veneer of constitutionalism had worn away. Liberals were being driven out of politics and into a near illegal status.

The French Bourbons were restored to the throne in 1815 but would rule only until 1830. This picture shows Louis XVIII, seated, second from left, and his brother, the count of Artois, who would become Charles X, standing on the left. Notice the bust of Henry IV in the background, placed there to associate the restored rulers with their popular late-sixteenth–early-seventeenth-century forebear. Bildarchiv Preussischer Kulturbesitz/Art Resource, NY

The Spanish Revolution of 1820

When the Bourbon Ferdinand VII of Spain (r. 1814–1833) was placed on his throne after Napoleon's downfall, he had promised to govern according to a written constitution. Once in power, however, he ignored his pledge, dissolved the *Cortés* (the parliament), and ruled alone. In 1820, army officers who were about to be sent to suppress revolution in Spain's Latin American colonies rebelled. In March, Ferdinand once again announced he would abide by the provisions of the constitution. For the time being, the revolution had succeeded.

Almost at the same time, in July 1820, revolution erupted in Naples, where the king of the Two Sicilies quickly accepted a constitution. There were other, lesser revolts in Italy, but none of them succeeded.

These events frightened the ever-nervous Metternich. Italian disturbances were especially troubling to him. Austria hoped to dominate the peninsula to provide a buffer against the spread of revolution on its own southern flank. Britain, however, opposed joint intervention in either Italy or Spain. Metternich turned to Prussia and Russia, the other members of the Holy Alliance formed in 1815, for support. The three eastern powers, along with unofficial delegations from Britain and France, met at the Congress of Troppau in late October 1820. Led by Tsar Alexander, the members of the Holy Alliance issued the Protocol of Troppau. This declaration asserted that stable governments might intervene to restore order in countries experiencing revolution. Yet even Russia hesitated to authorize Austrian intervention in Italian affairs. That decision was finally reached in January 1821 at the Congress of Laibach. Shortly thereafter, Austrian troops marched into Naples and restored the absolutist rule of the king of the Two Sicilies. From then on, Metternich attempted to foster policies that would improve the efficient administration of the various Italian governments so as to increase their support among their subjects.

The final postwar congress took place in October 1822 at Verona. Its primary purpose was to resolve the situation in Spain. Once again, Britain balked at joint action. Shortly before the meeting, Castlereagh had committed suicide. George Canning (1770–1827), the new foreign minister, was much less sympathetic to Metternich's goals. At Verona, Britain, in effect, withdrew from continental affairs. Austria, Prussia, and Russia agreed to support French intervention in Spain. In April 1823, a French army crossed the Pyrenees and within a few months suppressed the Spanish revolution. French troops remained in Spain to prop up King Ferdinand until 1827.

What did not happen in Spain, however, was as important for the new international order as what did happen. France did not use its intervention as an excuse to aggrandize its power or increase its territory. The same had been true of all the other interventions under the congress system. The great powers authorized these interventions to preserve or restore conservative regimes, not to conquer territory for themselves. Their goal was to maintain the international order established at Vienna. Such a situation stood in sharp contrast to the alliances to invade or confiscate territory that the European powers had made during the eighteenth century and the wars of the French Revolution and Napoleon. This new mode of international restraint through formal and informal consultation prevented war among the great powers until the middle of the century and averted a general European conflict until 1914. As one historian has commented, "The statesmen of the Vienna generation . . . did not so much fear war because they thought it would bring revolution as because they had learned from bitter experience that war was revolution."[2]

The Congress of Verona and the Spanish intervention had a second diplomatic result. The new British foreign minister, George Canning, was much more interested in British commerce and trade than Castlereagh had been. Thus Canning sought to prevent the extension of European reaction to Spain's colonies in Latin America, which were then in revolt (see page 640). He intended to exploit these South American revolutions to break Spain's old trading monopoly with its colonies and gain access for Britain to Latin American trade. To that end, he supported the American Monroe Doctrine in 1823, prohibiting further colonization and intervention by European powers in the Americas. Britain soon recognized the Spanish colonies as independent states. Through the rest of the century, British commercial interests dominated Latin America. Canning may thus be said to have brought the War of Jenkins's Ear (1739) to a successful conclusion.

▼ The Conservative Order Shaken in Europe

In the first years following the Congress of Vienna, the restored conservative order had, in general, successfully resisted the forces of liberalism. Beginning in the mid-1820s, however, challenges to conservative governments intensified. The Ottoman Empire was unable to prevent successful nationalist uprisings in Greece and Serbia. Conservative regimes in Russia, France, and Great Britain faced new political discontent. (See Map 20–1.) In Russia the result was suppression; in France, revolution; and in Britain, accommodation. Belgium emerged as a newly independent state.

View the **Map** "Map Discovery: Unrest of the 1820s and 1830s: Centers of Revolutionary Action" on **MyHistoryLab.com**

[2]Paul W. Schroeder, *The Transformation of European Politics, 1763–1848* (Oxford, UK: Clarendon Press, 1994), p. 802.

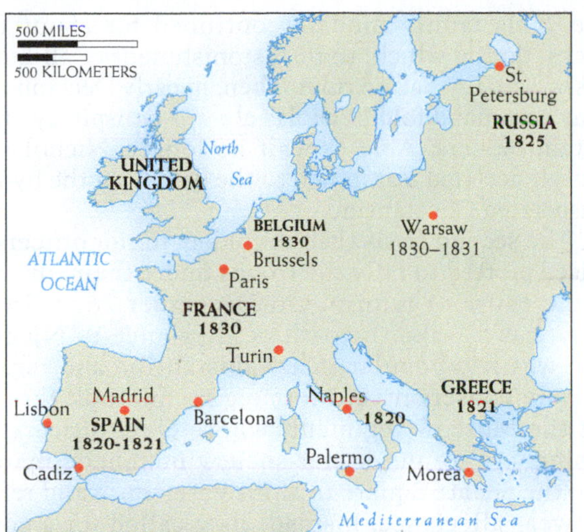

Map 20–1 **CENTERS OF REVOLUTION, 1820–1831** The conservative order imposed by the great powers in post-Napoleonic Europe was challenged by various uprisings and revolutions, beginning in 1820–1821 in Spain, Naples, and Greece and spreading to Russia, Poland, France, and Belgium later in the decade.

Revolt Against Ottoman Rule in the Balkans

The Greek Revolution of 1821 While the powers were plotting conservative interventions in Italy and Spain, a third Mediterranean revolt erupted—in Greece. The Greek revolution became one of the most famous of the century because it attracted the support and participation of many illustrious writers. Liberals throughout Europe, who were seeing their own hopes crushed at home, imagined that the ancient Greek democracy was being reborn. Lord Byron went to fight in Greece and died there in 1824 (of cholera). Philhellenic ("pro-Greek") societies were founded in nearly every major country. The struggle was posed in the eighteenth-century Enlightenment terms of Western liberal Greek freedom against the Asian oriental despotism of the Ottoman Empire.

View the **Closer Look** "An English Poet Appears as an Albanian" on **MyHistoryLab.com**

As discussed in Chapter 13, the Ottoman Empire had not changed its fundamental political or economic structures during the eighteenth century even as the major European states grew richer and more powerful. Ottoman weakness and instability troubled European diplomacy throughout the nineteenth century, raising what was known as "the Eastern Question": What should the European powers do about the Ottoman inability to ensure political and administrative stability in its possessions in and around the eastern Mediterranean? Most of the major powers had a keen interest in those territories. Russia and Austria coveted land in the Balkans. France and Britain were concerned with the empire's commerce and with control of key naval positions in the eastern Mediterranean. Also at issue was the treatment of the Christian inhabitants of the empire and access to the Christian shrines in the Holy Land. The goals of the great powers often conflicted with the desire for independence of the many national groups in the Ottoman Empire. Yet, because the powers had little desire to strengthen the empire, they were often more sympathetic to nationalistic aspirations there than elsewhere in Europe.

These conflicting interests, as well as mutual distrust, prevented any direct intervention in Greek affairs for several years. Eventually, however, Britain, France, and Russia concluded that an independent Greece would benefit their strategic interests and would not threaten their domestic security. In 1827, they signed the Treaty of London, demanding Turkish recognition of Greek independence, and sent a joint fleet to support the Greek revolt. In 1828, Russia sent troops into the Ottoman holdings in what is today Romania, ultimately gaining control of that territory in 1829 with the Treaty of Adrianople. The treaty also stipulated the Turks would allow Britain, France, and Russia to decide the future of Greece. In 1830, a second Treaty of London declared Greece an independent kingdom. Two years later, Otto I (r. 1832–1862), the son of the king of Bavaria, was chosen to be the first king of the new Greek kingdom.

Serbian Independence The year 1830 also saw the establishment of a second independent state on the Balkan peninsula. Since the late eighteenth century, some Serbians had sought independence from the Ottoman Empire. During the Napoleonic wars, Serbia's fate had been linked to Russian policy and Russian relations with the Ottoman Empire. Between 1804 and 1813, a remarkable Serbian leader, Kara George (1762–1817), had led a guerrilla war against the Ottomans. This ultimately unsuccessful revolution helped develop a greater sense of national belonging among some Serbs and attracted the interest of the great powers.

View the **Map** "The Ottoman Empire in the Late 18th Century" on **MyHistoryLab.com**

In 1815 and 1816, a new leader, Miloš Obrenović (1780–1860), succeeded in negotiating greater administrative autonomy for some Serbian territory, but most Serbs lived outside the borders of this new entity. In 1830, the Ottoman sultan formally granted independence to Serbia, and by the late 1830s, the major powers granted it diplomatic recognition. Serbia's political structure, however, remained in doubt for many years.

In 1833, Obrenović, now a hereditary prince, pressured the Ottoman authorities to extend the borders of Serbia, which they did. These new boundaries persisted until 1878. Serbian leaders continued to seek additional territory, however, creating tensions with Austria. The status of minorities, particularly Muslims, within Serbian territory was also a problem.

In the mid-1820s, Russia, which like Serbia was a Slav state and Eastern Orthodox in religion, became Serbia's formal protector. In 1856, Serbia came under the collective protection of the great powers, but the special relationship between Russia and Serbia would continue until World War I and would play a decisive role in the outbreak of that conflict.

Russia: The Decembrist Revolt of 1825

Tsar Alexander I had come to the throne in 1801 after a palace coup against his father, Tsar Paul (r. 1796–1801). After flirting with Enlightenment ideas, Alexander turned permanently away from reform. Both at home and abroad, he took the lead in suppressing liberalism and nationalism. There would be no significant challenge to tsarist autocracy until his death.

Unrest in the Army As Russian forces drove Napoleon's army across Europe and then occupied defeated France, many Russian officers were exposed to the ideas of the French Revolution and the Enlightenment. Some of them, realizing how economically backward and politically stifled their own nation remained, developed reformist sympathies. Unable to express themselves openly because of Alexander's repressive policies, they formed secret societies. One of these, the Southern Society, led by an officer named Pestel, advocated representative government and the abolition of serfdom. Pestel himself even favored limited independence for Poland and democracy. Another secret society, the Northern Society, was more moderate. It favored constitutional monarchy and the abolition of serfdom but wanted to protect the interests of the aristocracy. Both societies were small and often in conflict with each other. They agreed only that Russia's government must change. Sometime during 1825, they apparently decided to carry out a *coup d'état* in 1826.

Dynastic Crisis In late November 1825, Tsar Alexander I died unexpectedly. His death created two crises. The first was dynastic. Alexander had no direct heir. His brother Constantine (1779–1831), the next in line to the throne and at the time the commander of Russian forces in occupied Poland, had married a Roman Catholic Polish woman who refused to convert to Orthodoxy. He had thus excluded himself from the throne and was more than willing to renounce any claim to it. Through a series of secret instructions made public only after his death, Alexander had named his younger brother, Nicholas (r. 1825–1855), as the new tsar.

Once Alexander was dead, the legality of these instructions became uncertain. Constantine acknowledged Nicholas as tsar, and Nicholas acknowledged Constantine. This family muddle continued for about three weeks, during which, to the astonishment of all Europe, Russia actually had no ruler. Then, in early December, the army command told Nicholas about a conspiracy among certain officers. Able to wait no longer, Nicholas had himself declared tsar, much to the delight of the by-now-exasperated Constantine.

The second crisis then unfolded. Junior officers had indeed plotted to rally the troops under their command to the cause of reform. On December 26, 1825, the army was to take the oath of allegiance to Nicholas, who was less popular than Constantine and regarded as more conservative. Most regiments took the oath, but the Moscow regiment, whose chief officers, surprisingly, were not secret society members, marched into the Senate Square in Saint Petersburg and refused to swear allegiance. Instead, they called for a constitution and Constantine as tsar. Attempts to settle the situation peacefully failed. Late in the afternoon, Nicholas ordered the cavalry and the artillery to attack the insurgents. More than sixty people were killed. Early in 1826, Nicholas himself presided over the commission that investigated the Decembrist Revolt and the secret army societies. Five of the plotters were executed, and more than a hundred others were exiled to Siberia.

Although the Decembrist Revolt failed completely, it was the first rebellion in modern Russian history whose instigators had had specific political goals. They wanted a constitutional government and the abolition of serfdom. As the century passed, the political martyrdom of the Decembrists came to symbolize the yearnings of the never numerous Russian liberals.

The Autocracy of Nicholas I Although Nicholas was neither an ignorant nor a bigoted reactionary, he came to symbolize the most extreme form of nineteenth-century autocracy. He knew economic growth and social improvement in Russia required reform, but he was afraid of change. In 1842, he told his State Council, "There is no doubt that serfdom, in its present form, is a flagrant evil which everyone realizes, yet to attempt to remedy it now would be, of course, an evil more disastrous."[3] To remove serfdom would necessarily, in his view, have undermined the nobles' support of the tsar. So Nicholas turned his back on this and practically all other reforms. Literary and political censorship and a widespread system of surveillance by secret police flourished throughout his reign. Nicholas hoped that strict censorship would prevent liberal west European ideas from penetrating Russia. There was little attempt to forge even an efficient and honest administration. Nicholas's only significant reform was a codification of Russian law, published in 1833.

[3]Michael T. Florinsky, *Russia: A History and an Interpretation*, Vol. 2 (New York: Macmillan, 1953), p. 755.

A Closer LOOK

View the Closer Look on MyHistoryLab.com

AN UNSUCCESSFUL MILITARY COUP IN RUSSIA

When the Moscow regiment refused to swear allegiance to the new tsar, Nicholas I, instead demanding his brother Constantine be proclaimed tsar and that a constitution be issued, Nicholas ordered the cavalry and artillery to attack them. Although a total failure, the Decembrist Revolt came to symbolize the yearnings of all Russian liberals in the nineteenth century for a constitutional government.

Although the uprising was witnessed by a large crowd of civilians, the rebels failed to reach out to the broader public. Their plans for insurrection remained secret, their aims little understood and involvement in the uprising limited to only a few hundred participants.

Like the supporters of the new tsar, Nicholas I, who suppressed the uprising, the insurrectionaries were all members of the military. Although the tsar attempted to defeat the rebels using a cavalry attack, it was the less romantic artillery that succeeded in ending the rebellion.

The insurrection took place beneath a statue of Peter the Great that had been erected by Catherine II in 1782. The famous Russian poet, Alexander Pushkin, who was sympathetic to the Decembrists, wrote a poem about the statue called the Bronze Horseman, which called forth the ambiguous relationship between the tsar as protector of and threat to the Russian people: "Whither do you gallop, haughty steed, And where will you plant your hooves?"

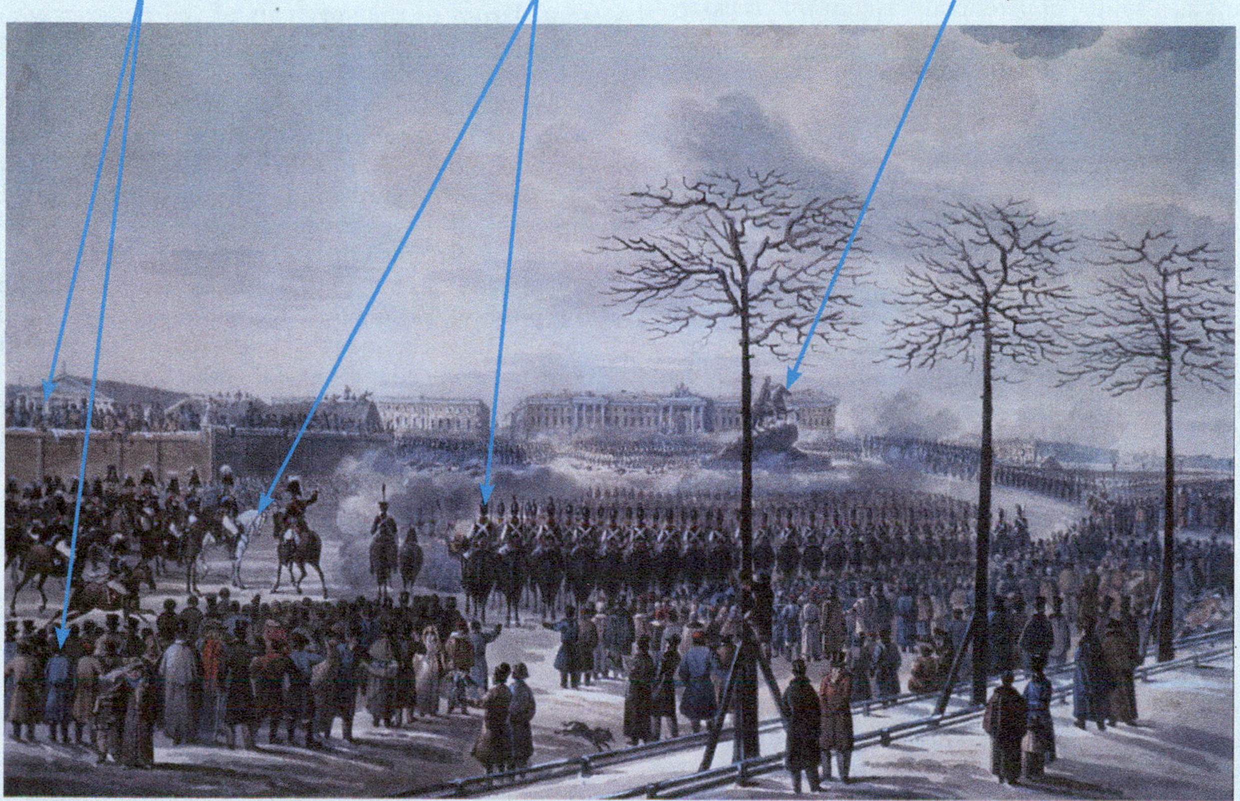

Karl Kolman (1786–1846), *The Insurrection of the Decembrists at Senate Square, St. Petersburg on 14th December, 1825* (w/c on paper) by Russian School (nineteenth century). Private Collection/Archives Charmet/Bridgeman Art Library

What is the role of the civilian population in this image? In what ways does the presence of civilians make the uprising seem less harmful?

What is the significance of the location of the insurrection?

Is it easy to tell what is happening in this painting? Why or why not?

Official Nationality In place of reform, Nicholas and his closest advisers embraced a program called Official Nationality. Presiding over this program was Count S. S. Uvarov, minister of education from 1833 to 1849. Its slogan, published repeatedly in government documents, newspapers, journals, and schoolbooks, was "Orthodoxy, Autocracy, and Nationalism." The Russian Orthodox church was to provide the basis for morality, education, and intellectual life. The church, which, since the days of Peter the Great, had been an arm of the secular government, controlled the schools and universities. Young Russians were taught to accept their place in life and to spurn social mobility.

Autocracy meant the unrestrained power of the tsar as the only authority that could hold the vast expanse of Russia and its peoples together. Political writers stressed that only under the autocracy of Peter the Great, Catherine the Great, and Alexander I had Russia prospered and exerted a major influence on world affairs.

Through the glorification of Russian nationality, Russians were urged to see their religion, language, and customs as a source of perennial wisdom that separated them from the moral corruption and political turmoil of the West. This program alienated serious Russian intellectuals from the tsarist government.

Revolt and Repression in Poland Nicholas I was also extremely conservative in foreign affairs, as became apparent in Poland in the 1830s. A large part of former Poland, which had been partitioned in the late eighteenth century and ceased to exist as an independent state, remained under Russian domination after the Congress of Vienna but was granted a constitutional government with a parliament, called the diet, that had limited powers. Under this arrangement, the tsar also reigned as king of Poland. Both Alexander and Nicholas delegated their brother, the Grand Duke Constantine, to run Poland's government. Although both tsars frequently infringed on the constitution and quarreled with the Polish diet, this arrangement held through the 1820s. Nevertheless, Polish nationalists continued to agitate for change.

In late November 1830, after news of the French and Belgian revolutions of that summer had reached Poland, a small insurrection of soldiers and students broke out in Warsaw. Disturbances soon spread throughout the country. On December 18, the Polish diet declared the revolution a nationalist movement. Early the next month, the diet deposed Nicholas as king of Poland. The tsar sent troops into the country and suppressed the revolt. In February 1832, Nicholas issued the Organic Statute, declaring Poland to be an integral part of the Russian Empire. Although this statute guaranteed certain Polish liberties, in practice, the Russian government systematically ignored them. The Polish uprising had confirmed the tsar's worst fears. Henceforth Russia and Nicholas became the gendarme of Europe, ever ready to provide troops to suppress liberal and nationalist movements.

View the **Image** "The Clemency of the Russian Monster, British Cartoon, 1832" on **MyHistoryLab.com**

Revolution in France (1830)

The Polish revolt was the most distant of several disturbances that flowed from the overthrow of the Bourbon dynasty in France during July 1830. When Louis XVIII had died in 1824, his brother, the count of Artois, the leader of the ultraroyalist faction, succeeded him as Charles X (r. 1824–1830). The new king was a firm believer in rule by divine right.

The Reactionary Policies of Charles X Charles X's first action was to have the Chamber of Deputies in 1824 and 1825 indemnify aristocrats who had lost their lands in the revolution. He did this by lowering the interest rates on government bonds to create a fund to pay an annual sum to the survivors of the *émigrés* who had forfeited land. Middle-class bondholders, who had lost income, resented this measure. Charles also restored the rule of primogeniture, whereby only the eldest son of an aristocrat inherited the family domains. To support the Roman Catholic Church, he enacted a law that punished sacrilege with imprisonment or death. Liberals disapproved of all these measures.

In the elections of 1827, the liberals gained enough seats in the Chamber of Deputies to compel the king to compromise. He appointed a less conservative ministry. Laws against the press were eased as was government dominance of education. Liberals, however, wanted a genuinely constitutional regime and remained unsatisfied. In 1829, the king replaced his moderate ministry with an ultraroyalist cabinet headed by the Prince de Polignac (1780–1847). The opposition, in desperation, opened negotiations with the liberal Orléans branch of the royal family.

The July Revolution In 1830, Charles X called for new elections, in which the liberals scored a stunning victory. Instead of accepting the new Chamber of Deputies, the king and his ministers decided to attempt a royalist seizure of power. In June and July 1830, Polignac sent a naval expedition against Algiers, which was nominally under Ottoman rule but had in fact become a pirate state whose ships preyed on the merchant vessels of all nations. News of the capture of Algiers and the founding of a French Empire in North Africa reached Paris on July 9. Taking advantage of the euphoria this victory created, Charles issued the Four Ordinances on July 25, 1830, staging what amounted to a royal *coup d'état*. These ordinances restricted freedom of the press, dissolved the recently elected Chamber of Deputies, limited the

On July 5, 1830, French forces captured Algiers, which France would continue to rule until 1962. Note how this drawing contrasts the power and modernity of the French conquerors with the almost medieval appearance of the Algerian defenses. Snark/Art Resource, NY

franchise to the wealthiest people in the country, and called for new elections.

The Four Ordinances provoked swift and decisive popular reaction. Liberal newspapers called on the nation to reject the monarch's actions. The workers of Paris, burdened since 1827 by an economic downturn, erected barricades in the streets. The king called out troops, and although more than 1,800 people died during the ensuing battles, the army was not able to gain control of Paris.

On August 2, Charles X abdicated and went into exile in England. The Chamber of Deputies named a new ministry composed of constitutional monarchists. In an act that finally ended the rule of the Bourbon dynasty, it also proclaimed Louis Philippe (r. 1830–1848), the duke d'Orléans, the new king instead of the Count de Chambord, the infant grandson of Charles X in whose favor Charles had abdicated.

In the Revolution of 1830, the liberals of the Chamber of Deputies had filled a power vacuum the Paris uprising and the failure of effective royal action had created. Had Charles X provided himself with sufficient troops in Paris, the outcome could have been different. Moreover, had the liberals, who favored a constitutional monarchy, not acted quickly, the workers and shopkeepers of Paris might have attempted to form a republic. By seizing the moment, the middle class, the bureaucrats, and the moderate aristocratic liberals overthrew the restoration monarchy and still avoided a republic. These liberals feared a new popular revolution such as the one that had swept France in 1792. They had no desire for another *sans-culotte* republic. A fundamental political and social tension thus underlay the new monarchy. The revolution had succeeded thanks to a temporary alliance between hard-pressed laborers and the prosperous middle class, but these two groups soon realized that their basic goals were different.

Monarchy Under Louis Philippe Politically, the *July Monarchy*, as the new regime was called, was more liberal than the restoration government. Louis Philippe was called the "king of the French" rather than "king of France." The tricolor flag of the revolution replaced the white flag of the Bourbons. The new constitution was regarded as a right of the people rather than as a concession of the monarch. Catholicism became the religion of a majority of the people rather than "the official religion." The new government was strongly anticlerical. Censorship was abolished. The franchise became wider but remained restricted. The king had to cooperate with the Chamber of Deputies; he could not dispense with laws on his own authority.

Socially, however, the Revolution of 1830 proved conservative. The hereditary peerage was abolished in 1831, but the everyday economic, political, and social influence of the landed oligarchy continued. Money was the path to power and influence in the government. There was much corruption.

Most importantly, the liberal monarchy displayed little or no sympathy for the lower and working classes. In 1830, the workers of Paris had called for the protection of jobs, better wages, and the preservation of the traditional crafts, rather than for the usual goals of political liberalism. The government of Louis Philippe ignored their demands and their plight. The laboring classes of Paris and the provincial cities seemed just one more possible source of disorder. In late 1831, troops suppressed a workers' revolt in Lyons. In July 1832, an uprising occurred in Paris during the funeral of a popular Napoleonic general. Again the government called out troops, and more than eight hundred people were killed or wounded. In 1834, a large strike by silk workers in Lyons was crushed. Such discontent might be smothered for a time, but unless the government addressed the social and economic conditions that created it, new turmoil would eventually erupt.

The new French government of 1830 was only too happy to retain the control of the city of Algiers that Charles X had achieved less than a month before his overthrow. The occupation of Algeria gave French merchants in Marseilles new economic ties to North Africa. Moreover, the French quickly dismantled the structures of the Ottoman government that had survived in Algeria and set out to conquer and administer the interior of the country, which was larger than France itself and where Ottoman rule had never penetrated. By the 1850s, the French had extended their rule, after constant warfare against Muslim tribesmen, as far as the northern Sahara desert. France now had a vast new empire, and French citizens and other Europeans also began to settle in Algeria in large numbers, especially in the cities. In the second half of the nineteenth century, the French government came to regard Algeria, despite its overwhelmingly Muslim population, as not a colony but an integral part of France itself. This was to have serious repercussions after World War II when a pro-independence movement developed among Muslim Algerians.

Belgium Becomes Independent (1830)

The July Revolution in Paris sent sparks to other political tinder on the Continent. The revolutionary fires first flared in neighboring Belgium. The former Austrian Netherlands, Belgium had been merged with the kingdom of Holland in 1815. The two countries differed in language, religion, and economy, however, and the Belgian upper classes never reconciled themselves to Dutch rule.

On August 25, 1830, disturbances broke out in Brussels after the performance of an opera about a rebellion in Naples against Spanish rule. To end the rioting, the municipal authorities and people from the propertied classes formed a provisional national government. When compromise between the Belgians and the Dutch failed, King William I of Holland (r. 1815–1840) sent troops and ships against Belgium. By November 10, 1830, the Dutch had been defeated. A national congress then wrote a liberal Belgian constitution, which was issued in 1831.

Although the major powers saw the revolution in Belgium as upsetting the boundaries the Congress of Vienna had established, they were not inclined to intervene to reverse it. Russia was preoccupied with the Polish revolt. Prussia and the other German states were suppressing small uprisings in their own domains. The Austrians were busy putting down disturbances in Italy. Under Louis Philippe, France hoped to dominate an independent Belgium. Britain could tolerate a liberal Belgium, as long as it was free of foreign domination.

In December 1830, Lord Palmerston (1784–1865), the British foreign minister, persuaded representatives of the powers in London to recognize Belgium as an independent and neutral state. In July 1831, Prince Leopold of Saxe-Coburg (r. 1831–1865), who had connections to the British royal family and had married the daughter of Louis Philippe, became king of the Belgians. The Convention of 1839 guaranteed Belgian neutrality, which remained an article of faith in European international relations for almost a century.

Both Belgium and Serbia gained independence in 1830, and ironically, diplomatic crises involving both nations led to World War I. The assassination of an Austrian archduke by a Serbian nationalist in Sarajevo in 1914 triggered the war, and Germany's violation of Belgian neutrality brought Britain into it.

The Great Reform Bill in Britain (1832)

In Great Britain, the revolutionary year of 1830 saw the election of a House of Commons that debated the first major bill to reform Parliament. The death of George IV (r. 1820–1830) and the accession of William IV (r. 1830–1837) required the calling of a parliamentary election, held in the summer of 1830. Historians once believed the July revolution in France influenced voting in Britain, but close analysis of the time and character of individual county and borough elections has shown otherwise. The passage of the Great Reform Bill, which became law in 1832, was the result of a series of events different from those that occurred on the Continent. In Britain, the forces of conservatism and reform accommodated each other.

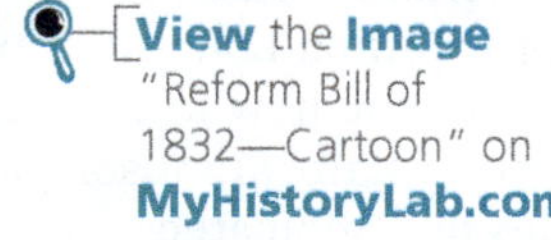
View the Image "Reform Bill of 1832—Cartoon" on MyHistoryLab.com

Political and Economic Reform Several factors contributed to this spirit of compromise. First, the commercial and industrial class was larger in Britain than in other countries. No government could ignore their economic interests without damaging British prosperity. Second, Britain's liberal Whig aristocrats, who regarded themselves as the protectors of constitutional liberty, had a long tradition of favoring moderate reforms that would make revolutionary changes unnecessary. Early Whig sympathy for the French Revolution reduced their influence. After 1815, however, they reentered the political arena. Finally, British law, tradition, and public opinion all showed a strong respect for civil liberties.

In 1820, the year after the passage of the notorious Six Acts, Lord Liverpool shrewdly reshaped his cabinet. Although they were conservatives, the new members of the government also believed it had to accommodate itself to the changing social and economic life of the nation. They favored greater economic freedom and repealed the Combination Acts that had prohibited labor organizations.

Catholic Emancipation Act English determination to maintain the union with Ireland brought about another key reform. England's relationship to Ireland was similar to that of Russia to Poland or Austria to its several national groups. In 1800, fearful that Irish nationalists might again rebel as they had in 1798 and perhaps turn Ireland into a base for a French invasion, William Pitt the Younger had persuaded Parliament to pass the Act of Union between Ireland and England. Ireland now sent a hundred members to the House of Commons. Only Protestant Irishmen, however, could be elected to represent their overwhelmingly Roman Catholic nation.

During the 1820s, under the leadership of Daniel O'Connell (1775–1847), Irish nationalists organized the Catholic Association to agitate for Catholic emancipation. In 1828, O'Connell secured his own election to Parliament, where he could not legally take his seat. The duke of Wellington, who was now prime minister, realized that henceforth Ireland might elect an overwhelmingly Catholic delegation. If they were not seated, civil war might erupt across the Irish Sea. Consequently, in 1829, Wellington and Robert Peel steered the Catholic Emancipation Act through Parliament. Roman Catholics could now become members of Parliament. This measure, together with the repeal in 1828 of restrictions against Protestant nonconformists, ended the Anglican monopoly on British political life.

Catholic emancipation was a liberal measure passed for the conservative purpose of preserving order in Ireland. It included a provision raising the property qualification to vote in Ireland, so that only the wealthier Irish could vote. Nonetheless, this measure alienated many of Wellington's Anglican Tory supporters in the House of Commons. The election of 1830 returned many supporters of parliamentary reform to Parliament. Even some Tories supported reform because they thought only a corrupt House of Commons could have passed Catholic emancipation. The Tories, consequently, were badly divided, and the Wellington ministry soon fell. King William IV then turned to the leader of the Whigs, Earl Grey (1764–1845), to form a government.

Legislating Change The Whig ministry presented the House of Commons with a major reform bill that had two broad goals. The first was to replace "rotten boroughs," or boroughs that had few voters, with representatives for the previously unrepresented manufacturing districts and cities. Second, the number of voters in England and Wales was to be increased by about 50 percent through a series of new franchises. In 1831, the House of Commons narrowly defeated the bill. Grey called for a new election and won a majority in favor of the bill. The House of Commons passed the reform bill, but the House of Lords rejected it. Mass meetings were held throughout the country. Riots broke out in several cities. Finally, William IV agreed to create enough new peers to give a third reform bill a majority in the House of Lords. Under this pressure, the measure became law in 1832.

The **Great Reform Bill** expanded the size of the English electorate, but it was not a democratic measure. It increased the number of voters by more than 200,000, or almost 50 percent, but it kept a property qualification for the franchise. (Gender was also a qualification. No thought was given to enfranchising women.) Some members of the working class actually lost the right to vote because certain old franchise rights were abolished. New urban boroughs were created to allow the growing cities to have a voice in the House of Commons. Yet the passage of the reform act did not, as was once thought, constitute the triumph of middle-class interests in England: For every new urban electoral district, a new rural

Beginning in the 1820s Daniel O'Connell revolutionized the organization of Irish politics. He created a grassroots organization and collected funds to finance Irish nationalist activities. He was also known as one of the great public speakers of his generation.

EVENTS ASSOCIATED WITH LIBERAL REFORM AND REVOLUTION

1824	Charles X becomes king of France
1825	Decembrist Revolt in Russia
1828	Repeal of restrictions against British Protestant nonconformists
1829	Catholic Emancipation Act passed in Great Britain; Ottoman Sultan grants independence to Serbia
1830 (July 9)	News of French colonial conquest in Algeria reaches Paris
1830 (July 25)	Charles X issues the Four Ordinances
1830 (August 2)	Charles X abdicates; Louis Philippe proclaimed king
1830 (August 25)	Belgian revolution
1830 (November 29)	Polish revolution
1832	Organic Statute makes Poland an integral part of Russian Empire
1832	Great Reform Bill passed in Great Britain

district was also drawn, and the aristocracy was expected to dominate rural elections. What the bill permitted was a wider variety of property to be represented in the House of Commons.

The success of the reform bill reconciled previously unrepresented property owners and economic interests to the political institutions of the country. The act laid the groundwork for further orderly reforms of the church, municipal government, and commercial policy. By admitting into the political forum people who sought change and giving them access to the legislative process, it made revolution in Britain unnecessary. Great Britain thus maintained its traditional institutions of government while allowing an increasingly diverse group of people to influence them.

▼ The Wars of Independence in Latin America

The wars of the French Revolution and, more particularly, those of Napoleon sparked movements for independence from European domination throughout Latin America. In less than two decades, between 1804 and 1824, France was driven from Haiti, Portugal lost control of Brazil, and Spain was forced to withdraw from all of its American empire except Cuba and Puerto Rico. Three centuries of Iberian colonial government over the South American continent ended. These wars brought to a conclusion the era of European political domination and direct economic exploitation of the American continents that had begun with the encounter between the peoples of the New World and Spain at the end of the fifteenth century. The period of transatlantic history beginning with the American Revolution and ending with the Latin American Wars of Independence thus constituted the first era of decolonization from European rule. (See Map 20–2.)

Watch the Video "Revolutions and Their Impact in Modern Latin America" on **MyHistoryLab.com**

Wars of Independence on the South American Continent

Haiti's revolution, which was described in Chapter 19, involved the popular uprising of a repressed social group. It proved to be the great exception in the Latin American drive for liberty from European masters. Generally speaking, on the South American continent, the Creole elite—merchants, landowners, and professional people of Spanish descent but who were born in the colonies—led the movements against Spain and Portugal. Few Native Americans, Africans or their descendents, or people of mixed race, whether enslaved or free, became involved in or benefited from the end of Iberian rule. Indeed, the example of the Haitian slave revolt haunted the Creoles, as did the revolts of Indians in the Andes in 1780 and 1781. The Creoles were determined that any drive for political independence from Spain and Portugal should not cause social disruption or the loss of their own privileges. In this respect, the Creole revolutionaries were not unlike American revolutionaries in the southern colonies, who wanted to reject British rule but keep their slaves, or French revolutionaries, who wanted to depose the king but not to extend liberty to the French working class.

View the Map "Interactive Map: Latin Americans Obtain Independence" on **MyHistoryLab.com**

Creole Discontent Creole discontent with Spanish colonial government had many sources. (The Brazilian situation will be discussed separately. See page 643.) Latin American merchants wanted to trade more freely within the region and with North American and European markets. They wanted commercial regulations that would benefit them rather than Spain. They had also resented increases in taxation by the Spanish crown.

Creoles resented Spanish policies that favored *peninsulares*—white people born in Spain—for political patronage, including appointments in the colonial government, church, and army. Seen in this light, the royal patronage system represented another device with which Spain extracted wealth and income from America to benefit its own people in Europe rather than its colonial subjects.

Map 20–2 LATIN AMERICA IN 1830 By 1830 most of Latin America had been liberated from Europe. This map shows the initial borders of the states of the region with the dates of their independence. The United Provinces of La Plata formed the nucleus of what later became Argentina.

Creole leaders had read the Enlightenment philosophes and regarded their reforms as potentially beneficial to the region. They were also well aware of the events and the political philosophy of the American Revolution. To transform Creole discontent into revolt against the Spanish government required more, however, than reform programs and revolutionary examples. That transforming event occurred in Europe when Napoleon invaded Portugal in 1807 and made his own brother king of Spain in 1808. Napoleon's overthrow of the Spanish

Bourbon monarchy created an imperial political vacuum throughout Spanish Latin America that encouraged Creole leaders to act.

The Creole elite feared a liberal Napoleonic monarchy in Spain would attempt to impose reforms in Latin America that would harm their economic and social interests. They also feared a French-controlled Spain would try to drain the region of the wealth and resources Napoleon needed for his wars. To protect their interests and to seize the opportunity to direct their own political destiny, between 1808 and 1810 Creole *juntas*, or political committees, claimed the right to govern different regions of Latin America. Many of them insincerely declared they were ruling in the name of the deposed Spanish Bourbon monarch Ferdinand VII. After the establishment of these local *juntas*, Spain never effectively reestablished its authority in South America, although it would take ten years or more of politically and economically exhausting warfare before Latin American independence became permanent. The establishment of the *juntas* also ended the privileges of the *peninsulares*, whose welfare had always depended on the favors of the Spanish crown. Creoles now took over positions in the government and army.

San Martín in Río de la Plata The vast size of Latin America, its geographical barriers, its distinct regional differences, and the absence of an even marginally integrated economy meant there would be several different paths to independence. The first region to assert itself was the Río de la Plata, or modern Argentina. The center of revolt was the city of Buenos Aires, whose citizens, as early as 1806, had fought off a British invasion and thus had learned they could protect themselves without Spanish assistance. In 1810, the *junta* in Buenos Aires not only thrust off Spanish authority, but also sent forces into Paraguay and Uruguay to liberate them from Spain. These armies were defeated, but Spain nevertheless lost control of both areas. Paraguay asserted its own independence. Brazil took over Uruguay.

These early defeats did not discourage the Buenos Aires government, which determined to liberate Peru, the stronghold of royalist power and loyalty on the continent. By 1817, José de San Martín (1778–1850), the leading general of the Río de la Plata forces, led an army in a daring march over the Andes Mountains and occupied Santiago in Chile, where Chilean independence leader Bernardo O'Higgins (1778–1842) was established as the supreme dictator. From Santiago, San Martín organized a fleet that, in 1820, carried his army by sea to Peru. The next year, San Martín drove royalist forces from Lima and became Protector of Peru.

Simón Bolívar's Liberation of Venezuela While the army of San Martín had been liberating the southern portion of the continent, Simón Bolívar (1783–1830) had been pursuing a similar task in the north. Bolívar had been involved in the organization of a liberating *junta* in Caracas, Venezuela, in 1810. He was a firm advocate of both independence and a republic. Between 1811 and 1814, civil war broke out throughout Venezuela as both royalists, on one hand, and slaves and *llaneros* (Venezuelan cowboys), on the other, challenged the authority of the republican government. Bolívar had to go into exile first in Colombia and then in Jamaica. In 1816, with help from Haiti, he returned to the continent. He first captured Bogotá, capital of New Granada (including modern Colombia, Bolivia, and Ecuador), to secure a base for an attack on Venezuela. The tactic worked. By the summer of 1821, Bolívar's forces captured Caracas, and he was named president.

A year later, in July 1822, the armies of Bolívar and San Martín joined as they moved to liberate Quito, the capital of what is today Ecuador. At a famous meeting in Guayaquil, the two liberators sharply disagreed about the future political structure of Latin America. San Martín believed the peoples of the region required monarchies; Bolívar maintained his republicanism. Not long after the meeting, San Martín quietly retired from public life and went into exile in Europe. Meanwhile, Bolívar deliberately allowed the political situation in Peru to fall into

Simón Bolívar. Bolívar was the liberator of much of Latin America. He inclined toward a policy of political liberalism.
Pictorial Press Ltd/Alamy

confusion, and, in 1823, he sent in troops to establish his control. On December 9, 1824, at the Battle of Ayacucho, the liberating army crushed the main Spanish royalist forces. This battle marked the end of Spain's effort to retain its South American empire.

Independence in New Spain

The drive for independence in New Spain, which included present-day Mexico as well as Texas, California, and the rest of the southwest United States, illustrates better than in any other region the socially conservative outcome of the Latin American colonial revolutions. As elsewhere, a local governing *junta* was organized in 1808. Before it had undertaken any significant measures, however, a Creole priest, Miguel Hidalgo y Costilla (1753–1811), in 1810 issued a call for rebellion to the Indians in his parish. They and other repressed groups of black and mestizo urban and rural workers responded. Father Hidalgo set forth a program of social reform, including hints of changes in landholding. Soon he stood at the head of a loosely organized group of 80,000 followers, who captured several major cities and then marched on to Mexico City. Hidalgo's forces and the royalist army that opposed them committed many atrocities. In July 1811, the revolutionary priest was captured and executed. Leadership of his movement then fell to José María Morelos y Pavón (1765–1815), a mestizo priest. Far more radical than Hidalgo, he called for an end to forced labor and for substantial land reforms. He was executed in 1815, ending five years of popular uprising.

The uprising and its demand for fundamental social reforms united all conservative political groups in Mexico, both Creole and Spanish. These groups opposed any kind of reform that might diminish their privileges. In 1820, however, an unexpected challenge arose to their recently achieved security. As already discussed, the revolution in Spain had forced Ferdinand VII to accept a liberal constitution. Conservative Mexicans feared the new liberal monarchy would attempt to impose liberal reforms on Mexico. Therefore, for the most conservative of reasons, they rallied behind a former royalist general, Agustín de Iturbide (1783–1824), who declared Mexico independent of Spain in 1821. Shortly thereafter, Iturbide was declared emperor. His own regime did not last long, but he had created an independent Mexico, governed by groups determined to resist significant social reform.

Read the **Document** "The Plan of Iguala" on **MyHistoryLab.com**

Brazilian Independence

Brazilian independence, in contrast to that of Spanish Latin America, came relatively simply and peacefully. As already noted, the Portuguese royal family, along with several thousand government officials and members of the court, fled to Brazil in 1807. Their arrival immediately transformed Rio de Janeiro into a royal city. The prince regent João addressed many of the local complaints, equivalent to those of the Spanish Creoles, by, for example, taking measures that expanded trade. In 1815, he made Brazil a kingdom, which meant it was no longer to be regarded merely as a colony of Portugal. This change was in many respects long overdue, since Brazil was far larger and more prosperous than Portugal itself. Then, in 1820, a revolution occurred in Portugal, and its leaders demanded João's return to Lisbon. They also demanded the return of Brazil to colonial status. João, who had become King João VI in 1816 (r. 1816–1826), returned to Portugal but left his son Dom Pedro as regent in Brazil and encouraged him to be sympathetic to the political aspirations of the Brazilians. In September 1822, Dom Pedro embraced the cause of Brazilian independence against the recolonizing efforts of Portugal. By the end of the year, he had become emperor of an independent Brazil, which remained a monarchy under his son and successor Dom Pedro II (r. 1831–1889) until 1889. Thus, in contrast to virtually all other nations of Latin America, Brazil achieved independence in a way that left no real dispute as to where the center of political authority lay.

Two other factors aided the peaceful transition to independence in Brazil. First, the political and social elite of Brazil wanted to avoid the destruction that the wars of independence had unleashed in the Spanish American Empire. Second, these leaders had every intention of preserving slavery. The wars of independence elsewhere had generally led to the abolition of slavery or moved the new states closer to abolishing it. Warfare in Brazil might have caused social turmoil with similar consequences.

View the **Closer Look** "Imagining Brazilian Independence" on **MyHistoryLab.com**

In Perspective

The French Revolution and Napoleonic wars brought tremendous political and social instability to Europe. The Congress System, spearheaded by Metternich, set up a process for mediating conflicts among European powers without going to war. The first years after the Congress of Vienna saw a return to territorial and political stability in much of Europe. Although the great powers were able to negotiate their conflicts with one another peacefully, however, they faced increasing domestic pressure for reform. Nationalists demanded a realignment of political boundaries to reflect what they thought were meaningful cultural communities. Liberals demanded an end to the arbitrary rule of monarchs and the political dominance of the landed aristocracy through the introduction of constitutions. Many of the revolutionary disturbances in Europe were suppressed without substantial concessions.

Nonetheless, during the 1820s, liberal political ideas and some liberal political figures began to make inroads into the otherwise conservative domestic order. Although the Decembrist Uprising of 1825 in Russia only lasted a few hours, the Greek revolt that broke out in 1821 was successful. In 1830, revolution and reform again began to move across Europe. The French replaced the Bourbons with a more liberal monarchy. Belgium also achieved independence under a liberal government. Britain moved slowly toward a more liberal position. Popular pressures at home led the British aristocratic leadership to enact a moderate reform bill in 1832. Thereafter, Britain would be viewed as the leading liberal state in Europe and one that would support nationalistic causes.

At the same time that conservative regimes weathered these challenges within Europe, Spain and Portugal were pushed out of their colonies in the New World. Unlike the Haitian Revolution, however, the revolutions in Latin America were fundamentally socially conservative.

KEY TERMS

Concert of Europe (p. 617)
congress system (p. 617)
conservatism (p. 617)
Great Reform Bill (p. 639)
nationalism (p. 618)

REVIEW QUESTIONS

1. What is nationalism? What were the goals of nationalists? What difficulties did nationalists confront in realizing those goals? Why was nationalism a special threat to the Austrian Empire? What areas saw significant nationalist movements between 1815 and 1830? Which were successful and which unsuccessful?
2. What were the tenets of liberalism? Who were the liberals, and how did liberalism affect the political developments of the early nineteenth century? What is the relationship of liberalism to nationalism?
3. What difficulties did the conservatives in Austria, Prussia, and Russia face after the Napoleonic wars? How did they attempt to solve those difficulties at home and in international affairs? What were the aims of the Concert of Europe? How did the Congress of Vienna change international relations?
4. What were the main reasons for Creole discontent with Spanish rule, and to what extent did Enlightenment political philosophy influence the Creole leaders? Who were some of the primary leaders of Latin American independence? Why was Brazil's path to independence different from that of Spanish America?
5. What were the main provisions of the constitution of the restored monarchy in France? What did Charles X hope to accomplish? Why did revolution break out in France in 1830? What did this revolution achieve and what problems did it fail to resolve?
6. Why did Britain avoid a revolution in the early 1830s? What was the purpose of the Great Reform Bill? What did it achieve? Would you call it a "revolutionary" document?
7. By approximately 1830, how had European political ambitions and the ideas of liberalism and nationalism begun to undermine the Ottoman Empire? Which Ottoman territories were lost by that date?

SUGGESTED READINGS

B. Anderson, *Imagined Communities*, rev. ed. (2006). An influential and controversial discussion of nationalism.

M. S. Bell, *Toussaint Louverture: A Biography* (2007). An outstanding new biography.

M. Berdahl, *The Politics of the Prussian Nobility: The Development of a Conservative Ideology, 1770–1848* (1988). A major examination of German conservative outlooks.

A. Briggs, *The Making of Modern England* (1959). Classic survey of English history during the first half of the nineteenth century.

A. Craitu, *Liberalism under Siege: The Political Thought of the French Doctrinaires* (2003). An outstanding study of early nineteenth-century French liberalism.

M. F. Cross and D. Williams, eds., *French Experience from Republic to Monarchy, 1792–1824: New Dawns in Politics, Knowledge and Culture* (2000). Essays on French culture from the revolution through the restoration.

D. Dakin, *The Struggle for Greek Independence* (1973). An excellent explanation of the Greek independence question.

L. Dubois, *Avengers of the New World: The Story of the Haitian Revolution* (2004). An analytic narrative likely to replace others.

E. J. Evans, *Britain Before the Reform Act: Politics and Society, 1815–1832* (2008). Explores the forces that resisted and pressed for reform.

W. Fortescue, *Revolution and Counter-Revolution in France, 1815–1852* (2002). A helpful brief survey.

E. Gellner, *Nations and Nationalism* (1983). A classic theoretical work.

L. Greenfeld, *Nationalism: Five Roads to Modernity* (1992). A major comparative study.

R. Harvey, *Liberators: Latin America's Struggle for Independence* (2002). An excellent, lively treatment.

E. J. Hobsbawm, *Nations and Nationalism since 1780: Programme, Myth, Reality*, rev. ed. (1992). Emphasizes intellectual factors.

C. Jelavich and B. Jelavich, *The Establishment of the Balkan National States, 1804–1920* (1987). A standard survey.

G. A. Kelly, *The Humane Comedy: Constant, Tocqueville, and French Liberalism* (2007). The best introduction to the subject.

M. B. Levinger, *Enlightened Nationalism: The Transformation of Prussian Political Culture, 1806–1848* (2002). A clear and expansive overview on the most recent scholarship.

J. Lynch, *Simon Bolivar: A Life* (2006). Now the standard biography.

C. A. Macartney, *The Habsburg Empire, 1790–1918* (1971). Remains an important survey.

N. V. Riasanovsky, *Nicholas I and Official Nationality in Russia, 1825–1855* (1959). Remains a lucid discussion of the conservative ideology that made Russia the major opponent of liberalism.

J. Sheehan, *German History, 1770–1866* (1989). A long work that is now the best available survey of the subject.

A. Sked, *Metternich and Austria: An Evaluation* (2008). A thoughtful restoration of Metternich to the position of leading diplomat of his age.

A. B. Ulam, *Russia's Failed Revolutionaries* (1981). Contains a useful discussion of the Decembrists as a background for other nineteenth-century Russian revolutionary activity.

B. Wilson, *The Making of Victorian Values: Decency and Dissent in Britain: 1789–1837* (2007). A very lively overview of the cultural factors shaping early nineteenth-century British society.

MyHistoryLab™ MEDIA ASSIGNMENTS

Find these resources in the Media Assignments folder for Chapter 20 on **MyHistoryLab**.

QUESTIONS FOR ANALYSIS

1. How are the ideas of liberalism and romanticism illustrated in this image?

   ***Section:* The Wars of Independence in Latin America**

   View the **Closer Look** Imagining Brazilian Independence, p. 643

2. How does Smith view the impacts of industrialization?

   ***Section:* The Emergence of Nationalism and Liberalism**

   Read the **Document** Adam Smith, *The Wealth of Nations*, p. 624

3. How has this artist characterized the Reform Bill of 1832?

   ***Section:* The Conservative Order Shaken in Europe**

   View the **Image** Reform Bill of 1832—Cartoon, p. 638

4. What is the artist's aim in portraying Russia in this way?

   ***Section:* The Conservative Order Shaken in Europe**

   View the **Image** The Clemency of the Russian Monster, British Cartoon, 1832, p. 636

5. How does this map demonstrate some of the problems facing nationalistic movements?

***Section:* Conservative Restoration in Europe**

View the **Map** Map Discovery: Nationalities within the Habsburg Empire, p. 626

OTHER RESOURCES FROM THIS CHAPTER

The Conservative Order

View the **Map** Geographic Tour: Europe in 1815, p. 617

The Emergence of Nationalism and Liberalism

Read the **Compare and Connect** Mazzini and Lord Acton Debate the Political Principles of Nationalism, p. 620

Read the **Document** Laws of Population Growth (1798) Malthus, p. 625

Read the **Document** David Ricardo, Excerpt from *Principles of Political Economy and Taxation*, p. 625

The Conservative Orders Shaken in Europe

View the **Map** Map Discovery: Unrest of the 1820s and 1830s: Centers of Revolutionary Action, p. 632

View the **Closer Look** An English Poet Appears as an Albanian, p. 633

View the **Map** The Ottoman Empire in the Late 18th Century, p. 633

The Wars of Independence in Latin America

Watch the **Video** Revolutions and Their Impact in Modern Latin America, p. 640

View the **Map** Interactive Map: Latin Americans Obtain Independence, p. 640

Read the **Document** The Plan of Iguala, p. 643

Romanian peasants rally at Blaj in Transylvania on May 15, 1848. In 1848 Ana Ipatescu helped to lead Transylvanian revolutionaries against Russian rule. Transylvania is part of present-day Romania. The revolutions of 1848 in Eastern Europe were primarily uprisings of nationalist groups. Although generally repressed in the revolutions of that year, subject nationalities would prove a source of political upheaval and unrest in the region throughout the rest of the century, ultimately providing the spark for the outbreak of World War I. The Rally of the Romanian Peasants at Blaj in Transylvania on the 15th of May, 1848 (colour lithograph). Hungarian School/Private Collection/Archives Charmet/The Bridgeman Art Library International

Listen to the Chapter Audio on MyHistoryLab.com

21

Economic Advance and Social Unrest (1830–1850)

▼ **Toward an Industrial Society**
Population and Migration • Railways

▼ **The Labor Force**
The Emergence of a Wage-Labor Force • Working-Class Political Action: The Example of British Chartism

▼ **Family Structures and the Industrial Revolution**
The Family in the Early Factory System

▼ **Women in the Early Industrial Revolution**
Opportunities and Exploitation in Employment • Changing Expectations in the Working-Class Marriage

▼ **Problems of Crime, Order, and Poverty**
New Police Forces • Prison Reform • Government Policies Based on Classical Economics

▼ **Early Socialism**
Utopian Socialism • Anarchism • Marxism

▼ **1848: Year of Revolutions**
France: The Second Republic and Louis Napoleon • The Habsburg Empire: Nationalism Resisted • Italy: Republicanism Defeated • The German Confederation: Liberalism Frustrated

▼ **In Perspective**

LEARNING OBJECTIVES

How did industrialization spread across Europe?

How did industrialization change the European labor force?

How did industrialization affect European families?

What role did women play in the Industrial Revolution?

How did the establishment of police forces and the reform of prisons change society?

What were the key assumptions of classical economic theory?

How did socialism challenge classical economics?

Why did a series of revolutions erupt across Europe in 1848?

BY 1830, EUROPE was headed toward an industrial society. Only Great Britain had already attained that status, but the pounding of new machinery and the grinding of railway engines soon began to echo across much of the Continent. Yet what characterized the second quarter of the century was not the triumph of industrialism but the final protests of those economic groups who opposed it. Intellectually, the period saw the formulation of the major creeds supporting and criticizing the newly emerging society.

These were years of uncertainty for almost everyone. Even the most confident entrepreneurs knew the trade cycle could bankrupt them within weeks. For the industrial workers and the artisans, unemployment became a haunting and recurring problem. For peasants and agricultural workers, the question was sufficiency of food. It was a period of self-conscious transition that culminated in 1848 with a continent-wide outbreak of revolution. People knew one mode of life was passing, but no one knew what would replace it.

▼ Toward an Industrial Society

The Industrial Revolution had begun in eighteenth-century Great Britain with the advances in textile production described in Chapter 15. Natural resources, adequate capital, native technological skills, a growing food supply, a social structure that allowed considerable mobility, the tremendously profitable slave trade, and strong foreign and domestic demand for goods had given Britain an edge in achieving a vast new capacity for production in manufacturing. British factories and recently invented machines allowed producers to furnish customers with a greater number of consumer products of a higher quality and for lower prices than those of any competitors. Also, the French Revolution and the wars of Napoleon had finally destroyed the French Atlantic trade and thus disrupted continental economic life for two decades. The Latin American wars of independence opened the markets of South America to British goods. In North America, both the United States and Canada demanded British products. Through its control of India, Britain commanded the markets of southern Asia. British banks similarly dominated the international financial markets.

View the Map "Interactive Map: Europe Industrialization" on **MyHistoryLab.com**

The British textile industry was a vast worldwide economic network. For much of its supply of raw cotton, this industry depended on the labor of American slaves, although abolitionists had succeeded in outlawing direct British participation in the slave trade in 1807. In turn, the finished textiles were shipped all over the world along sea-lanes the British navy protected. The wealth that Britain gained through textile production and its other industries of iron making, shipbuilding, china production, and the manufacture of other finished goods was invested all over the world, but especially in the United States and Latin America. This enormous activity provided the economic foundation for British dominance of the world scene throughout the nineteenth century.

Despite their economic lag, the continental nations were beginning to make material progress. By the 1830s, in Belgium, France, and the German states, the number of steam engines in use was growing steadily. Exploitation of the coalfields of the Ruhr and the Saar basins had begun. Coke was replacing charcoal in iron and steel production.

Although there were pockets of production—such as Lyons, Rouen, and Lille in France and Liege in Belgium—in Western Europe, most continental manufacturing still took place in the countryside. New machines were integrated into the existing domestic system. The slow pace of continental imitation of the British example meant that, at midcentury, peasants and urban artisans remained more important politically than industrial factory workers.

Population and Migration

While the process of industrialization spread, the population of Europe continued to grow on the base of the eighteenth-century population explosion. The number of people in France rose from 32.5 million in 1831 to 35.8 million in 1851. During approximately the same period, the population of the German states rose from 26.5 million to 33.5 million and that of Britain from 16.3 million to 20.8 million. More and more of the people of Europe lived in cities. By midcentury, one-half of the population of England and Wales and one-quarter of the population of France and the German states had become town dwellers. Further to the east and south, by contrast, Europeans continued to live overwhelmingly in rural settings, with little industrial manufacturing.

View the Map "Map Discovery: Population Growth in Europe, 1800–1850" on **MyHistoryLab.com**

The sheer numbers of human beings put considerable pressure on the physical resources of the cities. Migration from the countryside meant that existing housing, water, sewers, food supplies, and lighting were completely inadequate. Slums with indescribable filth grew, and disease, especially cholera, ravaged the population. Crime increased and became a way of life for those who could make a living in no other manner. Human misery and degradation in many early-nineteenth-century cities seemed to have no bounds.

The situation in the countryside was scarcely better. During the first half of the century, the productive use of the land remained the basic fact of life for most Europeans. The enclosures of the late eighteenth century, the land redistribution of the French Revolution, and the emancipation of serfs in Prussia and later throughout Austria (1848) and Russia (1861) commercialized landholding. Liberal reformers had hoped the legal revolution in ownership would transform peasants into progressive, industrious farmers. Instead, most peasants became conservative landholders without enough land to make agricultural innovations or, oftentimes, even to support themselves.

It is important to note the differing dates of rural emancipation across Europe. In England, France, and the Low Countries, persons living in the countryside could move freely between country and town. In many of the German states, Austria, and Russia, such migration was difficult until the serfs were emancipated. Even when emancipation did occur, as throughout the German states early in the century, it did not make migration simple. Where there was no fluid market for free labor moving to the cities, the pace of industrialization was slower.

The specter of poor harvests still haunted Europe. The worst such experience of the century was the Irish famine of 1845 to 1847. Perhaps as many as half a million Irish peasants with no land or small plots simply starved when disease blighted the potato crop. Hundreds of thousands emigrated. (See "Encountering the Past: The Potato and the Great Hunger in Ireland," page 649.) By midcentury, the revolution in landholding led to greater agricultural production. It also resulted in a vast uprooting of people from the countryside into cities and from Europe into the rest of the world. The countryside thus provided many of the workers for the new factories, as well as people with few economic skills who slowly emigrated to cities in hope of finding work.

Railways

Industrial advance itself had also contributed to this migration. The 1830s and 1840s opened the first great age of railway building. The Stockton and Darlington Line opened in England in 1825. By 1830, another major line had been built between Manchester and Liverpool and had several hundred passengers a day. Belgium had undertaken railway construction by 1835. The first French line opened in 1832, but serious construction came only in the 1840s. The German states entered the railway age in 1835. At midcentury, Britain had 9,797 kilometers of railway, France 2,915, and the German states 5,856. (See Map 21–1.)

View the **Map** "Map Discovery: Great Britain: Railroads, ca. 1850" on **MyHistoryLab.com**

The railroads, plus canals and improved regular roads, meant people could leave the place of their birth more easily than ever before. The improvement in transportation also allowed cheaper and more rapid passage of raw materials and finished products.

Map 21–1 **EUROPEAN RAILROADS IN 1850** At midcentury Britain had the most extensive rail network and the most industrialized economy in Europe, but rail lines were expanding rapidly in France, the German states, and Austria. Southern and eastern Europe had few railways, and the Ottoman Empire had none.

ENCOUNTERING THE *Past*

THE POTATO AND THE GREAT HUNGER IN IRELAND

ANY AGRICULTURAL ECONOMY that depends on a single product is in a precarious position. If the people that economy supports also depend on a single source of food, they also stand on the edge of catastrophe—they have nothing to fall back on if their only source of food fails. That kind of catastrophe occurred in Ireland, which was under British rule in the 1840s when the potato crop failed.

During the eighteenth century, almost half of the Irish population came to depend on the potato, which had been brought to Europe from South America in the seventeenth century, as virtually their only food. On less than one acre, an Irish peasant could raise enough potatoes to feed ten other people for a year and pay his rent (few Irish peasants owned their own land).

Before the 1840s, there had been isolated potato failures in parts of Ireland, but never a general failure. Then in 1845, a mysterious blight, caused by a fungus, struck potato crops across Ireland. The potato vines withered in the fields, and potatoes in storage became moldy and inedible. Half the crop was lost. The Irish, with modest aid from the British government, survived, but in 1846 the blight reappeared and destroyed the entire crop. The crop of 1847 was better, but the blight came again in 1848.

This series of Irish potato crop failures was the worst agricultural disaster to strike nineteenth-century Europe. Without potatoes, Irish tenants could not pay their rent. Landlords drove starving tenants off their farms. Disease spread, and tens of thousands died.

In 1846, in response to the Irish famine, the British government repealed the tariffs on imported grain known as the Corn Laws and enacted a program of public works to employ the dispossessed, but the help was inadequate. Most economists and politicians believed government aid caused more harm than good, and the government was reluctant to provide charity. The 1847 Irish Poor Relief Act required anyone who occupied more than one-quarter acre of land to enter a government-run workhouse before receiving poor relief, but the scale of the disaster overwhelmed the workhouses.

To escape the famine, soon known as The Great Hunger, many of the Irish poor emigrated, primarily to the United States and Britain itself. Much of Ireland became depopulated. The census of 1841 counted 8,197,000 people in Ireland; ten years later, death and emigration had cut the population by more than 1.5 million. By 1901, more waves of emigration had reduced it to 4,459,000. The population had still not recovered to prefamine levels at the dawn of the twenty-first century: In 2000, the combined population of the Irish Republic and British-ruled Northern Ireland was only 5,460,000. Alone among the nations of Europe, Ireland has fewer inhabitants today than it did in the nineteenth century.

Sources: R. N. Salaman, *The History and Social Influence of the Potato* (Cambridge, UK: Cambridge University Press, 1985); Cecil Woodham-Smith, *The Great Hunger: Ireland 1845–1849* (New York: Harper & Row, 1962).

Why was the failure of the potato crop such a disaster for Ireland?

How did the famine affect the Irish population?

Painter George Frederick Watts' 1850 depiction of a scene set during the Irish Potato Famine. So many people starved during the famine that workhouses could not shelter them all. © Trustees of the Watts Gallery, Compton, Surrey, UK/The Bridgeman Art Library

George Stephenson (1781–1848) invented the locomotive in 1814, but the "Rocket," his improved design shown here, did not win out over other competitors until 1829. In the following two decades the spread of railways transformed the economy of Western Europe. Image Works/Mary Evans Picture Library Ltd.

Railways epitomized the character of the industrial economy during the second quarter of the century. They represented investment in capital goods rather than in consumer goods. Consequently, there was a shortage of consumer goods at cheap prices. This favoring of capital over consumer production was one reason the working class was often unable to purchase much for its wages. The railways, which embodied the most dramatic application of the steam engine, in and of themselves also brought about still more industrialization. Rails and railway cars sharply increased demand for iron and steel, fabrics, glass, and wood. Preparing the ground for tracks, laying the tracks, and constructing railroad stations were major construction projects that created jobs and required skilled labor. The new iron and steel capacity soon permitted the construction of ironclad ships and iron machinery rather than ships and machinery made of wood. These new capital industries led to the formation of vast industrial fortunes that would be invested in still newer enterprises. Industrialism had begun to grow on itself.

▼ The Labor Force

The composition and experience of the early nineteenth-century labor force was varied. No single description could include all the factory workers, urban artisans, domestic craftspeople, household servants, miners, countryside peddlers, farm workers, or railroad workers. Some of the workforce was reasonably well off and enjoyed steady employment and decent wages. Other workers were the "laboring poor," who held jobs, but earned little more than subsistence wages. Then there were those, such as the women and children who worked nearly naked in the mines of Wales, whose conditions of life shocked Europe when a parliamentary report in the 1840s publicized them. Furthermore, the conditions of workers varied from decade to decade and from industry to industry within any particular decade.

Although historians have traditionally emphasized the role and experience of industrial factory workers, only the textile-manufacturing industry became thoroughly mechanized and moved into the factory setting during the first half of the century. Far more of the nonrural, nonagricultural workforce consisted of skilled artisans living in cities or small towns. They were attempting to maintain the value of their skills and control over their trades in the face of changing features of production. All these working people faced possible unemployment, with little or no provision for their security. During their lives, they confronted the dissolution of many of the traditional social ties of custom and community.

The Emergence of a Wage-Labor Force

During the nineteenth century, artisans as well as factory workers eventually came to participate in a wage-labor force in which their labor became a commodity of the labor marketplace. This process has often been termed *proletarianization*. In the process of becoming wage laborers, artisans gradually lost both significant ownership of the means of production, such as tools and equipment, and of control over the conduct of their own trades. The process occurred most rapidly wherever the factory system arose, displacing previous skilled labor. The factory owner provided the financial capital to construct the factory, to purchase the machinery, and to secure the raw materials. The factory workers contributed their labor for a wage. The process could also occur outside the factory setting if a new invention, such as a mechanical printing press, could do the work of several artisans within an urban or rural workshop setting.

Factory workers also had to submit to various kinds of factory discipline that was virtually always unpopular and difficult to impose. This discipline meant the demands for a smooth operation of the machinery largely determined working conditions. Closing of factory gates to late workers, fines for such lateness, dismissal for drunkenness, and public scolding of faulty laborers were attempts to create human discipline that would match the mechanical regularity of the cables, wheels, and pistons. The factory worker had no direct say about the quality of the product or its price. (See "Compare and

Connect: Andrew Ure and John Ruskin Debate the Conditions of Factory Production," pages 652–653.)

For all the difficulties of workers in factory conditions, however, their economic situation was often better than that of textile workers, who resisted the factory mode of production. In particular, English hand-loom weavers, who continued to work in their homes, experienced decades of declining trade and growing poverty in their failing attempt to compete with power looms.

Urban artisans in the nineteenth century entered the wage-labor force more slowly than factory workers, and machinery had little to do with the process. The emergence of factories in and of itself did not harm urban artisans. Many even prospered from the development. For example, the construction and maintenance of the new machines generated major demand for metalworkers, who consequently did well. The actual erection of factories and the expansion of cities benefited all craftspeople in the building trades, such as carpenters, roofers, joiners, and masons. The lower prices for machine-made textiles aided artisans involved in making clothing, such as tailors and hatters, by reducing the costs of their raw materials. Where the urban artisans encountered difficulty and where they found their skills and livelihood threatened was in the organization of production.

In the eighteenth century, a European town or city workplace had usually consisted of a few artisans laboring for a master. They labored first as apprentices and then as journeymen, according to established guild regulations and practices. The master owned the workshop and the larger equipment, and the apprentices and journeymen owned their tools. The journeyman could expect eventually to become a master. This guild system had allowed workers to exercise a considerable degree of control over labor recruitment and training, the pace of production, the quality of the product, and its price. The guild functioned to protect the integrity of the craft and the prosperity of the craftsmen.

In the nineteenth century, it became increasingly difficult for artisans to exercise corporate or guild direction and control over their trades. The legislation of the French Revolution had outlawed such organizations in France. Across Europe, political and economic liberals disapproved of labor and guild organizations and attempted to ban them. These thinkers believed guilds raised the price of both labor and products to the disadvantage of owners of capital and consumers.

Other destructive forces were also at work. The masters often found themselves under increased competitive pressure from larger, more heavily capitalized establishments or from the introduction of machine production into a previously craft-dominated industry. In many workshops masters began to follow a practice, known in France as *confection*, whereby goods, such as shoes, clothing, and furniture, were produced in standard sizes and styles rather than by special orders for individual customers.

This practice increased the division of labor in the workshop. Each artisan produced a smaller part of the more-or-less uniform final product. Thus, less skill was required of each artisan, and the particular skills a worker possessed became less valuable. To increase production and reduce costs, masters also tried to lower the wages they paid for piecework. Those attempts often led to work stoppages or strikes. Migrants from the countryside or small towns into the cities created, in some cases, a surplus of relatively unskilled workers. They were willing to work for lower wages or under less favorable and protected conditions than traditional artisans. This situation made it much more difficult for urban journeymen ever to hope to become masters in charge of their own workshops. Increasingly, these artisans became lifetime wage laborers whose skills were simply bought and sold in the marketplace.

Working-Class Political Action: The Example of British Chartism

By midcentury, such artisans, proud of their skills and frustrated in their social and economic expectations, became the most radical political element in the European working class. From at least the 1830s onward, these artisans took the lead in one country after another in attempting to formulate new ways to protect their social and economic interests.

By the late 1830s, many British workers linked the solution of their economic plight to a program of political reform known as **Chartism**. In 1836, William Lovett (1800–1877) and other London radical artisans formed the London Working Men's Association. In 1838, the group issued the Charter, demanding six specific reforms. The Six Points of the Charter included universal male suffrage, annual election of the House of Commons, the secret ballot, equal electoral districts, and the abolition of property qualifications for and the payment of salaries to members of the House of Commons.

Read the **Document** "Chartist Movement: The People's Petition of 1838" on **MyHistoryLab.com**

For more than ten years, the Chartists, who were never tightly organized, agitated for their reforms. On three occasions the Charter was presented to Parliament, which refused to pass it. Petitions with millions of signatures were presented to the House of Commons. Strikes were called. The Chartists published a newspaper, the *Northern Star*. Feargus O'Connor (1794–1855), the most important Chartist leader, made speeches across Britain. Despite this vast activity, Chartism as a national movement failed. Its ranks were split between those who advocated violence and those who wanted to use peaceful tactics. On the local level, however, the Chartists scored several successes and controlled the city councils in Leeds and Sheffield.

COMPARE AND CONNECT Andrew Ure and John Ruskin Debate the Conditions of Factory Production

Read the **Compare and Connect** on **MyHistoryLab.com**

THE FACTORY WAS itself as much an invention of the Industrial Revolution as were the new machines the factory often housed. The factory required a new organization of labor. It also made possible the production of vast new quantities of manufactured goods. From its inception the factory system provoked both praise and criticism. Andrew Ure saw much positive good arising from factory production whereas John Ruskin became a vehement critic. How might the women of Todmorden (see page 659) have replied to both writers?

QUESTIONS

1. **Why does Ure emphasize the willingness of workers to be employed in factories?**
2. **How does Ure portray the factory system as creating the possibility of new abundance?**
3. **How does Ruskin see the use of machinery reducing workers to a machine?**
4. **Is Ruskin's criticism of the division of labor a correct analysis or simply a well-crafted metaphorical criticism?**
5. **How might Ure have replied to Ruskin?**

I. Andrew Ure Praises the Factory System

Andrew Ure (1778–1857) was a Scottisch physician and a great proponent of the benefits of the factory system. In 1835 he published The Philosophy of Manufactures, which went through many editions from then until late in the century. He saw factories as increasing productivity and also providing a healthier environment than agricultural work or mining.

The term Factory, in technology, designates the combined operation of many orders of work—people, adult and young, in tending with assiduous skill a system of productive machines continuously impelled by a central power. This definition includes such organizations as cotton-mills, flax-mills, silk-mills, woolen-mills, and certain engineering works. . . . I conceive that this title, in its strictest sense, involves the idea of a vast automaton, composed of various mechanical and intellectual organs, acting in uninterrupted concert for the production of a common object, all of them being subordinated to a self-regulated moving force. . . .

In its precise acceptation, the Factory system is of recent origin, and may claim England for its birthplace. . . .

When the first water-frames for spinning cotton were erected at Cromford, in the romantic valley of the Derwent, about sixty years ago, mankind were little aware of the mighty revolution which the new system of labor was destined by Providence to achieve, not only in the structure of British society, but in the fortunes of the world at large.

Arkwright alone had the sagacity to discern, and the boldness to predict in glowing language, how vastly productive human industry would become, when no longer proportioned in its results to muscular effort, which is by its nature fitful and capricious, but when made to consist in the task of guiding the work of mechanical fingers and arms, regularly impelled with great velocity by some indefatigable physical power. . . .

In my recent tour, continued during several months, through the manufacturing districts, I have seen tens of thousands of old, young, and middle-aged of both sexes, many of them too feeble to get their daily bread by any of the former modes of industry, earning abundant food, raiment, and domestic accommodation, without perspiring at a single pore, screened meanwhile from the summer's sun and the winter's frost, in apartments more airy and salubrious than those of the metropolis, in which our legislative and fashionable aristocracies assemble. In those spacious halls the benignant power of steam summons around him his myriads of willing menials, and assigns to each the regulated task, substituting for painful muscular effort on their part, the energies of his own gigantic arm, and demanding in return only attention and dexterity to correct such little aberrations as casually occur in his workmanship. . . . Such is the factory system, replete with prodigies in mechanics and political economy, which promises, in its future growth, to become the great minister of civilization to the terraqueous globe, enabling this country, as its heart, to diffuse along with its commerce, the life-blood of science and religion to myriads of people still lying "in the region and shadow of death." ■

Sources: Andrew Ure, *The Philosophy of Manufactures; or, An Exposition of the Scientific, Moral, and Commercial Economy of the Factory System* (London, 1835), pp. 13 ff., as quoted in Mack Walker, ed., *Metternich's Europe* (New York: Walker and Company, 1968), pp. 275–276, 278–279.

II. John Ruskin Decries the Impact of Industrial Production on Workers

Englishman John Ruskin (1819–1900) was the foremost mid-nineteenth-century critic of art and architecture. He commenced his career interested primarily in painting and then moved to architecture. In the course of that transition he became increasingly sensitive to the working conditions of the craftsmen who constructed the buildings he studied. Over time he became a major social critic of the new industrial order. His earliest statement of social criticism occurred in a chapter titled "The Nature of Gothic" in his 1851 book The Stones of Venice. *Here Ruskin passionately attacked the mechanical routine of work associated with industrial machinery. He also attacked the concept of increasing work through the division of labor, which had been conceptualized by Adam Smith in* The Wealth of Nations *(1776). Smith had illustrated the division of labor by describing a pin factory. Ruskin here responds to Smith's analysis.*

You must either make a tool of the creature, or a man of him. You cannot make both. Men were not intended to work with the accuracy of tools, to be precise and perfect in all their actions. If you will have that precision out of them, and make their fingers measure degrees like cog-wheels, and their arms strike curves like compasses, you must unhumanize them. All the energy of their spirits must be given to make cogs and compasses of themselves. All their attention and strength must go to the accomplishment of the mean act. . . . On the other hand, if you will make a man of the working creature, you cannot make a tool. Let him but begin to imagine, to think to try to do anything worth doing; and the engine-turned precision is lost at once. Out come all his roughness, all his dulness, all his incapability; shame upon shame, failure upon failure, pause after pause: but out comes the whole majesty of him also; . . .

It is verily this degradation of the operative into a machine, which, more than any other evil of the times, is leading the mass of the nations everywhere into vain, incoherent, destructive struggling for a freedom of which they cannot explain the nature to themselves. . . . It is not that men are ill read, but that they have no pleasure in the work by which they make their bread, and therefore look to wealth as the only means of pleasure. . . .

It is not, truly speaking, the labour that is divided; but the men:—Divided into mere segments of men—broken into small fragments and crumbs of life; so that all the little pieces of intelligence that is left in a man is not enough to make a pin, or a nail, but exhausts itself in making the point of a pin or the head of a nail. . . . And all the evil to which that cry is urging our myriads can be met only in one way: not by teaching nor preaching, for to teach them is but to show them their misery, and to preach to them, if we do nothing more than preach, is to mock at it. It can be met only by a right understanding, on the part of all classes, of what kinds of labour are good for men, raising them, and making them happy; by a determined sacrifice of such convenience, or beauty, or cheapness as is to be got only by the degradation of the workman; and by equally determined demand for the products and results of healthy and ennobling labour. ■

From J. Ruskin, *The Stones of Venice, Vol. 2* (New York: Lovell, Coryell, and Co., n.d.), pp. 162, 164, 165–166.

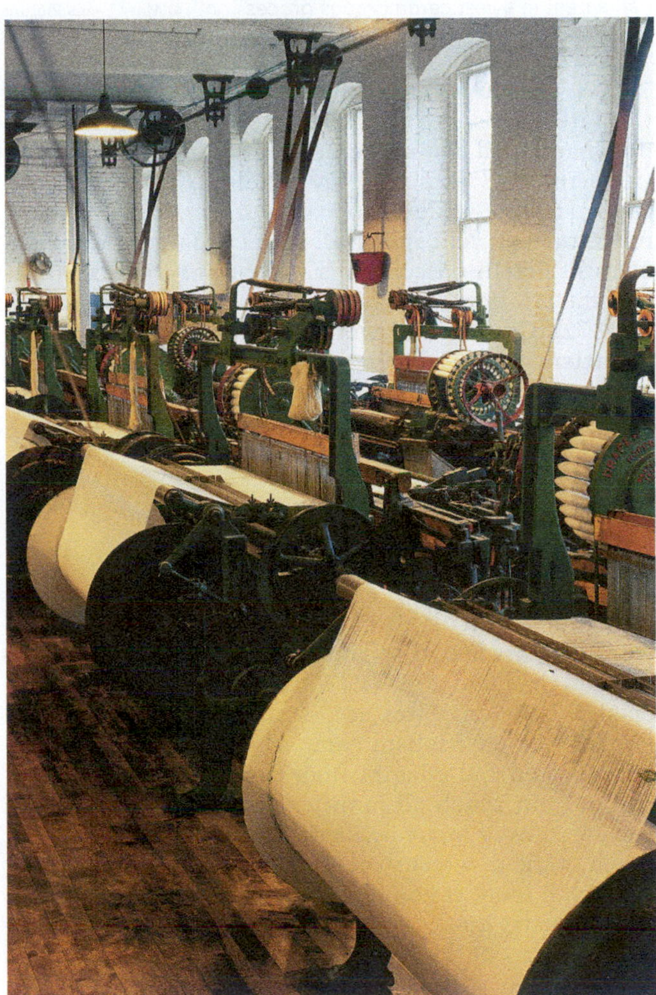

Power looms used in the mass production of textiles during the Industrial Revolution. Dorling Kindersley Medical Library/David Lyons © Dorling Kindersley. Courtesy of the Boott Cotton Mills Museum, Lowell, Massachusetts

In the 1830s and 1840s, the Chartists circulated petitions throughout Britain demanding political reform. Here the petitions are being taken to Parliament in a vast ceremonious procession. © Mary Evans Picture Library/Alamy

As prosperity returned after the depression of the late 1830s and early 1840s, many working people abandoned the movement. Chartists' demonstrations in 1848 fizzled. Nevertheless, Chartism was the first large-scale European working-class political movement. It had specific goals and largely working-class leadership. Eventually, several of the Six Points became law (for example, the secret ballot was enacted in 1872). Continental working-class observers saw in Chartism the kind of mass movement that workers must eventually adopt if they were to improve their situation.

▼ Family Structures and the Industrial Revolution

It is more difficult to generalize about the European working-class family structure in the age of early industrialism than under the Old Regime. Industrialism developed at different rates across the Continent, and the impact of industrialism cannot be separated from that of migration and urbanization. Furthermore, industrialism did not touch all families directly; the structures and customs of many peasant families changed little for much of the nineteenth century.

Much more is known about the relationships of the new industry to the family in Great Britain than elsewhere. Many of the British developments foreshadowed those in other countries as the factory system spread.

The Family in the Early Factory System

Contrary to what historians and other observers once believed, the adoption of new machinery and factory production did not destroy the working-class family. Before the late-eighteenth-century revolution in textile production in England, the individual family involved in textiles was the chief unit of production. The earliest textile-related inventions, such as the spinning jenny, did not change that situation. As noted in Chapter 15, the new machine was initially simply brought into the home to spin the thread. It was the mechanization of weaving that led to the major change. The father who became a machine weaver was then employed in a factory. His work was thus separated from his home. Although the departure of the father for the factory led to changes in family life, the structure of early English factories enabled the father to preserve certain of his traditional family roles as they had existed before the factory system.

In the domestic system of the family economy, the father and mother had worked with their children in textile production as a family unit. They had trained and disciplined the children within the home setting. Their home life and their economic life were largely the same. Moreover, in the home setting, the wife who worked as a spinner might have earned as much or even more than her husband. Early factory owners and supervisors permitted the father to employ his wife and children as his assistants. Thus, parental training and discipline could be transferred from the home into the early factory. In some cases, in both Britain and France, whole families would move near a new factory so that the family as a unit could work there. Despite those accommodations to family life, family members still had to face the new work discipline of the factory setting. Moreover, women assisting their husbands in the factory often did less skilled work than they had in their homes.

A major shift in this family and factory structure began in the mid-1820s in England and had been more or less completed by the mid-1830s. As spinning and weaving were put under one roof, the size of factories and of the machinery grew. These newer machines required fewer skilled operators, but many relatively unskilled attendants. This became the work of unmarried women and children. Factory owners found these workers would accept lower wages and were less likely than adult men to try to form worker organizations or unions.

Factory wages for the more skilled adult males, however, became sufficiently high to allow some fathers to remove their children from the factory and send them to school. The children who were left working in the factories as assistants were often the children of the economically depressed hand-loom weavers. The wives of the skilled operatives also usually no longer worked in the factories. So the original links of the family in the British textile factory that had existed for well over a quarter century largely disappeared. Men were supervising women and children who did not belong to their families.

THE GREAT EXHIBITION IN LONDON

THE GREAT EXHIBITION of 1851 was held in London to celebrate progress in industry and commerce achieved through the new industrial order. Its organizers invited governments and businesses from around the globe to display the products they manufactured. The organizers generally supported free trade and believed the displays would demonstrate the value of peaceful commerce.

Note the construction of the building known as the Crystal Palace. The structural iron symbolized the possibility of using new kinds of building materials. The vast quantities of glass demonstrated that a once scarce luxury good could now be produced in large quantities for everyday consumption. In the past such structures of iron and glass had been used only for small greenhouses to raise plants on aristocratic estates.

The crowds in the picture and the even larger crowds who actually attended the Great Exhibition demonstrated that, after a quarter century of social turmoil and political discontent in Europe, large numbers of people could gather peacefully in public.

The classical statues to the left were present to show that the new consumer goods industrialism made possible was compatible with an ongoing culture of elite art. Flags to the left labeled "India" and "Silk" recall India, Britain's most important colony.

London's Crystal Palace during the International Exhibition of 1851. Victoria & Albert Museum, London, Great Britain/ Art Resource, NY

How does this image promote the British Empire?

What role does this image suggest that women play in Britain's commercial society?

What tools does the artist use to depict British prosperity?

Concern for Child Labor At this point in the 1830s, workers became concerned about the plight of child laborers because parents were no longer exercising discipline over their own children in the factories. The English Factory Act of 1833 forbade the employment of children under age nine, limited the workday of children aged nine to thirteen to nine hours a day, and required the factory owner to pay for two hours of education a day for these children. The effect was further to divide work and home life. The workday for adults and older teenagers remained twelve hours. Younger children often worked in relays of four or six hours. Consequently, the parental link was thoroughly broken. The education requirement began the process of removing nurturing and training from the home and family to a school, where a teacher rather than the parents was in charge of education.

Read the Document "British Parliament, 'Inquiry: Child Labor' " on **MyHistoryLab.com**

After passage of the English Factory Act, many British workers demanded shorter workdays for adults. They desired to reunite, in some manner, the workday of adults with that of their children or at least to allow adults to spend more time with their children. In 1847, Parliament mandated a ten-hour workday. By present standards, this was long. At that time, however, it allowed parents and children more hours together as a domestic unit, since their relationship as a work or production unit had ceased wherever the factory system prevailed. By the mid-1840s, in the lives of industrial workers, the roles of men as breadwinners and as fathers and husbands had become distinct in the British textile industry. Furthermore, reformers' concerns about the working conditions of women in factories and in mines arose in part from the relatively new view that the place of women was in the home rather than in an industrial or even agrarian workplace.

Changing Economic Role for the Family What occurred in Britain presents a general pattern for what would happen elsewhere with the spread of industrial capitalism and public education. The European family was passing from being the chief unit of both production and consumption to becoming the chief unit of consumption alone. This development did not mean the end of the family as an economic unit. Parents and children, however, now came to depend on sharing wages often derived from several sources, rather than on sharing work in the home or factory.

Ultimately, the wage economy meant that families were less closely bound together than in the past. Because wages could be sent over long distances to parents, children might now move farther away from home. Once they moved far away, the economic link was, in time, often broken. In contrast, when a family settled in an industrial city, the wage economy might, in that or the next generation, actually discourage children from leaving home as early as they had in the past. Children could find wage employment in the same city and then live at home until they had accumulated enough savings to marry and begin their own household. That situation meant children often remained with their parents longer than in the past.

▼ Women in the Early Industrial Revolution

As noted in Chapter 15, the industrial economy ultimately produced an immense impact on the home and family life of women. First, it eventually took most productive work out of the home and allowed many families to live on the wages of the male spouse. That transformation prepared the way for a new concept of gender-determined roles in the home and in domestic life generally. Women came to be associated with domestic duties, such as housekeeping, food preparation, childrearing and nurturing, and household management, or with poorly paid, largely unskilled cottage industries. Men came to be associated almost exclusively with the financial support of the family. Children were raised to conform to these expected gender patterns. Previously, this domestic division of labor into separate male and female spheres had prevailed only among the relatively small middle class and the gentry. During the nineteenth century, that division came to characterize the working class as well.

Opportunities and Exploitation in Employment

Because the early Industrial Revolution had begun in textile production, women and their labor were deeply involved from the start. Although both spinning and weaving were still domestic industries, women usually worked in all stages of production. Hand spinning was virtually always a woman's task. At first, when spinning was moved into factories and involved large machines, men often displaced women. Furthermore, the higher wages male cotton-factory workers commanded allowed many married women not to work or to work only to supplement their husbands' wages.

Women in Factories With the next generation of machines in the 1820s, however, unmarried women rapidly became employed in the factories, where they often constituted the majority of workers. Their new jobs, however, often demanded fewer skills than those they had previously exercised in the home production of textiles. Women's factory work also required fewer skills than most work men did. Tending a machine required less skill than spinning or weaving or acting as forewoman. There was thus a certain paradox in the impact of the factory on women: It opened many new jobs to them but lowered the level of skills they needed to have. The supervisors of women were almost invariably men.

As textile production became increasingly automated in the nineteenth century, textile factories required fewer skilled workers and more unskilled attendants. To fill these unskilled positions, factory owners turned increasingly to unmarried women and widows, who worked for lower wages than men and were less likely to form labor organizations. Courtesy of the Library of Congress

Moreover, almost always, the women in the factories were young, single women or widows. Upon marriage or perhaps after the birth of the first child, young women usually found their husbands earned enough money for them to leave the factory. Sometimes the factory owners, who disliked employing married women because of the likelihood of pregnancy, the influence of their husbands, and the duties of childrearing, no longer wanted them. Widows might return to factory work because they lacked their husbands' former income.

Read the Document "Industrial Society and Factory Conditions (early 1800s)" on **MyHistoryLab.com**

Work on the Land and in the Home In Britain and elsewhere by midcentury, industrial factory work still accounted for less than half of all employment for women. The largest group of employed women in France continued to work on the land. In England, they were domestic servants. Throughout Western Europe, domestic cottage industries, such as lace making, glove making, garment making, and other kinds of needlework, employed many women. In almost all such cases, their conditions of labor were harsh, whether they worked in their homes or in sweatshops. It cannot be overemphasized that all work by women commanded low wages and involved low skills. They had virtually no effective modes to protect themselves from exploitation. The charwoman, hired by the day to do rough house cleaning or washing, was a common sight across the Continent and symbolized the plight of working women.

The low wages of female workers in all areas of employment sometimes led them to become prostitutes to supplement their wage income. This situation prevailed across Europe throughout the century. In 1844, Louise Aston (1814–1871), a German political radical, portrayed this situation in a poem looking at the experience of a Silesian weaver as she confronts a factory owner on whom her family depends to purchase the cloth they have woven:

The factory owner has come,
And he says to me: "My darling child,
I know your people
Are living in misery and sorrow;
So if you want to lie with me
For three or four nights,
See this shiny gold coin!
It's yours immediately."[1]

Such sexual exploitation of women was hardly new to European society, but the particular pressures of the transformation of the economy from one of skilled artisans to that of unskilled factory workers made many women especially vulnerable. (See the Document, "Women Industrial Workers Explain Their Economic Situation," page 659.)

Changing Expectations in the Working-Class Marriage

Moving to cities and entering the wage economy gave women wider opportunities for marriage. Cohabitation before marriage was not uncommon. Parents had less to do with arranging marriages than in the past. Marriage now usually meant a woman would leave the workforce to live on her husband's earnings. If all went well, that arrangement

[1]Lia Secci, "German Women Writers and the Revolution of 1848," in John C. Fout, ed., *German Women in the Nineteenth Century: A Social History* (New York: Holmes & Meier, 1984), p. 162.

might improve her situation. If the husband became ill or died, however, or if he deserted his wife, she would have to reenter the market for unskilled labor at an advanced age.

Despite these changes, many of the traditional practices associated with the family economy survived into the industrial era. As a young woman came of age, both family needs and her desire to marry still directed what she would do with her life. The most likely early occupation for a young woman was domestic service. A girl born in the country normally migrated to a nearby town or city for such employment, often living initially with a relative. As in the past, she would try to earn enough in wages to give herself a dowry, so she might marry and set up her own household. If she became a factory worker, she would probably live in a supervised dormitory. These dormitories helped attract young women to work in a factory by convincing parents their daughters would be safe.

The life of young women in the cities was more precarious than earlier. There were fewer family and community ties. There were also perhaps more available young men. These men, who worked for wages rather than in the older apprenticeship structures, were more mobile, so relationships between men and women often were more fleeting. In any case, illegitimate births increased; fewer women who became pregnant before marriage found the father willing to marry them.

Marriage in the wage industrial economy was also different in certain respects from marriage in earlier times. It still involved starting a separate household, but the structure of gender relationships within the household was different. Marriage was less an economic partnership. The husband's wages might well be able to support the entire family. The wage economy and the industrialization separating workplace from home made it difficult for women to combine domestic duties with work. When married women worked, it was usually in the nonindustrial sector of the economy. More often than not, the children rather than the wife were sent to work. This may help explain the increase in the number of births within marriages, as children in the wage economy usually were an economic asset. Married women worked outside the home only when family needs, illness, or widowhood forced them to.

In the home, working-class women were by no means idle. Their domestic duties were an essential factor in the family wage economy. If work took place elsewhere, someone had to be directly in charge of maintaining the home. Homemaking came to the fore when a life at home had to be organized separately from the place of work. Wives were concerned primarily with food and cooking, but they were also often in charge of the family's finances. The role of the mother expanded when the children still living at home became wage earners. She was now providing home support for her entire wage-earning family. She created the environment to which the family members returned after work. The longer period of home life of working children may also have increased and strengthened familial bonds of affection between those children and their hardworking homebound mothers. In all these respects, the culture of the working-class marriage and family tended to imitate the family patterns of the middle and upper classes, whose members had often accepted the view of separate gender spheres set forth by Rousseau and popularized in hundreds of novels, journals, and newspapers.

▼ Problems of Crime, Order, and Poverty

Throughout the nineteenth century, the political and economic elite in Europe was profoundly concerned about social order. The revolutions of the late eighteenth and early nineteenth centuries made them fearful of future disorder and threats to life and property. Industrialization and urbanization also contributed to this problem of order. Thousands of Europeans migrated from the countryside to the towns and cities. There, they often encountered poverty or unemployment and general social frustration and disappointment. Cities became associated with criminal activity, especially crimes against property, such as theft and arson. Throughout the

London policeman. Professional police forces did not exist before the early nineteenth century. The London police force was created in 1829. A Sergeant of 1865 (colour litho), Fosten, Bryan (b.1928)/Private Collection/Peter Newark Pictures/The Bridgeman Art Library

Document

WOMEN INDUSTRIAL WORKERS EXPLAIN THEIR ECONOMIC SITUATION

In 1832, there was much discussion in the British press about factory legislation. Most of that discussion concerned the employment of children, but The Examiner *newspaper suggested that factory laws should also, in time, eliminate women's employment in factories. That article provoked the following letter to the editor, composed by or on behalf of women factory workers, which stated why women needed such employment and the unattractive alternatives.*

How do these women explain their need to hold manufacturing jobs? What changes in production methods have led women from the home to the factory? How does the situation of these women relate to the possibility of their marrying?

Sir,

Living as we do, in the densely populated manufacturing districts of Lancashire, and most of us belonging to that class of females who earn their bread either directly or indirectly by manufactories, we have looked with no little anxiety for your opinion on the Factory Bill. . . . You are for doing away with our services in manufactories altogether. So much the better, if you had pointed out any other more eligible and practical employment for the surplus female labour, that will want other channels for a subsistence. If our competition were withdrawn, and short hours substituted, we have no doubt but the effects would be as you have stated, "not to lower wages, as the male branch of the family would be enabled to earn as much as the whole had done," but for the thousands of females who are employed in manufactories, who have no legitimate claim on any male relative for employment or support, and who have, through a variety of circumstance, been early thrown on their own resources for a livelihood, what is to become of them?

In this neighbourhood, hand-loom has been almost totally superseded by power-loom weaving, and no inconsiderable number of females, who must depend on their own exertions, or their parishes for support, have been forced, of necessity into the manufactories, from their total inability to earn a livelihood at home.

It is a lamentable fact that, in these parts of the country, there is scarcely any other mode of employment for female industry, if we except servitude and dressmaking. Of the former of these, there is no chance of employment for one-twentieth of the candidates that would rush into the field, to say nothing of lowering the wages of our sisters of the same craft; and of the latter, galling as some of the hardships of manufactories are (of which the indelicacy of mixing with the men is not the least), yet there are few women who have been so employed, that would change conditions with the ill-used genteel little slaves, who have to lose sleep and health, in catering to the whims and frivolities of the butterflies of fashion.

We see no way of escape from starvation, but to accept the very tempting offers of the newspapers, held out as baits to us, fairly to ship ourselves off to Van Dieman's Land [Tasmania] on the very delicate errand of husband hunting, and having safely arrived at the "Land of Goshen," jump ashore, with a "Who wants me?". . .

The Female Operatives of Todmorden

From *The Examiner*, February 26, 1832, as quoted in Ivy Pinchbeck, *Women Workers and the Industrial Revolution, 1750–1850* (New York: Augustus M. Kelley, 1969), pp. 199–200.

first sixty years of the nineteenth century, crime appears to have increased slowly but steadily before more or less reaching a plateau.

Historians and social scientists are divided about the reasons for this rise in the crime rate. So little is known about crime in rural settings that comparisons with the cities are difficult. Moreover, crime statistics in the nineteenth century are problematic. No two nations kept them in the same manner. Different legal codes and systems of judicial administration were in effect in different

In many prisons, treadmills like these were the only source of exercise available to English prisoners. Bildarchiv Preussischer Kulturbesitz/Art Resource, NY

areas of the Continent, thus giving somewhat different legal definitions of what constituted criminal activity. The result has been confusion, difficult research, and tentative conclusions.

New Police Forces

From the propertied, elite classes, two major views about containing crime and criminals emerged during the nineteenth century: better systems of police and prison reform. The result of these efforts was the triumph in Europe of the idea of a policed society in which a paid, professionally trained group of law-enforcement officers keeps order, protects property and lives, investigates crime, and apprehends offenders. These officers are distinct from the army and are charged specifically with domestic security. It is to them that the civilian population normally turns for law enforcement. A key feature of the theory of a policed society is that the visible presence of law-enforcement officers may prevent crime. These police forces, again at least in theory, did not perform a political role, although many countries often ignored that distinction. Police forces also became one of the largest groups of municipal government employees.

Professional police forces did not really exist until the early nineteenth century. They differed from one country to another in both authority and organization, but their creation proved crucial to the emergence of an orderly European society. The prefect of Paris, who was the chief administrative official of that city, set forth the principles that lay behind the founding of all of these new police units when he announced that "Safety by day and night, free traffic movement, clean streets, the supervision of and precaution against accidents, the maintenance of order in public places, the seeking out of offences and their perpetrators. . . . The municipal police is a parental police."[2]

Professional police forces appeared in Paris in 1828. The next year, the British Parliament passed legislation sponsored by Sir Robert Peel (1788–1850) that placed police on London streets. They were soon known as *bobbies* or, more disparagingly, as Peelers, after the sponsor of the legislation. Berlin deployed similar police departments after the Revolution of 1848. All of these forces were distinguished by an easily recognizable uniform. Police on the Continent carried guns; those in Britain did not.

Although citizens sometimes viewed police with suspicion, especially in Britain where many people opposed the creation of a professional police force as a threat to traditional British liberties, by the end of the century, most Europeans regarded the police as their protectors. Persons from the upper and middle classes felt police made their property more secure. Persons from the working class also frequently turned to the police to protect their lives and property and to aid them in emergencies. Of course, most

[2]Clive Emsley, *Policing and Its Context, 1750–1870* (London: Macmillan, 1983), p. 58.

people hated and feared political or secret police wherever governments, especially in Russia, created them.

Prison Reform

Before the nineteenth century, European prisons were local jails or state prisons, such as the Bastille. Governments also sent criminals to prison ships, called *hulks*. Some Mediterranean nations sentenced prisoners to naval galleys, where, chained to their benches, they rowed until they died or were eventually released. In prisons, inmates lived under wretched conditions. Men, women, and children were housed together. Persons guilty of minor offenses were left in the same room with those guilty of the most serious offenses.

Beginning in the late eighteenth century, the British government sentenced persons convicted of the most serious offenses to transportation. Transportation to the colony of New South Wales in Australia was regarded as an alternative to capital punishment, and the British used it until the mid-nineteenth century, when the colonies began to object. Thereafter, the British government housed long-term prisoners in public works prisons in Britain.

By the close of the eighteenth century and in the early nineteenth century, reformers, such as John Howard (1726–1790) and Elizabeth Fry (1780–1845) in England and Charles Lucas (1803–1889) in France, exposed the horrendous conditions in prisons and demanded change. Reform came slowly because of the expense of constructing new prisons and a lack of sympathy for criminals.

In the 1840s, however, both the French and the English undertook several bold efforts at prison reform. These efforts would appear to indicate a shift in opinion whereby crime was seen not as an assault on order or on authority but as a mark of a character fault in the criminal. Thereafter, part of the goal of imprisonment was to rehabilitate or transform the prisoner. The result of this change was the creation of exceedingly repressive prison systems designed according to the most advanced scientific modes of understanding criminals and criminal reform.

Read the **Document** "Leon Faucher, 'Prison Rules' " on **MyHistoryLab.com**

Europeans used various prison models originally established in the United States. All these experiments depended on separating prisoners from each other. One was known as the *Auburn system* after Auburn Prison in New York State. According to it, prisoners were separated from each other during the night but could associate while working during the day. The other was the *Philadelphia system*, in which prisoners were rigorously kept separated from each other at all times.

The chief characteristics of these systems were an individual cell for each prisoner and long periods of separation and silence among prisoners. The most famous example of this kind of prison in Europe was Pentonville Prison near London. There, each prisoner occupied a separate cell and was never allowed to speak to or see another prisoner. Each prisoner wore a mask when in the prison yard; in the chapel, each had a separate stall. The point of the system was to induce self-reflection in which the prisoners would think about their crimes and eventually decide to repudiate their criminal tendencies. As time passed, the system became more relaxed because the intense isolation often led to mental collapse.

In France, imprisonment became more repressive as the century passed. The French constructed prisons similar to Pentonville in the 1840s. In 1875, the French also adopted a firm, general policy of isolating inmates. France constructed sixty prisons based on this principle by 1908. Prisoners were supposed to be trained in a trade or skill while in prison so they could reemerge as reformed citizens.

The vast increase in repeat offenses led the French government in 1885, long after the British had abandoned the practice, to sentence serious repeat offenders to transportation to places such as the infamous Devil's Island off the coast of South America. Transportation was intended literally to purge the nation of its worst criminals and to ensure they would never return.

These attempts to create a police force and to reform prisons illustrate the concern about order and stability by European political and social elites that developed after the French Revolution. On the whole, their efforts succeeded. By the end of the century, an orderly society had been established, and the new police and prisons had no small role in that development.

Government Policies Based on Classical Economics

The principles of classical economics (see Chapter 20) contributed to cooperation between the middle classes and governments, both of whom were threatened by the demands of the working class for more fundamental change. Louis Philippe (1773–1850) and his minister François Guizot (1787–1874) told the French to go forth and enrich themselves. People who simply displayed sufficient energy need not be poor. A number of the French middle class did just that. The July Monarchy (1830–1848) saw the construction of major capital-intensive projects, such as roads, canals, and railways. Little, however, was done about the poverty in the cities and the countryside.

In the German states, the middle classes also made headway. After the Napoleonic wars, the Prussian reformers had seen the desirability of abolishing internal tariffs that impeded economic growth. In 1834, all the major German states, except Austria, formed the *Zollverein*, or free trading union. Classical economics was moderated in the German states by the tradition dating from the enlightened absolutism of state direction

MAJOR WORKS OF ECONOMIC AND POLITICAL COMMENTARY

1776	Adam Smith, *The Wealth of Nations*
1798	Thomas Malthus, *Essay on the Principle of Population*
1817	David Ricardo, *Principles of Political Economy*
1830s	Harriet Martineau, *Illustrations of Political Economy*
1839	Louis Blanc, *The Organization of Labor*
1845	Friedrich Engels, *The Condition of the Working Class in England*
1848	Karl Marx and Friedrich Engels, *The Communist Manifesto*

of economic development. German economist Friedrich List (1789–1846) argued for this approach to economic growth during the second quarter of the century. He was convinced that only strong state support would allow German states to catch up to Britain, which had begun the process of industrialization earlier.

Britain was the home of the major classical economists, and their policies were widely accepted. The utilitarian thought of Jeremy Bentham (1748–1832) increased their influence. Although **utilitarianism** did not originate with him, Bentham sought to create codes of scientific law that were founded on the principle of utility, that is, the greatest happiness for the greatest number. In his *Fragment on Government* (1776) and *The Principles of Morals and Legislation* (1789), Bentham explained the application of the principle of utility would overcome the special interests of privileged groups who prevented rational government. He regarded the existing legal and judicial systems as burdened by traditional practices that harmed the very people the law should serve. The application of reason and utility would remove the legal clutter that prevented justice from being realized. He believed the principle of utility could be applied to other areas of government administration.

Bentham gathered around him political disciples who combined his ideas with those of classical economics. In 1834, the reformed House of Commons passed a new Poor Law that followers of Bentham had prepared. This measure established a Poor Law Commission that set out to make poverty the most undesirable of all social situations. Government poor relief was to be disbursed only in workhouses. Life in the workhouse was consciously designed to be more unpleasant than life outside. Husbands and wives were separated, the food was bad, and the enforced work was distasteful. The social stigma of the workhouse was even worse. The law and its administration presupposed that people would not work because they were lazy. The laboring class, not unjustly, regarded the workhouses as new "bastilles."

The second British monument to applied classical economics was the repeal of the **Corn Laws** in 1846. The Anti–Corn Law League, organized by manufacturers, had sought this goal for more than six years. The League wanted to abolish the tariffs protecting the domestic price of grain. That change would lead to lower food prices, which would then allow lower wages at no real cost to the workers. In turn, the prices on British manufactured goods could also be lowered to strengthen their competitive position in the world market.

The actual reason for Sir Robert Peel's repeal of the Corn Laws in 1846 was the Irish famine. Peel had to open British ports to foreign grain to feed the starving Irish. He realized the Corn Laws could not be reimposed. Peel accompanied the abolition measure with a program for government aid to modernize British agriculture and to make it more efficient. The repeal of the Corn Laws was the culmination of the lowering of British tariffs that had begun during the 1820s. It marked the opening of an era of free trade that continued until the twentieth century.

▼ Early Socialism

During the twentieth century, the socialist movement, in the form of either communist or social democratic political parties, constituted one of the major political forces in Europe. Less than 150 years ago, the advocates of socialism lacked any meaningful political following, and their doctrines appeared blurred and confused to most of their contemporaries. It is important to understand their early ideas and then to see (as shall be seen in later chapters) how those ideas, which for many years appeared on the margins of European political life, came to assume great importance in the late nineteenth century and beyond.

The early socialists generally applauded the new productive capacity of industrialism. They denied, however, that the free market could adequately produce and distribute goods the way the classical economists claimed. In the capitalist order, the socialists saw primarily mismanagement, low wages, misdistribution of goods, and suffering arising from the unregulated industrial system. Moreover, the socialists thought human society should be organized as a community, rather than merely as a conglomerate of atomistic, selfish individuals.

Utopian Socialism

Among the earliest people to define the social question was a group of writers whom their critics called the **utopian socialists**. They were considered utopian because their ideas were often visionary and because they frequently advocated the creation of ideal communities. They were called socialists because they questioned the structures and values of the existing capitalistic framework. In some cases, they actually deserved neither

Robert Owen, a Scottish industrialist and early socialist, created an ideal industrial community at New Lanark, Scotland. He believed deeply in the power of education and saw that the children of workmen received sound educations. © Mary Evans Picture Library/Alamy

description. A significant factor in the experience of almost all of these groups was the discussion, and sometimes the practice, of radical ideas about sexuality and the family. People who might have been sympathetic to their economic concerns were profoundly unsympathetic to their views on free love and open family relationships.

Saint-Simonianism Count Claude Henri de Saint-Simon (1760–1825) was the earliest of the socialist pioneers. As a young, liberal French aristocrat, he had fought in the American Revolution. Later he welcomed the French Revolution, during which he made and lost a fortune. By the time of Napoleon's ascendancy, he had turned to a career of writing and social criticism and a concern for order.

Above all else, Saint-Simon believed modern society would require rational management. Private wealth, property, and enterprise should be subject to an administration other than that of its owners. His ideal government would have consisted of a large board of directors organizing and coordinating the activity of individuals and groups to achieve social harmony. In a sense, he was the ideological father of technocracy. Not the *redistribution* of wealth but its *management* by experts would alleviate the poverty and social dislocation of the age.

When Saint-Simon died in 1825, he had persuaded only a handful of people his ideas were correct. Nonetheless, Saint-Simonian societies were always centers for lively discussion of advanced social ideals. Some of the earliest debates in France over feminism took place within these societies. During the late 1820s and 1830s, the Saint-Simonians became well known for advocating sexuality outside marriage. Several of Saint-Simon's disciples also became leaders in the French railway industry during the 1850s.

Owenism The major British contributor to the early socialist tradition was Robert Owen (1771–1858), a self-made cotton manufacturer. In his early twenties, Owen became a partner in one of the largest cotton factories in Britain at New Lanark, Scotland. Owen was a firm believer in the environmentalist psychology of the Enlightenment that had flowed from the thought of John Locke. If human beings were placed in the correct surroundings, they and their character could be improved. Moreover, Owen saw no incompatibility between creating a humane industrial environment and making a good profit.

At New Lanark, he put his ideas into practice. Workers were provided with good quarters. Recreational possibilities abounded, and the children received an education. There were several churches, although Owen himself was a notorious freethinker on matters of religion and sex. In the factory itself, rewards were given for good work. His plant made a fine profit. Visitors flocked from all over Europe to see what Owen had done through enlightened management.

Read the **Document** "Robert Owen, Excerpt from *Address to the Workers of New Lanark, 1816*" on **MyHistoryLab.com**

In numerous articles and pamphlets, as well as in letters to influential people, Owen pleaded for a reorganization of industry based on his own successful model. He envisioned a series of communities shaped like parallelograms in which factory workers and farm workers might live together and produce their goods in cooperation. During the 1820s, Owen sold his New Lanark factory and then went to the United States, where he established the community of New Harmony, Indiana. When quarrels among the members led to the community's failure, he refused to give up his reformist causes. He returned to Britain, where he became the moving force behind the organization of the Grand National Union, an attempt to draw all British trade unions into a single body. It collapsed along with other labor organizations during the early 1830s.

Fourierism Charles Fourier (1772–1837) was Owen's French intellectual counterpart. He was a commercial salesperson who never succeeded in attracting the same kind of public attention as Owen. He wrote his books and articles and waited at home each day at noon, hoping to meet a patron who would undertake his program. No one ever arrived to meet him. Fourier believed the industrial order ignored the passionate side of human nature. Social discipline ignored all the pleasures that human beings naturally seek.

Fourier advocated the construction of communities, called *phalanxes*, in which liberated living would replace the boredom and dullness of industrial existence. Agrarian rather than industrial production would predominate in these communities. Sexual activity would be relatively free, and marriage was to be reserved only for later life. Fourier also urged that no person be required to perform the same kind of work for the entire day. People would be both happier and more productive if they moved from one task to another. Through his emphasis on the problem of boredom, Fourier isolated one of the key difficulties of modern economic life.

Saint-Simon, Owen, and Fourier expected some existing government to carry out their ideas. They failed to confront the political difficulties their envisioned social transformations would arouse. Other figures paid more attention to the politics of the situation. In 1839, Louis Blanc (1811–1882) published *The Organization of Labor*. Like other socialist writers, this Frenchman demanded an end to competition, but he did not seek a wholly new society. He called for political reform that would give the vote to the working class. Once so empowered, workers could use the vote to turn the political processes to their own economic advantage. A state controlled by a working-class electorate would finance workshops to employ the poor. In time, such workshops might replace private enterprise, and industry would be organized to ensure jobs. Blanc recognized the power of the state to improve life and the conditions of labor. The state itself could become the great employer of labor.

Anarchism

Other writers and activists of the 1840s, however, rejected both industry and the dominance of government. These were the **anarchists**. They are usually included in the socialist tradition, although they do not exactly fit there. Some favored programs of violence and terrorism; others were peaceful. Auguste Blanqui (1805–1881) was a major spokesperson for terror. He spent most of his adult life in jail. Seeking to abolish both capitalism and the state, Blanqui urged the development of a professional revolutionary vanguard to attack capitalist society. His ideas for the new society were vague, but in his call for professional revolutionaries, he foreshadowed Lenin.

Pierre-Joseph Proudhon (1809–1865) represented the other strain of anarchism. In his most famous work *What Is Property?* (1840), Proudhon attacked the banking system, which rarely extended credit to small-property owners or the poor. He wanted credit expanded to allow such people to engage in economic enterprise that would not involve unfair or unearned profits. Society should be organized on the basis of mutualism, which amounted to a system of small businesses and other cooperative enterprises among which there would be peaceful cooperation and exchanges of goods based on mutual recognition of the labor each area of production required. With such a social system, the state as the protector of property would be unnecessary. Later in the century, anarchists would favor a wide variety of cooperative businesses whose point was to favor the community good over that of the individual as well as to afford an essential fairness in exchange. Proudhon's ideas later influenced the French labor movement, which was generally less directly political in its activities than the labor movements in Britain and the German states.

Marxism

The mode of socialist thought that eventually exerted more influence over modern European history than any other was **Marxism**. During the late nineteenth century, its ideas permeated the major continental socialist parties. With the Bolshevik Revolution of November 1917, Vladimir Lenin's interpretation of Marxist thought came to dominate the Soviet Union and, after World War II, Eastern Europe and revolutionary movements in the colonial and post-colonial world. After the collapse of the Soviet Union and of the communist governments in Eastern Europe in the last twenty years of the twentieth century, it is difficult for many people to recapture the power that Marx's political and social vision exerted over Europe and other parts of the world for more than a hundred years.

Too often, the history of European socialism has been regarded as a linear development leading naturally or necessarily to the late-nineteenth-century triumph of Marxism within the major socialist political parties. Nothing could be further from the truth. Marxist ideas came to define what "socialism" meant to many people, but only through competition with other socialist formulas and largely as a result of the political situation in Germany during the last quarter of the nineteenth century. At midcentury, the ideas of Karl Marx were simply one more contribution to a heady mixture of concepts

Karl Marx's communist philosophy became the most widespread of the many varieties of socialism, but his monumental work became subject to varying interpretations, criticisms, and revisions that continue to this day. Library of Congress

and programs criticizing the emerging industrial capitalist society. Marxism differed from its competitors in its claims to scientific accuracy, its rejection of liberal reform, its harsh criticism of other contemporary socialist platforms, and its call for revolution, though the character of that revolution was not well defined. Furthermore, Marx set the emergence of the industrial workforce in the context of a world historical development from which he drew sweeping political conclusions.

Karl Marx (1818–1883) was born in the Prussian Rhineland. His father's family had been Jewish, but his father had converted to Lutheranism, and Judaism played no role in his education. Marx's middle-class parents sent him to the University of Berlin, where he became deeply involved in Hegelian philosophy and radical politics. In 1842 and 1843, he edited the radical *Rhineland Gazette* (*Rheinische Zeitung*). Soon the Prussian authorities drove him into exile. He lived in poverty, first in Paris, then in Brussels, and finally, after 1849, in London.

Partnership with Engels In 1844, Marx met Friedrich Engels (1820–1895), another young middle-class German, whose father owned a textile factory in Manchester, England. The next year Engels published *The Condition of the Working Class in England*, which presented a devastating picture of industrial life. The two men became fast friends. Late in 1847, they were asked to write a pamphlet for a newly organized and ultimately short-lived secret Communist League. *The Communist Manifesto*, published in German, appeared early in 1848. Marx, Engels, and the League had adopted the name *communist* because it was much more self-consciously radical than socialist. Communism implied the outright abolition of private property, rather than a less extensive rearrangement of society. Neither Marx nor his thought had any effect on the revolutionary events of 1848, which is discussed more fully later in this chapter. Only later would the *Manifesto*, a work of fewer than fifty pages, earn its status as one of the most influential political tracts in modern European history.

Read the Document "Capitalism Challenged: *The Communist Manifesto* (1848)" on **MyHistoryLab.com**

Sources of Marx's Ideas Marx derived the major ideas of the *Manifesto* and of his later work, including *Capital* (Vol. 1, 1867), from German Hegelianism, French utopian socialism, and British classical economics. Marx applied to concrete historical, social, and economic developments Hegel's abstract philosophical concept that thought develops from the clash of thesis and antithesis into a new intellectual synthesis. For Marx, the conflict between dominant and subordinate social groups led to the emergence of a new dominant social group. These new social relationships, in turn, generated new discontent, conflict, and development. The French utopian socialists had depicted the problems of capitalist society and had raised the issue of property redistribution. Both Hegel and Saint-Simon led Marx to see society and economic conditions as developing through historical stages. The classical economists had produced the analytical tools for an empirical, scientific examination of the industrial capitalist society.

Using the intellectual tools that Hegel, the French utopian socialists, and the British classical economists provided, Marx fashioned a philosophy that gave a special role or function to the new industrial workforce as the single most important driving force of contemporary history. Marx later explained to a friend:

> What I did that was new was to prove: (1) that the existence of classes is bound up with particular historical phases in the development of production; (2) that the class struggle necessarily leads to the dictatorship of the proletariat; (3) that this dictatorship itself only constitutes the transition to the abolition of all classes and to a classless society.[3]

In the *Communist Manifesto* and his numerous other writings, Marx equated the fate of the proletariat—that is, the new industrial labor force—with the fate of humanity itself. According to Marx, as the proletariat came to liberate itself from its bondage to the capitalist mode of industrial production, such liberation would eventually amount to the liberation of all humanity. It was this utopian vision of human emancipation, no matter how much the actual later development of the European and

[3]Albert Fried and Ronald Sanders, eds., *Socialist Thought: A Documentary History* (Garden City, NY: Anchor Doubleday, 1964), p. 295.

world economy failed to conform to Marx's predictions, that drew many people from Europe and elsewhere to embrace much of his thought and to base their political actions on their understanding of his philosophy. Besides this wider vision, however, the details of Marx's argument were also important for later nineteenth-century and twentieth-century European political life.

Revolution through Class Conflict In the *Communist Manifesto*, Marx and Engels contended that human history must be understood rationally and as a whole. History is the record of humankind's coming to grips with physical nature to produce the goods necessary for survival. That basic productive process determines the structures, values, and ideas of a society. Historically, the organization of the means of production has always involved conflict between the classes that owned and controlled the means of production and the classes that worked for them. That necessary conflict has provided the engine for historical development; it is not an accidental by-product of mismanagement or bad intentions. Thus, piecemeal reforms cannot eliminate the social and economic evils inherent in the very structures of production. To achieve that, a radical social transformation is required. The development of capitalism will make such a revolution inevitable.

In Marx's and Engels's eyes, the class conflict that had characterized previous Western history had become simplified during the early nineteenth century into a struggle between the bourgeoisie and the proletariat, or between the middle class associated with industry and commerce, on the one hand, and the workers, on the other. The character of capitalism itself ensured the sharpening of the struggle. Capitalist production and competition would steadily increase the size of the unpropertied proletariat. Large-scale mechanical production crushed both traditional and smaller industrial producers into the ranks of the proletariat. As the business structures grew larger and larger, the competitive pressures would squeeze out smaller middle-class units. Competition among the few remaining giant concerns would lead to more intense suffering for the proletariat. The process also meant the proletariat itself would continue to expand to include more and more people. As this ever-expanding body of workers suffered increasingly from the competition among the ever-enlarging firms, Marx contended, they would eventually begin to foment revolution. Finally, they would overthrow the few remaining owners of the means of production. For a time, the workers would organize the means of production through a dictatorship of the proletariat. This would eventually give way to a propertyless and classless communist society.

This proletarian revolution was inevitable, according to Marx and Engels. The structure of capitalism required competition and consolidation of enterprise. Although the class conflict involved in the contemporary process resembled that of the past, it differed in one major respect: The struggle between the capitalistic bourgeoisie and the industrial proletariat would culminate in a wholly new society that would be free of class conflict. The victorious proletariat, by its very nature, could not be a new oppressor class: "The proletarian movement is the self-conscious, independent movement of the immense majority, in the interest of the immense majority."[4] The result of the proletarian victory would be "an association in which the free development of each is the condition for the free development of all."[5] The victory of the proletariat over the bourgeoisie would represent the culmination of human history. For the first time in human history, one group of people would not be oppressing another. (See the Document, "Karl Marx and Friedrich Engels Describe the Class Struggle," page 667.)

The economic environment of the 1840s had conditioned Marx's analysis. The decade had seen much unemployment and deprivation. During the later part of the century, however, European and American capitalism did not collapse as he had predicted, nor did the middle class become proletarianized. Rather, the industrial system benefited more and more people. Nonetheless, within a generation of the publication of the *Communist Manifesto*, Marxism had captured the imagination of many socialists, especially in German-speaking Europe, and large segments of the working class. Marxist doctrines appeared to be based on the empirical evidence of hard economic fact. Marxism's scientific claim helped spread the ideology as science became more influential during the second half of the century. At its core, however, the attraction of the ideology was its utopian vision of ultimate human liberation, no matter how illiberal or authoritarian the governments that embraced the Marxist vision in the twentieth century were.

▼ 1848: Year of Revolutions

In 1848, a series of liberal and nationalist revolutions erupted across the Continent. (See Map 21–2, p. 668.) No single factor caused this general revolutionary groundswell; rather, similar conditions existed in several countries. News from other parts of Europe, however, influenced both the revolutionaries and the conservative forces who opposed them. Severe food shortages had prevailed since 1846. Grain and potato harvests had been poor. The famine in Ireland was simply the worst example of a more widespread situation. The commercial and industrial economy was also depressed. Unemployment was widespread. Systems of poor relief were overburdened. These difficulties, added to the wretched living

[4]Robert C. Tucker, ed., *The Marx-Engels Reader* (New York: W. W. Norton, 1972), p. 353.

[5]Tucker, *The Marx-Engels Reader*, p. 353.

Document

KARL MARX AND FRIEDRICH ENGELS DESCRIBE THE CLASS STRUGGLE

The Communist Manifesto *(1848) is arguably the most influential political pamphlet of modern European history. In that relatively brief document, Karl Marx and Friedrich Engels portrayed human history as developing from ancient times to the present through a series of economic class struggles. In the contemporary world, they saw the complex struggles of the past reduced to a head-on economic, political, and social clash between the bourgeoisie, or capital-owning class, and the proletariat, or workers. Both groups had emerged in the course of history. The bourgeoisie had arisen from medieval townsmen asserting their liberty against feudal landowners and then against other groups of aristocrats. In turn, as the bourgeoisie came to dominate the economy and invest their capital in modern industry, they produced the contemporary wage-labor force. Over time this labor force came to see that its interests opposed those of its economic masters. The result was to be the final class conflict of history because, as Marx and Engels argued, the proletariat, unlike any previous group seeking to establish its liberty, was so large that its victory was also the victory of humanity itself.*

Whom do Marx and Engels portray as the previous enemies of the bourgeoisie? How did bourgeois economic development and dominance lead to a society based on the "cash nexus"? Why is the bourgeoisie responsible for the emergence of the proletariat? Why is the victory of the proletariat inevitable?

The history of all hitherto existing society is the history of class struggles. . . .

Our epoch, the epoch of the bourgeoisie, possesses, however, this distinctive feature: it has simplified the class antagonisms. Society as a whole is more and more splitting up into two great hostile camps, into two great classes directly facing each other: Bourgeoisie and Proletariat. . . .

Each step in the development of the bourgeoisie was accompanied by a corresponding political advance of that class. . . .

The bourgeoisie, wherever it has gotten the upper hand, has put an end to all feudal, patriarchal, idyllic relations. It has pitilessly torn asunder the motley feudal ties that bound man to his "natural superiors," and has left remaining no other nexus between man and man than naked self-interest, than callous "cash payment.". . .

The proletariat goes through various stages of development. With its birth begins its struggle with the bourgeoisie. . . .

But with the development of industry the proletariat not only increases in number; it becomes concentrated in greater masses, its strength grows, and it feels that strength more. The various interests and conditions of life within the ranks of the proletariat are more and more equalized, in proportion as machinery obliterates all distinctions of labour, and nearly everywhere reduces wages to the same low level. . . .

The bourgeoisie finds itself involved in a constant battle. . . .

Of all the classes that stand face to face with the bourgeoisie today, the proletariat alone is a really revolutionary class. . . .

All previous historical movements were movements of minorities, or in the interest of minorities. The proletarian movement is the self-conscious, independent movement of the immense majority, in the interest of the immense majority. . . .

The advance of industry, whose involuntary promoter is the bourgeoisie, replaces the isolation of the labourers, due to competition, by their revolutionary combination, due to association. The development of Modern Industry, therefore, cuts from under its feet the very foundation on which the bourgeoisie produces and appropriates products. What the bourgeoisie, therefore, produces, above all, is its own grave-diggers. Its fall and the victory of the proletariat are equally inevitable. . . .

The proletarians have nothing to lose but their chains. They have a world to win.

From Karl Marx and Friedrich Engels, *The Communist Manifesto*, in Lawrence H. Simon, ed., *Karl Marx, Selected Writings* (Indianapolis, IN: Hackett Publishing Company, Inc., 1994), pp. 158, 159, 160, 161, 165, 166–167, 168, 169, 186.

Map 21–2 **CENTERS OF REVOLUTION IN 1848–1849** The revolution that toppled the July Monarchy in Paris in 1848 soon spread to Austria and many of the other German and Italian states. Yet by the end of 1849, most of these uprisings had been suppressed.

conditions in the cities and increasing doubts about the capabilities of various rulers, heightened the frustration and discontent of the urban artisan and laboring classes. People expected their governments to intervene to alleviate the economic crisis. Government inaction, either because of a principled opposition to intervention or because of confusion about what policies would help, fueled popular anger and a loss of faith in the wisdom and legitimacy of rule.

The dynamic force for change in 1848 originated, however, not with the working classes, but with the political liberals, who were generally drawn from the middle classes. Throughout the Continent, liberals were pushing for their program of a more representative government, civil liberty, and unregulated economic life. The repeal of the English Corn Laws and the example of peaceful agitation by the Anti–Corn Law League encouraged them. The liberals on the Continent wanted to pursue similar peaceful tactics. To put additional pressure on their governments, however, they began to appeal for the support of the urban working classes. The latter, however, wanted improved working and economic conditions, rather than a more liberal government. Moreover, their tactics were frequently violent rather than peaceful. The temporary alliance of liberals and workers in several states overthrew or severely shook the old order; then the allies began to fight each other.

Finally, outside France, nationalism was an important common factor in the uprisings. Germans, Hungarians, Italians, Czechs, and smaller national groups in eastern Europe sought to either create independent national states that would reorganize or replace existing political entities or, in some cases, achieve substantial national autonomy within larger empires. This brought them into conflict not only with existing states, but also with other nationalist movements. The Austrian Empire, as usual, was the state most profoundly endangered by nationalism.

The immediate results of the 1848 revolutions were stunning. Never in a single year had Europe known so many major uprisings. The French monarchy fell, and other thrones were shaken. Yet the revolutions proved to be a false spring for progressive Europeans. Without exception, the revolutions failed to establish genuinely liberal or national states. The conservative order proved stronger and more resilient than anyone had expected. Moreover, the liberal middle-class political activists in each country discovered they could no longer push for political reform without also raising the social question. The liberals refused to follow political revolution with social reform and thus isolated themselves from the working classes. Once separated from potential mass support, the liberal revolutions became easy prey for the armies of the reactionary classes.

France: The Second Republic and Louis Napoleon

As had happened twice before, the revolutionary tinder first blazed in Paris. The liberal political opponents of the corrupt regime of Louis Philippe and his minister Guizot organized a series of political banquets. They used these occasions to criticize the government and demand further admission for them and

During the February days of the French Revolution of 1848, crowds in Paris burned the throne of Louis Philippe. Bildarchiv Preussischer Kulturbesitz/Art Resource, NY

their middle-class supporters to the political process. The poor harvests of 1846 and 1847 and the resulting high food prices and unemployment brought working-class support to the liberal campaign. On February 21, 1848, the government forbade further banquets. A large one had been scheduled for the next day. On February 22, disgruntled Parisian workers paraded through the streets demanding reform and Guizot's ouster. The next morning the crowds grew, and by afternoon, Guizot had resigned. The crowds erected barricades, and numerous clashes occurred between the citizenry and the municipal guard. On February 24, 1848, Louis Philippe abdicated and fled to England.

The National Assembly and Paris Workers The liberal opposition, led by the poet Alphonse de Lamartine (1790–1869), organized a provisional government. The liberals intended to call an election for an assembly that would write a republican constitution. The various working-class groups in Paris, however, had other ideas: They wanted a social as well as a political revolution. Led by Louis Blanc, they demanded representation in the cabinet. Blanc and two other radical leaders became ministers. Under their pressure, the provisional government organized national workshops to provide work and relief for thousands of unemployed workers.

On Sunday, April 23, an election based on universal male suffrage chose the new National Assembly. The result was a legislature dominated by moderates and conservatives. In the French provinces, many people resented the Paris radicals and were frightened by their ideas. The church and the local notables still exercised considerable influence. Peasants feared that Parisian socialists would confiscate their small farms. The new conservative National Assembly had little sympathy for the expensive national workshops, which they incorrectly perceived to be socialistic.

Throughout May, government troops and the unemployed workers and artisans of Paris clashed. As a result, the assembly closed the workshops to new entrants and planned to eject many enrolled workers. By late June, barricades again appeared in Paris. On June 24, under orders from the government, General Louis Cavaignac (1802–1857), with troops drawn largely from the conservative countryside, moved to destroy the barricades and quell disturbances. During the next two days, more than four hundred people were killed. Thereafter, troops hunted down another 3,000 persons in street fighting. The drive for social revolution had ended.

Emergence of Louis Napoleon The so-called June Days confirmed the political predominance of conservative property holders in French life. They wanted a state that was safe for small property. Late in 1848, the election for president confirmed this search for social order. The new president was Louis Napoleon Bonaparte (1808–1873), a nephew of the great emperor. For most of his life, he had been an adventurer living outside of France. Twice he had attempted to lead a coup against the July Monarchy. The disorder of 1848 gave him a new opportunity to enter French political life. After the corruption of Louis Philippe and the turmoil of the early months of the Second Republic, the voters turned to the name of Bonaparte as a source of stability and greatness.

View the **Image** "Louis Napoleon v. General Cavaignac—British Cartoon, 1848" on **MyHistoryLab.com**

THE REVOLUTIONARY CRISIS OF 1848–1851

	1848
February 22–24	Revolution in Paris forces the abdication of Louis Philippe
February 26	National workshops established in Paris
March 3	Kossuth attacks the Habsburg domination of Hungary
March 13	Revolution in Vienna
March 15	The Habsburg emperor accepts the Hungarian March Revolution Laws
March 18	Frederick William IV of Prussia promises a constitution; revolt against Austria in Milan
March 19	Frederick William IV is forced to salute the corpses of slain revolutionaries in Berlin
March 22	Piedmont declares war on Austria
April 23	Election of the French National Assembly
May 15	Worker protests in Paris lead the National Assembly to close the national workshops
May 17	Habsburg emperor Ferdinand flees from Vienna to Innsbruck
May 18	The Frankfurt Assembly gathers to prepare a German constitution
June 2	Pan-Slavic Congress gathers in Prague
June 17	Austrian troops suppress a Czech revolution in Prague
June 23–26	Troops of the National Assembly suppress a workers' insurrection in Paris
July 24	Austria defeats Piedmont
September 17	General Jelačić invades Hungary
October 31	Vienna falls to General Windischgraetz
November 15	Papal minister Rossi is assassinated in Rome
November 16	Revolution in Rome
November 25	Pope Pius IX flees Rome
December 2	Habsburg Emperor Ferdinand abdicates and Francis Joseph becomes emperor
December 10	Louis Napoleon is elected president of the Second French Republic
	1849
January 5	General Windischgraetz occupies Budapest
February 2	The Roman Republic is proclaimed
March 12	War is resumed between Piedmont and Austria
March 23	Piedmont is defeated, and Charles Albert abdicates the crown of Piedmont in favor of Victor Emmanuel II
March 27	The Frankfurt Parliament completes a constitution for Germany
March 28	The Frankfurt Parliament elects Frederick William IV of Prussia to be emperor of Germany
April 21	Frederick William IV of Prussia rejects the crown offered by the Frankfurt Parliament
June 18	Troops disperse the remaining members of the Frankfurt Parliament
July 3	French troops overthrow the Roman Republic
August 9–13	Austria, aided by Russian troops, defeats the Hungarians
	1851
December 2	*Coup d'état* of Louis Napoleon

The election of the "Little Napoleon" doomed the Second Republic. Louis Napoleon was dedicated to his own fame rather than to republican institutions. He was the first of the modern dictators who, by playing on unstable politics and social insecurity, changed European life. He quarreled with the National Assembly and claimed that he, rather than they, represented the will of the nation. In 1851, the assembly refused to amend the constitution to allow the president to run for reelection. Consequently, on December 2, 1851, the anniversary of the great Napoleon's victory at Austerlitz, Louis Napoleon seized power. Troops dispersed the assembly, and the president called for new elections. More than two hundred people died resisting the coup, and more than 26,000 persons were arrested throughout the country. Almost 10,000 persons who opposed the coup were transported to Algeria.

Yet, in the plebiscite of December 21, 1851, more than 7.5 million voters supported the actions of Louis Napoleon and approved a new constitution that consolidated his power. Only about 600,000 citizens dared to vote against him. A year later, in December 1852, an empire was proclaimed, and Louis Napoleon became Emperor Napoleon III. Again a plebiscite approved the action. For the second time in just over fifty years, France had turned from republicanism to Caesarism.

Frenchwomen in 1848 The years between the February Revolution of 1848 and the Napoleonic coup of 1851 saw major feminist activity by Frenchwomen. Especially in Paris, women seized the opportunity of the collapse of the July Monarchy to voice demands for reform of their social conditions. They joined the wide variety of political clubs that emerged in the wake of the revolution. Some of these clubs emphasized women's rights. Some women even tried unsuccessfully to vote in the elections of 1848. Both middle-class and working-class women were involved in these activities. The most radical group of women called themselves the Vesuvians, after the volcano in Italy. They claimed it was time for the demands of women to erupt like pent-up lava. They demanded full domestic household equality between men and women,

Chez Aubert, Pl. de la Bourse
Camille, je vais au Club,
– Soignez le pot au feu et couchez ma fille de bonne heure ...... si elle crie, vous lui donnerez à téter. – Avec quoi, Bobonne? – Avec le biberon, imbécile! ....

Women who hoped the principles of 1848 would apply to their own political rights were sorely disappointed. Fear that women's political participation would lead to the emasculation of their husbands played into a strong backlash against nascent feminism. In this 1848 cartoon, a woman tells her husband she's going to the club, leaving him to care for their infant daughter. © Photos 12/Alamy

the right of women to serve in the military, and similarity in dress for both sexes. They also conducted street demonstrations. The radical character of their demands and actions lost them the support of more moderate women.

Certain Parisian women quickly attempted to use for their own cause the liberal freedoms that suddenly had become available. They organized the *Voix des femmes* (*The Women's Voice*), a daily newspaper that addressed issues of concern to women. The newspaper insisted that improving the lot of men would not necessarily improve the condition of women. They soon organized a society with the same name as the newspaper. Many of the women involved in the newspaper and society had earlier been involved in Saint-Simonian or Fourierist groups. Members of the *Voix des femmes* group were relatively conservative feminists. They cooperated with male political groups, and they urged the integrity of the family and fidelity in marriage. They furthermore warmly embraced the maternal role for women but tried to use it to raise the importance of women in society. Because motherhood and childrearing are so important to a society, they argued, women must receive better education, economic security, equal civil rights, property rights, and the rights to work and vote. The provisional government made no move to enact these rights, although some members of the assembly supported the women's groups. The emphasis on family and motherhood represented, in part, a defensive strategy to prevent conservative women and men from accusing the advocates of women's rights of seeking to destroy the family and traditional marriage.

The fate of French feminists in 1848 was similar to that of the radical workers. They were thoroughly defeated and their efforts wholly frustrated. Once the elections were held that spring, the new government expressed no sympathy for their causes. The closing of the national workshops adversely affected women workers as well as men and blocked one outlet that women had used to make their needs known. The conservative crackdown on political clubs closed another arena in which women had participated. Women were soon specifically forbidden to participate in political clubs either by themselves or with men. These repressive actions repeated what had happened to politically active Frenchwomen and their organizations in 1793.

At this point, women associated with the *Voix des femmes* attempted to organize workers' groups to improve the economic situation for working-class women. Two leaders of this effort, Jeanne Deroin (d. 1894) and Pauline Roland (1805–1852), were arrested, tried, and imprisoned for these activities. The former eventually left France; the latter was sent off to Algeria during the repression after the coup of Louis Napoleon. By 1852, the entire feminist movement that had sprung up in 1848 had been eradicated.

The Habsburg Empire: Nationalism Resisted

The events of February 1848 in Paris immediately reverberated throughout the Habsburg domains. The empire was susceptible to revolutionary challenge on every score. Its government rejected liberal institutions. Its borders cut across national lines that more people found meaningful than ever before. Its society perpetuated serfdom. In 1848, the regime confronted rebellions in Vienna, Prague, Hungary, and its Italian holdings. The disturbances that broke out in many German cities also threatened Habsburg predominance. In the initial months, rebels appeared to work together in their demands for reform. By the fall, however, fundamental differences in their priorities became apparent. While some demands focused on national autonomy, others concerned liberal political priorities, like a constitution. Workers' interest in

View the **Map** "The Nationalities of Austria-Hungary, 1867" on **MyHistoryLab.com**

radical social and economic change was not shared by liberal revolutionaries.

The Vienna Uprising The Habsburg troubles began on March 3, 1848, when Louis Kossuth (1802–1894), a Hungarian nationalist and member of the Hungarian diet, attacked Austrian domination, called for the independence of Hungary, and demanded a responsible ministry under the Habsburg dynasty. Ten days later, inspired by Kossuth's speeches, students led a series of disturbances in Vienna. The army failed to restore order. Metternich resigned and fled the country. The feeble-minded Emperor Ferdinand (r. 1835–1848) promised a moderately liberal constitution. Unsatisfied, the radical students then formed democratic clubs to press the revolution further. On May 17, the emperor and the imperial court fled to Innsbruck. The government of Vienna at this point lay in the hands of a committee of more than two hundred persons concerned primarily with alleviating the economic plight of the city's workers.

Read the Document "Metternich on the Revolutions of 1848" on **MyHistoryLab.com**

What the Habsburg government most feared was not the urban rebellions but an uprising of the serfs in the countryside. Already a few serfs had invaded manor houses and burned property records. Consequently, almost immediately after the Vienna uprising, the imperial government emancipated the serfs in much of Austria. The Hungarian diet also abolished serfdom in March 1848. These actions smothered the most serious potential threat to order in the empire. The emancipated serfs now had little reason to support the revolutionary movement in the cities. These emancipations were one of the most important permanent results of the Revolutions of 1848.

The Hungarian Revolt The Vienna revolt had emboldened the Hungarians. The Hungarian leaders of the March Revolution were primarily liberals supported by nobles who wanted their aristocratic liberties guaranteed against the central government in Vienna. The Hungarian diet passed the March Laws, which mandated equality of religion, jury trials, the election of the lower chamber of the diet, a relatively free press, and payment of taxes by the nobility. Emperor Ferdinand approved these measures because in the spring of 1848 he could do little else.

Hungarian nationalists also hoped to establish a separate Hungarian state within the Habsburg domains. They would exercise local autonomy while Ferdinand remained their emperor. As part of this scheme for a partially independent state, the Hungarians attempted to annex Transylvania, Croatia, and other eastern territories of the Habsburg Empire. That annexation would have brought Romanians, Croatians, and Serbs under Hungarian government. These national groups resisted the drive toward Magyarization (based on the Hungarian word for Hungarian, *Magyar*), especially the imposition on them, for the purposes of the government and administration, of the Hungarian language. The national groups whom the Hungarians were now repressing believed the Habsburgs offered them a better chance to preserve their national or ethnic identity, their languages, and their economic self-interest. In late March, the Vienna government sent Count Josip Jelačić (1801–1859) to aid the national groups who were rebelling against the rebellious Hungarians. By early September 1848, he was invading Hungary with the support of the national groups who were resisting Magyarization. These events in Hungary represented a prime example of the clash between liberalism and nationalism. The Hungarian March Laws

Louis Kossuth, a Hungarian nationalist, seeking to raise troops to fight for Hungarian independence during the revolutionary disturbances of 1848. Bildarchiv Preussischer Kulturbesitz/Art Resource, NY

would have created a state that was liberal in political structure but would not have allowed autonomy to non-Hungarian-speaking peoples within Hungary's borders.

Czech Nationalism In mid-March 1848, with Vienna and Budapest in revolt, Czech nationalists demanded that the Czech provinces of Bohemia and Moravia be permitted to constitute an autonomous Slavic state within the empire similar to that just enacted in Hungary. Conflict immediately developed, however, between the Czechs and the Germans living in these regions. The Czechs summoned a congress of Slavs, including Poles, Ruthenians, Czechs, Slovaks, Croats, Slovenes, and Serbs, which met in Prague in early June. Under the leadership of Francis Palacky (1798–1876), this first Pan-Slavic Congress called for the national equality of Slavs within the Habsburg Empire. The manifesto also protested the repression of all Slavic peoples under Habsburg, Hungarian, German, and Ottoman domination. It did not, however, call for the full political independence of the Slavic nations. Palacky was convinced that the Czechs, Poles, and other Slavs were too small and weak to defend themselves against an aggressive Russia. (See the Document, "A Czech Nationalist Defends the Austrian Empire," page 674.) If Pan-Slavism were allowed to develop far enough to create a vast east European Slavic nation or federation of Slavic states that would extend from Poland south and eastward through Ukraine, it was clear that Russian interests would surely dominate it. Although such a state never came into being, the prospect of a unified Slavic people freed from Ottoman, Habsburg, and German control was an important political factor in later European history. Despite the fear many non-Russian Slavs had of Russia, Russia would use **Pan-Slavism** as a tool to attempt to gain the support of nationalist minorities in eastern Europe and the Balkans and to bring pressure against both the Habsburg Empire and Germany.

On June 12, the day the Pan-Slavic Congress closed, a radical insurrection broke out in Prague. General Prince Alfred Windischgraetz (1787–1862), whose wife had been killed by a stray bullet, moved his troops against the uprising. The Prague middle class was happy to see the radicals suppressed, which was finalized by June 17. The Germans in the area approved the smothering of Czech nationalism. The policy of "divide and conquer" had succeeded.

Rebellion in Northern Italy While repelling the Hungarian and Czech bids for autonomy, the Habsburg government also faced war in northern Italy. A revolt against Habsburg domination began in Milan on March 18. Five days later, Austrian commander General Count Joseph Wenzel Radetzky (1766–1858) retreated from the city. King Charles Albert of Piedmont (r. 1831–1849), who wanted to annex Lombardy (the province of which Milan is the capital), aided the rebels. The Austrian forces fared badly until July, when Radetzky, reinforced by new troops, defeated Piedmont and suppressed the revolt. For the time being, Austria held its position in northern Italy.

Vienna and Hungary remained to be recaptured. In midsummer, the emperor returned to the capital. A newly elected assembly was trying to write a constitution, and within the city, the radicals continued to press for concessions. The imperial government decided to reassert its control. When a new insurrection occurred in October, the imperial army bombarded Vienna and crushed the revolt. On December 2, Emperor Ferdinand, clearly too feeble to govern, abdicated in favor of his young nephew Francis Joseph (r. 1848–1916). Real power now lay with Prince Felix Schwarzenberg (1800–1852), who intended to use the army with full force.

On January 5, 1849, troops occupied Budapest. By March the triumphant Austrian forces had imposed military rule over Hungary, and the new emperor repudiated the recent constitution. The Hungarian nobles attempted one last revolt. In August, Austrian troops, reinforced by 200,000 soldiers that Tsar Nicholas I of Russia (r. 1825–1855) happily furnished, finally crushed the Hungarians. Croatians and other nationalities that had resisted Magyarization welcomed the collapse of the revolt. The imperial Habsburg government survived its gravest internal challenge because of the divisions among its enemies and its own willingness to use military force with a vengeance.

Italy: Republicanism Defeated

The brief war between Piedmont and Austria in 1848 marked only the first stage of the Italian revolution. Many Italians hoped King Charles Albert of Piedmont would drive Austria from the peninsula and thus prepare the way for Italian unification. The defeat of Piedmont was a sharp disappointment to them. Liberal and nationalist hopes then shifted to the pope. Pius IX (r. 1846–1878) had a liberal reputation. He had reformed the administration of the Papal States. Nationalists believed a united Italian state might emerge under his leadership.

In Rome, however, as in other cities, political radicalism was on the rise. On November 15, 1848, a democratic radical assassinated Count Pelligrino Rossi (r. 1787–1848), the liberal minister of the Papal States. The next day, popular demonstrations forced the pope to appoint a radical ministry. Shortly thereafter, Pius IX fled to Naples for refuge. In February 1849, the radicals proclaimed the Roman Republic. Republican nationalists from all over Italy, including Giuseppe Mazzini (1805–1872) and Giuseppe Garibaldi (1807–1882), two of the most prominent, flocked to Rome. They hoped to use the new republic as a base of operations to unite the rest of Italy under a republican government.

Read the Document "Giuseppe Mazzini, *Life and Writings of Giuseppe Mazzini, 1805–1872*" on **MyHistoryLab.com**

Document

A Czech Nationalist Defends the Austrian Empire

Czech historian and linguist František Palacky (1798–1876) was invited to represent Bohemia at the Frankfurt Parliament in the spring of 1848 by German nationalists who did not consider Czechs to be members of a separate nation. In his letter of response, Palacky explained why he did not think Czechs were members of the German nation. First he distinguished an alliance of princes between a union of peoples—although Czechs had been ruled by German princes, this did not make the Czech people German themselves. Then he turned his attention to Austria. At the same time that he argued that only Austria could protect the small nations of Europe from Russian aggression, he insisted that Austrian policy toward minority nationalities must change. The German nation, he suggested, threatened Austria's integrity, and therefore the safety of the Czech nation.

How does Palacky's notion of the difference between a federation of princes and a unified nation reflect the new importance of popular nationalism? What threat from the East does Palacky fear? Why does he think the Austrian Empire is essential to European peace? What is the difference between the demands he makes of Austria and full independence for the Czech nation?

I can neither accept your invitation, gentleman, on my own behalf nor by delegating another "reliable patriot." Allow me to explain, as briefly as possible, my reasons.

The declared goal of your assembly is to substitute a confederation of the German nation for the hitherto existing confederation of princes, to bring the German nation to real unity, to strengthen German national feeling, and to thus increase Germany's internal and external power. . . .

I am not a German, at least I don't feel myself to be one. . . . I am a Bohemian of Slavic origin, and I have dedicated myself, with all the little I possess and am capable of, completely and forever to

In March 1849, radicals in Piedmont forced Charles Albert to renew the patriotic war against Austria. After the almost immediate defeat of Piedmont at the Battle of Novara, the king abdicated in favor of his son, Victor Emmanuel II (r. 1849–1878). The defeat meant the Roman Republic must defend itself alone. The troops that attacked Rome and restored the pope came from France. The French wanted to prevent the rise of a strong, unified state on their southern border. Moreover, protection of the pope was good domestic politics for the French Republic and its president, Louis Napoleon. In early June 1849, 10,000 French soldiers laid siege to Rome. By the end of the month, the Roman Republic had dissolved. Garibaldi attempted to lead an army north against Austria, but he was defeated. On July 3, Rome fell to the French forces, which stayed there to protect the pope until 1870.

Pius IX renounced his liberalism. He became one of the arch conservatives of the next quarter century. Leadership for Italian unification would have to come from another direction.

The German Confederation: Liberalism Frustrated

The revolutionary contagion had also spread rapidly through the German states. Insurrections calling for liberal government and greater German unity erupted in Wurtemburg, Saxony, Hanover, and Bavaria where King Ludwig I (r. 1825–1848) was forced to abdicate in favor of his son. The major revolution, however, occurred in Prussia. Prussia's king, Frederick William IV, had long opposed the introduction of any constitution.

Revolution in Prussia By March 15, 1848, large popular disturbances had erupted in Berlin. Frederick William IV (r. 1840–1861), believing the trouble stemmed from foreign conspirators, refused to turn his troops on the Berliners. He even announced limited reforms. Nevertheless, on March 18, several citizens were killed when troops cleared a square near the palace.

The monarch was still hesitant to use his troops forcefully, and the government was divided and confused. The

the service of my nation. That nation is admittedly a small one, but has always been a separate one, existing for itself; its rulers have participated in the confederation of German princes for centuries, but it never considered itself to be part of the German nation, and was never, at any point over the course of centuries, considered part of the German nation by others. The entire bond tying Bohemia first to the Holy Roman Empire and then to the German Confederation was always a purely dynastic one, of which the Bohemian nation, the Bohemian estates hardly took any notice. . . .

The second reason that prohibits me from participating in your proceedings is the fact that you, of necessity, both wish to and will fatally weaken Austria as an independent empire; yes, you will even render its existence impossible. [Austria is] a state whose preservation, integrity, and strengthening are and must be a primary and important matter not only for my own nation, but for all of Europe—yes even for all of humanity and civilization itself.

You know what Power holds the entire Eastern portion of our continent. . . . Since I, for all my love of my own nation, have always set the interests of humanity and science above those of nationality, there is no greater opponent and antagonist of even the mere possibility of a Russian universal monarchy than I—not because it would be Russian, but because it would be universal.

You know that the southeast of Europe, all along the border of the Russian Empire, is populated by many peoples who differ markedly in their origin, language, history, and culture—Slavs, Romanians, Hungarians, and Germans, not to mention Greeks, Turks, and Albanians—none of whom is, on its own, powerful enough to successfully resist their superior neighbor to the East for all time. That is something they can only do when united with one another by a firm bond. . . . Truly, if the Austrian state had not long since come into existence, one would have to create it as quickly as possible, in the interest of Europe, in the interest of humanity itself. . . .

Why, then, did we see this state in the critical moment . . . anchorless and well nigh helpless? Because [Austria], in unfortunate blindness, has for a long time failed to recognize and even denied the actual legal and moral foundation of its own existence: the basic principle of complete equality of rights and mutual regard for all the nationalities and religions united under its scepter. The law of nations is a true natural law. . . .

As soon as I direct my gaze beyond the borders of Bohemia, natural and historical considerations oblige me to look not towards Frankfurt but towards Vienna, and to seek there the center that is suited and destined to guarantee and protect the peace, freedom, and rights of my nation.

From František Palacky, "Eine Stimme über Österreichs Ansclụß an Deutschland," in *Oesterreichs Staatsidee* (Prague: J.L. Kober, 1866, 80–84). [Translation by Alison Frank]

king called for a Prussian constituent assembly to write a constitution. The next day, as angry Berliners crowded around the palace, Frederick William IV appeared on the balcony to salute the corpses of his slain subjects. He made further concessions and implied that henceforth Prussia would help unify Germany. For all practical purposes, the Prussian monarchy had capitulated.

Frederick William IV appointed a cabinet headed by David Hansemann (1790–1864), a widely respected moderate liberal. The Prussian constituent assembly, however, proved to be radical and democratic. As time passed, the king and his conservative supporters decided to ignore the assembly. The liberal ministry resigned and a conservative one replaced it. In April 1849, the assembly was dissolved, and the monarch proclaimed his own constitution. One of its key elements was a system of three-tier voting. All adult males were allowed to vote. They voted, however, according to three classes arranged by ability to pay taxes. Thus the largest taxpayers, who constituted only about 5 percent of the population, elected one-third of the Prussian Parliament. This system prevailed in Prussia until 1918. In the revised Prussian constitution of 1850, the ministry was responsible to the king alone. Moreover, the Prussian army and officer corps swore loyalty directly to the monarch.

The Frankfurt Parliament While Prussia was moving from revolution to reaction, other events were unfolding in the German Confederation as a whole. On May 18, 1848, representatives from all the German states gathered in Saint Paul's Church in Frankfurt to revise the organization of the German Confederation. The Frankfurt Parliament intended to write a moderately liberal constitution for a united Germany. The liberal character of the Frankfurt Parliament alienated both German conservatives and the German working class. The very existence of the parliament, representing as it did a challenge to the existing political order, offended the conservatives. The Frankfurt Parliament's refusal to restore the protection the guilds had once afforded cost it the support of the industrial workers and artisans. The liberals were too attached to the concept of a free labor market to offer meaningful legislation to workers. This failure marked the beginning of a profound split between German liberals and the German working class. For the rest of the century, German conservatives would be able to play on that division.

As if to demonstrate its disaffection from workers, in September 1848, the Frankfurt Parliament called in troops of the German Confederation to suppress a radical insurrection in the city. The liberals in the parliament wanted nothing to do with workers who erected barricades and threatened the safety of property.

The Frankfurt Parliament also floundered on the issue of unification. Members differed over whether to include Austria in a united Germany. The "large German [*grossdeutsch*] solution" favored Austria's inclusion, whereas the "small German [*kleindeutsch*] solution" advocated its exclusion. Although it was an uncle of the Austrian Emperor, Archduke John, who was asked to be regent of the German nation, the rest of the Habsburg dynasty rejected the whole notion of German unification, which raised too many other nationality problems within the Habsburg domains. Consequently, the Frankfurt Parliament looked to Prussian, rather than Austrian, leadership.

On March 27, 1849, the parliament produced its constitution. Shortly thereafter, its delegates offered the crown of a united Germany to Frederick William IV of Prussia. He rejected the offer, referring to the crown as a "dog collar" and asserting that kings ruled by the grace of God rather than by the permission of man-made constitutions. Upon his refusal, the Frankfurt Parliament began to dissolve. Not long afterward, troops drove off the remaining members.

German liberals never fully recovered from this defeat. The Frankfurt Parliament had alienated the artisans and the working class without gaining any compensating support from the conservatives. The liberals had proved themselves to be awkward, hesitant, unrealistic, and ultimately dependent on the armies of the monarchies. They had failed to unite Germany or to confront effectively the realities of political power in the German states. The various revolutions did manage to extend the franchise in some of the German states and to establish conservative constitutions. The gains were not negligible, but they were a far cry from the hopes of March 1848.

In Perspective

The first half of the nineteenth century witnessed unprecedented social change in Europe. The foundations of the industrial economy were laid. That emerging economy changed virtually every existing institution. Railways crossed the Continent. New consumer goods became available. Family patterns changed, as did the social and economic expectations of women. The crowding of cities presented new social and political problems. The new concern about crime and the establishment of police forces brought issues of social order to the foreground. An urban working class became one of the chief facts of both political and social life. The ebb and flow of the business cycle increased economic anxiety for workers and property owners alike.

While all these fundamental social changes took place, Europe was also experiencing continuing political strife. The turmoil of 1848 through 1850 ended the era of liberal revolution that had begun in 1789. Liberals and nationalists discovered that rational argument and small, local insurrections would not achieve their goals. The political initiative passed for a time to the conservative political groups. Henceforth, nationalists were less romantic and more hardheaded. Railways, commerce, guns, soldiers, and devious diplomacy, rather than language and cultural heritage, became the future weapons of national unification. The working class also adopted new tactics and a new organization. The era of the riot and urban insurrection was ending; in the future, workers would turn to trade unions and political parties to achieve their political and social goals.

Perhaps most importantly after 1848, the European middle class ceased to be revolutionary. It became increasingly concerned about protecting its property against radical political and social movements associated with socialism and, as the century passed, with Marxism. The middle class remained politically liberal only as long as liberalism seemed to promise economic stability and social security for its own style of life.

Finally, as will be seen more fully in the next chapter, the revolutions of 1848 also changed European conservatism. Metternich's conservative policies had not prevented the upheavals of 1848. In the following decades, European conservatives would find new ways to adapt some of the new forces of European politics to their ends. They would embrace their own forms of nationalism and even democratic structures to ensure that they remained dominant over much of Europe.

KEY TERMS

anarchists (p. 664)
Chartism (p. 651)
Corn Laws (p. 662)
Marxism (p. 664)
Pan-Slavism (p. 673)
utilitarianism (p. 662)
utopian socialists (p. 662)

REVIEW QUESTIONS

1. What inventions were particularly important in the development of industrialism? How did industrialism change society? Why were the years covered in this chapter so difficult for artisans? How was the European labor force transformed into a wage-labor workforce?
2. How did the industrial economy change the working-class family? What roles and duties did various family members assume? How did the role of women change in the new industrial era?
3. What were the goals of the working class in the new industrial society, and how did they differ from middle-class goals? Why did the working class and the middle class pursue different goals?
4. Why did European states create police forces in the nineteenth century? How and why did prisons change during this era?
5. How would you define socialism? What were the chief ideas of the early socialists? How did the ideas of Karl Marx differ from those of the socialists? What historical role did Marx assign to the proletariat?
6. What factors, old and new, led to the widespread outbreak of the revolutions in 1848? Were the causes in the various countries essentially the same, or did each have its own particular set of circumstances? Why did these revolutions fail throughout Europe? What roles did liberals and nationalists play in the revolutions? Why did they sometimes clash?

SUGGESTED READINGS

B. S. Anderson and J. P. Zinsser, *A History of Their Own: Women in Europe from Prehistory to the Present*, Vol. 2 (1988). A wide-ranging survey.

I. Berlin, *Karl Marx: His Life and Environment*, 4th ed. (1996). A classic introduction.

R. B. Carlisle, *The Proffered Crown: Saint-Simonianism and the Doctrine of Hope* (1987). The best treatment of the broad social doctrines of Saint-Simonianism.

J. Coffin, *The Politics of Women's Work* (1996). Examines the subject in France.

I. Deak, *The Lawful Revolution: Louis Kossuth and the Hungarians, 1848–1849* (1979). The most significant study of the topic in English.

R. J. Evans, *The Revolutions in Europe, 1848–1849: From Reform to Reaction* (2002). A series of essays by major experts.

J. F. C. Harrison, *Quest for the New Moral World: Robert Owen and the Owenites in Britain and America* (1969). The standard work.

D. I. Kertzer and M. Barbagli, eds., *Family Life in the Long Nineteenth Century, 1789–1913: The History of the European Family* (2002). Wide-ranging collection of essays.

K. Kolakowski, *Main Currents of Marxism: Its Rise, Growth, and Dissolution*, 3 vols. (1978). A classic, comprehensive survey.

D. Landes, *The Unbound Prometheus: Technological Change and Industrial Development in Western Europe from 1750 to the Present* (1969). Classic one-volume treatment of technological development in a broad social and economic context.

H. Perkin, *The Origins of Modern English Society, 1780–1880* (1969). A provocative attempt to look at the society as a whole.

J. D. Randers-Pehrson, *Germans and the Revolution of 1848–1849* (2001). An exhaustive treatment of the subject.

W. H. Sewell, Jr., *Work and Revolution in France: The Language of Labor from the Old Regime to 1848* (1980). A fine analysis of French artisans.

J. Sperber, *The European Revolution, 1841–1851* (2005). An excellent synthesis.

E. P. Thompson, *The Making of the English Working Class* (1964). A classic work.

F. Wheen, *Karl Marx: A Life* (2001). An accessible work that emphasizes the contradictions in Marx's career and personality.

D. Winch, *Riches and Poverty: An Intellectual History of Political Economy in Britain, 1750–1834* (1996). A superb survey from Adam Smith through Thomas Malthus.

MyHistoryLab™ MEDIA ASSIGNMENTS

Find these resources in the Media Assignments folder for Chapter 21 on **MyHistoryLab**.

QUESTIONS FOR ANALYSIS

1. What was the goal of the Great Exhibition?

    ***Section:* Family Structures and the Industrial Revolution**

    View the **Closer Look** The Great Exhibition in London, p. 655

2. What portions of Austria-Hungary appear most liable to fragmentation?

    Section: 1848: Year of Revolutions

    View the **Map** The Nationalities of Austria-Hungary, 1867, p. 671

3. What areas of Europe had the first railroad systems?

    ***Section:* Toward an Industrial Society**

    View the **Map** Interactive Map: Europe Industrialization, p. 647

4. Comparing this map to the map of industrialization in Europe, what correlations do you see?

Section: **Toward an Industrial Society**

View the Map Map Discovery: Population Growth in Europe, 1800–1850, p. 647

5. What influenced Mazzini in his life's work?

Section: **1848: Year of Revolutions**

Read the Document Giuseppe Mazzini, *Life and Writings of Giuseppe Mazzini, 1805–1872*, p. 673

OTHER RESOURCES FROM THIS CHAPTER

Toward an Industrial Society

View the Map Map Discovery: Great Britain: Railroads, ca. 1850, p. 648

The Labor Force

Read the Document Chartist Movement: The People's Petition of 1838, p. 651

Read the Compare and Connect Andrew Ure and John Ruskin Debate the Conditions of Factory Production, p. 652

Family Structures and the Industrial Revolution

Read the Document British Parliament, "Inquiry: Child Labor," p. 656

Women in the Early Industrial Revolution

Read the Document Industrial Society and Factory Conditions (early 1800s), p. 657

Problems of Crime, Order, and Poverty

Read the Document Leon Faucher, "Prison Rules," p. 661

Early Socialism

Read the Document Robert Owen, Excerpt from *Address to the Workers of New Lanark, 1816*, p. 663

Read the Document Capitalism Challenged: *The Communist Manifesto* (1848), p. 665

1848: Year of Revolutions

View the Image Louis Napoleon v. General Cavaignac—British Cartoon, 1848, p. 669

Read the Document Metternich on the Revolutions of 1848, p. 672

The Abolition of Slavery in the Transatlantic Economy

ONE OF THE most important developments during the age of Enlightenment and revolution was the opening of a crusade to abolish chattel slavery in the transatlantic economy. The antislavery movement constituted the greatest and most extensive achievement of liberal reformers during the eighteenth and nineteenth centuries. Indeed, it marked the first time in the history of the world that a society actually tried to abolish slavery. This achievement came as the result of the impact of Christian ethics, Enlightenment ideals, slave revolts, revolutionary wars in America and Europe, civil war in the United States, and economic dislocation in the slave economies themselves. In 1750, almost no one seriously questioned the existence of slavery, but, by 1888, the institution no longer existed in the transatlantic economy.

Chattel slavery—the ownership of one human being by another—had existed in the West as well as elsewhere in the world since ancient times and had received intellectual and religious justification throughout the history of the West. Both Plato and Aristotle provided arguments for slavery based on the assertion that persons in bondage were intended by nature to be slaves. Christian writers similarly accommodated themselves to the institution. They contended that the most harmful form of slavery was the enslavement of the soul to sin rather than the enslavement of the physical body. They also argued that genuine freedom was realized through one's relationship to God and that problems relating to the injustices of inequality would be solved in the hereafter. Christian scholastic thinkers in the Middle Ages portrayed slavery as part of the natural and necessary hierarchy of the universe.

Slavery Spreads to the Americas

A vast slave trade existed throughout the Mediterranean world through the end of the Middle Ages, but—to the extent that serfdom can be distinguished from slavery—slavery was no longer a dominant institution on the European continent or within the European economy. The European encounter with America at the end of the fifteenth century radically transformed this situation. The American continent and the West Indies presented opportunities for achieving great wealth, but a major labor shortage existed in these regions. Eventually slavery provided the means to resolve this labor shortage.

The establishment and maintenance of slavery in the transatlantic economy drew Europeans and Americans into various relationships with Africa. About the same time as the encounter with America, Europeans made contact with areas of West Africa where slavery already existed. This region became the chief source of slaves imported into the Americas. Four centuries later, during the antislavery movement, Europeans used their commitment to ending the African economy's dependence on the slave trade to justify imperialist intervention in the continent. Those efforts led to the penetration of Africa by European traders, missionaries, and finally colonial forces and administrators.

Although at one time or another slaves labored throughout the Americas, the system of slavery became primarily identified with the plantation economy stretching from Maryland south to Brazil, where tropical products, initially primarily sugar, were produced by slave labor. This plantation economy existed from approximately the late sixteenth through the late nineteenth centuries. The slaves on whose labor this economy was based included Native Americans enslaved within both the Spanish Empire and North America, and Africans forcibly imported into the Americas. Slaves were virtually always defined by their masters as belonging to a different race, even if one of their parents was a slaveholder. Race itself soon became part of the justification for the social hierarchy of the plantation world. In and of itself, the fact of slavery in the Americas was not unusual to the Western experience or to that of other societies in Africa or Asia. Slavery had existed at most times and places in human history. Far more unusual in the history of the West, and for that matter in the experience of all other societies that had held and continued to hold slaves, was the emergence after 1760 of an international movement to abolish chattel slavery in the transatlantic economy.

The Crusade Against Slavery

The eighteenth-century crusade against slavery originated in a profound change in the religious and intellectual outlooks on slavery among small but influential groups in both America and Europe. The entire thrust of Enlightenment reasoning to the extent that it challenged or questioned the wisdom of existing institutions gnawed away at the older defenses of slavery, most particularly the concept of an unchanging social hierarchy. Although some writers associated with the Enlightenment, including John Locke, were reluctant to question slavery and even defended it, the general Enlightenment rhetoric of equality stood in sharp contrast to the radical inequality of slavery. Montesquieu sharply satirized slavery in *The Spirit of the Laws* (1748). Similarly, the emphasis of Adam Smith in *The Wealth of Nations* (1776) on free labor and efficiency of free markets undermined defenses of slavery.

Within much eighteenth-century literature, there emerged a tendency to idealize primitive peoples living in cultures very different from those of Europe. Previously such peoples had been regarded as backward and rebellious. Now numerous writers portrayed them as embodying a lost human virtue. This expanding body of literature transformed the way many people thought about slavery and allowed some Europeans to look on African slaves in the Americas as having been betrayed and robbed of an original innocence. Additionally, much eighteenth-century European ethical thinking, as well as later romantic poetry, emphasized empathy and feeling. In such a climate, attitudes toward slavery were transformed. Once considered to be the natural and deserved result of some deficiency in slaves themselves, slavery now grew to be regarded as undeserved and unacceptable. The same kind of ethical thinking led reformers to believe that by working against slavery, for virtually the first time defined as an unmitigated evil, they would realize their own highest ethical character.

Religious movements became the single most important cultural force to foster the antislavery crusade. The evangelical religious revival associated with Methodism and with other forms of Protestant preaching emphasized the conversion experience and the change of heart as a sign of having received salvation. In 1774, John Wesley, the founder of Methodism, attacked slaveholding in *Thoughts on Slavery*. Turning against slaveholding and slave trading by plantation owners and slave traders served to illustrate one clear example of such a change of heart. Some slaveholders and slave traders feared they might be endangering their own salvation by their association with the institution. John Newton, a former slave trader who underwent an evangelical conversion, wrote the hymn "Amazing Grace."

The initial religious protest against slavery originated among English Quakers, a radical Protestant religious group founded by George Fox in the seventeenth century. By the early eighteenth century, it had solidified itself into a small but relatively wealthy sect in England. Members of Quaker congregations at that time actually owned slaves in the West Indies and participated in the transatlantic slave trade. During the Seven Years' War (1756–1763), however, many Quakers experienced economic hardship. Furthermore, the war created other difficulties for the English population as a whole. Certain Quakers decided the presence of the evil of slavery in the world explained these troubles. They then sought to remove this evil from their own lives and that of their congregations and began to take action against the whole system of slavery that characterized the transatlantic economy.

Just as the slave system was a transatlantic affair, so was the crusade against it. Quakers in both Philadelphia and England soon moved against the institution. The most influential of the early antislavery writers was Anthony Benezet, a Philadelphia Quaker, whose most important publications were *Some Considerations on the Keeping of Negroes* (1754) and *A Short Account of That Part of Africa Inhabited by the Negroes* (1762). The latter work emphasized the manner in which the slave trade degraded African society itself. Benezet also drew heavily on Montesquieu. This may not be

After 1833, the British Royal Navy patrolled the African coasts attempting to intercept slave-trading ships. In 1868, the British ship HMS *Daphne* captured a slaving ship and freed the slaves. A British lieutenant, John Armstrong Challice, included photographs of the freed slaves in his report to the Foreign Office as part of his efforts to apply pressure to ending the slave trade out of Zanzibar. National Archives (UK) Catalogue reference: FO 84/1310 (b)

surprising because Enlightenment writers often admired the English Quakers as exemplifying a religion of tolerance and reason.

By the earliest stages of the American Revolution a small group of reformers, normally spearheaded by Quakers, had established an antislavery network. They published pamphlets, sermons, and books on the subject. The Society for the Relief of Free Negroes Illegally Held in Bondage, the first antislavery society in the world, was founded in Philadelphia in 1775 and, when reorganized in 1784 as the Pennsylvania Abolition Society, Benjamin Franklin became its president. In 1787, the Committee for the Abolition of the Slave Trade was organized in England. In France, the Société des Amis des Noirs was founded in 1778.

The turmoil of the American Revolution and the founding of the American republic gave these groups the occasion for some of their earliest successes. Emancipation gradually, but nonetheless steadily, spread among the northern states. In 1787, the Continental Congress forbade the presence of slavery in the newly organized Northwest Territory north of the Ohio River. What is important so far as the crusade against slavery is concerned is the disappearance of slavery in approximately half of the new nation and the commitment not to extend it to an important new territory. Despite these American developments, Great Britain became and remained the center for the antislavery movement. In 1772, a decision by the chief justice affirmed that slaves brought into Great Britain could not forcibly be removed. The decision, though of less immediate importance than some thought at the time, gave further impetus to the small but growing group of antislavery reformers.

During the early 1780s, the antislavery reformers in Great Britain decided to work toward ending the slave trade rather than the institution of slavery. The horrors of the slave trade caught the public's attention in 1783 when the captain of the slave ship *Zong* threw more than 130 slaves overboard in order to collect insurance. For the reformers, attacking the trade rather than the institution appeared a less radical and a more achievable reform. To many, the slave trade appeared to be a more obvious crime than the holding of slaves, which seemed a more nearly passive act. Furthermore, attacking slavery itself involved serious issues of property rights that might alienate potential supporters of the abolition of the slave trade. The antislavery groups also believed that if the trade was ended, planters would have to treat their remaining slaves more humanely.

By the end of the 1780s, the English Quakers were joined by evangelical Christians from the Church of England to form the Society for the Abolition of the Slave Trade. The most famous of the new leaders was William Wilberforce who, for the rest of his life, fought the slave trade. Year after year, he introduced a bill to abolish the slave trade. Finally, in 1807, he saw it passed.

Slave Revolts

While the British reformers worked for the abolition of the slave trade, slaves themselves in certain areas took matters into their own hands. The largest emancipation of slaves to occur in the eighteenth century came on the island of Saint Domingue (Haiti), France's wealthiest colony, as a result of the slave revolt of 1794 led by Toussaint L'Ouverture and Jean-Jacques Dessalines. The revolt in Haiti and Haiti's eventual independence in 1804 stood as a warning to slave owners throughout the West Indies. (See Chapter 19.) There would be other slave revolts such as those in Virginia led by Gabriel Prosser in

The slave revolt on the French island of St. Domingue achieved the largest emancipation of slaves in the eighteenth century. In this print, Toussaint L'Ouverture leads the revolt. CORBIS/Bettmann

1800 and by Nat Turner in 1831, in South Carolina led by Denmark Vesey in 1822, in British-controlled Demarra in 1823 and 1824, and in Jamaica in 1831. Each of these was brutally suppressed.

Economic Pressures

Through the conclusion of the Seven Years' War, the West Indies interest group had been one of the most powerful in the British Parliament. During the second half of the eighteenth century and beyond, new and different economic interest groups began to displace the influence of that group. Within the West Indies themselves the planters were experiencing soil exhaustion and new competition from newly tilled islands controlled by France and other new islands opened for sugar cultivation. Some older plantations were being abandoned while others operated with low profitability. Now with the new islands under cultivation there was a glut of sugar on the market, and as a consequence the price was falling.

Under these conditions some British West Indies planters, for reasons that had nothing to do with religion or humanitarianism, began to favor curtailing the slave trade. Without new slaves, French planters would lack the labor they needed to exploit their islands. During the Napoleonic Wars, the British captured a number of the valuable French islands. In order to protect the planters on the older British West Indies islands, in 1805, the British cabinet issued Orders in Council, which forbade the importation of slaves into the newly acquired French islands. By 1807, the abolition sentiment was strong enough for Parliament to pass Wilberforce's measure prohibiting slave trading from any British port.

The suppression of this trade through the navy became one of the fundamental pillars of nineteenth-century British foreign policy. Throughout the rest of the Napoleonic era the British attempted to draw allies into a policy of forbidding the slave trade. They also attempted unsuccessfully to incorporate the abolition of the slave trade into the settlement of the Congress of Vienna. In addition, the British navy maintained squadrons of ships around the coast of West Africa to halt slave traders. Although the French and Americans also patrolled the West African coast, neither was deeply committed to ending the slave trade. Nonetheless, in 1824, the American Congress made slave trading a capital offense.

The French invasion of Spain in 1808, as discussed in Chapter 20, provided the spark for the Latin American wars of independence. The leaders of these movements had been influenced by the liberal ideas of the Enlightenment and were, thus, generally predisposed to disapprove of slavery. The political groups seeking independence from Spain also sought the support of slaves by promises of emancipation. Furthermore, the newly independent nations needed good relations with Britain to support their economies, and, consequently, most of them very quickly freed their slaves to gain such support. The actual freeing of slaves was gradual and often came some years after the emancipation legislation. In Brazil, slavery continued into the 1880s. Except for Brazil, slavery would gradually disappear by approximately the middle of the nineteenth century from all of the newly independent nations of Latin America.

Abolishing Slavery in the New World

British reformers gradually recognized that the abolition of the slave trade had not actually improved the lot of slaves. In 1823, they adopted as a new goal the gradual emancipation of slaves. The chief voices calling for this change were those of William Wilberforce and Thomas Clarkson, who were active in founding the Abolition Society. The savagery with which West Indian planters put down slave revolts in 1823 and 1824 and again in 1831 strengthened the resolve of the antislavery reformers. By 1830, the reformers had abandoned the goal of gradual abolition and demanded the complete abolition of slavery. In 1833, after the passage of the Reform Bill in Great Britain, they achieved that goal when Parliament abolished the right of British subjects to hold slaves. In the British West Indies, 750,000 slaves were freed within a few years.

The other old colonial powers in the New World tended to be much slower in their own abolition of slavery. Portugal did little or nothing about slavery in Brazil, and when that nation became independent of Portugal, its new government continued slavery. Portugal ended slavery elsewhere in its American possessions in 1836; the Swedes, in 1847; the Danes, in 1848; but the Dutch not until 1863. France had witnessed a significant antislavery movement throughout the first half of the century, but slavery was not abolished in its West Indian possessions until the revolution of 1848.

During the first thirty years of the nineteenth century, the institution of slavery revived and achieved strong new footholds in the transatlantic world. These areas were the lower south of the United States for the cultivation of cotton, Brazil for the cultivation of coffee, and Cuba for the cultivation of sugar. World demand for these products made the slave system economically viable in these regions. Consequently, despite the drive to emancipation, which had succeeded in the northern states of the United States, slavery persisted in much of the Caribbean and in most of Latin America.

An antislavery movement had existed in the United States since the end of the eighteenth century, but it took on a new life in the early 1830s. The British abolition of slavery in the West Indies served as an inspiration to a new generation of American antislavery leaders, the most famous of whom was William Lloyd Garrison. He and other American abolitionists raised the question of slavery throughout the 1830s and 1840s. It was, however, the disposition of lands the United States had acquired in the Mexican War of 1847 that placed slavery at the heart of the American political debate. For over a decade the question of slavery sharply divided Americans. The election of Lincoln in 1860 brought those sectional tensions to a head, and the American Civil War erupted in the spring of 1861. In 1863, Lincoln issued the Emancipation Proclamation, which ended slavery in the combatant states. The passage of the Thirteenth Amendment to the American Constitution in 1865 abolished slavery in the United States.

The end of slavery in the United Sates left both Cuba, the most important remaining possession of the Spanish Empire in the Americas, and Brazil with slave economies. In 1868, an insurgency against Spanish colonial policy broke out in Cuba and lasted for ten years. This war disrupted much of the Cuban economy and saw some planters move toward using free labor. The Spanish forces attacked other planters by freeing their slaves. In 1870, the Spanish government passed a measure for gradual emancipation of slaves in both Cuba and Puerto Rico. In subsequent years, the sugar economy collapsed, making slavery unprofitable. Abolitionist agitation grew in Spain, and slavery was abolished in its New World colonies in 1886.

Brazil, under British pressure, had effectively ended the slave trade in 1850, but the question of the abolition of slavery was postponed for many years. In 1871, as a result of abolitionist agitation and because the Emperor Pedro II opposed slavery, a law providing for an extremely gradual abolition of slavery was passed. During the next two decades, abolitionist sentiment grew, and public figures from across the political spectrum voiced opposition to slavery. In 1888, Isabel Christiana, then regent while her father Pedro II was in Europe for medical treatment, signed a law abolishing slavery in Brazil without any form of compensation to the slave owners.

The abolition of slavery in Brazil ended a system of forced labor that had characterized the transatlantic economy for almost four hundred years. Wherever slavery had existed, however, its presence left and would continue to leave long-term consequences for the realization of equality and social justice. The end of slavery, consequently, did not end the problems that slavery created in the transatlantic world.

Africa and the End of Slavery

The transatlantic slave trade itself had adversely affected the life of Africa both through the vast loss of population over the centuries as well as through the undermining of African society through the internal slave trade. Similarly, the crusade against transatlantic slavery had drawn Europeans much more deeply into the affairs of the African continent. The various efforts by antislavery groups began to impact Africa in the first half of the nineteenth century. Their goal was to transform the African economy by substituting new peaceful trade in tropical goods for the slave trade. The reformers hoped to spread both free trade and Christianity into Africa. "Christianity and civilization" and "Christianity and commerce" were popular slogans of the day. Missionaries and traders saw themselves as natural allies in the cause.

The first effort in this direction was the resettlement of black slaves or children of black slaves into Africa. In 1787, the British established a colony of poor free blacks from Britain in Sierra Leone. The effort went badly, but a few years later former slaves once owned by British loyalists in America were settled there. Then former slaves from the Caribbean were brought to Sierra Leone. The colony became relatively successful only after 1807, when the British navy landed slaves rescued from captured slave trading ships. Sierra Leone, though quite small, became a place on the coast of West Africa where Christianity and commerce rather than the slave trade flourished. The French established a smaller experiment at Libreville in Gabon. The most famous and lasting attempt to resettle former black slaves in Africa was the establishment of Liberia by the efforts of the American Colonization Society after 1817. Liberia became an independent republic in 1847. All these efforts to move former slaves back to Africa had only modest success, but they did affect the life of West Africa.

Other antislavery reformers were less interested in establishing outposts for the settlement of former slaves than in transforming the African economy itself. In 1841, the African Civilization Society under the leadership of Thomas Fowell Buxton sent a group of paddle steamers up the Niger River in the hope of creating the basis for new trade with Africa. The goal was to establish free trade between Britain and Africa in which the manufactured goods of the former, most particularly textiles, would be exchanged for tropical agricultural goods produced by Africans. The expedition failed because most of its members died of disease. Yet the impulse to penetrate Africa for purposes of spreading trade and Christianity would continue for the rest of the century.

The antislavery movement marked the first of the intrusions of the European powers well beyond the coast of West Africa into the heart of the continent. After the American Civil War finally halted any large-scale demand for slaves from Africa, the antislavery reformers began to focus on ending the slave trade in East Africa and the Indian Ocean. This drive against slavery and the slave trade in Africa itself became one of the rationales for European interference in Africa during the second half of the nineteenth century and served as one of the foundations for the establishment of the late-century colonial empires.

The crusade against slavery in the transatlantic economy eventually touched most of the world. It radically transformed the economies and societies of both North and South America. It led to a transformation of the African economy and eventually to a significant European presence in the life of African societies. Efforts to eradicate slavery, particularly the efforts by British reformers, caused the spread of the reform movement into Asia. Slavery has not been abolished throughout the world, and antislavery societies still exist, though they receive little publicity. Yet the abolition of slavery in the transatlantic world stands as one of the most permanent achievements of the forces of eighteenth-century Enlightenment and revolution.

What were the justifications of slavery prior to the eighteenth century? What religious and intellectual developments led some Europeans and some Americans to question and criticize the institution of slavery? Why did antislavery reformers first concentrate on the abolition of the slave trade? How did both slavery and antislavery lead Americans and Europeans to become involved with Africa? How did that involvement change between approximately 1600 and 1870?

Watch the Video Atlantic Connections: Sugar, Smallpox and Slavery on **MyHistoryLab.com**

View the Closer Look African Slaves in America on **MyHistoryLab.com**

View the Closer Look The Slave Ship Brookes on **MyHistoryLab.com**

William I, the new emperor of Germany, lays the cornerstone of the Reichstag (German parliament) building in Berlin. Although William I was head of state, it is Bismarck who stands out, as usual, in his white uniform. ullstein bild/The Granger Collection, NYC—

Listen to the **Chapter Audio** on **MyHistoryLab.com**

22 The Age of Nation-States

▼ **The Crimean War (1853–1856)**
Peace Settlement and Long-Term Results

▼ **Reforms in the Ottoman Empire**

▼ **Italian Unification**
Romantic Republicans • Cavour's Policy • The New Italian State

▼ **German Unification**
Bismarck • The Franco-Prussian War and the German Empire (1870–1871)

▼ **France: From Liberal Empire to the Third Republic**
The Paris Commune • The Third Republic

▼ **The Habsburg Empire**
Formation of the Dual Monarchy • Unrest of Nationalities

▼ **Russia: Emancipation and Revolutionary Stirrings**
Reforms of Alexander II • Revolutionaries

▼ **Great Britain: Toward Democracy**
The Second Reform Act (1867) • Gladstone's Great Ministry (1868–1874) • Disraeli in Office (1874–1880) • The Irish Question

▼ **In Perspective**

LEARNING OBJECTIVES

Why was the Crimean War fought?

How did the Ottoman Empire attempt to reform itself?

How did Italy achieve unification?

How did Bismarck use war as a tool for achieving German unification?

What event led to the establishment of a Third Republic in France?

Why was nationalism such a threat to the Habsburg Empire?

Why did reform in Russia fail to produce political stability?

What forces led to the expansion of democracy in Great Britain?

THE REVOLUTIONS OF 1848 collapsed in defeat for both liberalism and nationalism. In the 1850s, conservative regimes were entrenched across the Continent. Yet only a quarter century later, many of the major goals of early-nineteenth-century liberals and nationalists appeared to have been reached. Italy and Germany were each united under constitutional monarchies, albeit conservative ones. The Habsburg emperor accepted constitutional government and granted wide-ranging autonomy to Hungary. In Russia, the tsar emancipated the serfs. France had become a republic. Liberalism and even democracy flourished in Great Britain. The Ottoman Empire also undertook major reforms.

Paradoxically, most of these developments occurred under conservative political leadership. War and competition with other states compelled some governments to pursue new policies at home as well as abroad. They had to find novel methods to maintain the loyalty of their subjects. Some conservative leaders preferred to carry out a popular policy on their own terms so that they, rather than the liberals, would receive credit. Other leaders acted as they did because they had no choice. Across Europe, the franchise was extended to an ever larger number of men, irrespective of their income. Political rights became increasingly linked to adulthood and manhood, rather than status, inherited privilege, or wealth.

▼ The Crimean War (1853–1856)

As has so often been true in modern European history, the impetus for change originated in war. The Crimean War (1853–1856) was rooted in the long-standing desire of Russia to extend its influence over the Ottoman Empire (see Map 22–1). Two disputes led to the conflict. First, as noted in Chapter 17, the Russians had, since the time of Catherine the Great (r. 1762–1796), been given protective oversight of Orthodox Christians in the Empire, and France had similar oversight of Roman Catholics. In 1851, yielding to French pressure, the Ottoman sultan had assigned care of certain holy places in Palestine to Roman Catholics. This decision angered the Russians and damaged Russian prestige. Second, Russia wanted to extend its control over the Ottoman provinces of Moldavia and Walachia (now in Romania). In the summer of 1853, the Russians used their right to protect Orthodox Christians in the Ottoman Empire as the pretext to occupy the two provinces. Shortly thereafter, the Ottoman Empire declared war on Russia.

View the **Map** "Map Discovery: The Crimean War, 1853–1856" on **MyHistoryLab.com**

Of far more significance to the great powers than the protection of Christian sites in Palestine was the fate of the weak Ottoman Empire. The Russian government envisioned the eventual breakup of the empire and hoped to extend its influence at Ottoman expense. France, Britain, and Austria, though recognizing the difficulties of the Ottoman government and using it to their own advantage when the opportunity presented itself, opposed Russian expansion in the eastern Mediterranean, where they had extensive naval and commercial interests. The French emperor Napoleon III (r. 1852–1870) also thought an activist foreign policy would shore up domestic support for his regime.

View the **Map** "The Decline of the Ottoman Empire, 1800–1913" on **MyHistoryLab.com**

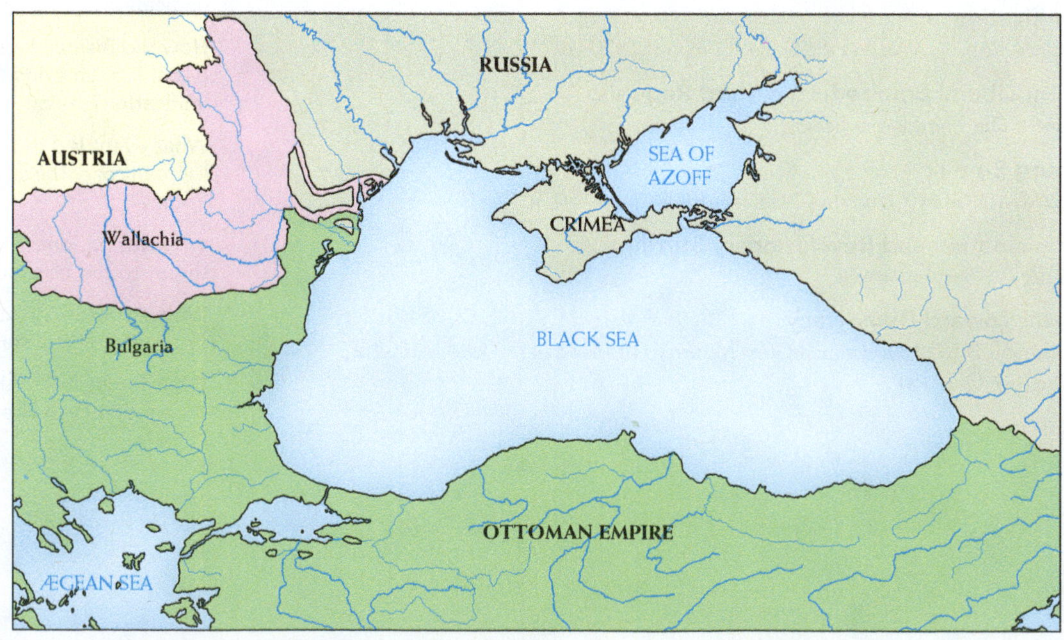

Map 22–1 **THE CRIMEAN WAR** Although named after the Crimean Peninsula, the Crimean War was actually fought across the entire northern and eastern coasts of the Black Sea.

In this painting, completed two decades after the war, Elizabeth Thomson, Lady Butler, emphasizes the suffering of ordinary troops as well as their comradeship. Lady Elizabeth Thompson Butler (1846–1933), *The Roll Call: Calling the Roll after an Engagement, Crimea.* The Royal Collection © 2005, Her Majesty Queen Elizabeth II. Photo by SC

On March 28, 1854, France and Britain declared war on Russia in alliance with the Ottomans. Much to the disappointment of Tsar Nicholas I, Austria and Prussia remained neutral. Prussia proceeded cautiously until its own foreign policy interest in the matter became clearer. Austria, concerned about its own interests in the Balkans, mobilized troops as a symbol of support of Britain and France's move, but did not declare war.

Both sides conducted the conflict ineptly, a fact that became widely known in Western Europe because the Crimean War was the first to be covered by war correspondents and photographers. The ill-equipped and poorly commanded armies became bogged down along the Crimean coast of the Black Sea. In March 1855, the Russian tsar Nicholas I died, and his son, Alexander II, took the throne. Alexander II was more open to ending the conflict than his father had been. In September 1855, after a long siege, the Russian fortress of Sevastopol fell to the French and British. Thereafter, both sides moved to end the war.

View the **Closer Look** "The Crimean War Recalled" on **MyHistoryLab.com**

Peace Settlement and Long-Term Results

In March 1856, a conference in Paris concluded the Treaty of Paris. This treaty required Russia to surrender territory near the mouth of the Danube River, to recognize the neutrality of the Black Sea, and to renounce its claims to protect Orthodox Christians in the Ottoman Empire. Even before the conference, Austria had forced Russia to withdraw from Moldavia and Walachia. The image of an invincible Russia that had prevailed across Europe since the close of the Napoleonic Wars was shattered. The new Russian tsar, Alexander II, undertook far-reaching reforms intended to address the fundamental weakness he believed the Crimean War had revealed. The Ottoman Empire over whose fate the Crimean War had been fought undertook reforms.

Also shattered was the Concert of Europe (see Chapter 20) as a means of dealing with international relations on the Continent. Following the successful repression of the 1848 uprisings, the great powers feared revolution less than they had earlier in the century, and, consequently, they displayed much less reverence for the Vienna settlement. As historian Gordon Craig put it, "After 1856, there were more powers willing to fight to overthrow the existing order than there were to take up arms to defend it."[1] As a result, for about twenty-five years after the Crimean War, European affairs were unstable, producing a period of adventurism in foreign policy. Although Russia was the formal loser of the Crimean War, in some ways it was Austria's position that was most fatefully weakened. Russia felt betrayed by Austria's lack of support following Russia's assistance in suppressing the Hungarian revolt of 1848–1849. The Western powers were not satisfied with Austria's half-hearted and noncommittal expressions of sympathy. Austria thus became isolated diplomatically, making it seem vulnerable to domestic political pressure.

[1]*The New Cambridge Modern History*, Vol. 10 (Cambridge, UK: Cambridge University Press, 1967), p. 273.

Reforms in the Ottoman Empire

The short-lived Napoleonic invasion of the Ottoman province of Egypt in 1798–1799 (see Chapter 19) sparked a drive for change in the Ottoman Empire. The Ottomans never gained true control over Egypt, and the viceroy of Egypt's own embrace of reform threatened to make Egypt an alternative source of power in the Eastern Mediterranean (see "A Closer Look: The Suez Canal," page 689). In 1839, under pressure from imperial bureaucrats who had studied in Europe, the Ottoman sultan issued a decree, called the *Hatt-i Sharif of Gülhane*, that attempted to reorganize the empire's administration and military along European lines. This decree opened what became known as the *Tanzimat* (meaning "reorganization") era of the Ottoman Empire, lasting from 1839 to 1876. The reforms, which were drawn up by administrative councils and not issued arbitrarily by the sultan, liberalized the economy, ended the practice of tax farming, and sought to eliminate corruption. The *Hatt-i Sharif* was particularly remarkable for extending civic equality to Ottoman subjects regardless of their religion. Muslims, Christians, and Jews were now equal before the law. The empire also made it much easier for Muslims to enter into commercial agreements with non-Muslims, both within the empire and from abroad.

Watch the Video "Video Lectures: The Ottoman Tanzimat Period (1839–1876): The Middle East Confronts Modernity" on **MyHistoryLab.com**

Another reform decree, called the *Hatti-i Hümayun*, was promulgated in 1856 at the close of the Crimean War. Under the influence of Britain and France, it spelled out the rights of non-Muslims more explicitly, giving them equal obligations with Muslims for military service and equal opportunity for state employment and admission to state schools. The decree also abolished torture and allowed foreigners to acquire some forms of property. In time, printing presses and Western-oriented schools appeared in the empire mainly via Christian missionaries, many of whom were Americans. For the first time in its long history, the Ottoman Empire actually sought to copy European legal and military institutions and the secular values flowing from liberalism.

The imperial government took these steps to gain the loyalty of its Christian subjects at a time when nationalism was making increasing inroads among them. In effect, during this reform era the Ottoman government broke down the millet system and sought to define all its citizens as Ottoman subjects rather than as members of particular religious communities.

Read the Document "An Ottoman Government Decree Defines the Official Notion of the 'Modern' Citizen, June 19, 1870" on **MyHistoryLab.com**

However, putting these reforms into practice proved difficult. In some regions of the empire, especially in Egypt and Tunis, local rulers were virtually independent of Istanbul. They carried out their own modernizing reforms, often working closely with European powers. In the capital itself, power struggles developed among courtiers, European-oriented administrators and army officers, merchants who prospered from the changes, and the *ulama*, which sought to maintain the rule of Islamic law. Because of these tensions, as well as growing nationalism in various regions, the Ottoman Empire failed to achieve genuine political strength and stability. Many Ottomans—including local leaders in parts of "European Turkey" like Bosnia—questioned the wisdom of Tanzimat and warned that replacing long-standing Islamic institutions with European ones would lead to disaster.

The Balkan wars of the late 1870s, which resulted in either the independence of, or Russian or Austrian

Ottoman reformers established a parliament in 1877, but the sultan retained most political authority. *Illustrated London News* of April 14, 1877. Mary Evans Picture Library Ltd.

View the Closer Look on MyHistoryLab.com

THE SUEZ CANAL

UNTIL THE third quarter of the nineteenth century, ships sailing between the Indian Ocean and the Mediterranean Sea or Atlantic Ocean had to navigate all the way around Africa, or to portage their goods overland across the Suez Isthmus, which separated the Red Sea from the Mediterranean Sea. In the mid-1850s, the viceroy of Egypt agreed to a bold plan: the Frenchman Ferdinand de Lesseps, using plans drawn up by Tyrolian engineer Alois Negrelli, proposed to dig a canal across the isthmus and open it to traffic from all nations. The canal's construction began in 1859, and was completed ten years later. The construction of the canal came to symbolize European technological superiority at the same time that British critics condemned Egypt's use of slave labor. In promoting the canal, Ferdinand Lesseps said that anyone "preoccupied with questions of civilization and progress cannot look at a map and not be seized with a powerful desire to make disappear the only obstacle interfering with the flow of the commerce of the world."[1]

The canal, although not yet completed in 1864, is portrayed as if already busy with traffic. From the start, the project was characterized by great optimism and faith in the inevitable progress, despite financial difficulties that plagued its backers and the opposition of Great Britain to the whole undertaking.

Port Said, to the left, was a new city constructed to manage exports out of the canal.

The artist ignores classic rules of perspective in order to portray an image of the canal that emphasizes the grandeur of scale.

The rocks in the foreground emphasize the obstacles to transit. The travelers riding on camels suggest the slow progress of overland transportation.

Albert Rieger (1832–1905), *The Suez Canal* (1864; oil on canvas). Museo Civico Rivoltello, Trieste, Italy/ Alinari/The Bridgeman Art Library International

This painting was commissioned by a financial backer of the Suez Canal. How does the image serve to promote the canal?

What sort of image of Egypt does this painting evoke? How is it consistent or inconsistent with reforms sweeping across the Ottoman Empire in this time period?

[1]Zachary Karabell, *Parting the Desert: The Creation of the Suez Canal* (New York: Knopf, 2003), p. 78.

dominance over, most of the empire's European holdings, demonstrated the inability of the Ottoman Empire to master its own destiny. (See Chapter 26.) The response to these foreign defeats resulted in greater efforts to modernize the army and the economy and to build railways and telegraphs. In 1876, reformers persuaded the sultan to proclaim an Ottoman constitution on the grounds that European political arrangements as well as technology accounted for European strength. The constitution called for a parliament consisting of an elected chamber of deputies and an appointed senate (these met for the first time in 1877) but left the sultan's power mostly intact. Nonetheless, a new sultan soon rejected even these limited steps toward constitutionalism and dismissed the parliament. In 1908, military officers carried out a revolution against the authority, though not the person, of the sultan. Another group of reformist officers, known as the *Young Turks*, came to the fore with another program to modernize the empire. They were still in charge when World War I broke out, and their decision to enter the war on the side of the Central Powers in November 1914 led to the empire's defeat and collapse. (See Chapter 26.)

One of the underlying themes of all these attempts at reform and modernization from 1839 to 1914 was the increasing secularization of the government, which sought less to question the Islamic foundations of society than to reduce the influence of the Muslim religious authorities on the state.

Italian Unification

In the mid-nineteenth century, the Italian peninsula consisted of nearly a dozen independent states, many of them under the direct or indirect rule of the Habsburgs. Nationalists had long wanted to unite the small, mostly absolutist principalities of the Italian peninsula into a single state. During the first half of the century, however, opinion differed about how to achieve Italian unification.

View the **Map** "The Unification of Italy, 1859–1870" on **MyHistoryLab.com**

Romantic Republicans

One approach to the issue was *romantic republicanism*. After the Congress of Vienna, secret republican societies were founded throughout Italy, the most famous of which was the Carbonari ("charcoal burners"). They were widely feared, but ineffective.

After the failure of nationalist uprisings in Italy in 1831, the leadership of romantic republican nationalism passed to Giuseppe Mazzini (1805–1872). He became the most important nationalist leader in Europe and brought new fervor to the cause. He once declared, "Nationality is the role assigned by God to a people in the work of humanity. It is its mission, its task on earth, to the end that God's thought may be realized in the world."[2] In 1831, he founded the Young Italy Society to drive Austria from the peninsula and establish an Italian republic.

During the 1830s and 1840s, Mazzini and his fellow republican Giuseppe Garibaldi (1807–1882) led insurrections. Both were involved in the ill-fated Roman Republic of 1849. Throughout the 1850s, they continued to conduct what amounted to guerrilla warfare. Because both men spent much time in exile, they became well known across the Continent and in the United States.

Republican nationalism frightened moderate Italians, who wanted to rid themselves of Austrian domination but not to establish a republic. For a time, these people had hoped the papacy would sponsor unification. That solution became impossible after the experience of Pius IX with the Roman Republic in 1849. Consequently, at midcentury, "Italy" remained, in the words of the Austrian foreign minister, Prince Metternich, "a geographical expression" rather than a political entity.

Yet by 1860, the Italian peninsula was transformed into a nation-state under a constitutional monarchy. Count Camillo Cavour (1810–1861), the prime minister of Piedmont—not romantic republicans—made this possible. His method was to combine force of arms with secret diplomacy.

Cavour's Policy

Piedmont (officially styled the Kingdom of Sardinia), in northwestern Italy, was the most independent state on the peninsula. The Congress of Vienna had restored the kingdom as a buffer between French and Austrian ambitions. During 1848 and 1849, King Charles Albert of Piedmont, after having promulgated a conservative constitution, twice fought Austria unsuccessfully (see Chapter 21). After the second defeat, he abdicated in favor of his son, Victor Emmanuel I (r. 1849–1878). In 1852, the new monarch chose Cavour as his prime minister.

A cunning statesman, Cavour had begun political life as a conservative but had gradually moved toward a moderately liberal position. He had made a fortune by investing in railroads, reforming agriculture on his estates, and editing a newspaper. He was deeply imbued with the ideas of the Enlightenment, classical economics, and utilitarianism. Cavour was a nationalist of a new breed who had no respect for Mazzini's ideals. A strong monarchist, Cavour rejected republicanism. He favored a unified state on the Italian peninsula because he believed it was necessary for economic and material progress, not romantic ideals.

Cavour believed that the first step toward independence was proving to the great powers that Italians were efficient and economically progressive. As premier of

[2] William L. Langer, *Political and Social Upheaval, 1832–1852* (New York: Harper Torchbooks, 1969), p. 115.

Count Camillo Cavour (1810–1861), whom the Russian thinker Alexander Herzen once called a "fat bespectacled little bourgeois of genius," used an opportunistic alliance with France against Austria and military interventions in the Papal States and southern Italy to secure Italian unification under King Victor Emmanuel II of Piedmont, rather than as the republic that Mazzini and Garibaldi had advocated. He was not, in fact, bourgeois, but was the son of a count.

Piedmont, he promoted free trade, railway construction, expansion of credit, and agricultural improvement. He believed that such material and economic bonds, rather than fuzzy romantic yearnings, must unite the Italians. Cavour also recognized the need to capture the loyalties of those Italians who believed in other varieties of nationalism. He thus fostered the Nationalist Society, which established chapters in other Italian states to press for unification under the leadership of Piedmont. Finally, Cavour believed the Habsburgs would never agree to Italian unification, and that consequently an alliance with France was necessary to defeat Austria. The accession of Napoleon III in France seemed to open the way for such aid.

French Sympathies Cavour used the Crimean War to bring the Italian question to the attention of the great powers. In 1855, Piedmont sent 10,000 troops to help France and Britain capture Sebastopol. At the same time that Piedmont had assisted France and Great Britain, Austria had remained neutral. Piedmont's small but significant participation in the war allowed Cavour to raise the question of unification at the Paris conference. He left Paris with no immediate reward, but his intelligence and political capacity had impressed everyone, especially Napoleon III. During the rest of the decade, he achieved further international respectability for Piedmont by opposing Mazzini, who was still attempting to lead nationalist uprisings. By 1858, Cavour represented a moderate, monarchist alternative to both republicanism and reactionary absolutism in Italy.

Cavour bided his time. Then, in January 1858, an Italian named Felice Orsini attempted to assassinate Napoleon III. The incident heightened the emperor's interest in the Italian issue. He saw himself continuing his more famous uncle's liberation of the peninsula. He also saw Piedmont as a potential ally against Austria. In July 1858, Cavour and Napoleon III met at Plombières in southern France. Riding alone in a carriage, with the emperor at the reins, the two men plotted to provoke a war in Italy that would permit them to defeat Austria. A formal treaty in December 1858 confirmed the agreement.

War with Austria In early 1859, tension grew between Austria and Piedmont as Piedmont mobilized its army. Austria played right into Cavour's hands. On April 22, Austria demanded that Piedmont demobilize. That allowed Piedmont to claim that Austria was provoking a war. France intervened to aid its ally. On June 4, the Austrians were defeated at Magenta, and on June 24 at Solferino. Meanwhile, revolutions had broken out in Tuscany, Modena, Parma, and the Romagna provinces of the Papal States.

With the Austrians in retreat and the new revolutionary regimes calling for union with Piedmont, Napoleon III feared too extensive a Piedmontese victory. On July 11, he concluded peace with Austria at Villafranca. Piedmont received Lombardy, but Venetia remained under Austrian control. Cavour felt betrayed by France, but the war had driven Austria from most of northern Italy. Later that summer, Parma, Modena, Tuscany, and the Romagna voted to unite with Piedmont. (See Map 22–2, p. 692.)

Garibaldi's Campaign At this point, the forces of romantic republican nationalism compelled Cavour to pursue the complete unification of northern and southern Italy. In May 1860, Garibaldi landed in Sicily with more than 1,000 troops, who had been outfitted in the north. He captured Palermo and prepared to attack the mainland. By September he controlled the city and kingdom of Naples, probably the most

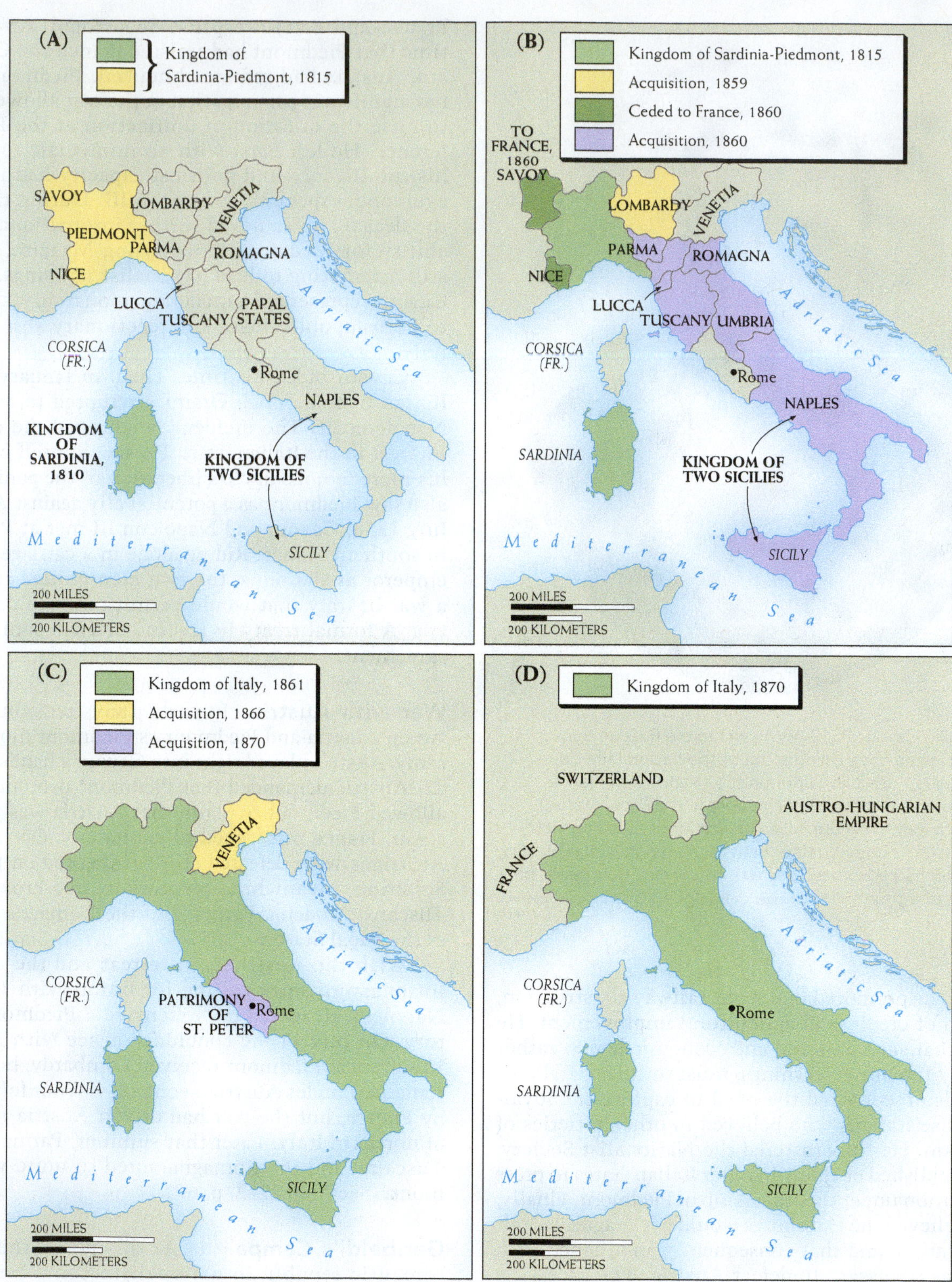

Map 22–2 **THE UNIFICATION OF ITALY** Beginning with the association of Sardinia and Piedmont by the Congress of Vienna in 1815, unification was achieved through the expansion of Piedmont between 1859 and 1870. Both Cavour's statesmanship and the campaigns of ardent nationalists played large roles.

corrupt example of Italian absolutism. For more than two decades Garibaldi had hoped to form a republican Italy, but Cavour forestalled him. He rushed Piedmontese troops south to confront Garibaldi. On the way, they conquered the rest of the Papal States except the area around Rome, which French troops saved for the pope. Recognizing that to persist would guarantee further bloodshed and a protracted civil war, Garibaldi's nationalism won out over his republicanism, and he accepted Piedmontese domination and a monarchical, rather than republican, Italy. In late 1860, Naples and Sicily voted to join the Italian kingdom. In response to the help received from France and Napoleon III's concern over the new large nation-state on his borders, Piedmont ceded Savoy and Nice, where much of the population spoke French, to France. (See "Compare and Connect: Nineteenth Century Nationalism: Two Sides," pages 694–695.)

RIGHT LEG IN THE BOOT AT LAST.

GARIBALDI. "IF IT WON'T GO ON, SIRE, TRY A LITTLE MORE POWDER."

In this Punch cartoon from November 1860, Garibaldi's decision to accept Victor Emmanuel as king of Italy is portrayed as submission. Garibaldi ultimately decided that achieving Italian unification—and avoiding Civil War—was more important than pursuing his radical social and political goals. © World History Archive/Alamy

The New Italian State

In March 1861, Victor Emmanuel II was proclaimed king of Italy. Three months later Cavour died. The new state more than ever needed his skills because Piedmont had, in effect, not so much united Italy as conquered it. The republicans resented the treatment of Garibaldi. The clericals were appalled at the conquest of the Papal States. In the south, armed resistance against the imposition of Piedmontese-style administration continued until 1866. The economies and societies of north and south Italy were incompatible. The south was rural, poor, and backward. The north was industrializing, and its economy was increasingly linked to that of the rest of Europe. The social structures of the two regions reflected these differences, with large landholders and peasants dominant in the south and an urban working class emerging in the north.

The political framework of the united Italy could not overcome these problems. The constitution, which was that promulgated for Piedmont in 1848, provided for a conservative constitutional monarchy. Parliament consisted of two houses: a senate appointed by the king and a chamber of deputies elected on a narrow franchise. Ministers were responsible to the monarch, not to Parliament. These arrangements did not foster vigorous parliamentary life. Political leaders often simply avoided major problems. In place of efficient, progressive government, such as Cavour had brought to Piedmont, a system called *transformismo* developed. Bribery, favors, or a seat in the cabinet "transformed" political opponents into government supporters. Italian politics became a byword for corruption.

The unification was not complete. Many Italians believed other territories should be added to their nation. The most important of these were Venetia and Rome. The former was gained in 1866 in return for Italy's alliance with Prussia in the Austro-Prussian War. French troops continued to guard Rome and the papacy until the troops were withdrawn during the Franco-Prussian War of 1870. The Italian state then annexed Rome and made it the capital. The papacy confined itself to the Vatican and remained hostile to the Italian state until the Lateran Accord of 1929. (See Chapter 27.)

By 1870, the only areas with large Italian-speaking populations that remained outside Italy were the province of Trent, or Southern Tyrol, and the city of Trieste. Both were ruled by Austria, and neither was inhabited solely by people who considered themselves Italian or even spoke Italian. Conflicts in these areas between Italians, Germans, Slovenes, and people who had no national affiliation fueled the continued hostility of Italian nationalists toward Austria. The desire to liberate *Italia irredenta*, or "unredeemed Italy," was one reason for the Italian support of the Allies against Austria and Germany during World War I.

COMPARE AND CONNECT

Nineteenth-Century Nationalism: Two Sides

Read the Compare and Connect on MyHistoryLab.com

THE SECOND QUARTER of the nineteenth century witnessed the unification first of Italy and then of Germany. Both processes involved warfare. The Kingdom of Sardinia conquered and united northern Italy, and then Garibaldi led his "Red Shirts" to conquer the south. Prussia united Germany in a series of wars against Denmark, Austria, and France. These two documents illustrate different justifications for the call to military action for unifying each nation. Garibaldi presents his forces as liberators against tyranny. Treitschke makes an argument for the German annexation of Alsace and Lorraine on the grounds of national security and history.

QUESTIONS

1. **How does Garibaldi's manifesto turn the war for unification in southern Italy into a popular campaign?**
2. **How does Garibaldi portray the struggle for unification as a battle against tyranny?**
3. **On what grounds does Treitschke base the German claim to Alsace and Lorraine?**
4. **Why does Treitschke contend it is proper to ignore the wishes of the people involved?**
5. **How could one nationalist, Garibaldi, see his goal as one of popular liberation while another, Treitschke, see his as reclaiming lost regions of a national homeland? Are these two views compatible or distinctly different?**

I. Garibaldi Calls Italians to Act to Unify Their Nation

Garibaldi was the most charismatic figure in the drive for Italian unification. He was the leader of guerrilla military forces known as the Red Shirts. In May 1860 after northern Italy had been united under the Kingdom of Sardinia whose monarch was Victor Emmanuel, Garibaldi landed his force of about a thousand men in Sicily and from there they crossed into southern Italy to conquer the kingdom of Naples and make it part of a united Italian state. Garibaldi was himself a republican, but he reconciled himself to supporting Victor Emmanuel. Before leaving Sicily for the mainland, Garibaldi issued this call to arms demanding that the Italians of southern Italy rise against the kingdom of Naples. The various geographical areas he mentions were located from the south northward to Rome. The Tincino River lay in northern Italy and Garibaldi is recalling the participation of his troops in the war that unified the north.

Italians! The Sicilians are fighting against the enemies of Italy and for Italy. To help them with money, arms, and especially men, is the duty of every Italian.

Let the Marches, Umbria, Sabine, the Roman Campagna, and the Neapolitan territory rise, so as to divide the enemy's forces.

If the cities do not offer a sufficient basis for insurrection, let the more resolute throw themselves into the open country. A brave man can always find a weapon. In the name of Heaven, hearken not to the voice of those who cram themselves at well-served tables. Let us arm. Let us fight for our brothers; tomorrow we can fight for ourselves.

A handful of brave men, who have followed me in battles for our country, are advancing with me to the rescue. Italy

General Giuseppe Garibaldi (1807–1882).
Universal Images Group/Getty Images

knows them; they always appear at the hour of danger. Brave and generous companions, they have devoted their lives to their country; they will shed their last drop of blood for it, seeking no other reward than that of a pure conscience.

"Italy and Victor Emmanuel!"—that was our battle-cry when we crossed the Tincino; it will resound into the very depths of Aetna [the volcanic mountain]. As this prophetic battle-cry re-echoes from the hills of Italy to the Tarpeian Mount, the tottering thrones of tyranny will fall to pieces, and the whole country will rise like one man. ■

From "History," *The Annual Register . . . 1860* (London, 1861), p. 221, as quoted in Raymond Phineas Stearns, *Pageant of Europe: Sources and Selections from the Renaissance to the Present Day* (New York: Harcourt, Brace & Company, 1948), pp. 583–584.

II. Heinrich von Treitschke Demands the Annexation of Alsace and Lorraine

The Franco-Prussian War witnessed outbursts of extreme nationalist rhetoric on both sides. One such voice was that of German historian Heinrich von Treitschke (1834–1896). In a newspaper article, he demanded the annexation of Alsace and Lorraine from France. He did so even though the population of Alsace wished to remain part of France and German was not the dominant language in the region. He appealed to an earlier time when the region had been German in language and culture, and he asserted that "might makes right" to assure German domination.

The sense of justice to Germany demands the lessening of France. . . .

What is demanded by justice is, at the same time, absolutely necessary for our security. . . .

Every State must seek the guarantees of its own security in itself alone. . . .

In view of our obligation to secure the peace of the world, who will venture to object that the people of Alsace and Lorraine do not want to belong to us? The doctrine of the right of all the branches of the German race to decide on their own destinies, the plausible solution of demagogues without a fatherland, shiver to pieces in presence of the sacred necessity of these great days. These territories are ours by the right of the sword, and we shall dispose of them in virtue of a higher right—the right of the German nation, which will not permit its lost children to remain strangers to the German Empire. We Germans, who know Germany and France, know better than these unfortunates themselves what is good for the people of Alsace. . . . Against their will we shall restore them to their true selves. We have seen with joyful wonder the undying power of the moral forces of history, manifested far too frequently in the immense changes of these days, to place much confidence in the value of a mere popular disinclination. The spirit of a nation lays hold, not only of the generation which lives beside it, but of those who are before and behind it. We appeal from the mistaken wishes of the men who are there today to the wishes of those who were there before them. We appeal to all those strong German men who once stamped the seal of our German nature on the language and manners, the art and the social life of the Upper Rhine. Before the nineteenth century closes, the world will recognize that . . . we were only obeying the dictates of national honor when we made little account of the preferences of the people who live in Alsace today. . . .

At all times the subjection of a German race to France has been an unhealthy thing; today it is an offence against the reason of History—a vassalship of free men to half-educated barbarians. . . .

There is no perfect identity between the political and national frontier of any European country. Not one of the great Powers, and Germany no more than the rest of them, can ever subscribe to the principle that "language alone decides the formation of States." It would be impossible to carry that principle into effect. . . .

The German territory which we demand is ours by nature and by history. . . . In the tempests of the great Revolution the people of Alsace, like all the citizens of France, learned to forget their past. . . .

Most assuredly, the task of reuniting there the broken links between the ages is one of the heaviest that has ever been imposed upon the political forces of our nation. . . .

The people of Alsace are already beginning to doubt the invincibility of their nation, and at all events to divine the mighty growth of the German Empire. Perverse obstinacy, and a thousand French intrigues creeping in the dark, will make every step on the newly conquered soil difficult for us: but our ultimate success is certain, for on our side fights what is stronger than the lying artifices of the stranger—nature herself and the voice of common blood. ■

From Heinrich von Treitschke, "What We Demand from France" (1870), in Heinrich von Treitschke, *Germany, France, Russia and Islam* (New York: G. P. Putnam's Sons, 1915), pp. 100, 102, 106, 109, 120, 122, 134–135, 153, 158.

▼ German Unification

German unification was the most important political development in Europe between 1848 and 1914. (See Map 22–3.) It transformed the balance of economic, military, and international power. Moreover, the way it was created largely determined the character of the new German state. Germany's unification was masterminded by the conservative prime minister of Prussia, who wanted to outflank Prussian liberals and prevent a more radical version of a unified Germany from being imposed by revolution from below. The prime minister was aided by the army and the monarchy. Although he had no master plan for German unification, he used every opportunity to secure the continued dominance of Prussia within Germany and the power of the Prussian monarch. A unified Germany, which two generations of German liberals had sought, was actually achieved for the most illiberal of reasons.

View the Map "Map Discovery: The Unification of Germany, 1866–1871" on MyHistoryLab.com

During the 1850s, German unification seemed remote. The political structure of the German-speaking lands was the German Confederation, which had been established at the Congress of Vienna. It was a loose federation of thirty-nine states of differing size and strength whose appointed representatives met in a central diet in Frankfurt. The two by far strongest states were Austria and Prussia. During the 1850s, Austria presided over the diet of the German Confederation. The major states continued to trade with each other through the *Zollverein* (tariff union), and railways linked their economies. Frederick William IV of Prussia had rejected overtures toward unification under Prussian leadership. Austria continued to oppose any union. If a union included Austrian Germans, the empire would be split in half; if it excluded them, Austria's influence within Germany would diminish. Liberal nationalists had not recovered from the humiliations of 1848 and 1849, and did not have the political power to push for unification. What quickly overturned this static situation was a series of domestic political changes and problems within Prussia.

In 1858, Frederick William IV was adjudged insane, and his brother William assumed the regency. William I (r. 1861–1888), who became king in his own right in 1861, was less idealistic than his brother and more of

Map 22–3 **THE UNIFICATION OF GERMANY** Under Bismarck's leadership, and with the strong support of its royal house, Prussia used diplomatic and military means, on both the German and international stages, to unify the German states into a strong national entity.

a Prussian patriot. In the usual Hohenzollern tradition, his first concern was to strengthen the Prussian army. In 1860, his war minister and chief of staff proposed to enlarge the army, to increase the number of officers, and to extend the period of conscription from two to three years. The Prussian Parliament, created by the Constitution of 1850, refused to approve the necessary taxes. The liberals, who dominated the body, sought to avoid placing additional power in the hands of the monarchy. For two years, monarch and Parliament were deadlocked.

Bismarck

In September 1862, William I turned for help to the person who, more than any other single individual, shaped the next thirty years of European history: Otto von Bismarck (1815–1898). Bismarck came from Junker (noble landlord) stock. During the 1840s, he was elected to the provincial diet, where he was so reactionary he disturbed even the king. Yet he had made his mark. From 1851 to 1859, Bismarck served as the Prussian representative to the German Confederation. There he was an outspoken opponent of Austria. Later he became Prussian ambassador to Russia and was ambassador to France when William I appointed him prime minister.

Upon becoming prime minister in 1862, Bismarck immediately moved against the liberal Parliament. He contended that even without new financial levies, the Prussian constitution permitted the government to carry out its functions on the basis of previously granted taxes. Therefore, taxes could be collected and spent despite the parliamentary refusal to vote them. The army and most of the bureaucracy supported this interpretation of the constitution. In 1863, however, new elections sustained the liberal majority in the Parliament. Bismarck had to find a way to attract popular support away from the liberals and toward the monarchy and the army. He, therefore, set about uniting Germany through the conservative institutions of Prussia. In effect, Bismarck embraced the cause of German nationalism as a strategy to enable Prussian conservatives to outmaneuver Prussian liberals.

Although Bismarck never abandoned his fundamental conservatism, he did recognize that the only successful way to prevent the change he did not want was to lead Prussia towards change that was compatible with his basic values: monarchism and Prussian strength. Because the transformations in German history that he oversaw amounted to a revolution with the aim of protecting core conservative values, he has been called a "white revolutionary."[3] He opposed parliamentary government, but not a constitutionalism that preserved a strong monarchy. He understood that Prussia—and later, Germany—must have a strong industrial base. His years in Frankfurt arguing with his Austrian counterpart had hardened his Prussian patriotism. In politics, he was a pragmatist who put more trust in power and action than in ideas.

As he declared in his first speech as prime minister, "Germany is not looking to Prussia's liberalism but to her power. . . . The great questions of the day will not be decided by speeches and majority decisions—that was the mistake of 1848–1849—but by iron and blood."[4] After German unification, Bismarck became a dedicated advocate of preserving European peace. He served as an important check on the ambitions of his king. But during the process of unification, Bismarck was willing to go to war to achieve his goals. Germany was unified over the course of three wars, each of which Bismarck could have prevented had he not considered them useful.

The Danish War (1864) Bismarck's vision of a united Germany did not include all German-speaking lands. That is to say, he pursued a *kleindeutsch*, or small German, solution to unification. He intended to exclude Austria from any future united German state. This goal required complex diplomacy.

The Schleswig-Holstein problem gave Bismarck an opportunity to antagonize Austria. The kings of Denmark had long ruled these two northern duchies, which had never actually become part of Denmark itself, and which were inhabited by both Germans and Danes. Holstein, where Germans predominated, belonged to the German Confederation. In 1863, the Danish Parliament moved to incorporate both duchies into Denmark. The smaller states of the German Confederation proposed an all-German war to halt this move. Bismarck proposed a war against Denmark waged by Prussia allied with Austria, excluding the smaller German states. Together, the two large states easily defeated Denmark in 1864. The Danish defeat increased Bismarck's personal prestige and strengthened his political hand. This apparent cooperation led to multiple opportunities for Prussia to pick fights with Austria over the administration of the provinces.

Over the next two years, Bismarck managed to maneuver Austria into war with Prussia. In August 1865, the two powers negotiated the Convention of Gastein, which put Austria in charge of Holstein and Prussia in charge of Schleswig. Bismarck then needed to prepare a second, more decisive conflict with Austria. First, he prepared international support for Prussia. He had gained Russian sympathy in 1863 by supporting Russia's suppression of a Polish revolt, and he persuaded Napoleon III to promise neutrality in an Austro-Prussian conflict. In April 1866, Bismarck promised Venetia to the new Kingdom of Italy if

[3]Henry Kissinger, "The White Revolutionary: Reflections on Bismarck," *Daedalus* 97 (Summer 1968): 888.

[4]Otto Pflanze, *Bismarck and the Development of Germany: The Period of Unification: 1815–1871* (Princeton, NJ: Princeton University Press, 1963), p. 177.

The proclamation of the German Empire in the Hall of Mirrors at Versailles, January 18, 1871, after the defeat of France in the Franco-Prussian War. Kaiser Wilhelm I is standing at the top of the steps under the flags. The viewer's eye, however, is drawn to Bismarck, who stands in the center in a white uniform. Anton von Werner, "Die Proklamierung des Deutschen Kaiserreiches," Bildarchiv Preussischer Kulturbesitz/Art Resource, NY

it attacked Austria in support of Prussia when war broke out. Now Bismarck had to provoke his war.

The Austro–Prussian War (1866) Constant Austro–Prussian tensions had arisen over the administration of Schleswig and Holstein. Bismarck ordered the Prussian forces to be as obnoxious as possible to the Austrians. On June 1, 1866, Austria appealed to the German Confederation to intervene in the dispute. Bismarck claimed that this request violated the 1864 alliance and the Convention of Gastein. The result was the Seven Weeks' War, which began in the summer of 1866. Nationalists were horrified by this German "civil war." Although the smaller German states sided with Austria, Prussia decisively defeated Austria and its allies at Königgrätz in Bohemia.

Read the Document "A Letter from Bismarck (1866)" on **MyHistoryLab.com**

The Treaty of Prague, which ended the conflict on August 23, was lenient toward Austria, which only lost Venetia, ceded as promised to Napoleon III, who in turn ceded it to Italy. Austria refused to give Venetia directly to Italy because the Austrians had crushed the Italians during the war. The treaty permanently excluded the Austrian Habsburgs from German affairs. Prussia had thus established itself as the only major power among the German states. The same nationalists who had objected to Bismarck's fostering of conflict with Austria now celebrated "the god of the moment: success."[5]

[5]Jonathan Steinberg, *Bismarck: A Life* (Oxford, UK: Oxford University Press, 2011), p. 263.

The North German Confederation In 1867, Prussia annexed Hanover, Hesse-Kassel, Nassau, and the city of Frankfurt, all of which had supported Austria during the war, and deposed their rulers. Under Prussian leadership, all the German states north of the Main River now formed the North German Confederation. Each state retained its own government, but all military forces were under federal control. The president of the federation was the king of Prussia, represented by his chancellor, Bismarck. A legislature consisted of two houses: a federal council, or *Bundesrat*, composed of members appointed by the governments of the states, and a lower house, or *Reichstag*, chosen by universal male suffrage.

Bismarck, the great conservative chancellor, unlike German liberals, actually embraced a democratic franchise because he anticipated that the peasants would vote for conservatives. Moreover, the *Reichstag* had little real power because the ministers were responsible only to the monarch. The *Reichstag* could not even originate legislation. The chancellor had to propose all laws. The legislature did have the right to approve military budgets, but these were usually submitted to cover several years at a time. The constitution of the North German Confederation, which, after 1871, became the constitution of the German Empire, possessed some of the appearances, but none of the substance, of liberalism. Germany was, in effect, a conservative monarchy supported by the landed aristocracy and the military.

Bismarck's spectacular successes overwhelmed the liberal opposition in the Prussian Parliament. The liberals were split between those who prized the principles of liberalism and those whose primary goal was national unification. In the end, nationalism proved more attractive. In 1866, the Prussian Parliament retroactively approved the military budget that it had rejected earlier. Bismarck had crushed the Prussian liberals by making the monarchy and the army the most popular institutions in the country. The drive toward German national unification had achieved his domestic Prussian political goal.

The Franco-Prussian War and the German Empire (1870–1871)

Bismarck now wanted to complete unification by bringing the states of southern Germany—Bavaria, Württemberg, Baden, and Hesse-Darmstadt—into the newly established confederation. Spain gave him the excuse. In 1868, a military coup deposed the corrupt Bourbon queen of Spain, Isabella II (r. 1833–1868). To replace her, the Spaniards chose Prince Leopold of Hohenzollern-Sigmaringen, a Catholic cousin of William I of Prussia. On June 19, 1870, Leopold accepted the Spanish crown with Prussian blessings. Bismarck knew that France would object strongly to a Hohenzollern Spain.

On July 2, the Spanish government announced Leopold's acceptance, and the French reacted as expected. France sent its ambassador, Count Vincent Benedetti (1817–1900), to consult with William I, who was vacationing at Bad Ems. They discussed the matter at several meetings. On July 12, Leopold's father renounced his son's candidacy for the Spanish throne, fearing the issue would cause war between Prussia and France. William was relieved that conflict had been avoided, and he had not had to order Leopold to renounce the Spanish throne.

The matter might have rested there had it not been for the impetuosity of the French and the guile of Bismarck. On July 13, the French government instructed Benedetti to ask William for assurances he would tolerate no future Spanish candidacy for Leopold. The king refused but said he might take the question under further consideration. Later that day he sent Bismarck, who was in Berlin, a telegram reporting the substance of the meeting. The peaceful resolution of the controversy had disappointed the chancellor, who desperately wanted a war with France to complete unification. The king's telegram gave him a new opportunity to provoke war. Bismarck released an edited version of the dispatch. The revised Ems telegram made it appear that William had insulted the French ambassador. The idea was to goad France into declaring war.

The French government fell for Bismarck's bait and declared war on July 19. Napoleon III was sick and not eager for war, but his government believed victory over the North German Confederation would renew popular support for the empire. Once the conflict erupted, the southern German states, honoring treaties of 1866, joined Prussia against France, whose defeat was not long in coming. On September 1, at the Battle of Sedan, German forces not only beat the French army but also captured Napoleon III. By late September, Paris was besieged; it finally capitulated on January 28, 1871.

Ten days earlier, in the Hall of Mirrors at the Palace of Versailles, the German Empire had been proclaimed. The German princes requested William to accept the title of German emperor. The princes remained heads of their respective states within the new empire. Through

GERMAN AND ITALIAN UNIFICATION

1854	Crimean War opens
1855	Cavour leads Piedmont into the war on the side of France and Britain
1856	Treaty of Paris concludes the Crimean War
1858 (January 14)	Attempt to assassinate Napoleon III
1858 (July 20)	Secret conference between Napoleon III and Cavour at Plombières
1859	War of Piedmont and France against Austria
1860	Garibaldi lands his forces in Sicily and invades southern Italy
1861 (March 17)	Proclamation of the Kingdom of Italy
1861 (June 6)	Death of Cavour
1862	Bismarck becomes prime minister of Prussia
1864	Danish War
1865	Convention of Gastein
1866	Seven Weeks' War between Prussia and Austria
1866	Austria cedes Venetia to Italy
1867	North German Confederation formed
1870 (June 19–July 12)	Crisis over Hohenzollern candidacy for the Spanish throne
1870 (July 13)	Bismarck publishes the edited Ems dispatch
1870 (July 19)	France declares war on Prussia
1870 (September 1)	German forces defeat France at Sedan and capture Napoleon III
1870 (September 4)	French Republic proclaimed
1870 (October 2)	Italian state annexes Rome
1871 (January 18)	Proclamation of the German Empire at Versailles
1871 (March 28–May 28)	Paris Commune
1871 (May 23)	Treaty of Frankfurt ratified between France and Germany

the peace settlement with France, Germany annexed Alsace and part of Lorraine and forced the French to pay a large indemnity. (See the Document "Heinrich von Treitschke Demands the Annexation of Alsace and Lorraine," page 695.)

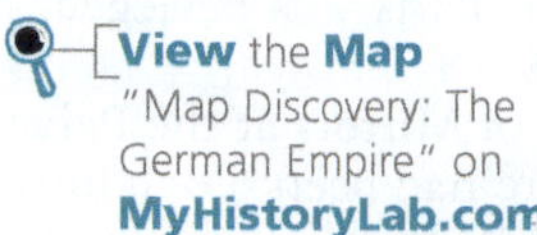
View the **Map** "Map Discovery: The German Empire" on **MyHistoryLab.com**

Both the fact and the manner of German unification produced long-range effects in Europe. A powerful new state had been created in north central Europe. It was rich in natural resources and talented citizens, and had an advanced educational system. Militarily and economically, the German Empire would be far stronger than Prussia had been alone. The unification of Germany was also a blow to European liberalism because the new state was a conservative creation. Conservative politics were now backed not by a weak Austria or an economically underdeveloped Russia, but by the strongest military and economic state on the Continent.

The two nations most immediately affected by German and Italian unification were France and Austria. The emergence of the two new unified states revealed French and Habsburg weakness. Each had to change. France returned to republican government, and the Habsburgs undertook a major domestic restructuring.

Read the **Document** "Fustel de Coulanges, *Letter to German Historian Theodor Mommsen, 1870*" on **MyHistoryLab.com**

▼ France: From Liberal Empire to the Third Republic

Historians divide the reign of Napoleon III (r. 1852–1870) into the years of the authoritarian empire and those of the liberal empire. The year of division is 1860. After the coup in December 1851, Napoleon III had controlled the legislature, censored the press, and harassed political dissidents. His support came from the army, property owners, the French Catholic Church, peasants, and businesspeople. They approved the security he ensured for property, his protection of the pope, and his economic program. French victory in the Crimean War had confirmed the emperor's popularity.

From the late 1850s onward, Napoleon III began to modify his authoritarian policy. In 1860, he concluded a free-trade treaty with Britain and permitted freer debate in the legislature. By the late 1860s, he had relaxed the press laws and permitted labor unions. In 1870, he allowed the leaders of the moderates in the legislature to form a ministry, and he also agreed to a liberal constitution that made the ministers responsible to the legislature.

Napoleon III's liberal concessions sought to shore up domestic support to compensate for his failures in foreign policy. By 1860, he had lost control of the diplomacy of Italian unification. Between 1861 and 1867, he had supported a disastrous military expedition against Mexico led by Archduke Ferdinand Maximilian of Austria, who became Emperor Maximilian I of Mexico. The French intervention ended in defeat and Maximilian's execution. In 1866, France had watched passively while Bismarck and Prussia reorganized German affairs. The Franco–Prussian War of 1870 had been the French government's last and most disastrous attempt to demonstrate strength in international affairs in order to secure domestic popularity.

The Second Empire came to an inglorious end with the Battle of Sedan in September 1870. The emperor was captured and then allowed to go to England, where he died in 1873. Shortly after news of Sedan reached Paris, a republic was proclaimed and a government of national defense established. Paris itself was soon under Prussian siege, and the government moved to Bordeaux. Paris finally surrendered in January 1871, but France had been ready to sue for peace long before.

The Paris Commune

The division between the provinces and Paris became sharper after the fighting with Germany stopped. Monarchists dominated the new National Assembly elected in February. For the time being, the assembly gave executive power to Adolphe Thiers (1797–1877), who had been active in French politics since 1830. He negotiated a settlement with Prussia (the Treaty of Frankfurt), which was officially ratified on May 23.

Many Parisians, having suffered during the siege, resented what they regarded as a betrayal by the monarchist National Assembly sitting at Versailles. The Parisians elected a new municipal government, called the *Paris Commune*, which was formally proclaimed on March 28, 1871. The Commune intended to administer Paris separately from the rest of France. Radicals and socialists of all stripes participated in the Commune. In April, the National Assembly surrounded Paris with an army. On May 8, this army bombarded the city. On May 21, it broke through the city's defenses. During the next seven days, the troops killed about 20,000 inhabitants while the communards shot scores of hostages.

View the **Map** "Map Discovery: The Paris Commune, 1871" on **MyHistoryLab.com**

The Paris Commune became a legend throughout Europe. Marxists regarded it as a genuine proletarian government that the French bourgeoisie had suppressed. This interpretation is mistaken. The Commune, though of shifting composition, was dominated by petty bourgeois members. The socialism of the Commune had its roots in Blanqui's and Proudhon's anarchism rather than in Marx's concept of class conflict. The Commune wanted not a workers' state, but a nation of relatively independent, radically democratic enclaves. Its suppression thus represented not only the protection of property, but also the triumph of the centralized nation-state. Just as the armies of Piedmont and Prussia had united the small states of Italy and Germany, the army of the French National Assembly destroyed the particularistic political tendencies of Paris and, by implication, those of any other French community.

The Third Republic

The National Assembly backed into a republican form of government against its will. Its monarchist majority was divided in loyalty between the House of Bourbon and the House of Orléans. They could have surmounted this problem because the Bourbon claimant, the count of Chambord, had no children and agreed to accept the Orléanist heir as his successor. Chambord refused to become king, however, if France retained the revolutionary tricolor flag; the white flag of the Bourbons, however, symbolized extreme political reaction and was unacceptable to even conservative monarchists.

While the monarchists quarreled among themselves, events marched on. By September 1873, the indemnity had been paid, and the Prussian occupation troops had withdrawn. Thiers was ousted from office because he had displayed clear republican sentiments. A conservative army officer, Marshal Patrice MacMahon (1808–1893), was elected president and expected to prepare for a monarchist restoration. In 1875, the National Assembly, still monarchist in sentiment but unable to find a king, adopted a law that provided for a Chamber of Deputies elected by universal male suffrage, a senate chosen indirectly, and a president elected by the two legislative houses. This rather simple republican system had resulted from the bickering and frustration of the monarchists.

After numerous quarrels with the Chamber of Deputies, MacMahon resigned in 1879. His departure meant that dedicated republicans controlled the national government despite lingering opposition from the church, wealthy families, and a part of the army.

The political structure of the Third Republic proved much stronger than many citizens suspected at the time. It survived challenges from persons such as General Georges Boulanger (1837–1891), who would have imposed stronger executive authority. It also survived several scandals, such as those involving sales of awards of the Legion of Honor and widespread corruption of politicians and journalists by a company that tried to construct a canal in Panama, that made its politics appear increasingly corrupt. The institutions of the republic, however, allowed new ministers to replace those whose corruption was exposed without revolution.

▼ The Habsburg Empire

At the beginning of the nineteenth century, Austria was still considered the most powerful state in central Europe. A series of defeats and mismanaged diplomatic conflicts had revealed Austria's weakness relative to France, Russia, Germany, and even Italy, and left it isolated. An ungenerous critic remarked that a standing army of soldiers, a kneeling army of priests, and a crawling army of informers supported the empire. In the age of national states, liberal institutions, and industrialism, the Habsburg domains remained primarily dynastic, absolutist, and agrarian. The Habsburg response to the revolts of 1848–1849 had been to reassert absolutism. Emperor Francis Joseph (r. 1848–1916) was honest, conscientious, and hardworking,

Francis Joseph (1830–1916) ruled Austria and then Austria-Hungary from 1848 until his death. In this 1865 photo, the young emperor is shown in military gala attire, one of his preferred uniforms. His devotion to the Austrian army made it difficult for him to share control over the military with parliament, which contributed to chronic underfunding.

Document

MARK TWAIN DESCRIBES THE AUSTRIAN PARLIAMENT

Mark Twain (1835–1910) visited Austria in the fall of 1897 and witnessed a parliamentary debate during the discussions of renewal of the Compromise agreement between Austria and Hungary. The specific content of the debate did not interest Twain, but he was very taken with the way it illustrated the paralysis of the Austrian parliament. German nationalists were so outraged by a recent agreement to allow Czech to be used in government offices in Bohemia that they were determined to prevent any parliamentary business from taking place. Their methods of obstruction included noisemaking and continual interruptions.

How would a stenographic protocol taken of the parliamentary session that Twain attended reflect the atmosphere in the chamber? How did parliamentary government function in Austria in 1897? What prevented it from functioning? What tools did representatives use to communicate their political positions? Did they rely on parliamentary rights and responsibilities, or on ignoring them, or both?

At 8.45, on the evening of the 28th of October . . . Dr. Lecher was granted the floor. . . .

Then burst out such another wild and frantic and deafening clamor as has not been heard on this planet . . . Yells from the Left, counter-yells from the Right, explosions of yells from all sides at once. . . . Out of the midst of this thunder and turmoil and tempest rose Dr. Lecher, serene and collected, and the providential length of him enabled his head to show out above it. He began his twelve-hour speech. At any rate, his lips could be seen to move, and that was evidence. On high sat the President imploring order, with his long hands put together as in prayer, and his lips visibly but not hearably speaking. At intervals he grasped his bell and swung it up and down with vigor, adding its keen clamor to the storm weltering there below.

Dr. Lecher went on with his pantomime speech, contented, untroubled. . . . One of the interrupters who made himself heard was . . . Wolf. . . . Out of him came early this thundering peal, audible above the storm:

"I demand the floor. I wish to offer a motion."

In the sudden lull which followed, the President answered, "Dr. Lecher has the floor."

Wolf. "I move the close of the sitting!"

P. "Representative Lecher has the floor." [Stormy outburst from the Left—that is, the Opposition.]

Wolf. I demand the floor for the introduction of a formal motion. [Pause.] Mr. President, are you going to grant it, or not? [Crash of approval from the Left.] I will keep on demanding the floor till I get it.

P. "I call Representative Wolf to order. Dr. Lecher has the floor."

Wolf. "Mr. President, are you going to observe the Rules of this House?" [Tempest of applause and confused ejaculations from the Left—a boom and roar which long endured, and stopped all business for the time being.] . . .

For answer the President . . . began to jangle his bell with energy at the moment that that wild pandemonium of voices burst out again.

Wolf (hearable above the storm). "Mr. President, I demand the floor."

. . . The President blandly answered that Dr. Lecher had the floor. Which was true; and he was speaking, too, calmly, earnestly, and argumentatively; and the official stenographers had left their places and were at his elbows taking down his words, he leaning and orating into their ears—a most curious and interesting scene.

From Mark Twain, "Stirring Times in Austria," *Harper's New Monthly Magazine* 96 (March 1898): 530–535.

but unimaginative and deeply committed to dynastic tradition. He did not have an advisor like Bismarck or Cavour who could show him the path to managing inevitable change. Instead, he held on to tradition as long as possible, only reacting to events as he was forced to do so.

During the 1850s, his ministers attempted to impose a centralized administration on the empire. The Vienna government abolished internal tariffs in the empire. It divided Hungary, which had been so revolutionary in 1848, into military districts. The Roman Catholic Church acquired control of education. In a country in which traditional local privileges held by powerful aristocratic interests had so much historical power, these attempts to increase central power encountered tremendous resentment. They eventually floundered because of setbacks in foreign affairs.

Austrian refusal to support Russia during the Crimean War meant the new tsar Alexander II (r. 1855–1881) would no longer help preserve Habsburg rule in Hungary, as Nicholas I had done in 1849. Austria lost Russian support without gaining the support of France or Great Britain. The Austrian defeat in 1859 at the hands of France and Piedmont, the subsequent loss of territory in Italy, and, later, the defeat at the hands of Prussia in 1866 confirmed the necessity for a new domestic policy. The emperor, his civil servants, aristocrats, and politicians tried to construct a viable system of government that would maintain the integrity of the empire while meeting regional demands for some self-governance.

MAJOR DATES IN THE LATE-NINETEENTH-CENTURY HABSBURG EMPIRE

1848	Francis Joseph becomes emperor at age 18
1859	Defeat by France and Piedmont
1860	October Diploma
1861	February Patent
1866	Defeat by Prussia
1867	Compromise between emperor and Hungary, establishing the Dual Monarchy
1897	Ordinances giving equality of language between Germans and Czechs in Austria
1907	Universal male suffrage introduced for Austria

Formation of the Dual Monarchy

In 1860, Francis Joseph backed off of his attempts at centralization and issued the October Diploma, which created a federation among the states and provinces of the empire. There were to be local diets dominated by the landed classes and a single imperial parliament. The Hungarian nobility, however, rejected the plan.

Consequently, in 1861, the emperor issued the February Patent, which set up an entirely different form of government. It established a bicameral imperial parliament, or *Reichsrat*, with an upper chamber appointed by the emperor and an indirectly elected lower chamber. Again, the Hungarians refused to cooperate in a system that denied them full control over historic Hungarian territory. Nevertheless, for six years, the February Patent governed the empire. Ministers were responsible to the emperor, not the *Reichsrat*, and civil liberties were not guaranteed. Armies could be levied and taxes raised without parliamentary consent. When the *Reichsrat* was not in session, the emperor could rule by decree.

Meanwhile, secret negotiations between the emperor and the Hungarians produced no concrete result until the Prussian defeat of Austria in the summer of 1866 and the consequent exclusion of Austria from German affairs. Francis Joseph now had to come to terms with the Hungarians. The subsequent *Ausgleich*, or Compromise, of 1867 transformed the Habsburg Empire into a dual monarchy known as Austria-Hungary.

Francis Joseph was crowned king of Hungary in Budapest in 1867. Except for the common monarch, army, and foreign relations, Austria and Hungary became almost wholly separate states. They shared ministers of foreign affairs, defense, and finance, but the other ministers were different for each state. There were also separate parliaments. Each year, sixty parliamentary delegates from each state met to discuss mutual interests. Every ten years, Austria and Hungary renegotiated their trade relationship. This cumbersome machinery, unique in European history, reconciled the Hungarians to Habsburg rule.

Unrest of Nationalities

The Compromise of 1867 introduced two different principles of political legitimacy into the two sections of the Habsburg Empire. In Hungary, political loyalty was based on nationality because Hungary had been recognized as a distinct part of the monarchy on the basis of nationalism. At the same time that Hungarian nationalists praised nationalism in their conflict with the Habsburg emperor and the Germans within Austria, they denied any kind of national rights to people living in Hungary who did not consider themselves Hungarian, including Romanians and Croats. In the rest of the Habsburg domains, the principle of legitimacy meant dynastic loyalty to the emperor. Nationalists who claimed to represent other peoples within the empire wished to achieve the same type of settlement that the Hungarians had won, or to govern themselves, or as time went on, to unite with fellow nationals who lived outside the empire.

View the **Map** "The Nationalities of Austria-Hungary, 1867" on **MyHistoryLab.com**

Nationalists claiming to represent Czechs, Poles, Ukrainians, Romanians, Croats, and Italians complained that the Compromise of 1867 permitted the German-speaking Austrians and the Hungarians to dominate all other nationalities within their respective "halves" of the empire. The most vocal critics were the Czechs of Bohemia. They favored a policy of "trialism," or triple monarchy, in which the Czechs would have a position similar to that of the Hungarians. In 1871, Francis Joseph

NATIONALITIES WITHIN THE HABSBURG EMPIRE. The Habsburg census forced residents to choose one single "language of daily use." The many bilingual people in the empire were thus statistically presented as members of a single nationality. As a result, in ethno-linguistic maps the empire appeared as a patchwork of many different nationalities. This both underestimated the sense of unity within the empire and overestimated the homogeneity of the various "national" regions. This map, taken from a 1905 French school textbook, is typical of that phenomenon. Map of the Austro-Hungarian empire, illustration from a French geography school textbook, 1905 (colour litho), French School (20th century). Private Collection/Archives Charmet/The Bridgeman Art Library International

was willing to accept this concept. The Hungarians, however, vetoed it lest they be forced to make similar concessions to their own subject nationalities. Furthermore, German-speakers in Bohemia were afraid the Czech language would be imposed on them.

At the same time that the Compromise between Austria and Hungary was introduced, the emperor proclaimed a new constitution, called the "Basic Law," that would apply in Austria. It guaranteed Austrians basic civil rights. The liberal provisions of the constitution, however, did not satisfy nationalists within the empire. By the 1890s, however, Czech nationalism was particularly strident. In 1897, Francis Joseph's prime minister, Count Casimir Badeni, made the Czech and German languages equal in Bohemia. This would in effect require that all civil servants in Bohemia be bilingual. Both German and Czech nationalists in the Austrian *Reichsrat* opposed these measures by disrupting Parliament. By the turn of the century, this obstructionism, which included the playing of musical instruments in the *Reichsrat*, had paralyzed parliamentary life. With parliament unable to pass legislation, the emperor ruled by imperial decree through the bureaucracy. In 1907, Francis Joseph introduced universal male suffrage in Austria (but not in Hungary), but this action did not eliminate the chaos in the *Reichsrat*. Parliament's problems diminished many Austrians' faith in the effectiveness of constitutional rule.

Interest in nationalism became more widespread during the last quarter of the nineteenth century, but even then many Austrians continued to place greater importance in dynastic loyalty, religion, or local identity. Language became the single most important factor in defining a nation. The expansion of education made this possible. In all countries where nationalist groups prospered, their membership was dominated by intellectuals, students, and educated members of the middle class, all of whom were familiar with the literary version of particular national languages.

The agitation of nationalists within the Habsburg Empire not only caused internal political difficulties, it also became a major source of political instability for all of central and eastern Europe. Each of the nationality problems normally had ramifications for both foreign and domestic policy. Although some nationalists complained about the domination of the German population of Austria, German nationalism was no more compatible with the multinational empire than any other nationalism. Some Germans in Austria yearned to join the new German Empire. Some Poles wanted an independent state in union with their fellow nationals who lived in the Russian Empire and Germany. Even Poles who argued for autonomy within the Austrian Empire used nationalist language that seemed to undermine the idea of a unified empire. It was not in the Austrian emperor's power to authorize greater links between the various parts of the former Polish–Lithuanian Commonwealth. Italian nationalists in Trieste and Southern Tyrol/Trent demanded unification with the Kingdom of Italy, exacerbating tensions between Austria and Italy. Many of the Slavic nationalities, especially in the South, looked to Russia to protect their interests or influence the government in Vienna. Romania was concerned about the Romanian minority in Hungary. Serbia sought to expand its borders to include Serbs who lived within Habsburg or Ottoman territory. Out of these Balkan tensions emerged much of the turmoil that would spark World War I.

At the same time that national tensions within Austria-Hungary were a significant contributor to the political instability of the empire and the international tensions that led to the outbreak of World War I, they should not be overestimated. Nationalists dominated the press and politics, but their views were not universally shared. Many subjects of the Habsburg emperor remained loyal to the dynasty and the idea of a multinational empire until the very last months of World War I.

Whatever the private sentiments of the citizenry, however, nationality problems touched all four of the great central and eastern European empires—the German, the Russian, the Austrian, and the Ottoman. All four contained many minority groups, including, in the case of the first three, large Polish populations. The weakness of the Ottoman Empire allowed both Austria and Russia to compete in the Balkans for influence and thus further inflame nationalist resentments. Such nationalist stirrings affected the fate of all four empires from the 1860s through the outbreak of World War I. The government of each of these empires would be overturned during the war, and the Habsburg monarchy and the Ottoman Empire would disappear.

▼ Russia: Emancipation and Revolutionary Stirrings

Russia changed remarkably during the last half of the nineteenth century. The government finally addressed the long-standing problem of serfdom and undertook a broad range of administrative reforms. During the same period, however, radical revolutionary groups began to organize. These groups tried to draw the peasants into revolutionary activity and assassinated government officials, including the tsar. The government's response was renewed repression.

Watch the **Video** "Russian Terrorism" on **MyHistoryLab.com**

Reforms of Alexander II

Russia's defeat in the Crimean War and its humiliation in the Treaty of Paris compelled the government to reconsider its domestic policies. Nicholas I died in 1855 during the conflict. His son Alexander II (r. 1855–1881), who had traveled extensively in Russia and been well prepared to rule, was familiar with the difficulties the empire faced. The debacle of the war had made reform both necessary and possible. Alexander II took advantage of this turn of events to institute the most extensive restructuring of Russian society and administration since Peter the Great. Like Peter, Alexander imposed his reforms from the top.

Abolition of Serfdom In every area of economic and public life, a profound cultural gap separated Russia from the rest of Europe. Nowhere was this more apparent than in the survival of serfdom. In Russia, the institution had changed little since the eighteenth century, although every other nation on the continent had abandoned it. Russian landowners still had a free hand with their serfs, and the serfs had little recourse against the landlords. In March 1856, at the conclusion of the Crimean War, Alexander II announced his intention to abolish serfdom. He had decided that its abolition was necessary if Russia was to remain a great power.

View the **Map** "Map Discovery: Russian Serfs" on **MyHistoryLab.com**

Serfdom was economically inefficient. There was always the threat of revolt, and the serfs forced into the army had performed poorly in the Crimean War. Moreover, nineteenth-century moral opinion condemned serfdom. For five years, government commissions wrestled over how to implement the tsar's desire. Finally, in February 1861, despite opposition from the nobility and the landlords, Alexander II ended serfdom.

Read the **Document** "Emancipation Manifesto (1861)" on **MyHistoryLab.com**

The actual emancipation law was a disappointment, however, because land did not accompany freedom. Serfs immediately received the personal right to marry without their landlord's permission, as well as the rights to buy and sell property, to sue in court, and to pursue trades. What they did not receive was free title to their land. They had to pay the landlords over a period of forty-nine years for allotments of land that were frequently too small to support them. The former serfs, who were now free peasant farmers, made the payments to the government, which had already reimbursed the landlords for their losses. The peasants would not receive title to the land until the debt was paid. Although peasants were no longer personally bonded to their landlords, restrictions

MAJOR DATES IN LATE-NINETEENTH-CENTURY RUSSIA

1855	Alexander II becomes tsar
1856	Defeat in Crimean War
1861	Serfdom abolished
1863	Suppression of Polish rebellion
1864	Reorganization of local government
1864	Reform of judicial system
1874	Military enlistment period reduced
1878	Attempted assassination of military governor of Saint Petersburg
1879	Land and Freedom splits
1881	The People's Will assassinates Alexander II
1881	Alexander III becomes tsar
1894	Nicholas II becomes tsar

on individual freedom continued. What the landlord no longer controlled was now controlled by the communes and the elders who oversaw their management and governance. Redemption payments, taxes, and rights to land use were all collective and controlled by village elders, whose permission was even required if a peasant wanted to leave the commune.

The procedures were so complicated and the results so limited that many serfs believed real emancipation was still to come. The redemption payments led to almost unending difficulty. Poor harvests made it impossible for many peasants to make the payments, and they fell increasingly behind in their debt. The situation was not remedied until 1906, when, during the widespread revolutionary unrest following the Japanese defeat of Russia in 1905, the government grudgingly canceled the remaining debts.

Reform of Local Government, the Judicial System, and the Military The abolition of serfdom required the reorganization of local government and the judicial system. The authority of village communes replaced that of the landlord over the peasant. The village elders settled family quarrels, imposed fines, issued internal passports that were legally required for peasants to move from one locale to another, and collected taxes. Often the village commune, not individual peasants, owned the land. The nobility were given a larger role in local administration through a system of provincial and county *zemstvos*, or councils, organized in 1864. These councils were to oversee local matters, such as bridge and road repair, education, and agricultural improvement. The *zemstvos* were underfunded and many of them remained ineffective.

In 1864, Alexander II issued a new statute on the judiciary that for the first time introduced Western European legal principles into Russia. These included equality before the law, impartial hearings, uniform procedures, judicial independence, and trial by jury. The new system was far from perfect. The judges were not genuinely independent, and the tsar could increase as well as reduce sentences. Nonetheless, the new courts were both more efficient and less corrupt than the old system.

The government also reformed the army. Russia possessed the largest army on the continent, but it had floundered badly in the Crimean War. The usual period of service for a soldier was twenty-five years. Villages had to provide quotas of serfs to serve in the army. Once in the army, recruits rarely saw their homes again. Life in the army was harsh, even by the brutal standards of most midcentury armies. In the 1860s, the army lowered the period of service to fifteen years and relaxed discipline slightly. In 1874, the enlistment period was lowered to six years of active duty and nine years in the reserves. All males were subject to military service after the age of twenty.

Repression in Poland Alexander's reforms became more measured shortly after the Polish January Insurrection of 1863. As in 1830, Polish nationalists attempted to overthrow Russian dominance. Once again the Russian army suppressed the rebellion. Alexander II then moved to Russify Poland. In 1864, he emancipated the Polish serfs to punish the politically restive Polish nobility. Russian law, language, and administration were imposed on all areas of Polish life.

As the Polish suppression demonstrated, Alexander II was a reformer only within the limits of his own autocracy. His changes in Russian life failed to create new loyalty to, or gratitude for, the government among his subjects. The serfs felt their emancipation had been inadequate. The nobles and the wealthier educated segments of Russian society resented the tsar's persistent refusal to allow them a meaningful role in government and policymaking. Consequently, although Alexander II became known as the Tsar Liberator, he was never popular. He became even more indecisive and closed-minded after an attempt was made on his life in 1866. Thereafter, Russia increasingly became a police state. This new repression fueled the activity of radical groups within Russia. Their actions, in turn, made the autocracy more reactionary.

Revolutionaries

Many critics, both inside and outside Russia, targeted the tsarist regime. One of the most prominent was Alexander Herzen (1812–1870), who lived in exile. From London, he published a reformist newspaper called *The Bell*. Russian students and intellectuals who had greeted Alexander II's initial reforms enthusiastically soon became discontented with their limited character. Drawing on the ideas of Herzen and other radicals, these students formed a revolutionary movement known as *populism*. They sought a social revolution based on the communal life of the Russian peasants. The chief radical society was called *Land and Freedom*.

In the early 1870s, hundreds of young Russian men and women took their revolutionary message into the countryside. They intended to live with the peasants, to gain their trust, and to teach them about the peasant's role in the coming revolution. The bewildered and distrustful peasants turned most of the youths over to the police. In the winter of 1877–1878, almost two hundred students were tried. Most were acquitted or given light sentences because they had been held for months in preventive detention and because the court believed a display of mercy might lessen public sympathy for the young revolutionaries. The court even suggested the tsar might wish to pardon those students given heavier sentences. The tsar refused and let it be known he favored heavy penalties for all persons involved in revolutionary activity.

Thereafter, the revolutionaries decided the tsarist regime must be attacked directly. They adopted a policy of terrorism. In January 1878, Vera Zasulich (1849–1919) attempted to assassinate the military governor of Saint Petersburg. A jury acquitted her because the governor she had shot had a reputation for brutality. Some people also believed Zasulich had a personal rather than a political grievance against her victim. Nonetheless, the verdict further encouraged the terrorists.

In 1879, a group known as *The People's Will* split off from Land and Freedom. It was dedicated to the overthrow of the autocracy. Its members decided to assassinate the tsar himself. (See the Document, "The People's Will Issues a Revolutionary Manifesto," page 708.) Several attempts failed, but on March 1, 1881, a bomb hurled by a member of The People's Will killed Alexander II. Four men and two women were sentenced to death for the deed. All of them had been willing to die for their cause. The emergence of such dedicated revolutionary opposition was as much a part of the reign of Alexander II as were his reforms.

The reign of Alexander III (r. 1881–1894) strengthened that pessimism. He possessed all the autocratic and repressive characteristics of his grandfather, Nicholas I. Alexander III sought primarily to roll back his father's reforms. He favored the centralized bureaucracy over the *zemstvos*. He strengthened the secret police and increased censorship of the press. In effect, he confirmed all the evils that the revolutionaries saw as inherent in autocratic government. His son, Nicholas II (r. 1894–1917), would discover that autocracy could not survive the pressures of the twentieth century.

▼ Great Britain: Toward Democracy

While the continental nations became unified and struggled toward internal political restructuring, Great Britain symbolized the confident liberal state. Britain faced its own difficulties and domestic conflicts, but it seemed able to deal with them through its existing political institutions. The general prosperity of the third quarter of the century mitigated the social hostility of the 1840s. Even the leaders of trade unions during these years asked mainly to receive more of the fruits of prosperity and to have their social respectability acknowledged. Parliament itself remained an institution through which new groups and interests were absorbed into the existing political processes. (See "Encountering the Past: The Arrival of Penny Postage," page 710.)

The Second Reform Act (1867)

By the early 1860s, most observers realized the franchise would again have to be expanded. Many politicians came to believe that the only way to win over the workers' loyalty to the existing system was to accept their demands for the right to vote. Organizations such as the Reform League, led by John Bright (1811–1889), agitated for parliamentary action. In 1866, Lord Russell's Liberal ministry introduced a reform bill that a coalition of traditional Conservatives and antidemocratic Liberals defeated. Russell resigned, and the Conservative Lord Derby (1799–1869) replaced him.

The Conservative ministry, led in the House of Commons by Benjamin Disraeli (1804–1881), introduced its own reform bill in 1867. As the debate proceeded, Disraeli accepted one amendment after another and expanded the electorate well beyond the limits the Liberals had earlier proposed. The final measure increased the number of voters from approximately 1,430,000 to 2,470,000. Although Britain was not a democracy, the admission of large numbers of male working-class voters represented a large step in that direction. As was the case elsewhere in Europe

Tsar Alexander II (r. 1855–1881) was assassinated on March 1, 1881. The assassins first threw a bomb that wounded several Imperial guards. When the tsar stopped his carriage to see the wounded, the assassins threw a second bomb, killing him. Bildarchiv Preussischer Kulturbesitz/ Art Resource, NY

Document

THE PEOPLE'S WILL ISSUES A REVOLUTIONARY MANIFESTO

In the late 1870s, an extreme revolutionary movement appeared in Russia calling itself The People's Will. It advocated the overthrow of the tsarist government and the election of an Organizing Assembly to form a government based on popular representation. It directly embraced terrorism as a path toward its goal of the Russian people governing themselves. Members of this group assassinated Alexander II in 1881.

Which of the group's seven demands might be associated with liberalism, and which go beyond liberalism in their radical intent? Why does the group believe it must engage in terrorism as well as propaganda? Would any reforms by the Russian government have satisfied this group or dissuaded them from terrorist action?

Although we are ready to submit wholly to the popular will, we regard it as none the less our duty, as a party, to appear before the people with our program. . . . It is as follows:

1. Perpetual popular representation . . . having full power to act in all national questions.
2. General local self-government, secured by the election of all officers, and the economic independence of the people.
3. The self-controlled village commune as the economic and administrative unit.
4. Ownership of the land by the people.
5. A system of measures having for their object the turning over to the laborers of all mining works and factories.
6. Complete freedom of conscience, speech, association, public meeting, and electioneering activity.
7. The substitution of a territorial militia for the army. . . .

In view of the stated aim of the party its operations may be classified as follows:

1. Propaganda and agitation. Our propaganda has for its object the popularization, in all social classes, of the idea of a political and popular revolution as a means of social reform, as well as popularization of the party's own program. Its essential features are criticism of the existing order of things, and a statement and explanation of revolutionary methods. The aim of agitation should be to incite the people to protest as generally as possible against the present state of affairs, to demand such reforms as are in harmony with the party's purposes, and, especially, to demand the summoning of an Organizing Assembly. . . .
2. Destructive and terroristic activity. Terroristic activity consists in the destruction of the most harmful persons in the Government, the protection of the party from spies, and the punishment of official lawlessness and violence in all the more prominent and important cases in which such lawlessness and violence are manifested. The aim of such activity is to break down the prestige of Governmental power, to furnish continuous proof of the possibility of carrying on a contest with the Government, to raise in that way the revolutionary spirit of the people and inspire belief in the practicability of revolution, and, finally, to form a body suited and accustomed to warfare.

From George Kennan, *Siberia and the Exile System*, Vol. 2 (New York: The Century Co., 1891), pp. 495–499.

where the franchise was extended, however, women continued to have no political rights. Across Europe, the franchise was becoming a male prerogative instead of an upper-class one.

Like his contemporary Bismarck, Disraeli thought democracy could be a conservative tool. He thought that eventually significant portions of the working class would support Conservative candidates who were responsive to social issues. Because reform was inevitable, it was best for the Conservatives to enjoy the credit for it. He also thought the growing suburban middle class would become more conservative. In the long run, his intuition proved correct. The Conservative Party dominated British politics in the twentieth century.

The immediate election of 1868, however, dashed Disraeli's hopes. William Gladstone (1809–1898) became the new prime minister. Gladstone had begun political life in 1833 as a strong Tory, but over the next thirty-five years, he became steadily more liberal. He had supported Robert Peel, free trade, repeal of the Corn Laws, and efficient administration. As chancellor of the exchequer (finance minister) during the 1850s and early 1860s, he had lowered taxes and government expenditures. In 1866, he had been Russell's spokesperson in the House of Commons for the unsuccessful Liberal reform bill.

View the **Image** "Gladstone and Disraeli—Punch Cartoon" on **MyHistoryLab.com**

Gladstone's Great Ministry (1868–1874)

Gladstone's ministry of 1868 to 1874 witnessed the culmination of classical British liberalism. Those institutions that remained the preserve of the aristocracy and the Anglican church were opened to people from other classes and religious denominations. In 1870, competitive examinations for the civil service replaced patronage. In 1871, the purchase of officers' commissions in the army was abolished. The same year, Anglican religious requirements for the faculties of Oxford and Cambridge universities were removed. The Ballot Act of 1872 introduced voting by secret ballot.

The most momentous measure of Gladstone's first ministry was the Education Act of 1870. For the first time in British history, the government assumed the responsibility for establishing and running elementary schools. Previously, British education had been a task relegated to the religious denominations, which received small amounts of state support for the purpose. Henceforth, the government would establish schools where religious denominations had not done so.

These reforms were typically liberal. They sought to remove abuses without destroying institutions and to permit all able citizens to compete on the grounds of ability and merit. They tried to avoid the potential danger to a democratic state of an illiterate citizenry. At the same time, they reinforced loyalty to the nation by abolishing sources of discontent.

Disraeli in Office (1874–1880)

Disraeli succeeded Gladstone as prime minister in 1874. The two men differed on most issues. Whereas Gladstone looked to individualism, free trade, and competition to solve social problems, Disraeli believed in paternalistic legislation to protect the weak and ease class antagonisms.

Disraeli had few specific programs or ideas. The significant social legislation of his ministry stemmed primarily from the efforts of his home secretary, Richard Cross (1823–1914). The Public Health Act of 1875

A House of Commons Debate. William Ewart Gladstone, standing on the right, is attacking Benjamin Disraeli, who sits with legs crossed and arms folded. Gladstone served in the British Parliament from the 1830s through the 1890s. Four times the Liberal Party prime minister, he was responsible for guiding major reforms through Parliament. Disraeli, regarded as the founder of modern British conservatism, served as prime minister from 1874 to 1880. Mary Evans Picture Library

ENCOUNTERING THE *Past*

THE ARRIVAL OF PENNY POSTAGE

WHILE THE ARMIES of the great powers were redrawing the map of Europe during the middle of the nineteenth century, new forms of administration were drawing people closer together. One of the most important of these innovations was the development of postal systems for delivering mail inexpensively. The British government took the lead.

Sending letters and newspapers through the mail had become increasingly expensive, and the British postal service ran large deficits. Other countries had similar problems. At that time the weight of the item to be mailed and the distance over which it had to be carried determined how much it cost to mail it. Furthermore, the person receiving the letter or packet, not the sender, had to pay the postage. Many officials had the privilege of franking their letters and thus paying nothing. The system encouraged schemes to avoid paying postage. Some people could not afford the postage on letters sent to them. Others put symbols on the outside of a letter, so the recipient could refuse to accept the letter but still "get the message."

Rowland Hill (1795–1879), an English reformer, proposed a simple new procedure in 1837. The price of postage would be lowered, would be uniform for most letters and newspapers regardless of distance, and would be prepaid by the sender. Franking by government officials would also end.

In 1840, the system, known as the Uniform Penny Post, began. Within two years the volume of British mail grew from approximately 75 million items to 196.5 million and, by 1849, to 329 million. The reduced cost of postage meant almost everyone could afford to send letters and postcards. It also led to a huge increase in the size of the government workforce. In Britain and most other countries, the number of postal workers was soon rivaled only by the number of soldiers and sailors.

Hill had also suggested a small, self-adhesive stamp be attached to a letter to indicate the postage had been paid. The first such stamp bore only the words POSTAGE ONE PENNY. It paid for letters up to one-half ounce. A two-penny stamp was used for letters that weighed an ounce.

Other nations soon issued their own stamps. It became as important for governments to prevent the forging of postage stamps as currency. Consequently, stamps were printed from engraved steel plates to which small changes were made from time to time. Those changes, introduced to prevent fraud or to commemorate famous people and events, together with the sheer number of national postal systems with their own stamps, gave rise to the hobby of stamp collecting.

The rise of the modern postal system also fostered international cooperation. A treaty signed in Berne, Switzerland, in 1874, established what became the Universal Postal Union, which is still functioning. It mandates that the postage paid in the sender's nation assures delivery of a letter or package anywhere in the world.

Sources: M. J. Daunton, "Rowland Hill and the Penny Post," *History Today,* August 1985; "Post, and Postal Service," *Encyclopedia Britannica,* 11th ed.

What changes did Rowland Hill introduce into the British postal service?

How did those changes affect the quantity of mail and the size of the government workforce?

With the new British postal system, the volume of mail vastly increased, as did the number of postal workers involved in sorting and delivering it. Illustrated London News Ltd/Mary Evans Picture Library consolidated previous legislation on sanitation and reaffirmed the duty of the state to interfere with private property to protect health and physical well-being. Through the Artisan Dwelling Act of 1875, the government became actively involved in providing housing for the working class. That same year, in an important symbolic gesture, the Conservative majority in Parliament gave new protection to British trade unions and allowed them to raise picket lines. The Gladstone ministry, although recognizing the legality of unions, had refused such protection.

The Irish Question

From the late 1860s onward, Irish nationalists had sought to achieve **home rule** for Ireland, by which they meant Irish control of local government. The Irish Question became the major issue of the 1880s, during Gladstone's second ministry.

During his first ministry, Gladstone addressed the Irish question through two major pieces of legislation. In 1869, he disestablished the Church of Ireland, the Irish branch of the Anglican church. Henceforth, Irish Roman Catholics would not pay taxes to support the hated Protestant church, to which few of the Irish belonged. Second, in 1870, the Liberal ministry sponsored a land act that provided compensation to those Irish tenant farmers who were evicted and loans for those who wished to purchase their land. Throughout the 1870s, the Irish question continued to fester. Land remained the center of the agitation. The organization of the Irish Land League in the late 1870s led to intense agitation and intimidation of landlords, who were often Protestants of English descent. The leader of the Irish movement for a just land settlement and for home rule was Charles Stewart Parnell (1846–1891). In 1881, the second Gladstone ministry passed another Irish land act that strengthened tenant rights. It was accompanied, however, by a Coercion Act to restore law and order to Ireland.

By 1885, Parnell had organized eighty-five Irish members of the House of Commons into a tightly disciplined party that often voted as a bloc. They frequently disrupted Parliament to gain attention for the cause of home rule. In the election of 1885, the Irish Party emerged holding the balance of power between the English Liberals and Conservatives. Irish support could decide which party took office. In December 1885, Gladstone announced his support of home rule for Ireland and Parnell gave his votes to a Liberal ministry. The home rule issue then split the Liberal Party. In 1886, a group known as the Liberal Unionists joined with the Conservatives to defeat home rule. Gladstone called for a new election, but the Liberals were defeated. They remained divided, and Ireland remained firmly under English administration.

The new Conservative ministry of Lord Salisbury (1830–1903) attempted to reconcile the Irish to British rule through public works and administrative reform. The policy, which was tied to further coercion, had only marginal success. In 1892, Gladstone returned to power. A second Home Rule Bill passed the House of Commons but was defeated in the House of Lords. There the Irish question stood until after the turn of the century. The Conservatives sponsored a land act in 1903 that carried out the final transfer of land to tenant ownership. Ireland became a country of small farms. In 1912, a Liberal ministry passed the third Home Rule Bill. Under the provisions of the House of Lords Act of 1911, which curbed the power of the Lords, the bill had to pass the Commons three times over the Lords' veto to become law. The third passage occurred in the summer of 1914, but the implementation of home rule was suspended for the duration of World War I.

The Irish question affected British politics in a manner not unlike that of the Austrian nationalities problem. Normal British domestic issues could not be resolved because of the political divisions Ireland created. The split of the Liberal Party proved especially harmful to the cause of further social and political reform. People who could agree about reform could not agree about Ireland,

MAJOR DATES IN LATE-NINETEENTH-CENTURY BRITAIN

1867	Second Reform Act
1868	Gladstone becomes prime minister
1869	Disestablishment of Church of Ireland
1870	Education Act and first Irish Land Act
1871	Purchase of army officers' commissions abolished
1871	Religious tests abolished at Oxford and Cambridge
1872	Secret Ballot Act
1874	Disraeli becomes prime minister
1875	Public Health Act and Artisan Dwelling Act
1880	Beginning of Gladstone's second ministry
1881	Second Irish Land Act and Irish Coercion Act
1884	Third Reform Act
1885	Gladstone announces support of Irish home rule
1886	Home Rule Bill defeated and Lord Salisbury becomes the Conservative prime minister
1892	Gladstone begins his third ministry; second Irish Home Rule Bill defeated
1903	Third Irish Land Act
1912	Third Irish Home Rule Bill passed
1914	Provisions of Irish Home Rule Bill suspended because of the outbreak of World War I

and the Irish problem seemed more important. Because the two traditional parties failed to deal with the social questions by the turn of the century, a newly organized Labour Party began to fill the vacuum.

In Perspective

Between 1850 and 1875, the major contours of the political systems that would dominate Europe until World War I had been drawn. These systems and political arrangements solved, as far as such matters can be solved, many of the political problems that had troubled Europeans during the first half of the nineteenth century. On the whole, the concept of the nation-state had triumphed. Support for governments no longer stemmed from loyalty to dynasties, but from citizen participation. Moreover, the unity of nations was now based on cultural, linguistic, and historical bonds. Both parliamentary governments and monarchies had been compelled to recognize the force of nationalism and the larger role of citizens in political affairs. Only Russia failed to make such concessions. In Russia the only concession to popular opinion had been the emancipation of the serfs.

Future discontent would arise primarily from the demands of labor to enter the political processes and the unsatisfied aspirations of subject nationalities. These two sources of unrest would trouble Europe for the next forty years and would eventually undermine the political structures created during the late nineteenth century.

KEY TERM

home rule (p. 711)

REVIEW QUESTIONS

1. Why did the Ottoman Empire attempt to reform itself between 1839 and 1914? What was the result of these efforts?
2. Why was it so difficult to unify Italy? What groups wanted unification? Why did Cavour succeed? What did Garibaldi contribute to Italian unification?
3. How and why did Bismarck unify Germany? Why had earlier attempts failed? How did German unification affect the rest of Europe?
4. What events led to the establishment of the Third Republic in France? What were the objectives of the Paris Commune?
5. What problems did Austria share with other eastern European empires? Were they solved? Why did the Habsburgs agree to the Compromise of 1867? Was it a success?
6. What reforms did Alexander II institute in Russia? Did they solve Russia's domestic problems? Why did the abolition of serfdom not satisfy the peasants? What were the goals of *The People's Will*?
7. How did the policies of the British Liberal and Conservative parties differ between 1860 and 1890? Why was Irish home rule such a divisive issue in British politics?

SUGGESTED READINGS

V. Aksan, *Ottoman Wars, 1700–1870: An Empire Besieged* (2007). Explores the impact of war on the weakening of the Ottoman Empire.

R. Aldous, *The Lion and the Unicorn: Gladstone vs. Disraeli* (2008). An accessible volume tracing the great political rivalry of the mid-Victorian age.

P. Bew, *Ireland: The Politics of Enmity 1789–2006* (2007). A major, outstanding survey of the sweep of modern Irish history.

E. F. Biagini, *British Democracy and Irish Nationalism 1876–1906* (2007). Explores impact of the Irish question on British political structures themselves.

D. Blackbourn, *The Long Nineteenth Century: A History of Germany, 1780–1918* (1998). An outstanding survey.

R. Blake, *Disraeli* (1967). Remains the best biography.

J. Breuilly, *Austria, Prussia and Germany, 1806–1871* (2002). Examines the complex relations of these states leading up to German unification.

C. Clark, *Iron Kingdom: The Rise and Downfall of Prussia, 1600–1947* (2006). Now the standard survey.

M. Clark, *The Italian Risorgimento* (1998). A brief overview.

R. B. Edgerton, *Death or Glory: The Legacy of the Crimean War* (2000). Multifaceted study of a mismanaged war that transformed European politics.

C. J. Eichner, *Surmounting the Barricades: Women in the Paris Commune* (2004). Explores the impact of women's journalism and organizing in the Commune and wider radical political tradition.

B. Eklof and J. Bushnell, *Russia's Great Reforms, 1855–1881* (1994). A clear analysis.

R. Gildea, *Children of the Revolution: The French, 1799–1914* (2008). An important study of how the French Revolution affected the next century in French society and politics.
M. A. Hanioglu, *A Brief History of the Late Ottoman Empire* (2008). An accessible introduction.
R. Kee, *The Green Flag: A History of Irish Nationalism* (2001). A lively, accessible account.
D. Langewiesche, *Liberalism in Germany* (1999). A broad survey that is particularly good on the problems unification caused for German Liberals.
H. C. G. Matthew, *Gladstone, 1809–1898* (1998). A superb biography.
D. Moon, *Abolition of Serfdom in Russia: 1762–1907* (2001). Analysis with documents.
W. G. Moss, *Russia in the Age of Alexander II, Tolstoy and Dostoyevsky* (2002). Emphasizes the cultural background.
N. M. Naimark, *Terrorists and Social Democrats: The Russian Revolutionary Movement under Alexander III* (1983). Useful discussion of a complicated subject.
P. G. Nord, *The Republican Moment: Struggles for Democracy in Nineteenth-Century France* (1996). A major examination of nineteenth-century French political culture.
J. Parry, *The Politics of Patriotism: English Liberalism, National Identity and Europe, 1830–1886* (2006). An excellent overview of English Liberalism and how its values determined mid-Victorian relations with the Continent.
J. P. Parry, *The Rise and Fall of Liberal Government in Victorian Britain* (1994). An outstanding study.
O. Pflanze, *Bismarck and the Development of Germany*, 3 vols. (1990). A major biography and history of Germany for the period.
R. Price, *The French Second Empire: An Anatomy of Political Power* (2001). This volume along with the following title are the most comprehensive recent study.
R. Price, *People and Politics in France, 1848–1870* (2004). A clear survey.
E. Radzinsky, *Alexander II: The Last Great Tsar* (2005). An accessible biography.
L. Riall, *Garibaldi: Invention of a Hero* (2007). An exploration of a nationalist hero's reputation in his own day and later.
A. Scirocco, *Garibaldi: Citizen of the World: A Biography* (2007). An admiring account.
D. Shafer, *The Paris Commune: French Politics, Culture, and Society at the Crossroads of the Revolutionary Tradition and Revolutionary Socialism* (2005). Relates the Commune to previous and later revolutionary traditions.
A. Sked, *Decline and Fall of the Habsburg Empire 1815–1918* (2001). A major, accessible survey of a difficult subject.
D. M. Smith, *Cavour* (1984). An excellent biography.

MyHistoryLab™ MEDIA ASSIGNMENTS

Find these resources in the Media Assignments folder for Chapter 22 on **MyHistoryLab**.

QUESTIONS FOR ANALYSIS

1. What are some of the weaknesses of this painting as a historical source?

   ***Section:* The Crimean War (1853–1856)**
   View the **Closer Look** The Crimean War Recalled, p. 687

2. Why do the authors say that the countries most affected by German unification were France and Austria?

   ***Section:* German Unification**
   View the **Map** Map Discovery: The Unification of Germany, 1866–1871, p. 696

3. What do you consider the most profound change in the Ottoman Empire in the period of the Tanzimat?

   ***Section:* The Crimean War (1853–1856)**
   Watch the **Video** Video Lectures: The Ottoman Tanzimat Period (1839–1876): The Middle East Confronts Modernity, p. 688

4. What principles does the author place in opposition to Mommsen's nationalistic and historical principles?

   ***Section:* German Unification**
   Read the **Document** Fustel de Coulanges, *Letter to German Historian Theodor Mommsen, 1870*, p. 700

5. What do you consider the greatest weakness in the conditions for former serfs laid out by this document?

   ***Section:* Russia: Emancipation and Revolutionary Stirrings**
   Read the **Document** Emancipation Manifesto (1861), p. 705

OTHER RESOURCES FROM THIS CHAPTER

The Crimean War (1853–1856)

View the **Map** Map Discovery: The Crimean War, 1853–1856, p. 686

View the **Map** The Decline of the Ottoman Empire, 1800–1913, p. 686

Read the **Document** An Ottoman Government Decree Defines the Official Notion of the "Modern" Citizen, June 19, 1870, p. 688

Italian Unification

View the **Map** The Unification of Italy, 1859–1870, p. 690

Read the **Compare and Connect** Nineteenth-Century Nationalism: Two Sides, p. 694

German Unification

Read the **Document** A Letter from Bismarck (1866), p. 698

View the **Map** Map Discovery: The German Empire, p. 700

France: From Liberal Empire to the Third Republic

View the Map Map Discovery: The Paris Commune, 1871, p. 700

The Habsburg Empire

View the Map The Nationalities of Austria-Hungary, 1867, p. 703

Russia: Emancipation and Revolutionary Stirrings

Watch the Video Russian Terrorism, p. 705

View the Map Map Discovery: Russian Serfs, p. 705

Great Britain: Toward Democracy

View the Image Gladstone and Disraeli—Punch Cartoon, p. 709

Women laundry workers. Although new opportunities opened to them in the late nineteenth century, many working-class women, like these women ironing in a laundry, remained in traditional occupations. As the wine bottle suggests, alcoholism was a problem for women as well as men engaged in tedious work. Edgar Degas (1834–1917), "Two Laundresses" (c. 1884). Réunion des Musées Nationaux/Art Resource, NY

Listen to the **Chapter Audio** on **MyHistoryLab.com**

23

The Building of European Supremacy: Society and Politics to World War I

▼ Population Trends and Migration

▼ The Second Industrial Revolution
New Industries • Economic Difficulties

▼ The Middle Classes in Ascendancy
Social Distinctions within the Middle Classes

▼ Late-Nineteenth-Century Urban Life
The Redesign of Cities • Urban Sanitation • Housing Reform and Middle-Class Values

▼ Varieties of Late-Nineteenth-Century Women's Experiences
Women's Social Disabilities • New Employment Patterns for Women • Working-Class Women • Poverty and Prostitution • Women of the Middle Class • The Rise of Political Feminism

▼ Jewish Emancipation
Differing Degrees of Citizenship • Broadened Opportunities

▼ Labor, Socialism, and Politics to World War I
Trade Unionism • Democracy and Political Parties • Karl Marx and the First International • Great Britain: Fabianism and Early Welfare Programs • France: "Opportunism" Rejected • Germany: Social Democrats and Revisionism • Russia: Industrial Development and the Birth of Bolshevism

▼ In Perspective

LEARNING OBJECTIVES

Why were so many Europeans on the move in the late nineteenth century?

How did the second Industrial Revolution transform European life?

What explains the prominence of the middle class in late-nineteenth-century Europe?

What forces shaped the development of European cities?

What was life like for women in late-nineteenth-century Europe?

How did Jewish life in Europe change in the late nineteenth century?

What role did the socialist and labor movements play in late-nineteenth-century politics?

THE GROWTH OF industrialism between 1860 and 1914 increased Europe's productive capacity to unprecedented and unparalleled levels. New steel mills, railways, shipyards, and chemical plants reflected an expanding supply of capital goods in the second half of the nineteenth century. By the first decade of the twentieth century, the age of the automobile, the airplane, the bicycle, the refrigerated ship, the telephone, the radio, the typewriter, and the electric light bulb had dawned. The world's economies, based on the gold standard, became increasingly interdependent. Europe's political, economic, and cultural reach extended across much of the inhabited world as European empires established global empires (see Chapter 25). European manufactured goods and financial capital flowed into markets all over the globe. In turn, Europeans imported foreign raw materials and foodstuffs. Within Europe itself, the eastern and southern European countries tended to import finished goods from the west and the north and to export agricultural products. While European societies remained divided over questions like workers' and women's rights, most Europeans took pride in what they believed was their superior "civilization" compared to the peoples they encountered in Africa and Asia. Political leaders took advantage of the popularity of imperialism to distract the ever-expanding electorate from dissatisfaction at home.

Within Europe, nation-states with large electorates, political parties, and centralized bureaucracies emerged. Business adopted large-scale corporate structures, and the labor force organized itself into trade unions. The number of white-collar workers increased. Western Europe became predominantly urban. Socialism strongly affected the political life of all nations. The foundations of the welfare state and of vast military establishments were laid. Taxation increased accordingly.

Europe had also quietly become dependent on the resources and markets of the rest of the world. Changes in the weather in Kansas, Argentina, or New Zealand might now affect the European economy. Before World War I, however, Europe's industrial, military, and financial supremacy concealed that dependency. Many Europeans assumed their supremacy to be natural and permanent, but the twentieth century would reveal it to have been temporary.

▼ Population Trends and Migration

The proportion of Europeans in the world's total population was apparently greater around 1900—estimated at about 20 percent—than ever before or since. The number of Europeans had risen from approximately 266 million in 1850 to 401 million in 1900 and to 447 million in 1910. Thereafter, birth and death rates declined or stabilized in Europe and other developed regions, and population growth began to slow.

Watch the Video "The Big Picture: The World in 1914 C.E." on MyHistoryLab.com

Europe's peoples were on the move in the latter half of the century as never before (see Map 23–1). The midcentury emancipation of peasants made legal movement and migration easier. Railways, steamships, and better roads increased mobility. Cheap land and better wages accompanied economic development in parts of Europe, North America, Latin America, and Australia, enticing people to move from regions where they had little prospect of improving their lives to regions that held or seemed to hold opportunity. In Europe itself the main migration continued to be from the countryside into urban areas. During this era, Europeans also left their own continent in record numbers. Between 1846 and 1932, more than 50 million Europeans left their homelands. The major areas to benefit from this movement were the United States, Canada, Australia, South Africa, Brazil, Algeria, and Argentina. At midcentury, most of the emigrants were from Great Britain (especially Ireland), the German states, and Scandinavia. After 1885, migration from southern and eastern Europe rose. This exodus helped relieve the social and population pressures on the Continent. Although much of this migration was permanent, even Europeans who remained in the countries of their birth were more likely to move seasonally or temporarily than ever before.

▼ The Second Industrial Revolution

During the third quarter of the nineteenth century, the gap that had long existed between British and continental economic development closed. (See Map 23–2, p. 718.) The basic heavy industries of Belgium, France, and Germany expanded rapidly. In particular, the growth of German industry was stunning. German steel production surpassed Britain's in 1893 and was nearly twice that of Britain by the outbreak of World War I. The emergence of an industrial Germany was the major fact of European economic and political life at the turn of the century, and contributed to British fear of German power.

View the Map "Industrial Development in Key Regional Centers, ca. 1900" on MyHistoryLab.com

New Industries

Initially, the economic expansion of the third quarter of the century involved the spread of industries similar to those pioneered earlier in Great Britain. In particular, the expansion of railway systems on the Continent spurred economic growth. Thereafter, however, wholly new industries emerged. This latter development is usually termed the ***Second Industrial Revolution.*** The first Industrial Revolution was associated with textiles, steam, and iron; by contrast, the second was associated with steel, chemicals, electricity, and oil.

In the 1850s, Henry Bessemer (1830–1898), an English engineer, discovered a new process, named after him,

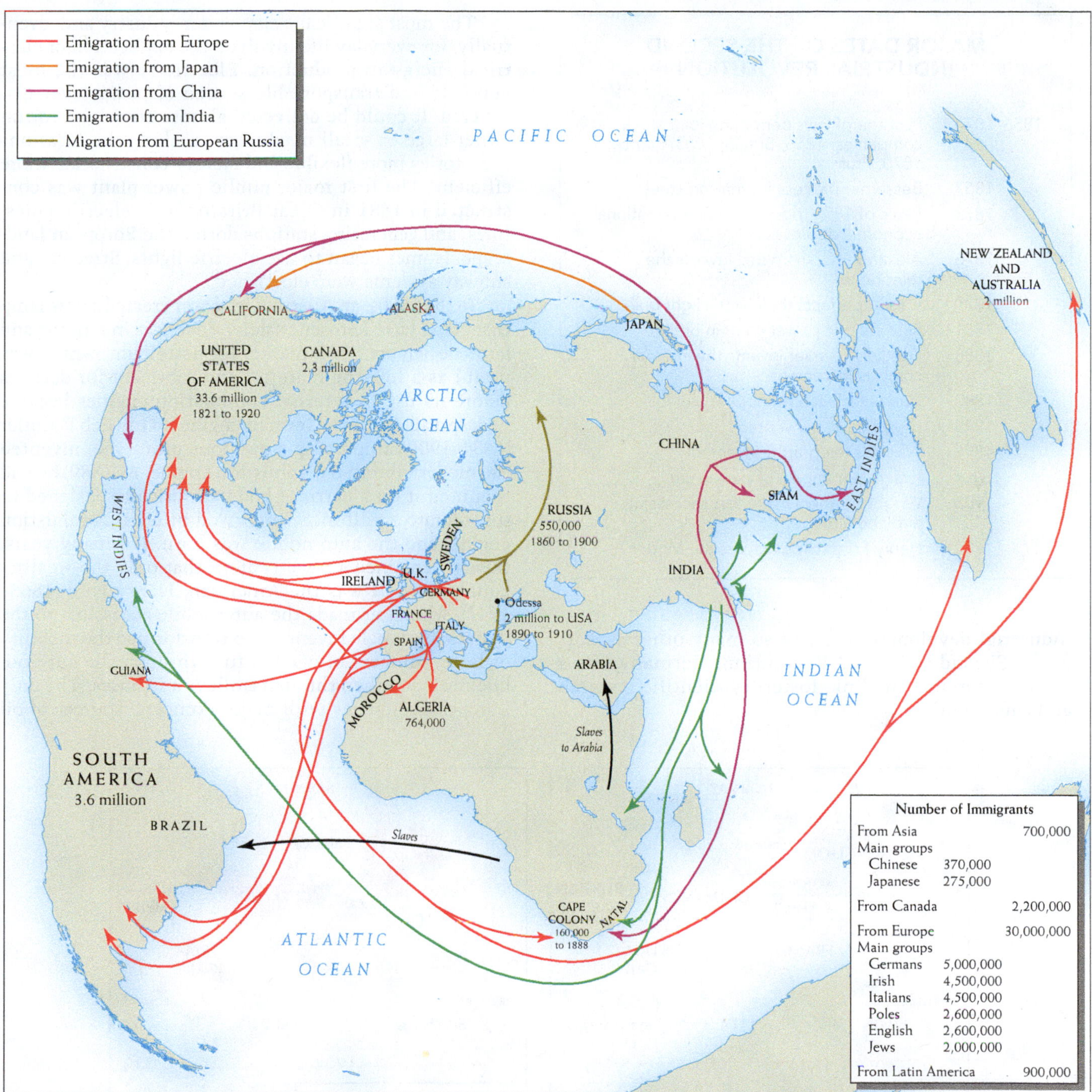

Map 23–1 **PATTERNS OF GLOBAL MIGRATION, 1840–1900** Emigration was a global process by the late nineteenth century, but more immigrants went to the United States than to every other nation combined.

for manufacturing steel cheaply in large quantities. In 1860, Great Britain, Belgium, France, and Germany combined produced 125,000 tons of steel. By 1913, the figure had risen to over 32 million tons.

The chemical industry also came of age during this period. The Solway process of alkali production allowed the recovery of more chemical by-products and permitted increased production of sulfuric acid and laundry soap. New dyestuffs and plastics were also developed. Formal scientific research played an important role in this growth of the chemical industry, marking the beginning of a direct link between science and

MAJOR DATES OF THE SECOND INDUSTRIAL REVOLUTION

1856–1870	Passage of laws permitting joint stock companies: 1856, Britain; 1863, France; 1870, Prussia
1857	Bessemer process for making steel
1873	Panic of 1873 triggers major international economic depression
1876	Alexander Graham Bell invents the telephone
1879	Edison perfects the electric light bulb
1881	First electric power plant in Britain
1885	Gottlieb Daimler invents the internal combustion engine
1889	Daimler's first automobile
1895	Diesel engine invented
1895	Wireless telegraphy invented
1890s	First major impact of petroleum
1903	Wright brothers make first successful airplane flight
1909	Henry Ford manufactures the Model T

industrial development. As in so many other aspects of the Second Industrial Revolution, Germany was a leader in forging this link, fostering scientific research and education.

The most significant change for industry and, eventually, for everyday life involved the application of electrical energy to production. Electricity was the most versatile and transportable source of power ever discovered. It could be delivered almost anywhere to run either large or small machinery, making the locations of factories more flexible and factory construction more efficient. The first major public power plant was constructed in 1881 in Great Britain. Soon electric poles, lines, and generating stations dotted the European landscape. Homes began to use electric lights. Streetcar and subway systems were electrified.

In the 1850s, an Austrian inventor created a new lamp that could burn kerosene safely. Advances in refining and lamp design created a market for petroleum, which was useful as a lighting material and lubricant for decades before its use in internal combustion engines became widespread. In 1885, German engineer Gottlieb Daimler (1834–1900), improving a previous prototype, invented the modern internal combustion engine. By 1889, he had mounted it on a carriage body specifically designed to incorporate a still more improved internal combustion engine, and the automobile was born. For many years, the car remained a novelty item that only the wealthy could afford. It was the American, Henry Ford (1863–1947), who later made the automobile accessible to the masses. No single invention so transformed the mobility of large numbers of people, first through the automobile itself and then through trolleys and buses. The only European countries with major domestic sources of oil

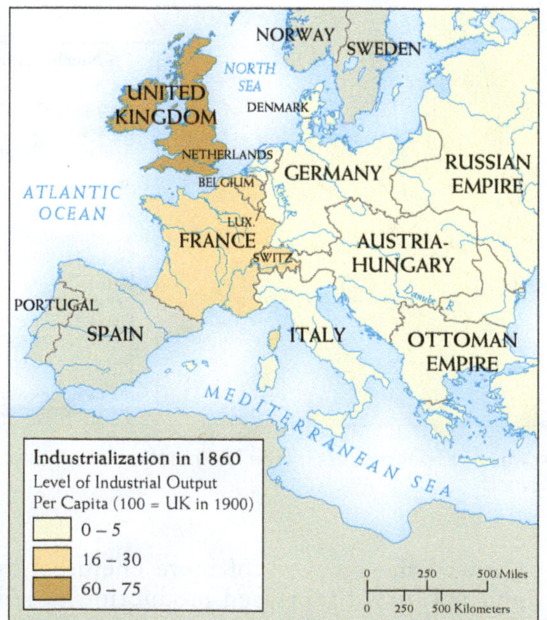

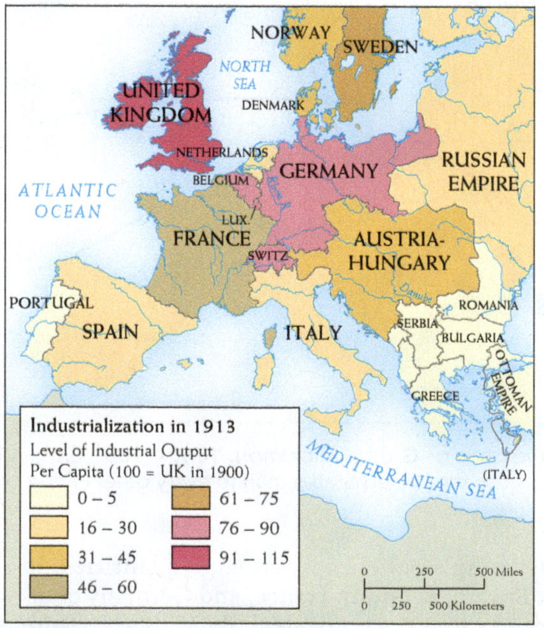

Map 23–2 **EUROPEAN INDUSTRIALIZATION, 1860–1913** In 1860 Britain was far more industrialized than other European countries. In the following half-century, industrial output rose significantly, if unevenly, across much of Western Europe, especially in the new German Empire. The economies of the Balkan states and the Ottoman Empire, however, remained largely agricultural.

The invention and commercialization of automobiles soon led to auto races in Europe and North America. Here Henri Fournier, the winner of the 1901 Paris to Berlin Motor Car Race, sits in his winning racing car manufactured by the Paris-based auto firm of Emile and Louis Mors. Getty Images Inc.–Hulton Archive Photos

production were Russia and Austria-Hungary. Then as now, Europe depended on imported supplies of oil. The major oil companies were Standard Oil of the United States, British Shell Oil, and Royal Dutch Petroleum.

Economic Difficulties

Despite the multiplication of new industries, the second half of the nineteenth century was not a period of uninterrupted or smooth economic growth. Both industry and agriculture generally prospered from 1850 to 1873, but in the last quarter of the century, economic advance slowed. Speculation and overexpansion, as well as Germany's abandonment of the silver standard, led to the first of many crises of modern capitalism. Bad weather and foreign competition put grave pressures on European agriculture and caused many European peasants to emigrate to other parts of the world.

As new farming regions developed in the United States, Canada, Argentina, Australia, and New Zealand, products from those areas challenged the market for home-produced European agricultural goods. Refrigerated ships could bring meat and dairy products to Europe from all over the world. Grain could be grown more economically on the plains of North America, Argentina, and Ukraine than it could in Western Europe, and railways and steamships made it easy and cheap to ship it across continents and oceans. These developments lowered the prices of consumer goods, but put great pressure on European agriculture.

Several large banks failed in 1873, and the rate of capital investment slowed. Some industries then entered a two-decade-long period of stagnation that many contemporaries regarded as a depression. Although the general standard of living in the industrialized nations improved in the second half of the nineteenth century, many workers still lived and labored in abysmal conditions. There were pockets of *unemployment* (a word that was coined during this period), and strikes and other forms of labor unrest were common. These economic difficulties fed the growth of trade unions and socialist political parties.

The new industries produced consumer goods, and expansion in consumer demand brought the economy out of stagnation by the end of the century. (See "Encountering the Past: Bicycles: Transportation, Freedom, and Sport," page 721.) Lower food prices eventually allowed all classes to spend more on consumer goods. Urbanization created larger markets by exposing people to more commodities than they would have encountered in the countryside. New forms of retailing and marketing appeared—department stores, chain stores, mail-order catalogs, and advertising—simultaneously stimulating and feeding consumer demand. (See the Document, "Paris Department Stores Expand Their Business," page 722.) Imperialism also opened new markets overseas for European consumer goods.

▼ The Middle Classes in Ascendancy

The sixty years before World War I were the age of the middle classes. The London Great Exhibition of 1851 held in the Crystal Palace displayed the products and the new material life they had forged. Thereafter, the middle classes became the arbiter of consumer taste. After the revolutions of 1848, the middle classes ceased to be a revolutionary group. Once the question of social equality and equality of property had been raised, large and small property owners across the Continent moved to protect what they possessed against demands from socialists and other working-class groups.

Social Distinctions within the Middle Classes

The middle classes, never perfectly homogeneous, grew increasingly diverse. Their most prosperous members—the owners and managers of great businesses and banks—lived in splendor that rivaled, and sometimes exceeded, that of the aristocracy. In Britain some of them, such as W. H. Smith (1825–1891), the owner of railway newsstands, were made members of the House of Lords. The Krupp family of Germany who owned huge steel works in the Rhineland were pillars of the state and were ennobled by the German emperor and received visits from the imperial court.

Only a few hundred families gained such wealth. Beneath them were the comfortable small entrepreneurs and professional people, whose incomes

Document

PRAISE AND CONCERNS REGARDING RAILWAY TRAVEL

In the nineteenth century, the superlative symbol of modern, industrial society was the railroad. At the same time that writers and travelers praised the new mobility made possible by rail travel, they also feared the moral, social, economic, and even physical effects this new invention would have on rural communities, innkeepers, and travelers themselves. These excerpts show both the excitement and the anxiety inspired by the new mode of travel. The first is from German poet Heinrich Heine's 1843 reflection on the opening of the railway lines from Paris to Rouen and Orléans. The second is from an 1884 medical text cautioning against the physical and psychological trauma of travel at great speeds by railway.

How did the railway make distant places seem closer together? What distinguished railway travel from the forms of travel that preceded it? Why was railway travel considered stressful? How does the railway symbolize the modern world?

"What changes must now occur, in our way of looking at things, in our notions! Even the elementary concepts of time and space have begun to vacillate. Space is killed by the railways, and we are left with time alone. . . . Now you can travel to Orléans in four and a half hours, and it takes no longer to get to Rouen. Just imagine what will happen when the lines to Belgium and Germany are completed and connected with their railways! I feel as if the mountains and forests of all countries were advancing on Paris. Even now, I can smell the German linden trees; the North Sea's breakers are rolling against my door."

"There is pulling at the eyeballs on looking out of the window; a jarring noise, the compound of continuous noise of wheels, and this conducted into the framework of the compartment; with the obligato [or persistent motif] of whistle and of the brake dashing in occasionally, and always carrying some element of annoyance, surprise, or shock; there is the swaying of the train from side to side, or the jolting over uneven rails and ill-adjusted points; and the general effect of these upon the temper, the muscles, and the moral nature. Let all that is especially, or accidentally, out of the order be left out of consideration, and suppose that all is as good as it can be, and yet there are the residua that have been mentioned. There are 'impressions' that are made, and that unavoidably, by the very conditions of the journey; and they involve fatigue. The eyes are strained, the ears are dinned, the muscles are jostled hither and thither, and the nerves are worried by the attempt to maintain order, and so comes weariness."

From Wolfgang Schivelbusch, *The Railway Journey: The Industrialization of Space and Time in the 19th Century* (Berkeley: University of California Press, 1986), pp. 37, 118.

permitted private homes, large quantities of furniture, pianos, pictures, books, journals, education for their children, and vacations. Also in this group were the shopkeepers, schoolteachers, librarians, and others who had either a bit of property or a skill derived from education that provided respectable nonmanual employment.

Finally, there was a wholly new element—"white-collar workers"—who formed the lower middle class, or ***petite bourgeoisie.*** They included secretaries, retail clerks, and lower-level bureaucrats in business and government. They often had working-class origins and might even belong to unions, but they had middle-class aspirations and consciously sought to distance themselves from a working-class lifestyle. They pursued educational opportunities and chances for even the slightest career advancement for themselves and their children. Many of them spent much of their disposable

ENCOUNTERING THE *Past*

BICYCLES: TRANSPORTATION, FREEDOM, AND SPORT

BEFORE THE CAR came the bicycle. Bicycles were the first mass-produced, affordable machines for individual travel. Between 1880 and 1900, they took Europe and North America by storm. For the first time in history, individual men and, significantly, women had a machine that enabled them to travel on their own for work or pleasure. Bicycles had an immense impact on Western society.

The first functioning bicycles had been invented in Germany about 1817, but they were clumsy and dangerous. Made of wood, these machines lacked pedals and tires. They had to be pushed along the ground, and their riders could not control their speed. It took another eighty years for the modern bicycle to take shape. Pedals were introduced in the 1860s. Metal frames, solid rubber tires, and chain drives, which increased speed, appeared in the 1870s. In the 1880s, the ride became much smoother when John Boyd Dunlop, an Irish physician, invented the pneumatic tire, and in France, the Michelin brothers introduced the inner tube. (Before then, the ride was so rough that bicycles were sometimes called "boneshakers.") By the 1890s, the "safety bicycle" with its now familiar triangular frame and chain drive attached to the pedal and back wheel was being mass-produced across Europe and North America, and men and women of the working class could afford them. By 1900, male workers of modest means across Europe were riding bicycles to work.

By increasing individual mobility, the bicycle made it easier to get to work, to hold a job farther from home, and to move about one's city or town or reach the countryside. New clothing designs, especially "bloomers," trousers worn under skirts (designed before the bicycle), permitted women to bicycle while maintaining modesty. In the 1890s, feminists like Marie Pognon in France and Susan B. Anthony in the United States hailed the "egalitarian and leveling bicycle" for the freedom it gave women.

By 1914, there were millions of cyclists across the transatlantic world. Europeans and Americans organized cycling clubs with distinctive uniforms. Some of these clubs, such as the English Clarion Cycling Clubs, the French Union Sportive du Parti Socialiste, and the German *Solidaritet*, used cycling trips to spread literature for left-wing causes. Other groups cycled for pleasure. The kinds of touring clubs that now exist for automobiles were first organized for cyclists, as were many of the early European travel guides such as the French *Guides Michelin*, which first appeared in 1900. Then as now, Michelin made tires and stood to sell more of them the more people toured the countryside.

Bicycle racing quickly became a competitive sport. The most famous professional racer in the world was Marshall Walter "Major" Taylor, an African American who raced in both the United States and Europe. Paris and other French cities built velodromes for indoor cycle racing, which was one of the official sports of the first modern Olympics in 1896. In 1903, *L'Auto*, a French sports paper, organized the first Tour de France race to increase its circulation. Six riders raced a 2,500-km course over nineteen days.

Sources: Eugen Weber, *France: Fin de Siècle* (Cambridge, MA: Harvard University Press, 1986), pp. 103–104, 195–206; Will and Terra Hanger, "Bicycles," *History Magazine* (October/November 2001).

Why did bicycles become so popular in Europe in the late nineteenth century?

What advantages did bicycles bring to women?

The bicycle helped liberate women's lives, but as this French advertising poster (c. 1905) suggests, it also was associated with glamour and sexual independence.

Document

PARIS DEPARTMENT STORES EXPAND THEIR BUSINESS

The department store in Europe and the United States became a major retailing institution in the last half of the nineteenth century. It was one of the reasons for the expansion in late-century consumer demand. This description, written by E. Levasseur in 1907, follows the growth of such stores in Paris and explains why they exerted such economic power. Note how many of their sales techniques stores still use today.

Why should French governments have favored the growth of department stores? Where did these stores stand in the process of economic production and sales? Why was the volume of sales so important? What kinds of people might have benefited from the jobs available in these stores? Why might these stores have hurt small retailers?

It was in the reign of Louis Philippe [1830–1848] that department stores for fashion goods and dresses . . . began to be distinguished. The type was already one of other notable developments of the Second Empire; it became one of the most important ones of the Third Republic. These stores have increased in number and several of them have become extremely large. Combining in their different departments all articles of clothing, toilet articles, furniture and many other ranges of goods, it is their special object so to combine all commodities as to attract and satisfy customers who will find conveniently together an assortment of a mass of articles corresponding to all their various needs. They attract customers by permanent display, by free entry into the shops, by periodic exhibitions, by special sales, by fixed prices, and by their ability to deliver the goods purchased to customers' homes, in Paris and to the provinces. Turning themselves into direct intermediaries between the producer and the consumer, even producing sometimes some of their articles in their own workshops, buying at lowest prices because of their large orders and because they are in a position to profit from bargains, working with large sums, and selling to most of their customers for cash only, they can transmit these benefits in lowered selling prices. They can even decide to sell at a loss, as an advertisement or to get rid of out-of-date fashions.

The success of these department stores is only possible thanks to the volume of their business, and this volume needs considerable capital and a very large turnover. Now capital, having become abundant, is freely combined nowadays in large enterprises. . . . [T]he large urban agglomerations, the ease with which goods can be transported by the railways, the diffusion of some comforts to strata below the middle classes, have all favoured these developments. . . .

According to the tax records of 1891, these stores in Paris, numbering 12, employed 1,708 persons and rated their site values at 2,159,000 francs; the largest had then 542 employees. These same stores had, in 1901, 9,784 employees; one of them over 2,000 and another over 1,600; their site value was doubled.

From Sidney Pollard and Colin Holmes, *Documents of European Economic History*, Vol. 3. (London: Edward Arnold, 1972), pp. 95–96.

income on consumer goods, such as stylish clothing and furniture, that were distinctively middle class in appearance.

Significant tensions and social anxieties marked relations among the various middle-class groups. Small shopkeepers resented the power of the great capitalists, with their department stores and mail-order catalogs. There is some evidence that the professions were becoming overcrowded. People who had only recently attained a middle-class lifestyle feared losing it in bad economic times.

▼ Late-Nineteenth-Century Urban Life

Europe became more urbanized than ever in the latter half of the nineteenth century as migration to the cities continued. Between 1850 and 1911, urban dwellers rose from 25 to 44 percent of the population in France and from 30 to 60 percent of the population in Germany. Similar increases occurred in other Western European countries.

SILBER AND FLEMING'S STERLING SILVER PLATE, GOLD AND SILVER JEWELLERY, AND WATCH AND CLOCK DEPARTMENTS, WOOD-STREET, LONDON.

Department stores, such as Silber and Fleming in London, allowed middle-class men and women to view the wide variety of new consumer goods. The Granger Collection, NYC—

The rural migrants to the cities were largely uprooted from traditional social ties. They often faced poor housing, social anonymity, and unemployment. People from different regional backgrounds, sometimes speaking different languages and practicing different religions, found themselves in proximity to one another and had difficulty mixing socially. Competition for jobs generated new varieties of political and social discontent, such as the anti-Semitism directed at the thousands of Russian Jews who had migrated to Western Europe. Indeed, much of the political anti-Semitism of the latter part of the century had its roots in the problems urban migration generated.

The Redesign of Cities

The inward urban migration placed new social and economic demands on already strained city resources and gradually transformed the patterns of urban living. National and municipal governments redesigned the central portions of many large European cities during the second half of the century. Previously, the central urban areas had been places where people from all social classes both lived and worked. From the middle of the century onward, planners transformed these districts into areas where businesses, government offices, large stores, and theaters were located, but where fewer people resided. Commerce, trade, government, and leisure activities now dominated central cities.

The New Paris The most famous and extensive transformation of a major city occurred in Paris. Like many other European cities, Paris had expanded from the Middle Ages onward with little or no planning. Great public buildings and squalid hovels stood near each other. The Seine River was an open sewer. The streets were narrow, crooked, and crowded. It was impossible to cross easily from one part of the city to another either on foot or by carriage. In 1850, an accurate map of the city did not even exist. Of more concern to the government of Napoleon III (r. 1852–1870), the city's streets had provided battlegrounds for urban insurrections that had threatened or toppled French governments on numerous occasions, most recently in 1848.

Napoleon III personally determined to redesign Paris. He appointed Baron Georges Haussmann (1809–1891), who, as prefect of the Seine from 1853 to 1870, oversaw a vast urban reconstruction program. Whole districts were destroyed to open the way for the broad boulevards and streets that became the hallmark of modern Paris. Much, though not all, of the purpose of this street planning was political. The wide vistas not only were beautiful, but they also allowed for the quick deployment of troops to put down riots. The eradication of the many small streets and alleys removed areas where barricades could be, and had been, erected.

The project was also political in another sense. In addition to the new boulevards, parks such as the Bois de Boulogne and major public buildings such as the Paris Opera were also constructed or completed. These projects, along with the demolition and street building, created thousands of government jobs. Many other laborers found employment in the private construction that accompanied the public works.

Further rebuilding and redesign occurred under the Third Republic after the destruction that accompanied the suppression of the Paris Commune in 1871. Many department stores, office complexes, and largely middle-class apartment buildings were constructed. By the late 1870s, mechanical trams were operating in Paris. After much debate, construction of a subway system (the *métro*) began in 1895. Near the close of the century, new railway stations were also erected to link the refurbished central city to the suburbs.

The Eiffel Tower, shown under construction in this painting, was to become a symbol of the newly redesigned Paris and its steel structure a symbol of French industrial strength. The Construction of the Eiffel Tower, January 1889 (oil on canvas), Delance, Paul Louis (1848–1924)/Musee de la Ville de Paris, Musee Carnavalet, Paris, France/ Giraudon/The Bridgeman Art Library

GROWTH OF MAJOR EUROPEAN CITIES (FIGURES IN THOUSANDS)

	1850	1880	1910
Berlin	419	1,122	2,071
Birmingham	233	437	840
Frankfurt	65	137	415
London	2,685	4,470	7,256
Madrid	281	398	600
Moscow	365	748	1,533
Paris	1,053	2,269	2,888
Rome	175	300	542
Saint Petersburg	485	877	1,962
Vienna	444	1,104	2,031
Warsaw	160	339	872

In 1889, the Eiffel Tower was built, originally as a temporary structure for the international trade exposition of that year. Not all the new structures of Paris bespoke the impact of middle-class commerce and the reign of iron and steel, however. Between 1873 and 1914, the Roman Catholic Church oversaw the construction of the Basilica of the Sacred Heart (*Sacré Coeur*) high atop Montmartre as an act of national penance for the sins that had supposedly led to French defeat in the Franco–Prussian War (1870–1871). Those two landmarks—the Eiffel Tower and the Basilica of the Sacred Heart—symbolized the social and political divisions between liberals and conservatives in the Third Republic.

View the **Architectural Panorama** "Eiffel Tower" on **MyHistoryLab.com**

Development of Suburbs Commercial development, railway construction, and slum clearance displaced many city dwellers and raised urban land values and rents. Consequently, both the middle classes and the working class began to seek housing elsewhere. The middle classes looked for neighborhoods removed from urban congestion. The working class looked for affordable housing. The result, in virtually all countries, was the development of suburbs surrounding the city proper. These suburbs housed families whose breadwinners worked in the central city or in a factory located within the city limits.

The expansion of railways with cheap workday fares and the introduction of mechanical and, later, electric tramways, as well as subways, allowed tens of thousands of workers from all classes to move daily between the city and the outlying suburbs. For hundreds of thousands of Europeans, home and work became more physically separated than ever before.

Urban Sanitation

The efforts of governments and of the increasingly conservative middle classes to maintain public order after 1848 led to a growing concern with the problems of public health and housing for the poor. A widespread feeling arose that only when the health and housing of the working class were improved would middle-class health also be secure and the political order stable.

Impact of Cholera Concerns with health and housing first manifested themselves as a result of the great cholera epidemics of the 1830s and 1840s. Unlike many other common deadly diseases of the day that touched only the poor, cholera struck all classes, and the middle class demanded a solution. Before the development of the bacterial theory of disease late in the century, physicians and sanitary reformers believed that miasmas in the air spread the infections that led to cholera and other diseases. These miasmas, which could be detected by their foul odors, were believed to arise from filth. The way to get rid of the dangerous, foul-smelling air was to clean up the cities.

During the 1840s, many physicians and some government officials began to publicize the dangerous, unsanitary conditions associated with overcrowding in cities and with businesses, such as basement slaughterhouses. In 1840, Louis René Villermé (1782–1863) published his *Tableau de l'état physique et moral des ouvriers* (*Catalog of the Physical and Moral State of Workers*) about urban working-class conditions in France. In 1842, Edwin Chadwick's (1800–1890) *Report on the Sanitary Condition of the Labouring Population* shocked the English public. In Germany, Rudolf Virchow (1821–1902) published similar findings. These and various other private reports and those by public commissions closely linked the issues of wretched living conditions and public health. They also argued that sanitary reform would remove the dangers. Those reports now provide some of the best information available about working-class living conditions in the mid-nineteenth century.

Read the Document "Edwin Chadwick, *Summary from the Poor Law Commissioners*" on **MyHistoryLab.com**

New Water and Sewer Systems The proposed solution to the health hazard was cleanliness, to be achieved through new water and sewer systems. These facilities were constructed slowly, usually first in capital cities and then much later in provincial centers. Some major urban areas did not have good water systems until after 1900. Nonetheless, the building of such systems was one of the major health and engineering achievements of the second half of the nineteenth century. The sewer system of Paris was a famous part of Haussmann's rebuilding program. In London, the construction of the Albert Embankment along the Thames involved not only large sewers discharging into the river, but gas mains and water pipes as well; all were encased in thick walls of granite and concrete, one of the new building materials of the day. Wherever these sanitary facilities were installed, the mortality rate dropped considerably—not because they prevented miasmas, but because they disposed of human waste and provided clean water free of harmful bacteria for people to drink, cook with, and bathe in.

A major feature of the reconstruction of mid-nineteenth-century Paris under the Emperor Napoleon II was a vast new sewer system to provide for drainage in the city. Sewer workmen could travel the length of the structure on small rail cars. Even today tourists still may visit parts of the mid-city Paris sewer system. Nadar/Stringer/Hulton Archive/Getty Images

MAJOR DATES RELATING TO SANITATION REFORM

1830s and 1840s	Cholera epidemics
1840	Villermé's *Catalog of the Physical and Moral State of Workers*
1842	Chadwick's *Report on the Sanitary Condition of the Labouring Population*
1848	British Public Health Act
1851	French Melun Act

Expanded Government Involvement in Public Health The concern with public health led to an expansion of governmental power on various levels. In Britain the Public Health Act of 1848, in France the Melun Act of 1851, and various laws in the still independent German states, as well as later legislation, introduced new restraints on private life and enterprise. This legislation allowed medical officers and building inspectors to enter homes and businesses in the name of public health. The state could condemn private property for posing health hazards. Private land could be excavated to construct the sewers and water mains required to protect the public. New building regulations restrained the activities of private contractors.

Full acceptance at the close of the century of the bacterial theory of disease associated with the discoveries of Louis Pasteur (1822–1895) in France, Robert Koch (1843–1910) in Germany, and Joseph Lister (1827–1912) in Britain increased public concern about cleanliness. Throughout Europe, issues related to the maintenance of public health and the physical well-being of the population repeatedly opened the way for new modes of government intervention in the lives of citizens.

Housing Reform and Middle-Class Values

The newly available information about working-class living conditions also led to heated debates over the housing problem. The wretched dwellings of the poor were themselves a cause of poor sanitation and thus became a newly perceived health hazard. Furthermore, the domestic arrangements of the poor, whose large families might live in a single room without any personal privacy, shocked middle-class reformers and bureaucrats. A single toilet might serve a whole block of tenements. After the revolutions of 1848, the overcrowding in housing and the social discontent that it generated were also seen to pose a political danger.

Document

A Doctor Learns How to Prevent Childbed Fever

Until the nineteenth century, women frequently died in childbirth. While women who gave birth in hospitals (which affluent women avoided) could benefit from the assistance of an obstetrician in a difficult delivery, statistical evidence that childbirth on the street was safer than in the Vienna General Hospital led to a medical crisis in that city. One young doctor, Ignaz Semmelweis (1818–1865), noticed that mortality rates were much higher in the clinic where obstetricians were trained (the "first clinic") than in the clinic where only midwives were trained (the "second clinic"). His conclusion—that doctors' research on cadavers caused them to infect patients in the maternity ward—was extremely controversial. Many doctors considered that, since they were "gentlemen," the suggestion that their hands were "dirty" was an insult.[1] *Only after Semmelweis' death and the popularization of Pasteur's germ theory would the benefits of disinfecting doctors' hands through washing become widely accepted.*

How did physicians explain puerperal, or "childbed," fever before Semmelweis' experiments? How was it possible to explain the fever before the knowledge of germ theory? Why were obstetricians more likely to infect maternity patients than midwives? Why would affluent women have avoided giving birth in hospitals?

Medicine's highest duty is saving threatened human life, and obstetrics is the branch of medicine in which this duty is most obviously fulfilled. . . . Unfortunately the number of cases in which the obstetrician achieves such blessings vanishes in comparison with the number of victims to whom his help is of no avail. This dark side of obstetrics is childbed fever.

. . . From the time the first clinic began training only obstetricians until June 1847, the mortality rate in the first clinic was consistently greater than in the second clinic, where only midwives were trained. . . . The additional mortality in the first clinic consisted of many hundreds of maternity patients, some of whom I saw die from puerperal processes, but for whose deaths I could find no explanation in the existing etiology. . . . It has not been questioned and has been expressed thousands of times that the horrible ravages of childbed fever are caused by . . . atmospheric-cosmic-terrestrial changes, as yet not precisely defined, that often extend over whole countrysides, and by which childbed fever is generated in persons predisposed by the puerperal state. But if the atmospheric-cosmic-terrestrial conditions of Vienna cause puerperal fever in predisposed persons, how is it that for many years these conditions have affected persons in the first clinic while sparing similarly predisposed persons in the second?

I was convinced that the greater mortality rate at the first clinic was due to an endemic [that is, something "due to causes limited by the boundaries of the hospital"] but as yet unknown cause. . . . I was aware of many facts for which I had no explanation. . . . Everything was in question; everything seemed inexplicable; everything was doubtful. Only the large number of deaths was an unquestionable reality. . . .

On 20 March [1847], Professor [of Forensic Medicine, Jakob] Kolletschka died. Kolletschka . . . often conducted autopsies. During one such exercise, his finger was pricked by a student with the same knife that was being used in the autopsy. . . . I could see clearly that the disease from which Kolletschka died was identical to that from which so many hundred maternity patients had also died. . . . Not the wound, but contamination of the wound by the cadaverous particles caused his death. . . . Because of the anatomical orientation of the Viennese medical school, professors, assistants, and students [but not midwives] have frequent opportunity to contact cadavers. . . . In the examination of pregnant or delivering maternity patients, the hands, contaminated with cadaverous particles, are brought into contact with [these patients]. . . . To destroy cadaverous matter adhering to hands . . . both the students and I were required to wash before examinations. . . . In 1846, before washing with chlorine was introduced, of 4,010 patients cared for in the first clinic, 459 died (11.4 percent). . . . In 1848, chlorine washings were employed throughout the year and of 3,556 patients, 45 died (1.27 percent).

[1] Richard Wertz and Dorothy Wertz, *Lying-In: A History of Childbirth in America* (New Haven, CT: Yale University Press, 1989), p. 122.

From Ignaz Semmelweis, *The Etiology, Concept, and Prophylaxis of Childbed Fever*, translated and edited with an introduction by K. Codell Carter (Madison: University of Wisconsin Press, 1983), pp. 63–89.

Many urban working-class families lived in cramped quarters without indoor plumbing, such as this apartment in Berlin. Deutsches Historisches Museum

Middle-class reformers thus turned to housing reform to solve the medical, moral, and political dangers slums posed. Decent housing would foster a good home life, in turn leading to a healthy, moral, and politically stable population. As A. V. Huber, one of the early German housing reformers, declared,

> Certainly it would not be too much to say that the home is the communal embodiment of family life. Thus the purity of the dwelling is almost as important for the family as is the cleanliness of the body for the individual. Good or bad housing is a question of life and death if ever there was one.[2]

Later advocates of housing reform, such as Jules Simon (1814–1896) in France, saw good housing as leading to good family life and, ultimately, to strong patriotic feeling. It was widely believed that providing the poor and the working class with adequate, respectable, cheap housing would alleviate social and political discontent. It was also believed that the personal saving and investment that were required to own a home would lead the working class to adopt the thrifty habits of the middle classes.

Private philanthropy funded the first initiatives to address the housing problem. Companies operating on low profit margins or making low-interest loans encouraged housing for the poor. Firms such as the German Krupp Armaments concern, which sought to ensure a contented, healthy, and stable workforce, constructed model housing projects and industrial communities.

By the mid-1880s, the migration into cities had made housing a political issue. Legislation in England in 1885 lowered the interest rates to construct cheap housing, and soon thereafter local governments began public housing projects. In Germany, action on housing came later in the century through the initiative of local municipalities. In 1894, France made inexpensive credit available to construct housing for the poor. None of these governments, however, adopted widescale housing experiments.

Nonetheless, by 1914, the housing problem had been fully recognized if not adequately addressed. The goal of housing reform across Western Europe came to be to provide homes for the members of the working class that would allow them to enjoy a family life more or less like that of the middle class. Such a home would be in the form of a detached house or an affordable city apartment with several rooms, a private entrance, and separate toilet facilities.

▼ Varieties of Late-Nineteenth-Century Women's Experiences

Late-nineteenth-century women and men led lives that reflected their social rank. Yet, within each rank, the experience of women was distinct from that of men. Women had no voting rights, and limited opportunities to assert their economic and legal rights. They remained, generally speaking, economically dependent on men, whatever their social class.

Women's Social Disabilities

In the mid-nineteenth century, virtually all European women faced social and legal disabilities in three areas: property rights, family law, and education. By the close of the century, there had been some improvement in each area.

Women and Property Until the last quarter of the century in most European countries, married women could not own property in their own names, no matter what their social class. For all practical purposes, upon marriage, women lost to their husbands' control any property they owned or that they might inherit or earn by their own labor. Their legal identities were subsumed in their husbands' identities, and they had no independent standing before the law. The courts saw the theft of a woman's purse as a theft of her husband's property. Because private property and wage earning were the bases of European society, these disabilities put married women at a great disadvantage, limiting their freedom to work, to save, and to move from one location to another.

Reform of women's property rights came slowly. By 1882, Great Britain had passed the Married Woman's

[2]Nicholas Bullock and James Read, *The Movement for Housing Reform in Germany and France, 1840–1914* (Cambridge, UK: Cambridge University Press, 1985), p. 42.

Property Act, which allowed married women to own property in their own right. In France, however, a married woman could not even open a savings account in her own name until 1895, and married French women did not gain possession of the wages they earned until 1907. In 1900, Germany allowed women to take jobs without their husbands' permission, but except for her wages, a German husband retained control of most of his wife's property. Similar laws prevailed elsewhere in Europe.

Family Law European family law also disadvantaged women. Legal codes required wives to "give obedience" to their husbands. The Napoleonic Code and the remnants of Roman law still in effect made women legal minors throughout Europe. Divorce was difficult everywhere for most of the century. In England before 1857, each divorce required a separate act of Parliament. Thereafter, couples could divorce, with difficulty, through the Court of Matrimonial Causes. Most nations did not permit divorce by mutual consent. French law forbade divorce between 1816 and 1884. Thereafter, the majority of nations recognized a legal cause for divorce—cruelty or injury—which had to be proven in court. In Great Britain, adultery was the usual cause for divorce, but to obtain a divorce, a woman had to prove her husband's adultery plus other offenses, whereas a man only had to prove his wife's adultery. In Germany, only adultery or serious maltreatment were recognized as reasons for divorce. Across Europe, some version of the double standard prevailed whereby husbands' extramarital sexual relations were tolerated to a much greater degree than those of wives. Everywhere, divorce required hearings in court and the presentation of legal proof, making the process expensive and more difficult for women, who did not control their own property.

The authority of husbands also extended to children. A husband could take children away from their mother and give them to someone else to rear. Only a father, in most countries, could permit his daughter to marry. In some countries, he could virtually force his daughter to marry the man of his choice. In cases of divorce and separation, courts normally awarded the husband authority over and custody of children, no matter how he had treated them previously.

Issues surrounding the sexual and reproductive rights of women could hardly be discussed in the nineteenth century. Until well into the twentieth century, both contraception and abortion were illegal. The law surrounding rape normally worked to the disadvantage of women. Wherever they turned with their problems—whether to physicians or lawyers—women confronted an official or legal world that men almost wholly populated and controlled.

Educational Barriers Throughout the nineteenth century, women had less access to education than men had and what was available to them was inferior to that available to men. Not surprisingly, there were many more illiterate women than men. Most women were educated only enough for the domestic lives they were expected to lead.

University and professional education remained reserved for men until at least the third quarter of the century. In Switzerland, the University of Zurich first opened its doors to women in the 1860s. The University of London admitted women for degrees in 1878. Women's colleges were founded at Cambridge during the last quarter of the century. Women could take Oxford and Cambridge university examinations but were not awarded degrees at Oxford until 1920 and at Cambridge until 1921. In France, women could not attend lectures at the Sorbonne until 1880. Just before the turn of the century, universities and medical schools in the Austrian Empire allowed women to matriculate, but Prussian universities did not admit women until after 1900. Russian women did not attend universities before 1914, but other institutions that awarded degrees were open to them. Italian universities proved themselves more open to both women students and women instructors than similar institutions elsewhere in Europe. In many countries, more foreign than native women attended university classes. This was especially the case in Zurich, where many Russian women studied for medical degrees. Many of the American women who founded or taught in the first women's colleges in the United States studied at European universities.

The absence of a system of secondary education for women prevented most of them from gaining the qualifications they needed to enter a university whether or not the university prohibited them. Educated, professional men feared that admitting women would overcrowd their professions. Women who attended universities and medical schools, like the young Russian women who studied medicine at Zurich, were sometimes labeled political radicals.

By the turn of the century, some men in the educated elites feared the challenge educated women posed to traditional gender roles in the home and workplace. Restricting women's access to secondary and university education helped bar them from social and economic advancement. Women would benefit only marginally from the expansion of professional employment that occurred during the late nineteenth and early twentieth centuries. Very few women did enter the professions, particularly medicine. Most nations refused to allow women to become lawyers until after World War I.

School teaching at the elementary level, which had come to be seen as a "female job" because of its association with the nurturing of children, became a professional haven for women. Trained at institutions designed particularly for elementary schoolteachers, usually known as normal schools, women schoolteachers at the elementary level were regarded as educated, but not as university educated. Higher education remained largely the province of men.

The few women who pioneered in the professions and on government commissions and school boards or who dispersed birth control information faced social obstacles, humiliation, and often outright bigotry. These women and their male supporters were challenging the clear separation into male and female spheres that had emerged in middle-class European social life during the nineteenth century. Women themselves were often hesitant to support feminist causes or expanded opportunities for females because they had been so thoroughly acculturated into the recently stereotyped roles. Many women, as well as men, saw a real conflict between family responsibilities and feminism.

New Employment Patterns for Women

During the Second Industrial Revolution, two major developments affected the economic lives of women. The first was the large-scale expansion in the variety of jobs available to women outside the better-paying learned professions. The second was the withdrawal of many married women from the workforce. These two seemingly contradictory developments require explanation.

Availability of New Jobs The expansion of governmental bureaucracies, the emergence of corporations and other large businesses, and the vast growth of retail stores opened many new employment opportunities for women. The need for elementary school teachers, usually women, grew as governments adopted compulsory education laws. Technological inventions and innovations, such as the typewriter and, eventually, the telephone exchange, also fostered female employment. Women by the thousands became secretaries and clerks for governments and private businesses. Thousands more became shop assistants.

Although these jobs did open new and often better employment opportunities for women, they nonetheless required low-level skills and involved minimal training. They were occupied primarily by unmarried women or widows. Women rarely occupied more prominent positions.

Employers continued to pay women low wages because, they argued, although they often knew better, that a woman did not need to live on what she herself earned but could expect additional financial support from her father or her husband. Consequently, a woman who did need to support herself independently could seldom find a job that paid an adequate income—or a position that paid as well as one a man who was supporting himself held.

In the late nineteenth century, up until World War I, the most common occupation for urban working-class women remained domestic service. These women are employed in the kitchen of a middle-class household in Germany. Bildarchiv Preussischer Kulturbesitz/Art Resource, NY

Women working in the London Central Telephone Exchange. The invention of the telephone opened new employment opportunities for women. Image Works/Mary Evans Picture Library Ltd.

Withdrawal from the Labor Force Most of the women filling the new service positions were young and unmarried. Upon marriage, or certainly after the birth of her first child, a woman normally withdrew from the labor force. Either she did not work or she worked at some occupation that she could pursue at home. This pattern was not new, but it had become significantly more common by the end of the nineteenth century. The kinds of industrial occupations that women had filled in the mid-nineteenth century, especially textile and garment making, were shrinking. Married or unmarried women thus had fewer opportunities for employment in those industries. Employers in offices and retail stores preferred young, unmarried women whose family responsibilities would not interfere with their work.

The cultural dominance of the middle class established a pattern of social expectations, especially for wives. The more prosperous a working-class family became, the less involved in employment its women were supposed to be. Indeed, the less income-producing work a wife did, the more prosperous and stable the family was considered.

Yet behind these generalities stands the enormous variety of social and economic experiences late-nineteenth-century women actually encountered. As might be expected, the chief determinant of these individual experiences was social class.

Working-Class Women

Although the textile industry and garment making were much less dominant than earlier in the century, they continued to employ many women. The German clothing-making trade illustrates the kind of vulnerable economic situation that women could encounter as a result of their limited skills and the way the trade was organized. The system of manufacturing mass-made clothes of uniform sizes in Germany was designed to require minimal capital investment by manufacturers and to protect them from risk. A major manufacturer would produce clothing through what was called a *putting-out system*. The manufacturer would purchase the material and then put it out for tailoring. Usually, numerous independently owned small sweatshops or women working in their homes made the clothing. It was seldom made in a factory.

Read the **Document** "Adelheid Popp, 'Finding Work: Women Factory Workers' " on **MyHistoryLab.com**

In Berlin in 1896, this system employed more than 80,000 garment workers. When business was good and demand strong, employment for these women was high. As the seasons shifted or business slackened, however, less and less work was put out, idling many of them. In effect, the workers who actually sewed the clothing carried much of the risk of the enterprise.

The expectation of separate social and economic spheres for men and women and the definition of women's chief work as pertaining to the home contributed mightily to the exploitation of women workers outside the home. Because their wages were regarded merely as supplementing their husbands' wages, they became particularly vulnerable to the kind of economic exploitation that characterized the German putting-out system for clothing production and similar systems elsewhere. Women were nearly always treated as casual workers everywhere in Europe.

Poverty and Prostitution

A major, but little recognized, social fact of most nineteenth-century cities was the presence of a surplus of working women who did not fit the stereotype of wife or daughter

Working-class women were often portrayed as violating middle-class norms of good "feminine" behavior. In this 1886 etching, tobacco workers in a factory protest the dismissal of one of their colleagues. Austrian National Image Library, 460.376-B

supplementing a family's income. Almost always many more women were seeking employment than there were jobs. The economic vulnerability of women and the consequent poverty many of them faced were among the chief causes of prostitution. Every major late-nineteenth-century European city had thousands of prostitutes.

Read the Document "George Bernard Shaw, *Mrs. Warren's Profession*" on **MyHistoryLab.com**

On the Continent, prostitution was generally legalized and subject to governmental and municipal regulations that male legislatures and councils passed and male police and physicians enforced. In Britain, prostitution received only minimal regulation.

Many myths and misunderstandings have surrounded the subject of prostitution. The most recent studies of prostitution in England emphasize that most prostitutes were active on the streets for only a few years, from their late teens to about age twenty-five. Many were poor women who had recently migrated from nearby rural areas. Others were born in the towns where they became prostitutes. Certain cities—those with large army garrisons or naval bases or those, like London, with large transient populations—attracted prostitutes. Far fewer prostitutes worked in manufacturing towns, where there were more opportunities for steady employment and community life was more stable.

Women who became prostitutes usually came from families of unskilled workers and had minimal skills and education themselves. Many had been servants. They also often were orphans or came from broken homes. Working-class women were always potentially subject to sexual exploitation, whether they became prostitutes or not.

Women of the Middle Class

A vast social gap separated poor working-class women from their middle-class counterparts. As their fathers' and husbands' incomes permitted, middle-class women participated in the vast expansion of consumerism and domestic comfort that marked the late nineteenth and the early twentieth centuries. They filled their homes with

Realist Norwegian painter Christian Krogh (1852–1925) believed that art should portray contemporary social issues. In this painting, "Albertine in the Police Doctor's Waiting Room," he shows a roomful of prostitutes waiting to be checked for venereal disease. While most are garishly dressed, the simply dressed "Albertine" (being gestured into the next room by a policeman) suggests the poverty that drew many women to prostitution. The Granger Collection, NYC—

manufactured items, including clothing, china, furniture, carpets, drapery, wallpaper, and prints. They enjoyed all the improvements of sanitation and electricity. They could command the services of numerous domestic servants. They moved into the fashionable new houses being constructed in the rapidly expanding suburbs.

The Cult of Domesticity For the middle classes, the distinction between work and family, defined by gender, had become complete and constituted the model for all other social groups. Middle-class women, if at all possible, did not work. More than any other women, they became limited to the roles of wife and mother. As a result, they might enjoy great domestic luxury and comfort, but their lives, talents, ambitions, and opportunities for applying their intelligence were sharply circumscribed.

Middle-class women became, in large measure, the product of a particular understanding of social life. Home life was to be a private place of refuge from the life of business and the marketplace.

As studies of the lives of middle-class women in northern France have suggested, this image of the middle-class home and of the role of women in the home is different from the one that had existed earlier in the nineteenth century. During the first half of the century, many middle-class wives contributed directly to their husbands' business, handling accounts or correspondence. These women also frequently left the task of rearing their children to nurses and governesses. The reasons for the change during the century are not certain, but it appears that men began to insist on doing business exclusively with other men. Magazines and books for women began to praise motherhood, domesticity, religion, and charity as the proper work of women in accordance with the concept of separate spheres. Rearing and nurturing her children were a woman's chief tasks. Her only experience or training was for the role of dutiful daughter, wife, and mother.

Within the home, a middle-class woman largely directed the household. She oversaw virtually all domestic management and child care. She was in charge of the home as a unit of consumption, which is why so much advertising was directed toward women. All this domestic activity, however, occurred within the bounds of the approved middle-class lifestyle that set strict limits on a woman's initiative. In her conspicuous position within the home and family, a woman symbolized first her father's and then her husband's worldly success.

Religious and Charitable Activities Throughout Europe, religion and religious activities became part of the expected work of women. They internalized those portions of the Christian religion that stressed meekness and passivity. This close association between religion and a strict domestic life for women was one reason for later tension between feminism and religious authorities.

Another important role for middle-class women was the administration of charity. Women were considered especially qualified for this work because of their presumed innate spirituality and their capacity to instill domestic and personal discipline. Middle-class women were often in charge of clubs for poor youth, societies to protect poor young women, schools for infants, and societies for visiting the poor. Women were supposed to be particularly interested in the problems of poor women, their families, and their children. By the end of the century, middle-class women seeking to expand their spheres of activity became social workers for the church, for private charities, or for the government. These vocations were a natural extension of the roles society assigned to them.

The following obituary of a French lady who died in the late nineteenth century illustrates how these vocations and virtues received public praise for women who fulfilled them:

> The poor were the object of her affectionate interest, especially the shameful poor, the fallen people. She sought them out and helped them with perfect discretion which doubled the value of her benevolent interest. To those whom she could approach without fear of bruising their dignity, she brought, along with alms to assure their existence, consolation of the most serious sort—she raised their courage and their hopes. To others, each Sunday, she opened all the doors of her home, above all when her children were still young. In making them distribute these alms with her, she hoped to initiate them early into practices of charity.[3]

Many ideas and social forces would challenge the values this obituary celebrates, but the role for upper-middle-class women that it illustrates would dominate European life for decades to come.

Sexuality and Family Size Historians have come to realize that the world of the middle-class wife and her family was much more complicated than they once thought. Neither all wives nor their families conformed to the stereotypes. Recent studies suggest that the middle classes of the nineteenth century enjoyed sexual relations within marriage far more than was once thought. Diaries, letters, and even early medical and sociological sex surveys indicate that sexual enjoyment rather than sexual repression was fundamental to middle-class marriages. Much of the inhibition about sexuality stemmed from the dangers of childbirth, which, in an age of limited sanitation and anesthesia, were widely and rightly feared, rather than from any dislike or disapproval of sex itself.

One of the major changes in this regard during the second half of the century was the acceptance of a small family size among the middle classes. The birthrate in

[3]Bonnie G. Smith, *Ladies of the Leisure Class: The Bourgeoises of Northern France in the Nineteenth Century* (Princeton, NJ: Princeton University Press, 1981), pp. 147–148. Copyright © 1981 by Princeton University Press. Reprinted by permission of Princeton University Press.

France dropped throughout the nineteenth century. It began to fall in England steadily from the 1870s onward. During the last decades of the century, new contraceptive devices became available, which middle-class couples used. One of the reasons for the apparently conscious decision of couples to limit their family size was to maintain a relatively high level of material consumption.

The Rise of Political Feminism

Liberal society and its values had neither automatically nor inevitably improved the lot of women. In particular, they did not give women the vote or access to political activity. In Catholic countries, male liberals feared that granting the vote to women would benefit political conservatives because men thought that priests exercised undue control over women. A similar apprehension existed about the alleged influence of the Anglican clergy over women in England and Protestant pastors in parts of Germany. Consequently, anticlerical liberals often refused to cooperate with feminists.

Obstacles to Achieving Equality Many women were reluctant to support feminist causes. Political issues relating to gender were only one of several priorities for women. Some were sensitive to their class and economic interests. Others subordinated feminist political issues to national unity and patriotism. Still others would not support particular feminist organizations because they objected to their tactics. The various social and tactical differences among women often led to sharp divisions within the feminists' own ranks. Except in England, it was often difficult for working-class and middle-class women to cooperate. Roman Catholic feminists were uncomfortable with radical secularist feminists. There were other disagreements about which goals were most important for improving women's legal and social conditions.

Although liberal society and law presented women with many obstacles, they also provided feminists with many of their intellectual and political tools. As early as 1792 in Britain, Mary Wollstonecraft (1759–1797), in *The Vindication of the Rights of Woman*, had applied the revolutionary doctrines of the rights of man to the predicament of the members of her own sex (see Chapter 17). John Stuart Mill (1806–1873) and Harriet Taylor (1804–1858) extended the logic of liberal freedom to the position of women in *The Subjection of Women* (1869). The arguments for utility and efficiency so dear to middle-class liberals could be used to expose the human and social waste implicit in the inferior role assigned to women.

Read the Document "John Stuart Mill, *The Subjection of Women*" on **MyHistoryLab.com**

Furthermore, the socialist criticism of capitalist society often, though by no means always, included a harsh indictment of the social and economic position to which women had been relegated. The earliest statements in support of feminism arose from critics of the existing order who were often people who had unorthodox opinions about sexuality, family life, and property. This hardened resistance to the feminist message.

Votes for Women in Britain Europe's most dynamic women's movement was in Britain. There, Millicent Fawcett (1847–1929) led the moderate National Union of Women's Suffrage Societies. She believed Parliament would grant women the vote only if it were convinced they would be respectable and responsible in their political activity. In 1908, the National Union could rally almost half a million women in London. Fawcett's husband, Henry Fawcett (1833–1884), was a Liberal Party cabinet minister and economist who also supported women's suffrage. Her tactics were those of English liberals.

Watch the Video "British Women's Suffrage" on **MyHistoryLab.com**

MAJOR DATES IN LATE-NINETEENTH-CENTURY AND EARLY-TWENTIETH-CENTURY WOMEN'S HISTORY

1857	Revised English divorce law
1865	University of Zurich admits women for degrees
1869	John Stuart Mill's *The Subjection of Women*
1878	University of London admits women as candidates for degrees
1882	English Married Woman's Property Act
1894	Union of German Women's Organizations founded
1901	National Council of French Women founded
1903	British Women's Social and Political Union founded
1907	Norway permits women to vote on national issues
1910	British suffragettes adopt radical tactics
1918	Vote extended to some British women
1919	Weimar constitution allows German women to vote
1920	Ratification of Nineteenth Amendment grants women right to vote in United States
1920–1921	Oxford and Cambridge Universities award degrees to women
1922	French Senate defeats bill extending vote to women
1928	Britain extends vote to women on same basis as men

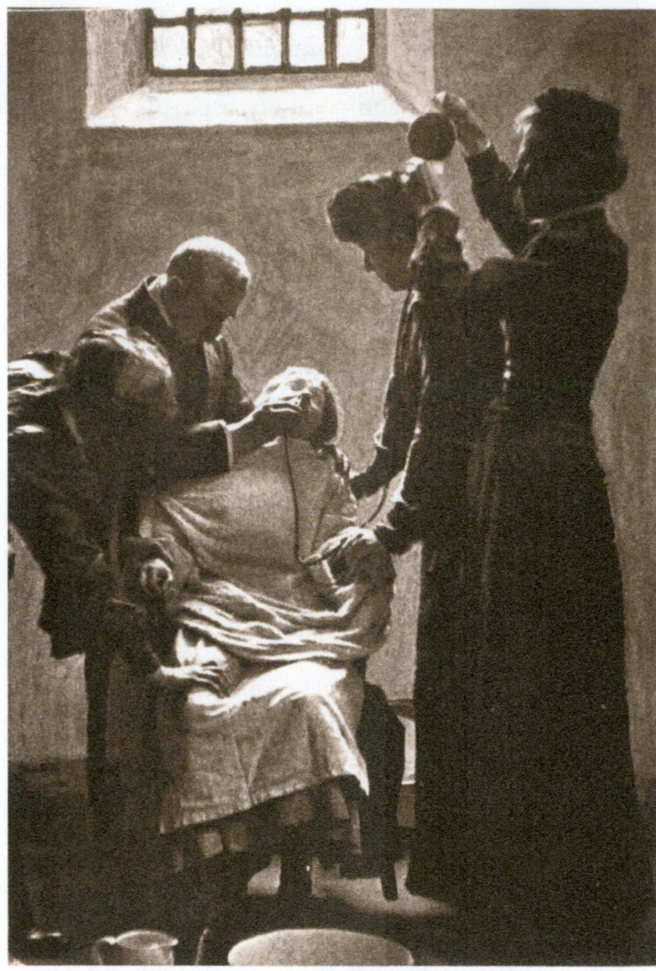

When advocates of women's suffrage went on hunger strike, they were forcibly fed in prison. When they refused to open their mouths, feeding tubes were inserted into their nostrils, as in this 1909 photograph taken in Holloway Prison in London. Suffragette being force-fed with the nasal tube in Holloway Prison, 1909 (sepia photo), English photographer (20th century). Private Collection/The Stapleton Collection/ The Bridgeman Art Library International

Emmeline Pankhurst (1858–1928) led a much more radical branch of British feminists. Pankhurst's husband, who died near the close of the century, had been active in both labor and Irish nationalist politics. Irish nationalists had developed numerous disruptive political tactics. Early labor politicians had also sometimes confronted the police over the right to hold meetings. In 1903, Pankhurst and her daughters, Christabel and Sylvia, founded the Women's Social and Political Union. For years they and their followers, known derisively as **suffragettes**, lobbied publicly and privately for extending the vote to women. By 1910, having failed to move the government, they turned to the violent tactics of arson, breaking windows, and sabotage of postal boxes. (See the Document, "Emmeline Pankhurst Defends Militant Suffragette Tactics," page 735.) They marched en masse on Parliament. The Liberal government of Prime Minister Herbert Asquith (1852–1928) imprisoned demonstrators and force-fed those who went on hunger strikes in jail. The government refused to extend the franchise. Only in 1918, and then as a result of their contribution to the war effort in World War I, did British women over age thirty receive the vote. (Men could vote at age twenty-one.)

Emmeline Pankhurst (1857–1928) was frequently arrested for forcibly advocating votes for British women. Jimmy Sime/Stringer/ Hulton Archive/Getty Images

Read the Document "'Freedom or Death' (1913) Emmeline Pankhurst" on **MyHistoryLab.com**

The Influence of the British Suffrage Movement Abroad Nowhere was the British suffrage movement more influential than in the United States. The radical tactics of British suffragists influenced leaders of the U.S. movement like Alice Paul and Lucy Burns, both of whom worked together with the Pankhursts in Britain. Like suffragists in Britain, Paul, Burns, and the members of their organization, the National Women's Party, chose to demand full political rights instead of aiming for a more peaceful, gradual expansion of rights. They, too, used tactics that attracted publicity, such as hunger strikes during imprisonment.

Political Feminism on the Continent Women's movements on the Continent tended to be much smaller than in Britain. In France, when Hubertine Auclert (1848–1914) began campaigning for the vote in the 1880s, she stood virtually alone. During the 1890s, several women's organizations emerged. In 1901, the National Council of French Women (CNFF) was organized among upper-middle-class women, but it did not support the vote for women for several years. French Roman Catholic feminists such as Marie Mauguet (1844–1928) supported the franchise. Almost all French feminists, however, rejected violence and believed women could achieve the vote through careful legalism. In 1919, the French Chamber of Deputies passed a bill granting the vote to women, but in 1922, the French Senate defeated the bill. French women did not receive the right to vote until after World War II.

Document

EMMELINE PANKHURST DEFENDS MILITANT SUFFRAGETTE TACTICS

Emmeline Pankhurst (1858–1928) led the most radical wing of early-twentieth-century British feminists in their demand for the vote. In 1910 she called for militant tactics against the Liberal government of Prime Minister Henry Asquith. In her autobiography of 1914, Mrs. Pankhurst explains why she undertook such tactics. A partial franchise for women was not enacted in Britain until 1918. Today a statue of Mrs. Pankhurst stands not far from the Houses of Parliament.

What are Pankhurst's assumptions about the factors that would move the British government to enact the franchise for women? Why do you think the government responded so fiercely to the attack on postal boxes? How might these tactics have backfired on the movement?

I had called upon women to join me in striking at the Government through the only thing that governments are really very much concerned about—property—and the response was immediate. Within a few days the newspapers rang with the story of the attack made on letter boxes in London, Liverpool, Birmingham, Bristol, and half a dozen other cities. In some cases the boxes, when opened by postmen, mysteriously burst into flame; in others the letters were destroyed by corrosive chemicals; in still others the addresses were rendered illegible by black fluids. Altogether it was estimated that over 5,000 letters were completely destroyed and many thousands more were delayed in transit.

It was with a deep sense of their gravity that these letter-burning protests were undertaken, but we felt that something drastic must be done in order to destroy the apathy of the men of England who view with indifference the suffering of women oppressed by unjust laws. . . .

In only a few cases were the offenders apprehended, and one of the few women arrested was a helpless cripple, a woman who could move about only in a wheeled chair. She received a sentence of eight months in the first division, and, resolutely hunger striking, was forcibly fed with unusual brutality, the prison doctor deliberately breaking one of her teeth in order to insert a gag. In spite of her disabilities and her weakness the crippled girl persisted in her hunger strike and her resistance to prison rules, and within a short time had to be released. The excessive sentences of the other pillar box destroyers resolved themselves into very short terms because of the resistance of the prisoners, every one of whom adopted the hunger strike. . . .

It was at this time, February, 1913, less than two years ago as I write these words, that militancy, as it is now generally understood by the public, began—militancy in the sense of continued, destructive, guerilla warfare against the Government through injury to private property. . . . We had tried every other measure . . . and our years of work and suffering and sacrifice had taught us that the Government would not yield to right and justice. . . . Now our task was to show the Government that it was expedient to yield to the women's just demands. In order to do that we had to make England and every department of English life insecure and unsafe. We had to make English law a failure and the courts farce comedy theatres; we had to discredit the Government and Parliament in the eyes of the world; we had to spoil English sports, hurt business, destroy valuable property, demoralise the world of society, shame the churches, upset the whole orderly conduct of life.

That is, we had to do as much of this guerilla warfare as the people of England would tolerate.

From Emmeline Pankhurst, *My Own Story* (New York: Hearst International Library, 1914), pp. 270–271, 279–280.

In Germany, feminist awareness and action faced great challenges. Louise Otto (1819–1895) had pioneered the German women's movement in the 1840s, but was forced to withdraw from political life during the backlash after 1848. German law actually forbade German women from engaging in political activity. In 1894, Otto's friend, Auguste Schmidt (1833–1902), together with several other women, founded the Union of German Women's Organizations (BDF). By 1902, the German women's movement, which had begun with demands for better education for women, was supporting the right to vote. But its main concern remained improving women's social conditions, increasing their access to education, and extending their right to other protections. The BDF also tried to gain women's admittance to political or civic activity on the municipal level. Its work usually included education, child welfare, charity, and public health. The German Social Democratic Party supported women's suffrage, but the German authorities and German Roman Catholics so disdained the socialists that its support only made suffrage more suspect in their eyes. Women received the vote in Germany only in 1919, under the constitution of the Weimar Republic after the German defeat in war and revolution at home.

Throughout Europe before World War I, women demanded rights widely and vocally. Their tactics and the success they achieved, however, varied from country to country depending on political and class structures. Before World War I, only Norway (1907) and Finland (1906) allowed women to vote on national issues.

▼ Jewish Emancipation

The emancipation of European Jews from the narrow life of the ghetto into a world of equal or nearly equal citizenship and social status was a major accomplishment of political liberalism and had an enduring impact on European life. Emancipation, slow and never fully completed, began in the late eighteenth century and continued throughout the nineteenth. It moved at different paces in different countries.

Differing Degrees of Citizenship

In 1781 and 1782, Joseph II, the Habsburg emperor, issued decrees that placed Jews, Orthodox Christians, and Protestants in his empire under more or less the same laws as Catholics. In France, the National Assembly recognized Jews as French citizens in 1789. During the turmoil of the Napoleonic Wars, Jewish communities in Italy and the German states were allowed to mix on a generally equal footing with the Christian population. These steps toward political emancipation were always uncertain and were frequently limited or abrogated when rulers or governments changed. Certain freedoms were granted, only to be partially withdrawn later. Even countries that had given Jews political rights did not permit them to own land and often subjected them to discriminatory taxes. Nonetheless, during the first half of the century, Jews began to gain equal or more nearly equal citizenship.

In Russia, and in Poland under Russian rule, the traditional modes of prejudice and discrimination continued unabated until World War I. Russian rule treated Jews as aliens. The government undermined Jewish community life, limited the publication of Jewish books, restricted areas where Jews could live, required Jews to have internal passports to move about the country, banned Jews from many forms of state service, and excluded Jews from many institutions of higher education. The state allowed the police and right-wing nationalist groups to conduct ***pogroms***—organized riots—against Jewish neighborhoods and villages. The tsar of Russia, Nicholas II, was himself an ardent anti-Semite.

Broadened Opportunities

After the revolutions of 1848, European Jews saw a general improvement in their situation that lasted for several decades. In various German states, Italy, the Low Countries, and Scandinavia, Jews attained full citizenship. After 1858, Jews in Great Britain could sit in Parliament. Austria-Hungary extended full legal rights to Jews in 1867. Indeed, from about 1850 to 1880, relatively little organized or overt prejudice was expressed against Jews in non-Russian Europe. They entered the professions and other occupations once closed to them. They participated fully in literary and cultural life. They were active in

Because many major financial institutions of nineteenth-century Europe were owned by wealthy Jewish families, anti-Semitic political figures often blamed them for economic hard times. The most famous such family was the Rothschilds, who controlled banks in several countries. The head of the London branch was Lionel Rothschild (1808–1879). He was elected to Parliament several times but was not seated because he would not take the required Christian oath. After the requirement of that oath was abolished in 1858, he sat in Parliament from 1858 until 1874. Hulton Archive/Stringer/Archive Photos/Getty Images the arts and music. They became leaders in science and education. Jews intermarried freely with non-Jews as legal, secular prohibitions against such marriages were repealed during the last quarter of the century.

Outside of Russia, Jewish politicians entered cabinets and served in the highest offices of the state. Politically, Jews often were aligned with liberal parties because these groups had championed equal rights. Later in the century, especially in eastern Europe, many Jews became associated with socialist parties.

The prejudice that had been associated with Christian religious attitudes toward Jews seemed to have largely dissipated. Hundreds of thousands of European Jews migrated from Russia's Pale of Settlement (the only part of Russia where Jews were permitted to live) to Western Europe and the United States. Almost anywhere in Europe, Jews might encounter prejudice on a personal level. Yet in England, France, Italy, Germany, the Low Countries, and Austria, the legalized persecution and discrimination that had so haunted Jews in the past seemed to have ended.

View the Map "Map Discovery: Jewish Migration" on **MyHistoryLab.com**

That newfound security began to erode during the last two decades of the nineteenth century. Anti-Semitic voices began to be heard in the 1870s, attributing the economic stagnation of the decade to Jewish bankers and financial interests. In the 1880s, organized **anti-Semitism** erupted in Germany, as it did in France at the time of the Dreyfus affair (see Chapter 24). Most Jewish leaders believed the attacks on Jewish life were merely temporary recurrences of older forms of prejudice; they felt their communities would remain safe under the liberal legal protections that had been extended during the century.

▼ Labor, Socialism, and Politics to World War I

The late-century industrial expansion further changed the life of the labor force. In all industrializing continental countries, the numbers of the urban proletariat rose. The proportion of artisans and highly skilled workers declined, and for the first time, factory wage earners predominated. The number of unskilled workers in shipping, transportation, and building also grew.

Workers still had to look to themselves to improve their lot. After 1848, however, European workers stopped rioting in the streets to voice their grievances. After midcentury, workers turned to new institutions and ideologies. Chief among these were trade unions, democratic political parties, and socialism.

Trade Unionism

Trade unionism came of age when governments extended legal protections to unions during the second half of the century. Unions became fully legal in Great Britain in 1871 and were allowed to picket in 1875. The Third French Republic fully legalized unions in 1884. In Germany, unions were permitted to function with little disturbance after 1890. As long as the representatives of the traditional governing classes looked after labor interests, members of the working class rarely sought office themselves.

Unions directed their midcentury organizational efforts toward skilled workers and the immediate improvement of wages and working conditions. By the close of the century, industrial unions for unskilled workers were being organized. Employers intensely

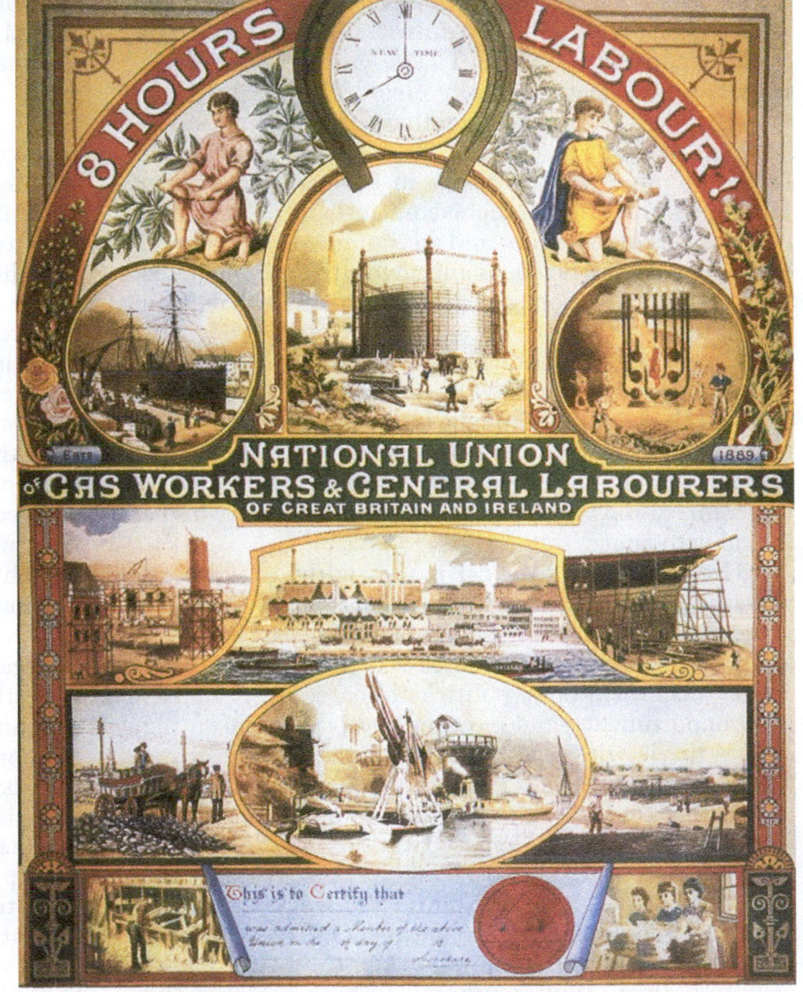

Trade unions continued to grow in late-nineteenth-century Great Britain. The effort to curb the unions eventually led to the formation of the Labour Party. The British unions often had quite elaborate membership certificates, such as this one for the National Union of Gas Workers and General Labourers of Great Britain and Ireland. The Granger Collection opposed these large unions of thousands of workers. Unions frequently had to engage in long strikes to convince employers to accept their demands. Europe experienced a rash of strikes in the decade before World War I as unions sought to keep wages in line with inflation. Despite union advances, however, and the growth of union membership (in 1910 to approximately 3 million in Britain, 2 million in Germany, and 977,000 in France), most of Europe's labor force was never unionized in this period. What the unions did represent for workers was a new collective form of association to confront economic difficulties and improve security.

Democracy and Political Parties

Except for Russia, all the major European states adopted broad-based, if not perfectly democratic, electoral systems in the late nineteenth century. Great Britain passed its second voting reform act in 1867 and its third in 1884. Bismarck brought universal male suffrage to the German Empire in 1871. The French Chamber of Deputies was democratically elected. Universal male suffrage was adopted in Switzerland in 1879, in Spain in 1890, in Belgium in 1893, in the Netherlands in 1896, in Norway in 1898, in Austria in 1907, and in Italy in 1912. The broadened franchise meant politicians could no longer ignore workers, and discontented groups could now voice their grievances and advocate their programs within the institutions of government rather than from the outside.

The advent of democracy brought organized mass political parties to Europe for the first time. The expansion of the electorate brought into the political process many people whose level of political consciousness, awareness, and interest was low. This electorate had to be organized and taught about power and influence in the liberal democratic state.

The organized political party—with its workers, newspapers, offices, social life, and discipline—was the vehicle that mobilized the new voters. The largest single group in these mass electorates was the working class. The democratization of politics presented the socialists with opportunities and required the traditional ruling classes to vie with the socialists for the support of the new voters.

During these years, socialism as a political ideology and plan of action opposed nationalism. The problems of class were supposed to be transnational, and socialism was supposed to unite the working classes across national borders. European socialists, however, badly underestimated the emotional drawing power of nationalism. Many workers had both socialist and nationalist sympathies, which were rarely in conflict with each other. When the outbreak of war in 1914 did bring them into conflict, however, nationalist feelings prevailed.

The major question for late-century socialist parties throughout Europe was whether revolution or democratic reform would improve the life of the working class. This question sharply divided all socialist parties and especially those whose leadership adhered to the intellectual legacy of Karl Marx. The Bolshevik Revolution of November 1917 would transform socialist debates and actions and render many of the prewar disputes moot.

Karl Marx and the First International

Karl Marx himself took into account the new realities that developed during the third quarter of the century. Although he continued to predict the disintegration of capitalism, his practical, public political activity reflected a different approach.

In 1864, a group of British and French trade unionists founded the International Working Men's Association. Known as the First International, its membership encompassed a vast array of radical political types, including socialists, anarchists, and Polish nationalists. In the inaugural address for the First International, Marx approved workers' and trade unions' efforts to reform the conditions of labor within the existing political and economic processes. In his private writings he often criticized such reformist activity, but these writings were not made public until near the end of the century, years after his death.

The violence involved in the rise and suppression of the Paris Commune (see Chapter 22), which Marx had declared a genuine proletarian uprising, cast a pall over socialism throughout Europe. British trade unionists, who received legal protections in 1871, wanted no connection with the events in Paris. The French authorities used the uprising to suppress socialist activity. Under these pressures, the First International held its last European congress in 1873. It soon transferred its offices to the United States, where it was dissolved in 1876.

The short-lived First International had a disproportionately great impact on the future of European socialism. Throughout the late 1860s, the organization gathered statistics, kept labor groups informed of mutual problems, provided a forum to debate socialist doctrine, and overstated its own influence over contemporary events. From these debates and activities, Marxism emerged as the single most important strand of socialism. Marx and his supporters defeated or drove out anarchists and advocates of other forms of socialism. The apparently scientific character of Marxism made it attractive at a time when science was more influential than at any previous period in European history. Marx's thought deeply impressed German socialists, who were to establish the most powerful socialist party in Europe and became the chief vehicle for preserving and developing it. The full development of German socialism, however, also involved the influence of non-Marxist socialists in Great Britain.

Great Britain: Fabianism and Early Welfare Programs

Neither Marxism nor any other form of socialism made significant progress in Great Britain, the most industrial society of the day. Trade unions grew steadily, and their members normally supported Liberal Party candidates. The "new unionism" of the late 1880s and the 1890s organized the dockworkers, the gas workers, and similar unskilled groups. In 1892, Keir Hardie (1856–1915) became the first independent working man to be elected to Parliament. Until 1901, labor's general political activity remained limited. In that year, however, the House of Lords, which also acts as Britain's highest court, removed the legal protection previously accorded union funds through the Taff Vale decision. The Trades Union Congress responded by launching the Labour Party. In the election of 1906, the fledgling party sent twenty-nine members to Parliament. Although the British labor movement became more militant in this period, its goals did not include socialism. In scores of strikes before the war, workers fought for wages to meet the rising cost of living. The government took a larger role than ever before in mediating these strikes, which in 1911 and 1912 involved the railways, the docks, and the coal mines.

British socialism itself remained primarily the preserve of non-Marxist intellectuals. The Fabian Society, founded in 1884, was Britain's most influential socialist group. The society took its name from Q. Fabius Maximus (d. 203 B.C.E.), the Roman general whose tactics against Hannibal involved avoiding direct conflict that might lead to defeat. Its leading members were Sidney Webb (1859–1947), Beatrice Webb (1858–1943), H. G. Wells (1866–1946), Graham Wallas (1858–1932), and George Bernard Shaw (1856–1950). Many Fabians were civil servants who believed the problems of industry could be solved and achieved gradually, peacefully, and democratically. They sought to educate the country about the rational wisdom of socialism. They were particularly interested in modes of collective ownership on the municipal level, so-called gas-and-water socialism.

The British government responded slowly to these pressures. After 1906, the Liberal Party, led by Sir Henry Campbell-Bannerman (1836–1908) and, after 1908, by Herbert Asquith, pursued a two-pronged policy. Fearful of losing seats in Parliament to the new Labour Party, they restored the former protection of the unions. Then, after 1909, under the leadership of Chancellor of the Exchequer David Lloyd George (1863–1945), the Liberal ministry undertook a broad program of social legislation that included establishing labor exchanges; regulating certain trades, such as tailoring and lace making; and passing the National Insurance Act of 1911, which provided unemployment benefits and health care.

The financing of these programs brought the Liberal majority in the House of Commons into conflict with the Conservative-dominated House of Lords. The result was the Parliament Act of 1911, which allowed the Commons to override the legislative veto of the upper chamber. The new taxes and social programs meant that in Britain, the home of nineteenth-century liberalism, the state was taking on an expanded role in the life of its citizens. The early welfare legislation was only marginally satisfactory to labor, many of whose members still thought they could gain more from the direct action of strikes.

Beatrice and Sidney Webb. These most influential British Fabian Socialists, shown in a photograph from the 1920s, wrote many books on governmental and economic matters, served on special parliamentary commissions, and agitated for the enactment of socialist policies. Hulton Archive/Stringer/Getty Images

France: "Opportunism" Rejected

French socialism was a less united and more politically factionalized movement than socialism in other countries. At the turn of the century, Jean Jaurès (1859–1914) and Jules Guesde (1845–1922) led the two major factions of French socialists. Jaurès believed socialists should cooperate with middle-class Radical ministries to ensure the enactment of needed social legislation. Guesde opposed this policy, arguing that socialists could not, with integrity, support a bourgeois cabinet they were theoretically dedicated to overthrowing.

The Second International had been founded in 1889 in a new effort to unify the various national socialist parties and trade unions. By 1904, the Amsterdam Congress of the Second International debated the issue of *opportunism*, as such participation by socialists in cabinets was termed. The Congress condemned opportunism in France and ordered French socialists to form a single party. Jaurès accepted the decision. Thereafter French socialists began to work together, and, by 1914, the recently united Socialist Party had become the second largest group in the Chamber of Deputies. Jaurès was assassinated in 1914 in a Paris café at the outbreak of World War I. In the throes of wartime patriotism, French socialist leaders participated in the wartime cabinet.

The French labor movement, with deep roots in anarchism, was uninterested in either politics or socialism. French workers usually voted socialist, but the unions themselves, unlike those in Britain, avoided active political participation. The main labor union, Confédération Générale du Travail, founded in 1895, regarded itself as a rival to the socialist parties. Its leaders sought to improve the workers' conditions through direct action. They embraced the doctrines of *syndicalism*, which had been most persuasively expounded by Georges Sorel (1847–1922) in *Reflections on Violence* (1908). This book enshrined the general strike as a device to unite workers and gain them power. The strike tactic often conflicted with the socialist belief in aiding labor through state action. Strikes were common in France between 1905 and 1914, and the middle-class Radical ministry repeatedly used troops to suppress them.

Germany: Social Democrats and Revisionism

The negative judgment the Second International rendered against French socialist participation in bourgeois ministries reflected a policy of permanent hostility to nonsocialist governments that the German Social Democratic Party, or SPD, had already adopted. The organizational success of this party, more than any other single factor, kept Marxist socialism alive during the late nineteenth and early twentieth centuries.

The SDP had been founded in 1875. Its origins lay in the labor agitation of Ferdinand Lasalle (1825–1864), who wanted workers to participate in German politics. Wilhelm Liebknecht (1826–1900) and August Bebel (1840–1913), who were Marxists who opposed reformist politics, soon joined the party. Thus, from its founding, the SPD was divided between those who advocated reform and those who advocated revolution.

Read the Document "Socialism: The Gotha Program (1875)" on **MyHistoryLab.com**

Bismarck's Repression of the SPD Twelve years of persecution under Bismarck forged the character of the SPD. The so-called Iron Chancellor believed socialism would undermine German politics and society. He used an assassination attempt on Emperor William I (r. 1861–1888) in 1878, in which the socialists were not actually involved, to steer antisocialist laws through the *Reichstag*. The measures suppressed the organization, meetings, newspapers, and other public activities of the SPD. Thereafter, to remain a socialist meant to remove oneself from the mainstream of respectable German life and possibly to lose one's job. The antisocialist legislation proved politically counterproductive. Even under the repressive laws, members of the SPD could sit in the *Reichstag*. From the early 1880s onward, the SPD steadily polled more and more votes in elections to the *Reichstag*.

As simple repression failed to wean German workers from socialist loyalties, Bismarck undertook a program of social welfare legislation. In 1883, the German Empire adopted a health insurance measure. The next year the *Reichstag* enacted accident insurance legislation. Finally, in 1889, Bismarck sponsored a plan for old age and disability pensions. These programs, to which both workers and employers contributed, represented a paternalistic, conservative alternative to socialism. The state itself would organize a system of social security that did not require any change in the system of property holding or politics. Germany became the first major industrial nation to employ and benefit from this kind of welfare program.

The Erfurt Program After forcing Bismarck's resignation mainly because of differences over foreign policy, Emperor William II (r. 1888–1918) allowed the antisocialist legislation to expire, hoping to build new political support among the working class. With the repressive measures lifted, the party needed to decide what attitude to assume toward the German Empire.

The answer came in the Erfurt Program of 1891, formulated under the political guidance of Bebel and the ideological tutelage of Karl Kautsky (1854–1938). The program insisted on the necessity of socialist ownership of the means of production. The party intended to pursue these goals through legal political participation rather than by revolutionary activity. Kautsky argued that because capitalism by its very nature must collapse, the immediate task for socialists was to improve workers' lives rather than work for revolution, which was inevitable. So, although in theory the SPD was vehemently hostile to the German Empire, in practice the party functioned within the Empire's institutions. The SPD members of the *Reichstag* maintained clear political consciences by refusing to enter the cabinet (to which they were not invited anyway) and by refraining for many years from voting in favor of the military budget. In this way, they hoped to use their political positions to benefit the workers they represented, without strengthening the political and economic system they opposed.

The Debate over Revisionism The dilemma of the SPD, however, generated the most important challenge within the socialist movement to the orthodox Marxist analysis of capitalism and the socialist revolution. The author of this socialist heresy, Eduard Bernstein (1850–1932), had lived in Britain and was familiar with the Fabians. Bernstein questioned whether Marx and his later orthodox followers, such as Kautsky, had been correct in their pessimistic appraisal of capitalism and the necessity of revolution. In *Evolutionary Socialism* (1899), Bernstein pointed to conditions that did not meet orthodox Marxists' expectations. The standard of living was rising in Europe. Stockholding was making the ownership of capitalist industry more widespread. The inner contradictions of capitalism had not developed the way Marx had predicted. Moreover, the extension of the franchise to the working class meant that parliamentary methods might achieve revolutionary social change. For Bernstein, social reform through democratic institutions replaced revolution as the path to a humane socialist society. (See "Compare and Connect: Bernstein and Lenin Debate the Tactics of European Socialism," pages 744–745.)

Bernstein's doctrines, known as *Revisionism*, generated heated debate among German socialists, who finally condemned them. His critics argued that evolution toward social democracy might be possible in liberal, parliamentary Britain, but not in conservative Germany, with its feeble *Reichstag*. Nonetheless, while still calling for revolution, the SPD pursued a course of action similar to what Bernstein advocated. Its trade union members, prospering within the German economy, did not want revolution. Its grassroots members wanted to be patriotic Germans as well as good socialists. Its leaders feared anything that might renew the persecution they had experienced under Bismarck.

Consequently, the SPD worked for electoral gains, expansion of its membership, and short-term political and social reform. It prospered and became one of the most important institutions of imperial Germany. Even middle-class Germans voted for it to oppose the illiberal institutions of the empire. In August 1914, after long debate among themselves, the SPD members of the *Reichstag* unanimously voted for the war credits that would finance Germany's participation in World War I.

Russia: Industrial Development and the Birth of Bolshevism

In the 1890s, Russia entered the industrial age and confronted many of the problems that other nations of the Continent had experienced fifty or seventy-five years earlier. Unlike those other countries, Russia had to deal with political discontent and economic development simultaneously. Russian socialism reflected that peculiar situation.

Witte's Program for Industrial Growth Tsar Alexander III (r. 1881–1894) and, after him, Nicholas II (r. 1894–1917) were determined that Russia should become an industrial power. Only by doing so, they believed, could the country maintain its position as a great power. Count Sergei Witte (1849–1915) led Russia into the industrial age. After a career in railways and other private business, he was appointed first minister of communications and then finance minister in 1892. Witte, who pursued a policy of planned economic development, protective tariffs, high taxes, putting Russia's currency on the gold standard, and efficiency in government and business, epitomized the nineteenth-century modernizer. He established a strong financial relationship with the French money market, which enabled Russia to finance its modernization program with French loans and which later led to diplomatic cooperation and an alliance between Russia and France.

View the Image "Early Russian Factory" on **MyHistoryLab.com**

Witte favored heavy industries. Between 1890 and 1904, the Russian railway system grew from 30,596 to 59,616 kilometers. The 5,000-mile-long Trans-Siberian Railroad was completed in 1903. Coal output more than tripled during the same period. Pig-iron production increased from 928,000 tons in 1890 to 4,641,000 tons in 1913. During the same period, steel production rose from 378,000 to 4,918,000 tons. Textile manufacturing continued to expand and was still the single largest industry. The factory system spread extensively.

Industrialism, however, also brought social discontent to Russia, as it had elsewhere. Landowners felt that foreign capitalists were earning too much of the profit. The peasants saw their grain exports and tax payments finance development that did not measurably improve their lives. A small, but significant, industrial proletariat emerged. In 1900, Russia had approximately 3 million factory workers. Their working and living conditions were poor. They enjoyed little state protection, and trade unions were illegal. In 1897, Witte did enact an 11.5-hour workday, but needless to say, discontent and strikes continued.

Read the Document "M. I. Pokzovskaya, *Working Conditions of Women in the Factories*" on **MyHistoryLab.com**

Similar social and economic problems arose in the countryside. Russian agriculture had not prospered after the emancipation of the serfs in 1861. The peasants remained burdened with redemption payments for the land they farmed, local taxes, excessive national taxes, and falling grain prices. Peasants did not own their land as individuals, but communally through the *mir*, or village. They farmed the land inefficiently through strip farming or by tilling small plots. Many free peasants with too little land to support their families had to work on large estates owned by nobles or for more prosperous peasant farmers, known as *kulaks*. Between 1860 and 1914, the population of European Russia rose from about 50 million to around 103 million people. Land hunger and discontent spread among the peasants and sparked frequent uprisings in the countryside.

New political developments accompanied economic changes. The membership and intellectual roots of the Social Revolutionary Party, founded in 1901, reached back to the Populists of the 1870s. The new party opposed industrialism and looked to the communal life of rural Russia as a model for the future. In 1903, the Constitutional Democratic Party, or Cadets, was formed. This liberal party drew its members from those who participated in local councils called *zemstvos*. Modeling themselves on the liberal parties of Western Europe, the Cadets wanted a constitutional monarchy under a parliamentary regime with civil liberties and economic progress.

Lenin's Early Thought and Career The situation of Russian socialists differed radically from that of socialists in other major European countries. Russia had no representative institutions and only a small working class. The compromises and accommodations achieved elsewhere were meaningless in Russia where socialists believed that in both theory and practice they must be revolutionary. The repressive policies of the tsarist regime required the Russian Social Democratic Party, founded in 1898, to function in exile. The party members greatly admired the German Social Democratic Party and adopted its Marxist ideology.

The leading late-nineteenth-century Russian Marxist was Gregory Plekhanov (1857–1918), who wrote from exile in Switzerland. At the turn of the century, his chief disciple was Vladimir Ilyich Ulyanov (1870–1924), who later took the name of Lenin. The future leader of the communist revolution was the son of a high bureaucrat. His older brother, while a student in Saint Petersburg, had become involved in radical politics; arrested for participating in a plot against Alexander III, he was executed in 1887. In 1893, Lenin moved to Saint Petersburg, where he studied law. Soon he, too, was drawn to the revolutionary groups among the factory workers. He was arrested in 1895 and exiled to Siberia. In 1900, after his release, Lenin left Russia for the West. He spent most of the next seventeen years in Switzerland.

Сестрорѣцкій Оружейн. Заводъ.

№

Предъявителю сего Константину Петровичу Иванову

Разрѣшается входъ въ Магазин Завода до 1 Января 1918 года.

Примѣчаніе:

1) Билетъ всегда имѣть при себѣ и предъявлять по первому требованію администраціи завода.

2) Билетъ долженъ быть предъявленъ въ контору завода для записи въ книгу.

Помощникъ Начальника Сестр. Оруж. Завода по технической части

Lenin had been banned from Russia, and had to return to St. Petersburg using an assumed name and in disguise. He traveled using this passport, issued to him under the assumed name of Konstantin Petrovich Ivanov.

There, Lenin became deeply involved in the disputes of the exiled Russian Social Democrats. They all considered themselves Marxists, but they differed on what a Marxist revolution would mean for primarily rural Russia and on how to structure their own party. The Social Democrats favored industrial development and did not idolize Russia's agricultural past. Most Russian Social Democrats believed Russia had to develop a large proletariat before the Marxist revolution could come. They also hoped to build a mass political party like the German SPD.

Lenin dissented from both these ideas. In *What Is to Be Done?* (1902), he condemned any cooperation with existing governments, such as those the German SPD had made as well as trade unionism that settled for short-term reformist gains. Lenin further rejected the concept of a mass democratic party composed of workers. Instead, he declared that revolutionary consciousness would not arise spontaneously from the working class. Rather, "people who make revolutionary activity their profession" must carry that consciousness to the workers.[4] Only a small, tightly organized elite party could possess the proper dedication to revolution and resist penetration by police spies. The guiding principle of that party should be "the strictest secrecy, the strictest selection of members, and the training of professional revolutionaries."[5] Lenin thus rejected both Kautsky's view that revolution was inevitable and Bernstein's view that democratic means could achieve revolutionary goals. Lenin substituted the small, professional, nondemocratic revolutionary party for Marx's proletariat as the instrument of revolutionary change. (See "Compare and Connect: Bernstein and Lenin Debate the Tactics of European Socialism," pages 744–745.)

In 1903, at the London Congress of the Russian Social Democratic Party, Lenin forced a split in the party ranks. He and his followers lost many votes on questions put before the congress, but near its close they mustered a slim majority. Thereafter Lenin's faction assumed the name **Bolsheviks**, meaning "majority," and the other, more moderate, democratic revolutionary faction came to be known as the **Mensheviks**, or "minority." There was, of course, a considerable public relations advantage to the name *Bolshevik*.

A fundamental organizational difference had existed between the two chief factions of the Russian Social Democratic Party. The Mensheviks wanted a party with a mass membership, similar to the German SDP and other West European socialist parties, which would function democratically. The Bolsheviks intended the party to consist of elite professional revolutionaries who would provide centralized leadership for the working class.

In 1905, Lenin complemented his organizational theory with a program for revolution in Russia. In *Two Tactics of Social Democracy in the Bourgeois-Democratic Revolution*, he urged the socialist revolution to unite the proletariat and the peasantry. Lenin grasped better than any other revolutionary the profound discontent in the Russian countryside. He believed the tsarist government probably could not suppress an alliance of workers and peasants in rebellion.

Lenin's two principles—an elite party and a dual social revolution—guided later Bolshevik activity. In 1912, the Bolsheviks organized themselves as a separate party. The Bolsheviks ultimately seized power in November 1917, transforming the political landscape of the twentieth century, but they did so only after the turmoil of World War I had undermined support for the tsar and only after other political forces had already toppled the tsarist government in February 1917. Before World War I, the Bolsheviks constituted the odd man out in European socialist politics; they exerted no significant prewar influence on members of other socialist groups. For their part, the Bolsheviks responded by scorning the West European socialist parties that worked within their nations' political systems.

The Revolution of 1905 and Its Aftermath The quarrels among the exiled Russian socialists and Lenin's doctrines had no immediate influence on events in Russia. Industrialization continued to stir resentment. In 1903, Nicholas II dismissed Witte, hoping to quell the criticism. The next year, in response to conflicts over Manchuria and Korea, Russia went to war against Japan, partly in hopes the conflict would rally public opinion to the tsar. Instead, the Russians lost the war, and the government faced an internal political crisis. The Japanese captured Port Arthur, Russia's naval base on the coast of China, early in 1905. A few days later, on January 22, a Russian Orthodox priest named Father George Gapon led several hundred workers to present a petition to the tsar to improve industrial conditions. The petitioners did not know that the tsar was not even in Saint Petersburg, but as they approached the Winter Palace, troops opened fire, killing approximately forty people and wounding hundreds of others. As word of this massacre spread, and large, angry crowds gathered elsewhere in the city, the military shot more people. The final death toll was approximately two hundred killed and eight hundred wounded, though at the time rumors made the numbers much larger. The day, soon known as Bloody Sunday, marked a turning point. Vast numbers of ordinary Russians came to believe they could no longer trust the tsar or his government.

During the next ten months, revolutionary disturbances spread throughout Russia. Sailors mutinied, workers went on strike, peasants revolted, and property was attacked. The uncle of Nicholas II was assassinated

[4] Albert Fried and Ronald Sanders, eds., *Socialist Thought: A Documentary History* (Garden City, NY: Anchor Doubleday, 1964), p. 459.

[5] Fried and Sanders, *Socialist Thought*, p. 468.

COMPARE AND CONNECT Bernstein and Lenin Debate the Tactics of European Socialism

Read the Compare and Connect on MyHistoryLab.com

BY THE CLOSE of the nineteenth century the European Socialist movement found itself sharply divided over its future goals and tactics. Some socialists, including Eduard Bernstein, came to reject Karl Marx's emphasis on a proletarian revolution, and embraced democratic politics as the best way to realize their goals of improving the life of the working class. A minority, including Lenin, rejected democracy and embraced the concept of violent revolution achieved by a small professional elite rather than by a spontaneous proletarian uprising. After the 1917 Bolshevik Revolution in Russia, those divisions would play themselves out in an enormously hostile conflict between democratic socialist parties in Western Europe and Communists in the Soviet Union and Communist parties in Western Europe dominated by the Soviet Union. (See Chapters 26 and 27.)

QUESTIONS

1. **According to Bernstein, what specific predictions in the *Communist Manifesto* failed to materialize?**
2. **Why is the advance of democracy important to Bernstein's argument? Why does he renounce the concept of a "dictatorship of the proletariat"?**
3. **What does Lenin mean by "professional revolutionaries"? Why does Russia need such revolutionaries?**
4. **How does Lenin reconcile his antidemocratic views to the goal of aiding the working class?**
5. **How could the ideas of both Bernstein and Lenin be seen as departures from Marx's own thinking?**

I. Eduard Bernstein Urges Socialists to Embrace Democracy

Eduard Bernstein was responsible for the emergence of Revisionism within the German Social Democratic Party. He was a dedicated socialist, but was convinced that Marx's Communist Manifesto *(1848) had not predicted the actual future of the European working classes. Bernstein believed the capitalist system would not suddenly collapse and that socialists should change their tactics to achieve democratic political rights and pursue reform instead of revolution. (Compare this document with the passages from* The Communist Manifesto *in Chapter 21.)*

Social conditions have not developed to such an acute opposition of things and classes as is depicted in the [*Communist*] *Manifesto*. . . . The number of members of the possessing classes is today not smaller but larger. The enormous increase of social wealth is not accompanied by a decreasing number of large capitalists but by an increasing number of capitalists of all degrees. . . .

In all advanced countries we see the privileges of the capitalist bourgeoisie yielding step by step to democratic organizations. . . .

The conquest of political power by the working classes, the expropriation of capitalists, are not ends in themselves but only means for the accomplishment of certain aims and endeavours. . . .

Democracy is in principle the suppression of class government, though it is not yet the actual suppression of classes. . . . The right to vote in a democracy makes its members virtually partners in the community, and this virtual partnership must in the end lead to real partnership. . . .

Universal franchise is, from two sides, the alternative to a violent revolution. But universal suffrage is only a part of democracy, although a part which in time must draw the other parts after it as the magnet attracts to itself the scattered portions of iron. It certainly proceeds more slowly than many would wish, but in spite of that it is at work. And social democracy cannot further this work better than by taking its stand unreserved only the theory of democracy—on the ground of universal suffrage with all the consequences resulting therefrom to its tactics. . . .

Is there any sense . . . in maintaining the phrase of the 'dictatorship of the proletariat' at a time when in all possible places representatives of social democracy have placed themselves practically in the arena of Parliamentary work, have declared for the proportional representation of the people, and for direct legislation—all of which is inconsistent with a dictatorship.

The phrase is to-day so antiquated that it is only to be reconciled with reality by stripping the word dictatorship of its actual meaning and attaching to it some kind of weakened interpretation. The whole practical activity of social democracy is directed towards creating circumstances and conditions which shall render possible and secure a transition (free from convulsive outbursts) of the modern social order to a higher one. ■

From Eduard Bernstein, *Evolutionary Socialism: A Criticism and Affirmation, 1899* (New York: Schocken Books, 1961), pp. xxiv–xxv, xxix, 143–146.

II. Lenin Argues for the Necessity of a Secret and Elite Party of Professional Revolutionaries

Social democratic parties in Western Europe had mass memberships and were generally democratic organizations. In this passage from What Is to Be Done? *(1902), Lenin explains why the autocratic political conditions of Russia demanded a different kind of organization for the Russian Social Democratic Party. Lenin's ideas became the guiding principles of Bolshevik organization. Lenin departed from Marx's own thought by urging the necessity of fulminating revolution rather than waiting for it to occur as a necessary result of the collapse of capitalism.*

I assert that it is far more difficult [for government police] to unearth a dozen wise men than a hundred fools. This position I will defend, no matter how much you instigate the masses against me for my "anti-democratic" views, etc. As I have stated repeatedly, by "wise men," in connection with organization, I mean professional revolutionaries, irrespective of whether they have developed from among students or working men. I assert: (1) that no revolutionary movement can endure without a stable organization of leaders maintaining continuity; (2) that the broader the popular mass drawn spontaneously into the struggle, which forms the basis of the movement and participates in it, the more urgent the need for such an organization, and the more solid this organization must be . . . ; (3) that such an organization must consist chiefly of people professionally engaged in revolutionary activity; (4) that in an autocratic state [such as Russia], the more we confine the membership of such an organization to people who are professionally engaged in revolutionary activity and who have been professionally trained in the art of combating the political police, the more difficult will it be to unearth the organization; and (5) the greater will be the number of people from the working class and from other social classes who will be able to join the movement and perform active work in it. . . .

The only serious organization principle for the active workers of our movement should be the strictest secrecy, the strictest selection of members, and the training of professional revolutionaries. ■

By the close of the nineteenth century, European socialists had come to doubt whether the industrial proletariat around the world, such as these workers in the Krupp steel works around 1910, would or could actually bring about a revolution as predicted by Marx. Eduard Bernstein thought democratic social change would improve the lot of workers. Lenin believed an elite revolutionary party would produce such radical change. Krupp was one of many Germany companies that introduced paternalistic benefits to workers, such as modern housing projects subsidized by the company, in an effort to show that cooperation did more to improve workers' lives than violent revolution would. Stringer/Hulton Archive/Getty Images

From Albert Fried and Ronald Sanders, eds. *Socialist Thought: A Documentary History* (Garden City, NY: Anchor Doubleday, 1964), pp. 460, 468.

MAJOR DATES IN THE DEVELOPMENT OF SOCIALISM

1864	International Working Men's Association (the First International) founded
1875	German Social Democratic Party founded
1876	First International dissolved
1878	German antisocialist laws passed
1884	British Fabian Society founded
1889	Second International founded
1891	German antisocialist laws permitted to expire
1891	German Social Democratic Party's Erfurt Program
1895	French Confédération Générale du Travail founded
1899	Eduard Bernstein's *Evolutionary Socialism*
1902	The British Labour Party founded
1902	Lenin's *What Is to Be Done?*
1903	Bolshevik–Menshevik split
1904	"Opportunism" rejected at the Amsterdam Congress of the Second International

in Moscow. Liberal leaders of the Constitutional Democratic Party from the *zemstvos* demanded political reform. University students went on strike. Social Revolutionaries and Social Democrats agitated among urban working groups. In early October 1905, strikes broke out in Saint Petersburg, and for all practical purposes, worker councils, called *soviets*, controlled the city. Nicholas II issued the October Manifesto, which promised Russia a constitutional government.

Early in 1906, Nicholas II announced the creation of a representative body, the *Duma*, with two chambers. He reserved to himself, however, ministerial appointments, financial policy, and military and foreign affairs. The April elections returned a highly radical group of representatives. The tsar appointed Piotr Stolypin (1862–1911), who had little sympathy for parliamentary government, as prime minister. Stolypin persuaded Nicholas to dissolve the Duma. A second assembly was elected in February 1907. Again, cooperation proved impossible, and the tsar dissolved that Duma in June. A third Duma, elected in late 1907 on the basis of a more conservative franchise, proved sufficiently pliable for the tsar and Stolypin. Thus, within two years of the 1905 Revolution, Nicholas II had recaptured much of the ground he had conceded.

Stolypin set about repressing rebellion, removing some causes of the revolt, and rallying property owners behind the tsarist regime. Early in 1907, special field courts-martial condemned almost seven hundred rebellious peasants to death. Before undertaking this repression, Stolypin, in November 1906, had canceled any redemptive payments that the peasants still owed the government from the emancipation of the serfs in 1861. He took this step to encourage peasants to assume individual proprietorship of the land they farmed and to abandon the communal system of shared village ownership. Stolypin believed farmers would be more productive working for themselves. Combined with a program to instruct peasants on how to farm more efficiently, this policy improved agricultural production. However, many peasant small-holders sold their land and joined the industrial labor force.

The moderate liberals who sat in the Duma approved of the new land measures promoting competition and individual property ownership. The Constitutional Democrats wanted a more genuinely parliamentary mode of government, but they compromised out of fear of new revolutionary disturbances. Hatred of Stolypin was still widespread, however, among the country's older conservative groups, and industrial workers remained antagonistic to the tsar. In 1911, Stolypin was assassinated by a Social Revolutionary, who may have been a police agent

MAJOR DATES IN TURN-OF-THE-CENTURY RUSSIAN HISTORY

1892	Witte appointed finance minister
1895	Lenin arrested and sent to Siberia
1897	11.5-hour workday established
1898	Russian Social Democratic Party founded
1900	Lenin leaves Russia for western Europe
1901	Social Revolutionary Party founded
1903	Constitutional Democratic Party (Cadets) founded
1903	Bolshevik–Menshevik split
1903	Witte dismissed
1904	Russo-Japanese War begins
1905 (August)	Japan defeats Russia
1905 (January 22)	Revolution breaks out in Saint Petersburg after Bloody Sunday
1905 (October 20)	General strike
1905 (October 26)	October Manifesto establishes constitutional government
1906 (May 10)	First Duma meets
1906 (June)	Stolypin appointed prime minister
1906 (July 21)	Dissolution of first Duma
1906 (November)	Land redemption payments canceled for peasants
1907 (March 5–16)	Second Duma seated and dismissed in June
1907	Franchise changed and a third Duma elected, which sits until 1912
1911	Stolypin assassinated by a Social Revolutionary
1912	Fourth Duma elected
1914	World War I breaks out

BLOODY SUNDAY, ST. PETERSBURG, 1905

ON BLOODY SUNDAY, January 22, 1905, troops of Tsar Nicholas II fired on a peaceful procession of workers at the Winter Palace who sought to present a petition for better working and living conditions. The scene in a Saint Petersburg square portrayed here, which can still be visited today, depicts one of the enduring images of events leading to the subsequent Russian Revolutions of 1905 and 1917. It figured in at least two movies: the 1925 antitsarist Soviet silent film called *The Ninth of January*, and *Nicholas and Alexandra*, the lavish 1971 movie that was sympathetic to the tsar and blamed Bloody Sunday on frightened and incompetent officials. While Nicholas had not ordered the troops to fire and was not even in St. Petersburg on Bloody Sunday, the event all but destroyed any chance of reconciliation between the tsarist government and the Russian working class.

The workers are visibly defenseless in the face of the rifles being fired at them.

Although the square before the Winter Palace toward the right of the troops is large and might have allowed an escape route of sorts for the workers' procession, the troops forced the crowd into an area of narrow escape.

The view is the one that officials in the Winter Palace, which lay behind the row of troops with rifles, would have seen.

Bildarchiv Preussischer Kulturbesitz/Art Resource. NY

How did the invention of photography and the making of movies transform the recording and interpretation of the past?

Do you think the firing on the crowd in 1905 was as orderly as this still from a later Bolshevik film made it appear?

How did the ongoing recollection and reenactment of this dramatic, violent moment in the Revolution of 1905 serve to continue to discredit the tsarist government and to champion the later Bolshevik Revolution?

in the pay of conservatives. Nicholas II found no worthy successor. His government simply muddled along.

Meanwhile, at court, the monk Grigory Efimovich Rasputin (1871?–1916) gained ascendancy with the tsar and his wife because of his alleged power to heal the tsar's hemophilic son Alexis, the heir to the throne, when medicine proved unable to help the boy. Popular resentment of Rasputin's undue influence, as well as continued social discontent and conservative resistance to any further liberal reforms, undermined the position of the tsar and his government after 1911. Once again, as in 1904, Nicholas II and his ministers thought that some bold move in foreign policy might bring the regime the popular support it desperately needed.

In Perspective

From 1860 through 1914, two apparently contradictory developments emerged in European social life. On one hand, the lifestyle of the urban middle classes became the model to which much of society aspired. The characteristics of this lifestyle included a relatively small family living in its own house or large apartment, servants, and a wife who did not earn an income. The middle classes, in general, benefited from the many material comforts that the Second Industrial Revolution had generated.

During the same period, the forces of socialism and labor unions assumed a new and major role in European political life. Their leaders demanded greater social justice and a fairer distribution of the vast quantities of consumer goods Europe was producing. Some socialists sought in one way or another to work within existing political systems. Others—particularly, those in Russia—advocated revolution. The growth in wealth and the availability of new goods and services magnified the injustices the poor suffered, and the contrast between them and the middle classes made the demands of labor and the socialists more strident. In Russia, the strains of the early stages of industrialization intensified social unrest. These strains, compounded by the humiliating defeat in a war against Japan, triggered the unsuccessful revolution of 1905.

The working class, however, was not alone in seeking change. Women, for the first time in European history, began in significant ways to demand a political role and to protest the gender inequalities embedded in law and family life. They were beginning to enter the professions and were taking a significant role in the service economy, such as the new telephone companies. These changes, as much as the demands of socialists, would, in time, raise questions about the adequacy of the much admired late-nineteenth-century middle-class lifestyle.

KEY TERMS

anti-Semitism (p. 737)
Bolsheviks (p. 743)
Mensheviks (p. 743)
petite bourgeoisie (p. 720)
pogroms (p. 736)
Second Industrial Revolution (p. 716)
suffragettes (p. 734)

REVIEW QUESTIONS

1. How did the Second Industrial Revolution transform European society? What new industries developed, and which do you think had the greatest impact in the twentieth century? Why did European economic growth slacken in the second half of the nineteenth century?
2. Why were European cities redesigned during the late nineteenth century? Why were housing and health key issues for urban reform?
3. What was the status of European women in the second half of the nineteenth century? Why did they grow discontented with their lot? What factors led to change? To what extent had they improved their position by 1914? What tactics did they use to effect change? Was the emancipation of women inevitable? How did women approach their situation differently from country to country?
4. What were the major characteristics of Jewish emancipation in the nineteenth century?
5. What was the status of the European working classes in 1860? Had it improved by 1914? Why did trade unions and organized mass political parties grow? Why were the debates over "opportunism" and "revisionism" important to the Western European socialist parties?
6. What were the benefits and drawbacks of industrialization for Russia? Were the tsars wise to attempt to modernize their country, or should they have left it as it was? How did Lenin's view of socialism differ from that of the socialists in Western Europe?

SUGGESTED READINGS

A. Ascher, *P. A. Stolypin: The Search for Stability in Late Imperial Russia* (2000). A broad-ranging biography based on extensive research.

P. Birnbaum, *Jewish Destinies: Citizenship, State, and Community in Modern France* (2000). Explores the subject from the French Revolution to the present.

J. Bush, *Women Against the Vote: Female Anti-Suffragism in Britain* (2007). An important study of British women opposed to the extension of the vote to women.

T. W. Clyman and J. Vowles, *Russia through Women's Eyes: Autobiographies from Tsarist Russia* (1996). A splendid collection of relatively brief memoirs.

G. Crossick and S. Jaumain, eds., *Cathedrals of Consumption: The European Department Store, 1850–1939* (1999). Essays on the development of a new mode of distribution of consumer goods.

D. Ellenson, *After Emancipation: Jewish Religious Responses to Modernity* (2004). A volume that explores numerous examples of this response across Europe.

A. Geifman, *Thou Shalt Kill: Revolutionary Terrorism in Russia, 1894–1917* (1993). An examination of political violence in late imperial Russia.

R. F. Hamilton, *Marxism, Revisionism, and Leninism: Explication, Assessment, and Commentary* (2000). A contribution by a historically minded sociologist.

J. Harsin, *Policing Prostitution in Nineteenth-Century Paris* (1985). A major study of this significant subject in French social history.

G. Himmelfarb, *Poverty and Compassion: The Moral Imagination of the Late Victorians* (1991). The best examination of late Victorian social thought.

E. Hobsbawm, *The Age of Empire, 1875–1914* (1987). A stimulating survey that covers cultural as well as political developments.

S. S. Holton, *Feminism and Democracy: Women's Suffrage and Reform Politics in Britain, 1900–1918* (1986). An excellent treatment of the subject.

T. Hoppen, *The Mid-Victorian Generation, 1846–1886* (1998). The most extensive treatment of the subject.

S. Kovin, *Slumming: Sexual and Social Politics in Victorian London* (2004). Explores the complexities of the extension of charity and social services in late Victorian London.

M. Malia, *Russia under Western Eyes: From the Bronze Horseman to the Lenin Mausoleum* (2000). A brilliant work on how Western intellectuals understood Russia.

E. D. Rappaport, *Shopping for Pleasure: Women in the Making of London's West End* (2001). A study of the rise of department stores in London.

H. Rogger, *Jewish Policies and Right-Wing Politics in Imperial Russia* (1986). A learned examination of Russian anti-Semitism.

M. L. Rozenblit, *The Jews of Vienna, 1867–1914: Assimilation and Identity* (1983). Covers the cultural, economic, and political life of Viennese Jews.

R. Service, *Lenin: A Biography* (2002). Based on new sources and will no doubt become the standard biography.

D. Sorkin, *The Transformation of German Jewry, 1780–1840* (1987). An examination of Jewish emancipation in Germany.

G. P. Steenson, *Not One Man! Not One Penny!: German Social Democracy, 1863–1914* (1999). An extensive survey.

N. Stone, *Europe Transformed* (1984). A sweeping survey that emphasizes the difficulties of late-nineteenth-century liberalism.

A. Thorpe, *A History of the British Labour Party* (2001). From its inception to the twenty-first century.

J. R. Walkowitz, *Prostitution and Victorian Society: Women, Class, and the State* (1980). A work of great insight and sensitivity.

MyHistoryLab™ MEDIA ASSIGNMENTS

Find these resources in the Media Assignments folder for Chapter 23 on **MyHistoryLab**.

QUESTIONS FOR ANALYSIS

1. What similarities exist between this event and the uprising in Egypt of 2010–2011?

   ***Section:* Labor, Socialism, and Politics to World War I**

   View the **Closer Look** Bloody Sunday, St. Petersburg 1905, p. 747

2. What major concerns of the age does this report reflect?

   ***Section:* Late-Nineteenth-Century Urban Life**

   Read the **Document** Edwin Chadwick, *Summary from the Poor Law Commissioners*, p. 725

3. What was the relationship between population growth and industrialization in the 1800s?

   ***Section:* Population Trends and Migration**

   Watch the **Video** The Big Picture: The World in 1914 C.E., p. 716

4. What do you consider the main principles on which Pankhurst claims equal rights for women?

   ***Section:* Varieties of Late-Nineteenth-Century Women's Experiences**

   Read the **Document** "Freedom or Death" (1913) Emmeline Pankhurst, p. 734

5. What new experiences and difficulties accompanied her first job for this writer?

   ***Section:* Varieties of Late-Nineteenth-Century Women's Experiences**

   Read the **Document** Adelheid Popp, "Finding Work: Women Factory Workers," p. 730

OTHER RESOURCES FROM THIS CHAPTER

The Second Industrial Revolution

View the **Map** Industrial Development in Key Regional Centers, ca. 1900, p. 716

Late-Nineteenth-Century Urban Life

View the **Architectural Panorama** Eiffel Tower, p. 724

Varieties of Late-Nineteenth-Century Women's Experiences

Read the **Document** George Bernard Shaw, *Mrs. Warren's Profession*, p. 731

Read the **Document** John Stuart Mill, *The Subjection of Women*, p. 733

Watch the **Video** British Women's Suffrage, p. 733

Jewish Emancipation

View the **Map** Map Discovery: Jewish Migration, p. 737

Labor, Socialism, and Politics to World War I

Read the **Document** Socialism: The Gotha Program (1875), p. 740

View the **Image** Early Russian Factory, p. 741

Read the **Document** M. I. Pokzovskaya, *Working Conditions of Women in the Factories*, p. 741

Read the **Compare and Connect** Bernstein and Lenin Debate the Tactics of European Socialism, p. 744

Darwin's theories about the evolution of humankind from the higher primates aroused enormous controversy. This caricature shows him with a monkey's body holding a mirror to an apelike creature. National History Museum, London, UK/Bridgeman Art Library

Listen to the Chapter Audio on MyHistoryLab.com

24

The Birth of Modern European Thought

▼ **The New Reading Public**
Advances in Primary Education • Reading Material for the Mass Audience

▼ **Science at Midcentury**
Comte, Positivism, and the Prestige of Science • New Theories of Evolution: Lamark, Lyell, Darwin, Wallace • Science and Ethics: Social Darwinism

▼ **Christianity and the Church Under Siege**
Intellectual Skepticism • Conflict Between Church and State • Areas of Religious Revival • The Roman Catholic Church and the Modern World • Islam and Late-Nineteenth-Century European Thought

▼ **Toward a Twentieth-Century Frame of Mind**
Science: The Revolution in Physics • Literature: Realism and Naturalism • Modernism in Literature • The Coming of Modern Art • Friedrich Nietzsche and the Revolt Against Reason • The Birth of Psychoanalysis • Retreat from Rationalism in Politics • Racism • Anti-Semitism and the Birth of Zionism

▼ **Women and Modern Thought**
Antifeminism in Late-Century Thought • New Directions in Feminism

▼ **In Perspective**

LEARNING OBJECTIVES

What effect did state-financed education have on literacy in late-nineteenth-century Europe?

What role did science play in the second half of the nineteenth century?

What challenges did European Christianity face in the late nineteenth century?

How did developments in art, psychology, and science reflect a profound shift in Western thought?

How did women challenge gender stereotypes in the late nineteenth and early twentieth centuries?

DURING THE SAME period that the modern nation-state developed and the Second Industrial Revolution laid the foundations for modern life, the ideas that marked European thought for much of the twentieth century and beyond took shape. Like previous intellectual changes, these arose from earlier patterns of thought. The Enlightenment provided late-nineteenth-century Europeans with a heritage of rationalism, toleration, cosmopolitanism, and an appreciation of science. Romanticism led them to value feelings, imagination, national identity, and the autonomy of the artistic experience.

By 1900, these strands of thought had become woven into a new fabric. Many of the traditional intellectual signposts were disappearing. Christianity had experienced the most severe intellectual attack in its history. The picture of the physical world that had prevailed since Newton had undergone major modification. Darwin and Freud had challenged the special place that Western thinkers had assigned to humankind. Writers began to question rationality. The humanitarian ideals of liberalism and socialism gave way to aggressive nationalism. European intellectuals were more daring than ever before, but they were also probably less certain and optimistic.

▼ The New Reading Public

The social context of intellectual life changed in the latter part of the nineteenth century. For the first time in Europe, a mass reading public came into existence as more people than ever before became drawn into the world of print culture. In 1850, about half the population of Western Europe and a much higher proportion of Russians were illiterate. That situation changed during the next half-century.

Advances in Primary Education

Literacy on the Continent improved steadily from the 1860s onward as governments financed education. Austria mandated elementary education in 1775, Hungary provided elementary education in 1868, Britain in 1870, Switzerland in 1874, Italy in 1877, and France between 1878 and 1881. The already advanced education system of Prussia was extended throughout the German Empire after 1871. By 1900, in Britain, France, Belgium, the Netherlands, Germany, and Scandinavia, approximately 85 percent or more of the people could read. Literacy rates in Austria-Hungary varied from very high in certain urban areas to very low in the eastern and southernmost provinces. Italy, Spain, Russia, and the Balkans had illiteracy rates of between 30 and 60 percent.

The new primary education in the basic skills of reading, writing, and elementary arithmetic reflected and generated social change. Both liberals and conservatives regarded such minimal training as necessary for orderly political behavior by the newly enfranchised voters. They also hoped that literacy would create a more productive labor force.

The school-teaching profession grew rapidly in numbers and, as noted in Chapter 23, became a major area for the employment of women. Having created systems of primary education, the major nations had to give further attention to secondary education by the time of World War I. In another generation, the question would become one of democratic university instruction.

Public education became widespread in Europe during the second half of the nineteenth century and women came to dominate the profession of school teaching, especially at the elementary level. This 1905 photograph shows English schoolchildren going through morning drills.

Reading Material for the Mass Audience

The expanding literate population created a vast market for new reading material. The number of newspapers, books, magazines, mail-order catalogs, and libraries grew rapidly. Cheap mass-circulation newspapers, such as *Le Petit Journal* of Paris and the *Daily Mail* of London, enjoyed their first heyday. Such newspapers carried advertising that alerted readers to new consumer products. Other publishers produced newspapers with specialized political or religious viewpoints. The number of monthly and quarterly journals for families, women, and freethinking intellectuals increased. Probably more people with different ideas could get into print in the late nineteenth century than ever before in European history.

Many of the new readers were only marginally literate and ill-informed about many subjects. Cheap newspapers prospered on stories of sensational crimes and political scandal and on pages of advertising. Religious journals depended on denominational rivalry. A brisk market existed for pornography. Newspapers with editorials on the front page became major factors in the emerging mass politics.

Critics pointed to the low level of public taste, but the new education, the new readers, and the myriad new books and journals permitted a popularization of knowledge that has become a hallmark of our world. The new literacy was the intellectual parallel of the railroad and the steamship. People could leave their original intellectual surroundings because literacy is not an end in itself but leads to other skills and other knowledge.

▼ Science at Midcentury

In about 1850, learned persons regarded the physical world as rational, mechanical, and dependable. Experiment and observation could reveal its laws objectively. Scientific theory purportedly described physical nature as it really existed. Moreover, by 1850, science had a strong institutional life in French and German universities and in new professional societies. William Whewell of Cambridge University had invented the word "scientist" in the early 1830s, and it was in common use by the end of the century. (See "Encountering the Past: The Birth of Science Fiction," page 754.)

Comte, Positivism, and the Prestige of Science

During the early nineteenth century, science had continued to establish itself as the model for all human knowledge. French philosopher Auguste Comte (1798–1857) developed **positivism**, a philosophy of human intellectual development that culminated in science. In *The Positive Philosophy* (1830–1842), Comte argued that human thought had developed in three stages. In the first, or theological, stage, physical nature was explained in terms of the action of divinities or spirits. In the second, or metaphysical, stage, abstract principles were regarded as the operative agencies of nature. In the final, or positive, stage, explanations of nature were based on exact description of phenomena.

Read the **Document** "Auguste Comte, 'Course of Positive Philosophy' (France), 1830–1842" on **MyHistoryLab.com**

Comte believed that positive laws of social behavior could be discovered in the same fashion as laws of physical nature. He is, thus, generally regarded as the father of sociology. Works like Comte's helped convince learned Europeans that all knowledge must resemble scientific knowledge.

New Theories of Evolution: Lamarck, Lyell, Darwin, Wallace

The first modern European thinker to develop a comprehensive theory of evolutionary change was Jean-Baptiste Lamarck (1744–1829). Lamarck denied the possibility of extinction, that geological forms changed gradually over time, and that living organisms had to match their environments. From these premises, the notion that living organisms also changed gradually over time seemed a necessary conclusion. Organisms were forced to change their habits in response to changes in their environments, and new habits led to new forms. Lamarck is best remembered today for his idea that acquired characteristics could be inherited, that is, that a blacksmith's son could be born with a stronger arm because of his father's lifelong muscular use of that arm. While this notion has since been largely rejected, Lamarck's broader ideas about evolutionary change proved very influential.

Another major contributor to new theories of evolution in the nineteenth century was geologist Charles Lyell (1797–1875). Lyell published *Principles of Geology* in three volumes between 1830 and 1833. In it, he developed the older theory of "uniformitarianism." Uniformitarianism holds that the same natural laws that govern the universe in the present have always governed the universe, and that they are consistent across both time and space. It also holds that change is gradual and uniform. Lyell's theory of gradual change and of using present-day observation to explain phenomenon in the deep past profoundly influenced Charles Darwin (1809–1882), who wrote in 1844 that "I always feel as if my books came half out of Lyell's brains."[1]

In 1859, Darwin published *On the Origin of Species*, which carried the mechanical interpretation of physical nature into the world of living things. The book was one of the seminal works of Western thought. Both Darwin and his book have been much misunderstood. He did not originate the concept of evolution, which had been discussed widely before he wrote. Alfred Russel Wallace (1823–1913) came to many of the same conclusions as Darwin independently and based on his own field research. Both men, separately, formulated variations of the principle of natural selection, which explained how species had changed or evolved over time. Earlier writers had believed evolution might occur; Darwin and Wallace explained how it could occur.

Read the **Document** "*Origin of Species*, Charles Darwin (1859)" on **MyHistoryLab.com**

Drawing on Malthus, the two scientists contended that more living organisms come into existence than can survive in their environment. Those organisms with a marginal advantage in the struggle for existence live long enough to propagate. This principle of survival of the fittest Darwin called **natural selection**. It was naturalistic and mechanistic, requiring no guiding mind behind the development in organic nature. What neither Darwin nor anyone else in his day could explain was the origin of those chance variations that provided some living things with the marginal chance for survival. Only after 1900, when the work on heredity of Austrian monk Gregor Mendel (1822–1884) received public attention, did the mystery of those variations begin to be unraveled.

Darwin and Wallace's theory represented the triumph of naturalistic explanation, which removed the idea of purpose from organic nature. Eyes were not made for seeing according to the rational wisdom and purpose of God, but had developed mechanistically over time. Thus, the theory of evolution through natural selection not only contradicted the biblical narrative of the Creation but also undermined both the deistic argument for the existence of God from the design of the universe and the whole concept of fixity in nature or the universe at

[1]Stephen Jay Gould, *The Structure of Evolutionary Theory* (Cambridge, MA: Harvard University Press, 2002), p. 94.

THE BIRTH OF SCIENCE FICTION

DURING THE RENAISSANCE many European writers composed works about fantasy voyages to distant lands. In the seventeenth century, authors published some two hundred accounts of trips to the moon. Throughout the nineteenth century, other authors told tales of fantastic voyages into space or beneath the earth. Mary Shelley's *Frankenstein* displayed many of the characteristics of science fiction, with themes pushing the boundary of what was technologically possible at the time it was written.

However, the real father of today's works of popular science fiction was Jules Verne (1828–1905). His *Five Weeks in a Balloon* (1863), a tale of a balloon trip across Africa, sold so well that a French publisher immediately gave Verne a contract to write two such stories each year for a magazine. In 1865, he published a fanciful story about a trip to the moon in a projectile launched from a cannon, *From the Earth to the Moon*. This story influenced the work of another pioneer in science fiction, French filmmaker George Méliès, whose 1902 film *A Trip to the Moon* is indebted to Verne. So influential was Verne's image of the future that the United States named its first atomic submarine the *Nautilus* after the vessel the mysterious Captain Nemo commanded in Verne's *Twenty Thousand Leagues under the Sea* (1870).

Verne prided himself on his scientific veracity. He also located his stories in his own age. Readers felt they were experiencing a contemporary adventure.

Toward the turn of the century, science fiction found another master in English novelist H. G. Wells (1866–1946), who in 1895 published *The Time Machine* in which the characters travel through time. Wells's first success was rapidly followed by *The Island of Dr. Moreau* (1896) about a mad surgeon's inhuman experiments on animals, and *The War of the Worlds* (1898) about a Martian invasion of the earth. Wells invented many of the devices, such as new stars appearing near the solar system, Martians and other planetary creatures unfriendly to humans, machinery that goes astray, and strange diseases, that would become the stock in trade for later science fiction writers.

Verne, Wells, and their many imitators published their stories in cheap illustrated magazines with mass circulations. Consequently, science fiction immediately entered popular culture. Throughout the twentieth century popular movies and television series were made based on the stories of both Verne and Wells. In 1938, when Orson Welles (1915–1985) broadcast *War of the Worlds* over the radio, many Americans actually believed Martians had landed in New Jersey. The works of Verne and Wells continue to influence the writing of science fiction.

Sources: P. Nichols and J. Clute, *The Encyclopedia of Science Fiction* (New York: St. Martin's Press, 1995); Dieter Wuckel and Bruce Cassidy, *The Illustrated History of Science Fiction* (New York: Ungar, 1986); David Kyle, *A Pictorial History of Science Fiction* (London: Hamlyn, 1976).

The interior of the projectile.

The interior of the projectile launched to the moon is shown in this illustration from an early edition of *From the Earth to the Moon.* The Granger Collection, NYC—All rights reserved

Why is Jules Verne considered the father of modern science fiction?

What enduring plot devices did H. G. Wells introduce?

Why did science fiction become so popular?

large. The idea that physical and organic nature might be constantly changing allowed people to believe that society, values, customs, and beliefs should also change.

In 1871, in *The Descent of Man*, Darwin applied the principle of evolution by natural selection to human beings. Darwin was not the first person to treat human beings as animals, but he contended that humankind's moral nature and religious sentiments, as well as its physical frame, had developed naturalistically largely in response to the requirements of survival. Neither the origin nor the character of humankind, in Darwin's view, required the existence of a god for their explanation.

Darwin's theory of evolution by natural selection was controversial from the moment *On the Origin of Species* appeared. It encountered criticism from both the religious and the scientific communities. By the end of the century, scientists widely accepted the concept of evolution, but not yet Darwin's mechanism of natural selection. The acceptance of the latter really dates from the 1920s and 1930s, when Darwin's theory was combined with modern genetics.

Science and Ethics: Social Darwinism

One area in which science came to have a new significance was social thought and ethics. Philosophers applied the concept of the struggle for survival to human social relationships. The phrase "survival of the fittest" predated Darwin and reflected the competitive outlook of classical economics. Darwin's use of the phrase gave it the prestige associated with advanced science.

The most famous advocate of evolutionary ethics was Herbert Spencer (1820–1903), a British philosopher. Spencer, a strong individualist, believed human society progresses through competition. If the weak receive too much protection, the rest of humankind is the loser. In Spencer's work, struggle against one's fellow human beings became a kind of ethical imperative. The concept could be (and was) applied to justify not aiding the poor and the working class or to justify the domination of colonial peoples or to advocate aggressive competition among nations. Evolutionary ethics and similar concepts, all of which are usually termed ***Social Darwinism***, often came close to saying that "might makes right."

Read the Document "Herbert Spencer, Social Darwinism, from *The Data of Ethics* (1857)" on **MyHistoryLab.com**

One of the chief opponents of such thinking was Thomas Henry Huxley, the great defender of Darwin. In 1893, Huxley declared that the physical process of evolution was at odds with human ethical development. The struggle in nature only showed how human beings should not behave. (See "Compare and Connect: The Debate over Social Darwinism," pages 756–757.) Despite Huxley's arguments, the ideas of Social Darwinism continued to influence thought and public policy on both sides of the Atlantic.

▼ Christianity and the Church Under Siege

The nineteenth century was one of the most difficult periods in the history of organized Christian churches. Many European intellectuals left the faith. Secular, liberal nation-states attacked the influence of the church. The expansion of population and the growth of cities challenged its organizational capacity. Yet during all this turmoil, the Protestant and Catholic churches continued to draw popular support and personal religious devotion. The same decades marked by skepticism among many European intellectuals saw the burgeoning of the Christian missionary movement around the globe (see Chapter 25). Nonetheless, the development of an overwhelmingly secular European society had its roots in the late nineteenth century.

Intellectual Skepticism

The intellectual attack on Christianity challenged its historical credibility, its scientific accuracy, and its morality. The philosophes of the Enlightenment had delighted in pointing out contradictions in the Bible. The historical scholarship of the nineteenth century brought new issues to the foreground.

History In 1835, David Friedrich Strauss (1808–1874) published *The Life of Jesus*, in which he questioned whether the Bible provides any genuine historical evidence about Jesus. Strauss contended the story of Jesus is a myth that arose from the particular social and intellectual conditions of first-century Palestine. Jesus' character and life represent the aspirations of the people of that time and place, rather than events that actually occurred.

During the second half of the century, scholars such as Julius Wellhausen (1844–1918) in Germany, Ernst Renan (1823–1892) in France, and Matthew Arnold (1822–1888) in Great Britain contended that human authors had written and revised the books of the Bible with the problems of Jewish society and politics in mind. In the scholarship of these writers the Bible appeared, like the Homeric epics, a book that had been written by normal human beings in a primitive society. This questioning of the historical validity of the Bible caused more literate men and women to lose faith in Christianity than any other single cause.

Read the Document "Matthew Arnold, Excerpt from *Dover Beach*" on **MyHistoryLab.com**

COMPARE AND CONNECT The Debate over Social Darwinism

Read the **Compare and Connect** on **MyHistoryLab.com**

DURING THE LATE nineteenth and early twentieth centuries scientists as well as other social commentators debated the question of whether the concept of "survival of the fittest" on which Charles Darwin had based his concept of evolution by natural selection should apply to human society and the competition between nations. Some commentators, such as Herbert Spencer, had advocated generally unbridled economic competition with little or no help to the poor and others who fared badly as a result of such competition. In 1893 T. H. Huxley rejected that view. However, a few years later Karl Pearson, another distinguished British scientist who supported the idea of evolution, argued that Social Darwinism should and did govern the relationships among nations.

QUESTIONS

1. **Why does Huxley equate "social progress" with the "ethical process"?**
2. **In this passage, does Huxley present human society as part of nature or as something that may be separate from nature?**
3. **How does Pearson connect Darwin's ideas to the concept of human progress?**
4. **How might Pearson's ideas justify imperial expansion, which will be considered in the next chapter? How could these arguments foster a climate of international violence?**
5. **How might Huxley's ideas be used to support broadly beneficial social welfare programs enacted to produce national populations healthy enough to compete in the international rivalry envisioned by Pearson?**

I. T. H. Huxley Criticizes Evolutionary Ethics

T. H. Huxley (1825–1895) was a British scientist who had been among Darwin's strongest defenders. Huxley, however, became a major critic of Social Darwinism, which attempted to deduce ethical principles from evolutionary processes involving struggle in nature. Drawing a strong distinction between the cosmic process of evolution and the social process of ethical development, he argued in Evolution and Ethics *(1893) that human ethical progress occurs through combating the cosmic process.*

Men in society are undoubtedly subject to the cosmic process. As among other animals, multiplication goes on without cessation, and involves severe competition for the means of support. The struggle for existence tends to eliminate those less fitted to adapt themselves to the circumstances of their existence. The strongest, the most self-assertive, tend to tread down the weaker. But the influence of the cosmic process on the evolution of society is the greater the more rudimentary its civilization. Social progress means a checking of the cosmic process at every step and the substitution for it of another, which may be called the ethical process; the end of which is not the survival of those who may happen to be the fittest, in respect of the whole of the conditions which obtain, but of those who are ethically the best.

As I have already urged, the practice of that which is ethically best—what we call goodness or virtue—involves a course of conduct which, in all respects, is opposed to that which leads to success in the cosmic struggle for existence. In place of ruthless self-assertion it demands self-restraint; in place of thrusting aside, or treading down, all competitors, it requires that the individual shall not merely respect, but shall help his fellows; its influence is directed, not so much to the survival of the fittest, as to the fitting of as many as possible to survive. It repudiates the gladiatorial theory of existence.

It is from neglect of these plain considerations that the fanatical individualism of our time attempts to apply the analogy of cosmic nature to society. . . .

Let us understand, once for all, that the ethical progress of society depends, not on imitating the cosmic process, still less in running away from it, but in combating it. ■

From T. H. Huxley, *Evolution and Ethics* (London: Macmillan & Co., 1893), as quoted in Franklin L. Baumer, *Main Currents of Western Thought: Readings in Western European Intellectual History from the Middle Ages to the Present*, 3rd ed., rev. (New York: Alfred A. Knopf, 1970), pp. 561–562.

II. Social Darwinism and Imperialism

T. H. Huxley's assault did not end the influence of Social Darwinism. Debates about competition among nations for trade, military superiority, and empire dominated much turn-of-the-twentieth-century political thought. The idea of biological competition became applied to nations and races and produced substantial impact on public opinion and among policymakers. In the selection that follows, Karl Pearson (1857–1936), an English scientist, attempts to connect concepts from evolutionary theory—the struggle for survival and the survival of the fittest—to the development of human societies.

PEARS
PEARS' SOAP
The first step towards lightening
"The White Man's Burden"
is through teaching the virtues of cleanliness.
Pears' Soap
is a potent factor in brightening the dark corners of the earth as civilization advances, while amongst the cultured of all nations it holds the highest place—it is the ideal toilet soap.
All sorts of people use it, all sorts of stores sell it.

Racism was often a by-product of Social Darwinist theory. At the turn of the twentieth century, racism permeated many facets of popular life. This ad for Pears' Soap caters to the racist attitudes held by many whites during this time. Library of Congress/*Colliers*, October 4, 1899

History shows me one way, and one way only, in which a state of civilisation has been produced, namely, the struggle of race with race, and the survival of the physically and mentally fitter race. This dependence of progress on the survival of the fitter race, terribly black as it may seem to some of you, gives the struggle for existence its redeeming features; it is the fiery crucible out of which comes the finer metal. You may hope for a time when the sword shall be turned into the ploughshare, when American and German and English traders shall no longer compete in the markets of the world for raw materials, for their food supply, when the white man and the dark shall share the soil between them, and each till it as he lists. But, believe me, when that day comes mankind will no longer progress; there will be nothing to check the fertility of inferior stock; the relentless law of heredity will not be controlled and guided by natural selection. Man will stagnate. . . . The path of progress is strewn with the wreck of nations; traces are everywhere to be seen of the hecatombs of inferior races, and of victims who found not the narrow way to the greater perfection. Yet these dead peoples are, in very truth, the stepping stones on which mankind has arisen to the higher intellectual and deeper emotional life of today. ■

From Karl Pearson, *National Life from the Standpoint of Science*, 2nd ed. (Cambridge, UK: Cambridge University Press, 1907), pp. 21, 26–27, 64.

Science Nineteenth-century science also undermined Christianity and faith in the validity of biblical narratives, although eighteenth-century writers had led Christians to believe the scientific examination of nature buttressed their faith. The geology of Charles Lyell suggested the earth is much older than the biblical records contend. By looking to natural causes to explain floods, mountains, and valleys, Lyell removed the miraculous hand of God from the physical development of the earth. Darwin's theory cast doubt on the Creation. Anthropologists, psychologists, and sociologists proposed that religious sentiments are just one more set of natural phenomena.

Morality Other intellectuals questioned the morality of Christianity. The issue of immoral biblical stories was again raised. The morality of the Old Testament God, his cruelty and unpredictability, did not fit well with the tolerant, rational values of liberals. They also wondered about the morality of the New Testament God, who would sacrifice for his own satisfaction the only perfect being ever to walk the earth. Even some clergy began to wonder if they could preach doctrines they felt to be immoral.

From another direction, writers like Friedrich Nietzsche (1844–1900) in Germany portrayed Christianity as a religion that glorified weakness rather than the strength life required. Christianity demanded a useless and debilitating sacrifice of the flesh and spirit, rather than heroic living and daring. Nietzsche once observed, "War and courage have accomplished more great things than love of neighbor."[2]

These skeptical currents created a climate in which Christianity lost much of its intellectual respectability. Fewer educated people joined the clergy. Many people found they could live with little or no reference to Christianity. The secularism of everyday life proved as harmful to the faith as the direct attacks. This situation was especially prevalent in the cities, which were growing faster than the capacity of the churches to meet the challenge. Whole generations of the urban poor grew up with little or no experience of the church as an institution or of Christianity as a religious faith.

Conflict Between Church and State

The secular states of late-nineteenth-century Europe clashed with both the Protestant and the Roman Catholic churches. Liberals, including those who were religiously observant, disliked the dogma and the political privileges of the established churches. National states were often suspicious of the supranational character of the Roman Catholic Church. The primary area of conflict between the state and the churches, however, was education. Previously, most education in Europe had taken place in church schools. The churches feared that future generations would emerge from the new state-financed schools without any religious teaching. From 1870 through the turn of the century, all the major countries debated religious education.

Great Britain In Great Britain, the Education Act of 1870 provided for state-supported schools run by elected school boards, whereas earlier the government had given small grants to religious schools. The new schools were to be built in areas where the religious denominations did not provide satisfactory education. All the churches opposed improvements in education because these increased the costs of church schools. In the Education Act of 1902, the government provided state support for both religious and nonreligious schools but imposed the same educational standards on each.

France France had a dual system of Catholic and public schools. Under the Falloux Law of 1850, local priests provided religious education in public schools. Between 1878 and 1886, a series of educational laws sponsored by Jules Ferry (1832–1893) replaced religious instruction in the public schools with civic training. The number of public schools was expanded, and members of religious orders could no longer teach in them. After the Dreyfus affair (discussed later in this chapter), the French Catholic Church paid a price for its reactionary politics. The Radical government of Pierre Waldeck-Rousseau (1846–1904), drawn from pro-Dreyfus groups, suppressed the religious orders. In 1905, church and state were formally separated.

Germany and the *Kulturkampf* The most extreme and violent church–state conflict occurred in Germany during the 1870s. The ***Kulturkampf*** (clash of civilizations), as it was called, pitted Bismarck and German liberals against the Catholic Church in Germany. From the start, the conflict was more political than religious. Bismarck and German liberals had different reasons for being suspicious of the power of the Roman Catholic Church in Germany. Bismarck was suspicious of the loyalties of the many Polish-speaking Catholics in Prussia. Liberals were appalled by the Pope's pronouncement of papal infallibility in 1870, and thought Catholics represented a "backward" opposition to progress. They both feared the power of the Catholic Center party, a political party dedicated to protecting the liberty of the Catholic Church within unified Germany. In 1870 and 1871, Bismarck removed the clergy from overseeing local education in Prussia. This secularization of education represented the beginning of a concerted attack on the Catholic Church in Germany.

View the **Closer Look** "Conflict between Church and State in Germany" on **MyHistoryLab.com**

[2]Walter Kaufmann, ed. and trans., *The Portable Nietzsche* (New York: Viking, 1967), p. 159.

The "May Laws" of 1873, which applied to Prussia but not to the entire German Empire, required priests to be educated in German schools and universities and to pass state examinations. The state could veto the appointments of priests. The legislation abolished the disciplinary power of the pope and the church over the clergy and transferred it to the state. Many of the clergy refused to obey, and new laws allowed their property to be seized, their pay to be stopped, and for them to be held in prison. Thousands of priests and bishops were arrested or exiled from Prussia.

By the end of the 1870s, Bismarck had abandoned his attack on the Catholic Church. He had gained state control of education and civil laws governing marriage only at the price of provoking Catholic resentment against the German state. He also found that the Center Party made an even better ally than the liberals. The resistance of Catholics to measures taken against their priests made the *Kulturkampf* unwinnable; a realignment of German politics made winning it unnecessary.

Areas of Religious Revival

The German Catholic resistance to the intrusions of the secular state illustrates the continuing vitality of Christianity during this period of intellectual and political hardship for the church. In Great Britain, both the Anglican Church and the Nonconformist denominations expanded and raised vast sums for new churches and schools. In Ireland, the 1870s saw a Catholic devotional revival. In France, after the defeat by Prussia, priests organized special pilgrimages to shrines for thousands of penitents who believed France had been defeated because of their sins. The cult of the miracle of Lourdes grew during these years.

The last half of the nineteenth century witnessed the final great effort to Christianize Europe. It was well organized, well led, and well financed. It failed only because the population of Europe had outstripped the resources of the churches.

The Roman Catholic Church and the Modern World

The most striking feature of Christian religious revival was the resilience of the papacy. The brief hope for a liberal pontificate from Pope Pius IX (r. 1846–1878) vanished when he fled the turmoil of Rome in November 1848. In the 1860s, embittered by the process of Italian unification, he launched a counteroffensive against liberalism. In 1864, he issued the *Syllabus of Errors*, in which he described as false the statement that "the Roman Pontiff can, and ought to, reconcile himself, and come to terms with, progress, liberalism and modern civilization."[3]

[3]W. F. Hogan, "Syllabus of Errors," *The New Catholic Encyclopedia*, Vol. 13, 2nd edition (Detroit, MI: Gale, 2003), p. 652.

In 1869, the pope summoned the First Vatican Council. The next year, the council promulgated the dogma of **papal infallibility** when speaking officially on matters of faith and morals. No earlier pope had asserted such centralized authority within the church. The First Vatican Council ended in 1870, when Italian troops occupied Rome at the outbreak of the Franco–Prussian War. Thereafter the territory of the papacy was limited to the Vatican City, but the papacy made no formal accommodation to the Italian state until 1929. The spiritual authority of the papacy became a substitute for its lost political and temporal authority.

Pius IX was succeeded by Leo XIII (r. 1878–1903). Leo, who was sixty-eight years old at the time of his election, sought to make accommodations to the modern age and to address its great social questions. Leo XIII's most important pronouncement on public issues was the encyclical *Rerum Novarum* (1891). In that document, he defended private property, religious education, and religious control of the marriage laws, and he condemned socialism and Marxism, but he also declared that employers should treat their employees justly, pay them proper wages, and permit them to organize labor unions. The pope urged that modern society be organized in corporate groups that would include people from various classes who would cooperate according to Christian principles. The corporate society, based on medieval social organization, was to be an alternative to both socialism and competitive capitalism. On the basis of Leo XIII's pronouncements, democratic Catholic political parties and Catholic trade unions were founded throughout Europe. (See the Document "Leo XIII Considers the Social Question in European Politics," page 762.)

Read the **Document** "Pope Leo XIII, *Rerum Novarum* (*Of New Things*), 1891" on **MyHistoryLab.com**

His successor Pius X (r. 1903–1914) hoped to resist modern thought and restore traditional devotional life. Between 1903 and 1907, he condemned Catholic modernism, a movement of modern biblical criticism within the church, and in 1910 he required all priests to take an anti-Modernist oath. The struggle between Catholicism and modern thought was resumed.

Islam and Late-Nineteenth-Century European Thought

The few European thinkers who wrote about Islam in the late nineteenth century discussed it using the same scientific and naturalistic scholarly methods they applied to Christianity and Judaism. They interpreted Islam as a historical phenomenon without any reference to the supernatural, and the Qur'an received the same kind of critical historical analysis that was being directed toward the Bible. In the works of scholars such as influential

POPULAR RELIGION AND PILGRIMAGE

THE NINETEENTH CENTURY WAS A PERIOD of great challenge for the Roman Catholic Church in Europe, but it also witnessed a revival in popular religiosity, and in particular in the practice of pilgrimage. Pilgrimage had been common in the medieval and early modern periods, but had come under attack during the Enlightenment. The formal proclamation of the doctrine of the Immaculate Conception in 1854 contributed to a dramatic increase in Marian pilgrimage. After a fourteen-year old girl saw an apparition of a woman claiming to be the immaculate conception in Lourdes in 1858, the Church authorized the creation of a pilgrimage site on the spot. Lourdes became the second-most visited pilgrimage destination in Europe, after Rome.

Pilgrims traveled from all parts of Europe. While pilgrimage sites could take on a national character, they were overwhelmingly supranational. Long-distance travel to pilgrimage sites was made more feasible by the introduction of the railroad and the spread of railroad networks into the provinces.

Women featured prominently in pilgrimages. Although often separated by sex during their journey, pilgrimages represented an opportunity for men and women to mingle outside the confines of the family home.

Many pilgrims hoped that infirmities such as blindness or lameness could be cured through the intercession of a saint to whom they could pray most effectively at a pilgrimage site.

PILGRIMAGES IN FRANCE—DEPARTURE FROM A PROVINCIAL STATION OF "SACRED HEART" PILGRIMS FOR LOURDES.

This 1873 wood engraving shows pilgrims who have arrived in a train station near Lourdes, and are preparing to proceed to their destination on foot. The Granger Collection, NYC—

How is the diversity of pilgrims represented in this image? What sort of people went on pilgrimage?

What is the mood of the pilgrims as they anticipate their arrival in Lourdes?

What sort of journey could nineteenth-century pilgrims expect, and how had it changed since the medieval and early modern periods?

French writer Ernest Renan, Islam was, like Judaism, a manifestation of the ancient Semitic mentality, which had given rise to a powerful monotheistic vision. Renan and sociologists such as Max Weber also falsely described Islam as a religion and culture incapable of developing science. Renan's views were opposed in a French journal by Jamal al-Din al-Afghani (1839–1897), an Egyptian intellectual, who argued that over time Islam, which had arisen six hundred years after Christianity, would eventually produce cultures as modern as those in Europe. The European racial and cultural outlooks that denigrated nonwhite peoples and their civilizations were also directed toward the Arab world.

Read the Document "Sayyid Jamal al-Din al-Afghani, 'Lecture on Teaching and Learning' " on **MyHistoryLab.com**

Christian missionaries reinforced these anti-Islamic attitudes. They blamed Islam for Arab economic backwardness, for mistreating women, and for condoning slavery. Missionaries founded schools and hospitals, hoping these Christian foundations would eventually lead some Muslims to Christianity. Few Muslims converted, but these institutions did educate young Arabs in Western science and medicine, and many of their students became leaders in the Middle East. Eventually, as missionary families came to live for long periods of time among Arabs, they became more sympathetic to Arab political aspirations.

Within the Islamic world, and especially in the decaying Ottoman Empire, as political leaders continued to champion Western scientific education and technology, they confronted a variety of responses from religious thinkers. Some of these thinkers sought to combine modern thought with Islam. For example, the Salafi, or the salafiyya movement, believed there was no inherent contradiction between science and Islam. They believed Muhammad had wisely and properly addressed the issues of his day, and a reformed Islamic faith could do so again. The Arab world should cease imitating the West and modernize itself on the basis of a pure, restored Islamic faith. The Salafi emphasized a rational reading of the Qur'an and saw Ottoman decline as the result of Muslim religious error. This outlook, which had originally sought to reconcile Islam with the modern world, eventually led many Muslims in the twentieth century to oppose Western influence.

Other Islamic religious leaders simply rejected the West and modern thought. They included the Mahdist movement in Sudan, the Sanussiya in Libya, and the Wahhabi movement in the Arabian peninsula. Such religious-based opposition was strongest in those portions of the Middle East where the European presence was least direct, which is to say outside of Morocco, Algeria, Egypt, and Tunisia, which for all intents and purposes were under the control of Western powers by 1900, and Turkey, where Ottoman leaders had long been deeply involved with the West.

▼ Toward a Twentieth-Century Frame of Mind

The last quarter of the nineteenth century and the first decade of the twentieth century were the crucible of modern Western thought. Philosophers, scientists, psychologists, and artists began to portray physical reality, human nature, and society in ways different from those of the past. Their new concepts challenged the major presuppositions of mid-nineteenth-century science, rationalism, liberalism, and bourgeois morality.

Science: The Revolution in Physics

The changes in the scientific worldview originated within the scientific community itself. By the late 1870s, discontent existed over the excessive realism of midcentury science. It was thought that many scientists believed their mechanistic models, solid atoms, and absolute time and space actually described the real universe.

In 1883, Ernst Mach (1838–1916) published *The Science of Mechanics*, in which he urged that scientists consider their concepts descriptive not of the physical world, but of the sensations the scientific observer experiences. Scientists could describe only the sensations, not the physical world that underlay those sensations. In line with Mach, French scientist Henri Poincaré (1854–1912) urged that the theories of scientists be regarded as hypothetical constructs of the human mind rather than as true descriptions of nature. In 1911, Hans Vaihinger (1852–1933) suggested the concepts of science be considered "as if" descriptions of the physical world. By World War I, few scientists believed they could portray the "truth" about physical reality. Rather, they saw themselves as recording the observations of instruments and as offering useful hypothetical or symbolic models of nature.

X-Rays and Radiation Discoveries in the laboratory paralleled the philosophical challenge to nineteenth-century science. With those discoveries, the comfortable world of supposedly "complete" nineteenth-century physics vanished forever. In December 1895, Wilhelm Roentgen (1845–1923) published a paper on his discovery of X-rays, a form of energy that penetrated various opaque materials. Major steps in the exploration of radioactivity followed within months of the publication of his paper.

In 1896, Henri Becquerel (1852–1908) discovered that uranium emitted a similar form of energy. The next year, J. J. Thomson (1856–1940), at Cambridge University, formulated the theory of the electron. The interior world of the atom had become a new area for human exploration. In 1902, Ernest Rutherford (1871–1937) explained the cause of radiation through the disintegration of the atoms of radioactive materials. Shortly thereafter, he speculated on the immense store of energy present in the atom.

Document

Leo XIII Considers the Social Question in European Politics

In his 1891 encyclical Rerum Novarum, *Pope Leo XIII provided the Catholic Church's answer to secular calls for social reforms. The pope denied the socialist claim that class conflict is the natural state of affairs. He urged employers to seek just and peaceful relations with workers.*

How does Leo XIII reject the concept of class conflict? What responsibilities does he assign to the rich and to the poor? Are the responsibilities of the two classes equal? What kinds of social reform might emerge from these ideas?

The great mistake that is made in the matter now under consideration is to possess oneself of the idea that class is naturally hostile to class; that rich and poor are intended by Nature to live at war with one another. So irrational and so false is this view that the exact contrary is the truth. . . . Each requires the other; capital cannot do without labour, nor labour without capital. Mutual agreement results in pleasantness and good order; perpetual conflict necessarily produces confusion and outrage. Now, in preventing such strife as this, and in making it impossible, the efficacy of Christianity is marvelous and manifold. . . . Religion teaches the labouring man and the workman to carry out honestly and well all equitable agreements freely made; never to injure capital, or to outrage the person of an employer; never to employ violence in representing his own cause, or to engage in riot or disorder; and to have nothing to do with men of evil principles, who work upon the people with artful promises and raise hopes which usually end in disaster and in repentance when too late. Religion teaches the rich man and the employer that their work people are not their slaves; that they must respect in every man his dignity as a man and as a Christian; that labour is nothing to be ashamed of, if we listen to right reason and to Christian philosophy, but is an honourable employment, enabling a man to sustain his life in an upright and creditable way; and that it is shameful and inhuman to treat men like chattels to make money by, or to look upon them merely as so much muscle or physical power. Thus, again, Religion teaches that, as among the workman's concerns are Religion herself and things spiritual and mental, the employer is bound to see that he has time for the duties of piety; that he be not exposed to corrupting influences and dangerous occasions; and that he be not led away to neglect his home and family or to squander his wages. Then, again, the employer must never tax his work people beyond their strength, nor employ them in work unsuited to their sex or age. His great and principal obligation is to give every one that which is just.

From F. S. Nitti, *Catholic Socialism*, trans. by Mary Mackintosh (London: S. Sonnenschein, 1895), p. 409.

Theories of Quantum Energy, Relativity, and Uncertainty The discovery of radioactivity and discontent with the existing mechanical models led to revolutionary theories in physics. In 1900, Max Planck (1858–1947) pioneered the articulation of the quantum theory of energy, according to which energy is a series of discrete quantities, or packets, rather than a continuous stream. In 1905, Albert Einstein (1879–1955) published his first epoch-making papers on relativity in which he contended that time and space exist not separately, but rather as a combined continuum. Moreover, the measurement of time and space depends on the observer as well as on the entities being measured.

In 1927, Werner Heisenberg (1901–1976) set forth his uncertainty principle, according to which the behavior of subatomic particles is a matter of statistical probability rather than of exactly determinable cause and effect. Much that had seemed unquestionable about the physical universe had now become ambiguous.

The mathematical complexity of twentieth-century physics meant science would rarely be successfully popularized. At the same time, science affected daily living more than ever before. Scientists from the late nineteenth

Read the **Document** "Werner Heisenberg, 'Uncertainty' (Germany), 1927" on **MyHistoryLab.com**

Marie Skłodowska Curie (1869–1934) and Pierre Curie (1859–1906) were two of the most important figures in the advance of physics and chemistry. Skłodowska Curie was born in Warsaw (Russian Poland) but worked in France for most of her life. She is credited with the discovery of radium, for which she was awarded the Nobel Prize in Chemistry in 1911. The Granger Collection, New York

century onward became the most successful group of Western intellectuals in gaining the financial support of governments and private institutions for the pursuit of their research. They did so by relating the success of science to the economic progress, military security, and the health of their nations.

Literature: Realism and Naturalism

Between 1850 and 1914, the moral certainties of middle-class Europeans changed no less radically than their concepts of the physical universe. The realist movement in literature portrayed the hypocrisy, brutality, and the dullness that underlay bourgeois life. By using the midcentury cult of science so vital to the middle class, **realist** writers confronted readers with the harsh realities of life. Realism rejected the romantic idealization of nature, the poor, love, and polite society and instead portrayed the dark side of life.

Earlier writers, including Charles Dickens (1812–1870) and Honoré de Balzac (1799–1850), had portrayed the cruelty of industrial life and of a society based on money. Other authors, such as George Eliot (born Mary Ann Evans, 1819–1880), paid close attention to the details of her characters. These authors' work had, however, included imagination and artistry, and a belief that a better morality was possible through Christian or humane values.

The major figures of late-century realism examined the dreary and unseemly side of life without being certain whether a better life was possible. They portrayed human beings as subject to the passions, the materialistic determinism, and the pressures of the environment like any other animals. Most of them, however, also saw society itself as perpetuating evil.

Flaubert and Zola Critics have often considered Gustave Flaubert's (1821–1880) *Madame Bovary* (1857), with its story of colorless provincial life and a woman's hapless search for love in and outside of marriage, as the first genuinely realistic novel. The work portrayed life without heroism, purpose, or even civility.

The author who turned realism into a movement, however, was Emile Zola (1840–1902). He found artistic inspiration in Claude Bernard's (1813–1878) *Introduction to the Study of Experimental Medicine* (1865). Zola argued that he could write an experimental novel in which he would observe and report the characters and their actions as the scientist might relate a laboratory experiment. He once declared, "I have simply done on living bodies the work of analysis which surgeons perform on corpses."[4] He believed absolute physical and psychological determinism ruled human events in the way it did the physical world.

Between 1871 and 1893, Zola published twenty novels exploring subjects normally untouched by writers: alcoholism, prostitution, adultery, labor strife. He refused to turn his readers' thoughts away from the ugly aspects of life. Nothing in his purview received the light of hope or the aura of romance. Although critics faulted his taste and moralists condemned his subject matter, Zola enjoyed a worldwide following. As is described later in this chapter, he took a leading role in the defense of Captain Dreyfus.

Read the **Document** "Emile Zola, *Nana*" on **MyHistoryLab.com**

Ibsen and Shaw Norwegian playwright Henrik Ibsen (1828–1906) carried realism into the dramatic presentation of domestic life. He sought to strip away the illusory

[4]George J. Becker, *Documents of Modern Literary Realism* (Princeton, NJ: Princeton University Press, 1963), p. 159.

mask of middle-class morality. His most famous play is *A Doll's House* (1879). Its chief character, Nora, has a narrow-minded husband who cannot tolerate independence of character or thought on her part. She finally leaves him, slamming the door behind her. In *Ghosts* (1881), a respectable woman must deal with a son suffering from syphilis inherited from her husband. In *The Master Builder* (1892), an aging architect kills himself while trying to impress a young woman. Ibsen's works were controversial. He dared to attack sentimentality, the ideal of the female "angel of the house," and the cloak of respectability that hung so insecurely over the middle-class family.

Read the **Document** "Henrik Ibsen, from *A Doll's House*, Act Three" on **MyHistoryLab.com**

One of Ibsen's greatest champions was Irish writer George Bernard Shaw (1856–1950), who spent most of his life in England. Shaw defended Ibsen's work and made his own realistic onslaught against romanticism and false respectability. In *Mrs. Warren's Profession* (1893), he dealt with prostitution. In *Arms and the Man* (1894) and *Man and Superman* (1903), he heaped scorn on the romantic ideals of love and war, and in *Androcles and the Lion* (1913), he pilloried Christianity.

Realist writers believed it their duty to portray reality and the commonplace. In dissecting what they considered the "real" world, they helped change the moral perception of the good life. They refused to let public opinion dictate what they wrote about or how they treated their subjects. By presenting their audiences with unmentionable subjects, they sought to remove the veneer of hypocrisy that had forbidden such discussion. They hoped to destroy illusions and compel the public to face reality. Few of the realist writers who raised these problems posed solutions to them. They often left their readers unable to sustain old values and uncertain about where to find new ones.

Modernism in Literature

From the 1870s onward throughout Europe, a new multifaceted movement, usually called **modernism**, touched all the arts. Like realism, modernism was critical of middle-class society and morality. Modernism, however, was not deeply concerned with social issues. What drove the modernists was a concern for the aesthetic or the beautiful. Across the spectrum of the arts, modernists tried to break the received forms and to create new forms. English essayist Walter Pater (1839–1903) set the tone of the movement when he declared in 1877 that all art "constantly aspires to the condition of music."

Among the chief proponents of modernism in England were the members of the Bloomsbury Group, including authors Virginia Woolf (1882–1941) and Leonard Woolf (1880–1969), artists Vanessa Bell (1879–1961) and Duncan Grant (1885–1978), historian and literary critic Lytton Strachey (1880–1932), and economist John Maynard Keynes (1883–1946). These authors challenged the values of their Victorian forebears. In *Eminent Victorians* (1918), Strachey used a series of biographical sketches to heap contempt on his subjects. Keynesian economics eventually challenged much of the structure of nineteenth-century economic theory. In both personal practice and theory, the Bloomsbury Group rejected what they regarded as the repressive sexual morality of their parents' generation.

Read the **Document** "John Maynard Keynes, from *The End of Laissez-Faire*" on **MyHistoryLab.com**

No one charted these changing sensibilities with more eloquence than Virginia Woolf. Her novels, such as *Mrs. Dalloway* (1925) and *To the Lighthouse* (1927), portrayed individuals seeking to make their way in a world with most of the nineteenth-century social and moral certainties removed.

On the Continent, one of the major practitioners of modernism in literature was Marcel Proust (1871–1922). In his seven-volume novel *In Search of Time Past* (*A la Recherche du Temps Perdu*), published between 1913 and 1927, he adopted a stream-of-consciousness

Marcel Proust's multivolume *In Search of Time Past* (*A la Recherche du Temps Perdu*), which was published between 1913 and 1927, was one of the most significant modernist novels.

format that allowed him to explore his memories. He would concentrate on a single experience or object and then allow his mind to wander through all the thoughts and memories it evoked. In Germany, Thomas Mann (1875–1955), through a long series of novels, the most famous of which were *Buddenbrooks* (1901) and *The Magic Mountain* (1924), explored both the social experience of middle-class Germans and how they dealt with the intellectual heritage of the nineteenth century. In *Ulysses* (1922), James Joyce (1882–1941), who was born in Ireland but spent much of his life on the Continent, transformed not only the novel, but also the structure of the paragraph.

Modernism in literature arose before World War I and flourished after the war, nourished by the turmoil and social dislocation it created. The war removed many of the old political structures and social expectations. After its appalling violence, readers found themselves much less shocked by upheavals in literary forms and the moral content of novels and poetry.

The Coming of Modern Art

The last quarter of the nineteenth century witnessed a series of new departures in Western art that transformed painting and later sculpture in a revolutionary manner that has continued to the present day.

Impressionism This fundamental change in European painting arose primarily in Paris. Two major characteristics marked this new style of painting. First, instead of portraying religious, mythological, and historical themes, painters began to depict modern life itself, focusing on the social life and leisure activities of the urban middle and lower middle classes. Second, many of these artists were fascinated with light, color, and the representation through painting itself of momentary, largely unfocused, visual experience. Contemporaries called these paintings *impressionistic* and considered them curious and artistically shocking when they were first displayed in Paris. During the twentieth century these paintings would

Édouard Manet (1832–1883), *A Bar at the Folies-Bergère*, 1882. Oil on canvas, 96 × 130 cm/Peter Barritt/SuperStock/Alamy

become the most popular works visited in both European and American art museums.

The new paintings of modern life by the impressionists, including Édouard Manet (1837–1883), Claude Monet (1840–1926), Camille Pissaro (1830–1903), Pierre-Auguste Renoir (1841–1919), and Edgar Degas (1834–1917), recorded Parisians attending cafés, dance halls, concerts, picnics, horse races, boating excursions, and beach parties. The backdrop for these works was Paris as it had been reconstructed under Napoleon III (r. 1852–1870) into a city of wide boulevards, parks, and places for middle-class leisure.

View the **Closer Look** "Monet's *Water Lilies*" on **MyHistoryLab.com**

The sites included in these paintings allowed people from different classes to mix socially while pursuing a leisure activity. One such meeting place was the Folies-Bergère, one of many Parisian cafés/concert halls where patrons could enjoy a variety of popular entertainment, including singers, musicians, dancers, gymnasts, and animal shows.

In *A Bar at the Folies-Bergère*, first displayed in 1882, Édouard Manet painted a young barmaid standing behind a table holding liquor and wine bottles and in front of a large mirror that reflects the activity occurring in front of her. (Manet actually painted this picture in his studio with a woman who worked as a barmaid posing as his model.) The table, together with its bottles, fruit, vase, and flowers, constitutes a formal still-life composition, but unlike traditional still lifes, this one shows objects of commercial consumption in a setting where leisure itself is commercially consumed. The mirror reflects the table and its contents, the music hall itself with the legs of a trapeze artist appearing in the top left corner, the audience for the performance, the back of the barmaid, and a man she is serving. Manet took great pains to paint the interior light of the hall, which appears to be coming from the newly invented electric light bulbs.

One of the great questions of the painting is the meaning and expression of the barmaid. The hubbub and restlessness of the reflected audience and the noise and excitement of the performance do not register on her face. The barmaid's expression may suggest the anonymity of so many social encounters in modern urban life. Because it was commonly assumed in Paris that many barmaids and shop girls needed to supplement their meager wages through prostitution, scholars have suggested that the woman in this painting, like the liquor and the fruit, is simply another object of commerce.

Postimpressionism By the 1880s, the impressionists had had an enormous impact on contemporary art. Their work was followed by that of younger artists who drew upon their techniques but also attempted often to relate the achievement of impressionism to earlier artistic traditions. Form and structure rather than the effort to record the impression of the moment played a major role in their work. This later type of art has been described as ***Postimpressionism***, though it should best be understood as a continuation of the previous movement rather than a reaction against it. The chief figures associated with Postimpressionism are Georges Seurat, Paul Cézanne, Vincent Van Gogh, and Paul Gauguin.

Georges Seurat, *A Sunday Afternoon on the Island of La Grande Jatte*, 1884–1886. Oil on canvas. 81 3/4 × 121 1/4 in. (2.07 × 3.08 m). Helen Birch Bartlett Memorial Collection. 1926.224. Reproduction, The Art Institute of Chicago. Photograph ©, The Art Institute of Chicago—All rights reserved

Georges Seurat (1859–1891) was a young French painter who read extensively in contemporary scientific works about light, color, and vision. These studies led him to a technique of painting known as pointillism whereby the artist applied small dots or points of paint to the canvas. Through this laborious process he hoped to decompose colors into their basic units, leaving it to the eye of the viewer to mix those dots into the desired color or shade of color. Seurat is counted among the first Postimpressionists because he saw himself bringing the new painting of modern life back into touch with earlier artistic traditions.

Seurat also introduced implicit social commentary into the previous impressionist portrayal of leisured activity. The Grande Jatte was an island in the Seine beyond Paris where on Sundays Parisians would gather. In Seurat's painting, *A Sunday Afternoon on the Island of La Grande Jatte*, shadows in the foreground suggest that all is not entirely sunny for the largely middle-class afternoon crowd. The boatman smoking the pipe indicates a brooding working-class presence in the foreground of their lives. All the figures resemble the mannequins that appeared in the fashionable new Paris department stores. Except for the one child who is running, the figures appear almost mechanical, like the manufacturing processes that produced their clothing and their other domestic consumer goods. These figures, compared by one contemporary critic to lead soldiers, stand bored and perhaps puzzled by their situation of comfort, leisure, and ease.

View the **Closer Look** "Sunday on La Grande Jatte" on **MyHistoryLab.com**

In reaction to the impressionists' fascination with light, Paul Cézanne (1839–1906), working largely in isolation, attempted to bring form and solidity back into his paintings of still life and of the landscape of Provence. Displaying a new sensitivity to non-Western peoples and their art, Paul Gauguin (1848–1903) produced works portraying peoples living in the South Pacific. Other artists collected African masks or studied such objects in the anthropological museum in Paris. Whereas Cézanne had given artists a new way of looking at and then shaping reality, the art of Africa and of the Pacific gave artists examples of remarkable works that had no relationship to the long-standing Western artistic tradition.

Cubism The single most radical new departure in early-twentieth-century Western art was ***cubism,*** a term first coined to describe the paintings of Pablo Picasso (1881–1973) and Georges Braque (1882–1963).

For over five hundred years, painting in the West had sought to reproduce the appearance of reality. From the time of the Renaissance, paintings functioned as a kind of window on an artistic depiction of the real world. Even the impressionists and postimpressionists essentially stood in this tradition.

Beginning in 1907, Picasso and Braque rejected the idea of a painting as constituting a window onto the real world. Rather, they saw painting as an autonomous realm of art

Georges Braque, *Violin and Palette* 1909–1910. Autumn 1909. Oil on canvas. 91.7 × 42.8 cm (36 1/8 × 16 7/8 inches). Solomon R. Guggenheim Museum, New York, 54.1412. Photograph by Lee B. Ewing © The Solomon R. Guggenheim Foundation, New York. © 2004 Artists Rights Society (ARS), New York/ADAGP, Paris itself with no purpose beyond itself. Braque once commented, "The painter thinks in forms and colors. The aim is not to reconstitute an anecdotal fact but to constitute a pictorial fact. . . . One does not imitate the appearance; the appearance is the result."[5] Echoing the art of ancient Egypt, medieval primitives, and Africa, Picasso and Braque represented only two dimensions in their painting. They made little or no effort to go beyond the flatness of the surface itself. They attempted to include at one time on a single surface as many different perspectives, angles, or views of the object painted as possible. "Reality" was the construction of their experience of multiple perceptions. The space in the paintings was literally the space of two dimensions filled with geometric shapes as well as geometric voids. The shapes stand dismantled, set in new and usually unexpected positions, communicating a sense of dislocation.

Braque's still life *Violin and Palette* (1909 and 1910) represents the cubist determination to present "a new, completely non-illusionistic and non-imitative method of depicting the visual world."[6] Various shapes seem to flow into other shapes. Portions of the violin and of the palette are recognizable, but as shapes, not as objects in and of themselves. The violin appears at one moment from a host of perspectives. As we move to the right of the painting, no elements reproduce a recognizable object. Throughout the painting Braque is literally taking apart the violin and other objects, so that he and the viewer can analyze them. As one commentator explained in 1919 in regard to cubism, "[T]he true picture will constitute an individual object, which will possess an existence of its own apart from the subject that has inspired it."[7] The elements of the palette, the violin, and the notes of a musical score floating on folded paper tents hold interest and meaning in this painting only because they are in the painting, not because they are imitations of a violin, a palette, or a musical score.

Watch the Video "The Art of Pablo Picasso" on **MyHistoryLab.com**

The cubist painters sought to redirect the artistic portrayal of reality in the same manner that modernists in literature had reshaped the portrayal of social and moral experience and the new physics had reconceptualized nature itself.

Friedrich Nietzsche and the Revolt Against Reason

During the second half of the century, philosophers began to question the adequacy of rational thinking to address the human situation. No writer better exemplified this new attitude than German philosopher Friedrich Nietzsche (1844–1900). He was wholly at odds with the values of the age and attacked Christianity, democracy, nationalism, rationality, science, and progress. He sought less to change values than to probe their sources in the human character.

His first important work was *The Birth of Tragedy* (1872) in which he urged that the nonrational aspects of human nature are as important and noble as the rational characteristics. He insisted on the positive function of instinct and ecstasy in human life. To limit human activity to strictly rational behavior was to impoverish human life. In Nietzsche's view, the strength for the heroic life and the highest artistic achievement arises from sources beyond rationality.

In later works, such as the prose poem *Thus Spake Zarathustra* (1883), Nietzsche criticized democracy and Christianity. Both would lead only to the mediocrity of sheepish masses. He announced the death of God and proclaimed the coming of the *Superman* (Übermensch), who would embody heroism and greatness. The term was frequently interpreted as some mode of super human or super race, but such was not Nietzsche's intention. He was critical of contemporary racism and anti-Semitism. He sought a return to the heroism that he associated with Greek life in the Homeric age. He thought the values of Christianity and of bourgeois morality prevented humankind from achieving life on a heroic level.

Two of Nietzsche's most profound works are *Beyond Good and Evil* (1886) and *The Genealogy of Morals* (1887). Nietzsche sought to discover not what is good and what is evil, but the social and psychological sources of the judgment of good and evil. He declared, "There are no moral phenomena at all, but only a moral interpretation of phenomena."[8] He dared to raise the question of whether morality itself was valuable: "We need a critique of moral values; the value of these values themselves must first be called in question."[9] In Nietzsche's view, morality was a human convention that had no independent existence. For Nietzsche, this discovery liberated human beings to create life-affirming values instead. Christianity, utilitarianism, and middle-class respectability could, in good conscience, be abandoned. Human beings could create a new moral order that would glorify pride, assertiveness, and strength rather than meekness, humility, and weakness.

Read the Document "Friedrich Nietzsche, *Beyond Good and Evil*" on **MyHistoryLab.com**

In his appeal to feelings and emotions and in his questioning of the adequacy of rationalism, Nietzsche drew on the Romantic tradition. The kind of creative impulse that earlier Romantics had considered the gift of artists Nietzsche saw as the burden of all human beings. The character of the human situation that this philosophy urged on its contemporaries was that of an ever-changing flux in which nothing but change itself was permanent.

[6]Edward F. Fry, *Cubism* (New York: McGraw-Hill, 1966), p. 38.

[5]Max Kozloff, *Cubism/Futurism* (New York: Charterhouse, 1973), p. 11.

[7]Maurice Raynal, "Some Intentions of Cubism," 1919, as quoted in Fry, *Cubism*, p. 153.

[8]*The Basic Writings of Nietzsche*, ed. and trans. by Walter Kaufman (New York: The Modern Library, 1968), p. 275.

[9]Kaufman, *The Basic Writings of Nietzsche*, p. 456.

DATES OF MAJOR WORKS OF FICTION

1857	Flaubert, *Madame Bovary*
1877	Zola, *L'Assommoir*
1879	Ibsen, *A Doll's House*
1880	Zola, *Nana*
1881	Ibsen, *Ghosts*
1892	Ibsen, *The Master Builder*
1893	Shaw, *Mrs. Warren's Profession*
1894	Shaw, *Arms and the Man*
1901	Mann, *Buddenbrooks*
1903	Shaw, *Man and Superman*
1913	Shaw, *Androcles and the Lion*
1913	Proust, first volume of *In Search of Time Past*
1922	Joyce, *Ulysses*
1924	Mann, *The Magic Mountain*
1925	Woolf, *Mrs. Dalloway*
1927	Woolf, *To the Lighthouse*

In 1909 Freud and his then-devoted disciple Carl Jung visited Clark University in Worcester, Massachusetts, during Freud's only trip to the United States. Here Freud sits on the right holding a cane. Jung is sitting on the far left. Archives of the History of American Psychology—The University of Akron. Courtesy Clark University, Special Collections

Human beings had to forge from their own will and determination the values that were to exist in the world.

The Birth of Psychoanalysis

A determination to probe beneath the surface or public appearance united the major figures of late-nineteenth-century science, art, and philosophy. They sought to discern the undercurrents, tensions, and complexities that lay beneath the calm surfaces of hard atoms, respectable families, rationality, and social relationships. As a result of their theories and discoveries, educated Europeans could never again view the surface of life with complacency or even with much confidence. No intellectual development more exemplified this trend than psychoanalysis through the work of Sigmund Freud (1856–1939).

Development of Freud's Early Theories Freud was born in Moravia into an Austrian Jewish family that settled in Vienna. He planned to become a lawyer but soon moved to study physiology and medicine. In 1886, he opened his medical practice in Vienna, where he lived until the Nazis drove him out in 1938. Freud sought to apply the critical method of science to the study of psychic disorders. He collaborated with another physician, Josef Breuer (1842–1925), and in 1895, they published *Studies in Hysteria.*

In the mid-1890s, Freud abandoned the hypnosis he had learned during a year in Paris and allowed his patients to talk freely and spontaneously about themselves. He found that they associated their particular neurotic symptoms with experiences related to earlier experiences, going back to childhood. He also noted that sexual matters were significant in his patients' problems. For a time, he thought that perhaps sexual incidents during childhood accounted for their illnesses.

By 1897, however, Freud had rejected this view. In its place he formulated a theory of infantile sexuality, according to which sexual drives and energy already exist in infants and do not simply emerge at puberty. Freud thus questioned in the most radical manner the concept of childhood innocence.

Freud's Concern with Dreams During the same decade, Freud also examined the psychic phenomena of dreams. Romantic writers had taken dreams seriously, but few psychologists had examined them scientifically. Freud believed the seemingly irrational content of dreams must have a reasonable, scientific explanation. He concluded that dreams allow unconscious wishes, desires, and drives that had been excluded from everyday conscious life to enjoy freer play in the mind. "The dream," he wrote, "is the [disguised] fulfillment of a [suppressed, repressed] wish."[10] During the waking hours, the mind represses or censors certain wishes, which are as important to the individual's psychological makeup as conscious thought is. Freud developed these concepts and related them to his idea of infantile sexuality in his most important book, *The Interpretation of Dreams,* published in 1900.

[10] *The Basic Writings of Sigmund Freud,* trans. by A. A. Brill (New York: The Modern Library, 1938), p. 235.

Freud's Later Thought In later books and essays, Freud developed a new model of the internal organization of the mind as an arena of struggle and conflict among three entities: the id, the superego, and the ego. The **id** consists of amoral, irrational, driving instincts for sexual gratification, aggression, and general physical and sensual pleasure. The **superego** embodies the external moral imperatives and expectations imposed on the personality by society and culture. The **ego** mediates between the impulses of the id and the asceticism of the superego and allows the personality to cope with the inner and outer demands of its existence. Consequently, everyday behavior displays the activity of the personality as its inner drives are partially repressed through the ego's coping with external moral expectations, as interpreted by the superego.

In his acknowledgment of the roles of instinct, will, dreams, and sexuality, Freud reflected the Romantic tradition of the nineteenth century. In other respects, however, he was a son of the Enlightenment. Like the philosophes, he was a realist who wanted human beings to live free of fear and illusions by rationally understanding themselves and their world. He saw the personalities of human beings as being determined by finite physical and mental forces in a finite world. He was hostile to religion and spoke of it as an illusion. Freud, like the writers of the eighteenth century, wished to see civilization and humane behavior prevail. More fully than those predecessors, however, he understood the immense sacrifice of instinctual drives required for rational civilized behavior. It has been a grave misreading of Freud to see him as urging humankind to thrust off all repression. He did indeed believe that excessive repression could lead to a mental disorder, but he also believed civilization and the survival of humankind required some repression of sexuality and aggression. Freud thought the sacrifice and struggle were worthwhile, but he was pessimistic about the future of civilization in the West.

Divisions in the Psychoanalytic Movement By 1910, Freud had gathered around him a small group of disciples. Several of his early followers soon moved toward theories of which Freud disapproved. The most important of these dissenters was Carl Jung (1875–1961), a Swiss whom for many years Freud regarded as his most promising student. Jung questioned the primacy of sexual drives in forming personality and in contributing to mental disorder. He also put less faith in reason.

Jung believed the human subconscious contains inherited memories from previous generations. These collective memories, as well as the personal experience of an individual, constitute his or her soul. Jung regarded human beings in the twentieth century as alienated from these useful collective memories. Freud was highly critical of most of Jung's work. If Freud's thought derived primarily from the Enlightenment, Jung's was more dependent on Romanticism.

By the 1920s, the psychoanalytic movement had become even more fragmented. Nonetheless, it influenced not only psychology, but also sociology, anthropology, religious studies, and literary theory.

Retreat from Rationalism in Politics

Nineteenth-century liberals and socialists agreed that rational analysis could discern the problems of society and prepare solutions. These thinkers felt that, once given the vote, individuals would behave according to their rational political self-interest. Education would improve the human condition. By 1900, these views had come under attack. Political scientists and sociologists painted politics as frequently irrational. Racial theorists questioned whether rationality and education could affect human society at all.

Weber German sociologist Max Weber (1864–1920) regarded the emergence of rationalism throughout society as the major development of human history. Such rationalization displayed itself in the rise of both scientific knowledge and bureaucratic organization.

Weber saw bureaucratization as the basic feature of modern social life. He used this view to oppose Marx's concept of the development of capitalism as the driving force in modern society. Bureaucratization involved the division of labor as each individual fit into a particular role in much larger organizations. Furthermore, Weber believed that in modern society people derive their own self-images and sense of personal worth from their positions in these organizations.

Weber also contended—again, in contrast to Marx—that noneconomic factors might account for major developments in human history. For example, in his best known essay, *The Protestant Ethic and the Spirit of Capitalism* (1905), Weber traced much of the rational character of capitalist enterprise to the ascetic religious doctrines of Puritanism. The Puritans, in his opinion, worked for worldly success less for its own sake than to assure themselves that they stood among the elect of God. The theory has generated historical research and debate from its publication to the present.

Theorists of Collective Behavior In his emphasis on the individual and on the dominant role of rationality, Weber differed from many contemporary social scientists who explored the activity of crowds and mobs. In *Reflections on Violence* (1908), Georges Sorel (1847–1922) argued that people do not pursue rationally perceived goals but are led to action by collectively shared ideals. Émile Durkheim (1858–1917) and Graham Wallas (1858–1932) became deeply interested in the necessity of shared values and activities in a society. Besides playing down the function of reason in society, all these theorists emphasized the role of collective groups in politics rather than that of the individual, formerly championed by liberals.

Racism

The same tendencies to question or even to deny the constructive activity of reason in human affairs and to sacrifice the individual to the group manifested themselves in theories of race. **Racism** had long existed in Europe. Renaissance explorers had displayed prejudice against nonwhite peoples. Since at least the eighteenth century, biologists and anthropologists had classified human beings according to the color of their skin, their language, and their stage of civilization. After late-eighteenth-century linguistic scholars observed similarities between many of the European languages and Sanskrit, they postulated the existence of an ancient race called the Aryans, who had spoken the original language from which the rest derived. During the Romantic period, writers had called the different cultures of Europe "races."

The debates over slavery in the European colonies and the United States had given further opportunity for the development of racial theory. In the late nineteenth century, however, race emerged as a single dominant explanation of the history and the character of large groups of people. What transformed racial thinking at the end of the century was its association with the biological sciences. The prestige associated with biology and science in general became transferred to racial thinking, whose advocates now claimed to possess a materialistic, scientific basis for their thought. They argued that racial science could support a hierarchy of superior and inferior races within Europe and among the various peoples outside Europe.

Gobineau Count Arthur de Gobineau (1816–1882), a reactionary French diplomat, enunciated the first important theory of race as the major determinant of human history. In his four-volume *Essay on the Inequality of the Human Races* (1853–1854), Gobineau portrayed the troubles of Western civilization as the result of the long degeneration of the original white Aryan race. He claimed it had unwisely intermarried with the inferior yellow and black races, thus diluting the greatness and ability that originally existed in its blood. Gobineau saw no way to reverse this degeneration.

Gobineau's essay remained little known for years. However, a growing literature by anthropologists and explorers spread racial thinking. In the wake of Darwin's theory, thinkers applied the concept of survival of the fittest to races and nations. The recognition of the animal nature of humankind made the racial idea all the more persuasive.

Chamberlain At the close of the century, Houston Stewart Chamberlain (1855–1927), an Englishman who settled in Germany, drew together these strands of racial thought into the two volumes of his *Foundations of the Nineteenth Century* (1899). He championed the concept of biological determinism through race but believed that through genetics the human race could be improved and even that a superior race could be developed.

Chamberlain was anti-Semitic. He pointed to the Jews as the major enemy of European racial regeneration. Chamberlain's book and the works on which it drew aided the spread of anti-Semitism in European political life.

Late-Century Nationalism Racial thinking was one part of a wider late-century movement toward more aggressive nationalism. Previously, nationalism had in general been a movement among European literary figures and liberals (see Chapter 20). The former had sought to develop what they regarded as the historically distinct qualities of particular national literatures. The liberal nationalists had hoped to redraw the map of Europe to reflect what they thought were national boundaries. The drive for the unification of Italy and Germany had been major goals, as had been the liberation of Poland from foreign domination. The various national groups of the Habsburg Empire had also sought political and cultural autonomy, if not independence.

From the 1870s onward, however, nationalism became a movement with mass support, well-financed organizations, and political parties. Nationalists often redefined nationality in terms of race and blood. The new nationalism opposed the internationalism of both liberalism and socialism. The ideal of nationality was used to overcome the pluralism of class, religion, and geography. The nation became a secular religion in the hands of state schoolteachers, who were replacing the clergy as the instructors of youth. Nationalism of this aggressive, racist variety became the most powerful ideology of the early twentieth century.

Some Europeans also used racial theory to support harsh, condescending treatment of colonial peoples in the late nineteenth and early twentieth centuries. They were convinced that white Europeans were racially superior to the peoples of color whom they governed. Similar racial theory also informed attitudes toward peoples of color in the West itself, as was the case with the inferiority ascribed to African Americans and Native Americans in the United States.

Anti-Semitism and the Birth of Zionism

Political and racial anti-Semitism, which cast such dark shadows across the twentieth century, developed, in part, from the prevailing atmosphere of racial thought and the retreat from rationality in politics. Religious anti-Semitism dated from at least the Middle Ages. Since the French Revolution, West European Jews had gradually gained entry into civil life. Popular anti-Semitism, however, survived, with the Jewish community being identified with money and banking interests. During the last third of the century, as finance capitalism changed the economic structure of Europe, many non-Jewish

Document

ÉMILE ZOLA ACCUSES THE ENEMIES OF DREYFUS OF SELF-INTEREST AND ILLEGAL ACTIONS

On January 13, 1898, Émile Zola, the leading French novelist of his day and a strong defender of Captain Alfred Dreyfus, published perhaps the most famous newspaper article of the century in France. The format of the article was a letter to the president of the French Republic. Under a large-type banner headline "J'accuse" ("I accuse"), Zola accused a series of high military officers and others of illegally and dishonestly persecuting Dreyfus. Zola knew he could possibly face charges and convictions of libel. Eventually he fled France for political refuge in England.

What are the accusations that Zola brings against Dreyfus's enemies? How does Zola see Dreyfus's enemies as protecting their own institutions and self-interest? How does Zola put his own reputation and fame on the line in defending Dreyfus?

I accuse Lt-Col du Paty de Clam of having been the diabolical agent of a miscarriage of justice (though unwittingly, I am willing to believe) and then of having defended his evil deed for the past three years through the most preposterous and most blameworthy machinations.

I accuse General Mercier of having been an accomplice, at least by weak-mindedness, to one of the most iniquitous acts of this century.

I accuse General Billot of having had in his hands undeniable proof that Dreyfus was innocent and of having suppressed it, of having committed this crime against justice and against humanity for political purposes, so that the General Staff, which had been compromised, would not lose face.

I accuse Generals de Boisdeffre and Gonse of having been accomplices to this same crime, one out of intense clerical conviction, no doubt, and the other perhaps because of the esprit de corps which makes the War Office the Holy of Holies and hence unattackable. . . .

I accuse the three handwriting experts . . . of having submitted fraudulent and deceitful reports—unless a medication examination concludes that their eyesight and their judgment were impaired.

I accuse the War Office of having conducted an abominable campaign in the press . . . in order to cover up its misdeeds and lead public opinion astray.

Finally, I accuse the first court martial of having violated the law by sentencing a defendant on the basis of documents which remained secret, and I accuse the second court martial of having covered up that illegal action, on order, by having, in its own turn, committed the judicial crime of knowingly acquitting a guilty man.

In making these accusations, I am fully aware that my action comes under Articles 30 and 31 of the law of 29 July 1881 on the press, which makes libel a punishable offence. I deliberately expose myself to that law.

As for the persons I have accused, I do not know them: I have never seen them: I feel no rancour or hatred towards them. To me, they are mere entities, mere embodiments of social malfeasance. And the action I am taking here is merely a revolutionary means to hasten the revelation of truth and justice.

. . . Let them dare to summon me before a court of law! Let the inquiry be held in broad daylight!

I am waiting.

Émile Zola Letter to M. Félix Faure, President of the Republic, published in *L'Aurore*, January 13, 1898, trans. by Eleanor Levieux, in Alain Pagés, ed., *Émile Zola, The Dreyfus Affair: "J'accuse" and Other Writings* (New Haven, CT: Yale University Press, 1996), pp. 52–53.

Europeans threatened by the changes became hostile toward the Jewish community.

The Dreyfus Affair In Vienna, Mayor Karl Lueger (1844–1910) used anti-Semitism as a major attraction for his Christian Socialist Party. In Germany, ultraconservative Lutheran chaplain Adolf Stoecker (1835–1909) revived anti-Semitism. Nowhere, however, did nineteenth-century anti-Semitism create a greater political crisis than the one caused by the Dreyfus affair in France.

On December 22, 1894, a French military court found Captain Alfred Dreyfus (1859–1935) guilty of passing secret information to the German army. The evidence against him was flimsy and was later revealed to have been forged. Someone in the officer corps had been passing documents to the Germans, and it suited the army investigators to accuse Dreyfus, who was Jewish. Even after Dreyfus was sent to Devil's Island, a notorious prison in French Guiana, however, secrets continued to flow to the German army. In 1896, a new head of French counterintelligence reexamined the Dreyfus file and found evidence of forgery. A different officer was implicated, but a military court acquitted him of all charges.

By then the affair had provoked near-hysterical public debate. The army, the French Catholic Church, political conservatives, and vehemently anti-Semitic newspapers contended that Dreyfus was guilty despite mounting evidence of his innocence. Anti-Dreyfus opinion was dominant at the beginning of the affair. In 1898, however, the novelist Émile Zola (1840–1902) published a newspaper article, *"J'accuse"* ("I accuse"), in which he contended that the army had denied due process to Dreyfus and had suppressed or forged evidence. Zola was convicted of libel and fled to England to avoid serving a one-year prison sentence.

0088923 ALFRED DREYFUS (1859-1935).
Credit: Rue des Archives / The Granger Collection, New York

Photographs of Alfred Dreyfus taken in January 1895, after his sentencing to life imprisonment for treason in 1894. The photograph shows him in uniform, but stripped of all the signs and insignia of his rank. The trial and conviction of Captain Dreyfus provoked the most serious crisis of the Third Republic. Rue des Archives/The Granger Collection, NYC—All rights reserved

Zola was only one of numerous liberals, radicals, and socialists who had begun to demand a new trial for Dreyfus. Although these forces of the political left had come to Dreyfus's support rather slowly, they soon realized his cause could aid their own public image. They portrayed the conservative institutions of the nation as having denied Dreyfus the rights belonging to any citizen of the republic. They also claimed, and properly so, that Dreyfus had been framed to protect the guilty persons, who were still in the army. In August 1898, further evidence of forged material came to light. The officer responsible for those forgeries committed suicide in jail, but a new military trial again convicted Dreyfus. The president of France immediately pardoned him and eventually, in 1906, a civilian court set aside the results of both military trials.

The Dreyfus case divided France as no issue had done since the Paris Commune. By its conclusion, the conservatives were on the defensive. The military, and by extension the conservatives who supported them, had persecuted an innocent person and manufactured false evidence against him to protect themselves from disclosure. They had also embraced violent anti-Semitism. On the political left, radicals, republicans, and socialists developed an informal alliance, which outlived the Dreyfus case itself. These groups realized that the political left had to support republican institutions to achieve its goals. Nonetheless, the political and religious divisions and suspicions growing out of the Dreyfus affair continued to divide the Third Republic until France's defeat by Germany in 1940.

To this ugly atmosphere, racial thought contributed the belief that no matter to what extent Jews assimilated

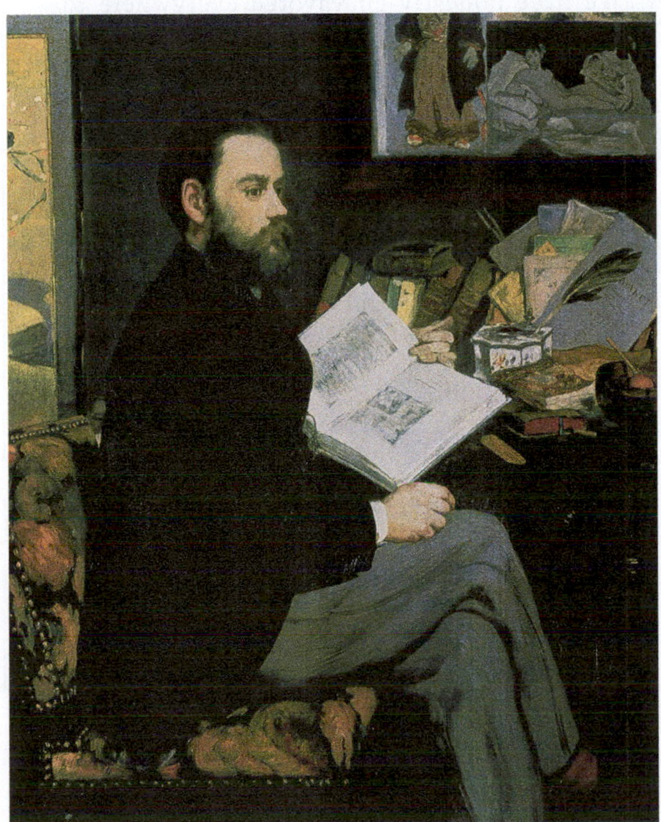

Émile Zola of France was the master of the realistic novel. Oil on canvas, 146.5 × 114 cm. Réunion des Musées Nationaux/Art Resource, Inc.

Document

HERZL ADVOCATES JEWISH NATIONALISM

Theodor Herzl (1860–1904) was one of the most successful journalists in German-speaking Europe. In his youth, Herzl, who was Jewish, believed that religion was a private matter, and that Jews could successfully assimilate into the societies in which they lived. He wrote essays for the leading Viennese daily newspaper, the Neue Freie Presse (New Free Press)*, and became the paper's Paris correspondent in time to witness the Dreyfus affair firsthand. In 1895, he began writing* The Jewish State *(which was first published in 1896). In it, Herzl abandoned the notion of Jews' assimilation into societies that seemed determined to reject them, and advocated the formation of a new political Jewish nation. Although scholars now believe that Herzl was most strongly influenced by anti-Semitism in Vienna, Herzl himself attributed his "conversion" to Zionism to the trauma of the Dreyfus affair.*

How does Herzl relate anti-Semitism to the failure of the Enlightenment? Why does he highlight anti-Semitism in France and England, rather than Austria or Russia? How is Herzl's Jewish nationalism similar to other forms of nationalism, and in what ways does it differ?

This century has given the world a wonderful renaissance by means of its technical acquisitions; but at the same time its miraculous improvements have not been employed in the service of humanity. . . .

Now, I am of the opinion that electric light was not invented for the purpose of illuminating the drawing-rooms of a few snobs, but rather for the purpose of throwing light on some of the dark problems of humanity. One of these problems, and not the least of them, is the Jewish question. In solving it, we are working not only for ourselves, but for many other over-burdened and oppressed beings also.

The Jewish question . . . is a remnant of the Middle Ages, which civilized nations do not even yet seem able to shake off, try as they will. . . . The Jewish question exists wherever Jews live in perceptible numbers. Where it does not exist, it is carried by Jews in the course of their migrations. We naturally move to those places where we are not persecuted, and there our presence produces persecution. This is the case in every country, and will remain so, even in those most highly civilized—France itself being no exception—till the Jewish question finds a solution on a political basis. . . .

We have honestly endeavored everywhere to merge ourselves in the social life of surrounding communities, and to preserve only the faith of our fathers. It has not been permitted to us. In vain are we loyal patriots, our loyalty in some places running to extremes; in vain do we make the same sacrifices of life and property as our fellow citizens; in vain do we strive to increase the fame of our native land in science and art, or her wealth by trade and commerce. In countries where we have lived for centuries we are still cried down as strangers, and often by those whose ancestors were not yet domiciled in the land where Jews had already made experience of suffering. The majority may decide which are the strangers; for this, as indeed every point which arises in the commerce of nations, is a question of might. . . . In the world of today, and for an indefinite period it will probably remain so, might precedes right. Therefore it is useless for us to be loyal patriots.

From Theodor Herzl, *The Jewish State: An Attempt at a Modern Solution of the Jewish Question* (New York: Maccabæan, 1904), pp. 3–5.

themselves into the culture of their country, their Jewishness—and thus their alleged danger to society—would remain. For racial thinkers, the problem of race was not in the character, but in the blood of the Jew. An important Jewish response to this new, rabid outbreak of anti-Semitism was the launching in 1896 of the **Zionist** movement to found a separate Jewish state. Its founder was the Austro-Hungarian Theodor Herzl (1860–1904).

Herzl's Response The conviction in 1894 of Captain Dreyfus in France and the election of Karl Lueger in 1895 as mayor of Vienna, as well as personal experiences of

Theodor Herzl's visions of a Jewish state would eventually lead to the creation of the state of Israel in 1948. Hulton Archive/Getty Images

discrimination, convinced Herzl that liberal politics and the institutions of the liberal state could not protect the Jews in Europe or ensure that they would be treated justly. In 1896, Herzl published *The Jewish State*, in which he called for a separate state in which all Jews might be assured of those rights and liberties that they should be enjoying in the liberal states of Europe. Furthermore, Herzl followed the tactics of late-century mass democratic politics by directing his appeal particularly to the poor Jews who lived in the ghettos of Eastern Europe and the slums of Western Europe. The original call to Zionism thus combined a rejection of the anti-Semitism of Europe and a desire to realize some of the ideals of both liberalism and socialism in a state outside Europe. (See the Document "Herzl Calls for a Jewish State," page 774.)

▼ Women and Modern Thought

The ideas that so shook Europe from the publication of *The Origin of Species* through the opening of World War I produced, at best, mixed results for women. Within the often radically new ways of thinking about the world, views of women and their roles in society often remained remarkably unchanged.

Antifeminism in Late-Century Thought

The influence of biology on the thinking of intellectuals during the late nineteenth century and their own interest in the nonrational side of human behavior led many of them to sustain what had become stereotyped views of women. The emphasis on biology, evolution, and reproduction led intellectuals to concentrate on women's mothering role. Their interest in the nonrational led them to reassert the traditional view that feeling and the nurturing instinct are basic to women's nature. Many late-century thinkers and writers of fiction also often displayed fear and hostility toward women, portraying them as creatures susceptible to overwhelming and often destructive feelings and instincts. A genuinely misogynist strain emerged in late-century fiction and painting.

Much of the biological thought that challenged religious ideas and the accepted wisdom in science actually reinforced the traditional view of women as creatures weaker and less able than men. Darwin himself held such views of women, and he expressed them directly in his scientific writings. Medical thought of the late century similarly sustained these views. Whatever social changes were to be wrought through science, significant changes in the organization of the home and the relationship between men and women were not among them.

This conservative and hostile perception of women manifested itself in several ways within the scientific community. In London in 1860, the Ethnological Society excluded women from its discussions on the grounds that the subject matter of the customs of primitive peoples was unfit for women and that women were amateurs whose presence would lower the level of the discussion. T. H. Huxley took the lead in this exclusion, as he had in a previous exclusion of women from meetings of the Geological Society. Male scientists also believed women should not discuss reproduction or other sexual matters. Huxley, in public lectures, claimed to have found scientific evidence of the inferiority of women to men. Karl Vogt (1817–1895), a leading German anthropologist, held similar views about the character of women. Darwin would repeat the ideas of both Huxley and Vogt in his *Descent of Man*. Late-Victorian anthropologists tended likewise to assign women, as well as nonwhite races, an inferior place in the human family. Still, despite their otherwise conservative views on gender, both Darwin and Huxley supported the expansion of education for women.

Freud, too, portrayed women as incomplete human beings who might be inevitably destined to unhappy mental lives. He saw the natural destiny of women as motherhood and the rearing of sons as their greatest fulfillment. The first psychoanalysts were trained as medical doctors, and their views of women reflected contemporary medical education, which, like much of the scientific establishment, tended to portray women as inferior. Distinguished women psychoanalysts, such as Karen Horney (1885–1952) and Melanie Klein (1882–1960), would later challenge Freud's views on women, and other writers would try to establish a psychoanalytic basis for feminism. Nonetheless, the psychoanalytic profession would remain dominated by men, as would academic psychology. Because psychology increasingly influenced childrearing and domestic relations law in the twentieth century, it, ironically, gave men a large impact in the one area of social activity that women had dominated.

The social sciences of the late nineteenth and early twentieth centuries similarly reinforced traditional gender roles. Most major theorists believed that women's role in reproduction and child rearing demanded a social position inferior to men. Auguste Comte, whose thought in this area owed much to Rousseau, portrayed women as biologically and intellectually inferior to men. Herbert Spencer, although an advocate for improving women's lot, thought they could never achieve equality with men. Émile Durkheim portrayed women as creatures of feeling and family rather than of intellect. Max Weber favored improvements in the condition of women but did not really support significant changes in their social roles or in their relationship to men. Virtually all of the early sociologists took a conservative view of marriage, the family, childrearing, and divorce.

New Directions in Feminism

The close of the century witnessed a revival of feminist thought in Europe. The role of feminist writers during these years was difficult. Many women's organizations, as seen in Chapter 23, concentrated on achieving the vote for women, but feminist writers and activists raised other questions as well. Some organizations redefined ways of thinking about women and their relationships to men and society. Few of these groups were large, and their victories were rare. Nonetheless, by the early 1900s, they had defined the issues that would become more fully and successfully explored after World War II.

Sexual Morality and the Family In various nations, middle-class women began to challenge the double standard of sexual morality and the traditional male-dominated family. This often meant challenging laws about prostitution.

Between 1864 and 1886, English prostitutes were subject to the Contagious Diseases Acts. The police in certain cities with naval or military bases could require any woman identified as, or suspected of being, a prostitute to undergo an immediate internal medical examination for venereal disease. Those found to have a disease could be confined for months to locked hospitals without legal recourse. The law took no action against their male customers. Indeed, the purpose of the laws was to protect men, presumably sailors and soldiers, and not the women themselves, from infection.

These laws angered English middle-class women who believed the harsh working conditions and the poverty imposed on so many working-class women were the true causes of prostitution. They framed the issue in the context of their own efforts to prove that women are as human and rational as men and thus properly subject to equal treatment. They saw poor women being made victims of the same kind of discrimination that prevented women of their class from entering the universities and professions. The Contagious Diseases Acts assumed that women were inferior to men and treated them as less than rational human beings. The laws literally put women's bodies under the control of male customers, male physicians, and male law-enforcement personnel. They denied to poor women the freedoms that all men enjoyed in English society.

By 1869, the Ladies' National Association for the Repeal of the Contagious Diseases Acts, a distinctly middle-class organization led by Josephine Butler (1828–1906), began actively to oppose those laws. The group achieved the suspension of the acts in 1883 and their repeal in 1886. Government and police regulation of prostitution roused similar movements in other nations, which adopted the English movement as a model. In Vienna during the 1890s, the General Austrian Women's Association, led by Auguste Fickert (1855–1910), combated the legal regulation of prostitution, which would have put women under the control of police authorities. In Germany, women's groups divided between those who would have penalized prostitutes and those who saw them as victims of male society. By the turn of the century, the latter had come to dominate, although tensions between the groups would remain for some time.

The feminist groups that demanded the abolition of laws that punished prostitutes without questioning the behavior of their customers were challenging the double standard and, by extension, the traditional relationship of men and women in marriage. In their view, marriage should be a free union of equals, with men and women sharing responsibility for their children. In Germany, the Mothers' Protection League (*Bund für Mutterschutz*) contended that both married and unmarried mothers required the help of the state, including leaves for pregnancy and child care. This radical group emphasized the need to rethink all sexual morality. In Sweden, Ellen Key (1849–1926), in *The Century of the Child* (1900) and *The Renaissance of Motherhood* (1914), maintained that motherhood is so crucial to society that the government, rather than husbands, should support mothers and their children. Virtually all turn-of-the-century feminists in one way or another supported wider sexual freedom for women, often claiming it would benefit society as well as improve women's lives.

Read the **Document** "Ellen Key, from *The Century of the Child*" on **MyHistoryLab.com**

Women Defining their Own Lives For Josephine Butler and Auguste Fickert, as well as other continental feminists, achieving legal and social equality for women would

PUBLICATION DATES OF MAJOR NONFICTION WORKS

1830	Lyell, *Principles of Geology*
1830–1842	Comte, *The Positive Philosophy*
1835	Strauss, *The Life of Jesus*
1853–1854	Gobineau, *Essay on the Inequality of the Human Races*
1859	Darwin, *The Origin of Species*
1864	Pius IX, *Syllabus of Errors*
1865	Bernard, *An Introduction to the Study of Experimental Medicine*
1871	Darwin, *The Descent of Man*
1872	Nietzsche, *The Birth of Tragedy*
1883	Mach, *The Science of Mechanics*
1883	Nietzsche, *Thus Spake Zarathustra*
1891	Leo XIII, *Rerum Novarum*
1893	Huxley, *Evolution and Ethics*
1896	Herzl, *The Jewish State*
1899	Chamberlain, *The Foundations of the Nineteenth Century*
1900	Freud, *The Interpretation of Dreams*
1900	Key, *The Century of the Child*
1905	Weber, *The Protestant Ethic and the Spirit of Capitalism*
1908	Sorel, *Reflections on Violence*
1929	Woolf, *A Room of One's Own*
1933	Jung, *Modern Man in Search of a Soul*

be one step toward transforming Europe from a male-dominated society to one in which both men and women could control their own destinies. Fickert wrote, "Our final goal is therefore not the acknowledgement of rights, but the elevation of our intellectual and moral level, the development of our personality."[11] Increasingly, feminists would concentrate on freeing and developing women's personalities through better education and government financial support for women engaged in traditional social roles, whether or not they had gained the vote.

Some women also became active within socialist circles. There they argued that the socialist transformation of society should include major reforms for women. Socialist parties usually had all-male leadership. By the close of the century, most male socialist leaders, including Lenin and later Stalin, were intolerant of demands for changes in the family or greater sexual freedom for either men or women. Nonetheless, socialist writings began to include calls for improvements in the economic situation of women that were compatible with more advanced feminist ideals.

It was within literary circles, however, that feminist writers often most clearly articulated the problems that they now understood themselves to face. Distinguished women authors were actually doing, on a more or less equal footing, something that men had always done, leading some to wonder whether simple equality was the main issue. Virginia Woolf's *A Room of One's Own* (1929) became one of the fundamental texts of twentieth-century feminist literature. In it, she meditated first on the difficulties that women of both brilliance and social standing encountered in being taken seriously as writers and intellectuals. She concluded that a woman who wishes to write requires both a room of her own, meaning a space not dominated by male institutions, and an adequate independent income. Woolf was concerned with more than asserting the right of women to

Read the **Document** "Virginia Woolf, from *A Room of One's Own* (Great Britain), 1929" on **MyHistoryLab.com**

Virginia Woolf charted the changing sentiments of a world with most of the nineteenth-century social and moral certainties removed. In *A Room of One's Own*, quoted in the document selection on p. 778, she also challenged some of the accepted notions of feminist thought, asking whether women writers should bring to their work any separate qualities they possessed as women, and concluding that men and women writers should strive to share each other's sensibilities. George C. Beresford/Hulton Archive/Getty Images

[11]Harriet Anderson, *Utopian Feminism: Women's Movements in Fin-de-Siècle Vienna* (New Haven, CT: Yale University Press, 1992), p. 13.

Document

VIRGINIA WOOLF URGES WOMEN TO WRITE

In 1928, Virginia Woolf, an English novelist, delivered two papers at women's colleges at Cambridge University that became the basis for A Room of One's Own, *published a year later. There, discussing the difficulty a woman writer confronted in finding women role models, she outlined obstacles that women faced in achieving the education, the time, and the income that would allow them to write. In the passage that follows, which closes her essay, she urges women to begin to write so future women authors would have models. She then presents an image of Shakespeare's sister, who, lacking such models, had not written anything, but who, through the collective efforts of women, might in the future emerge as a great writer because she would have the literary models of the women Woolf addressed to follow and to imitate.*

How does Woolf's fiction of Shakespeare's sister establish a benchmark for women writers? What does Woolf mean by the common life through which women will need to work to become independent writers? Why does she emphasize the need for women to have both income and space if they are to become independent writers?

A thousand pens are ready to suggest what you should do and what effect you will have. My own suggestion is a little fantastic, I admit; I prefer, therefore, to put it in the form of fiction.

I told you in the course of this paper that Shakespeare had a sister; but do not look for her in Sir Sidney Lee's life of the poet. She died young—alas, she never wrote a word. She lies buried where the omnibuses now stop, opposite the Elephant and Castle [a London intersection]. Now my belief is that this poet who never wrote a word and was buried at the cross-roads still lives. She lives in you and in me, and in many other women who are not here to-night, for they are washing up the dishes and putting the children to bed. But she lives; for great poets do not die; they are continuing presences; they need only the opportunity to walk among us in the flesh. This opportunity, as I think, it is now coming within your power to give her. For my belief is that if we live another century or so—I am talking of the common life which is the real life and not of the little separate lives which we live as individuals—and have five hundred [pounds income] a year each of us and rooms of our own; if we have the habit of freedom and the courage to write exactly what we think; if we escape a little from the common sitting-room and see human beings not always in their relation to each other but in relation to reality; and the sky, too, and the trees or whatever it may be in themselves; . . . if we face the fact, for it is a fact, that there is no arm to cling to, but that we go alone and that our relation is to the world of reality and not only to the world of men and women, then the opportunity will come and the dead poet who was Shakespeare's sister will put on the body which she has so often laid down. Drawing her life from the lives of the unknown who were her forerunners, as her brother did before her, she will be born. As for her coming without that preparation, without that effort on our part, without that determination that when she is born again she shall find it possible to live and write her poetry, that we cannot expect, for that would be impossible. But I maintain that she would come if we worked for her, and that so to work, even in poverty and obscurity, is worthwhile.

From Virginia Woolf, *A Room of One's Own* (London: The Hogarth Press, 1974), pp. 170–172.

participate in intellectual life, however. Establishing a new stance for feminist writers, she asked whether women, as writers, must imitate men or whether they should bring to their endeavors the separate intellectual and psychological qualities they possessed as women. As she had challenged some of the literary conventions of the traditional novel in her fiction, she challenged some of the accepted notions of feminist thought in *A Room of One's Own* and concluded that male and female writers must actually be able to think as both men and women and share the sensibilities of each. In this sense, she sought to open the whole question of gender definition. (See the Document "Virginia Woolf Urges Women to Write," page 778.)

By World War I, feminism in Europe, fairly or not, had become associated in the popular imagination with challenges to traditional gender roles and sexual morality and with either socialism or political radicalism. So when extremely conservative political movements arose between the world wars, their leaders often emphasized traditional roles for women and traditional ideas about sexual morality. (See Chapter 27.)

In Perspective

By the opening of the twentieth century, European thought had achieved contours that seem familiar to us today. Science had revolutionized thinking about nature. Physicists had transformed the traditional views of matter and energy as they probed the mysteries of the atom. Evolutionary biology had revealed that human beings are not distinct from the natural order. Many believed science would provide a new basis for ethics and morality. Christianity had experienced its most severe challenge in modern times from science, history, philosophy, and the secular national states.

Nonreligious thinkers and writers also assailed the primacy of reason. Nietzsche and Freud, in their different ways, questioned whether human beings are rational creatures at all. Weber and other social and political theorists doubted that politics could ever be entirely rational. All these developments challenged the rational values of the Enlightenment.

The racial theorists questioned whether mind and character were as important as racial characteristics allegedly carried in the blood. Racial thinking also allowed some Europeans to believe they were inherently superior to non-Europeans, Jews, and ethnic minorities in Europe itself.

Turn-of-the-century feminists demanded equal treatment for women under the law and contended that the relationship between men and women within marriage required rethinking. They set forth much of the feminist agenda for the twentieth century.

KEY TERMS

cubism (p. 767)
ego (p. 770)
id (p. 770)
Kulturkampf (p. 758)
modernism (p. 764)
natural selection (p. 753)
papal infallibility (p. 759)
positivism (p. 753)
Postimpressionism (p. 766)
racism (p. 771)
realist (p. 763)
Social Darwinism (p. 755)
superego (p. 770)
Zionist (p. 774)

REVIEW QUESTIONS

1. Why was science dominant in the second half of the nineteenth century? How did the scientific outlook change between 1850 and 1914? What was positivism? How did Darwin and Wallace's theory of natural selection affect ethics, Christianity, and European views of human nature?
2. Why was Christianity attacked in the late nineteenth century? Why was Leo XIII regarded as a liberal pope? Why was the papacy itself so resilient?
3. Why did Europeans feel superior toward Islam? How did Islamic thinkers respond to the European challenge?
4. How did social conditions of literature change in the late nineteenth century? What was the significance of the explosion of literary matter? How did the realists undermine middle-class morality? How did literary modernism differ from realism?
5. What were the major movements associated with the rise of modern art?
6. How did Nietzsche and Freud challenge traditional morality?
7. Why were many late-nineteenth-century intellectuals afraid of and hostile to women? How did Freud view the position of women? What social and political issues affected women in the late nineteenth and early twentieth centuries? What new directions did feminism take?
8. What was the character of late-nineteenth-century racism? How did it become associated with anti-Semitism?
9. How did many ideas associated with modernism conflict with feminist goals? What were new departures in turn-of-the-century feminism?

SUGGESTED READINGS

C. Allen, *The Human Christ: The Search for the Historical Jesus* (1998). A broad survey of the issue for the past two centuries.

M. D. Biddis, *Father of Racist Ideology: The Social and Political Thought of Count Gobineau* (1970). Sets the subject in the more general context of nineteenth-century thought.

P. Bowler, *Evolution: The History of an Idea* (2003). An outstanding survey.

J. Browne, *Charles Darwin*, 2 vols. (1995, 2002). A stunning biography.

J. Burrow, *The Crisis of Reason: European Thought, 1848–1914* (2000). The best overview available.

F. J. Coppa, *The Modern Papacy since 1789* (1999). A straightforward survey.

F. J. Coppa, *Politics and Papacy in the Modern World* (2008). A broad-ranging exploration.

B. Denvir, *Post-Impressionism* (1992). A brief introduction.

T. Dixon, *The Invention of Altruism: Making Moral Meanings in Victorian Britain* (2008). An outstanding study of the changing ideas regarding social improvement in the wake of the ideas of Comte, Darwin, and Spencer.

M. Francis, *Herbert Spencer and the Invention of Modern Life* (2007). Now the standard biography.

P. Gay, *Modernism: The Lure of Heresy* (2007). A broad interdisciplinary exploration.

R. Harris, *Lourdes: Body and Soul in a Secular Age* (1999). A sensitive discussion of Lourdes in its religious and cultural contexts.

R. Helmstadter, ed., *Freedom and Religion in the Nineteenth Century* (1997). Major essays on the relationship of church and state.

J. Hodge and G. Radick, *The Cambridge Companion to Darwin* (2003). A far-ranging collection of essays with a good bibliography.

A. Hourani, *Arab Thought in the Liberal Age 1789–1939* (1967). A classic account, clearly written and accessible to the nonspecialist.

J. Köhler, *Zarathustra's Secret: The Interior Life of Friedrich Nietzsche* (2002). A controversial new biography.

W. Lacqueur, *A History of Zionism* (2003). The most extensive one-volume treatment.

M. Levenson, *The Cambridge Companion to Modernism* (1999). Excellent essays on a wide range of subjects.

B. Lightman, *Victorian Popularizers of Science: Designing Nature for New Audiences* (2007). A study that adds numerous new dimensions to the subject.

G. Makari, *Revolution in Mind: The Creation of Psychoanalysis* (2008). A major, multidimensional survey.

A. Pais, *Subtle Is the Lord: The Science and Life of Albert Einstein* (1983). The most accessible biography.

P. G. J. Pulzer, *The Rise of Political Anti-Semitism in Germany and Austria* (1989). A sound discussion of anti-Semitism and Central European politics.

F. Quinn, *The Sum of All Heresies: The Image of Islam in Western Thought* (2008). An interesting and clear overview of this important subject.

R. Rosenblum, *Cubism and 20th Century Art* (2001). A well-informed introduction.

M. Ruse and R. J. Richards, *The Cambridge Companion to the "Origin of Species"* (2008). Excellent essays based on the most recent scholarship.

C. E. Schorske, *Fin de Siècle Vienna: Politics and Culture* (1980). Classic essays on the creative intellectual climate of Vienna.

W. Smith, *Politics and the Sciences of Culture in Germany, 1840–1920* (1991). A major survey of the interaction between science and the social sciences.

F. M. Turner, *Contesting Cultural Authority: Essays in Victorian Intellectual Life* (1993). Explorations in issues relating to Victorian science and religion.

D. Vital, *A People Apart: The Jews in Europe 1789–1939* (1999). A broad and deeply researched volume.

A. N. Wilson, *God's Funeral* (1999). Explores the thinkers who contributed to religious doubt during the nineteenth and twentieth centuries.

MyHistoryLab™ MEDIA ASSIGNMENTS

Find these resources in the Media Assignments folder for Chapter 24 on **MyHistoryLab**.

QUESTIONS FOR ANALYSIS

1. What tools are used by the two chess players in furthering their goals?

   ***Section:* Christianity and the Church Under Siege**

   View the **Closer Look** Conflict Between Church and State in Germany, p. 758

2. How has Spencer moved beyond Darwin's ideas in applying them to human society?

   ***Section:* Science at Midcentury**

   Read the **Document** Herbert Spencer, Social Darwinism, from *The Data of Ethics* (1857), p. 755

3. How does this work relate to other intellectual and scientific developments of its time?

   ***Section:* Toward a Twentieth-Century Frame of Mind**

   View the **Closer Look** Sunday on La Grande Jatte, p. 767

4. Why do you think the ideas of Heisenberg had such a wide impact?

   ***Section:* Toward a Twentieth-Century Frame of Mind**

   Read the **Document** Werner Heisenberg, "Uncertainty" (Germany), 1927, p. 762

5. What does Key mean by the "holiness of generation"?

Section: **Women and Modern Thought**

Read the **Document** Ellen Key, from *The Century of the Child*, p. 776

OTHER RESOURCES FROM THIS CHAPTER

Science at Midcentury

Read the **Document** Auguste Comte, "Course of Positive Philosophy" (France), 1830–1842, p. 753

Read the **Document** *Origin of Species*, Charles Darwin (1859), p. 753

Christianity and the Church Under Siege

Read the **Document** Matthew Arnold, Excerpt from *Dover Beach*, p. 755

Read the **Compare and Connect** The Debate over Social Darwinism, p. 756

Read the **Document** Pope Leo XIII, *Rerum Novarum* (*Of New Things*), 1891, p. 759

Read the **Document** Sayyid Jamal al-Din al-Afghani, "Lecture on Teaching and Learning," p. 761

Toward a Twentieth-Century Frame of Mind

Read the **Document** Emile Zola, *Nana*, p. 763

Read the **Document** Henrik Ibsen, from *A Doll's House*, Act Three, p. 764

Read the **Document** John Maynard Keynes, from *The End of Laissez-Faire*, p. 764

View the **Closer Look** Monet's *Water Lilies*, p. 766

Watch the **Video** The Art of Pablo Picasso, p. 768

Read the **Document** Friedrich Nietzsche, *Beyond Good and Evil*, p. 768

Women and Modern Thought

Read the **Document** Virginia Woolf, from *A Room of One's Own* (Great Britain), 1929, p. 777

The global British Empire dominated the nineteenth-century European imperial experience. The empire was popularized in newspapers, books, and novels, as well as in thousands of illustrations and photographs. This illustration seeks to portray the worldwide reach of the British Empire and the varied peoples whom it governed abroad and, at the same time, as seen in the caption, how it sought to build domestic pride in the imperial achievement. Similar illustrations could be found portraying the empires of France, Germany, the Netherlands, Belgium, and Russia. "Citizens of the British Empire, the Greatest Empire the world has ever known . . . " 1911, *London Illustrated News*. Mary Evans Picture Library

Listen to the **Chapter Audio** on **MyHistoryLab.com**

25

The Age of Western Imperialism

- **The Close of the Age of Early Modern Colonization**
- **The Age of British Imperial Dominance**
  The Imperialism of Free Trade • British Settler Colonies
- **India—The Jewel in the Crown of the British Empire**
- **The "New Imperialism," 1870–1914**
- **Motives for the New Imperialism**
- **The Partition of Africa**
  Algeria, Tunisia, Morocco, and Libya • Egypt and British Strategic Concern about the Upper Nile West Africa • The Belgian Congo • German Empire in Africa • Southern Africa
- **Russian Expansion in Mainland Asia**
- **Western Powers in Asia**
  France in Asia • The United States' Actions in Asia, the Pacific, and Latin America • The Boxer Rebellion
- **Tools of Imperialism**
  Steamboats • Conquest of Tropical Diseases • Firearms
- **The Missionary Factor**
  Missionary Movements • Tensions Between Missionaries and Imperial Administrators • Missionaries and Indigenous Religious Movements
- **Science and Imperialism**
  Botany • Zoology • Medicine • Anthropology
- **In Perspective**

LEARNING OBJECTIVES

How did early modern colonization differ from nineteenth-century Western imperialism?

How did Britain use its economic might to extend its influence around the world?

Why was India such an important part of the British Empire?

What was new about the "New Imperialism" and what role did economic motives play in nineteenth-century imperialism?

How did European politics contribute to the "Scramble for Africa"?

How did Russia come to control a vast and diverse Asian empire and what developments facilitated Western penetration and control of Asia?

How did technological innovations make nineteenth-century imperialism possible?

What was the relationship between missionaries and their home governments?

How did science help imperialism capture the imagination of domestic audiences in Europe?

THE HALF-CENTURY between the opening of the American Revolution and the end of the Latin American Wars of Independence (1775–1830) marked the end of the early modern era of European interaction with the wider world that had begun in the late fifteenth century. The second and third quarters of the nineteenth century witnessed the high age of the British Empire. During that time other European nations had fewer interests in the non-Western world. For a variety of reasons, this situation began to change in the 1870s, however, with the dawn of the period historians call the **New Imperialism**. For the next half-century, until the outbreak of World War I in 1914, European powers brought much of the world under their dominance and direct control. During this period the United States and Japan also first appeared as major players on the world stage.

The word ***imperialism*** is now used so loosely in political debate that it has almost lost meaning. To analyze events in the nineteenth century, it may be useful to define imperialism as "the policy of extending a nation's authority by territorial acquisition or by establishing economic and political hegemony over other nations."[1] That definition seems to apply equally well to ancient Egypt and Mesopotamia and to European domination in the nineteenth century, but the latter case had new elements. Previous imperialisms had either seized land and settled it with the conqueror's people or established trading centers to exploit the resources of the dominated area. Nineteenth-century Western imperialism did not abandon these methods, but it introduced new ones. Moreover, modern Western imperial powers benefited from the advanced economies and technologies that they had developed since the late eighteenth century.

Nonetheless, as we shall see, the age of modern imperialism and the interactions of Western nations with other parts of the world displayed many of the themes we have discussed in this book. The challenges of governing and administering empires brought to the fore constitutional issues. The technology that enabled Europeans to build empires displayed the impact of scientific knowledge on Western society and industry and Westerners' ability to use that knowledge to dominate other parts of the world. The activities of missionaries and their frequent conflict with colonial administrators reflected the struggles that had long disturbed church-state relations in their home countries. The criticism of imperial ventures by some Westerners manifested the critical spirit that has informed so much of the Western experience. The economic exploitation of and cultural disrespect for other peoples reflected the limits of Europeans' commitment to equality.

The legacies of nineteenth-century Western imperialism still affect our world today. The emergence of independent states in Asia and Africa from former colonies after World War II, the Vietnam War, the establishment of Communism in China, the rise and fall of apartheid in South Africa, and the turbulence in the Middle East all flow directly from the imperial encounters of the nineteenth and early twentieth centuries. So does much of the present-day economic structure and agricultural production of the non-Western world. Furthermore, the current tensions between Christian churches of the northern and southern hemispheres would not exist if missionaries had not planted new Christian communities in Africa and Asia during the nineteenth century. The existence of Canada, Australia, and New Zealand as self-governing nations is also the result of nineteenth-century British imperial policy. Consequently, the subjects discussed in this chapter are important for understanding both the political rivalries among European nations that led to World War I and the world in which we find ourselves today.

[1]*American Heritage Dictionary of the English Language*, 3rd ed. (New York: Houghton Mifflin, 1993), p. 681.

▼ The Close of the Age of Early Modern Colonization

The era of early modern European expansion that lasted from the late fifteenth to the late eighteenth centuries had witnessed the encounter, conquest, settlement, and exploitation of the American continents by the Spanish, Portuguese, French, and English; the establishment of modest trading posts by European countries in Africa and Asia; Dutch dominance in the East Indies (modern Indonesia); and British domination of India. During these three centuries, the European powers had largely conducted their colonial rivalries within the context of the mercantilist economic assumptions we discussed in Chapter 16. Each empire was, at least in theory and largely in fact, closed to the commerce of other nations. Furthermore, in the Americas, from New England to the Caribbean and then throughout Latin America, slavery was a major fact of economic life, with most slaves imported from Africa.

Early European colonial rivalry had occurred primarily within the transatlantic world. By the early eighteenth century, the following patterns of European domination prevailed in the Americas. The Spanish Empire extended from California and Texas to Argentina. The Spanish also claimed Florida. Portugal controlled Brazil. The Dutch, French, Spanish, and British exploited the rich sugar islands of the Caribbean. France loosely controlled the Saint Lawrence and Mississippi River Valleys and the upper Atlantic coast. The British had settled the Atlantic coast from Maine to Georgia.

Between the mid-eighteenth and the early nineteenth centuries, a vast political transformation occurred in these regions. The French lost their North

American empire to the British. The American Revolution drove the British from their Atlantic coastal colonies, which became the United States. Thousands of American loyalists fled to Canada, which developed a closer relationship with Britain. Warfare shifted the ownership of the Caribbean islands from one country to another, with Haiti by 1804 establishing its independence from France. (See Chapter 20.) In 1803, Napoleon sold the vast Louisiana Territory to the United States. In the 1820s Latin America shook off Spanish and Portuguese control. Except for Canada, the Caribbean islands, and a few toeholds on the coasts of Central and South America, European rule in the Americas had ended. The Monroe Doctrine, which the United States announced in 1823 and the British navy enforced, closed the Americas to European colonialism.

The most striking result of these events was the collapse of Spain, Portugal, and (temporarily) France as significant colonial powers. Although Spain retained Cuba, Puerto Rico, Guam, and the Philippines until 1898 and Portugal had colonies in Africa until the 1970s and in Asia until 1999, neither country would ever again be a major colonial or European power. France, by contrast, remained a great European power and by 1914, it again controlled a vast overseas empire, second in size and population only to Britain's.

View the **Map** "Interactive Map: World Colonial Empires 1900" on **MyHistoryLab.com**

In contrast to early modern European empires, slavery was absent from those of the nineteenth century. In 1807 Britain had banned the slave trade and had abolished slavery itself in its own colonies in 1833–1834. (See "The West and the World: The Abolition of Slavery in the Transatlantic Economy,." page 679.) Thereafter, the British navy worked to close down the slave trade of other nations (and often used this self-imposed moral duty as an excuse to interfere with foreign shipping). Consequently, although economic inequality and forced labor were common in the European empires of the late nineteenth century, the institution of slavery, which had been the chief characteristic of the earlier imperial transatlantic plantation economies, had disappeared. Africa would play a different role in modern imperialism than it had when it had served as the chief source of slaves for the Americas.

Roman Catholicism had been the driving religious influence among the early modern transatlantic empires. Almost from the moment Europeans first reached the Americas in the 1490s, Catholic priests, friars, and nuns had worked relentlessly to convert the indigenous peoples of the Caribbean, Latin America, and French Canada. These regions remain overwhelmingly Catholic. The largely Protestant settlers of the British colonies had been religiously zealous, but their missionary impulse was less strong, and there were fewer indigenous people along the Atlantic seaboard for them to convert. By contrast, during the nineteenth century, evangelical Protestants from Britain and the societies that backed them set the pace for missionary enterprises that other Western nations imitated, including those that sponsored Roman Catholic missions.

▼ The Age of British Imperial Dominance

During the first half of the nineteenth century, no one doubted that Great Britain was the only power that could exert its influence virtually around the world. During this half-century, Britain fostered the settlements that became the nations of Canada, Australia, and New Zealand and expanded its control of India. The early nineteenth-century British Empire also included smaller colonies and islands in the Caribbean and the Pacific and Indian Oceans. However, until the 1860s and 1870s, except in India and western Canada, Britain did not seek additional territory. Rather, it extended its influence through what historians call the **Imperialism of Free Trade.**

View the **Closer Look** "An Allegory of the British Empire" on **MyHistoryLab.com**

The Imperialism of Free Trade

Nineteenth-century British imperial economic ideas differed sharply from the mercantilist doctrines that had dominated previous centuries. Mercantile economic doctrine had asserted that a nation measured its wealth in terms of the amount of gold and silver it amassed and that the amount of trade was finite: If one nation's trade increased, another nation's trade had to decrease. But in the 1770s, economic thinkers such as Adam Smith (see Chapter 17) argued that empires would best prosper by abandoning closed imperial systems in favor of free trade, that is, by fostering the exchange of goods across borders and oceans with minimal government regulation and tariff barriers. Free traders argued that this would allow trade to grow upon itself—that the amount of trade was potentially infinite—and would assure consumers the lowest prices. This outlook still dominates economic theory in the West and provides the theoretical foundation for economic globalism.

As a result of the productive energies that the Industrial Revolution of the late eighteenth and early nineteenth centuries unleashed, Britain became "the workshop of the world." It produced more manufactured goods than its population could absorb on its own, and it did so more cheaply than anyone else. To dominate a foreign market, British merchants needed only the ability to trade without government interference in the form of tariffs, subsidies, or price controls. Until at least the 1870s, free trade alone allowed Britain to dominate economically one region of the world after another without the need to establish a formal colonial administration.

Although nineteenth-century liberals believed that free trade fostered peace, it could and did lead to warfare. The most important example of this concerned the opium trade between British merchants operating out of India and their potential Chinese customers. China had never been an extensive market for Western goods. Nonetheless, Europeans and Americans wanted to import Chinese goods, especially tea, silk, and porcelain, in large quantities. With the Chinese uninterested in buying Western manufactured goods, British merchants looked for another product to sell to the Chinese market. They found it in the opium produced in India. The Chinese government resisted the import of opium to prevent addiction among its people. (See the Document "A Chinese Official Appeals to Queen Victoria to Halt the Opium Trade,." page 786.)

Read the **Document** "Letter to Queen Victoria (1839) Lin Zexu" on **MyHistoryLab.com**

Between 1839 and 1842 and again between 1856 and 1860, the British went to war to impose a free trade in opium on China. At the conclusion of the first of these Opium Wars, the British gained control of Hong Kong, and forced the Chinese to allow Christian missionaries to operate in China, to open various ports to British merchants who remained subject to British rather than Chinese law, and to pay substantial reparations. During the Second Opium War, Britain, in alliance with France, forced the Chinese to allow foreign envoys to establish embassies in Beijing, to open more ports and areas to foreign trade, and to permit Christian missionaries to operate even more freely in China. The British were prepared to enforce free trade and their merchants' access to foreign markets even if the products those merchants sold poisoned buyers.

British Settler Colonies

During the early nineteenth century, Britain oversaw the settlement and economic development of three regions that had come under its domination in the eighteenth century: Canada, Australia, and New Zealand. Warfare had won Canada. Captain James Cook's voyages of exploration in the 1770s established British claims to Australia and New Zealand. Australia was first settled as a colony for British convicts. Missionaries led the colonization of New Zealand. The settlement of these lands, which attracted millions of immigrants from Britain and other European nations, resembled the westward movement in the United States during the same period. In both cases, native peoples paid the cost—in land, lives, and liberty—for European settlement.

The British assumed that eventually these regions would have some form of self-government and be a market for British goods. And in fact during the nineteenth century, each of these colonies did establish self-government based on British law and political institutions. The British system of self-government based on an increasingly inclusive franchise was thus transferred to large parts of the world.

▼ India—The Jewel in the Crown of the British Empire

Except for Canada, nineteenth-century British colonial interest shifted from the Atlantic world to Asia and the Indian and Pacific Oceans. During the same years that Britain had

Armed Chinese junks were no match for British warships during the first Opium War. The war ended in 1842 with the Treaty of Nanjing. The Granger Collection, NYC—

Document

A Chinese Official Appeals to Queen Victoria to Halt the Opium Trade

In 1839 the emperor of China became deeply concerned about the illegal opium trade between his country and British merchants, who are termed "barbarians," meaning foreigners, in the letter. He designated one of his officials to investigate the trade in Canton and to take steps to halt it. Among other things, this official, Lin Tse-hsü, wrote a strongly worded letter to Queen Victoria, the British monarch, whom he addressed late in the letter as "O King." He noted that all Chinese exports including tea, rhubarb, and woolens benefited the people who received them and did no harm. He appealed to the queen's conscience to halt the opium trade. He also indicated the new penalties that would be imposed on Chinese subjects and foreign merchants who engaged in the trade while appealing to those merchants not to risk the penalties. The letter produced no success for China because except for opium the country needed few products that the British could trade with them. Late in 1839 the British under the guise of enforcing free trade undertook what became known as the First Opium War, defeated China, and imposed a treaty that permitted opium to enter China.

How does Lin Tse-hsü appeal to the mutual Chinese and British recognition of the harm posed by opium? How might the penalties imposed by China serve to frighten off British merchants? How did British naval technology make China easily victimized by Britain? How does the opium trade of the middle of the nineteenth century compare with the international drug trafficking of the early twentieth century?

. . . after a long period of commercial intercourse, there appear among the crowd of barbarians [that is, foreigners trading in China] both good persons and bad, unevenly. Consequently there are those who smuggle opium to seduce the Chinese people and so cause the spread of the poison to all provinces . . . His Majesty the Emperor, upon hearing of this, is in a towering rage. . . .

The wealth of China is used to profit the barbarians. . . . By what right do they then in return use the poisonous drug to injure the Chinese people? . . . Let us ask, where is your conscience? I have heard that smoking of opium is very strictly forbidden by your country; that is because the harm caused by opium is clearly understood. Since it is not permitted to do harm to your own country, then even less should you let it be passed on to the harm of other countries—how much less to China! Of all that China exports to foreign countries, there is not a single thing which is not beneficial to people. . . .

Even if you do not sell opium, you still have this threefold profit. How can you bear to go further, selling products injurious to others in order to fulfill your insatiable desire? . . .

Now we have set up regulations governing the Chinese people. He who sells opium shall receive the death penalty and he who smokes it also the death penalty. . . . [I]n the new regulations, in regard to those barbarians who bring opium to China, the penalty is fixed at decapitation or strangulation. This is what is called getting rid of a harmful thing on behalf of mankind. . . .

The barbarian merchants of your country, if they wish to do business for a prolonged period, are required to obey our statutes respectfully and to cut off permanently the source of opium. They must by no means try to test the effectiveness of the law with their lives. May you, O King, check your wicked and sift your vicious people before they come to China, in order to guarantee the peace of your nation . . . to let the two countries enjoy together the blessings of peace.

Lin Tse-hsü to Queen Victoria, summer 1839, as quoted in Ssu-yü Teng and John K. Fairbank, *China's Response to the West: A Documentary Survey, 1839–1923* (Cambridge, MA: Harvard University Press, 1954), pp. 24–27.

lost its North American colonies (1775–1783), it had established itself as the ruler of India. British India encompassed what is today India, Pakistan, and Bangladesh. From the late eighteenth century until its independence in 1947, India was the most important part of the British Empire and provided the base for British military and economic power throughout Asia. The protection of the commercial and military routes to India would be the chief concern of British imperial strategy during the nineteenth century. Other nations, particularly Russia, believed they could threaten Britain by bringing military pressure to bear on India. As we shall see later in the chapter, Britain largely became involved in Africa in the late nineteenth century to protect India.

Control of India meant that Britain had to dominate and govern not a land of settler-farmers, most of whom had emigrated from Britain and shared British values, but rather a vast heterogeneous nonwhite population with numerous political allegiances, complex economic and social conditions, and non-Western religions, particularly Islam and Hinduism.

In theory until 1857, India was still ruled by the Mughal Empire, which had governed the region since the 1500s. But that empire was only a shadow of its former self. Local rulers, called nawabs or maharajahs, paid little attention to the Mughal emperor who still resided in Delhi, the old imperial capital.

Initially the British achieved their domination of India through the East India Company, which was a private company of merchants chartered by Parliament in 1600. In the late eighteenth and early nineteenth centuries, the Company expanded its authority across India by warfare and negotiation. In some cases its armies, which were composed mostly of Indian troops led by British officers and paid from taxes the Company collected, defeated rulers who resisted it and seized their territory. In others, it supported one Indian ruler against another. If an Indian prince died without clear heirs or lost control of his state, the Company might annex it. By the 1830s, British control over India was essentially complete. The willingness of Indians to defer to British authority rather than accept the dominance of other Indians made British rule possible. Like the Romans, the British had perfected the imperial art of dividing and conquering (see Map 25–1).

Read the **Document** "Dadabhai Naoroji, *The Benefits of British Rule in India*, 1871" on **MyHistoryLab.com**

The rationale for British rule in India changed over time. The East India Company essentially saw India as a place to make money through economic exploitation. By the early nineteenth century, while still hoping to make India profitable, the British saw themselves as bringing wise administration to a subcontinent where local authority was in disarray. In 1813, Parliament permitted British Christian missionaries to work in India. Their presence meant that for the first time Britons would challenge the religious customs of Indian Hindus and Muslims. Some British administrators began to cooperate with missionaries to bring the "enlightenment" of Western values to India. For example, the British prohibited the practice of *suttee* (Hindu widows burning themselves to death on their husband's funeral pyres). English became the official administrative language of

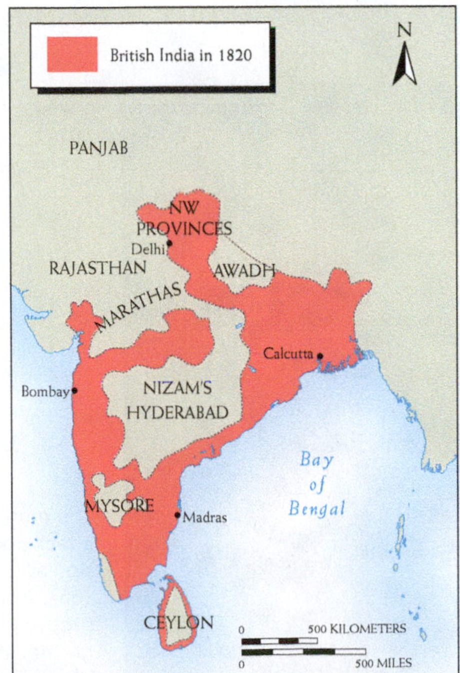

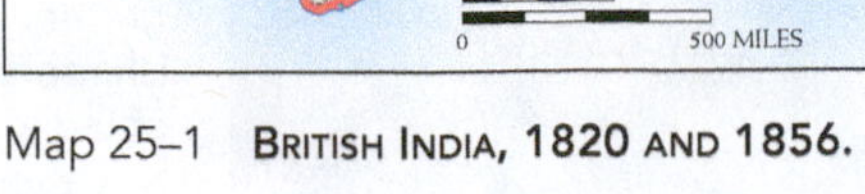

Map 25–1 **BRITISH INDIA, 1820 AND 1856.**

India. These and other intrusions suggested that British administrators believed they could raise India to what they considered to be a higher rung on the ladder of civilization. In their own colonial empire, the French would later call this belief in the spread of Western values "the civilizing mission."

In 1857, however, India witnessed the most extensive resistance against any European power that occurred in the nineteenth century. The sepoy rebellion or mutiny (Indian troops were called sepoys) was all the more frightening to the British because it occurred within the Indian Army itself. The precipitating cause of the mutiny was the Company's introduction of new cartridges for its soldiers' muskets that the sepoys believed (falsely, the cartridges were in fact coated with vegetable oil) were lubricated with pork or beef fat. Soldiers had to bite off the end of the cartridge to use it. This would have offended both Muslims, for whom the pig was unclean, and Hindus, to whom the cow was sacred. Some Indian troops feared that the British wanted to use the religious pollution that biting pork- and beef-coated cartridges would have caused to force them to convert to Christianity. There was also simmering anger over the way the Company treated native rulers and with the Company's policy of paying British troops more than it paid Indians.

Read the **Document** "The Indian Revolt (1857)" on **MyHistoryLab.com**

With support from native rulers, the British harshly suppressed the rebels. Their tactics became even more ruthless after sepoys massacred British women and children. Tens of thousands of Indians and more than 10,000 Britons were killed. By June 1858, the British were firmly back in control.

The immediate British political response to the mutiny was passage of the Government of India Act in 1858, which transferred political authority from the East India Company to the British Crown. Many company officials became British Crown administrators. The British also restrained their efforts to change India or to move it "toward civilization." Instead, the British administration sought to refrain from interfering with Indian religion and became distrustful of missionary efforts to convert Indians to Christianity. The British also worked more closely with Indian rulers. One-third of India remained under the rule of Indian princes who swore allegiance to the British Crown and were "advised" by British officials. More British troops were also stationed in India, and Indian troops were not allowed artillery. Finally in 1877, Prime Minister Benjamin Disraeli pushed through an Act of Parliament that declared Queen Victoria (r. 1837–1901) to be Empress of India.

Indians did not sit passively by while Britain revised its policies. In 1885, Hindus founded the Indian National Congress with the goals of modernizing Indian life and liberalizing British policy. Muslims organized the Muslim League in 1887, which for a time cooperated with the National Congress, but eventually sought an independent Muslim state. After World War I, the Indian nationalist movement grew stronger, in part because of British blunders, but more because Indian leaders pursued effective strategies, which we discuss in Chapter 29.

Read the **Document** "Amrita Lal Roy, *English Rule in India, 1886*" on **MyHistoryLab.com**

The mutinous sepoy cavalry attacking a British infantry division at the Battle of Cawnpore in 1857. Although the uprising was suppressed, it was not easily forgotten. In its aftermath the British reorganized the government of India. The Granger Collection, New York

Document

GANDHI QUESTIONS THE VALUE OF ENGLISH CIVILIZATION

Mohandas Karamchand Gandhi (1869–1948), best known by the honorific Mahatma Gandhi, was a leader of the anticolonial movement in India, and one of the principle theorists of nonviolent resistance. His most important work, Hind Swaraj *(1910), advocated self-rule for India. In it, he outlined both a criticism of modern civilization and what he considered should rightly be the "canonical aims of life." In particular, he criticized modern civilization's separation of bodily and spiritual welfare, and its concentration on the former at the expense of the latter. Gandhi translated the original text, written in his native Gujarati, into English himself, intending for it to be read throughout the British empire.*

On what grounds does Gandhi criticize modern European (and more specifically British) civilization? What sort of image does he paint of the past? What does he suggest are the greatest values in life? Are they compatible with civilization? What are the political implications of this attitude for Indian politics during the colonial period? Europeans often used women's subjugation as an excuse to intervene in non-European states and societies. How does Gandhi turn this line of reasoning on its head?

Let us first consider what state of things is described by the word 'civilisation.' Its true test lies in the fact that people living in it make bodily welfare the object of life. The people of Europe today live in better built houses than they did a hundred years ago. This is considered an emblem of civilisation, and this is also a matter to promote bodily happiness. Formerly, they wore skins, and used as their weapons spears. Now they wear long trousers, and for embellishing their bodies, they wear a variety of clothing, and, instead of spears, they carry with them revolvers. . . . If people of a certain country, who have hitherto not been in the habit of wearing much clothing, boots, etc., adopt European clothing, they are supposed to have become civilised out of savagery. . . . Formerly, when people wanted to fight with one another, they measured between them their bodily strength; now it is possible to take away thousands of lives by one man working behind a gun from a hill. This is civilization. Formerly, men worked in the open air only as much as they liked. Now thousands of workmen meet together and for the sake of maintenance work in factories or mines. Their condition is worse than that of beasts. They are obliged to work, at the risk of their lives, at most dangerous occupations, for the sake of millionaires. Formerly, men were made slaves under physical compulsion. Now they are enslaved by temptation of money and of luxuries that money can buy. Formerly, people had two or three meals consisting of home-made bread and vegetables; now, they require something to eat every two hours so that they have hardly leisure for anything else. . . . These are all true tests of civilization. . . . Even a child can understand that in all I have described above there can be no inducement to morality. Civilisation seeks to increase bodily comforts, and it fails miserably even in doing so.

This civilization is irreligion, and it has taken such a hold on the people in Europe that those who are in it appear to be half mad. They lack real physical strength or courage. They keep up their energy by intoxication. They can hardly be happy in solitude.

Women, who should be the queens of households, wander in the streets or they slave away in factories. For the sake of a pittance, half a million women in England alone are labouring under trying circumstances in factories or similar institutions. This awful fact is one of the causes of the daily growing suffragette movement.

This civilization is such that one has only to be patient and it will be self-destroyed. . . . Civilization is not an incurable disease, but it should never be forgotten that the English are at present afflicted by it.

From M. K. Gandhi, *Hind Swaraj and Other Writings*, Centenary Edition, edited by Anthony Parel (Cambridge, UK: University of Cambridge Press, 2009), pp. 34–37.

The "New Imperialism," 1870–1914

Whereas in the first three-quarters of the nineteenth century Britain had largely dominated the world stage, between 1870 and 1914 other Western powers undertook colonial ventures with remarkable results. During this half-century, Western nations including the United States and Japan, which had industrialized and modernized its government and armed forces along Western lines between the 1860s and the 1880s, achieved unprecedented influence and control over the rest of the world and provoked intense colonial rivalries with each other. Between 1870 and 1900, Western states spread their control over some 10 million square miles and 150 million people—about one-fifth of the world's land area and one-tenth of its population. During this period, imperial expansion went forward with great speed, and empire was regarded as necessary for a great power. Because of the numerous actors, the speed, the extent, and the many nations involved, historians regard this era as constituting a "New Imperialism" that was different from the imperialism of the early nineteenth century. New Imperialism is a term of convenience that covered many diverse and even conflicting actions, ideas, and activities.

Watch the **Video** "New Imperialism" on **MyHistoryLab.com**

Why were the imperial encounters of this era perceived to be "new"? First, they were more intentionally imperial and involved direct political and administrative control of non-Westerners by the Western powers. With a few notable exceptions, including Western influence over China and European and American economic dominance in Latin America, free-trade imperialism and informal empire were abandoned. In their place arose a variety of devices for formal empire or imperial control through **protectorates** and **spheres of influence**. In a protectorate a Western nation placed officials in a foreign state to oversee its government without formally assuming responsibility for administration. In other instances, a European state, the United States, or Japan established "spheres of influence" in which it received special commercial and legal privileges in part of an Asian or African state without direct political involvement. These late-century imperial changes encompassed the British Crown taking over direct administration of India, the British and French establishing protectorates over Egypt and Tunisia, respectively, the establishment of direct French rule in Vietnam, the division of Africa into colonies ruled by half a dozen European powers, the division of Persia (Iran) into Russian- and British-dominated zones, Japanese annexation of Korea and Taiwan, and the United States annexing Hawaii and taking control of the Philippines from Spain.

Second, the New Imperialism occurred over a relatively brief period and involved an unprecedented number of nations. In addition to the older imperial powers—Britain, France, Russia, the Netherlands, Spain, and Portugal—the newly united Germany and Italy and the

President Theodore Roosevelt at the controls of a steam shovel during construction of the Panama Canal in 1906. The Panama Canal serves as an example of U.S. imperialist ventures in the Western Hemisphere. Library of Congress

Belgian monarchy, which had only existed since 1830, sought to achieve empires as did the United States and Japan.

Third, virtually none of the numerous imperial ventures of this era involved significant numbers of immigrants as settlers. Rather, Westerners came to govern directly or indirectly vast numbers of non-European peoples. Fourth, during these decades Europeans at home and in colonial settings exhibited a cultural confidence and racial arrogance that marked a departure from previous eras when many persons associated with European empires esteemed indigenous cultures or assumed that these cultures could be raised on the ladder of civilization. (See the Document "Social Darwinism and Imperialism,." page 759.) Fifth, despite its worldwide scope and especially the establishment of French rule in Indochina, the New Imperialism focused to an unprecedented degree on Africa, with the European powers partitioning Africa among themselves. The boundaries they established still determine Africa's political divisions.

Read the **Document** "Karl Pearson, 'Social Darwinism and Imperialism' " on **MyHistoryLab.com**

Two other points should be noted about the New Imperialism. First, the actual number of Westerners involved in carrying it out was relatively small. Except for soldiers and sailors, only a few thousand administrators, merchants, and missionaries were associated with empire. Second, the empires created by the New Imperialism were short-lived, in most cases lasting less than a century.

▼ Motives for the New Imperialism

Because the New Imperialism cast such a long shadow over colonial peoples during the twentieth century and beyond, historians and politicians have fiercely debated its character and motives. These disputes have often reflected debates over the relationship of the West to the non-Western world. The debates also embody the capacity for self-criticism and self-questioning that has marked Western civilization since the ancient Greeks.

Until the mid-twentieth century, the predominant interpretation of the motives for the New Imperialism was economic. This view originated in a book titled *Imperialism: A Study* published in 1902 by English economist and journalist J. A. Hobson (1858–1940). Hobson had opposed Britain's conquest of the Dutch-speaking, white-ruled Afrikaner republics in South Africa during the Boer War (1899–1902), which he blamed on the influence of capitalists and bankers. He saw the same influences behind the imperialist ambitions of other European states. According to Hobson, capitalist economies overproduced, which caused manufacturers, bankers, and financiers to press governments into imperial ventures to provide new markets for their excess goods and capital. Hobson declared, "Thus we reach the conclusion that Imperialism is the endeavor of our great controllers of industry to broaden the channel for the flow of their surplus weal by seeking foreign markets and foreign investments to take off the goods and capital they cannot sell or use at home."[2] Hobson, who was a radical but not a Marxist critic of capitalism, believed that European economies should be restructured to make imperialism as he understood it unnecessary.

In 1916 Lenin adopted and modified Hobson's ideas in his book *Imperialism, the Highest Stage of Capitalism*. There Lenin maintained, "Imperialism is the monopoly stage of capitalism," the last stage of a dying system.[3] He argued that competition inevitably eliminates inefficient capitalists and therefore leads to monopoly. Powerful industrial and financial capitalists soon run out of profitable investments in their own countries and persuade their governments to gain colonies in "less developed" countries. Here they can find higher profits, new markets for their products, and safe sources of raw materials. For Lenin, as we saw in Chapter 23, capitalism could not be reformed. Revolution was needed. Lenin's concept of imperialism after the Russian Revolution of 1917 became dogma in the Soviet Bloc and influenced the thinking of Marxist historians in Western countries for decades.

Read the **Document** "Vladimir Lenin, *Imperialism, the Highest Stage of Capitalism*" on **MyHistoryLab.com**

Hobson and Lenin presumed that something inherent in the economic and political character of capitalist states caused them to undertake imperial ventures. Each writer developed a broad theory about the New Imperialism that was based on their need to support their own political agenda—opposition to the Boer War for Hobson and the necessity for revolution for Lenin.

The history of the Western imperial advance, as we will see in subsequent sections of this chapter, does not support the theories of Hobson and Lenin. European powers did invest considerable capital abroad and did seek markets, but not in a way that fits the Hobson-Lenin model. Britain, for example, made heavier investments abroad before 1875, when it was not actively acquiring new colonies, than during the next two decades when it was expanding its empire. Only a small percentage of British and European overseas investments, moreover, went to their new colonies. Most capital went into other European countries or to older, well-established states like the United States and Argentina and to the settler colonies of Canada, Australia, and New Zealand. Even when Western countries did invest in new colonies, they often did not invest in their own colonies.

[2] J. A. Hobson, *Imperialism: A Study* (London: James Nisbet, 1902), p. 85, as quoted in H. L. Wesseling, *The European Colonial Empires* (London: Longman, 2004), p. 129.

[3] V. I. Lenin, *Imperialism, the Highest Stage of Capitalism* (New York: International Publishers, 1939), p. 88.

The facts are equally discouraging for those who try to explain the New Imperialism by emphasizing the need for markets and raw materials. While some European businesspeople and politicians hoped that colonial expansion would cure the great depression of 1873 to 1896, few colonies were important markets for the great imperial nations. All these states were forced to rely on areas that they did not control as sources of vital raw materials. It is not even clear that control of the new colonies was particularly profitable, with the notable exception of India. Nevertheless, as one of the leading students of the subject has said, "No one can determine whether the accounts of empire ultimately closed with a favorable cash balance."[4] That is true of the European imperial nations collectively, but it is certain that for some of them, like Italy and Germany, empire was a losing proposition. Some individuals (such as King Leopold II of the Belgians in the Congo) and companies, of course, made great profits from particular colonial ventures, but such people and firms were not always able to influence national policy. Economics certainly played a part, but a full understanding of the New Imperialism requires a search for other motives as well.

At the time, advocates of imperialism justified it in various ways. Some, embracing what they called the **"civilizing mission,"** argued that the European nations had a duty to bring the benefits of their higher culture and superior civilization to "backward" peoples. Religious groups demanded that Western governments support Christian missionaries politically and even militarily. Some politicians and diplomats supported imperialism as a tool of social policy. In Germany, for instance, conservative nationalists hoped that imperial expansion would deflect public interest away from demands for social reform. Yet Germany acquired few colonies, and such considerations played little, if any, role in its colonial policy. In Britain, Joseph Chamberlain (1836–1914), the colonial secretary from 1895 to 1903, argued for the empire as a source of profit and economic security that would finance a great program of domestic reform, but he made these arguments well after Britain had acquired most of its empire. Another apparently plausible justification for imperialism was that colonies would attract a European country's surplus population. But most continental European emigrants went to the Americas and Australia, areas their home countries did not control.

Read the **Document** "Arthur James Balfour, 'Problems with Which We Have to Deal in Egypt,' 1910" on **MyHistoryLab.com**

Three motives seem to have strongly influenced the imperial policies of each of the major European nations.

First, after 1870, many political leaders came to believe that the possession of colonies or of imperial influence was an important and even necessary characteristic of a great European power. Here they were clearly following the British example. By the 1880s French politicians believed that colonies could compensate for France's loss of prestige and territory in the Franco–Prussian War of 1870–1871. Similar motives drove Russia's advance into Asia following its defeat in the Crimean War (1854–1856). As a result, vast French and Russian empires were created. Two newly created European states also embraced imperial ventures: Italy believed it must secure colonies to prove that it was a great power but did so with only modest success; Germany created a more significant, if short-lived, empire. The United States at the time of the Spanish-American War in 1898 also came to believe that possession of colonies was essential to its world status. So did Japan, which became a major imperial power in Asia, acquiring Taiwan in 1895 after defeating China and annexing the independent kingdom of Korea in 1910.

Second, much of the territorial acquisitions associated with the New Imperialism as well as subsequent Western involvement in the Middle East arose in anticipation of the decay of the Ottoman Empire (see Chapter 22). In European diplomacy this became known as the Eastern Question. The Ottoman Empire at its height in the seventeenth century had extended from Algeria to the Balkans, Mesopotamia, and the Arabian Peninsula. Throughout the nineteenth century, however, the Ottoman government in Istanbul slowly but steadily lost province after province to Western powers or nationalist revolts. European powers were anxious that their rivals might profit from the weakness of the Ottoman Empire, and became directly involved in both precipitating and trying to control the course of the loss of Ottoman authority. Tension between the Russian and Austrian empires over former Ottoman territory in the Balkans, for example, provided the catalyst of the outbreak of World War I, and the turmoil that has characterized much of the Middle East since 1945 originated in the collapse of Ottoman power in that area.

Western powers exploited similar weakness in the Qing dynasty in China to ensure access to Chinese markets and resources and to protect foreign nationals working in China, including missionaries. Mutual rivalries, however, prevented the imperial powers from carving up China into actual colonies until Japan attempted to conquer the country in the 1930s (see Chapter 28).

Third, the geopolitical assumptions of European statesmen led them to deeper and deeper involvements from the eastern Mediterranean to Africa. European powers often intruded into other regions of the world to protect what they regarded as their strategic interest and then had to decide how to manage the necessity of administering them.

One final comment should be made about the motives for the New Imperialism. Western governments

[4]D. K. Fieldhouse, *The Colonial Empires* (New York: Delacorte, 1966), p. 393.

THE FRENCH IN MOROCCO

MANY IMPERIALISTS—EUROPEAN, American, and Asian—claimed altruistic motives for their acquisition of colonies. The French took pride in bringing "French civilization" to the lands France ruled. This cover of a magazine appeared in November 1911, the year when the French decision to extend and tighten their control of Morocco sparked an international crisis. It illustrates (literally) how France justified its colonial empire as a "mission civilisatrice," a vocation to bring civilization to "backward" peoples.

The central figure on the cover is a shining Marianne, the symbol of the French Republic, carrying a horn of plenty from which gold coins spill out. Marianne is far larger than the Moroccans, who look at her in wonder and admiration at the benefits that French rule will bring.

The illustration reveals the arrogance of such imperial pretensions. In the top right-hand corner, a French officer in a pith helmet gives orders to a saluting African soldier.

The message at the bottom of the page says, "France will be able to freely bring civilization, prosperity, and peace to Morocco."

Le Petit Journal

5 CENT. SUPPLÉMENT ILLUSTRÉ 5 CENT.

DIMANCHE 19 NOVEMBRE 1911

LA FRANCE VA POUVOIR PORTER LIBREMENT AU MAROC LA CIVILISATION LA RICHESSE ET LA PAIX

The Granger Collection, New York

What is the intended audience for this image?

How does this image of the effect of French imperialism serve France's domestic political interests?

What are the trappings of civilization emphasized in this image?

COMPARE AND CONNECT Two Views of Turn-of-the-Twentieth-Century Imperial Expansion

Read the Compare and Connect on MyHistoryLab.com

THROUGHOUT THE AGE of the most active European expansion, political and popular opinion was divided over whether imperialism was desirable and morally right for the major European powers. Gustav Schmoller, a German political economist, sets forth the argument in favor of imperial expansion about 1900; four years later French socialist novelist Anatole France attacked imperialism.

QUESTIONS

1. **What are the characteristics that Schmoller ascribes to other contemporary imperial powers?**
2. **What are the benefits Schmoller sees arising from colonies?**
3. **Why does France equate imperialism with barbarism?**
4. **Why does France believe that virtually no benefits result from imperialism?**
5. **How could writers looking at the European imperial enterprise come to such different conclusions about it? What values inform the views of each writer?**

I. Gustav Schmoller Makes the Case for German Imperial Expansion

Gustav Schmoller (1838–1917) was a highly respected German economist and active political figure who served in the Prussian Privy Council and as a member of the Upper Chamber in the Prussian Diet. In this lecture from around the turn of the century, Schmoller presents Germany as surrounded on the world scene by aggressive imperial powers. He argues that Germany must imitate them and create its own strong navy and overseas empire. Note the importance he attached to the victory of the United States in the Spanish-American War and the manner in which he portrays Spain as an unsuccessful imperial power.

In various States, arrogant, reckless, cold-blooded daring bullies, men who possess the morals of a captain of pirates . . . push themselves more and more forward into the Government. . . . We must not forget that it is in the freest States, England and North America, where the tendencies of conquest, Imperial schemes, and hatred against new economic competitors are growing up amongst the masses. The leaders of these agitations are great speculators, who have the morals of a pirate, and who are at the same time party leaders and Ministers of State. . . . The conquest of Cuba and the Philippines by the United States alters their political and economical basis. Their tendency to exclude Europe from the North and South American markets must needs lead to new great conflicts. . . . These bullies, these pirates and speculators *à la* Cecil Rhodes, act like poison within their State. They buy the press, corrupt ministers and the aristocracy, and bring on wars for the benefit of a bankrupt company or for the gain of filthy lucre. . . . We mean to extend our trade and industries far enough to enable us to live and sustain a growing population. We mean to defend our colonies, and, if possible, to acquire somewhere agricultural colonies. We mean to prevent extravagant mercantilism everywhere, and to prevent the division of the earth among the three world powers, which would exclude all other countries and destroy their trade. In order to attain this modest gain we require to-day so badly a large fleet. The German Empire must become the centre of a coalition of States, chiefly in order to be able to hold the balance in the death-struggle between Russia and England, but that is only possible if we possess a stronger fleet than that of today. . . . We must wish that at any price a German country, peopled by twenty to thirty million Germans, should grow up in Southern Brazil. Without the possibility of energetic proceedings on the part of Germany our future over there is threatened. . . . We do not mean to press for an economic alliance with Holland, but if the Dutch are wise, if they do not want to lose their colonies someday, as Spain did, they will hasten to seek our alliance. ■

Source: Gustav Schmoller lecture of about 1900, quoted in J. Ellis Barker, *Modern Germany: Her Political and Economic Problems, Her Foreign and Domestic Policy, Her Ambitions, and the Causes of Her Success*, 2nd ed. (London: Smith, Elder, & Co., 1907), pp. 139–140.

II. Anatole France Denounces Imperialism

Anatole France (1844–1924) was a famous late-century French novelist who was also active in the French socialist movement. Many socialists across Europe criticized the imperial ventures of their governments. In this passage France provides both a moral and a utilitarian critique of French imperialism around the world. He associates it with ambitious military figures, greedy businessmen, and corrupt politicians. He also contends that it brings nothing of value to France. Critiques of similar character appeared among other liberal, socialist, and radical politicians and political commentators across Europe and also in the United States. Criticism of imperialism of this character would continue until the close of the colonial age during the last quarter of the twentieth century. Notice that like Schmoller, France sees imperialism as something characterizing all the major powers.

Imperialism is the most recent form of barbarism, the end of the line for civilization. I do not distinguish between the two terms—imperialism and barbarism—for they mean the same thing.

We Frenchmen, a thrifty people, who see to it that we have no more children than we are able to support easily, careful of adventuring into foreign lands, we Frenchmen who hardly ever leave our own gardens, for what in the world do we need colonies? What can we do with them? What are the benefits for us? It has cost France much in lives and money so that the Congo, Cochinchina, Annam, Tonkin, Guinea, and Madagascar may be able to buy cotton from Manchester, liquors from Danzig, and wine from Hamburg. For the last seventy years France has attacked and persecuted the Arabs so that Algeria might be inhabited by Italians and Spaniards!

The French people get nothing from the colonial lands of Africa and Asia. But their government finds it profitable. Through colonial conquest the military people get promotions, pensions, and awards, in addition to the glory gained by quelling the natives. Shipowners, army contractors, and shady politicians prosper. The ignorant mob is flattered because it believes that an overseas empire will make the British and Germans green with envy.

Will this colonial madness never end? I know well that nations are not reasonable. Considering their composition, it would be strange, indeed, if they were. But sometimes they know instinctively what is bad for them. Through long and bitter experience they will come to see the mistakes they have made. And, one day, they will realize that colonies bring only danger and ruin. ■

Arrival in Saigon of Paul Beau (1857–1927), governor general of Indo-China 1902–1907, from *Le Petit Journal*, November 1902.

Arrival in Saigon of Paul Beau (1857–1927), Governor General of Indo-China 1902–07, from 'Le Petit Journal', November 1902 (colour engraving), Dufresne, Charles Georges (1876–1938)/Private Collection/Archives Charmet/The Bridgeman Art Library

Source: Anatole France, "The Colonial Folly," (1904), as quoted in Louis L. Snyder, *The Imperialism Reader: Documents and Readings on Modern Expansionism* (New York: D. Van Nostrand Company, Inc., 1962), pp. 155–156.

often found themselves reacting to events on the spot rather than determining an action in advance. In one region after another, a colonial administrator, military commander, group of missionaries, or business concern would act without prior authorization from the governments in Europe. This then created a situation to which those governments had to respond and often led to greater involvement in an area than European governments had ever wanted or intended. (See "Compare and Connect: Two Views of Turn-of-the-Twentieth-Century Imperial Expansion," pages 794–795.)

▼ The Partition of Africa

For almost fifty years inter-European rivalries played out in regions far away from Europe itself and nowhere more intensely than in Africa. During the so-called "Scramble for Africa," which occurred between the late 1870s and about 1912, the European powers sought to maximize their strategic control of African territory, markets, and raw materials. Motivated by intense competition, the imperial powers eventually divided almost the entire continent among themselves (see Map 25–2). The short- and long-term consequences were devastating for the Africans. Among the long-term effects was that European control forcibly integrated largely agrarian African societies into the modern world industrial economy. In the process, new forms of agrarian production, market economies, social organizations, political structures, and religious allegiances emerged that would form the basis for the postcolonial African nations (see Map 25–3, p. 798).

The European partition of Africa was not based on a universal policy, and each power acquired and administered its new possessions in different ways. Their goals, however, were the same: to gain control, or at least dominance, through diplomacy or force and then either to place Europeans directly in charge of administering the territories or to compel local rulers to accept European "advisers" who would exercise real authority.

Algeria, Tunisia, Morocco, and Libya

France left the Congress of Vienna in 1815 with only a few small colonies and trading posts. For a time French popular opinion seems to have resisted further colonial ventures. Then in 1830, as we saw in Chapter 20, the government of Charles X (r. 1824–1830) launched a military expedition against Algiers. Following the Revolution of 1830, which deposed Charles, France did not pull back from Algeria. French governments saw Algeria's fertile coastal regions as providing land for a settler colony. By 1871, more than 275,000 French settlers lived there. Over the decades, France pushed beyond the coast into the Sahara Desert where its forces established their authority over various nomadic Muslim peoples. The French came to regard Algeria as an integral part of France, and the European inhabitants there were French citizens who elected representatives to the parliament in Paris. Civilian French officials administered the coastal districts of Algeria, where most of the Europeans lived, as if they were part of France itself. Algeria was the most important portion of the French Empire, and it was the part of Africa that a European nation most fully and directly ruled.

In 1881–1882, the French also established a protectorate over Tunisia, which was nominally a province of the Ottoman Empire, and then between 1901 and 1912, set up another protectorate in Morocco. In both Tunisia and Morocco, the French retained the local rulers as puppet monarchs.

Italy, having failed to conquer Ethiopia in 1896, seized Libya from Turkey in 1911–1912, establishing its most important colony. These French and Italian colonial advances in North Africa demonstrated the profound weakness of the Ottoman Empire. Thus, by the outbreak of World War I, all of North Africa lay under some form of European control. In each of these cases a Western power dominated a largely Muslim population.

Egypt and British Strategic Concern about the Upper Nile

Like Tunisia, Egypt, the richest and most populous region of North Africa, was a semi-independent province of the Ottoman Empire under the hereditary rule of a Muslim dynasty. After the failed Napoleonic invasion in 1798, the Khedives, as Egyptian rulers were titled, had tried to modernize Egypt by building new harbors, roads, and a modern army. Egypt also sought to expand its rule into the Sudan. To pay for these projects, the Khedives borrowed money from European creditors. To earn the money to repay these loans, they forced farmers to plant cash crops, particularly cotton, which could be sold on the international market. This proved a mixed blessing. When cotton prices were high, for example, during the American Civil War (1861–1865), which cut off supplies of cotton from the southern states to British and French mills, the Egyptian economy boomed, and government revenues soared. When cotton prices fell, as they did after the Civil War, so did Egyptian revenue. The Egyptian government became utterly dependent on European creditors for new loans at exorbitant rates of interest. The construction of the Suez Canal was the final blow to Egypt's finances.

The Suez Canal, as we saw in Chapter 22, was opened in 1869. Built by French engineers with European capital, it was one of the most remarkable engineering feats of the day. The canal connected the Mediterranean to the Red Sea, which meant that ships from Europe no longer had to sail around Africa to reach Asia. In particular, the canal reduced the shipping distance from India to Britain from about 12,000 miles to 7,000 miles. The canal increased the speed of international contacts and, by reducing shipping costs, made many goods

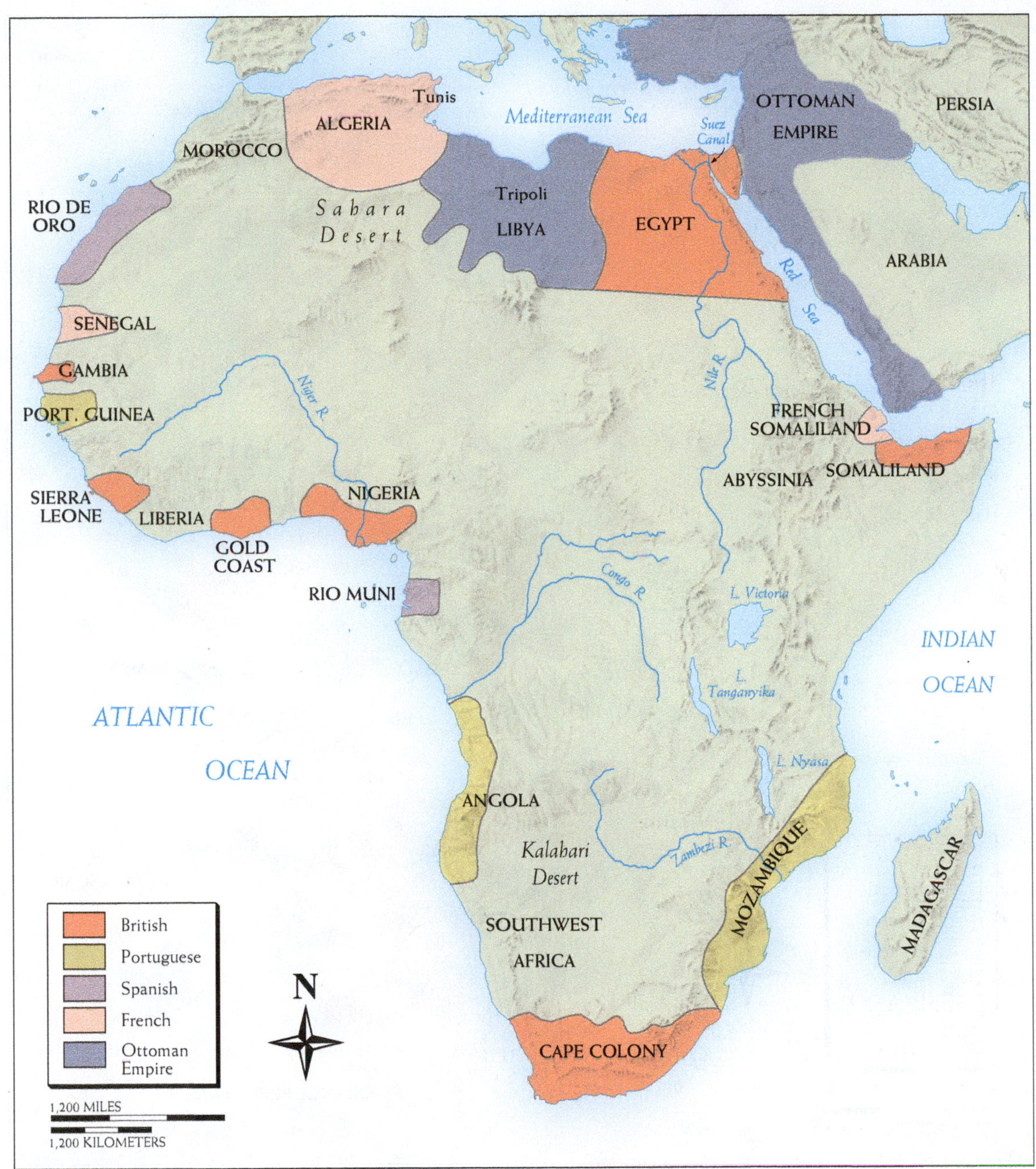

Map 25–2 **IMPERIAL EXPANSION IN AFRICA TO 1880** Until the 1880s, few European countries held colonies in Africa, mostly on its fringes.

on the world market more affordable. India thus became an even more important market for British goods. Yet the tangible benefits to Egypt itself were not immediately clear. By 1875, the Khedive was bankrupt, and that year Prime Minister Benjamin Disraeli purchased the Khedive's shares in the canal to give the British government a controlling interest in its management. Egypt's European creditors were taking more than 50 percent of Egyptian revenue each year to repay their loans, and they forced the Egyptian government to increase taxes to raise more revenue. This provoked a nationalist rebellion, and, in 1881, the Egyptian army took over the government to defend Egypt from foreign exploitation. An uncooperative, nationalist Egypt was, however, not in the interests of the European powers. So Britain in 1882 sent a fleet and army to Egypt that easily defeated the Egyptians and established seventy years of British supremacy in the country. A European power was thus drawn into the Middle East as never before.

View the **Image** "Disraeli Purchasing Controlling Interest in the Suez Canal" on **MyHistoryLab.com**

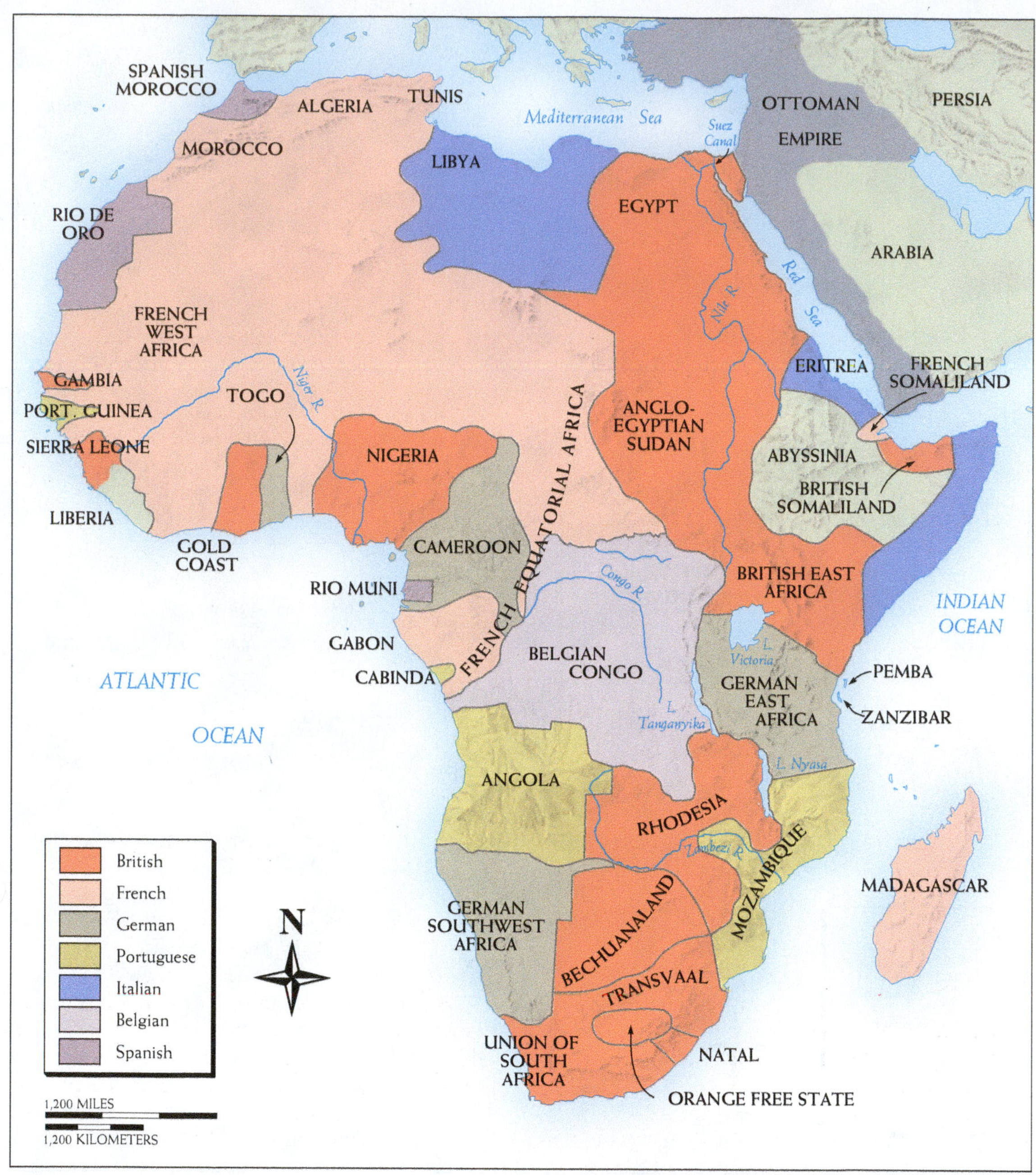

Map 25–3 **PARTITION OF AFRICA, 1880–1914** Before 1880, the European presence in Africa was largely the remains of early exploration by old imperialists and did not penetrate the heart of the continent. By 1914, the occupying powers included most large European states; only Liberia and Abyssinia (Ethiopia) remained independent.

Egypt was never an official part of the British Empire. The Khedives, who became kings after Egypt severed its ties with Turkey during World War I, continued to reign, but a small number of British officials dominated the Egyptian administration. The British used their experience "advising" the Indian princes to run Egypt behind the facade of the Khedive's government.

Britain's primary goal in Egypt was political and military stability. Egypt had to repay its debts, and Britain was to retain control of the Suez Canal. The British built a naval base at Alexandria and installed a large garrison in Cairo. They established municipal governments that were responsible for taxation and public services and further expanded cotton cultivation. They also prevented the Egyptians from establishing a textile industry that would compete with Britain's own mills.

Economically, this meant that while the Egyptian economy grew and tax revenues increased, per capita

The opening of the Suez Canal in 1869, linking Asia and Europe, was a major engineering achievement. It also became a major international waterway, reducing the distance from London to Bombay by half. The Inauguration Procession of the Suez Canal at El-Guisr in 1865, from 'Voyage Pittoresque a travers l'Isthme de Suez' by Marius Fontane, engraved by Jules Didier (1831–c.80) 1869–70 (colour litho), Riou, Edouard (1833–1900)/Bibliotheque des Arts Decoratifs, Paris, France/Archives Charmet/ The Bridgeman Art Library

income actually declined among Egyptians, most of whom were peasants who owned little or no land. Politically, it led to the growth of Egyptian nationalism, to Islamic militancy, and to demands that the British leave Egypt. Egyptian Islamic militants, organized into the Muslim Brotherhood in the late 1920s, would provide many of the anti-Western ideas that inspire radical Islam today.

The British occupation of Egypt quickly drew Britain even deeper into Africa along the Nile. Control of the upper Nile had been understood to be essential to the security of Egypt since ancient times. The collapse of the Khedive's authority in Cairo in 1881 had led to a similar collapse of Egyptian authority in the Sudan. In 1883 Muhammad Ahmad, a radical Muslim leader who claimed to be the Mahdi, a Muslim messiah, annihilated an Egyptian expeditionary force led by British officers. The British then sent General Charles Gordon to the Sudan, but Gordon, a hero in Britain, was killed in 1885 when the Mahdi's forces captured Khartoum, the Sudan's capital. The Mahdi himself died shortly thereafter, but his followers established a strict Islamic state. The Sudan remained in turmoil until 1898 when an Anglo-Egyptian army under General Sir Herbert, later Lord, Kitchener (1850–1916) conquered it in a remarkably violent campaign during which 11,000 Sudanese troops were killed and 16,000 were wounded by modern weaponry in a single battle at Omdurman. The British lost only 48 men in the battle. (See the Document "Winston Churchill Reports on the Power of Modern Weaponry," page 800.) The number of casualties at Omdurman would not be matched in a single day until European armies turned modern weapons upon each other during World War I.

The British determination to secure the upper Nile and the Sudan led to one of the major crises of the imperial age. Although the French had refused to participate when British forces invaded Egypt in 1882, they retained large investments there and still hoped to influence Egyptian affairs by controlling the upper Nile. In the summer of 1898, a small French military force from West Africa reached the upper Nile at an unimportant location called Fashoda. As Kitchener's forces moved south, he confronted the French. War seemed possible until Paris ordered the French to withdraw. Instead of fighting, France and Britain eventually resolved their imperial rivalries. France acquiesced in Britain's domination of Egypt, and Britain agreed to support French ambitions in Morocco. The peaceful resolution of the Fashoda incident and other imperial disputes was essential to the formation of the loose alliance called the Anglo-French Entente in 1904 and to the two countries fighting as allies in World War I.

West Africa

France could surrender hope of dominating Egypt because it already controlled much of sub-Saharan Africa. West Africa, in particular, was a key area for French imperialism. In 1895 French West Africa included 12 million inhabitants and was eight times larger than France itself.

The British had four West African colonies: Sierra Leone, which was originally a home for freed slaves, Gambia, the Gold Coast (now Ghana), and Nigeria, the largest and most populous black African colony that any European power possessed. British slavers had worked on the Nigerian coast during the eighteenth century, and

Document

WINSTON CHURCHILL REPORTS ON THE POWER OF MODERN WEAPONRY AGAINST AN AFRICAN ARMY

In 1898 an army of approximately 25,000 British and Egyptian troops led by General Sir Horatio Kitchener invaded the Sudan to reassert British control against the forces of Abdullah al-Taashi, a Muslim military leader who succeeded the Mahdi. The Sudanese troops were called dervishes. The British and Egyptians were armed with modern rifles, machine guns, and artillery and were accompanied by gunboats on the Nile River. The dervishes also had guns, but they were less advanced technologically. One of the largest battles in colonial history occurred on September 2, 1898, at Omdurman, near Khartoum, the capital of Sudan. The dervish force consisted of approximately 50,000 well-disciplined troops and cavalry. Within hours, however, they were routed because of the firepower advantage enjoyed by the British and Egyptian troops. Winston Churchill, who was serving in a cavalry regiment, later described the battle in a book on the war. Historians now believe more than 11,000 dervish troops died that day and approximately 16,000 were wounded while British casualties amounted to around 48 dead and fewer than 400 wounded. Observers at the time, as well as historians later, believed Kitchener used greater force and caused far more deaths and casualties than were necessary.

How does Churchill indicate his respect for the courage of the dervish forces? Why might the kind of warfare made possible by advanced weapons be termed "industrial warfare"? How does Churchill convey the fearfulness of this battle?

Great clouds of smoke appeared all along the front of the British and Soudanese brigades. One after another four batteries opened on the enemy at a range of about 3,000 yards. The sound of the cannonade rolled up to us on the ridge, and was re-echoed by the hills. Above the heads of the moving masses shells began to burst, dotting the air with smoke-balls and the ground with bodies. But a nearer tragedy impended. The 'White Flags' were nearly over the crest. In another minute they would become visible to the batteries. Did they realise what would come to meet them? . . . It was a matter of machinery. . . . In a few seconds swift destruction would rush on these brave men. . . . Forthwith the gunboats . . . and other guns . . . opened on them. . . . The white banners toppled over in all directions. . . . It was a terrible sight, for as yet they had not hurt us at all, and it seemed an unfair advantage to strike thus cruelly when they could not reply. . . .

The infantry fired steadily and stolidly, without hurry or excitement, for the enemy were far away and the officers careful. . . . The empty cartridge-cases, tinkling to the ground, formed a small but growing heap beside each man. And all the time out on the plain on the other side bullets were shearing through flesh, smashing and splintering bone; blood spouted from terrible wounds; valiant men were struggling on through a hell of whistling metal, exploding shells, and spurting dust—suffering, despairing, dying. . . .

. . . at the critical moment the gunboat arrived on the scene and began suddenly to blaze and flame from Maxim guns, quick-firing guns, and rifles. The range was short; the effect tremendous. The terrible machine, floating gracefully on the waters—a beautiful white devil—wreathed itself in smoke. . . .

. . . the great Dervish army, who had advanced at sunrise in hope and courage, fled in utter rout, pursued by the Egyptian cavalry, harried by the 21st Lancers, and leaving more than 9,000 warriors dead and even greater numbers wounded behind them.

Thus ended the battle of Omdurman—the most signal triumph ever gained by the arms of science over barbarians.

From Winston Spencer Churchill, *The River War: An Historical Account of the Reconquest of the Soudan*, ed. F. Rhodes, new rev. ed. (London: Longmans, Green, and Co., 1902), pp. 272–273, 274, 279, 300.

The battle of Omdurman, fought on September 2, 1898, and described in the Churchill feature on page 800, demonstrated the capacity of European forces armed with the most modern weapons—in this case, a British army composed of British, Egyptian, and Sudanese troops, commanded by Major General Sir Horatio Kitchener—to decimate a vast Sudanese force armed with less advanced weapons. In the battle, which occurred near Khartoum, the British encircled the Sudanese forces. Approximately 10,000 African warriors were killed, while British losses numbered forty-eight men. The 21st Lancers lead the battle against the Arab stronghold at Omdurman in 1897, Tacconi, Ferdinando (1922–2006). Private Collection/© Look and Learn/The Bridgeman Art Library International

Britain had moved steadily into the Nigerian interior since the 1840s, seeking to establish trade and acquire tropical products, especially palm oil and cotton. The British annexed the port of Lagos in 1861. Various British trading companies operated on the Niger River with the Royal Niger Company, the most important of them, founded in 1886. Over time the British established protectorates over the Muslim emirates in northern Nigeria and direct control over other areas. In 1914, they combined all these territories into a single administrative unit, which they called the colony of Nigeria. To prevent indigenous resistance, British officials ran the country through local rulers, a policy known as indirect rule. Nigeria also became one of the most successful regions for British missionaries and has one of the largest Christian populations in Africa.

The Belgian Congo

Perhaps the most remarkable story in the European scramble for Africa was the acquisition of the Belgian Congo. In the 1880s, the lands drained by the vast Congo River and its tributaries became the personal property of King Leopold II of Belgium (r. 1865–1909). As a young monarch, he had become determined that Belgium, despite its small territory, must acquire colonies. No doubt he was inspired by the great commercial wealth that the neighboring Netherlands had accumulated from its long history of trade and empire in the East Indies.

The Belgian government, however, had no interest in colonies. So despite being a constitutional monarch, Leopold used his own wealth and political guile to realize his colonial ambitions. He did so under the guise of humanitarian concern for Africans. In 1876, he gathered explorers, geographers, and antislavery reformers in Brussels and formed the International African Association. He then recruited English-born journalist and explorer Henry Morton Stanley (1841–1904) to undertake an expedition into the Congo. Stanley had previously made a great reputation by crossing Africa from east to west. Between 1879 and 1884, he explored the Congo and on Leopold's behalf made "treaties" with African rulers who had no idea what they were signing. Leopold then won diplomatic recognition for those treaties and for his own allegedly humanitarian efforts in the region, first from the United States and then in 1884–1885 from a conference in Berlin to allocate African territory among the European powers (see next section). The larger, stronger European states, particularly France, Britain, and Germany, were willing to let Leopold govern the Congo to keep one another out. Leopold, thus, personally became the ruler of an African domain that was over seventy times the size of Belgium.

View the **Image** "Belgian King Crushing the Congo Free State—Cartoon" on **MyHistoryLab.com**

Although Leopold cultivated the image of a humanitarian ruler by sponsoring antislavery conferences and manipulating public relations, his goal in the Congo was brutal economic exploitation. Leopold's administrators used slave labor, intimidation, torture, mutilation, and mass murder to extract rubber and ivory from what became known as the Congo Free State. Eventually, beginning with African American reporter George Washington Williams (1849–1891) and culminating with an international outcry led by English journalist E. D. Morel (1873–1924) and diplomat Roger Casement (1864–1916), Leopold's crimes were exposed, and he formally turned the Congo over to Belgium in 1908, the year before he died.

The cruelties in the Congo, which became the basis for Joseph Conrad's classic novel *Heart of Darkness* (1902), were recorded in photographs, eyewitness

Ivory was a prized possession used for decorative purposes and jewelry. Caravan with Ivory, French Congo, (now the Republic of the Congo). Robert Visser (1882–1894). c. 1890–1900, postcard, collotype. Publisher unknown, c. 1900. Postcard 1912. Image No. EEPA 1985-140792. Eliot Elisofon Photographic Archives. National Museum of African Art, Smithsonian Institution

accounts, and newspaper articles and by an official Belgian commission. The most responsible historical estimates suggest that Leopold's exploitation halved the population of the Congo in about thirty years. Millions of Africans were murdered or died from overwork, starvation, and disease.

German Empire in Africa

German chancellor Otto von Bismarck appears to have pursued an imperial policy, however briefly, from coldly political motives and with only modest enthusiasm. Bismarck had initially been dismissive of colonial ventures. By the mid-1880s, however, he had changed his mind. In 1884 and 1885, Germany declared protectorates over South-West Africa (today the country of Namibia), Togoland, and the Cameroons in West Africa, and Tanganyika in East Africa. None of these places was particularly valuable or strategically important. Bismarck acquired colonies chiefly to improve Germany's diplomatic position in Europe and to divert France into colonial expansion and away from hostility to Germany. He also used German colonial activities in Africa to pressure the British to be reasonable about European affairs.

Read the **Document** "Carl Peters, 'A Manifesto for German Colonization' " on **MyHistoryLab.com**

Bismarck called the Berlin Conference in 1884 (not to be confused with the Congress of Berlin, which sought to settle the Eastern Question in 1879). At the Berlin Conference the major European powers decided on a process of power-sharing in Africa that would eventually lead to the formal partition of nearly the entire continent. That was not, however, their intent. The diplomatic representatives sat in a room where a

PUNCH, OR THE LONDON CHARIVARI.—NOVEMBER 28, 1906.
IN THE RUBBER COILS.
SCENE—The Congo "Free" State.

In this 1906 cartoon, King Leopold II is depicted as a snake squeezing a Congolese rubber worker to death in his coils. In the background, a woman flees in horror, clutching a baby. Leopold's policies in Belgium led directly to the death of half of the native population of his territory in only thirty years. © Mary Evans Picture Library/Alamy large map of Africa hung on a wall, and that has led to a myth that they glanced at the map and divided up their interests in the continent. It is true that by 1890 almost all the continent had been parceled out. Great powers and small ones expanded into areas neither profitable nor strategic for reasons that were less calculating and rational than Bismarck's. But at the Berlin Conference itself, representatives of the assembled powers thought they were setting guidelines that would bring civilization, Christianity, and commerce to Africa without formal partitions. Just how mistaken they were would be revealed by the terrible fate of Congo in the hands of Leopold II.

Germany's proved to be the shortest lived of any of the European colonial ventures. German imperialism involved few Germans and produced no significant economic returns. At the end of World War I, the Allies stripped Germany of its colonial holdings. This meant that Germany was the only major West European state not drawn into the struggles of decolonization after World War II. But the German entry into the arena of imperial competition did contribute to the tensions that led to World War I (see Chapter 26). (See the Document "Gustav Scholler Makes the Case for German Imperial Expansion," page 794.)

Genocide in South-West Africa The German Empire lasted for only about three decades, but in that time German administrators carried out a major atrocity against indigenous peoples in German South-West Africa. The Germans had occupied the region because the British were not interested in it and because parts of it appeared suitable for settlement. As German administrators seized more land and used natives as virtual slave labor, resistance mounted and German settlers were killed.

In 1904 the Herero people in the colony revolted, and the Germans decided to take severe action. They announced that the Hereros had to leave their land, and German commander General Lothar von Trotha authorized the killing of all male Hereros. Germans drove Herero women and children into the desert. (See the Document "General von Trotha Demands that the Herero People Leave Their Land," page 804.) Herero prisoners were placed in concentration camps where the death rates from disease were high, although the Germans ran the camps with meticulous bureaucratic attention to detail. A United Nations report in 1985 concluded that by the time the Germans suppressed the revolt in 1908, 80 percent of the Herero population had died.

Southern Africa

Except for coastal Algeria, only South Africa had attracted large numbers of European settlers. The Dutch had begun to settle there in the mid-1600s. By 1800, Cape Town had become an important port for ships on their way to Asia. During the Napoleonic Wars the British captured Cape Town from the Dutch. Soon thereafter, British settlers began to arrive, and British economic and cultural influence soon predominated on the Cape. Even though the British abolished slavery throughout the empire in 1834, African workers at the Cape remained subject to strict discriminatory legislation.

Not unsurprisingly, the Dutch resented British control. During the 1830s and 1840s, the Boers or Afrikaners, as the descendants of the Dutch were known, undertook the **Great Trek** during which they moved north and east of the Cape. This migration became the key moment in the forging of Afrikaner national consciousness. They founded states outside British control that would become Natal, Transvaal, and the Orange Free State. During the Great Trek the Boers also fought the Zulu people, who were themselves building an empire over other Africans. In 1843 the British annexed Natal, but the other two Boer republics remained independent.

In 1886 gold was discovered in the Transvaal, and 50,000 miners rushed to Johannesburg. There were now more non-Boer white settlers in the Transvaal than Boers, but the government refused to allow non-Boers the right to vote. In 1895, Cecil Rhodes (1853–1902), prime minister of the Cape Colony, supported a conspiracy to install a British government in the Transvaal. The conspiracy failed and Rhodes was forced to resign, but tensions mounted between Britain and the Boers. In 1899 war broke out. Although the British finally won the Boer War in 1902, they were surprised by the strength of Boer resistance. When the Boers resorted to guerilla tactics, the British gathered Boer women and children into what they called **concentration camps** where many died from disease and exposure. (In the 1890s, the Spanish had also set up such camps when seeking to suppress a rebellion in Cuba.)

View the **Image** "The Boer War and Queen Victoria—Dutch Caricature" on **MyHistoryLab.com**

In 1910, the British combined the colonies in South Africa into a confederation whose constitution guaranteed the rule of the European minority over the majority black and nonwhite population. Africans and people of mixed race whom the British referred to as "colored" were forbidden to own land, denied the right to vote, and excluded from positions of power. To preserve their political power and economic privileges, the white elite of South Africa eventually enforced a policy of racial **apartheid**—"separateness"—that turned the country into a totally segregated land until the 1990s. The result was decades of oppression, racial tensions, and economic exploitation.

Document

GENERAL VON TROTHA DEMANDS THAT THE HERERO PEOPLE LEAVE THEIR LAND

In 1904 Germany moved to repress the Herero people of South-West Africa who were resisting German rule. General Lothar von Trotha was in charge of the campaign. During his war against the Herero, he issued the following proclamation, which displays the outlook that led him and his troops to undertake a campaign of genocide against the Herero. The campaign had already, through warfare, disease, and forcing women and children into the desert, killed many Herero.

How does this proclamation indicate frustration at the incapacity of the Germans to control the Herero? How might this proclamation support the charge of genocide? What assumptions about racial superiority might lie behind this proclamation?

I, the great general of the German soldiers, send this letter to the Herero people. Herero are no longer German subjects. They have murdered, stolen, cut off the ears, and noses and other body parts from wounded soldiers, and now out of cowardice refuse to fight. I say to the people: anyone delivering a captain to one of my stations as a prisoner will receive one thousand [German] marks. . . . The Herero people must leave this land. If they do not, I will force them to do so by using the great gun [artillery]. Within the German border every male Herero, armed or unarmed, with or without cattle, will be shot to death. I will no longer receive women or children but will drive them back to their people or have them shot. These are my words to the Herero people.

A German soldier guards Herero women and children in a prison camp in German South-West Africa in 1906. ullstein bild/The Granger Collection, NYC—All rights reserved

General Lothar von Trotha, Proclamation of October 2, 1904, as quoted in Isabel V. Hull, *Absolute Destruction: Military Culture and the Practices of War in Imperial Germany* (Ithaca, NY: Cornell University Press, 2005), p. 56.

Diamond mining in South Africa took off in the late 1860s. By 1880 Kimberly, the biggest mine in the region, had 30,000 people, second only to Cape Town. Whites monopolized the well-paid, skilled jobs, while black Africans undertook dangerous work in the mines. This photograph was taken around 1900, when the De Beers diamond mines employed nearly 4,000 people. © Chris Howes/Wild Places Photography/ Alamy

EXPANSION OF EUROPEAN POWER AND THE NEW IMPERIALISM

1869	Suez Canal completed
1875	Britain gains control of the Suez Canal
1879–1884	Leopold II establishes his personal rule in the Congo
1882	France controls Tunisia
1880s	Britain establishes protectorate over Egypt
1884–1885	Germany establishes protectorate over Southwest Africa (Namibia), Togoland, the Cameroons, and East Africa (Tanzania)
1895	Japan seizes Taiwan from China
1898	Spanish-American War: United States acquires Puerto Rico, Philippines, and Guam, annexes Hawaiian Islands, and establishes virtual protectorate over Cuba
1899	United States proposes Open Door Policy in Far East
1899–1902	Boer War in South Africa
1908	Belgium takes over the Congo from Leopold II
1905–1912	France establishes protectorate over Morocco
1910	Japan annexes Korea
1912	Italy conquers Libya from Turkey

▼ Russian Expansion in Mainland Asia

The British presence in India was intimately related to Russian expansion across mainland Asia in the nineteenth century, which eventually brought huge territories and millions of people of a variety of ethnicities and religions under tsarist rule. This expansion of Russian imperialism is one of the chief sources of tensions that exist today between the Russian Federation and Chechnya and other parts of the Caucasus.

During the early eighteenth century, the tsars had consolidated their control around the Baltic Sea. Catherine the Great (r. 1762–1796) had gained much of southern Ukraine and opened the regions around the Black Sea to Russian control at the cost of Ottoman influence. The partitions of Poland had extended Russian authority toward the west (see Chapter 17). During the nineteenth century the Russian government would look to the east where no major state could oppose its advance and where the weakness of the Ottoman Empire and China worked to Russian advantage.

Even during the eighteenth century, the tsarist government had ruled extremely diverse groups of people who were not Russian by language, religion, or cultural heritage. The Russians had generally approached these peoples in a pragmatic way, tolerating their religions and recognizing their social elites in exchange for loyalty to the tsar.

Beginning in the late eighteenth century, however, the tsarist government began to regard the nomadic societies or communities who lived in the mountainous regions to the south and east as "inorodtsy," meaning foreigners. Moreover, the government drew upon the Enlightenment four-stage theory of social development, discussed in Chapter 17, to distinguish sedentary peoples as superior to those who lived as hunters, gatherers, fishermen, or nomads. One of the purposes thereafter of Russian expansion was, like that of early Victorian British administrators in India, to raise these people on the ladder of civilization. Russian governors would henceforth rarely, if ever, consider conquered peoples to be their social or cultural equals.

The nineteenth century saw Russia extend its authority in three distinct areas of mainland Asia. The first was in the Transcaucasus. This expansion came at the cost of Persia and the Ottoman Empire. The tsarist government presented these conquests as moves to protect Christian Georgians and Armenians from Muslim rule. It never securely incorporated these regions into the Russian Empire because their elites were not willing to be co-opted. By the late nineteenth century, nationalist unrest was rising among Georgians, Armenians, and Azerbaijanis.

The Russians were also only modestly successful in subjugating the Muslim peoples living in the Caucasus regions of Chechnya, Dagestan, and Circassia. Between 1817 and 1865, the Russians had to fight a brutal guerilla war in these areas led by Imam Shamil (1797–1871). Once the Russian government had suppressed this resistance, it pursued its usual policy of seeking to gain the support of local aristocrats by recognizing their privileges and not disturbing their religion. Again this policy was only partially successful.

The second prong of Russian imperial advance occurred in the vast steppes of Central Asia where various nomadic peoples, including Kazakhs, lived.

The final area of Russian imperial conquest occurred in southern Middle Asia from the 1860s to the 1880s. (See the Document "The Russian Foreign Minister Explains the Imperatives of Expansion in Asia,." page 807.) This is the region of present-day Uzbekistan, Turkistan, and the areas bordering Afghanistan, all of which are primarily Muslim. Here the Russians established protectorates under the nominal authority of the local rulers known as khans. Expansion in this area followed Russia's defeat in the Crimean War and sought to demonstrate that Russia could still exert imperial influence in Asia and counter the British presence in India. The Russian-British rivalry over these regions, particularly over Afghanistan, became known in journalism and fiction as "the Great Game." It sometimes brought Russia and Britain to the edge of war until the early twentieth century when both powers became more concerned about German influence in the Ottoman Empire that they were about one another. The Anglo-Russian Convention of 1907 ended their Central Asian rivalry and gave each power spheres of influence in Persia. Like the settlement of colonial claims between Britain and France, the end of this particular imperial contest also opened the way for Britain and Russia to become allies against Germany during World War I.

Though the Russians largely subdued the Caucasus region by the 1860s—with a Muslim separatist movement led by Imam Shamil put down only after decades of struggle—the many ethnic groups of this rugged mountain region remained largely autonomous until well into the twentieth century. This photograph, most likely taken around 1890, shows a group of chain-clad warriors from the Khevsureti region of Georgia (which had been incorporated into the Russian Empire early in the nineteenth century). With their primitive firearms, swords, and shields, these fighting men may appear to be no match for mechanized firepower, but the people of this region nevertheless remained largely free of governmental authority until well into the twentieth century. Courtesy of the Library of Congress

▼ Western Powers in Asia

France in Asia

While merchants had established the British interest in India and South Asia, French interest in Indochina arose because of the activity of Roman Catholic missionaries. The French domain in Indochina eventually consisted of Vietnam, Cambodia, and Laos.

French missionaries had been active in Vietnam as early as the seventeenth century. However, with papal support, they gained ground in Indochina and elsewhere in Asia in the 1830s and 1840s. Persecution soon followed. In 1856, Napoleon III (r. 1852–1870), whose troops protected the Pope in Rome and whose wife was a fervent Roman Catholic, sent forces to Vietnam to protect the missionaries and give France a base from which the French navy could operate in the Far East and French commerce could expand in Asia. By 1862, French forces controlled Saigon and the area around it. By the 1880s, France controlled all of Vietnam and had made Cambodia a protectorate. In 1896, Laos also became a French protectorate. Missionary work continued throughout Indochina, especially in Vietnam where Catholics became and remain a significant minority.

Document

THE RUSSIAN FOREIGN MINISTER EXPLAINS THE IMPERATIVES OF EXPANSION IN ASIA

Prince Alexander M. Gorchakov (1798–1883) served as Russian foreign minister from 1856 to 1882. This was the period in which Russia conquered most of Central Asia. In this passage he justifies those conquests by asserting a Russian civilizing mission and strategic concerns. Note how he emphasizes what he regards as the superior civilization of Russia over the Asians it seeks to conquer.

How does Gorchakov equate semi-savage states with potential disorder? Why does he believe civilized states must move against the semi-savage states? How does he emphasize Russia's status as a great power by associating its problems and reasons for imperial conquest with those of other colonial nations?

The situation of Russia in Middle Asia is that of all civilized states which come into contact with semi-savage and itinerant ethnic groups without a structured social organization. In such a case the interest in the security of one's borders and in trade relations always makes it imperative that the civilized state should have a certain authority over its neighbors, who as a result of their wild and impetuous customs are very disconcerting. Initially it is a matter of containing their attacks and raids. In order to stop them, one is usually compelled to subjugate the adjoining ethnic groups more or less directly. Once this has been achieved, their manners become less unruly, though they in turn are now subjected to attacks by more distant tribes. The state is duty-bound to protect them against such raids, and punish the others for their deeds. From this springs the necessity of further protracted periodic expeditions against an enemy who, on account of his social order, cannot be caught. . . . For this reason the state has to decide between two alternatives. Either it must give up this unceasing work and surrender its border to continual disorder . . . or it must penetrate further and further into the wild lands . . . This has been the fate of all states which have come up against this kind of situation. The United States in America, France in Africa, Holland in its colonies, Britain in eastern India—all were drawn less by ambition and more by necessity along this path forwards on which it is very difficult to stop once one has started.

Prince Alexander M. Gorchakov, as quoted in Andreas Kappeler, *The Russian Empire: A Multiethnic History*, tr. Alfred Clayton (London: Longman, 2001), p. 194.

The United States' Actions in Asia, the Pacific, and Latin America

In 1853, a United States naval squadron under Commodore Matthew C. Perry (1794–1858) arrived in Japanese waters to open Japanese markets to American goods. In 1867, American interest in the Pacific again manifested itself when the United States bought Alaska from Russia. For the next twenty-five years, the United States assumed a fairly passive role in foreign affairs, but it had established its presence in the Pacific.

Cuba's revolt against Spain in the 1890s ended this passivity and provided the impetus for the creation of an American empire. Sympathy for the Cuban cause, investments on the island, the desire for Cuban sugar, and concern over Cuba's strategic importance all helped drive the United States to fight Spain.

Victory in the brief Spanish-American War of 1898 brought the United States an informal protectorate over Cuba, and the annexation of Puerto Rico ended four hundred years of Spanish rule in the Western Hemisphere. The United States also forced Spain to sell it the Philippines and Guam, while Germany bought the other Spanish islands in the Pacific. The United States and Germany divided Samoa between them. In 1898 the United States also annexed Hawaii, five years after an American-backed coup had overthrown the native Hawaiian monarchy. In 1903,

President Theodore Roosevelt supported United States efforts to acquire the rights to build and control the Panama Canal. When Colombia refused to ratify an agreement granting these rights to the United States, Roosevelt supported Panama's separation from Colombia. A treaty was subsequently signed with a representative of the new independent state of Panama, and the United States commenced building, using equipment purchased from an earlier French effort, in 1904. This burst of activity made the United States an imperial power. This status was confirmed when Roosevelt sent an American fleet around the world between 1907 and 1909 and when the U.S.-built Panama Canal opened in 1914.

The Boxer Rebellion

By the close of the nineteenth century, Western powers had forced the Chinese government to give them privileged status in Chinese markets. With the backing of their governments, Christian missionaries were operating in much of China. The Qing Dynasty, which had ruled China since 1644, was in a state of near collapse, and its decay both enabled Western penetration and was exacerbated by it.

The United States feared that the European powers and Japan would soon carve up China and close its lucrative markets and investment opportunities to American interests. In 1899, to prevent this, the United States proposed the Open Door Policy, which was designed to prevent formal foreign annexations of Chinese territory and to allow businesspeople from all nations to trade in China on equal terms. Although all the powers except Russia eventually agreed to this policy in principle, they nonetheless carved out spheres of influence in China, and France, Britain, Germany, and Russia established naval bases on the Chinese coast (see Map 25–4).

Although the Qing government was too feeble to resist Western bullying, hatred of foreigners and resentment at their presence were strong. From late 1899 through the autumn of 1901, a Chinese group called The Righteous and Harmonious Society of Fists, better known in the West as the Boxers, attempted to resist the Western incursions. The Boxers, who were supported by a faction at the Qing court, hated missionaries whom they saw as agents of the imperial powers and killed thousands of their Chinese converts.

For the imperial powers, the key moment in the Boxer Rebellion was the attacks on the foreign diplomatic missions in Beijing, which lasted off and on for three months in 1900 until an international army occupied the Chinese capital in August 1900. For the second time in less than half a century, Western troops had seized Beijing. In September 1901, the Chinese government agreed to execute officials who had helped the Boxers and pay large reparations to the Western powers and Japan.

The suppression of the Boxer Rebellion had demonstrated that even without formal empire Western powers could freely intervene in China. It set the stage for the collapse of the Qing dynasty in 1912 and opened China to decades of internal turmoil, foreign invasion, civil war, and eventually in 1949 a Communist Revolution.

In 1900, an international force composed of troops drawn from Austria-Hungary, the French Third Republic, the German Empire, Italy, Japan, Russia, the United Kingdom, and the United States invaded China to put down the Boxer Rebellion, which had endangered Western missionaries and Western interests in China. In August 1900 these forces occupied Beijing. This contemporary print presents the image of a romanticized heroic assault by these foreign troops. Courtesy of the Library of Congress

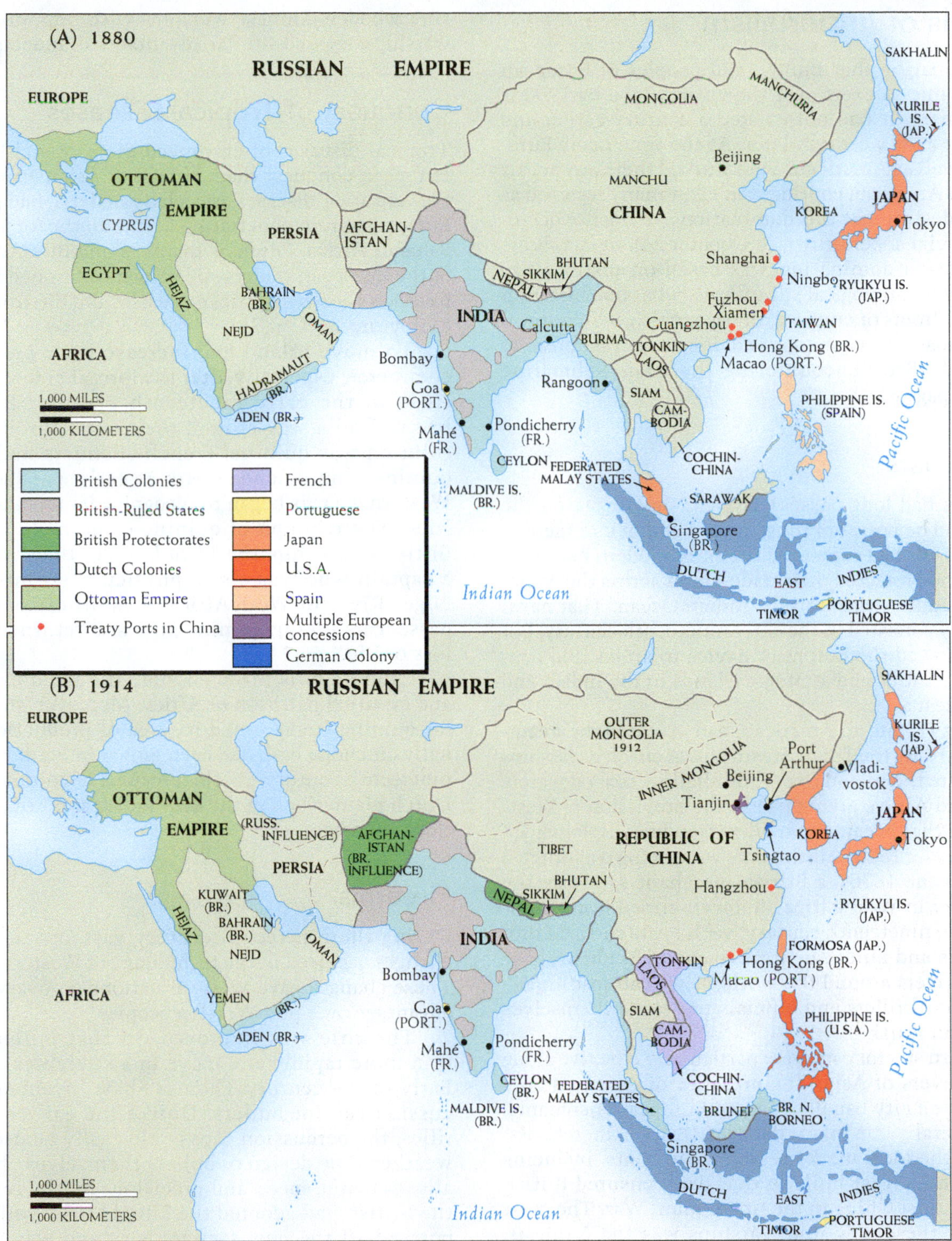

Map 25–4 **ASIA, 1880–1914** As in Africa, the decades before World War I saw imperialism spread widely and rapidly in Asia. Two new powers, Japan and the United States, joined the British, French, and Dutch in extending control both to islands and to the mainland and in exploiting an enfeebled China.

Tools of Imperialism

The domination that Europe and peoples of European descent came to exert over the entire globe by 1900 is extraordinary. It had not existed a century earlier and would not exist a century later. At the time many Europeans as well as Americans who worked their way across the North American continent in what many regarded as manifest destiny saw this domination as evidence of cultural or racial superiority (see Chapter 24). In fact, however, Western domination was based on distinct and temporary technological advantages, what one historian called the "tools of empire."[5] These tools gave Westerners the capacity to conquer and dominate vast areas of the world. (See "Encountering the Past: Submarine Cables,." page 811.)

Steamboats

Europeans had long possessed naval superiority on the high seas. The power of those navies and of commercial sailing vessels had supported the early modern European empires and protected their trade routes across the Atlantic and around Africa into the Indian Ocean. That naval superiority persisted in the early nineteenth century, but it only allowed the European navies to attack and control coastal cities and strategic islands in the Indian and Pacific Oceans.

Robert Fulton, an American, had invented the steamboat in 1807. By the 1830s, steam power enabled warships to penetrate the inland rivers and shallow coastal waters of Asia and Africa, giving rise to the projection of Western power that became known as "gunboat diplomacy."

By the late 1820s, steamboats were being constructed of iron. In the 1830s, a British merchant sailed up the Niger River in West Africa on a well-armed iron steamship. In the nineteenth century, such boats carried European goods and European arms to ensure trade in those goods up rivers around the world. It was almost impossible for local rulers and officials to defend themselves against iron warships.

Western steamboats were particularly effective along the vast rivers of Asia. The presence of gunboats on a river beside a city usually ensured European merchants, and, especially for many decades, British merchants, access to the local markets. Iron steamboats, including some of the largest built to that date, ensured British success against China in the first Opium War. The most famous of these new iron warships was the *Nemesis*, which was 184 feet long and employed two sixty-horsepower engines. This single ship armed with cannon and rockets was able to silence the guns of Chinese forts and sink wooden Chinese warships with impunity. French warships enjoyed similar advantages in Indochina.

Conquest of Tropical Diseases

Tropical diseases often proved more of an obstacle to European conquest than African or Asian armed forces. For centuries, diseases, especially malaria, had prevented Europeans from penetrating deep into the forests of sub-Saharan Africa. Often as many as one-third to one-half of the European traders and soldiers stationed in trading bases on the West African coast would die from disease each year.

To move inland and increase their profits from commerce, especially after the formal end of the slave trade in the early nineteenth century, Europeans had to find a way around the malaria problem. The solution was quinine. French chemists had isolated quinine from cinchona bark as early as 1820. Slowly Western doctors began to recognize its medicinal qualities. The triumph of quinine came in 1854 when a British steamship, the *Pleiad*, under the command of a captain who was also a physician, steamed up the Niger River in West Africa with all of its crew and passengers taking quinine pills and returned with no loss of life.

Quinine pills made possible the rapid exploration and eventual partition of Africa. Moreover, the demand for quinine transformed its area of production. Originally cinchona bark had been grown in Peru. By the late nineteenth century, its chief regions of cultivation were Dutch plantations in the East Indies and British plantations in India.

Firearms

During the nineteenth century vast and momentous changes occurred in the technology of Western firearms. These changes gave Western nations an overwhelming advantage over non-Western peoples.

The rifle was improved, so that bullets would spin more rapidly and move in a straighter direction. Early in the century Thomas Shaw invented the percussion cap for bullets. Unlike the earlier flintlock rifles, the percussion caps could easily be used in wet weather. The design of bullets themselves changed to allow greater speed and precision. By the mid-1850s, the British had adopted the Enfield rifle, which incorporated all the new technologies and was manufactured with interchangeable parts. These guns were accurate at several hundred yards. The invention of the breechloader in the 1860s brought still greater distance and precision in firepower for both rifles and artillery. Later in the century smokeless gunpowder and repeating mechanisms further enhanced accuracy and firepower.

[5]Daniel Headrick, *Tools of Empire: Technology and European Imperialism in the Nineteenth Century* (New York: Oxford University Press, 1981). The authors wish to acknowledge their indebtedness to Headrick's scholarship in this section.

ENCOUNTERING THE *Past*

SUBMARINE CABLES

UNDERWATER TELEGRAPHIC cables were among the important inventions of the mid-nineteenth century utilizing then new electrical technology. Submarine cables amazed people of that era and the early twentieth century much as the Internet does today. These cables also allowed for unprecedented international communication.

The first submarine cable was laid between Great Britain and France in 1850, and the first transatlantic cable was installed successfully in 1866. Thereafter to a remarkable extent, made evident by the accompanying world map of the early twentieth century, the imperial strategic, military concerns of the British government determined the pattern of the installation of these cables of the Eastern Associated Telegraph Companies founded in 1872. It was a case of imperial expansion determining the application of an exciting new technology using electricity. The route of the original Eastern cable of 1872 traced the coast of Western Europe, then across the Mediterranean through the Red Sea into the Indian Ocean to India, then overland in India, then eastward underwater to northern Australia and Hong Kong. By 1922, as seen in the map, cables linked all the areas of the British Empire acquired in the previous half-century as well as the important markets for British trade in Latin America. The company oversaw approximately 130,000 miles of cable. These submarine cables thus reflected late-nineteenth-century British imperial expansion and also provided essential communication allowing the empire to function economically, politically, and militarily.

In 1922 the Eastern Associated Telegraph Companies of Great Britain published a celebratory fiftieth anniversary volume. It opened by declaring, "On the world's oceans, surrounded by forests of vegetation, faintly reflected in the waving seaweeds of shallow shores, amidst the haunts of creatures which never see the light of the sun, where the skeletons of the wrecked ships of to-day and yesterday loom like phantom far and near, lie the great submarine ropes with which man has encircled the earth. Through the dark underworld of the sea, across submerged continents, and over valleys, plains and mountains, trodden in an ageless past by the forerunners of mankind, these electrified ropes carry the messages of man to man." Eastern Associated Telegraph described their cables as "the nervous system of the civilized world" and boasted, "There is hardly any spot in the more developed parts of the British Empire and of the world which cannot speedily be reached by a message marked 'via Eastern.' "

Source: *Fifty Years of "Via Eastern": A Souvenir and Record of the Celebrations in Connection with the Jubilee of the Eastern Associated Telegraph Companies MXMXII* (privately printed, 1922), pp. 13, 16.

FTL Design

The Maxim was the first wholly portable machine gun, pictured here with its American-born inventor Hiram Stevens Maxim (1840–1916), who became a British citizen. Technological superiority in weaponry and naval ships accounted in large measure for the success of Western imperialism in the nineteenth century. © 2005 Roger Viollet/The Image Works

All these technological changes were incorporated into the development of the machine gun. By 1900, the machine gun had become arguably the single most important weapon in colonial warfare and accounted for the deaths of tens of thousands of non-European peoples. Europeans also used dum-dum bullets, which exploded inside a wound, against native peoples when they would not use them against other Europeans.

Repeatedly in late-century colonial military campaigns, native peoples' guns, when they had any, were no match for European weapons. European nations also attempted to prevent new kinds of guns from being sold in Africa or other parts of the imperial world. A relatively small European force armed with the new rifles, cannon, and machine guns could overcome local armies that vastly outnumbered them. Such weaponry permitted Kitchener's overwhelming victory in the Sudan in 1898. Often Europeans ascribed their victories to their supposedly advanced civilization or racial superiority rather than recognizing that they owed their triumphs to superior firepower.

When African and Asian states did secure advanced weapons, they could either defeat European armies or carry out prolonged resistance. For example, in 1896, an Ethiopian army armed in part with modern rifles purchased from the French annihilated an invading Italian force at the Battle of Aduwa.

▼ The Missionary Factor

The modern Western missionary movement, which continues to the present day, originated in Great Britain in the late eighteenth century as a direct outgrowth of the rise of evangelical Christianity. Evangelicalism, which influenced Protestant communities from Central Europe to the United States, emphasized the authority of the Bible, the importance of a personal conversion experience, and the duty to spread the Gospel. Many Evangelicals were also concerned to prepare the world for the Second Coming of Jesus by carrying the message of Christian redemption to peoples who had not heard it. British Evangelicals first looked to unchurched groups in their own nation as the primary field for bearing Christian witness, but by the close of the eighteenth century, in a largely new departure for Protestants, small groups of Evangelicals began to be active in the non-Western world. Roman Catholics later copied these early Protestant missionary efforts. The result of this widespread nineteenth-century missionary campaign was the establishment of large Christian communities in Africa and Asia.

Missionary Movements

Evangelical Protestant Missionaries The chief moving forces in the British missionary movement were the Baptist Missionary Society, the London Missionary Society, the Edinburgh and Glasgow Missionary Societies, and the Church [of England] Missionary Society, all founded in the 1790s. American Protestant missionary societies soon followed. One of the most influential publications urging missionary work was the Baptist William Carey's "An Enquiry into the Obligations of Christians, to use Means for the Conversion of the Heathen" (1792), which made the then novel argument that British Christians must carry their faith to non-Western peoples overseas. A year after publishing his tract, Carey himself went to India. He and others of his persuasion believed they dwelled in a providential moment of history for the expansion of Christianity. This coincided with the consolidation of British control of India and the opening of what would become a century of unprecedented imperial expansion. Initially the missionary societies, who often competed with each other along denominational lines, floundered and attracted little support, but by the mid-1820s, they were firmly established and growing enterprises. By 1900, British missionary societies employed approximately 10,000 missionaries.

View the **Image** "Christian Missionary in China, circa 1900" on **MyHistoryLab.com**

German Protestants also embraced the missionary impulse. The earliest German societies such as the Leipzig Mission, founded in 1836, devoted their efforts to India. The Rhenish Missionary Society, founded in 1828, established itself in East Africa and supported German colonial claims there in the 1880s. As early as 1833, the Berlin Missionary Society sent missionaries to South Africa; by 1869, it was also working in China.

Roman Catholic Missionary Advance The nineteenth-century French Roman Catholic missionary effort was also enormous. It reflected the resurgence of the Catholic Church in France in the decades following the French Revolution and Napoleon. The Society for the Propagation of the Faith, the largest French missionary society, was founded in 1822. By the 1860s, it had over a million members. Its earliest missionaries went to China and Vietnam. Over time, however, French Catholic missionaries worked on every continent, including the islands of the Pacific. The White Fathers, so named because of their flowing white robes, were founded in 1868 to send missionaries to Africa, including Muslim North Africa.

Women and Missionary Activity As Europeans traveled around the world, they often commented on the status and treatment of women in other societies. In the Ottoman Empire, affluent women lived in separate portions of the house called harems. In India, *sati*, a practice whereby widows immolated themselves on their deceased husbands funeral pyres, existed in some communities. In China, some young girls were encouraged to bind their feet to prevent their full growth, leading to painful, deformed feet and limited mobility. European observers made broad generalizations about the position of women in other societies based on their limited understanding of these practices. They often believed that their "civilizing" interventions in other societies would be particularly beneficial to women and girls. Much of the activity intended to improve the status and quality of life of women was led by missionaries. In India, for example, missionaries founded women's colleges. As missionary groups became more directly associated with education, the number of women missionaries in India grew, and by the early twentieth century, most missionaries there were women. Women also played a large role in missionary activity in Africa and elsewhere. This missionary activity gave married and unmarried women the opportunity to travel and experience the world outside Europe firsthand. Some of these women carried their impressions back to their home countries and tried to take a larger role in politics.

Tensions Between Missionaries and Imperial Administrators

The mission societies and their missionaries had a complex relationship with their home governments. Missionary work did not necessarily support imperial missions. Missionaries from both Europe and America often settled in regions their governments did not control, and missionary societies often employed missionaries who came from a country other than the one sponsoring their mission. Nonetheless, the missionaries did develop many links with Western governments. The British missionary movement often saw the expansion of the British Empire as opening the way for the spread of the Gospel. They saw the spread of Western commerce as both financially beneficial for missions and as opening up new areas for the missionary enterprise. During the Opium Wars, for example, the missionary societies demanded that the British government negotiate access for missionaries as well as traders and merchandise into China. Missionaries and advocates of free trade imperialism thus could have a mutually supportive relationship. This relationship softened toward the close of the century when the missionary societies defined themselves more strictly in terms of the spiritual mission of bearing witness to the Gospel.

Colonial administrators frequently resisted the introduction of missionaries into their territories for fear the missionaries would prove a destabilizing force

Women played a prominent role as teachers in the Western foreign missionary effort. Miss Emily Hartwell was a turn-of-the-century, American-born Protestant missionary to the Foochow Mission in Fuzhou Shi, China. Here, in a photo from the missionary magazine *Light and Life*, she is pictured with one of her Bible classes composed of Chinese women. Her letters home spoke of the disadvantages of women in Chinese culture. Courtesy of the Library of Congress as they challenged traditional religions and cultural values. Missionaries might defend the rights of native peoples against official imperial policy or commercial interests' efforts to increase their profits. In the settlement colonies missionaries often clashed with the settlers who wanted to prevent native peoples from gaining the skills that would enable them to compete with whites. Colonial officials were also concerned about conflicts between Christian converts from different denominations. Furthermore, missionaries frequently educated persons from the lower levels of society who might resent colonial rule and the authority of native elites. The Christian vision of equality before God could, though it did not always, undermine the hierarchies of colonial authority. As one historian has commented, in India "there were always prominent missionaries prepared to challenge or ignore the imperial system and their own ecclesiastical authorities."[6]

But even when colonial officials disliked them, missionaries nonetheless provided much of the educational infrastructure of imperialism, particularly in India. At the village level their schools provided instruction in the local languages and English. Some of these schools received government financial support and hence became part of the administrative system. Missionaries also established institutions of higher education, including Serampore College (1818), Bishops College (1824) in Calcutta, and Forman Christian College (1865) in Lahore. These colleges trained primarily members of the Indian elite, both Hindu and Muslim. Instruction was invariably in English because the elites realized that knowing English was essential to their status in imperial India.

The relationship of French Roman Catholic missionaries to imperialism was complicated because the governments of the Third Republic in France were usually anticlerical after the 1870s. Yet although the republican government often clashed with the Catholic Church in France, it frequently supported missionary activity abroad as a way of extending French national interests. For example, France remained the official protector of Roman Catholics in the Ottoman Empire even after the French government broke diplomatic ties with the Vatican in 1905. In some cases the government in Paris or local colonial administrators encouraged French missionary activity to make native peoples sympathetic to French rule or to block the advance of other European powers. By teaching the French language, French missionaries also made it easier for French commercial interests to operate in a territory.

By 1900, approximately 58,000 French priests, religious brothers, and nuns were involved in the missionary enterprise. Like their British and German counterparts, French missionaries also often experienced tense relations with colonial administrators. Sometimes the colonial government pressed the civilizing mission through secular physicians, teachers, and agricultural consultants to counter the religious influence of missionaries. At the same time, however, the success of the French Catholic missionary effort meant that colonial officials in Vietnam and parts of Africa and the Pacific had to deal with large numbers of native Roman Catholics who supported and admired the missionaries. Yet by the early twentieth century, French missionaries increasingly saw their role not only as winning converts but also as molding native cultures in the image of France. As one historian has written, "Spreading civilization, which missionaries had long considered simply a fortunate by-product of evangelizing, came to the fore in Catholic propaganda as the movement's chief goal. From the 1890s forward, missionary publications increasingly chronicled the lives and tribulations of missionaries committed not only to God but also to the *patrie* [the French fatherland] and a specifically French civilizing mission."[7]

However sympathetic missionaries might become to indigenous peoples, they remained spokespersons for Western civilization. Because missionaries wished to convert indigenous peoples to Western Christianity, they implicitly shared with colonial officials the general cultural assumption of the superiority of things Western. Yet the very concern to bring Christian truth to non-Christian groups meant that Western missionaries had to engage native cultures in ways that colonial administrators did not. Missionaries had to learn local languages to translate the Bible and in doing so probably preserved some languages from extinction. They often needed to understand indigenous customs before seeking to change them. Some missionaries thus became amateur anthropologists. Nonetheless, even when missionaries were not formal agents of empire, they introduced Western cultural values, manners, and outlooks. While colonial governments might be associated with more advanced military and transportation technology, missionaries might be associated with more advanced medicine or agriculture in the hospitals and mission stations they ran. And missionaries, like colonial officials, generally assumed that native peoples were inferior to Westerners. While a few missionaries by 1900 believed that Christians and persons of other religions could learn from each other, most missionaries regarded non-Christians simply as heathens. That outlook, like the attitudes of secular administrators, generated its own sets of reactions.

[6]J. P. Daughton, *Empire Divided: Religion, Republicanism, and the Making of French Colonialism, 1880–1914* (New York: Oxford University Press, 2006), p. 18.

[7]Robert Frykenberg, "Christian Missions and the Raj," in Norman Etherington, ed., *Missions and Empire* (New York: Oxford University Press, 2005), p. 129.

Missionaries and Indigenous Religious Movements

Just as the presence of colonial administrations during the nineteenth century gave rise to various nationalist movements or movements that promoted the rights and interests of native peoples, the missionary activities gave rise to Asian and African religious movements that challenged the dominance of Western missionaries. The founding of new African and Asian Christian churches occurred as a result of the rejection of the racial and cultural assumptions of Western missionaries and as a means of reconciling Christianity with long-standing cultural practices, such as polygamy in Africa. The most important fact about the independent churches of Africa was that their leaders were African. For example, in 1888 David Brown Vincent established the Native Baptist Church in Lagos, Nigeria, after leaving the American-founded Baptist Church there. Not long thereafter, in South Africa Mangena Makone broke with the Methodists to found the Ethiopian Church. In Kenya, Christian members of the Kikuyu tribe split with the Church of Scotland Mission. In the early twentieth century, Christian Pentecostal groups arose among African Christians, as did other churches associated with gifts of healing or prophecy. These independent religious movements are the roots from which has sprung the current divide between Christian Churches of the northern and southern hemispheres, which we discuss more fully in Chapter 30.

In summary, how may one describe the interrelationship of the missionary movement and colonialism? First, it was dynamic and changed during the nineteenth century as missionary goals and sensibilities changed from one generation to another. Second, the missionary movement spawned an enormous amount of printed publicity in the form of newspaper and journal articles, missionary society publications, and missionary narratives and autobiographies. These materials publicized the vision of empire and raised interest in the West about the non-Western world. They also strongly influenced popular culture at a time when the churches were more influential than they are today, especially in Europe. Third, the missionary societies and the churches with which they were associated became skilled at pressuring their governments. Initially they directed their efforts toward permitting and protecting missionary activities. By the early twentieth century, however, many missionaries were supporting native peoples in their opposition to colonial authorities. Fourth, the religious effects of the missions were a two-way street. While Westerners brought Christianity to Africa and Asia, by 1900, non-Western Christians were beginning to move Christianity away from its dominance by Europeans and Americans. This process is still going on today. Finally, the missionary movement of the nineteenth century made Christianity a genuinely worldwide religion for the first time. The spread of Christianity, like the development of self-government in the British settler colonies, was thus one of the major elements of the extension of Western civilization around the globe.

▼ Science and Imperialism

The early modern European encounter with the non-Western world from the fifteenth-century voyages of discovery onward had been associated with the expansion of natural knowledge. The same would be true of Western imperialism in the nineteenth and early twentieth centuries. Commencing in 1768, Captain James Cook (1728–1779) had undertaken his famous voyages to the South Pacific under the patronage of the Royal Society of London to observe the transit of the planet Venus. Sir Joseph Banks (1744–1820), later president of the Royal Society, went with him to collect specimens of plants and animals unknown in Europe. Other British, French, and Spanish naval expeditions also carried scientists with their crews. Scientific societies often cooperated with military forces to carry out their research. For example, dozens of French scholars accompanied Napoleon's invasion of Egypt in 1798.

Geography was an expanding scientific discipline in the nineteenth century. Explorers wrote of their discoveries and adventures in Africa and Asia. Some explorers, such as Scottish Presbyterian David Livingstone (1813–1873) and French Jesuit Armand David (1829–1900), were also missionaries. Explorers portrayed themselves as pioneers who opened wild and savage spaces for commerce, religion, and ultimately civilization. Consequently, scientific and geographical societies generally supported their nations' imperialist goals and saw their research as benefiting from it. Scientific institutes, especially astronomical observatories, were set up in colonies. Moreover, the colonial administrations employed large numbers of engineers who planned and oversaw the construction of railways, roads, bridges, harbors, dams, and telegraph lines throughout the European empires. Geologists working for governments and private companies surveyed the mineral resources of newly acquired empires. As one British historian put it, "Natural scientists formed . . . [an] important . . . category of professional 'collaborators': an interest group central to the weaving of Africa, Asia, and the Americans into the fabric of national life."[8]

Four areas of scientific research deserve particular mention because they demonstrate how imperialism could filter into the wider European culture and capture

[8]Richard Drayton, *Nature's Government: Science, Imperial Britain, and the "Improvement" of the World* (New Haven, CT: Yale University Press, 2000), p. 171.

the imagination of domestic audiences who never set foot outside Europe. These are botany, zoology, medicine, and anthropology.

Botany

Botany was the nineteenth-century colonial science par excellence, reflecting and nurturing the vast expansion of agriculture around the globe. This expansion brought millions of acres of new land under cultivation in the Americas, Australia, New Zealand, and Algeria. Colonial officials and Western investors also forced or induced colonial peoples, mainly in the tropics, to grow cash crops—such as coffee, sugar, tea, rubber, jute, cotton, bananas, and cocoa—for export to Europe.

European botanists were intensely interested in the plants they might discover abroad. Their interest ranged from the discovery of previously unknown specimens through the development of new crops that would improve agriculture. Changes in taste, like the spread of tea and coffee drinking, and in technology, like the demand for rubber for bicycle and motorcar tires, could create demands for colonial agricultural products. Gutta-percha, a latex from trees in southeast Asia, came to fulfill a host of uses, from insulating electrical wires to providing material for flooring. Palm oil from West Africa was used in cooking, industrial lubrication, soaps, and cosmetics.

Kew Garden near London was the center of a vast network of botanical research. Joseph Dalton Hooker, its director, persuaded collectors from around the world to send specimens to Kew. Tropical plants were grown in its greenhouse, where British citizens could visit the grounds and see the plants that populated the far regions of the British empire. This photo shows Kew Palace, located in Kew Garden. Dorling Kindersley © Jamie Marshall

British colonies almost invariably had a large botanical garden to develop useful plants. The Royal Botanical Garden at Kew, near London, was the hub in a vast network of imperial gardens dedicated to the advancement of agriculture.

Gardens such as Kew and the *Jardin des Plantes* in Paris also allowed the general public to encounter a soft and inviting side of empire. Visitors could experience different parts of the empire in a pleasant setting as they strolled along flowerbeds, under trees, or through greenhouses. These great gardens made empire appear benign and far removed from the difficulties of its administration, the oppression of its indigenous peoples, or the havoc that empire may have wreaked on the peasant farmers of faraway places. These gardens and the new products and foods that Europeans and Americans consumed persuaded them that empire was part of the general progress of the age, which they associated with science.

The gardens with their research staffs also were devices for transforming economies. The same spirit of agricultural improvement that had begun in Britain in the eighteenth century was carried throughout the empire. Botanists worked as economic innovators to achieve intercontinental transfers of plants to secure products for their home countries and to develop colonial economies. In India, the British pushed farmers to grow cotton, hemp, tea, and cinchona trees. French botanists helped change the agricultural economy of Algeria from producing grain, which France already had in abundance, to growing wine grapes, fruit, and olives, which had ready markets in France.

One of the most important contributions British botanists made was to introduce rubber trees to British colonies. Until the 1890s the British had had to import rubber from wild trees that grew in the Amazon jungles of Brazil and Peru. To get around this expensive monopoly, British botanists in 1876 smuggled seeds from these wild trees to Kew where plants were grown for the eventual production of rubber in British tropical colonies. By the early twentieth century, British Malaya in southeast Asia had become a major producer of rubber, as did parts of the Gold Coast colony in Africa. The French and Dutch then created rubber plantations in Indochina and the East Indies. As a result, the market for wild South American rubber all but collapsed, ruining the economy of the Amazon.

As plant commodities fell in value in one part of the British Empire, British administrators and merchants would contact Kew Garden for suggestions of other profitable crops. The botanists thus profited from empire by establishing themselves as the experts for the economic development of colonies after they had been annexed or after the crops that had once supported them were no longer profitable. Planters associations in the European colonies also established their own experimental stations to improve existing crops or develop new ones for cultivation.

Zoology

In the eighteenth century some European monarchs, such as the Habsburg emperors in Vienna and the French kings in Paris, had established collections of exotic animals. In the nineteenth century zoos and zoological gardens were founded in major European and American cities. These zoos displayed animals from around the world that expeditions acquired from the regions that European imperialism was penetrating.

Other scientists would collect specimens of animals, particularly birds, which they killed and brought back from the colonies to Europe to be placed in natural history museums. These museums became increasingly popular in the late nineteenth century.

Medicine

Medical science was an integral part of the imperial enterprise on several different levels. As already noted, Westerners had to overcome various tropical diseases, especially malaria, that prevented them from surviving in the tropics. But Western medicine also became a fundamental feature of the civilizing mission of colonial administrators and missionaries, many of whom were physicians. The spread of Western medicine justified colonial rule and helped win converts. The primary diseases that Western doctors sought to battle in the tropical colonies were yellow fever, sleeping sickness, small pox, hookworm, and leprosy.

Missionaries had pioneered the introduction of Western medicine into the colonial setting. They presented themselves as people who sought to heal both body and soul. Some missionaries thought they could convert native peoples to Christianity by first demonstrating the power of Western medicine. In Africa various forms of surgery and the removal of cataracts, which restored sight, became powerful tools of conversion.

Physicians and medical researchers sought to win government financial support by demonstrating that modern medicine could cure the endemic diseases that ravaged colonial peoples. Among the most influential colonial medical institutions were the Pasteur Institutes, named after Louis Pasteur (1822–1895), the French scientist who had found a cure for rabies and other diseases. The first overseas Pasteur Institute was founded in Saigon in 1891; others followed across the French Empire.

One of the most famous cases of a cure for a tropical disease that followed an imperial involvement was the conquest of yellow fever. After U.S. forces occupied Cuba in 1898, a yellow fever epidemic struck Havana and hundreds of American troops died. The Surgeon General of the United States sent a medical commission headed by Dr. Walter Reed to Cuba to address the problem. A Cuban physician, Carlos Finley, persuaded Reed to look to an insect source for the disease. Experiments convinced Reed that yellow fever was mosquito borne. Steps were taken to eradicate mosquitoes in Havana, and the epidemic ceased. The conquest of yellow fever opened the way for the later construction of the Panama Canal during which etymologists protected workers from mosquito bites.

In general in the colonial world, Western science became a vehicle for what is often termed *cultural imperialism*. Medical advances allowed Western penetration of the tropics and then underpinned Western cultural and political domination. European medical institutions controlled research in the colonies. Westerners seldom had respect for Asian and African medical personnel no matter how well they were trained. At the same time, Western medicine either eradicated or lessened the impact of diseases that had ravaged the non-Western world for centuries.

Anthropology

Almost immediately from Christopher Columbus's first encounter with the Americas in 1492, European observers began to record and analyze the character of the non-European peoples they confronted and conquered. This interest never ceased, but in the late nineteenth century, the study of non-Western peoples became associated with the science of anthropology.

Anthropological societies were founded in Paris (1859), London (1863), and Berlin (1870). The leaders of these new societies were convinced of the multiple origins of the races of humankind (a theory termed *polygenesis*) and of the inherent inequality of races. The concept of multiple origins had originated earlier in the nineteenth century in the United States where it had been an argument in defense of slavery. Polygenesis was one of many scientific theories that supported a hierarchy of unequal races at the top of which Westerners always placed the white races.

Many anthropologists believed that such factors as skull type determined human character, another idea originating in the United States. Paul Broca (1824–1880), a French physician who specialized in the brain, measured the skulls of human beings from different races and

Peoples from colonized nations were transported to various world's fairs and similar exhibitions during the late nineteenth and early twentieth centuries. They constituted living exhibitions, where they were expected to portray "native customs" or the like. Here at the St. Louis World's Fair of 1904 African Pygmies demonstrated beheading. In this and other similar examples, native peoples were frequently presented in demeaning roles that filled the expectations of spectators to see "exotic" behavior. Such performances and exhibitions served to convince the Western spectators of the superiority of their civilization over that of the peoples living in the colonized world. Courtesy of the Library of Congress

assigned them intellectual capacity on the basis of brain size. Other European and American scientists followed his lead. Anthropologists who studied colonial societies carried these ideas with them.

Anthropology as a social science infused with racial thinking (see Chapter 24) had become organized in Western Europe on the eve of the Scramble for Africa. Anthropologists from then through World War II rode the wave of imperial enthusiasm. They worked closely with colonial administrations and encouraged expeditions to explore Africa. Even anthropologists who opposed colonialism cooperated with colonial administrators once the colonial empires had been created. Moreover, whatever their private doubts about racial theory may have been, anthropologists eagerly sought university professorships in the colonies and government funding for research on the grounds that their research supported colonialism. In fact, however, colonial officials rarely sought anthropologists' advice. Instead, anthropologists influenced imperial policies through their books, lectures, and university classes. European and American readers and students were invariably told that non-Western peoples were inferior, that their economies were underdeveloped, that their societies were corrupt, decadent, or primitive, and that their religions were dangerous and false. All this proved the need for Western administration and control.

Many of these same attitudes informed the creation of the great anthropological museums in Europe and the United States. The most famous of these was and remains the Museum of Mankind (Musée de l'Homme) in Paris, which began in 1878 as a Museum of Ethnography. But one of the most remarkable is the Royal Museum for Central Africa that Leopold II established in 1897 in Brussels to showcase his Congolese empire. Leopold's museum had begun earlier that year as an exhibit at a World's Fair that also boasted an African village on its grounds with more than fifty Africans living in it. These museums, which were very popular, often presented artifacts of African and Asian culture that explorers or other travelers or researchers had brought home. These exhibitions, like the botanical gardens, zoos, and museums of natural history, introduced Western audiences to what they considered to be the exotic features and otherness of non-Western peoples and cultures.

The idea of museums or zoos to display exotic creatures was also extended to human beings in both Europe and the United States. Showmen such as the American P. T. Barnum would exhibit Africans, Asians, and Native Americans. Carl Hagenbeck, a German, brought Polynesians, Sudanese, and Inuits from Canada to live in "native villages" in the Hamburg Zoo. In the thirty years before World War I, the Paris zoo staged over twenty-five such exhibitions. At World's Fairs, millions of Europeans and Americans paid to view native peoples. As late as 1958 the Brussels World's Fair, like that of Leopold II sixty years earlier, boasted a village of Congolese people.

In Perspective

Western imperialism during the nineteenth and early twentieth centuries reshaped the world in ways that still affect us today. The productive capacity, military superiority, and technological prowess first of the European powers and later of the United States allowed those nations to dominate the world as they had never been able to do before. For some Europeans, the ability to rule others was all the justification for rule that was required. Their dominance would last for about a century. Western influence arose from decades of free-trade imperialism in the early nineteenth century that was marked in general by the absence of formal imperial government except for Britain in India and its settler colonies. The New Imperialism began in the 1870s largely as a result of the political changes that had occurred in Europe since the 1850s—the defeat of Russia in the Crimean War, the unification of Italy and Germany, and the defeat of France by Germany in 1870—that upset the balance of power and heightened tensions and competition among the great powers who increasingly sought to reassure themselves and assert their power by expanding into the non-Western world. The New Imperialism thus involved the creation of formal empires as a sign of great power status, the protection of what were seen as vital geopolitical interests, an assertion of white racial superiority, and the partition of Africa. All these ideas and events led the European powers into overseas imperial rivalries that contributed to the tensions resulting in the outbreak of World War I in 1914.

Western imperialism found many supporters. Manufacturers and merchants sought markets for their goods and sources of tropical raw materials. Missionaries sought to evangelize the parts of Africa and Asia previously closed to Christianity. Scientists saw the imperial mission as creating networks for research and a new appreciation of their own efforts as supporters of their national governments. Army and navy officers looked to colonial wars as avenues for professional advancement.

For over a century, from the 1830s to the 1940s, the peoples of the non-Western world found themselves generally acted upon by foreign political, economic, and military forces that they could not effectively resist. Many of these non-Western peoples sought to work with Westerners for their own advantage. Indeed, the Western colonial empires could not have functioned without African and Asian collaborators. By the outbreak of World War I, however, discontent was stirring throughout the colonial world, and the leaders of the post–World War II movement for decolonization and independence had begun to emerge.

KEY TERMS

apartheid (p. 803)
civilizing mission (p. 792)
concentration camps (p. 803)
Great Trek (p. 803)
imperialism (p. 783)
Imperialism of Free Trade (p. 784)
New Imperialism (p. 783)
protectorates (p. 790)
spheres of influence (p. 790)

REVIEW QUESTIONS

1. How did European imperial interests shift geographically in the nineteenth century? How was free trade related to the expansion of European influence around the globe?
2. What was the New Imperialism? How was it different from free-trade imperialism? Why was Britain the dominant world power until the late nineteenth century? What were the Opium Wars?
3. How did the British come to dominate India? What were the causes of the Indian rebellion of 1857? How did British rule in India change after the rebellion? Why was India so important to Britain?
4. What were the motives of the New Imperialism? To what extent was the New Imperialism related to the capitalist search for higher profits and new markets? How did colonial officials and businesspeople influence the growth of colonial empires?
5. Why was Algeria the most important part of the French Empire? What parts of the Ottoman Empire fell under European rule between the 1880s and 1914? Why did Britain come to dominate Egypt? Why did Germany and Italy acquire colonies? Why did Leopold II build an empire in the Congo? What was the Scramble for Africa?
6. How did France gain control of Indochina? How did the United States become an imperial power? Where did Russia expand in mainland Asia? What were the consequences of Western imperialism in China?
7. What were the "tools of imperialism"? Why was quinine so important for the spread of empires? What technological improvements enabled Western powers to dominate so much of the non-Western world? Why were the new colonial empires so short-lived?
8. Why did Western missionary efforts expand in the nineteenth century? Why was the relationship between Western missionaries and colonial officials so

complicated? Why did Africans want to found their own churches? How has the spread of Christianity in the non-Western world affected the Christian churches?

9. How did Westerners justify imperialism? What was the civilizing mission? What sciences were most associated with the New Imperialism? What role did racism play in the New Imperialism?

SUGGESTED READINGS

M. Adas, *Machines as the Measure of Men: Science, Technology, and Ideologies of Western Dominance* (1989). The best single volume on racial thinking and technological advances as forming ideologies of European colonial dominance.

R. Aldrich, *Greater France: A History of French Overseas Expansion* (1996). Remains the best overview.

C. Bayly, *Imperial Meridian: The British Empire and the World: 1780–1830* (1989). Places the British expansion in India into larger imperial contexts.

D. Brower, *Turkestan and the Fate of the Russian Empire* (2003). A concise treatment of a case study in Russian imperialism in Asia.

A. Burton, *Burdens of History: British Feminists, Indian Women, and Imperial Culture, 1865–1915* (1994). Explores the relationship of women in Britain's Indian empire.

A. Conklin, *A Mission to Civilize: The Republican Idea of Empire in France and West Africa, 1895–1930* (2000). An in-depth analysis of a case history of the civilizing mission.

F. Cooper and A. L. Stoler, eds., *Tensions of Empire: Colonial Cultures in a Bourgeois World* (1997). Explores difficulties of accommodating ideas and realities of empire to domestic middle-class values and outlooks.

J. Cox, *Imperial Fault Lines: Christianity and Colonial Power in India, 1818–1940* (2002). The best treatment of British missionaries in India.

J. P. Daughton, *An Empire Divided: Religion, Republicanism, and the Making of French Colonialism, 1880–1914* (2008). A superb discussion of the interaction of religion, empire, and domestic French politics.

N. P. Dirks, *The Scandal of Empire: India and the Creation of Imperial Britain* (2006). An elegant study of the interaction of British political sensibilities and the emergence of the British Empire in India.

R. Drayton, *Nature's Government: Science, Imperial Britain, and the "Improvement" of the World* (2000). The best volume on the relationship of science and imperialism.

M. H. Edney, *Mapping an Empire: The Geographical Construction of British India, 1765–1843* (1997). Discusses how the science of cartography contributed to the British domination of India.

N. Etherington, ed., *Missions and Empire* (2005). An excellent collection of essays.

D. Headrick, *The Tools of Empire: Technology and European Imperialism in the Nineteenth Century* (1981). Remains an important work of analysis.

A. Hochschild, *King Leopold's Ghost: A Study of Greed, Terror, and Heroism in Colonial Africa* (1999). A well-informed account of a tragedy.

I. Hull, *Absolute Destruction: Military Culture and the Practices of War in Imperial Germany* (2006). Excellent account of destructive German actions in East Africa.

R. Hyam, *Britain's Imperial Century 1815–1914: A Study of Empire and Expansion* (2002). The single best one-volume analysis.

T. Jeal, *Livingstone* (2001). This and the following title recount the lives of the two persons most associated in the popular mind with the exploration of Africa.

T. Jeal, *Stanley: The Impossible Life of Africa's Greatest Explorer* (2008).

A. Kappeler, *The Russian Empire: A Multiethnic History* (2001). A straightforward overview that is very clear on the concepts behind Russian expansionist policy.

D. C. Lievan, *The Russian Empire and Its Rivals* (2001). Explores the imperial side of Russian government.

K. E. Meyer and S. B. Brysa, *Tournament of Shadows: The Great Game and the Race for Empire in Central Asia* (1999). A lively account of the conflict between Great Britain and Russia.

W. J. Mommsen, *Theories of Imperialism* (1980). A study of the debate on the meaning of imperialism.

M. A. Osborne, *Nature, the Exotic, and the Science of French Colonialism* (1994). Explores the impact of French horticultural gardens and imperialism.

L. Pyenson, *Civilizing Mission: Exact Sciences and French Overseas Expansion, 1830–1940* (1993). A major work of the history of both science and imperialism.

B. Porter, *The Absent-Minded Imperialists: Empire, Society, and Culture in Britain* (2006). Discusses the relatively few people actually involved in British imperialism and how imperialism often had a low profile in the British Isles.

B. Porter, *The Lion's Share: A Short History of British Imperialism, 1850–2004* (2004). A lively narrative.

R. Robinson, J. Gallagher, and A. Denny, *Africa and the Victorians: The Official Mind of Imperialism* (2000). A classic analysis that continues to bear rereading.

P. J. Tuck, *French Catholic Missionaries and the Politics of Imperialism in Vietnam, 1857–1914* (1987). Includes both narrative and documents.

H. L. Wesseling, *Divide and Rule: The Partition of Africa, 1889–1914* (1996). A clear narrative and analysis of a complicated topic.

H. L. Wesseling, *The European Colonial Empires: 1815–1919* (2004). The best recent overview of the entire nineteenth-century European colonial ventures.

E. R. Wolf, *Europe and the People Without History* (1990). A classic, highly critical account.

A. Zimmerman, *Anthropology and Antihumanism in Imperial Germany* (2001). Discusses the manner in which anthropology in conjunction with imperialism challenged humanistic ideas in German intellectual life.

MyHistoryLab™ MEDIA ASSIGNMENTS

Find these resources in the Media Assignments folder for Chapter 25 on **MyHistoryLab**.

QUESTIONS FOR ANALYSIS

1. In this image, what is the relationship between the French and the people of Morocco?

   ***Section:* Motives for the New Imperialism**

   View the **Closer Look** The French in Morocco, p. 793

2. How would you summarize the author's view of British rule in India?

   ***Section:* India—the Jewel in the Crown of the British Empire**

   Read the **Document** Amrita Lal Roy, *English Rule in India, 1886*, p. 788

3. What are some of the causes for a shift to the "new imperialism"?

   ***Section:* The "New Imperialism," 1870–1914**

   Watch the **Video** New Imperialism, p. 790

4. What is the role of nationalism in Peters' argument?

   ***Section:* The Partition of Africa**

   Read the **Document** Carl Peters, "A Manifesto for German Colonization," p. 802

5. In this political cartoon, what is the queen's attitude toward the deaths caused by the war?

   ***Section:* The Partition of Africa**

   View the **Image** The Boer War and Queen Victoria—Dutch Caricature, p. 803

OTHER RESOURCES FROM THIS CHAPTER

The Close of the Age of Early Modern Colonization

View the **Map** Interactive Map: World Colonial Empires 1900, p. 784

The Age of British Imperial Dominance

View the **Closer Look** An Allegory of the British Empire, p. 784

Read the **Document** Letter to Queen Victoria (1839) Lin Zexu, p. 785

India—The Jewel in the Crown of the British Empire

Read the **Document** Dadabhai Naoroji, *The Benefits of British Rule in India*, 1871, p. 787

Read the **Document** The Indian Revolt (1857), p. 788

The "New Imperialism," 1870–1914

Read the **Document** Karl Pearson, "Social Darwinism and Imperialism," p. 791

Motives for the New Imperialism

Read the **Document** Vladimir Lenin, *Imperialism, the Highest Stage of Capitalism*, p. 791

Read the **Document** Arthur James Balfour, "Problems with Which We Have to Deal in Egypt," 1910, p. 792

Read the **Compare and Connect** Two Views of the Turn-of-the-Twentieth-Century Imperial Expansion, p. 794

The Partition of Africa

View the **Image** Disraeli Purchasing Controlling Interest in the Suez Canal, p. 797

View the **Image** Belgian King Crushing the Congo Free State—Cartoon, p. 801

The Missionary Factor

View the **Image** Christian Missionary in China, circa 1900, p. 812

THE WEST & THE WORLD

Imperialism: Ancient and Modern

THE CONCEPT OF "empire" does not win favor today, and the word *imperialism*, derived from it, has carried an increasingly pejorative meaning since it was coined in the nineteenth century. Both words imply forcible domination by a nation or a state that exploits an alien people for its own benefit. Although, in our time, the charge of imperialism arises whenever a large and powerful nation influences weaker ones, exertion of influence alone is not imperialism. To be true to historical experience, one nation's actions toward another are imperialistic only if the dominant nation exerts both political and military control over the weaker one. In that sense, the last great empire in the modern world was the conglomeration of republics and ostensibly independent satellite states dominated by Russia prior to the USSR's collapse, but the Russians and the other imperial powers after World War II took no public pride in their domination. In our day, ruling an "empire" or engaging in "imperialism" is generally considered among the worst acts a nation can commit.

Such views are rare, perhaps unique, in the history of civilization. A major source for this opinion is the Christian religious tradition, especially parts of the New Testament that deprecate power and worldly glory and praise humility. In fact, Christianity was not hostile to power and empire, for it took control of the Roman Empire in the fourth century C.E. and has lived comfortably with "empire" until our own century. The rise of democracy and nationalism in the last two centuries may have been more influential in changing attitudes toward imperialism because these movements exalt the freedom and autonomy of a people. Perhaps the modern disdain for empire building has its principal origins in the extraordinary horror of modern warfare and the historical knowledge that competition for empire has often led to war.

If, however, we are to understand the widespread experience of empire throughout history, we must be alert to the great gap that separates the views of most people throughout history from our current opinions. The earliest empires go back more than 4,000 years to the valleys of the Nile and the Tigris-Euphrates, and empires arose later in China, Japan, India, Iran, and Central and South America, among other areas. Typically, they were led by rulers who were believed to be gods or the representatives of gods, or at least were godlike in their ability to rule over many people. To their own people they brought wealth and prosperity, power, and reflected glory, all considered highly desirable. No one appears to have questioned the propriety of conquering another people and taking their lands, property, and persons to benefit the conquerors. Empire seemed to be part of the order of things—good for the rulers, usually bad for the ruled.

The Greeks: Ambiguities of Power

In most respects, the Greeks resembled other ancient peoples in their attitudes toward power, conquest, empire, and the benefits that came with them. Their Olympian gods held sway over earth, heaven, and the underworld because of victorious wars over other deities, and they gloried in their rule. The heroes in the epic poems that formed the Greek system of values won glory and honor through battle, conquest, and rule over other people. They viewed the world as a place of intense competition in which victory and domination, which brought fame and glory, were the highest goals, whereas defeat and subordination brought ignominy and shame.

When the legendary world of aristocratic heroes gave way to the world of city-states (*poleis*), competition was elevated from contests among individuals, households, and clans to contests and wars among *poleis*. In 416 B.C.E., more than a decade after the death of Pericles (c. 490–429 B.C.E.), Athenian spokesmen explained to some Melian officials their view of international relations: "Of the gods we believe, and of men we know, that by a necessity of their nature they always rule wherever they have the power."[9] Although their language was shockingly blunt, it reflected the views of most Greeks.

Yet this was also a dramatic presentation of the morally problematic status of the Athenian Empire. The Athenians' harsh statement would have struck a sympathetic chord among the Greeks. They appreciated power and the security and glory it can bring, but their own historical experience was different from that of other ancient nations. Their culture had been shaped by small, autonomous, independent city-states, and they considered freedom natural for people raised in such an environment. Citizens, they believed, should be free in their persons; free to maintain their own constitutions, laws, and customs; and their city-states should be free to conduct their own foreign relations and to compete for power and glory. The free, autonomous *polis*, they thought, was greater than the mightiest powers in the world, and the sixth-century B.C.E. poet Phocylides was prepared to compare it to the great Assyrian Empire: "A

[9]Thucydides 5.105

little *polis* living orderly in a high place is greater than block-headed Nineveh" (Fragment 5).

When *poleis* fought one another, the victor typically took control of a piece of borderland that was usually the source of the dispute. They did not normally enslave the defeated enemy or annex and occupy its land. In these matters, as in many others, the Greeks distinguished themselves from alien peoples who did not speak Greek and were not shaped by the Greek cultural tradition. These people were called barbarians, *barbaroi*, because their speech sounded to the Greeks like "bar bar." Because they had not been raised as people in free communities but lived as subjects to a ruler, they were, it seemed, slaves by nature. To the Greeks, then, dominating and enslaving such people was perfectly acceptable. Greeks, however, viewed themselves as naturally free, as they demonstrated by creating and living in the free institutions of the *polis*. To rule over such people, to deny them their freedom and autonomy, would be wrong—so the Greeks thought, but they did not always act accordingly. The early Spartans, for instance, had changed the status of the conquered Greeks of Laconia and Messenia to *Helots*, or slaves of the state.

The Greeks shared still another belief that interfered with the comfortable acceptance of great power and empire: They thought any good thing amassed by humans to excess, beyond moderation, eventually led to *hubris*, a condition of wanton violence arising from arrogant pride in one's greatness. Those overcome by hubris were thought to have overstepped the limits established for human beings, to have shown contempt for the gods, and, thereby, to have incurred *nemesis*, or divine anger and retribution. The great example to the Greeks of the fifth century B.C.E. of the workings of hubris and nemesis was the fate of Xerxes (r. 486–465 B.C.E.), Great King of the Persian Empire. His power became so great, it filled him with a blind arrogance that led him to try to extend his rule over the Greek mainland and thus brought disaster to himself and his people. When, therefore, the Athenians undertook the leadership of a Greek alliance after the Persian War, and that leadership brought them wealth and power and, in fact, turned into what was frankly acknowledged to be an empire, their response was ambiguous and contradictory. These developments were a source of pride and gratification, but also of embarrassment and, to some Athenians, shame.

The Macedonian conquest of the Greek city-states in 338 B.C.E. marked a return to an older attitude toward empire. Alexander the Great (r. 340–323 B.C.E.) conquered the vast Persian Empire, itself the successor of empires that had stretched from the Nile to the Indus valley. The death of Alexander led to its division and eventual absorption by the emergent Roman Empire by the second century B.C.E.

The ancient world was fascinated by the clash of empires that marked its history. The Romans created the grandest of the ancient empires, but they knew theirs had been preceded by others. On the walls of the House of the Faun in Pompeii, there resides an ancient mosaic depicting the Battle of Issus (333 B.C.E.), when the Macedonian Alexander the Great defeated the Persian Empire ruled by Darius III. Alexander appears on the left of the mosaic and Darius appears on his chariot. The mosaic, based on a still more ancient lost painting, probably dates from the second century B.C.E. and was rediscovered in 1831. Alinari/Art Resource, NY

The Romans: A Theory of Empire

The Romans had fewer hesitations about the desirability of imperial power than the Greeks. Their culture, which arose from a world of farmers accustomed to hard work, deprivation, and subordination to authority, venerated the military virtues. Roman society valued power, glory, and the responsibilities of leadership, even domination, without embarrassment. In time, the Romans formulated a theory of empire that claimed Roman rule brought great advantages to its subjects: prosperity, justice, the rule of law, and, most valuable of all, peace. In the words of their great epic poet Virgil (70–19 B.C.E.), it was the Roman practice "to humble the arrogant and be sparing to their subjects."[10] These claims had considerable foundation, and the Romans could not have ruled so vast an empire with a relatively small army for more than half a millennium if their subjects had not enjoyed these benefits. Some of the conquered had a different viewpoint, however. As one British chieftain put it in the first century C.E.: "They make a wilderness and call it peace."[11]

Muslims, Mongols, and Ottomans

The rise of Islam in the seventh century C.E. produced a new kind of empire that derived its energy from religious zeal. Bursting out of Arabia, the Muslim armies swiftly gained control of most of the territory held by the old Persian Empire, North Africa, and Spain.

In the twelfth and thirteenth centuries, the great Mongol Empire, at its height, dominated Eurasia from the Pacific to central Europe, ruling Russia for more than two centuries. As in most ancient empires, the Mongols demanded taxes and military service from the conquered. They also imposed their rule over the mighty and long-standing Chinese Empire, parts of India, and much of the Islamic world before their power declined.

Still another great empire that spanned Europe and Asia was that of the Ottomans, a Turkish people, originally from central Asia. In the fourteenth century, they established a kingdom in Anatolia (Asia Minor) and soon conquered the ancient Byzantine Empire, seizing Constantinople in 1453. In the next century, the Ottoman Empire dominated southeastern Europe, the Black Sea, North Africa from Morocco to Egypt, Palestine, Syria and Arabia, Mesopotamia and Iraq, and Kurdistan and Georgia in the Caucasus. As late as 1683, Ottoman armies threatened to take Vienna and push into western Europe. Over the next two centuries, however, Ottoman power declined as the European national states grew stronger. Russia, in particular, inflicted defeats that left Turkey in the late nineteenth century, "the sick man of Europe."

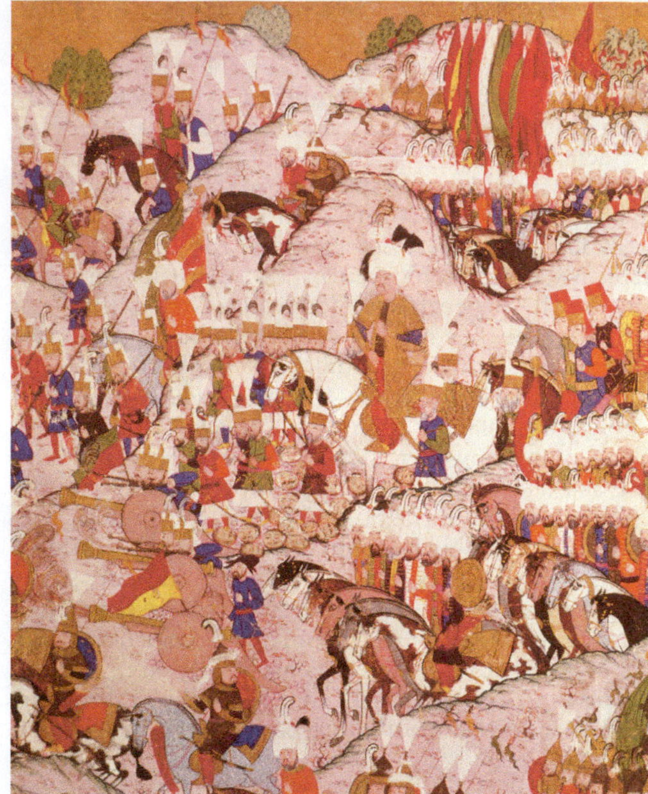

The Ottoman Turks began to overrun the Balkans in the mid-1300s. In 1526, Sultan Suleyman the Magnificent destroyed a Hungarian army at the Battle of Mohacs. The Ottoman Empire ruled most of the Balkans until the late nineteenth century. Suleyman I the Magnificent (1494–1566). Sultan Suleyman at the Battles of Mahocs (detail). Lokman, The Military Campaigns of Suleyman the Magnificent. Hunername manuscript. Ottoman dynasty, Istanbul. Topkapi Palace Museum, Istanbul, Turkey. Bridgeman-Giraudon/Art Resource, NY

European Expansion

Europe, divided first by feudalism, then by the emergence of multiple nascent national states, had been the victim of Islamic imperial expansion during the Middle Ages, first at the hands of the Arabs, then the Turks. The crusades had produced small and transitory conquests. It was only in the late 1400s that Europeans began the economic and political expansion that culminated in their command of much of the planet by 1900. The first phase of European expansion involved the "discovery," exploration, conquest, exploitation, and settlement of the Americas. It was made possible by important developments in naval and military technology, the dynamism inherent in early commercial and financial capitalism, and the freedom to compete for wealth and power unleashed by the division into separate states.

Spain and Portugal took the lead, founding empires in Central and South America, sometimes conquering existing empires ruled by native peoples. In Central America, the Aztecs exacted labor and taxes from their subject peoples, using some of them as human sacrifices. In the Andes, the Incas ruled a great empire that also required military service and forced labor from its subjects. Both Native American empires were overthrown by Spain, which then established a vast American empire whose resources, especially gold and silver, formed the basis of the great Spanish Empire in Europe. Portugal exploited

[10]Virgil *Aeneid* 6.850

[11]Tacitus *Agricola* 30

the agricultural and mineral riches of Brazil using slaves imported from Africa.

The seventeenth century saw the establishment of European trading posts and then colonies on the Indian subcontinent and in the East Indies, chiefly by the Dutch, British, and French. In North America, Spain held Mexico, Florida, and California. Of more lasting significance were French and British settlements in Canada and what was to become the United States. The British colonies, especially, represented a special kind of European overseas settlement in which concern for commerce was less important than the acquisition of land for farming.

The wars of the eighteenth century ultimately cleared North America and India of French competition, leaving both as British monopolies and important bases of what would become a worldwide British Empire. The largest and most populous empire in the history of the world, it included colonies of one sort or another on all the inhabited continents; "the sun," as the saying went, "never set on the British Empire." Whether European colonialism was profitable for the imperial powers is still controversial, but Great Britain certainly benefited more than the others. Unlike most colonial powers, the British imported great quantities of natural resources from their colonies and carried on a high percentage of their trade with them. Even more singular, the British Empire included such self-governing areas as Canada, Australia, New Zealand, and South Africa, ruled by emigrants from Britain who remained loyal to the mother country and were willing to assist it in wartime. "The jewel in Britain's imperial crown," as another saying went, "was India." With a population of some 300 million, it contained perhaps 80 percent of the empire's subjects and provided much of the imperial profit.

At the height of its power in the mid-nineteenth century, it is remarkable how little money and effort Britain needed to spend to maintain these desired conditions. The cost of its armed services, including its great navy, during these years was only about 2–3 percent of its gross national product—a low figure compared with other nations, and incredibly low considering Britain's status as the world's greatest empire. The British army was the smallest among the European powers: By 1880 it numbered fewer than a quarter of a million men—less than half the size of France's and barely a quarter of Russia's.

France returned to its imperial pursuits after its defeat in the Napoleonic Wars, especially in North Africa and Southeast Asia, and in the last quarter of the century, Germany and Italy joined the competition for colonies. The latter part of the century brought the European partition of Africa and the establishment of European economic and political power throughout Asia. Modernized Japan, too, became a colonial power, modeling itself on the imperialist policies of the European powers. (See Chapter 26.)

By the next century, European dominance had created a single global economy and had made events in any corner of the world significant thousands of miles away. The possession of colonies became part of the definition of a great power, and the competition for colonies helped bring on World War I.

European imperialism ultimately rested on the willingness to use force. When anti-British agitation mounted in India after World War I, General Reginald Dyer's troops fired on unarmed Indian demonstrators at Amritsar. More than three hundred Indians were killed. UPI/CORBIS/Bettmann

Toward Decolonization

The weakening of the European colonial powers in World War II began the process of decolonization. The economic value of most colonies had proved to be much smaller than anticipated, and the colonial powers lacked both the capacity and the incentive to restore their former rule. Nationalist movements in the old colonies, moreover, would make such attempts costly and unpleasant. These movements flourished under the banner of national self-determination, self-government, and independence, ideas that came from and were cherished by the European colonial powers themselves. The example of Nazi Germany, moreover, had discredited theories of racial superiority that had justified much of European imperial rule. For European imperialism the handwriting was on the wall, although some colonial powers held on more fiercely than others. The French, for instance, fought at great cost—but in vain—to retain Algeria and Indochina. By the 1970s, a postcolonial world had emerged, and the concept of empire had become unclean. (See Chapter 29.)

What were the major ancient attitudes toward imperialism? What are the major modern attitudes? How do you account for the differences? What justifications and explanations have modern people used in connection with imperialism? Which do you think are the most important? Do you think ancient and modern reasons for imperialism are fundamentally different?

Read the **Document** Herodotus: Demaratus Explains Greek Freedom to Xerxes, c. 430 B.C.E. on **MyHistoryLab.com**

Listen to the **Audio** Creating the Roman Empire on **MyHistoryLab.com**

View the **Image** Mosaic of Alexander the Great on **MyHistoryLab.com**

View the **Image** British Empire poster, "Growing Markets for our Goods" on **MyHistoryLab.com**

World War I produced unprecedented destruction and loss of life. Rather than a war of rapid movement, much combat occurred along stationary trenches dug in both Western and Eastern Europe. Here, Austro-Hungarian troops fight from trenches on the eastern front wearing gas masks. The use of poison gas was one of the innovations of the war and was generally condemned after the war. National Archives and Records Administration

Listen to the Chapter Audio on MyHistoryLab.com

26

Alliances, War, and a Troubled Peace

▼ **Emergence of the German Empire and the Alliance Systems (1873–1890)**
Bismarck's Leadership • Forging the Triple Entente (1890–1907)

▼ **World War I**
The Road to War (1908–1914) • Sarajevo and the Outbreak of War (June–August 1914) • Strategies and Stalemate: 1914–1917

▼ **The Russian Revolution**
The Provisional Government • Lenin and the Bolsheviks • The Communist Dictatorship

▼ **The End of World War I**
Germany's Last Offensive • The Armistice • The End of the Ottoman Empire

▼ **The Settlement at Paris**
Obstacles the Peacemakers Faced • The Peace • World War I and Colonial Empires • Evaluating the Peace

▼ **In Perspective**

LEARNING OBJECTIVES

Why did the alliance system fail?

How did conflict in the Balkans lead to the outbreak of general war in Europe?

What factors made the rise of the Bolsheviks to power in Russia possible?

What were the immediate consequences of the end of World War I?

What were the key weaknesses of the Paris peace settlement?

IN THE SUMMER of 1914, the Archduke Francis Ferdinand, heir to the throne of Austria-Hungary, was assassinated in Sarajevo, Bosnia. This act of political violence set off a crisis that concluded with the outbreak of a European war that eventually became a worldwide conflict involving numerous colonies of the European imperial powers and the United States of America. Originally known as the Great War, World War I witnessed unprecedented loss of life and destruction of property. The war constituted the defining event of the twentieth century from which followed revolution first in Russia and later in Germany and Austria. The Ottoman Empire would also collapse. Thereafter from that time to the present day the vast semicircle of territories commencing in Germany in central Europe then passing through eastern Europe and the Balkans into Turkey and then across northeastern Africa into the Arab Peninsula has for almost a century witnessed violent shifts in political power and political ideologies.

Moreover, the deeply flawed peace settlement that ended World War I planted the seeds of ongoing European international tension, economic dislocation, and conflict. That settlement treated Germany harshly, though presumably no more harshly than Germany would have treated its foes if it had been victorious. Despite the severity of the settlement toward Germany, the new international system failed to provide realistic and effective safeguards against a return to power of a vengeful Germany. The withdrawal of the United States into a disdainful isolation from world affairs further destroyed the basis for keeping the peace on which the hopes of Britain and France relied. The economic consequences of the peace settlement produced domestic economic problems that played into the hands of extreme political parties that wished to overturn the post–World War I peace settlement.

World War I, which produced these extensive ongoing destructive results, originated in the domestic unrest among subject nationalities on the Continent and the imperial rivalries among the great powers that built up in the decades after the unification of Germany and Italy. The ferocity of the conflict was the result of the modern armament of European nations made possible by the Second Industrial Revolution. The conflict reached its worldwide extent because of the empires created by European states in the nineteenth century and the rise to the status of a great power by the United States.

For over two decades after 1871 European diplomats and political leaders through various alliances had been able to contain and resolve those domestic and international tensions while Europe prospered and exerted vast global influence. After 1890, however, Europe witnessed a series of international crises that might have but did not lead to war. It also witnessed important diplomatic realignments. Then in the summer of 1914 the crisis in the Balkans following the assassination of heir to the throne of Austria-Hungary erupted into a conflict of previously unimaginable extent, destruction, and political upheaval that lasted until 1918.

▼ Emergence of the German Empire and the Alliance Systems (1873–1890)

Prussia's victories over Austria and France and its creation of a large, powerful German Empire in 1871 revolutionized European diplomacy. A vast new political unit had united the majority of Germans to form a nation of great and growing population, wealth, industrial capacity, and military power. Its sudden appearance created new problems and upset the balance of power that the Congress of Vienna had forged. Britain and Russia retained their positions, although the Crimean War had weakened the latter.

View the Map "The German Empire" on MyHistoryLab.com

Austria, however, had been severely weakened, and the forces of nationalism threatened it with disintegration. The Franco-Prussian War and the German annexation of Alsace-Lorraine badly damaged French power and prestige. The French were afraid of their powerful new neighbor as well as resentful of their defeat, their loss of territory, and the loss of France's traditional position as the dominant Western European power.

Bismarck's Leadership

Until 1890, Bismarck continued to guide German policy. After 1871, he insisted Germany was a satisfied power and wanted no further territorial gains, and he meant it. He wanted to avoid a new war that might undo his achievement. He tried to assuage French resentment by pursuing friendly relations and by supporting French colonial aspirations. He also prepared for the worst. If France could not be conciliated, it must be isolated. Bismarck sought to prevent an alliance between France and any other European power—especially Austria or Russia—that would threaten Germany with a war on two fronts.

War in the Balkans Bismarck's first move was to establish the Three Emperors' League in 1873. The League brought together the three great conservative empires of Germany, Austria, and Russia. The league soon collapsed over Austro-Russian rivalry in the Balkans that arose from the Russo-Turkish War that broke out in 1877. The tottering Ottoman Empire was held together chiefly because the European powers could not agree about how to partition it. Ottoman weakness encouraged Serbia and Montenegro to come to the aid of their fellow Slavs in Bosnia and Herzegovina when they revolted against Turkish rule. Soon the rebellion spread to Bulgaria.

Then Russia entered the fray and turned it into a major international crisis. The Russians hoped to pursue their traditional policy of expansion at Ottoman expense and especially to achieve their most cherished goal: control of Constantinople and the Dardanelles. Russian intervention also reflected the influence of the Pan-Slavic movement, which sought to unite all the Slavic peoples, even those under Austrian or Ottoman rule, under the protection of Holy Mother Russia.

The Ottoman Empire was soon forced to sue for peace. The Treaty of San Stefano of March 1878 was a Russian triumph. The Slavic states in the Balkans were freed of Ottoman rule, and Russia itself obtained territory and a large monetary indemnity. The settlement, however, alarmed the other great powers. Austria feared that the Slavic victory and the increase in Russian influence in the Balkans would threaten its own Balkan provinces. The British were alarmed both by the effect of the Russian victory on the European balance of power and by the possibility of Russian control of the Dardanelles, which would make Russia a Mediterranean power and threaten Britain's control of the Suez Canal. Disraeli was determined to resist, and British public opinion supported him. A music-hall song that became popular gave the language a new word for super patriotism: *jingoism*.

We don't want to fight,
But by jingo if we do,
We've got the men,
We've got the ships,
We've got the money too!
The Russians will not have Constantinople!

The Congress of Berlin Britain and Austria forced Russia to agree to an international conference at which the other great powers would review the provisions of San Stefano. The resulting Congress of Berlin met in June and July 1878 under the presidency of Bismarck. The choice of site and presiding officer were a clear recognition of Germany's new importance and of Bismarck's claim that Germany wanted no new territory and sought to preserve the peace.

Bismarck referred to himself as an "honest broker," and the title was justified. He wanted to avoid a war between Russia and Austria into which he feared Germany would be drawn with nothing to gain and much to lose. From the collapsing Ottoman Empire, he wanted nothing. "The Eastern Question," he said, "is not worth the healthy bones of a single Pomeranian musketeer."[1]

The decisions of the congress were a blow to Russian ambitions. Bulgaria, a Russian client, was reduced in size by two-thirds and deprived of access to the Aegean Sea. Austria-Hungary was given Bosnia and Herzegovina to "occupy and administer," although those provinces remained formally under Ottoman rule. Britain received Cyprus, and France was encouraged to occupy Tunisia. These territories were compensation for the gains that Russia was permitted to keep. Germany asked for nothing, but still earned Russian resentment. The Russians believed they had saved Prussia in 1807 from complete destruction by Napoleon and had expected German gratitude. They were bitterly disappointed, and the Three Emperors' League was dead.

The Berlin settlement also annoyed the Balkan states. Romania wanted Bessarabia, which Russia kept; Bulgaria wanted the borders of the Treaty of San Stefano; and Greece wanted more Ottoman territory. The major trouble spot, however, was in the south Slavic states of Serbia and Montenegro. They resented the Austrian occupation of Bosnia and Herzegovina, as did many of the natives of those provinces. The south Slavic question, no less than the estrangement between Russia and Germany, was a threat to the peace of Europe.

View the **Map** "Congress of Berlin" on **MyHistoryLab.com**

German Alliances with Russia and Austria For the moment, Bismarck could ignore the Balkans, but he could not ignore the breach in his eastern alliance system. With Russia alienated, he concluded a secret treaty with Austria in 1879. This Dual Alliance provided that Germany and Austria would come to each other's aid if Russia attacked either of them. If another country attacked one of them, each promised at least to maintain neutrality.

The treaty was for five years and was renewed regularly until 1918. As the anchor of German policy, it was criticized at the time, and in retrospect, some have considered it an error. It appeared to tie German fortunes to those of the troubled Austro-Hungarian Empire and thus to borrow trouble for Germany. That is, Germany was much more likely to be drawn into aiding Austria-Hungary than the reverse. In addition, by isolating the Russians, the Dual Alliance pushed them to seek alliances in the West.

Bismarck was fully aware of these dangers but discounted them with good reason. He personally never allowed the alliance to drag Germany into Austria's Balkan quarrels. As he put it, in any alliance there is a horse and a rider, and he meant Germany to be the rider. He made it clear to the Austrians that the alliance was purely defensive and Germany would never be a party to an attack on Russia. "For us," he said, "Balkan questions can never be a motive for war."

Bismarck believed that monarchical, reactionary Russia would not seek an alliance either with republican, revolutionary France or with increasingly democratic Britain. In fact, he expected the Austro-German negotiations to frighten Russia into seeking closer relations with Germany, and he was right. By 1881, he had renewed the Three Emperors' League on a firmer basis. The three powers promised to maintain friendly neutrality in case a fourth power attacked any of them. Other clauses included the right of Austria to annex Bosnia-Herzegovina whenever it wished and the support of all three powers for closing the Dardanelles to all nations in case of war.

The agreement allayed German fears of a Russian–French alliance and Russian fears of a combination of Austria and Britain against it, of Britain's fleet sailing into the Black Sea, and of a hostile combination of Germany and Austria. Most importantly, the agreement reduced the tension in the Balkans between Austria and Russia.

[1]Hajo Holborn, *A History of Modern Germany, 1840–1945* (New York: Knopf, 1969), p. 239.

The Triple Alliance In 1882, Italy, ambitious for colonial expansion and angered by the French occupation of Tunisia, asked to join the Dual Alliance. The provisions of its entry were defensive and directed against France. Bismarck's policy was now a complete success. He was allied with three of the great powers and friendly with the other, Great Britain, which held aloof from all alliances. France was isolated and no threat. Bismarck's diplomacy was a great achievement, but an even greater challenge was to maintain this complicated system of secret alliances in the face of the continuing rivalries among Germany's allies. Despite a war in 1885 between Serbia and Bulgaria that again estranged Austria and Russia, Bismarck succeeded.

Although the Three Emperors' League lapsed, the Triple Alliance (Germany, Austria, and Italy) was renewed for another five years. To restore German relations with Russia, Bismarck negotiated the Reinsurance Treaty of 1887, in which both powers promised to remain neutral if either was attacked. All seemed smooth, but a change in the German monarchy upset Bismarck's arrangements.

In 1888, William II (r. 1888–1918) came to the German throne. He was twenty-nine years old, ambitious, and impetuous. He was imperious by temperament and believed he ruled by divine right. An injury at birth had left him with a withered left arm. He compensated for this disability with vigorous exercise, a military bearing, and an often embarrassingly bombastic rhetoric.

Like many Germans of his generation, William II was filled with a sense of Germany's destiny as the leading power of Europe. He wanted recognition of at least equality with Britain, the land of his mother and of his grandmother, Queen Victoria. To achieve a "place in the sun," he and his contemporaries wanted a navy and colonies like Britain's. These aims, of course, ran counter to Bismarck's limited continental policy. When William argued for a navy as a defense against a British landing in North Germany, Bismarck replied, "If the British should land on our soil, I should have them arrested." This was only one example of the great distance between the young emperor, or kaiser, and his chancellor. In 1890, William used a disagreement over domestic policy to dismiss Bismarck.

As long as Bismarck held power, Germany was secure, and the great European powers remained at peace. Although he made mistakes, there was much to admire in his understanding and management of international relations in the hard world of reality. He had a clear and limited idea of his nation's goals. He resisted pressures for further expansion with few and insignificant exceptions. He understood and used the full range of diplomatic weapons: appeasement and deterrence, threats and promises, secrecy and openness. He understood the needs and hopes of other countries and, where possible, tried to help them satisfy their needs or used those countries to his own advantage. His system of alliances created a stalemate in the Balkans and ensured German security.

Bismarck and the young Kaiser William II meet in 1888. The two disagreed over many issues, and in 1890 William dismissed the aged chancellor. © Classic Image/Alamy

During Bismarck's time, Germany was a force for European peace and was increasingly understood to be so. This position would not, of course, have been possible without its great military power. It also required, however, the leadership of a statesman who was willing and able to exercise restraint and who understood what his country needed and what was possible.

Forging the Triple Entente (1890–1907)

Franco–Russian Alliance Almost immediately after Bismarck's retirement, his system of alliances collapsed. His successor was General Leo von Caprivi (1831–1899), who had once asked, "What kind of jackass will dare to be Bismarck's successor?" Caprivi refused the Russian request to renew the Reinsurance Treaty, in part because he felt incompetent to continue Bismarck's complicated policy and in part because he wished to draw Germany closer to Britain, but Britain remained aloof, and Russia was alienated.

Even Bismarck had assumed that ideological differences would prevent a Franco–Russian alliance. Political isolation and the need for foreign capital, however, drove the Russians toward France. The French, who were even more isolated, encouraged their investors to pour capital into Russia if such investment would help produce security against Germany. In 1894, France and Russia signed a defensive alliance against Germany.

Britain and Germany Britain now became the key to the international situation. Colonial rivalries pitted the British against the Russians in Central Asia and against the French in Africa. (See Chapter 25.) Traditionally, Britain had also opposed Russian control of Constantinople and the Dardanelles and French control of the Low Countries. There was no reason to think Britain would soon become friendly to its traditional rivals or abandon its accustomed friendliness toward the Germans.

Yet within a decade of William II's accession, Germany had become the enemy in British minds. Before the turn of the century, popular British thrillers about imaginary wars portrayed the French as the invader; after the turn of the century, the enemy was usually Germany. This remarkable transformation has often been attributed to economic rivalry between Germany and Britain, in which Germany challenged and even overtook British production in various materials and markets. Certainly, Germany made such gains, and many Britons resented them. Yet the economic problem was not a serious cause of hostility, and it waned during the first decade of the century. The real problem lay in the foreign and naval policies of the German emperor and his ministers.

William II admired Britain's colonial empire and mighty fleet. At first, Germany tried to win the British over to the Triple Alliance, but when Britain clung to its "splendid isolation," German policy changed. The idea was to demonstrate Germany's worth as an ally by withdrawing support and even making trouble for Britain. This odd manner of gaining an ally reflected the kaiser's confused feelings toward Britain, which mixed dislike and jealousy with admiration. Many Germans, especially in the intellectual community, shared these feelings. Like William, they were eager for Germany to pursue a "world policy" rather than Bismarck's limited one that confined German interests to Europe. They, too, saw England as the barrier to German ambitions. Their influence in the schools, the universities, and the press guaranteed popular approval of hostility to Britain.

In Africa, the Germans blocked British attempts to build a railroad from Cape Town to Cairo. They also openly sympathized with the Boers of South Africa in their resistance to British expansion. In 1896, William congratulated Paul Kruger (1825–1904), president of the Boer Transvaal Republic, for repulsing a British raid "without having to appeal to friendly powers [i.e., Germany] for assistance." (See Chapter 25.)

In 1898, William began to realize his dream of a German navy with the passage of a naval law providing for the construction of nineteen battleships. In 1900, a second law doubled that figure. The architect of the new navy was Admiral Alfred von Tirpitz (1849–1930), who openly proclaimed that Germany's naval policy was aimed at Britain. His "risk" theory argued that Germany could build a fleet strong enough not to defeat the British, but to do enough damage to make the British navy inferior to that of other powers like France or the United States. The theory was, in fact, absurd because as Germany's fleet became menacing, the British would certainly build enough ships to maintain their advantage, and Britain had greater financial resources than Germany.

The naval policy, therefore, was doomed to failure. Its main results were to waste German resources and to begin a great naval race with Britain. Eventually, the threat the German navy posed so antagonized and alarmed British opinion that the British abandoned their traditional policies of avoiding alliances.

At first, however, Britain was not unduly concerned. The general hostility of world opinion during the Boer War (1899–1902), in which their great empire crushed a rebellion by South African farmers, embarrassed the British, and their isolation no longer seemed so splendid. The Germans had acted with restraint during the war. Between 1898 and 1901, Joseph Chamberlain, the colonial secretary, made several attempts to conclude an alliance with Germany. The Germans, confident that a British alliance with France or Russia was impossible, refused and held out for greater concessions.

The Entente Cordiale The first breach in Britain's isolation came in 1902, when it concluded an alliance with Japan to defend British interests in the Far East against Russia. Next, Britain abandoned its traditional antagonism toward France and in 1904 concluded a series of agreements with the French, collectively called the Entente Cordiale. It was not a formal treaty and had no military provisions, but it settled all outstanding colonial differences between the two nations. In particular, Britain gave France a free hand in Morocco in return for French recognition of British control over Egypt. The Entente Cordiale was a long step toward aligning the British with Germany's great potential enemy.

Britain's new relationship with France was surprising, but in 1904, hardly anyone believed the British whale and the Russian bear would ever come together. The Russo–Japanese War of 1904–1905 made such a development seem even less likely because Britain was allied with Russia's enemy, but Britain had behaved with restraint, and their unexpected defeat, which also led to the Russian Revolution of 1905, humiliated the Russians. Although the revolution was put down, it weakened Russia and reduced British apprehensions about Russian power. The British also became concerned that Russia might again drift into the German orbit.

The First Moroccan Crisis At this point, Germany decided to test the new understanding between Britain and France. In March 1905, Emperor William II landed at Tangier, made a speech in favor of Moroccan independence, and by implication asserted Germany's right to participate in Morocco's destiny. This speech was a challenge to France. Germany's chancellor, Prince Bernhard von Bülow (1849–1929), intended to show France how weak it was. He also hoped to gain colonial concessions.

The Germans demanded an international conference to show their power more dramatically. The conference met in 1906 at Algeciras in Spain. Austria sided with its German ally, but Spain, which also had claims in Morocco, Italy, Russia, and the United States, voted with Britain and France. The Germans had overplayed their hand, receiving trivial concessions, and the French position in Morocco was confirmed. German bullying had, moreover, driven Britain and France closer together. In the face of the threat of a German attack on France, Sir Edward Grey (1862–1933), the British foreign secretary, without making a firm commitment, authorized conversations between the British and French general staffs. Their agreements became morally binding as the years passed. By 1914, French and British military and naval plans were so mutually dependent that the two countries were effectively, if not formally, allies.

British Agreement with Russia Britain's fear of Germany's growing naval power, its concern over German ambitions in the Near East (as represented by the German-sponsored plan to build a railroad from Berlin to Baghdad), and its closer relations with France made it desirable for Britain to become more friendly with France's ally, Russia. With French support, in 1907 the British concluded an agreement with Russia much like the Entente Cordiale with France. It settled Russo–British quarrels in Central Asia and opened the door for wider cooperation. The Triple Entente, an informal, but powerful, association of Britain, France, and Russia, was now ranged against the Triple Alliance. Italy was an unreliable ally, however, which meant two great land powers and Great Britain encircled Germany and Austria-Hungary.

William II and his ministers had turned Bismarck's nightmare of the prospect of a two-front war with France and Russia into a reality. They had made it more horrible by adding Britain to their foes. The equilibrium that Bismarck had worked so hard to achieve was destroyed. Britain would no longer support Austria in restraining Russian ambitions in the Balkans. Germany, increasingly alarmed by a sense of being encircled, was less willing to restrain the Austrians for fear of alienating them, too. In the Dual Alliance of Germany and Austria, the rider was now less clear.

Bismarck had built his alliance system to maintain peace, but the new alliance increased the risk of war and made the Balkans a likely spot for it to break out. Bismarck's diplomacy had left France isolated and impotent. The new arrangement associated France with the two greatest powers in Europe besides Germany. The Germans could rely only on Austria, and Austria's troubles made it less likely to provide aid than to need it.

View the Map
"European Alliances on the Eve of World War I" on MyHistoryLab.com

World War I

The Road to War (1908–1914)

The weak Ottoman Empire still controlled the central strip of the Balkan Peninsula running west from Constantinople to the Adriatic. North and south of it were the independent states of Romania, Serbia, Montenegro, and Greece, as well as Bulgaria, technically still part of the empire but legally autonomous and practically independent. The Austro-Hungarian Empire included Croatia and Slovenia and, since 1878, had "occupied and administered" Bosnia and Herzegovina.

View the Map "Interactive Map: The Decline of the Ottoman Empire" on MyHistoryLab.com

Except for the Greeks and the Romanians, most of the inhabitants of the Balkans spoke variants of the same Slavic language and felt a cultural and historical kinship with one another. For centuries Austrians, Hungarians, or Turks had ruled them, and the nationalism that characterized late-nineteenth-century Europe made many of them eager for independence. The more radical among them longed for a union of the south Slavic, or Yugoslav, peoples in a single nation. They looked to independent Serbia as the center of the new nation and hoped to detach all the Slavic provinces (especially Bosnia, which bordered on Serbia) from Austria. Serbia believed its destiny was to unite the Slavs at the expense of Austria, as Piedmont had united the Italians and Prussia the Germans.

In 1908, a group of modernizing reformers called the Young Turks seized power in the Ottoman Empire. Their actions threatened to breathe new life into the empire and to interfere with the plans of the European jackals to pounce on the Ottoman corpse. These events brought on the first of a series of Balkan crises that would eventually lead to war.

View the Map "Diplomatic Crises, 1905–1914" on MyHistoryLab.com

The Bosnian Crisis In 1908, the Austrian and Russian governments decided to act quickly before Turkey became strong enough to resist. They struck a bargain in which Russia agreed to support the Austrian annexation of Bosnia and Herzegovina in return for Austrian backing for opening the Dardanelles to Russian warships.

Austria, however, declared the annexation before the Russians could act. The British and French, eager for the favor of the Young Turks, refused to agree to the Russian demand to open the Dardanelles. The Russians were humiliated and furious, but too weak to do anything but protest. The Austrian annexation of Bosnia enraged Russia's "little brothers," the Serbs.

Germany had not been warned in advance of Austria's plans and was unhappy because the action threatened their relations with Russia and Turkey. Germany felt so dependent on the Dual Alliance, however, that it nevertheless assured Austria of its support. Austria had been given a free hand, and to some extent, Vienna was now making German policy. It was a dangerous precedent. Also, the failure of Britain and France to support Russia strained the Triple Entente. This made it harder for them to oppose Russian interests in the future if they were to keep Russian friendship.

The Second Moroccan Crisis The second Moroccan crisis, in 1911, emphasized the French and British need for mutual support. When France sent an army to Morocco, Germany took the opportunity to "protect German interests" there as a means to extort colonial concessions in the French Congo. To add force to their demands, the Germans sent the gunboat *Panther* to the Moroccan port of Agadir, purportedly to protect German citizens there. Once again, as in 1905, the Germans went too far. The *Panther*'s visit to Agadir provoked a strong reaction in Britain. For some time Anglo-German relations had been growing worse, chiefly because the naval race had intensified. In 1907, Germany had built its first dreadnought, a new type of battleship that Britain had launched in 1906. In 1908, Germany had passed still another naval law that accelerated the challenge to British naval supremacy.

These actions threatened Britain's security. Britain had to increase taxes to pay for new armaments just when its liberal government was launching its expensive program of social legislation. Negotiations failed to persuade William II and Tirpitz to slow down naval construction.

In this atmosphere, the British heard of the *Panther*'s arrival in Morocco. They wrongly believed the Germans meant to turn Agadir into a naval base on the Atlantic. The crisis passed when France yielded some insignificant bits of the Congo and Germany recognized the French protectorate over Morocco. Britain drew closer to France. The British made plans to send an expeditionary force to defend France in case Germany attacked, and the British and French navies agreed to cooperate. Without any formal treaty, the German naval construction and the Agadir crisis had turned the Entente Cordiale into a de facto alliance. If Germany attacked France, Britain must defend the French, for its own security was inextricably tied up with that of France.

War in the Balkans The second Moroccan crisis also provoked another crisis in the Balkans. Italy sought to gain colonies and to take its place among the great powers. It wanted Libya, which, though worth little before the discovery of oil in the 1950s, was at least available. Italy feared that the recognition of the French protectorate in Morocco would encourage France to move into Libya also. So, in 1911, Italy attacked the Ottoman Empire to preempt the French, and forced Turkey to cede Libya and the Dodecanese Islands in the Aegean. The Italian victory encouraged the Balkan states to try their luck. In 1912, Bulgaria, Greece, Montenegro, and Serbia jointly attacked the Ottoman Empire and won easily. (See Map 26–1.) After this First Balkan War, the victors fell out among themselves over the division of Macedonia, and in 1913 a Second Balkan War erupted. This time, Turkey and Romania joined Serbia and Greece against Bulgaria and stripped away much of what the Bulgarians had gained in 1878 and 1912.

View the **Image** "European Leaders Attempt to Quell the Balkan Crises—Punch Cartoon" on **MyHistoryLab.com**

After the First Balkan War, the alarmed Austrians were determined to limit Serbian gains and especially to prevent the Serbs from gaining a port on the Adriatic. This policy meant keeping Serbia out of Albania, but the Russians backed the Serbs, and tensions mounted. An international conference sponsored by Britain in early 1913 resolved the dispute in Austria's favor and called for an independent principality of Albania. Austria, however, felt humiliated by the public airing of Serbian demands, and the Serbs defied the powers and continued to occupy parts of Albania. Finally, in October 1913, Austria issued an ultimatum, and Serbia withdrew its forces from Albania.

During this crisis, many officials in Austria had wanted an all-out attack on Serbia to remove its threat to the empire once and for all. Emperor Francis Joseph and the heir to the throne, Archduke Francis Ferdinand, had resisted those demands. At the same time, Pan-Slavic sentiment in Russia pressed Tsar Nicholas II to take a firm stand, but Russia once again let Austria have its way with Serbia. Throughout the crisis, Britain, France, Italy, and Germany restrained their allies, although each worried about appearing to be too reluctant to help its friends.

The lessons learned from this crisis of 1913 influenced behavior in the final crisis in 1914. As in 1908, the Russians had been embarrassed by their passivity, and

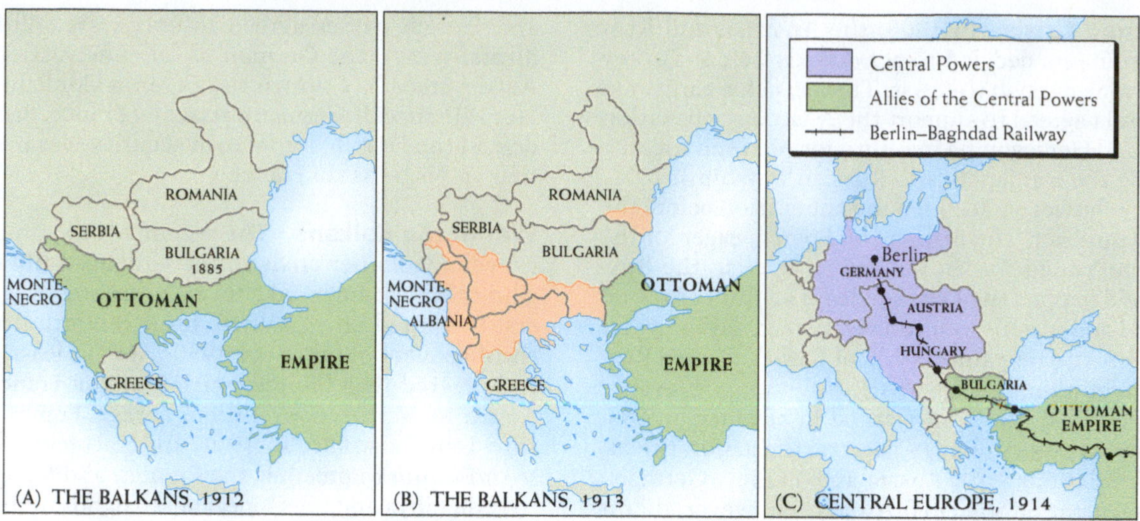

Map 26–1 **THE BALKANS, 1912–1913** Two maps show the Balkans (a) before and (b) after the two Balkan wars; note the Ottoman retreat. In (c), we see the geographical relationship of the Central Powers and their Bulgarian and Turkish allies.

their allies were more reluctant to restrain them again. The Austrians were embarrassed by the results of accepting an international conference and were determined not to do it again. They had gotten better results from threatening to use force; they and their German allies did not miss the lesson.

Sarajevo and the Outbreak of War (June–August 1914)

The Assassination On June 28, 1914, a nineteen-year-old Serbian nationalist shot and killed Archduke Francis Ferdinand, heir to the Austrian throne, and his wife as they drove in an open car through the Bosnian capital of Sarajevo. The assassin was a member of a conspiracy hatched by a political terrorist society called Union or Death, better known as the Black Hand. The chief of intelligence of the Serbian army's general staff had helped plan and prepare the crime. Though his role was not known at the time, it was generally believed throughout Europe that Serbian officials were involved. The glee of the Serbian press after the assassination lent support to that belief.

Read the Document "Borijove Jevtic, *The Murder of Archduke Franz Ferdinand at Sarajevo* (28 June 1914)" on **MyHistoryLab.com**

The archduke was not popular in Austria, and his funeral evoked little grief. He had been known to favor a form of federal government for Austria that would have raised the status of the Slavs in the empire. This position alienated the conservatives among the

Watch the Video "Video Lectures: The Outbreak of World War I" on **MyHistoryLab.com**

THE COMING OF WORLD WAR I

1871	The end of the Franco-Prussian War; creation of the German Empire; German annexation of Alsace-Lorraine
1873	The Three Emperors' League (Germany, Russia, and Austria-Hungary)
1877–1878	The Russo–Turkish War
1878	The Congress of Berlin
1879	The Dual Alliance between Germany and Austria
1881	The Three Emperors' League is renewed
1882	Italy joins Germany and Austria in the Triple Alliance
1888	William II becomes the German emperor
1890	Bismarck is dismissed
1894	The Franco–Russian alliance
1898	Germany begins to build a battleship navy
1899–1902	Boer War
1902	The British alliance with Japan
1904	The Entente Cordiale between Britain and France
1904–1905	The Russo–Japanese War
1905–1906	The first Moroccan crisis
1907	The British agreement with Russia
1908–1909	The Bosnian crisis
1911	The second Moroccan crisis
1911	Italy attacks Turkey
1912–1913	The First and Second Balkan Wars
1914	Outbreak of World War I

Top: The Austrian archduke Francis Ferdinand and his wife in Sarajevo on June 28, 1914. Later in the day the royal couple was assassinated by young revolutionaries trained and supplied in Serbia, igniting the crisis that led to World War I. *Bottom:* Moments after the assassination the Austrian police captured one of the assassins. © Pictorial Press/Alamy

Habsburg officials and the Hungarians. It also threatened the radical nationalists' dream of an independent south Slav state.

Germany and Austria's Response News of the assassination produced outrage everywhere in Europe except in Serbia. To those Austrians who had long favored an attack on Serbia, the opportunity seemed irresistible, but it was never easy for the Dual Monarchy to make a decision. Conrad von Hotzendorf (1852–1925), chief of the Austrian general staff, urged an attack, as he had often done before. Count Stefan Tisza (1861–1918), speaking for Hungary, resisted. Count Leopold von Berchtold (1863–1942), the Austro-Hungarian foreign minister, felt the need for strong action, but he knew German support would be required in the likely event that Russia should intervene to protect Serbia. Moreover, nothing could be done without Tisza's approval, and only German support could persuade the Hungarians to accept a war. The question of peace or war against Serbia, therefore, had to be answered in Berlin.

William II and Chancellor Theobald von Bethmann-Hollweg (1856–1921) readily promised German support for an attack on Serbia. It has often been said that they gave the Austrians a "blank check," but their message was more specific than that. They urged the Austrians to move swiftly while the other powers were still angry at Serbia. They also made the Austrians feel they would view a failure to act as evidence of Austria-Hungary's weakness and uselessness as an ally. Therefore, the Austrians never wavered in their determination to make war on Serbia. They hoped, with the protection of Germany, to fight Serbia alone, but they were prepared to risk a general European conflict. The Germans also knew they risked a general war, but they too hoped to "localize" the fight between Austria and Serbia.

Some scholars believe Germany had long been plotting war, and some even think a specific plan for war in 1914 was set in motion as early as 1912. The vast body of evidence on the crisis of 1914, however, gives little support to such notions. The German leaders plainly reacted to a crisis they had not foreseen and just as plainly made decisions in response to events. The decision to support Austria, however, made war difficult, if not impossible, to avoid. The emperor and chancellor made that decision without significant consulting of either their military or diplomatic advisers.

William II reacted violently to the assassination. He was moved by his friendship for the archduke and by outrage at an attack on royalty. A different provocation would probably not have moved him so much. Bethmann-Hollweg was less emotional, but under severe pressure. To resist the decision would have meant flatly opposing the emperor. The German army suspected the chancellor of being soft. It would have been difficult for him to take a conciliatory position. Important military leaders, especially General Helmut von Moltke (1848–1916), Chief of the General Staff since 1906, had come to believe that the growing power of Russia threatened Germany. Moltke repeatedly spoke of the need for a decisive war against Russia, and its allies if necessary, "the sooner the better." His influence would be important at key moments in the crisis.

Bethmann-Hollweg, like many other Germans, also feared for the future. Russia was recovering its strength and would reach a military peak in 1917. The Triple Entente was growing closer and more powerful, and Germany's only reliable ally was Austria. The chancellor recognized the danger of supporting Austria, but he

Document

THE AUSTRIAN AMBASSADOR GETS A "BLANK CHECK" FROM THE KAISER

It was at a meeting at Potsdam on July 5, 1914, that the Austrian ambassador received from the Kaiser assurance that Germany would support Austria in the Balkans, even at the risk of war.

Was the Kaiser's reply a blank check? If not, how would you characterize his message?

After lunch, when I again called attention to the seriousness of the situation, the Kaiser authorised me to inform our gracious Majesty that we might in this case, as in all others, rely upon Germany's full support. He must, as he said before, first hear what the Imperial Chancellor has to say, but he did not doubt in the least that Herr von Bethmann-Hollweg would agree with him. Especially as far as our action against Serbia was concerned. But it was his [Kaiser Wilhelm's] opinion that this action must not be delayed. Russia's attitude will no doubt be hostile but to this he had been for years prepared, and should a war between Austria-Hungary and Russia be unavoidable, we might be convinced that Germany, our old faithful ally, would stand at our side. Russia at the present time was in no way prepared for war, and would think twice before it appealed to arms. But it will certainly set other powers on to the Triple Alliance and add fuel to the fire in the Balkans. He understands perfectly well that His Apostolic Majesty [the Austrian Emperor Franz Josef] in his well-known love of peace would be reluctant to march into Serbia; but if we had really recognised the necessity of warlike action against Serbia, he [Kaiser Wilhelm] would regret if we did not make use of the present moment which is all in our favour.

From *Outbreak of the World War: German Documents Collected by Karl Kautsky*, eds. Max Montgelas and Walther Schücking (New York, Carnegie Endowment for International Peace, 1924), p. 76.

believed it to be even more dangerous to withhold that support. If Austria did not crush Serbia, it might collapse before the onslaught of Slavic nationalism backed by Russia. If Germany did not defend its ally, the Austrians might look elsewhere for help. His policy was one of calculated risk.

Unfortunately, the calculations proved to be incorrect. Bethmann-Hollweg hoped the Austrians would strike swiftly and present the powers with a fait accompli while the outrage of the assassination was still fresh, and he hoped German support would deter Russia. Failing that, he was prepared for a continental war against France and Russia. This policy, though, depended on British neutrality, and the German chancellor convinced himself the British would stand aloof.

The Austrians, however, were slow to act. They did not even deliver their deliberately unacceptable ultimatum to Serbia until July 23, when the general hostility toward Serbia had begun to subside. Serbia further embarrassed the Austrians by returning so soft and conciliatory an answer that even the mercurial German emperor thought it removed all reason for war, but the Austrians were determined not to turn back. (See "Compare and Connect: The Outbreak of World War I," pages 838–840.) On July 28, they declared war on Serbia, even though the army would not be ready to attack until mid-August.

The Triple Entente's Response The Russians, previously so often forced to back off, responded angrily to the Austrian demands on Serbia. The most conservative elements of the Russian government feared that war would lead to revolution, as it had in 1905, but nationalists, Pan-Slavs, and most of the politically conscious classes in general demanded action. The government responded by ordering partial mobilization, against Austria only. This policy was militarily impossible, but its intention was to put diplomatic pressure on Austria to refrain from attacking Serbia.

Mobilization of any kind, however, was a dangerous weapon because it was generally understood to be equivalent to an act of war. In fact, only Germany's war plan made mobilization the first and irrevocable start of a war.

It required a quick victory in the west before the Russians were ready to act. Even partial Russian mobilization seemed to jeopardize this plan and put Germany in great danger. From this point on, the general staff pressed for German mobilization and war. Their claim of military necessity soon became irresistible.

France and Britain were not eager for war. France's president and prime minister were on their way back from a long-planned state visit to Russia when the crisis flared on July 23. The Austrians had, in fact, delivered their ultimatum to the Serbs precisely when these two men would be at sea. Had they been in Paris, they might have tried to restrain the Russians. In their absence and without consulting his government, the French ambassador to Russia gave the Russians the same assurances of support that Germany had given Austria. The British worked hard to resolve the crisis by traditional means: a conference of the powers. Austria, still smarting from its humiliation after the London Conference of 1913, would not hear of it. The Germans privately supported the Austrians but publicly took on a conciliatory tone to placate the British.

Soon, however, Bethmann-Hollweg realized what he should have known from the first: If Germany attacked France, Britain must fight. Until July 30, his public appeals to Austria for restraint were a sham. Thereafter, he sincerely tried to persuade the Austrians to negotiate and avoid a general war, but it was too late. The Austrians could not turn back without losing their own self-respect and the respect of the Germans.

On July 30, Austria ordered mobilization against Russia. Bethmann-Hollweg resisted the enormous pressure to mobilize, not because he hoped to avoid war, but because he wanted Russia to mobilize against Germany first and appear to be the aggressor. Only in that way could he win the support of the German nation for war, especially the backing of pacifist Social Democrats. His luck was good for a change. The news of Russian general mobilization came only minutes before Germany would have mobilized in any case. Germany then declared war on Russia on August 1. The Schlieffen Plan went into effect. The Germans occupied Luxembourg on August 2 and invaded Belgium, which resisted, on August 3—the same day Germany declared war on France. The invasion of Belgium violated the treaty of 1839 in which the British had joined the other powers in guaranteeing Belgian neutrality. This factor undermined sentiment in Britain for neutrality and united the nation against Germany, which then invaded France. On August 4, Britain declared war on Germany.

View the **Map** "Map Discovery: The Schlieffen Plan and France's Plan XVII, ca. 1905–1914" on **MyHistoryLab.com**

The Great War had begun. As Sir Edward Grey, the British foreign secretary, put it, the lights were going out all over Europe. They would come on again, but Europe would never be the same.

Although debate on the causes of the war continues, the most common opinion today is that German ambitions for a higher place in the international order under the new kaiser William II led to a new challenge to the status quo. German bullying resulted in a series of crises that led to the final crisis in July 1914, when Germany supported—indeed, pushed—its only reliable ally Austria into a war against Serbia that touched off the world war.

The deeper causes of that war are seen to be Germany's new ambitions to become a world power like Great Britain and to become the dominant power on the European continent. Germany's decision to build a battleship navy threatened Britain's interests and security. In response, the British launched an expensive and unwelcome naval race to maintain their superiority at sea and abandoned their cherished "splendid isolation" and long-standing competitions with France and Russia. In an unprecedented reversal of policy, they made an alliance with Japan and agreements with France and Russia to form the "Triple Entente," which grew from a set of colonial accords to an informal, but visible, check on German ambitions. This new international configuration alarmed Germany, which complained that jealous and hostile forces were "encircling" it. The Germans feared the growing power of the country's enemies, but Germany did not seriously attempt to ease the tension. Instead, a new arms race ensued, and Germany assumed a rigid stance in the final crisis that ended in war.

Watch the **Video** "The Origins of World War I" on **MyHistoryLab.com**

Strategies and Stalemate: 1914–1917

Throughout Europe, jubilation greeted the outbreak of war. No general war had been fought since Napoleon, and few understood the horrors of modern warfare. The dominant memory was of Bismarck's swift and decisive campaigns, in which the costs and casualties were light and the rewards great. After years of crises and resentments, war came as a release of tension. The popular press had increased public awareness of, and interest in, foreign affairs and had fanned the flames of patriotism. The prospect of war moved even a rational man of science like Sigmund Freud to say, "My whole libido goes out to Austria-Hungary."

The Triple Entente powers—or the Allies, as they called themselves—held superiority in numbers and financial resources, as well as command of the sea. (See Figure 26–1, p. 841.) Germany and Austria, the Central Powers, had the advantages of possessing internal lines of communication and having launched their attack first.

A New Style of War Both sides expected a war of movement, like the European wars of the later nineteenth century, that would end quickly with not more than a few battles, which would prove decisive. The American Civil War, where improved weapons produced enormous

COMPARE AND CONNECT The Outbreak of World War I

Read the **Compare and Connect** on **MyHistoryLab.com**

IN THE CENTURY between the Congress of Vienna and the events at Sarajevo, Europe had overcome one crisis after another without recourse to a major war. Yet the assassination of the Archduke Francis Ferdinand, heir to the Austro-Hungarian Empire, in a Bosnian town on June 28, 1914, produced a crisis that led to a general and catastrophic war. It is interesting to focus attention on the crisis of July 1914 and to trace the steps that turned a Balkan incident into a major disaster. Austria's ultimatum to Serbia and the answer of the Serbians were critical events in bringing on the war.

QUESTIONS

1. **Which of the demands were the most difficult for the Serbians to meet?**
2. **Why did the Austrians fix so short a time for response?**
3. **Which demands did the Serbians fail to grant? Why?**
4. **Was the Austrian immediate declaration of war justified?**

I. The Austrian Ultimatum

On the afternoon of July 23, after an investigation of the assassination of the Archduke Franz Ferdinand at Sarajevo, the Austrians presented a list of demands to Serbia, and the Serbs were given forty-eight hours to reply. The Austrian ambassador to Belgrade was instructed to leave the country and break off diplomatic relations unless the demands were met without reservations. The Serbians knew that some officials of the Serbian government took part in the plot.

The results brought out by the inquiry no longer permit the Imperial and Royal Government to maintain the attitude of patient tolerance which it has observed for years toward those agitations which center at Belgrade and are spread thence into the territories of the Monarchy. Instead, these results impose upon the Imperial and Royal Government the obligation to put an end to those intrigues, which constitute a standing menace to the peace of the Monarchy.

In order to attain this end, the Imperial and Royal Government finds itself compelled to demand that the Serbian Government give official assurance that it will condemn the propaganda directed against Austria-Hungary, that is to say, the whole body of the efforts whose ultimate object it is to separate from the Monarchy territories that belong to it; and that it will obligate itself to suppress with all the means at its command this criminal and terroristic propaganda. . . .

1. to suppress every publication which shall incite to hatred and contempt the Monarchy, and the general tendency of which shall be directed against the territorial integrity of the latter;
2. to proceed at once to the dissolution of the Narodna Odbrana [a Serbian nationalist propaganda and paramilitary organization], confiscate all of its means of propaganda, and in the same manner to proceed against the other unions and associations in Serbia which occupy themselves with propaganda against Austria-Hungary; the Royal Government will take such measures as are necessary to make sure that the dissolved associations may not continue their activities under other names in other forms;
3. to eliminate without delay from public instruction in Serbia, everything, whether connected with the teaching corps or with the methods of teaching, that serves or may serve to nourish the propaganda against Austria-Hungary;
4. to remove from the military and administrative service in general all officers and officials who have been guilty of carrying on the propaganda against Austria-Hungary, whose names the Imperial and Royal Government reserve the right to make known to the Royal Government . . . ;
5. to agree to the cooperation in Serbia of the organs of the Imperial Royal Government in the suppression of the subversive movement directed against the integrity of the Monarchy;
6. to institute a judicial inquiry against every participant in the conspiracy of the twenty-eighth of June who may be found in Serbian territory; the organs of the Imperial and Royal Government delegated for this purpose will take part in the proceedings held for this purpose;
7. to undertake with all haste the arrest of Major Voislav Tankositch and of one Milan Ciganovitch, a Serbian official, who have been compromised by the results of the inquiry . . . ;

This ethnographic map of the Balkan Peninsula, made by a Serbian nationalist named Jovan Cviji'cin in 1918, served as inspiration for the campaign of ethnic cleansing that would devastate the region once known as Yugoslavia. Library of Congress

10. to inform the Imperial and Royal Government without delay of the execution of the measures comprised in the foregoing points.

The Imperial and Royal Government awaits the reply of the Royal Government by Saturday, the twenty-fifth instant, at 6 P.M., at the latest. ■

From "The Austrian Ultimatum," in *Outbreak of the World War*, German documents collected by Karl Kautsky and ed. by Max Montgelas and Walther Schucking, trans. by the Carnegie Endowment for International Peace. Division of International Law, Supplement I (1924) (New York: Oxford University Press, 1924), pp. 604–605.

II. The Serbian Response

The reply of the Serbians was remarkably reasonable. In his first reaction to it the German Kaiser said:

"After reading over the Serbian reply, which I received this morning, I am convinced that on the whole the wishes of the Danube Monarchy have been acceded to. The few reservations that Serbia makes in regard to individual points could, according to my opinion, be settled by negotiation. But it contains the announcement orbi et urbi of a capitulation of the most humiliating kind, and as a result, every cause for war falls to the ground." *But it was not unconditional acceptance of the ultimatum.*

The royal Servian government have received the communication of the Imperial and Royal Government of the 10th instant, and are convinced that their reply will remove any misunderstanding which may threaten to impair the good neighbourly relations between the Austro-Hungarian Monarchy and the Kingdom of Servia. . . .

The Royal Government have been pained and surprised at the statements, according to which members of the Kingdom of Servia are supposed to have participated in the preparations for the crime committed at Serajevo; the Royal Government expected to be invited to collaborate in an investigation of all that concerns this crime, and they were ready, in order to prove the entire correctness of their attitude, to take measures against any persons concerning whom representations were made to them. Falling in, therefore, with the desire of the Imperial and Royal Government, they are prepared to hand over for trial any Servian subject, without regard to his situation or rank, of whose complicity in the crime of Serajevo proofs are forthcoming, and more especially they undertake to cause to be published on the first page of the] "Journal officiel," on the date of the 13th (26th) July, the following declaration:

The Royal Government of Servia condemn all propaganda which may be directed against Austria-Hungary, that is to say, all such tendencies as aim at ultimately detaching from the Austro-Hungarian Monarchy territories which form part thereof and they sincerely deplore the baneful consequences of these criminal movements. The Royal Government regret that, according to the communication from the Imperial and Royal Government, certain Servian officers and officials should have taken part in the above-mentioned propaganda and thus compromised the good neighbourly relations to which the Royal Servian Government was solemnly engaged by the declaration of the 31st March, 1909, which declaration disapproves and repudiates all idea or attempt at interference with the destiny of the inhabitants of any part whatsoever of Austria-Hungary, and they consider it their duty formally to warn the officers, officials, and entire population of the kingdom that henceforth they will take the most rigorous steps against all such persons as are guilty of such acts, to prevent and to repress which they will use their utmost endeavour. . . .

The Royal Government further undertake:—

1. To introduce at the first regular convocation of the Skuptchina a provision into the press law providing for the most severe punishment of incitement to hatred or contempt of the Austro-Hungarian Monarchy, and for taking action against any publication the general tendency of which is directed against the territorial integrity of Austria-Hungary. . . .
2. The Royal Government will accept the demand of the Imperial and Royal Government, and will dissolve the "Narodna Odbrana" Society and every other society which may be directing its efforts against Austria-Hungary.
3. The Royal Servian Government undertake to remove without delay from their public educational establishments in Servia all that serves or could serve to foment propaganda against Austria-Hungary, whenever the Imperial and Royal Government furnish them with facts and proofs of this propaganda.
4. The Royal Government also agree to remove from military service all such persons as the judicial enquiry may have proved to be guilty of acts directed against the integrity of the territory of the Austro-Hungarian Monarchy, and they expect the Imperial and Royal Government to communicate to them at a later date the names and the acts of these officers and officials for the purposes of the proceedings which are to be taken against them.
5. The Royal Government must confess that they do not clearly grasp the meaning or the scope of the demand made by the Imperial and Royal Government that Servia shall undertake to accept the collaboration of the organs of the Imperial and Royal Government upon their territory, but they declare that they will admit such collaboration as agrees with the principle of international law, with criminal procedure, and with good neighbourly relations.
6. It goes without saying that the Royal Government consider it their duty to open an enquiry against all such persons as are, or eventually may be, implicated in the plot of the 15th June, and who happen to be within the territory of the kingdom. As regards the participation in this enquiry of Austro-Hungarian agents or authorities appointed for this purpose by the Imperial and Royal Government, the Royal Government cannot accept such an arrangement, as it would be a violation of the Constitution and of the law of criminal procedure; nevertheless, in concrete cases communications as to the results of the investigation in question might be given to the Austro-Hungarian agents.
7. The Royal Government proceeded, on the very evening of the delivery of the note, to arrest Commandant Voislav Tankossitch. As regards Milan Ziganovitch, who is a subject of the Austro-Hungarian Monarchy and who, up to the 15th June was employed (on probation) by the directorate of railways, it has not yet been possible to arrest him. . . .
10. The Royal Government will inform the Imperial and Royal Government the execution of the measures comprised under the above heads, in so far as this has not already been done by the present note, as soon as each measure has been ordered and carried out.

If the Imperial and Royal Government are not satisfied with this reply, the Servian Government, considering that it is not to the common interest to precipitate the solution of this question, are ready, as always, to accept a pacific understanding, either by referring this question to the decision of the International Tribunal of The Hague, or to the Great Powers which took part in the drawing up of the declaration made by the Servian Government on the 18th (31st) March 1909.

Belgrade, July 12 (25), 1914. ■

From "Serbia's Answer to Ultimatum," from *British Diplomatic Correspondence in Collected Diplomatic Documents Relating to the Outbreak of the European War*, No. 39 (London: H.M. Stationery Office, 1915), pp. 31–37.

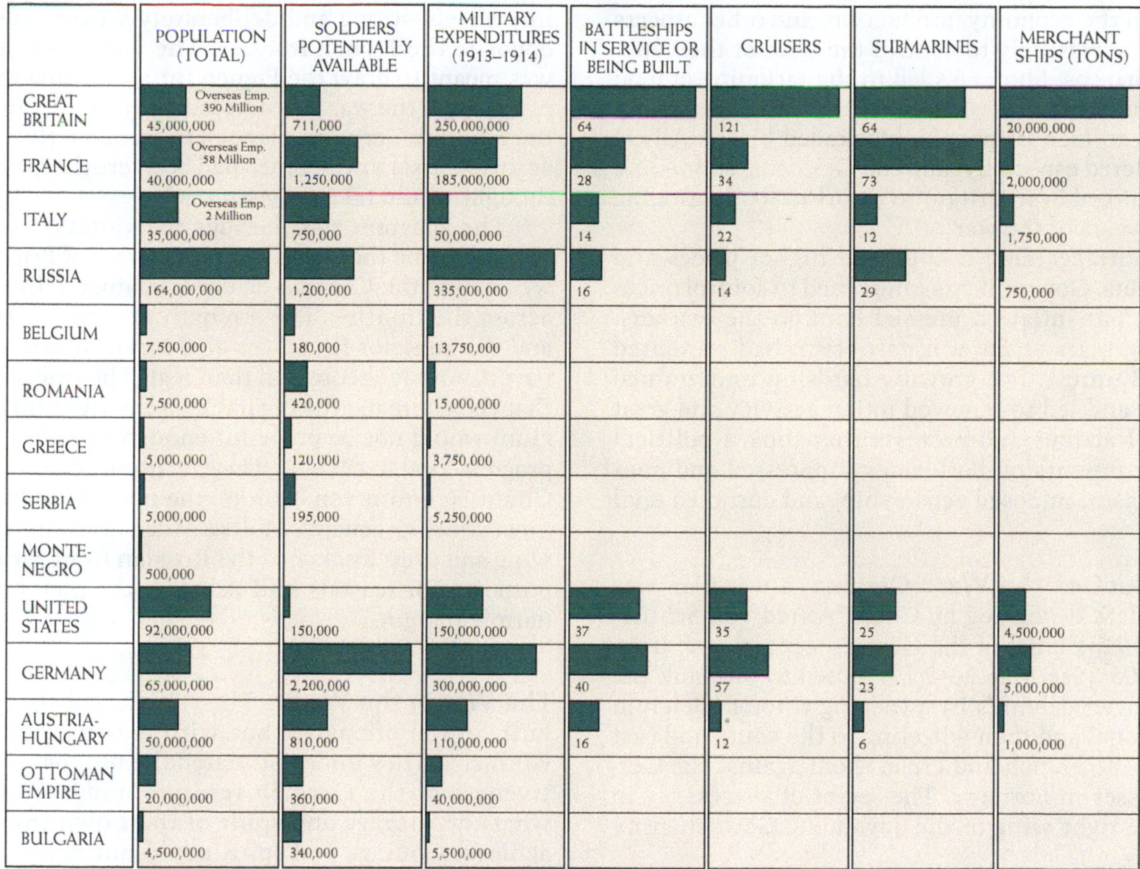

POPULATION (TOTAL)
SOLDIERS POTENTIALLY AVAILABLE
MILITARY EXPENDITURES (1913–1914)
BATTLESHIPS IN SERVICE OR BEING BUILT
CRUISERS
SUBMARINES
MERCHANT SHIPS (TONS)
GREAT BRITAIN
Overseas Emp. 390 Million
45,000,000
711,000
250,000,000
64
121
64
20,000,000
FRANCE
Overseas Emp. 58 Million
40,000,000
1,250,000
185,000,000
28
34
73
2,000,000
ITALY
Overseas Emp. 2 Million
35,000,000
750,000
50,000,000
14
22
12
1,750,000
RUSSIA
164,000,000
1,200,000
335,000,000
16
14
29
750,000
BELGIUM
7,500,000
180,000
13,750,000
ROMANIA
7,500,000
420,000
15,000,000
GREECE
5,000,000
120,000
3,750,000
SERBIA
5,000,000
195,000
5,250,000
MONTE-NEGRO
500,000
UNITED STATES
92,000,000
150,000
150,000,000
37
35
25
4,500,000
GERMANY
65,000,000
2,200,000
300,000,000
40
57
23
5,000,000
AUSTRIA-HUNGARY
50,000,000
810,000
110,000,000
16
12
6
1,000,000
OTTOMAN EMPIRE
20,000,000
360,000
40,000,000
BULGARIA
4,500,000
340,000
5,500,000

Figure 26–1 Relative strengths of the combatants in World War I.

casualties that, in turn, caused the armies to dig lines of trenches and erect field fortifications, was a terrible war that lasted for four years. The Europeans took little notice. Both sides continued to believe in the decisiveness of the offensive and planned for a quick victory. The development of ever more powerful artillery, rifles with greater range and accuracy, and, especially, machine guns, however, gave the advantage to the defense. The German offensive in the west failed to break the allied forces; both sides were forced to dig deep trenches protected by barbed wire and machine guns. Over time, airplanes and tanks were introduced, bringing warfare into the machine age, and casualties were terribly numerous. The armies were raised by conscription, even in Britain for the first time, making the conflict a total war. This new kind of warfare affected not only the combatants but the civilian population, as well. The heavy cost in lives and wounds of the fighting forces was terrible, but the burden on the civilian population was also enormous.

View the Closer Look "Trench Warfare" on MyHistoryLab.com

The Home Front As the war continued, the demand for foodstuffs, supplies, and other necessities and their destruction on land and sea made it a war of exhaustion as well as of annihilation. Dangers and shortages of every kind plagued the people at home and forced important changes in their lives. Women, especially, encountered new opportunities and faced great challenges. With so many men off in the armed services, many of them had to take on the responsibilities of the head of the household as well as their own usual duties. Soon, more and more women were drawn into jobs away from home, such as conducting street cars, that were more demanding than the traditional limited sphere thought suitable for women but also better paying. As the demand for greater production grew, women were hired to do hard manual labor in munitions plants and other factories that had been thought to be work for men only. These wartime experiences surely helped change the society's view of the proper role of women.

Government Control Early in the war, business and production continued in the usual way, but within months its inefficiency and inadequacy to deal with the new demands became obvious. Shortages, especially in munitions and other military needs, led governments to intervene in the economy, production, and other aspects of life and increasingly to control the lives of their subjects and citizens. Shortages led to the rationing of food and other needed items. Germany, which relied heavily on imports to feed its people, blockaded by the Allies' navies, suffered especially, and the Germans' submarine campaign forced even Britain to resort to food rationing in the last years of the war.

The shortages also encouraged higher prices and black markets. Governments intervened to control prices and wages, but inflation pressed hard on the workers. In the early years of the war patriotism had prevented strikes and unrest, but growing hardship undermined class unity and led to renewed union activity and great numbers of strikes and protests that took a political turn. Governments on both sides suppressed and punished criticism, imposed censorship, and curtailed civil liberties.

The Conduct of the War Germany's war plan was based on ideas developed by Count Alfred von Schlieffen (1833–1913), chief of the German general staff from 1891 to 1906. (See Map 26–2.) It aimed to outflank the French frontier defenses by sweeping through Belgium to the Channel and then wheeling to the south and east to envelop the French and crush them against the German fortresses in Lorraine. The secret of success lay in making the right wing of the advancing German army immensely strong and deliberately weakening the left opposite the French frontier. The weakness of the left was meant to draw the French into attacking the wrong place while the war was decided on the German right. In the east, the Germans planned to stand on the defensive against Russia until France had been crushed, a task they thought would take only six weeks.

Map 26–2 **THE SCHLIEFFEN PLAN OF 1905** Germany's grand strategy for quickly winning the war against France in 1914 is shown by the wheeling arrows on the map. In the original plan, the crushing blows at France were to be followed by the release of troops for use against Russia on Germany's eastern front. The plan, however, was not adequately implemented, and the war on the western front became a long contest in place.

The apparent risk, besides the violation of Belgian neutrality and the consequent alienation of Britain, lay in weakening the German defenses against a direct attack across the frontier. The strength of German fortresses and the superior firepower of German howitzers made that risk more theoretical than real. The true danger was that the German striking force on the right through Belgium would not be powerful enough to make the swift progress vital to success. The execution of the plan fell to Count Helmuth von Moltke, the nephew of Bismarck's most effective general. Moltke added divisions to the left wing and even weakened the Russian front for the same purpose. For reasons still debated, the plan failed by a narrow margin.

The War in the West The French had also put their faith in the offensive, but with less reason than the Germans. They underestimated the numbers and effectiveness of the German reserves and overestimated what the courage and spirit of their own troops could achieve. Courage and spirit could not defeat machine guns and heavy artillery. The French offensive on Germany's western frontier failed totally. This defeat probably was preferable to a partial success because it released troops for use against the main German army. As a result, the French and the British were able to stop the German advance on Paris at the Battle of the Marne in September 1914. (See Map 26–3 and Map 26–4, p. 844.)

Thereafter, the nature of the war in the west became one of position instead of movement. Both sides dug in behind a wall of trenches protected by barbed wire that stretched from the North Sea to Switzerland. Strategically placed machine-gun nests made assaults difficult and dangerous. Both sides, nonetheless, attempted massive attacks preceded by artillery bombardments of unprecedented and horrible force and duration. Still, the defense was always able to recover and to bring up reserves fast enough to prevent a breakthrough.

Assaults that cost hundreds of thousands of lives produced advances of only hundreds of yards. Even poison gas proved ineffective. In 1916, the British introduced the tank, which eventually proved to be the answer to the machine gun. The Allied command was slow to understand this, however, and until the end of the war, defense was supreme. For three years after its establishment, the western front moved only a few miles in either direction.

Map 26–3 **World War I in Europe** Despite the importance of military action in the Far East, in the Arab world, and at sea, the main theaters of activity in World War I were in the European areas.

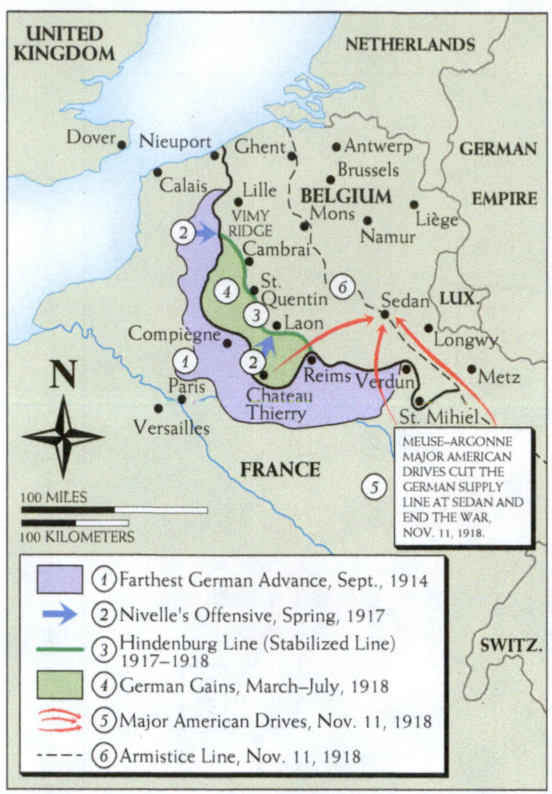

Map 26–4 **THE WESTERN FRONT, 1914–1918** This map shows the crucial western front in detail.

The War in the East In the east, the war began auspiciously for the Allies. The Russians advanced into Austrian territory and inflicted heavy casualties, but Russian incompetence and German energy soon reversed the situation. A junior German officer, Erich Ludendorff (1865–1937), under the command of the elderly general Paul von Hindenburg (1847–1934), destroyed or captured an entire Russian army at the Battle of Tannenberg and defeated another one at the Masurian Lakes. In 1915, the Central Powers pressed their advantage in the east and drove into the Baltic states and Russian Poland, inflicting more than 2 million casualties in a single year.

As the battlelines hardened, both sides sought new allies. Turkey (because of its hostility to Russia) and Bulgaria (the enemy of Serbia) joined the Central Powers. Both sides bid for Italian support with promises of the spoils of victory. Because the Austrians held what the Italians wanted most, the Allies could promise more. In a secret treaty of 1915, they agreed to deliver to Italy after victory most of *Italia irredenta* (i.e., the South Tyrol, Trieste, and some of the Dalmatian Islands), plus colonies in Africa and a share of the Turkish Empire. By the spring of 1915, Italy was engaging Austrian armies. The Italian campaign weakened Austria and diverted some German troops, but the Italian alliance never produced significant results. Romania joined the Allies in 1916 but was quickly defeated and driven from the war.

British tanks moving toward the Battle of Cambrai in Flanders late in 1917. Tanks were impervious to machine-gun fire. Had they been used in great numbers, they might have broken the stalemate in the west. Bildarchiv Preussischer Kulturbesitz/Art Resource, NY

THE DEVELOPMENT OF THE ARMORED TANK

WARFARE FREQUENTLY PROVES a source of technological innovation. Such was true of World War I, which witnessed the development of numerous new weapons. Among the most important of these was the tank—an armored vehicle using a caterpillar track rather than wheels for transport. The caterpillar track had been invented in Great Britain but was then purchased by the American Holt tractor company, which devised a caterpillar tractor in the first decade of the century to cultivate areas with either wet or loose earth where a wheeled vehicle would sink into the ground. During World War I the British modified the caterpillar tractor by introducing a heavily armored closed compartment for a crew armed with machine guns. These early slow-moving tanks could drive over trenches, small hills, and rough terrain and through mud and thus bring mobility to the combat zones where trench warfare had made any kind of effective assault on enemy troops difficult. The tank was used primarily by Britain, France, and the United States in relatively small numbers in World War I, but later rapidly moving tanks became one of the major weapons of later twentieth-century warfare.

Note that the design of the driver's area of the tractor was intended to allow the driver a wide area of vision and also was fully exposed.

Note how the caterpillar track on the tractor would allow it to move over difficult or wet ground without sinking.

Library of Congress

The armament of the tank was intended to protect the tank crew from small-arms fire while the opening on the top permitted the mounting of a machine gun.

The interior of the tank allowed for a small crew working in an extremely hot climate with little or no chance for escape if the tank was hit by a large artillery round or became bogged down in enemy territory.

Topical Press Agency/Stringer/Hulton Archive/Getty Images

What technological developments prior to World War I made tank warfare possible? What military developments made it desirable?

What advantages does tank warfare offer?

How do tanks interact with other military units to achieve success?

What devices and tactics have modern armies developed to combat the tank?

In the Far East, Japan honored its alliance with Britain and entered the war. The Japanese quickly overran the German colonies in China and the Pacific and used the opportunity to put pressure on China. Both sides also appealed to nationalistic sentiment in areas the enemy held. The Germans supported nationalist movements among the Irish, the Flemings in Belgium, and the Poles and Ukrainians under Russian rule. They even tried to persuade the Turks to lead a Muslim uprising against the British in Egypt and India, and against the French and Italians in North Africa. The Allies made the same appeals with greater success. They sponsored movements of national autonomy for the Czechs, the Slovaks, the south Slavs, and against the Poles who were under Austrian rule. They also favored a movement of Arab independence from Turkey. Guided by Colonel T. E. Lawrence (1888–1935), this last scheme proved especially successful later in the war.

In 1915, the Allies tried to break the deadlock on the western front by going around it. The idea came chiefly from Winston Churchill (1874–1965), first lord of the British admiralty. He proposed to attack the Dardanelles and capture Constantinople. This policy supposedly would knock Turkey from the war, bring help to the Balkan front, and ease communications with Russia. The plan was daring, but promising, and in its original form, it presented little risk. British naval superiority and the element of surprise might force the straits and capture Constantinople by purely naval action. Even if the scheme failed, the fleet could just sail away.

The success of Churchill's plan depended on timing, speed, and daring leadership, but all of these were lacking. Worse, the execution of the attack was inept and overly cautious. Troops were landed, and as Turkish resistance continued, the Allied commitment increased. Before the campaign was abandoned, the Allies lost almost 150,000 men and diverted three times that number from more useful occupations.

Return to the West Both sides turned back to the west in 1916. General Erich von Falkenhayn (1861–1922), who had succeeded Moltke in September 1914, attacked the French stronghold of Verdun. His plan was not to break through the French line, but to inflict enormous casualties on the French, who would have to defend Verdun against superior firepower from several directions. He, too, underestimated the superiority of the defense. The French held Verdun with comparatively few men and inflicted almost as many casualties as they suffered. The commander of Verdun, Henri Pétain (1856–1951), became a national hero, and "They shall not pass" became a slogan of national defiance.

The Allies tried to end the impasse by launching a major offensive along the River Somme in July. Aided by a Russian attack in the east that drew off some German strength and by an enormous artillery bombardment, they hoped at last to break through. Once again, the defense was superior. Enormous casualties on both sides brought no result. The war on land dragged on with no end in sight.

The War at Sea As the war continued, control of the sea became more important. The British ignored the distinction between war supplies (which were contraband according to international law) and food or other peaceful cargo (which was not subject to seizure). They imposed a strict blockade meant to starve out the enemy, regardless of international law. The Germans responded with submarine warfare meant to destroy British shipping and starve the British. They declared the waters around the British Isles a war zone, where even neutral ships would not be safe. Both policies were unwelcome to neutrals, and especially to the United States, which conducted extensive trade in the Atlantic. Yet the sinking of neutral ships by German submarines was both more dramatic and more offensive than the British blockade.

In May 1915, a German submarine torpedoed the British liner *Lusitania*. Among the 1,200 who drowned were 118 Americans. President Woodrow Wilson (1856–1924) warned Germany that a repetition would have grave consequences; the Germans desisted for the time being, rather than further anger the United States. This development gave the Allies a considerable advantage. The German fleet that had cost so much money and had caused so much trouble played no significant part in the war. The only major battle it fought was at Jutland in 1916. The battle resulted in a standoff and confirmed British domination of the surface of the sea.

America Enters the War In December 1916, President Wilson intervened to try to bring about a negotiated peace. Neither side, however, was willing to renounce war aims that its opponent found acceptable. The war seemed likely to continue until one or both sides reached exhaustion.

Two events early in 1917 changed the situation radically. On February 1, the Germans announced the resumption of unrestricted submarine warfare, which led the United States to break off diplomatic relations. On April 6, the United States declared war on Germany. One of the deterrents to an earlier American intervention had been the presence of the autocratic tsarist Russia among the Allies. Wilson could conceive of the war only as an idealistic crusade "to make the world safe for democracy." That problem was resolved in March 1917 by a revolution in Russia that overthrew the tsarist government.

The use of poison gas (by both sides) during World War I and its dreadful effects—blinding, asphyxiation, burned lungs—came to symbolize the horrors of modern war. This painting shows a group of British soldiers being guided to the rear after they were blinded by mustard gas on the western front. *Gassed*, an oil study, 1918–19 (oil on canvas), Sargent, John Singer (1856–1925). Private Collection/ Photo © Christie's Images/The Bridgeman Art Library International.

▼ The Russian Revolution

Many unexpected consequences flowed from World War I, reshaping both Europe and the rest of the world in ways that virtually no one could have anticipated in 1910. For the rest of European history in the twentieth century no such unexpected event produced so many long-term results as the revolution that occurred in Russia in 1917. That revolution changed the course of the war and the future course of Europe by setting a Communist government in charge of a major European state and empire.

The Russian Revolution of 1917, which ultimately produced impacts over the years around the globe, went through two distinct stages. In March of that year the government of Tsar Nicholas II collapsed in the wake of popular demonstrations against the war, its casualties, and the economic and social conditions flowing from Russian participation in the conflict. Then in November a second unforeseen event occurred. The previously largely obscure and ignored Bolshevik Party led by Lenin (see Chapter 23) seized power from the provisional government. The Bolsheviks would quickly take Russia out of the war and then proceed to establish their own domestic Communist Party dictatorship.

No political faction planned or led the March Revolution in Russia. It was the result of the collapse of the monarchy's ability to govern. Although public opinion in Russia had strongly supported the country's entry into the war, the conflict overtaxed Russia's resources and the efficiency of the tsarist government.

Nicholas II was weak and incompetent and suspected of being under the domination of his German wife and the insidious peasant faith healer Rasputin, whom a group of Russian noblemen assassinated in 1916. Military and domestic failures produced massive casualties, widespread hunger, strikes by workers, and disorganization in the army. The peasant discontent that had plagued the countryside before 1914 did not subside during the conflict. In 1915, the tsar took personal command of the armies on the German front, which kept him away from the capital. In his absence, corrupt and incompetent ministers increasingly discredited the government even in the eyes of conservative monarchists. All political factions in the Duma, Russia's parliament, were discontented.

The Provisional Government

In early March 1917, strikes and worker demonstrations erupted in Petrograd, as Saint Petersburg had been renamed. The ill-disciplined troops in the city refused to fire on the demonstrators. (See the Document "The Outbreak of the Russian Revolution," page 849.) The tsar abdicated on March 15. The government of Russia fell into the hands of members of the Duma, who soon formed a provisional government composed chiefly of Constitutional Democrats (Cadets) with Western sympathies.

At the same time, the various socialist groups, including both Social Revolutionaries and Social Democrats of the Menshevik wing, began to organize soviets, councils of workers and soldiers. Initially, they allowed the provisional government to function without actually supporting it. As relatively orthodox Marxists, the Mensheviks believed that Russia had to have a bourgeois stage of development before it could have a revolution of the proletariat. They were willing to work temporarily with the Constitutional Democrats in a liberal regime, but they became estranged when the Cadets failed to

Petrograd munitions workers demonstrating in 1917. Ria-Novosti/Sovfoto/Eastfoto

control the army or to purge "reactionaries" from the government.

In this climate, the provisional government decided to remain loyal to Russia's alliances and continue the war. The provisional government thus accepted tsarist foreign policy and associated itself with the main source of domestic suffering and discontent. The collapse of the last Russian offensive in the summer of 1917 sealed its fate. Disillusionment with the war, shortages of food and other necessities at home, and the peasants' demands for land reform undermined the government. This occurred even after moderate socialist Alexander Kerensky (1881–1970) became prime minister. Moreover, discipline in the army had disintegrated.

Lenin and the Bolsheviks

Ever since April, the Bolshevik wing of the Social Democratic Party had been working against the provisional government. The Germans, in their most successful attempt at subversion, had rushed the brilliant Bolshevik leader V. I. Lenin (1870–1924) in a sealed train from his exile in Switzerland across Germany to Petrograd. They hoped he would cause trouble for the revolutionary government.

View the **Closer Look** "Bolshevik Revolution Propaganda Poster" on **MyHistoryLab.com**

Lenin saw the opportunity to achieve the political alliance of workers and peasants he had discussed before the war. In speech after speech, he hammered away on the theme of peace, bread, and land. The Bolsheviks demanded that all political power go to the soviets, which they controlled. The failure of the summer offensive encouraged them to attempt a coup, but the effort was a failure. Lenin fled to Finland, and his chief collaborator, Leon Trotsky (1879–1940), was imprisoned.

Read the **Document** "Bolshevik Seizure of Power, 1917" on **MyHistoryLab.com**

The failure of a right-wing countercoup gave the Bolsheviks another chance. Trotsky, released from prison, led the powerful Petrograd soviet. Lenin returned in October, insisted to his doubting colleagues that the

Document

THE OUTBREAK OF THE RUSSIAN REVOLUTION

The Russian Revolution of March 1917 started with a series of ill-organized demonstrations in Petrograd. These actions and the ineffectuality of the government's response are described in the memoirs of Maurice Paléologue (1859–1944), the French ambassador.

What elements contributing to the success of the March Revolution emerge from this selection? Why might the army have been unreliable? Why did the two ambassadors think a new ministry should be appointed? What were the grievances of the revolutionaries? Why is there no discussion of the leaders of the revolution? What role did the emperor (tsar) play in these events?

MONDAY, MARCH 12, 1917

At half-past eight this morning, just as I finished dressing, I heard a strange and prolonged din which seemed to come from the Alexander Bridge. I looked out: there was no one on the bridge, which usually presents such a busy scene. But, almost immediately, a disorderly mob carrying red flags appeared at the end which is on the right bank of the Neva, and a regiment came towards it from the opposite side. It looked as if there would be a violent collision, but on the contrary the two bodies coalesced. The army was fraternizing with revolt.

Shortly afterwards, someone came to tell me that the Volhynian regiment of the Guard had mutinied during the night, killed its officers and was parading the city, calling on the people to take part in the revolution and trying to win over the troops who still remain loyal.

At ten o'clock there was a sharp burst of firing, and flames could be seen rising somewhere on the Liteïny Prospekt which is quite close to the embassy. Then silence. Accompanied by my military attaché, Lieutenant-Colonel Lavergne, I went out to see what was happening. Frightened inhabitants were scattering through the streets. There was indescribable confusion at the corner of the Liteïny. Soldiers were helping civilians to erect a barricade. Flames mounted from the Law Courts. The gates of the arsenal burst open with a crash. Suddenly the crack of machine-gun fire split the air: it was the regulars who had just taken up position near the Nevsky Prospekt. The revolutionaries replied. I had seen enough to have no doubt as to what was coming. Under a hail of bullets I returned to the embassy with Lavergne who had walked calmly and slowly to the hottest corner out of sheer bravado.

About half-past eleven I went to the Ministry for Foreign Affairs, picking up Buchanan [the British ambassador to Russia] on the way.

I told Pokrovski [the Russian foreign minister] everything I had just witnessed.

"So it's even more serious than I thought," he said.

But he preserved unruffled composure, flavoured with a touch of skepticism, when he told me of the steps on which the ministers had decided during the night:

"The sitting of the Duma has been prorogued to April and we have sent a telegram to the Emperor, begging him to return at once. With the exception of M. Protopopov [the Minister of the Interior, in charge of the police], my colleagues and I all thought that a dictatorship should be established without delay; it would be conferred upon some general whose prestige with the army is pretty high, General Russky for example."

I argued that, judging by what I saw this morning, the loyalty of the army was already too heavily shaken for our hopes of salvation to be based on the use of the "strong hand," and that the immediate appointment of a ministry inspiring confidence in the Duma seemed to me more essential than ever, as there is not a moment to lose. I reminded Pokrovski that in 1789, 1830, and 1848, three French dynasties were overthrown because they were too late in realizing the significance and strength of the movement against them. I added that in such a grave crisis the representative of allied France had a right to give the Imperial Government advice on a matter of internal politics.

Buchanan endorsed my opinion.

Pokrovski replied that he personally shared our views, but that the presence of Protopopov in the Council of Ministers paralyzed action of any kind.

I asked him:

"Is there no one who can open the Emperor's eyes to the real situation?"

He heaved a despairing sigh.

"The Emperor is blind!"

Deep grief was writ large on the face of the honest man and good citizen whose uprightness, patriotism and disinterestedness I can never sufficiently extol.

From Maurice Paléologue, *An Ambassador's Memoirs* (London: Doubleday & Company, Inc., and Hutchinson Publishing Group, Ltd., 1924), pp. 221–225.

time was ripe to take power, and by the extraordinary force of his personality persuaded them to act. Trotsky organized the coup that took place on November 6 and concluded with an armed assault on the provisional government. The Bolsheviks, almost as much to their own astonishment as to that of the rest of the world, had come to rule Russia. (See the Document "An Eyewitness Account of the Bolsheviks' Seizure of Power," below.)

The Communist Dictatorship

The victors moved to fulfill their promises and to ensure their own security. The provisional government had decreed an election for late November to select a Constituent Assembly. The Social Revolutionaries won a large majority over the Bolsheviks. When the assembly gathered in January, it met for only a day before the Red Army, controlled by the Bolsheviks, dispersed it. All other political parties also ceased to function in any meaningful fashion. In November and January, the Bolshevik government nationalized the land and turned it over to its peasant proprietors. Factory workers were put in charge of their plants. The state seized banks and repudiated the debt of the tsarist government. Property of the church reverted to the state.

The Bolshevik government also took Russia out of the war, which they believed benefited only capitalism. They signed an armistice with Germany in December 1917 and in March 1918 accepted the Treaty of Brest-Litovsk, by which Russia yielded Poland, Finland, the Baltic states, and Ukraine. Some territory in the Transcaucasus region went to Turkey. The Bolsheviks also agreed to pay a heavy war indemnity.

These terms were a high price to pay for peace, but Lenin had no choice. Russia was incapable of renewing the war effort, and the Bolsheviks needed time to impose their rule. Moreover, Lenin believed that the war and the Russian example would soon lead to communist revolutions across Europe.

The new Bolshevik government met major domestic resistance. Civil war erupted between Red Russians,

Document

An Eyewitness Account of the Bolsheviks' Seizure of Power

John Reed was an American newspaperman who was in Russia during the Revolution of 1917, an enthusiastic convert to Communism, a supporter of the Bolsheviks, and an ardent admirer of Lenin. In the following selections from his account of the Bolshevik revolution, he described Lenin's qualities and the part Lenin played in overthrowing the provisional government.

What was the provisional government? How did it come into being? Why was it under pressure in November 1917? Which groups were vying for power? What program gave victory to the Bolsheviks?

Thursday, Oct. 26/Nov. 8

The Congress was to meet at one o'clock, and long since the great meeting-hall had filled, but by seven there was yet no sign of the presidium. . . . The Bolshevik and Left Social Revolutionary factions were in session in their own rooms. All the livelong afternoon Lenin and Trotzky had fought against compromise. A considerable part of the Bolsheviki were in favour of giving way so far as to create a joint all-Socialist government. "We can't hold on!" they cried. "Too much is against us. We haven't got the men. We will be isolated, and the whole thing will fall." So Kameniev, Riazanov and others.

But Lenin, with Trotzky beside him, stood firm as a rock. "Let the compromisers accept our programme and they can come in! We won't give way an inch. If there are comrades here who haven't the courage and the will to dare what we dare, let him leave with the rest of the cowards and conciliators! Backed by the workers and soldiers we shall go on."

At five minutes past seven came word from the left Socialist Revolutionaries to say that they would remain in the Military Revolutionary Committee. "See!" said Lenin, "They are following.". . .

It was just 8:40 when a thundering wave of cheers announced the entrance of the presidium with Lenin—great Lenin—among them. A short, stocky figure, with a big head set down in his shoulders, who supported the revolution, and White Russians, who opposed it. In the summer of 1918, the Bolsheviks murdered the tsar and his family. Loyal army officers continued to fight the revolution and received aid from Allied armies. Under the leadership of Trotsky, however, the Red Army eventually overcame the domestic opposition. By 1921, Lenin and his supporters were in firm control.

▼ The End of World War I

The collapse of Russia and the Treaty of Brest-Litovsk were the zenith of German success. The Germans controlled eastern Europe and its resources, especially food, and by 1918 they were free to concentrate their forces on the western front. These developments would probably have been decisive without American intervention. Still, American troops would not arrive in significant numbers for about a year, and both sides tried to win the war in 1917.

An Allied attempt to break through in the west failed disastrously. Losses were heavy and the French army mutinied. The Austrians, supported by the Germans, defeated the Italians at Caporetto and threatened to overrun northern Italy, until they were checked with the aid of Allied troops. The deadlock continued, but time was running out for the Central Powers.

Germany's Last Offensive

In March 1918, the Germans decided to gamble everything on one last offensive. (This decision was taken chiefly by Ludendorff, second in command to Hindenburg, but the real leader of the army.) The German army reached the Marne again but got no farther. They had no more reserves, and the entire nation was exhausted. In contrast, the arrival of American troops in ever-increasing numbers bolstered the Allies. An Allied counteroffensive proved irresistible. As the exhausted Austrians collapsed in Italy, and Bulgaria and Turkey dropped out

bald and bulging. Little eyes, a snubbish nose, wide, generous mouth, and heavy chin; clean-shaven now, but already beginning to bristle with the well-known beard of his past and future. Dressed in shabby clothes, his trousers much too long for him. Unimpressive, to be the idol of a mob, loved and revered as perhaps few leaders in history have been. A strange popular leader—a leader purely by virtue of intellect; colourless, humourless, uncompromising and detached, without picturesque idiosyncrasies—but with the power of explaining profound ideas in simple terms, of analysing a concrete situation. And combined with shrewdness, the greatest intellectual audacity.

. . .

Other speakers followed, apparently without any order. A delegate of the coal-miners of the Don Basin called upon the Congress to take measures against Kaledin, who might cut off coal and food from the capital. Several soldiers just arrived from the Front brought the enthusiastic greetings of their regiments.

. . . Now Lenin, gripping the edge of the reading stand, letting his little winking eyes travel over the crowd as he stood there waiting, apparently oblivious to the long-rolling ovation, which lasted several minutes. When it finished, he said simply, "We shall now proceed to construct the Socialist order!" Again that overwhelming human roar.

"The first thing is the adoption of practical measures to realise peace. . . . We shall offer peace to the peoples of all the belligerent countries upon the basis of the Soviet terms—no annexations, no indemnities, and the right of self-determination of peoples. At the same time, according to our promise, we shall publish and repudiate the secret treaties. . . . The question of War and Peace is so clear that I think that I may, without preamble, read the project of a Proclamation to the Peoples of All the Belligerent Countries. . . ."

His great mouth, seeming to smile, opened wide as he spoke; his voice was hoarse—not unpleasantly so, but as if it had hardened that way after years and years of speaking—and went on monotonously, with the effect of being able to go on forever. . . . For emphasis he bent forward slightly. No gestures. And before him, a thousand simple faces looking up in intent adoration. . . .

It was exactly 10:35 when Kameniev asked all in favour of the proclamation to hold up their cards. One delegate dared to raise his hand against, but the sudden sharp outburst around him brought it swiftly down. . . . Unanimous.

At two o'clock the Land Decree was put to vote, with only one against and the peasant delegates were wild with joy. . . . So plunged the Bolsheviki ahead, irresistible, over-riding hesitation and opposition—the only people in Russia who had a definite programme of action while the others talked for eight long months. . . .

From John Reed, *Ten Days That Shook the World* (New York: Boni and Liveright, 1919), pp. 123–129.

of the war, the German high command knew the end was imminent.

Ludendorff was determined to make peace before the German army was thoroughly defeated in the field and to make civilians responsible for ending the war. For some time, he had been the effective ruler of Germany under the aegis of the emperor. He now allowed a new government to be established on democratic principles and to seek peace immediately. The new government, under Prince Max of Baden, asked for peace on the basis of the **Fourteen Points** that President Wilson had declared as the American war aims. These were idealistic principles, including self-determination for nationalities, open diplomacy, freedom of the seas, disarmament, and the establishment of the League of Nations to keep the peace. Wilson insisted he would deal only with a democratic German government because he wanted to be sure he was dealing with the German people and not merely their rulers.

Read the **Document** "Woodrow Wilson, *The Fourteen Points* (1918)" on **MyHistoryLab.com**

The Armistice

The disintegration of the German army forced William II to abdicate on November 9, 1918. The majority branch of the Social Democratic Party proclaimed a republic to prevent their radical Leninist wing from setting up a soviet government. Two days later, this republican, socialist-led government signed the armistice that ended the war by accepting German defeat. The German people were, in general, unaware their army had been defeated and was crumbling. No foreign soldier stood on German soil. Many Germans expected a negotiated and mild settlement. The real peace was different and embittered the Germans. Many of them came to believe Germany had not been defeated but had been tricked by the enemy and betrayed—even stabbed in the back—by republicans and socialists at home.

The victors rejoiced, but they also had much to mourn. The casualties on all sides came to about 10 million dead and twice as many wounded. The economic and financial resources of the European states were badly strained. The victorious Allies, formerly creditors to the world, became debtors to the new American colossus, which the calamities of war had barely touched.

The Great War, as contemporaries called it, World War I to those who lived through its horrible offspring, lasted more than four years, doing terrible damage. Battle casualties alone counted more than 4 million dead and 8.3 million wounded among the Central Powers and 5.4 million dead and 7 million wounded from their opponents; millions of civilians died from the war and causes arising from it. Among the casualties also were the German, Austro-Hungarian, Russian, and Turkish Empires. The American intervention in 1917 thrust the United States into European affairs with a vengeance, and the collapse of the Russian autocracy brought the Bolshevik Revolution and the reality of a great communist state. Disappointment, resentment, and economic dislocations caused by the war brought various forms of fascism to Italy, Germany, and other countries. The comfortable nineteenth-century assumptions of inevitable progress based on reason, science and technology, individual freedom, democracy, and free enterprise gave way in many places to cynicism, nihilism, dictatorship, statism, official racism, and class warfare. It is widely agreed that the First World War was the mother of the Second and to most of the horrors of the rest of the century.

These kinds of changes affected the colonial peoples the European powers ruled, and overseas empires would never again be as secure as they had seemed before the war. Europe was no longer the center of the world, free to interfere when it wished or to ignore the rest of the world if it chose. The memory of that war lived on to shake the nerve of the victorious Western powers as they faced the new conditions of the postwar world.

MAJOR CAMPAIGNS AND EVENTS OF WORLD WAR I

August 1914	Germans attack in West
August–September	First Battle of the Marne
1914	Battles of Tannenberg and the Masurian Lakes
April 1915	British land at Gallipoli, start of Dardanelles campaign
May 1915	Germans sink British ship *Lusitania*
February 1916	Germans attack Verdun
May–June 1916	Battle of Jutland
July–November 1916	Battle of the Somme
February 1917	Germans declare unrestricted submarine warfare
March 1917	Russian Revolution
April 1917	United States enters war
November 1917	Bolsheviks seize power in Russia
March 1918	Treaty of Brest-Litovsk
March 1918	German offensive in the West
November 1918	Armistice

The End of the Ottoman Empire

World War I witnessed the end of the German, Austrian, and Russian Empires in the heart of Europe. The conflict also brought about the collapse of the Ottoman Empire, the ramifications of which also persist to the present day.

Women munitions workers in England. World War I demanded more from the civilian populations than had previous wars, resulting in important social changes. The demands of the munitions industries and a shortage of men (so many of whom were in uniform) brought many women out of traditional roles at home and into factories and other war-related work. Stringer/Hulton Archive/Getty Images

At the outbreak of World War I in August 1914, the Ottoman Empire was neutral, but many military officers, the so-called Young Turks who had taken control of the Ottoman government in 1909, were pro-German. After hesitating for three months, the Turks decided to enter the war on the German side in November 1914. This decision ultimately brought about the end of the Ottoman Empire. Early victories gave way to defeat after defeat at the hands of the Russians and the British, the latter assisted by Arabs from the Arabian Peninsula and neighboring lands, most notably Hussein (1856–1931), *sherif* (ruler or emir) of Mecca, the city of Muhammad. The British drove the Ottomans out of Palestine and advanced deep into Mesopotamia, as far north as the oil fields of Mosul in modern Iraq. By October 30, 1918, Turkey was out of the war. In November, an Allied fleet sailed into the harbor of Constantinople and landed troops who occupied the city. The Ottoman government was helpless.

View the **Closer Look** "Young Turks Overthrow Abdülhamid II, 1908" on **MyHistoryLab.com**

The peace treaty signed in Paris in 1920 between Turkey and the Allies dismembered the Ottoman Empire, placing large parts of it, particularly the areas Arabs inhabited, under the control of Britain and France. In Mesopotamia the British created the state of Iraq, which, along with Palestine, became British mandates. Syria and Lebanon became French mandates. (**Mandates** were territories that were legally administered under the auspices of the League of Nations but were in effect ruled as colonies.) A Greek invasion of the Turkish homeland in Anatolia in 1919 provoked a nationalist reaction, bringing the young general Mustafa Kemal (1881–1938), who later took the name Ataturk, meaning "Father of the Turks," to power. He drove the Greeks out of Anatolia and compelled the victorious powers to make a new arrangement sealed by the treaty of Lausanne in 1923. Ataturk abolished the Ottoman sultanate and deposed the last caliph. The new Republic of Turkey abandoned most of the old Ottoman Empire but became fully independent of control by the European powers and sovereign in its Anatolian homeland. Under Ataturk and his successors, Turkey, although its population was overwhelmingly Muslim, became a secular state and a force for stability in the region.

The Arab portions of the old empire, however, were a different story. Divided into a collection of artificial states that had no historical reality, governed or

The Allies promoted Arab efforts to secure independence from Turkey in an effort to remove Turkey from the war. Delegates to the peace conference of 1919 in Paris included British colonel T. E. Lawrence, who helped lead the rebellion, and representatives from the Middle Eastern region. Prince Feisal, the third son of King Hussein, stands in the foreground of this picture; Colonel T. E. Lawrence is in the middle row, second from the right; and Brigadier General Nuri Pasha Said of Baghdad is second from the left. CORBIS/Bettmann

Ataturk (1881–1938), the father of the Turkish Republic, sought to modernize his country by forcing Turks to adopt Western ways, including the Latin alphabet. Here he is shown teaching the alphabet as president in 1928. akg-images/Newscom

dominated as client regimes by the British and French, they were relatively quiet during the 1920s and 1930s. The weakening of Britain and France during and after World War II, however, and their subsequent abandonment of control in the Middle East would create problems in the latter part of the century.

Watch the Video "Video Lectures: The Continuing Legacy of World War I in the Middle East" on **MyHistoryLab.com**

▼ The Settlement at Paris

The representatives of the victorious states gathered at Versailles and other Parisian suburbs in the first half of 1919. Wilson speaking for the United States, David Lloyd George (1863–1945) for Britain, Georges Clemenceau (1841–1929) for France, and Vittorio Emanuele Orlando (1860–1952) for Italy made up the Big Four. Japan also had an important part in the discussions. The diplomats who met in Paris had a far more difficult task than those who had sat at Vienna a century earlier. Both groups attempted to restore order to the world after long and costly wars. At the earlier conference, however, Metternich and his associates could confine their thoughts to Europe. France had acknowledged defeat and was willing to take part in and uphold the Vienna settlement. The diplomats at Vienna were not much affected by public opinion, and they could draw the new map of Europe along practical lines determined by the realities of power and softened by compromise.

View the **Closer Look** "Peace at Versailles" on **MyHistoryLab.com**

"The Big Four" attending the Paris peace conference in 1919: Vittorio Orlande, premier of Italy; David Lloyd George, prime minister of Great Britain; Georges Clemenceau, premier of France; and Woodrow Wilson, president of the United States (left to right). National Archives and Records Administration

Obstacles the Peacemakers Faced

The negotiators at Paris in 1919 were less fortunate. They represented constitutional, generally democratic governments, and public opinion had become a mighty force. Though there were secret sessions, the conference often worked in the full glare of publicity. Nationalism had become almost a secular religion, and Europe's many ethnic groups could not be relied on to remain quiet while the great powers distributed them on the map. Moreover, propaganda and especially the intervention of Woodrow Wilson had transformed World War I into a moral crusade to achieve a peace that would be just as well as secure. (See "Encountering the Past: War Propaganda and the Movies," page 856.) The Fourteen Points set forth the right of nationalities to self-determination as an absolute value, but in fact no one could draw the map of Europe to match ethnic groups perfectly with their homelands. All these elements made compromise difficult.

Wilson's idealism, moreover, came into conflict with the more practical war aims of the victorious powers and with many of the secret treaties that had been made before and during the war. The British and French people had been told that Germany would be made to pay for the war. Russia had been promised control of Constantinople in return for recognizing the French claim to Alsace-Lorraine and British control of Egypt. Romania had been promised Transylvania at the expense of Hungary.

View the **Image** "Woodrow Wilson on His Way to Versailles, 1919" on **MyHistoryLab.com**

Some of the agreements contradicted others. Italy and Serbia had competing claims in the Adriatic. During the war, the British had encouraged Arab hopes of an independent Arab state carved out of the Ottoman Empire. Those plans, however, contradicted the Balfour Declaration (1917), in which the British seemed to accept Zionist ideology and to promise the Jews a national home in Palestine. Both of these plans conflicted with an Anglo-French agreement to divide the Near East between themselves.

The continuing national goals of the victors presented further obstacles to an idealistic "peace without victors." France was painfully conscious of its numerical inferiority to Germany and of the low birthrate that

ENCOUNTERING THE *Past*

WAR PROPAGANDA AND THE MOVIES: CHARLIE CHAPLIN

THE VAST SCOPE of World War I required support. As the war stretched on and its costs increased, all the competing nations intensified propaganda campaigns to justify the huge expenditure of lives and resources. Sometimes this took the form of painting the enemy in brutal and lurid colors to provoke hatred, and sometimes it took the form of sympathetic images of patriotism and sacrifice for a noble cause. These efforts, sponsored both by government and private agencies, saturated the lives of everyone—men, women, and even children—while the war lasted.

At first, most of the propaganda came in the form of writing—newspaper articles and pamphlets—justifying the war and demonizing the enemy. Soon, however, verbal efforts gave way to more emotionally powerful visual devices such as posters, cartoons, and caricatures. By the middle of the war, however, the relatively new medium of film became the most powerful weapon of propaganda. Graphically and dramatically, movies showed the enemy as either horrible or ridiculous and one's own soldiers and people as brave and noble. Such images could reach rich and poor, literate and illiterate, young and old, with great emotional effect.

Charlie Chaplin in *Shoulder Arms.* © Sunset Boulevard/CORBIS Sygma

Both sides produced films that became enormously popular, but none more so than those Charlie Chaplin (1889–1977) did for the Allies. Born in England, he came to America as a vaudeville star in 1914 and was already famous when the war broke out. His tragicomic character, the tramp, in many variations, had universal appeal. His wartime films had amazing effects: They helped sell great quantities of Liberty Bonds (which the American government used to help pay for its involvement in the war), raised the morale of civilians, and even eased the miseries of shell-shocked soldiers.

Chaplin's 1918 movie *Shoulder Arms* was his greatest wartime success. It gave a comic picture of the difficulties of basic training for American recruits and portrays the Germans as bumbling fools. In the film, Chaplin's character, exhausted by the rigors of drilling, falls asleep. He wakes up at the front, where he deceives the enemy by pretending to be a tree and captures first a German unit and finally the kaiser, all by himself.

The Germans, too, soon learned the propaganda value of films, which were more completely in the hands of the government than those made in the Allied states. The German army made comedies, melodramas, and newsreels and showed them both to the troops and the civilian public. The German government thought movies so important that even during the freezing, brutal winter of 1917–1918 when fuel supplies were at a premium, it gave movie theaters special priority to use coal and electricity—but there was no German Charlie Chaplin.

What were the purposes of propaganda in the war?

What were the advantages of using movies in the war effort?

would keep it inferior. So France was naturally eager to weaken Germany permanently and preserve French superiority. Italy continued to seek *Italia irredenta*, Britain looked to its imperial interests, and Japan pursued its own advantage in Asia. The United States insisted on freedom of the seas, which favored American commerce, and on its right to maintain the Monroe Doctrine.

Finally, the peacemakers of 1919 faced a world still in turmoil. The greatest immediate threat appeared to be the spread of Bolshevism. While civil war distracted Lenin and his colleagues, the Allies landed small armies in Russia to help overthrow the Bolshevik regime. The revolution seemed likely to spread as communist governments were established in Bavaria and Hungary. A communist uprising led by the "Spartacus group" had to be suppressed in Berlin. The worried Allies even allowed an army of German volunteers to fight the Bolsheviks in the Baltic states.

Fear of the spread of communism affected the diplomats at Versailles, but it was far from dominant. The Germans played on such fears to get better terms, but the Allies, especially the French, would not hear of it. Fear of Germany remained the chief concern for France. More traditional and more immediate interests governed the policies of the other Allies.

The Peace

The Paris settlement consisted of five separate treaties between the victors and the defeated powers. Formal sessions began on January 18, 1919, and the last treaty was signed on August 10, 1920. (See Map 26–5.) Wilson arrived in Europe to unprecedented popular acclaim. Liberals and idealists expected a new kind of international order achieved in a new and better way, but they were soon disillusioned. "Open covenants openly arrived at" soon gave way to closed sessions in which Wilson, Clemenceau, and Lloyd George made arrangements that seemed cynical to outsiders.

The notion of "a peace without victors" became a mockery when the Soviet Union (as Russia was now called) and Germany were excluded from the peace conference. The Germans were simply presented with a treaty and compelled to accept it, fully justified in their complaint that the treaty had been dictated, not negotiated. The principle of national self-determination was violated many times and was unavoidable. Still, their exclusion from decisions angered the diplomats from the small nations. The undeserved adulation accorded Wilson on his arrival gradually turned into equally undeserved scorn. He had not abandoned his ideals lightly but had merely given way to the irresistible force of reality.

The League of Nations Wilson could make unpalatable concessions without abandoning his ideals because he put great faith in a new instrument for peace and justice: the **League of Nations**. Its covenant was an essential part of the peace treaty. The league was to be not an international government, but a body of sovereign states that agreed to pursue common policies and to consult in the common interest, especially when war threatened. The members promised to submit differences among themselves to arbitration, an international court, or the League Council. Refusal to abide by the results would justify economic sanctions and even military intervention by the league. The league was unlikely to be effective, however, because it had no armed forces at its disposal. Furthermore, any action required the unanimous consent of its council, consisting permanently of Britain, France, Italy, the United States, and Japan, as well as four other states that had temporary seats. The Covenant of the League bound its members to "respect and preserve" the territorial integrity of all its members; this was generally seen as a device to ensure the security of the victorious powers. The exclusion of Germany and the Soviet Union from the League Assembly further undermined its claim to evenhandedness.

Read the **Document** "The Covenant of the League of Nations" on **MyHistoryLab.com**

Members of the League of Nations remained fully sovereign and continued to pursue their national interests. Only Wilson put much faith in the league's future ability to produce peace and justice. To get the other states to agree to the league, he approved territorial settlements that violated his own principles.

Germany In the West, the main territorial issue was the fate of Germany. Although a united Germany was less than fifty years old, no one seems to have thought of undoing Bismarck's work and dividing the country into its component parts. The French wanted to set the Rhineland up as a separate buffer state, but Lloyd George and Wilson would not permit it. Still, they could not ignore France's need for protection against a resurgent Germany. France received Alsace-Lorraine and the right to work the coal mines of the Saar for fifteen years. Germany west of the Rhine and fifty kilometers east of it was to be a demilitarized zone. Allied troops could stay on the west bank for fifteen years.

The treaty also provided that Britain and the United States would help France if Germany attacked it. Such an attack was made more unlikely by the permanent disarmament of Germany. Its army was limited to 100,000 men on long-term service, its fleet was reduced to a coastal defense force, and it was forbidden to have warplanes, submarines, tanks, heavy artillery, or poison gas. As long as these provisions were observed, France would be safe.

The East The settlement in the East reflected the collapse of the great defeated empires that had ruled it for

Map 26–5 **WORLD WAR I PEACE SETTLEMENT IN EUROPE AND THE MIDDLE EAST** The map of central and eastern Europe, as well as that of the Middle East, underwent drastic revision after World War I. The enormous territorial losses suffered by Germany, Austria-Hungary, the Ottoman Empire, Bulgaria, and Russia were the other side of the coin represented by gains for France, Italy, Greece, and Romania and by the appearance or reappearance of at least eight new independent states from Finland in the north to Yugoslavia in the south. The mandate system for former Ottoman territories outside Turkey proper laid foundations for several new, mostly Arab, states in the Middle East. In Africa, the mandate system placed the former German colonies under British, French, and South African rule. (See Map 25–3.)

centuries. Germany lost part of Silesia, and East Prussia was cut off from the rest of Germany by a corridor carved out to give the revived state of Poland access to the sea. The Austro-Hungarian Empire disappeared entirely, giving way to five small successor states. Most of its German-speaking people were gathered in the Republic of Austria, cut off from the Germans of Bohemia and forbidden to unite with Germany.

The Magyars were left with the much-reduced kingdom of Hungary. The Czechs of Bohemia and Moravia joined with the Slovaks and Ruthenians to the east to form Czechoslovakia, and this new state included several million unhappy Germans plus Poles, Magyars, and Ukrainians. The southern Slavs were united in the Kingdom of Serbs, Croats, and Slovenes, or Yugoslavia. Italy gained Trentino, which included tens of thousands of German speakers, and the port of Trieste. Romania was enlarged by receiving Transylvania from Hungary and Bessarabia from Russia. Bulgaria lost territory to Greece and Yugoslavia. Russia lost vast territories in the west. Finland, Estonia, Latvia, and Lithuania became independent states, and most of Poland was carved out of formerly Russian soil.

Reparations Perhaps the most debated part of the peace settlement dealt with reparations for the damage Germany did during the war. Before the armistice, the Germans promised to pay compensation "for all damages done to the civilian population of the Allies and their property." The Americans judged the amount would be between \$15 billion and \$25 billion and that Germany would be able to pay that amount. France and Britain, however, who worried about repaying their war debts to the United States, were eager to have Germany pay the full cost of the war, including pensions to survivors and dependents.

There was a general agreement that Germany could not afford to pay such a huge sum, whatever it might be, and the conference did not specify an amount. In the meantime, Germany was to pay \$5 billion annually until 1921. At that time, a final figure would be set, which Germany would have to pay in thirty years. The French did not regret the outcome. Either Germany would pay and be bled into impotence, or Germany would refuse to pay and French intervention would be warranted.

To justify these huge reparation payments, the Allies inserted the notorious **war guilt clause** (Clause 231) into the treaty:

> The Allied and Associated Governments affirm, and Germany accepts, the responsibility of Germany and her allies for causing all the loss and damage to which the Allied and Associated Governments and their nationals have been subjected as a consequence of the war imposed upon them by aggression of Germany and her allies.

The Germans, of course, did not believe they were solely responsible for the war and bitterly resented the charge. They had lost territories containing badly needed natural resources. Yet they were presented with an astronomical and apparently unlimited reparations bill. To add insult to injury, they were required to admit to a war guilt they did not feel.

Finally, to heap insult upon insult, they were required to accept the entire treaty as the victors wrote it, without negotiation. Germany's prime minister Philipp Scheidmann (1865–1939) spoke of the treaty as the imprisonment of the German people and asked, "What hand would not wither that binds itself and us in these fetters?" There was no choice, however. The Social Democrats and the Catholic Center Party formed a new government, and their representatives signed the treaty. These parties formed the backbone of the Weimar government that ruled Germany until 1933. They never overcame the stigma of having accepted the Treaty of Versailles.

World War I and Colonial Empires

World War I and the peace settlement introduced numerous changes and transformations into the European colonial world.

Redistribution of Colonies into Mandates The rivalries over empire that had predated the outbreak of the war and that had contributed so mightily to prewar tensions continued throughout the conflict. Through secret treaties of 1915 the Allies planned for the eventual dismemberment of the German Empire and the distribution of its colonies to allied victors. The German government had similarly envisioned taking colonial spoils had it won the conflict. In effect, the war had opened the possibility for whoever won it to expand their empires at the cost of the defeated powers. As a result, the single most important imperial consequence of World War I was Germany being stripped of its colonies and the Ottoman Empire of regions it had formerly governed.

The Covenant of the League of Nations established mandates within these former colonies and regions. These mandates, located in the Middle East, Africa, and the Pacific, were placed under the "tutelage" of one of the great powers under League of Nations supervision and encouraged to advance toward independence. Britain and France became the chief mandate administrators and were consequently drawn more deeply into new regions of the world, most particularly, the Middle East. In effect, the mandates became colonies of the administering powers. Some mandates, most notably Iraq, became independent between the wars. Other mandates became independent often with considerable conflict from the closing years of World War II through the third quarter of the twentieth century. These latter mandates included Palestine, Syria, Lebanon, Transjordan, Tanganyka, Kamerun, Southwest Africa, and German New Guinea, to mention only some of the major areas.

Colonial Participation Colonial peoples themselves had played a significant role in World War I. Germany itself did not call upon troops from its colonies. The war led Britain and France, however, to view their empires in new ways as sources of military as well as economic support. The French government recruited tens of thousands of Algerians into its armed forces and over 150,000 West Africans. It is estimated that more than 2.5 million British colonial troops participated in the war. More than 1.25 million Indian troops were involved either directly in combat or as laborers working for cheap wages. Canada, Australia, New Zealand, and South Africa sent hundreds of thousands of troops into the war and experienced very significant losses. The presence of so many non-European troops on the European continent even before the arrival of U.S. troops was one of the factors that made the war a genuinely world conflict. Both colonial troops of color and United States troops of color encountered significant racial prejudice in Europe.

What Europeans had learned from the wartime experience was the value of their colonies in terms of troops to be recruited and natural resources to be devoted to the war effort, and they tended to seek ways to draw them into closer relations. In this respect, the years after the war were in some ways the period of most extensive direct colonial involvement by Great Britain and France and the ongoing desire for empire on the part of Italy. When World War II broke out, both nations would encounter much more nationalist resistance that after the war would culminate in decolonization. (See Chapter 29.)

Impact of the Peace Settlement on Future Colonial Relations Many native colonial leaders in Africa and Asia had supported the allied war effort in the hope that their peoples would be rewarded with greater independence and better economic relations with Europe. Wilson's Fourteen Points and his emphasis on self-determination had also contributed to raising such expectations. These hopes were dashed at the peace conference and in the years thereafter. Numerous later leaders of anticolonial nationalist movements were either in Paris at the time of the conference or closely followed its events. These colonial leaders had hoped they might be allowed to put their case for independence or major administrative reform before the conference, and they had been denied that opportunity. Their disappointment led them over the years to reject engagement with the existing international order and to move in various new directions of disruptive and ultimately successful national anticolonialism.

The European powers themselves had directly contributed to these developments in another fashion. They had sought to stir nationalist uprisings in the lands of their opponents. Here the most significant effort took place among Arab peoples governed by the Ottoman Empire, which had sided with Germany. The British led Arab nationalist groups to believe that they might achieve independence in the wake of an allied victory. T. E. Lawrence, later known popularly as Lawrence of Arabia, led much of this effort on behalf of the British. For their part the Germans had attempted to stir unrest in northern Africa.

A glance at the new map of the post–World War I world could give the impression that the old imperial nations, especially Britain and France, were more powerful than ever, but that impression would be superficial and misleading. The great Western European powers had paid an enormous price in lives, money, and will for their victory in the war. Colonial peoples pressed for the rights that the West proclaimed as universal but denied to their colonies, and some influential minorities in the countries that ruled those colonies sympathized with colonial aspirations for independence. Tension between colonies and their ruling nations was a cause of serious instability in the world the Paris treaties of 1919 created.

Evaluating the Peace

Few peace settlements have undergone more severe attacks than the one negotiated in Paris in 1919. It was natural that the defeated powers should object to it, but the peace soon came under bitter criticism in the victorious countries as well. Many of the French objected that the treaty tied French security to promises of aid from the unreliable Anglo-Saxon countries. In England and the United States, a wave of bitter criticism arose in liberal quarters because the treaty seemed to violate the idealistic and liberal aims that the Western leaders had professed.

It was not a peace without victors. It did not put an end to imperialism but attempted to promote the national interests of the winning nations. It violated the principles of national self-determination by leaving significant pockets of minorities outside the borders of their national homelands.

The Economic Consequences of the Peace The most influential economic critic of the treaty was John

Maynard Keynes (1883–1946), a brilliant British economist who took part in the peace conference. He resigned in disgust when he saw the direction it was taking. His book *The Economic Consequences of the Peace* (1920) was a scathing attack, especially on reparations and the other economic aspects of the peace. It was also a skillful assault on the negotiators and particularly on Wilson, whom Keynes depicted as a fool and a hypocrite. Keynes argued that the Treaty of Versailles was both immoral and unworkable. He called it a Carthaginian peace, referring to Rome's destruction of Carthage after the Third Punic War. He argued that such a peace would bring economic ruin and war to Europe unless it was repudiated.

Keynes's argument had a great effect on the British, who were already suspicious of France and glad of an excuse to withdraw from continental affairs. The decent and respectable position came to be one that supported revision of the treaty in favor of Germany. In the United States, the book fed the traditional tendency toward isolationism and gave powerful weapons to Wilson's enemies. Wilson's own political mistakes helped prevent American ratification of the treaty. Thus, America was out of the League of Nations and not bound to defend France. Britain, therefore, was also free from its obligation to France. France was left to protect itself without adequate means to do so for long.

Many of the attacks on the Treaty of Versailles are unjustified. It was not a Carthaginian peace. Germany was neither dismembered nor ruined. Reparations could be and were scaled down. Until the great world depression of the 1930s, the Germans recovered prosperity. Complaints against the peace should also be measured against the peace that the victorious Germans had imposed on Russia at Brest-Litovsk and their plans for a European settlement if they had won. Both were far more severe than anything enacted at Versailles. The attempt to achieve self-determination for nationalities was less than perfect, but it was the best effort Europe had ever made to do so.

Divisive New Boundaries and Tariff Walls The peace, nevertheless, was unsatisfactory in important ways. The elimination of the Austro-Hungarian Empire, however inevitable, created serious problems. Economically, it was disastrous. New borders and tariff walls separated raw materials from manufacturing areas and producers from their markets. In hard times, this separation created friction and hostility that aggravated other quarrels the peace treaties also created. Poland contained unhappy German, Lithuanian, and Ukrainian minorities, and Czechoslovakia and Yugoslavia were collections of nationalities that did not find it easy to live together. Territorial disputes in Eastern Europe promoted further tension.

Moreover, the peace rested on a victory that Germany did not admit. The Germans felt cheated rather than defeated. The high moral principles the Allies proclaimed undercut the validity of the peace, for it plainly fell far short of those principles.

Failure to Accept Reality Finally, the great weakness of the peace was its failure to accept reality. Germany and Russia must inevitably play an important part in European affairs, yet the settlement and the League of Nations excluded them. Given the many discontented parties, the peace was not self-enforcing, yet no satisfactory machinery to enforce it was established. The League of Nations was never a serious force for this purpose. It was left to France, with no guarantee of support from Britain and no hope of help from the United States, to defend the new arrangements. Finland, the Baltic states, Poland, Romania, Czechoslovakia, and Yugoslavia were expected to be a barrier to the westward expansion of Russian communism and to help deter a revival of German power. Most of these states, however, would have to rely on France in case of danger, and France was simply not strong enough to protect them if Germany revived.

The tragedy of the Treaty of Versailles was that it was neither conciliatory enough to remove the desire for revision, even at the cost of war, nor harsh enough to make another war impossible. The only hope for a lasting peace was that Germany would remain disarmed while the more obnoxious clauses of the peace treaty were revised. Such a policy required continued attention to the problem, unity among the victors, and farsighted leadership; but none of these was consistently present during the next two decades.

In Perspective

The unification of Germany in 1871 transformed the European international order. For twenty years a series of alliances and an ongoing process of shrewd negotiation on the part of Bismarck had brought a fragile stability to European diplomatic relations. In the years after Bismarck was forced from office in 1890, Kaiser Wilhelm and the German military pursued expansively aggressive policies that destabilized European diplomatic relations. Germany became overly dependent upon its alliance with Austria. Britain, France, and Russia by the first decade of the twentieth century had come to forge the very kind of friendly diplomatic understandings that Bismarck had sought to avoid.

The first fifteen years of the twentieth century saw a number of European diplomatic crises related to imperial concerns and rivalries in the Balkan Peninsula. These crises increased distrust between Germany and other European powers and worked to cement the understandings among Britain, France, and Russia. The assassination of Archduke Francis Ferdinand in the summer of 1914 sparked a Balkans crisis that could not be contained. The initial conflict between Serbia and Austria-Hungry soon drew in Russia in support of the former and Germany in support of the latter. Thereafter, the other alliances and understandings of mutual support came into play. The war plans of the various powers quickly led to the most extensive war Europe had experienced in a century.

Other unexpected transformative events followed the military stalemate. In March 1917 revolution overthrew the tsarist government of Russia. The next month the United States entered the war. In November 1917 the Bolsheviks seized power in Russia and rapidly withdrew Russia from the conflict. By November 1918 Germany surrendered. In both Germany and Austria-Hungary the governments that had led their nations into the war had collapsed.

At the Paris Peace Conference of 1919 the victorious allies redrew the map of Europe, rearranged much of the European colonial world, established the League of Nations, and imposed a war guilt clause and high reparations on Germany. The United States refused to ratify the treaty and for two decades largely withdrew from European affairs. The peace settlement itself planted the seeds of ongoing resentment and nationalist unrest in Europe.

KEY TERMS

Fourteen Points (p. 852) League of Nations (p. 857) mandates (p. 853) war guilt clause (p. 859)

REVIEW QUESTIONS

1. What role in the world did Bismarck envisage for the new Germany after 1871? How successful was he in carrying out his vision? Was he wise to tie Germany to Austria-Hungary?
2. Why and in what stages did Britain abandon its policy of "splendid isolation" at the turn of the century? Were the policies it pursued instead wise ones, or should Britain have followed a different course altogether?
3. How did developments in the Balkans lead to the outbreak of World War I? What was the role of Serbia? Of Austria? Of Russia? What was the aim of German policy in July 1914? Did Germany want a general war?
4. Why did Germany lose World War I? Could Germany have won, or was victory never a possibility? What were the benefits of Versailles to Europe, and what were its drawbacks? Was the settlement too harsh or too conciliatory? Could it have secured lasting peace in Europe? How might it have been improved?
5. Why did Lenin succeed in establishing Bolshevik rule in Russia? What role did Trotsky play? Was it wise policy for Lenin to take Russia out of the war?
6. How had imperialism contributed to pre–World War I rivalries? How did the war and the peace settlement change European colonialism and plant seeds for further colonial discontent?

SUGGESTED READINGS

L. Albertini, *The Origins of the War of 1914*, 3 vols. (1952, 1957). Discursive, but invaluable.

V. R. Berghahn, *Germany and the Approach of War in 1914* (1973). Stresses the importance of Germany's naval program.

S. B. Fay, *The Origins of the World War*, 2 vols. (1928). The best and most influential of the revisionist accounts.

O. Figes, *A People's Tragedy: The Russian Revolution: 1891–1924* (1998). The best recent analytic narrrative.

F. Fischer, *Germany's Aims in the First World War* (1967). An influential interpretation that stirred an enormous controversy by emphasizing Germany's role in bringing on the war.

D. Fromkin, *Europe's Last Summer: Who Started the Great War in 1914?* (2004). A lively and readable account of the outbreak of the war.

D. Fromkin, *A Peace to End All Peace: The Fall of the Ottoman Empire and the Creation of the Modern Middle East* (1989). A well-informed narrative of a complicated process.

R. F. Hamilton and H. H. Herwig, *The Origins of World War I* (2003). An extensive collection of essays examining the subject from a number of differing perspectives.

H. Herwig, *The First World War: Germany and Austria, 1914–18* (1997). A fine study of the war from the losers' perspective.

J. N. Horne, *Labour at War: France and Britain, 1914–1918* (1991). Examines a major issue on the home fronts.

J. Joll, *The Origins of the First World War* (2006). Most recent revision of a classic study.

P. Kennedy, *The Rise of the Anglo-German Antagonism, 1860–1914* (1980). An unusual and thorough analysis of the political, economic, and cultural roots of important diplomatic developments.

D. C. B. Lieven, *Russia and the Origins of the First World War* (1983). A good account of the forces that shaped Russian policy.

M. Macmillan, *Paris 1919: Six Months That Changed the World* (2003). The most extensive recent treatment.

E. Manela, *The Wilsonian Moment: Self Determination and the International Origins of Anticolonial Nationalism* (2007). A major exploration of how Wilson's foreign policy at Versailles raised colonial expectations and revolts in Egypt, India, China, and Korea.

A. Mombauer, *The Origins of the First World War: Controversies and Consensus* (2002). A discussion and evaluation of historians' shifting views regarding the responsibility for the outbreak of the war.

R. O. Paxton and J. Hessler, *Europe in the Twentieth Century*, 5th ed. (2011). A fine general account.

R. Pipes, *A Concise History of the Russian Revolution* (1996). A readable account by a master historian.

Z. Steiner, *Britain and the Origins of the First World War* (2003). A perceptive and informed account of British foreign policy before the war.

D. Stevenson, *Cataclysm: The First World War as Political Tragedy* (2004). Analyzes the bankruptcy of reason that precipitated the war and kept it going.

N. Stone, *The Eastern Front 1914–1917* (2004). A study of the often neglected region of the war.

H. Strachan, *The First World War* (2004). A one-volume version of the massive three-volume magisterial account now underway.

S. R. Williamson, Jr., *Austria-Hungary and the Origins of the First World War* (1991). A valuable study of a complex subject.

MyHistoryLab™ MEDIA ASSIGNMENTS

Find these resources in the Media Assignments folder for Chapter 26 on **MyHistoryLab**.

QUESTIONS FOR ANALYSIS

1. How did tanks change the nature of warfare, beginning with World War I?

   ***Section:* World War I**
   View the **Closer Look** The Development of the Armored Tank, p. 845

2. How have historians changed their explanations for the origins of World War I?

   ***Section:* World War I**
   Watch the **Video** The Origins of World War I, p. 837

3. Of the legacies of World War I, which do you think is the most important today?

   ***Section:* The End of World War I**
   Watch the **Video** Video Lectures: The Continuing Legacy of World War I in the Middle East, p. 854

4. How does this represent the response of European leaders to the crises in the Balkans, and the likely success of that response?

   ***Section:* World War I**
   View the **Image** European Leaders Attempt to Quell the Balkan Crises—Punch Cartoon, p. 833

5. What is this document's attitude toward nationalist principles?

   ***Section:* The End of World War I**
   Read the **Document** Woodrow Wilson, *The Fourteen Points* (1918), p. 852

OTHER RESOURCES FROM THIS CHAPTER

Emergence of the German Empire and the Alliance Systems (1873–1890)

View the **Map** The German Empire, p. 828

View the **Map** Congress of Berlin, p. 829

View the **Map** European Alliances on the Eve of World War I, p. 832

World War I

View the **Map** Interactive Map: The Decline of the Ottoman Empire, p. 832

View the **Map** Diplomatic Crises, 1905–1914, p. 832

Read the **Document** Borijove Jevtic, *The Murder of Archduke Franz Ferdinand at Sarajevo* (28 June 1914), p. 834

Watch the **Video** Video Lectures: The Outbreak of World War I, p. 834

View the **Map** Map Discovery: The Schlieffen Plan and France's Plan XVII, ca. 1905–1914, p. 837

Read the **Compare and Connect** The Outbreak of World War I, p. 838

View the **Closer Look** Trench Warfare, p. 841

The Russian Revolution

View the **Closer Look** Bolshevik Revolution Propaganda Poster, p. 848

Read the **Document** Bolshevik Seizure of Power, 1917, p. 848

The End of World War I

View the **Closer Look** Young Turks Overthrow Abdülhamid II, 1908, p. 853

The Settlement at Paris

View the **Closer Look** Peace at Versailles, p. 854

View the **Image** Woodrow Wilson on His Way to Versailles, 1919, p. 855

Read the **Document** The Covenant of the League of Nations, p. 857

This poster shows an idealized Soviet collective farm on which tractors owned by the state have replaced peasant labor. In reality, collectivization provoked fierce resistance and caused famines in which millions of peasants died. Poster concerning the first Five Year Plan with a photograph of Joseph Stalin (1879–1953), "At the end of the Plan, the basis of collectivisation must be completed," 1932 (colour litho.) by Klutchis (fl. 1932). Deutsches Plakat Museum, Essen, Germany/Archives Charmet/The Bridgeman Art Library

Listen to the Chapter Audio on MyHistoryLab.com

The Interwar Years: The Challenge of Dictators and Depression

▼ **After Versailles: Demands for Revision and Enforcement**

▼ **Toward the Great Depression in Europe**
Financial Tailspin • Problems in Agricultural Commodities • Depression and Government Policy in Britain and France

▼ **The Soviet Experiment**
War Communism • The New Economic Policy • The Third International • Stalin versus Trotsky • The Decision for Rapid Industrialization • The Collectivization of Agriculture • The Purges

▼ **The Fascist Experiment in Italy**
The Rise of Mussolini • The Fascists in Power

▼ **German Democracy and Dictatorship**
The Weimar Republic • Depression and Political Deadlock • Hitler Comes to Power • Hitler's Consolidation of Power • Anti-Semitism and the Police State • Racial Ideology and the Lives of Women • Nazi Economic Policy

▼ **Trials of the Successor States in Eastern Europe**
Economic and Ethnic Pressures • Poland: Democracy to Military Rule • Czechoslovakia: A Viable Democratic Experiment • Hungary: Turn to Authoritarianism • Austria: Political Turmoil and Nazi Occupation • Southeastern Europe: Royal Dictatorships

▼ **In Perspective**

LEARNING OBJECTIVES

Why did the Paris settlement fail to bring peace and prosperity to Europe?

What key factors combined to produce the Great Depression?

What was the relationship between politics and economics in the early decades of the Soviet Union?

What did fascism mean to Mussolini and his supporters?

Why did democracy fail to thrive in postwar Germany?

What shared challenges faced the successor states in eastern Europe?

DURING THE TWO decades that followed the Paris settlement, Europe saw bold experiments in politics and economic life. Two broad sets of factors accounted for these experiments. First, the war, the Russian Revolution, and the peace treaty had transformed the political face of Europe. New political regimes had emerged in the wake of the collapse of the monarchies of Germany, Austria-Hungary, and Russia. These were the Weimar Republic in Germany, a host of successor states to the Austro-Hungarian and Russian Empires, and the Communist Soviet Union. In Great Britain, most of Ireland established itself as, in effect, an independent nation. These new governments immediately faced the problems of postwar reconstruction, economic dislocation, and nationalistic resentment. Most of these nations also included large groups who questioned the legitimacy of their governments. All the governments and societies of both Western and Eastern Europe believed themselves profoundly threatened by the Soviet Union. The Russian Revolution was thus a pivotal factor in the rise of right-wing and fascist dictators, who often justified their power on the basis of their firm opposition to the "Red Menace" and to the growing popularity of socialism and communism in many European countries during the economic crisis of the 1930s.

Second, beginning in the early twenties, economic dislocations that led to the economic downturn that became known as the Great Depression began to spread across the world. The economic troubles were caused by financial turmoil in the industrialized nations and a collapse of commodity prices that hurt the economies of the countries that exported raw materials. Faced with political instability and economic crisis, governments contrived various responses. The Great Depression itself, which began in 1929, was the most severe downturn capitalist economies had ever experienced. High unemployment, low production, financial instability, and shrinking trade arrived and would not depart. Business and political leaders despaired over the market's seeming inability to resolve the crisis. Marxists and, indeed, many other observers thought the final downfall of capitalism was at hand.

European voters looked for new ways out of the doldrums, and politicians sought to escape the pressures that the Depression had brought on them. One result of the fight for economic security was the establishment of the Nazi dictatorship in Germany. Another was the piecemeal construction of what became known as the mixed economy; that is, governments became directly involved in making economic decisions alongside business and labor. In both cases, most of the political and economic guidelines of nineteenth-century liberalism were abandoned, and so were decency and civility in political life. Authoritarianism and aggression were not the inescapable destiny of Europe. They emerged from the failure to secure alternative modes of democratic political life and stable international relations and from the inability to achieve long-term economic prosperity.

▼ After Versailles: Demands for Revision and Enforcement

The Paris settlement fostered both resentments and discontent. Those resentments counted among the chief political factors in Europe for the next two decades. Germany had been humiliated. The arrangements for reparations led to endless haggling over payments. Many national groups in the successor states of the Austro-Hungarian Empire felt that their rights to self-determination had been violated or ignored. There were strident demands for further border adjustments because significant national minorities, particularly Germans and Magyars, resided outside the national boundaries drawn in Paris. On the other side, the victorious powers, especially France, often believed that the provisions of the treaties were being inadequately enforced. Consequently, throughout the 1920s and into the 1930s, demands either to revise or to enforce the Paris treaties contributed to domestic political turmoil across the Continent. Many political figures were willing

View the **Image** "The Mask Falls—German Cartoon Reacting to Treaty of Versailles" on **MyHistoryLab.com**

The French invasion of the German Ruhr (1923) began a crisis that brought strikes and rampant inflation in Germany. Here French troops have commandeered a German locomotive during one of the strikes. UPI/CORBIS/Bettmann

to fish in these troubled international waters for a large catch of domestic votes.

▼ Toward the Great Depression in Europe

Along with the move toward political experimentation and the demands for revision of the new international order, there was a widespread yearning to return to the economic prosperity of the prewar years. After 1918, however, it was impossible to restore in the economic realm what U.S. president Warren Harding (1865–1923) would term *normalcy*. During the Great War, Europeans had turned the military and industrial power that they had created during the previous century against themselves. What had been "normal" in economic and social life before 1914 could not be reestablished.

The casualties from the war numbered in the millions. (See Table 27–1.) This represented not only a waste of human life and talent, but also the loss of producers and consumers.

Three factors originating in the 1920s combined to bring about the intense severity and the extended length of the **Great Depression**. First, a financial crisis stemmed directly from the war and the peace settlement. To this was added a crisis in the production and distribution of goods in the world market. These two problems became intertwined in 1929, and in Europe they reached the breaking point in 1931. Finally, both of these difficulties became worse than they might have been because no major Western European country or the United States provided strong, responsible economic leadership that might have resulted in some form of cooperation to face the challenge of the Depression.

TABLE 27–1 TOTAL CASUALTIES IN THE FIRST WORLD WAR

Country	Dead	Wounded	Total Killed as a Percentage of Population
France	1,398,000	2,000,000	3.4
Belgium	38,000	44,700	0.5
Italy	578,000	947,000	1.6
British Empire	921,000	2,090,000	1.7
Romania	250,000	120,000	3.3
Serbia	278,000	133,000	5.7
Greece	26,000	21,000	0.5
Russia	1,811,000	1,450,000	1.1
Bulgaria	88,000	152,000	1.9
Germany	2,037,000	4,207,000	3.0
Austria-Hungary	1,100,000	3,620,000	1.9
Turkey	804,000	400,000	3.7
United States	114,000	206,000	0.1

Source: Niall Ferguson, *The Pity of War* (New York: Basic Books, 1998).

Financial Tailspin

As one of the chief victors in the war, France was determined to collect reparations from Germany for the destruction the war had caused in northern France. The United States was no less determined that its allies repay the money it had lent them during the war. The European allies also owed debts to each other. German reparations were to provide the means of repaying all these debts. Most of the money that the Allies collected from each other also went to the United States.

The quest for payment of German reparations caused one of the major diplomatic crises of the 1920s; that crisis itself resulted in further economic upheaval. In early 1923 the Allies—France in particular—declared Germany to be in technical default of its reparation payments. On January 11, to ensure receipt of the hard-won reparations, French and Belgian troops occupied the Ruhr mining and manufacturing district. The **Weimar Republic** ordered passive resistance that amounted to a general strike in Germany's largest industrial region. Confronted with this tactic, the French sent technicians and engineers to run the German mines and railroads. France got its way. The Germans paid, but its victory cost France dearly. The British were alienated by the French heavy-handedness and took no part in the occupation. Britain became more suspicious of France and more sympathetic to Germany. The cost of the Ruhr occupation, moreover, vastly increased French as well as German inflation and damaged the French economy.

The political and economic turmoil of the Ruhr invasion led to international attempts to ease the German payment of reparations. At the same time, American investment capital was pouring into Europe. However, by 1928 this investment decreased as American money became diverted into the booming New York stock market. The crash of Wall Street in October 1929—the result of virtually unregulated financial speculation—saw the loss of large amounts of money. Credit sharply contracted in the United States as numerous banks failed. Thereafter, little American capital was available for investment in Europe.

As American credit for Europe began to run out, a major financial crisis struck the Continent. In May 1931 the Kreditanstalt bank in Austria collapsed. The

Kreditanstalt was a primary financial institution for much of central and eastern Europe. Its collapse put severe pressure on the German banking system, which was saved only through government guarantees. As the German difficulties increased, U.S. president Herbert Hoover (1874–1964) announced in June 1931 a one-year moratorium on all payments of international debts. The Hoover moratorium was a prelude to the end of reparations. The Lausanne Conference in the summer of 1932 brought, in effect, the era of reparations to a close. The next year the debts owed to the United States were settled either through small token payments or simply through default.

[**View** the **Map** "The Great Depression in Europe" on **MyHistoryLab.com**

Problems in Agricultural Commodities

In the 1920s the market demand for European goods shrank, leaving much of the Continent's productive capacity idle or underused. This problem originated both within and outside Europe. In both instances the difficulty arose from agriculture. Better methods of farming, improved strains of wheat, expanded acreage under the plow, and more extensive transport facilities vastly increased the quantity of grain produced by farmers around the world. World wheat prices fell to record lows. Although this helped consumers, it decreased the income of European farmers. At the same time, higher industrial wages raised the cost of the industrial goods that farmers or peasants used. Consequently, they had great difficulty paying off their mortgages and loans for normal operating costs. These problems were especially acute in central and eastern Europe and increased farmers' disillusionment with liberal politics. German farmers, for example, would become prime supporters of the National Socialist Workers Party (Nazis).

Outside Europe similar problems affected other producers of agricultural commodities. The prices they received for their products plummeted. Government-held reserves of raw materials reached record levels. This glut of major world commodities involved wheat, sugar, coffee, rubber, wool, and lard. The people who produced these goods in underdeveloped nations could no longer make enough money to buy goods from industrial Europe. As world credit collapsed, the economic position of these commodity producers worsened. Commodity production had simply outstripped world demand.

The results of the collapse in the agricultural sector of the world economy and the financial turmoil were stagnation and depression for European industry. Coal, iron, and textiles had depended largely on international markets. Unemployment spread from these industries to those producing consumer goods. Persistent unemployment in Great Britain and, to a lesser extent, in Germany during the 1920s had created "soft" domestic markets. The policies of reduced spending with which the governments confronted the Depression further weakened domestic demand. By the early 1930s the Depression was feeding on itself.

Depression and Government Policy in Britain and France

The Depression did not mean absolute economic decline or total unemployment. But the economic downturn spread potential as well as actual insecurity. People in nearly all walks of life feared the loss of their economic security. The Depression also frustrated normal social and economic expectations. Even the employed often seemed to make no progress; and their anxieties created a major source of discontent.

The governments of the late 1920s and the early 1930s were not well suited in either structure or ideology to confront these problems. The electorates demanded action. The governments' responses depended largely on the severity of the Depression in a particular country and on the self-confidence of the nation's political system.

Great Britain and France, which because of their vast empires commanded very large economies, undertook moderate political experiments. In 1924 the Labour Party in Great Britain established itself as a viable governing party by forming a short-lived government. It again formed a ministry in 1929. Under the pressure of the Depression and at the urging of King George V (r. 1910–1936), Labour prime minister Ramsay MacDonald (1866–1937) organized a National Government, which was a coalition of the Labour, Conservative, and Liberal Parties. It remained in power until 1935, when a Conservative ministry led by Stanley Baldwin (1867–1947) replaced it. (See the Document "John Maynard Keynes Calls for Government Investment to Create Employment," pages 870–871.)

The 1920s also saw the establishment of an independent Irish state. On Easter Monday in April 1916, a nationalist uprising occurred in Dublin, the only rebellion of a national group against any government engaged in World War I. The British suppressed the uprising but made martyrs of its leaders by executing several of them. Leadership of the nationalist cause quickly shifted from the Irish Party in Parliament to the extremist *Sinn Fein*, or "Ourselves Alone," movement. In the election of 1918, Sinn Fein won all but four of the Irish parliamentary seats outside Ulster. They refused to go to the Parliament at Westminster. Instead, they constituted themselves into a *Dail Eireann*, or Irish Parliament. On January 21, 1919, they declared Irish independence. Thereafter a civil war broke out between the military wing of Sinn Fein, which became the Irish Republican Army (IRA), and the British army. The conflict ended with a treaty in December 1921, which established the Irish Free State as one of the dominions in the British Commonwealth. The six, predominantly

Protestant, counties of Ulster, or Northern Ireland, were permitted to remain part of what was now called the United Kingdom of Great Britain and Northern Ireland, with provisions for home rule. In the 1920s and 1930s, the Free State gradually severed its ties to Britain. It remained neutral during World War II and declared itself an independent republic in 1949.

Read the **Document** "Irish National Identity: (a) Irish Declaration of Independence; (b) Ulster's Solemn League and Covenant; (c) Eamon de Valera, radio broadcast" on **MyHistoryLab.com**

The most important French interwar political experiment was the **Popular Front** Ministry, which came to office in 1936. It was composed of Socialists, Radicals, and Communists—the first time that Socialists and Communists had cooperated in a ministry. They did so because they feared right-wing political groups in France and saw the threat of such regimes elsewhere in Europe. Despite fierce resistance from business and conservative groups, the Popular Front enacted major social and economic reforms, including the forty-hour week, paid vacations for workers, and compulsory arbitration of labor disputes. But its parliamentary support gradually faded until its final collapse in October 1938.

The political changes in Britain and France were essentially of domestic significance. But the political experiments of the 1920s and 1930s that reshaped world history and civilization involved the establishment of a Soviet government in Russia, a Fascist regime in Italy, and a Nazi dictatorship in Germany.

▼ The Soviet Experiment

The consolidation of the Bolshevik Revolution in Russia established the most extensive and durable of all twentieth-century authoritarian governments. The Communist Party of the Soviet Union retained power from 1917 until the end of 1991, and its presence influenced the political history of Europe and much of the rest of the world, as did no other single factor. Unlike the Italian Fascists or the German National Socialists, the Bolsheviks seized power violently through revolution. For several years they confronted civil war, and their leaders long felt insecure about their hold on the country. The Communist Party was neither a mass party nor a nationalistic one. Its early membership rarely exceeded more than 1 percent of the Russian population. The Bolsheviks confronted a much less industrialized economy than that in Italy or Germany. They believed in and practiced the collectivization of economic life. The Marxist–Leninist ideology had vastly more international appeal than the nationalism of the Fascists and the racism of the Nazis. Communism was an exportable commodity. The Communists regarded their government and their revolution not as part of the national history of Russia, but as epoch-making events in the history of the world and the development of humanity. (See "Compare and Connect: The Soviets and the Nazis Confront the Issues of Women and the Family,." pages 890–891.) Fear of communism and determination to stop its spread became one of the leading political forces in Western Europe and the United States for most of the rest of the century. Policies flowing from that opposition would influence European and American relationships with much of the rest of the world.

War Communism

Within the Soviet Union the Red Army under the organizational genius of Leon Trotsky (1879–1940) had suppressed internal and foreign military opposition to the new government during the civil war that raged from 1918 to 1920. Within months of the revolution, a new secret police, known as *Cheka*, appeared. Throughout the civil war Lenin (1870–1924) had declared that the Bolshevik Party,

Anxiety over the spread of the Bolshevik Revolution was a fundamental factor of European politics during the 1920s and 1930s. Images like this Soviet portrait of Lenin as a heroic revolutionary conjured fears among people in the rest of Europe of a political force determined to overturn their social, political, and economic institutions. Bildarchiv Preussischer Kulturbesitz/Art Resource, NY

Document

JOHN MAYNARD KEYNES CALLS FOR GOVERNMENT INVESTMENT TO CREATE EMPLOYMENT

Since at least the late nineteenth century, European social critics had questioned whether capitalistic economies could function without major crises that resulted in unemployment and other social disruptions. Virtually all economists, however, believed that given enough time capitalistic economies would correct themselves. Consequently, when the Great Depression struck the worldwide economy, the governments of Western Europe and the United States initially undertook relatively modest actions to address it. They were doing what most economists at the time advocated. Socialists, of course, had long advocated government intervention. In 1936, however, John Maynard Keynes, a prominent British economist, published The General Theory of Employment, Interest and Money. *Keynes, who was not a socialist, believed that the Great Depression demonstrated that economic crises could be so severe that private investment would simply not take place and thus could not generate new economic activity that would revive employment and lift the economy out of depression. In the passage, Keynes explains that although he believes in individual initiative, there are times it will not occur. Under those conditions he calls for the "socialisation of investment," which was his term for government spending to spark new economic activity that would expand employment. In the second paragraph, he argues that the role of such government investment or spending is to provide employment for those workers whom the private economy cannot employ. Keynes's book did not influence many policies during the Great Depression, but after World War II, many Western governments devised economic policies along the lines he advocated.*

as the vanguard of the revolution, was imposing the dictatorship of the proletariat. Political and economic administration became highly centralized. All major decisions flowed from the top in a nondemocratic manner. Under the economic policy of **War Communism**, the revolutionary government confiscated and then operated the banks, the transport facilities, and heavy industry. The state also forcibly requisitioned grain and shipped it from the countryside to feed the army and the urban workers. The Bolsheviks used the need to fight the civil war as justification for suppressing any resistance to these economic policies.

War Communism helped the Red Army defeat its opponents. The revolution had survived and triumphed. The policy, however, generated domestic opposition to the Bolsheviks, who in 1920 numbered only about 600,000. The alliance of workers and peasants forged in 1917 by the Bolsheviks' slogan of "Peace, Bread, and Land" had begun to dissolve. Many Russians were no longer willing to make the sacrifices demanded by the central party bureaucrats. In 1920 and 1921, serious strikes occurred. Peasants were discontented and resisted the requisition of grain. In March 1921, the sailors mutinied at the Kronstadt naval base on the Baltic. The Red Army crushed the rebellion with grave loss of life. Each of these acts of opposition suggested that the proletariat itself was opposing the dictatorship of the proletariat. Also, by late 1920 it had become clear that revolution was not going to sweep across the rest of Europe. For the time being the Soviet Union would constitute a vast island of revolutionary socialism in the larger sea of world capitalism.

The New Economic Policy

Under these difficult conditions Lenin made a strategic retreat. In March 1921, following the Kronstadt mutiny, he outlined the **New Economic Policy**, or NEP. Apart from what he termed "the commanding heights" of banking, heavy industry, transportation, and international commerce, considerable private economic enterprise was allowed. In particular, peasants could farm for a profit. They would pay taxes like other citizens, but they could sell their surplus grain on the open market. The NEP was consistent with Lenin's earlier conviction that the Russian peasantry held the key to the success of the revolution, but the changes came too late to avert the famine of 1921–1922 in which perhaps 5 million people died. After 1921 the countryside did become more stable, and a secure food supply seemed assured for the cities.

Why does Keynes believe the private economy will not always provide sufficient employment? Why does he call government spending the "socialisation of investment"? How much of his argument is analytical? How much political?

In some respects the foregoing theory is moderately conservative in its implications. For whilst it indicates the vital importance of establishing certain central controls in matters which are now left in the main to individual initiative, there are wide fields of activity which are unaffected. The State will have to exercise a guiding influence on the propensity to consume partly through its scheme of taxation, partly by fixing the rate of interest, and partly, perhaps, in other ways. Furthermore, it seems unlikely that the influence of banking policy on the rate of interest will be sufficient by itself to determine an optimum rate of investment. I conceive, therefore, that a somewhat comprehensive socialisation of investment will prove the only means of securing an approximation to full employment; though this need not exclude all manner of compromises and of devices by which public authority will co-operate with private initiative. But beyond this, no obvious case is made out for a system of State Socialism which would embrace most of the economic life of the community. It is not the ownership of the instruments of production which it is important for the State to assume. If the State is able to determine the aggregate amount of resources devoted to augmenting the instruments and the basic rate of reward to those who own them, it will have accomplished all that is necessary. . . .

To put the matter concretely, I see no reason to suppose that the existing system seriously misemploys the factors of production which are in use. There are, of course, errors of foresight; but these would not be avoided by centralizing decisions. When 9,000,000 men are employed out of 10,000,000 willing and able to work, there is no evidence that the labour of these 9,000,000 men is misdirected. The complaint against the present system is not that these 9,000,000 men ought to be employed on different tasks, but that tasks should be available for the remaining 1,000,000 men. It is in determining the volume, not the direction, of actual employment that the existing system has broken down.

From John Maynard Keynes, *The General Theory of Employment, Interest and Money* (London: Macmillan & Co., Ltd., 1960), p. 379.

Similar free enterprise flourished within light industry and the domestic retail trade. By 1927 industrial production had reached its 1913 level. The revolution seemed to have transformed Russia into a land of small farms and privately owned shops and businesses.

View the **Image** "Bolshevik Revolution poster" on **MyHistoryLab.com**

The Third International

The onset and consolidation of the Bolshevik Revolution in Russia was a transforming event for the history of socialism as well as for Russia and international affairs. The revolution stunned West European socialists. In the West, before the war, as discussed in Chapter 23, social democratic parties had regarded the Russian Bolsheviks as eccentric, politically marginal Marxist extremists. The Bolshevik victory forced West European social democrats to rethink their position within the world of international socialism. For their part, the Bolsheviks intended to establish themselves as the international leaders of Marxism and regarded reformist social democrats as enemies and rivals.

In 1919, the Soviet communists founded the Third International of the European socialist movement, better known as the *Comintern*. The Comintern worked to make the Bolshevik model of socialism, as Lenin had developed it, the rule for all socialist parties outside the Soviet Union. In 1920, the Comintern imposed its Twenty-one Conditions on any socialist party that wished to join it. These conditions included acknowledging Moscow's leadership, rejecting reformist or revisionist socialism, repudiating previous socialist leaders, and adopting the Communist Party name. In effect, the Comintern sought to destroy democratic socialism, which it accused of having betrayed the working class through reform policies and parliamentary accommodation.

The decision whether to accept these conditions split every major European socialist party. As a result, separate communist and social democratic parties emerged in most countries and they fought each other more intensely than they fought either capitalism or conservative political parties. Their fierce conflict was one of the fundamental features of the interwar European political landscape.

These Comintern polices and the resulting divisions of the socialist parties directly affected the rise of the fascists and the Nazis in Western Europe. It is difficult to overestimate the fears that Soviet political rhetoric and Communist Party activity aroused in Europe during the 1920s and 1930s. Conservative and right-wing political groups manipulated and exaggerated these fears. The presence of separate communist parties in Western Europe meant that right-wing politicians always had a convenient target they could justly accuse of seeking to overthrow the government and to impose Soviet-style political, social, and economic systems in their nations. Furthermore, right-wing politicians also accused the democratic socialists of supporting policies that might facilitate a communist takeover. The divisions between Communists and democratic socialists also meant that right-wing political movements rarely had to confront a united left.

Stalin versus Trotsky

The NEP had caused sharp disputes within the Politburo, the highest governing committee of the Communist Party. The partial return to capitalism seemed to some members nothing less than a betrayal of sound Marxist principles. These frictions increased as Lenin's firm hand disappeared. In 1922 he suffered a stroke and never again dominated party affairs; in 1924 he died. In the ensuing power vacuum, an intense struggle for leadership of the party commenced. Two factions emerged. One was led by Trotsky; the other by Joseph Stalin (1879–1953), who had become general secretary of the party in 1922. Shortly before his death Lenin had criticized both men. He was especially harsh toward Stalin. However, as general secretary Stalin's base of power lay with the party membership and with the daily management of party affairs, he was able to withstand the posthumous criticism of Lenin.

Each faction wanted to control the party and thus also the state, but the struggle was fought over the question of Russia's path toward industrialization and the future of the Communist revolutionary movement. Trotsky, speaking for what became known as the left wing, urged rapid industrialization and looked to voluntary collectivization of farming by poor peasants as a means of increasing agricultural production. He further argued that the revolution in Russia could succeed only if new revolutions took place elsewhere. Russia needed the skills and wealth of other nations to build its own economy. As Trotsky's influence within the party began to wane, he also demanded that party members be permitted to criticize the policies of the government and the party. Trotsky, however, was a latecomer to the advocacy of open discussion. When he had controlled the Red Army, he had been a harsh and unflinching disciplinarian.

A right-wing faction opposed Trotsky, and Stalin was its true political manipulator. In the mid-1920s this group pressed for the continuation of Lenin's NEP and relatively slow industrialization.

Stalin was the ultimate victor in these intraparty rivalries. Unlike the other early Bolshevik leaders, he had not spent a long exile in Western Europe. He was much less an intellectual and internationalist. He was also much more brutal. His handling of various recalcitrant national groups within Russia after the revolution had shocked even Lenin. Stalin's power lay in his command of bureaucratic and administrative methods. He was neither a brilliant writer nor an effective public speaker; however, he mastered the crucial, if dull, details of party structure, including admission, promotion, and rewards. That mastery meant that he could draw on the support of the lower levels of the party apparatus when he clashed with other leaders.

In the mid-1920s Stalin supported Bukharin's position on economic development. In 1924 he also enunciated, in opposition to Trotsky, the doctrine of "socialism in one country." He urged that socialism could be achieved in Russia alone. Russian success did not depend on the fate of the revolution elsewhere. Stalin thus nationalized the previously international scope of the Marxist revolution. He cunningly used the apparatus of the party and his control over its Central Committee to edge out Trotsky and his supporters. By 1927 Trotsky had been removed from all his offices, ousted from the party, and exiled. In 1929 he was expelled from Russia and eventually moved to Mexico, where he was murdered in 1940 by one of Stalin's agents. With the removal of Trotsky, Stalin was firmly in control of the Soviet state. It remained to be seen what "socialism in one country" would mean in practice.

The Decision for Rapid Industrialization

In 1927 the Party Congress decided to push for rapid industrialization. As implemented through what has been termed "industrialization by political mobilization," this policy marked a sharp departure from the NEP and a rejection of the pockets of relatively free-market operations within the larger Soviet economy.[1]

Stalin's goal was to have the Soviet Union overtake the productive capacity of its enemies, the capitalist nations. This policy required the rapid construction of heavy industries, such as iron, steel, and machine tool making; building electricity-generating stations; and manufacturing tractors. Stalin's organizational vehicle for industrialization was a series of five-year plans, starting in 1928. The State Planning Commission, or *Gosplan*, set goals for production in every area of economic life and attempted to organize the economy to meet them. The task of coordinating all facets of production was immensely complicated. Deliveries of materials from mines or factories had to be assured before the next unit could carry out its part of the plan. Enormous economic disruption occurred as the *Gosplan* built power plants and

[1]Vladimir Andrle, *A Social History of Twentieth-Century Russia* (London: Arnold, 1994), p. 161.

steel mills and increased the output of mines. The plans consistently favored capital projects over the production of consumer goods. The number of centralized agencies and ministries involved in planning soared, and they often competed with each other.

Read the Document "Joseph Stalin, *Five Year Plan*" on MyHistoryLab.com

The rapid expansion of the industrial base created the first genuinely large factory labor force in what had been Russia. Workers were recruited from the countryside and from the urban unemployed. New cities and industrial districts in existing cities arose. Most workers were crowded into shoddy buildings with inadequate sanitation, living space, and nourishment. Their lives were as bad as or worse than anything Marx and Engels had decried in the nineteenth century.

The government and the Communist Party undertook a vast program of propaganda to sell the five-year plans to the Russian people and to elicit their cooperation. The government boasted of the sheer size of the plants and new towns being constructed. Such propaganda was necessary because most industrial workers were displaced peasants who had never worked in a factory and often resisted industrial discipline. The party appealed to the idealism of the young in proclaiming its goals of rapidly modernizing the nation. Workers, such as a legendary coal miner named Stakhanov, who exceeded their assigned goals received rewards and publicity.

View the Image "Stalinist Poster" on MyHistoryLab.com

The results were impressive. Soviet industrial production rose approximately 400 percent between 1928 and 1940. Industries that had never existed in Russia challenged their foreign counterparts. Hundreds of thousands of people populated new industrial cities. The social and human cost of this effort had, however, been appalling.

Magnitogorsk was a city that became a monument to Stalin's drive toward rapid industrialization. Located in the Ural Mountains near a vast supply of iron ore, the city became the site of major iron and steel production. It was one of the new industrial cities founded under the Five Year Plan designed to challenge the capitalist production of the Western nations. National Archives and Records Administration

The Collectivization of Agriculture

Agricultural productivity had always been a core problem for the emerging Soviet economy. Under the NEP the government purchased a certain amount of grain at prices it set itself. The rest of the grain was then supposed to be sold at market prices, which were higher than the government-set prices. Many peasant farmers of all degrees of wealth tried to circumvent this system, often by keeping grain off the market in hopes that its price would rise. The scarcity of consumer goods available for purchase in the countryside also encouraged hoarding. With little to buy from what they earned by selling their grain, farmers had little incentive to sell it. Instead, many of them refused to sell grain to the government at the low prices it set and insisted on selling it at the market price, which the government refused to accept. In 1928 and 1929, as a result, the Soviet government confronted shortfalls of grain on the market and the prospect of food shortages in the cities and social unrest.

Stalin therefore decided to reverse the agricultural policies of the NEP. Toward the end of the 1920s, Soviet economists and party officials devised an explanation for the difficulties they confronted in the agricultural sector. First, they asserted that the traditional peasant holdings were too small to produce enough grain to meet the country's needs. Second, they claimed that a class-enemy was responsible for the hoarding and for what they regarded as speculation in the grain trade. This enemy was the group of relatively prosperous peasants, known as *kulaks,* who numbered somewhat less than 5 percent of the rural population and were often the most productive and efficient farmers. On the basis of these ideas, Stalin decided that Soviet agriculture must be collectivized to produce enough grain for domestic food and foreign export. **Collectivization**—the replacement of private peasant farms with huge state-run and state-owned farms called collectives—would also put the Communist Party firmly in control of the farm sector of the economy and free up peasant labor to work in the expanding industrial sector. To carry out this policy, Stalin portrayed the *kulak*s as the fundamental cause of the agricultural problems.

Party officials carried out the initial campaign of dekulakization and collectivization. Usually they would seek first to remove *kulaks* from a village while confiscating their land and would then attempt to coerce the remaining peasants into organizing a collective farm. Enormous turmoil and violence resulted. In March 1930, Stalin called a brief halt to the process, justifying the slowdown on the grounds of "dizziness from success." After the harvest of that year had been secured, however, the drive to collectivize the farms was renewed with vehemence.

Peasants determined to keep their land, often with women in the lead, had sabotaged collectivization by slaughtering millions of livestock between 1929 and 1933. Peasants who resisted were killed outright. Others starved to death on their own farms when all the grain that they had produced was seized. Over 2 million peasants were forcibly removed from their homes and deported to distant areas of the Soviet Union or to prison camps where many died from disease, exposure, and malnutrition. Even if they survived that ordeal, they then had to patch together some kind of life as industrial workers or miners in Siberia or another inhospitable province. Their children were treated as class-enemies and political traitors. Much of the violence of collectivization occurred in Ukraine, where Stalin used the process not only to restructure agricultural production but also to crush any vestiges of Ukrainian nationalism, and many millions of lives were lost as a result.

Stalin used intimidation and propaganda to support his drive to collectivize Soviet agriculture. Communist Party agitators led groups of peasants such as these to demand the seizure of the farms worked by the better-off and more successful farmers known as *kulaks.* AP/Wide World Photos

During the drive toward collectivization, the Communist Party also targeted priests of the Russian Orthodox Church. The Party, atheistic in its ideology, had always opposed religion, but only with collectivization were many rural priests attacked and churches closed or vandalized. Between 1926 and 1937, the number of priests recorded in the Soviet census dropped by more than one-half. Rabbis, Catholic priests, Protestant ministers, and mullahs received the same harsh treatment.

By 1937, over 90 percent of Soviet grain production had been collectivized. The violent transformation of Soviet agriculture meant producers on collective farms could no longer decide what crops to produce or how much to sell them for. The government organized Motor-Tractor Stations that supplied the seed and equipment for several collective farms in a region and oversaw the collection and sale of grain. The heads of these stations were Party political operatives, and they determined what payments the farmers eventually received for the grain they had produced. Alongside the state-run collective farms, by the mid-1930s, the government allowed farmers small household plots to grow fruit and vegetables for their families and for local sale. These plots became an important part of Soviet agriculture because peasants tended them so carefully and productively.

At the cost of millions of peasant lives, Stalin and the Communist Party had won the battle of the grain fields, but they had not solved the problem of producing enough food. That difficulty would plague the Soviet Union until its collapse in 1991 and remains a problem for its successor states.

The Purges

In 1933, with turmoil in the countryside and economic dislocation caused by industrialization, Stalin and others in the central Soviet bureaucracy began to fear they were losing control of the country and the party apparatus and that effective rivals to their power and policies might emerge. These apprehensions were largely a figment of Stalin's own paranoia and lust for power, but they resulted in the **Great Purges**, which remain one of the most mysterious and horrendous political events of the twentieth century. Few observers understood the purges at the time, and despite the recent opening of Soviet archives, they have still not been fully comprehended, either inside or outside the former Soviet Union.

The pretext for the onset of the purges was the assassination on December 1, 1934, of Sergei Kirov (1888–1934), the popular party chief of Leningrad and a member of the Politburo. In the wake of the shooting, thousands of people were arrested, and still more were expelled from the party and sent to labor camps. At the time, many thought that opponents of the regime had murdered Kirov, and Stalin routinely accused those whom he attacked of complicity in the crime. Today, many scholars believe that Stalin himself authorized Kirov's assassination because he was afraid of him. The available documentary evidence does not allow us to know for sure whether Stalin was involved, but he quickly used Kirov's death for his own purposes. Under Stalin, the Soviet Communist Party had already shown it could punish dissent within its ranks. The debates of the 1920s within the party and the expulsion of Trotsky had established a clear precedent for exercising firm discipline, and in the confusion surrounding the implementation of the five-year plans, persons accused of sabotage and disloyalty had been executed. The purges, however, went far beyond any of these precedents.

The purges that took place immediately after Kirov's death were just the beginning of a larger and longer process. Between 1936 and 1938, a series of spectacular show trials were held in Moscow. Former high Soviet leaders, including members of the Politburo, such as Bukharin, publicly confessed to political crimes and were convicted and executed. It is still not certain why they made their palpably false confessions, although this seems to have been the kind of ritual confession of faults and shortcomings that had long characterized internal Communist Party life. They had also been interrogated under the most difficult conditions, including torture, and feared for their families' lives. (Stalin regularly arrested the wives, children, siblings, and in-laws of "traitors" and had them shot or sent to die in labor camps.) Other lower-level party members were tried in private and shot. Hundreds of thousands, perhaps millions, of ordinary Soviet citizens received no trial at all and were either executed or deported to slave labor camps where many died. Within the party itself, thousands of members were expelled, and applicants for membership were removed from the rolls. After the civilian party members and leaders had been purged, the prosecutors turned against the government bureaucracy and the Soviet army and navy, convicting and executing thousands of officials and officers, including heroes of the civil war. The exact number of executions, imprisonments, interrogations, and expulsions is unknown, but it ran well into the millions. While the purges went on, no one in the Soviet Union, except Stalin himself, was safe.

The rational explanations of the purges—to the extent that mass murder can ever be rationally explained—probably lie in two directions. First, over the several years the purges lasted, different portions of the party leadership moved against others. Initially, Stalin and the central Moscow leadership used the purges to settle old scores and to discipline and gain more control over lower levels of the party in the far-flung regions of the Soviet Union. In addition to increasing Stalin's authority, these central bureaucratic groups wanted to eliminate any opposition to their own positions or policies. By 1937, however, Stalin seems to have become distrustful of the central party elite, his own supporters, and began to find or pretend to

By the mid-1930s, Stalin's purges had eliminated many leaders and other members from the Soviet Communist Party. This photograph of a meeting of a party congress in 1936 shows a number of the surviving leaders with Stalin, who sits fourth from the right in the front row. To his left is Vyacheslav Molotov, longtime foreign minister. The first person on the left in the front row is Nikita Khrushchev, who headed the Soviet Union in the late 1950s and early 1960s. Itar-Tass/Sovfoto/Eastfoto

find enemies within its ranks. Moreover, by that date, local communist groups were allowed to designate their own victims with little direction from Moscow. Thereafter, a self-destructive cascade of accusations, imprisonments, and executions occurred throughout the party and within its highest levels. The Communist Party leadership at all levels appeared to be consuming itself in an atmosphere of terror for its own sake. This situation has been termed "centrally authorized chaos."[2]

Second, no matter how much tension and rivalry there were among the different levels and regions of the Communist Party, Stalin's primary motive in the purges was almost certainly fear for his own power and a ruthless determination to preserve and increase it. He and the deputies whom he allowed to survive the purges personally selected certain victims and determined the fate of their families. In effect, the purges created a new Communist Party that was absolutely subservient and loyal to Stalin. The "old Bolsheviks" of the October Revolution in 1917 were among his earliest targets. They and others active in the first years of the revolution knew how far Stalin had moved from Lenin's policies. New, younger recruits replaced the party members who were executed or expelled. The newcomers knew little about old Russia or the ideals of the original Bolsheviks. They had not been loyal to Lenin, Trotsky, Bukharin, or any other Soviet leader except Stalin himself.

The internal difficulties of collectivization and industrialization and his worries about internal opposition led Stalin to make an important shift in foreign policy. In 1934, he began to fear the nation might be left isolated against aggression by Nazi Germany. The Soviet Union was not yet strong enough to withstand such an attack. So that year he ordered the Comintern to permit communist parties in other countries to cooperate with noncommunist parties against Nazism and fascism. This reversed the Comintern policy Lenin established as part of the Twenty-One Conditions in 1919. The new Stalinist policy allowed the Popular Front Government in France to come to power.

▼ The Fascist Experiment in Italy

The first authoritarian political experiment in Western Europe that arose in part from fears of the spread of bolshevism beyond the Soviet Union occurred in Italy. The

[2]J. Arch Getty and Oleg V. Naumov, *The Road to Terror: Stalin and the Self-Destruction of the Bolsheviks, 1932–1939*, trans. by Benjamin Sher (New Haven, CT: Yale University Press, 1999), p. 583.

general term *fascist*, which has been used to describe the various right-wing dictatorships that arose between the wars, was derived from the Italian Fascist movement of Benito Mussolini (1883–1945).

While scholars still dispute the exact meaning of ***fascism*** as a political term, the governments regarded as fascist were antidemocratic, anti-Marxist, antiparliamentary, and frequently anti-Semitic. They hoped to hold back the spread of bolshevism, which seemed a real threat at the time. They sought a world that would be safe for the middle class, small businesses, owners of moderate amounts of property, and small farmers. The fascist regimes rejected the political inheritance of the French Revolution and of nineteenth-century liberalism. (See the Document "Mussolini Heaps Contempt on Political Liberalism,." page 878.) Their adherents believed that normal parliamentary politics and parties sacrificed national honor and greatness to petty party disputes. They wanted to overcome the class conflict of Marxism and the party conflict of liberalism by consolidating the various groups and classes within the nation for great national purposes. As Mussolini declared in 1931, "The fascist conception of the state is all-embracing, and outside of the state no human or spiritual values can exist, let alone be desirable."[3] Fascist governments were usually single-party dictatorships characterized by terrorism against and police surveillance of both opponents and the general citizenry. These dictatorships were rooted in the base of mass political parties.

The Rise of Mussolini

The Italian *Fasci di Combattimento* ("Band of Combat") was founded in 1919 in Milan. Most of its members were war veterans who felt that the sacrifices Italy had made in World War I had been in vain. They resented Italy's failure to gain the city of Fiume, toward the northern end of the Adriatic Sea, and other territories at the Paris conference. They feared socialism, inflation, and labor unrest.

Read the Document "Benito Mussolini, 'The Political and Social Doctrine of Fascism' " on **MyHistoryLab.com**

Their leader or ***Duce,*** Benito Mussolini, was the son of a blacksmith. After having been a schoolteacher and a day laborer, he became active in Italian Socialist politics and by 1912 had become editor of the socialist newspaper *Avanti*. In 1914 Mussolini broke with the Socialists and supported Italian entry into the war on the side of the Allies. His interventionist position lost him the editorship of *Avanti*. He then established his own paper, *Il Popolo d'Italia*. Later he served in the army and was wounded. In 1919 Mussolini was just another Italian politician. His *Fasci* organization was one of many small political groups in a country characterized by such entities. As a politician, Mussolini was an opportunist par excellence. He could change his ideas and principles to suit every new occasion. Action for him was always more important than thought or rational justification. His one real rule was political survival.

Postwar Italian politics was a muddle. During the war the Italian Parliament had virtually ceased to function. Ministers had ruled by decree. However, many Italians were dissatisfied with the parliamentary system as it then existed. They felt that Italy had emerged from the war as less than a victorious nation, had not been treated as a great power at the peace conference, and had not received the rewards it deserved. The main spokesman for this discontent was extreme nationalist writer Gabriele D'Annunzio (1863–1938). In 1919 he captured Fiume with a force of patriotic Italians. The Italian army, enforcing the terms of the Versailles Treaty, eventually drove him out. D'Annunzio had provided the example of the political use of a nongovernmental military force. Removing him from Fiume made the parliamentary ministry seem unpatriotic.

Between 1919 and 1921 Italy was also wracked by social turmoil. Numerous industrial strikes occurred, and workers occupied factories. Peasants seized uncultivated land from large estates. Parliamentary and constitutional government seemed incapable of dealing with this unrest. The Socialist Party had captured a plurality of seats in the Chamber of Deputies in 1919. A new Catholic Popular Party had also done well. Both appealed to the working and agrarian classes. However, neither party would cooperate with the other, and parliamentary deadlock resulted. Under these conditions, many Italians honestly—and still others conveniently—believed that a Communist revolution might break out.

Initially, Mussolini was uncertain which way the political winds were blowing. He first supported the factory occupations and land seizures. Never one to be concerned with consistency, however, he soon reversed himself. He had discovered that many upper- and middle-class Italians who were hurt by inflation and who feared the loss of their property had no sympathy for the workers or the peasants. They wanted order rather than some vague social justice that might harm their own interests. Consequently, Mussolini and his Fascists took direct action in the face of the government's inaction. They formed local squads who terrorized Socialists. They attacked strikers and farm workers and protected strikebreakers. Conservative land and factory owners were grateful to the terrorists. The officers of the law simply ignored these crimes. By early 1922 the Fascists controlled local government in many parts of northern Italy.

In 1921 Mussolini and thirty-four of his followers had been elected to the Chamber of Deputies. Their importance grew as the local Fascists gained more direct power.

[3]Denis Mack Smith, *Italy: A Modern History* (Ann Arbor: University of Michigan Press, 1959), p. 412.

Document

MUSSOLINI HEAPS CONTEMPT ON POLITICAL LIBERALISM

The political tactics of the Italian Fascists wholly disregarded the liberal belief in the rule of law and the consent of the governed. In 1923 Mussolini explained why the Fascists so hated and repudiated these liberal principles. Note his emphasis on the idea of the twentieth century as a new historical epoch requiring a new kind of politics and his undisguised praise of force in politics.

Who would be some nineteenth-century liberal political leaders included in Mussolini's attack? Why might Mussolini's audience have been receptive to these views? What events or developments within liberal states allowed Mussolini to portray liberalism as so corrupt and powerless?

Liberalism is not the last word, nor does it represent the definitive formula on the subject of the art of government. . . . Liberalism is the product and the technique of the nineteenth century. . . . It does not follow that the Liberal scheme of government, good for the nineteenth century, for a century, that is, dominated by two such phenomena as the growth of capitalism and the strengthening of the sentiment of nationalism, should be adapted to the twentieth century, which announces itself already with characteristics sufficiently different from those that marked the preceding century. . . .

I challenge Liberal gentlemen to tell if ever in history there has been a government that was based solely on popular consent and that renounced all use of force whatsoever. A government so constructed there has never been and never will be. Consent is an ever-changing thing like the shifting sand on the sea coast, it can never be permanent: It can never be complete. . . . If it be accepted as an axiom that any system of government whatever creates malcontents, how are you going to prevent this discontent from overflowing and constituting a menace to the stability of the State? You will prevent it by force. By the assembling of the greatest force possible. By the inexorable use of this force whenever it is necessary. Take away from any government whatsoever force—and by force is meant physical, armed force—and leave it only its immortal principles, and that government will be at the mercy of the first organized group that decides to overthrow it. Fascism now throws these lifeless theories out to rot. . . . The truth evident now to all who are not warped by [liberal] dogmatism is that men have tired of liberty. They have made an orgy of it. Liberty is today no longer the chaste and austere virgin for whom the generations of the first half of the last century fought and died. For the gallant, restless and bitter youth who face the dawn of a new history there are other words that exercise a far greater fascination, and those words are: order, hierarchy, discipline. . . .

Know then, once and for all, that Fascism knows no idols and worships no fetishes. It has already stepped over, and if it be necessary it will turn tranquilly and step again over, the more or less putrescent corpse of the Goddess of Liberty.

From Benito Mussolini, "Force and Consent" (1923), as trans. in Jonathan F. Scott and Alexander Baltzly, eds., *Readings in European History Since 1814* (New York: F. S. Crofts, 1931), pp. 680–682.

The Fascist movement now had hundreds of thousands of supporters. In October 1922 the Fascists, dressed in their characteristic black shirts, began a march on Rome. Intimidated, King Victor Emmanuel III (r. 1900–1946) refused to authorize using the army against the marchers. No other single decision so ensured a Fascist seizure of power. The cabinet resigned in protest. On October 29 the monarch telegraphed Mussolini in Milan and asked him to become prime minister. The next day Mussolini arrived in Rome by sleeping car and, as head of the government, greeted his followers when they entered the city.

Technically, Mussolini had come into office by legal means. The monarch did have the power to appoint the prime minister. Mussolini, however, had no majority in the Chamber of Deputies. Behind the legal façade of his assumption of power lay months of terrorist disruption and intimidation and the threat of the Fascists' October march.

Benito Mussolini became famous for bombastic public speeches delivered in settings surrounded by his Fascist followers and military supporters. AP Wide World Photos

The Fascists in Power

Mussolini had not really expected to be appointed prime minister. He moved cautiously to consolidate his power. He succeeded because of the impotence of his rivals, his effective use of his office, his power over the masses, and his sheer ruthlessness. On November 23, 1922, the king and Parliament granted Mussolini dictatorial authority for one year to bring order to the lower levels of the government. Wherever possible, Mussolini appointed Fascists to office. Late in 1924, at Mussolini's behest, Parliament changed the election law. Previously parties had been represented in the Chamber of Deputies in proportion to the popular vote cast for them. According to the new election law, the party that gained the largest popular vote (with a minimum of at least 25 percent) received two-thirds of the seats in the chamber. Coalition government, with all its compromises and hesitations, would no longer be necessary. In the election of 1924 the Fascists won a great victory and complete control of the Chamber of Deputies. They used that majority to end legitimate parliamentary life. A series of laws passed in 1925 and 1926 permitted Mussolini, in effect, to rule by decree. In 1926 all other political parties were dissolved, and Italy was transformed into a single-party, dictatorial state.

The Italian dictator made one important domestic departure that brought him significant political dividends. Through the Lateran Accord he signed with the Vatican in February 1929, the Roman Catholic Church and the Italian state made peace with each other. Ever since the armies of Italian unification had seized papal lands in the 1860s, the church had been hostile to the state. The popes had virtually secluded themselves in the Vatican after 1870. The agreement of 1929 recognized the pope as the temporal ruler of the mini-state of Vatican City. The Italian government agreed to pay an indemnity to the papacy for confiscated land. The state also recognized Catholicism as the religion of the nation, exempted church property from taxes, and allowed church law to govern marriage. The Lateran Accord brought further respectability to Mussolini's authoritarian regime.

▼ German Democracy and Dictatorship

The Weimar Republic

The Weimar Republic was born from the defeat of the imperial army, the revolution of 1918 against the Hohenzollerns, and the hopes of German Liberals and Social Democrats. Its name derived from the city in which its constitution was written and promulgated in August 1919. While the constitution was being debated, the republic, headed by the Social Democrats, accepted the humiliating terms of the Versailles Treaty. Although its officials had signed only under the threat of an Allied invasion, the republic was nevertheless permanently associated with the national disgrace and the economic burdens of the treaty. Throughout the 1920s the government of the republic was required to fulfill the economic and military provisions imposed by the Paris settlement. It became all too easy for nationalists and military figures whose policies had brought on the tragedy and defeat of the war to blame the young republic and the Socialists for the results of the conflict. In Germany, more than in other countries, the desire to revise the treaty was closely related to a desire to change the mode of domestic government.

The Weimar Constitution was a highly enlightened document. It guaranteed civil liberties and provided for direct election, by universal suffrage, of the ***Reichstag*** and the president. It also, however, contained crucial structural flaws that eventually allowed it to be overthrown. Seats in the *Reichstag* were allotted according to a complicated system of proportional representation. This made it relatively easy for small political parties to gain seats and resulted in shifting party combinations that led to eleven governments in thirteen years. Ministers were technically responsible to the *Reichstag*, but the president appointed and removed the chancellor, the head of the cabinet. Perhaps most important, Article 48 allowed the president, in an emergency, to rule by decree.

The constitution thus permitted the possibility of presidential dictatorship.

The new government suffered major and minor humiliations as well as considerable economic instability. In March 1920 the right-wing Kapp Putsch, or armed insurrection, erupted in Berlin. Led by a conservative civil servant and supported by army officers, the attempted coup failed, but only after government officials had fled the city and workers had carried out a general strike. In the same month, strikes took place in the Ruhr mining district. The government sent in troops. Such extremism from both the left and the right would haunt the republic for all its days. In May 1921 the Allies presented a reparations bill for 132 billion gold marks. The German Republican government accepted this preposterous demand only after new Allied threats of occupation. Throughout the early 1920s there were numerous assassinations or attempted assassinations of important Republican leaders. Violence was the hallmark of the first five years of the republic.

Invasion of the Ruhr and Inflation Inflation brought on the major crisis of this period. The financing of the war and continued postwar deficit spending generated an immense rise in prices. Consequently, the value of German currency fell. By early 1921 the German mark traded against the American dollar at a ratio of 64 to 1, compared with a ratio of 4.2 to 1 in 1914. The German financial community contended that the value of the currency could not be stabilized until the reparations issue had been solved. In the meantime, the printing presses kept pouring forth paper money, which was used to redeem government bonds as they fell due.

The French invasion of the Ruhr in January 1923, to secure the payment of reparations, and the German response of passive economic resistance produced cataclysmic inflation. The Weimar government paid subsidies to the Ruhr labor force, who had laid down their tools. Unemployment soon spread from the Ruhr to other parts of the country, creating a new drain on the treasury and also reducing tax revenues. The printing presses by this point had difficulty providing enough paper currency to keep up with the daily rise in prices. Money was literally not worth the paper it was printed on. Stores were unwilling to exchange goods for the worthless currency, and farmers withheld produce from the market.

The moral and social values of thrift and prudence were thoroughly undermined. Middle-class savings, pensions, and insurance policies were wiped out, as were investments in government bonds. Simultaneously, debts and mortgages could not be paid off. Speculators in land, real estate, and industry made fortunes. Union contracts generally allowed workers to keep up with rising prices. Thus, inflation was not a disaster for everyone. To the middle and lower middle classes, however, the inflation was another trauma coming hard on the heels of the military defeat and the peace treaty. Only when the social and economic upheaval of these months is grasped can one understand the German desire for order and security at almost any cost.

In 1923, Germany suffered from cataclysmic inflation. Paper money became worthless and people used it as fuel for kitchen stoves. Library of Congress

Read the **Document** "Heinrich Hauser, 'With Germany's Unemployed' " on **MyHistoryLab.com**

Hitler's Early Career Late in 1923 Adolf Hitler (1889–1945) made his first significant appearance on the German political scene. The son of a minor Austrian customs official, he had gone to Vienna, where his hopes of gaining admission to an elite art school were soon dashed. He lived off money sent by his widowed mother and later off his Austrian orphan's allowance. He also painted postcards for further income and later found work as a day laborer. In Vienna he encountered Mayor Karl Lueger's (1844–1910) Christian Socialist Party, which prospered on an ideology of anti-Semitism and from the social anxieties of the lower middle class. Hitler absorbed the rabid German nationalism and extreme anti-Semitism that flourished in Vienna. He came to hate Marxism, which he associated with Jews. During World War I Hitler fought in the German army, was wounded, rose to the rank of corporal, and won the Iron Cross for bravery. The war gave him his first sense of purpose.

After the conflict, Hitler settled in Munich, and during the two years after the war firmly and frequently voiced anti-Semitism as a fundamental part of his political outlook. He soon became associated with a small nationalistic, anti-Semitic political party that in 1920 adopted the name of National Socialist German Workers Party, better known simply as the **Nazis**. In the same year the group began to parade under a red-and-white banner with a black swastika. It issued a platform, or program, of Twenty-Five Points. Among other things, this platform called for the repudiation of the Versailles Treaty, the unification of Austria and Germany, the exclusion of Jews from German citizenship, agrarian reform, the prohibition of land speculation, the confiscation of war profits, state administration of the giant cartels, and the replacement of department stores with small retail shops. Originally the Nazis had called for a broad program of nationalization of industry in an attempt to compete directly with the Marxist political parties for the vote of the workers. As the tactic failed, the Nazis redefined the meaning of the word *socialist* in the party name, so that it suggested a nationalistic outlook. In 1922, Hitler said,

> Whoever is prepared to make the national cause his own to such an extent that he knows no higher ideal than the welfare of his nation; whoever has understood our great national anthem, *Deutschland, Deutschland, über Alles* ["Germany, Germany, over All"], to mean that nothing in the wide world surpasses in his eyes this Germany, people and land, land and people—that man is a Socialist.[4]

This definition, of course, had nothing to do with traditional German socialism. The "socialism" that Hitler and the Nazis had in mind was not state ownership of the means of production, but the subordination of all economic enterprise to the welfare of the nation. It often implied protection for small economic enterprises. Increasingly, the Nazis discovered their party appealed to virtually any economic group that was at risk and under pressure. They often tailored their messages to the particular local problems these groups confronted in different parts of Germany. The Nazis also found considerable support among war veterans, who faced economic and social displacement in Weimar society.

Soon after the promulgation of the Twenty-Five Points, the storm troopers, or **SA** (*Sturm Abteilung*), were organized under the leadership of Captain Ernst Roehm (1887–1934). It was a paramilitary organization that initially provided its members with food and uniforms and, later in the decade, with wages. In the mid-1920s the SA adopted its famous brown-shirted uniform. The storm troopers were the chief Nazi instrument for terror and intimidation before the party controlled the government. They were a law unto themselves. The organization constituted a means of preserving military discipline and values outside the small army permitted by the Paris settlement. The existence of such a private party army and of a similar one run by the Communists was a sign of the potential for violence in the Weimar Republic and the widespread contempt for the law and the institutions of the republic.

The social and economic turmoil following the French occupation of the Ruhr and the German inflation gave the fledgling party an opportunity for direct action against the Weimar Republic, which seemed incapable of providing military or economic security. By this time, because of his immense oratorical skills and organizational abilities, Hitler personally dominated the Nazi Party. As he established his dominance within the party, he clearly had the model of Mussolini in mind and spoke of the Italian dictator's accomplishments in glowing terms. Both men recruited from disillusioned veterans of the World War. Both adopted paramilitary modes of organization. Both disparaged liberal politics as incapable of achieving great national ends and righting the wrongs of the peace settlement. Both exalted the principle of obedience to the heroic leader. In late 1923, with the memory of Mussolini's march on Rome still fresh, Hitler attempted to seize power by force.

Watch the **Video** "Video Lectures: Conformity and Opposition in Nazi Germany" on **MyHistoryLab.com**

On November 9, 1923, Hitler and a band of followers, accompanied by General Erich Ludendorff (1865–1937), attempted an unsuccessful putsch from a beer hall in Munich. When the local authorities crushed the rising, sixteen Nazis were killed. Hitler and Ludendorff were arrested and tried for treason. The general was acquitted. Hitler used the trial to make himself into a national figure. He condemned the republic, the Versailles Treaty, the Jews, and the weakened condition of his adopted country. He was convicted and sentenced to five years in prison. He actually spent only a few months in jail before being paroled. During this time, he dictated ***Mein Kampf*** ("My Struggle"), from which he eventually made a good deal of money. In this book, not taken seriously enough at the time, he outlined key political views from which he never swerved, including a fierce racial anti-Semitism; opposition to Bolshevism, which he associated with Jews; and a conviction that Germany must expand eastward into Poland and Ukraine to achieve greater "living space." Such expansion assumed the resurgence of German military might. In effect, Hitler transferred the foreign policy goals and racial outlooks previously associated with German overseas imperialism to the politics of central and eastern Europe. The natural targets of implementing these ideas would be Jews, the successor states of eastern Europe,

[4]Alan Bullock, *Hitler: A Study in Tyranny*, rev. ed. (New York: Harper & Row, 1964), p. 76.

Document

HITLER DENOUNCES THE VERSAILLES TREATY

Demands for revision of the Versailles Treaty of 1919 existed in many European nations during the 1920s, but such demands were especially fundamental to German politics and constituted a fundamental platform of the National Socialist Movement. Hitler and his followers made denunciation of the treaty their single most uncompromising declaration. In this speech of April 17, 1923, Hitler explained how the treaty had undermined the German nation.

How might the French invasion of the Ruhr and the resulting inflation have made this speech particularly effective? To what extent was Hitler's condemnation of the control the Versailles Treaty imposed on Germany correct? How does Hitler contrast his young Nazi movement with the young Weimar Republic? Why does the one appear a strong and the other a weak supporter of German national goals?

With the armistice begins the humiliation of Germany. If the Republic on the day of its foundation had appealed to the country: "Germans, stand together! Up and resist the foe! The Fatherland, the Republic expects of you that you fight to your last breath," then millions who are now the enemies of the Republic would be fanatical Republicans. Today they are the foes of the Republic not because it is a Republic but because this Republic was founded at the moment when Germany was humiliated, because it so discredited the new flag that men's eyes must turn regretfully towards the old flag.

It was no Treaty of Peace which was signed, but a betrayal of Peace.

The Treaty was signed which demanded from Germany that she should perform what was for ever impossible of performance. But that was not the worst; after all that was only a question of material values. This was not the end: Commissions of Control were formed! For the first time in the history of the modern world there were planted on a State agents of foreign Powers to act as Hangmen and German soldiers were set to serve the foreigner. And if one of these Commissions was "insulted," a company of the German army had to defile before the French flag. We no longer feel the humiliation of such an act; but the outside world says, "What a people of curs!"

So long as this Treaty stands there can be no resurrection of the German people: no social reform of any kind is possible! The Treaty was made in order to bring 20 million Germans to their deaths and to ruin the German nation. But those who made the Treaty cannot set it aside. At its foundation our Movement formulated three demands;

1. Setting aside of the Peace Treaty.
2. Unification of all Germans.
3. Land and soil to feed our nation.

Our Movement could formulate these demands, since it was not our Movement which caused the War, it has not made the Republic, it did not sign the Peace Treaty.

There is thus one thing which is the first task of this Movement: it desires to make the German once more National, that his Fatherland shall stand for him above everything else. It desires to teach our people to understand afresh the truth of the old saying: He who would not be a hammer must be an anvil. An anvil are we today, and that anvil will be beaten until out of the anvil we fashion once more a hammer, a German sword!

From a speech delivered in Munich on April 17, 1923, by Adolph Hitler, from *The Speeches of Adolf Hitler, April 1922–August 1939*, trans. by Norman H. Baynes (London and New York: Oxford University Press, 1942), pp. 56–57.

the Soviet Union, and any groups within Germany that opposed Hitler's vision of national unity and purpose. In the mid-1920s, most observers discounted the likelihood of any German political party carrying out such policies.

Read the Document "Adolf Hitler, Excerpt from *Mein Kampf*" on **MyHistoryLab.com**

During his imprisonment, Hitler reached two other decisions. First, it appears that this was the moment when he came to see himself as the leader who could transform Germany from a position of weakness to strength. Second, he decided that he and the party must pursue power by legal means, but as Hitler emerged

During a Nazi Party rally in Nuremberg in 1927, Adolf Hitler stops his motorcade to receive the applause of the surrounding crowd. In the late 1920s, the Nazi movement was only one of many bringing strife to the Weimar Republic. Heinrich Hoffman/ Bildarchiv Preussischer Kulturbesitz

from his imprisonment, he was still a regional politician (albeit one who was transforming himself into a national figure).

The Stresemann Years The officials of the republic were attempting to repair the damage from the inflation. Gustav Stresemann (1878–1929) was responsible primarily for reconstruction of the republic and for its achievement of a sense of self-confidence. Stresemann abandoned the policy of passive resistance in the Ruhr. The country simply could not afford it. Then, with the aid of banker Hjalmar Schacht (1877–1970), he introduced a new German currency. The rate of exchange was 1 trillion of the old German marks for one new Rentenmark. Stresemann also moved against challenges from both the left and the right. He supported the crushing of both Hitler's abortive putsch and smaller Communist disturbances. In late November 1923, after four months as chancellor, he resigned to become foreign minister, a post he held until his death in 1929. In that office he continued to influence the affairs of the republic.

In 1924 the Weimar Republic and the Allies renegotiated the reparation payments. The Dawes Plan lowered the annual payments and allowed them to fluctuate according to the fortunes of the German economy. The last French troops left the Ruhr in 1925. (See Map 27–1.) The same year, Field Marshal Paul von Hindenburg (1847–1934), a military hero and a conservative monarchist, was elected president of the republic. He governed in strict accordance with the constitution, but his election suggested that German politics had become more conservative. Conservative Germans seemed reconciled to the republic. This conservatism was in line with the prosperity of the latter 1920s. Foreign capital flowed into Germany, and employment, which had been poor throughout most of the postwar years, improved smartly. Giant industrial combines spread. The prosperity helped to establish broader acceptance and appreciation of the republic.

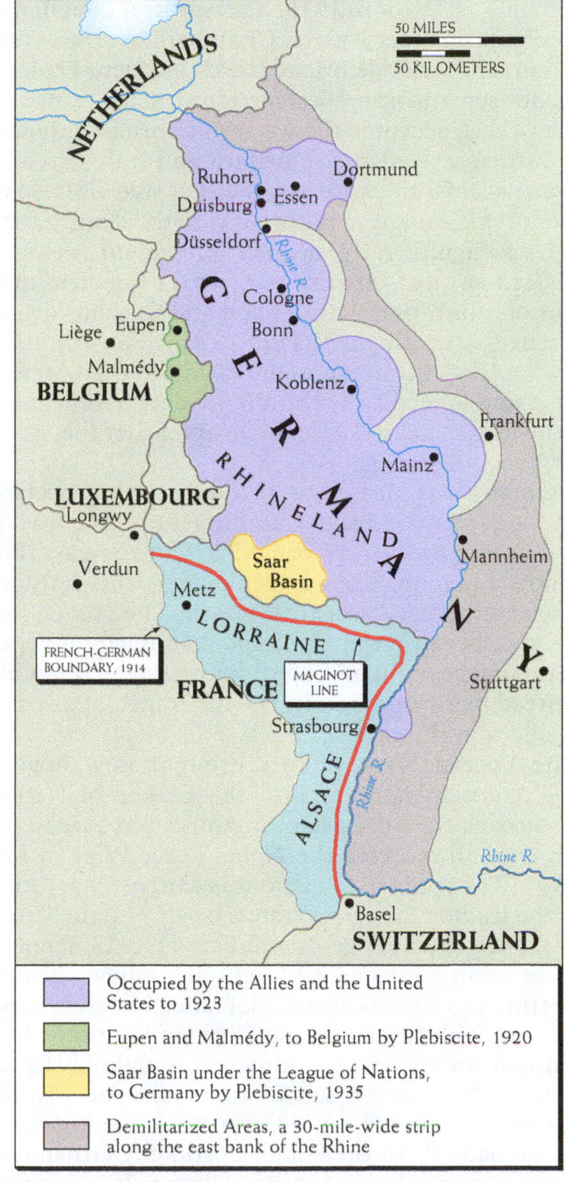

Map 27–1 **GERMANY'S WESTERN FRONTIER** The French–Belgian–German border area between the two world wars was sensitive. Despite efforts to restrain tensions, there were persistent difficulties related to the Ruhr, Rhineland, Saar, and Eupen-Malmédy regions that required strong defenses.

In foreign affairs, Stresemann pursued a conciliatory course. He fulfilled the provisions of the Versailles Treaty even as he attempted to revise it by diplomacy. He was willing to accept the settlement in the west but was a determined, if sometimes secret, revisionist in the east. He aimed to recover German-speaking territories lost to Poland and Czechoslovakia and possibly to unite with Austria, chiefly by diplomatic means. The first step, however, was to achieve respectability and economic recovery. That goal required a policy of accommodation and "fulfillment," for the moment at least.

Locarno These developments gave rise to the Locarno Agreements of October 1925. The spirit of conciliation led foreign ministers Austen Chamberlain (1863–1937) for Britain and Aristide Briand (1862–1932) for France to accept Stresemann's proposal for a fresh start. France and Germany both accepted the western frontier established at Versailles as legitimate. Britain and Italy agreed to intervene against the aggressor if either side violated the frontier or if Germany sent troops into the demilitarized Rhineland. Significantly, no such agreement was made about Germany's eastern frontier, but the Germans made treaties of arbitration with Poland and Czechoslovakia, and France strengthened its ties with those countries. France supported German membership in the League of Nations and agreed to withdraw its occupation troops from the Rhineland in 1930, five years earlier than specified at Versailles.

Germany was pleased to have achieved respectability and a guarantee against another Ruhr occupation, as well as the possibility of revision in the east. Britain enjoyed playing a more evenhanded role. Italy was glad to be recognized as a great power. The French were happy, too, because the Germans voluntarily accepted the permanence of their western frontier, which was also guaranteed by Britain and Italy, and France maintained its alliances in the east.

The Locarno Agreements brought new hope to Europe. Germany's entry into the League of Nations was greeted with enthusiasm. Chamberlain, Briand, and Stresemann all received the Nobel Peace Prize in 1925 and 1926. The spirit of Locarno was carried even further when the leading European states, Japan, and the United States signed the Kellogg-Briand Pact in 1928, renouncing "war as an instrument of national policy." The joy and optimism were not justified. France had merely recognized its inability to coerce Germany without help. Britain had shown its unwillingness to uphold the settlement in the east. Austen Chamberlain declared that no British government would ever "risk the bones of a British grenadier" for the Polish Corridor. Germany was not reconciled to the eastern settlement. It maintained clandestine military connections with the Soviet Union and planned to continue to press for revision.

In both France and Germany, moreover, the conciliatory politicians represented only a part of the nation. In Germany especially, most people continued to reject Versailles and regarded Locarno as only an extension of it. When the Dawes Plan ran out in 1929 it was replaced by the Young Plan, which lowered the reparation payments, put a term on how long they must be made, and removed Germany entirely from outside supervision and control. The intensity of the outcry in Germany against the continuation of any reparations showed how far the Germans were from accepting their situation. Despite these problems, war was by no means inevitable. Europe, aided by American loans, was returning to prosperity. German leaders like Stresemann would certainly have continued to press for change, but there is little reason to think that they would have resorted to force, much less to a general war. Continued prosperity and diplomatic success might have won the loyalty of the German people for the Weimar Republic and moderate revisionism, but the Great Depression of the 1930s brought new forces to power.

Depression and Political Deadlock

The outflow of foreign, and especially American, capital from Germany that began in 1928 undermined the economic prosperity of the Weimar Republic. The resulting economic crisis brought parliamentary government to a halt. In 1928 a coalition of center parties and the Social Democrats governed. All went reasonably well until the Depression struck. Then the coalition partners differed sharply on economic policy. The Social Democrats refused to reduce social and unemployment insurance. The more conservative parties, remembering the inflation of 1923, insisted on a balanced budget. The coalition dissolved in March 1930. To resolve the parliamentary deadlock in the *Reichstag*, President von Hindenburg appointed Heinrich Brüning (1885–1970) as chancellor. Lacking a majority in the *Reichstag*, the new chancellor governed through emergency presidential decrees, as authorized by Article 48 of the constitution. Party divisions prevented the *Reichstag* from overriding the decrees. The Weimar Republic had become a presidential dictatorship.

German unemployment rose from 2,258,000 in March 1930 to over 6,000,000 in March 1932. There had been persistent unemployment during the 1920s, but nothing of such magnitude or duration. The economic downturn and the parliamentary deadlock worked to the advantage of the more extreme political parties. In the election of 1928 the Nazis had won only 12 seats in the *Reichstag*, and the Communists had won 54 seats. Two years later, after the election of 1930, the Nazis held 107 seats and the Communists 77.

The power of the Nazis in the streets was also on the rise. The unemployment fed thousands of men into the storm troopers, which had 100,000 members in 1930 and almost 1 million in 1933. The SA freely and viciously attacked Communists and Social Democrats. For the

Nazis, politics meant the capture of power through terror and intimidation as well as through elections. Decency and civility in political life vanished. Nazi rallies resembled secular religious revivals. The Nazis paraded through the streets and the countryside. They gained powerful supporters and sympathizers among businessmen, military officers, and newspaper owners. Some intellectuals were also sympathetic. The Nazis transformed this discipline and enthusiasm born of economic despair and nationalistic frustration into impressive electoral results.

Hitler Comes to Power

For two years Brüning continued to govern with the backing of Hindenburg. The economy did not improve, and the political situation deteriorated. In 1932 the eighty-three-year-old president stood for reelection. Hitler ran against him and forced a runoff. The Nazi leader garnered 30.1 percent of the vote in the first election and 36.8 percent in the second. Although Hindenburg was returned to office, the vote convinced him that Brüning had lost the confidence of conservative German voters. In May 1932 he dismissed Brüning and appointed Franz von Papen (1878–1969) in his place. The new chancellor was one of a small group of extremely conservative advisers on whom the aged Hindenburg had become dependent. Others included the president's son and several generals. With the continued paralysis in the *Reichstag*, their influence over the president amounted to control of the government. Consequently, the crucial decisions of the next several months were made by only a handful of people.

Papen and the circle around the president wanted to draw the Nazis into cooperation with them without giving Hitler effective power. The government needed the popular support on the right that only the Nazis seemed able to generate. The Hindenburg circle decided to convince Hitler that the Nazis could not come to power on their own. Papen removed the ban on Nazi meetings that Brüning had imposed and then called a *Reichstag* election for July 1932. The Nazis won 230 seats and polled 37.2 percent of the vote. Hitler would only enter the Cabinet if he were made chancellor. Hindenburg refused. Another election was called in November, partly to wear down the Nazis' financial resources. The Nazis won only 196 seats, and their percentage of the popular vote dipped to 33.1 percent. The advisers around Hindenburg still refused to appoint Hitler to office.

In early December 1932 Papen resigned, and General Kurt von Schleicher (1882–1934) became chancellor. People were now afraid of civil war between the extreme left and the far right. Schleicher decided to try and fashion a broad-based coalition of conservative groups and trade unionists. The prospect of such a coalition, including groups from the political left, frightened the Hindenburg circle even more than the prospect of Hitler. They did not trust Schleicher's motives, which have never been clear. Consequently, they persuaded Hindenburg to appoint Hitler chancellor. To control him and to see that he did little mischief, Papen was named vice chancellor, and other traditional conservatives were appointed to the Cabinet. On January 30, 1933, Adolf Hitler became the chancellor of Germany.

It is important to emphasize that this outcome had not been inevitable. As his most distinguished biographer has observed, "Hitler's rise from humble beginnings to 'seize' power by 'triumph of the will' was the stuff of Nazi legend. In fact, political miscalculation by those with regular access to the corridors of power rather than any actions on the part of the Nazi leader played a larger role in placing him in the Chancellor's seat."[5] Hitler did not come to office on the tide of history, but through the blunders of conservative German politicians who hated the Weimar Republic and its rejection of traditional German political elites and who feared the domestic political turmoil the Depression had spawned.

Like Mussolini, Hitler had, however, technically become head of the government by legal means. All the proper legal forms and procedures had been observed. As a result, the civil service, the courts, and the other agencies of the government could support him in good conscience. He had forged a rigidly disciplined party structure and had mastered the techniques of mass politics and propaganda. (See "Encountering the Past: Cinema of the Political Left and Right,." page 886.) He understood how to touch the raw social and political nerves of the electorate. His support appears to have come from across the social spectrum and not, as historians once thought, just from the lower middle class. Pockets of resistance appeared among Roman Catholic voters in the countryside and small towns. Otherwise, support for Hitler was particularly strong among groups such as farmers, war veterans, and the young, whom the insecurity of the 1920s and the Depression of the early 1930s had badly hurt. Hitler promised them security against communists and socialists, effective government in place of the petty politics of the other parties, and a strong, restored, purposeful Germany.

German big business once received much of the blame for the rise of Hitler. There is little evidence, however, that business contributions made any crucial difference to the Nazis' success or failure. Hitler's supporters were frequently suspicious of big business and capitalism. They wanted a simpler world, one in which small property would be safe from both socialism and big business. These people supported Hitler and the Nazis rather than the Social Democrats because the latter were not sufficiently nationalistic. The Nazis won out over other conservative nationalistic parties because, unlike those conservatives, the Nazis did address social insecurities.

[5] Ian Kershaw, *Hitler 1889–1936: Hubris* (New York: W. W. Norton & Company, 1999), p. 424.

CINEMA OF THE POLITICAL LEFT AND RIGHT

BEFORE THE INVENTION of television, the cinema was the most powerful cultural vehicle for political regimes to project their power. Film directors of genius were drawn to the authoritarian governments of both the left and the right, and the films they made for these regimes, especially those of Soviet Russia and Nazi Germany, still impress moviegoers.

During the 1920s, the Soviet Union promoted the cinema as a propaganda tool. The greatest Soviet film director was Sergei Eisenstein (1898–1948). His most famous film, *The Battleship Potemkin*, which critics regard as one of the most important films of all time, depicts a mutiny on a warship during the Russian Revolution of 1905. In *Potemkin*, Eisenstein portrayed the working class itself as the hero of both the film and, true to Marxist doctrine, of history itself.

As Stalin gained more and more power from the mid-1920s onward, he imposed rigid censorship on the arts. To work in the Soviet Union, Eisenstein had to make films that pleased Stalin, and this he did. However, such was Eisenstein's genius that he also made two movies that many film scholars consider masterpieces: *Alexander Nevsky*, which depicts the victory of a medieval Russian prince over invading Germans, and *Ivan the Terrible*, which some see, in its depiction of the sixteenth-century despotic tsar whom Stalin admired, as Eisenstein's surrender to Stalin and others as a portrayal of tyranny.

Leni Riefenstahl (1902–2003) was by the early 1930s the most skilled documentary filmmaker in Germany and perhaps the world—an extraordinary accomplishment for a woman in a field dominated by men. Adolf Hitler asked her to make a documentary extolling the Third Reich after the Nazis took power in 1933. The results were *Triumph of the Will* (1934), about a Nazi Party rally, and *Olympia* (1938), about the Olympic Games held in Berlin in 1936. Both films display innovative, dramatically effective cinematic techniques and also the skilled political theatricality of the Nazi regime. These films dazzled audiences and are still shown in film classes as major works of twentieth-century cinematic art. Yet despite her artistry, Riefenstahl became marked—no matter how much she protested that she was a "pure" artist—as a producer of Nazi propaganda films. No American film studio would distribute her films to U.S. audiences.

After the defeat of Germany in 1945, Riefenstahl was imprisoned by the Allies under their de-Nazification program before being released in 1949. Thereafter, she attempted to rescue her career as a filmmaker, but the Nazi taint proved indelible. Instead, she became a noted photographer, especially of underwater photography. To the end of her life, Riefenstahl defends her films for the Third Reich as art, not propaganda.

Leni Riefenstahl filming the 1936 Olympic Games in Berlin with Hitler on the reviewing stand.

Why were the Soviet and Nazi regimes so interested in the cinema?

How did Leni Riefenstahl's films of Hitler and Nazi rallies affect her later career?

Hitler's Consolidation of Power

Once in office, Hitler consolidated his control with almost lightning speed. This process had three facets: the capture of full legal authority, the crushing of alternative political groups, and the purging of rivals within the Nazi Party itself. On February 27, 1933, a mentally ill Dutch Communist set fire to the *Reichstag* building in Berlin. The Nazis quickly turned the incident to their own advantage by claiming that the fire proved the existence of an immediate Communist threat against the government. To the public, it seemed plausible that the Communists might attempt some action against the state now that the Nazis were in power. Under Article 48, Hitler issued an Emergency Decree suspending civil liberties and proceeded to arrest Communists or alleged Communists. This decree remained in force as long as Hitler ruled Germany.

In early March another *Reichstag* election took place. The Nazis still received only 43.9 percent of the vote. However, the arrest of the newly elected Communist deputies and the political fear aroused by the fire meant that Hitler could control the *Reichstag*. On March 23, 1933, the *Reichstag* passed an Enabling Act that permitted Hitler to rule by decree. Thereafter, there were no legal limits on his exercise of power. The Weimar Constitution was never formally repealed or amended. It had simply been supplanted by the February Emergency Decree and the March Enabling Act, which together made the constitution a dead letter.

The *Reichstag* fire in 1933 provided Hitler with an excuse to consolidate his power. Bildarchiv Preussischer Kulturbesitz

Perhaps better than anyone else, Hitler understood that he and his party had not inevitably come to power. His potential opponents had been divided between 1929 and 1933. He intended to prevent them from regrouping. In a series of complex moves, Hitler outlawed or undermined various German institutions that might have served as rallying points for opposition. In early May 1933 the offices, banks, and newspapers of the free trade unions were seized, and their leaders arrested. The Nazi Party itself, rather than any government agency, undertook this action. In late June and early July, the other German political parties were outlawed. By July 14, 1933, the National Socialists were the only legal party in Germany. During the same months the Nazis had taken control of the governments of the individual federal states in Germany. By the close of 1933, all major institutions of potential opposition had been eliminated.

The final element in Hitler's personal consolidation of power involved the Nazi Party itself. By late 1933 the SA consisted of approximately 1 million active members and a larger number of reserves. The commander of this party army was Ernst Roehm, a possible rival to Hitler himself. The German army officer corps, on whom Hitler depended to rebuild the national army, was jealous of the SA. Consequently, to protect his own position and to shore up support with the regular army, on June 30, 1934, Hitler ordered the murder of key SA officers, including Roehm. Others killed between June 30 and July 2 included former chancellor von Schleicher and his wife. The exact number of purged victims is unknown, but it has been estimated to have exceeded one hundred. The German army, which was the only institution in the nation that might have prevented the murders, did nothing. A month later, on August 2, 1934, President

Hindenburg died. Thereafter, the offices of chancellor and president were combined. Hitler was now the ***Führer***, or sole ruler, of Germany and of the Nazi Party.

Anti-Semitism and the Police State

Terror and intimidation had helped propel the Nazis to office. As Hitler consolidated his power, he oversaw the organization of a police state. The chief vehicle of police surveillance was the **SS** (*Schutzstaffel*), or security units, commanded by Heinrich Himmler (1900–1945). This group had originated in the mid-1920s as a bodyguard for Hitler and had become a more elite paramilitary organization than the larger SA. In 1933 the SS had approximately 52,000 members. It was the instrument that carried out the blood purges of the party in 1934. By 1936 Himmler had become head of all police matters in Germany.

Read the Document "Heinrich Himmler, 'Speech to SS Officers' " on **MyHistoryLab.com**

Attack on Jewish Economic Life The police character of the Nazi regime was all-pervasive, but the people who most consistently experienced its terror were the German Jews. Anti-Semitism had been a key plank of the Nazi program—anti-Semitism based on biological racial theories stemming from late-nineteenth-century thought rather than from religious discrimination. Before World War II the Nazi attack on the Jews went through three stages of increasing intensity. In 1933, shortly after assuming power, the Nazis excluded Jews from the civil service. For a time they also attempted to enforce boycotts of Jewish shops and businesses. The boycotts won relatively little public support.

Soon after seizing power, the Nazi government began harassing German Jewish businesses. Non-Jewish German citizens were urged not to buy merchandise from shops owned by Jews. Art Resource/Bildarchiv Preussischer Kulturbesitz

Racial Legislation Then in 1935, a series of measures known as the Nuremberg Laws robbed German Jews of their citizenship. The professions and the major occupations were closed to those defined as Jews. Marriage and sexual intercourse between Jews and non-Jews were prohibited. Legal exclusion and humiliation of the Jews became the order of the day. The definition of who was a Jew in this law was both confusing and complex because the Nazis could not produce regulations based solely on a racial concept. The Nazi legal definitions of who was a Jew took into account the number of Jewish parents or grandparents, as well as whether a person practiced Judaism. All persons with at least three Jewish grandparents were defined as Jews, but persons with two Jewish grandparents were considered Jewish only if they practiced Judaism, or if they were married to a Jew, or if they had been born to a marriage with one Jewish parent, or if they had been born out of wedlock with one Jewish parent.

Kristallnacht The persecution of the Jews increased again in 1938. Business careers were forbidden. In November 1938, under orders from the Nazi Party, thousands of Jewish stores and synagogues were burned or otherwise destroyed. The Jewish community itself had to pay for the damage that occurred on this ***Kristallnacht*** ("Night of Smashed Glass") because the government confiscated the insurance money. In many other ways, large and petty, the German Jews were harassed. This persecution allowed the Nazis to inculcate the rest of the population with the concept of a master race of pure German "Aryans" and also to display their own contempt for civil liberties.

The Final Solution After the war broke out, Hitler decided in 1942 to destroy the Jews in Europe. It is thought that over 6 million Jews, mostly from eastern European nations, died as a result of that staggering decision, unprecedented in its scope and implementation. This subject is more fully treated in the next chapter.

Racial Ideology and the Lives of Women

Hitler and other Nazis were less interested in increasing the national population, which was Mussolini's policy in Italy, than in producing racially pure Germans. In their role as mothers, German women had the special task of preserving racial purity and giving birth to pure Germans who were healthy in mind and body. According to this view, women were to breed strong sons and daughters for the German nation. Nazi journalists often compared the role of women in childbirth to that of men in battle. Each served the state in particular social and gender roles. In both cases, the good of the nation was more important than that of the individual. (See "Compare and Connect: The Soviets and the Nazis Confront the Issues of Women and the Family," pages 890–891.)

Nazi racial ideology focused on women as the carriers and bearers of both the desired and undesired races. Nazi policy favored motherhood only for those whom its adherents regarded as racially fit for it. As early as late 1933, the government raised the issue of what kind of persons were fit to bear children for the nation. This policy disapproved of fostering motherhood among those people Nazi racism condemned—particularly the Jews, but also Slavs and Gypsies. During the mass executions of Jews in the Holocaust, Jewish women were specifically targeted for death, in part to prevent them from bearing a new generation.

Read the **Document** "Gertrud Scholtz-Klink, 'Speech to the Nazi Women's Organization' (Germany), 1935" on **MyHistoryLab.com**

Nazi theorists also discriminated between the healthy and unhealthy, the desirable and undesirable, in the German population itself. The government sought to prevent "undesirables" from reproducing, a policy that led to both the sterilization and death of many women, often because of an alleged mental "degeneracy." Some pregnant women were forced to have abortions. The Nazis' population policy was, in effect, one of selective breeding, or antenatalism, that profoundly affected the lives of women.

To support motherhood among those whom they believed should have children, the Nazis provided loans to encourage early marriage, tax breaks for families with children, and child allowances. In this respect, Nazi legislation resembled that passed elsewhere in Europe during the decade. The subsidies and other family payments were sent to husbands rather than wives, to make married fatherhood seem preferable to bachelorhood. Furthermore, these policies were administered on the premise that only racially and physically desirable children received support.

Although Nazi ideology emphasized motherhood, in 1930 the party vowed to protect the jobs of working women, and the number of women working in Germany rose steadily under the Nazi regime. The Nazis recognized that in the midst of the Depression many women needed to work, but the party urged them to pursue employment that was "natural" to their character as women. Such employment included agricultural labor, teaching, nursing, social service, and domestic service. The Nazis also intended women to be educators of the young. In that role, whether as mothers or as members of the serving professions, women became special protectors of German cultural values. Through cooking, dress, music, and stories, mothers were to instill a love for the nation in their children. As consumers for the home, women were to support German-owned shops, buy German-made goods, and boycott Jewish merchants.

Nazi Economic Policy

Besides consolidating political authority and pursuing anti-Semitic policies, Hitler still had to confront the Great Depression. German unemployment had helped propel him to power. The Nazis attacked this problem with a success that astonished and frightened Europe. By 1936, while the rest of the European economy remained stagnant, the specter of unemployment and other difficulties associated with the Great Depression no longer haunted Germany.

As far as the economic crisis was concerned, Hitler had become the most effective political leader in Europe. This success was perhaps the most important reason Germans supported his tyrannical regime. The Nazi success against the Great Depression gave the regime credibility. Behind the direction of both business and labor stood the Nazi terror and police. The Nazi economic experiment proved that, by sacrificing all political and civil liberty, destroying a free trade-union movement, limiting the private exercise of capital, and ignoring consumer satisfaction, a government could achieve full employment to prepare for war and aggression.

Nazi economic policies supported private property and private capitalism but subordinated all significant economic enterprise and decisions about prices and investment to the goals of the state. Hitler reversed the deflationary policy of the cabinets that had preceded him. He instituted a massive program of public works and vast military spending. From the earliest years of the Nazi regime, government spending and other economic policies served to pursue the cause of rearmament. The government built canals, reclaimed land, and constructed an extensive highway system with clear military uses. It also sent unemployed workers back to farms if they had originally come from them. Other laborers were not permitted to change jobs without official permission.

In 1935, the renunciation of the military provisions of the Versailles treaty led to open rearmament and military expansion with little opposition, as explained in Chapter 28. These measures essentially restored full employment. In 1936, Hitler instructed Hermann Göring (1893–1946), who had headed the air force since 1933, to undertake a four-year plan to prepare the army and the economy for war. The government determined that Germany must be economically self-sufficient. Armaments received top priority. This economic program satisfied both the yearning for social and economic security and the desire for national fulfillment.

COMPARE AND CONNECT The Soviets and the Nazis Confront the Issues of Women and the Family

Read the Compare and Connect on MyHistoryLab.com

BOTH THE SOVIET and Nazi dictatorships intruded deeply into the private lives of their citizens. Some Communist writers in the Soviet Union imagined utopian changes to traditional family life and traditional roles for women. In Germany the state imposed policies on women that would make their roles of wives and mothers serve the larger political and ideological goals of the Nazi Party. Different and opposed as were these policies of the two dictatorships, both challenged the social roles of women that were emerging in Western Europe and in the United States.

QUESTIONS

1. **Why did Kollontai see the restructuring of the family as essential to the establishment of a new kind of Communist society? Would these changes make people loyal to that society?**
2. **What changes in society does the kind of economic independence Kollontai seeks for women presuppose? What might childhood be like in this society?**
3. **What are the social tasks Hitler assigns to women? How does he attempt to subordinate the lives of women to the supremacy of the state?**
4. **Why does Hitler associate the emancipation of women with Jews and intellectuals?**
5. **Why was the present and future role of women such an important topic for both the Communist and the Nazi governments?**

I. A Communist Woman Demands a New Family Life

While Lenin sought to consolidate the Bolshevik Revolution against internal and external enemies, there existed within the young Soviet Union a vast utopian impulse to change and reform virtually every social institution that had existed before the revolution or those Communists associated with capitalist society. Alexandra Kollontai (1872–1952) was a spokesperson of the extreme political left within the early Soviet Union. There had been much speculation on how the end of bourgeois society might change the structure of the family and the position of women. In this passage written in 1920, Kollontai states one of the most radically utopian visions of this change. During the years immediately after the revolution, extreme rumors circulated in both Europe and America about sexual and family experimentation in the Soviet Union. Statements such as this fostered such rumors. Kollontai herself later became a supporter of Stalin and a Soviet diplomat.

There is no escaping the fact: the old type of family has seen its day. It is not the fault of the Communist State, it is the result of the changed conditions of life. The family is ceasing to be a necessity of the State, as it was in the past; on the contrary, it is worse than useless, since it needlessly holds back the female workers from more productive and far more serious work. . . . But on the ruins of the former family we shall soon see a new form rising which will involve altogether different relations between men and women, and which will be a union of affection and comradeship, a union of two equal members of the Communist society, both of them free, both of them independent, both of them workers. No more domestic "servitude" of women. No more inequality within the family. No more fear on the part of the woman lest she remain without support or aid with little ones in her arms if her husband should desert her. The woman in the Communist city no longer depends on her husband but on her work. It is not her husband but her robust arms which will support her. There will be no more anxiety as to the fate of her children. The State of the Workers will assume responsibility for these. Marriage will be purified of all its material elements, of all money calculations, which constitute a hideous blemish on family life in our days. . . .

The woman who is called upon to struggle in the great cause of the liberation of the workers—such a woman should know that in the new State there will be no more room for such petty divisions as were formerly understood: "These are my own children, to them I owe all my maternal solicitude, all my affection; those are your children, my neighbour's children; I am not concerned with them. I have enough to do with my own." Henceforth the worker-mother, who is conscious of her social function, will rise to a point where she no longer differentiates between yours and mine; she must remember that there are henceforth only our children, those of the Communist State, the common possession of all the workers.

The Worker's State has need of a new form of relation between the sexes. The narrow and exclusive affection of the mother for her own children must expand until it embraces all the children of the great proletarian family. In place of the indissoluble marriage based on the servitude of woman, we shall see rise the free union, fortified by the love and mutual respect of the two members of the Workers' State, equal in their rights and in their obligations. In place of the individual and egotistic family there will arise a great universal family of workers, in which all the workers, men and women, will be, above all, workers, comrades. ■

From Alexandra Kollontai, *Communism and the Family*, as reprinted in Rudolf Schlesinger, ed. and trans., *The Family in the USSR* (London: Routledge and Kegan Paul, 1949), pp. 67–69. Reprinted by permission.

II. Hitler Rejects the Emancipation of Women

According to Nazi ideology, women's place was in the home producing and rearing children and supporting their husbands. In this speech, Hitler urges this view of the role of women. He uses anti-Semitism to discredit those writers who had urged the emancipation of women from their traditional roles and occupations. Hitler returns here to the "separate spheres" concept of the relationship of men and women. His traditional view of women was directed against views that were associated with the Soviet experiment during the interwar years. Contrast this Nazi outlook on women and the family with the Bolshevik position described by Alexandra Kollontai in the previous document. Ironically, once World War II began, the Nazi leadership demanded that women leave the home and work in factories to support the war effort.

The slogan "Emancipation of women" was invented by Jewish intellectuals and its content was formed by the same spirit. In the really good times of German life the German woman had no need to emancipate herself. She possessed exactly what nature had necessarily given her to administer and preserve; just as the man in his good times had no need to fear that he would be ousted from his position in relation to the woman. . . .

If the man's world is said to be the State, his struggle, his readiness to devote his powers to the service of the community, then it may perhaps be said that the woman's is a smaller world. For her world is her husband, her family, her children, and her home. But what would become of the greater world if there were no one to tend and care for the smaller one? How could the greater world survive if there were no one to make the cares of the smaller world the content of their lives? No, the greater world is built on the foundation of this smaller world. This great world cannot survive if the smaller world is not stable. Providence has entrusted to the woman the cares of that world which is her very own, and only on the basis of this smaller world can the man's world be formed and built up. The two worlds are not antagonistic. They complement each other, they belong together just as man and woman belong together.

We do not consider it correct for the woman to interfere in the world of the man, in his main sphere. We consider it natural if these two worlds remain distinct. To the one belongs the strength of feeling, the strength of the soul. To the other belongs the strength of vision, of toughness, of decision, and of the willingness to act. In the one case this strength demands the willingness of the woman to risk her life to preserve this important cell and to multiply it, and in the other case it demands from the man the readiness to safeguard life. . . .

So our women's movement is for us not something which inscribes on its banner as its programme the fight against men, but something which has as its programme the common fight together with men. For the new National Socialist national community acquires a firm basis precisely because we have gained the trust of millions of women as fanatical fellow-combatants, women who have fought for the common life in the service of the common task of preserving life. . . .

Whereas previously the programmes of the liberal, intellectualist women's movements contained many points, the programme of our National Socialist Women's movement has in reality but one single point, and that point is the child, that tiny creature which must be born and grow strong and which alone gives meaning to the whole life-struggle. ■

This Soviet poster illustrates the role of women in communist society as key players in industrial and agricultural development and progress. This differs greatly from the traditional role assigned to women in Nazi ideology. CORBIS/Bettmann © Swim Inc./CORBIS

From J. Noakes and G. Pridham, eds., *Nazism, 1919–1945*, Vol. 2, *State, Economy and Society, 1933–39: A Documentary Reader*, Exeter Studies in History No. 8 (University of Exeter Press, 1984), pp. 449–450.

THE NAZI PARTY RALLY

YOUNG WOMEN WERE enthusiastic supporters among the crowd extending the Nazi salute in a 1938 rally.

The Nazi Party had used what later became the ever-present Swastika (or hooked cross) symbol since 1920. Hitler himself claimed to have chosen the symbol, which he and other Nazis associated with an allegedly racially pure Aryan past. In fact, many cultures had used the Swastika as a symbol. The Nazis adopted the Swastika as the German national flag in 1935.

Nazi rallies were intended to generate nationalistic group solidarity that would demonstrate that whatever other divisions might exist in the nation, loyalty to the Nazi Party and to the nation would be more important than any other group loyalty.

The image in the photo illustrates the gender divisions Nazi ideology fostered. Men were portrayed as defenders of the homeland. Women were to pursue traditional domestic roles and to bear children for the nation.

Bildarchiv Preussischer Kulturbesitz

How might the holding of rallies serve to give the sense that loyalty to the Nazi Party and the nation overrode all other social and political loyalties?

How could the experience of attending Nazi rallies or viewing them through movies or news reels convey to the German and non-German public throughout Europe a sense of inevitable Nazi success and widespread support?

What events or experiences at Nazi rallies might not have been captured in photographs? How could photographs be used to shape the news in the 1930s and later?

With the crushing of the trade unions in 1933, strikes became illegal. There was no genuine collective bargaining. The government handled labor disputes through compulsory arbitration. It also required workers and employers to participate in the Labor Front, an organization intended to demonstrate that class conflict had ended. The Labor Front sponsored a "Strength Through Joy" program that provided vacations and other forms of recreation for workers and farmers.

MAJOR POLITICAL EVENTS OF THE 1920s AND 1930s

1919 (August)	Constitution of the Weimar Republic promulgated
1920	Kapp Putsch in Berlin
1921 (March)	Kronstadt mutiny leads Lenin to initiate his New Economic Policy
1922 (October)	Fascist march on Rome leads to Mussolini's assumption of power
1923 (January)	France invades the Ruhr
1923 (November)	Hitler's Beer Hall Putsch
1924	Death of Lenin
1925	Locarno Agreements
1928	Kellogg-Briand Pact; first Five-Year Plan launched in USSR
1929 (January)	Trotsky expelled from USSR
1929 (February)	Lateran Accord between the Vatican and the Italian state
1929 (April)	Bukharin expelled from his offices in the Soviet Union; Stalin's central position thus affirmed
1929 (October)	New York stock market crash
1930 (March)	Brüning government begins in Germany
	Stalin calls for moderation in his policy of agricultural collectivization because of "dizziness from success"
1930 (September)	Nazis capture 107 seats in German *Reichstag*
1931 (August)	National Government formed in Britain
1932 (March 13)	Hindenburg defeats Hitler for German presidency
1932 (May 31)	Franz von Papen forms German Cabinet
1932 (July 31)	German *Reichstag* election
1932 (November 6)	German *Reichstag* election
1932 (December 2)	Kurt von Schleicher forms German cabinet
1933 (January 30)	Hitler made German chancellor
1933 (February 27)	*Reichstag* fire
1932 (March 5)	*Reichstag* election
1932 (August)	Enabling Act consolidates Nazi power
1934 (June 30)	Blood purge of the Nazi Party
1934 (August 2)	Death of Hindenburg
1934 (December 1)	Assassination of Kirov leads to the beginning of Stalin's purges
1936 (May)	Popular Front government in France
1936 (July–August)	Most famous of public purge trials in Russia

▼ Trials of the Successor States in Eastern Europe

It had been an article of faith among nineteenth-century liberals sympathetic to nationalism that only good could flow from the demise of Austria-Hungary, the restoration of Poland, and the establishment of nation-states throughout eastern Europe. These new states were to embody the principle of national self-determination and to provide a buffer against the westward spread of Bolshevism. They were, however, in trouble from the beginning.

View the **Map** "Map Discovery: Eastern Europe and the Soviet Union, 1919–1939" on **MyHistoryLab.com**

Economic and Ethnic Pressures

All the new states faced immense postwar economic difficulties. None of them possessed the kind of strong economy that nation-states such as France and Germany had developed in the nineteenth century. Indeed, political independence disrupted the previous economic relationships that each of them had developed as part of one of the prewar empires. None of the new states was financially independent; except for Czechoslovakia, all of them depended on foreign loans to finance economic development. Nationalistic antagonisms often prevented these states from trading with each other, and as a consequence, most became highly dependent on trade with Germany. The successor states of eastern Europe were poor and overwhelmingly rural nations in an industrialized world. The Depression hit them especially hard because they had to import finished goods for which they paid with agricultural exports whose value was falling sharply.

Finally, throughout eastern Europe, the collapse of the old German, Russian, and Austrian empires allowed various ethnic groups—large and small—to pursue nationalistic goals unchecked by any great power or central political authority. The major social and political groups in these countries were generally unwilling to make compromises lest they undermine their nationalist identity and independence. Each state included minority groups that wanted to be independent or to become part of a different nation in the region. Again, except for Czechoslovakia, all these states succumbed to some form of domestic authoritarian government.

Poland: Democracy to Military Rule

The nation whose postwar fortunes probably most disappointed liberal Europeans was Poland. For more than a hundred years, the country had been erased from the map.

(See Chapter 17.) An independent Poland had been one of Woodrow Wilson's Fourteen Points. When the country was restored in 1919, nationalism proved an insufficient bond to overcome political disagreements stemming from class differences, diverse economic interests, and regionalism. Furthermore, large Ukrainian, Jewish, Lithuanian, and German minorities distrusted the Polish government and resented attempts to force them to adopt Polish culture. The new Poland had been constructed from portions governed by Germany, Russia, and Austria for over a century. Each of those regions of partitioned Poland had different administrative systems and laws, different economies, and different degrees of experience with electoral institutions. A host of small political parties bedeviled the new Polish Parliament, and the executive was weak. In 1926, Marshal Josef Pilsudski (1867–1935) carried out a military coup. Thereafter, he ruled, in effect, personally until his death, when the government passed into the hands of a group of his military followers. The government became increasingly anti-Semitic, and non-Polish minorities suffered various forms of discrimination.

Czechoslovakia: A Viable Democratic Experiment

Only one central European successor state escaped the fate of self-imposed authoritarian government. Czechoslovakia possessed a strong industrial base, a substantial middle class, and a tradition of liberal values. During the war, Czechs and Slovaks had cooperated to aid the Allies. They had learned to work together and generally to trust each other. After the war, the new government had broken up large estates in favor of small peasant holdings. In the person of Thomas Masaryk (1850–1937), the nation possessed a gifted leader of immense integrity and fairness. The country had a real chance of becoming a viable modern nation-state.

There were, however, tensions between the Czechs and the Slovaks, who were poorer and more rural. Moreover, other non-Czech national groups, including Poles, Magyars, Ukrainians, and especially the Germans of the Sudetenland, which the Paris settlement had placed within Czech borders, resented being part of Czechoslovakia. The parliamentary regime might have been able to work through these problems, but extreme German nationalists in the Sudetenland looked to Hitler, who wanted to expand into eastern Europe, for help. In 1938, at Munich, the great powers first divided liberal Czechoslovakia to appease Hitler's aggressive instincts and then watched passively in early 1939 as he occupied much of the country, gave parts to Poland and Hungary, and manipulated a Slovak puppet state.

Hungary: Turn to Authoritarianism

Hungary was one of the defeated powers of World War I. In that defeat, it achieved its long-desired separation from Austria, but at a high political and economic price. In Hungary during 1919, Bela Kun (1885–1937), a communist, established a short-lived Hungarian Soviet Republic, which received socialist support. The Allies authorized an invasion by Romanian troops to remove the communist danger. The Hungarian landowners then established Admiral Miklós Horthy (1868–1957) as regent for the Habsburg monarch who could not return to his throne—a position Horthy held until 1944. After the collapse of the Kun government, thousands of Hungarians were either executed or imprisoned. It was, in part, in reaction to Kun's cooperation with socialists that Lenin ordered the Comintern to reject such cooperation in the future. Kun himself fled to Russia where Stalin later had him killed.

The Hungarians also deeply resented the territory Hungary had lost in the Paris settlement. The largely agrarian Hungarian economy suffered from a general stagnation. During the 1920s, the effective ruler of Hungary was Count Stephen Bethlen (1874–1947). He presided over a government that was parliamentary in form, but aristocratic in character. In 1932, he was succeeded by General Julius Gömbös (1886–1936), who pursued anti-Semitic policies and rigged elections. No matter how the popular vote turned out, the Gömbös party controlled Parliament. After his death in 1936, anti-Semitism lingered in Hungarian politics.

Austria: Political Turmoil and Nazi Occupation

Austria's situation was little better than that of the other successor states. A quarter of the 8 million Austrians lived in Vienna. Viable economic life was almost impossible, and the Paris settlement forbade union with Germany. Throughout the 1920s, the leftist Social Democrats and the conservative Christian Socialists contended for power. Both groups employed small armies to terrorize their opponents and to impress their followers.

In 1933, Christian Socialist Engelbert Dollfuss (1892–1934) became chancellor. He tried to steer a course between the Austrian Social Democrats and the German Nazis, who had surfaced in Austria. In 1934, he outlawed all political parties except the Christian Socialists, the agrarians, and the paramilitary groups that composed his own Fatherland Front. He used troops against the Social Democrats but was murdered later that year during an unsuccessful Nazi coup. His successor, Kurt von Schuschnigg (1897–1977), presided over Austria until Hitler annexed it in 1938.

Southeastern Europe: Royal Dictatorships

In southeastern Europe, revision of the arrangements in the Paris settlement was less of an issue. Parliamentary government floundered there nevertheless. Yugoslavia had been founded by the Corfu Agreement of 1917 and was known as the Kingdom of the Serbs, Croats, and Slovenes until 1929. Throughout the interwar period, the Serbs dominated the government and were opposed by the Croats. The two groups clashed violently, but the Serbs had the advantage of having had an independent state with an army prior to World War I, whereas the Croats and Slovenes had been part of the Austro-Hungarian Empire. The Croats generally were Roman Catholic, better educated, and accustomed to reasonably incorrupt government administration. The Serbs were Orthodox, less well educated, and considered corrupt administrators by the Croats. Furthermore, although each group predominated in certain areas of the country, each had isolated enclaves in other parts of the nation. Bosnia-Herzegovina, in addition to Serbs and Croats, had a significant Muslim population. The Slovenes, Muslims, Albanians, and other small national groups often played the Serbs and the Croats against each other. All the political parties except the small Communist Party represented a particular ethnic group rather than the nation of Yugoslavia. The violent clash of nationalities eventually led to a royal dictatorship in 1929 under King Alexander I (r. 1921–1934), himself a Serb. He outlawed political parties and jailed popular politicians. Alexander was assassinated in 1934, but the authoritarian government continued under a regency for his son.

Other royal dictatorships were imposed elsewhere in the Balkans: in Romania by King Carol II (r. 1930–1940) and in Bulgaria by King Boris III (r. 1918–1943). They regarded their own illiberal regimes as preventing the seizure of power by more extreme antiparliamentary movements and as quieting the discontent of the varied nationalities within their borders. In Greece, the parliamentary monarchy floundered amid military coups and calls for a republic. In 1936, General John Metaxas (1871–1941) instituted a dictatorship under King George II (r. 1935–1947) that, for the time being, ended parliamentary life in Greece.

In Perspective

By the mid-1930s, dictators of the right and the left had established themselves across much of Europe. Political tyranny was hardly new to Europe, but several factors combined to give these rulers unique characteristics. They drew their immediate support from well-organized political parties. Except for the Bolsheviks, these were mass parties. The roots of support for the dictators lay in nationalism, the social and economic frustration of the Great Depression, and political ideologies that promised to transform the social and political order. As long as the new rulers seemed successful, they did not lack support. Many citizens believed these leaders had ended the pettiness of everyday politics.

After coming to power, the dictators possessed a practical monopoly over mass communications. Through armies, police forces, and party discipline, they also monopolized terror and coercive power. They could propagandize large populations and compel people to obey them and their followers. Finally, as a result of the Second Industrial Revolution, they commanded a vast amount of technology and a capacity for immense destruction. Earlier rulers in Europe may have shared the ruthless ambitions of Hitler, Mussolini, and Stalin, but they had lacked the ready implements of physical force to impose their wills.

Mass political support, the monopoly of police and military power, and technological capacity meant the dictators of the 1930s held more extensive sway over their nations than any other group of rulers who had ever governed on the Continent. Soon the issue would become whether they would be able to maintain peace among themselves and with their democratic neighbors.

KEY TERMS

collectivization (p. 874)
Duce (p. 877)
fascism (p. 877)
Führer (p. 888)
Great Depression (p. 867)
Great Purges (p. 875)
Kristallnacht (p. 888)
Mein Kampf (p. 881)
Nazis (p. 881)
New Economic Policy (NEP) (p. 870)
Popular Front (p. 869)
Reichstag (p. 879)
SA (p. 881)
SS (p. 888)
War Communism (p. 870)
Weimar Republic (p. 867)

REVIEW QUESTIONS

1. What caused the Great Depression? Why was it more severe and why did it last longer than previous economic downturns? Could it have been avoided?
2. How did Stalin achieve supreme power in the Soviet Union? Why did he decide that Russia had to industrialize rapidly? Why did this require the collectivization of agriculture? Was the policy a success? How did it affect the Russian people? Why did Stalin carry out the great purges?
3. Why was Italy dissatisfied and unstable after World War I? How did Mussolini achieve power? What were the characteristics of the Fascist state?

4. Why did the Weimar Republic collapse in Germany? How did Hitler come to power? Which groups in Germany supported Hitler and why were they pro-Nazi? How did he consolidate his power? Why was anti-Semitism central to Nazi policy?
5. What characteristics did the authoritarian regimes in the Soviet Union, Italy, and Germany have in common? What role did terror play in each?
6. Why did liberal democracy fail in the successor states of Eastern Europe?

SUGGESTED READINGS

L. Ahamed, *Lords of Finance: The Bankers Who Broke the World* (2009). A lively narrative of the banking collapse leading to the Great Depression.

W. S. Allen, *The Nazi Seizure of Power: The Experience of a Single German Town, 1930–1935*, rev. ed. (1984). A classic treatment of Nazism in a microcosmic setting.

A. Applebaum, *Gulag: A History* (2003). A superbly readable account of Stalin's system of persecution and resulting prison camps.

I. T. Berend, *Decades of Crisis: Central and Eastern Europe before World War II* (2001). The best recent survey of the subject.

R. J. Bosworth, *Mussolini* (2002). A major biography.

R. J. B. Bosworth, *Mussolini's Italy: Life Under the Fascist Dictatorship, 1915–1945* (2007). A broad-based study of both fascist politics and the impact of those politics on Italian life.

M. Burleigh and W. Wipperman, *The Racial State: Germany 1933–1945* (1991). Emphasizes the manner in which racial theory influenced numerous areas of policy.

R. Conquest, *The Great Terror: A Reassessment* (2007). A pioneering and definitive study of Stalin's purges.

I. Deutscher, *The Prophet Armed* (1954), *The Prophet Unarmed* (1959), and *The Prophet Outcast* (1963). Remains the major biography of Trotsky.

B. A. Engel and A. Posadskaya-Vanderbeck, *A Revolution of Their Own: Voices of Women in Soviet History* (1998). Long interviews and autobiographical recollections by women who lived through the Soviet era.

R. Evans, *The Coming of the Third Reich* (2004) and *The Third Reich in Power, 1933–1939* (2005). A superb narrative.

G. Feldman, *The Great Disorder: Politics, Economics, and Society in the German Inflation, 1914–1924* (1993). The best work on the subject.

S. Fitzpatrick, *Stalin's Peasants: Resistance and Survival in the Russian Village After Collectivization* (1994). A pioneering study.

F. Furet, *The Passing of an Illusion: The Idea of Communism in the Twentieth Century* (1995). A brilliant account of how communism shaped politics and thought outside the Soviet Union.

R. Gellately, *Lenin, Stalin, and Hitler: The Age of Social Catastrophe* (2007). A major new study of the Soviet and Nazi dictatorships.

R. Gellately and N. Stoltzfus, *Social Outsiders in Nazi Germany* (2001). Important essays on Nazi treatment of groups the party regarded as undesirables.

J. A. Getty and O. V. Naumov, *The Road to Terror: Stalin and the Self-Destruction of the Bolsheviks, 1932–1939* (1999). A remarkable collection of documents and commentary on Stalin's purges.

R. Hamilton, *Who Voted for Hitler?* (1982). An examination of voting patterns and sources of Nazi support.

J. Jackson, *The Popular Front in France: Defending Democracy, 1934–1938* (1988). An extensive treatment.

P. Kenez, *The Birth of the Propaganda State: Soviet Methods of Mass Mobilization, 1917–1929* (1985). An examination of the manner in which the Communist government inculcated popular support.

B. Kent, *The Spoils of War: The Politics, Economics, and Diplomacy of Reparations, 1918–1932* (1993). A comprehensive account of the intricacies of the reparations problem of the 1920s.

I. Kershaw, *Hitler*, 2 vols. (2001). Replaces all previous biographies.

C. Kindleberger, *The World in Depression, 1929–1939* (1986). A classic, accessible analysis.

M. Kitchen, *Europe Between the Wars*, 2nd ed. (2006). A good general account.

R. J. Overy, *The Inter-War Crisis*, rev. 2nd ed. (2009). A brief and lively analysis of the period.

R. Pipes, *The Unknown Lenin: From the Secret Archives* (1996). A collection of previously unpublished documents that indicated the repressive character of Lenin's government.

P. Pulzer, *Jews and the German State: The Political History of a Minority, 1848–1933* (1992). A detailed history by a major historian of European minorities.

R. Service, *Stalin: A Biography* (2005). The strongest of a host of recent biographical studies.

J. Stephenson, *Women in Nazi Germany* (2001). Analysis with documents.

Z. S. Steiner, *The Lights that Failed: European International History 1919–1933* (2007). The definitive study of the European states in these years.

A. Tooze, *The Wages of Destruction: The Making and Breaking of the Nazi Economy* (2006). A wide-ranging, accessible study of the politics and ideology behind Nazi economic policy.

E. Weber, *The Hollow Years: France in the 1930s* (1995). Examines France between the wars.

L. Yahil, *The Holocaust: The Fate of European Jewry, 1932–1945* (1990). A major study of this fundamental subject in twentieth-century history.

MyHistoryLab™ MEDIA ASSIGNMENTS

Find these resources in the Media Assignments folder for Chapter 27 on **MyHistoryLab**.

QUESTIONS FOR ANALYSIS

1. Why do you think Hitler had such a strong appeal among young Germans?

   ***Section:* German Democracy and Dictatorship**
   View the **Closer Look** The Nazi Party Rally, p. 892

2. Why has this artist used an image of Lenin and of industrialization in this poster?

   ***Section:* The Soviet Experiment**
   View the **Image** Stalinist Poster, p. 873

3. What do you consider the most important considerations in understanding the appeal of Hitler?

   ***Section:* German Democracy and Dictatorship**
   Watch the **Video** Video Lectures: Conformity and Opposition in Nazi Germany, p. 881

4. What is the relationship between nationalism and Fascism?

   ***Section:* The Fascist Experiment in Italy**
   Read the **Document** Benito Mussolini, "The Political and Social Doctrine of Fascism," p. 877

5. How did Germany's experience in World War I seem to have influenced Himmler's attitude toward those he considers non-German?

   ***Section:* German Democracy and Dictatorship**
   Read the **Document** Heinrich Himmler, "Speech to SS Officers," p. 888

OTHER RESOURCES FROM THIS CHAPTER

After Versailles: Demands for Revision and Enforcement

View the **Image** The Mask Falls—German Cartoon Reacting to Treaty of Versailles, p. 866

Toward the Great Depression in Europe

View the **Map** The Great Depression in Europe, p. 868

Read the **Document** Irish National Identity: (a) Irish Declaration of Independence; (b) Ulster's Solemn League and Covenant; (c) Eamon de Valera, radio broadcast, p. 869

The Soviet Experiment

View the **Image** Bolshevik Revolution poster, p. 871

Read the **Document** Joseph Stalin, *Five Year Plan*, p. 873

German Democracy and Dictatorship

Read the **Document** Heinrich Hauser, "With Germany's Unemployed," p. 880

Read the **Document** Adolf Hitler, Excerpt from *Mein Kampf*, p. 882

Read the **Document** Gertrud Scholtz-Klink, "Speech to the Nazi Women's Organization" (Germany), 1935, p. 889

Read the **Compare and Connect** The Soviets and the Nazis Confront the Issues of Women and the Family, p. 890

Trials of the Successor States in Eastern Europe

View the **Map** Map Discovery: Eastern Europe and the Soviet Union, 1919–1939, p. 893

In August 1945, the United States exploded atomic bombs on the Japanese cities of Hiroshima and Nagasaki. A week later Japan surrendered. Without the bombs the United States would almost certainly have had to invade Japan, and tens of thousands of Americans would have been killed. Still, the decision to use the bomb remains controversial.

Listen to the Chapter Audio on MyHistoryLab.com

28 World War II

▼ **Again the Road to War (1933–1939)**

Hitler's Goals • Italy Attacks Ethiopia • Remilitarization of the Rhineland • The Spanish Civil War • Austria and Czechoslovakia • Munich • The Nazi–Soviet Pact

▼ **World War II (1939–1945)**

The German Conquest of Europe • The Battle of Britain • The German Attack on Russia • Hitler's Plans for Europe • Japan and the United States Enter the War • The Tide Turns • The Defeat of Nazi Germany • Fall of the Japanese Empire • The Cost of War

▼ **Racism and the Holocaust**

The Destruction of the Polish Jewish Community • Polish Anti-Semitism Between the Wars • The Nazi Assault on the Jews of Poland • Explanations of the Holocaust

▼ **The Domestic Fronts**

Germany: From Apparent Victory to Defeat • France: Defeat, Collaboration, and Resistance • Great Britain: Organization for Victory • The Soviet Union: "The Great Patriotic War"

▼ **Preparations for Peace**

The Atlantic Charter • Tehran: Agreement on a Second Front • Yalta • Potsdam

▼ **In Perspective**

LEARNING OBJECTIVES

How did World War I sow the seeds of World War II?

In what ways was World War II a "total" war?

What was the Holocaust?

What impact did World War II have on European society?

How did the Allies prepare for a postwar Europe?

THE MORE IDEALISTIC survivors of World War I, especially in the United States and Great Britain, thought of it as "the war to end all wars" and a war "to make the world safe for democracy." Only thus could they justify the slaughter, expense, and upheaval of that terrible conflict. How appalled they would have been had they known that only twenty years after the peace treaties a second great war would break out, more global than the first. In this war, the democracies would be fighting for their lives against militaristic, nationalistic, authoritarian, and totalitarian states in Europe and Asia, and they would be allied with the communist Soviet Union in the struggle. The defeat of the militarists and dictators would not bring the peace they longed for, but the Cold War, in which the European states would become powers of the second class, subordinate to two new superpowers, partially or fully non-European: the Soviet Union and the United States.

▼ Again the Road to War (1933–1939)

World War I and the Versailles treaty had only a marginal relationship to the world depression of the 1930s. In Germany, however, where the reparations settlement had contributed to the vast inflation of 1923, economic and social discontent focused on the Versailles settlement as the cause of all ills. Throughout the late 1920s, Adolf Hitler and the Nazi Party denounced Versailles as the source of all of Germany's troubles. The economic woes of the early 1930s seemed to bear them out. Nationalism and attention to the social question, along with party discipline, had been the sources of Nazi success. They continued to influence Hitler's foreign policy after he became chancellor in January 1933. Moreover, the Nazi destruction of the Weimar constitution and of political opposition meant that Hitler himself totally dominated German foreign policy. Consequently, it is important to know what his goals were and how he planned to achieve them.

Hitler's Goals

From the first expression of his goals in a book written in jail, *Mein Kampf* (*My Struggle*), to his last days in the underground bunker in Berlin where he killed himself, Hitler's racial theories and goals were at the center of his thought. He meant to go far beyond Germany's 1914 boundaries, which were the limit of the vision of his predecessors. He meant to bring the entire German people—the *Volk*—understood as a racial group, together into a single nation.

Read the Document "Adolf Hitler, *Mein Kampf*" on **MyHistoryLab.com**

The new Germany would include all the Germanic parts of the old Habsburg Empire, including Austria. This virile and growing nation would need more space to live, or ***Lebensraum***, that would be taken from the Slavs, who, according to Nazi theory, were a lesser race, fit only for servitude. The removal of the Jews, another inferior race according to Nazi theory, would purify the new Germany. The plans required the conquest of Poland and Ukraine as the primary areas for German settlement and for providing badly needed food. Neither *Mein Kampf* nor later statements of policy were blueprints for action. Rather, Hitler was a brilliant improviser who exploited opportunities as they arose. He never lost sight of his goal, however, which would almost certainly require a major war.

Germany Rearms When Hitler came to power, Germany was far too weak to permit a direct approach to reach his aims. The first problem he set out to resolve was to shake off the fetters of Versailles and to make Germany a formidable military power. In October 1933, Germany withdrew from an international disarmament conference and also from the League of Nations. Hitler argued that because the other powers had not disarmed as they had promised, it was wrong to keep Germany helpless. These acts alarmed the French but were merely symbolic. In January 1934, Germany signed a nonaggression pact with Poland that was of greater concern to France, for it undermined France's chief means of containing the Germans. At last, in March 1935, Hitler formally renounced the disarmament provisions of the Versailles treaty with the formation of a German air force, and soon he reinstated conscription, which aimed at an army of half a million men.

The League of Nations Fails Growing evidence that the League of Nations could not keep the peace and that collective security was a myth made Hitler's path easier. In September 1931, Japan occupied Manchuria. China appealed to the League of Nations. The league dispatched a commission under a British diplomat, the earl of Lytton (1876–1951). The *Lytton Report* condemned the Japanese for resorting to force, but the powers were unwilling to impose sanctions. Japan withdrew from the League and kept control of Manchuria.

When Hitler announced his decision to rearm Germany, the League formally condemned that action, but it took no steps to prevent it. France and Britain felt unable to object forcefully because they had not carried out their own promises to disarm. Instead, they met with Mussolini in June 1935 to form the so-called Stresa Front, promising to use force to maintain the status quo in Europe. This show of unity was short-lived, however. Britain, desperate to maintain superiority at sea, violated the spirit of the Stresa accords and sacrificed French security needs to make a separate naval agreement with Hitler. The pact allowed him to rebuild the German fleet to 35 percent of the British navy. Hitler had taken a major step toward his goal without provoking serious opposition. Italy's expansionist ambitions in Africa, however, soon brought it into conflict with the Western powers.

Italy Attacks Ethiopia

In October 1935, Mussolini, using a border incident as an excuse, attacked Ethiopia. This attack made the impotence of the League of Nations and the timidity of the Allies clear. Mussolini's purposes were to avenge a humiliating defeat that the Italians had suffered in Ethiopia in 1896, to restore Roman imperial glory, and, perhaps, to distract Italian public opinion from domestic problems.

View the Closer Look "An Ethiopian View of the Battle of Adowa" on MyHistoryLab.com

France and Britain were eager to appease Mussolini to offset the growing power of Germany. They were prepared to allow him the substance of conquest if he would maintain Ethiopia's formal independence. For Mussolini, however, the form was more important than the substance. His attack outraged opinion in the West, and the French and British governments were forced to at least appear to resist.

The League of Nations condemned Italian aggression and, for the first time, voted economic sanctions. It imposed an arms embargo that limited loans and credits to, and imports from, Italy. To avoid alienating Mussolini, however, Britain and France refused to embargo oil, the one economic sanction that could have prevented Italian victory. Even more important, Britain allowed Italian troops and munitions to reach Ethiopia through the Suez Canal. The results of this policy were disastrous. The League of Nations and collective security were discredited, and Mussolini was alienated. He now turned to Germany, and by November 1, 1936, he spoke publicly of a Rome–Berlin **Axis**.

Remilitarization of the Rhineland

The Ethiopian affair also convinced Hitler that the Western powers were too timid to oppose him forcefully. On March 7, 1936, he took his greatest risk yet, sending a small armed force into the demilitarized Rhineland. This was a breach not only of the Versailles treaty, but also of the Locarno Agreements of 1925—agreements Germany had made voluntarily. It also removed a crucial element of French security. France and Britain had every right to resist, and the French especially had a claim to retain the only element of security left to them after the failure of the Allies to guarantee France's defense. Yet neither power did anything but register a feeble protest with the League of Nations. British opinion would not permit support for France, and the French would not act alone. Internal division and a military doctrine that stressed defense and shunned the offensive paralyzed them. A growing pacifism further weakened both countries.

In retrospect, the Allies lost a great opportunity in the Rhineland to stop Hitler before he became a serious menace. The failure of his gamble, taken against his generals' advice, might have led to his overthrow; at the least, it would have made German expansion to the east dangerous if not impossible. Nor is there reason to doubt that the French army could easily have routed the tiny German force in the Rhineland. As the German general Alfred Jodl (1890–1946) said some years later, "The French covering army would have blown us to bits."[1]

A Germany that was rapidly rearming and had a defensible western frontier presented a completely new problem to the Western powers. Their response was the policy of **appeasement**, based on the assumption that Germany had real grievances and that Hitler's goals were limited and ultimately acceptable. They set out to negotiate and make concessions before a crisis could lead to war.

Behind this approach was the universal dread of another war. Memories of the horrors of the last war were still vivid, and the prospect of aerial bombardment made the thought of a new war even more terrifying. A firmer policy, moreover, would have required rapid rearmament. British leaders especially were reluctant to pursue this path because of the expense and the widespread belief that the arms race had been a major cause of the last war. As Germany armed, the French huddled behind their newly constructed defensive wall, the Maginot Line, and the British hoped for the best.

The Spanish Civil War

The Spanish Civil War, which broke out in July 1936, made the new European alignment that found the Western democracies on one side and the fascist states on the other clearer. (See Map 28–1.) In 1931, the monarchy had collapsed, and Spain became a democratic republic. The new government followed a program of moderate reform that antagonized landowners, the Catholic Church, nationalists, and conservatives without satisfying the demands of peasants, workers, Catalán separatists, or radicals. Elections in February 1936 brought to power a Spanish Popular Front government ranging from republicans of the left to communists and anarchists. The losers, especially the Falangists, the Spanish fascists, would not accept defeat at the polls. In July, the army, later led by General Francisco Franco (1892–1975), invaded from Spanish Morocco and began a civil war against the republic.

Read the Document "Speech to Spaniards (1936) Francisco Franco" on MyHistoryLab.com

The Spanish Civil War, which lasted almost three years, cost hundreds of thousands of lives and provided a training ground for World War II. Germany and Italy supported Franco with troops, airplanes, and supplies. The Soviet Union sent equipment and advisers to the republicans. Liberals and leftists from Europe and America volunteered to fight in the republican ranks against fascism.

The civil war, fought on blatantly ideological lines, profoundly affected world politics. It brought Germany and Italy closer together, leading to the Rome–Berlin Axis Pact in 1936. Japan joined the Axis powers in the Anti-Comintern Pact, ostensibly directed against international

[1]W. L. Shirer, *The Collapse of the Third Republic* (New York: Simon & Schuster, 1969), p. 281.

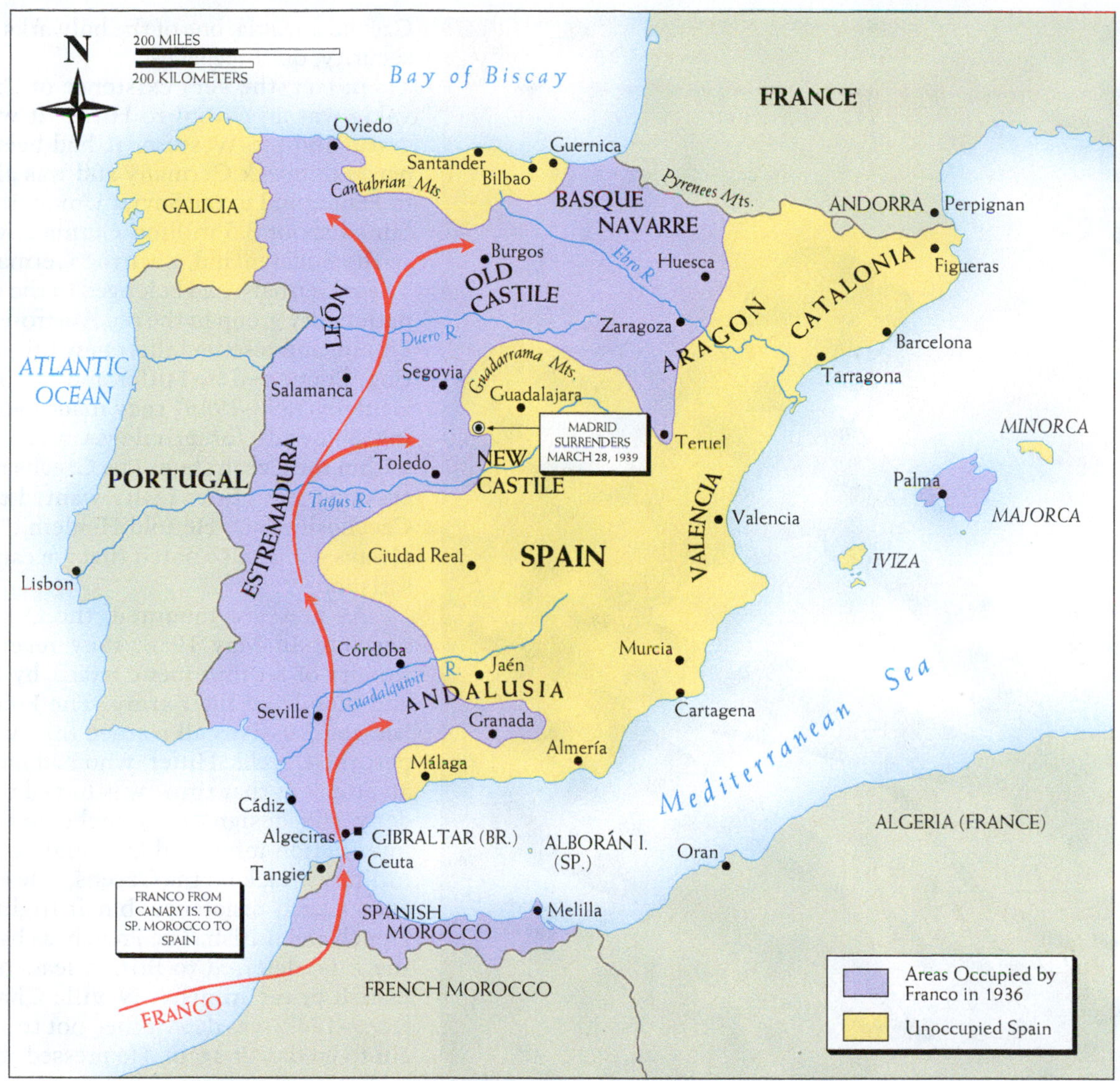

Map 28–1 **THE SPANISH CIVIL WAR, 1936–1939** The purple area on the map shows the large portion of Spain quickly overrun by Franco's insurgent armies during the first year of the war. In the next two years, progress came more slowly for the fascists as the war became a kind of international rehearsal for the coming World War II. Madrid's fall to Franco in the spring of 1939 had been preceded by that of Barcelona a few weeks earlier.

communism, but really a new and powerful diplomatic alliance. Western Europe, especially France, had a great interest in preventing Spain from falling into the hands of a fascist regime closely allied with Germany and Italy. Appeasement reigned, however. Although international law permitted the sale of weapons and munitions to the legitimate republican government, France and Britain forbade the export of war materials to either side, and the United States passed new neutrality legislation to the same end. When Barcelona fell to Franco early in 1939, the fascists had won effective control of Spain.

View the **Image** "Spanish Civil War poster" on **MyHistoryLab.com**

Austria and Czechoslovakia

Hitler made good use of his new friendship with Mussolini. He had always planned to annex his native Austria. In 1934, the Nazi Party in Austria assassinated the prime minister and tried to seize power. Mussolini had not yet allied with Hitler and was suspicious of German intentions. He quickly moved an army to the Austrian border, thus preventing German intervention and causing the coup to fail.

In 1938, the new diplomatic situation encouraged Hitler to try again. He perhaps hoped to achieve his goal by propaganda, bullying, and threats, but Austrian

This poster supports General Francisco Franco's Nationalists in the bloody Spanish Civil War, which lasted almost three years and claimed hundreds of thousands of lives. Courtesy of the Library of Congress

chancellor Kurt von Schuschnigg (1897–1977) refused to be intimidated. Schuschnigg announced a plebiscite for March 13, in which the Austrian people themselves could decide whether to unite with Germany. To forestall the plebiscite, Hitler sent his army into Austria on March 12. To his relief, Mussolini did not object, and Hitler rode to Vienna amid the cheers of his Austrian sympathizers.

The ***Anschluss***, or union of Germany and Austria, was another clear violation of Versailles. The treaty, however, was now a dead letter, and the West remained passive. The *Anschluss* had great strategic significance, however, because Germany now surrounded Czechoslovakia, one of the bulwarks of French security, on three sides.

In fact, the very existence of Czechoslovakia was an affront to Hitler. It was democratic and pro-Western; it had been created partly to check Germany and was allied both to France and to the Soviet Union. It also contained about 3.5 million Germans who lived in the Sudetenland, near the German border. These Germans had belonged to the dominant nationality group in the old Austro-Hungarian Empire and resented their new minority position. Supported by Hitler and led by Konrad Henlein (1898–1945), they made ever-increasing demands for privileges and autonomy within the Czech state. The Czechs made concessions, but Hitler really wanted to destroy Czechoslovakia. He told Henlein, "We must always demand so much that we can never be satisfied."[2]

As pressure mounted, the Czechs grew nervous. In May 1938, they received false rumors of an imminent attack by Germany and mobilized their army. The French, British, and Russians all warned they would support the Czechs. Hitler, who had not planned an attack at that time, was forced to publicly deny any designs on Czechoslovakia. The humiliation infuriated him, and he planned a military attack on the Czechs. The affair stiffened Czech resistance, but it frightened the French and British. The French, as had become the rule, deferred to British leadership. The British prime minister Neville Chamberlain (1869–1940) was determined not to allow Britain to go to war again. He pressed the Czechs to make concessions to Germany, but no concession was enough.

On September 12, 1938, Hitler made a provocative speech at the Nuremberg Nazi Party rally. His rhetoric led to rioting in the Sudetenland, and the Czechs declared martial law. German intervention seemed imminent. Chamberlain, aged sixty-nine, who had never flown before, made three flights to Germany between September 15 and September 29 in an attempt to appease Hitler at Czech expense and thus to avoid war. At Hitler's mountain retreat, Berchtesgaden, on September 15, Chamberlain accepted the separation of the Sudetenland from Czechoslovakia, and he and the French premier, Edouard Daladier (1884–1970), forced the Czechs to agree by threatening to abandon them if they did not. A week later, Chamberlain flew yet again to Germany, only to find that Hitler had raised

[2]Alan Bullock, *Hitler, a Study in Tyranny* (New York: Harper & Row, 1962), p. 443.

his demands. He wanted cession of the Sudetenland in three days and immediate occupation by the German army.

Munich

Chamberlain returned to England, and France and Britain prepared for war. At Chamberlain's request and at the last moment, Mussolini proposed a conference of Germany, Italy, France, and Britain. It met on September 29 at Munich. Hitler received almost everything he had demanded. (See Map 28–2.) The Sudetenland, the key to Czech security, became part of Germany, thus depriving the Czechs of any chance of self-defense. In return, Hitler agreed to spare the rest of Czechoslovakia. He promised, "I have no more territorial demands to make in Europe." Chamberlain returned to England with the Munich agreement and told a cheering crowd that he had brought "peace with honour. I believe it is peace for our time."

View the Image "Hitler and Chamberlain, 1938" on MyHistoryLab.com

Even in the short run, the appeasement of Hitler at Munich was a failure. Czechoslovakia did not survive. Soon Poland and Hungary tore more territory from it, and the Slovaks demanded a state of their own. Finally, on March 15, 1939, Hitler broke his promise and occupied Prague, putting an end to the Czech state and to illusions that his only goal was to restore Germans to the Reich. Defenders of the appeasers have argued that their policy bought valuable time in which the West could prepare for war, but the appeasers themselves, who thought they were achieving peace, did not make that argument, nor does the evidence support it.

View the Map "The Partitions of Czechoslovakia and Poland 1938–1939" on MyHistoryLab.com

If the French and the British had been willing to attack Germany from the west while the Czechs fought in their own defense, their efforts might have been successful. High officers in the German army were opposed to Hitler's risky policies and might have overthrown him. Even failing such developments, a war begun in October 1938 would have forced Hitler to fight without the friendly

Map 28–2 **PARTITIONS OF CZECHOSLOVAKIA AND POLAND, 1938–1939** The immediate background of World War II is found in the complex international drama unfolding on Germany's eastern frontier in 1938 and 1939. Germany's expansion inevitably meant the victimization of Austria, Czechoslovakia, and Poland. With the failure of the Western powers' appeasement policy and the signing of a German–Soviet pact, the stage for the war was set.

COMPARE AND CONNECT The Munich Settlement

Read the Compare and Connect on MyHistoryLab.com

ON SEPTEMBER 29–30, 1938, Germany's dictator Adolf Hitler met with British prime minister Neville Chamberlain, Italy's dictator Benito Mussolini, and France's prime minister Edouard Daladier to settle the fate of Czechoslovakia. The Czechs were not permitted to take part. It was the height of the Western democracies' effort to appease the dictators and resulted in the partition of Czechoslovakia; the region called the Sudetenland was handed over to Germany, leaving the Czechs without a viable defense. Although Hitler promised to stop there, he took over the rest of the country without firing a shot on March 15, 1939. The following documents present opposite views on the achievement at Munich.

QUESTIONS

1. **Why did Chamberlain think the meeting at Munich was a success for Britain?**
2. **How would he defend his policy of appeasement?**
3. **What were Churchill's objections to the Munich agreement?**
4. **What critique would he make of the appeasement policy?**
5. **Who do you think was right? Why?**

I. Chamberlain's Evaluation

The following is an account of Chamberlain's return to England the day after the conference. He was greeted like a hero at the airport by a big crowd. Later that day he stood outside Number 10 Downing Street where again he read from the document and declared that he had brought back "peace with honour. I believe it is peace for our time."

Various shots of Mrs Chamberlain waving and shaking hands with crowds around Downing Street who are offering their support. M/S as Chamberlain's aeroplane finishes its return journey after the conference, taxis and comes to a stop at Heston. M/S of newsreel cameras filming his return from a roof at the aerodrome. M/S as Chamberlain emerges smiling from the door of a British Airways aeroplane to the cheers of the crowd. He shakes hands with a man waiting for him. L/S of crowds watching.

C/U as he makes a speech on the airfield—"The settlement of the Czech problem, which has now been achieved, is, in my view only the prelude to a larger settlement in which all Europe may find peace" (people cheer at this). "This morning I had another talk with the German Chancellor Herr Hitler and here is the paper which bears his name upon it as well as mine" (he holds paper up and waves it about, people cheer again). "Some of you perhaps have already heard what it contains, but I would just like to read it to you." (He reads—'We, the German Fuhrer and Chancellor and the British Prime Minister, have had a further meeting today and are agreed in recognising that the question of Anglo-German relations is of the first importance for the two countries, and for Europe. We regard the agreement signed last night and the Anglo-German naval agreement, as symbolic of the desire of our two peoples never to go to war with one another again' (everyone cheers) 'We are resolved that the method of consultation shall be the method adopted' (lots of "hear hears") 'to deal with any other questions that may concern our two countries, and we are determined to continue our efforts to remove possible sources of difference and thus to contribute to assure the peace of Europe.'") Everyone cheers and someone shouts "three cheers for Chamberlain" which they all do as he walks away and gets into the car. Everyone waves as he drives away.

Various shots as his car drives through the crowds to Buckingham Palace, people wave as he passes. M/S as King George VI and Queen Elizabeth (later the Queen Mother) come out onto the balcony of the palace with Neville Chamberlain and his wife. L/S as they wave and crowds wave back. L/S of cars and people blocking the street outside the palace. ■

From British Pathe.com Peace Four Power Conference 983.14.

II. Churchill's Response to Munich

In the parliamentary debate that followed the Munich conference at the end of September 1938, Winston Churchill was one of the few critics of what had been accomplished. In the following selections from his speech, he expresses his concerns.

I will begin by saying what everybody would like to ignore or forget but which must nevertheless be stated, namely, that we have sustained a total and unmitigated defeat, and that France has suffered even more than we have. . . .

We really must not waste time after all this long Debate upon the difference between the positions reached at Berchtesgaden, at Godesberg and at Munich. They can be very simply epitomized, if the House will permit me to vary the metaphor. One pound was demanded at the pistol's point. When it was given, £2 were demanded at the pistol's point. Finally, the dictator consented to take £1 17s. 6d. and the rest in promises of good will for the future. . . .

All is over. Silent, mournful, abandoned, broken, Czechoslovakia recedes into the darkness. She has suffered in every respect by her association with the Western democracies and with the League of Nations, of which she has always been an obedient servant. . . .

We have been reduced in these five years from a position of security so overwhelming and so unchallengeable that we never cared to think about it. We have been reduced from a position where the very word "war" was considered one which could be used only by persons qualifying for a lunatic asylum. We have been reduced from a position of safety and power—power to do good, power to be generous to a beaten foe, power to make terms with Germany, power to give her proper redress for her grievances, power to stop her arming if we chose, power to take any step in strength or mercy or justice which we thought right—reduced in five years from a position safe and unchallenged to where we stand now. . . .

[T]he responsibility must rest with those who have had the undisputed control of our political affairs. They neither prevented Germany from rearming, nor did they rearm ourselves in time. They quarreled with Italy without saving Ethiopia. They exploited and discredited the vast institution of the League of Nations and they neglected to make alliances and combinations which might have repaired previous errors, and thus they left us in the hour of trial without adequate national defense or effective international security. . . .

We are in the presence of a disaster of the first magnitude which has befallen Great Britain and France. Do not let us blind ourselves to that. It must now be accepted that all the countries of Central and Eastern Europe will make the best terms they can with the triumphant Nazi power. The system of alliances in Central Europe upon which France has relied for her safety has been swept away, and I can see no means by which it can be reconstituted. The road down the Danube Valley to the Black Sea, the road which leads as far as Turkey, has been opened. ■

From *Parliamentary Debates*, 5th series, vol. 339 (1938).

Agreement at Munich. On September 29–30, 1938, Hitler met with the leaders of Britain and France at Munich to decide the fate of Czechoslovakia. The Allied leaders abandoned the small democratic nation in a vain attempt to appease Hitler and avoid war. From left to right in the foreground: British Prime Minister Neville Chamberlain, French Prime Minister Edouard Daladier, Adolf Hitler, Benito Mussolini, and Italian Minister of Foreign Affairs (and Mussolini's son-in-law), Count Ciano. National Archives and Records Administration

Document

Winston Churchill Warns of the Effects of the Munich Agreement

Churchill delivered a speech on the Munich Agreement before the House of Commons on October 5, 1938. Following are excerpts from it.

What was decided at Munich? Why were the representatives of Czechoslovakia not at the meeting? Why did Chamberlain think the meeting was successful? Munich was the high point of the policy called "appeasement." How would its advocates defend this policy? Churchill was a leading opponent of appeasement. What are his objections to it?

The Chancellor of the Exchequer [Sir John Simon] said it was the first time Herr Hitler had been made to retract—I think that was the word—in any degree. We really must not waste time after all this long Debate upon the difference between the positions reached at Berchtesgaden, at Godesberg and at Munich. They can be very simply epitomized, if the House will permit me to vary the metaphor. One pound was demanded at the pistol's point. When it was given, £2 were demanded at the pistol's point. Finally, the dictator consented to take £1 17s. 6d. and the rest in promises of good will for the future. . . .

I do not grudge our loyal, brave people, who were ready to do their duty no matter what the cost, who never flinched under the strain of last week—I do not grudge them the natural, spontaneous outbursts of joy and relief when they learned that the hard ordeal would no longer be required of them at the moment; but they should know the truth. They should know that there has been gross neglect and deficiency in our defenses; they should know that we have sustained a defeat without a war, the consequences of which will travel far with us along our road; they should know that we have passed an awful milestone in our history, when the whole equilibrium of Europe has been deranged, and that the terrible words have for the time being been pronounced against the Western democracies: "Thou art weighed in the balance and found wanting." And do not suppose that this is the end. This is only the beginning of the reckoning. This is only the first sip, the first foretaste of a bitter cup which will be proffered to us year by year unless, by a supreme recovery of moral health and martial vigor, we arise again and take our stand for freedom as in the olden time.

neutrality and material assistance of the Soviet Union—and without the resources of Eastern Europe that became available to him as a result of appeasement and Soviet cooperation. If, moreover, the West ever had a chance of concluding an alliance with the Soviet Union against Hitler, the exclusion of the Russians from Munich and the appeasement policy helped destroy it. Munich remains an example of shortsighted policy that helped bring on war in disadvantageous circumstances because of the very fear of war and the failure to prepare for it. (See "Compare and Connect: The Munich Settlement," pages 904–905.)

Hitler's occupation of Prague discredited appeasement in Britain. In the summer of 1939, a Gallup poll showed that three-quarters of the British public believed it was worth a war to stop Hitler. Though Chamberlain himself had not lost all faith in his policy, he felt he had to respond to public opinion, and he responded to excess.

Poland was the next target of German expansion. In the spring of 1939, the Germans put pressure on Poland to restore the formerly German city of Danzig and to allow a railroad and a highway through the Polish Corridor to connect East Prussia with the rest of Germany. When the Poles would not yield, the usual propaganda campaign began, and the pressure mounted. On March 31, Chamberlain announced a Franco–British guarantee of Polish independence. Hitler appears to have expected to fight a war with Poland, but not with the Western allies, for he did not take their guarantee seriously. He had come to hold their leaders in contempt. He knew both countries were unprepared for war and that large segments of their populations opposed fighting for Poland.

Read the **Document** "Adolf Hitler, 'The Obersalzberg Speech' " on **MyHistoryLab.com**

Moreover, France and Britain had no means to get effective help to the Poles. The French, still dominated by the defensive mentality of the Maginot Line, had no intention of attacking Germany. The only way to defend Poland was to bring Russia into the alliance against Hitler, but a Russian alliance posed many problems. Each side was profoundly suspicious of the other. The French and the British were hostile to communism, and since Stalin's purge of the Red Army, they were skeptical of the military value of a Russian alliance. Besides, the Russians could not help Poland without being given the right to enter Poland and Romania. Both nations, suspicious of Russian intentions—and with good reason—refused to grant these rights. As a result, Western negotiations for an alliance with Russia made little progress.

The Nazi–Soviet Pact

The Russians had at least equally good reason to hesitate. They resented being left out of the Munich agreement. The low priority that the West gave to negotiations with Russia, compared with the urgency with which Britain and France dealt with Hitler, annoyed them. The Russians feared, rightly, that the Western powers meant them to bear the burden of the war against Germany. As a result, they opened negotiations with Hitler, and on August 23, 1939, the world was shocked to learn of a Nazi–Soviet nonaggression pact.

The secret provisions of the pact, which were easily guessed and soon carried out, divided Poland between the two powers and allowed Russia to occupy the Baltic states and to take Bessarabia from Romania. The most bitter ideological enemies had become allies. Communist parties in the West changed their line overnight from ardently advocating resistance to Hitler to a policy of peace and quiet. Ideology gave way to political and military reality. The West offered the Russians immediate danger without much prospect of gain. Hitler offered Stalin short-term gain without immediate danger. There could be little doubt about Stalin's decision.

The Nazi–Soviet pact sealed the fate of Poland, and the Franco–British commitment guaranteed a general war. On September 1, 1939, the Germans invaded Poland. Two days later, Britain and France declared war on Germany. World War II had begun.

▼ World War II (1939–1945)

World War II was truly global. Fighting took place in Europe, North Africa, and Asia, on the Atlantic and the Pacific Oceans, and in the northern and southern hemispheres. The demand for the fullest exploitation of material and human resources for increased production, the use of blockades, and the intensive bombing of civilian targets made the war of 1939 even more "total"—that is, comprehensive and intense—than that of 1914.

The German Conquest of Europe

The German attack on Poland produced swift success. The new style of "lightning warfare," or ***blitzkrieg,*** employed fast-moving, massed armored columns supported by airpower. The Poles had few planes and fewer tanks, and their defense soon collapsed. The speed of the German victory astonished the Russians, who hastened to collect their share of the booty before Hitler could deprive them of it.

On September 17, Russia invaded Poland from the east, dividing the country with the Germans. The Red Army then occupied the encircled Baltic countries. By July 1940, Estonia, Latvia, and Lithuania had become puppet republics within the Soviet Union. In June 1940, the Russians forced Romania to cede Bessarabia. In November 1939, the Russians invaded Finland, but the Finns resisted fiercely for six months. Although they were finally worn down and compelled to yield territory and bases to Russia, the Finns remained independent. Russian expansionism and the poor performance of the

THE COMING OF WORLD WAR II

1919 (June)	The Versailles Treaty
1923 (January)	France occupies the Ruhr
1925 (October)	The Locarno Agreements
1931 (Spring)	Onset of the Great Depression in Europe
1931 (September)	Japan occupies Manchuria
1933 (January)	Hitler comes to power
1933 (October)	Germany withdraws from the League of Nations
1935 (March)	Hitler renounces disarmament, starts an air force, and begins conscription
1935 (October)	Mussolini attacks Ethiopia
1936 (March)	Germany reoccupies and remilitarizes the Rhineland
1936 (July)	Outbreak of the Spanish Civil War
1936 (October)	Formation of the Rome–Berlin Axis
1938 (March)	*Anschluss* with Austria
1938 (September)	The Munich conference and the partition of Czechoslovakia
1939 (March)	Hitler occupies Prague; France and Great Britain guarantee Polish independence
1939 (August)	The Nazi–Soviet pact
1939 (September 1)	Germany invades Poland
1939 (September 3)	Britain and France declare war on Germany

Red Army in Finland may well have encouraged Hitler to invade the Soviet Union in June 1941, just twenty-two months after the 1939 treaty.

Until the spring of 1940, the western front was quiet. The French remained behind the Maginot Line while Hitler and Stalin swallowed Poland and the Baltic states. Britain rearmed hastily, and the British navy blockaded Germany. Cynics in the West called it the phony war, or *Sitzkrieg*, but Hitler shattered the stillness in the spring of 1940. In April, without warning and with swift success, the Germans invaded Denmark and Norway. Hitler's northern front was secure, and he now had both air and naval bases closer to Britain. A month later, a combined land and air attack struck Belgium, the Netherlands, and Luxembourg. German airpower and armored divisions were irresistible. The Dutch surrendered in a few days; the Belgians, though aided by the French and the British, gave up less than two weeks later.

The British and French armies in Belgium were forced to flee to the English Channel to seek escape on the beaches of Dunkirk. The heroic efforts of hundreds of Britons manning small boats saved more than 200,000 British and 100,000 French soldiers. Casualties, however, were high, and valuable equipment was abandoned.

The Maginot Line ran from Switzerland to the Belgian frontier. Until 1936, the French had expected the Belgians to continue the fortifications along their German border. After Hitler remilitarized the Rhineland without opposition, the Belgians lost faith in their French alliance and proclaimed their neutrality, leaving the Maginot Line exposed on its left flank. Hitler's swift advance through Belgium, therefore, circumvented France's main line of defense.

The French army, poorly and hesitantly led by aged generals who did not understand how to use tanks and planes, collapsed. Mussolini, eager to claim the spoils of victory when he thought it was safe to do so, invaded southern France on June 10. Less than a week later, the new French government, under the ancient hero of Verdun, Marshal Henri Philippe Pétain (1856–1951), asked for an armistice. In two months Hitler had accomplished what Germany had failed to achieve in four years of bitter fighting in the previous war.

Read the **Document** "Marc Bloch, from *Strange Defeat*" on **MyHistoryLab.com**

The Battle of Britain

The fall of France left Britain isolated, and Hitler expected the British to come to terms. He was prepared to allow Britain to retain its empire in return for a free hand for

Adolf Hitler receives news of Marshal Pétain's request for an armistice following the fall of Paris in June 1940. National Archives and Records Administration

Germany on the Continent. The British had never been willing to accept such an arrangement and had fought the long and difficult war against Napoleon to prevent a single power from dominating the Continent. If there was any chance the British would consider such terms, it disappeared when Winston Churchill (1874–1965) replaced Chamberlain as prime minister in May 1940.

Churchill had been an early and forceful critic of Hitler, the Nazis, and the policy of appeasement. He was a descendant and biographer of the duke of Marlborough (1650–1722), who had fought Louis XIV in the eighteenth century. Churchill's sense of history, his feeling for British greatness, and his hatred of tyranny and love of freedom made him reject any compromise with Hitler. His skill as a speaker and a writer enabled him to inspire the British people with his own courage and determination and to undertake what seemed a hopeless fight. Hitler and his allies, including the Soviet Union, controlled all of Europe. Japan was having its way in Asia. The United States was neutral, dominated by isolationist sentiment, and determined to avoid involvement outside the western hemisphere.

Read the Document "Winston Churchill, 'Their Finest Hour' (Great Britain), 1940" on **MyHistoryLab.com**

One of Churchill's greatest achievements was establishing a close relationship with U.S. president Franklin D. Roosevelt (1882–1945). Roosevelt found ways to help the British despite strong political opposition. In 1940 and 1941, before the United States was at war, America sent military supplies, traded badly needed warships for leases on British naval bases, and even convoyed ships across the Atlantic to help the British survive.

As weeks passed and Britain remained defiant, Hitler was forced to contemplate an invasion, and that required control of the air. The first strikes by the German air force (*Luftwaffe*), directed against the airfields and fighter planes in southeast England, began in August 1940. If these attacks had continued, Germany might have gained control of the air and, with it, the chance of a successful invasion.

In August 1941, President Franklin Roosevelt and Prime Minister Winston Churchill met at sea and agreed on a broad program of liberal peace aims, called the Atlantic Charter, in the spirit of Woodrow Wilson's Fourteen Points (see page 930). The Granger Collection

In early September, however, seeking revenge for some British bombing raids on German cities, the *Luftwaffe* switched its main attacks to London. For two months, it bombed London every night. Much of the city was destroyed, and about 15,000 people were killed. The theories of victory through airpower alone, however, proved false. Casualties were much fewer than expected, and morale was not shattered. In fact, the bombings united the British people and made them more resolute.

The Royal Air Force (RAF) inflicted heavy losses on the *Luftwaffe*. Aided by the newly developed radar and excellent communications, the British Spitfire and Hurricane fighter planes destroyed more than twice as many enemy planes as the RAF lost. Hitler had lost the Battle of Britain in the air and was forced to abandon his plans for invasion.

The German Attack on Russia

The defeat of Russia and the conquest of the Ukraine to provide *Lebensraum*, or "living space," for the German people had always been a major goal for Hitler. Even before the assault on Britain, he had informed his staff of his intention to attack Russia as soon as conditions were favorable. In December 1940, even while the bombing of England continued, he ordered his generals to prepare to invade Russia by May 15, 1941. (See Map 28–3, p. 910.) He apparently thought a *blitzkrieg* victory in the east would also destroy the British hope of resistance.

Operation Barbarossa, the code name for the invasion of Russia, was aimed to destroy Russia before winter could set in. Success depended, in part, on an early start, but here Hitler's Italian alliance proved costly. Mussolini was jealous of Hitler's success and annoyed by how the German dictator had treated him. His invasion of France was a fiasco, even though the Germans were simultaneously crushing the main French forces. Hitler did not allow Mussolini to annex French territory in Europe or North Africa. Mussolini instead attacked the British in Egypt and drove them back some sixty miles. Encouraged by this success, he also invaded Greece from his base in Albania (which he had seized in 1939). As he told his son-in-law, Count Ciano: "Hitler always faces me with a fait accompli. This time I am going to pay him back in his own coin. He will find out in the newspapers that I have occupied Greece."[3]

In North Africa, however, the British counterattacked and invaded Libya. The Greeks themselves

[3]Gordon Wright, *The Ordeal of Total War, 1939–1945* (New York: Harper & Row, 1968), pp. 35–36.

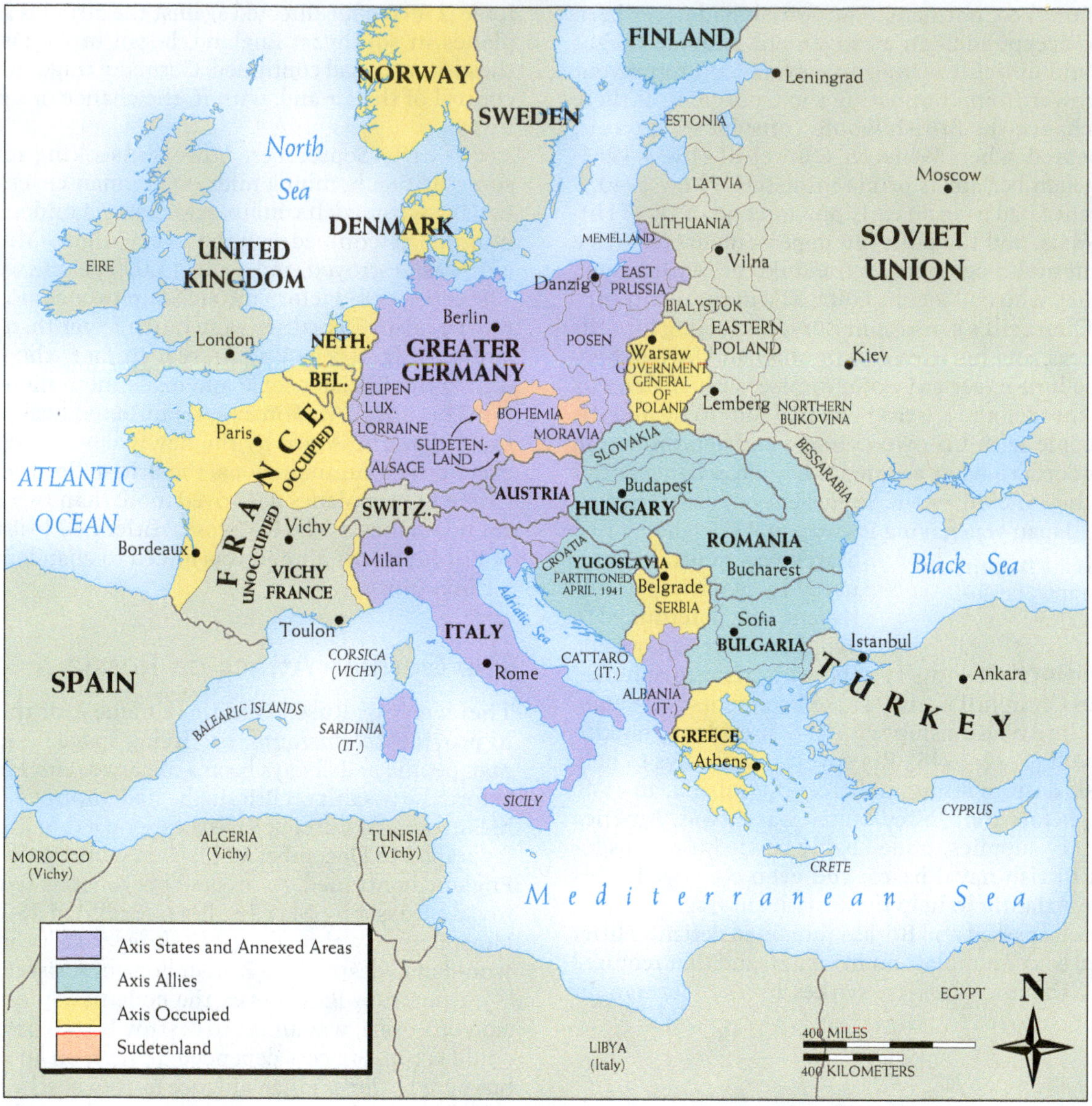

Map 28–3 **AXIS EUROPE, 1941** On the eve of the German invasion of the Soviet Union, the Germany–Italy Axis bestrode most of Western Europe by annexation, occupation, or alliance—from Norway and Finland in the north to Greece in the south and from Poland to France. Britain, the Soviets, a number of insurgent groups, and, finally, America, had before them the long struggle of conquering this Axis "fortress Europe."

pushed into Albania. In March 1941, the British sent help to the Greeks, and Hitler was forced to divert his attention to the Balkans and Africa. General Erwin Rommel (1891–1944), later to earn the title of "Desert Fox," went to Africa and soon drove the British back into Egypt. In the Balkans, the German army swiftly occupied Yugoslavia and crushed Greek resistance. The price, however, was a delay of six weeks. The diversion Mussolini's vanity caused proved to be costly the following winter in the Russian campaign.

Operation Barbarossa was launched against Russia on June 22, 1941, and it almost succeeded. Despite their deep suspicion of Germany (and the excuse apologists for the Soviet Union later offered that the Nazi–Soviet pact was meant to give Russia time to prepare), the Russians were taken quite by surprise. Stalin appears to have panicked. He had not fortified his frontier, nor did he order his troops to withdraw when attacked. In the first two days, the Germans destroyed 2,000 Russian planes on the ground. By November, the German army stood at the gates of Leningrad, on the outskirts of Moscow, and on the Don

View the **Image** "Nazis Executing Russian Civilians" on **MyHistoryLab.com**

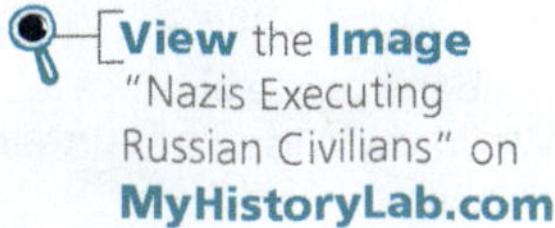

River. Of the 4.5 million troops with which the Russians had begun the fighting, they had lost 2.5 million; of their 15,000 tanks, only 700 were left. Moscow was in panic, and a German victory seemed imminent.

Yet the Germans could not deliver the final blow. In August, they delayed their advance while Hitler decided strategy. The German general staff wanted to take Moscow before winter. This plan probably would have brought victory. Unlike in Napoleon's time, Moscow was the hub of the Russian transportation system. Hitler, however, diverted a significant force to the south. By the time he was ready to return to the offensive near Moscow, it was too late. Winter devastated the German army, which was not equipped to face it.

Given precious time, Stalin restored order and built defenses for the city. Even more importantly, troops arrived from Siberia, where they had been placed to check a possible Japanese attack. In November and December, the Russians counterattacked. The *blitzkrieg* had turned into a war of attrition, and the Germans began to have nightmares of duplicating Napoleon's retreat.

Hitler's Plans for Europe

Hitler often spoke of the "new order" that he meant to impose after he had established his **Third Reich** (empire) throughout Europe. The first two German empires were those of Charlemagne in the ninth century and Bismarck in the nineteenth. Hitler predicted that his own would last for a thousand years. If his organization of Germany before the war is a proper guide, he had no single plan of government but relied on intuition and pragmatism. His organization of a conquered Europe had the same patchwork characteristics. Some conquered territory was annexed to Germany, some was not annexed but administered directly by German officials, and other lands were nominally autonomous but ruled by puppet governments.

Hitler's regime was probably unmatched in history for carefully planned terror and inhumanity. His plan of giving *Lebensraum* to the Germans was to be accomplished at the expense of people he deemed to be inferior. Hitler established colonies of Germans in parts of Poland, driving the local people from their land and employing them as cheap, virtually slave labor. He had similar plans on an even greater scale for Russia. The Russians would be driven back to Central Asia and Siberia. Frontier colonies of German war veterans would keep them in check while Germans settled European Russia.

Hitler's long-range plans included germanization as well as colonization. In lands people racially akin to the Germans inhabited, like the Scandinavian countries, the Netherlands, and Switzerland, the German nation would absorb the natives. Such peoples would be reeducated and purged of dissenting elements, but there would be little or no colonization. Hitler even had plans to adopt selected people from the lesser races into the master race. For example, the Nazis planned to bring half a million Ukrainian girls to Germany as servants and find German husbands for them.

Hitler regarded the conquered lands as a source of plunder. From Eastern Europe, he removed everything useful, including entire industries. In Russia and Poland, the Germans simply confiscated the land itself. In the West, the conquered countries had to support the occupying army at a rate several times above the real cost. The Germans used the profits to buy up everything desirable, stripping the conquered peoples of most necessities. The Nazis were frank about their policies. One of Hitler's high officials said, "Whether nations live in prosperity or starve to death interests me only insofar as we need them as slaves for our culture."[4]

Japan and the United States Enter the War

The American government was pro-British. The assistance that Roosevelt gave Britain would have justified a German declaration of war. Hitler, however, held back. The U.S. government might not have overcome isolationist sentiment and entered the war in the Atlantic if war had not been thrust on America in the Pacific.

Since the Japanese conquest of Manchuria in 1931, American policy toward Japan had been suspicious and unfriendly. The outbreak of the war in Europe emboldened the Japanese to accelerate their drive to dominate Asia. They allied themselves with Germany and Italy, made a treaty of neutrality with the Soviet Union, and forced defeated France to give them bases in Indochina. They also continued their war in China and planned to gain control of Malaya and the East Indies (Indonesia) at the expense of beleaguered Britain and the conquered Netherlands. The only barrier to Japanese expansion was the United States.

The Americans had temporized, unwilling to cut off vital supplies of oil and other materials for fear of provoking a Japanese attack on Southeast Asia and the East Indies. The Japanese occupation of Indochina in July 1941 changed that policy, which had already begun to stiffen. The United States froze Japanese assets and cut off oil supplies; the British and Dutch did the same. Japanese plans for expansion could not continue without the conquest of the Indonesian oil fields and Malayan rubber and tin.

In October, a war faction led by General Hideki Tojo (1885–1948) took power in Japan and decided to risk a war rather than yield. On Sunday morning, December 7, 1941, while Japanese representatives were in Washington to discuss a settlement, Japan launched an air attack on

[4]Wright, *The Ordeal of Total War*, p. 117.

Pearl Harbor, Hawaii, the chief American naval base in the Pacific. The technique was similar to the one Japan had used against the Russian fleet at Port Arthur in 1904, and it caught the Americans equally by surprise. The attack destroyed much of the American fleet and many airplanes. The American capacity to wage war in the Pacific was negated for the time being. The next day, the United States and Britain declared war on Japan. Three days later, Germany and Italy declared war on the United States.

Watch the **Video** "Video: FDR on Winning the War" on **MyHistoryLab.com**

The Tide Turns

The potential power of the United States was enormous, but America was ill prepared for war. The army was tiny, inexperienced, and poorly supplied. American industry was not ready for war. The Japanese swiftly captured Guam, Wake Island, and the Philippine Islands. By the spring of 1942, they had conquered Hong Kong, Malaya, Burma, and the Dutch East Indies. They controlled the southwest Pacific as far as New Guinea and were poised for an attack on Australia. It seemed that nothing could stop them.

In 1942, the Germans also advanced deeper into Russia, while in Africa Rommel drove the British back into Egypt until they stopped him at El Alamein, only seventy miles from Alexandria. Relations between the democracies and their Soviet ally were not close. German submarine warfare was threatening British supplies. The Allies were being thrown back on every front, and the future looked bleak.

The first good news for the Allied cause in the Pacific came in the spring of 1942. A naval battle in the Coral Sea sank many Japanese ships and gave security to Australia. A month later, the United States defeated the Japanese

The successful Japanese attack on the American base at Pearl Harbor in Hawaii on December 7, 1941, together with simultaneous attacks on other Pacific bases, brought the United States into war against the Axis powers. This picture shows the battleships USS *West Virginia* and USS *Tennessee* in flames as a small boat rescues a man from the water. U.S. Army Photo in a fierce air and naval battle off Midway Island. This victory blunted the chance of another assault on Hawaii and did enough damage to halt the Japanese advance. Soon American marines landed on Guadalcanal in the Solomon Islands and began to reverse the momentum of the war. The war in the Pacific was far from over, but the check to Japan allowed the Allies to concentrate their efforts on Europe.

More than twenty nations located all over the world were opposed to the Axis powers. The main combatants, however, were Great Britain, the Soviet Union, and the United States. The two Western democracies cooperated to an unprecedented degree, but suspicion between them and the Soviet Union continued. The Russians accepted all the aid they could get. Nevertheless, they did not trust their allies, complained of inadequate help, and demanded that the democracies open a "second front" on the mainland of Europe.

In 1942, American preparation and production were inadequate to invade Europe. German submarines made it dangerous to ship the vast numbers of troops such an invasion needed across the Atlantic. Not until 1944 were conditions right for the invasion, but in the meantime other developments forecast the doom of the Axis. (See "Encountering the Past: Rosie the Riveter and American Women in the War Effort," page 915.)

Allied Landings in Africa, Sicily, and Italy In November 1942, an Allied force landed in French North Africa. (See Map 28–4.) Even before that landing, after stopping Rommel at El Alamein, British field marshal Bernard Montgomery (1887–1976) had begun a drive to the west. Now, the Americans pushed eastward through Morocco and Algeria. The two armies caught the German army between them in Tunisia and crushed it. The Allies now controlled the Mediterranean and could attack southern Europe.

In July and August 1943, the Allies took Sicily. A coup toppled Mussolini, but the Germans occupied Italy. The Allies landed in Italy, and Marshal Pietro Badoglio (1871–1956), the leader of the new Italian government, declared war on Germany. Churchill had spoken of Italy as the "soft underbelly" of the Axis, but the Germans there resisted fiercely. Still, the need to defend Italy weakened the Germans on other fronts.

Battle of Stalingrad The Russian campaign became especially demanding. In the summer of 1942, the Germans resumed the offensive on all fronts but were unable to get far except in the south. (See Map 28–5, p. 914.) Their goal was the oil fields near the Caspian Sea. Stalingrad, on the Volga, was a key point on the flank of the German army in the south. Hitler was determined

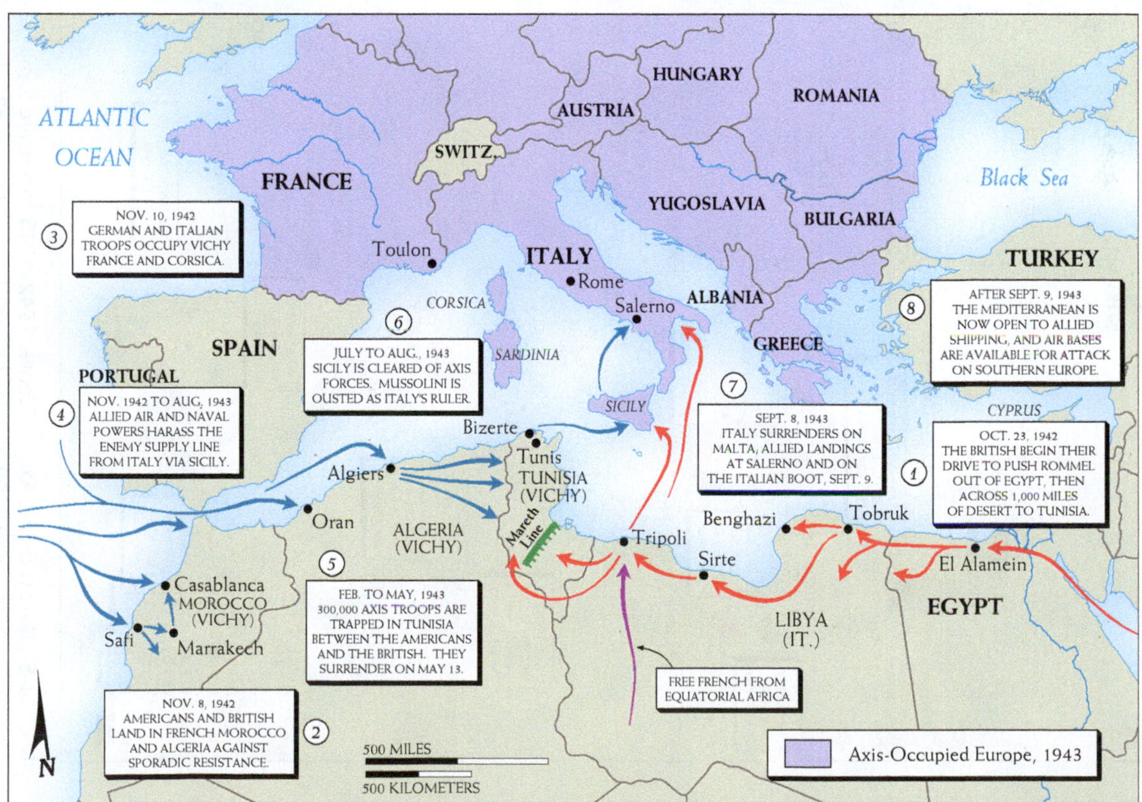

Map 28–4 **NORTH AFRICAN CAMPAIGNS, 1942–1945** Control of North Africa would give the Allies access to Europe from the south. The map illustrates this theater of the war from Morocco to Egypt and the Suez Canal.

Map 28–5 **Defeat of the Axis in Europe, 1942–1945** Here are some of the major steps in the progress toward Allied victory against Axis Europe. From the south through Italy, the west through France, and the east through Russia, the Allies gradually conquered the Continent to bring the war in Europe to a close.

ENCOUNTERING THE *Past*

ROSIE THE RIVETER AND AMERICAN WOMEN IN THE WAR EFFORT

THE INDUCTION OF millions of men into the armed forces created a demand for new workers, especially in the defense industries. In response, millions of women entered the labor force, some of them taking jobs in defense plants to do work only men usually did. Economic pressures caused by the Great Depression of the 1930s had already brought many more women into the workforce than had been common before. Most came from poor families and worked in white-collar jobs to support themselves or to help their families eke out a living. Even so, the heavy burden of housework and the widespread hostility to women working outside the home kept most women at home.

America's entry into the war changed things quickly. The need for vast amounts of equipment to wage the war called for and attracted new groups to seek work in the many enlarged and new factories. African Americans from the south came to northern and western cities to seek well-paying jobs, and women, too, came forward in greater numbers than ever before. Prejudices of various kinds had kept them from many opportunities, but the needs of war were too important. In October 1942, President Roosevelt made the new situation clear: "In some communities employers dislike to hire women. In others they are reluctant to hire Negroes. We can no longer afford to indulge such prejudice."

Many women changed jobs to work in the defense industries; others entered the workforce for the first time, lured less by wages than by patriotism. Their brothers and boyfriends were risking their lives for their country and its ideals of freedom and democracy. They were eager to do their part to support them, to be, in the words of a current song, the woman "behind the man behind the gun." Another popular song, "Rosie the Riveter," told of a young woman working in an aircraft factory to provide protection for her boyfriend in the Marines. Rosie became one of the best-known symbols of the war effort when she appeared on the cover of the *Saturday Evening Post* in a painting by Norman Rockwell. With her rivet gun on her lap she stamps on a copy of Hitler's *Mein Kampf*, the hated symbol of the evil enemy.

How did the war change women's place in American society?

What attitudes did it need to overcome?

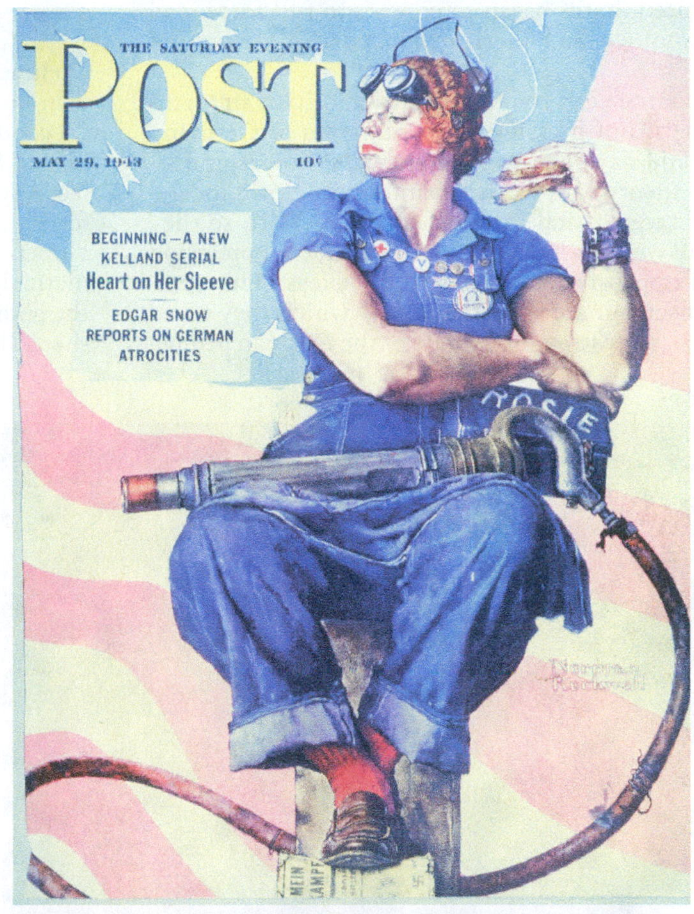

Rosie the Riveter was one of the best-known symbols of the U.S. war effort in World War II. Printed by permission of the Norman Rockwell Family Agency/*The Saturday Evening Post* masthead TM SEPS licensed by Curtis Licensing to take the city, and Stalin was equally determined to hold it. The Battle of Stalingrad raged for months with unexampled ferocity. The Russians lost more men in this one battle than the Americans lost in combat during the entire war, but their heroic defense prevailed. Because Hitler again overruled his generals and would not allow a retreat, he lost an entire German army at Stalingrad.

Stalingrad marked the turning point of the Russian campaign. Thereafter, the Americans provided material help. Even more importantly, increased production from their own industry allowed the Russians to gain and keep the offensive. As the Germans' resources dwindled, the Russians inexorably advanced westward.

Strategic Bombing In 1943, the Allies also gained ground in production and logistics. The industrial might of the United States began to come into full force, and new technology and tactics reduced the submarine menace.

In the same year, the American and British air forces began a series of massive bombardments of Germany by night and day. The Americans were more committed to the theory of "precision bombing" of military and industrial targets vital to the enemy war effort, so they flew the day missions. The British considered precision bombing impossible and therefore useless. They preferred indiscriminate "area bombing," which they could do at night, to destroy the morale of the German people.

In the battle of Stalingrad, Russian troops contested every street and building. Although the city was all but destroyed in the fighting and Russian casualties were enormous, the German army in the east never recovered from the defeat it suffered there. Hulton Archives/Getty Images, Inc.

Neither kind of bombing had much effect on the war until 1944, when the Americans introduced long-range fighters that could protect the bombers and allow accurate missions by day.

By 1945, the Allies could bomb at will. Concentrated attacks on industrial targets, especially communication centers and oil refineries, did extensive damage and helped shorten the war. Terror bombing continued, too, with no useful result. The bombardment of Dresden in February 1945 was especially savage and destructive. It was much debated within the British government and has raised moral questions since. Whatever else it accomplished, the aerial war over Germany took a heavy toll of the German air force and diverted German resources from other military purposes.

The Defeat of Nazi Germany

On June 6, 1944 ("D-Day"), American, British, and Canadian troops landed in force on the coast of Normandy. The "second front" was opened. General Dwight D. Eisenhower (1890–1969), the commander of the Allied armies, faced a difficult problem. The European coast was heavily fortified. Amphibious assaults, moreover, are especially vulnerable to wind and weather. Success depended on meticulous planning, heavy bombing, and feints to mask the point of attack. The German defense was strong, but the Allies established a beachhead and then broke out of it. In mid-August, the Allies also landed in southern France. By the beginning of September, France had been liberated.

View the **Image** "Eisenhower and U.S. Troops before D-Day" on **MyHistoryLab.com**

The Battle of the Bulge All went smoothly until December, when the Germans launched a counterattack in Belgium and Luxembourg through the Ardennes Forest. Because the Germans pushed forward into the Allied line, this was called the Battle of the Bulge. Although the Allies suffered heavy losses, the Bulge was the last gasp for the Germans in the West. The Allies crossed the Rhine in March 1945, and German resistance crumbled. This time there could be no doubt the Germans had lost the war on the battlefield.

The Capture of Berlin In the east, the Russians swept forward no less swiftly, despite fierce German resistance. By March 1945, they were near Berlin. Because the Allies insisted on unconditional surrender, the Germans fought on until May. Hitler committed suicide in an underground bunker in Berlin on April

American soldiers land at Omaha Beach in Normandy on D-Day, June 6, 1944. Courtesy of the Library of Congress

30, 1945. The Russians occupied Berlin by agreement with their Western allies. The Third Reich lasted only a dozen years instead of the thousand Hitler had predicted.

Fall of the Japanese Empire

The war in Europe ended on May 8, 1945, and by then, victory over Japan was also in sight. The original Japanese attack on the United States had been a calculated risk against the odds. Japan was inherently weaker than the United States. The longer the war lasted, the more American superiority in industrial production and population counted.

Americans Recapture the Pacific Islands In 1943, the American forces, still small in number, began a campaign of "island hopping." They did not try to recapture every Pacific island the Japanese held but selected major bases and strategic sites along the enemy supply line. (See Map 28–6, p. 918.) Starting from the Solomon Islands, they moved northeast toward Japan itself. By June 1944, they had reached the Mariana Islands, usable as bases to bomb the Japanese in the Philippines, China, and Japan itself.

In October of the same year, the Americans recaptured most of the Philippines and drove the Japanese fleet back into its home waters. In 1945, Iwo Jima and Okinawa fell, despite fierce Japanese resistance that included kamikaze attacks, suicide missions in which pilots deliberately flew their explosive-filled planes into American warships. From these new bases, closer to Japan, the Americans launched a terrible wave of bombings that destroyed Japanese industry and disabled the Japanese navy. Still, the Japanese government, dominated by a military clique, refused to surrender.

Confronted with Japan's determination, the Americans made plans for a frontal assault on the Japanese homeland. They calculated it might cost a million American casualties and even greater losses for the Japanese. At this point, science and technology presented the Americans with another choice.

The Atomic Bomb Since early in the war, a secret program had been in progress. Its staff, many of whom were exiles from Hitler's Europe, was working to use atomic energy for military purposes. On August 6, 1945, an American plane dropped an atomic bomb on the Japanese city of Hiroshima. The city was destroyed, and

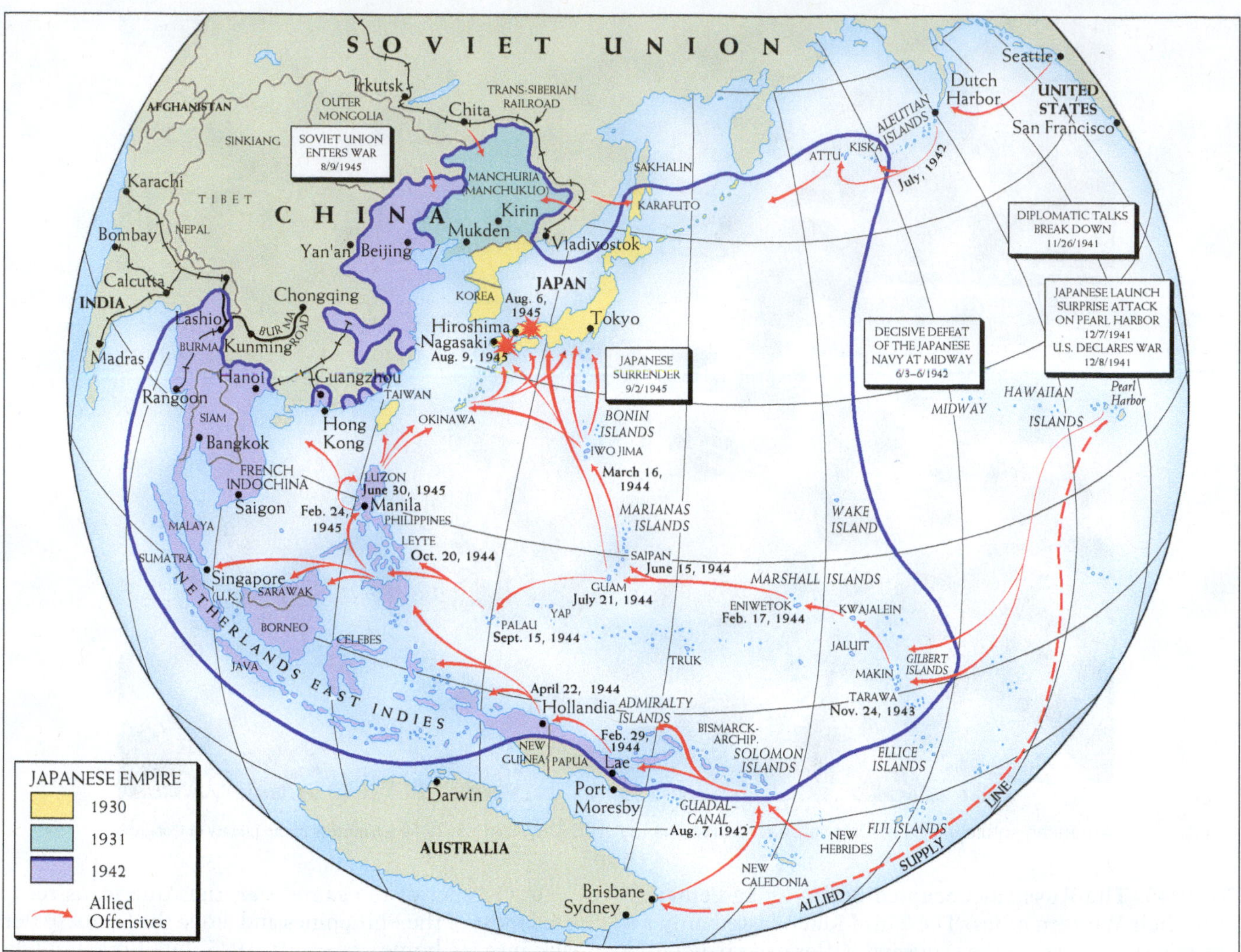

Map 28–6 **WORLD WAR II IN THE PACIFIC** As in Europe, the Pacific war involved Allied recapture of areas that had been quickly taken earlier by the enemy. The enormous area represented by the map shows the initial expansion of Japanese holdings to cover half the Pacific and its islands, as well as huge sections of eastern Asia, and the long struggle to push the Japanese back to their homeland and defeat them by the summer of 1945.

more than 70,000 of its 200,000 residents were killed. Two days later, the Soviet Union declared war on Japan and invaded Manchuria. The next day, a second atomic bomb hit Nagasaki. Even then, the Japanese cabinet was prepared to face an invasion rather than give up.

Read the Document "An Eyewitness to Hiroshima (1945)" on **MyHistoryLab.com**

The unprecedented intervention of Emperor Hirohito (r. 1926–1989) finally forced the government to surrender on August 14 on the condition that Japan retain the emperor. Although the Allies had continued to insist on unconditional surrender, President Harry S. Truman (1884–1972), who had come to office on April 12, 1945, upon the death of Franklin D. Roosevelt, accepted the condition. Peace was formally signed aboard the USS *Missouri* in Tokyo Bay on September 2, 1945.

Revulsion at the use of atomic bombs, as well as hindsight arising from the Cold War, have made the decision to use the bomb against Japanese cities controversial. Some have suggested the bombings were unnecessary to win the war and their main purpose was to frighten the Russians into a more cooperative attitude after the war. Others have emphasized the bureaucratic, almost automatic nature of the decision, once it had been decided to develop the bomb. To the decision makers and their contemporaries, however, matters were simpler. The bomb was a way to end the war swiftly and save American lives. The decision to use it was conscious, not automatic, and required no ulterior motive.

The Cost of War

World War II was the most terrible war in history. Military deaths are estimated at some 15 million, and at least as many civilians were killed. If we include deaths linked indirectly to the war, from disease, hunger, and other causes, the number of victims might reach 40 million. Most of Europe and large parts of Asia were devastated. Yet the end of so terrible a war brought little opportunity to relax. The dawn of the atomic age made people conscious that another major war might extinguish humanity. Everything depended on concluding a stable peace, but even as the fighting ended, conflicts among the victors made the prospects of a lasting peace doubtful.

▼ Racism and the Holocaust

The most horrible aspect of the Nazi rule in Europe arose not from military or economic necessity but from the inhumanity and brutality inherent in Hitler's racial doctrines. These were applied to several groups of people in Eastern Europe.

Hitler considered the Slavs *Untermenschen*, subhuman creatures like beasts who need not be treated as people. In parts of Poland, the upper and professional classes were entirely removed—jailed, deported, or killed. Schools and churches were closed. The Nazis limited marriage to keep down the Polish birthrate and imposed harsh living conditions.

In Russia, things were even worse. Hitler spoke of his Russian campaign as a war of extermination. Heinrich Himmler (1900–1945), head of Hitler's elite SS formations, planned to eliminate 30 million Slavs to make room for Germans; he formed extermination squads for this purpose. Six million Russian prisoners of war and deported civilians may have died under Nazi rule.

Hitler, however, had envisioned a special fate for the Jews. He meant to make all Europe *Judenrein*, or "free of Jews." For a time, he considered sending them to the island of Madagascar. Later, he arrived at the "final solution of the Jewish problem"—extermination. The Nazis built extermination camps in Germany and Poland and used the latest technology to achieve the most efficient means to kill millions of men, women, and children simply because they were Jews. (See the Document "Mass

World War II resulted in the near-total destruction of the Jews of Europe, victims of the Holocaust spawned by Hitler's racial theories of the superiority and inferiority of particular ethnic groups. Hitler placed special emphasis on the need to exterminate the Jews, to whom he attributed particular wickedness. This picture shows Hungarian Jewish women, after "disinfection" and head shaving, marching to the concentration or death camp at Auschwitz-Birkenau, Poland. Library of Congress/Photo by Bernhard Walter; source: National Archives and Records Administration

Murder at Belsen," pages 922–923.) The most extensive destruction occurred in Eastern Europe and Russia, but the Nazis and their collaborators in occupied areas of Western Europe, including France, the Netherlands, Italy, and Belgium, also deported Jews from these nations to almost certain death in the east. Before the war was over, perhaps 6 million Jews had died in what has come to be called the **Holocaust**. Only about a million European Jews remained alive, most of them in pitiable condition. (See Map 28–7.)

It is difficult to comprehend the massive Nazi effort to eradicate the Jews of Europe. This destruction took different forms in different regions of the Continent. To explore this central event of twentieth-century European history, we examine the fate of the Polish Jewish community, which before World War II was the largest in Europe, consisting of 10 percent of Poland's population.

The Destruction of the Polish Jewish Community

A large Jewish community had dwelled within Poland for centuries, often in a climate of religious and cultural anti-Semitism. As a result of this anti-Semitism, Polish Jews had long lived in their own villages and later in their own urban neighborhoods. After the late-eighteenth-century partitions of Poland and the Congress of Vienna, most of Poland came under Russian rule. Through the policy of Official Nationalism (see Chapter 21), the nineteenth-century tsars identified loyalty to their government with membership in the Russian Orthodox Church. Other Christian groups, such as Lutherans and Roman Catholics, were often treated with suspicion. Jews were treated worse and were subject to a wide variety of discriminatory legislation. Polish Jews did not experience any of the forms of Jewish emancipation that occurred in Western Europe. (See Chapter 24.)

Language, food, dress, and place of residence as well as religion distinguished Jews from the rest of the Polish population, almost all of whom were Roman Catholics. Hebrew was the Polish Jews' chief written language, and Yiddish their primary spoken language. Many Jews, particularly older ones, wore distinctive dress. They ate food different from that of most Poles. Many Polish Jews also moved to cities, and Jews were regarded as an urban people in a predominantly rural nation. Moreover, Jews were among the poorest people in Poland, often working as self-employed merchants, peddlers, and craftspeople, or in industries, such as textiles, clothing, and paper, that other Poles identified as Jewish-dominated. Few Polish Jews belonged to trade unions. These conditions made them vulnerable during the economic turmoil of the 1920s and especially of the 1930s.

Map 28–7 **THE HOLOCAUST** The Nazi policy of ethnic cleansing—targeting Jews, Gypsies, political dissidents, and "social deviants"—began with imprisoning them in concentration camps, but by 1943 the *Endlösung*, or Final Solution, called for the systematic extermination of "undersirables."

Polish Anti-Semitism Between the Wars

After the restoration of Poland following World War I, Polish leaders were divided about the role of Jews in Polish national life. Jozef Pilsudski (1867–1935), who dominated the interwar era, favored including Jews within the civic definition of the nation, and the constitution allowed Jews to participate in political life. After Pilsudski's death, political groups that equated citizenship with Polish ethnicity and embraced anti-Semitism came to the fore. Their ideology, no less than that of tsarist Russian Orthodoxy, defined Jews as outside the Polish nation.

No matter which political outlook dominated, discrimination against Jews existed throughout the culture and politics of interwar Poland. During those years, the Polish government, supported by spokesmen for the Polish Roman Catholic Church, pursued policies that were anti-Semitic. The Polish government nationalized the matches, salt, tobacco, and alcohol industries and then enacted legislation that discriminated against hiring Jews for these government monopolies. Other laws made it difficult for Jews to observe the Sabbath while keeping their jobs. Regulations requiring businesses to be closed on Sunday meant Jewish shops had to close two days of the week. By the late 1930s, as ethnic nationalism became stronger, the government required businesses to display their owners' names prominently, which made it easy for people to avoid Jewish shops. Because Jews were excluded from the civil service, they moved into law and medicine, which provoked further resentment.

The path of assimilation into the larger culture that many European Jewish leaders had advocated during the nineteenth century hit a dead end in Poland because many Poles refused to regard even secular, assimilated Jews as fellow Poles. Nonetheless, many Jews attempted to embrace the social practices, dress, and language of the Polish majority without actually expecting to be considered Polish. They saw themselves as moving from a traditional style of life to a more modern and Polish one. Jewish newspapers and other magazines began to be published in Polish. Jews took advantage of their right to political participation, but they were divided into different factions and could not agree on how to defend Jewish life and culture in Poland. These divisions made the Jews of Poland more vulnerable when World War II broke out in 1939.

Whatever active anti-Semitism existed in Poland before the German invasion of 1939, it was the Nazis who tried to destroy the Polish Jewish community and Jewish communities elsewhere in Europe that fell under German control. In that respect, the Holocaust constitutes an event driven by German policy within the larger event of World War II.

The Nazi Assault on the Jews of Poland

The joint German–Soviet invasion of Poland brought millions of Jews under either German or Soviet authority. By conquering Poland, the Nazi government could carry out the destruction of Jewish communities to an extent far beyond anything possible in Germany itself. From the Nazi standpoint, the destruction of the Polish Jewish community held special importance. Polish Jewry was large and had produced many religious, cultural, and political leaders. It also constituted the single most important source for Jewish emigration beyond Eastern Europe. For the Nazis, Poland was the chief breeding ground for world Jewry.

By late autumn 1939, the Germans had begun to move against Polish Jews. The Nazi government first thought it might herd virtually all the Jews of occupied Europe into the Lublin region of Poland. By early 1940, the Nazis decided to move as many Jews as possible into ghettos, where they would be separated from the rest of the Polish population. The largest ghettos were Lodz and Warsaw, each of which had populations of several hundred thousand. The Nazis moved Jews from all over Poland and, eventually, other occupied regions by rail into these ghettos and then sealed them off with police guards and walls. Jewish councils, which were torn between responsibility to their communities and the need to respond to German orders, administered the ghettos. The Nazis confiscated and sold the personal property and businesses of the Jews who were herded into the ghettos. Jewish laborers were sent out to work as contract labor while their families remained in the ghettos. By 1941, the Polish Jews had lost their civic standing and property. They had been located in segregated communities within Poland where disease was rampant and the food supply meager. Approximately 20 percent of the population of both the Lodz and Warsaw ghettos died of disease and malnourishment.

The German invasion of the Soviet Union in June 1941 made the situation of Jews in Poland even worse. The advancing German forces killed tens of thousands of Jews in the Soviet Union during 1941 and hundreds of thousands more the next year. Bolsheviks and Jews became conflated in German thinking and propaganda. During the second half of 1941, the Nazi government decided to exterminate the Jews of Europe. From late 1941 through 1944, the Germans transported Jews from the ghettos by rail to death camps in Poland, including Kulmhof, Belzen, Sobibor, Treblinka, Birkenau, and Auschwitz. One or more of the camps were in operation from 1941 to 1944, with Auschwitz being the last closed. In these camps, Jews were systematically killed in gas chambers.

By 1945, approximately 90 percent of the pre-1939 Jewish population of Poland had been destroyed. The tiny minority of Polish Jews who had survived faced bitter anti-Semitism under the postwar Soviet-dominated government. Many immigrated to Israel, leaving only a few thousand Jews within the borders of a nation where they had numbered in the millions and where they had created a rich religious, cultural, and political community. The largest Jewish community in Europe had virtually ceased to exist.

Document

MASS MURDER AT BELSEN

Hitler's calculated plan to wipe out Europe's Jews, along with millions of other people he considered undesirable for racial and other reasons, was not widely known during the war. Care was taken to keep the mass murders secret. Even when news of them leaked out, many people were reluctant to believe what they heard, and participants in the crimes were naturally not eager to talk about them. Kurt Gerstein, a colonel in the SS, was part of the apparatus of extermination. However, unlike most people involved and at great risk to himself, he tried to tell the world what was taking place. The following is an account of what he saw at the death camp at Belsen in 1942.

What were the reasons for Hitler's policy of exterminating millions of men, women, and children? Why did many Germans take part in the process? Why did so conscientious a man as Colonel Gerstein not resist?

A train arrived from Lemberg [Lvov]. There were forty-five cars containing 6,700 people, 1,450 of whom were already dead. Through the gratings on the windows, children could be seen peering out, terribly pale and frightened, their eyes filled with mortal dread. . . . The train entered the station, and two hundred Ukrainians wrenched open the doors and drove the people out of the carriages with their leather whips. Instructions came through a large loudspeaker telling them to remove all their clothing, artificial limbs, glasses, etc. They were to hand over all objects of value at the counter. . . . Shoes were to be carefully tied together, for otherwise no one would ever again have been able to find shoes belonging to each other in a pile that was a good eighty feet high. Then the women and girls were sent to the barber who, with two or three strokes of his scissors, cut off all their hair and dropped it into potato sacks. "That's for some special purpose or other on U-Boats, for packing or something like that," I was told by an SS-Unterscharfuhrer. . . .

Then the column moved off. Headed by an extremely pretty young girl, they walked along the avenue, all naked, men, women, and children, with artificial limbs removed. I myself was stationed up on the ramp between the [gas] chambers with Captain Wirth.

Explanations of the Holocaust

As interest in the Holocaust has grown since the 1960s, so has debate about its character and meaning. Was it a unique event of unprecedented and unparalleled evil, or was it one specific instance of a more general human wickedness that has found expression throughout history? Are its roots to be found in flaws in human nature as a whole, or are they unique to the experience of the West or, perhaps, to the German people? Some scholars point to the horrible mass murders committed in the twentieth century by communist regimes under Stalin in the Soviet Union and under Mao in China, each of which killed many more people than did Hitler, as evidence of the more general character of the phenomenon. Others argue that the Holocaust was unique because its goal was the annihilation of a whole people, from infants to the aged, just because of who they were. Some focus on the wickedness personified by Hitler, who was driven by his fixation on the myth of Jewish power and evil.

Perhaps we should think of the problem from the standpoint of two questions: Why were the Jews the main target of Hitler's policy of extermination? How was it possible to carry out such a vast mass murder? Surely, an essential part of an answer to the first question is the persistence of anti-Semitism in Christianity and Western culture, from the Church Fathers to Luther and to the teachings of churches in modern times. Some would combine this religious and historical anti-Semitism with the coming of the Enlightenment and the social sciences, which gave rise to pseudoscientific racial theories that lent a new twist to the old hatred of the Jews. Pseudoscientific racism appears to have been the most powerful influence on Hitler, but it could not have found widespread support without deeply rooted religious and social anti-Semitism.

Mothers with babies at their breasts came up, hesitated, and entered the chambers of death. At the corner stood a burly SS man with a priest-like voice. "Nothing at all is going to happen to you!" he told the poor wretches. "All you have to do when you get into the chambers is to breathe in deeply. That stretches the lungs. Inhaling is necessary to prevent disease and epidemics." When asked what would be done with them, he replied: "Well, of course, the men will have to work building houses and roads, but the women won't need to work. They can do housework or help in the kitchen, but only if they want to." For some of these poor creatures, this was a small ray of hope that was enough to make them walk the few steps to the chambers without resistance. Most of them knew what was going on. The smell told them what their fate was to be. They went up the small flight of steps and saw everything. Mothers with their babies clasped to their breasts, small children, adults, men, women, all naked; they hesitated, but they entered the chambers of death, thrust forward by the others behind them or by the leather whips of the SS [Storm Troopers]. Most went in without a word. . . . Many were saying prayers. I prayed with them. I pressed myself into a corner and cried aloud to my God and theirs. How gladly I should have gone into the chambers with them; how gladly I should have died with them. Then they would have found an SS officer in uniform in their gas chambers; they would have believed it was an accident and the story would have been buried and forgotten. But I could not do that yet. First, I had to make known what I had seen here. The chambers were filling up. Fill them up well—that was Captain Wirth's order. The people were treading on each other's feet. There were 700–800 of them in an area of 270 square feet, in 1,590 cubic feet of space. The SS crushed them together as tightly as they possibly could. The doors closed. Meanwhile, the rest waited out in the open, all naked. "It's done exactly the same way in winter," I was told. "But they may catch their death!" I said. "That's what they're here for," an SS man said. . . . The Diesel exhaust gases were intended to kill those unfortunates. But the engine was not working. . . . The people in the gas chambers waited, in vain. I heard them weeping, sobbing. . . . After 2 hours and 49 minutes, measured by my stop watch, the Diesel started. Up to that moment, men and women had been shut up alive in those four chambers, four times 750 people in four times 1,590 cubic feet of space. Another twenty-five minutes dragged by. Many of those inside were already dead. They could be seen through the small window when the electric light went on for a moment and lit up the inside of the chamber. After twenty-eight minutes, few were left alive. At the end of thirty-two minutes, all were dead.

For example, in at least one instance in Poland, Poles turned against their Jewish neighbors in outbursts of localized anti-Semitic violence. In July 1941, in the town of Jedwabne, in northeast Poland, non-Jewish Poles killed approximately 1,600 of their Jewish fellow townspeople. This horrendous incident suggests that although the Nazis carried out most of the atrocities against the Jews, a climate of either indifference or outright support existed in Poland as well as in other parts of Nazi-occupied Europe. Yet it must also be noted that between 1942 and 1945 the Council for Aid to Jews in Occupied Poland, known as ZEGOTA and sponsored by the Polish government in exile, protected and aided the escape of many thousands of Polish Jews.

As to how it was possible to murder 6 million people, part of the answer must lie in the parochial nationalism that arose during and after the French Revolution. For many people, nationalism divided the world into one's fellow nationals and all others. It encouraged, excused, and even justified terrible and violent acts performed on behalf of one's homeland. Another part of the answer may derive from the utopian visions also unleashed by some Enlightenment writers, who promised to achieve perfect societies through social engineering, regardless of the human cost. To this were added the scientific and technological advances that gave the modern state new power to command its people, to persuade them to obey by controlling the media of propaganda, and to enforce its will with efficient brutality. All of these permitted the creation of a totalitarian state that, for the first time in history, could conduct mass murder on the scale of the Holocaust.

These questions and their possible answers are but suggestions meant to encourage further and deeper thought in what will surely be a continuing debate among scholars and the general public. World War II

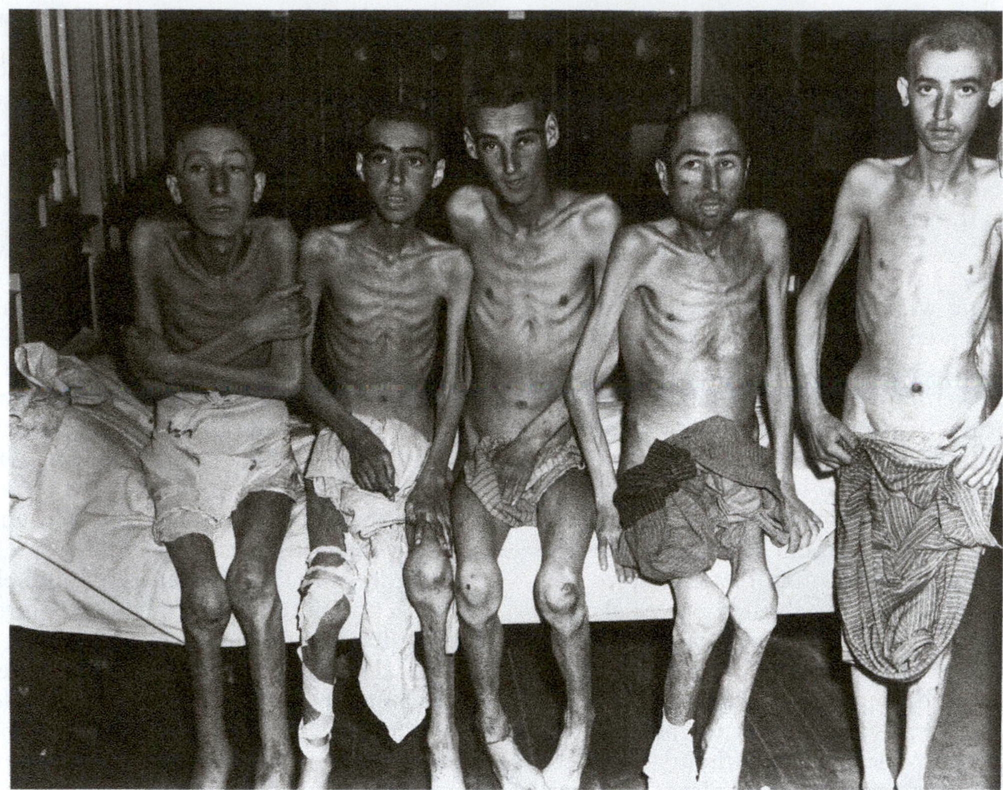

Male inmates, emaciated and freezing, at a German concentration camp in 1945. Library of Congress

MAJOR CAMPAIGNS AND EVENTS OF WORLD WAR II

September 1939	Germany and the Soviet Union invade Poland
November 1939	The Soviet Union invades Finland
April 1940	Germany invades Denmark and Norway
May 1940	Germany invades Belgium, the Netherlands, Luxembourg, and France
June 1940	Fall of France
August 1940	Battle of Britain begins
June 1941	Germany invades the Soviet Union
July 1941	Japan takes Indochina
December 1941	Japan attacks Pearl Harbor; United States enters war against Axis powers
June 1942	Battle of Midway Island
November 1942	Battle of Stalingrad begins
July–August 1943	Allies take Sicily, land in Italy
June 1944	Allies land in Normandy
May 1945	Germany surrenders
August 1945	Atomic bombs dropped on Hiroshima and Nagasaki
September 1945	Japan formally surrenders

was unmatched in cruelty in modern times. When Stalin's armies conquered Poland and entered Germany, they raped, pillaged, and deported millions to the east. The British and American bombing of Germany killed thousands of civilians, and the atomic bombs dropped on Japan killed and maimed tens of thousands more. The bombings, however, were thought of as acts of war that would help defeat the enemy. Stalin's atrocities were not widely known in the West at the time or even today.

The victorious Western allies were shocked by what they saw when they came upon the Nazi extermination camps and their pitiful survivors. Little wonder it was that they were convinced the effort to resist the Nazis and all the pain it had cost were well worth it.

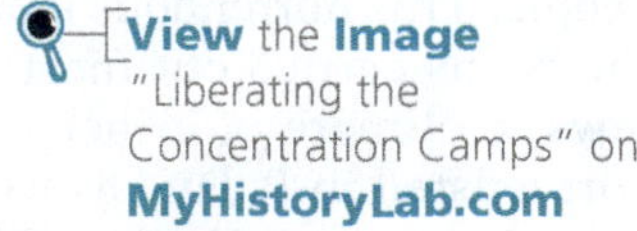

View the **Image** "Liberating the Concentration Camps" on **MyHistoryLab.com**

▼ The Domestic Fronts

World War II represented an effort at total war by all the belligerents. Never in European or world history had so many men and women and such resources been devoted to military effort. One result was the carnage that occurred during the fighting. Another was an unprecedented organization of civilians on the home fronts.

Each domestic effort and experience was different, but few escaped the impact of the conflict. Everywhere there were shortages, propaganda campaigns, and new political developments.

The war powerfully affected the daily lives of the people at home, and the organization of the home front was crucial for the course of the war. Governments intruded into many areas of private life, including what and how much people could eat, what work they did, and how they could be protected from attack. Survival and victory depended heavily on the efforts and morale of the civilian population.

Germany: From Apparent Victory to Defeat

Hitler had expected to defeat all his enemies by rapid strokes, or *blitzkriegs*. Such campaigns would have required little change in Germany's society and economy. During the first two years of the war, in fact, Hitler demanded few sacrifices from the German people. Spending on domestic projects continued, and food was plentiful; the economy was not on a full wartime footing. Germany's failure to quickly overwhelm the Soviet Union changed everything. Food was no longer available from the east in needed quantities, Germany had to mobilize for total war, and the government demanded major sacrifices.

A great expansion of the army and of military production began in 1942. As minister for armaments and munitions, Albert Speer (1905–1981) directed the economy, and Germany met its military needs. The government sought the cooperation of major German businesses to increase wartime production. Between 1942 and late 1944, the output of military products tripled. As the war went on, more men were drafted from industry into the army, and military production suffered.

As the manufacture of armaments replaced the production of consumer goods, shortages of everyday products became serious. Prices and wages were controlled, but the standard of living of German workers fell. Food rationing began in April 1942, and shortages were severe until the Nazi government seized more food from occupied Europe. Teenagers, women, and workers of retirement age were compelled to work in factories.

Bombing of Cologne. The Allied campaign of aerial bombardment did terrible damage to German cities. This photograph shows the devastation it delivered to the city of Cologne on the Rhine. United States Signal Corps

To preserve their own home front, the Nazis passed on the suffering to their defeated neighbors. They seized machines and equipment from the nations they conquered and extorted money from them. Millions of defeated opponents, soldiers, and civilians served as forced labor in Germany, many dying from the grim conditions of their lives.

By 1943, labor shortages became severe. The Nazis required German teenagers and retired men to work in the factories, and many women joined them. To achieve total mobilization, the Germans closed retail businesses, raised the age of eligibility of women for compulsory service, shifted non-German domestic workers to wartime industry, moved artists and entertainers into military service, closed theaters, and reduced such basic public services as mail and railways. Finally, the Nazis compelled thousands of non-Germans to do forced labor in Germany.

Hitler assigned women a special place in the war effort. The celebration of motherhood continued, with an emphasis on women who were the mothers of important military figures. Films portrayed ordinary women who became brave and patriotic during the war and remained faithful to their husbands who were at the front. Women were shown as mothers and wives who sent their sons and husbands off to war. The government pictured other wartime activities of women as the natural fulfillment of their maternal roles. As air-raid wardens, they protected their families; as factory workers in munitions plants, they aided their sons on the front lines. Women working on farms were providing for their soldier sons and husbands; as housewives, they were helping to win the war by conserving food. Finally, by their faithful chastity, German women were protecting racial purity. They were not to marry or to have sex with non-Germans. During the war domestic political propaganda went beyond what occurred in other countries. Hitler and other Germans genuinely believed that weak domestic support had led to Germany's defeat in World War I; they were determined not to let this happen again. Nazi propaganda blamed the outbreak of the war on the British and the Jews and its prolongation on Germany's opponents. It also stressed the power of Germany and the inferiority of its foes.

Propaganda minister Josef Goebbels (1897–1945) used both radio and films to boost the Nazi cause. Movies of the collapse of Poland, Belgium, Holland, and France showed German military might. Throughout the conquered territories, the Nazis used the same mass media to frighten inhabitants about the possible consequences of an Allied victory. Later in the war, Goebbels broadcast exaggerated claims of Nazi victories. As the German armies were checked on the battlefield, especially in Russia, propaganda became a substitute for victory. To stiffen German resolve, propaganda now aimed to frighten Germans about the consequences of defeat.

After May 1943, when the Allies began their major bombing offensive over Germany, the German people had much to fear. The bombing devastated one German city after another but did not undermine German morale. The bombing may even have increased German resistance by seeming to confirm the regime's propaganda about the ruthlessness of Germany's opponents.

World War II increased the power of the Nazi Party in Germany. Every area of the economy and society came under the direct influence or control of the party. The Nazis were determined that they, rather than the traditionally honored German officer corps, would profit from the new authority the war effort was giving to the central government. There was virtually no serious opposition to Hitler or his ministers. In July 1944, a group of army officers attempted to assassinate Hitler; the effort failed, and there was little popular support for this act.

The war brought great changes to Germany, but what transformed the country most was the experience of physical destruction, invasion, and occupation. Hitler and the Nazis had brought Germany to such a complete and disastrous defeat that only a new kind of state with new political structures could emerge.

France: Defeat, Collaboration, and Resistance

The terms of the 1940 armistice between France, under Pétain, and Germany, signed June 22, allowed the Germans to occupy more than half of France, including the Atlantic and English Channel coasts. To prevent the French from continuing the fight from North Africa, and even more to prevent them from turning their fleet over to Britain, Hitler left southern France unoccupied until November 1942. Marshal Pétain set up a dictatorial regime at the resort city of Vichy and collaborated with the Germans in hopes of preserving as much autonomy as possible.

Some of the collaborators believed the Germans were sure to win the war and wanted to be on the victorious side. A few sympathized with Nazi ideas and plans. Many conservatives regarded the French defeat as a judgment on what they saw as the corrupt, secularized, liberal Third Republic. Most of the French were not active collaborators but were demoralized by defeat and German power.

Many conservatives and extreme rightists saw in the Vichy government a way to reshape the French national character and to halt the decadence they associated with political and religious liberalism. The Roman Catholic clergy, which had lost power and influence under the Third Republic, gained status under Vichy. The church supported Pétain, and his government restored religious instruction in the state schools and increased financial support for Catholic schools. Vichy adopted the church's views on the importance of family and spiritual values. The government made divorce difficult and forbade it entirely during the first three years of marriage. The state encouraged and subsidized large families.

A Closer LOOK

THE VICHY REGIME IN FRANCE

AFTER THEIR SURPRISINGLY swift conquest of France in 1940, the Germans ruled one part of it directly from Paris, leaving the rest unoccupied until 1942, but firmly under the control of a collaborationist French government under Marshal Henri Philippe Pétain (1856–1951; see Map 28–3). This regime, based in the city of Vichy, pursued a reactionary policy, turning away from the democratic ways of the defeated Third Republic. The "Propaganda Centers of the National Revolution" published the poster shown in the photo. "The National Revolution" was the name the Vichy regime gave to its program to remake France.

The house on the left, representing the Third Republic, carries the name "France and Company," which implies that the Third Republic was run like a corrupt business firm. It tilts precariously on shaky supports: egoism, radicalism, capitalism, communism, Jewry, antimilitarism, parliament, and disorder. These, in turn, rest on what Vichy considered the Republic's basic flaws: laziness, demagogy, and internationalism instead of French patriotism.

The house on the right represents the Vichy government. Its name is "France," pure and simple. It sits, safe, strong, neat, and orderly, on solid columns: school, craftsmanship, the peasantry, and the military. These rest on equally firm bases: discipline, order, thrift, and courage. Underlying all are the three basic values—work, family, and fatherland—which Vichy made its national slogan to replace the liberty, equality, and fraternity that had been the motto of French republican regimes since the French Revolution.

Photo 12/Alamy

What were the political differences between the Vichy regime and its critics?

Why would they want to replace the traditional slogans of the French Revolution with the ones they introduced?

What events in the twentieth century might seem to justify the change?

The Vichy regime also encouraged an intense, chauvinistic nationalism. It exploited prejudice against foreigners working in France and fostered resentment even against French men and women whom it regarded as not genuinely "French," especially French Jews. Anti-Semitism was not new in France, as the Dreyfus affair had demonstrated. Even before Germany undertook Hitler's "final solution" in 1942, the French had begun to remove Jews from positions of influence in government, education, and publishing. In 1941, the Germans began to intern Jews living in occupied France; soon they murdered individual Jews and imposed large fines collectively on the Jews of the occupied zone. In the spring of 1942, they began to deport Jews from France—ultimately more than 60,000—to the extermination camps of Eastern Europe. The Vichy government had no part in these decisions, but it made no protest, and its own anti-Semitic policies made the whole process easier to carry out. The great majority of Frenchmen, who were not Jewish, also suffered greatly.

The absence of some 2 million men who were prisoners of war compelled the women of France to carry on much of the labor normally done by men. All the French suffered shortages of all consumer goods under a strict and mismanaged rationing system. The Germans seized about 20 percent of the French food production, and French farm production fell by half because of lack of fuel, fertilizer, and workers. Food shortages were most acute in large cities. Farmers did better, but the official ration provided starvation-level diets of 1,300 or fewer calories a day.

Some French men and women, notably General Charles de Gaulle (1890–1969), fled to Britain after the defeat of France. There they organized the French National Committee of Liberation, or "Free French." Until the end of 1942, the Vichy government controlled French North Africa and the navy, but the Free French began operating in Central Africa. From London, they broadcast hope and defiance to their compatriots in France. Serious internal resistance to the German occupiers and the Vichy government, however, began to develop only late in 1942. The Germans tried to force young people in occupied France to work in German factories; some of them joined the Resistance, but the number of all the resisters was small. Fear of German retaliation deterred many. Others disliked the violence that resistance to a powerful ruthless nation inevitably entailed. As long as it appeared the Germans would win the war, moreover, resistance seemed imprudent and futile. For these reasons, the organized Resistance never attracted more than 5 percent of the adult French population.

By early 1944, the tide of battle had shifted. The Allies seemed sure to win, and the Vichy government would clearly not survive; only then did a large-scale active movement of resistance assert itself. General de Gaulle spoke confidently for Free France from his base in London and urged the French people to resist their conquerors and the German lackeys in the Vichy government. Within France, Resistance groups joined forces to plan for a better day. From Algiers on August 9, 1944, the Committee of National Liberation declared the authority of Vichy illegitimate. French soldiers joined in the liberation of Paris and established a government for Free France. On October 21, 1945, France voted to end the Third Republic and adopted a new constitution as the basis of the Fourth Republic. The French people had experienced defeat, disgrace, deprivation, and suffering. Hostility and quarrels over who had done what during the occupation and under Vichy divided them for decades.

Great Britain: Organization for Victory

On May 22, 1940, the British Parliament gave the government emergency powers. Together with others already in effect, this measure allowed the government to institute compulsory military service, rationing, and economic controls.

To deal with the crisis, all British political parties joined in a national government under Winston Churchill. Churchill and the British war cabinet moved as quickly as possible to mobilize the nation. Perhaps the most pressing immediate need was to produce airplanes to fight the Germans in the Battle of Britain. Lord Beaverbrook (1879–1964), one of Britain's most important newspaper publishers, led this effort. The demand for more planes and other armaments inspired a campaign to reclaim scrap metal. Wrought-iron fences, kitchen pots and pans, and every conceivable metal object were collected for the war effort. This was only one successful example of the many ways the civilian population enthusiastically engaged in the struggle.

By the end of 1941, British production had already surpassed Germany's. To meet the heavy demands on the labor force, factory hours were extended and many women joined the workforce. Unemployment disappeared, and the working classes had more money to spend than they had enjoyed for many years. To avoid inflation caused by increased demand for an inadequate supply of consumer goods, savings were encouraged, and taxes were raised to absorb the excess purchasing power.

The "blitz" air attacks in 1940–1941 were the most immediate and dramatic experience of the war for the British people. The German air raids killed thousands of people and left many others homeless. Once the bombing began, many families removed their children to the countryside. Ironically, the rescue effort improved the standard of living of many of the children, for the government paid for their food and medication. The government issued gas masks to thousands of city dwellers, who were frequently compelled to take shelter from the bombs in the London subways.

After the spring of 1941, Hitler needed most of his air force on the Russian front, but the bombing of Britain continued, killing more than 30,000 people by the end of the war. Terrible as it was, this toll was much smaller

Fire engulfs a building in London, England, during the German air raids. Despite many casualties and widespread devastation, the German bombing of London did not break British morale or prevent the city from functioning. Getty Images

than the number of Germans Allied bombing killed. In England, as in Germany, however, the bombing may have made people more determined.

The British made many sacrifices. Transportation facilities were strained simply from carrying enough coal to heat homes and run factories. Food and clothing for civilians were scarce and strictly rationed. Every scrap of land was farmed, increasing the productive portion by almost 4 million acres. Gasoline was scarce, and private vehicles almost vanished.

The British established their own propaganda machine to influence the Continent. The British Broadcasting Company (BBC) sent programs to every country in Europe in the local language to encourage resistance to the Nazis. At home, the government used the radio to unify the nation. Soldiers at the front heard the same programs their families did at home. The most famous program, second only to Churchill's speeches, was *It's That Man Again*, a humorous broadcast filled with imaginary figures that the entire nation came to treasure.

Strangely, for the broad mass of the population, the standard of living improved during the war. The general health of the nation also improved, for reasons that are still not clear. These improvements should not be exaggerated, but they did occur, and many connected them with the active involvement of the government in the economy and in the lives of the citizens. This wartime experience may have contributed to the Labour Party's victory in 1945; many feared a return to Conservative Party rule would also mean a return to the economic problems and unemployment of the 1930s.

The Soviet Union: "The Great Patriotic War"

The war against Germany came as a great surprise to Stalin and the Soviet Union. The German attack violated the 1939 pact with Hitler and put the government of the Soviet Union on the defensive militarily and politically. It showed the failure of Stalin's foreign policy and the ineptness of his preparation for war. He claimed the pact had given the nation an extra year and a half to prepare for war, but this was clearly a lame and implausible excuse in light of the ease of Germany's early victories. Within days, German troops occupied much of the western Soviet Union. The communist government feared that Soviet citizens in the occupied zones—many of whom were not ethnic Russians—might welcome the Germans as liberators. The Stalinist regime had harshly oppressed these Soviet citizens.

No nation suffered more during World War II than the Soviet Union. Perhaps as many as 16 million people were killed, and vast numbers of Soviet troops were taken prisoner. Hundreds of cities and towns and well over half of the industrial and transportation facilities of the country were devastated. From 1942, thousands of Soviet prisoners worked in German factories as forced labor. The Germans also seized grain, mineral resources, and oil from the Soviet Union.

Stalin conducted the war as the virtual chief of the armed forces, and the State Committee for Defense provided strong central coordination. In the decade before the war, Stalin had already made the Soviet Union a highly centralized state; he had tried to manage the entire economy from Moscow through the Five Year Plan, the collectivization of agriculture, and the purges. The country was thus already on what amounted to a wartime footing long before the conflict erupted. When the war began, millions of citizens entered the army, but the army itself did not grow in influence at the expense of the state and the Communist Party—that is, of Stalin. He was suspicious of the generals, though he had presumably eliminated officers of doubtful loyalty in the purges of the late 1930s. As the war continued, however, the army gained more freedom of action, and eventually the generals were no longer subservient to party commissars. The power of Stalin and the nature of Soviet government and society, however, still sharply limited the army.

Soviet propaganda was different from that of other nations. Because the Soviet government distrusted the loyalty of its citizens, it confiscated radios to prevent the people from listening to German or British propaganda. In cities, the government broadcast to the people over loudspeakers in place of radios. During the war, Soviet propaganda emphasized Russian patriotism rather than traditional Marxist themes that stressed class conflict. The struggle against the Germans was called "The Great Patriotic War."

The regime republished great Russian novels of the past and printed more than half a million copies of Tolstoy's *War and Peace*, which was set during Napoleon's invasion of Russia, during the siege of Leningrad (Saint Petersburg). Authors wrote straightforward propaganda fostering hatred of the Germans. Serge Eisenstein (1898–1948), the great filmmaker (see "Encountering the Past: Cinema of the Political Left and Right," Chapter 27), produced a vast epic titled *Ivan the Terrible*, which glorified this brutal sixteenth-century tsar. Composers wrote music to evoke heroic emotions. The most important of these was Dimitri Shostakovich's (1906–1975) *Leningrad Symphony*.

The pressure of war led Stalin to make peace with the Russian Orthodox Church, and the Patriarch of Moscow urged resistance to the Germans. Stalin hoped this new policy would increase his support at home and in Eastern Europe, where the Orthodox Church predominated.

Within occupied portions of the western Soviet Union, an active resistance movement harassed the Germans. The swiftness of the German invasion had stranded thousands of Soviet troops behind German lines. Some escaped and carried on guerrilla warfare behind enemy lines. Stalin supported partisan forces in lands the enemy held for two reasons: He wanted to cause as much difficulty as possible for the Germans, and Soviet-sponsored resistance reminded the peasants that the Soviet government had not disappeared. Stalin feared the peasants' hatred of the communist government and collectivization might lead them to collaborate with the invaders. When the Soviet army moved westward, it incorporated the partisans into the regular army.

As its armies reclaimed the occupied areas and then moved across Eastern and Central Europe, the Soviet Union established itself as a world power second only to the United States. Stalin had entered the war a reluctant belligerent, but he emerged a major victor. In that respect, the war and the extraordinary patriotic effort and sacrifice it generated consolidated the power of Stalin and the party more effectively than the political and social policies of the previous decade.

▼ Preparations for Peace

The split between the Soviet Union and its wartime allies should cause no surprise. As the self-proclaimed center of world communism, the Soviet Union was openly dedicated to the overthrow of the capitalist nations. The Soviets muted this message, however, when the occasion demanded. On the other side, the Western allies were no less open about their hostility to communism and its chief purveyor, the Soviet Union. Although they had been friendly in the early stages of the 1917 Russian Revolution, they had intervened to try to overthrow the Bolshevik regime during the resulting civil war. The United States did not grant formal recognition to the USSR until 1933. The Western powers' exclusion of the Soviets from the Munich conference and Stalin's pact with Hitler did nothing to improve relations between them during the war.

Nonetheless, the need to cooperate against a common enemy and strenuous propaganda efforts helped improve Western feeling toward the Soviet ally. Still, Stalin remained suspicious and critical of the Western war effort, and Churchill was determined to contain the Soviet advance into Europe. Roosevelt perhaps had been more hopeful that the Allies could continue to work together after the war, but even he was losing faith by 1945. Differences in historical development and ideology, as well as traditional conflicts over political power and influence, soon dashed hopes of a mutually satisfactory peace settlement and continued cooperation to uphold it.

The Atlantic Charter

In August 1941, even before the Americans were at war, Roosevelt and Churchill met on a ship off Newfoundland and agreed to the Atlantic Charter. This broad set of principles in the spirit of Wilson's Fourteen Points provided a theoretical basis for the peace they sought. When Russia and the United States joined Britain in the war, the three powers entered a purely military alliance in January 1942, leaving all political questions aside. The first political conference was the meeting of foreign ministers in Moscow in October 1943. The ministers reaffirmed earlier agreements to fight on until the enemy surrendered unconditionally and to continue cooperating after the war in a united-nations organization.

Read the **Document** "Franklin D. Roosevelt and Winston Churchill, 'The Atlantic Charter' " on **MyHistoryLab.com**

Tehran: Agreement on a Second Front

The first meeting of the leaders of the "Big Three" (the USSR, Britain, and the United States) took place at Tehran, the capital of Iran, in 1943. Western promises to open a second front in France the next summer (1944) and Stalin's agreement to fight Japan when Germany was defeated created an atmosphere of goodwill in which to discuss a postwar settlement. Stalin wanted to retain what he had gained in his pact with Hitler and to dismember Germany. Roosevelt and Churchill were conciliatory but made no firm commitments.

NEGOTIATIONS AMONG THE ALLIES

August 1941	Churchill and Roosevelt meet off Newfoundland to sign Atlantic Charter
October 1943	American, British, and Soviet foreign ministers meet in Moscow
November 1943	Churchill, Roosevelt, and Stalin meet at Tehran
October 1944	Churchill meets with Stalin in Moscow
February 1945	Churchill, Roosevelt, and Stalin meet at Yalta
July 1945	Attlee, Stalin, and Truman meet at Potsdam

The most important decision was the one that chose Europe's west coast as the main point of attack instead of the Mediterranean. That meant, in retrospect, that Soviet forces would occupy Eastern Europe and control its destiny. At Tehran in 1943, the Western allies did not foresee this clearly, for the Russians were still fighting deep within their own frontiers, and military considerations were paramount.

Churchill and Stalin By 1944, the situation had changed. In August, Soviet armies were before Warsaw, which had revolted against the Germans in expectation of liberation, but the Russians halted and turned south into the Balkans, allowing the Germans to annihilate the Poles. The Russians gained control of Romania, Bulgaria, and Hungary, advances that centuries of expansionist tsars had only dreamed of achieving. Alarmed by these developments, Churchill went to Moscow and met with Stalin in October. They agreed to share power in the Balkans on the basis of Soviet predominance in Romania and Bulgaria, Western predominance in Greece, and equality of influence in Yugoslavia and Hungary. These agreements were not enforceable without American approval, and the Americans were hostile to such un-Wilsonian devices as "spheres of influence."

Germany The three powers easily agreed on Germany—its disarmament, de-Nazification, and division

In February 1945, Churchill, Roosevelt, and Stalin met at Yalta in the Crimea to plan for the organization of Europe after the end of the war. The Big Three are seated. Standing behind President Roosevelt is Admiral William D. Leahy. Behind the prime minister are Admiral Sir Andrew Cunningham and Air Marshal Portal. U.S. Army Photograph into four zones of occupation by France and the Big Three. Churchill, however, began to balk at Stalin's demand for $20 billion in reparations as well as forced labor from all the zones, with Russia to get half of everything. These matters festered and caused dissension in the future.

Eastern Europe The settlement of Eastern Europe was equally thorny. Everyone agreed the Soviet Union deserved to have friendly neighboring governments, but the West insisted they also be autonomous and democratic. The Western leaders, particularly Churchill, were not eager to see Russia dominate Eastern Europe. They were also, especially Roosevelt, committed to democracy and self-determination.

Stalin, however, knew that independent, freely elected governments in Poland, Hungary, and Romania would not be friendly to Russia. He had already established a puppet government in Poland in competition with the Polish government-in-exile in London. Under pressure from the Western leaders, however, he agreed to include some Poles friendly to the West in it. He also signed a Declaration on Liberated Europe, promising self-determination and free democratic elections.

Stalin may have been eager to avoid conflict before the war with Germany was over. He was always afraid the Allies would make a separate peace with Germany and betray him, and he probably thought it worth endorsing some hollow principles as the price of continued harmony. In any case, he wasted little time violating these agreements.

Yalta

The next meeting of the Big Three was at Yalta in Crimea in February 1945. The Western armies had not yet crossed the Rhine, but the Soviet army was within a hundred miles of Berlin. (See Map 28–8.) The war with Japan continued, and no atomic explosion had yet taken place. Roosevelt, faced with a prospective invasion of Japan and heavy losses, was eager to bring the Russians into the Pacific war as soon as possible. As a true Wilsonian, he also suspected Churchill's determination to maintain the British Empire and Britain's colonial advantages. The Americans thought Churchill's plan to set up British spheres of influence in Europe would encourage the Russians to do the same and would lead to friction and war. To encourage Russian participation in the war against Japan, Roosevelt and Churchill made extensive concessions to Russia, ceding the Soviets Sakhalin and the Kurile Islands, and accommodating some of their desires in Korea and in Manchuria.

Watch the **Video** "The Big Three Confer—Yalta Conference" on **MyHistoryLab.com**

Map 28–8 **YALTA TO THE SURRENDER** "The Big Three"—Roosevelt, Churchill, and Stalin—met at Yalta in the Crimea in February 1945. At the meeting, concessions were made to Stalin concerning the settlement of Eastern Europe because Roosevelt was eager to bring the Russians into the Pacific war as soon as possible. This map shows the positions held by the victors when Germany surrendered.

Again in the tradition of Wilson, Roosevelt emphasized a united-nations organization: "Through the United Nations, he hoped to achieve a self-enforcing peace settlement that would not require American troops, as well as an open world without spheres of influence in which American enterprise could work freely."[5] Soviet agreement on these points seemed worth concessions elsewhere.

Potsdam

The Big Three met for the last time in the Berlin suburb of Potsdam in July 1945. Much had changed since the previous conference. Germany had been defeated, and

[5]Robert O. Paxton, *Europe in the Twentieth Century* (New York: Harcourt Brace Jovanovich, 1975), p. 487.

news of the successful explosion of an atomic weapon reached the American president during the meetings. The cast of characters was also different: President Truman replaced the deceased Roosevelt, and Clement Attlee (1883–1967), leader of the Labour Party that had just won a general election, replaced Churchill as Britain's spokesperson during the conference. Previous agreements were reaffirmed, but progress on undecided questions was slow.

Russia's western frontier was moved far into what had been Poland and included most of German East Prussia. In compensation, Poland was allowed "temporary administration" over the rest of East Prussia and Germany east of the Oder-Neisse River, a condition that became permanent. In effect, Poland was moved about a hundred miles west, at the expense of Germany, to accommodate the Soviet Union. The Allies agreed to divide Germany into occupation zones until the final peace treaty was signed. Germany remained divided until 1990.

View the Map "Interactive Map: Post World War II Division of Austria and Germany" on **MyHistoryLab.com**

A Council of Foreign Ministers was established to draft peace treaties for Germany's allies. Growing disagreements made the job difficult, and Italy, Romania, Hungary, Bulgaria, and Finland did not sign treaties until February 1947. The Russians were dissatisfied with the treaty that the United States made with Japan in 1951 and signed their own agreements with the Japanese in 1956. These disagreements were foreshadowed at Potsdam.

In Perspective

The second great war of the twentieth century (1939–1945) grew out of the unsatisfactory resolution of the first. In retrospect, the two wars appear to some people to be one continuous conflict, a kind of twentieth-century "Thirty Years' War," with two main periods of fighting separated by an uneasy truce. To others, that point of view oversimplifies by implying the second war was the inevitable result of the first and its inadequate peace treaties. The latter opinion seems more sound, for, whatever the flaws of the treaties of Paris, the world suffered an even more terrible war than the first because of failures of judgment and will by the victorious democratic powers.

Between the two wars, the United States, which had become the wealthiest and potentially the strongest nation in the world, disarmed almost entirely and withdrew into a shortsighted and foolish isolation. Therefore, it played no important part in restraining the angry and ambitious dictators who brought on the war. Britain and France refused to face the threat the Axis powers posed until the most deadly war in history was required to put it down. If the victorious democracies had remained strong, responsible, and realistic, they could have remedied whatever injustices or mistakes arose from the treaties without endangering the peace.

The second war itself was so plainly a world war that little need be said to indicate its global character. If the Japanese occupation of Manchuria in 1931 was not technically a part of that war, it was a significant precursor. Moreover, there were Italy's attack on the African nation of Ethiopia in 1935; the Italian, German, and Soviet interventions in the Spanish Civil War (1936–1939); and Japan's attack on China in 1937. These acts revealed that aggressive forces were on the march around the globe and the defenders of the world order lacked the will to stop them. The formation of the Axis incorporating Germany, Italy, and Japan guaranteed that when the war came, it would be fought around the world.

There was fighting and suffering in Asia, Africa, the Pacific islands, and Europe, and men and women from all the inhabited continents took part in them. The use of atomic weapons brought the frightful struggle to a close. Still, what are called conventional weapons did almost all the damage; their level of destructiveness threatened the survival of civilization, even without the use of atomic or nuclear devices.

World War II ended not with unsatisfactory peace treaties, but with no treaty at all in the European arena, where the war had begun. The world quickly split into two unfriendly camps: the western, led by the United States, and the eastern, led by the Soviet Union. This division, among other things, hastened the liberation of former colonial territories. The bargaining power of the new nations that emerged from them was temporarily increased as the two rival superpowers tried to gain their friendship or allegiance. It became customary to refer to these nations as "the Third World" or "developing countries," with the former Soviet Union and the United States and their respective allies being the first two. Time has shown that the differences among Third World nations are so great that the term is all but meaningless.

The surprising treatment the defeated powers of World War II received was also largely the result of the emergence of the Cold War. Instead of holding them back, the Western powers installed democratic governments in Italy, West Germany, and Japan, took them into the Western alliances designed to contain communism, and helped them recover economically. All three are now among the richest nations in the world.

KEY TERMS

Anschluss (p. 902)
appeasement (p. 900)
Axis (p. 900)
blitzkrieg (p. 907)
Holocaust (p. 920)
Lebensraum (p. 899)
Luftwaffe (p. 909)
Third Reich (p. 911)

REVIEW QUESTIONS

1. What were Hitler's foreign policy aims? Was he bent on conquest, or did he simply want to return Germany to its 1914 boundaries?
2. Why did Britain and France adopt a policy of appeasement in the 1930s? Did the West buy valuable time to rearm at Munich in 1938?
3. How was Hitler able to defeat France so easily in 1940? Why did the air war against Britain fail? Why did Hitler invade Russia? Could the invasion have succeeded?
4. Why did Japan attack the United States at Pearl Harbor? How important was American intervention in the war? Why did the United States drop atomic bombs on Japan? Was President Truman right to use the bombs?
5. How did experiences on the domestic front in Britain differ from those in Germany and France? What impact did "The Great Patriotic War" have on the people of the Soviet Union?
6. What was Hitler's "final solution" to the Jewish question? Why did he want to eliminate Slavs as well? To what extent can it be said the Holocaust was the defining event of the twentieth century?

SUGGESTED READINGS

O. Bartov, *Mirrors of Destruction: War, Genocide, and Modern Identity* (2000). Remarkably penetrating essays.
A. Beevor, *The Spanish Civil War* (2001). Particularly strong on the political issues.
R. S. Botwinick, *A History of the Holocaust*, 2nd ed. (2002). A brief, but useful account of the causes, character, and results of the Holocaust.
C. Browning, *The Origins of the Final Solution: The Evolution of the Nazi Jewish Policy* (2004). The story of how Hitler's policy developed from discrimination to annihilation.
W. S. Churchill, *The Second World War*, 6 vols. (1948–1954). The memoirs of the great British leader.
A. Crozier, *The Causes of the Second World War* (1997). An examination of what brought on the war.
J. C. Fest, *Hitler* (2002). A fine Hitler biography.
R. B. Frank, *Downfall: The End of the Imperial Japanese Empire* (1998). A thorough, well-documented account of the last months of the Japanese Empire and why it surrendered.
J. L. Gaddis, *We Now Know: Rethinking Cold War History* (1998). A fine account of the early Cold War using new evidence emerging since the collapse of the Soviet Union.
J. L. Gaddis, P. H. Gordon, and E. May eds., *Cold War Statesmen Confront the Bomb: Nuclear Diplomacy since 1945* (1999). Essays on the effect of atomic and nuclear weapons on diplomacy since World War II.
M. Gilbert, *The Holocaust: A History of the Jews of Europe during the Second World War* (1985). The best and most comprehensive treatment.
M. Hastings, *The Second World War: A World in Flames* (2004). A fine account by a leading student of contemporary warfare.
A. Iriye, *Pearl Harbor and the Coming of the Pacific War* (1999). Essays on how the Pacific war came about, including a selection of documents.
W. F. Kimball, *Forged in War: Roosevelt, Churchill, and the Second World War* (1998). A study of the collaboration between the two great leaders of the West.
M. Knox, *Common Destiny, Dictatorship, Foreign Policy, and War in Fascist Italy and Nazi Germany* (2000). A brilliant comparison between the two dictatorships.
M. Knox, *Mussolini Unleashed* (1982). An outstanding study of fascist Italy in World War II.
W. Murray, *The Change in the European Balance of Power 1938–1939* (1984). A brilliant study of the relationship among strategy, foreign policy, economics, and domestic politics.
W. Murray and A. R. Millett, *A War to Be Won: Fighting the Second World War* (2000). A splendid account of military operations.
P. Neville, *Hitler and Appeasement: The British Attempt to Prevent the Second World War* (2005). A defense of the British appeasers of Hitler.
R. Overy, *Why the Allies Won* (1997). An analysis of the reasons for the Allied victory with emphasis on technology.
N. Rich, *Hitler's War Aims*, 2 vols. (1973–1974). The best study of the subject in English.
A. Roberts, *The Storm of War: A New History of the Second World War* (2011). A concise, yet comprehensive up-to-date history.
D. Vital, *A People Apart: The Jews in Europe, 1789–1939* (1999). A major survey with excellent discussions of the interwar period.
Z. S. Steiner, *The Triumph of the Dark: European International History, 1933–1939* (2011). A masterly narrative and analysis of the years leading to war.
R. Wade, *The Russian Revolution, 1917* (2000). A fine account that includes political and social history.
G. L. Weinberg, *A World at Arms: A Global History of World War II*, 2nd ed. (2005). An excellent narrative.

MyHistoryLab™ Media Assignments

Find these resources in the Media Assignments folder for Chapter 28 on MyHistoryLab.

QUESTIONS FOR ANALYSIS

1. To what extent do the three principles underpinning the solid "house" of France reflect Nazi values?

   ***Section:* The Domestic Fronts**
   View the **Closer Look** The Vichy Regime in France, p. 927

2. What imagery does Franco use in this speech to appeal to the Spanish people?

   ***Section:* Again the Road to War (1933–1939)**
   Read the **Document** Speech to Spaniards (1936) Francisco Franco, p. 900

3. How does this film clip add to your understanding of the meeting of the "Big Three"?

   ***Section:* Preparations for Peace**
   Watch the **Video** The Big Three Confer—Yalta Conference, p. 932

4. How does the author account for the defeat of France?

   ***Section:* World War II (1939–1945)**
   Read the **Document** Marc Bloch, from *Strange Defeat*, p. 908

5. Is this document primarily a reaction to Nazi aggression, or does it have broader aims?

   ***Section:* Preparations for Peace**
   Read the **Document** Franklin D. Roosevelt and Winston Churchill, "The Atlantic Charter," p. 930

OTHER RESOURCES FROM THIS CHAPTER

Again the Road to War (1933–1939)

Read the **Document** Adolf Hitler, *Mein Kampf*, p. 899

View the **Closer Look** An Ethiopian View of the Battle of Adowa, p. 900

View the **Image** Spanish Civil War poster, p. 901

View the **Image** Hitler and Chamberlain, 1938, p. 903

View the **Map** The Partitions of Czechoslovakia and Poland 1938–1939, p. 903

Read the **Compare and Connect** The Munich Settlement, p. 904

Read the **Document** Adolf Hitler, "The Obersalzberg Speech," p. 906

World War II (1939–1945)

Read the **Document** Winston Churchill, "Their Finest Hour" (Great Britain), 1940, p. 909

View the **Image** Nazis Executing Russian Civilians, p. 910

Watch the **Video** Video: FDR on Winning the War, p. 912

View the **Image** Eisenhower and U.S. Troops before D-Day, p. 916

Read the **Document** An Eyewitness to Hiroshima (1945), p. 918

Racism and the Holocaust

View the **Image** Liberating the Concentration Camps, p. 924

Preparations for Peace

View the **Map** Interactive Map: Post World War II Division of Austria and Germany, p. 933

A statue of Queen Victoria is removed from the front of the Supreme Court building in Georgetown, former capital of the British colony of Guyana, in February 1970, in preparation for the transition to independence. Decolonization represented as dramatic a transition in world political relations as had the establishment of European empires in the nineteenth-century Victorian age. Bettmann/CORBIS—

Listen to the **Chapter Audio** on **MyHistoryLab.com**

29

The Cold War Era, Decolonization, and the Emergence of a New Europe

▼ **The Emergence of the Cold War**
Containment in American Foreign Policy • Soviet Domination of Eastern Europe • The Postwar Division of Germany • NATO and the Warsaw Pact • The Creation of the State of Israel • The Korean War

▼ **The Khrushchev Era in the Soviet Union**
Khrushchev's Domestic Policies • The Three Crises of 1956

▼ **Later Cold War Confrontations**
The Berlin Wall • The Cuban Missile Crisis

▼ **The Brezhnev Era**
1968: The Invasion of Czechoslovakia • The United States and Détente • The Invasion of Afghanistan • Communism and Solidarity in Poland • Relations with the Reagan Administration

▼ **Decolonization: The European Retreat from Empire**
Major Areas of Colonial Withdrawal • India • Further British Retreat from Empire

▼ **The Turmoil of French Decolonization**
France and Algeria • France and Vietnam • Vietnam Drawn into the Cold War • Direct United States Involvement

▼ **The Collapse of European Communism**
Gorbachev Attempts to Reform the Soviet Union • 1989: Revolution in Eastern Europe • The Collapse of the Soviet Union • The Yeltsin Decade

▼ **The Collapse of Yugoslavia and Civil War**

▼ **Putin and the Resurgence of Russia**

▼ **The Rise of Radical Political Islamism**
Arab Nationalism • The Iranian Revolution • Afghanistan and Radical Islamism

▼ **A Transformed West**

▼ **In Perspective**

LEARNING OBJECTIVES

What were the origins of the Cold War?

How did the Berlin Wall and the Cuban Missile Crisis strain relations between the United States and the Soviet Union?

What impact did Brezhnev have on the Soviet Union and Eastern Europe?

How did World War II serve as a catalyst for decolonization?

Why was France so reluctant to decolonize?

Why did European communism collapse?

How did ethnic tensions lead to civil war in Yugoslavia?

What vision does Putin have of Russia's place in the world?

What forces gave rise to radical political Islamism?

How did the events of September 11, 2001, transform the West?

SINCE THE END of World War II in 1945, two often interrelated sets of fundamental, international political relationships have shaped the experience of Europe, the United States, and the wider global community. These were the Cold War between the United States and the Soviet Union and the long process of **decolonization**, whereby the peoples of those regions of the world formally or informally dominated by European nations and later by the United States have rejected that domination.

From the end of World War II in 1945 until the collapse of communist regimes in Eastern Europe between 1989 and 1991, the Soviet Union and the United States—two nuclear-armed superpowers—confronted each other in a simmering conflict known as the **Cold War**. While it lasted, this conflict dominated global politics and threatened the peace of Europe, which stood divided between the U.S.-dominated North Atlantic Treaty Organization (**NATO**) and the Soviet-dominated **Warsaw Pact**.

Decolonization very rapidly became enmeshed with the Cold War. As the nations of Europe retreated from empire, the rivalry between the two superpowers expanded into a contest for dominance in the postcolonial world. Superpower intervention aggravated local conflicts on every continent. In its efforts to limit communism, the United States became embroiled in bitter wars in Korea and Vietnam. The struggle between Israel and the Arab nations likewise became an arena of superpower conflict.

In the almost two decades since the collapse of the Soviet Union, the United States has remained the world's single superpower. It has become symbolically identified as embodying the political, economic, and cultural values of modern Western civilization. In this role, it has replaced Europe as the object of anti-Western resistance. One of the numerous results of this new situation is the clash between the United States and radical political Islamism. The result has been the terrorist attacks on the United States on September 11, 2001, and the subsequent American intervention in Afghanistan and Iraq.

One way to think of the past sixty years is to see the history of Western civilization as entering a new global era. Europe and later the United States had been active across the world scene since the end of the fifteenth century. Europe had created formal and informal regions of empire by the early twentieth century. However, commencing strongly in the 1930s and continuing to the present day, those once colonially dominated areas of the world have actively impacted upon the international relations and domestic politics of many European nations and of the United States rather than remaining regions largely subject to Western economic, political, and military influence. The give and take of political, economic, military, and cultural power has become far more reciprocal between the West and the rest of the global community.

▼ The Emergence of the Cold War

The tense relationship between the United States and the Soviet Union began in the closing months of World War II. Some scholars attribute the hardening of the atmosphere between the two countries to Harry Truman's assumption of the presidency in April 1945, after the death of the more sympathetic Franklin Roosevelt, and to the American possession of an effective atomic bomb. Evidence suggests, however, that Truman was trying to carry Roosevelt's policies forward and that Soviet actions in Eastern Europe had begun to distress Roosevelt himself. Some have also argued that Truman did not use the atomic bomb to try to keep Russia out of the Pacific. On the contrary, he worked hard to ensure Russian intervention against Japan in 1945. In part, the coldness between the Allies arose from the mutual feeling that each had violated previous agreements. The Russians were plainly asserting permanent control of Poland and Romania under puppet communist governments. The United States was taking a harder line about German reparation payments to the Soviet Union.

In retrospect, however, and as more information emerges from the previously closed Soviet archives, it appears unlikely that friendlier styles on either side could have avoided a split that arose from basic differences of ideology and interest. The Soviet Union's attempt to extend its control westward into central Europe and the Balkans and southward into the Middle East continued the general thrust of the foreign policy of tsarist Russia. Britain had traditionally tried to restrain Russian expansion into these areas, and the United States inherited that task as Britain's power waned.

Beyond considerations of traditional power politics and international rivalries lay the special problem posed by contradictory ideologies firmly held by the two great victorious nations. The Soviet Union was a communist autocracy that had long proclaimed its intention to bring its economic, social, and political system to the rest of the world and to eliminate the democratic, capitalistic world order. The United States was no less eager to encourage and foster democracy and free enterprise and especially to prevent the Soviets from dominating Europe. In light of that conflict it is hard to see how serious competition could have been avoided. What is truly remarkable is that such a contest could go on for decades without a direct military conflict between the antagonists.

The Americans made no attempt to roll back Soviet power where it existed at the close of World War II. (See Map 29–1, p. 938.) At the time, American military forces were the greatest in U.S. history, American industrial power was unmatched in the world, and atomic weapons were an American monopoly. In less than a year from the war's end, the Americans had reduced their forces in Europe from 3.5 million to 500,000. The speed of the withdrawal reflected domestic pressure to "get the boys

Map 29–1 **TERRITORIAL CHANGES IN EUROPE AFTER WORLD WAR II** The map shows the shifts in territory that followed the defeat of the Axis. No treaty of peace formally ended the war with Germany.

home" but was also fully in accord with America's peacetime plans and goals, which included support for self-determination, autonomy, and democracy in the political sphere, and free trade, freedom of the seas, no barriers to investment, and an Open Door policy in the economic sphere. These goals reflected American principles and served American interests well. As the strongest, richest nation in the world—the one with the greatest industrial base and the strongest currency—the United States would benefit handsomely from an international order based on such goals.

Although postwar American hostility to colonial empires created tensions with France and Britain, the main conflict lay with the Soviet Union. The growth in France and Italy of large popular communist parties taking orders from Moscow led the Americans to believe that Stalin was engaged in a worldwide plot to subvert capitalism and democracy. From the Soviet perspective, extending the borders of the USSR and dominating the formerly independent successor states of Eastern Europe would provide needed security and compensate for the fearful losses the Soviet people had endured in the war. The Soviets could thus see American resistance to their expansion as a threat to their security and their legitimate aims. They considered American objections to Soviet actions in Poland and other states as an effort to undermine regimes friendly to Russia and to encircle the Soviet Union with hostile neighbors. The Soviets could also use this point of view to justify their own attempts to overthrow regimes friendly to the United States in Western Europe and elsewhere.

Evidence of the new mood of postwar hostility between the former allies was soon apparent. In February 1946, both Stalin and his foreign minister, Vyacheslav Molotov (1890–1986), publicly spoke of the Western democracies as enemies. A month later, Churchill gave a speech in Fulton, Missouri, in which he declared that an "Iron Curtain" had descended on Europe, dividing a free and democratic West from an East under totalitarian rule. He warned against communist subversion and urged Western unity and strength against the new menace. In this atmosphere, difficulties grew.

Read the **Document** "Joseph Stalin, Excerpts from the 'Soviet Victory' Speech, 1946" on **MyHistoryLab.com**

Read the **Document** "Winston Churchill, from the Iron Curtain Speech, 1946" on **MyHistoryLab.com**

Containment in American Foreign Policy

The resistance of Americans and Western Europeans to what they increasingly perceived as Soviet intransigence and communist plans for subversion and expansion took a clearer form in 1947. The American policy became known as one of **containment**, the purpose of which was to resist the extension of Soviet expansion and influence in the expectation that eventually the Soviet Union would collapse from internal pressures and the burdens of its foreign oppression. This strategy, which American policymakers devised in the late 1940s, would direct the broad outlines of American foreign policy for the next four decades, until the Soviet Union did collapse from exactly such pressures. Containment marked a major departure in American foreign policy and transformed the international situation during the second half of the twentieth century. The execution of the policy led the United States to enter overseas alliances, to make formal and informal commitments of support to regimes around the world it perceived as being anticommunist, to undertake enormous military expenditures, and to send large amounts of money abroad. In all these respects, the United States assumed unprecedented long-term foreign policy responsibilities. The United States thus became a permanent player in European international relations and in areas of the world where only European nations had been involved earlier in the century. (See "Compare and Connect: The Soviet Union and the United States Draw the Lines of the Cold War,." pages 942–943.)

The Truman Doctrine Since 1944, civil war had been raging in Greece between the royalist government restored by Britain and insurgents supported by the communist countries, chiefly Yugoslavia. In 1947, Britain informed the United States it could no longer financially support its Greek allies. On March 12, President Truman asked Congress to provide funds to support Greece and Turkey, which was then under Soviet pressure to yield control of the Dardanelles, and Congress complied. In a speech to Congress that gave these actions much broader significance, the president set forth what came to be called the Truman Doctrine. He advocated a policy of support for "free people who are resisting attempted subjugation by armed minorities or by outside pressures," by implication, anywhere in the world.

The Marshall Plan American aid to Greece and Turkey took the form of military equipment and advisers. For Western Europe, where postwar poverty and hunger fueled the menacing growth of communist parties, the Americans devised the European Recovery Program. Named the **Marshall Plan** after George C. Marshall (1880–1959), the secretary of state who introduced it, this program provided broad economic aid to European states on the sole condition that they work together for their mutual benefit. The Soviet Union and its satellites were invited to participate. Finland and Czechoslovakia were willing to do so, and Poland and Hungary showed interest. The Soviets, however, forbade them to take part.

The Marshall Plan restored prosperity to Western Europe and set the stage for Europe's unprecedented postwar economic growth. In addition to the vast program of American economic aid, the strong Christian Democratic movement that dominated the politics of Italy, France, and West Germany worked to keep communist influence at bay outside the Soviet sphere in Eastern Europe.

Following the declaration of the Truman Doctrine and the announcement of the Marshall Plan, the Soviet Union defined a new era of conflict between the United

President Harry Truman greets Secretary of State George Marshall returning from Europe. Truman and Marshall were the architects of American foreign policy during the early years of the Cold War. Hulton Archive Photos/Getty Images, Inc.

States and itself. (See "Compare and Connect: The Soviet Union and the United States Draw the Lines of the Cold War," pages 942–943.)

Soviet Domination of Eastern Europe

The Soviet determination to control Eastern Europe had both historical and ideological roots. Western European powers had invaded Russia twice in the nineteenth century (under Napoleon in 1812 and during the Crimean War of 1854–1856) and already twice more in the twentieth century. Tsarist Russia had governed most of Poland from the 1790s to 1915 and had intervened at the request of the Austrian Empire to put down the Hungarian revolution in 1849. Russia's interests in Turkey and the lands around the Black Sea were similarly long-standing. Given this history and the Soviet Union's extraordinary losses in World War II, it is not surprising that Soviet leaders sought to use their Eastern European satellites as a buffer against future invasions.

View the Map "Interactive Map: Shifting Borders: Eastern Europe" on **MyHistoryLab.com**

Stalin may have seen containment as a renewed Western attempt to isolate and encircle the USSR. In Eastern Europe, the Soviet Union found numerous supporters among those segments of the population who had opposed the various right-wing movements in those countries before the war and who had fought the Nazis during the war. In the autumn of 1947, Stalin called a meeting in Warsaw of all communist parties from around the globe. There they organized the Communist Information Bureau (Cominform), a revival of the old Comintern, dedicated to spreading revolutionary communism throughout the world. In Western Europe the establishment of the Cominform officially ended the era of the popular front during which communists had cooperated with noncommunist parties. Hard-liners who supported the Soviet line on every issue replaced communist leaders in the West who favored collaboration and reform.

In February 1948, in Prague, Stalin gave a brutal display of his new policy of bringing the governments of Eastern Europe under direct Soviet control. The communists expelled the democratic members of what had been a coalition government and murdered Jan Masaryk (1886–1948), the foreign minister and son of the founder of Czechoslovakia, Thomas Masaryk. President Edvard Beneš (1884–1948) was forced to resign, and Czechoslovakia was brought fully under Soviet rule. There and elsewhere in Eastern Europe, it was clear there would be no multiparty political system.

During the late 1940s, the Soviet Union required the other subject governments in Eastern Europe to impose Stalinist policies, including one-party political systems, close military cooperation with the Soviet Union, the collectivization of agriculture, Communist Party domination of education, and attacks on the churches. Longtime Communist Party officials were purged and condemned in show trials like those that had taken place in Moscow during the late 1930s. The catalyst for this harsh tightening probably was the success of Marshal Josip (Broz) Tito (1892–1980), the leader of communist Yugoslavia, in freeing his country from Soviet domination. Stalin wanted to prevent other Eastern European states from following the Yugoslav example.

MAJOR DATES OF EARLY COLD WAR YEARS

1945	Yalta Conference
1945	Founding of the United Nations
1946	Churchill's Iron Curtain speech
1947 (March)	Truman Doctrine regarding Greece and Turkey
1947 (June)	Announcement of Marshall Plan
1948	Communist takeover in Czechoslovakia
1948	Communist takeover in Hungary
1948–1949	Berlin blockade
1949	NATO founded
1949	East and West Germany emerge as separate states
1950–1953	Korean conflict
1955	Warsaw Pact founded

The Postwar Division of Germany

Soviet actions, especially those in Czechoslovakia, increased the determination of the United States to go ahead with its own arrangements in Germany.

Disagreements over Germany During the war, the Allies had never decided how to treat Germany after its defeat. At first they all agreed it should be dismembered, but they differed on how. By the time of Yalta, Churchill had come to fear Russian control of Eastern and central Europe and began to oppose dismemberment.

The Allies also differed on economic policy. The Russians swiftly dismantled German industry in the eastern zone, but the Americans acted differently in the western zone. They concluded that if they followed the Soviet policy, the United States would have to support Germany economically for the foreseeable future. It would also cause chaos and open the way for communism. They preferred, therefore, to try to make Germany self-sufficient, and this meant restoring, rather than destroying, its industrial capacity. To the Soviets, the restoration of a powerful industrial Germany, even in the western zone only, was frightening. The same difference of approach hampered agreement on reparations. The Soviets claimed the right to the industrial equipment in all the zones, and the Americans resisted their demands.

Berlin Blockade When the Western powers agreed to go forward with a separate constitution for the western sectors of Germany in February 1948, the Soviets walked out of the joint Allied Control Commission. In the summer of that year, the Western powers issued a new currency in their zone. All four powers governed Berlin, though it was well within the Soviet zone. The Soviets feared the new currency, which was circulating in Berlin at better rates than their own currency. They chose to seal the city off by closing all railroads and highways that led from Berlin to West Germany. Their purpose was to drive the Western powers out of Berlin.

The Western allies responded to the Berlin blockade by airlifting supplies to the city for almost a year. In May 1949, the Russians were forced to reopen access to Berlin. The incident, however, was decisive. It increased tensions and suspicions between the opponents and hastened the separation of Germany into two states. West Germany formally became the German Federal Republic in September 1949, and the eastern region became the German Democratic Republic a month later. Ironically, Germany had been dismembered in a way no one had planned or expected. The two Germanys and the divided city of Berlin, isolated within East Germany, would remain central fixtures in the geopolitics of the Cold War until 1989. (See Map 29–2.)

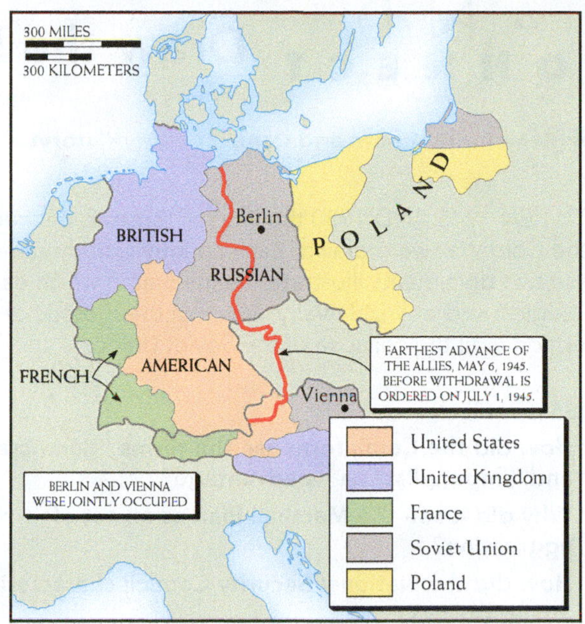

Map 29–2 **OCCUPIED GERMANY AND AUSTRIA** At the war's end, defeated Germany, including Austria, was occupied by the victorious Allies in the several zones shown here. Austria, by prompt agreement, was reestablished as an independent, neutral state, no longer occupied. The German zones hardened into an "East" Germany (the former Soviet zone) and a "West" Germany (the former British, French, and American zones). Berlin, within the Soviet zone, was similarly divided.

NATO and the Warsaw Pact

Meanwhile, the nations of Western Europe had been drawing closer together. The Marshall Plan encouraged international cooperation. In March 1948, Belgium, the Netherlands, Luxembourg, France, and Britain signed the Treaty of Brussels, providing for cooperation in economic and military matters. In April 1949, these nations joined with Italy, Denmark, Norway, Portugal, and Iceland to sign a treaty with Canada and the United States that formed the North Atlantic Treaty Organization (NATO), which committed its members to mutual assistance if any of them was attacked. The NATO treaty transformed the West into a bloc. A few years later, West Germany, Greece, and Turkey joined the alliance. For the first time in history, the United States was committed to defend allies outside the western hemisphere.

A series of bilateral treaties providing for close ties and mutual assistance in case of attack governed Soviet relations with the states of Eastern Europe. In 1949, these states formed the Council of Mutual Assistance (COMECON) to integrate their economies. Unlike the NATO states, the Soviets directly dominated the Eastern alliance system through local communist parties controlled from Moscow and the presence of the Red Army. The Warsaw Pact of May 1955, which included Albania, Bulgaria, Czechoslovakia, East Germany, Hungary, Poland, Romania, and the Soviet Union, gave formal recognition to this system. Europe was divided into two unfriendly blocs. The Cold War had taken firm shape in Europe. (See Map 29–3, p. 944.)

The strategic interests of the United States and the Soviet Union would not, however, permit the Cold War to be limited to the European continent. Major flash points would erupt around the world during the decades that followed, particularly in the Middle East and Asia. The establishment of a communist government in Cuba after 1959 would bring the conflict to the American hemisphere as well. In each case, the Cold War rivalry transformed what might otherwise have been regional conflicts into superpower strategic concerns.

The Creation of the State of Israel

One of the areas of ongoing regional conflict that became a major point of Cold War rivalry was the Middle East. Following World War I, Great Britain had exercised the chief political influence in the region under various mandates from the League of Nations. After World War II, both the Zionist movement, which sought to establish an independent Jewish state, and Arab nationalists, who sought to achieve self-determination, challenged British authority and influence.

COMPARE AND CONNECT The Soviet Union and the United States Draw the Lines of the Cold War

Read the **Compare and Connect** on **MyHistoryLab.com**

BETWEEN 1945 AND 1950 the lines of tensions between the United States and the Soviet Union that became known as the Cold War were drawn. Each country quickly came to define the other as its principal enemy on the world scene. These two documents illustrate the manner in which each nation set its conflict with the other into a larger framework of ideological and political rivalry. Much of the rhetoric of these two documents would characterize the Cold War from its inception until the collapse of the Soviet Union.

QUESTIONS

1. **How did the Cominform use the terms "democratic" and "imperialist" to its advantage?**
2. **Why did it see the Marshall Plan as an act of aggression?**
3. **How did the National Security Council characterize Soviet policy?**
4. **What were the goals of containment?**
5. **Why did the Council urge that the Soviet Union always be given opportunity to save face and to back down with dignity?**
6. **How does each document indicate that both the Soviet Union and the United States regarded their tensions and conflict as part of a wider global political scene?**

I. The Cominform Defines Conflict between the Soviet Union and the United States

In 1947, under the leadership of the Soviet Union, the leaders of the Soviet and East European Communist Parties formed the Communist Information Bureau, which became known as the Cominform. It was organized in the wake of the Truman Doctrine and Marshall Plan. In September 1947, the Communist Parties constituting the Cominform issued a statement that set forth their view of the emerging conflict between the Soviet bloc and the United States. In doing so, they not only attacked the United States, but also the democratic socialist parties of Western Europe that the Soviet Union had seen as an enemy since the days of Lenin.

Fundamental changes have taken place in the international situation as a result of the Second World War and in the post-war period.

These changes are characterized by a new disposition of the basic political forces operating in the world arena, by a change in the relations among the victor states in the Second World War, and their realignment.

. . . The Soviet Union and the other democratic countries regarded as their basic war aims the restoration and consolidation of democratic order in Europe, the eradication of fascism and the prevention of the possibility of new aggression on the part of Germany, and the establishment of a lasting all-round cooperation among the nations of Europe. The United States of America, and Britain in agreement with them, set themselves another aim in the war: to rid themselves of competitors on the markets (Germany and Japan) and to establish their dominant position. . . .

Thus two camps were formed—the imperialist and anti-democratic camp having as its basic aim the establishment of world domination of American imperialism and the smashing of democracy, and the anti-imperialist and democratic camp having as its basic aim the undermining of imperialism, the consolidation of democracy, and the eradication of the remnants of fascism. . . .

. . . the imperialist camp and its leading force, the United States, are displaying particularly aggressive activity. . . . The Truman-Marshall Plan is only a constituent part . . . of the general plan for the policy of global expansion pursued by the United States in all parts of the World. . . .

To frustrate the plan of imperialist aggression the efforts of all the democratic anti-imperialist forces of Europe are necessary. The right-wing Socialists are traitors to this cause. . . . and primarily the French Socialists and the British Labourites . . . by their servility and sycophancy are helping American capital to achieve its aims, provoking it to resort to extortion and impelling their own countries on to a path of vassal-like dependence on the United States of America.

This imposes a special task on the Communist Parties. They must take into their hands the banner of defense of the national independence and sovereignty of their countries. . . .

The principle danger for the working class today lies in underestimating their own strength and overestimating the strength of the imperialist camp. ■

From United States Senate, 81st Congress, 1st Session, Document No. 48, *North Atlantic Treaty: Documents Relating to the North Atlantic Treaty* (Washington, DC: U.S. Government Printing Office, 1949), pp. 117–120, as quoted in Katharine J. Lualdi, *Sources of the Making of the West: Peoples and Culture*, Vol. 2 (Boston: Bedford/St. Martin's Press, 2009), pp. 248–250.

II. The United States National Security Council Proposes to Contain the Soviet Union

In response to the domination of Eastern Europe by Communist Parties dominated by the Soviet Union and the occupation of these nations by Soviet troops, the United States government in 1950 adopted a policy of "containment" of the Soviet Union. This policy had been debated for many months and had for all practical purposes been in effect since the declaration of the Truman Doctrine in 1947. It was formally set forth after a period of implementation in what became known as the National Security Council Paper 68, arguably the most important statement of American foreign policy of the mid-twentieth century. The paper presented the Soviet Union as a nation determined to pursue an expansionist foreign policy and ideological struggle and as a long-term solution to that challenge proposed a policy of containing the influence of the Soviet Union diplomatically and militarily.

The fundamental design of those who control the Soviet Union and the international communist movement is to retain and solidify their absolute power, first in the Soviet Union and second in the areas now under their control. . . .

The design, therefore, calls for the complete subversion or forcible destruction of the machinery of government and structure of society in the countries of the non-Soviet world and their replacement by an apparatus and structure subservient to and controlled from the Kremlin. . . .

Our overall policy at the present time may be described as one designed to foster a world environment in which the American system can survive and flourish. It therefore rejects the concept of isolation and affirms the necessity of our positive participation in the world community.

This broad intention embraces two subsidiary policies. One is a policy which we would probably pursue even if there were no Soviet threat. It is a policy of attempting to develop a healthy international community. The other is the policy of "containing" the Soviet system. . . .

As for the policy of "containment," it is one which seeks by all means short of war to (1) block further expansion of Soviet power, (2) expose the falsities of Soviet pretensions, (3) induce a retraction of the Kremlin's control and influence, and (4) in general, so foster the seeds of destruction within the Soviet system that the Kremlin is brought at least to the point of modifying its behavior to conform to generally accepted international standards. . . .

One of the most important ingredients of power is military strength. . . . Without superior aggregate military strength . . . a policy of "containment"—which is in effect a policy of calculated and gradual coercion—is no more than a policy of bluff.

At the same time, it is essential to the successful conduct of a policy of "containment" that we always leave open the possibility of negotiation with the USSR . . .

In "containment" it is desirable to exert pressure in a fashion which will avoid so far as possible directly challenging Soviet prestige, to keep open the possibility for the USSR to retreat before pressure with a minimum loss of face and to secure political advantage from the failure of the Kremlin to yield or take advantage of the openings we leave it. ■

The Allied airlift in action during the Berlin Blockade. Every day for almost a year Western planes supplied the city until Stalin lifted the blockade in May 1949. Art Resource/Bildarchiv Preussischer Kulturbesitz

From National Security Council, Paper Number 68, *Foreign Relations of the United States* (Washington, DC: U.S. Government Printing Office, 1977), Sections: III, IV, VI, as cited on www.seattleu.edu/artsci/history/us1945/docs/nsc68-1.htm.

Map 29–3 **MAJOR COLD WAR EUROPEAN ALLIANCE SYSTEMS** The North Atlantic Treaty Organization, which includes both Canada and the United States, stretches as far east as Turkey. By contrast, the Warsaw Pact nations were the contiguous Communist states of Eastern Europe, with the Soviet Union, of course, as the dominant member.

British Balfour Declaration The modern state of Israel was the achievement of the world Zionist movement, founded in 1897 by Theodor Herzl (see Chapter 24) and later led by Chaim Weizmann (1874–1952). In 1917, during World War I, Arthur Balfour (1846–1930), the British foreign secretary, declared that Britain favored establishing a national home for the Jewish people in Palestine, which was then under Ottoman rule. Between the wars, thousands of Jews, mainly from Europe, immigrated to what had become British-ruled Palestine. During this period, the *Yishuv*, or Jewish community in Palestine, developed its own political parties, press, labor unions, and educational system. Arabs already living in Palestine considered the Jewish settlers intruders, and violent conflicts ensued. The British tried, but failed, to mediate these clashes.

This situation might have prevailed longer, except for the outbreak of World War II and Hitler's attempt to exterminate the Jews of Europe. The Nazi persecution united Jews throughout the world behind the Zionist ideal of a Jewish state in Palestine, and it touched the conscience of the United States and other Western powers. It seemed morally right to do something for the Jewish refugees from Nazi concentration camps.

The U.N. Resolution In 1947, the British turned over to the United Nations the problem of the relationship of Arabs and Jews in Palestine. That same year, the United Nations passed a resolution dividing the territory into two states, one Jewish and one Arab. The Arabs in Palestine and the surrounding Arab states resisted this resolution. Not unnaturally, they resented the influx of new settlers. Many Palestinian Arabs were displaced and became refugees themselves.

Israel Declares Independence In May 1948, the British officially withdrew from Palestine, and the Yishuv declared the independence of a new Jewish state called *Israel* on May 14. Two days later, the United States, through the personal intervention of President Truman, recognized the new nation, whose first prime minister was David Ben-Gurion (1886–1973). Almost immediately, Lebanon, Syria, Jordan, Egypt, and Iraq invaded Israel. The fighting continued throughout 1948 and 1949. By the end of its war of independence against the Arabs, Israel had expanded its borders beyond the limits the United Nations had originally set forth. Jerusalem was divided between Jordan and Israel. By 1949, Israel had secured its existence, but not the acceptance of its Arab neighbors. As long as Egypt, Jordan, Syria, Lebanon, Iraq, and Saudi Arabia, to name those nations closest, withheld diplomatic recognition from Israel, the peace was only an armed truce. (See Map 29–4.)

Map 29–4 **ISRAEL AND ITS NEIGHBORS IN 1949** The territories gained by Israel in 1949 did not secure peace in the region. In fact, the disposition of those lands and the Arab refugees who live there has constituted the core of the region's unresolved problems to the present day.

The Arab–Israeli conflict would inevitably draw in the superpowers. The dispute directly involved Europe because many of the citizens of Israel had emigrated from there, and Europe, like the United States, was highly dependent on oil from Arab countries. Furthermore, both the United States and the Soviet Union believed they had major strategic and economic interests in the region.

By 1949, the United States had established itself as a firm ally of Israel. Gradually, the Soviet Union began to furnish aid to the Arab nations. The bipolar tensions that had settled over Europe were thus transferred to the Middle East. Furthermore, the existence of the state of Israel would become one of the major points of contention between the United States and the governments of the various Arab states and later one of the chief complaints of radical political Islamists against the United States.

The Korean War

While early stages of the Cold War took place in Europe and the Arab–Israeli conflict developed in the Middle East, the United States confronted armed aggression in Asia. As part of a UN police action, it intervened militarily in Korea, following the same principle of containment that directed its actions in Europe.

Between 1910 and 1945, Japan, as an Asian colonial power, had occupied and exploited the formerly independent kingdom of Korea, but at the close of World War II, the United States and the Soviet Union expelled the Japanese and divided Korea into two parts along the thirty-eighth parallel of latitude. Korea was supposed to be reunited. By 1948, however, two separate states had emerged: the Democratic People's Republic of Korea in the north, supported by the Soviet Union, and the Republic of Korea in the south, supported by the United States.

In late June 1950, after border clashes, North Korea invaded South Korea across the thirty-eighth parallel. The United States intervened, at first unilaterally and then under the authority of a UN resolution. Great Britain, Turkey, Australia, and other countries sent token forces. The Korean police action was technically a UN-sponsored venture to halt aggression. (It had been made possible when Stalin ordered the Soviet ambassador to boycott the United Nations when the key vote was taken.) For the United States, the point of the Korean conflict was to contain the spread and halt the aggression of communism.

Late in 1950, the Chinese, responding to the approach of UN forces near their border, sent troops to support North Korea. The American forces had to retreat. The U.S. policymakers believed, mistakenly, that the Chinese, who, since 1949, had been under the communist government of Mao Zedong (1893–1976), were simply Soviet puppets. Accordingly, the Americans viewed the movement of Chinese troops into Korea as another example of communist pressure against a noncommunist state, similar to what had previously happened in Europe. Today it is clear that Mao disliked Stalin and that tension existed between Moscow and the People's Republic of China, but that was little understood at the time.

On June 16, 1953, the Eisenhower administration concluded an armistice ending the Korean War and restoring the border near the thirty-eighth parallel. (See Map 29–5.) Thousands of American troops, however, are still stationed in Korea. The United States seemed to have successfully applied the lessons of the Cold War it had learned in Europe to Asia. The Korean War confirmed the American government's faith in containment. It also transformed the Cold War into a global rivalry that ranged well beyond Europe.

The formation of NATO and the Korean conflict capped the first round of the Cold War. In 1953, Stalin's death and the armistice in Korea fostered hopes that international tensions might ease. In early 1955, Soviet occupation forces left Austria after that nation accepted neutral status. Later that year, the leaders of France, Great Britain, the Soviet Union, and the United States held a summit conference in Geneva. Nuclear weapons and the future of a divided Germany were the chief items on the agenda. Despite public displays of friendliness, the meeting produced few substantial agreements, and the Cold War soon resumed.

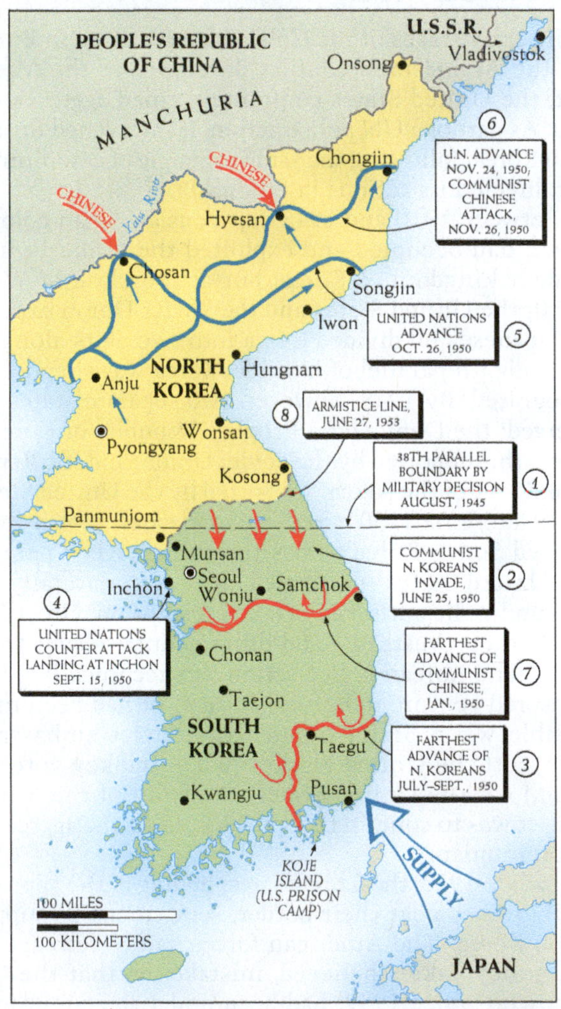

Map 29–5 **KOREA, 1950–1953** This map indicates the major developments in the bitter three-year struggle that followed the North Korean invasion of South Korea in 1950.

▼ The Khrushchev Era in the Soviet Union

No other nation had suffered greater losses or more deprivation during World War II than the Soviet Union. Many Russians had hoped the end of the war would signal a reduction in the scope of the police state and a redirection of the economy away from heavy industry to consumer products. They were disappointed. Stalin did little or nothing to modify the character of the regime he had created. If anything, his determination to centralize his authority and a desire to undertake a new wave of internal purges continued until his death on March 6, 1953.

For a time, no single leader replaced Stalin. Rather, the *presidium* (the renamed Politburo) pursued a policy of collective leadership. Gradually, however, power and influence began to devolve on Nikita Khrushchev (1894–1971), who had been named party secretary in 1953. Three years later, he became premier. Khrushchev's rise ended collective leadership, but he never commanded the extraordinary powers of Stalin.

Khrushchev's Domestic Policies

The Khrushchev era, which lasted until the autumn of 1964, witnessed a retreat from Stalinism, though not from authoritarianism. Khrushchev sought to reform the Soviet system but to maintain the dominance of the Communist Party. Intellectuals were somewhat freer to express their opinions. Although Boris Pasternak (1890–1960), the author of *Dr. Zhivago* (1957), was not permitted to receive the Nobel prize for literature in 1958, another dissident author, Aleksandr Solzhenitsyn (b. 1918), could publish *One Day in the Life of Ivan Denisovich* (1963), a grim account of life in a Soviet labor camp under Stalin. Khrushchev also made modest efforts to meet the demand for more consumer goods and decentralize economic planning. In agriculture, he removed many of the more restrictive regulations on private cultivation and sought to expand the area available for growing wheat. At first, this program led to record grain production, but inappropriate farming techniques soon reduced yields. The Soviet Union had to import vast

MAJOR DATES OF THE EARLY KHRUSHCHEV ERA

1953	Death of Stalin
1955	Austria established as a neutral state
1955	Geneva summit
1956 (February)	Khrushchev's secret speech denouncing Stalin
1956 (Autumn)	Polish crisis
1956 (October)	Suez crisis
1956 (October)	Hungarian uprising
1957	*Sputnik* launched

quantities of grain each year from the United States and other countries.

The Secret Speech of 1956 In February 1956, Khrushchev made an extraordinary departure from expected practice by directly attacking the policies of the Stalin years. At the Twentieth Congress of the Communist Party, Khrushchev gave a secret speech (later published outside the Soviet Union) in which he denounced Stalin and his crimes against socialist justice during the purges of the 1930s. The speech stunned party circles, but it also opened the way for genuine, if limited, internal criticism of the Soviet government and for many of the changes in intellectual and economic life cited earlier. Gradually, Khrushchev removed the strongest supporters of Stalinist policies from the presidium. By 1958, all of Stalin's former supporters were gone, and none had been executed. (See the Document "Khrushchev Denounces the Crimes of Stalin: The Secret Speech,." page 948.)

Khrushchev's speech, however, had repercussions well beyond the borders of the Soviet Union. Communist leaders in Eastern Europe took it as a signal that they could govern with greater leeway than before and retreat from Stalinist policies. Indeed, Khrushchev's speech was simply the first of a number of extraordinary events in 1956.

The Three Crises of 1956

The Suez Intervention In July 1956, President Gamal Abdel Nasser (1918–1970) of Egypt nationalized the Suez Canal. Great Britain and France, who had controlled the private company that had run the canal, feared that this action would close the canal to their supplies of oil in the Persian Gulf. In October 1956, war broke out between Egypt and Israel. The British and French seized the opportunity to intervene militarily; however, the United States refused to support their action. The Soviet Union protested vehemently. The Anglo-French forces had to be withdrawn, and Egypt retained control of the canal.

Watch the Video "Video Lectures: Cold War Connections: Russia, America, Berlin, and Cuba" on **MyHistoryLab.com**

The Suez intervention proved that without the support of the United States the nations of Western Europe could no longer impose their will on the rest of the world. It also appeared that the United States and the Soviet Union had restrained their allies from undertaking actions that might have resulted in a wider conflict. The fact that neither of the superpowers wanted war constrained both Egypt and the Anglo-French forces.

Read the Document "Gamal Abdel Nasser, Speech on the Suez Canal (Egypt), 1956" on **MyHistoryLab.com**

Polish Efforts Toward Independent Action The autumn of 1956 also saw important developments in Eastern Europe that demonstrated similar limitations on independent action among the Soviet bloc nations. When the prime minister of Poland died, the Polish Communist Party leaders refused to replace him with Moscow's nominee, despite considerable pressure from the Soviets. In the end, Wladyslaw Gomulka (1905–1982) emerged as the new Communist leader of Poland. He was the choice of the Poles, and he proved acceptable to the Soviets because he promised continued economic and military cooperation, and particularly because he continued Polish membership in the Warsaw Pact. Within those limits he halted the collectivization of Polish agriculture and improved relations with the Polish Roman Catholic Church.

The Hungarian Uprising Hungary provided the third trouble spot for the Soviet Union. In late October, demonstrations of sympathy for the Poles in Budapest led to street fighting. The Hungarian communists installed a new ministry headed by former premier Imre Nagy (1896–1958). Nagy was a Communist who sought a more independent position for Hungary. He went much further in his demands than Gomulka and directly appealed for political support from noncommunist groups in Hungary. Nagy called for the removal of Soviet troops and the ultimate neutralization of Hungary. He even called for Hungarian withdrawal from the Warsaw Pact. These demands were wholly unacceptable to the Soviet Union. In early November, Soviet troops invaded Hungary; deposed Nagy, who was later executed; and imposed Janos Kadar (1912–1989) as premier.

The events of 1956 in the Middle East and Eastern Europe solidified the position of the United States and the Soviet Union as superpowers. In different ways and to differing degrees, the two superpowers had demonstrated this new political reality to their allies. The nations of Western Europe would be able to make independent policy among themselves within Europe but were generally curtailed from independent action on the broader international scene. For approximately twenty-five years,

Document

KHRUSHCHEV DENOUNCES THE CRIMES OF STALIN: THE SECRET SPEECH

In 1956, Khrushchev denounced Stalin in a secret speech to the Party Congress. The New York Times *published a text of that speech, smuggled from Russia.*

What specific actions by Stalin did Khrushchev denounce? Why does Khrushchev pay so much attention to Stalin's creation of the concept of an "enemy of the people"? Why does Khrushchev distinguish between the actions of Stalin and those of Lenin?

Stalin acted not through persuasion, explanation, and patient cooperation with people, but by imposing his concepts and demanding absolute submission to his opinion. Whoever opposed this concept or tried to prove his viewpoint and the correctness of his position was doomed to removal from the leading collective [group] and to subsequent moral and physical annihilation. . . .

Stalin originated the concept of "enemy of the people." This term automatically rendered it unnecessary that the ideological errors of a man or men engaged in a controversy be proved; this term made possible the usage of the most cruel repression violating all norms of revolutionary legality, against anyone who in any way disagreed with Stalin, against those who were only suspected of hostile intent, against those who had bad reputations.

This concept "enemy of the people" actually eliminated the possibility of any kind of ideological fight or the making of one's views known on this or that issue, even those of a practical character. In the main, and in actuality, the only proof of guilt used, against all norms of current legal science, was the "confession" of the accused himself; and, as a subsequent probing proved, "confessions" were acquired through physical pressures against the accused. . . .

Lenin used severe methods only in the most necessary cases, when the exploiting classes were still in existence and were vigorously opposing the revolution, when the struggle for survival was decidedly assuming the sharpest forms, even including civil war.

Stalin, on the other hand, used extreme methods and mass repressions at a time when the revolution was already victorious, when the Soviet State was strengthened, when the exploiting classes were already liquidated and Socialist relations were rooted solidly in all phases of national economy, when our party was politically consolidated and had strengthened itself both numerically and ideologically. It is clear that here Stalin showed in a whole series of cases his intolerance, his brutality and his abuse of power. Instead of proving his political correctness and mobilizing the masses, he often chose the path of repression and physical annihilation, not only against actual enemies, but also against individuals who had not committed any crimes against the party and the Soviet Government.

From "Krushchev Denounces the Crimes of Stalin: The Secret Speech," *New York Times*, June 5, 1956, pp. 13–16.

the nations of Eastern Europe would be permitted virtually no autonomous actions in either the domestic or the international sphere.

▼ Later Cold War Confrontations

After 1956, the Soviet Union began to talk about "peaceful coexistence" with the United States. With the 1957 launch of *Sputnik*, the first satellite to orbit the earth, the Soviet Union appeared to have achieved an enormous technological superiority over the West. In 1958, the two countries began negotiations toward limiting the testing of nuclear weapons. By 1959, tensions had relaxed sufficiently for Western leaders to visit Moscow and for Khrushchev to tour the United States. A summit meeting was scheduled for May 1960, and President Eisenhower was to go to Moscow.

Just before the Paris Summit Conference, the Soviet Union shot down an American U-2 aircraft that was flying reconnaissance over Soviet territory. Khrushchev demanded an apology from Eisenhower for this air surveillance. Eisenhower accepted full responsibility for the surveillance policy but refused to apologize publicly. Khrushchev then refused to take part in the summit conference, just as the participants arrived in the French capital. The conference, as well as Eisenhower's proposed trip to the Soviet Union, was thus aborted.

The Soviets did not scuttle the summit meeting on the eve of its opening simply because of the American spy flights. They had long been aware of these flights and had other reasons for protesting them when they did. By 1960, the communist world itself had split between the Soviets and the Chinese, who were portraying the Russians as lacking revolutionary zeal. Destroying the summit was, in part, a way to demonstrate the Soviet Union's hard-line attitude toward the capitalist world.

The Berlin Wall

The aborted Paris conference opened the most difficult period of the Cold War. In 1961, the new U.S. president, John F. Kennedy (1917–1963), and Premier Khrushchev met in Vienna with inconclusive results.

Throughout 1961, thousands of refugees from East Germany crossed the border into West Berlin. This outflow of people embarrassed East Germany, hurt its economy, and demonstrated the Soviet Union's inability to control Eastern Europe. Consequently, in August 1961, the East Germans, with Soviet support, erected a concrete wall along the border between East and West Berlin, separating the two parts of the city. Despite speeches and symbolic support from the West, the wall halted the flow of refugees and brought the U.S. commitment to West Germany into doubt.

Watch the Video "Video: Escaping the Berlin Wall" on **MyHistoryLab.com**

The Cuban Missile Crisis

The most dangerous days of the Cold War occurred during the Cuban missile crisis of 1962. This event represented another facet of the globalization of the Cold War, on this occasion, into the Americas. Cuba lies less than 100 miles off the Florida coast, and the United States had dominated the island since the Spanish-American War in 1898. In 1957, Fidel Castro (b. 1926) launched an insurgency in Cuba, which toppled the dictatorship of Flugencio Batista (1901–1973) on New Year's Day of 1959. Thereafter Castro established a communist government, and Cuba became an ally of the Soviet Union. These events caused enormous concern within the United States.

In 1962, the Soviet Union secretly began to place nuclear missiles in Cuba. In response, the American government, under President Kennedy, blockaded Cuba, halted the shipment of new missiles, and demanded the removal of existing installations. After a tense week, during which nuclear war seemed a real possibility, the Soviets backed down, and the crisis ended. This adventurism in foreign policy undermined Khrushchev's credibility in the ruling circles of the Soviet Union and caused other non-European communist regimes to question the Soviet commitment to their security and survival. It also increased the influence of the People's Republic of China in communist circles and convinced Soviet military leaders of the need to strengthen their forces so that they would be as strong as, or stronger than, those of the United States in any future confrontation.

If the Cuban missile crisis had led to war, the United States could have launched missiles over Europe or from European bases into the Soviet Union. The crisis thus threatened Europe directly, but it was the last major Cold War confrontation to do so. In 1963, the United States and the Soviet Union concluded a nuclear test ban treaty. This agreement marked the beginning of a lessening in the overt tensions between the two powers.

MAJOR DATES OF LATER COLD WAR YEARS

1959	Khrushchev's visit to the United States
1960	Failed Paris Summit
1961	East Germany erects Berlin Wall
1962	Cuban missile crisis
1963	Test Ban Treaty between Soviet Union and the United States
1964	Khrushchev falls from power
1968	Soviet invasion of Czechoslovakia
1972	Strategic Arms Limitation Treaty

▼ The Brezhnev Era

By 1964, many in the Soviet Communist Party had concluded that Khrushchev had tried to do too much too soon and had done it poorly. On October 16, 1964, Khrushchev was forced to resign. He was replaced by Alexei Kosygin (1904–1980) as premier and Leonid Brezhnev (1906–1982) as party secretary. Brezhnev eventually emerged as the dominant figure.

1968: The Invasion of Czechoslovakia

In 1968, during what became known as the Prague Spring, the government of Czechoslovakia, under Alexander Dubcek (1921–1992), began to experiment with a

During the Cuban missile crisis of 1962, the American ambassador to the United Nations displayed photographs to persuade the world of the threat to the United States less than one hundred miles from its own shores. © CORBIS

more liberal communism. Dubcek expanded freedom of discussion and other intellectual rights at a time when the Soviet Union was suppressing them. In the summer of 1968, the Soviet government and its allies in the Warsaw Pact sent troops into Czechoslovakia and replaced Dubcek with communist leaders more to its own liking.

At the time of the invasion, Soviet party chairman Brezhnev, in what came to be termed the ***Brezhnev Doctrine,*** declared the right of the Soviet Union to interfere in the domestic politics of other communist countries. Whereas the Truman Doctrine of 1947 had supported democratic governments and offered help to resist further communist penetration in Europe, the Brezhnev Doctrine of 1968 sought to sustain the communist governments of Eastern Europe and prevent any liberalization in the region. No further direct Soviet interventions occurred in Eastern Europe after 1968, yet the invasion of Czechoslovakia showed that any attempt at a greater liberalization could trigger Soviet military repression.

The United States and Détente

Foreign policy under Brezhnev combined attempts to reach an accommodation with the United States with continued efforts to expand Soviet influence and maintain Soviet leadership of the communist movement.

Although the Soviet Union sided with North Vietnam in its war with the United States, which is discussed later in this chapter, Soviet support was restrained. Under President Richard Nixon (1969–1974), the United States began a policy of **détente** with the Soviet Union, and the two countries concluded agreements on trade and on reducing strategic arms. Despite these agreements, Soviet spending on defense, and particularly on its navy, grew, damaging the consumer sectors of the economy.

During Gerald Ford's presidency (1974–1977), both the United States and the Soviet Union along with other European nations signed the Helsinki Accords. The accords recognized the Soviet sphere of influence in Eastern Europe, but they also recognized the human rights of the signers' citizens, which every government, including the Soviet Union, agreed to protect. President Jimmy Carter (1977–1981), a strong advocate of human rights, sought to induce the Soviet Union to comply with this commitment, a policy that cooled relations between the two countries.

Throughout this period of détente, in addition to its military presence in Eastern Europe, the Soviet Union pursued an activist foreign policy around the world. During the 1970s, it financed Cuban military intervention in Angola, Mozambique, and Ethiopia. Soviet funds flowed to the Sandinista forces in Nicaragua and to Vietnam, which permitted the Soviets to use naval bases after

In the summer of 1968, Soviet tanks rolled into Czechoslovakia, ending that country's experiment in liberalized communism. This picture shows defiant flag-waving Czechs on a truck rolling past a Soviet tank in the immediate aftermath of the invasion. Hulton Archive Photos/Getty Images, Inc.

North Vietnam conquered the south in 1975. The Soviet Union also provided funds and weapons to various Arab governments for use against Israel.

Each of these actions represented either Soviet support for what it viewed as its own strategic interests or an attempt to weaken the interests of the United States. Even more importantly, following its backing down in the Cuban missile crisis, the Soviet government was determined to build up its military forces. By the early 1980s, the Soviet Union possessed the largest armed force in the world and had achieved virtual nuclear parity with the United States.

The Invasion of Afghanistan

It was at this moment of great military strength in 1979 that the Brezhnev government decided to invade Afghanistan, a strategic decision of enormous long-range consequences for the future of the Soviet Union as well as the United States. Although the Soviet Union already had a presence in Afghanistan, the Brezhnev government, for reasons that remain unclear, determined to send in troops to ensure its influence in central Asia and to install a puppet Afghan government.

The invasion brought a sharp response from the United States. The U.S. Senate refused to ratify a second Strategic Arms Limitation agreement that President Carter had signed earlier that year. The United States also embargoed grain shipments to the Soviet Union, boycotted the 1980 Olympic Games in Moscow, and sent aid to the Afghan rebels through various third parties, as did Pakistan, Saudi Arabia, and other Islamic nations. The U.S. Central Intelligence Agency became directly involved with the Afghan resistance forces, some of whom were radical Muslims. China, which felt threatened by the invasion, also helped the rebels.

Eventually, the Soviet forces bogged down in Afghanistan and could not defeat their guerrilla enemies. The Afghans killed thousands of Soviet troops a year and inflicted many other casualties. The morale and prestige of the Soviet army plummeted. At first, few Soviets knew about the problems in Afghanistan, but during the 1980s, the military failure became common knowledge in the Soviet Union. Although the Afghan war did not make daily headline news in the Western press, it sapped Soviet strength for ten years and demoralized the Soviet Union not unlike the way the Vietnam conflict did the United States.

Communism and Solidarity in Poland

Events in Poland commencing in 1980—a time when the Soviet government was becoming increasingly rigidified and involved in Afghanistan—challenged both the authority of the Polish Communist Party and the influence of the Soviet Union.

After the events of late 1956, when the Polish Communist Party had accommodated itself to Soviet domination, chronic economic mismanagement and persistent shortages of food and consumer goods plagued Poland for twenty-five years. In 1978, the election of Karol Wojtyla, cardinal archbishop of Kraków, as Pope John Paul II (d. 2005) proved important for Polish resistance to communist control and Soviet domination. An outspoken Polish opponent of communism now occupied a position of authority and enormous public visibility well beyond the reach of Soviet or communist control. The new pope visited his homeland in 1979 and received a tumultuous welcome.

In July 1980, the Polish government raised meat prices, leading to hundreds of protest strikes across the country. On August 14, workers occupied the Lenin shipyard at Gdansk on the Baltic coast. The strike soon spread to other shipyards, transport facilities, and factories connected with the shipbuilding industry. The strikers, led by Lech Walesa (b. 1944), refused to negotiate through any of the government-controlled unions. The Gdansk strike ended on August 31 after the government promised the workers the right to organize an independent union called Solidarity. In September, the head of the Polish Communist Party was replaced, the Polish courts recognized Solidarity as an independent union, and the state-controlled radio broadcast a Roman Catholic mass for the first time in thirty years.

The summer of 1981 saw events that were no less remarkable occur within the Polish Communist Party itself. For the first time in any European communist state, secret elections for the party congress were permitted with real choices among the candidates. A single party continued to govern Poland, but for the time being, the party congress permitted real debate within its ranks.

MAJOR DATES OF THE BREZHNEV ERA

1974	Solzhenitsyn expelled
1975	Helsinki Accords
1979	Soviet invasion of Afghanistan
1980	U.S. Olympic Games boycott
1981	Martial law declared in Poland in response to Solidarity
1982	Death of Brezhnev

This extraordinary Polish experiment, however, ended abruptly. In 1981, General Wojciech Jaruzelski (b. 1923) became head of the Polish Communist Party, and the army imposed martial law in December. The leaders of Solidarity were arrested. The Polish military acted to preserve its own position and perhaps to prevent a Soviet invasion similar to the one in Czechoslovakia in 1968. Martial law remained in effect until late in 1983, but the Polish Communist Party could not solve Poland's major economic problems.

Relations with the Reagan Administration

Early in the administration of President Ronald Reagan (1981–1989), the United States relaxed its grain embargo on the Soviet Union and placed less emphasis on human rights. At the same time, however, Reagan intensified Cold War rhetoric, famously describing the Soviet Union as an "evil empire." More importantly, the Reagan administration increased U.S. military spending, slowed arms limitation negotiations, deployed a new missile system in Europe, and proposed the Strategic Defense Initiative (dubbed "Star Wars" by the press), involving a high-technology space-based defense against nuclear attack. The Star Wars proposal, although controversial in the United States, was a major issue in later arms control negotiations with the Soviet Union. Star Wars and the Reagan defense spending forced the Soviet Union to increase its own defense spending when it could ill afford to do so and contributed to the economic problems that helped bring about its collapse. Yet even during Reagan's first term (1981–1985), no major transformation of the Soviet Union seemed to be in the offing.

Meanwhile throughout these four decades of the Cold War between the United States and the Soviet Union, extraordinary events had been occurring in Africa and Asia.

▼ Decolonization: The European Retreat from Empire

The transformation of much of Africa and Asia from colonial domains into independent nations was the most remarkable global political event of the second half of the twentieth century. The numbers of people involved alone reveals the magnitude of the change. At the founding of the United Nations in 1945, approximately one-third of the population of the world was subject to the government of colonial powers. Since that time, more than eighty of those then non-self-governing territories have been admitted to UN membership as independent states. (See Map 29–6.)

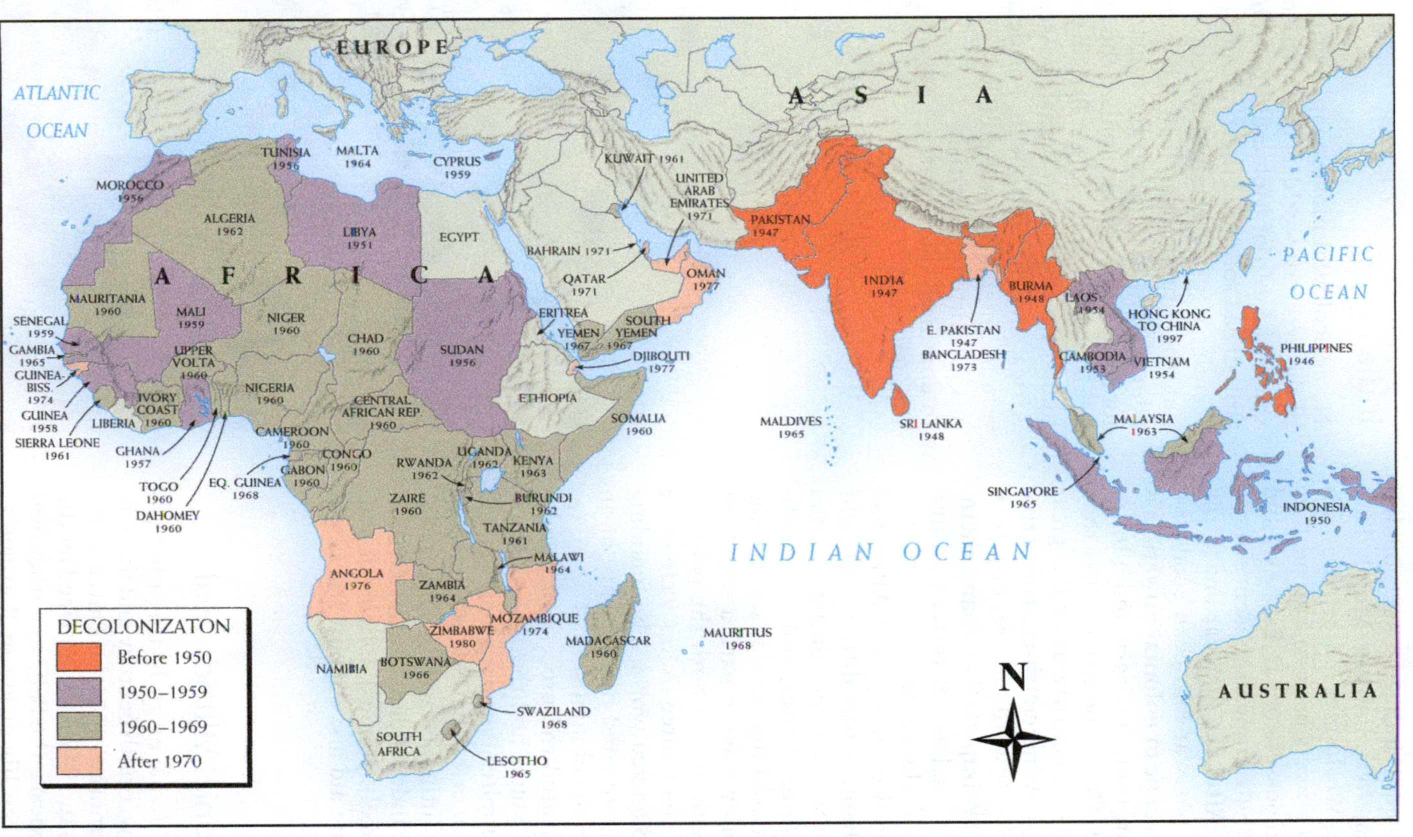

Map 29–6 **Decolonization Since World War II** The Western powers' rapid retreat from imperialism after World War II is graphically shown on this outline map covering half the globe—from West Africa to the southwest Pacific.

During the interwar years the European colonial powers had confronted a variety of revolts or nationalist movements, which they had been able to contain either by military force or modest reforms. The war itself and the opportunities it provided to indigenous nationalist movements within Africa, Asia, and the Middle East transformed the situation. World War II drew the military forces of the colonial powers back to Europe. The Japanese overran European possessions in East Asia and demonstrated thus that the European presence there might not be permanent. After the dislocations of the war came the immediate postwar European economic collapse, which left the European colonial powers less able to afford to maintain their military and administrative positions abroad. Consequently, in less than a century after the great nineteenth-century drive toward empire, European imperialists found themselves in retreat around the globe.

View the **Map** "Map Discovery: Decolonization" on **MyHistoryLab.com**

The liberal-democratic war aims of the Allies had also undermined colonialism. It was difficult to fight against tyranny in Europe while maintaining colonial dominance abroad. The United States, and in particular Franklin Roosevelt, opposed the continuation of the colonial empires. This policy was, in part, a matter of principle, but it also recognized that both the political and economic interests of the United States were more likely to prosper in a decolonized world. The founding of the United Nations also ensured the presence of an international body opposed to colonialism.

The Cold War complicated the process of decolonization. Both the United States and the Soviet Union opposed the old colonial empires, but both also worried about the potential alignment of the new nations and moved to create spheres of influence and, in some cases, alliances with the newly independent states. Certain nations, such as India, fiercely pursued policies of neutrality in hopes of receiving aid and support from both sides.

Major Areas of Colonial Withdrawal

Decolonization was a worldwide event lasting throughout the second half of the twentieth century and beyond. It involved such dramatic moments as the Dutch being forced from the East Indies in 1949 to be replaced by the independent nation of Indonesia, the Belgian withdrawal from the Congo in 1960, the liberation of Portuguese Mozambique and Angola in 1974 and 1975, and the end of all-white rule in Rhodesia (Zimbabwe) in 1979 and most remarkably in South Africa in 1994.

Each of these events was important, especially to the peoples involved, but the two largest colonial empires were the British and the French. Their retreat from empire produced the most far-reaching repercussions not only in former colonial nations, but in both Europe and the United States as well.

India

No anticolonial movement so gripped the imagination of the Western world as that carried out in India under the leadership of Mohandas Gandhi (1869–1948). The British had solidified their rule of India in the mid-eighteenth century extending and consolidating it throughout the nineteenth. (See Chapter 25.) The British administration required the Indians themselves to pay for British rule. India supplied the raw materials for the British cotton mills. Other British policies pushed many Indians to migrate to British possessions in East Asia, Africa, and the Caribbean. For decades, the religious, ethnic, linguistic, and political divisions among Indians permitted the British to dominate the country through a divide-and-rule strategy.

Watch the **Video** "Video Lectures: Gandhi in India" on **MyHistoryLab.com**

Ghandi led India from colonialism to independence. Part of his appeal was the simplicity of his life and dress. CORBIS/Bettmann

As early as 1885, politically active Hindu Indians founded the Indian National Congress with the goals of modernizing Indian life and liberalizing British policy. Muslims organized the Muslim League in 1887, which for a time cooperated with the National Congress but eventually sought an independent Muslim nation. After World War I, the Indian nationalist movement grew steadily in strength, in part because of British blunders, but more importantly because remarkable leaders pursued effective strategies.

Chief among these leaders was Gandhi, who had studied law in Britain and there began to encounter the ideas of liberal Western thinkers, including the American Henry David Thoreau (1817–1862) from whom he learned the concept of passive resistance. After being called to the bar in London in 1891, he returned briefly to India and then in 1893 went to South Africa where for over twenty years he worked on behalf of Indian immigrants. During those years he continued to read widely and became convinced of the power of passive resistance. Gandhi returned to India in 1915 and soon distinguished himself as a leader of Indian nationalism by his insistence on religious toleration. From the 1920s to the mid-1940s, he inspired a growing movement of passive resistance to British rule in India. In 1930, he led a famous march to break the British salt monopoly by collecting salt from the sea. He was repeatedly arrested and jailed by the British authorities. To embarrass the British during these imprisonments and to gain worldwide publicity, he undertook long protest fasts during which he nearly died. In 1942, during World War II, Gandhi called on the British Government to leave India. In 1947, the British Labor government, weary of the incessant agitation and uncertain of its ability to maintain control in India, decided to do so.

Gandhi became and remains the most famous anticolonial leader of the twentieth century. His career demonstrates how such a leader could use ideas taken from the West against colonial regimes. His use of passive resistance became a model for Dr. Martin Luther King, Jr. (1929–1968) during the civil rights movement in the United States during the late 1950s and 1960s. (See the Document "Gandhi Explains His Doctrine of Nonviolence," page 956.)

Gandhi and the Congress Party succeeded in forcing the British from India. However, they did not succeed in creating a single nation. Parallel to Gandhi's drive for an India characterized by diverse religions living in mutual toleration, the Muslim League led by Ali Jinnah (1876–1948) sought a distinctly Muslim state. What occurred in 1947 as the British left India was a partition of the country into the states of India and Pakistan. Intense sectarian warfare and hundreds of thousands of deaths marked the partition. A Hindu extremist assassinated Gandhi himself in 1948. It should also be noted that despite partition a vast Muslim population remained in India. Pakistan was initially a nation of two parts separated geographically by hundreds of miles of Indian territory. In 1971, East Pakistan broke away to become independent Bangladesh. As will be seen later in this chapter, the founding of Pakistan would be important for the emergence of political Islamism.

The partition of India and Pakistan illustrates an often-neglected factor in the process of decolonization. In many colonial regions, the retreat of the colonial powers opened the way for new or renewed conflicts among different ethnic and religious groups within the former colonial empires. For example, since partition, India and Pakistan have disputed the ownership of Kashmir in repeated armed clashes. Another example is the conflict over the former Portuguese colony of East Timor whose people have asserted a right to independence against the government of Indonesia, which occupied it for twenty years after Portugal withdrew in 1975.

Further British Retreat from Empire

The British surrender of India marked the beginning of a long, steady retreat from empire. Generally speaking, the British accepted the loss of empire as inevitable. British decolonization sought first to maintain whatever links were economically and politically possible without conflict. Indeed, during the 1940s and 1950s, the British undertook various development programs in their remaining Asian, African, and Caribbean colonies. These investments paradoxically made the British government and public more aware of the actual costs of empire and may have led both to accept more easily the end of empire. Second, throughout decolonization the British hoped to oversee the creation of institutions in their former colonies that would ensure representative self-government once they had departed.

In 1948, Burma and Sri Lanka (formerly Ceylon) became independent. As already observed, the formation of the state of Israel and Arab nationalist movements forced Britain to withdraw from Palestine. During the 1950s, the British tried, belatedly, to prepare their tropical colonies for self-government. Ghana (formerly the Gold Coast) and Nigeria—which became self-governing in 1957 and 1960, respectively—were the major examples of planned decolonization. In other areas, such as Cyprus, Kenya, and Aden (now part of Yemen), the British withdrew under the pressure of militant nationalist movements. In many areas, violence between the British and the forces demanding independence hastened this retreat.

The development of these former colonies in the second half of the twentieth century has followed two distinct paths. In general, political instability and poverty have characterized the history of the independent states in Africa. By contrast, Asia has been an area of overall political stability and remarkable economic growth, challenging the economies of both the United States and Western Europe.

Document

GANDHI EXPLAINS HIS DOCTRINE OF NONVIOLENCE

The most famous device Indian nationalists used against British colonial rule in India was Gandhi's doctrine of nonviolence. He had come to believe in its power during his years in South Africa. Gandhi wrote this description of the meaning of nonviolence during World War II. Yet even while enunciating its meaning, he refused to associate himself with nonviolence in international relations. This reluctance may have stemmed from his recognition that the war against the Axis powers was a war against Nazi racism and Japanese imperialism, both of which were dangerous for colonial peoples of color.

Why does Gandhi see nonviolence as evidence of strength? How does he refrain from extending nonviolence to external relations? How was Gandhi's doctrine transferable to other political movements, such as the American civil rights struggle?

I do believe that, where there is only a choice between cowardice and violence, I would advise violence. . . .

But I believe that non-violence is infinitely superior to violence, forgiveness is more manly than punishment. . . .

Non-violence is the law of our species as violence is the law of the brute. The spirit lies dormant in the brute, and he knows no law but that of physical might. The dignity of man requires obedience to a higher law—to the strength of the spirit.

I have therefore ventured to place before India the ancient law of self-sacrifice. . . .

Non-violence in its dynamic condition means conscious suffering. It does not mean meek submission to the will of the evil-doer, but it means the pitting of one's whole soul against the will of the tyrant. Working under this law of our being, it is possible for a single individual to defy the whole might of an unjust empire to save his honour, his religion, his soul, and lay the foundation for that empire's fall or its regeneration. . . .

I have not the capacity for preaching universal non-violence to the country. I preach, therefore, non-violence restricted strictly for the purpose of winning our freedom and therefore perhaps for preaching the regulation of international relations by non-violent means. But my incapacity must not be mistaken for that of the doctrine of non-violence. I see it with my intellect in all its effulgence. My heart grasps it. But I have not yet the attainments of preaching universal non-violence with effect. . . .

I do justify entire non-violence, and consider it possible in relation between man and man and nation and nation; but it is not "a resignation from all fighting against wickedness." On the contrary, the non-violence of my conception is a more active, more real fighting against wickedness than retaliation whose very nature is to increase wickedness. I contemplate a mental, and therefore a moral, opposition to immoralities. I seek entirely to blunt the edge of the tyrant's sword, not by putting up against it a sharper-edged weapon, but by disappointing his expectations that I should be offering physical resistance. . . .

Non-violence, therefore, presupposes ability to strike. It is a conscious deliberate restraint put upon one's desire for vengeance.

From "Gandhi Explains His Doctrine of Non-Violence," in M. K. Gandhi, *Non-Violence in Peace and War* (Navajivan Publishing, 1942). Reprinted by permission of the Navajivan Trust.

▼ The Turmoil of French Decolonization

Although the British retreat from empire involved violence, at no point did the British "make a stand." Moreover, many groups in Britain, including the leadership of the Labour Party, had long been critical of colonialism. Such was not the case with France. Having been defeated by the Nazis and then liberated by the allied forces, France believed it must reassert its position as a great power. This determination led it into two disastrous attempts to maintain its colonial empire, in Algeria and Vietnam. As will be seen, the situation in Vietnam, because of the intervention of the United States, drew French decolonization directly into the tensions of the Cold War.

France and Algeria

France had conquered the pirate's nest of Algiers in 1830 as Charles X (r. 1824–1830) futilely hoped the invasion would increase support for his monarchy. (See Chapter 20.) In late 1848, the French government made Algeria an integral part of France, establishing three administrative departments that were administered like those in France itself. Over the decades, as France consolidated and extended its position in Algeria, French soldiers and hundreds of thousands of Europeans from France and other Mediterranean countries settled there, primarily in the cities and on small farms. By the close of World War I, approximately 20 percent of the population was of European descent. Collectively these immigrants were termed the *pieds noirs* (meaning "black feet," a derogatory term). The voting structure was set up to give the French settlers as large a voice as the majority Arab Muslim population. The further one moved toward the south away from the coast and into the Sahara Desert, the greater the influence of the French military. Algerian Muslims were not given posts in the administration. Shortly after World War I, the French extended the rights of full French citizenship to Algerian Muslims who had fought in the war, who were literate in French, or who owned land, but this rewarded only a few thousand of them.

During World War II, the forces of Free France dominated Algeria after 1942 while the Vichy regime still governed metropolitan France. The Free French government did little to change the colonial status quo. Moreover, in May 1945, during celebrations of the Allied victory in World War II, a violent clash broke out at Sétif between Muslims and French settlers. Matters rapidly got out of hand, and people on both sides were killed, but the French repressed the Muslims with a considerable loss of life. The Muslims of Algeria saw this incident the same way the Russian working classes viewed Bloody Sunday in 1905. (See Chapter 23.) It robbed the French administration of legitimacy and marked the beginning of conscious Algerian nationalism. Thereafter, many Algerian Muslims supported independence. To placate Muslim opinion, in 1947, the French established a structure for limited political representation of the Muslim population and undertook economic reforms. Not unsurprisingly, these steps proved ineffective.

Algerian nationalists soon founded the National Liberation Front (FLN). In late 1954, insurrections and soon open civil war broke out in Algeria as the FLN undertook highly effective guerrilla warfare. The government of the Fourth French Republic that had been founded in 1945 adamantly declared Algeria an integral part of France and refused to compromise with the insurgents. Thereafter a war lasting until 1962 ground on between the Algerian nationalists and the French. Both sides committed atrocities; hundreds of thousands of Algerians were killed. The war divided France itself with many French citizens, often of left-wing political opinion, objecting to the war,

In 1959, Charles de Gaulle, as president of the French Republic, visited Algiers to great acclaim from its European inhabitants, known as *colons*. By 1962, however, he had sponsored a referendum that led to Algerian independence and the flight of most of those people. Loomis Dean/Getty Images, Inc.

and the French military, still smarting from its defeats in World War II and in Indochina, determined to fight on. The presence of more than 1 million European settlers in Algeria, who saw any settlement with the nationalists as a betrayal, exacerbated the situation. The French government itself became paralyzed and lost control of the army. There was fear of civil war in France itself or of a military takeover. In Algeria, violence was spreading.

Read the **Document** "Frantz Fanon, from *The Wretched of the Earth*" on **MyHistoryLab.com**

In the midst of this turmoil, General Charles de Gaulle (1890–1970), who had led the Free French forces during World War II and had briefly governed France immediately after the war, reentered French political life largely at the urging of the military. His condition for taking office was the end of the Fourth Republic and the promulgation of a new constitution, which enhanced the power of the president and created the Fifth Republic. The voters ratified this, and de Gaulle became president of France in December 1958. He then undertook a long strategic retreat from Algeria. The process was neither peaceful nor easy. In 1961, for example, it looked as if a group of officers known as the OAS (Organisation Armée Secrète) would attempt a coup in Paris. There were bombings, murders, and attempts on de Gaulle's life. In 1962, however, de Gaulle held a referendum in Algeria on independence, which passed overwhelmingly. Algeria became independent on July 3, 1962.

Once the FLN took over Algeria under the presidency of Mohammed Ben Bella (b. 1919), however, a second factor came into play in French domestic life. Hundreds of thousands of *pied noirs* settlers fled Algeria for France, as did many Muslims who had supported the French and had good cause to fear reprisals. (Thousands of pro-French Muslims who did not flee were massacred.) The emigration of this latter group marked the beginning of a large, and largely unwelcome, Muslim population in France.

France and Vietnam

One of the reasons for the strong French stand against Algerian independence had been the loss of its south Asian empire in Indochina just before the Algerian insurrection broke out in 1954. Whereas the Algerian drive toward independence essentially involved only France and the populations of Algeria, the Indochina problem eventually drew the United States into war in Vietnam.

In its push for empire, France had occupied Indochina (which contained Laos, Cambodia, and Vietnam) between 1857 and 1893. By 1930, Ho Chi Minh (1892–1969) had turned a nationalist movement against French colonial rule into the Indochina Communist Party, which the French, for a time, succeeded in suppressing. World War II, however, provided new opportunities for Ho Chi Minh and other nationalists as they fought both the Japanese who occupied Indochina in 1941 and the pro-Vichy French colonial administration that collaborated with the Japanese until 1945. The war thus established Ho Chi Minh as a major anticolonial, nationalist leader. He was a communist to be sure, but he had achieved his position in Vietnam during the war without the support of Chinese or Soviet communists.

In September 1945, Ho Chi Minh declared the independence of Vietnam under the Viet Minh, a coalition of nationalists that the communists soon dominated. By 1947, a full-fledged civil war had erupted in Vietnam. (Cambodia and, to a lesser extent, Laos remained quiescent under pro-French or neutralist monarchies.)

Until 1949, the United States displayed minimal concern about the Indochina war. The establishment of the Communist People's Republic of China that year dramatically changed the U.S. outlook. The United States now saw the French colonial war against Ho Chi Minh as an integral part of the Cold War conflict. The U.S. support for France in southeast Asia also served to gain French support for the establishment of NATO. Even though the United States supported the French effort in Vietnam financially, it was not prepared, despite divisions among policymakers, to intervene militarily. In the spring of 1954, during an international conference in Geneva on the future of Vietnam, the French military stronghold of Dien Bien Phu fell to Viet Minh forces after a prolonged siege. France lost the will to continue the struggle, which had become increasingly unpopular with the French people.

By late June, a complicated and unsatisfactory peace accord divided Vietnam at the seventeenth parallel of latitude. North of the parallel, centered in Hanoi, the Viet Minh were in charge; below it, centered in Saigon, the French were in charge. This was to be a temporary border. By 1956, elections were to be held to reunify the country. In effect, the conference attempted to transform a military conflict into a political one.

Vietnam Drawn into the Cold War

Unhappy with these arrangements, the United States, in September 1954, formed the Southeast Asia Treaty Organization (SEATO), a collective security agreement that somewhat resembled the European NATO alliance, but without the integration of military forces or inclusion of all states in the region. Its membership consisted of the United States, Great Britain, France, Australia, New Zealand, Thailand, Pakistan, and the Philippines.

By 1955, American policymakers had begun to think about Indochina, and particularly Vietnam, largely in terms of the Korean example. The U.S. government assumed, incorrectly, that, like the government of North Korea, the government in North Vietnam was basically a communist puppet of the Soviets and the Chinese. That same year, French troops began to withdraw from South Vietnam. As they left, the various Vietnamese political groups began to fight for power among themselves.

The United States stepped into the turmoil in Vietnam with military and economic aid. Among the Vietnamese politicians it chose to support was Ngo Dinh Diem (1901–1963), a strong noncommunist nationalist who had not collaborated with the French. Because the United States had been publicly and deeply committed to the French, however, Vietnamese nationalists would view any government it supported with suspicion. In October 1955, Diem established a Republic of Vietnam in the territory for which the Geneva conference had made France responsible. Diem announced that the Geneva agreements would not bind his newly established government and that elections would not be held in 1956. The American government, which had not signed the Geneva documents, supported his position.

In 1960, the National Liberation Front was founded, with the goals of overthrowing Diem, unifying the country, reforming the economy, and ousting the Americans. It was anticolonial, nationalist, and communist. Its military arm was called the Viet Cong and was aided by the government of North Vietnam. Diem, a Roman Catholic, also faced mounting criticism from Buddhists and the army. His response to these pressures was further repression and dependence on an ever-smaller group of advisers.

MAJOR DATES IN THE VIETNAM CONFLICT

1945	Ho Chi Minh proclaims Vietnamese independence from French rule
1947–1954	War between France and Vietnam
1950	U.S. financial aid to France
1954	Geneva conference on Southeast Asia opens
1954	French defeat at Dien Bien Phu
1954	Southeast Asia Treaty Organization (SEATO) founded
1955	Diem establishes Republic of Vietnam in the south
1960	Founding of National Liberation Front to overthrow the Diem government
1961	Six hundred American troops and advisers in Vietnam
1963	Diem overthrown and assassinated
1964	Gulf of Tonkin Resolution
1965	Major U.S. troop commitment
1969	Nixon announces policy of Vietnamization
1973	Ceasefire announced
1975	Saigon falls to North Vietnamese troops

Direct United States Involvement

The Eisenhower and Kennedy administrations continued to support Diem while demanding reforms in his government. The American military presence grew from about 600 advisers in early 1961 to more than 16,000 troops in late 1963. The political situation in Vietnam became increasingly unstable. On November 1, 1963, an army coup in which the United States was deeply involved overthrew and murdered Diem. The United States hoped a new government in South Vietnam would generate popular support. Thereafter, the United States sought to find a leader who could fulfill that hope. It finally settled on Nguyen Van Thieu (1923–2001), who governed South Vietnam from 1966 to 1975.

President Kennedy was assassinated on November 22, 1963. His successor, Lyndon Johnson (1963–1969), vastly expanded the commitment to South Vietnam. In August 1964, after an attack on an American ship in the Gulf of Tonkin, Johnson authorized the first bombing of North Vietnam. In February 1965, major bombing attacks began. They continued, with only brief pauses, until early in 1973. The land war grew until more than 500,000 Americans were stationed in South Vietnam.

In 1969, President Richard Nixon began a policy known as *Vietnamization*, which involved the gradual withdrawal of American troops from Vietnam while the South Vietnamese army took over the full military effort. Peace negotiations had begun in Paris in the spring of 1968, but a ceasefire was not finally arranged until January 1973. American troops left South Vietnam, and North Vietnam released its American prisoners of war. In early 1975, an evacuation of South Vietnamese troops from the northern part of their country turned into a rout when they were attacked by the North Vietnamese. On April 30, 1975, Saigon (renamed Ho Chi Minh City) fell to the Viet Cong and the North Vietnamese army. Vietnam was finally united. (See Map 29–7, p. 961.)

The U.S. intervention in Vietnam, which grew out of a power vacuum left by French decolonization, affected the entire Western world. For a decade after the Cuban missile crisis, Vietnam largely diverted the attention of the United States from Europe. American prestige suffered, and the U.S. policy in Southeast Asia made many Europeans question the wisdom of the American government and its commitment to Western Europe. Many young Europeans and many people in the former colonial world as well as many Americans came to regard the United States not as a protector of liberty, but as an ambitious, aggressive, and cruel power trying to keep colonialism alive after the end of the colonial era. Within the United States, the Vietnam conflict produced enormous divisions and debates over American involvement in the rest of the world that persist to the present day.

U.S. troops engaged in combat in Vietnam. At the war's peak, more than 500,000 American troops were stationed in South Vietnam. The United States struggled in Vietnam for more than a decade, seriously threatening its commitment to Western Europe. U.S. Army Photo

The Collapse of European Communism

The withdrawal of Soviet influence from Eastern Europe and the internal collapse of the Soviet Union are the most important European historical events of the second half of the twentieth century. They had virtually no parallel in modern European history. All of the other major governments that had disappeared in Europe earlier in the century had fallen either as the result of domestic revolution brought on by military defeat, as happened in tsarist Russia, Germany, and Austria after World War I and Italy during World War II, or military defeat followed by military occupation, as was the case with Germany after 1945 and the Third Republic in France in 1940. By contrast, the Soviet Union essentially imploded and then divided into separate successor states. There was no foreign invasion, no military defeat, and no internal revolution. Many of the factors leading to the Soviet collapse remain murky, but here is a relatively clear narrative of what occurred.

Under Brezhnev, who governed from 1964 to 1982, the Soviet government became markedly more repressive at home, suggesting a return to Stalinist policies. In 1974, the government expelled Aleksandr Solzhenitsyn. It also began to harass Jewish citizens, creating bureaucratic obstacles for those who wanted to emigrate to Israel. This internal repression gave rise to a dissident movement. Certain Soviet citizens dared to criticize the regime in public and accused the government of violating the human rights provision of the 1975 Helsinki Accords. The dissidents included prominent citizens, such as the Nobel Prize–winning physicist Andrei Sakharov (1921–1989). The Soviet government responded with further repression, placing some opponents in psychiatric hospitals and others under what amounted to house arrest. During the same period the structures of the Communist Party became both rigidified and corrupt, which increasingly demoralized younger Soviet bureaucrats and party members.

Gorbachev Attempts to Reform the Soviet Union

Although economic stagnation, party corruption, and the lingering Afghan war had long been undermining Soviet authority, what brought these forces to a head and began the dramatic collapse of the Soviet Empire was the

Map 29–7 **VIETNAM AND ITS SOUTHEAST ASIAN NEIGHBORS** The map identifies important locations associated with the war in Vietnam.

accession to power of Mikhail S. Gorbachev (b. 1931) in 1985 after both of Brezhnev's two immediate successors, Yuri Andropov (1914–1984) and Konstantin Chernenko (1911–1985), died within thirteen months of each other. In what proved to be the last great attempt to reform the Soviet system, Gorbachev immediately began the most remarkable changes that the Soviet Union had witnessed since the 1920s. These reforms loosed forces that, within seven years, would force him to retire from office and would end both communist rule and the Soviet Union as it had existed since the Bolshevik Revolution of 1917. (See "Encountering the Past: Rock Music and Political Protest,." page 962.)

Economic *Perestroika* Gorbachev's primary goal was to revive the Russian economy to raise the country's standard of living. Initially, he and his supporters, most of whom he had appointed himself, challenged traditional party and bureaucratic management of the Soviet government and economy. Under the policy of ***perestroika***, or "restructuring," they reduced the size and importance of the centralized economic ministries.

During these same years, Gorbachev confronted significant labor discontent. A major strike by coal miners occurred in July 1989 in Siberia. Gorbachev had to settle their grievances quickly, because the economy desperately needed their output. He promised them better wages and wider political liberties.

By early 1990, in a clear abandonment of traditional Marxist ideology, Gorbachev began to advocate private ownership of property and liberalization of the economy toward free market mechanisms. Despite many organizational changes, the Soviet economy remained stagnate and even declined. The failure of Gorbachev's economic policies affected his political policies. To some extent, he pursued bold political reform because he failed to achieve economic progress.

Read the **Document** "Mikhail Gorbachev on the Need for Economic Reform (1987)" on **MyHistoryLab.com**

Glasnost Gorbachev allowed an extraordinary public discussion and criticism of Soviet history and Soviet Communist Party policy. This development was termed ***glasnost***, or openness. The contributions to Soviet history of such figures from the 1920s and 1930s as Nikolai Bukharin, whom Stalin had executed in 1938, received official public recognition. Workers were permitted to criticize party officials and the economic plans of the party and the government. Censorship was relaxed and free expression encouraged. Dissidents were released from prison. In the summer of 1988, Gorbachev presided over a party congress that witnessed full debates.

Gorbachev soon applied *perestroika* to the political arena. In 1988, a new constitution permitted openly contested elections. After real political campaigning—a new experience for the Soviet Union—the Congress of People's Deputies was elected in 1989. One of the new members of the congress was Andrei Sakharov, the dissident physicist whom Brezhnev had persecuted. After lively debate, the Supreme Soviet, another elected body—although one the Communist Party dominated—formally elected Gorbachev president in 1989.

The policy of open discussion allowed national minorities within the Soviet Union to demand political autonomy. Throughout its history, the Soviet Union had remained a vast empire of subject peoples. The tsars had conquered some of those groups and Stalin had incorporated others, such as the Baltic states, into the Soviet Union. *Glasnost* quickly brought to the foreground the discontent of all such peoples, no matter how or when they had been subjugated. Gorbachev proved inept in addressing these ethnic complaints. He badly underestimated the unrest that internal national discontent could generate.

ROCK MUSIC AND POLITICAL PROTEST

ROCK MUSIC, WHICH epitomizes popular culture throughout the Western world, was a form of entertainment with a loud antiestablishment political message. Rock originated in the United States in the 1950s with African American musicians and working-class and country music singers. By the early 1960s, rock also included folk singers who used their music to champion the civil rights movement and protest the war in Vietnam.

European rock groups both embraced and transformed American rock music. The most spectacularly successful European group was the Beatles. Though sporting long hair and attracting the politically active young, the Beatles' lyrics were more laid back than political.

During the 1970s, in both the United States and Europe, punk rock groups, with provocative names such as the Sex Pistols, became popular. Punk rock was deeply antiestablishment, but Western society, which was increasingly pluralistic, took punk rock in its stride.

The Russian rock group Dynamic performs in Moscow in 1987. R. Podemi/TASS/Sovfoto/Eastfoto

In Eastern Europe and the Soviet Union, however, punk rock was literally revolutionary. There the ever more radical rock music of the 1970s and 1980s became a major vehicle for social and political criticism. In the face of communist cultural conformity, rock stars symbolized daring and personal heroism. Lyrics openly criticized communist governments, as in this example from "Get Out of Control," sung at a rock concert in Leningrad (now St. Petersburg) in 1986:

We were watched from the days of kindergarten.
Some nice men and kind women
Beat us up. They chose the most painful places
And treated us like animals on the farm.
So we grew up like a disciplined herd.
We sing what they want and live how they want
And we look at them downside up, as if we're trapped.
We just watch how they hit us
Get out of control!
Get out of control!
And sing what you want
And not just what is allowed
We have a right to yell![1]

This song became popular throughout Eastern Europe. It revealed how alienated the youth of the region had become from the official culture of the communist regimes. Rock music expressed and helped spread the disaffection that contributed to the collapse of communism throughout Eastern Europe at the end of the 1980s.

How did rock music evolve into an antiestablishment form of entertainment?

Why was rock music considered subversive in the Eastern bloc nations?

[1] Artemy Troitsky, *Back in the USSR: The True Story of Rock in Russia* (Boston: Faber & Faber, 1987), p. 127, as cited in Sabrina P. Ramet, ed., *Social Currents in Eastern Europe: The Sources and Meaning of the Great Transformation* (Durham, NC: Duke University Press, 1991), p. 239.

President Ronald Reagan and Premier Mikhail Gorbachev confer at a summit meeting in December 1987. AP Wide World Photos

1989: Revolution in Eastern Europe

Solidarity Reemerges in Poland In the early 1980s, Poland's government relaxed martial law, and it eventually released all the Solidarity prisoners, although Jaruzelski remained president. In 1988, new strikes surprised even the leaders of Solidarity. This time, the communist government could not reimpose control. After consultations between the government and Solidarity, the union was legalized. Lech Walesa again took center stage, as a kind of mediator between the government and the more independent elements of the trade union movement he had founded.

Jaruzelski began some political reforms with the tacit consent of the Soviet Union. He promised free elections to a parliament with increased powers. When elections were held in 1989, the communists lost overwhelmingly to Solidarity candidates. Late in the summer, Jaruzelski, unable to find a communist who could forge a majority coalition in Parliament, turned to Solidarity and appointed the first noncommunist prime minister of Poland since 1945. Gorbachev expressly approved the appointment.

Toward Hungarian Independence Throughout 1989, as these events unfolded within Poland, one Soviet-dominated state after another in Eastern Europe moved toward independence. Early in the year, the Hungarian government opened its border with Austria, permitting free travel between the two countries. This breach in the Iron Curtain immediately led thousands of East Germans to move through Hungary and Austria to West Germany. In May, Janos Kadar, who had been installed after the Soviet intervention in 1956, was stripped of his position as president of the Hungarian Communist Party. Thousands of Hungarians gave an honorary burial to the body of Imre Nagy, whom Kadar had executed in 1958. The Hungarian Communist Party changed its name to the Socialist Party, permitted other parties to engage openly in politics, and promised free elections by October.

German Reunification In the autumn of 1989, popular demonstrations erupted in East German cities. Adding to the pressure, Gorbachev told the leaders of the East German Communist Party that the Soviet Union would not use force to support them. With startling swiftness, the East German government resigned, making way for a younger generation of communist leaders who remained in office for only a few weeks. In November 1989, in one of the most emotional moments in European history

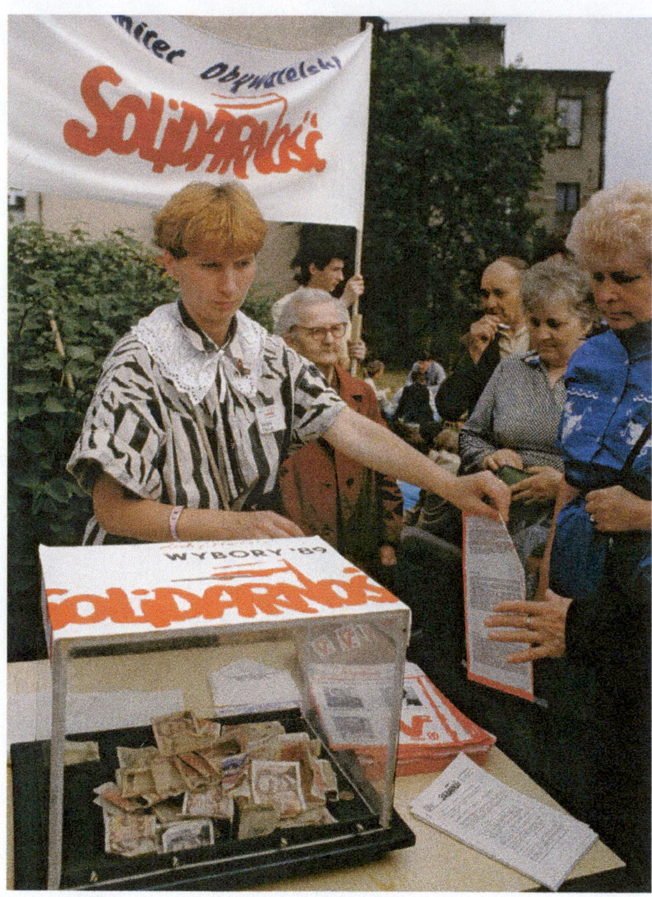

The Polish trade union "Solidarity" in 1989 successfully forced the Polish communist government to hold free elections. In June of that year Solidarity, whose members here are collecting funds for their campaign, won overwhelmingly. Bernard Bisson/CORBIS/Bettmann

since 1945, the government of East Germany ordered the opening of the Berlin Wall. That week, tens of thousands of East Berliners crossed into West Berlin to celebrate, to visit their families, and to shop with money the West German government gave them. Shortly thereafter, free travel began between East and West Germany. (See Map 29–8.)

Within days of these dramatic events, West Germany and the other Western nations faced the issue of German reunification. Helmut Kohl (b. 1930), the chancellor of West Germany, became the leading force in moving toward full unification. Late in 1989, the European Economic Community accepted, in principle, the unification of Germany. By February 1990, some form of reunification had become a foregone conclusion, accepted by the United States, the Soviet Union, Great Britain, and France.

The Velvet Revolution in Czechoslovakia Revolution in Czechoslovakia rapidly followed the breach of the Berlin Wall. The popular new Czech leader who led the forces against the party was Václav Havel (b. 1936), a playwright of international standing whom the communist government had imprisoned. In December 1989, the tottering communist government, together with the Soviet Union and other Warsaw Pact states, acknowledged that the invasion of 1968 had been a mistake. Shortly thereafter, Havel's group, known as Civic Forum, forced Gustav Husak (b. 1913), who had been president of Czechoslovakia since 1968, to resign. On December 28, 1989, Alexander Dubcek became chairman of the Parliament, and the next day, Havel was elected president.

Violent Revolution in Romania The only revolution of 1989 that involved significant violence occurred in Romania. There, in mid-December, the forces of President Nicolae Ceausescu (1918–1989), who had governed without opposition since 1965, fired on crowds that were protesting conditions in the country. By December 22, Bucharest was in full revolt. Ceausescu and his wife attempted to flee, but were captured, secretly tried, and shot on December 25.

The Soviet Stance on Revolutionary Developments None of the revolutions of 1989 could have taken place unless the Soviet Union had refused to intervene militarily, in contrast to 1956 and 1968. As events unfolded, it became clear that Gorbachev would not rescue the old-line communist governments and party leaderships in Eastern Europe. In October 1989, he formally renounced the Brezhnev Doctrine. For the first time since the end of World War II, Eastern Europeans could shape their own political destiny without the fear of Soviet military intervention. Once they realized the Soviets would not act, thousands of ordinary citizens took to the streets to denounce Communist Party domination and assert their desire for democracy. The major question facing the Soviet Union became the peaceful withdrawal of its troops from Eastern Europe. The haphazard nature of that withdrawal and the general poverty to which those troops returned were other factors undermining the Soviet armed forces.

The peaceful character of most of these revolutions was not inevitable. It may, in part, have resulted from the shock with which much of the world responded to the violent repression of pro-democracy protesters in Beijing's Tiananmen Square by the People's Republic of China in May 1989. The Communist Party officials of Eastern Europe and the Soviet Union clearly decided in 1989 that they could not offend world opinion with a similar attack on democratic demonstrators.

The Collapse of the Soviet Union

Gorbachev clearly believed, as his behavior toward Eastern Europe in 1989 showed, that the Soviet Union could no longer afford to support communist governments in

Map 29–8 **THE BORDERS OF GERMANY IN THE TWENTIETH CENTURY** Map A shows the borders of imperial Germany at the outbreak of World War I. Map B shows the borders of Germany after the Versailles peace settlement. Map C shows the borders of Germany after Hitler's invasion of the Rhineland, the Anschluss with Austria, the Munich Pact, the invasion of Czechoslovakia, and the invasion of Poland. Map D illustrates the division of Germany into the German Federal Republic (West Germany) and the German Democratic Republic (East Germany) in the aftermath of World War II. Map E illustrates the borders of Germany after reunification in 1990.

that region or intervene to uphold their authority while seeking to restructure its own economy. He also had concluded that the Communist Party in the Soviet Union must restructure itself and its relationship to the Soviet state and society.

Renunciation of Communist Political Monopoly In early 1990, Gorbachev formally proposed to the Central Committee of the Soviet Communist Party that the party abandon its monopoly of power. After intense debate, the committee abandoned the Leninist position that only a single elite party could act as the vanguard of the revolution and forge a new Soviet society.

New Political Forces Gorbachev confronted challenges from three major political forces by 1990. One consisted of those groups—considered conservative in the Soviet context—whose members wanted to preserve the influence of the Communist Party and the Soviet army. The country's economic stagnation and political and social turmoil deeply disturbed them. They appeared to control significant groups in the economy and society. During late 1990 and early 1991, Gorbachev, who himself seems to have been disturbed by the nation's turmoil, began to appoint members of these factions to key positions in the government. In other words, he seemed to be making a strategic retreat.

Gorbachev initiated these moves because he was now facing opposition from a second group—those who wanted much more extensive and rapid change. Their leading spokesman was Boris Yeltsin (1931–2007). He and his supporters wanted to move quickly to a market economy and a more democratic government. Like Gorbachev, Yeltsin had risen through the ranks of the Communist Party and had then become disillusioned with its policies. Throughout the late 1980s, he had been critical of Gorbachev. In 1990, he was elected president of the Russian Republic, the largest and most important of the Soviet Union's constituent republics. In the new political climate, that position gave him a firm political base from which to challenge Gorbachev's authority and increase his own.

The third force that came into play from 1989 onward was growing regional unrest in some of the republics of the Soviet Union. These republics had experienced considerable discontent in the past, but the military and the Communist Party had always managed to repress it. Initially, the greatest unrest came from the three Baltic republics of Estonia, Latvia, and Lithuania, which had been independent states until 1940 when the Soviet Union had occupied them in accord with secret provisions of the Soviet–German nonaggression pact of 1939. That pact with Nazi Germany provided the only seemingly legal basis for the Soviet Union's continued control. In these republics, many local communist leaders began to see themselves as national leaders rather than as party stalwarts.

MAJOR EVENTS IN THE REVOLUTIONS OF 1989

January 11	Independent parties permitted in Hungary
April 5	Solidarity legalized in Poland and free elections accepted by government
May 2	Hungary dismantles barriers along its borders
May 8	Janos Kadar removed from office in Hungary
May 17	Polish government recognizes Roman Catholic Church
June 4	Solidarity victory in Polish parliamentary elections
July 25	Solidarity asked to join coalition government
August 24	Solidarity member appointed premier in Poland
October 18	Erich Honecker removed from office in East Germany
October 23	Hungary proclaims itself a republic
October 25	Gorbachev renounces Brezhnev Doctrine
November 9	Berlin Wall opened
November 17	Large antigovernment demonstration in Czechoslovakia crushed by police
November 19	Czechoslovak opposition groups organize into Civic Forum and demand resignation of communist leaders responsible for 1968 invasion
November 24	Czechoslovak communist leadership resigns
December 1	New Czechoslovak communist leaders denounce 1968 invasion; Soviet Union and Warsaw Pact express regret over 1968 invasion
December 3	Czechoslovak government announces ministry with noncommunist members
December 16–17	Massacre of civilians in Timisoara, Romania
December 22	Ceausescu government overthrown in Romania with many casualties
December 25	Announcement of Ceausescu's execution
December 28	Alexander Dubcek elected chairman of Czechoslovak Parliament
December 29	Václav Havel elected president of Czechoslovakia

During 1989 and 1990, the parliaments of the Baltic republics tried to decrease Soviet control, and Lithuania actually declared independence. Gorbachev used military force to resist these moves. Discontent also arose in the Soviet Islamic republics in Central Asia and the Caucasus. Riots broke out in Azerbaijan and Tajikistan,

COLLAPSE OF THE BERLIN WALL

NO SINGLE STRUCTURE so illustrated the divisions of the Cold War as the Berlin Wall, which was erected in 1961. The most symbolic moment in the collapse of communism across Eastern Europe came in November 1989 when that wall was breached.

R. Bossu/Sygma/CORBIS

The sight of hundreds of Germans standing on top of the wall would have been unthinkable just days before. Armed East German and Soviet guards had for over a quarter century prevented Germans from crossing the wall except at a few heavily guarded checkpoints.

English graffiti had been placed on the wall to ensure that an international television audience, which was largely English-speaking, would understand the aspirations of those people who wanted the wall to come down.

The overwhelmingly youthful crowd indicates the repudiation by the new generation of Germans and Europeans of the Cold War divisions.

How did the vast numbers of photographs of this event, as well as amateur movies and videos, illustrate that the manner in which the dispersal of information could no longer be controlled by governments?

In June 1989, the Chinese government had violently suppressed a vast rally in Tiananmen Square in Beijing. How does this picture from Berlin about six months later illustrate the decision of the Soviet and East German governments to behave differently in the face of popular opposition?

What does this picture both reveal and fail to reveal about the motives of the East Germans who crossed the Berlin Wall in November 1989?

where the army was used as a police force against Soviet citizens. Throughout 1990 and 1991, Gorbachev sought to negotiate new constitutional arrangements between the republics and the central government. His failure to effect such arrangements may have been the single most important reason for the rapid collapse of the Soviet Union.

The August 1991 Coup The turning point in all of these events came in August 1991, when the conservative forces that Gorbachev had brought into the government attempted a coup. Troops occupied Moscow, and Gorbachev was placed under house arrest while on vacation in Crimea. The forces of political and economic reaction—led by people who, at the time, were associated with Gorbachev—had at last tried to seize control. The day of the coup, Boris Yeltsin climbed on a tank in front of the Russian Parliament building to denounce the coup and ask the world for help to maintain the Soviet Union's movement toward democracy.

Within two days, the coup collapsed. Gorbachev returned to Moscow, but in humiliation, having been victimized by the groups to whom he had turned for support. One of the largest public demonstrations in Russian history—perhaps even the largest—celebrated the failure of the coup in Moscow. From that point on, Yeltsin steadily became the dominant political figure in the nation. The Communist Party, compromised by its participation in the coup, collapsed as a political force. The constitutional arrangements between the central government and the individual republics were revised. In December 1991, the Soviet Union ceased to exist, Gorbachev left office, and the Commonwealth of Independent States came into being. (See Map 29–9.)

The collapse of European communism in the Soviet Union and throughout Eastern Europe has closed the era in which Marxism dominated European socialism that began in the 1870s with the German socialists' adoption of Marxist thought. The Bolshevik victory in the Russian

Map 29–9 **THE COMMONWEALTH OF INDEPENDENT STATES** In December 1991, the Soviet Union broke up into its fifteen constituent republics. Eleven of these were loosely joined in the Commonwealth of Independent States. Also shown is the autonomous region of Chechnya, which has waged two bloody wars with Russia in the last decade. Because the borders of Soviet republics were drawn not so much as to promote stability but instability among the many ethnic groups of the Soviet Union, long-simmering disputes flared up once the empire collapsed. The many conflicts Georgia has faced since it regained its independence in 1991 are representative: It fought unsuccessful wars in the early 1990s to keep the break-away regions of Abkhazia and South Ossetia, both of whose populations were heavily non-Georgian, under its control. In August 2008, when Georgia attempted to reassert its sovereignty over South Ossetia after Russian provocation, it was quickly repulsed by a massive invasion from Russia that resulted in hundreds of fatalities and billions of dollars of damage.

Revolution seemed to validate Marxism, and the policies of Lenin and Stalin sought to extend it around the world. Now the Soviet Union and the communist governments of Eastern Europe—heirs to the Bolshevik Revolution—have vanished, and the economies they built have collapsed. As a result, Marxist socialism has been discredited, and socialism in general may find itself on the defensive in the future.

View the **Closer Look** "Statue of Lenin Toppled During Soviet Collapse" on **MyHistoryLab.com**

The Yeltsin Decade

Boris Yeltsin emerged as the strongest leader within the new commonwealth. As president of Russia, he was head of the largest and most powerful of the new states. His popularity was high both in Russia and in the commonwealth in 1992, but within a year, he faced serious economic and political problems. The Russian Parliament, most of whom were former communists, opposed Yeltsin personally and his policies of economic and political reform. Relations between the president and Parliament reached an impasse, crippling the government. In September 1993, Yeltsin suspended Parliament, which responded by deposing him. Parliament leaders tried to incite popular uprisings against Yeltsin in Moscow. The military, however, backed Yeltsin, and he surrounded the Parliament building with troops and tanks. On October 4, 1993, after pro-Parliament rioters rampaged through Moscow, Yeltsin ordered the tanks to attack the Parliament building, crushing the opposition.

These actions consolidated Yeltsin's authority. The major Western powers, deeply concerned by the turmoil in Russia, supported him. In December 1993, Russians voted for a new Parliament and approved a new constitution. By 1994, the central government found itself at war in the Islamic province of Chechnya in the Caucasus. Under Yeltsin, Russian forces held off a rebel victory, but the war reached no clear conclusion.

During the mid-1990s, to dismantle the Soviet state and economy, former state-owned industries were privatized. This complicated process involved much corruption and opportunism by individuals determined to profit from the emerging economic organization. One result was the creation of a small group of enormously wealthy individuals, whom the press dubbed "the oligarchs." While these people amassed vast wealth, the general Russian economy remained stagnant. In 1998, Russia defaulted on its international debt payments. Political assassinations occurred and have continued to the present time. The economic downturn contributed to further political unrest. In the face of these problems and in declining health, Yeltsin resigned the presidency in a dramatic gesture just as the new century opened. His hand-picked successor was Vladimir Putin (b. 1952), a relatively unknown figure at the time. Putin would lead the Russian Federation in new economic and political directions. Before considering Putin's role, it is necessary

A Chechen fighter points his rifle at the head of a Russian prisoner of war outside the Chechen capital Grozny in August 1996. Mindaugas Kulbis/AP Wide World Photos

to examine the events that occurred during the 1990s in southeastern Europe.

▼ The Collapse of Yugoslavia and Civil War

Yugoslavia was created after World War I. Its borders included seven major national groups—Serbs, Croats, Slovenes, Montenegrins, Macedonians, Bosnians, and Albanians—among whom there have been ethnic disputes for centuries. The Croats and Slovenes are Roman Catholic and use the Latin alphabet. The Serbs, Montenegrins, and Macedonians are Eastern Orthodox and use the Cyrillic alphabet. The Bosnians and Albanians are mostly Muslims. Most members of each group reside in a region with which they are associated historically—Serbia, Croatia, Slovenia, Montenegro, Macedonia, Bosnia-Herzegovina, and Kosovo—and these regions constituted individual republics or autonomous areas within Yugoslavia. Many Serbs, however, lived outside Serbia proper.

Tito (1892–1980) had acted independently of Stalin in the late 1940s and pursued his own foreign policy. To mute ethnic differences, he encouraged a cult of personality around himself and instituted complex political power-sharing among these different groups. After his death, economic difficulties undermined the authority of the central government, and Yugoslavia gradually dissolved into civil war.

In the late 1980s, the old ethnic differences came to the foreground again in Yugoslav politics. Nationalist leaders—most notably Slobodan Milosevic (b. 1941–2006) in Serbia and Franjo Tudjman (b. 1922) in Croatia—gained authority. The Serbs contended that Serbia did not exercise sufficient influence in Yugoslavia and that

THE BREAKUP OF YUGOSLAVIA

June 1991	Slovenia declares independence; Croatia declares independence
September 1991	Macedonia declares independence
April 1992	War erupts in Bosnia and Herzegovina after Muslims and Croats vote for independence
April 1992	Serbia and Montenegro proclaim a new Federal Republic of Yugoslavia
November 1995	Peace agreement reached in Dayton, Ohio
March 1998	War breaks out in Kosovo, a province of Serbia
March 1999	NATO bombing of Serbia begins
February 2008	Kosovo declares independence

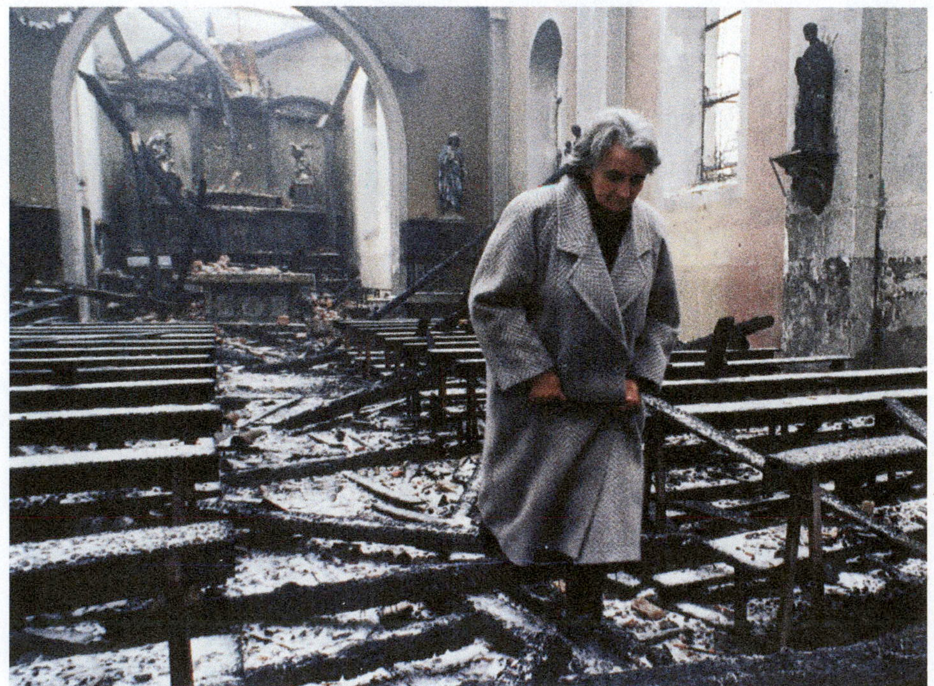

Destruction of Sarajevo. An elderly parishioner walks through the ruins of St. Mary's Roman Catholic Church in Sarajevo. The church was destroyed by Serb shelling in May 1992. Reuters/CORBIS/Bettmann

Serbs living in Yugoslavia but outside Serbia encountered systematic discrimination, especially from Croats and Albanians. Ethnic tension and violence resulted. During the summer of 1990, in the wake of the changes in the former Soviet bloc nations, Slovenia and Croatia declared independence from the central Yugoslav government, and several European nations, including, most importantly, Germany, immediately granted them recognition. The full European community soon did likewise.

From this point on, violence escalated. Serbia—concerned about Serbs living in Croatia and about the loss of lands and resources there—was determined to maintain a unitary Yugoslav state that it would dominate. Croatia was equally determined to secure independence. Croatian Serbs demanded safeguards against discrimination and violence, providing the Serbian army with a pretext to move against Croatia. By June 1991, full-fledged war had erupted between the two republics. Serbia accused Croatia of reviving fascism; Croatia accused Serbia of maintaining a Stalinist regime. At its core, however, the conflict was ethnic; as such, it highlights the potential for violent ethnic conflict within the former Soviet Union.

View the **Map** "The Former Yugoslavia after 1991" on **MyHistoryLab.com**

The conflict took a new turn in 1992 when Croatian and Serbian forces determined to divide Bosnia-Herzegovina. The Muslims in Bosnia—who had lived alongside Serbs and Croats for generations—soon became crushed between the opposing forces. The Serbs in particular, pursuing a policy called "ethnic cleansing," a euphemism redolent of some of the worst horrors of World War II, killed or forcibly removed many Bosnian Muslims.

More than any other single event, the unremitting bombardment of Sarajevo, the capital of Bosnia-Herzegovina, brought the violence of the Yugoslav civil war to the attention of the world. The United Nations attempted unsuccessfully to mediate the conflict and imposed sanctions that had little effect. Early in 1994, however, a shell exploded in the marketplace in Sarajevo, killing dozens of people. Thereafter, NATO forced the Serbs to withdraw their artillery from around Sarajevo.

View the **Map** "Map Discovery: Balkans" on **MyHistoryLab.com**

The events of the civil war came to a head in 1995 when NATO forces carried out strategic air strikes. Later that year, under the leadership of the United States, the leaders of the warring forces negotiated a peace agreement in Dayton, Ohio. The agreement was of great complexity but recognized an independent Bosnia. NATO troops, including those from the United States, have enforced the terms of the agreement.

Toward the end of the 1990s, Serbian aggression against ethnic Albanians in the province of Kosovo again drew NATO into Yugoslav affairs. For months, through television and other media, the world watched the Serbian military deport Albanians from Kosovo where Albanians constituted a majority of the population. The tactics closely resembled those the Serbs previously used in Bosnia. There were many casualties, atrocities, and deaths. Early in 1999, NATO again carried out an air campaign and sent troops into Kosovo to safeguard the ethnic Albanians. This air campaign was the largest military action in Europe since the close of World War II. In 2000, a revolution overthrew Slobodan Milosevic. The new Yugoslav government turned the former leader over to the International War Crimes Tribunal at the Hague; however, Milosevic died in 2006 before his trial reached completion.

The disintegration of the former Yugoslavia took still another important turn in February 2008 when Kosovo, with its Albanian majority population, declared its independence from Serbia. The United States, a majority of the nations composing the European Union, and all Kosovo's neighbors except Serbia have recognized the independence of Kosovo. The Russian Federation, a longtime supporter of Serbia, immediately and strongly condemned the independence of Kosovo. The issue of Kosovo's independence, as will be seen in the next section, led to Russian military actions in the region of the Black Sea later in 2008.

▼ Putin and the Resurgence of Russia

Vladimir Putin, who had become president of the Russian Federation in 2000, immediately moved to establish his position as a national and nationalistic leader of the federation. He vigorously renewed the war against the rebels in Chechnya, which resulted in heavy casualties and enormous destruction there, but also strengthened Putin's political support in Russia itself. The ongoing Chechen war spawned one of the major acts of recent terrorism in Russia. In September 2003, a group of Chechens captured an elementary school in Beslan, a community in the Russian republic of North Ossetia (in the north Caucasus) on the opening day of the term. Approximately 1,200 students, teachers, and parents were held hostage for several days. When government troops stormed the school, approximately 330 of the hostages were killed. By the middle of the decade, however, Russian forces had clearly established the upper hand over the Chechen rebels and the drive toward independence was firmly checked at a very high cost in lives on both sides.

In the wake of the Chechen war and as part of his determination that the central government will dominate Russia's economy and political life, Putin has sought to diminish local autonomy and centralize power in his own hands. The central government has also moved against leading oligarchs and other businessmen, with some being imprisoned. Putin used the attacks on these enormously wealthy and economically powerful figures to generate support from the broad Russian public who regard the oligarchs as thieves and one of the causes of the economic hardship of the 1990s. Putin also imprisoned political critics and opponents as well as moved against independent newspapers and television stations.

During Putin's presidency the Russian economy genuinely began to improve. Foreign debts were paid. The Russian ruble came to be regarded as a serious currency. Many more consumer goods were available. Much of this relative prosperity was the result of the oil resources available to the Russian Federation and the rising price of oil on the world market. Under Putin a clear trade-off occurred between political freedom and economic and political stability. In 2008 Putin left the elected presidency at the end of his second four-year term, turning the office over to his own handpicked successor Dmitri Medvedev (b. 1965). At the same time, however, Putin assumed the office of prime minister and clearly remained the chief political figure in the country.

Putin both as president and now prime minister has been determined to use the nation's economic recovery and new wealth to allow Russia to reassert its position as a major power on both the regional and world scene. After the terrorist attacks on the United States in September 2001, Putin supported the American assault on Afghanistan, largely because the Russian government was afraid that Islamic extremism would spread beyond Chechnya to other regions in Russia and to the largely Muslim nations that bordered Russia in Central Asia and the Caucasus. This period of cooperation proved short-lived. Putin became one of the leading voices against the American-led invasion of Iraq and has continued to criticize American policy in the region. Putin has also been sharply critical of the ongoing expansion of NATO, which has embraced nations directly bordering the Russian Federation. His government continued to attempt to exert influence in various new nations, such as the former Soviet republics of Ukraine and Georgia, that came into existence with the collapse of the former Soviet Union. (See the Document "Vladimir Putin Outlines a Vision of the Russian Future," page 973.)

This determination to assert Russian domination over recently independent nations once part of the former Soviet Union dramatically displayed itself in August 2008. That month troops of the Russian Federation invaded the republic of Georgia. What had provoked this attack was Georgia's having shortly before sent troops into South Ossetia. Russian troops first drove the Georgians out of South Ossetia, and then continued into Georgia itself. South Ossetia, itself a part of the former Soviet Union, had been divided into regions dominated by Russia and Georgia. Georgia sought to assert further influence, only to be immediately and overwhelmingly blocked by Russian forces. Russia eventually withdrew after a ceasefire but had succeeded in demonstrating its power in the region and in creating potential instability in postwar Georgia.

The aftermath of an attack by a Russian warplane on an apartment block in Gori, Georgia, during the conflict in South Ossetia in August 2008. Here a Georgian man cradles the body of a relative killed during the bombing, which killed at least five people. © Gleb Garanich/Reuters/America LLC

Document

VLADIMIR PUTIN OUTLINES A VISION OF THE RUSSIAN FUTURE

Vladimir Putin served as president of the Russian Federation from 1998 to 2008 when he moved to the office of prime minister. In one of his last presidential speeches he outlined his view of a democratic Russian future as well as his concerns about the relationship of the Russian Federation to NATO. His speech embraced a strong rhetoric of democracy but at the same time placed very considerable limits on the kind of activity and criticism that democratic parties might exercise. Note that he made no provision about who might decide if they were behaving in a fashion dangerous to the national interest. In his own time in office he imprisoned numerous political opponents. Also note his concerns about the future place in the world of the Russian Federation and his strong commitment to expansion of its military defense capacities.

How does Putin seem to embrace democratic reform? What are the limits that he places on democratic activity? How might those limits lead to government interference with the activity of political parties? What are Putin's concerns regarding NATO and the place of the Russian Federation in world affairs?

The desire of millions of our citizens for individual freedom and social justice is what defines the future of Russia's political system. The democratic state should become an effective instrument for civil society's self-organization. . . .

Russia's future political system will be centered on several large political parties that will have to work hard to maintain or affirm their leading positions, be open to change and broaden their dialogue with the voters.

Political parties must not forget their immense responsibility for Russia's future, for the nation's unity and for our country's stable development.

No matter how fierce the political battles and no matter how irreconcilable the differences between parties might be, they are never worth so much as to bring the country to the brink of chaos.

Irresponsible demagogy and attempts to divide society and use foreign help or intervention in domestic political struggles are not only immoral but are illegal. They belittle our people's dignity and undermine our democratic state. . . .

No matter what their differences, all of the different public forces in the country should act in accordance with one simple but essential principle: do nothing that would damage the interests of Russia and its citizens and act only for Russia's good, act in its national interests and in the interest of the prosperity and security of all its people. . . .

It is now clear that the world has entered a new spiral in the arms race. This does not depend on us and it is not we who began it. . . .

NATO itself is expanding and is bringing its military infrastructure ever closer to our borders. We have closed our bases in Cuba and Vietnam, but what have we got in return? New American bases in Romania and Bulgaria, and a new missile defense system with plans to install components of this system in Poland and the Czech Republic soon it seems. . . .

We are effectively being forced into a situation where we have to take measures in response, where we have no choice but to make the necessary decisions. . . .

Russia has a response to these new challenges and it always will. Russia will begin production of new types of weapons over these coming years, the quality of which is just as good and in some cases even surpasses those of other countries.

From Validmir Putin, Speech at Expanded Meeting of the State Council on Russia's Development Strategy through 2020, February 8, 2008, President of Russia, Official Web Portal, www.kremlin.ru/eng/text/speeches/2008/02/08/1137_type82912type82913_159643.shtml.

The Russian invasion of Georgia marked a new departure in post–Soviet Russian foreign policy and a resurgence of Russian international influence following the collapse of the Soviet Union nearly twenty years earlier. During that period both the European Union and NATO had moved to increase their memberships by expanding into Eastern Europe and into regions previously dominated by or part of the former Soviet

Union. The Russian Federation found itself compelled to watch over these expansions without being able to stop them or otherwise significantly influence them. Discussions had taken place about the possibility of bringing both Ukraine and Georgia into NATO. The United States had indicated support for such inclusion. Putin and other leaders of the Russian Federation had witnessed the manner in which various regions of the former Yugoslavia, most recently Kosovo in February 2008, had broken away from Serbia and established their own independence. The Russia Federation feared the example of Kosovo and the international recognition its independence had achieved might serve as a pattern for potential break-away regions in the Russian Federation. It also feared encirclement by NATO member nations where the United States might locate military bases. The action taken against Georgia served to demonstrate the ability of the Russian Federation to take military action on its borders and to give warning to other nations in the region of its capacity to intervene. At the same time the absence of any effective resistance to Russian actions in Georgia from either the United States or the European Union nations raised doubts about the capacity of either to influence events in the region of the Black Sea. Therefore, though the Russian incursion into Georgia was relatively brief, it demonstrated that the classic issues of European great power politics remain alive in the new Europe. Moreover, the action also demonstrated Russian willingness to take advantage of American involvement in Iraq and Afghanistan to reassert its potential authority in those regions it has dominated since the wars of Catherine the Great in the eighteenth century.

In late 2008 another question suddenly confronted Russia. As one element in the worldwide financial crisis, commodity prices dropped sharply. These included the price of oil on the world market. It remains to be seen whether Russia will be able to maintain its economic growth and political resurgence in the face of dropping income from the sale of oil, which has financed its new international influence during the past decade.

▼ The Rise of Radical Political Islamism

On September 11, 2001, Islamic terrorists attacked the United States, crashing hijacked civilian domestic aircraft into the Twin Towers of the World Trade Center in New York City, the Pentagon in Washington, DC, and a Pennsylvania field with a vast loss of life and property. These events and those flowing from them not only transformed American foreign policy toward the Middle East but have also changed European relations with the United States.

In retrospect, we can see that those attacks were the result of forces that had been affecting not only the United States but the Western world as well for at least a half-century. The end of the Cold War has been succeeded by a new political world in which both the United States and the nations of Europe, including the Russian Federation, are endangered by terrorist attacks from nongovernmental or non-state-based organizations. These groups are guided by ideologies in the Islamic world that have filled a political and ideological vacuum left by the end of the Cold War.

Radical Islamism is the term scholars use to describe an interpretation of Islam that came to have a significant impact in the Muslim world during the decades of decolonization. It is only one—and by no means the most popular—interpretation of Islam. The ideas informing radical Islamism extend back to the 1930s and resistance to British rule in Egypt, but for many years, those had little impact on the politics of the Middle East.

Arab Nationalism

Radical Islamism arose primarily in reaction to the secular Arab nationalism that developed in countries like Egypt and Syria in the 1920s and 1930s. Although Arab and other Middle Eastern nationalists, like nineteenth-century modernizers in the Ottoman Empire, believed that the path to independence and strength lay in adopting the technology and imitating the political institutions of the West, these advocates of radical Islam wanted to reject Western ideas and create a society based on a rigorous interpretation of Islam and its teachings. (See Chapter 22.)

In the wake of World War II, many of the foremost leaders of Arab nationalism against Western direct and indirect dominance, such as Gamal Abdul Nasser of Egypt, were sympathetic to socialism or to the Soviet Union. Because socialism and communism were Western ideologies, left-leaning Arab nationalism was no less Western in its orientation than were nationalists friendly to the United States. Moreover, Soviet communism was overtly atheistic and hence doubly offensive to devout Arab Muslims.

Nationalism forged by nondemocratic Middle Eastern governments, usually traditional monarchies or authoritarian regimes dominated by the military, brought different results to the various Arab nations. Oil made Saudi Arabia wealthy and powerful and the small Gulf states, such as Kuwait, rich but not powerful. Other states, such as Jordan, Syria, and Egypt, which lacked oil, remained burdened by large impoverished populations.

Arab governments defining themselves according to the values of nationalism worked out arrangements with local Muslim authorities. For example, the Saudi royal family turned over its educational system to adherents of a rigorist, puritanical form of Islam called *Wahhabism* while modernizing the country's infrastructure. The Egyptian government attempted to play off different Islamic groups against one another. These governments retained the support of prosperous, devout middle-class Muslims while doing little about the plight of the poor. In general, Muslim religious leaders were hostile to the Soviet Union and its influence in the Islamic world.

The Iranian Revolution

The Iranian Revolution of 1979 transformed the Middle East. The Ayatollah Ruhollah Khomeini (1902–1989) managed to unite both the middle and lower classes of a major Middle Eastern nation to overthrow a repressive but a modernizing government that had long cooperated with the United States. For the first time, a religiously dominated government defining itself and its mission in distinctly Islamic, as well as nationalistic, terms took control of a major state. Iran's revolutionary government was a theocracy; that is, there was no separation of religion and government or, in European terms, of church and state. The Iranian constitution gave the clergy, acting on behalf of God, the final say in all matters.

By challenging the Westernization of Iranian society, the Iranian Revolution shocked the world. It also challenged the largely secular presuppositions of Arab nationalists in states such as Egypt, Saudi Arabia, and Algeria that had failed to satisfy the needs of their own underclasses. In the mid-twentieth century, Arabs and other Middle Eastern peoples had turned to nationalism in reaction against European colonial powers. Those who grew up under nationalist leadership and still found themselves politically and economically disadvantaged, however, reacted against nationalism. The Iranian Revolution, which many thought would spread throughout the Islamic world, attracted them.

The Iranian Revolution both embodied and emboldened the forces of what is commonly called Islamic *fundamentalism*, but it is more correctly termed Islamic or Muslim *reformism*. This is the belief that a reformed or pure Islam must be established in the contemporary world. Most adherents of this point of view would emphasize personal piety and religious practice. However, a minority wish to see their states strictly governed the way Iran purports to be by Islamic law or the Shari'a. In fact, the Iranian clergy made numerous compromises to the practical demands of everyday government and the oil industry, but their public message to the world was that Iran is a strict Islamic state hostile to the West in general and the United States—"the Great Satan"—in particular. The Iranian Revolution also opposed the state of Israel on both religious and nationalistic grounds.

Watch the Video "Video Lectures: The 1979 Islamic Revolution in Iran: A Turning Point for the Middle East and the World" on **MyHistoryLab.com**

The conservative Arab governments feared the Iranian Revolution would challenge their legitimacy. They consequently began to pay much more attention to their own religious authorities and cracked down on radical reformist or fundamentalist Muslims. In Egypt, such actions followed the assassination in 1981 of President Anwar Sadat (b. 1918) by a member of the Muslim Brotherhood.

Afghanistan and Radical Islamism

The Russian invasion of Afghanistan of 1979, discussed earlier in this chapter, introduced a major new component into this already complicated picture, illustrating the convergence of Cold War and Islamist politics. The Soviet Union sought to impose a communist, and hence both Western and atheist, government in Afghanistan. Muslim religious authorities declared ***jihad,*** literally meaning "a struggle" but commonly interpreted as a religious war, against the Soviet Union. The Afghan resistance to the Soviets thus became simultaneously nationalistic, universalistic, and religious.

Thousands of Muslims, mostly fundamentalist in outlook, arrived in Afghanistan from across the Islamic world to oust the Soviets and their Afghan puppets. Conservative Arab states and the United States supported this effort, which succeeded when all Soviet forces withdrew in 1989. The conservative Arab states saw the Afghan war as an opportunity both to resist Soviet influence and to divert the energies of their own religious extremists. The United States saw the Afghan war as another round in the Cold War. The militant Muslim fundamentalists saw it as a religious struggle against an impious Western power.

The Taliban and Al Qaeda The Soviet withdrawal created a power vacuum in Afghanistan that lasted almost a decade. By 1998, however, rigorist Muslims known as the *Taliban* had seized control of the country. They imposed their own version of Islamic law, which involved strict regimentation of women and public executions, floggings, and mutilations for criminal, religious, and moral offenses. The Taliban also allowed groups of Muslim terrorists known as *Al Qaeda*, which means "Base," to establish training camps in their country. The terrorists who attacked the United States on September 11, 2001, came from these camps.

The ideology of these groups had emerged over several decades from different regions of the Islamic world but had been inculcated in Pakistan. The Pakistani government had long assigned considerable control over education to Islamic schools, or *madrasas*, that taught reformed Islam, rejection of liberal and nationalist secular values, intolerance toward non-Muslims, repudiation

Taliban fighters brandish their weapons in the main bazaar of Kandahar, Afghanistan, in late 2001. Reuters/Mian Kursheed

of Western culture, hostility to Israel, and hatred of the United States.

***Jihad* Against the United States** Once the *jihad* against the Soviet Union had succeeded, radical Muslims, largely educated in these Pakistani schools, turned their attention to the United States, the other great Western power. The event that brought about this redirection was the Persian Gulf War of 1991. The occasion for that conflict was the invasion of Kuwait by Iraq, under Saddam Hussein (1937–2006). The conservative Arab governments, most importantly Saudi Arabia, not only supported the United States but also permitted it to construct military bases on their territory. Islamic extremists who had fought in Afghanistan, one of whom was Osama bin Laden (b. 1957), saw the establishment of U.S. bases in Saudi Arabia, which was the home of the prophet Muhammad and contains Islam's two holiest cities, Mecca and Medina, as a new invasion by Western Crusaders. The bases added a new grievance to the already long list of radical Muslim complaints against the United States.

The United States became a target because of its secular public morality, its international wealth and power, its military strength, its ongoing support for Israel, and its adherence to the UN sanctions imposed on Iraq after the Gulf War. Certain Muslim religious authorities declared a *jihad* against the United States, thus transforming opposition to American policies and culture into a religious war. Through the 1990s, terrorist attacks were directed against targets in or associated with the United States. These included bombings of the World Trade Center in New York City in 1993, of a U.S. army barracks in Saudi Arabia in 1996, of U.S. embassies in East Africa in 1998, and of the USS *Cole* in the Yemeni port of Aden in 2000. These attacks resulted in a considerable loss of life.

▼ A Transformed West

The attacks on the United States on September 11, 2001, transformed and redirected American foreign policy into what the administration of President George W. Bush (b. 1946) termed "a war on terrorism." In late 2001, the United States attacked the Taliban government of Afghanistan, rapidly overthrowing it. The defeat of the Taliban destroyed Al Qaeda's Afghan bases but not its leadership, which survived, although it was dispersed and remains in hiding. By 2008 there was evidence that the Taliban had regrouped and again become active.

Following the Afghan campaign, the Bush administration set forth a policy of preemptive strikes and intervention against potential enemies of the United States. The administration argued that the danger of weapons of mass destruction developed by governments such as that of Iraq falling into the hands of international terrorist organizations posed so severe a danger to the security of the United States that the nation could not wait to respond to an attack but must take preemptive action. This argument, which aroused controversy both at home and abroad, marked a major departure from previous

United States foreign policy. It is a direct result of the attacks on the United States that occurred on September 11.

In 2002, the Bush administration turned its attention to Saddam Hussein's government in Iraq. Since the defeat of Iraq in 1991 by an international coalition led by the United States, Saddam Hussein, contrary to widespread expectations, had remained in power and had continued to oppress his own people. Throughout the 1990s, the Iraqi government had also resisted the work of United Nations inspectors charged with discovering and destroying weapons of mass destruction found in Iraq or facilities capable of manufacturing such weapons. The Iraqis eventually expelled the United Nations inspectors in 1998, and the United Nations was unable to reinsert them for almost five years.

The United States government adopted a policy of regime change in Iraq during the last years of the Clinton administration (1993–2001), although it did little to carry out that policy. In the wake of the September 11, 2001, attacks, however, the Bush administration determined to overthrow Saddam Hussein and remove any threat from supposed Iraqi weapons of mass destruction. In late 2002 and early 2003, the United States and British governments sought to obtain passage of United Nations Security Council resolutions that would require Iraq to disarm on its own or to be disarmed by military force. These efforts failed. France and Russia threatened to veto the measure, and a majority of the Security Council voted against it. Nonetheless, the United States and Great Britain, backed by token forces or other support from over thirty other nations, invaded Iraq in late March 2003. After three weeks of fighting, the Iraqi army and with it the government of Saddam Hussein collapsed. The announced goals of the invasion, in addition to toppling the Iraqi regime, were to destroy Iraq's capacity to manufacture or deploy weapons of mass destruction and to bring consensual government to the Iraqi people. The latter goal has remained elusive as Iraq has been violently split by deadly internal political conflict.

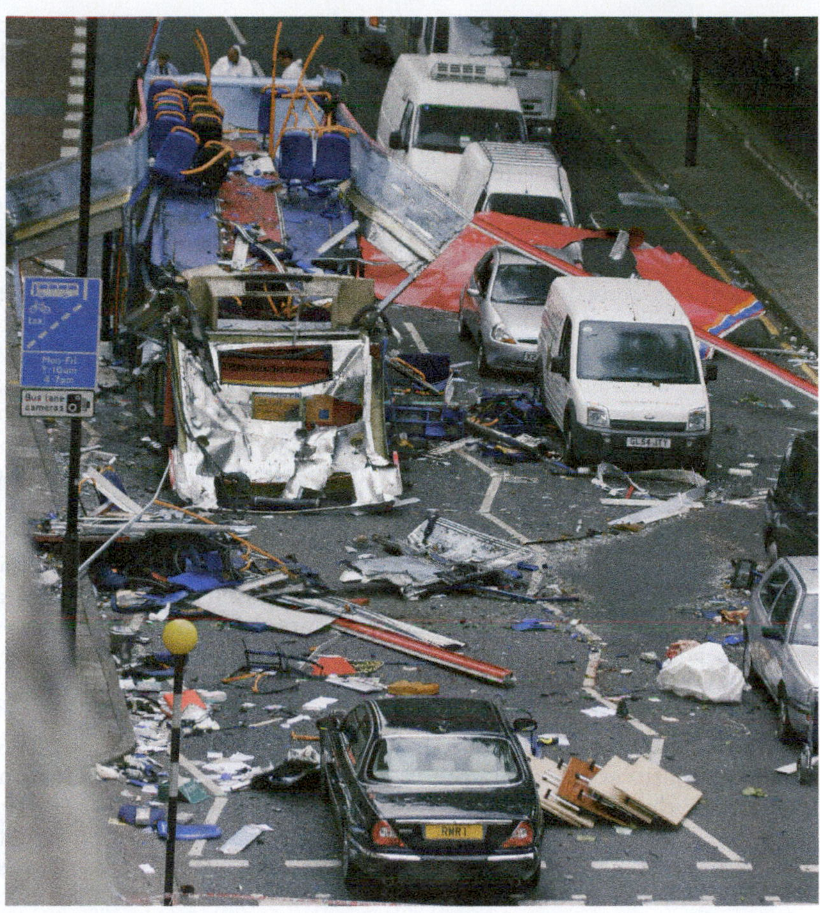

On July 7, 2005, a series of bombs rocked the London transport system, with the loss of over fifty lives. This photo shows the remains of a London bus on which a suicide bomber took more than a dozen lives near Russell Square, London. Sion Touhig/CORBIS/Bettmann

The invasion of Iraq was undertaken in the face of considerable opposition from France, Germany, and Russia. It also provoked large antiwar demonstrations in the United States and throughout the world. Both the war and the diplomatic difficulties preceding it disrupted the long-standing Atlantic alliance. Moreover, French and German opposition to the war created strains within Europe and particularly within NATO and the European Union, as other European governments either strongly supported or opposed the United States and Britain. As a result, the war in Iraq marked a new and divisive era in relations between the United States and Europe, and between the United States and the rest of the world.

Read the Document "Statement from Chancellor Schröder on the Iraq Crisis" on **MyHistoryLab.com**

Once the invasion of Iraq had been carried out and the occupation commenced, Al Qaeda terrorists struck in Europe itself. On March 11, 2004, at least 190 people were killed in train bombings in Madrid, Spain. The terrorist attack occurred just before the Spanish election. The Spanish government, which had supported the American invasion of Iraq, unexpectedly lost the election. The new government then soon withdrew Spanish troops from Iraq. The Madrid bombings were the largest act of terrorism against civilians in Europe since World War II. The attack demonstrated that terrorist attacks can directly influence European political processes.

The Iraq war and the bloody insurgency that followed generated enormous controversy. The coalition forces found no weapons of mass destruction in Iraq. Government commissions in the United States and

Britain have criticized the intelligence information used to justify the invasion. In 2004, however, President Bush was reelected. In March 2005, thousands of Iraqis braved threats to vote in the first meaningful election held in Iraq since the 1950s; later in October 2005 they would vote to ratify a new constitution. In 2006 Saddam Hussein was tried and executed for crimes against humanity. Meanwhile in May 2005, the British government of Prime Minister Tony Blair was also reelected, though with a much reduced parliamentary majority. However, on July 7, 2005, terrorist bombings struck the London bus and subway system with a considerable loss of life. Once more, as in Spain, terrorism struck a major European city. The British government, unlike the Spanish, continued to retain its armed forces in Iraq.

The Iraq war, which has witnessed the death of more than 4,000 American troops and thousands of Iraqis, continued to cause controversy in the United States and between the United States and its NATO allies. However, in early 2007 the Bush administration increased the number of troops committed to Iraq. The purpose of the increase in troops, called "the surge" in the press, was to bring about greater internal stability in the country and most particularly in Baghdad. Over the months the level of violence did subside. By 2008 the United States under the Bush administration and the Iraq government were negotiating the future status of American troops in Iraq with the goal of significantly reducing their numbers in upcoming years. Somewhat surprisingly, issues of the economy more than those of Middle East involvement dominated the 2008 U.S. presidential campaign. Early in 2009 after assuming the presidency, President Barack Obama undertook a policy to establish an orderly withdrawal of most American forces from Iraq by the late summer of 2010. In the next year he announced that all American combat troops would be gone by the end of 2011. Critics argued that events in Iraq suggested that its government and society were ill-prepared to maintain themselves against the growing involvement of Iran, which seemed to be close to developing nuclear weapons.

In Perspective

In 1900, the major European nations dominated the world. Their wealth in terms of manufacturing, investment banking, and consumer demand profoundly influenced the lives of millions of people on every continent. Their military power, particularly their navies, and their colonial administrators controlled most of Africa and much of Asia. Many Europeans were emigrating, especially to the Americas. Wherever Europeans traveled or governed, they could expect that people on other continents would look to Europe as a model for industrial development, accumulation of wealth, and high culture in the arts and sciences. It was the apex of the European era that began at the close of the fifteenth century. In 1900, almost no one could have predicted the enormous human tragedies that would occur in Europe during the next half-century or the retreat from world dominance that would mark the European experience during the rest of the twentieth century.

World War II resulted in the political collapse of Europe. In the wake of the war, the United States and the Soviet Union emerged as two superpowers, both of them equipped with nuclear weapons. From that time until the collapse of the Soviet Union in 1991, the U.S.–Soviet rivalry dominated world affairs. Local flash points became regions for rivalry and conflict between the two nuclear powers.

While the Cold War profoundly influenced international relations, the process of decolonization spread around the globe. One nation after another in Africa and Asia became free of direct European colonial rule. Scores of new nations emerged. Both the Soviet Union and the United States frequently filled the political, economic, and military vacuum the departure of the European colonial rulers left. This situation led each nation into major military interventions—the United States in Vietnam and the Soviet Union in Afghanistan—that had significant domestic consequences in each nation.

By the middle of the 1980s, the economy and political structures of the Soviet Union could no longer bear the burden of the Cold War. The effort to reform Soviet structures Mikhail Gorbachev commenced concluded with the surrender of political monopoly by the Soviet Communist Party. Simultaneously the Soviet Union retreated from Eastern Europe, and the states that the Soviet-controlled Communist Party formerly dominated achieved independence. By 1991, the Soviet Union had collapsed internally. The loosely structured Confederation of Independent States replaced it. Many former Soviet republics became completely independent states, some of which were hostile to Russia.

Since the collapse of the Soviet Union, the United States has remained the single superpower. Just after the turn of the new century, the United States suffered a major and unprecedented terrorist attack on its soil. Thereafter, the United States responded with unprecedented intervention in the Middle East. The political structures of that region were themselves the result of the decisions the Western powers took after World War I at the Versailles peace conference in 1919. In that regard, the conflict between the United States and many groups in the Middle East, most prominently radical political Islamists, represents one more chapter in the long, unfolding twentieth-century story of the global interaction between regions of the world European power once dominated and the West. The ongoing ramifications of decolonization have continued in the wake of the end of the Cold War.

KEY TERMS

Brezhnev Doctrine (p. 950)
Cold War (p. 937)
containment (p. 938)
decolonization (p. 937)
détente (p. 950)
glasnost (p. 961)
jihad (p. 975)
Marshall Plan (p. 939)
NATO (p. 937)
perestroika (p. 961)
Warsaw Pact (p. 937)

REVIEW QUESTIONS

1. How did the United States and the Soviet Union come to dominate Europe after 1945? How would you define the policy of *containment*? In what areas of the world did the United States specifically try to contain Soviet power from 1945 to 1982? Why were 1956 and 1962 crucial years in the Cold War?
2. How did Khrushchev's policies and reforms change the Soviet state after the repression of Stalin? Why did many people consider Khrushchev reckless?
3. Why did the nations of Europe give up their empires? How did World War II affect the movement toward decolonization? How did Gandhi lead India toward independence? How did French decolonization policies differ from Britain's? How did the United States become involved in Vietnam?
4. What internal political pressures did the Soviet Union experience in the 1970s and early 1980s? What steps did the Soviet government take to repress those protests? What role did Gorbachev's attempted reforms play in the collapse of the Soviet Union? What were the major events in Eastern Europe—particularly Poland—that contributed to the collapse of communism? What are the major domestic challenges for the new Confederation of Independent States?
5. Was the former Yugoslavia a national state? Why did it break apart and slide into civil war? How did the West respond to this crisis?
6. What were the major difficulties that the Russian Federation faced in the 1990s and beyond? How did the policies of Yeltsin and Putin address them? How has Putin attempted to preside over a resurgence of Russian great power influence? How do his goals in part reflect concern over the example of the political disintegration of Yugoslavia?
7. How did the American response to the attacks of September 11, 2001, divide the NATO alliance? Why do some European nations feel able to dissent from the U.S. position in the Middle East when they rarely did so during the Cold War?
8. What were the major causes for the rise of radical political Islamism? In what ways is the present U.S. intervention in the Middle East a result of decolonization and in what ways are other factors at work?

SUGGESTED READINGS

A. Ahmed, *Discovering Islam: Making Sense of Muslim History and Society*, rev. ed. (2003). An excellent and readable overview of Islamic–Western relations.

C. Bayly, *Forgotten Wars: Freedom and Revolution in Southeast Asia* (2007). An important volume on decolonization by a master historian of the region.

R. F. Betts, *Decolonization*, 2nd ed. (2004). A wide-ranging study of the process of decolonization after World War II.

A. Brown, *The Gorbachev Factor* (1996). Reflections by a thoughtful observer.

C. Elkins, *Imperial Reckoning: The Untold Story of Britain's Gulag in Kenya* (2005). A study of the violence involved in Britain's eventual departure from Kenya.

M. Ellman and V. Kontorovich, *The Disintegration of the Soviet Economic System* (1992). An overview of the economic strains in the Soviet Union during the 1980s.

G. Fuller, *The Future of Political Islam* (2003). A good overview of Islamist ideology by a former CIA staff member.

J. L. Gaddis, *Strategies of Containment: A Critical Appraisal of American National Security Policy during the Cold War* (2005). A thorough critical analysis of the invention and development of America's strategy toward the Soviet Union.

M. Glenny, *The Balkans, 1804–1999: Nationalism, War and the Great Powers* (1999). A lively narrative by a well-informed journalist.

M. I. Goldman, *Petrostate: Putin, Power, and the New Russia* (2008). A thoughtful, but critical analysis.

D. Halberstam, *The Coldest Winter: America and the Korean War* (2007). A superb narrative by a gifted journalist.

W. Hitchcock, *Struggle for Europe: The Turbulent History of a Divided Continent, 1945–2002* (2003). The best overall narrative now available.

A. Horne, *A Savage War of Peace: Algeria 1954–1962* (1987). A now dated but still classic narrative.

R. Hyam, *Britain's Declining Empire: The Road to Decolonization, 1918–1968* (2007). The best one-volume treatment.

T. Judah, *The Serbs: History, Myth and the Destruction of Yugoslavia* (1997). A clear overview of a complex event.

J. Keay, *Sowing the Wind: The Seeds of Conflict in the Middle East* (2003). A thoughtful account.

N. R. Keddie, *Modern Iran: Roots and Results of Revolution* (2003). Chapters 6 to 12 focus on Iran from 1941 through the 1978 revolution.

J. Keep, *Last of the Empires: A History of the Soviet Union, 1945–1991* (1995) (2007). An outstanding one-volume survey.

G. Kepel, *Jihad: The Trail of Political Islam* (2002). An extensive treatment by a leading French scholar.

Y. Khan, *The Great Partition: The Making of India and Pakistan* (2008). An important recent study of a difficult issue.

P. Khanna, *The Second World: Empires and Influence in the New Global Order* (2008). A volume that seeks to provide a broad global analysis of recent events.

W. R. Louis, *Ends of British Imperialism: The Scramble for Empire, Suez, and Decolonization* (2007). A major study that captures the intensity and passions of the events.

R. Mann, *A Grand Delusion: America's Descent into Vietnam* (2001). The best recent narrative.

K. E. Meyer and S. B. Brysac, *Kingmakers: The Invention of the Modern Middle East* (2008). A lively narrative of the past two centuries of British and then American influence in the Middle East.

D. E. Murphy, S. A. Kondrashev, and G. Bailey, *Battleground Berlin: CIA vs. KGB in the Cold War* (1997). One of the best of a vast literature on Cold War espionage.

W. E. Odom, *The Collapse of the Soviet Military* (1999). A study more wide ranging than the title suggests.

M. Oren, *Power, Faith, and Fantasy: America in the Middle East: 1776 to the Present* (2007). A thoughtful, balanced analysis.

B. Parekh, *Gandhi: A Very Short Introduction* (2001). A useful introduction to Gandhi's ideas.

T. R. Reid, *The United States of Europe: The New Superpower and the End of American Supremacy* (2004). A journalist's exploration of the impact of the European Union on American policy.

T. Shepard, *The Invention of Decolonization: The Algerian War and the Remaking of France* (2008). Explores the impact of the Algerian War on French politics.

L. Shevtsova, *Russia—Lost in Transition: The Yeltsin and Putin Legacies* (2007). A major analysis and meditation on the past two decades.

J. Springhall, *Decolonization since 1945: The Collapse of European Empires* (2001). Systematic treatment of each major former colony.

B. Stanley, *Missions, Nationalism, and the End of Empire* (2003). Discusses the often ignored role of Christian missions and decolonization.

M. Thomas, *The French Empire Between the Wars: Imperialism, Politics and Society* (2005). Useful background to postwar decolonization.

M. Viorst, *In the Shadow of the Prophet: The Struggle for the Soul of Islam* (2001). Explores the divisions in contemporary Islam.

L. Wright, *The Looming Tower: Al Qaeda and the Road to 9/11* (2007). A compelling narrative.

MyHistoryLab™ MEDIA ASSIGNMENTS

Find these resources in the Media Assignments folder for Chapter 29 on **MyHistoryLab**.

QUESTIONS FOR ANALYSIS

1. Why did this wall—which survived for less than thirty years—loom so large in the division between eastern and western Europe?

   ***Section:* The Collapse of European Communism**
   View the **Closer Look** Collapse of the Berlin Wall, p. 967

2. What were Schröder's objections to attacking Iraq?

   ***Section:* A Transformed West**
   Read the **Document** Statement from Chancellor Schröder on the Iraq Crisis, p. 977

3. Does this map help you understand such developments as the formation of NATO and the Marshall Plan?

   ***Section:* The Emergence of the Cold War**
   View the **Map** Interactive Map: Shifting Borders: Eastern Europe, p. 940

4. How did the standoff over Cuba illustrate Cold War tensions and Cold War strategies?

   ***Section:* The Khrushchev Era in the Soviet Union**
   Watch the **Video** Video Lectures: Cold War Connections: Russia, America, Berlin, and Cuba, p. 947

5. How does Nasser use the principles of the Atlantic Charter against the countries that drew up that agreement?

   ***Section:* The Khrushchev Era in the Soviet Union**
   Read the **Document** Gamal Abdel Nasser, Speech on the Suez Canal (Egypt), 1956, p. 947

OTHER RESOURCES FROM THIS CHAPTER

The Emergence of the Cold War

Read the **Document** Joseph Stalin, Excerpts from the "Soviet Victory" Speech, 1946, p. 938

Read the **Document** Winston Churchill, from the Iron Curtain Speech, 1946, p. 938

Read the **Compare and Connect** The Soviet Union and the United States Draw the Lines of the Cold War, p. 942

Later Cold War Confrontations

Watch the **Video** Video: Escaping the Berlin Wall, p. 949

Decolonization: The European Retreat from Empire

View the **Map** Map Discovery: Decolonization, p. 954

Watch the **Video** Video Lectures: Gandhi in India, p. 954

The Turmoil of French Decolonization

Read the **Document** Frantz Fanon, from *The Wretched of the Earth*, p. 958

The Collapse of European Communism

Read the **Document** Mikhail Gorbachev on the Need for Economic Reform (1987), p. 961

View the **Closer Look** Statue of Lenin Toppled During Soviet Collapse, p. 969

The Collapse of Yugoslavia and Civil War

View the **Map** The Former Yugoslavia after 1991, p. 971

View the **Map** Map Discovery: Balkans, p. 971

The Rise of Radical Political Islamism

Watch the **Video** Video Lectures: The 1979 Islamic Revolution in Iran: A Turning Point for the Middle East and the World, p. 975

The most important accomplishment of the European Community was the launching on January 1, 1999, of the Euro, a single monetary unit that replaced the national currencies of most of its member nations. In Frankfurt, Germany, people crowded around a symbol of the new currency. The world financial crisis that commenced in 2008 has placed many internal pressures on the European Community and upon its currency. AP Wide World Photos

Listen to the **Chapter Audio** on **MyHistoryLab.com**

30

Social, Cultural, and Economic Challenges in the West through the Present

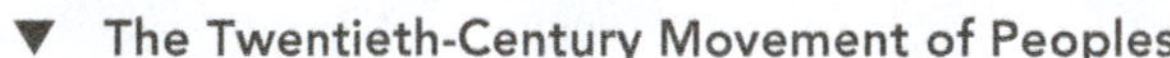

▼ **The Twentieth-Century Movement of Peoples**
Displacement Through War • External and Internal Migration • The New Muslim Population • European Population Trends

▼ **Toward a Welfare State Society**
Christian Democratic Parties • The Creation of Welfare States • Resistance to the Expansion of the Welfare State

▼ **New Patterns in Work and Expectations of Women**
Feminism • More Married Women in the Workforce • New Work Patterns • Women in the New Eastern Europe

▼ **Transformations in Knowledge and Culture**
Communism and Western Europe • Existentialism • Expansion of the University Population and Student Rebellion • The Americanization of Europe • A Consumer Society • Environmentalism

▼ **Art Since World War II**
Cultural Divisions and the Cold War

▼ **The Christian Heritage**
Neo-Orthodoxy • Liberal Theology • Roman Catholic Reform

▼ **Late-Twentieth-Century Technology: The Arrival of the Computer**
The Demand for Calculating Machines • Early Computer Technology • The Development of Desktop Computers

▼ **The Challenges of European Unification**
Postwar Cooperation • The European Economic Community • The European Union • Discord over the Union

▼ **New American Leadership and Financial Crisis**
European Debt Crisis

▼ **In Perspective**

LEARNING OBJECTIVES

How has migration changed the face of Europe?

What effect did the Great Depression and World War II have on the way Europeans viewed the role of government in social and economic life?

How did the status of women in business, politics, and the professions change in Europe in the second half of the twentieth century?

How was cultural and intellectual life transformed in Europe during the twentieth century?

How did the Cold War shape Western art in the second half of the twentieth century?

How has the Christian heritage of the West been affected by events of the twentieth century?

What impact has the computer had on twentieth-century society?

What led to Western European unification following World War II?

Was the year 2008 a turning point in the relationship between the United States and Europe?

THE COLD WAR defined the life of the West during most of the second half of the twentieth century. This conflict affected not only political developments and military alliances, but also the lives of millions of Europeans and Americans. For almost half a century, the easy travel throughout the world that many people take for granted today and that enriches the lives of thousands of American students every year was impossible. Vast areas were closed off. The Iron Curtain separated families. Most of Eastern Europe developed separately from Western Europe, with consequences in the quality of life, approaches to the relationship between states and their citizenry, and attitudes about gender, social responsibility, the environment, and the future.

Nevertheless, European society in both Eastern and Western Europe changed remarkably after World War II, as did, of course, the United States. Western Europe enjoyed unprecedented prosperity, peace, and technological advances. During the same years, Europe also took unprecedented steps toward economic cooperation and political union.

▼ The Twentieth-Century Movement of Peoples

In the twentieth century, the movement of peoples transformed European society and the character of many European communities. The Soviets' and Nazis' forced migrations, deportations, and, in some cases, mass executions were only the most dramatic examples of this kind of demographic change through violence. World War II and the subsequent economic transformation of the Continent brought extensive migrations. The most pervasive trend in this movement of peoples was the continuing shift from the countryside to the cities. Today, except for Albania, at least one-third of the population of every European nation lives in large cities. In Western Europe, city dwellers are approximately 75 percent of the population.

Watch the Video "Video Lectures: Identity Politics: Notting Hill Carnival" on **MyHistoryLab.com**

Other vast forced movements of peoples by governments, however, were little discussed during the Cold War. During the twentieth century, millions of Germans, Hungarians, Poles, Ukrainians, Bulgarians, Serbs, Finns, Chechens, Armenians, Greeks, Turks, Estonians, Latvians, Lithuanians, Bosnian Muslims, and other peoples were displaced.

These forced displacements transformed parts of Europe. Stalin moved whole nationalities from one area of the Soviet Union and its satellite states to another. Millions of people were killed in the process. The Nazis first displaced the Jews and then sought to exterminate them. Throughout Eastern Europe, cities that once had large Jewish populations and a vibrant Jewish religious and cultural life lost any Jewish presence. The displacement of Germans from Eastern Europe back into Germany immediately after World War II transformed cities that had had large German populations into places almost wholly populated by self-identified Czechs, Poles, or Russians.

Displacement Through War

World War II created a vast refugee problem. An estimated 46 million people were displaced in central and Eastern Europe and the Soviet Union alone between 1938 and 1948. Many cities in Germany and in central and Eastern Europe had been bombed or overrun by invading armies. The Nazis had moved hundreds of thousands of foreign workers into Germany as slave laborers. Millions more were prisoners of war. Some of these people returned to their homeland willingly; others, particularly Soviet prisoners fearful of being executed by Stalin, had to be forced to go back, and many were executed. Hundreds of thousands of Baltic, Polish, and Yugoslav prisoners found asylum in Western Europe.

View the Map "Map Discovery: Events in Eastern Europe, 1989–1990" on **MyHistoryLab.com**

Changes in political borders after the war also uprooted many people. For example, Poland, Czechoslovakia, and Hungary forcibly expelled millions of ethnic Germans from their territories to Germany. This transfer of over 12 million Germans in effect "solved" the problem of German minorities living outside of Germany's national boundaries that had been one of Hitler's excuses for aggression against neighboring countries, but at tremendous cost for those involved. In another case of forced migration, hundreds of thousands of Poles were transferred from territory the Soviet Union annexed to Poland's new western territories, acquired from Germany. Other minorities, such as Ukrainians in Poland and Italians on the Yugoslav coast, were driven back into what were presented as their "homelands," although many had never set foot on the territory of Ukraine or Italy before. As one historian has commented, "War, violence, and massive social dislocation turned Versailles's dream of national homogeneity into realities."[1]

External and Internal Migration

Between 1945 and 1960, approximately half a million Europeans left Europe each year. This was the largest outward migration since the 1920s, when around 700,000 persons had left annually. In the second half of the nineteenth century, most immigrants had been from rural areas. After World War II, they often included educated city dwellers. Immediately after the war, some governments encouraged migration because they were afraid

[1]Mark Mazower, *Dark Continent: Europe's Twentieth Century* (New York: Knopf, 1999), p. 218.

that, as in the 1930s, their economies would not be able to provide adequate employment for all their citizens.

Decolonization in the postwar period led many European colonials to return to Europe from overseas. The most dramatic example of this phenomenon was the more than one million French colonials who moved to France after the end of the Algerian war in 1962 (see Chapter 29). Britons returned from parts of the British Empire; Dutch returned from Indonesia in the late 1940s; Belgians from the Congo in the 1960s; and Portuguese from Mozambique and Angola in the 1970s.

Decolonization also led non-European inhabitants of the former colonies to migrate to Europe. Great Britain, for example, received thousands of immigrants from its former colonies in the Caribbean, Africa, and the Indian subcontinent. France received many immigrants from its empire in Africa, Indochina, and the Arab world. This influx has proved to be a long-term source of social tension and conflict. In Britain, racial tensions were high during the 1980s. France faced similar difficulties, which contributed to the emergence of the National Front, an extreme right-wing group led by Jean-Marie Le Pen (b. 1928) that sought to exploit the resentment many working-class voters felt toward North African immigrants. In 2002, Le Pen won enough votes to become one of the two candidates in the run-off election for the French presidency, although he lost overwhelmingly to Jacques Chirac (b. 1932) in the final ballot. Similar pressures have arisen in Germany, Austria, Italy, the Netherlands, Denmark, Switzerland, and elsewhere. Such tension did not result only from immigration from Africa and Asia; internal European migration—from the Balkans, Turkey, and the former Soviet Union, often of people in search of jobs—also changed the social and economic face of the Continent and led to a backlash. In recent years, internal immigration within the European Union has seen the movement of significant numbers of people. However, the growing Muslim presence in Europe has produced some of the most serious ethnic and political tensions.

The New Muslim Population

As recounted earlier in this textbook, well into the twentieth century the European relationship with most of the Muslim world was fraught with misinformation and misunderstanding. Muslims from the Ottoman Empire, the greatest Muslim state, rarely traveled in Europe, and few Europeans traveled in the empire. Europeans encountered Muslims mainly as subjects, in colonies such as Algeria, Egypt, the Indian subcontinent, sub-Saharan Africa, and the East Indies. In all these regions from at least the mid-nineteenth century onward, Christian missionaries often clashed with Muslim religious teachers.

At the same time, most Europeans, except for a few communities in the Balkans and the former Soviet Empire, regarded themselves and their national cultures as either Christian or secular. Indeed, until recently most Europeans paid little direct attention to Islam as a domestic matter.

That indifference began to change in the 1960s and had dissolved by the end of the twentieth century as a sizable Muslim population settled in Europe. This highly diverse immigrant community had become an issue in Europe even before the events of September 11, 2001.

Read the Document "Justin Vaisse, from 'Veiled Meaning' (France) 2004" on **MyHistoryLab.com**

The immigration of Muslims into Europe, and particularly Western Europe, arose from two chief sources: European economic growth and decolonization. As the economies of Western Europe began to recover in the quarter century after World War II,

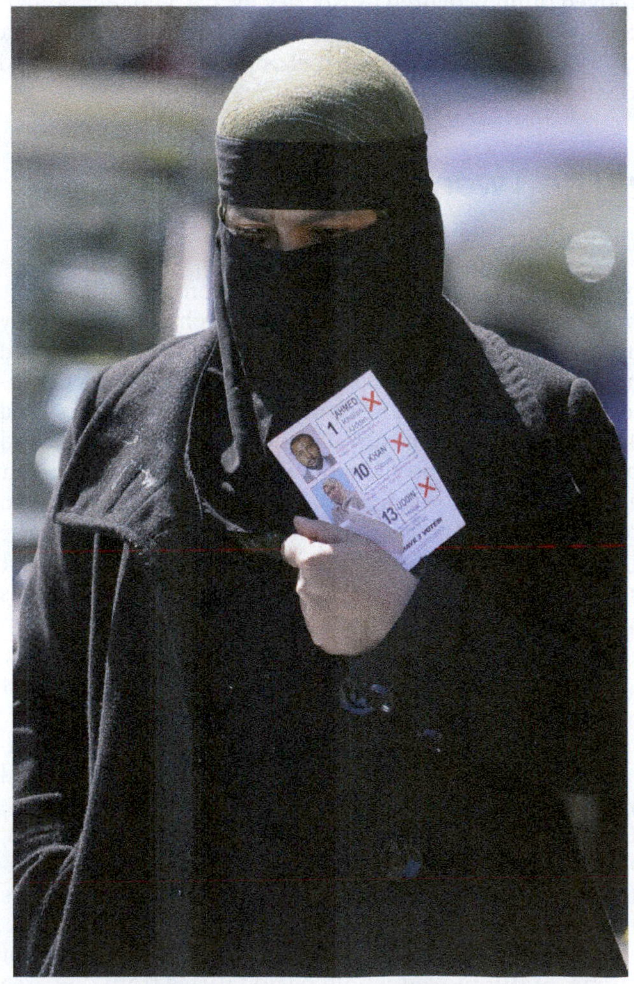

A woman carrying an election leaflet walks past a polling station in the east end of London. The presence of foreign-born Muslims whose labor is necessary for the prosperity of the European economy is an important issue in contemporary Europe. Many of these Muslims live in self-contained communities. Paul Hackett/Reuters a labor shortage developed. To fill this demand, Western Europe imported laborers, many of whom came from Muslim nations. For example, Turkish "guest workers" were invited to move to West Germany—on a temporary basis, it was presumed—in the 1960s, and Britain welcomed Pakistanis. The aftermath of decolonization and the quest for a better life led Muslims from East Africa and the Indian subcontinent to settle in Great Britain. The Algerian war brought many Muslims to France. Today there are approximately 1.3 million Muslims in Great Britain, 3.2 million in Germany, and 4.2 million in France. Smaller but still significant numbers have settled in Italy, Spain, Sweden, Denmark, and the Netherlands.

These Muslim immigrant communities share certain social and religious characteristics. Originally, many Muslims came to Europe expecting they would eventually return to their homes, an expectation their host countries shared. Neither the immigrants nor the host nations gave much thought to assimilation. Moreover, except for Great Britain, where all immigrants from the Commonwealth may vote immediately upon settling there, European governments made it difficult for Muslim or any other immigrants to take part in civic life. Unlike the United States, few European countries had any experience dealing with large-scale immigration. The Muslim communities have, therefore, generally remained unassimilated and self-contained. This segregation has provided internal community support for Muslim immigrants but has also prevented them from fully engaging with the societies in which they live. Many of their children have not learned European languages well, and Muslim women face challenges from both their own communities and the host communities when they try to become professionally or politically active outside the home.

Yet the world around these communities has changed. Many of the largely unskilled jobs that the immigrants originally filled have disappeared. Most of the Muslim immigrants to Europe, unlike many who have settled in the United States and Canada, were neither highly skilled nor professionally educated. As a result, they and their adult children who may have grown up in Europe find it difficult to get jobs in the modern service economy. Furthermore, as European economic growth has slowed, European Muslims have become the target of politicians, such as Le Pen in France, who seek to blame the immigrants for a host of problems, from crime to unemployment.

Read the **Document** "Jörg Haider, from *The Freedom I Mean* (Austria), 1995" on **MyHistoryLab.com**

The radicalization of parts of the Islamic world has also touched the Muslim communities in Europe. Although Turkish Muslims living in Germany come from a nation that has been secularized since the 1920s and thus tend to be less religiously observant than Pakistani Muslims dwelling in Great Britain, Muslims from both countries have been involved in radical Islamic groups. The July 7, 2005, suicide bombings in London were carried out by four young Muslims, three of whom had been born in the United Kingdom and one in Jamaica. By contrast, the French government has exerted more control over its Muslim population. However, that policy appeared to have failed badly when in the autumn of 2005 immigrant youth, largely Muslim, carried out riots in various parts of France. These were the most serious civil disturbances in France since 1968. Subsequent riots have occurred in Paris. There have also been sharp disputes in France over attempts by the government to forbid young Muslim women from wearing headscarves while attending secular government schools. The controversy over headscarves in France, which opponents say violates the French principle of a secular republic, has become so heated that a feminist candidate representing a far-left political group, the Nouveau Parti Anti-capitaliste, in 2010 has been attacked for wearing a headscarf despite her public support of secularism and feminism.

Nonetheless, European Muslims are not a homogeneous group. They come from different countries, have different class backgrounds, and espouse different Islamic traditions. Many European Muslims and Muslim clerics disagree strongly with each other. At the same time, these Muslim communities, so often now marked by deep poverty and unemployment, have become a major concern for European social workers, who disagree among themselves about how their governments should respond to them. What has become clear, however, is that European governments cannot regard their Muslim populations as passive communities; rather, European governments and societies must engage them as a permanent fact in the life of early twenty-first-century Europe.

European Population Trends

During the past quarter century, the European birthrate has stabilized in a manner that has deeply disturbed many observers. Europeans are having so few children that they are no longer replacing themselves. Whereas in the 1950s European women on average bore 2.1 children (the minimum replacement level), that rate fell to 1.9 in the 1980s, 1.47 in the early 2000s, and has rebounded slightly to 1.6 at present. In some countries, including Austria, Germany, Hungary, Italy, Portugal, and Spain, the rate is even lower. In the early twenty-first century, the United States fertility rate reached its lowest level in a century, 2.0, but was still substantially higher than European rates. If the current rates more or less hold, by the middle of this century, the United States will have more people than Europe for the first time in history.

There is no consensus on why the European birthrate has declined. One reason often cited is that women are postponing having children until later in their childbearing years. Another is that the economic crises of the past

COMPARE AND CONNECT Muslim Women Debate France's Ban on the Veil

Read the Compare and Connect on MyHistoryLab.com

IN APRIL 2011, a French law banning the wearing of certain types of veils in public went into effect. The ban applied to a covering that exposed only a woman's eyes, known outside of France as a niqab, but referred to as a burqa in the French debate. The 2011 law was only one further step in an extended debate about the place of public displays of religious piety, women's rights, the role of Muslims in French public life, and France's secular tradition. In 2004, France had already banned the wearing of veils in public schools. In June 2009, French president Nicolas Sarkozy explained his support of a more thorough ban: "We cannot accept to have in our country women who are prisoners behind netting, cut off from all social life, deprived of identity. . . . That is not the idea that the French republic has of women's dignity. The burqa is not a sign of religion, it is a sign of subservience. It will not be welcome on the territory of the French republic." In the months preceding and following the ban, France's public conversations about the veil exposed the complexity of a subject that involves feminists, Muslims, and advocates of minority rights in France, with representatives of each group often on both sides of the debate.

QUESTIONS

1. **How and why is the debate about the veil particularly fierce in France? What elements of French history and identity are challenged by the veil?**
2. **How does Eltahawy distinguish between Muslims' rights and the right to wear a veil?**
3. **Why might feminists be divided over the issue of the veil? In what ways are women's rights involved in this debate, and who claims to speak on behalf of women?**
4. **What are the different reasons cited for women's wearing of the veil? Are all of them related to religious piety?**
5. **What larger issues about the role of Muslims in France are exposed by this debate?**

I. Mona Eltahawy Argues Women's Rights Trump Cultural Relativism

Defenders of the French ban on the veil include some prominent Muslim women. Mona Eltahawy, an award-winning columnist born in Egypt and currently living in New York City, calls herself a "proud liberal Muslim." Her opposition to the veil is based not on fear of Islam, but on her belief that representing the veil as a necessary sign of Muslim feminine piety stems from a misinterpretation of the Koran. Her commentary shows the complexity of a debate that includes topics as diverse as xenophobia, cultural relativism, feminism, secularism, and a deep conflict about the nature of individual freedom.

Some have likened this issue to Switzerland's move last year to ban the construction of minarets. . . .

Underlying both bans is a dangerous silence: liberal refusal to robustly discuss what it means to be European, what it means to be Muslim, and racism and immigration. Liberals decrying the infringement of women's rights should acknowledge that the absence of debate on these critical issues allowed the political right and the Muslim right to seize the situation.

Europe's ascendant political right is unapologetically xenophobic. It caricatures the religion that I practice and uses those distortions to fan Islamophobia. But ultra-conservative strains of Islam, such as Salafism and Wahhabism, also caricature our religion and use that Islamophobia to silence opposition. . . .

The strains of Islam that promote face veils do not believe in the concept of a woman's right to choose and describe women as needing to be hidden to prove their "worth." . . . There is no choice in such conditioning. That is not a message Muslims learn in our holy book, the Koran, nor is the face veil prescribed by the majority of Muslim scholars.

The French ban has been condemned as anti-liberal and anti-feminist. Where were those howls when niqabs began appearing in European countries, where for years women fought for rights? A bizarre political correctness tied the tongues of those who would normally rally to defend women's rights.

There are several ideological conflicts here: Within Islam, liberal and feminist Muslims refuse to believe that full-length veils are mandatory. . . . Feminist groups run by Muslim women in various Western countries fight misogynistic practices justified in the name of culture and religion. Cultural relativists, they say, don't want to "offend" anyone by protesting the disappearance of women behind the veil—or worse.

For example, French women of North African and Muslim descent launched Ni Putes Ni Soumises (Neither Whores Nor Submissives) in response to violence against women in housing projects and forced marriages of immigrant women in France. That group supports the ban and has denounced the racism faced in France by immigrant women and men.

Cultural integration has failed, or not taken place, in many European countries, but women shouldn't pay the price for it. ■

From Mona Eltahawy, "From Liberals and Feminists, Unsettling Silence on Rending the Muslim Veil," *Washington Post*, Saturday, July 17, 2010, available at http://www.washingtonpost.com/wp-dyn/content/article/2010/07/16/AR2010071604356.html.

II. Kenza Drider Defends Her Right to Wear the Veil in Public

Kenza Drider was an ordinary French citizen before the debate about the public wearing of the veil took over French politics and society. A housewife and mother of four, Drider insists that wearing the veil is an expression of her personal freedom, and not a reflection of pressure coming from her husband, father, or any religious authority. Her husband, Allal, told a reporter that his response when he first saw his wife in a full-body niqab was "Are you really going out dressed like that?" When two women were fined for violating the French ban in September 2011, Kenza Drider announced her largely symbolic candidacy for president against incumbent President Sarkozy.

I will be going about my business in my full veil as I have for the last 12 years and nothing and nobody is going to stop me. . . . This whole law makes France look ridiculous. . . . I never thought I'd see the day when France, my France, the country I was born in and I love, the country of *liberté, égalité, fraternité*, would do something that so obviously violates people's freedom.

Kenza Drider, a French housewife from the town of Avignon, appears in public in a niqab, a face covering that reveals only her eyes, despite a 2011 ban on such veils in France. © Reuters

I'll be getting on with my life and if they want to send me to prison for wearing the niqab then so be it. One thing's for sure: I'm not taking it off.

[Wearing a veil] is not a religious constraint since it is not laid down in Islam or the Qur'an that I have to wear a full veil. It is my personal choice. . . .

I would never encourage others to do it just because I do. That is their choice. My daughters can do what they like. As I tell them, this is my choice, not theirs. . . .

I never covered my head when I was young. I came from a family of practising Muslims, but we were not expected to even wear a headscarf. Then I began looking into Islam and what it meant to be a Muslim and decided to wear a headscarf. Afterwards in my research into the wives of the Prophet I saw they wore the full veil and I liked this idea and decided to wear it. Before, I had felt something was missing. Then I put it on and I felt serene and complete. It pleased me and it has become a part of me. . . .

When President Sarkozy said: 'The burqa is not welcome in France', the president, my president, opened the door for racism, aggression and attacks on Islam. This is an attempt to stigmatise Islam and it has created enormous racism and Islamophobia that wasn't there before. . . .

This is about basic fundamental human rights and freedoms. I will go out in my full veil and I will fight. I'm prepared to go all the way to the European court of human rights and I will fight for my liberty.

Fines? They don't bother me. What is the state going to do, send a policeman outside my front door to give me a ticket every time I go out? For me this is women's liberty, the liberty to wear what I wish and not be punished for it.

If women want to walk around half-naked I don't object to them doing so. If they want to wear tight jeans where you can see their underwear or walk around with their breasts hanging out, I don't give a damn. But if they are allowed to do that, why should I not be allowed to cover up? ■

From Kim Willsher, " 'Burqa ban' in France: housewife vows to face jail rather than submit," *The Observer*, Saturday, April 9, 2011, available at http://www.guardian.co.uk/world/2011/apr/10/france-burqa-law-kenza-drider.

decade have made multiple children an indulgence some families feel they cannot afford. This demographic shift suggests that Europe may soon need new workers from outside its borders. Nevertheless, in response to public opinion, governments have been trying to limit immigration into Europe.

This falling birthrate means that Europe faces the prospect of an aging population, with fewer workers and more retirees. This puts tremendous financial stress on those European states that have traditionally provided strong state-funded support for retired persons. Postwar European prosperity has been tied to a strong welfare system, which the new demographics may make it impossible for states to continue to afford.

▼ Toward a Welfare State Society

In the second half of the twentieth century, the nations of Western Europe achieved unprecedented economic prosperity and maintained or inaugurated independent, liberal democratic governments. Most of them also confronted problems associated with decolonization and with maintaining economic growth.

The end of World War II saw vast constitutional changes in much of Western Europe, except for Portugal and Spain, which remained dictatorships until the mid-1970s. Before or during the war, Germany, Austria, Italy, and France had experienced authoritarian governments. The construction of stable, liberal, democratic political frameworks became a major goal of their postwar political leaders, as well as of the United States. All concerned recognized that the earlier political structures in those nations had failed to resist the rise of right-wing, antidemocratic movements. The Great Depression had shown that democracy requires a social and economic base, as well as a political structure. Most Europeans came to believe that government ought to ensure economic prosperity and social security. Success at doing so, they hoped, would stave off the kind of turmoil that had brought on tyranny and war.

Christian Democratic Parties

Democratic socialist parties faced challenges in the postwar era, in which they were opposed by both conservatives and communists. Some were successful, including the British Labour Party, and social democratic parties in Germany, Austria, and Scandinavia. On the continent, social democratic parties often shared power with various Christian democratic parties. Those Christian democratic parties, usually leading coalition governments, often introduced new policies that were also supported by social democrats.

Christian democratic parties were a major new feature of postwar politics. They were largely Roman Catholic in leadership and membership. Catholic parties had existed in Europe since the late nineteenth century. Until the 1930s, however, they had been conservative and had protected the social, political, and educational interests of the church. The postwar Christian democratic parties of Germany, France, Austria, and Italy, however, welcomed non-Catholic members. Democracy, economic growth, and anticommunism were their hallmarks. After 1947, in a policy that responded to United States pressure as well as internal conviction, communists were systematically excluded from Western European governments.

The Creation of Welfare States

The Great Depression, the rise of authoritarian states in the wake of economic dislocation and mass unemployment, and World War II, which involved more people in a war effort than ever before, changed how many Europeans thought about social welfare. Governments began to spend more on social welfare than they did on the military. This reallocation of funds was a reaction to the state violence of the first half of the century.

The modern European welfare state was broadly similar across the Continent. Before World War II, except in Scandinavia, the two basic models for social legislation were the German and the British. Bismarck had introduced social insurance in Germany during the 1880s to undermine the German Social Democratic Party. In effect, the imperial German government provided workers with social insurance and thus some sense of social security while denying them significant political participation. In early-twentieth-century Britain, where all classes had access to the political system, social insurance was targeted toward the poor. In both the German and British systems, workers were insured only against the risks from disease, injury on the job, and old age. Unemployment was assumed to be only a short-term problem and often one that workers brought on themselves. People higher up in the social structure could look out for themselves and did not need government help.

After World War II, the concept emerged that social insurance against predictable risks was a social right and should be available to all citizens. In Britain, William B. Beveridge (1879–1963) famously set forth this concept in 1942. Paradoxically, making coverage universal, as Beveridge recommended, appealed to conservatives as well as socialists. If medical care, old-age pensions, and other benefits were available to all, they would not become a device to redistribute income from one part of the population to another.

The first major European nation to begin to create a welfare state was Britain, in 1945 to 1951 under the Labour Party ministry of Clement Attlee (1883–1967). The most important element of this early legislation was the creation of the National Health Service. France and Germany did not adopt similar health care legislation until the 1970s because their governments initially refused to make coverage universal.

The spread of welfare legislation (including unemployment insurance) within Western Europe was related to both the Cold War and domestic political and economic policy. The communist states of Eastern Europe provided their people social security as well as full employment. The capitalist states came to believe they had to provide similar security for their people, in order to disarm a potential appeal of communism within their populations.

Resistance to the Expansion of the Welfare State

Western European attitudes toward the welfare state have reflected four periods that have marked economic life since the end of the war. The first period was one of reconstruction from 1945 through the early 1950s. It was followed by the second period—almost twenty-five years of generally steady and expanding economic growth. The third period brought first an era of inflation in the late 1970s and then one of relatively low growth and high unemployment from the 1990s to the early twenty-first century. We are now in the midst of a fourth period, in which financial crises have led to unstable economies and a questioning of the safety of allowing the market to self-regulate. During each of the first two periods, a general conviction existed, based on Keynesian economics, that the foundation of economic policy was government involvement in a mixed economy. From the late 1970s, more people came to believe the market should be allowed to regulate itself and that government should be less involved in, though not completely withdraw from, the economy. Most recently, the financial crises of the twenty-first century have led many Europeans to question their earlier abandonment of Keynesian economics.

The most influential political figure in reasserting the importance of markets and resisting the power of labor unions was Margaret Thatcher (b. 1925) of the British Conservative Party who served as prime minister from 1979 to 1990. She cut taxes and sought to curb inflation. She and her party were determined to roll back many of the socialist policies that Britain had enacted since the war. Her administration privatized many industries that Labour Party governments had nationalized. She also curbed the power of the trade unions in a series of bitter and often violent confrontations. Although her administration roused enormous controversy, she was able to push these policies through Parliament. Furthermore, over time the British Labour Party under the leadership of Tony Blair (b. 1953) itself largely came to accept what was at the time known as the Thatcher Revolution.

Read the **Compare and Connect** "Margaret Thatcher and Tony Blair Debate Government's Social Responsibility for Welfare" on **MyHistoryLab.com**

While Thatcher redirected the British economy, the government-furnished welfare services now found across continental Europe began to encounter resistance. The funding on which they are based assumed a growing population and low unemployment. As the proportion of the population consuming the services of the welfare state—the sick, the injured, the unemployed, and the elderly—increases relative to the number of able-bodied workers who pay for them, the costs of those services have risen.

The leveling-off of population growth in Europe discussed in the previous section has thus imperiled the benefits of the welfare state. Furthermore, during the past two decades, significant levels of unemployment in major Western European nations have increased welfare payments. The low fertility rates across the Continent mean the next working generation will have fewer people to support the retired elderly population, creating a challenge to the system that has been the hallmark of postwar European prosperity.

Margaret Thatcher, a shopkeeper's daughter who became the first female prime minister of Great Britain, served in that office from May 1979 through November 1990. Known as the "Iron Lady" of British politics, she led the Conservative Party to three electoral victories and carried out extensive restructuring of the British government and economy. In this photo, she greets the audience of the Conservative Party Conference in Brighton after an IRA bomb attack on her hotel earlier that day. © Bettmann/CORBIS

▼ New Patterns in Work and Expectations of Women

Since World War II, the work patterns and social expectations of European women have changed enormously. In all social ranks, women have begun to assume larger economic and political roles. More women have entered the "learned professions," and more are filling major managerial positions than ever before in European history. Yet, despite enormous gains during the second half of the twentieth century, and despite the collapse of those authoritarian governments whose social policies inhibited women from advancing into the mainstream of society, gender inequality remained a major characteristic of the social life of Europe at the opening of the twenty-first century.

Feminism

Since World War II, European feminism, although less highly organized than in America, has set forth a new agenda. The most influential postwar work on women's issues was Simone de Beauvoir's (1908–1986) *The Second Sex*, published in 1949. In that work, de Beauvoir explored the difference being a woman had made in her life. (See the Document "Simone de Beauvoir Urges Economic Freedom for Women," page 992.) She was part of the French intellectual establishment and thus wrote from a privileged position. Nonetheless, she and other European feminists argued that, at all levels, European women experienced distinct social and economic disadvantages. Divorce and family laws, for example, favored men. European feminists also called attention to the social problems that women faced, including spousal abuse.

In contrast to earlier feminism, recent feminism has been less a political movement pressing for specific rights than a social movement offering a broader critique of European culture. Several new feminist journals appeared during the 1970s, many of which are still published: *Courage*, *Emma—Magazine by Women for Women*, and *Spare Rib*. A statement in *Spare Rib*, an English magazine, captures the spirit of these publications:

> *Spare Rib* aims to reflect women's lives in all their diverse situations so that they can recognize themselves in its pages. This is done by making the magazine a vehicle for their writing and their images. Most of all, *Spare Rib* aims to bring women together and support them in taking control of their lives.[2]

This emphasis on women controlling their own lives may be the most important element of recent European feminism. Whereas in the past feminists sought and, in significant measure, gained legal and civil equality with men, they are now pursuing personal independence and issues that are particular to women. In this sense, feminism is an important manifestation of the critical tradition in Western culture.

[2]Bonnie S. Anderson and Judith P. Zinsser, *A History of Their Own: Women in Europe from Prehistory to the Present*, Vol. 2 (New York: HarperPerennial, 1988), p. 412.

Simone de Beauvoir was the major feminist writer in postwar Europe. Here she appears as a defense witness at the trial of a mother accused of helping her minor daughter receive an abortion. © Michel Artault/Apis/Sygma/CORBIS

More Married Women in the Workforce

Throughout the postwar period, the number of married women in the workforce has risen sharply. Both middle-class and working-class married women have sought jobs outside the home. Because of the low birthrate in the 1930s, there were fewer young single women in Europe in the years just after World War II. Married women entered the job market to replace them. Some factories changed their work shifts to accommodate the needs of married women. Consumer conveniences and improvements in health care also made it easier for married women to enter the workforce by reducing the demands child care and housekeeping made on their time. At the same time, all surveys indicate that the need to provide care for their children continues to be the most important difficulty women face in the workplace. Where child care is inadequate, unavailable, or unaffordable, women are more likely to remain in part-time employment. This contributes to income inequality for women and limited career opportunities relative to men in the same occupations and with the same qualifications.

In the twentieth century, children were no longer expected to contribute substantially to family income. They now spend more than a decade in compulsory education. Many families need more income than one worker can provide. Such financial necessity led many married women back to work. Evidence also suggests that married women began to work to escape the boredom and isolation of housework. Most often, however, working women continue to be responsible for maintaining the household and caring for children, leading to what has been called the "double burden," or work inside and outside the home.

Women in some European countries, such as Norway, have demanded that the state provide support for working mothers that will guarantee sufficient child care for them to work with the same degree of flexibility and opportunity as men with children. Advocates of enhanced child-care provisions used campaigns, protests, and rallies to pressure parliament to address the issue in the 1980s. Some Norwegians demanded equal access to child-care facilities, while others wanted state-funded home care allowances to pay for women to stay home with young children. Many feminists consider such home-care allowances to threaten gender equality in the workplace, and argue that they constitute pressure on women to stay home with young children.

New Work Patterns

The work pattern of European women has been far more consistent in the twentieth century than it had been in the nineteenth. Single women enter the workforce after their schooling and continue to work after marriage. They may stop working to care for their young children, but they return to work when the children begin school. For many women, however, returning to work is combined with fewer opportunities for professional advancement, limited hours, and unequal pay for the same work done by a male counterpart.

When women died relatively young, childrearing filled a large proportion of their lives. As a longer lifespan has shortened that proportion, women throughout the

Women and children participating in a women's liberation protest in London in 1971. Shepard Sherbell/CORBIS

Document

SIMONE DE BEAUVOIR URGES ECONOMIC FREEDOM FOR WOMEN

Simone de Beauvoir was the most important feminist voice of mid-twentieth-century Europe. In The Second Sex, *published in France in 1949, she explored the experience of women coming of age in a world of ideas, institutions, and social expectations shaped historically by men. Much of the book discusses the psychological strategies that modern European women had developed to deal with their status as "the second sex." Toward the end of her book, de Beauvoir argues that economic freedom and advancement for women are fundamental to their personal fulfillment.*

Why does de Beauvoir argue that economic freedom for women must accompany their achievement of civic rights? Why does the example of the small number of professional women illustrate issues for European women in general? How does she indicate that even professional women must overcome a culture in which the experience of women is fundamentally different from that of men? Do de Beauvoir's comments seem relevant for women at the opening of the twenty-first century? What similarities do you see to the views of Priscilla Wakefield (Chapter 15) and Mary Wollstonecraft (Chapter 17)?

According to French law, obedience is no longer included among the duties of a wife, and each woman citizen has the right to vote; but these civil liberties remain theoretical as long as they are unaccompanied by economic freedom. . . . It is through gainful employment that woman has traversed most of the distance that separated her from the male; and nothing else can guarantee her liberty in practice. Once she ceases to be a parasite, the system based on her dependence crumbles; between her and the universe there is no longer any need for a masculine mediator. . . .

When she is productive, active, she regains her transcendence; in her projects she concretely affirms her status as subject; in connection with the aims she pursues, with the money and the rights she takes possession of, she makes trial of and senses her responsibility. . . .

There are . . . a fairly large number of privileged women who find in their professions a means of economic and social autonomy. These come to mind when one considers woman's possibilities and her future. . . . [E]ven though they constitute as yet only a minority; they continue to be the subject of debate between feminists and antifeminists. The latter assert that the emancipated women of today succeed in doing nothing of importance in the world and that furthermore they have difficulty in achieving their own inner equilibrium. The former exaggerate the results obtained by professional women and are blind to their inner confusion. There is no good reason . . . to say they are on the wrong road; and still it is certain that they are not tranquilly installed in their new realm: as yet they are only halfway there. The woman who is economically emancipated from man is not for all that in a moral, social, and psychological situation identical with that of man. The way she carried on her profession and her devotion to it depends on the context supplied by the total pattern of her life. For when she begins her adult life she does not have behind her the same past as does a boy; she is not viewed by society in the same way; the universe presents itself to her in a different perspective. The fact of being a woman today poses peculiar problems for an independent human individual.

West are seeking ways to lead satisfying lives after their children have grown. Decisions about when to have children and how many have also shaped the late-twentieth-century work patterns for women. Many women have begun to limit the number of children they bear or to forgo childbearing and childrearing altogether. The age at which women have decided to bear children has risen, to the early twenties in Eastern Europe and to the late twenties in Western Europe. In urban areas, women have fewer children and have them later in life than rural women do.

Women in the New Eastern Europe

Under communism, women generally enjoyed social equality, as well as a broad spectrum of government-financed benefits. Most women (normally well over 50 percent) worked in these societies, both because they could and because they were expected to. No significant women's movements existed, however, because communist governments regarded them with suspicion, as they did all independent associations.

The new governments of the region are free but have shown little concern with women's issues. Indeed, the economic difficulties the new governments face may endanger their funding of health and welfare programs that benefit women and children. For example, a free market economy may limit the extensive maternity benefits upon which Eastern European women previously depended. Moreover, the high proportion of women in the workforce could leave them more vulnerable than men to the region's economic troubles. Women may be laid off before men and hired later than men for lower pay.

▼ Transformations in Knowledge and Culture

Knowledge and culture in Europe were rapidly transformed in the twentieth century. Institutions of higher education enrolled a larger and more diverse student body, making knowledge more widely available than ever before. Also, movements such as existentialism challenged traditional intellectual attitudes. Environmental concerns also raised new issues. Throughout this ferment, representatives of the Christian faith tried to keep their religion relevant.

Communism and Western Europe

Until the final decade of the twentieth century, Western Europe had large, organized communist parties, as well as groups of intellectuals sympathetic to communism. After the Bolshevik victory in the Russian Revolution and the subsequent civil war, the Western European socialist movement divided into independent democratic socialist parties and Soviet-dominated communist parties that followed the dictates of the Third International. In the 1920s and 1930s, those two groups fought each other with only rare moments of cooperation, such as that achieved during the French Popular Front in 1936.

The Intellectuals During the 1930s, as liberal democracies floundered in the face of the Great Depression and as right-wing regimes spread across the Continent, many people saw communism as a vehicle for protecting humane and even liberal values. European university students were often affiliated with the Communist Party. They and older intellectuals visited the Soviet Union and praised what they saw as Stalin's achievements. Many of these intellectuals did not know about Stalin's terror. Others simply closed their eyes to it, believing humane ends might come from inhumane methods. One group of former communists, writing after World War II, described their attraction toward, and later disillusionment with, communism in a book titled *The God That Failed* (1949).

Four events proved crucial to the intellectuals' disillusionment: the great Soviet public purge trials of the late 1930s, the Spanish Civil War (1936–1939), the Nazi–Soviet pact of 1939, and the Soviet invasion of Hungary in 1956. Arthur Koestler's (1905–1983) novel *Darkness at Noon* (1940) recorded a former communist's view of the purges. George Orwell (1903–1950), who had never been a communist but who had sympathized with the party, expressed his disappointment with Stalin's policy in Spain in *Homage to Catalonia* (1938). The Nazi–Soviet pact damaged Stalin's image as an opponent of fascism. Other intellectuals, such as French philosopher Jean-Paul Sartre (1905–1980), continued to believe in the Soviet Union during and after the war, but the Hungarian Revolution cooled their ardor. The Soviet-led invasion of Czechoslovakia in 1968 confirmed a general disillusionment with Soviet policies by left-wing Western European intellectuals.

Yet disillusionment with the Soviet Union or with Stalin did not mean disillusionment with Marxism or with radical socialist criticisms of European society. Some writers and social critics looked to the establishment of alternative communist governments based on non-Soviet models. During the decade after World War II, Yugoslavia provided such an example. Beginning in the late 1950s, radical students and a few intellectuals found inspiration in the Chinese Revolution. Other groups hoped a European Marxist system would

George Orwell (1903–1950), shown here with his son, was an English writer of socialist sympathies who wrote major works opposing Stalin and communist authoritarianism. Felix H. Man/ Bildarchiv Preussischer Kulturbesitz

develop. Among the more important contributors to this non-Soviet tradition was the Italian communist Antonio Gramsci (1891–1937), especially in his work *Letters from Prison* (published posthumously in 1947). The thinking of such non-Soviet communists became important to Western European communist parties, such as the Italian Communist Party, that hoped to gain office democratically.

Another way to accommodate Marxism within mid-twentieth-century European thought was to redefine the basic message of Marx himself. During the 1930s, many of Marx's previously unprinted essays were published. These books and articles, written before the *Communist Manifesto* of 1848, are abstract and philosophical. They show how the "young Marx" belonged more to the humanist than to the revolutionary tradition of European thought. Since World War II, works such as *Philosophic Manuscripts* of 1844 and *German Ideology* have been widely read. Today, many people are more familiar with them than with the *Manifesto* or *Capital*. They allowed people to separate Marxism from revolutionary violence or support of the Soviet Union. With the collapse of the communist governments of Eastern Europe and the Soviet Union, Marxism's influence on European intellectual life seemed to wane. The financial crisis of the twenty-first century has led some intellectuals to turn their attention back to Marx's critique of capitalism, even if they do not defend his vision of a communist alternative. Whether doubts about the functioning of the free market will lead to a resurgence in Marxism's influence remains uncertain.

Existentialism

The intellectual movement that perhaps best captured the predicament and mood of mid-twentieth-century European culture was **existentialism**. Like the modern Western mind in general, existentialism, which has been termed the "philosophy of Europe in the twentieth century," was badly divided; most of the philosophers associated with it disagreed with each other on major issues. The movement represented, in part, a continuation of the revolt against reason that began in the nineteenth century.

Roots in Nietzsche and Kierkegaard Friedrich Nietzsche (1844–1900), discussed in Chapter 24, was a major forerunner of existentialism. Another was Danish writer Søren Kierkegaard (1813–1855), who received little attention until after World War I. Kierkegaard was a rebel against both Hegelian philosophy and Danish Lutheranism. In works such as *Fear and Trembling* (1843), *Either/Or* (1843), and *Concluding Unscientific Postscript* (1846), he maintained that the truth of Christianity could be grasped only in the lives of those who faced extreme situations, not in creeds, doctrines, and church structures.

Kierkegaard also criticized Hegelian philosophy and, by implication, all academic rational philosophy. Philosophy's failure, he felt, was the attempt to contain life and human experience within abstract categories.

The intellectual and ethical crisis of World War I led many people to doubt whether human beings were actually in control of their own destiny. Its destructiveness challenged faith in human rationality and improvement. Indeed, the war's most terrible weapons—poison gas, machine guns, submarines, high explosives—were the products of rational technology. The pride in rational human achievement that had characterized nineteenth-century European civilization lay in ruins.

Questioning of Rationalism Existentialist thought thrived in this climate and received further support from the trauma of World War II. The major existential writers included the Germans Martin Heidegger (1889–1976) and Karl Jaspers (1883–1969) and the French Jean-Paul Sartre (1905–1980) and Albert Camus (1913–1960). Although they frequently disagreed with each other, they all questioned the primacy of reason and scientific understanding as ways to come to grips with the human situation. Heidegger, a philosopher deeply compromised by his association with the Nazis, argued, "Thinking only begins at the point where we have come to know that Reason, glorified for centuries, is the most obstinate adversary of thinking."[3]

The Romantic writers of the early nineteenth century had also questioned the primacy of reason, but their criticisms were much less radical than those of the existentialists. The Romantics emphasized the imagination and intuition, but the existentialists dwelled primarily on the extremes of human experience. Death, fear, and anxiety provided their themes. The titles of their works illustrate their sense of foreboding and alienation: *Being and Time* (1927), by Heidegger; *Nausea* (1938) and *Being and Nothingness* (1943), by Sartre; *The Stranger* (1942) and *The Plague* (1947), by Camus. The touchstone of philosophic truth became the experience of the individual under extreme conditions.

Watch the Video "The Big Picture: The World in 2015 C.E." on **MyHistoryLab.com**

[3]William Barrett, *Irrational Man* (Garden City, NY: Doubleday, 1962), p. 20.

According to the existentialists, human beings are compelled to formulate their own ethical values and cannot depend on traditional religion, rational philosophy, intuition, or social customs for ethical guidance. The opportunity and need to define values endow humans with a dreadful freedom. The existentialists protested against a world in which reason, technology, and politics produced war and genocide. Their thought reflected the uncertainty of social institutions and ethical values in the era of the two world wars.

Expansion of the University Population and Student Rebellion

As rapid changes in communications technology vastly expanded access to information, more Europeans received some form of university education. In 1900, only a few thousand people were enrolled in universities in any major European country, and only rarely were women allowed access to higher education. By 2010, that figure had risen to hundreds of thousands. Over one-third of Europeans in their thirties have had a university education, and women are more likely to attend university than men.

One of the most striking and unexpected results of this rising post–World War II population of students and intellectuals was the student rebellion of the 1960s. Student uprisings began in the early 1960s in the United States and grew with opposition to the war in Vietnam. The student rebellion then spread into Europe and other parts of the world. It was almost always associated with

Students and young people protested against the Vietnam War throughout Europe. This demonstration in Paris was led by a Communist organization that opposed both the United States action in the war and France's own imperialist history in former Indochina. © Bettmann/CORBIS

Document

SARTRE DISCUSSES HIS EXISTENTIALISM

Jean-Paul Sartre, dramatist, novelist, and philosopher, was the most important French existentialist. In the first paragraph of this 1946 statement, Sartre asserted that all human beings must experience a sense of anguish or the most extreme anxiety when undertaking a major commitment. That anguish arises because, consciously or unconsciously, they are deciding whether all human beings should make the same decision. In the second paragraph, Sartre argued that the existence or nonexistence of God would make no difference in human affairs. Humankind must discover the character of its own situation by itself.

How might the experiences of fascism in Europe and the fall of France to the Nazis have led Sartre to emphasize the need of human beings to choose? Why does Sartre believe existentialism must be related to atheism? Why did Sartre regard existentialism as optimistic?

The existentialist frankly states that man is in anguish. His meaning is as follows—When a man commits himself to anything, fully realizing that he is not only choosing what he will be, but is thereby at the same time a legislator deciding for the whole of mankind—in such a moment a man cannot escape from the sense of complete and profound responsibility. There are many, indeed, who show no such anxiety. But we affirm that they are merely disguising their anguish or are in flight from it. Certainly, many people think that in what they are doing they commit no one but themselves to anything: and if you ask them, "What would happen if everyone did so?," they shrug their shoulders and reply, "Everyone does not do so." But in truth, one ought always to ask oneself what would happen if everyone did as one is doing; nor can one escape from that disturbing thought except by a kind of self-deception. The man who lies in self-excuse, by saying, "Everyone will not do it" must be ill at ease in his conscience, for the act of lying implies the universal value which it denies. By its very disguise his anguish reveals itself.

Existentialism is nothing else but an attempt to draw the full conclusions from a consistently atheistic position. Its intention is not in the least that of plunging men into despair. And if by despair one means—as the Christians do—any attitude of unbelief, the despair of the existentialist is something different. Existentialism is not atheist in the sense that it would exhaust itself in demonstration of the nonexistence of God. It declares, rather, that even if God existed that would make no difference from its point of view. Not that we believe God does exist, but we think that the real problem is not that of His existence; what man needs is to find himself again and to understand that nothing can save him from himself, not even a valid proof of the existence of God. In this sense existentialism is optimistic. It is a doctrine of action, and it is only by self-deception, by confusing their own despair with ours, that Christians can describe us as without hope.

From Jean-Paul Sartre, *Existentialism and Humanism*, trans. by Philip Mairet (London: Methuen), in Walter Kaufman, ed., *Existentialism from Dostoyevsky to Sartre* (New York: Meridian Books, 1956), pp. 292, 310–311.

a radical political critique of the United States, although Eastern European students resented the Soviet Union even more. The movement was generally antimilitarist. Students also questioned middle-class values and traditional sexual mores and family life.

The student movement peaked in 1968, when American students demonstrated forcibly against U.S. involvement in Vietnam. In the same year, students at the Sorbonne in Paris almost brought down the government of Charles de Gaulle, and in Czechoslovakia, students were in the forefront of the liberal socialist experiment. These protests failed to have an immediate effect on the policies of the governments at which they were directed. The United States stayed in Vietnam until

1973, de Gaulle remained president of France for another year, and the Soviets suppressed the Czech experiment.

By the early 1970s, the era of student rebellion seemed to have passed. Students remained active in European movements against nuclear weapons and particularly against the placement of American nuclear weapons in Germany and elsewhere in Europe. From the mid-1970s, however, although often remaining political radicals, they generally abandoned the disruptive protests that had marked the 1960s.

The Americanization of Europe

During the past half-century, through the Marshall Plan, the leadership of NATO, the stationing of huge military bases, student exchanges, popular culture, and tourism, the United States has exerted enormous influence on Western Europe. The pejorative term *Americanization* refers, in part, to this economic and military influence, but also to concerns about cultural loss. Many Europeans feel that American popular entertainment, companies, and business methods threaten to extinguish Europe's unique qualities. Many American firms now have European branches. Large American corporations, such as McDonald's, Starbucks, Apple, and Gap, have outlets in European cities from Dublin to Moscow. American liquor companies and distilleries now sell their goods in Europe. Casual American clothing, such as blue jeans and baseball caps, is ubiquitous in Europe. Shopping centers and supermarkets, first pioneered in America, are displacing neighborhood markets in European cities. American television programs, movies, computer games, and rock and rap music are readily available. Furthermore, as Europe moves toward greater economic cooperation, English has become the common language of business, technology, and even some academic fields—and it is American English, not British. (See "Encountering, the Past: Toys from Europe Conquer the United States," page 998.)

Watch the Video "Video Lectures: Imperialism and the United States" on **MyHistoryLab.com**

A Consumer Society

Although European economies came under pressure during the 1990s and experienced high levels of unemployment, the consumer sector has expanded to an extraordinary degree during most of the last half-century.

The consumer orientation of the Western European economy emerged as one of the most important characteristics differentiating it from Eastern Europe. Those differences produced political results. In the Soviet Union and the nations it dominated in Eastern Europe, economic planning overwhelmingly favored capital investment and military production. These nations produced inadequate and low-quality consumer goods. Long lines for staples, such as food and clothing, were common. Automobiles were a luxury. Housing did not permit the luxury of privacy, and children were often forced to live with their parents well into adulthood.

By contrast, by the early 1950s, Western Europeans enjoyed an expansion of consumer goods and services. Automobile ownership has soared. Refrigerators, washing machines, electric ranges, televisions, microwaves, videocassette recorders, cameras, computers, CD players, DVD players, and other electronic consumer items are taken for granted. Like their American counterparts, Western Europeans now have a whole gamut of products, such as disposable diapers and prepared baby foods, to help them raise children. They take foreign vacations year round, prompting the expansion of ski resorts in the Alps and beach resorts on the Mediterranean.

This vast expansion of consumerism, which, as we noted in Chapter 15, began in the eighteenth century, became a defining characteristic of Western Europe in the late twentieth century. It stood in marked contrast to the consumer shortages in Eastern Europe. Yet through even the limited number of radios, televisions, movies, and videos available to them, people in the East grew increasingly aware of the discrepancy between their lifestyle and that of the West. They associated Western consumerism with democratic governments, free societies, and economic policies that favored the free market. Thus, the expansion of consumerism in the West, which many intellectuals and moralists deplored, helped generate the discontent that brought down communism in Eastern Europe and the Soviet Union.

Environmentalism

After World War II, shortages of consumer goods created a demand that fueled postwar economic reconstruction and growth into the 1950s and 1960s. In those expansive times, public debate about the ethics of economic expansion and efficiency and their effects on the environment was muted. Concerns about pollution began to grow in the 1970s, and by the 1980s, environmentalists had developed real political clout. Among the most important environmental groups were the German Greens. The Greens formed a political party in 1979 that immediately became an electoral force. During these same years, concern for environmental issues, such as global warming and the pollution of water and the atmosphere, commanded the attention of governments outside Europe and of the United Nations.

Read the Document "Towards a Green Europe, Towards a Green World" on **MyHistoryLab.com**

ENCOUNTERING THE *Past*

TOYS FROM EUROPE CONQUER THE UNITED STATES

TODAY MANY EUROPEANS criticize what they term *Americanization*—the intrusion of popular American products and restaurant chains onto the European scene. Yet over the past half-century one European toy—LEGO building blocks manufactured in Denmark—has shaped the experience of childhood for many children in the United States and the rest of the world, entering their lives and imaginations no less powerfully than the cartoon figures associated with the American Disney Corporation.

In 1932, in the midst of the depression, Ole Kirk Christiansen opened a small business in Billund, Denmark, that manufactured household goods and wooden toys. The toys sold so well that two years later the firm renamed itself LEGO from the Danish *LEg GOdt*, meaning "play well." The company remained small, producing only wooden toys, until 1947 when it began to make molded plastic toys. It only sold its products in Denmark.

In 1955, LEGO introduced LEGO Bricks—plastic building blocks of the familiar stud-and-tube type—that it sold in sets under the name LEGO System of Play. That system, which the firm patented in 1958, allowed children to combine LEGO Bricks in an almost endless number of ways, limited only by their own imaginations and that of their parents. The company also extended its market across and began to sell in the United States in 1961.

Thereafter, the success of LEGO as a toy and as a company fed on itself. The company added many new features to the original concept of interlocking building blocks. For example, wheels enabled children to use LEGO kits to build their own trucks, trains, and similar mobile toys.

In 1968, the LEGO Company, no doubt following the example of the Disney Corporation in the United States, opened an amusement park in Billund in which the rides were designed to look like huge LEGO toys. By the end of the century, LEGO had opened similar parks in England, the United States, and Germany.

However, the company remained focused on making toys for children. It designed new toys, such as plastic figures with human heads to ride in LEGO vehicles, and whole LEGO villages, castles, and pirate ships. By the 1990s, LEGO had become the largest toy manufacturer in Europe and a part of modern culture. Museums displayed LEGO products and art built from LEGO blocks. Contests were held to construct the largest or most unusual LEGO structures. In 1999, *Fortune* magazine included the LEGO Brick among the "Products of the Century," and in 2002, LEGO persuaded European and American management consultants that working with LEGO blocks would help business executives think more clearly about corporate planning. Perhaps most astonishing is that during a half-century of tumultuous change, children around the world have continued to play with these little pieces of plastic.

Children across the world play with LEGO toys. Tom Prettyman/PhotoEdit

Factual information derived from the official Lego Group Web site at www.lego.com/eng/info/history.

How has LEGO been an example of the European penetration of popular culture around the world?

Why has the influence of LEGO on children's toys been less controversial than the appearance of American fast-food chains in Europe?

Workers who participated in the clean-up after the Chernobyl disaster protest in front of riot police in Kiev, Ukraine, in November 2011. The government slashed the pensions and social benefits given to them after the clean-up. Sergey Dolzhenko/EPA/Newscom

Several developments lay behind this new concern for the environment. The Arab oil embargo of 1973–1974 pressed home two messages to the industrialized West: natural resources are limited, and foreign, potentially hostile, countries control critical resources. By the 1970s, too, the environmental consequences of three decades of economic expansion were becoming increasingly apparent. Fish were dying in the Thames River in England. Industrial pollution was destroying life in the Rhine River between Germany and France. Acid rain was killing trees from Sweden to Germany. Finally, long-standing worries about nuclear weapons merged with concerns about their environmental effects, strengthening antinuclear groups and generating opposition to the placement of nuclear weapons in Europe.

The German **Green movement** originated among radical student groups in the late 1960s. Like them, it was anticapitalist, blaming business for pollution. The Greens and other European environmental groups were also strongly antinuclear. Unlike the students of the 1960s, the Greens avoided violence and mass demonstrations, seeking instead to become a significant political presence through the electoral process.

Watch the Video "Video Lectures: British Petroleum Oil Spill—Environmental Disasters" on **MyHistoryLab.com**

The 1986 disaster at the Chernobyl nuclear reactor in the Soviet Union heightened concern about environmental issues and raised questions that no European government could ignore. The Soviet government had to confront casualties at the site and relocate tens of thousands of people. Radioactive fallout spread across Europe. Environmentalists had always contended that their issues transcended national borders. The Chernobyl fire proved them right.

After Chernobyl, European governments, East and West, began to respond to environmental concerns. Some observers believe the environment may become a major political issue across the Continent. In Western Europe, environmental groups command many votes. Economic and political integration opens the possibility of transnational cooperation on environmental matters. As the European Economic Community solidifies, it and its member nations will likely impose more environmental regulations on business and industry. The nations of Eastern Europe have been forced to face the cleanup of vast areas of industrial development polluted during the communist era and to try to combine environmental protection with economic growth.

▼ Art Since World War II

It is impossible to cover even briefly the expansive and varied world of Western art since the end of World War II. However, we can note how both the Cold War and the memory of the horrors of World War II influenced Western art.

Document

VOICES FROM CHERNOBYL

The nuclear disaster at Chernobyl, Ukraine, affected some towns in bordering Belarus as profoundly as it did parts of Ukraine. Journalist Svetlana Alexievich traveled through villages in the affected region in 1996, ten years after the disaster, and interviewed hundreds of survivors. The first of the two excerpts comes from an interview of the wife of a "liquidator," one of the firemen sent as first responders to put out the fire at the nuclear plant. She describes her husband's last days in a hospital in Moscow. The second excerpt comes from an interview with an elderly resident of one of the villages closest to the plant who refused to evacuate despite warnings that the area was unsafe.

Why was it difficult for people to understand the hazards of radiation? Why might someone choose to stay in Chernobyl? How might the memory of World War II have affected the way people responded to the catastrophe? What sort of information about the hazards of radiation was made available to local residents?

"I go back to the hospital and there's an orange on the bedside table. A big one, and pink. He's smiling: 'I got a gift. Take it.' Meanwhile the nurse is gesturing through the film that I can't eat it. It's been near him a while, so not only can you not eat it, you shouldn't even touch it. 'Come on, eat it,' he says. 'You like oranges.' I take the orange in my hand. Meanwhile he shuts his eyes and goes to sleep. They were always giving him shots to put him to sleep. The nurse is looking at me in horror. And me? I'm ready to do whatever it takes so that he doesn't think about death. And about the fact that his death is horrible, that I'm afraid of him. There's a fragment of some conversation, I'm remembering it. Someone is saying: 'you have to understand, this is not your husband anymore, not a beloved person, but a radioactive object with a strong density of poisoning. You're not suicidal. Get ahold of yourself.' And I'm like someone who's lost her mind."

—Lyudmilla Ignatenko

"We weren't too afraid of this radiation. We couldn't see it, and we didn't know what it was, maybe we were a little afraid, but once we'd seen it, we weren't so afraid. The police and the soldiers put up these signs. Some were next to people's houses, some were in the street—they'd write, 70 curie, 60 curie. We'd always lived off our potatoes, and then suddenly—we're not allowed to! For some people it was real bad for others it was funny. They advised us to work in our gardens in masks and rubber gloves. And then another big scientist came to the meeting hall and told us that we needed to wash our yards. Come on! I couldn't believe what I was hearing! They ordered us to wash our sheets, our blankets, our curtains. But they're in storage! In closets and trunks. There's no radiation in there! Behind glass? Behind closed doors? Come on! It's in the forest, in the field. They closed the wells, locked them up, wrapped them in cellophane. Said the water was 'dirty.' How can it be dirty when it's so clean? They told us a bunch of nonsense. You'll die. You need to leave. Evacuate. . . .

And then I hear about how the soldiers were evacuating one village, and this old man and woman stayed. Until then, when people were roused up and put on buses, they'd take their cow and go into the forest. They'd wait there. Like during the war, when they were burning down the villages. Why would our soldiers chase us? . . .

And why should I leave? It's nice here! Everything grows, everything blooming. From the littlest fly to the animals, everything's living."

—Zinaida Yevdokimovna Kovalenko

From Svetlana Alexievich, *Voices from Chernobyl*, trans. Keith Gessen (London: Dalkey Archive Press, 2005), pp. 15–16, 28–30.

Tatjiana Yablonskaya, *Bread*, 1949. Ria Novosti/Sovfoto/Eastfoto

Cultural Divisions and the Cold War

The stark differences between Soviet painter Tatjiana Yablonskaya's (b. 1917) sun-strewn *Bread* (1949) and the American Jackson Pollock's (1912–1956) dizzyingly abstract *One* (Number 31, 1950) mirror the cultural divisions of the early Cold War.

Jackson Pollock, *One* (Number 31, 1950). Oil and enamel on unprimed canvas, 8 ft. 10 in. × 17 ft. 5 5/8 in. (269.5 × 530.8 cm). The Museum of Modern Art/Licensed by Scala-Art Resource, NY. Sidney and Harriet Janis Collection Fund (by exchange). Photograph © 2000 The Museum of Modern Art, New York. 00007.68. © 2004 The Pollock-Krasner Foundation/Artists Rights Society (ARS), New York

View the Closer Look on MyHistoryLab.com

NAMELESS LIBRARY, VIENNA

BRITISH SCULPTOR Rachel Whiteread (b. 1963) is one of the leading artists of today's Europe. Her work illustrates how European art is breaking out of the modernist contours that were set at the beginning of the twentieth century. On one hand, Whiteread's art returns to what seem like familiar forms; on the other, it forces us to view these forms in ways that are as new to us as cubism was to the public in its day.

Whiteread's work is associated with minimalism in contemporary art. This movement, which originated in architecture and interior design, seeks to remove from the object being portrayed as many features as possible while retaining the object's form and the viewer's interest. Minimalist art aims to be as understated as possible. In Whiteread's hands, the minimal becomes the austere, and her work often exudes melancholy and loss.

Whiteread's most important public work, and one designed to endure, is *Nameless Library,* the Judenplatz Holocaust Memorial in Vienna, which commemorates the deaths of 65,000 Austrian Jews under the Nazis. This memorial, which resembles a vast haunting tomb, is cast in concrete and embodies the outline of books whose spines are turned inward, thus remaining forever unread and as unopenable as the library's huge concrete doors.

Whiteread has said the molded, unopened books, which have been compared to the ghost of a library, symbolize the loss both of Jewish contributions to culture and of Jewish lives in the Holocaust.

Who is the intended audience for this piece of work? Viennese? Tourists? How do you imagine different people respond to *Nameless Library?*

***Nameless Library* stands in Vienna's Judenplatz, in the center of its former Jewish district. It is surrounded by outdoor cafés and restaurants. What makes this an especially appropriate or inappropriate location for such a memorial?**

Bread, measuring over six feet high and twelve feet wide, is a monumental example of **socialist realism**. Established as the official doctrine of Soviet art and literature in 1934, socialist realism sought to create optimistic and easily intelligible scenes of a bold socialist future, in which prosperity and solidarity would reign. Manual laborers and prominent historical and political figures were painted in a traditional and often rigid figurative manner. Socialist realism became the dominant artistic model throughout the Soviet Union and Eastern Europe, only waning when Nikita Khrushchev liberalized Soviet cultural policy in the late 1950s.

Pollock's paintings are central documents of postwar American cultural life. Flinging paint from sticks and brushes onto his floor-bound canvas, Pollock freed his lines from representing any figure or outline. The result, in *One* (Number 31, 1950), which is over eight feet high and seventeen feet wide, is a writhing tangle of pure visual energy. In the politically charged atmosphere of the early Cold War, critics saw Pollock's exuberant "drip" paintings as the embodiment of American cultural freedom and celebrated the Wyoming-born Pollock as a kind of artist cowboy.

As skeptical as many viewers might have been about the merits of abstract art (*Time* magazine, for instance, dismissed Pollock as "Jack the dripper" in 1947), many people in the West saw it as the antithesis of the restrictions the dominance of socialist realism placed on individual creativity.

Indeed, New York City—not Paris—emerged as the international center of modern art after World War II. As the home of growing collections of twentieth-century art and dozens of European artists who had fled from the Nazis, New York became a fertile training ground for young artists such as Pollock. Just as American political and economic structures became models for the postwar redevelopment of Western Europe, so did American cultural developments. By the time Pollock's first posthumous retrospective toured Europe in 1958, much European painting resembled an elegant imitation of his frenetic lines.

Yablonskaya and Pollock together illustrate the two central poles of twentieth-century art: realism and abstraction. Although artistic style is no longer as closely associated with political programs as it once was, these two poles still frame the work of countless artists today.

▾ The Christian Heritage

In most ways, Christianity in Europe has continued to be as hard-pressed during the twentieth century as it had been in the late nineteenth. Material prosperity, political ideologies, environmentalism, gender politics, and simple indifference have replaced religious faith for many people. Still, despite the loss of much of their popular support and legal privileges and the low rates of church attendance, the European Christian churches continue to exercise social and political influence. In Germany, the churches were one of the few major institutions that the Nazis did not wholly subdue. Lutheran clergy, such as Martin Niemöller (1892–1984) and Dietrich Bonhoeffer (1906–1945), were leaders of the opposition to Hitler. After the war, most especially in Poland but also elsewhere in Eastern Europe, the Roman Catholic Church opposed communism. In Eastern and Western Europe, even in this most secular of ages, Christian churches have influenced state and society.

Neo-Orthodoxy

Liberal theologians of the nineteenth century often softened the concept of sin and portrayed human nature as close to the divine. The horror of World War I destroyed that optimistic faith. Many Europeans felt that evil had stalked the Continent.

The most important Christian response to World War I appeared in the theology of Karl Barth (1886–1968). In 1919, this Swiss pastor published *A Commentary on the Epistle to the Romans*, which reemphasized the transcendence of God and the dependence of humankind on the divine. Barth portrayed God as wholly other than, and different from, humankind. In a sense, Barth was returning to the Reformation theology of Luther, but the work of Kierkegaard had profoundly influenced his reading of the reformer. Those extreme moments of life Kierkegaard described provided the basis for a knowledge of humanity's need for God.

This view challenged much nineteenth-century writing about human nature. Barth's theology, which came to be known as neo-Orthodoxy, proved influential throughout the West in the wake of new disasters and suffering.

Liberal Theology

Neo-Orthodoxy did not, however, sweep away liberal theology, which had a strong advocate in Paul Tillich (1886–1965). This German American theologian tended to regard religion as a human, rather than a divine, phenomenon.

Other liberal theologians, such as Rudolf Bultmann (1884–1976), continued to work on the problems of naturalism and supernaturalism that had troubled earlier writers. Bultmann's major writing took place before World War II but was popularized after the war by the Anglican bishop John Robinson in *Honest to God* (1963). Another liberal Christian writer from Britain, C. S. Lewis (1878–1963), attracted millions of readers during and after World War II. This layman and scholar of medieval literature often expressed his thoughts on theology in the form of letters and short stories.

Roman Catholic Reform

Among Christian denominations, the most significant postwar changes have been in the Roman Catholic Church. Pope John XXIII (r. 1958–1963) initiated these changes, the most extensive in Catholicism for more than a century and, some would say, since the Council of Trent in the sixteenth century. In 1959, Pope John XXIII summoned the Twenty-First Ecumenical Council, which came to be called Vatican II. The council finished its work in 1965 under John's successor, Pope Paul VI (r. 1963–1978). Among many changes in Catholic liturgy the council introduced, Mass was now celebrated in the vernacular languages rather than in Latin. The council also encouraged freer relations with other Christian denominations, fostered a new spirit toward Judaism, and gave more power to bishops. In recognition of the growing importance to the church of the world outside Europe and North America, Pope Paul VI appointed several cardinals from the former colonial nations, transforming the church into a truly world body.

In contrast to these liberal changes, however, Pope Paul VI and his successors have firmly upheld the celibacy of priests, maintained the church's prohibition on contraception and abortion, and opposed moves to open the priesthood to women. The church's unyielding stand on clerical celibacy has caused many men to leave the priesthood and many men and women to leave religious orders. The laity has widely ignored the prohibition on contraception.

John Paul II, the former Karol Wojtyla, archbishop of Kraków in Poland, was elected in 1978 after the death of John Paul I, whose reign lasted only thirty-four days. The youngest pope since Pius IX (r. 1846–1878) and the first non-Italian pope since the sixteenth century, John Paul II (1920–2005) pursued a three-pronged policy during his long pontificate. First, he maintained traditionalist doctrine, stressing the authority of the papacy and attempting to limit doctrinal and liturgical experimentation.

Read the Document "Pope John Paul II, from *Centesimus Annus*" on **MyHistoryLab.com**

Throughout his pontificate John Paul II continued a close relationship with his native Poland to which he made several visits. The earliest of these, in June 1979, was important in demonstrating the authority of the church against Polish communist authorities. The Pope is shown here at one of several outdoor masses he held in Poland, this one in Czestochowa in southwestern Poland. In one of his sermons, he said "Poland in our time has become a land called to give an especially important witness." Associated Press

Second, taking a firm stand against communism, he supported resistance to the communist regimes in Eastern Europe. As a cardinal in Poland, he had clashed with the communist government. After his election, he visited Poland, lending support to Solidarity. His Polish origins helped make him an important factor in the popular resistance to Eastern Europe's communist governments that developed during the 1980s. He thus opened a new chapter in the relationship between church and state in modern Europe.

Third, John Paul II encouraged the growth of the church in the non-Western world, stressing the need for social justice but limiting the political activity of priests. The pope's concern for the expansion of Roman Catholicism beyond Europe and North America recognized and encouraged what appears to be a transformation in Christianity as a world religion. Whereas in Europe, Christian observance had declined sharply during the twentieth century, Christianity has grown rapidly and fervently in Africa and Latin America. By 2010, only about a quarter of the world's Christians lived in Europe; another quarter lived in sub-Saharan Africa, and well over one-third lived in North and South America. Recognizing these changes, John Paul II created more cardinals from non-Western nations.

John Paul II died in 2005. His successor was his closest collaborator, the German Cardinal Joseph Ratzinger (b. 1927), who took the name Benedict XVI. The new pope has followed his predecessor in his rigorous defense of orthodoxy. In September 2006 he delivered a speech in which he quoted a medieval writer criticizing Islam. The speech evoked considerable criticism in Europe and provoked riots in parts of the Islamic world. Pope Benedict XVI has also championed the role of religious freedom for Christians and other religiously observant peoples living in the midst of secular societies.

▼ Late-Twentieth-Century Technology: The Arrival of the Computer

During the twentieth century, technology crossed international borders the way popular culture did. As with other areas of European life and society, American technology had an unprecedented impact on the Continent, whether in the guise of the first airplanes or Henry Ford's method of producing affordable automobiles. It seems certain, however, that no single American technological achievement of the twentieth century will so influence Western life on both sides of the Atlantic, as well as throughout the rest of the world, as the computer.

The Demand for Calculating Machines

Beginning in the seventeenth century, thinkers associated with the scientific revolution—most famously, French mathematician and philosopher Blaise Pascal (1623–1662)—attempted to construct machines that would carry out mathematical calculations that human beings would find essentially impossible because of the tedium and the amount of time they involved. Starting in the late nineteenth century, the governments of the consolidating nation-states of Europe and of the United States confronted new administrative tasks that involved collecting and organizing vast amounts of data about national censuses, tax collection, economic statistics, and the administration of pensions and welfare legislation. During the same years, private businesses sought calculating machinery to handle and organize growing amounts of economic and business data. Such machines became technologically possible through the development of complex circuitry for electricity, the most versatile mode of energy in human history. Moreover, inventions that were dependent on electricity, including the telephone, the telegraph, underwater cables, and the wireless, created a new communications industry that also required the organization of large databases of customer information to deliver their services. By the late 1920s, companies like National Cash Register, Remington Rand, and International Business Machines Corporation (IBM) had begun to manufacture such business machinery.

Early Computer Technology

As has happened so often in history, warfare was the chief catalyst of change. After World War I and during World War II, the major powers developed new weapons that required exact mathematical ballistic calculations to strike targets with bombs delivered by aircraft or long-range guns.

The first machine genuinely recognizable as a modern digital computer was the Electronic Numerical Integrator and Computer (ENIAC), built and designed at Moore Laboratories of the University of Pennsylvania and put into use by the U.S. Army in 1946 for ballistics calculation. The ENIAC was an enormous piece of equipment with 40 panels, 1,500 electric relays, and 18,000 vacuum tubes. It also used thousands of punch cards, and a separate tabulator had to print the data from them. Further computer engineering occurred at the Institute for Advanced Research in Princeton, New Jersey, in laboratories at the Massachusetts Institute of Technology, and in other laboratories the U.S. government and private businesses, especially IBM, ran. The other primary sites for computer development were laboratories in Britain.

The earliest computers were very large. Here in a 1946 photograph, J. Presper Eckert and J. W. Mauchly stand by the Electronic Numerical Integrator and Computer (ENIAC), which was dedicated at the University of Pennsylvania Moore School of Electrical Engineering. CORBIS/Bettmann

The Development of Desktop Computers

During the 1950s, however, the transistor revolutionized electronics, permitting a miniaturization of circuitry that made vacuum tubes obsolete and allowed computers to become smaller. Computers still had to be programmed with difficult computer languages by persons expertly trained to use them.

By the late 1960s, however, two innovations transformed computing technology. First, control of the computer was transferred to a bitmap covering the screen of a computer monitor. The mouse, invented in 1964, eased the movement of the cursor around the computer screen. Second, engineers at the Intel Corporation—then a California start-up company—invented the microchip, which became the heart of all future computers.

The bitmap on the screen, operated through the mouse, in effect embedded complicated computer language in the machine, hidden from the user, who simply manipulated images on the screen with the mouse. Almost anyone could thus learn to operate computers. At the same time, the tiny microchip, itself a miniature computer or microprocessor, permitted computer technology to abandon the mainframe and move to still smaller computers. At the Xerox Corporation, engineers devised a small computer using a mouse, but the machine never achieved commercial success. By 1982, IBM had produced a small personal computer but temporarily lost the race for commercialization to a then small company called Apple Computer Corporation. The design features originally developed at Xerox informed the ideas of the Apple engineers, who, in early 1984, produced a small, highly accessible, commercially successful computer, known as the Macintosh, that would fit on a desktop in the home or office. IBM soon adopted the Apple concept with different engineering and marketing approaches and manufactured a product called the Personal Computer, or PC. By the mid-1980s, for a relatively modest cost (and one that has continued to drop), individuals had available for their own personal use in their offices or homes computers with far more power than the old mainframes. The Apple Macintosh and the IBM PC transformed computers into objects of everyday life and, in doing so, began to transform everyday life itself. Nonetheless, the chief contemporary users of computers remain governments followed by the telephone industry, banking and finance, automobile operation, and airline reservation systems.

Despite the potential democratizing character of computer technology, the computer revolution has also introduced new concepts of "haves" and "have-nots" to societies around the world. Computers, whatever their possible shortcomings, enable their users to do things that nonusers cannot do. Whether in poor school districts in the United States or in poor countries of the former Soviet bloc, students who graduate without computer skills will have difficulty making their way in the world's rapidly computerizing economy. Some commentators also fear that boys are more likely than girls to receive technological training in computers. Nations whose governments and businesses become networked into the world of computers will prosper more fully than those whose access to computer technology is deficient. In that regard, the possession of computers and the ability to use them will probably determine future economic competition, just as they have determined recent military competition.

▼ The Challenges of European Unification

The unprecedented steps toward economic cooperation and unity Western European nations took during the second half of the twentieth century were the single most important European success story of that era. The process originated from American encouragement in response to the Soviet domination of Eastern Europe and from the Western European states' own sense that they lacked effective political and economic power. Furthermore, leaders in France and Germany who recoiled from the disastrous peace that followed World War I were determined that something different would arise from the political collapse of Europe after World War II. They understood that cooperation, rather than revenge, must inform the future of Europe.

View the **Image** "European Union Flag" on **MyHistoryLab.com**

Postwar Cooperation

The mid-twentieth-century Western European movement toward unity could have occurred in at least three ways: politically, militarily, or economically. Economic cooperation, unlike military and political cooperation, involved little or no immediate loss of sovereignty by the participating nations. Furthermore, it brought material benefits to all the states involved, increasing popular support for their governments. Moreover, the administration of the Marshall Plan and the organization of NATO gave the countries involved new experience in working with each other and demonstrated the productivity and efficiency that mutual cooperation could achieve.

The first effort toward economic cooperation was the formation of the European Coal and Steel Community in 1951 by France, West Germany, Italy, and the Benelux countries (Belgium, the Netherlands, and Luxembourg). The community both benefited from and contributed to the immense growth of material production in Western Europe during this period. Its success reduced the suspicions of government and business groups about coordination and economic integration.

The European Economic Community

It took more than the prosperity of the European Coal and Steel Community to draw European leaders toward further unity, however. The unsuccessful Suez intervention of 1956 and the resulting diplomatic isolation of France and Britain persuaded many Europeans that only by acting together could they significantly influence the United States and the Soviet Union or control their own national and regional destinies. So, in 1957, through the Treaty of Rome, the six members of the Coal and Steel Community agreed to form a new organization: the **European Economic Community (EEC)**. The members of the Common Market, as the EEC was soon known, envisioned more than a free-trade union. They sought to achieve the eventual elimination of tariffs, a free flow of capital and labor, and similar wage and social benefits in all their countries.

The Common Market achieved stunning success during its early years. By 1968, well ahead of schedule, the six members had abolished all tariffs among themselves. Trade and labor migration among the members grew steadily. Moreover, nonmember states began to copy the EEC and, later, to seek to join it. In 1959, Britain, Denmark, Norway, Sweden, Switzerland, Austria, and Portugal formed the European Free Trade Area. By 1961, however, Britain had decided to join the Common Market. Twice, in 1963 and 1967, President Charles de Gaulle of France vetoed British membership. He argued that Britain was too closely tied to the United States to support the EEC wholeheartedly. Finally, in 1973, Great Britain, Ireland, and Denmark became members. Throughout the late 1970s, however, and into the 1980s, momentum for expanding EEC membership slowed. Norway and Sweden, with relatively strong economies, declined to join. Although in 1982, Spain, Portugal, and Greece applied for membership and were eventually admitted, sharp disagreements and a sense of stagnation within the EEC continued.

Read the **Document** "A Common Market and European Integration (1960)" on **MyHistoryLab.com**

The European Union

In 1988, the leaders of the EEC reached an important decision. By 1992, the EEC was to be a virtual free-trade zone with no trade barriers or other restrictive trade policies among its members. In 1991, the Treaty of Maastricht made a series of specific proposals that led to a unified EEC currency (the Euro) and a strong central bank. The treaty was submitted to referendums in several European states. Denmark initially rejected it, and it passed only narrowly in France and Great Britain, making clear that it needed wider popular support. When the treaty finally took effect in November 1993, the EEC was renamed the **European Union**.

Throughout the 1990s, the Union's influence grew. Its most notable achievement was the launching in early 1999 of the **euro**, which by 2002 had become the common currency in twelve of the member nations.

Read the Document "Treaty on European Union, 1992" on **MyHistoryLab.com**

In May 2004, the European Union added ten new nations, raising the total number of members to twenty-five. (See Map 30–1.) Membership in the European Union indicated that a nation had achieved economic stability and genuinely democratic institutions. At the time, some older member states worried that several of the new member states from the former Soviet bloc were relatively poor and would require much economic support from the Union. Ironically, it was states in Western and Southern Europe, not Eastern Europe, that plunged the EU into a debt crisis in 2010.

Discord over the Union

The 2004 expansion of the European Union may mark for some time the high point of European integration. During that year the leaders of the member nations adopted a new constitutional treaty for the Union. This treaty, generally known as the **European Constitution**, was a long, detailed, and highly complicated document involving a bill of rights and complex economic and political agreements among all the member states. It would have transferred considerable decision-making authority from the governments of the individual states to the central institutions of the European Union, many of which are located in Brussels, Luxembourg, and Strasbourg. To become effective, all the member states had to ratify the constitution either by their parliaments or through national referendums.

View the Map "European Union" on **MyHistoryLab.com**

To the surprise of many in the European elite, in the spring of 2005, referendums held in France and the Netherlands heavily defeated the new constitutional treaty. Britain, where support for further European integration was lukewarm at best, immediately postponed holding its own referendum. Public opinion in other nations also soured on the constitutional treaty. Furthermore, immediately after these events, discord erupted over the Union's internal budget. These events marked an

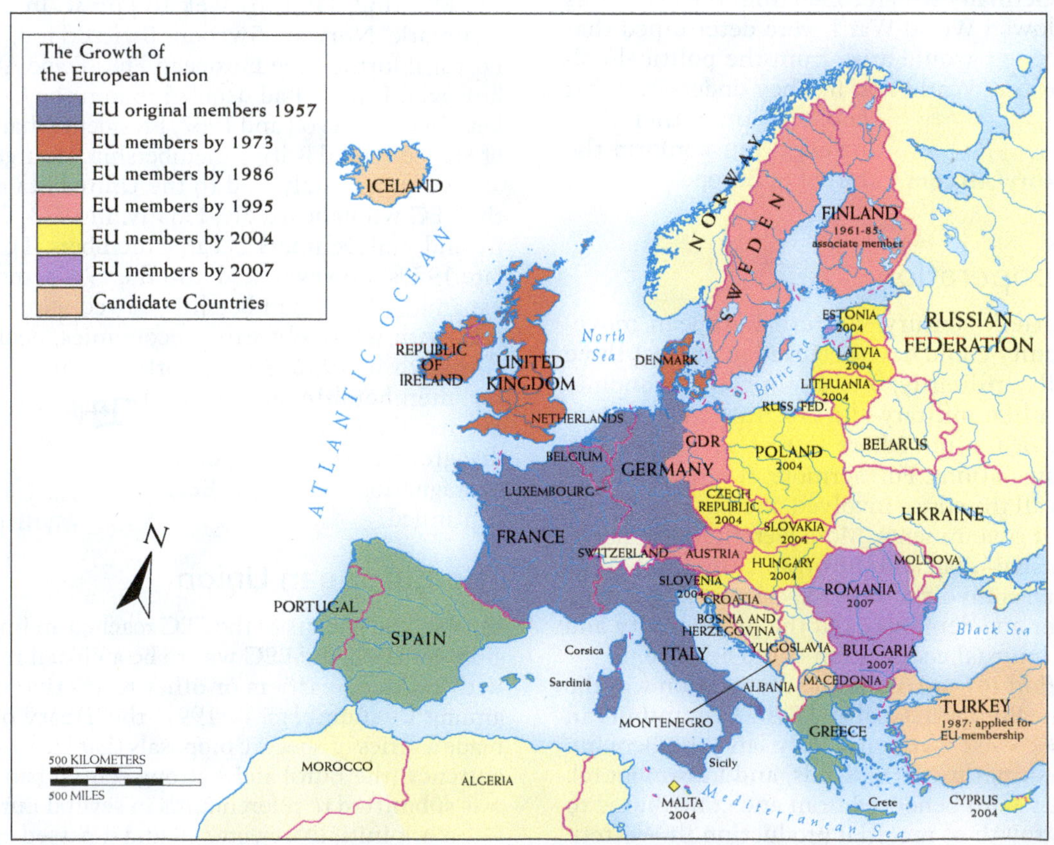

Map 30–1 THE GROWTH OF THE EUROPEAN UNION This map traces the growth of membership in the European Union from its founding in 1957 through the introduction of its newest members in 2007. Note that Turkey, though having applied for membership, has not yet been admitted.

A woman stands between a "yes" and a "no" campaign poster in reference to France's referendum on the EU constitution in a street of Rennes, western France, Friday May 27, 2005, two days before the vote. AP Wide World Photos

unprecedented crisis for the European Union and for the project of European integration. A similar crisis erupted in 2008 when a referendum in Ireland failed to support changes in the European Union that would create shared institutions of foreign policy formulation and military policy.

Several factors appear to have brought the European Union to this pass. First, for at least the past fifteen years, a gap has been growing between the European political elites who have led the drive toward unity and the European voting public. The former have either ignored the latter or have moved the project along with only narrow majorities. Second, the general Western European economy has stagnated for the last decade with relatively high rates of unemployment, especially among the young. Voting against the constitution was a way to voice discontent with this situation. Third, many of the smaller member states of the European Union have felt that France and Germany have either ignored them or taken them for granted. Fourth, some nations have come to believe that they were placed at an economic disadvantage when the Euro replaced their former national currencies because the rates of exchange were unfairly calculated. Fifth, many people in the various states, large and small, have become increasingly reluctant to cede national sovereignty and the authority to make economic decisions to the bureaucracy in Brussels. Britain, for example, would like to see less economic regulation. France, on the other hand, is loath to see the European Union gain the power to revise the French labor code with its extensive protections and benefits for workers.

Finally, another large issue has informed the internal skeptics of the current European Union. Over the past several years, the leaders of the major member states have grown more favorable to the eventual admission of Turkey as a member state. If Turkey were admitted, Europe would have to integrate into the Union a state whose population is larger and much poorer than that of any other member state. This would place enormous social and economic burdens on the other states. Furthermore, although the Turkish government has long been seen as adamantly secular, the Turkish people are overwhelmingly Muslim. This "Islamic factor" has become increasingly controversial among those Europeans who, whether they are religiously observant or not, believe European culture to be Christian, and among those secular Europeans who are deeply concerned about the political, economic, and social implications of the Continent's already significant Muslim population. These tensions grew after 2005 when a Danish newspaper published self-consciously irreverent cartoons insulting the Prophet Muhammad. Riots broke out in parts of the Islamic world and in subsequent years Danish businesses and embassies abroad became targets of Islamic attacks.

▼ New American Leadership and Financial Crisis

Much of the first decade of the twenty-first century witnessed considerable strain between the new post–Soviet Union Europe and the United States. As noted in Chapter 29, the immediate European reaction to the attacks on the United States on September 11, 2001, were sympathetic. The events leading up to the U.S. Iraq invasion in 2003 and the violence occurring since that invasion caused considerable strain between the United States and Europe, especially in terms of popular opinion. Europeans, through their press and to some extent through their governments, voiced much criticism over what they regarded as United States unilateral action in its foreign policy.

Three events in 2008 may have begun to change this situation and possibly to lessen those tensions. The first was the Russian invasion of Georgia, discussed in Chapter 29. The United States and the European Union agreed in condemning that action. Second, the American presidential election of 2008 saw the strong victory of Barack Obama, the Democratic Party candidate. Obama is the first African American to be elected to the presidency. He ran on a platform critical of the Iraq invasion and American unilateralism. Even though he also voiced strong support for the war in Afghanistan, Obama generated enormous popular support across Europe. Indeed, during the campaign he gave a speech in Berlin that drew a crowd of tens of thousands. Obama's victory in the presidential election and the expansion of Democratic Party majorities in Congress appear to

Document

AN ENGLISH BUSINESS EDITOR CALLS FOR EUROPE TO TAKE CHARGE OF ITS ECONOMIC FUTURE

Richard Lofthouse is the editor of CNBC European Business, *a magazine devoted to contemporary economic and business life. Educated in both Great Britain and the United States, Lofthouse brings a personal global perspective to his analysis. In the summer of 2008 he observed the tendency of Europeans to see their economic life as driven by global forces outside their control. In the face of such challenges, he called upon his readers to recall their cultural heritage and to embrace a spirit of entrepreneurship.*

Why are the challenges facing Europe and the West today international and global in contrast to the domestic political challenges of the third quarter of the twentieth century? What are the forces outside Europe impacting its economic life? What are the cultural qualities to which Lofthouse seeks to rally his readers?

In 1968, rioting across the US followed the assassination of Martin Luther King, while in France students and workers hoped to oust Charles de Gaulle's government. Broadly speaking these tumultuous events concerned generational conflict over prevailing values within the societies where the riots broke out. Forty years later, all the images of civil disobedience such as French fisherman dumping their catches and British hauliers blocking roads illustrate self-interest triggered by global forces rather than local ones, such as rising fuel and food prices.

If globalisation is a bus trip, then, Europe appears to have been steadily reduced in status from driver to conductor to helpless passenger. Almost none of the big issues currently shaping its future are European. In the past six months fear has intensified over China's economic rise and India has become the most seductive destination for entrepreneurial retailers. Most European banks have lost at least half of their value due to wildly misguided risk assessment in the US while most of the rise in the oil price reflects non-Western supply and demand habits.

One might paint Europe as the hapless victim of globalisation. Consideration of energy security suggests that the crunch will worsen as natural gas supplies evaporate (as if high oil prices weren't enough to keep you awake at night). Meanwhile, analysis of the future of retailing suggests that online retailing is set to soar, not least because even Americans are driving less in a bid to keep fuel costs down. Malls might have only just opened their doors in some emerging markets but in the West they face an uncertain future. The aviation industry believes that if oil remains at $135 a barrel, the world's airlines will lose $6.1bn this year.

It seems as if every business model in town is in the process of being wrecked by OPEC, or China's soaring resource demands, or greedy bankers; in reply, citizens protest that Congress or the European Union Commissioner or big oil companies should fix it and really, you know, it *is* someone else's fault. But that's not our view. In fact, it might be worth remembering Einstein's credo that "the significant problems we have cannot be solved at the same level of thinking with which we created them." This fragment is the basis of most of the entrepreneurship espoused in this publication, and it opens the door to creative solutions to problems that are invariably both global and local.

Europe has a leadership role to play in globalization, providing not just technological solutions to pressing problems such as climate change but perhaps more importantly offering a deep heritage of cultural intelligence and humanity arising from its eighteenth century Enlightenment.

There are hopeful signs to which one may point. A telemetry company is helping hauliers to cut their fuel consumption; an electric car project, backed by both Israel's government and Renault-Nissan, may herald the end of the internal combustion engine as we know it, and a book called *WASTEnomics* bristles with private sector solutions to excessive waste, the product of our extraordinary affluence.

Amended version of editorial published by Richard Lofthouse in *CNBC European Business* 39 (July–August 2008), p. 6. Published with the permission of the author.

have persuaded, at least for the moment, many Europeans that their assumptions about American culture were incorrect and that a new era of American foreign and domestic policy is at hand. Congressional resistance to many of President Obama's initiatives, however, have made his support in the American population seem much less assured than in the months immediately following his election.

Third, during the second half of 2008 a major international financial crisis potentially of the dimensions of that of the 1930s overwhelmed the American, transatlantic, and world economies. The crisis originated in the United States mortgage market where numerous major banks found themselves holding mortgages that could not be paid. Several major financial institutions in the United States failed, as did some banks in Europe. The United States and some European governments intervened deeply in areas of the economy where they had previously generally refrained from intervening. Stock markets around the world lost a third or more of their value. The interconnectedness of world markets demonstrated itself as never before, with financial panic displaying itself around the globe.

European Debt Crisis

From the start, European states with strong economies knew that there was a risk involved in sharing a common European currency with less affluent countries. The premise of the *Eurozone*, as the group of countries that shared the Euro came to be known, was that each country would control its deficits and maintain a stable economy. Countries like Greece and Italy had to lower their inflation rates and deficits in order to qualify for the Euro, and they had to promise to maintain those lower rates once they adopted the new currency. Participation in the Euro made countries appear to be safer investments, and Greece, Ireland, Spain, and Portugal were able to borrow money at favorable interest rates. In 2009, the new socialist government in Greece announced that the appearance of economic stability in Greece was based on the previous government's falsification of data: the deficit was, they announced, actually twice what it had been reported to be. Foreign investors withdrew not only from the Greek economy, but from other potentially risky economics like Spain, Portugal, and Ireland, and those countries' governments had trouble refinancing their substantial debts. In order to prevent the crisis from spilling over into other countries, Eurozone leaders like Germany have insisted on strict and unpopular austerity measures designed to lower deficits in Southern Europe. This has, in turn, raised issues over national sovereignty and the ability of individual member states to control their own economies. As has been the case in response to the financial crisis in the United States, some commentators argue that austerity measures, which include freezing or drastically reducing government spending, punish working-class Europeans for unscrupulous or speculative behavior on the part of economists, investors, and bankers. Debates about whether increased or reduced government spending

Outside the parliament building in February 2012, Greek citizens protest austerity measures aimed at reducing Greece's debt and securing loans from the European Union and other international organizations. This is just one battle in the fight to determine who should be responsible for rectifying the economic problems that had been mounting over the previous decade: the wealthy and big business through increased taxation or working people through reduced government services. Aristidis Vafeiadakis/ZUMA Press/Newscom would be more effective in ensuring economic recovery in Southern Europe are likely to continue for many years.

In ongoing debates about the wisdom of a common European currency, the fate of the Euro has been linked to the fate of the European Union itself. At the present, it is difficult to imagine that the effort to unify in Europe will either halt or be reversed. It also seems certain that all future developments will move much more slowly and will require increasingly complicated negotiations. Moreover, the future of the European Union has become enmeshed in often bitter and divisive debates within the member states over social policies, the future of their economies, and what role the state should play in economic affairs.

View the **Closer Look** "The Copenhagen Opera House" on **MyHistoryLab.com**

In Perspective

After decades of warfare and tension in the first half of the century, European society developed peacefully in the postwar period. France and Germany became natural allies, both working toward the common cause of European integration. Migration and the economic growth of the second half of the century reshaped the society of many European nations. Welfare systems provided an extensive social safety net. The role and opportunities for women in society expanded. More and more Europeans across the Continent attended universities. The end of Soviet domination began a process in which Eastern Europe increasingly came to participate in the affluence of the West with its myriad consumer goods.

By the close of the century, Europe, like much of the rest of the world, had entered a new technological revolution through the computer and advances in medical care. Economic growth slowed in the 1990s, but most of Europe outside the former communist-dominated regions continued to enjoy some of the highest standards of living in the world, under liberal democratic governments.

The efforts to unify Europe have transformed the Continent and the everyday lives of its citizens. The future of the European Union, however, now stands at a crossroads. The advancing financial crisis will only place new demands on the Union.

Europe no longer dominates global cultural or economic forces in the way that it did at the beginning of the twentieth century. In the twenty-first century, Europe is only one player in a global community of states that often look to their own traditions, rather than Europe, for models of how to organize societies, governments, and their interactions with one another.

KEY TERMS

euro (p. 1008)
European Constitution (p. 1008)
European Economic Community (EEC) (p. 1007)
European Union (p. 1007)
existentialism (p. 994)
Green movement (p. 999)
socialist realism (p. 1003)

REVIEW QUESTIONS

1. How did migration affect twentieth-century European social life? What internal and external forces led to migration?
2. In what specific ways was Europe Americanized in the second half of the twentieth century? How do you explain the trend toward a consumer society?
3. How has Islamic migration into Europe affected social tensions on the Continent? How did the migration come about? What are incidents occurring in Europe that have raised resentment within the Islamic world?
4. How did women's social and economic roles change in the second half of the twentieth century? What changes and problems have women faced since the fall of communism in Eastern Europe?
5. How did the pursuit and diffusion of knowledge change in the twentieth century? What have been the effects of the communications revolutions? Has Western intellectual life become more unified or less so? Why?
6. What were the technological steps in the emergence of the computer? What changes will computers bring in the next decade?
7. What were the major steps in the emergence of the European Union? Why is the Union now facing a crisis?

SUGGESTED READINGS

G. Ambrosius and W. H. Hubbard, *A Social and Economic History of Twentieth-Century Europe* (1989). An excellent one-volume treatment of the subject.

B. S. Anderson and J. P. Zinsser, *A History of Their Own: Women in Europe from Prehistory to the Present*, Vol. 2 (1988). A broad-ranging survey.

G. Bock and P. Thane, eds., *Maternity and Gender Politics: Women and the Rise of the European Welfare States, 1880s–1950s* (1991). Explores the emergence of welfare legislation.

E. Bramwell, *Ecology in the 20th Century: A History* (1989). Traces the environmental movement to its late-nineteenth-century origins.

P. E. Ceruzzi, *A History of Modern Computing* (2003). A comprehensive survey.

S. Collinson, *Beyond Borders: West European Migration Policy and the 21st Century* (1993). Explores a major contemporary European social issue.

R. Crossman, ed., *The God That Failed* (1949). Classic essays by former communist intellectuals.

D. Dinan, *Europe Recast: A History of the European Union* (2004). A major overview.

C. Fink, P. Gasert, and D. Junker, *1968: The World Transformed* (1998). The best collection of essays on a momentous year.

B. Graham, *Modern Europe: Place, Culture, Identity* (1998). Thoughtful essays on the future of Europe by a group of geographers.

H. S. Hughes, *Sophisticated Rebels: The Political Culture of European Dissent, 1968–1987* (1988). Thoughtful essays on recent cultural critics.

P. Jenkins, *Mrs. Thatcher's Revolution: The Ending of the Socialist Era* (1988). The best work on the subject.

P. Jenkins, *The Next Christendom: The Coming of Global Christianity* (2002). A provocative analysis.

T. Judt, *Past Imperfect: French Intellectuals, 1944–1956* (1992). An important study of French intellectuals and communism.

T. Judt, *Postwar: A History of Europe since 1945* (2005). The most recent authoritative overview.

R. Maltby, ed., *Passing Parade: A History of Popular Culture in the Twentieth Century* (1989). Essays on a topic just beginning to receive scholarly attention.

R. Marrus, *The Unwanted: European Refugees in the 20th Century* (1985). An important work on a disturbing subject.

D. Meyer, *Sex and Power: The Rise of Women in America, Russia, Sweden, and Italy* (1987). A lively, useful survey.

N. Naimark, *Fires of Hatred: Ethnic Cleansing in Twentieth-Century Europe* (2002). A remarkably sensitive treatment of a tragic subject.

M. Poster, *Existential Marxism in Postwar France* (1975). An excellent and clear work.

H. Rowley, *Tête-á-Tête: Simone de Beauvoir and Jean-Paul Sartre* (2005). A highly critical joint biography.

S. Strasser, C. McGovern, and M. Judt, *Getting and Spending: European and American Consumer Societies in the Twentieth Century* (1998). An extensive collection of comparative essays.

F. Thebaud, ed., *A History of Women in the West: Vol. 5. Toward a Cultural Identity in the Twentieth Century* (1994). A collection of wide-ranging essays of the highest quality.

MyHistoryLab™ MEDIA ASSIGNMENTS

Find these resources in the Media Assignments folder for Chapter 30 on **MyHistoryLab**.

QUESTIONS FOR ANALYSIS

1. What recent European developments are illustrated by this building?

   ***Section:* New American Leadership and Financial Crisis**

   View the **Closer Look** The Copenhagen Opera House, p. 1012

2. How does each of the two writers define freedom?

   ***Section:* The Twentieth-Century Movement of Peoples**

   Read the **Compare and Connect** Muslim Women Debate France's Ban on the Veil, p. 986

3. How did World War II influence intellectual trends in Europe in the late twentieth century?

   ***Section:* Transformations in Knowledge and Culture**

   Watch the **Video** The Big Picture: The World in 2015 C.E., p. 995

4. What rationale are given for supporting a ban on women wearing headscarves in France?

   ***Section:* The Twentieth-Century Movement of Peoples**

   Read the **Document** Justin Vaisse, from "Veiled Meaning" (France) 2004, p. 984

5. How do politics and environmental concerns intersect in this discourse?

   ***Section:* The Twentieth-Century Movement of Peoples**

   Read the **Document** Towards a Green Europe, Towards a Green World, p. 997

OTHER RESOURCES FROM THIS CHAPTER

The Twentieth-Century Movement of Peoples

Watch the **Video** Video Lectures: Identity Politics: Notting Hill Carnival, p. 983

View the **Map** Map Discovery: Events in Eastern Europe, 1989–1990, p. 983

Read the **Document** Jörg Haider, from *The Freedom I Mean* (Austria), 1995, p. 985

Toward a Welfare State Society

Read the **Compare and Connect** Margaret Thatcher and Tony Blair Debate Government's Social Responsibility for Welfare, p. 989

Transformations in Knowledge and Culture

Watch the **Video** Video Lectures: Imperialism and the United States, p. 997

Watch the **Video** Video Lectures: British Petroleum Oil Spill—Environmental Disasters, p. 999

The Christian Heritage

Read the **Document** Pope John Paul II, from *Centesimus Annus*, p. 1004

The Challenges of European Unification

View the **Image** European Union Flag, p. 1007

Read the **Document** A Common Market and European Integration (1960), p. 1007

Read the **Document** Treaty on European Union, 1992, p. 1008

View the **Map** European Union, p. 1008

Energy and the Modern World

NO SINGLE TECHNOLOGICAL factor so determines the social relationships and standard of living of human beings as energy. The more energy a society can command for each of its members, the stronger and more influential it will be. Throughout recorded human history, those societies that have found ways to improve their access to sources of energy, and have then effectively applied the energy, have dominated both their immediate environments and much of the world beyond. Indeed, the possession of, or the lack of powerful, inexpensive sources of energy in large measure determines which nations will be wealthy and which will be poor.

Animals, Wind, and Water

For civilization to advance technologically, energy had to be applied to tasks. The earliest source of such energy was animal power, which was used all over the world except among the peoples on the American continent prior to the arrival of the Europeans. Oxen, water buffalo, and horses were the major draft animals. Of these, horses were the most efficient.

Throughout the world until the eighteenth century, however, wind and water furnished most of the energy for machinery. Sailing ships had been used since ancient times for travel, fishing, and the transport of goods. The wind also worked mills that pumped water and ground grain. Waterwheels proved to be highly flexible machines and by the eighteenth century constituted the major sources of mechanical power in Europe and much of the rest of the world. But wind and water were uncertain sources of energy. The wind could cease; drought could dry up streams. Water-powered machinery had to be located near the stream furnishing the water. Consequently, most of the mills employing such machinery were located in the countryside.

Until the eighteenth century, sailing ships were powered by wind alone. In this fourteenth-century manuscript illustration, sailors navigate with the help of an astrolabe. Ms Fr 2810 f. 188 Navigators using an astrolabe in the Indian Ocean (vellum) by Boucicaut Master (fl. 1390–1430) (and workshop) Livre des Merveilles du Monde (c. 1410–1412). Bibliothèque Nationale, Paris, France/Bridgeman Art Library International

Although animals, wind, and water provided energy for relatively complicated machines capable of manufacturing and transporting high-quality goods, the economic and political transformations that have driven the history of the world for the past two and a half centuries could only have occurred through a qualitative as well as quantitative leap in the manner in which human beings commanded energy. The twin sources of this world-transforming energy have been fossil fuels and electricity.

Until the second half of the eighteenth century, fossil fuels—coal, petroleum, and, to a lesser extent, natural gas—contributed only a small portion of human energy requirements. Their use as meaningful sources of energy required a series of inventions that allowed the energy of heat to be changed into mechanical energy.

Steam Power and the Age of Coal

Although peoples living near coal deposits had used it as a household fuel for a very long time, only the invention of the steam engine, patented by James Watt in 1769, established a major industrial demand for coal. The steam engine first permitted the pumping of water from coal mines to increase production. But as the industrial uses for the steam engine grew, the invention itself drove the demand for greater quantities of coal as fuel.

Coal-fueled steam power changed the face of human society during the nineteenth century and continues to provide the energy for the most powerful turbogenerators at the dawn of the twenty-first century. Steam-powered machines could be made larger and more flexible than those powered by wind or water, and as long as coal was available, they could run steadily day and night. Steam engines, in contrast to waterwheels, were transportable. Factories could be moved away from streams in the countryside to urban areas where a ready workforce existed. And goods produced in factories powered by steam engines could be carried around the world by steam-powered locomotives and ships. Those expanding markets in turn called forth more steam-powered factories and even greater use of coal. Furthermore, steam-powered factories could also produce military weapons that could be placed on steam-powered naval vessels constructed of iron and steel in vast coal-fueled blast furnaces. When Theodore Roosevelt sent the U.S. fleet around the world, it was a testimony to the power of coal and steam as well as to the power of the American navy.

The age of steam was the age of coal. The nations possessing large coal deposits dominated much nineteenth-century economic life as the nations that possess oil reserves dominate much contemporary economic life. For many decades, Great Britain dominated the world's production and delivery of coal, which was transported over the entire world. Its domination was challenged only in the late nineteenth century as the United States and later Russia and China began to produce vast quantities of the fuel. Coal remained the chief fuel for the United States until after World War I and for Western Europe until after World War II. It remains the chief fuel for China.

Coal generated a rising standard of living in Europe and the expansion of European and later American power, but coal also generated a number of social and environmental problems. The most shocking conditions of exploited labor occurred in coal mines, where parliamentary reports of the 1840s described and illustrated half-clad women and children drawing coal carts from the depths of the mines to the surface. Throughout the nineteenth and twentieth centuries, thousands of miners died in mining disasters. Work in the mines injured the health of miners, as did the pollution sent into the atmosphere by coal fires from both factories and homes. By the early twentieth century, observers had begun to note the damage to the environment caused by strip mining of coal and the later abandonment of the regions.

The Internal Combustion Engine: The Age of Oil

As with coal, the impact of petroleum, the second major fossil fuel, also depended on the invention of machinery to use it. Originally, the use for oil was limited to kerosene, the fuel used for lighting around much of the world by 1900. It was upon the world demand for lamp oil that John D. Rockefeller founded the Standard Oil Company. The invention of the internal combustion engine in 1882 by Rudolf Daimler and the diesel engine in 1892 by Rudolf Diesel transformed the demand for oil. Toward the close of the nineteenth century, extensive oil production had begun in the United States, with Austria, Russia, Romania, Sumatra, Mexico, Iran, and Venezuela starting to tap their own oil resources before World War I.

Just as the steam engine had spurred the expansion of the coal industry, the internal combustion engine drove the oil industry. Fuel oil would begin to replace coal, not so much because it was cheaper but rather because it was more efficient, easier to store and transport, and cleaner to burn. Initially, fuel oil tended to be used in those countries where it could be produced relatively near the point of use. Until the end of World War II, the United States was the primary world producer and user of oil. As fuel for the internal combustion engine, oil became the driving force of automobiles, locomotives,

66
The Ladies' HOME JOURNAL
February, 1925
Cancel distance & conquer weather
The woman who drives her own Ford Closed Car is completely independent of road and weather conditions in any season.
It enables her to carry on all those activities of the winter months that necessitate travel to and fro—in or out of town. Her time and energy are conserved; her health is protected, no matter how bitterly cold the day, or how wet and slushy it is underfoot.
A Ford Sedan is always comfortable—warm and snug in winter, and in summer with ventilator and windows open wide, as cool and airy as an open car.
This seasonal comfort is combined with fine looks and Ford dependability; no wonder there is for this car so wide and ever-growing a demand.
FORD MOTOR COMPANY, DETROIT, MICHIGAN
TUDOR SEDAN, $580 ∴ FORDOR SEDAN, $660
COUPE, $520 ∴ ALL PRICES F. O. B. DETROIT
Ford
CLOSED CARS

Until 1924, Henry Ford had disdained national advertising for his cars. But as General Motors gained a competitive edge by making yearly changes in style and technology, Ford was forced to pay more attention to advertising. This ad was directed at "Mrs. Consumer," combining appeals to both female independence and motherly duties. Ford Motor Company

airplanes, ships, factory machinery, and electric generators. It revolutionized agricultural machinery and world food production, but as a fuel for transportation, it fostered a social transformation over much of the world.

Starting in the United States and then spreading elsewhere, owning an automobile introduced a new mobility factor into social relationships. People could move easily across long distances to join a new community or to start a new job. Inexpensive gasoline for cars and public transport buses permitted the development of suburbs ever farther removed from traditional urban centers. In turn, retailing moved away from city centers to shopping malls. At the same time, wherever the mechanization of farming through improved farm machinery took place, there usually followed a movement of people from farming communities to urban areas. The availability of cheap oil encouraged people to develop lifestyles that made them utterly dependent on that oil.

Electricity Increases the Demand for Oil

The manufacture of automobiles and other forms of transport using the internal combustion or diesel engine was central to all modern industrial life. As those industries expanded, so did the construction of extensive road systems. These in turn created new demands for fuel oil.

But the greatest demand for fuel oil arose from the application of electricity to the needs of everyday life. Electricity proved to be the most flexible and versatile source of energy for the twentieth century, and its generation provided the single greatest source of demand for both coal and oil. Electricity generation would also employ new modes of water power in the forms of hydroelectric generators.

The scientific basis for the production of electric energy was Michael Faraday's study of electromagnetic induction. In 1831, he demonstrated that mechanical energy under the proper conditions could be converted into electric energy. Even more important, the reverse was also true. Electricity could be generated in one location and applied far away wherever electrical lines could be extended. The applications of electrical power have appeared to be restricted only by the limitations of the inventive imagination.

During the second half of the nineteenth century, a whole host of inventors, such as Thomas Alva Edison, worked through the production and application of electrical power to service large regions. Electricity found applications across the spectrum of human society, actions, and enterprises. Access to electricity in the course of the twentieth century became the key factor for an improved standard of living. A fundamental moment in the decision by Japan to modernize during the late nineteenth century was the construction of the Tokyo Electric Light Company in 1888. The extension of electrical lines into the American countryside was one of the major accomplishments of Franklin Roosevelt's New Deal. Electrical power transformed the workplace, but even more strikingly it transformed homes. Without access to electrical power, domestic households could not make use of any of the growing array of labor-saving appliances such as electric washing machines, electric irons, electric stoves, and electric vacuum cleaners. Electric lights brightened whole cities. Electricity replaced both coal and oil as the source of power for many locomotives; it powered public tram systems and opened the way for the telegraph, the telephone, the wireless, the motion picture camera, and television. It planted the seeds for the computer revolution in communication and information. Electricity allowed manufacturing plants and office complexes to be built wherever electric lines could be carried. Indeed, the spread of access to electrical power has been the single best indication of economic advancement for any nation or region.

Yet within this era of ever-expanding electrification, coal and oil—the fundamental fossil fuels—would still provide the underpinnings of the world's energy. In fact, more oil and coal are used to generate electricity than for any other single purpose. Throughout the twentieth century, the demand for these fuels led to the refinement of their production techniques to permit the extraction of coal from ever-deeper seams and the strip mining of it from regions where previously it would have been economically unproductive to do so. The effort to discover, extract, and transport oil would have major consequences for the world's physical and geopolitical environment far into the twentieth century.

Oil and Global Politics in the Twentieth Century

As the twentieth century began, the United States was by far the largest producer and exporter of petroleum. Yet by the 1920s, the American government began to worry about running out of oil. So, too, did the British, who depended on imported oil for all of their military and industrial needs. During the 1920s and 1930s, both governments encouraged oil companies to forge agreements for the drilling and export of oil from the Middle East. These arrangements fit into the pattern of formal and informal colonialism that still characterized the interwar period.

After World War II, Western Europe, the Soviet Union, and the nations of the Warsaw Pact began to turn from coal to oil as the basis for economic growth. (Japan followed this course during the 1960s.) By 1947, the United States had begun to import more oil than it produced. These two developments—a new dependence on oil by the industrialized nations and the expanded search for oil by the West—formed the basis for the new role that the nations of the Middle East would play in the world economy as the chief oil exporters. Simultaneously, as the world's industrialized economies were growing dependent on Middle East oil production, nationalist leaders in that region were denouncing former colonial domination and rejecting relationships with the West and with Israel, a country that received strong political support from the United States and Western Europe. The stage was thus set for oil to play a new role in the geopolitical conflicts of the Cold War era.

Playing a major role in those conflicts was the Organization of Petroleum Exporting Nations (OPEC), founded in 1960. Regardless of their differences, OPEC members were united in two things: First, they deeply resented former colonial control of their oil supplies, and second, they were determined that their own governments, not foreign oil companies, would control those vital resources. (Mexico had brought its own petroleum industry under state control before World War II.) In 1973, during the Yom Kippur War, OPEC acted, sharply raising oil prices to nations whose governments supported Israel. The action caused severe economic consequences in the West and spurred new efforts to develop local oil reserves in politically safe locations such as in the North Sea. OPEC would attempt similar actions on other occasions, most successfully in 1979. In that year, a

In 1989, when a supertanker spilled 35,000 tons of crude oil into Alaska's Prince William Sound, rescue workers struggled to save the lives of seabirds and animals. Nevertheless, thousands died. ZUMA Press/Newscom

revolution in Iran overthrew the government, which had long been supported by the United States. OPEC cut off oil shipments to the West, causing severe dislocations. Concerns about securing oil supplies in the West were again sparked by the Persian Gulf War and other political tensions in the region.

In addition to the political problems associated with Middle East oil production, the industrial world's reliance on oil has had severe environmental consequences. Generally, when the United States dominated oil production, the oil refineries were located near the source of oil production. As the exploitation of oil reserves moved to the Middle East and then later in the century to Alaska and to the North Sea, oil refineries became separated from the drilling locations. Crude oil was shipped to refineries on enormous tankers. More than once, these supertankers have hit shoals or gone aground, causing large oil spills, calamitous to both animals and humans. Additionally, even when transported safely, the use of hydrocarbons like oil and coal contributes to air pollution and global warming, which scientists predict will have dire consequences for our planet's climate.

The Promise and Danger of Nuclear Energy

Following World War II, nuclear power became a new source for the generation of electrical energy. The power of the atom, first released in the 1940s for military purposes, held the promise of virtually infinite quantities of energy. The world would no longer be dependent on finite supplies of fossil fuel located in politically tense regions of the world. The generation of such energy, however, required the most complex sets of machinery ever devised to produce electrical energy. France and Great Britain began to build nuclear reactors in the 1950s, with the United States, the Soviet Union, and various other European nations following in the 1960s. Nations outside the West, such as India and Pakistan, looked to the construction of nuclear power stations as a means of moving more rapidly toward the achievements of industrialization and a rising standard of living through extensive electrification. Nations with limited supplies of fossil fuel, such as Japan, hoped nuclear energy would solve their energy supply problem. During its postwar occupation of Japan, the United States also encouraged the dissemination of information about the benefits of nuclear energy, and strictly prohibited the linking of nuclear energy with the atomic bomb attacks on Hiroshima and Nagasaki. There was little or no discussion of the dangers of nuclear energy. The oil shock of the mid-1970s brought new enthusiasm to the adoption of nuclear energy, but the economic downturn of the late 1970s and early 1980s slowed the construction of nuclear-generating stations. The construction of breeder reactors, which would produce their own fuel in the process of generating electrical energy, seemed to promise a world liberated from dependence on a finite supply of fossil fuels. Furthermore, unlike coal and oil, which have many uses besides that of fuel, uranium had no other economic use. The workers in the field of atomic energy were scientists and engineers rather than the kind of industrial labor force that produced coal and oil.

Yet the technology of nuclear energy production proved to be exceedingly dangerous. The atomic reactors produced spent radioactive waste that would remain hazardous for hundreds of years. In 1979, a meltdown at the Three Mile Island plant in Pennsylvania raised the specter of massive human and environmental devastation. In that case, the reactor was brought back under control without any demonstrated effect on human populations, but enthusiasm for nuclear energy in the United States diminished. In April 1986, a much more serious disaster at the Chernobyl nuclear generating plant in the Soviet Union caused enormous, lasting damage. Most recently, in March 2011 an earthquake and tsunami caused a meltdown at the Fukushima nuclear power plant in Japan, although the plant was supposed to have been designed to withstand exactly that sort of environmental challenge. Both the promise and danger of nuclear power continue to inform the political life of all nations using such power. It is wholly unclear, for example, what will be done with the radioactive spent fuel. Furthermore, the construction of nuclear generating plants has allowed nations that lack atomic weapons to train scientists and other experts who might be able to use that knowledge to develop atomic weapons. Whereas in the United States and Europe the military uses of atomic power came first and were followed by peaceful energy uses, the reverse has been the case in nations such as India and Pakistan. Despite its initial promise, nuclear power has contributed far less to energy production than we originally imagined.

The problem of energy remains with us in the new century. Environmental pollution and all the issues surrounding the nuclear generation of energy will demand increasing attention and expenditure of public funds. Similarly, the political pressures and tensions surrounding the oil supplies of the Middle East will not disappear, as advanced nations seek to secure and protect energy reserves while the nations that possess those reserves seek to secure a rising standard of living for themselves.

Trace the transformation of energy used in the West from wind and water to petroleum. How did coal transform both the industry and the military power of the West? How did inventions, such as the internal combustion engine, change the demands on sources of energy? Why did the rise of electrical power increase the need for petroleum? What opportunities and dangers has nuclear energy posed?

Read the **Document** The William Knox D'Arcy Oil Concession in Persia 1901 on **MyHistoryLab.com**

Read the **Document** Striking British Coal Miners, 1912 on **MyHistoryLab.com**

View the **Image** Cars on Daytona Beach, 1920s on **MyHistoryLab.com**

Read the **Document** Lenin Calls for Electrification of All Russia (1920) on **MyHistoryLab.com**

View the **Image** Edison's Vitascope on **MyHistoryLab.com**

Read the **Document** The Saudi-Aramco 50/50 Agreement (1950) on **MyHistoryLab.com**

GLOSSARY

Academy A center of philosophical investigation and a school for training statesmen and citizens that was founded by Plato in 386 B.C.E.

Acropolis (ACK-row-po-lis) The religious and civic center of Athens. It is the site of the Parthenon.

Act of Supremacy The declaration by Parliament in 1534 that Henry VIII, not the pope, was the head of the church in England.

agape (AG-a-pay) Meaning "love feast." A common meal that was part of the central ritual of early Christian worship.

agora (AG-o-rah) The Greek marketplace and civic center. It was the heart of the social life of the *polis*.

Agricultural Revolution The innovations in farm production that began in the eighteenth century and led to a scientific and mechanized agriculture.

Albigensians (Al-bi-GEN-see-uns) Thirteenth-century advocates of a dualist religion. They took their name from the city of Albi in southern France. Also called *Cathars*.

Anabaptists Protestants who insisted that only adult baptism conformed to Scripture.

anarchists Those who believe that government and social institutions are oppressive and unnecessary and society should be based on voluntary cooperation among individuals.

Anschluss (AHN-shluz) Meaning "union." The annexation of Austria by Germany in March 1938.

anti-Semitism Prejudice, hostility, or legal discrimination against Jews.

apartheid (a-PAR-tid) An official policy of segregation, assignment of peoples to distinct regions, and other forms of social, political, and economic discrimination based on race associated primarily with South Africa.

Apostolic Succession The Christian doctrine that the powers given by Jesus to his original disciples have been handed down from bishop to bishop through ordination.

appeasement The Anglo-French policy of making concessions to Germany in the 1930s to avoid a crisis that would lead to war. It assumed that Germany had real grievances and Hitler's aims were limited and ultimately acceptable.

Areopagus The governing council of Athens, originally open only to the nobility. It was named after the hill on which it met.

arete (AH-ray-tay) Manliness, courage, and the excellence appropriate to a hero. It was considered the highest virtue of Homeric society.

Arianism (AIR-ee-an-ism) The belief formulated by Arius of Alexandria (ca. 280–336 C.E.) that Jesus was a created being, neither fully man nor fully God, but something in between. It did away with the doctrine of the Trinity.

aristocratic resurgence Term applied to the eighteenth-century aristocratic efforts to resist the expanding power of European monarchies.

atomist School of ancient Greek philosophy founded in the fifth century B.C.E. by Leucippus of Miletus and Democritus of Abdera. It held that the world consists of innumerable, tiny, solid, indivisible, and unchangeable particles called *atoms*.

Attica (AT-tick-a) The region of Greece where Athens is located.

Augsburg Confession (AWGS-berg) The definitive statement of Lutheran belief made in 1530.

autocracy (AW-to-kra-see) Government in which the ruler has absolute power.

Axis The alliance between Nazi Germany and fascist Italy. Also called the *Pact of Steel*.

banalities Exactions that the lord of a manor could make on his tenants.

baroque (bah-ROWK) A style of art marked by heavy and dramatic ornamentation and curved rather than straight lines that flourished between 1550 and 1750. It was especially associated with the Catholic Counter-Reformation.

Beguines (bi-GEENS) Lay sisterhoods not bound by the rules of a religious order.

benefices Church offices granted by the ruler of a state or the pope to an individual. It also meant *fiefs* in the Middle Ages.

bishop Originally a person elected by early Christian congregations to lead them in worship and supervise their funds. In time, bishops became the religious and even political authorities for Christian communities within large geographical areas.

Black Death The bubonic plague that killed millions of Europeans in the fourteenth century.

blitzkrieg (BLITZ-kreeg) Meaning "lightning war." The German tactic early in World War II of employing fast-moving, massed armored columns supported by airpower to overwhelm the enemy.

Bolsheviks Meaning the "majority." Term Lenin applied to his faction of the Russian Social Democratic Party. It became the Communist Party of the Soviet Union after the Russian Revolution.

boyars The Russian nobility.

Brezhnev doctrine Statement by Soviet party chairman Brezhnev in 1968 that declared the right of the Soviet Union to interfere in the domestic policies of other communist countries.

Bronze Age The name given to the earliest civilized era, c. 4000 to 1000 B.C.E. The term reflects the importance of the metal bronze, a mixture of tin and copper, for the peoples of this age for use as weapons and tools.

Caesaropapism (SEE-zer-o-PAY-pi-zim) The direct involvement of the ruler in religious doctrine and practice as if he were the head of the church as well as the state.

caliphate (KAH-li-fate) The true line of succession to Muhammad.

categorical imperative According to Emmanuel Kant (1724–1804), the internal sense of moral duty or awareness possessed by all human beings.

catholic Meaning "universal." The body of belief held by most Christians enshrined within the church.

censor Official of the Roman republic charged with conducting the census and compiling the lists of citizens and members of the Senate. They could expel senators for financial or moral reasons. Two censors were elected every five years.

Chartism The first large-scale European working-class political movement. It sought political reforms that would favor the interests of skilled British workers in the 1830s and 1840s.

chiaroscuro (kyar-eh-SKEW-row) The use of shading to enhance naturalness in painting and drawing.

civilization A form of human culture marked by urbanism, metallurgy, and writing.

civilizing mission The concept that Western nations could bring advanced science and economic development to non-Western parts of the world that justified imperial administration.

clientage (KLI-ent-age) The custom in ancient Rome whereby men became supporters of more powerful men in return for legal and physical protection and economic benefits.

Cold War The ideological and geographical struggle between the United States and its allies and the USSR and its allies that began after World War II and lasted until the dissolution of the USSR in 1989.

collectivization The bedrock of Stalinist agriculture, which forced Russian peasants to give up their private farms and work as members of collectives, large agricultural units controlled by the state.

coloni (CO-loan-ee) Farmers or sharecroppers on the estates of wealthy Romans.

Commonwealthmen British political writers whose radical republican ideas influenced the American revolutionaries.

concentration camps Camps first established by Great Britain in South Africa during the Boer War to incarcerate noncombatant civilians; later, camps established for political prisoners and other persons deemed dangerous to the state in the Soviet Union and Nazi Germany. The term is now primarily associated with the camps established by the Nazis during the Holocaust.

Concert of Europe Term applied to the European great powers acting together (in "concert") to resolve international disputes between 1815 and the 1850s.

conciliar theory The argument that General Councils were superior in authority to the pope and represented the whole body of the faithful.

condottieri (con-da-TEE-AIR-ee) Military brokers who furnished mercenary forces to the Italian states during the Renaissance.

Congregationalists Congregationalists put a group or assembly above any one individual and prefer an ecclesiastical polity that allows each congregation to be autonomous, or self-governing.

congress system A series of international meetings among the European great powers to promote mutual cooperation between 1818 and 1822.

conquistadores (kahn-KWIS-teh-door-hez) Meaning "conquerors." The Spanish conquerors of the New World.

conservatism Support for the established order in church and state. In the nineteenth century, it implied support for legitimate monarchies, landed aristocracies, and established churches. Conservatives favored only gradual, or "organic," change.

Consulate French government dominated by Napoleon from 1799 to 1804.

consuls (CON-suls) The two chief magistrates of the Roman state.

consumer revolution The vast increase in both the desire and the possibility of consuming goods and services that began in the early eighteenth century and created the demand for sustaining the Industrial Revolution.

containment The U.S. policy during the Cold War of resisting Soviet expansion and influence in the expectation that the USSR would eventually collapse.

Convention French radical legislative body from 1792 to 1794.

Corn Laws British tariffs on imported grain that protected the price of grain grown within the British Isles.

Counter-Reformation The sixteenth-century reform movement in the Roman Catholic Church in reaction to the Protestant Reformation.

creed A brief statement of faith to which true Christians should adhere.

creoles (KRAY-ol-ez) Persons of Spanish descent born in the Spanish colonies.

Crusades Religious wars directed by the church against infidels and heretics.

cubism A radical new departure in early-twentieth-century Western art. This term was first coined to describe the paintings of Pablo Picasso and Georges Braque.

culture The ways of living built up by a group and passed on from one generation to another.

cuneiform (Q-nee-i-form) A writing system invented by the Sumerians that used a wedge-shaped stylus, or pointed tool, to write on wet clay tablets that were then baked or dried (*cuneus* means "wedge" in Latin). The writing was also cut into stone.

Curia (CURE-ee-a) The papal government.

Cynic School (SIN-ick) A fourth-century philosophical movement that ridiculed all religious observances and turned away from involvement in the affairs of the *polis*. Its most famous exemplar was Diogenes of Sinope (ca. 400–325 B.C.E.).

deacon Meaning "those who serve." In early Christian congregations, deacons assisted the presbyters, or elders.

decolonization The process of European retreat of colonial empires following World War II.

deism A belief in a rational God who had created the universe but then allowed it to function without his interference according to the mechanisms of nature and a belief in rewards and punishments after death for human action.

Delian League (DEE-li-an) An alliance of Greek states under the leadership of Athens that was formed in 478–477 B.C.E. to resist the Persians. In time the league was transformed into the Athenian Empire.

deme (DEEM) A small town in Attica or a ward in Athens that became the basic unit of Athenian civic life under the democratic reforms of Clisthenes in 508 B.C.E.

détente French for "relaxation," the easing of strained relations, especially in a political situation.

divine right of kings The theory that monarchs are appointed by and answerable only to God.

domestic system of textile production Method of producing textiles in which agents furnished raw materials to households whose members spun them into thread and then wove cloth, which the agents then sold as finished products.

Donatism The heresy that taught the efficacy of the sacraments depended on the moral character of the clergy who administered them.

Duce (DO-chay) Meaning "leader." Mussolini's title as head of the Fascist Party.

electors Nine German princes who had the right to elect the Holy Roman Emperor.

émigrés (em-ee-GRAYS) French aristocrats who fled France during the Revolution.

empiricism (em-PEER-ih-cism) The use of experiment and observation derived from sensory evidence to construct scientific theory or philosophy of knowledge.

enclosures The consolidation or fencing in of common lands by British landlords to increase production and achieve greater commercial profits. It also involved the reclamation of waste land and the consolidation of strips into block fields.

encomienda (en-co-mee-EN-da) The grant by the Spanish crown to a colonist of the labor of a specific number of Indians for a set period of time.

Enlightenment The eighteenth-century movement led by the *philosophes* that held that change and reform were both desirable through the application of reason and science.

Epicureans (EP-i-cure-ee-ans) School of philosophy founded by Epicurus of Athens (342–271 B.C.E.). It sought to liberate people from fear of death and the supernatural by teaching that the gods took no interest in human affairs and that true happiness consisted in pleasure, which was defined as the absence of pain. This could be achieved by attaining *ataraxia*, freedom from trouble, pain, and responsibility by withdrawing from business and public life.

equestrians (EE-quest-ree-ans) Literally "cavalrymen" or "knights." In the earliest years of the Roman Republic those who could afford to serve as mounted warriors. The equestrians evolved into a social rank of well-to-do businessmen and middle-ranking officials. Many of them supported the Gracchi.

Estates General The medieval French parliament. It consisted of three separate groups, or "estates": clergy, nobility, and commoners. It last met in 1789 at the outbreak of the French Revolution.

Etruscans (EE-trus-cans) A people of central Italy who exerted the most powerful external influence on the early Romans. Etruscan kings ruled Rome until 509 B.C.E.

Eucharist (YOU-ka-rist) Meaning "thanksgiving." The celebration of the Lord's Supper. Considered the central ritual of worship by most Christians. Also called *Holy Communion*.

euro The common currency created by the EEC in the late 1990s.

European Constitution A treaty adopted in 2004 by European Union member nations; it was a long, detailed, and highly complicated document involving a bill of rights and complex economic and political agreements among all the member states.

European Economic Community (EEC) The economic association formed by France, Germany, Italy, Belgium, the Netherlands, and Luxembourg in 1957. Also known as the *Common Market*.

European Union The new name given to the EEC in 1993. It included most of the states of Western Europe.

existentialism The post–World War II Western philosophy that holds human beings are totally responsible for their acts and that this responsibility causes them dread and anguish.

family economy The basic structure of production and consumption in preindustrial Europe.

fascism Political movements that tend to be antidemocratic, anti-Marxist, antiparliamentary, and often anti-Semitic. Fascists were invariably nationalists and exhalted the nation over the individual. They supported the interests of the middle class and rejected the ideas of the French Revolution and nineteenth-century liberalism. The first fascist regime was founded by Benito Mussolini (1883–1945) in Italy in the 1920s.

fealty An oath of loyalty by a vassal to a lord, promising to perform specified services.

feudal society (FEW-dull) The social, political, military, and economic system that prevailed in the Middle Ages and beyond in some parts of Europe.

fiefs Land granted to a vassal in exchange for services, usually military.

foederati (FAY-der-ah-tee) Barbarian tribes enlisted as special allies of the Roman Empire.

Fourteen Points President Woodrow Wilson's (1856–1924) idealistic war aims.

Fronde (FROHND) A series of rebellions against royal authority in France between 1649 and 1652.

Führer (FYOOR-er) Meaning "leader." The title taken by Hitler when he became dictator of Germany.

Gallican Liberties The ecclesiastical independence of the French crown and the French Roman Catholic church from papal authority in Rome.

Gaul (GAWL) Modern France.

ghettos Separate communities in which Jews were required by law to live.

glasnost (GLAZ-nohst) Meaning "openness." The policy initiated by Mikhail Gorbachev (MEEK-hail GORE-buh-choff) in the 1980s of permitting open criticism of the policies of the Soviet Communist Party.

Glorious Revolution The largely peaceful replacement of James II by William and Mary as English monarchs in 1688. It marked the beginning of constitutional monarchy in Britain.

Golden Bull The agreement in 1356 to establish a seven-member electoral college of German princes to choose the Holy Roman Emperor.

Great Depression A prolonged worldwide economic downturn that began in 1929 with the collapse of the New York Stock Exchange.

Great Purges The imprisonment and execution of millions of Soviet citizens by Stalin between 1934 and 1939.

Great Reform Bill (1832) A limited reform of the British House of Commons and an expansion of the electorate to include a wider variety of the propertied classes. It laid the groundwork for further orderly reforms within the British constitutional system.

Great Schism The appearance of two and at times three rival popes between 1378 and 1415.

Great Trek The migration by Boer (Dutch) farmers during the 1830s and 1840s from regions around Cape Town into the eastern and northeastern regions of South Africa that ultimately resulted in the founding of the Orange Free State and Transvaal.

Green movement A political environmentalist movement that began in West Germany in the 1970s and spread to a number of other Western nations.

guilds Associations of merchants or craftsmen that offered protection to their members and set rules for their work and products.

hacienda (ha-SEE-hen-da) A large landed estate in Spanish America.

Hegira (HEJ-ear-a) The flight of Muhammad and his followers from Mecca to Medina in 622 C.E. It marks the beginning of the Islamic calendar.

heliocentric theory (HE-li-o-cen-trick) The theory, now universally accepted, that the earth and the other planets revolve around the sun. First proposed by Aristarchos of Samos (310–230 B.C.E.). Its opposite, the geocentric theory, which was dominant until the sixteenth century C.E., held that the sun and the planets revolved around the earth.

Hellenistic A term coined in the nineteenth century to describe the period of three centuries during which Greek culture spread far from its homeland to Egypt and deep into Asia.

Helots (HELL-ots) Hereditary Spartan serfs.

heretics (HAIR-i-ticks) People whose beliefs were contrary to those of the Catholic Church.

hieroglyphics (HI-er-o-gli-phicks) The complicated writing script of ancient Egypt. It combined picture writing with pictographs and sound signs. Hieroglyph means "sacred carvings" in Greek.

Holocaust The Nazi extermination of millions of European Jews between 1940 and 1945. Also called the "final solution to the Jewish problem."

Holy Roman Empire The revival of the old Roman Empire, based mainly in Germany and northern Italy, that endured from 870 to 1806.

home rule The advocacy of a large measure of administrative autonomy for Ireland within the British Empire between the 1880s and 1914.

Homo sapiens (HO-mo say-pee-ans) The scientific name for human beings, from the Latin words meaning "Wise man." *Homo sapiens* emerged some 200,000 years ago.

honestiores (HON-est-ee-or-ez) The Roman term formalized from the beginning of the third century C.E. to denote the privileged classes: senators, equestrians, the municipal aristocracy, and soldiers.

***hoplite* phalanx** (FAY-lanks) The basic unit of Greek warfare in which infantrymen fought in close order, shield to shield, usually eight ranks deep. The phalanx perfectly suited the farmer-soldier-citizen who was the backbone of the *polis*.

hubris (WHO-bris) Arrogance brought on by excessive wealth or good fortune. The Greeks believed it led to moral blindness and divine vengeance.

Huguenots (HYOU-gu-nots) French Calvinists.

humanitas (HEW-man-i-tas) The Roman name for a liberal arts education.

humiliores (HEW-mi-lee-orez) The Roman term formalized at the beginning of the third century C.E. for the lower classes.

Hussites (HUS-Its) Followers of John Huss (d. 1415) who questioned Catholic teachings about the Eucharist.

iconoclasm (i-KON-o-kla-zoom) A heresy in Eastern Christianity that sought to ban the veneration of sacred images, or icons.

id, ego, superego The three entities in Sigmund Freud's model of the internal organization of the human mind. The id consists of the amoral, irrational instincts for self-gratification. The superego embodies the external morality imposed on the personality by society. The ego mediates between the two and allows the personality to cope with the internal and external demands of its existence.

***Iliad* and the *Odyssey*, The** (ILL-ee-ad) (O-dis-see) Epic poems by Homer about the "Dark Age" heroes of Greece who fought at Troy. The poems were written down in the eighth century B.C.E. after centuries of being sung by bards.

imperialism The extension of a nation's authority over other nations or areas through conquest or political or economic hegemony.

Imperialism of Free Trade The advance of European economic and political interests in the nineteenth century by demanding that non-European nations allow European nations, most particularly Great Britain, to introduce their manufactured goods freely into all nations or to introduce other goods, such as opium into China, that allowed those nations to establish economic influence and to determine the terms of trade.

imperium (IM-pear-ee-um) In ancient Rome, the right to issue commands and to enforce them by fines, arrests, and even corporal and capital punishment.

indulgence Remission of the temporal penalty of punishment in purgatory that remained after sins had been forgiven.

Industrial Revolution Mechanization of the European economy that began in Britain in the second half of the eighteenth century.

Inquisition A tribunal created by the Catholic Church in the mid-twelfth century to detect and punish heresy.

insulae (IN-sul-lay) Meaning "islands." The multistoried apartment buildings of Rome in which most of the inhabitants of the city lived.

Intolerable Acts Measures passed by the British Parliament in 1774 to punish the colony of Massachusetts and strengthen Britain's authority in the colonies. The laws provoked colonial opposition, which led immediately to the American Revolution.

investiture controversy The medieval conflict between the church and lay rulers over who would control bishops and abbots, symbolized by the ceremony of "investing" them with the symbols of their authority.

Ionia (I-o-knee-a) The part of western Asia Minor heavily colonized by the Greeks.

Islam (IZ-lahm) Meaning "submission." The religion founded by the prophet Muhammad.

Jacobins (JACK-uh-bins) The radical republican party during the French Revolution that displaced the Girondins.

Jacquerie (jah-KREE) Revolt of the French peasantry.

Jansenism A seventeenth-century movement within the Catholic Church that taught that human beings were so corrupted by original sin that they could do nothing good nor secure their own salvation without divine grace. (It was opposed to the Jesuits.)

jihad Literally meaning "a struggle," but commonly interpreted as a religious war.

Junkers (YOONG-kerz) The noble landlords of Prussia.

jus gentium (YUZ GEN-tee-um) Meaning "law of peoples." The body of Roman law that dealt with foreigners.

jus naturale (YUZ NAH-tu-rah-lay) Meaning "natural law." The Stoic concept of a world ruled by divine reason.

Ka'ba (KAH-bah) A black meteorite in the city of Mecca that became Islam's holiest shrine.

Kristallnacht (KRIS-tahl-NAHKT) Meaning "crystal night" because of the broken glass that littered German streets after the looting and destruction of Jewish homes, businesses, and synagogues across Germany on the orders of the Nazi Party in November 1938.

Kulturkampf (cool-TOOR-cahmff) Meaning the "battle for culture." The conflict between the Roman Catholic Church and the government of the German Empire in the 1870s.

laissez-faire (lay-ZAY-faire) French phrase meaning "allow to do." In economics the doctrine of minimal government interference in the working of the economy.

Late Antiquity The multicultural period between the end of the ancient world and the birth of the Middle Ages, 250–800 C.E.

latifundia (LAT-ee-fun-dee-a) Large plantations for growing cash crops owned by wealthy Romans.

Latium (LAT-ee-um) The region of Italy in which Rome is located. Its inhabitants were called *Latins*.

League of Nations The association of sovereign states set up after World War I to pursue common policies and avert international aggression.

Lebensraum (LAY-benz-rauhm) Meaning "living space." The Nazi plan to colonize and exploit the Slavic areas of Eastern Europe for the benefit of Germany.

levée en masse (le-VAY en MASS) The French revolutionary conscription (1792) of all males into the army and the harnessing of the economy for war production.

liberal arts The medieval university program that consisted of the *trivium* (TRI-vee-um): grammar, rhetoric, and logic, and the *quadrivium* (qua-DRI-vee-um): arithmetic, geometry, astronomy, and music.

Logos (LOW-goz) Divine reason, or fire, which according to the Stoics was the guiding principle in nature. Every human had a spark of this divinity, which returned to the eternal divine spirit after death.

Lollards (LALL-erds) Followers of John Wycliffe (d. 1384) who questioned the supremacy and privileges of the pope and the church hierarchy.

Lower Egypt The Nile delta.

Luftwaffe (LUFT-vaff-uh) The German air force in World War II.

Lyceum The name of the school founded by Aristotle when he returned to Athens in 336 B.C.E.

Magna Carta (MAG-nuh CAR-tuh) The "Great Charter" limiting royal power that the English nobility forced King John to sign in 1215.

mandates The assigning of the former German colonies and Turkish territories in the Middle East to Britain, France, Japan, Belgium, Australia, and South Africa as de facto colonies under the vague supervision of the League of Nations with the hope that the territories would someday advance to independence.

mannerism A style of art in the mid- to late-sixteenth century that permitted artists to express their own "manner" or feelings in contrast to the symmetry and simplicity of the art of the High Renaissance.

manors Village farms owned by a lord.

Marshall Plan The U.S. program named after Secretary of State George C. Marshall of providing economic aid to Europe after World War II.

Marxism The theory of Karl Marx (1818–1883) and Friedrich Engels (FREE-drick ENG-ulz) (1820–1895) that history is the result of class conflict, which will end in the inevitable triumph of the industrial proletariat over the bourgeoisie and the abolition of private property and social class.

Mein Kampf (MINE KAHMFF) Meaning *My Struggle*. Hitler's statement of his political program, published in 1924.

Mensheviks Meaning the "minority." Term Lenin applied to the majority moderate faction of the Russian Social Democratic Party opposed to him and the Bolsheviks.

mercantilism Term used to describe close government control of the economy that sought to maximize exports and accumulate as much precious metals as possible to enable the state to defend its economic and political interests.

Mesopotamia (MEZ-o-po-tay-me-a) Modern Iraq. The land between the Tigris and Euphrates Rivers where the first civilization appeared around 3000 B.C.E.

Messiah (MESS-eye-a) The redeemer whose coming Jews believed would establish the kingdom of God on earth. Christians considered Jesus to be the Messiah (*Christ* means Messiah in Greek).

Methodism An English religious movement begun by John Wesley (1703–1791) that stressed inward, heartfelt religion and the possibility of attaining Christian perfection in this life.

Minoan (MIN-o-an) The Bronze Age civilization that arose in Crete in the third and second millennia B.C.E.

modernism The movement in the arts and literature in the late nineteenth and early twentieth centuries to create new aesthetic forms and to elevate the aesthetic experience of a work of art above the attempt to portray reality as accurately as possible.

Monasticism A movement in the Christian church that arose first in the East in the third and fourth centuries C.E. in which first individual hermits and later organized communities of men and women (monks and nuns) separated themselves from the world to lead lives in imitation of Christ. In the West the Rule of St. Benedict (c. 480–547) became the dominant form of monasticism.

Monophysites (ma-NO-fiz-its) Adherents of the theory that Jesus had only one nature.

monotheism The worship of one universal God.

Mycenaean (MY-cen-a-an) The Bronze Age civilization of mainland Greece that was centered at Mycenae.

nationalism The belief that one is part of a nation, defined as a community with its own language, traditions, customs, and history that distinguish it from other nations and make it the primary focus of a person's loyalty and sense of identity.

NATO North Atlantic Treaty Organization. An alliance of countries from North America and Europe committed to fulfilling the goals of the North Atlantic Treaty signed on April 4, 1949.

natural selection The theory originating with Darwin that organisms evolve through a struggle for existence in which those that have a marginal advantage live long enough to propagate their kind.

Nazis The German Nationalist Socialist Party.

Neoclassicism An artistic movement that began in the 1760s and reached its peak in the 1780s and 1790s. This movement was a reaction against the frivolously decorative Rococo style that had dominated European art from the 1720s on.

Neolithic Age (NEE-o-lith-ick) The shift beginning 10,000 years ago from hunter-gatherer societies to settled communities of farmers and artisans. Also called the Age of Agriculture, it witnessed the invention of farming, the domestication of plants and animals, and the development of technologies such as pottery and weaving. The earliest Neolithic societies appeared in the Near East about 8000 B.C.E. "Neolithic" comes from the Greek words for "new stone."

Neoplatonism (KNEE-o-play-ton-ism) A religious philosophy that tried to combine mysticism with classical and rationalist speculation. Its chief formulator was Plotinus (205–270 C.E.).

New Economic Policy (NEP) A limited revival of capitalism, especially in light industry and agriculture, introduced by Lenin in 1921 to repair the damage inflicted on the Russian economy by the Civil War and war communism.

New Imperialism The extension in the late nineteenth and early twentieth centuries of Western political and economic dominance to Asia, the Middle East, and Africa.

nomes Regions or provinces of ancient Egypt governed by officials called *nomarchs*.

Old Regime Term applied to the pattern of social, political, and economic relationships and institutions that existed in Europe before the French Revolution.

optimates (OP-tee-ma-tes) Meaning "the best men." Roman politicians who supported the traditional role of the Senate.

orthodox Meaning "holding the right opinions." Applied to the doctrines of the Catholic Church.

Paleolithic (PAY-lee-o-lith-ick) The earliest period when stone tools were used, from about 1,000,000 to 10,000 B.C.E. From the Greek meaning "old stone."

Panhellenic (PAN-hell-en-ick) ("all-Greek") The sense of cultural identity that all Greeks felt in common with each other.

Pan-Slavism The movement to create a nation or federation that would embrace all the Slavic peoples of Eastern Europe.

papal infallibility The doctrine that the pope is infallible when pronouncing officially in his capacity as head of the church on matters of faith and morals, enumerated by the First Vatican Council in 1870.

Papal States Territory in central Italy ruled by the pope until 1870.

parlements (par-luh-MAHNS) French regional courts dominated by hereditary nobility. The most important was the *Parlement* of Paris, which claimed the right to register royal decrees before they could become law.

parliamentary monarchy The form of limited or constitutional monarchy set up in Britain after the Glorious Revolution of 1689 in which the monarch was subject to the law and ruled by the consent of parliament.

patrician (PA-tri-she-an) The hereditary upper class of early Republican Rome.

Peloponnesian Wars (PELL-o-po-knees-ee-an) The protracted struggle between Athens and Sparta to dominate Greece between 465 and Athens's final defeat in 404 B.C.E.

Peloponnesus (PELL-o-po-knee-sus) The southern peninsula of Greece where Sparta was located.

peninsulares (pen-in-SUE-la-rez) Persons born in Spain who settled in the Spanish colonies.

perestroika (pare-ess-TROY-ka) Meaning "restructuring." The attempt in the 1980s to reform the Soviet government and economy.

petite bourgeoisie (peh-TEET BOOSH-schwa-zee) The lower middle class.

pharaoh (FAY-row) The god-kings of ancient Egypt. The term originally meant "great house" or palace.

Pharisees (FAIR-i-sees) The group that was most strict in its adherence to Jewish law.

philosophes (fee-lou-SOPHS) The eighteenth-century writers and critics who forged the new attitudes favorable to change. They sought to apply reason and common sense to the institutions and societies of their day.

Phoenicians (FA-nee-shi-ans) The ancient inhabitants of modern Lebanon. A trading people, they established colonies throughout the Mediterranean.

physiocrats Eighteenth-century French thinkers who attacked the mercantilist regulation of the economy, advocated a limited economic role for government, and believed that all economic production depended on sound agriculture.

Platonism Philosophy of Plato that posits preexistent Ideal Forms of which all earthly things are imperfect models.

plebeian (PLEB-bee-an) The hereditary lower class of early Republican Rome.

pogroms (PO-grohms) Organized riots against Jews in the Russian Empire.

polis (PO-lis) (plural, *poleis*) The basic Greek political unit. Usually, but incompletely, translated as "city-state," the Greeks thought of the *polis* as a community of citizens theoretically descended from a common ancestor.

political absolutism A model of political development embodied by France in the seventeenth century. The French monarchy was able to build a secure financial base that was not deeply dependent on the support of noble estates, diets, or assemblies, and so it achieved absolute rule.

politiques Rulers or people in positions of power who put the success and well-being of their states above all else.

polytheists (PAH-lee-thee-ists) Those who worship many gods.

pontifex maximus (PON-ti-feks MAK-suh-muss) Meaning "supreme priest." The chief priest of ancient Rome. The title was later assumed by the popes.

Popular Front A government of all left-wing parties that took power in France in 1936 to enact social and economic reforms.

populares (PO-pew-lar-es) Roman politicians who sought to pursue a political career based on the support of the people rather than just the aristocracy.

positivism The philosophy of Auguste Comte that science is the final, or positive, stage of human intellectual development because it involves exact descriptions of phenomena, without recourse to unobservable operative principles, such as gods or spirits.

Postimpressionism A term used to describe European painting that followed impressionism; the term actually applies to several styles of art all of which to some extent derived from impression or stood in reaction to impressionism.

Pragmatic Sanction The legal basis negotiated by the Emperor Charles VI (r. 1711–1740) for the Habsburg succession through his daughter Maria Theresa (r. 1740–1780).

predestination The doctrine that God had foreordained all souls to salvation (the "elect") or damnation. It was especially associated with Calvinism.

presbyters (PRESS-bi-ters) Meaning "elder." People who directed the affairs of early Christian congregations.

Presbyterians Scottish Calvinists and English Protestants who advocated a national church composed of semiautonomous congregations governed by "presbyteries."

proconsulship (PRO-con-sul-ship) In Republican Rome, the extension of a consul's imperium beyond the end of his term of office to allow him to continue to command an army in the field.

protectorates (pro-TEC-tor-ates) Non-Western territories administered by Western nations without formal conquest or annexation, usually de facto colonies.

Ptolemaic systems (tow-LEM-a-ick) The pre-Copernican explanation of the universe, with the earth at the center of the universe, originated in the ancient world.

Puritans English Protestants who sought to "purify" the Church of England of any vestiges of Catholicism.

Qur'an (kuh-RAN) Meaning "a reciting." The Islamic bible, which Muslims believe God revealed to the prophet Muhammad.

racism The pseudoscientific theory that biological features of race determine human character and worth.

realist The style of art and literature that seeks to depict the physical world and human life with scientific objectivity and detached observation.

Reformation The sixteenth-century religious movement that sought to reform the Roman Catholic Church and led to the establishment of Protestantism.

regular clergy Monks and nuns who belong to religious orders.

Reichstag (RIKES-stahg) The German parliament, which existed in various forms, until 1945.

Reign of Terror The period between the summer of 1793 and the end of July 1794 when the French revolutionary state used extensive executions and violence to defend the Revolution and suppress its alleged internal enemies.

Rococo An artistic style that embraced lavish, often lighthearted decoration with an emphasis on pastel colors and the play of light.

Romanitas (row-MAN-ee-tas) Meaning "Roman-ness." The spread of the Roman way of life and the sense of identifying with Rome across the Roman Empire.

romanticism A reaction in early-nineteenth-century literature, philosophy, and religion against what many considered the excessive rationality and scientific narrowness of the Enlightenment.

SA The Nazi parliamentary forces, or storm troopers.

sans-culottes (SAHN coo-LOTS) Meaning "without knee-breeches." The lower-middle classes and artisans of Paris during the French Revolution.

Scholasticism Method of study based on logic and dialectic that dominated the medieval schools. It assumed that truth already existed; students had only to organize, elucidate, and defend knowledge learned from authoritative texts, especially those of Aristotle and the Church Fathers.

scientific revolution The sweeping change in the scientific view of the universe that occurred in the sixteenth and seventeenth centuries. The new scientific concepts and the method of their construction became the standard for assessing the validity of knowledge in the West.

scutage Monetary payments by a vassal to a lord in place of the required military service.

Second Industrial Revolution The emergence of new industries and the spread of industrialization from Britain to other countries, especially Germany and the United States, in the second half of the nineteenth century.

secular clergy Parish clergy who did not belong to a religious order.

Sejm (SHEM) The legislative assembly of the Polish nobility.

September Massacres The executions or murders of about 1200 people who were in the Paris city jails (mostly common criminals) by the Parisian mob in the first week of September 1792 during the French Revolution.

serf A peasant tied to the land he tilled.

Shi'a (SHE-ah) The minority of Muslims who trace their beliefs from the caliph Ali who was assassinated in 661 C.E.

Social Darwinism The application of Darwin's concept of "the survival of the fittest" to explain evolution in nature to human social relationships.

socialist realism Established as the official doctrine of Soviet art and literature in 1934, it sought to create optimistic and easily intelligible scenes of a bold socialist future, in which prosperity and solidarity would reign.

spheres of influence A region, city, or territory where a non-Western nation exercised informal administrative influence through economic, diplomatic, or military advisors.

spinning jenny A machine invented in England by James Hargreaves around 1765 to mass-produce thread.

SS The chief security units of the Nazi state.

Stoic (STOW-ick) A philosophical school founded by Zeno of Citium (335–263 B.C.E.) that taught that humans could only be happy with natural law. Human misery was caused by passion, which was a disease of the soul. The wise sought *apatheia*, freedom from passion.

studia humanitatis (STEW-dee-a hew-MAHN-ee-tah-tis) During the Renaissance, a liberal arts program of study that embraced grammar, rhetoric, poetry, history, philosophy, and politics.

Sturm und Drang (SHTURM und DRAHNG) Meaning "storm and stress." A movement in German romantic literature and philosophy that emphasized feeling and emotion.

suffragettes British women who lobbied and agitated for the right to vote in the early twentieth century.

Sunnis Those who follow the "tradition" (sunna) of the Prophet Muhammad. They are the dominant movement within Islam to which the vast majority of Muslims adhere.

symposium (SIM-po-see-um) The carefully organized drinking party that was the center of Greek aristocratic social life. It featured games, songs, poetry, and even philosophical disputation.

syncretism (SIN-cret-ism) The intermingling of different religions to form an amalgam that contained elements from each.

Table of Ranks An official hierarchy established by Peter the Great in imperial Russia that equated a person's social position and privileges with his rank in the state bureaucracy or army.

taille (TIE) The direct tax on the French peasantry.

ten lost tribes The Israelites who were scattered and lost to history when the northern kingdom of Israel fell to the Assyrians in 722 B.C.E.

Tertiaries (TER-she-air-ees) Laypeople affiliated with the monastic life who took vows of poverty, chastity, and obedience but remained in the world.

tetrarchy (TET-rar-key) Diocletian's (r. 306–337 C.E.) system for ruling the Roman Empire by four men with power divided territorially.

Thermidorian Reaction The reaction against the radicalism of the French Revolution that began in July 1794. Associated with the end of terror and establishment of the Directory.

Third Estate The branch of the French Estates General representing all of the kingdom outside the nobility and the clergy.

Third Reich (RIKE) Hitler's regime in Germany, which lasted from 1933 to 1945.

Thirty-Nine Articles (1563) The official statement of the beliefs of the Church of England. They established a moderate form of Protestantism.

three-field system A medieval innovation that increased the amount of land under cultivation by leaving only one third fallow in a given year.

transubstantiation The doctrine that the entire substances of the bread and wine are changed in the Eucharist into the body and blood of Christ.

tribunes (TRIB-unes) Roman officials who had to be plebeians and were elected by the plebeian assembly to protect plebeians from the arbitrary power of the magistrates.

ulema (oo-LEE-mah) Meaning "persons with correct knowledge." The Islamic scholarly elite who served a social function similar to the Christian clergy.

Upper Egypt The part of Egypt that runs from the delta to the Sudanese border.

utilitarianism The theory associated with Jeremy Bentham (1748–1832) that the principle of utility, defined as the greatest good for the greatest number of people, should be applied to government, the economy, and the judicial system.

utopian socialists Early-nineteenth-century writers who sought to replace the existing capitalist structure and values with visionary solutions or ideal communities.

vassal A person granted an estate or cash payments in return for accepting the obligation to render services to a lord.

Vulgate The Latin translation of the Bible by Jerome (348–420 C.E.) that became the standard bible used by the Catholic Church.

War Communism The economic policy adopted by the Bolsheviks during the Russian Civil War to seize the banks, heavy industry, railroads, and grain.

war guilt clause Clause 231 of the Versailles Treaty, which assigned responsibility for World War I solely to Germany.

Warsaw Pact An alliance of East European socialist states, dominated by the Soviet Union.

water frame A water-powered device invented by Richard Arkwright to produce a more durable cotton fabric. It led to the shift in the production of cotton textiles from households to factories.

Weimar Republic (Why-mar) The German democratic regime that existed between the end of World War I and Hitler's coming to power in 1933.

Zionist The movement to create a Jewish state in Palestine (the Biblical Zion).

INDEX

Italic page numbers refer to illustrations

A

Abolition Society, 681
Abortion
 19th century, 728
 20th century, 1004
Absolutism
 Enlightenment, 513, 538–547
 Hobbes on, *426*, 426–427
Academy of Experiments, 430
Act of Parliament (1877), 788
Act of Settlement (1701), 395
Act of Union (1707), 395
Act of Union (1798), 639
Acton, Lord, 620, 621
Addison, Joseph, 515
Aden, 955
Adrianople, Treaty of, 633
Advancement of Learning, The (Bacon), 423
Afghanistan
 radical Islamism and, 975–976, *976*
 Soviet invasion of, 951, 972
Africa
 decolonization, *936*, 955
 imperialism and, 796–804, *797*, *798*
 partition of, *798*
 slavery, 482–483, 486, 488–497, *489*, 683–684
 World War II, 913
African Colonization Society, 683
Afrikaners, 803
Agadir crisis, 833
Agriculture
 in the 1920s, 873–875
 collectivization, *865*, 873–875, *874*
 18th century, 453–455, 459–564
 enclosures replace open fields, 460–461
 exchange between Americas and Europe, 509–511
 Great Depression, 868
 Revolution, 459–464
Ahmad, Muhammad, 799
Aix-la-Chapelle, Treaty of (1668), 399
Aix-la-Chapelle, Treaty of (1748), 499
Al-Afghani, Jamal al-din, 761
Albanians, collapse of Yugoslavia and civil war, 971
Albertine in the Police Doctor's Waiting Room (Krogh), *731*
Aleksei, King of Russia, 411
Aleksei, son of Peter the Great, 412, 414
Alexander I, King of Yugoslavia, 895
Alexander I, Tsar of Russia, 592, 598, 600, 617, 632, 634–636
Alexander II, Tsar of Russia, 687, 703, 705–707, *707*, 708
Alexander III, Tsar of Russia, 707, 741, 742
Alexander Nevsky, 886
Alexander the Great (Alexander III), 823, *823*
Alexievich, Svetlana, 1000
Alexis, Tsar of Russia, 748
Algarotti, Francesco, 433
Algeria, French in, *637*, 638, 697, 796, 957
Almagest (Ptolemy), 419
Al Qaeda, 975–976, 976–977
Alsace, 695, 700
Alsace-Lorraine, 828, 857
American Colonization Society, 683
American Holt Company, 845
Americanization, 997, 998
American Revolution
 crisis and independence, 502–503
 events in England, 504–506
 impact of, 506
 key events/dates, *506*
 political ideas of Americans, 503–504
 resistance to British taxation, 501–502, *504*
Americas
 1763 map of, *502*
 diseases introduced, 489, *509*, 509–510
 European expansion, 824–825
 French-British rivalry, 484–485
 mining, *486*
 slavery in, 482–483, 486, 488–497, *489*, 679
 Spanish colonial system, 485–486
Amiens, Treaty of (1802), 590
Amritsar massacre, *825*
Amsterdam, 387, *387*
Anarchism, 664
Anatolia, 824, 853
Anatomy Lesson of Dr. Tulp, The (Rembrandt), *417*
Androcles and the Lion (Shaw), 764
Andropov, Yuri, 961
Anglicanism/Anglican Church, 388, 392, 394, 758
Anglo-Russian Convention (1907), 806
Angola, 954
Animals
 in Columbian exchange, 510–511
 domestication of, 1015
 as energy source, 1015
Anna, Empress of Russia, 453
Annals of Agriculture (Young), 460
Anne, Queen of England, 395
Anschluss, 902
Anthony, Susan B., 721
Anthropology, 817–818
Anti-Comintern Pact, 900–901
Anti-Corn Law League, 662, 668
Anti-Semitism, 723, 736, 737, 880–881, 888, *888*, 919–924, 928
 Dreyfus affair, 737, 772–775, 928
 holocaust, *919*, 919–924, *920*, 922–924
Antislavery societies, 680–681
Apartheid, 803
Appeasement policy, 900
Appert, Nicholas, 594, *594*
Apple Computer Corporation, 1006
Aquinas, Thomas, 427, 761
Arabian Nights, The, 612
Arab-Israeli conflict, 944–945
Arab nationalism, 974–975
Architecture
 Gothic, 608
 Rococo, 532
 Versailles, *397*, *445*, 446
Aristocracy. *See also* Social classes/society
 18th century, 451–453, *452*, 472, 473
 resurgence, 453
 urban, 472
Aristocratic resurgence, 453
Aristotle, 419, 427, 679
Arkwright, Richard, 466
Arms and the Man (Shaw), 764
Arndt, Ernest Moritz, 596, 597
Arnold, Matthew, 755
Arouet, Francois Marie. *See* Voltaire
Art/artisans, 473–458
 abstract, *1001*, 1003
 Baroque, *417*, 444–446, *444*, *445*
 cubism, *767*, 767–768
 Dutch, *417*
 Dwelling Act (1875), 711
 18th century, *449*, *456*, *469*, 473, 475, *475*, *476*
 German, Weimar Republic, 886
 impressionism, 765–766, *766*
 minimalist, 1002, 1003
 modernism, *765*, 765–768, *766*, 767
 19th century, *649*, 765–768
 post-impressionism, *766*, 766–767
 romanticism, 606–608, *608*
 Scientific Revolution, *417*, *422*, *431*
 socialist realism, *1001*, 1003
Articles of Confederation, 506
Artisan Dwelling Act (1875), 711
Artois, Count of, 563, 617, 631, 636
Aryans, 771
Asia, imperialism in, 805–809, *808*
Asquith, Herbert, 734, 735, 739
Assignats, 562–563, *563*, 568
Aston, Louise, 657
Astronomy
 Brahe, 419–421
 Copernicus, 418–419, *420*, 435
 Galileo, *421*, 421–422, 434–435, 438
 Kepler, 420–421
 Newton, *422*, 422–423
 Ptolemaic system, 419
 women in, 433–434
Ataturk, 853, *854*
Atlantic Charter, *909*, 930
Atlantic economy, 482–483, 490, 493
Atlantic Passage, 494–495
Atomic bomb, *898*, 918–919, 1020
Attlee, Clement, 933, 984
Auburn prison/system, 661
Auclert, Hubertine, 734
Auerstädt, Battle of (1806), 591
Augsburg
 League of (1686), 403
Augustine, St. (Bishop of Hippo), 402, 435
Augustinus (Jansen), 402

Ausgleich, 703
Austerlitz, Battle of (1805), 591, 595
Austria. *See also* Habsburg empire
  in the 1920s, 894
  alliances with England and Russia, 591
  aristocracy of 18th century, 451
  Congress of Vienna (1815), 599–601, *600*, 602, 618
  Dual Alliance, 829, 830
  Hitler's annexation of, 881, 901–902
  key events/dates, *408*
  Napoleon and, 585, 586, 591, 595–571
  parliament, 702
  peasant rebellion, 454
  Piedmont war with, 673, 674, 690, 691, 693
  Quadruple Alliance, 599, 600–601
  serfs in, 453
  Three Emperors' League (1873), 828–800
  Triple Alliance, 830
  World War I and, 834–836, 852
Austria-Hungary
  breakup of, 859
  formation of, 703, *704*
  map of, *834, 839*
  Triple Alliance, 830
  war in, 688, 828–829, *834*
  World War I, 850
Austrian Succession, war of (1740–1748), 498–499
Austro-Prussian War (1866), 698, *698*
Automobile, invention of, 718–719, *719*, 1016–1017, *1017*
Avanti, 877
Axis Europe, *910, 914*
Ayacucho, Battle of (1824), 643
Azerbaijan, 966
Aztecs, 824

B

Babeuf, Gracchus, 580
Bacon, Francis, 390, 423–425, *424*, 435
Baden, Max of, 852
Badoglio, Pietro, 913
Bailly, Jean-Sylvain, *556*
Bakewell, Robert, 460
Baldwin, Stanley, 868
Balfour, Arthur, 944
Balfour Declaration (1917), 855, 944
Balkans. *See also* World War I
  Congress of Berlin, 829
  map of, *834, 839*
  war in, 688–689, 828–829, *834*
Ballot Act (1872), 709
Balzac, Honoré de, 763
Banalities, 453
Bands of Jesus, 578–579
Bangladesh, 955
Banks, Joseph, 815
Baptist Missionary Society, 812
Bar at the Folies-Bergère, A (Manet), *765*, 766
Barnum, P. T., 818
Baroque architecture/art, *417*, 444–446, *444, 445*
Barth, Karl, 1003
Basel, treaties of (1795), 580
Bastille, fall of, 529, 550
Bathing, 474
Batista, Fulgencio, 949
Battle of Cawnpore, 788
Battle of Omdurman, 799, *801*
Battle of the Nations, 598
Battleship Potemkin, The, 886
BBC, 929
Beau, Paul, *795*
Beauvoir, Simone de, 990, *990*, 992
Beaverbrook, Lord, 928
Bebel, August, 740, 741
Beccaria, Cesare, 523–524
Becquerel, Henri, 761
Being and Nothingness (Sartre), 995
Being and Time (Heidegger), 995
Belgian Congo, 801–802, 954
Belgium, 638, 837, *841*, 842, 908
Bell, The, 706
Bell, Vanessa, 764
Belorussian Jews, 476, 477
Belsen, 922, 923
Ben Bella, Mohammed, 958
Benedetti, Vincent, 699
Benedict XVI, Pope (Joseph Ratzinger), 1005
Benes, Edvard, 940
Benezet, Anthony, 680
Ben-Gurion, David, 944–945
Bentham, Jeremy, 662
Berchtold, Leopold von, 834
Berlin
  Blockade, 941, *943*
  Congress of (1878), 829
  Decrees, 592
  18th century, 470
  Wall, 914–915, 963–964, 967, *967*
  World War II, 916–917
Berlin Academy of Science, 430
Berlin Conference (1884), 803
Berlin Missionary Society, 812
Bernadotte, French marshal, 598
Bernard, Claude, 763
Bernini, Gian Lorenzo, 444, *444*
Bernstein, Eduard, 741, 743, 744–745
Berri, Duke of, 617, 631
Bessarabia, 905
Bessemer, Henry, 716–717
Bethlen, Stephen, 894
Bethmann-Hollweg, Theobald von, 835, 836, 837
Beveridge, William B., 988
Beyle, Henri, 604
Beyond Good and Evil (Nietzsche), 768
Bibliothèque orientale (Oriental Library), 520
Bicycles, 721
Bill of Rights (England), 394
Bin Laden, Osama, 976
Birth control
  18th century, 459
  19th century, 657, 728, 732–733
Birth of Tragedy, The (Nietzsche), 768
Bishops College, 814
Bismarck, Otto von, *685*, 697, *698*, 758, 759, 803, 828–829, 830, *830*, 988
Black Hand, 834
Black Shirt March, 878
Blair, Tony, 978, 989
Blanc, Louis, 664, 669
Blanqui, Auguste, 664
Blitzkrieg, 905
Bloch, Marc, 908
Bloody Sunday, 743, 747, *747*
Bloomsbury Group, 764
Blücher, Marshal von, 600
Boers, 803
Boer War (1899–1902), 791, 831
Bohemia, 407, 454, 702
Bolívar, Simón, 642, *642*
Bolsheviks/Bolshevism, 741–743, 847, 850–851, 857, *869*, 869–870
Bonhoeffer, Dietrich, 1003
Book of Common Prayer (Cranmer), 391, 392
Book of Sports, 389
Boris III, King of Bulgaria, 895
Borodino, Battle of, 598
Bosnia, 833, 894, 970–971
Bosnia-Herzegovina, 894, 971
Bossuet, Jacques-Bénigne, 398, 400
Boston Massacre, 502
Botany, *816*, 816–817
Boucher, Francois, 532, *535*
Boulanger, Georges, 701
Boulton, Matthew, 468
Bourbons, 485–486, 585, 586, 595, 599, 631, *631*
Bourgeois, 473, 667
Boxer Rebellion, *795*, 808, 810
Boyars, 412, 413
Brahe, Tycho, 419–421
Brandenburg-Prussia, *409*
Brandt, Heinrich von, 596
Braque, Georges, *767*, 767–768
Brazil, 490, *491*, 643, 683
Bread (Yablonskaya), *1001*, 1003
Brest-Litovsk, Treaty of (1918), 850
Bretez, Louis, *463*
Breuer, Josef, 769
Brezhnev, Leonid, 949–952, 960
Brezhnev Doctrine, 950, 964
Briand, Aristide, 884
Brienne, Étienne Charles Loménie de, 553
Bright, John, 707
Britain. *See also* England
  in the 1920s, 758, 868
  African colonies, 785, 799, 801
  Battle of, 908–909
  British Emancipation Act, 638
  Chartism, 651, 653–654, *654*
  conflict between church and state, 758
  Crimean War (1853–1856), *686*, 686–687, *687*
  decolonization, 954–955
  Disraeli and, 707, 709, *709*, 711, 788, 796
  in Egypt, 796–799
  Fabianism and early welfare programs, 739
  general strike of 1929, 868
  Gladstone, 709, *709*, 711
  Great Depression in, 868–869
  Great Reform Bill of 1832, 638–640
  imperialism and, 782, 784–789, 824
  Industrial Revolution in, 465–466
  Irish problem, 619, 711–712
  key events/dates, *711, 891*
  Liverpool's ministry, 627, 630
  National Government, 868
  19th century, 647, 654, 656
  Peterloo Massacre and Six Acts, 630–631
  racial tensions in, 984
  Second Reform Act (1867), 707–709
  in Triple Entente (1890–1907), 830–832
  welfare state, 988–989
  World War I and, 833, *834*, 837–817, 846, 847, 853–854
  World War II and, 908–909, 928–929, *929*

British Conservative Party, *739*, 989
British Labour Party, 739, 868, 988, 989
British Settler Colonies, 785, 815
British Shell Oil, 719
Broca, Paul, 817–818
Brookes (ship), 495
Brüning, Heinrich, 884, 885
Brunswick, Duke of, 568
Brussels, Treaty of (1948), 941
Buckingham, Duke of, 388
Buddenbrooks (Mann), 764
Bukharin, Nikolai, 872, 875, 876, 961
Bulgaria, 829, 859, 895
Bulge, Battle of (1945), 916
Bülow, Bernhard von, 832
Bultmann, Rudolf, 1003
Bundesrat, 698
Bunker Hill, Battle of, 502
Burke, Edmund, 569–570, 571, 618
Burma, 955
Burns, Lucy, 734
Bush, George W., 976–977, 978
Bute, Earl of, 501, 504
Butler, Josephine, 776
Buxton, Thomas Fowell, 683
Byron, Lord, 604, 605, 606, *606*, 633

C

Cadets (Constitutional Democratic Party), 742, 746, 847–848
Cahiers de doléances, 554, 555
Calas, Jean, 519
Calonne, Charles Alexandre de, 552–553
Calvinism, 386
Cambodia, 958
Cambrai, Battle of, *844*
Campbell-Bannerman, Henry, 739
Campo Formio, Treaty of (1797), 585, 590
Camus, Albert, 995
Candide (Voltaire), 516
Cannibals, 440
Canning, George, 632–608
Cape Town, 803
Capital, Das (Marx), 665, 994
Caprivi, Leo von, 830–831
Caravaggio, Michelangelo, 444–445
Carbonari, 690
Carey, William, 812
Carlsbad Decrees, 627, 628, 629
Carlyle, Thomas, 613
Carnot, Lazare, 572
Carol II, King of Romania, 895
Carter, Jimmy, 950
Cartwright, Edmund, 468
Cartwright, John, 630
Casement, Roger, 801
Castlereagh, Viscount (Robert Stewart), 599, 601, 617, 632
Castro, Fidel, 949
Categorical imperative, 604
Catherine I, of Russia, 528, 544
Catherine II (the Great), 453, 476, 538, *544*, 544–546, 547, 570, 585, 686, 805
Catholic Center Party, 758, 859
Catholic Emancipation Act, 639
Catholicism
James II and fear of in England, 394–395
19th-century attack on, 758
Cato's Letters (Gordon), 504
Cato Street Company, 630–631
Caucasus, 805
Cavaignac, Louis, 669
Cavaliers, 392
Cavendish, Margaret, 432, *433*, 434
Cavour, Camillo, 690–691, *691*
Cawnpore, Battle, 788, *788*
Ceausescu, Nicolae, 964
Century of the Child, The (Key), 776
Cezanne, Paul, 766, 767
Chadwick, Edwin, 725
Challice, John Armstrong, *680*
Chamberlain, Austen, 884
Chamberlain, Houston Stewart, 771
Chamberlain, Joseph, 739, 792, 831
Chamberlain, Neville, 902–903, 906, *907*, 909
Chamber of Deputies, 617, 631, 636, 637, 701, 738, 878, 879
Chamber of Peers, 617, 631
Chambord, Count de, 637, 701
Chapelier Law (1791), 562
Chaplin, Charlie, 856, *856*
Charcot, Jean-Martin, 769
Charles Albert of Piedmont, 673, 674, 690
Charles I, King of England, 391–392, 445
Charles II, King of England, 392–393, 428
Charles II, King of Spain, 403
Charles III, King of Spain, 486, 488
Charles V, Holy Roman Emperor (Charles I of Spain), 540
Charles VI, King of Austria, 408–409, 412, 413
Charles VI, King of France, 408
Charles X, King of France, 636–638, *796*, 957
Charles XII, King of Sweden, 412
Charles XIV, King of Sweden, 598
Charter (England), 651
Charter (French), 617, 631
Charter of the Nobility, 453, 545
Chartism, 651, 653–654, *654*
Chateaubriand, Francois René de, 610, 611
Châtelet, Emilie du, 433, 513, *514*, 516, 521
Chattel slavery, 679
Chaumont, Treaty of (1814), 599
Chechen war, 971
Chechnya, 805, 806, 969, *969*, 971
Cheka, 869–870
Chemical industry, 717–718
Chernenko, Konstantin, 961
Chernobyl disaster, 999, *999*, 1000, 1020
Childbed fever, 726
Childbirth, dangers in, 726, 732
Childe Harold's Pilgrimage (Byron), 605
Child labor, 19th century, 656
Children. *See also* Family
in family economy of 18th century, *456*, 458–459
laborers, 459, 654, 656
19th century, 656
Chile, 642
China. *See also* People's Republic of China
Boxer Rebellion, 808, 810
imperialism and, 785, 786, 792
North Korea and, 945–946
Chirac, Jacques, 984
Cholera, 724–725
Christian Democratic parties, 939, 988
Christianity. *See also* Roman Catholicism
Caucasus, 805
Chechnya, 806
Circassia, 806
Enlightenment criticism of, 519–520
19th-century attack on, 755, 758–759
slaves conversion to, 496–497
20th century, 1003
Christianity Not Mysterious (Toland), 518
Christiansen, Ole Kirk, 998
Christian Socialist Party, 772–773, 880, 894
Christina of Sweden, Queen, 425, 432
Churchill, John, 403
Churchill, Winston, 800, 846, 907, 909, *909*, 913, 929, 930, 931, *931*, 932–933, 938, 940
Church of England, 518, 609
Church [of England] Missionary Society, 812
Church of Scotland Mission, 815
Ciano, Count, *907*, 909
Cinchona bark, 810
Cinema, Nazi and Soviet use of, 886
Circassia, 806
Cities/towns. *See also individual names of cities*
growth of, in 18th century, 470–476
growth of, in 19th century, 722–723
housing reform, 725, 727, *727*
19th century (late), 722–727, *724*
polis, 822
redesign of, 472, 723–724
sanitation in, 461, 724–725, *725*
urban riots, 475–476
urban social classes, 472–458
Civic Forum, 964
Civil Code (1804), 590
Civil Constitution of the Clergy, 563
Civilizing mission, 792
Civil Service Commission (Prussia), 539
Clarendon Code, 392
Clarkson, Thomas, 682
Clemenceau, Georges, 854, *855*, 857
Clemens, Samuel, 702
Clement XI, Pope, 402
Clergy
Civil Constitution of the Clergy, 563
Enlightenment and, 518–519
French Revolution and, 563
witchcraft and role of, 440–441
Clive, Robert, 485, 500, *500*
Coal, 1016
Cobbett, William, 630
Coercion Act (1817), 630
Coercion Act (1881), 711
Coffeehouses, 515, 517
Colbert, Jean-Baptiste, 398, *430*
Cold War
Afghanistan, Soviet invasion of, 951
Berlin blockade, 941, *943*

Cold War *(cont.)*
Berlin Wall, 949, 963–964, 967, *967*
Brezhnev era, 949–952
collapse of European communism, 960–964
containment policy, 938–940, 943
Cuban missile crisis, 949, *949*
Czechoslovakia, invasion of, 940, 950–951, *951*
decolonization, 952–955
détente, policy of, 950–951
emergence of, 937–946
European alliance systems, *944*
Germany, division of, 940–941, *941*
Gorbachev and, 960–961, *963*, 963–964
Hungarian uprising, 947
Israel, creation of, 941, 944–945
key events/dates, *940*, *949*
Khrushchev era, 946–948
Korean War (1950–1953), 945–946, *946*
NATO and Warsaw Pact, 937, 941, 947
Paris Summit Conference, 947
Polish autonomy, 947
Polish Solidarity, 952
Reagan administration, 952
Soviet assertion of domination of eastern Europe, 940
Suez crisis, 947
Vietnam and, 958–959
Coleridge, Samuel Taylor, 604
Collectivization, *865*, 873–875, *874*
Cologne, *925*
Columbian Exchange, 509–511
Columbus, Christopher, 390, 424, 491, 509, 510, 817
Combination Acts (1799), 630, 639
COMECON (Council of Mutual Assistance), 941
Cominform (Communist Information Bureau), 940, 942
Comintern (Third International), 839
Commentary on the Epistle to the Romans (Barth), 1003
Commerce
Spanish Casa de Contratación and Council of the Indies, 485–486
Committee for the Abolition of the Slave Trade, 681
Committee of General Security, 572
Committee of Public Safety, 572, 575, 577
Common Market, 1007
Common Sense (Paine), 502, 503
Commonwealthmen, 504
Commonwealth of Independent States, 968, *968*
Communism
collapse of European, 960–964
intellectuals, 993–994
in Poland, 950–951, *951*
in Soviet Union, 850–851, 869–876
use of term, 665
in Western Europe, 993
Communism and the Family (Kollontai), 892–893
Communist League, 665
Communist Manifesto, The (Marx and Engels), 665–666, 667, 744, 994
Communist party, in the Soviet Union, 869, 875–876, 964
Compagnie des Indes, 484
Compromise of 1867, 702, 703–704
Computers, 1005–1007, *1006*
Comte, Auguste, 753, 775
Concentration camps, 803. *See also* Holocaust
Concerning Germany (de Staël), 605
Concert of Europe, 617, 687
Concluding Unscientific Postscript (Kierkegaard), 994
Concord, Battle of, 502
Condition of the Working Class in England, The (Engels), 665
Condorcet, Nicolas de, 529
Confection, 651
Confédération Générale du Travail, 740
Confederation of the Rhine, 591
Congress of Berlin (1878), 829
Congress of Vienna (1815), 599–601, *600*, 602, 616, 618, 626, 682, *692*, 796
Congress system, 617
Conrad, Joseph, 801–802
Conservatism
in Belgium, 638
in Britain, 638–620
congress system, 617
in France, 636–638
in Greece, 633
in Latin America, 632, 640–642
19th century, 617–618
in Russia, 634–636
in Serbia, 633–634
in Spain, 632
Conspiracy of Equals, 580
Constable, John, 607, *608*
Constant, Benjamin, 622
Constantine of Russia (brother to Alexander II), 634, 636
Constantine of Russia (Grand Duke), 636
Constantinople, *520*, 846
Constitutional Convention (1787), 505
Constitutional Democratic Party. *See* Cadets
Constitution of 1791, 561
Constitution of the Year III, 580
Constitution of the Year VIII, 586
Consulate in France (1799–1804), 586–564
Consumerism, *464*, 464–465, 719, *723*, 997
Contagious Disease Acts (1864, 1886), 775
Continental Congress, 502, 681
Continental System, 592, *593*
Contratación (House of Trade), 485–486
Convention (French), 568, 572, 575, 577, 580, 638
Convention of Gastein (1865), 698
Convention of Westminister (1756), 499
Conversations on the Plurality of Worlds (Fontenelle), 433
Cook, James, 785, 815
Cooper, Anthony Ashley, 427–428
Copernicus, Nicholaus, 418–419, 435
Corfu Agreement (1917), 895
Corn Law (1815), 627, 649, 662, 668
Cornwallis, Lord, 502
Coromantee, 496
Cort, Henry, 469
Cortés, 632
Corvée, 453, *454*
Cottage industries, 470
Council for Aid to Jews in Occupied Poland (ZEGOTA), 923
Council of Elders, 580
Council of Five Hundred, 580
Council of Foreign Ministers, 933
Council of the Indies, 485
Council of Trent (1545–1563), 402, 434
Counterblast to Tobacco (James I), 390
Courage (journal), 990
Court of Matrimonial Causes, 728
Craig, Gordon, 687
Creoles, 486, 640–642
Crime, industrialization and, 658–661
Crimean War (1853–1856), *686*, 686–687, *687*, 792
Critique of Practical Reason, The (Kant), 603–604
Critique of Pure Reason, The (Kant), 603–604
Croatia/Croatians
in the 1920s, 895
collapse of Yugoslavia and civil war, 970–971
Compromise of 1867, 703–704
Habsburg, 407
Cromwell, Oliver, 392, *392*
Crosby, Alfred, 509
Cross, Richard, 709
Crown of Saint Stephen, 540
Crusades
Romanticism and, 611
Crystal Palace, 655, *655*, 719
Cuba
missile crisis, 949, *949*
slavery in, 683
Spanish-American War (1898), 792, 807
Cubism, *767*, 767–768
Cult of domesticity, 732
Cult of the Supreme Being, 577, *578*, 579
Cultural relativism, 529
Cunitz, Mary, 433–434
Curie, Marie, *763*
Curie, Pierre, *763*
Cvijicin, Jovan, *839*
Cyprus, 955
Czechoslovakia
in the 1920s, 894
collapse of communism, 951, 964
Compromise of 1867, 703–704
formation of, 859
Hitler's occupation of, 902–903
partition of, *903*, 906–907
revolution of 1848, 673, 674
Soviet invasion of, 940, 950–951, *951*, 993
under Soviet rule, 940

D

Dagestan, 806
Dail Eireann, 868
Daimler, Gottlieb, 718
Daimler, Rudolf, 1016
Daladier, Edouard, 902, 906, *907*
D'Alembert, Jean le Rond, 515, 523, 531
Danish War (1864), 697–698

D'Annunzio, Gabriele, 877
Dante Alighieri, 419
Danton, Jacques, 577
Daphne (ship), *680*
Darius III, *823*
Darkness at Noon (Koestler), 993
Darwin, Charles, *751*, 753, 755, 756–757, 775
D'Aubigne, Françoise, 402
David, Armand, 815
David, Jacques-Louis, 536–538, *537*, *556*, *576*, *589*
Dawes Plan, 883, 884
D-Day, 916, *917*, *918*
Decembrist revolt of 1825, 634–636, *635*
De-Christianization (French), 576
Declaration of Independence (1776), 502
Declaration of Indulgence (1672), 393
Declaration of Indulgence (1687), 394
Declaration of Pillnitz, 567
Declaration of the Rights of Man and Citizen, 557, 559, 561, 563, 564, 617, 622, 631
Declaration of the Rights of Woman, 561, 565, 576
Declaratory Act, 502
Decolonization, 826, *936*, 937, 952–955, *953*, 983–984
Degas, Edgar, *715*, 766
De Gaulle, Charles, 928, *957*, 958, 996–997, 1007
Deism, 518–519
Delacroix, Eugène, *616*
Democracy
  19th-century, 738, 744
De Montcalm, Louis Joseph, 500
Denmark, 941
Department stores, 722, 723
Depression. *See* Great Depression
Derby, Lord, 709
Deroin, Jeanne, 671
Descartes, René, 422, *425*, 425–426, 429, 432, 436–437
Descent of Man, The (Darwin), 755, 775
Description of a New World, Called the Blazing World (Cavendish), 433
Description of Egypt (Napoleon), 613
Dessalines, Jean-Jacques, 590, 681
Devil's Island, 661, 773
Devis, Arthur William, *591*
De Vries, Jan, 472
D'Herbelot, Barthélemy, 520
D'Holbach, Baron, 520
Dialogue on the Two Chief World Systems (Galileo), 435
Diamond mining, *805*
Dickens, Charles, 763
Dickinson, W., *517*
Diderot, Denis, 515, 523, *523*, 529, 530, 531, 538
Diem, Ngo Dinh. *See* Ngo Dinh Diem
Dien Bien Phu, 958
Diesel, Rudolf, 1016
Diplomatic Revolution of 1756, 499–480
Directory, establishment of French, 580
"Discourse on Happiness" (Châtelet), 521
Discourse on Method (Descartes), 425, 429, 436–437
Discourse on the Moral Effects of the Arts and Sciences (Rousseau), 527
Discourse on the Origin of Inequality (Rousseau), 527
Diseases
  conquest of tropical, 810
  Native Americans decimated by new, 489, *509*, 509–510
Disraeli, Benjamin, 707, 709, *709*, 711, 788, 797, 829
Divine Comedy (Dante), 419
Divine right of kings, 388, 398, 400, 636
Divorce
  Napoleonic Code and, 590
  19th century, 728
  Thermidorian Reaction and, 579
Dollfuss, Engelbert, 894
Doll's House (Ibsen), 764
Domestic system, 466
Dom Pedro, 643
Dom Pedro II, 643
Don Juan (Byron), 605
Dover, Treaty of (1670), 392, 399
Dreyfus, Alfred, 772–774
Dreyfus affair, 737, 772–775, 928
Dr. Zhivago (Pasternak), 946
Dual Alliance, 829, 830
Dubcek, Alexander, 949–950, 964
Duce. *See* Mussolini, Benito
Duma, 746, 847
Dumouriez, General, 569, 574
Dunlop, John Boyd, 721
Dupleix, Joseph, 485
Dupont de Nemours, Pierre, 524
Durkheim, Émile, 770, 776
Dutch, in Americas, 483
Dutch East Indies Company, 387, *387*
Dyer, Reginald, *825*

E

Eastern Associated Telegraph Companies, 811, *811*
Eastern question, 792
East India Company, 484, 500, 501, 502, 787
East Timor, 955
Eckert, J. Presper, *1006*
Economic Consequences of the Peace, The (Keynes), 861
Economy. *See also* Great Depression
  consumer, *464*, 464–465, 719, 997
  Enlightenment and, 524–526, 540
  family, 455–459
  financial crisis of 2008, 1009–1012
  four stage theory, 524–526
  French Revolution and, 561–563
  future for Europe, 1010
  imperialism and, 784–785
  inflation of 1923, 880, *880*
  key events/dates, *711*
  Keynesian economics, 764
  laissez-faire, 524, 661
  liberal goals, 624–625
  major works, 662
  mercantilist, 483–485, 524
  Nazi, 889–890, 891
  Netherlands, 386–387
  New Economic Policy, 870–871
  19th-century classical, 617–619, 624–625
  perestroika, 961
  plantation, 482–483
  post World War I, 866, 867–876, 881
  post World War II, 983
  second industrial revolution and, 719
  slave, 490–493, 679
Edict of Nantes (1598), 395–396, 402, 403, 404
Edinburgh and Glasgow Missionary Societies, 812
Edison, Thomas Alva, 1018
Education
  19th century, 728–729, 752, *752*
  Rousseau and, 603
  20th-century expansion of universities and student rebellions, *995*, 995–999
  of women (19th century), 728–729
Education Act (1870), 758
Education Act (1902), 758
Ego, 770
Egypt
  Arab-Israeli conflict, 944–945
  British in, 796–799
  Napoleon in, 585, *611*, 613
  Suez crisis, 947
  World War II, 909, 912, 913
Eiffel Tower, 724, *724*
Einstein, Albert, 762
Eisenhower, Dwight D., 916, 946, 947, 948, 959
Eisenstein, Sergei, 886, 930
Either/Or (Kierkegaard), 994
El Alamein, 912, 913
Electricity, 718, 1017–1018
Electronic Numerical Integrator and Computer, 1005, *1006*
Elements of the Philosophy of Newton (Voltaire), *514*, 516
Eliot, George, 763
Elizabeth I, Queen of England, 388
Elizabeth of Russia, 499, 544
Emancipation Act (1861), 706
Emancipation Proclamation, 497, 683
Émigrés, 563, 567, 585
Émile (Rousseau), 528, 531, 533, 603
Eminent Victorians (Strachey), 764
Emma—Magazine by Women for Women (journal), 990
Empiricism, 423–425
Employment
  Chartism, 651, 654
  family of 18th century, 457–459
  Industrial Revolution in 18th century and, 464–470
  Industrial Revolution in 19th century and, 650–651, 654, 656
  of women in the 18th century, 458
  of women in the 19th century, 656–658, 659, *729*, 729–730, *730*
  of women in the 20th century, 991–992, 993
Enabling Act (1933), 887
Encyclical, 759
Encyclopedia, The (Diderot), 523, *523*, 530, 531
Energy, modern world and, 1015–1020
Enfield rifle, 810
Engels, Friedrich, 665, 666, 667
Enghien, Duke of, 586

England. *See also* Britain
Age of Walpole, 395, *395*
agriculture in, 460
alliances with Austria and Russia, 591
American Revolution, 501–503
in Americas, 483, 484–485, 501–503
aristocracy of 18th century, 451
Austrian Succession, war of (1740–1748), 498–499
Charles I, 391
Charles II and restoration of the monarchy, 392–394
civil war, 391–392
compared with France, 388
Cromwell, 392, *392*
enclosure vs. open fields, 460–461
following American Revolution, 506
game laws, 455
Glorious Revolution, 394–395
Industrial Revolution, 465–466
James I, 390
James II, 394
key events/dates, *394*, *506*
Long Parliament, 391–392
parliamentary monarchy, 388
peasant rebellions in, 455
Quadruple Alliance, 599, 600–601
revival of monarchy, 392–394
romantic literature, 604–606
social reform, 538
suppression of reforms, following French Revolution, 570
toleration and political stability, 513–514
War of Jenkins's Ear, 498, 632
English Factory Act (1833), 656
ENIAC, 1005, *1006*
Enlightenment. *See also individual name of author or work*
absolutism in, 538–547
defined, 513, 516
Encyclopedia, The, 523, *523*, 530, 531
formative influences on, 513–515
major works of, *531*
philosophes, 515–518, 526–529
print culture, impact of, 513, 514–515
religion and, 518–519
society and, 523–526
women and, 529–532
"Enquiry into the Obligations of Christians, to Use Means for the Conversion of the Heathen, An" (Carey), 812
Entente Cordiale, 831–832
Environmentalism, 997, 999, 1000
nuclear energy and, 1020
oil spills and, 1019, *1019*
Erfurt Program, 740–741
Essay Concerning Human Understanding, An (Locke), 428, 429, 531
Essay on the Inequality of the Human Races (Gobineau), 771
Essay on the Principle of Population (Malthus), 624–625, *662*
Estates General, French, 553
becomes the National Assembly, 553–555
Louis XVI calls into session, 553
Esterhazy, Prince, 451
Estonia, 859, 966
Ethics (Spinoza), 522
Ethics and science, 755
Ethiopia, 899–900, 933, 950
Ethiopian Church, 815
Ethnic cleansing, 757, *757*, 971
Euro, *982*, 1008
Europe. *See also names of individual countries*
in 1714, *405*
expansion, 824–825
financial crisis, 1009–1012
territorial changes after World War II, *938*
unification of, 1007–1009
European Coal and Steel Community, 1007
European Coalition, 598
European Community (EC), *982*
European Constitution, 1008, *1009*
European Economic Community (EEC), 964, 1007
European Free Trade Area, 1007
European Union, 1007–1009, *1008*
Eurozone, 1011–1012
Evangelicalism, 812
Evangelical Protestant missionaries, 812
Evans, Mary Ann (George Eliot), 763
Evolution and Ethics (Huxley), 756
Evolutionary Socialism (Bernstein), 741
Executions, 472
Existentialism, 994–995, 996
Existentialism and Humanism (Sartre), 996
Exquemelin, Alexander, 488

F

Fabianism, 739, *739*
Fabius Maximus, Quintus, 739
Factories, 485, 650–651, 659
Falangists, 900
Falkenhayn, Erich von, 846
Falloux Law (1850), 758
Family
cult of domesticity, 732
economy, 455–459
18th century, 455–459
Nazi Germany, 893
19th century, 654, 656, 658, 663, 671, 775
Soviet Union, 892–893, *893*
20th century, 990, 993
Famine in Ireland, 511, 648, 649
Fanaticism, or Mohammed the Prophet (Voltaire), 520
Faraday, Michael, 1018
Fascism, in Italy, 876–879
Fashoda incident, 801
Faust (Goethe), 606
Fawcett, Millicent, 733
Fear and Trembling (Kierkegaard), 994
February Patent, 703
Feisal, Prince, *854*
Feminism/antifeminism
in France (1848), 670–671
late 19th century, 775–779
19th century, 733–736, 775–779
obstacles to equality, 733
rise of political, 733–736
sexual morality and the family, 732–733, 775–751
20th century, 990, 992
voting rights, 733–736, *734*, 776
Ferdinand, Francis (Archduke of Austria), 827, 834, *835*, 838
Ferdinand of Austria, 672, 674
Ferdinand VII, King of Spain, 632, 642
Ferry, Jules, 758
Festival of the Supreme Being, *578*
Fichte, J. G., 610
Fickert, Auguste, 776, 777
Final Act (1820), 627
Finland, 859, 905
Finley, Carlos, 817
Firearms, 810, 812, *812*
First Coalition, 572
First Continental Congress, 502
First International, 738
First Treatise of Government (Locke), 428
First Vatican Council, 759
FitzGerald, Edward, 612
Five Weeks in a Balloon (Verne), 754
Flaubert, Gustave, 763
Fleury, Cardinal, 406, 499
Flota system, 485
Folies-Bergère, *765*, 766
Fontenelle, Bernard de, 433
Food, introduction of canned, 594
Ford, Gerald, 950
Ford, Henry, 718, *1017*
Forman Christian College, 814
Foundations of the Nineteenth Century (Chamberlain), 771
Fourier, Charles, 664
Fournier, Henri, *719*
Four Ordinances, 636–637
Four-stage theory of economics, 524–526
Fourteen Points, 852, 855
Fox, Charles James, 505
Fox, George, 680
Fragment on Government (Bentham), 662
Fragonard, Jean-Honoré, 532
France. *See also* French Revolution
absolute monarchy, 395–406, *396*
African colonies, 801
agriculture, 461, 462–463
American Revolution and, 502
in Americas, 483, 484–485
aristocracy of 18th century, 451
Austrian Succession, war of (1740–1748), 498–499
Bourbon restoration, 485–486, 585, 595, 599, 631, *631*
compared with England, 388
conflict between church and state, 758
Consulate in (1799–1804), 586–588
Crimean War (1853–1856), 686
decolonization, 956–959
divine right of kings in, 398, 400
Dreyfus affair, 737, 772–775, 928
economy of, 396
Edict of Nantes, revocation of, 402–403, 404
18th century, 462–463, 557
Fourth Republic, 958
Franco-Prussian War (1870–1871), 699–700
Great Depression in, 868, 869

imperialism and, 793, *793*, 806, 824
Indochina and, 958–959
Jansenists, suppression of, 398, 402
Jews in, 736, 737
key events/dates, *398*
Louis XIII and Richelieu, 395
Louis XIV and Mazarin, 395
map of, in 1789, *562*
military, 398–399
Morocco, 793, *793*, 796
Napoleon's empire, 590–592
Netherlands invasion of, 386
Nine Years' War, 402, 403
Paris Commune, 700–701, 738
peasants in, 453, *454*
politics in 19th century, 739–740
racial tensions in, 984
revolution of 1830, 636–637, 796
revolution of 1848, *668*, 668–671
Ruhr, invasion of, *866*, 867, 880
Second Republic, 668–671
Third Republic, 701
Triple Entente (1890–1907), 830–832
Versailles, 396–398, *397*, 554, *555*
War of Devolution, 398–399
War of Spanish Succession, 403, *405*
World War I and, 841, *841*, 846, 853, *858*
World War II and, 908, 926–928
France, Anatole, 795
Franco, Francisco, 900, *902*
Franco-Prussian War (1870–1871), 792
Frankenstein: or, The Modern Prometheus (Shelley), 606
Frankfurt Parliament, 674, 675–676
Franklin, Benjamin, 538, 681
Frederick I, King of Prussia, 411
Frederick II (the Great), 552
Frederick William II, King of Prussia, 567, 570
Frederick William IV, King of Prussia, 675–676, 696
Freemasons, 515
French Academy of Science, 430, *430*
French and Indian War (1756–1763), 499
French National Committee of Liberation, 928
French Revolution
chronology of, *581*
Europe during, 569–572
monarchy pre-, 551–553
Paris Commune, 568
reconstruction of France, 560–567
Reign of Terror, 572–578
religion and, 576
resistance to taxation, 551–553
revolution of 1789, 553–560
second revolution, 567–569
Thermidorian reaction, 578–581
Freud, Sigmund, *769*, 769–770, 775–776, 837
Friedrich, Caspar David, 608, *609*
Fronde, 396, 402
Fry, Elizabeth, 661
Fukushima nuclear meltdown, 1020
Fulton, Robert, 810

G

Gainsborough, Thomas, *452*
Galileo Galilei, *421*, 421–422, 434–435, 438
Gallican liberties, 399, 402
Gandhi, Mohandas, 954, *954*, 955, 956
Gapon, George, 743
Garibaldi, Giuseppe, 603, 673, 674, 690, 691, *691*, *693*, *694*, 694–695
Garrison, William Lloyd, 683
Gastein, Convention of (1865), 698
Gauguin, Paul, 766, 767
Gay, Peter, 516
Gdansk, 952
Genealogy of Morals, The (Nietzsche), 768
General Austrian Women's Association, 776
General Motors, *1017*
General Theory of Employment, Interest, and Money (Keynes), 870, 871
Genius of Christianity (Chateaubriand), 610
Genocide, 803, 804
Geocentrism, 419
Geoffrin, Marie-Thérèse, 512, *512*, 529
Geography, 815
George I, King of England, 395
George II, King of England, 499, 895
George III, King of England, 501, 502, 503–506, 552
George IV, King of England, 638
George V, King of England, 868
Georgia (country), invasion of by Russian Federation, *972*, 972–974
German Confederation, 626, 627, *627*, 629, 676, 695
German Democratic Republic (East Germany), 941
German Federal Republic (West Germany), 941
German Ideology, 994
Germany. *See also* Hitler, Adolf; Nazis
African colonies, 802–803
after 1815, *601*
Austro-Prussian War (1866), 698, *698*
Berlin blockade, *943*
Berlin Wall, 949, 963–964, *967*
Bismarck's leadership, 828–829
borders of in 20th century, *965*
church and state conflict in, 758–759
Congress of Vienna (1815), 599–601, *602*, 618
Danish War (1864), 697–698
division into East and West, 940–941, *941*
Dual Alliance, 829, 830
map of, *601*
Napoleon and, 591, 599, 628
rearmament of, 899, 902
reparations for World War I, 859, 867–868, 880
reunification of East and West, 964–965, *965*
revolutions of 1848, *668*, 674–676
romantic literature, 605, 606
student nationalism and Carlsbad Decrees, 626–627
Three Emperors' League, 828–829
Triple Alliance, 830
Triple Entente, 830–832
unification of, *696*, 696–700
Weimar Republic, 867, 879–880
western frontier in, *883*
World War I, 834–836, 846, 851–852, 857, *858*, 880
World War II, 909–911, 925–926, 931–932
Germ theory, 726
Gerstein, Kurt, 922, 923
Ghana, 955
Ghettos, Jewish, 476–478
Ghosts (Ibsen), 764
Gibbon, Edward, 515, 519
Girondists, 567–569, 572, 574
Gladstone, William, 709, *709*, 711
Glasnost, 961
Glorious Revolution, 394–395
Gobineau, Arthur de, 771
God that Failed, The, 993
Goebbels, Josef, 926
Goethe, Johann Wolfgang von, 606
Gold Coast slave trade, 490, 493
Gömböm, Julius, 894
Gomulka, Wladyslaw, 947
Gorbachev, Mikhail S., 960–961, *963*, 963–964, 966–968
Gorchakov, Alexander M., 807
Gordon, Charles, 799
Gordon, George (1751–1793), 475
Gordon, George (1788–1824). *See* Byron, Lord
Gordon, Thomas, 504
Gordon riots, 475
Göring, Hermann, 889
Gosplan, 872–873
Gothic architecture, 608
Gouges, Olympe de, 561, 565, 576
Government
absolute monarchy in France, 388, 395–406
absolutism (Enlightenment), 538–547
absolutism (Hobbes), *426*, 426–427
absolutism vs. parliamentary monarcy, 388
Charles II and monarchy restoration, 393–394
divine right of kings, 388, 398, 400, 636
Great Depression and, 868–869
key events/dates, *670*
Long Parliament, 391–392
19th century, 735
Goya, Francisco de, *597*
Gramsci, Antonio, 994
Grand Alliance, 403
Grand Army of Napoleon, 598
Grand National Union, 664
Grant, Duncan, 764
Great Depression
agriculture and, 868
in Britain and France, 868–869
origins of, 867–868
Great Exhibition (1851), 655, *655*
Great Reform Bill (1832), 638–640
Green movement, 999
Greens (German), 997, 999
Grenville, George, 501
Grey, Earl, 639

Grey, Edward, 831, 832, 837
Grimm, Jakob, 610
Grimm, Wilhelm, 610
Gros, Antoine, *611*
Grounds of National Philosophy (Cavendish), 432
Guadalcanal, 912
Guam, 912
Guesde, Jules, 739
Guilds, 651
 18th century, 475
 in France, 561
Guizot, Francois, 661, 669
Gunboat diplomacy, 810
Gymnastics in Germany, 628, *628*

H

Habsburg Empire, 407, 485, 540
 Austrian Succession, war of, 498–499
 18th century, 407–409, *408*
 formation of dual monarchy, 703
 key events/dates, *703*
 nationalities within, 625–626, 703–705, *704*
 peasants/serfs in, 454, 540–522
 revolution of 1848, 671–673, *672*
Haeckel, Ernst, 753
Hagenbeck, Carl, 818
Haiti Revolution, 497, 588, *588*, 590, 681, *681*
Hall of Mirrors, *445*, *698*, 699
Hammer of Witches (Krämer & Sprenger), 442
Hampton Court Conference, 388
Hannibal, 739
Hanoverian dynasty, 395
Hansemann, David, 675
Hardenberg, Prince von, 595
Hardie, Keir, 739
Harding, Warren, 867
Hargreaves, James, 466, *466*
Hartwell, Emily, *813*
Harvey, William, 426
Hatti-I, Sharif of Gülhane, 688
Haussmann, Georges, 723
Havel, Václav, 964
Heart of Darkness (Conrad), 801–802
Hegel, G. W. F., 611, 612, 618, 665, 666
Heidegger, Martin, 995
Heine, Heinrich, 720
Heisenberg, Werner, 762
Heliocentric theory, 419
Helots, 823
Helsinki Accords, 950, 960
Henry IV, King of France (Henry of Navarre), 388, 395, 398, 631
Herder, Johann Gottfried, 529, 604, 610–611, 612
Herero people, 803, 804
Herzegovina, 833
Herzen, Alexander, 706
Herzl, Theodor, 774–775, *775*, 944
Hevelius, Elisabeth, 433
Hevelius, Johannes, 433
Hidalgo y Costilla, Miguel, 643
Higglers, 455
Hill, Rowland, 709
Himmler, Heinrich, 888, 919
Hindenburg, Paul von, 844, 851, 883, 884, 887–888
Hirohito, Emperor of Japan, 918
Hiroshima, *898*, 918–919, 1020
History of Ancient Art (Winckelmann), 535
History of the Peloponnesian War (Thucydides), 426
History of the Russian Empire under Peter the Great (Voltaire), 538
History of the Saracens (Ockley), 520
History of the Two Indies (Raynal), 530
Hitler, Adolf, *883*, *907*, *908*, 916. *See also* Nazis
 early career, 880–883
 goals of, 899
 plans for Europe, 901–903, 911
 Reichstag fire, 887, *887*
 remilitarization of Rhineland, 900
 rise to power, 884–885, 886
 women, role of, 888–889, *890*, 893
Hobbes, Thomas, *426*, 426–427, 429
Hobson, J. A., 791
Ho Chi Minh, 958
Hogarth, William, 472
Hohenzollerns, 406, 409–411, 699
Holland, 403, 638
Holocaust, *919*, 919–924, *920*, *924*, 1002, 1003
Holstein, 697
Holy Alliance (1815), *600*, 601, 632
Holy Synod, 413
Homage to Catalonia (Orwell), 993
Honest to God (Robinson), 1003
Hong Kong, 912
Hooker, Joseph Dalton, *816*
Hoover, Herbert, 868
Horney, Karen, 776
Horse, introduction to Americas, 510
Horthy, Miklós, 894
Hospitals, 726
Hotzendorf, Conrad von, 835
Houdon, Jean-Antoine, 516, 538
House of Commons, 391–392, 505, 506, 739
House of Hanover, 395, 403
House of Lords, 392, 711, 719, 739
Houses of Parliament (British), 608
Housing
 Artisan Dwelling Act (1875), 711
 reforms in 19th century, 725, *725*, 727
 slums, 724, 727, *727*
Howard, John, 661
Huber, A.V., 727
Hubertusburg, Treaty of (1763), 500
Hubris, 823
Hufton, Olwen, 458
Hugo, Victor, 604
Huguenots, 402
Hume, David, 463, 515, 519–520
Hundred Days, 600–601
Hungary/Hungarians
 in the 1920s, 894
 aristocracy of 18th century, 451
 Austria-Hungary, formation of, 703, *704*
 collapse of communism, 963
 Habsburg, 407, 671–673
 Magyars, 407, 499, 540, 544, 672–673, 703–704, 859, 894
 nationalism in, 625
 under Soviet control, 940, 941
 uprising of 1956, 947
 World War I, 834–835, *841*, 855
Hunt, Henry "Orator," 630
Husak, Gustav, 964
Hussein, Saddam, 976, 977
Hussein of Mecca, 853, *854*
Huxley, Thomas Henry, 753, 755, 756–757, 775

I

IBM, 1005, 1006
Ibsen, Henrik, 763
Id, 770
Idealism, German, 711
Ignatenko, Lyudmilla, 1000
Illustrations of Political Economy (Martineau), 625, 661
Immaculate Conception doctrine, 760
Imperial Hall, 532, *536*
Imperialism. *See also* New Imperialism
 defined, 783, 822
 European, 782–804
 of free trade, 784–785
 Greeks and, 822–823
 Muslims, Mongols, and Ottomans and, 824
 Roman, 823–824
 science and, 815–818
 tools of, 810
 Western, 782–826
Imperialism: A Study (Hobson), 791
Imperialism: The Highest Stage of Capitalism (Lenin), 791
Impositions, 388
Impressionism, 765–766, *766*
Incas, 824
Index of Prohibited Books, 435
India, 484
 British in, 785–789, *788*, 825, *825*, 954–955
 decolonization, 954–955
Indian National Congress, 788, 955
Indigenous religious movements, 815
Indirect rule, 801
Indochina, 958–959
Indochina Communist Party, 958
Indonesia, 954
Industrial Revolution, 18th century
 consumption of consumer goods, *464*, 464–465
 defined, 464
 in England, 465–466
 iron production, 468–469
 steam engine, 467–468
 textile production, 466–467
 women, impact on, *464*, 469–470
Industrial Revolution, 19th century
 1848 revolutions, 666, 668
 crime and order, 658–661
 economy, 661–662
 employment, 650–651
 family structures, 654, 656
 key events/dates, *618*, *670*
 map of, *668*, *718*
 new industries, 716–719
 population and migration, 647–648
 railways, 648, *648*, 650, *650*
 second, 617–619
 socialism, 662–666
 women in, 656–658
Infanticide, 443

Ingres, Jean, *584*
Innocent VIII, Pope, 442
Innocent X, Pope, 404
Innocent XI, Pope, 404
Inquiry into Human Nature (Hume), 519–520
Inquiry into the Nature and Causes of the Wealth of Nations (Smith), 524–526, 624
In Search of Time Past (A la Recherche du temps perdu) (Proust), 764
Institute for Advanced Research, 1005
Intel Corporation, 1006
Intellectuals, communism and, 993–994
Intendants, 486
Internal combustion engine, 718, 1016–1017
International African Association, 801
International Business Machines Corporation (IBM), 1005, 1006
International War Crimes Tribunal, 971
International Working Men's Association, 738
Interpretations of Dreams, The (Freud), 769
Intolerable Acts, 502
Introduction to the Study of Experimental Medicine (Bernard), 763
Ipatescu, Ana, *646*
Iran, revolution of 1979, 975
Iraq
  formation of, 859
  invasion of Kuwait, 976
  war against, 977–978
Ireland
  British and the Irish problem, 619, 711–712
  Catholic Emancipation Act, 639
  Charles I and, 391
  Cromwell and, 392, *392*
  famine of 1845-1847, 511, 648, 649
  Free State, 868–869
  Home Rule Bill, 711, 868
Irish Free State, 868–869
Irish Land League, 711
Irish Poor Relief Act (1847), 649
Irish Republican Army (IRA), 868
Iron, 468–469
Iron Curtain, 938
Isabel Christiana, 683
Isabella II, Queen of Spain, 699
Isabella of Castile, 485
Islam/Islamic. *See also* Muslims
  Enlightenment and, 520–522
  fundamentalism, 975
  imperialism and, 824
  late-19th century, 759, 761
  Muhammad, 520–521, 613, 761
  reformism, 975
  rise of radical political, 974–976
  Romanticism and, 611–613
  view by world, 611–613
Island of Dr. Moreau, The (Wells), 754
Israel
  Arab-Israeli conflict, 944–945
  creation of the state of, 941, 944–945, *945*
Israelites (Hebrews). *See* Jews
Issus, Battle of, *823*
Italia irredenta, 693, 844, 857
Italy
  attack on Ethiopia, 899–900
  fascism, 876–879
  revolution of 1848, *668*, 673–674
  Triple Alliance, 829–830
  unification of, 690–695, *692*
  World War I and, *834*, 846, 857, 859
  World War II and, 913
It's That Man Again, 929
Iturbide, Augustín de, 643
Ivan IV, the Terrible, 411
Ivan the Terrible, 886, 930
Ivan V, 411
Ivan VI, of Russia, 544
Ivory, 801

J

Jacobins, 567–568, 569, 574, 575–576, 578, 586
Jahn, Friedrich Ludwig, 628, *628*
James Edward, the Stuart pretender, 395
James I, King of England, 388–389, 445
James II, King of England, 394
Jamestown, 489
James VI, King of Scotland, 388
Jansen, Cornelius, 402, 403
Jansenists, 398, 402, 403, 435
Japan
  imperialism and, 790
  in Manchuria, 911
  nuclear meltdown in, 1020
  Russo-Japanese War (1904–1905), 831
  World War I and, 846, 854, 857
  World War II and, 911–912, 917–918
Jardin des Plantes, 816
Jaruzelski, Wojciech, 952, 963
Jaspers, Karl, 995
Jaurès, Jean, 739
Jefferson, Thomas, 538
Jellachich, Joseph, 672
Jena, Battle of (1806), 593
Jenkins, Robert, 498
Jenkins's Ear, War of (1739), 498, 632
Jerusalem: or, On Ecclesiastical Power and Judaism (Mendelsohn), 522
Jesuits, 402, 435
Jewish State, The (Herzl), 774, 775
Jews
  anti-Semitism, 736, 737, 771–775, 880–881, 888, *888*, 919–924, 928
  Belorussian, 476, 477
  18th century, 476–478
  Enlightenment and, 519, 522–523
  holocaust, *919*, 919–924, *920*, *924*, 1002, 1003
  19th century, 736–737
  pogroms, 736
Jihad, 976, 977
Jingoism, 829
Jinnah, Ali, 955
João VI, King of Brazil, 643
Jodl, Alfred, 900
John III Sobieski, King of Poland, 407
John Paul I, 1004
John Paul II, Pope (Karol Wojtyla), 435, 952, *1004*, 1004–1005
Johnson, Lyndon, 959
John XXIII, Pope, 1004
Joseph, brother to Napoleon, 595
Joseph I, of Austria, 408
Joseph II, of Austria, 538, 540–543, 547, 552, 736
Josephine de Beauharnais, 595, 598
Josephinism, 541
Joyce, James, 765
Judenplatz Holocaust Memorial, *1002*
July Monarchy (France), 637–638, 661
July Revolution, 636–637
Jung, Carl, 760, 769, *769*
Junkers, 410, 452, 595
Juntas, 642, 643

K

Kadar, Janos, 947, 963
Kant, Immanuel, 513, 515, 518, 520, 529, 530, 540, 593, 604–605
Kapp Putsch, 880
Kaunitz, Wenzel Anton, 499
Kautsky, Karl, 741
Kay, James, 466
Kazakhs, 806
Kellogg-Briand Pact (1928), 884
Kemal, Mustafa, 853
Kennedy, John F., 949, 959
Kenya, 955
Kepler, Johannes, 420–421, 423
Kerensky, Alexander, 848
Kew Garden, *816*, 816–817
Key, Ellen, 776
Keynes, John Maynard, 764, 861, 870, 871
Khedives, 796, 798
Khomeini, Ruhollah, 975
Khrushchev, Nikita, *876*, 946–948, 949, 1003
Kierkegaard, Soren, 994, 1003
Kikongo, 496
Kikuyu tribe, 815
King, Martin Luther, Jr., 955
Kingdom of Kongo, 490
Kingdom of the Serbs, Croats, and Slovenes, 859, 895
Kirch, Gottfried, 433
Kirov, Sergei, 875
Kitchener, Horatio, 799, 800, 801, *801*
Klein, Melanie, 776
Koch, Robert, 725
Koestler, Arthur, 994
Kohl, Helmut, 964
Kollontai, Alexandra, 892–893
Korean War (1950–1953), 945–946, *946*
Kosciuszko, Tadeusz, 570, 572
Kosovo, 971
Kossuth, Louis, 671, *672*
Kosygin, Alexei, 949
Kotzebue, August von, 627, *627*, 629
Kovalenko, Ainaida Yevdokimovna, 1000
Krämer, Heinrich, 442
Kreditanstalt, 867–868
Kristallnacht, 888
Krogh, Christian, *731*
Kruger, Paul, 831
Krupp family, 719
Kuchuk-Kainardji, Treaty of (1774), 546, 585
Kulaks, 742, 874, *874*
Kulturkampf, 758–759
Kun, Bela, 894
Kutuzov, Mikhail, 598
Kuwait, 974, 976

L

Labor. *See also* Employment
child, 656
factory workers in 19th century, 650–651, 656–657, *657*, 659
post World War I, 866
unions, *737*, 737–741
of women, *464*, 656–658, *657*, 729–731, *731*
Labor Front, 890
Labour Party (British), 739, 868
Lacombe, Claire, 575
Ladies' National Association for the Repeal of the Contagious Diseases Act, 776
Lafayette, Marquis de, 556–557
Laibach, congress of (1821), 632
Laissez-faire economics, 524, 661
Lamarck, Jean-Baptiste, 753
Lamartine, Alphonse de, 669
Land and Freedom, 706
Language(s). *See also individual languages*
nationalism and, 619
of slaves, 496
Laos, 958
Lasalle, Ferdinand, 740
Lateran Accord (1929), 693, 879
Latin America. *See also individual country names*
early exploration of, 482–463
map of, *641*
viceroyalties in, 485–486, *487*
wars of independence, 640–642
Latvia, 859, 966
Laud, William, 391
Lausanne Conference, 868
Law
Enlightenment and, 523–524
Napoleonic Code, 590, 624, 728
19th century and family, 728
Law, John, 403, *406*
Law of 22 Prairial, 577, 578
Lawrence, T. E., 846, *854*, 860
League of Augsburg (1686), 403
League of Nations, 847, 852, 857, 859, 861, 862, 884, 899, 900
Lectures on Dramatic Art and Literature (Schlegel), 604
Lectures on the Philosophy of History (Hegel), 611
Legislative Assembly, 560, 561, 567–568
LEGO Co., 998
Leipzig, Battle of, 598, 627
Leipzig Mission, 812
LeNain, Louis, 445
Lenin, Vladimir Ilyich Ulyanov, *742*, 742–743, 744–745, 791, 847, 850–851, *869*, 869–871
Leningrad Symphony (Shostakovich), 930
Léon, Pauline, 568, 575
Leopold I, of Austria, 403, 408, 411
Leopold II, of Austria, 544, 567
Leopold II, of Belgium, 801–802, *802*, 818
Leopold of Hohenzollern, 699
Leopold of Saxe-Coburg, 638
Leo XIII, Pope, 761, 762
Le Pen, Jean-Marie, 984
Lespinasse, Julie de, 529
Lesseps, Ferdinand de, 689
Lessing, Gotthold, 515, 519, 522, 593
Letter Concerning Toleration (Locke), 428–429
Letters from Prison (Gramsci), 994
Letters on a Regicide Peace (Burke), 571
Letters on Sunspots (Galileo), 421
Letters on the English (Voltaire), 516
Letter to the Grand Duchess Christina (Galileo), 435
Levasseur, E., 722
Levée en masse, 572, 580
Leviathan (Hobbes), *426*, 426–427, 429
Lewis, C. S., 1003
Lexington, Battle of, 502
Liberalism
early nineteenth century, 619, 622–624
economic goals, 624–625
fascism on, 878
political goals, 619, 622–625
relationship to nationalism, 618
Liberal theology, 1003–1004
Liberal Unionists, 711
Liberia, 683
Liberty Leading the People (Delacroix), *616*
Liberum veto, 407, 570
Libya, 796, 909
Liebknecht, Wilhelm, 740
Life of Jesus, The (Strauss), 755
Lincoln, Abraham, 683
Lin Tse-hsü, 786
List, Friedrich, 662
Lister, Joseph, 725
Literature. *See also individual name of work or author*
fiction, *769*
Lithuania, 859
for the mass audience in the 19th century, 752
modernism, 764–765
nonfiction works, 776
print culture, impact of, 513, 514–515
realism and naturalism, 763–764
romantic, 604–606
science fiction, 754
Lithuania, 966
Liverpool, Lord, 627, 630, 639
Livestock exchange between Americas and Europe, 510–511
Livingstone, David, 815
Livy, 536
Lloyd George, David, 739, 854, *855*, 857
Locarno Agreement (1925), 884, 900
Locke, John, 394, 400, 401, 427–429, *428*, 504, 513, 527, 531, 664, 680
Lodz, 921
Lofthouse, Richard, 1010
London
18th century, 465, 470, 472
terrorist attacks on, *977*, *978*
World War II, 909
London, treaties of (1827, 1830), 633
London Corresponding Society, 570
London Foundling Hospital, 459
London Missionary Society, 812
London Working Men's Association, 651
Long Parliament, 391–392
Lorraine, 695, 700
Louis Philippe, King of France, 637–638, 661, 669, *669*, 722
Louis XIII, King of France, *397*, 398
Louis XIV, King of France, 386, 388, 393, 394, 395–406, *396*, 403, 410, 429, 446, 511, 532, 551, 909
Louis XV, King of France, *406*, 499, 529, 532, 535, 538, 551, 552
Louis XVI, King of France, 535, 538, 551, *551*, 552–553, 554–555, 557, 559–560, 563–564, 567, *567*, 568, 569, *570*, 617, 631
Louis XVII, King of France, 631
Louis XVIII, King of France, 631, *631*, 636
Lourdes, 758, 760
L'Ouverture, Francois-Dominique Toussaint, 588, *588*, 590, 681, *681*
Lovett, William, 651
Lucas, Charles, 661
Lucinde (Schlegel), 606
Ludendorff, Erich, 844, 851, 852, 881
Ludwig II, King of Bavaria, 674
Lueger, Karl, 774, 880
Luftwaffe, 909
Luneville, Treaty of (1801), 586
Lusitania, 846
Luther, Martin, 399, 627
Luxembourg, 941
Lyell, Charles, 753, 758
Lytton, Earl of, 899
Lytton Report, 899

M

Maastricht, Treaty of (1991), 1007
MacDonald, Ramsay, 868
Macedon/Macedonians
collapse of Yugoslavia and civil war, 970–971
Mach, Ernest, 761
Machine gun, 810, *810*
Macintosh computer, 1006
MacMahon, Marshal, 701
Madame Bovary (Flaubert), 763
Madrid, terrorist attack on, 977
Magic Mountain, The (Mann), 765
Maginot Line, 900, 905, 908
Magnitogorsk, *873*
Magyars (Hungarians), 407, 499, 540, 544, 625, 672–673, 703–704, 859, 894
Mahdist movement, 761
Mahomet (Voltaire), *528*
Maintenon, Madame de, 402, *402*
Maize, 511
Malaria, 810
Malaya, 912
Malthus, Thomas, 624–625, *662*, 753
Man and Superman (Shaw), 764
Mandates, 853, 859–860
Manet, Edward, 766
Mangena Makone, 815
Mann, Thomas, 765
Mao Tse-tung, 945–946
March Laws (Hungary), 672–673
Maria Theresa, 409, *498*, 498–499, 499, 538, 540, 541, 542–543
Marie, Henrietta, 389
Marie Antoinette, 552, 556, 567, 568, 569, 576, *576*
Marie Louise, 595, 598
Marie Thérèse, 399
Marlborough, Duke of, 909
Marne, Battle of (1914), 842

Marriage. *See also* Divorce
18th century, *456*, 458
in Nazi Germany, 919
19th-century working-class, 657–658, 730, 732–733
in the Soviet Union, 892–893
20th century, 990, 993
Married Woman's Property Act (1882), 727–728
Marshall, George C., 939, *939*
Marshall Plan, *939*, 939–940, 997
Martineau, Harriet, 625, *662*
Marx, Karl, 664–666, *665*, 667, 738, 744, 968
Marxism, 664–666, 738, 743, 744–745, 770, 968–969, 993–994
Mary I, Queen of England, 386, 394
Mary II, Queen of England, 394
Mary Stuart, Queen of Scots, 388
Mary Tudor. *See* Mary I
Masaryk, Jan, 940
Masaryk, Thomas, 894, 940
Massachusetts Bay Colony, 388
Massachusetts Institute of Technology, 1005
Master Builder, The (Ibsen), 764
Masurian Lakes, Battle of (1914), 844
Mathematical Principles of Natural Philosophy (Newton), 422
Mathematics
metric system, 561, 566
Mauchly, J. W., *1006*
Mauguet, Marie, 734–735
Maupeou, René, 552
Maxim, Hiram Stevens, *812*
"Maxim" machine gun, *812*
Max of Baden, Prince, 852
May Laws, 759
Mazarin, Cardinal, 395, 396
Mazzini, Giuseppe, 620, 673, 690
Mecca, 976
Medicine, 726, 817–790
Medina, 976
Meditations (Descartes), 426
Medvedev, Dmitri, 971
Mein Kampf (My Struggle) (Hitler), 881, 899, 915, *915*
Melun Act (1851), 725
Mendel, Gregor, 753
Mendelsohn, Moses, *522*, 522–523, 540
Mensheviks, 743, 847–848
Mentenegro, World War I and, *841*
Mercantile empires, 483–485
Mercantilism, 483–485, 524
Merlini, Domenico, *536*
Metaxas, John, 895
Métayer system of farming, 462
Methodism, 609–610, 680
Metric system, 561, 566
Metternich, Klemens von, 598, 601, 617, 625, 626, *626*, 629, 632, 672, 854
Middle class. *See also* Social classes/society
18th-century urban, 472, 473
19th century, 719–720, 722
Middle East
romanticism and the, 611–613
Midway Island, 912–913
Midwives, 443, *443*, 458
Migrations
displacement through war, 983
19th century, 617, *618*, 647–648, *717*
20th century, 983–984
Milan Decree (1807), 592
Military/weaponry
atomic bombs, *898*, 918–919
British naval supremacy in, 590–591, *785*
Napoleonic, 586, 591, 596–597
New Model Army, Cromwell's, 392, *392*
poison gas, *827*, *847*
Russian, 706
tanks, introduction of, *844*, 845, *845*
trench warfare, 842, 845
World War I, *844*, 845, *845*, 846
World War II, 913, 915, 916, 918–919
Militia Ordinance, 392
Mill, Harriet Taylor, 733
Mill, John Stuart, 624, 733
Millerand, Alexander, 740
Millet system, 688
Milosevic, Slobodan, 970, 971
Missionaries, modern Western, 812–815
Mississippi Bubble, 403, 405
Mississippi Company, 403, 405
Modernism
Catholic, 759
in literature and art, 764–768, *767*
Modern Man in Search of a Soul (Jung), 770
Mohacs, Battle of, *824*
Molotov, Vyacheslav, *876*, 938
Moltke, Helmut von, 835, 842
Monarchies
absolute, in France, 388, 395–406
parliamentary, in England, 388
Monet, Claude, 766
Mongols, 824
Monroe Doctrine (1823), 632, 784
Montagu, Mary Wortley, 519
Montaigne, Michel de, 439
Montenegrins, collapse of Yugoslavia and civil war, 970–971
Montesquieu, Charles de Secondat, 515, 521–522, 526, 529, 530–531, 552, 680
Montgomery, Bernard, 913
Moravia/Moravians, 455, 610
Morel, E. D., 801
Morelos y Pavón, José María, 643
Morocco
crises in, 831, 833
French in, 793, *793*, 796
Mothers' Protection League, 776
Mountain (Jacobins), 569, 572
Mozambique, 950, 954
Mrs. Dalloway (Woolf), 764
Mrs. Warren's Profession (Shaw), 764
Mughal Empire, 787
Muhammad, 520–522, 613, 761
Munich agreement, 902–904, 906–907
Museum of Mankind, 818
Music Party, The (Watteau), *535*
Muslim Brotherhood, 975
Muslim League, 788, 955
Muslims, 955. *See also* Islam/Islamic
immigration and population changes, *984*, 984–985
Mussolini, Benito, 877–879, *879*, 881, 899–900, 901–902, 906, *907*, 908, 909, 913

N

Nagasaki, *898*, 918, 1020
Nagy, Imre, 947, 963
Nameless Library (Whiteread), 1002, *1002*
Nanjing, Treaty of (1842), *785*
Nantes, Edict of (1598), 395–396, 402, 404
Napoleon Bonaparte (Napoleon I), 566, 580, *584*, 590, *592*, 628
Consulate in France (1799–1804), 586–564
Continental System, 592, *593*
coronation of, 588, *589*
empire (1804–1814), 590–592, *599*, *603*
European response to, 592–598
Hundred Days, 600–601
Middle East and, *611*, 613
rise of, 585–586
Roman Catholicism and, 586–564
Napoleonic Code, 588, 624, 728
Napoleonic Concordat, 758
Napoleon II, 725
Napoleon III (Louis Napoleon Bonaparte), King of France, 668–671, 674, 686, 690, 691, 697, 699, 700, 723, 766, 806
Narva, Battle of (1700), 412
Nasser, Gamal Abdel, 947, 974
Nathan the Wise (Lessing), 519, 522
National Assembly, 553–555, 557–558, 564, 590, 669, 700–701
National Cash Register, 1005
National Constituent Assembly, 555–556, 557, 561, 563, 580
National Council of French Women, 734
National Front, 984
National Government (British), 868
National Guard (French), 556, 568
National Health Service (Britain), 988–989
National Insurance Act (1911), 739
Nationalism
Arab, 974–975
emergence of, 618–525
in Germany, 593, 595, 628
meaning of, 620–621
racism and, 771
relationship to liberalism, 618
romantic views of, 604–606
student, 626–627
Nationalist Society, 690
National Liberation Front, 957–958, 959
National Socialists. *See* Nazis
National Union of Gas Workers and General Labourers of Great Britain and Ireland, *737*
National Union of Women's Suffrage Societies, 733
National Women's Party, 734
Nationhood, 619
Native Americans, diseases introduced to, 489, *509*, 509–510
Native Baptist Church, 815
NATO (North Atlantic Treaty Organization), 937, 941, 958, 971, 972, 973, 974, 977, 1007

Naturalism, in literature, 608, 763–764
Natural philosophy, 418
Natural selection, *751*, 753, 755
Nature and the sublime, 608
Nature as mechanism, 423
Nausea (Sartre), 995
Nazis, 868
  annexation of Austria, 901–902
  assault on Jews of Poland, 921
  attack on Soviet Union, 909–910
  displacement of people, 983
  economic policy, 889–890, 891
  formation of, 880–883
  Great Depression and, 868, 884–885
  Hitler comes to power, 885
  Holocaust, *919*, 919–924, *920*, 922–924
  internal party purges, 887
  occupation of Czechoslovakia, 902–903, 906–907
  occupation of Poland, 903–904, 905
  partition of Poland, *903*
  police state and anti-Semitism, 888
  Reichstag fire, 887, *887*
  role of women, 888–889, *890*, 893
  Soviet pact, 905, 993
Necker, Jacques, 552, 553, 555, 605
Negrelli, Alois, 689
Nelson, Horatio, 585, 591, *591*
Nemesis (warship), 810
Nemo, captain, 754
Neoclassicism, 532, 535–536
Neolocalism, 456
Neo-Orthodoxy, 1003
Neoplatonism, 421
Netherlands
  agriculture in, 460
  Louis XIV, invasion of, 386, 398
  17th–18th century, 386–387
  World War II, 911
Neumann, Balthasar, 532
New Astronomy, The (Kepler), 421
New Atlantis (Bacon), 423
Newburn, Battle of (1640), 391
Newcomen, Thomas, 468
New Economic Policy (NEP), 870–871
New Imperialism
  defined, 783, 790–791
  key events/dates, *805*
  missionary factor, 812–815
  motives for, 791–796
  tools of, 810–784
New Spain, 485, 643
Newspapers, 19th century, 752
Newton, Isaac, *422*, 422–423, 439, 513, 516, 518
Newton, John, 680
Newtonianism for Ladies (Algarotti), 433
Ngo Dinh Diem, 958–959
Nguyen Van Thieu, 959
Nicaragua, 951
Nicholas and Alexandra, 747
Nicholas I, Tsar of Russia, 634, 636, 673, 687, 703, 705–707
Nicholas II, Tsar of Russia, 707, 741, 743, 746, 747, 748, 833, 847
Niemöller, Martin, 1003
Nietzsche, Friedrich, 758, 768–743, 994
Nigeria, 799, 801, 955
Nijmwegen, peace of (1678 and 1679), 399, 402
Ninety-five Theses, 627
Nine Years' War, 402, 403
Ninth of January, The, 747, *747*
Nixon, Richard, 950, 959
Nobility. *See* Aristocracy
Normandy, 916, *918*
North, Lord, 502, 504, 505
North Africa
  imperialism and, 796
  World War II, 909–910, 913, *913*, 926, 928
North Atlantic Treaty Organization. *See* NATO
North Briton, The (Wilkes), 504
Northern Ireland, formation of, 868, 869
Northern Society, 634
Northern Star, 651
North German Confederation, 698–699
Norway, 941
Novara, Battle of, 674
Novum Organum (Bacon), 423, *424*
Nuclear energy, 1019–1020
Nuremberg Laws, 888
Nuri Pasha Said, *854*
Nystad, peace of (1721), 412

O

OAS (Organisation Armée Secrète), 958
Oates, Titus, 393
Oath of the Horatii (David), 536, *537*
Obama, Barack, 974, 978, 1009, 1011
Obrenovitch, Milos, 633
Observations upon Experimental Philosophy (Cavendish), 432
Ockley, Simon, 520
O'Connell, Daniel, 639, *639*
O'Connor, Feargus, 651
October Manifesto, 746
Official Nationality, 636
Offray de la Mettrie, Julien, 520
O'Higgins, Bernado, 642
Oil, 718–719, 1016–1019, *1019*
Old Custom House Quay, *482*
Old Regime, 450, 505, 532
Olympia, 886
Olympic games, in Berlin (1936), 886, *886*
Omdurman, Battle of, 800, *801*
On Crimes and Punishments (Beccaria), 524
One Day in the Life of Ivan Denisovich (Solzhenitsyn), 946
One (Number 31, 1950) (Pollock), *1001*, 1003
On Heroes and Hero-Worship (Carlyle), 613
On the Origin of Species (Darwin), 753, 755
On the Revolutions of the Heavenly Spheres (Copernicus), 419, 435
OPEC, 1018–1019
Open Door Policy, 808
Operation Barbarossa, 909, 910
Opium wars, 785, *785*, 786
Oppenheimer, Samuel, 476
Opportunism, 740
Orders in Council, 682
Organic Articles (1802), 588
Organic Statute, 636
Organization of Labor, The (Blanc), 664
Organization of Petroleum Exporting Nations (OPEC), 1018–1019
Orlando, Vittorio Emanuele, 854, *855*
Orléans, Duke of, 403
Orsini, Felice, 691
Orwell, George, 993, *994*
Ossetia, 972, *972*
Otto, Louise, 736
Otto I, King of Greece, 633
Ottoman Empire, 486, *520*, 520–522, 633–634
  Crimean War (1853–1856), 686–687
  end of, 853–855
  end of expansion, 408
  imperialism and, 792, 824, *824*
  invasion by Russia, 545–546
  reforms in, 688–690
  role of the *ulama*, 688
  Russian war with, 412
  Russo-Turkish War, 828
  serfs in, 454
  in 17th century, 407
  World War I, 853–855
Ottoman Turks, 520–522, 545–546, 824, *824*
Owen, Robert, *663*, 663–664

P

Paine, Thomas, 502, 503, 569
Pakistan, 955, 975–976
Palacky, Francis, 673, 674, 675
Pale of Settlement, 737
Paléologue, Maurice, 849
Palestine, 944
Palmer, Robert, 540
Palmerston, Lord, 638
Panama Canal, *790*
Pankhurst, Emmeline, 734, *734*, 735
Pan-Slavic Congress, 673
Pantheon (Paris), 538
Panther (warship), 833
Papal infallibility, 759
Papen, Franz von, 885
Paraguay, 642
Pareto, Vilfredo, 771
Paris
  18th century, *463*, 470
  19th century, 723–724
  Paris Commune, 568, 578, 700–701, 738
  settlement of World War I in, 854–861, *858*, 866–867
Paris, Treaty of (1763), 500–501, 504
Paris, Treaty of (1783), 504
Paris, Treaty of (1856), 687
Paris Commune, 568, 578, 700–701, 738
Paris Foundling Hospital, 459
Paris Summit Conference, 947
Parlement/parlements, 396, 405–406, 476, 526, 551–552
  of Paris, 396, 513, 516, 552, 553
Parliament
  American Revolution and reform for, 505, 506
  Austrian, 702
  Charles I and, *391*, 391–392
  18th century, 453, 455
  James I and, 388
  James II and, 393
  Long, 391–392
  Short, 391
Parliament Act (1911), 739, 788
Parnell, Charles Stewart, 711
Pascal, Blaise, 435, 439, 1005
Pasternak, Boris, 946
Pasteur, Louis, 725, 726, 817
Patel the Elder, Pierre, *397*

Pater, Walter, 764
Paul, Alice, 734
Paul, Tsar of Russia, 634
Paul VI, Pope, 1004
Peace of Nijmwegen (1678 and 1679), 399, 402
Peace of Ryswick (1697), 403
Pearl Harbor, 911–912, *912*
Pearson, Karl, 757
Peasants/serfs
  abolition and serfdom in Russia, 705–706
  in 18th century, 454–455
  in France, 453, 454
  Pugachev Rebellion (1773–1775), 454, *454*, 547
  rebellions of 1762 and 1769, 454–455
Pedro I, Emperor of Brazil, 643
Pedro II, Emperor of Brazil, 643, 683
Peel, Robert, 639, 660, 662, 709
Peninsulares, 486
Pennsylvania Abolition Society, 681
Penny, Edward, *500*
Pensées (Pascal), 435
Pentonville Prison, 661
People's Republic of China, 964. *See also* China
People's Will, 707, 708
Percussion cap, 810
Perestroika, 961
Pericles, 822
Perry, Matthew C., 807
Persian Gulf War (1991), 976
Persian Letters, The (Montesquieu), 521, 526, 530
Personal computer, 1006–1007
Peru, 485, 642, 824
Pestel, 634
Pétain, Henri Philippe, 846, 908, 926, 927, *927*
Peter I (the Great), Tsar of Russia, *385*, 411–414, 452–453, 544, 546
Peter II, Tsar of Russia, 544
Peter III, Tsar of Russia, 453, 499, 544
Peterloo Massacre, 630–631
Petite bourgeoisie, 720
Petition of Right, 391
Petrograd, 847
Phalanx, 664
Phenomenology of Mind, The (Hegel), 611
Philadelphia system, 661
Philip of Anjou, 403
Philippine Islands, 912, 918
Philip V, King of Spain, 403
Philip VI, King of France, 485
Phillips, Thomas, 494–495
Philosophes, 513, 515–518, 526–529
Philosophical Dictionary (Voltaire), 520
Philosophic Manuscripts, 994
Philosophy. *See also individual authors or works*
  absolutism (Hobbes), *426*, 426–427
  empiricism (Bacon), 423–425, *424*, 435
  Enlightenment, 515–518
  liberty and toleration, 427–429
  19th century, 768–769
  rational deduction (Descartes), *425*, 425–426
Philosophy of Manufactures, The (Ure), 652
Physico-theology, 439–440
Physics, 761–763
Physiocrats, 524
Picasso, Pablo, 767
Piedmont, 673, 674, 690, 691, 693
Pilgrimage, 760
Pilgrimage to Isle of Cithera (Watteau), 532
Pilsudski, Marshal Josef, 894, 920
Piracy, 485, 488
Pissaro, Camille, 766
Pitt, William (the Elder), 500, 501, 504
Pitt, William (the Younger), 505–506, 570, 590–591, 639
Pius IX, Pope, 673, 690, 759
Pius VI, Pope, 563, 586
Pius VII, Pope, 587–588
Pius X, Pope, 761
Pizarro, Francisco, 511
Plague, The (Camus), 995
Planck, Max, 762
Plantation economy, 482
Plants, exchange between Americas and Europe, 510–511
Plassey, Battle of (1757), 500, *500*
Plato, 679
Pleiad (ship), 810
Plekhanov, Gregory, 742
Plymouth Colony, 388
Pognon, Marie, 721
Poincaré, Henri, 761
Pointillism, *766*, *767*
Poland
  in the 1920s, 891, 894
  aristocracy of 18th century, 451
  autonomy, 947
  destruction of Jewish communities, 920
  18th century, 406, 451
  Jews in, 920–921
  Jews in, *476*
  Nicholas I as ruler of, 636
  occupation of, in World War II, 905
  partition of (1939), *903*, 903–904
  partitions of (1772, 1793, 1795), 546, *546*, 547, 570–571
  Russian repression in, 636, 706
  Solidarity, 952, 963, *964*
Polar Sea, The (Friedrich), 608, *609*
Police forces, 19th-century formation of, *658*, 660–661
Polignac, Prince de, 636
Polis, 823
Polish Communist Party, 947, 952
Polish Patriots, 570
Polish Rebellion (1830), 706
Politburo, 875, 946
Political parties, 19th century, 738
Political Registrar (Cobbett), 630
Politics key events and dates, *891*
Pollock, Jackson, *1001*, 1003
Poltava, Battle of, 412
Polygenesis, 817
Pompadour, Madame de, 529, 532, *535*
Poor Law, 630, 662
Pope, Alexander, 515
Popish Plot, 394
Popolo d'Italia, Il, 877
Popular Front, 740, 869, 993
Population
  expansion in the 18th century, 461, 470, 472
  expansion in the 19th century, 617, 647–648
  Malthus on, *662*
  trends in the 20th century, 985, 988
  20th century, in Europe, 985, 988
Populism, 706
Portobello, 485
Portugal, 489, 517, 824–825
Positive Philosophy, The (Comte), 753
Positivism, 753
Postal systems, 709
Post-impressionism, *766*, 766–767
Potato, 511
Potosí, *486*
Potsdam Conference (1945), 932–933
Poverty, 471, 730–731
Pragmatic Sanction of Bourges, 408, 498
Prague, Treaty of (1866), 698
Predestination doctrine, 518
Presbyterians, 388, 391–392, 394
Presidium, 946
Pressburg, Treaty of, 591
Priestley, Joseph, 570
Principia Mathematica (Newton), 422, 433, 513
Principles of 1789, 624
Principles of Geology (Lyell), 754
Principles of Morals and Legislation, The (Bentham), 662
Principles of Political Economy (Ricardo), 625, *662*
Print culture, Enlightenment and, 513, 514–515
Prison reform, 19th century, *660*, 661
Proletarianization, 650–651, 666, 667, 745
Prosser, Gabriel, 681–682
Prostitution, 657, 730–731, *731*, 775–750
Protectorates, 790
Protestant Ethic and the Spirit of Capitalism (Weber), 770
Protestants, 812
Proudhon, Pierre-Joseph, 664
Proust, Marcel, 764, *764*
Prussia
  aristocracy of 18th century, 451–452
  army, 485
  Austrian Succession, war of (1740–1748), 498–499, 540
  Austro-Prussian War (1866), 698, *698*
  Congress of Vienna (1815), 599–601, *600*, 602, 617, 626
  defeat of reforms, 626
  Franco-Prussian War (1870–1871), 699–700
  Frederick II (the Great), 409, 411, 451, 498, 499–501, 516, 539–540, 546, 547, 552, 570
  Frederick William, the Great Elector, 409–411
  Frederick William I, 411
  Hohenzollerns and, 409–411
  Napoleon and, 591
  Quadruple Alliance, 599, 600–601
  revolution of 1848, 674–675
  serfs in, 461, 595
  17th–18th centuries, 409–411, 451–452, 453
  social reforms in, 595, 626

Prussian Civil Service Commission, 539
Psychoanalysis, 769–770
Ptolemaic system, 419
Ptolemy I, 419
Public Health Act (1848), 725
Public Health Act (1875), 709, 711
Public opinion, 515
Pugachev, Emelyan, 454, *454*
Pugachev Rebellion (1773–1775), 454, *454*, 547
Puritanism/Puritans, 388, 389, 391–392, 770
Putin, Vladimir, 969–970, 971–974
Putting-out system, 466, 730

Q

Qing dynasty, 808, 810
Quadruple Alliance, 599, 600–601, 617
Quakers, 680–681
Quebec, *481*, 500
Quebec Act, 502
Quesnay, Francois, 524
Quinine, 810
Qur'an, 520, 761, 975

R

Racine, Jean, 604
Racism
  anti-Semitism, 736, 737, 771–775, 880–881, 888, *888*, 919–924
  Chamberlain, views of, 771
  ethnic cleansing, 757, *757*, 971
  Gobineau, views of, 771
  Holocaust and, *919*, 919–924, *920*
  late-19th-century nationalism and, 771–775
Radetzky, Joseph Wenzel, 673
Radical Islamism, 974–975
Radio BBC, 929
Railways, 648, *648*, 650, *650*, 717, 720
Rain, Steam and Speed—The Great Western Railway (Turner), 608, *609*
Rasputin, Grigory Efimovich, 746, 748, 847
Rastatt, Treaty of (1714), 407
Ray, John, 440
Raymond, Julian, 564
Raynal, G.T., 530
Reagan, Ronald, 952, *963*
Realism, in literature, 763–764
Red Army, 850–851, 870, 905
Reed, John, 850
Reed, Walter, 817
Reflections on the Revolution in France (Burke), 569, 571
Reflections on Violence (Sorel), 740, 770
Reformation
  Council of Trent (1545–1563), 398, 433
Reform League, 709
Reichsrat, 703–704
Reichstag, *685*, 698, 740, 741, 879
  fire, 887, *887*
Reign of Terror, 572–578
Reinsurance, Treaty of (1887), 830
Relativity, theory of, 762
Religion. *see also* Reformation
  conflict between church and state, 758
  Enlightenment and, 518–519
  19th-century attack on, 755, 758–759
  19th-century women and, 732
  Romanticism and, 609–610
  Scientific Revolution and, 433–440
  of slaves, 496–497
  20th century, 1003–1005
Religion within the Limits of Reason (Kant), 520
Rembrandt van Rijn, 355, *417*
Remington Rand, 1005
Renaissance of Motherhood, The (Key), 776
Renan, Ernest, 755, 761
Renoir, Pierre-Auguste, 766
Report on the Sanitary Condition of the Labouring Population (Chadwick), 725
Republic of Virtue, 575
Rerum Novarum, 759, 762
Revisionism, 741
Rhenish Missionary Society, 812
Rhineland, remilitarization of, 900
Rhineland Gazette (Rheinische Zeitung), 665
Rhodes, Cecil, 803
Rhodesia, 954
Ricardo, David, 624, 625, *662*
Richelieu, Cardinal, 395, 396
Riefenstahl, Leni, 886, *886*
Rieger, Albert, *689*
Righteous and Harmonious Society of Fists, 808
Rights of Man, The (Paine), 569
"Rime of the Ancient Mariner, The" (Coleridge), 604
Río de la Plata, 486, 642
Riots, 18th century, 475–476
Robert Andrews and His Wife (Gainsborough), *452*
Robertson, William, 518
Robespierre, Maximilien, 575, 576, *577*, 577–578, *578*
Robinson, John, 1003
Rockefeller, John D., 1016
Rock music, 962
Rockwell, Norman, 915, *915*
Rococo art style, 532, 535–538
Roehm, Ernst, 881, 887
Roentgen, Wilhelm, 761
Roland, Pauline, 671
Roll Call: Calling the Roll after an Engagement, The, Crimea (Thompson), *687*
Roman Catholicism, 610, 988. *See also* Catholicism; Christianity
  Baroque art and, 444–446
  French Revolution and, 562, 563
  Joseph II, 540–541
  missionaries, 813, *813*
  modern world and, 759
  Napoleon and, 586–590
  20th century, 1004–1005
Roman Empire
  imperial power, 823–824
Romania
  in the 1920s, 895
  collapse of communism, 964
  Compromise of 1867, 703–704
  World War I, 829, 833, *841*, 846, 859
  World War II, 905
Romanov, Michael, 411
Romanov dynasty, 407, 411
Romanticism, 585, 602–613
  Islam, Middle East and, 611–613
  literature, 604–606, 995
  nationalism and history, view of, 610–613
  questioning of reason, 603–604
Romantic Republicanism, 690
Rome, Treaty of (1957), 1007
Rome-Berlin Axis, 900
Rome-Berlin Axis Pact (1936), 901
Rommel, Erwin, 910, 912, 913
Room of One's Own, A (Woolf), *777*, 777–779
Roosevelt, Franklin D., 909, *909*, 915, 918, 930, *931*, 932, 933, 937, 1018
Roosevelt, Theodore, *790*, 808, 1016
Rosetta Stone, 613
Rosie the Riveter, 915, *915*
Rossi, Pelligrino, 673
Rothschild, Lionel, *736*
Roundheads, 392
Rousseau, Jean-Jacques, 515, 517, *527*, 527–528, 531, 533, 559, 575, 603
Royal African Company of London, 494
Royal Air Force (RAF), 909
Royal Dutch Petroleum, 719
Royal Museum for Central Africa, 818
Royal Niger Company, 801
Royal Society of London, 430, 436, 815
Rubáiyát of Omar Kharyyám, 612
Rubber trees, 816
Rubens, Peter Paul, 445
Ruhr, French invasion of, *866*, 867, 880
Ruskin, John, 653
Russell, Lord, 707
Russia. *See also* Soviet Union
  Alexander I, Tsar of Russia, 592, 598, 600, 617, 632, 634–636
  Alexander II, reforms of, 705–706
  alliances with Austria and England, 591
  aristocracy of 18th century, 452–453
  Bolshevism, birth of, 741–743
  Catherine II (the Great), 453, 476, 544–546, 547, 570, 585, 686, 805
  Congress of Vienna (1815), 599–601, *600*, 602, 618
  Crimean War (1853–1856), 686–687
  Decembrist revolt of 1825, 634–636
  expansion of, 412–414, *545*
  Great Northern War, 412–413
  imperialism and, 805–806
  industrial growth in 19th century, 741–746
  invasion of Poland, 546
  Jews in, 476–478, 736–737
  key events/dates, *413*, *544*, *705*, *746*
  Napoleon's invasion of, 598
  navy, 412
  Peter I (the Great), *385*, 411–414, 452–453, 544, 546
  Quadruple Alliance, 599, 600–601
  resurgence of, 971–974
  revolutionaries, 706–707
  revolution of 1905, 743, *746*, 832
  revolution of 1917, 744, 791, 847–851
  Romanov dynasty, 411
  serfs in, 453, 705–706
  St. Petersburg, founding of, *412*, 412–413

streltsy and boyars, 412, 413
Three Emperors' League (1873), 828
Triple Entente (1890–1907), 830–832
World War I and, 833–834, 836–837, *841*, 844, 852, 857
Yeltsin decade, 969–970
Russian Federation
Georgia, invasion of, *972*, 972–974
Putin in, 971–974
Yeltsin decade, 969–970
Russian Orthodox Church, 413–414, 634, 875, 920
Russian Republic, 966, 971
Russo-Japanese War (1904–1905), 831
Russo-Turkish War (1875), 828
Ruthenians, 673
Rutherford, Ernest, 761
Ryswick, peace of (1697), 403

S

SA (storm troopers), 881, 884, 888
Sadat, Anwar, 975
Sailing ships, 1015, *1015*, 1016
Saint Domingue, 497, 564, 681, *681*
Saint-Simon, Claude Henri de, 663, 664, 752
Saint Teresa of Avila, 445
Sakharov, Andrei, 960
Salafi (Salafiyya) movement, 761
Sale, George, 520
Salisbury, Lord, 711
Salisbury Cathedral, from the Meadows (Constable), 607, *608*
Salon, 529
Sand, Karl, 627, *627*
Sanitation, 461, 474, *474*, 724–725, *725*
Sans-culottes, 568–569, 572, 575, 578, 579, 580, 581
San Stefano, Treaty of (1878), 828
Sanussiya movement, 761
Sarajevo, 834–835, *970*, 970–971
Sargent, John Singer, *847*
Sartre, Jean-Paul, 990, 993, 995, 996
Schacht, Hjalmar, 883
Scheidmann, Philipp, 859
Schlegel, August Wilhelm von, 604
Schlegel, Friedrich, 606
Schleicher, Kurt von, 885, 887
Schleiermacher, Friedrich, 610
Schleswig, 697
Schlieffen, Alfred von, 837
Schlieffen Plan, 837, *842*
Schmidt, Auguste, 736
Schmoller, Gustav, 794
Schönbrunn, Peace of, 595
Schuschnigg, Kurt von, 894, 902
Schwarzenberg, Felix, 673
Science
Comte, positivism, and the prestige of, 753
Darwin's theory of natural selection, *751*, 753, 755
ethics and, 755
imperialism and, 815–818
late-19th century, 761–763
mid-19th century, 752–755
Science fiction, 754
Science of Mechanics, The (Mach), 761
Sciences and the Arts, The (Stalbent), 431
Scientific induction, 426
Scientific Revolution
Bacon, 423–425, *424*, 435
Brahe, 419–421
Copernicus, 418–419, *420*, 435
Descartes, *425*, 425–426, 436–437
Galileo, *421*, 421–422, 434–435, 438
Hobbes, *426*, 426–427
institutions/societies, 429–432
Kepler, 420–421, 423
Locke, 427–429, *428*
major works of, *429*
Newton, *422*, 422–423
Pascal, 435, 439
religion and, 433–440
women and, 432–433
Scientists, use of term, 418, 753
Scotland, Charles I and, 391–392
Scott, Walter, 611
Scramble for Africa, 796
Second Coalition, 585
Second Continental Congress, 502
Second Estates, 553
Second Industrial Revolution, 617–619
Second International, 740
Second Reform Act (1867), 707–709
Second Sex, The (Beauvoir), 990, 992
Second Treatise of Government (Locke), 394, 401, 428
Sedan, Battle of (1870), 699, 700
Sejm, 407
Semmelweis, Ignaz, 726
Sepoy, 788, *788*
September 11, 2001 attacks, 937, 974, 976–977
September Massacres, 568, 576
Serampore College, 814
Serbia/Serbs
in the 1920s, 895
collapse of Yugoslavia and civil war, 970–971
independence (1830), 633–634
World War I, 833–834, *834*, *835*, 838–840
Serfs. *See* Peasants/serfs
Servant, defined, 456
Seurat, Georges, *766*, 766–767
Sevastopol, Battle of, 686
Seven Weeks' War, 698
Seven Years' War (1756–1763), 499–501, 544, 680
Sewer system, 725, *725*
Shaftesbury, Earl of, 393, 427–428
Shamil, Imam, 806, *806*
Shaw, George Bernard, 739, 764
Shaw, Thomas, 810
Shelley, Mary Godwin, 605–606
Shelley, Percy Bysshe, 606
Short Account of That Part of Africa Inhabited by the Negroes, A (Benezet), 680
Short Parliament, 391
Shostakovich, Dimitri, 930
Shoulder Arms (Chaplin), 856
Sicily, 913
Sierra Leone, 683
Siéyès, Abbé, 553, 586
Silber and Fleming, *723*
Silesia, 498, 499
Simon, Jules, *727*
Sinn Fein, 868
Siraj-ud-daulah, *500*
Six Acts (1819), 630, 639
Six Points of the Charter, 651, 654
Slavery, 674, 675
abolishing in the New World, 679, 682–683, 784
in the Americas, 482–483, 486, *486*, 488–497, *489*, *497*, 679
anthropology on, 817
crusade against, 679–681
end of, in Africa, 683–684
experience of, 493–497
in Haiti, 497, 588, *588*, 590, 681, *681*
revolts, 497, 681, *681*
ships, 494–495
transatlantic economy and, 482–483, 490–493, 679–684
Slavs, 673, 859
Slovenes, 895, 970–971
Smallpox, *509*, 510
Smith, Adam, 524–526, 528, 624, 653, 662, 680, 784
Smith, W. H., 719
Smoking, 390
Social classes/society
aristocracy of 18th century, 451–452, *452*
Enlightenment and, 523–526
middle class, 516, 719–720, 722
urban, 472–473
Social classes/society, in the Middle Ages
women, 731–733
Social Contract, The (Rousseau), 527, 528, 575
Social Darwinism, 755, 756–757, *757*, 776
Social Democratic Party (SPD), 740–741
Austrian, 894
German, 736, 740–741, 859, 879, 988
Russian, 742–743, 745, 850, 852
Socialism, 664
anarchism, 664
in Britain, 739
First International, 738
in Germany, 740–741
key events/dates, *746*
Marxism, 664–666, 738, 743, 744–745, 770, 968–969, 993–994
utopian, 662–664
Social Revolutionary Party, 742, 850
Social science, 523–524
Société des Amis des Noirs, 681
Society for the Abolition of the Slave Trade, 681
Society for the Relief and Free Negroes Illegally Held in Bondage, 681
Society of Jesus. *See* Jesuits
Society of Revolutionary Republican Women, 575–576, 578
Solidarity, 952, 963, *964*
Solomon Islands, 918
Solzhenitsyn, Aleksandr, 946, 960
Some Considerations on the Keeping of Negroes (Benezet), 680
Sons of Liberty, 502
Sorbonne, 728, 997
Sorel, Georges, 740, 770
Sorrows of Young Werther, The (Goethe), 606
South Africa, 791, 954
Southeast Asia Treaty Organization (SEATO), 958
Southern Society, 634
Soviet Communist Party, 871, 875–876, 964

Soviets, 746
Soviet Union. *See also* Cold War; Russia
  Afghanistan, invasion of, 951
  collapse of, 964, 966–970
  collectivization, *865*, 873–875, *874*
  Comintern (Third International), 871–872
  communism, 857
  coup of 1991, 967–968
  domination of eastern Europe, 939, 940
  family legislation, 888–889
  German attack on, 909–911
  Gorbachev, 960–961, *963*, 963–964, 966–968
  industrialization, 872–873
  Nazi-Soviet pact, 905
  New Economic Policy (NEP), 870–871
  purges, 875–876
  Stalin versus Trotsky, 872
  Third International, 871–872
  urban consumer shortages, 873
  war communism, 869–870
  women in, 890–891, *891*
  World War II, 892–893, *893*, 929–930
Spain
  in Americas, 483, 485–486, 590, 824, 825
  Civil War, *900*, 900–901, *902*, 993
  colonial system, 484–486
  Napoleon and, 590, 595
  revolution of 1820, 632
  terrorist attacks on, 977
  War of Jenkins's Ear, 498
Spanish-American War (1898), 792, 807
Spanish Succession, war of (1701–1714), 403, *405*, 485
Spare Rib (journal), 990
Spectator, The (Addison), 515
Speeches on Religion to Its Cultured Despisers (Schleiermacher), 610
Speer, Albert, 925
Spencer, Herbert, 755, 756–757, 775
Spheres of influence, 790
Spinning jenny, 466, *466*, 654
Spinoza, Baruch, 522–523
Spirit of the Laws (Montesquieu), 521–522, 526, 529, 680
Sprenger, Jacob, 442
Sputnik, 948
Sri Lanka, 955
SS (Schutzstaffel), 888
Staël, Madame de, 604, 605
Stakhanov, 873
Stalbent, Adriaen, *431*
Stalin, Joseph, 806, *865*, 872, *876*, 886, 910, 913, 916, 929–930, 931, *931*, 932, 933, 938, 940, 947, 948, 993
Stalingrad, Battle of (1942), 913, 916, *916*
Stamp Act, 501
Stamp Act Congress, 501, 505
Standard Oil Company, 719, 1016
Stanley, Henry Morton, 801
Starry Messenger (Galileo), 421
Steamboats, 810
Steam engine, 467–468, 1016
Steele, Richard, 515
Steel industry, 716–717
Stein, Baron von, 595
Stendhal, 604
Stephenson, George, *650*
Stewart, Robert (Viscount Castlereagh), 599, 600, 601, 617, 632
St. Louis World's Fair, *818*
Stockton and Darlington Line, 648
Stoecker, Adolf, 772–773
Stolypin, P. A., 746
Stones of Venice, The (Ruskin), 653
Stopes, Marie, 776
Storm troopers (SA), 881, 884, 888
St. Peter's Basilica, *444*, 445
St. Petersburg, *412*, 412–413, 470, 747, *747*
Strachey, Lytton, 764
Strafford, Earl of, 391
Stranger, The (Camus), 995
Strategic Arms Limitation, 951
Strategic Defense Initiative (Star Wars), 952
Strauss, David Friedrich, 755
Streltsy, 412, 413
Stresa Front, 899
Stresemann, Gustav, 883–884
Studies in Hysteria (Breuer and Freud), 769
Sturm and Drang, 603
Subjection of Women, The (Mill and Taylor), 733
Sublime and nature, 608
Submarine cables, 811, *811*
Suburbs, development, 723–724
Sudetenland, 902–903, 906
Suez Canal, 689, *689*, 796–797, *799*, 947
Suez Canal, The (Rieger), *689*
Suffrage for women, 670, 671, 733–736, *734*, 776
Suffragettes, 733–734
Sugar, 484, 489–492, *491*, *492*
Sugar Act, 501
Sugarcane, 511
Suleyman, sultan, 824
Sunday on the Grande-Jatte (Seurat), *766*, *767*
Superego, 770
Superman (Nietzsche), 768
Superstitution, 440–444
Supreme Soviet, 961
Suttee, 787
Swastika, 881, 890
Sweden
  Great Northern War, 412–413
Swift, Jonathan, 436, 437
Syllabus of Errors, 759
Syphilis, 510

T

Tableau de l'etat physique et moral des ouvriers (Villermé), 725
Table of Ranks, 413, 452
Taff Vale decision, 739
Taille, 451
Tajikistan, 966
Tales of the Crusades (Scott), 611
Taliban regime, 975–976, *976*
Talleyrand-Périgord, Charles Maurice de, 586, 600, *600*
Tannenberg, Battle of (1914), 844
Tanzimat, 686
Tatar. *See* Mongols
Taylor, Harriet, 624, 733
Taylor, Marshall Walter "Major," 721
Technology, 20th century, 1005–1007
Tehran Agreement (1943), 930–931
Tencin, Claudine de, 529
Tennis Court Oath, 554, 556
Terrorism, 937, 974, 976–977, 978
Test Act, 393
Textile production, 466–467, 647, 650, 651, *653*
Thatcher, Margaret, 989, *989*
Thermidorian reaction, 578–581
Thiers, Adolphe, 700
Third Coalition, 590–591
Third Estate, 553–554
Third International (Comintern), 871–872
Third of May, The (Goya), 597, *597*
Third Reich, 911
Third Voyage of Gulliver's Travels (Swift), *437*
Thirty Years' War (1618–1648)
  Treaty of Westphalia, 406
Thistlewood, Arthur, 631
Thompson, Elizabeth (Lady Butler), *687*
Thomson, J. J., 761
Thoreau, Henry David, 955
Thoughts on Slavery (Wesley), 680
Thoughts on the Imitation of Greek Works in Painting and Sculpture (Winckelmann), 535
Thousand and One Nights, The, 612
Three Emperors' League (1873), 828–829
Three Mile Island, 1020
Thucydides, 426
Thus Spake Zarathustra (Nietzsche), 768
Tiananmen Square, 964
Tiepolo, Gian Battista, 532
Tillich, Paul, 1003
Tilsit, Treaty of (1807), 592, 598
Time Machine, The (Wells), 754
Tirpitz, Alfred von, 831
Tisza, Stefan, 835
Tito, Josip, 940, 971
Tobacco, 390, *390*
Tojo, Hideki, 911
Tokyo Electric Light Company, 1018
Toland, John, 518, 519
Toleration Act (1689), 394
Tolstoy, Leon, 930
Tools of Imperialism, 810–812
Tories, 630
To the Lighthouse (Woolf), 764
Townsend, Charles, 460, 502
Toys, 998
Trafalgar, Battle of (1805), 591, *591*
Transcaucasus, 806
Transformismo, 693
Transportation and prison reform, *660*, 661
Transylvania, 455, *646*
Treaties. *See under names of treaties*
Treatise on Tolerance (Voltaire), 519
Treitschke, Heinrich von, 695
Trenchard, John, 504
Trent, Council of (1545–1563), 402, 434
Tribunals, 576–577
Triple Alliance, 399, 830
Triple Entente (1890–1907), 830–832, 835, 837
Triumph of the Will, 886
Troppau, congress and protocol of (1820), 632
Trotha, Lothar von, 803, 804
Trotsky, Leon, 850, 851, 869
Truman, Harry S., 918, 933, 937, 939, *939*, 944

Truman Doctrine, 846, 939, *939*, 949
Tudjman, Franjo, 970
Tull, Jethro, 460, *460*
Tulp, Nicholass, *417*
Tunisia, 796, 913
Turgot, Robert Jacques, 462–463
Turkey, 1009
Turkeys, 511
Turkish Embassy Letters (Montagu), 519
Turks, 520–522, 545–546
Turner, J. M. W., 608, *609*
Turner, Nat, 682
Turnvater Jahn, 628
Twain, Mark, 702
Twenty-Five Points (Nazis), 881
Twenty Thousand Leagues under the Sea (Verne), 754
Two Laundresses (Degas), *715*
Two Sicilies, 632
Two Tactics of Social Democracy in the Bourgeois-Democratic Revolution (Lenin), 743
Two-Thirds Law, 581

U

U-2 incident (1960), 948
Ulama, 688
Ultraroyalism, 617, 631
Ulyanov, Vladimir Ilyrich. *See* Lenin
Ulysses (Joyce), 765
Unemployment, 719, 868
Uniformitarianism, 753
Uniform Penny Post, 709
Unigenitus, 402
Union of German Women's Organization (BDFK), 736
Unions, *737*, 737–741, 890
United States. *See also* American Revolution; Cold War
- containment foreign policy, 938–940, 943
- imperialism and, 807–809
- Vietnam, 958–959, *960*
- World War I and, 846, 854, 857, 861–862
- World War II, 911–912, 916, 918–919

Universal Postal Union, 709
Urbanization. *See* Cities/towns
Urban VIII, Pope, 435, 445
Ure, Andrew, 652
Uruguay, 642
Utilitarianism, 662
Utopian socialism, 662–664
Utrecht, Treaty of (1713), 403, 483, 485, 499
Uvarov, 634

V

Vaihinger, Hans, 761
Valmy, Battle of, 568
Van Gogh, Vincent, 766
Varennes, 563, 567
Vatican City, 759, 879
Vatican II, 1004
Velvet Revolution (1989), 964
Venezuela, 642
Venice, 470
Verdun, Battle of (1916), 846
Vermuyden Cornelius, 460
Verne, Jules, 754
Verona, congress of, 632
Versailles, 396–399, *397*, 446
- Hall of Mirrors, *445*, *698*, 699

Versailles, Treaty of (1920), 854–861, 877, 880, 882, 884, 894
Vesey, Denmark, 682
Vesuvians, 670–671
Viceroyalties, 485–486, *487*
Vichy Regime, 926–928, 927, *927*, 957
Victor Emmanuel I, King of Italy, 690
Victor Emmanuel II, King of Italy, 674, 690, 691
Victor Emmanuel III, King of Italy, 878
Victoria, Queen of Britain, 786, 788, *936*
Vienna Congress of (1815), 599–601, *600*, 602, 616, 618, 626, 671, 682, *692*, 796
Vietnam, 958–959, *960*
Vietnamization, 959
Villermé, Louis René, 725
Vincent, David Brown, 815
Vindication of the Rights of Woman, A (Wollstonecraft), 531–532, 533, 534, 605, 733
Vingtième, 451
Violin and Palette (Braque), *767*, 768
Virchow, Rudolf, 725
Virgil, 824
Vogt, Karl, 775
Voix des femmes, 671
Voltaire, 433, *514*, 515, 516, 517, 518, 519, 520–521, *528*, 538
Voting rights for women, 670, 671, 733–736, *734*, 776

W

Wagram, Battle of, 595
Wahhabi movement, 761, 974–975
Wakefield, Priscilla, 470, 471
Wake Island, 912
Waldeck-Rousseau, René/Pierre, 740, 758
Walesa, Lech, 952, 963
Wallace, Alfred Russel, 753
Wallas, Graham, 739, 770
Wall Street crash (1929), 867
Walpole, Robert, 395, *395*, 498, 499, 504
War and Peace (Tolstoy), 930
War Communism, 869–870
Warfare/weaponry. *See* Military/weaponry
War guilt cause, World War I, 859
War of Austrian Succession (1740–1748), 498–499, 540
War of Devolution (1667–1668), 398–399
War of Jenkins's Ear, 498, 632
War of the Spanish Succession (1701–1714), 403, *405*, 485
War of the Worlds (Welles), 754
War reparations, 859, 867–868, 880
Warsaw, 470, 921
Warsaw Pact (1955), 937, 941, 947
Warton, Thomas, 604
Washington, George, 502
Water as energy source, *1015*, 1015–1016
Water frame, 466–467
Waterloo, Battle of (1815), 568, 600
Water system, 725
Watt, James, 468, 1016
Watteau, Jean-Antoine, 532, *535*
Watts, George Frederick, *649*
Wealth of Nations, The (Smith), 524–526, 528, 624, 653, *662*, 680
Webb, Beatrice, 739, *739*
Webb, Sidney, 739, *739*
Weber, Max, 761, 770, 776
Wedgewood, Josiah, 465
Weimar Republic, 867–868, 879–880
Weizmann, Chaim, 944
Welfare state, 988–989
Welles, Orson, 754
Wellesley, Arthur (Duke of Wellington), 500, 595, 598, 639
Wellhausen, Julius, 755
Wells, H. G., 739, 754
Welsey, Charles, 680
Wentworth, Thomas, 391
Wesley, Charles, 610
Wesley, John, 610, 680
Wesley, Susannah, 610
West, Benjamin, *481*
West Africa, 799, 801
Western Front, 844
Western Missionary Movement, 812
West Indies, 484, 489–490, 682
Westminister, Convention of (1756), 499
Westphalia, Treaty of (1648), 406
What Is Property? (Proudhon), 664
What Is the Third Estate? (Siéyés), 586
What Is to Be Done? (Lenin), 743, 745
Wheat, 511
Wheatley, Francis, *449*
Whewell, William, 753
Whigs, 393, 504, 638
White-collar workers, 716
Whiteread, Rachel, 1002
White Russians, 851
White Terror, 617, 631
Wilberforce, William, 681, 682
Wilhelm I, Kaiser, *698*
Wilkes, John, 504–505
"Wilkes and Liberty," *505*
Wilkinson, John, 468
William I, Emperor of Germany, *685*, 696–697, 699, 740
William I, King of Holland, 638
William II, Emperor of Germany, 740, 830, *830*, 835, 852
William III, King of England, 386, 387, 394, 398
William IV, King of England, 638–640
William of Orange (the Silent), 386, 394
Williams, George Washington, 801
Wilson, Woodrow, 846, 852, 854, 855, *855*, 857
Winckelmann, Johann Joachim, 535
Wind as energy source, *1015*, 1015–1016
Windischgraetz, Alfred, 673
Winkelmann, Maria, 433
Wisdom of God Manifested in His Works of Creation (Ray), 440
Witchcraft, 440–444
Witte, Sergei, 741–742, 743, 746
Wojtyla, Karol (John Paul II), 952
Wolfe, James, *481*, 500
Wollstonecraft, Mary, 531–532, *532*, 533, 534, 605–606, 733
Women
- in the 19th century, 727–736, 775–779
- in the 20th century, 990–993

Women *(cont.)*
cult of domesticity, 732
educational barriers, 728–729
employment patterns in 19th century, 656–658, *729*, 729–731, *730*
Enlightenment and, 529–532
family economy of 18th century and, 458
feminism, 670–671, 733–736, 775–779, 990
French (1848), 670–671
French Revolution and, 559–560, 568, 575–576, 579
Industrial Revolution (18th century), *449*, 469–470
Industrial Revolution (19th century), 656–658, *657*, 659
law and, 727–728
middle class, 731–733
as midwives, 443, *443*
Napoleonic Code and, 588, 728
Nazi Germany and role of, 888–889, 893, 925–926
pilgrimages by, 760
poverty/prostitution, 730–731, *731*
property rights, 727–728
Scientific Revolution and, 432–433
in the Soviet Union, 892–893
as teachers, 728–729, *752*
voting rights, 733–736, *734*, *776*
witchcraft and, *441*, 441–444
working-class, 656–658, *715*, 730, *731*
World War I and role of, *853*
World War II and role of, 915, *915*
Women's Social and Political Union, 734
Woolf, Leonard, 764
Woolf, Virginia, 764, *777*, *777–779*
Working-class women, 656–658, *715*, 730–731, *731*
World's Fairs, 818, *818*
World-Spirit, 612
World Trade Center, terrorist attacks on, 937, 974, 976–977
World War I (1914–1917), 827–828
casualties, 852, *867*
combatants, strength of, *841*
end of, 851–854
in Europe, *827*, *843*
major campaigns/events, *834*, *852*
naval battles, 846
origins of, 834–837
propaganda, 856, 926, 927, *927*, 929
Sarajevo and the outbreak of, 834–835
settlement at Paris, 854–861, *858*, 866–867
strategies and stalemate, 837, 841–847
U.S. enters, 846
Western Front, *844*
World War II (1939–1945)
allied landings in Africa, Sicily and Italy, 913
atomic bomb, *898*, 918–919
Battle of Britain, 908–909
Battle of Stalingrad, 913, 916, *916*
Battle of the Bulge, 916
in Britain, 908–909, 928– 929,*929*
cost of, 919
defeat of Germany, 916–917
defeat of Japan, 918–919
displacement of people, 983–984
events leading to, 899–905, *905*
in France, 926–928
German attack on Soviet Union, 909–911
German conquest/plans for Europe, 905
in Germany, 901–903, 925–926
Holocaust and racism, *919*, 919–924, *920*
Japan enters the war, 911–912
major campaigns/events, *914*, *924*
map of, *918*
preparations for peace, 930
in Soviet Union, 892–893, *893*, 929–930
strategic bombing, 916
U.S. enters the war, 911–912
Wright, Joseph, *469*
Wyvil, Christopher, 505

X

Xerox Corporation, 1006
Xerxes, 823
X-rays, 761

Y

Yablonskaya, Tatjiana, *1001*, 1003
Yalta Conference (1945), *931*, 932
Yellow fever, 817
Yeltsin, Boris, 966, 968, 969–970
Yorkshire Association Movement, 505–506
Yorktown, Battle of, 502
Young, Arthur, 460
Young Italy Society, 690
Young Plan, 884
Young Turks, 690, 833, 853
Yugoslavia
in the 1920s, 894–895
collapse of, and civil war, *970*, 970–971
ethnic composition of, 970–971
formation of, 859, 895
World War II, 909

Z

Zasulich, Vera, 706–707
Zedong, Mao, 945–946
Zemstvos, 706, 707, 742
Zionist movement, 771–775, 944
Zola, Émile, 763, 772, 773, *773*
Zollverein, 661, 696
Zong (ship), 681
Zoology, 817
Zurich, University of, 728